FROM THE OTHER SIDE OF THE CENTURY II

FROM THE OTHER SIDE OF THE CENTURY II

A New American Drama
1960–1995

Edited with Prefaces
by Douglas Messerli and Mac Wellman
With an Introduction
by Marc Robinson

SUN & MOON PRESS

LOS ANGELES · 1998

Sun & Moon Press
A Program of The Contemporary Arts Educational Project, Inc.
a nonprofit corporation
6026 Wilshire Boulevard, Los Angeles, California 90036
website: http://www.sunmoon.com

First Sun & Moon Press edition 1998
10 9 8 7 6 5 4 3 2 1
FIRST EDITION

This book was made possible, in part, through contributions to
The Contemporary Arts Educational Project, Inc., a nonprofiit corporation
and a matching grant from the National Endowment for the Arts,
a non-profit organization.

NATIONAL
ENDOWMENT
FOR ❤ THE
ARTS

Cover:Lorenzo Bonechi, *Giona (Jonah)*, 1984
oil on canvas
Design: Katie Messborn
Typography: Guy Bennett

LIBRARY OF CONGRESS CATALOGING IN PUBLICATION DATA
Messerli, Douglas and Mac Wellman, eds.
From the Other Side of the Century II:
A New American Drama 1960–1995
p. cm (Sun & Moon Classics:147 / ATL-American Theater in Literature)
ISBN: 1-55713-247-X
I. Title. II. Authors III. Editors IV. Series
811'.54_DC20

Printed in the United States of America on acid-free paper.

Contents

A Penny Universe

An anthology of this size and heft, unless it be viewed as a species of literary-dramatic door stop, has a lot to answer for. Why another big book of plays no one reads with the exception of the perfervid, desperate actor looking for audition material? Isn't it, after all, the business of drama critics to judge, in performance, what plays fly and which sink? Isn't drama, in the age of video and, increasingly, the cinema of titanic effects, clearly the dispensable medium? And, likewise, isn't theater, if we are to be fully honest, little more than a slightly embarrassing anachronism, a thing, aside from victim plays and British plays (which one is obliged to approve for political and cultural reasons) more than a little past ripeness?

One needs another big book because none of the other big books of plays really suffices; suffices to show the true diversity and wildness of American theater writing since the early sixties. I am not necessarily talking only of plays that have received honors and prizes, and earned their authors fame and riches; nor am I talking only of those that have done none of these things; but of the tradition of work that is essential and defining during these past, highly political and politicizing decades. Plays that defy formal conventions and the constraints imposed on the craft by mandarin opinion-makers in the press and academia who assume Higher Reason is theirs, and are jealous and suspicious of all American writers whose take on the stuff of what Greil Marcus has called "the old, weird America," is not imbued with the moral updraft these folk naively suppose to be the justification for all art.

To hell with that. These writers write plays that explore language and the dreams, lies, visions and visionary landscapes only writing—terrific writing—can bring into being. In that sense these plays are their own damned excuse for being what they are. Hence, they are not for everyone; in this sense, they are both democratic and elitist.

Douglas Messerli and I discussed all the plays included here, and many others we could not, for one reason or another, agree on; we argued, stamped and swore considerable. In the main, however, we did agree. For my part, I feel this project to be dedicated to the proposition that what one encounters on stage should be at least as wonderful, as surprising, as alive, as what one encounters on the street. And in the woods. And on the moon. And in the world that is the summation of the street, the woods, and all the ridiculous rest of it.

—MAC WELLMAN

A View from the Street

After completing and publishing my anthology of American poetry, *From the Other Side of the Century: A New American Poetry 1960–1995*, I determined to turn my attention to American drama—of all literary genres the most ignored in the publishing world. Theater had been my first love, and at one time—after a childhood in which I memorized the Burns-Mantle Best Play books—I could have stood toe to toe with the most knowledgeable of American theater historians. But over the past few decades, living in Washington, D.C. and Los Angeles, and focusing on other literary activities, I had lost touch with much of American theater. More importantly, although I had continued to read plays, I had not seen many of the seminal dramas and performances of the 1970s and 1980s. I needed someone knowledgeable who could help me with this enormous undertaking.

Over the years, Mac Wellman and I had talked incessantly about the state of American theater, and of the wonderful productions taking place in small theaters throughout the country. As early as 1985 Mac had edited an anthology, *Theatre of Wonders*, for Sun & Moon Press, a book that had been highly influential to American writers and readers, and resulted in part in the Sun & Moon Press publication of many contemporary playwrights. Mac was clearly the most likely of co-editors, and when he agreed, somewhat and understandably reluctantly, the massive task of reading quickly began.

We had few restrictions. Since our focus was on written texts, we gave preference to works that were centered in dramatic writing rather than in performance. Moreover, because we wanted to focus on the idea of what had occurred during these years to *American* theater, we chose plays with an American locale—a strange focus perhaps given the increasingly international thematics of contemporary playwrights, but also an interesting one, particularly if one compares the quality and diversity of the plays of these decades with the received lie that the great era of American theater existed from the 1930s through 1950s, represented by playwrights such as Eugene O'Neill, Arthur Miller, Tennessee Williams, William Inge, etc.

Throughout 1995, particularly over the summer of that year, I frequented theater bookshops in Los Angeles and New York, buying up every book by potential contributors. I met with numerous playwrights, directors, and actors seeking their suggestions. And I sought out hard-to-find plays recommended to me, every week it seemed, by Mac and others. Now that I look back on that year, what seemed to be an impossible burden at that moment is easily recalled with great joy.

As Mac has written, in our choices much stamping of feet, swearing of oaths, and sometimes even gentle persuasion ensued. But mostly we agreed: what an exciting and strange thing American drama was!—and, hopefully, continues to be. And that is, despite an anthology's obvious failures, all that editing such a book can truly hope to achieve: to reveal, to make manifest to an audience at large what a marvelous thing its subject is—that despite, perhaps, its frozen and frowning image captured, it is something beautiful and alive!

I am certain if Mac and I were to reedit this volume in 1999, some of the contents would be different. But that is precisely what has to happen to something so living, changing at every moment. Perhaps the best way to think of any anthology is, metaphorically speaking, as a photograph. What is caught in the instant of time contains, yes, what was there at that moment, but also reveals the biases and limitations of the photographers and their mechanisms. And a moment later the subject smiled.

The preparation of any such volume always involves the help and support of many. The editors of this anthology must thank the agents, publishers and authors who helped in making the selections affordable to a smaller publishing house, and in many cases provided newly typed and revised scripts. Our thanks also to the authors and directors who provided their suggestions.

My own staff deserves more than thanks for several years of hard work on this publication. Our typographer, Guy Bennett, patiently scanned and recast in drama format most of the plays in the volume; Diana Daves edited and proofread all thirty-eight dramas. Interns Thérèse Bachand and Angela Kang also proofread and offered valuable editorial advice, and Emily Salkin researched and wrote the short author biographies.

Mac and I originally planned a dialogue in the form of an introduction, but after two evenings of seemingly wonderful and enlightening communication, the tape recordings revealed an intriguing but at times so radically associative conversation that neither of us could easily untangle it. The brilliant writer on theater Marc Robinson produced an intelligent and far more readable introduction to our activities. Our sincere appreciation for his immense contribution.

—DOUGLAS MESSERLI

Introduction

If it does nothing else, this anthology should put to bed some tired words. "Experimental," "alternative," "avant-garde." Admirers of new American theater have used these adjectives so liberally over the past forty years that they have lost much of their force. They can no longer rouse a crowd of supporters nor alarm the guardians of tradition; and the day is long past when they adequately described an interesting play or playwright. Perhaps such terms meant something in the early days of American theater, when writers eager for success had to buckle under a dominant style. Then the naysayers were a tiny, if resilient, bunch. But now, after three generations of artists challenging assumptions about what constitutes a good play, the modes of innovation are too various to be summed up in a phrase and too energetic to be confined to the culture's margins. The alternative has itself become a tradition.

The old guard might be mortified, but this development is good news to all who make and chronicle theater—perhaps to no one more than its youngest artists. Gone is the romantic model of the avant-garde writer as solitary adventurer, deprived of a context for his or her experiments. Gone, too, the opposite (but no less romantic) notion of a single, amorphous "bohemia"—or "fringe," or "downtown"—to which were sent all outcasts, regardless of their idiosyncrasies. Now a writer dissatisfied with the status quo can choose to be schooled in one of many well-established communities unified by temperament and theatrical language, each eager to accommodate newcomers and breed namesakes. Playwrights who began their careers as pioneers, provocateurs, or delinquents now preside over extensive bloodlines, some of which stretch down to a generation that considers its founder a classic and nourishes itself on a shared history.

This anthology's table of contents reveals many robust family trees. Edward Albee encouraged Adrienne Kennedy to complete her first play, *Funnyhouse of a Negro,* and produced it soon after his own first works appeared in the toddler years of Off Broadway. Kennedy, in turn, can be heard in the echoes of Suzan-Lori Parks's theater, whose recent success has renewed critical interest in her neglected predecessor. Tony Kushner, for his part, traces his roots back through Maria Irene Fornes to Tennessee Williams. Erik Ehn happily acknowledges his debt to his onetime teacher John Guare and to Mac Wellman. Ed Bullins and Charles Ludlam once led entire artistic movements, in which styles of outrage and outrageousness were passed down from one writer to another. And every day it seems someone starts writing because he or she stumbled across a collection of Sam Shepard and couldn't believe it. The spirit of Shepard's early plays is kept alive by several of the youngest writers represented here.

Even the smallest of these families eventually acquires a name, occasionally self-declared but more often the invention of a sympathetic critic or editor. In this big book can be found several mini-anthologies honoring the Theaters of the Ridiculous and of the Absurd; the New Realists and the Neo-Formalists; Black theater and Gay theater; the Language writers and the Theater of Images. When these categories fail, geography is a fallback: Here are histories of Off-Off Broadway, of the California school and, more precisely, of such important incubators for new work as the Judson Poets' Theater, La Mama, and the Padua Hills Playwrights Festival. Some categories flash brightly, linger awhile, and then die, replaced by new names for similar groups of writers: At one time or another, readers of this anthology have probably surveyed the Theaters of Crisis, of Commitment, and of Protest; or the Theaters of Visions, of Wonders, and of the Marvelous. Tony Kushner once announced a new Theater of the Fabulous, in which he sat at the right hand of David Greenspan.

Granted, few of these names are specific enough, few expressive of the imaginative range within each group; and none do justice to the idiosyncrasies of individual writers. Indeed, in the effort to stake out territory, critics and editors often ignore what's least familiar about a particular writer in favor of the lowest common denominator. But at least such arguments are waged within the proper context—that of the new art itself. As admirers of Adrienne Kennedy wonder if she really has anything other than race in common with Amiri Baraka, and as Richard Foreman's partisans point out all the ways his self-referential work differs from that of Lee Breuer, the critical energy in the theatrical community undergoes a subtle but important change. The hated monolith known as "conventional theater" no longer seems relevant—it's a fair question whether it was ever possible to define such a thing. Anyone hoping to understand this art must now move beyond identifying only what their creators reject, and start examining what they offer in its place. All the usual prefixes—"anti," "post," "non," "off-off"—only point us in the right direction. Once we arrive at this rich theatrical territory, we have to devise a new language and draw our own maps.

That effort makes formalists of us all—if only so we draft our maps correctly, by first revisiting the basics of theater craft. Even in the plays that seem, on the surface, to correspond to established norms (those of farce, say, in Ludlam's *Reverse Psychology,* or of the battle-of-wills, in *The Zoo Story*), these playwrights encourage us to step back and linger over the elements of performance longer than we're used to, seeing how they contain clues to the largest meanings of the drama. The design of space, the passage of time, the rhythms of speech and movement: these "invisibles" of theater, once meant to disappear when stories or characters are compelling enough, instead emerge from the background to tell their own stories. It's as if we're being reeducated in the technique of seeing, mastering lessons we skipped over long ago because we mistakenly thought they would diminish the rapture of spectatorship.

We have to go back to school because the playwrights are already there. The most disciplined of them hope that by handling the materials of drama more rigorously and analytically than before—like a painter determined to relearn the mixing of pigments and the sizing of canvas, then the fundamentals of figure drawing and perspective—they will reveal truths that eluded them in the past. Plays with untroubled surfaces and impeccable poise are not necessarily the ideal: Too often, these writers realize, such style obscures a story's darker implications or a character's less patterned emotions. As the first step toward creating a fuller picture, these writers incorporate into their plays their questions about the form: The action seems powered by their desire to know the anatomy of a character, not just his or her personality, and to learn how far one can stretch dramatic language and movement. Other questions follow: What kind of charge is released when one character encounters another? What do we mean when we speak of stage presence? What defines the stage itself?

This last question is the hardest to answer, for many of these plays take place in a world where change is the only constant. The very setting seems to have a life of its own. Not in a sensational way: The landscape become an extension of its inhabitants, reflecting anxieties or ambitions only partly expressed in words. "The rooms besiege me" says Jean Peters in *A Movie Star Has to Star in Black and White,* and as she struggles against them, she reveals a hypersensitivity shared by many other characters in this anthology. Jeep fears the walls closing in on him in *Action.* Marion's spirit suffocates in her husband's townhouse in *Abingdon Square.* The different kinds of compartments in *Night Coil* (two adjacent chambers), *American Notes* (a motel room and lobby, a forest hideaway), and *Imperceptible Mutabilities in the Third Kingdom* (the hull of a slave ship, measured obsessively throughout the play) all serve as psychological pressure-cookers for their occupants. The more they know about the space, the less they feel able to control it. Intimacy, when this unrelieved, provides no security.

Outside, the landscape is just as restless, forcing characters to acknowledge emotions they would prefer to avoid. In Williams's *The Gnädiges Fräulein,* the houses look blown sideways by an unforgiving wind. In Breuer's *B. Beaver Animation,* a flood reduces the stage to a pile of planks, all that remain of B. Beaver's dam. Nature won't stay outdoors in Tina Howe's *One Shoe Off,* where roots break through the floorboards, branches wind themselves around the beams, and ivy crawls up the furniture. And consider how many writers—Constance Congdon, Len Jenkin, Eric Overmyer, Ronald Tavel, Murray Mednick, David Greenspan, John Steppling, Mac Wellman—set their plays in vast wastelands. A catastrophe seems imminent, or perhaps has just occurred. Either way, one senses that the space has won only a temporary reprieve from change—whether it comes in the form of urban warfare in *Native Speech,* nuclear holocaust in *No Mercy,* the death of the moon in *The Hyacinth Macaw,* or simply a surge of fear whenever the unseen dogs start barking in *Standard of the Breed,* or one's conversations sink into the midnight silences of *American Notes.* In each of these plays, an enormous sky stretches above measureless darkness. Characters use up all their emotional resources just keeping their small pools of light from dwindling away. All of them could be asking the question Rhoda asks in *Rhoda in Potatoland:* "How can I relate to this place?"

As we map this new theatrical territory, we will also have to acknowledge the effects of time, another element of performance we can no longer take for granted. When narrative is observed, its passage can be excruciating: In *The Zoo Story* and *Action,* one intensely felt minute gives way to another, just as unremitting, as if the present tense dilated to ensure that the subtlest gradations of experience are dramatized. Equally disorienting are those plays where the past won't remain in the background and the future won't wait its turn. The former aren't mere memory plays: OyamO, Holly Hughes, Congdon, and Kennedy each create a remembered world that is capable of sucking characters irretrievably into its vortex. And the latter aren't standard-issue fantasias: For Guare, Arnold Weinstein, Naomi Iizuka, and Richard Caliban (among others), the speculative selves available in dream or fantasy slip the leash of the characters who summoned them, wreaking havoc on the best-laid plans for narrative. In fact, it is the rare character in this anthology who doesn't exist in all three tenses at once. Time becomes an almost tangible element of the environment—groped through, wallowed in, pushed back—capable, like a tornado, of dispersing a character among numerous contexts; ready, like a flood, to overwhelm him all at once with worlds ordinarily visited one at a time. This ordeal is rarely as moving as in Suzan-Lori Parks's theater. Time *is* space for the travelers of the Middle Passage: On the African side of the ocean, and of the time elapsed since crossing, stands one version of a character; on the other, American side stands a later version: "I was wavin...at my uther me who I could barely see....Me hollering uhcross thuh cliffs at my Self....Come home come home dont stay out too late."

Self-division is epidemic in all this theater: It is as if stage-time acts as an acid on its inhabitants, breaking apart images valid only for the moment they are perceived, revealing the composition of personalities beneath the surface of ordinary behavior, and sometimes allowing us to see a self and its ramifications (the kind of person a character denies, fears, or hopes to become) at the same time. The spectacle is unsettling: The person on stage, fickle about his form, can't be trusted, nor can he trust himself. Shepard's Shooter identifies a condition known to many characters when he describes seeing a collection of limbs that, despite his best efforts, he can't claim: "When I look at my hand, I get terrified. The sight of my feet in the bathtub. The skin covering me. That's all that's covering me." He is "afraid to sleep for fear his body might do something without him knowing."

Standard psychological language is useless when it comes to describing such characters. They're not just "alienated," for instance, when the floor barely supports them, the walls close in, and their entire world sheds a skin just when it starts to seem familiar. ("I got no references for this," says Jeep, "Suddenly it's shifted.") "Ambivalence" doesn't begin to suggest their radical fracturing of will. (Kennedy's Clara sits in the margins watching movie stars "star in her life" and speak her thoughts.) "Nostalgic" or "idealistic" temperaments aren't to be found here; only characters so unmoored to a context that, like Fornes's Marion, they feel like they're "drowning in vagueness" and "have no character." Nor are they simply "insecure" or "confused," but rather suffer such an extreme form of self-consciousness that the self dissolves under the laser-like scrutiny of consciousness. (Foreman's Rhoda can't reconcile her body with her "body of knowledge.") Indeed, when we look at that place onstage where a character is supposed to be—a figure bearing the burden of biography on the road to realized choices—

instead we see phantoms and mannequins, and the debris of their struggle to become complete. There are figures like Dinah in *One Shoe Off*—donning and doffing costumes from famous plays, unable to find one that suits her self-image—and the heroine of Craig Lucas's *Reckless*, frequently changing her name and so, she hopes, her destiny. There are the malcontents in *Muzeeka, Red Eye of Love, Gallows Humor*, and *Rodents and Radios*, casting aside jobs and family roles in their quest for their essential identities. There are the characters in Bullins's and Hughes's theater, refusing to accept race and gender roles without irony. And finally there are the collages and force fields that stand in for character in the works of Kennedy, Breuer, and Foreman—everything that the critic Elinor Fuchs has called (in the major study of this development, *The Death of Character*) "ephemeral constellations of thought, vision, and action."

The world I've described might sound decadent—a soulless place biding its time until it grinds down to nothing. But it doesn't come across that way on either the page or the stage. Indeed, for all the instability of the theatrical landscape, its citizens seem neither helpless nor resigned to their fate—leading one to wonder if reports of the death of at least *these* characters have been exaggerated. What accounts for the liveliness? Few of these writers say so explicitly, but most of them protest a life (and an artistic representation of life) conditioned by habit—that "guarantee of a dull inviolability," as Beckett wrote in *Proust*, "the ballast that chains the dog to his vomit." These playwrights doubt that the surface of life—our social roles, daily routines, conversations, and manners—is a fair indication of its depths; doubt, also, that our standard explanations of what motivates behavior and comprises various emotional states are sufficiently comprehensive. How could they be, they argue, when we live in a world littered with obstacles to spontaneous action, genuine feeling, and daring thought? In the turmoil of these plays, readers can find a critique of the unexamined, unexamining life. The catalogue of error is extensive. We are enslaved to custom. Our yen for originality is helpless against our fidelity to what's typical—especially the typical appearance of originality. Radicals subscribe to a code of manners as rigid as that of the conservatives. Our anger and joy may erupt unexpectedly but soon they flow into well-traveled channels of expression. Even madness has its history of variations, exerting its pull on those who would have their passion seem incomparable. Where habit and history recede, the superego looms, reviving inhibitions we thought we had outgrown and creating new causes for hesitation, just when we feel least self-conscious. The rare individual who perseveres in the face of such obstruction still cannot break through the limits of his or her language. The kinds of speech we celebrate as natural or instinctive are no less the product of social conditioning than the most clichéd—and so control our imaginative access to what we experience. A similar burden—the gravity of approved grace—affects the body, limiting the eloquence available in movement.

Taking strength from their diagnosis, these writers direct most of their energy to our pretensions to self-knowledge, asking how well we can know ourselves, if all we know are the effects of habit. Couldn't there be another, more surprising self biding time out of sight, whom we have yet to acknowledge? What might we have become if we weren't trained to recognize only the parts of our personality that confirm our expectations—our impoverished sense of the possible?

Such skepticism, for all its breadth, is not cynical. It is rooted in faith—a faith that promises a fuller life to those who defy its conventions strongly enough. This blend of skepticism and faith cues the most passionate speeches in this anthology, fuels the brightest characters, and steers the plots that are the hardest to chart. In *The Zoo Story,* when Jerry declares he wants to "really talk"—and so break through the wall of pleasantness and caution keeping him from Peter—he sets the agenda for numerous future characters, who even though they stop short of Jerry's ultimate, suicidal attempt at contact, share his ambition. Phillip in *Gallows Humor* isn't content with "jogging in step with the rest"; he wants to recover a "healthy fear" of life. Jack Argue in *Muzeeka,* for his part, wants to smash the "clay pot [covering] our brain...deadening our instincts" and free us to dance like his beloved Estruscans. Only then will he be able to "connect in some way" with those he loves and with himself. Many characters try to answer the question Clara asks A *Movie Star Has to Star in Black and White:* "With what or with whom can I co-exist in a true union?"—a longing Rosalyn Drexler takes to its comic extreme in *Softly, and Consider the Nearness,* where night after night a woman talks romantically to her only faithful companion, the television. Shepard sums up the urgency of all these projects in *Action*—"You hunt for a way of being with anyone." Fornes, in *Abingdon Square,* notes the care needed to succeed: "You have to know how to enter another person's life."

This hunger for genuine contact, and for the security that contact promises, determines every aspect of these characters' lives. Few of these plays contain easygoing, tennis-style dialogue; instead, speech is more desperate, as characters try to find a language that will secure their listeners' devotion, or relieve an anxiety, or unravel a mystery, or simply insure their place in the play. Many characters, in fact, speak of speech as much as anything else: "Say it!" they tell themselves. "Take stock in what I say!" "Sing!"—anything to propel them closer to what fascinates them. In each case, characters hope to transform an impersonal landscape into a self-created one, to leave a "stain upon the silence."

Movement and stillness are just as charged. Like conversation, they are opportunities for putting down roots, if pursued emphatically enough. The Saxons in *Imperceptible Mutabilities* have their photographs taken repeatedly to prove their existence. Tavel's Toby won't leave his chair; neither will Shepard's Shooter, even though he wants to "lick the corners" of the room. The act of taking stage, along with the fear of losing ground, have never been so literal.

When contact with someone or someplace outside themselves fails, characters turn inward: B. Beaver hopes to unify the father and the writer in him, just as Clara wants to combine writer, daughter, wife, and sister; Rhoda wants to "go toward the source...the essence, to dig deeper into memory." Others move far beyond the world of their fellows: Spiritual needs—old-fashioned expressions of belief—are strongest in plays where the disarray is particularly severe. Speaking of *Turandot* in *Rodents and Radios,* one character says "There's just such a relentless, unstoppable faith behind it…that's what gets to me—that against all reason to believe in anything there nevertheless has always been this blind urge, like sap through the trees.…We persist and flourish." The world of these plays may be spinning centrifugally, but their characters are spinning centripetally—determined to reach more integrated and versatile versions of themselves.

The "blind urge" belongs to these playwrights as much as to their characters. For them, writing is a form of pushing against the screen of their own habits and preconceptions. On the other side of that screen, they believe, a character's suffering isn't obscured by euphemism; his or her lust isn't tamed into mere desire; other kinds of hunger aren't cut to fit familiar categories of greed and ambition. Such a world stretches to accommodate the outsized and ill-mannered character. It also finds a place for contradiction—everything one edits out in the attempt to assemble an intelligible personality.

These writers know that if they are to reach this world, they will first have to relinquish the appealing image of playwright-as-marionetteer, master of his creations. And so they do: In this collection, one senses that the playwright is never sure of his or her characters, who seem in the shifting landscape of a play to be more than merely the sum of their actions and utterances. The texture of much of this writing suggests that a passionate encounter is going on just beneath its surface, in which a playwright pursues rather than merely dramatizes lives and events. Each scene is another stab at knowledge, written less to prove a point or demonstrate a theme than to gather evidence. Some pages even read as if the playwrights are quarreling with their own styles, trying to elude habitual turns-of-phrase and signature rhythms. At such moments, one imagines the writers urging themselves to stick with difficult subjects or characters until they bend, past the point when they seem merely understood. Perhaps then something unexpected—and truly revelatory—will emerge. For a writer of such an analytic temperament, characters are propositions, meant to be tested against the writer's sense of the full force of thought and action. Staging becomes a form of inquiry; language and movement, the instruments of that inquiry. There is much to learn. What is the life behind the character? What is the true action beneath the apparent story? What is the vision towards which the speech is rushing, beyond the confines of conversation? Beneath, behind, within, beyond—the operative words for this drama. Is there a kind of theater that can answer those questions, that can resist the domesticating charms of the form's history so that the lives it dramatizes will retain their wildness? If so, such a play will show us not only who we are, but also who we can be, when we are shorn of habit, speaking openly, answering the prompting of a newly accessible psyche. If this drama is representational—and I think it is—then it represents this hoped for, possible life, one available to audiences willing to match the careering style of these characters. Writing, for the most anxious of these writers, becomes writing-towards.

"Tho' obscur'd," writes Blake in *America*, "this is the form of the Angelic land." Len Jenkin uses the passage as his epigraph to *American Notes*, but it could set the tone for a number of these plays. The America that Blake invokes, and that many of these playwrights recognize, is an inspiring idea resisting translation into a real place. Traditions and values may accumulate, and histories may be written—but none of that guarantees an individual a sense of home. As the restlessness of these characters proves, one may inhabit a place and still not feel master of it—or even welcome. Moreover, such "obscurity" may be permanent; at least that's how it seems in much of this drama: For all their determination to penetrate their mysterious surroundings and redeem the promise of the Angelic land, these characters never feel they arrive. Up to the last moment, their skepticism battles their faith: Individuals who began by scorning received definitions of their lives are careful not to settle for their own. They think there is always another corner of the setting to discover, another variation of their identity to try. Potential lives and future destinations remain more seductive than current experiences. Are such characters destined for days of self-contradiction—needing clarity and self-integration on the one hand; on the other, drawn to a life of continuous reinvention? Which state will make them feel more alive, not merely present? Which offers the most security, the most freedom? The questions are left hanging.

No wonder, then, that the most memorable passages in this anthology are the least conclusive. They point to something—a place, a quality, an image of oneself—that has yet to be experienced, something that remains invulnerable to cheapening and misunderstanding. Entire plays are summarized in these abbreviated lines: "I just wanted to be…," says Phillip in *Gallows Humor,* and as his voice trails off, the play opens up to reveal a picture of the need and sadness (and also the hope) behind the workings of the imagination. "I want to become—touch some part of—," says Jack Argue in *Muzeeka,* and here again speech arches forward, trying to reach the perfect expression and the perfect attitude, to present the most convincing incarnation of the self. By the time we get to *Action,* the state of expectation is familiar, but there are still no words for what's expected: "I'm looking forward to my life. I'm looking forward to uh—me….My true position…up for grabs." Another failed declaration? Or rather, a deliberate evasion of identity, for fear of it being interpreted too narrowly? So many characters are poised on similar precipices—wondering if the next sensation will be the one to illuminate the meaning of their lives, but also dreading its consequences. Revelation rarely comes, and perhaps that's why they sound ecstatic: The thrill is in the search, and in speaking of the search: "I roam," says one character. "I keep looking for the action!," says a second. From still another: "Let's keep pushing!"

In this context, the word "experimental" may not be meaningless after all. These lives mature by trial and error; their final form remains open to revision as the chase proceeds. Such theater encourages us to keep pace and, like its characters, to defer conclusions about what we see in order to see more.

—MARC ROBINSON

Edward Albee

❧

The Zoo Story

•

THE PLAYERS

PETER: A man in his early forties, neither fat nor gaunt, neither handsome nor homely. He wears tweeds, smokes a pipe, carries horn-rimmed glasses. Although he is moving into middle age, his dress and his manner would suggest a man younger.

JERRY: A man in his late thirties, not poorly dressed, but carelessly. What was once a trim and lightly muscled body has begun to go to fat; and while he is no longer handsome, it is evident that he once was. His fall from physical grace should not suggest debauchery; he has, to come closest to it, a great weariness.

THE SCENE

It is Central Park, a Sunday afternoon in summer, the present. There are two park benches. Behind them: foliage, trees, sky. At the beginning PETER *is seated on one of the benches.*

As the curtain rises, PETER *is seated on the* DS *bench. He is reading a book. He stops reading, cleans his glasses, goes back to reading.* JERRY *enters.*

JERRY: [*Enters* UR, *crosses* L *to* US *of* L *bench, then* DL *to* L *of* DS *bench.*] I've been to the zoo. [PETER *doesn't notice.*] I said, I've been to the zoo. MISTER, I'VE BEEN TO THE ZOO!

PETER: Hm?...What?...I'm sorry, were you talking to me?

JERRY: I went to the zoo, and then I walked until I came here. Have I been walking north?

PETER: [*Puzzled*] North? Why...I...I think so. Let me see.

JERRY: [*Pointing past the audience*] Is that Fifth Avenue?

PETER: Why, yes; yes, it is.

JERRY: And what is that cross street there; that one, to the right?

PETER: That? Oh, that's Seventy-Fourth Street.

JERRY: And the zoo is around Sixty-Fifth Street; so, I've been walking north.

PETER: [*Anxious to get back to his reading*] Yes; it would seem so.

JERRY: Good old north.

PETER: [*Lightly, by reflex*] Ha, ha.

JERRY: [*After a slight pause*] But not due north.

PETER: I...well, no, not due north; but, we...call it north. It's northerly.

JERRY: [*Watches as* PETER, *anxious to dismiss, him prepares his pipe. Crosses* DR, *then* L *to* R *of* DS *bench.*] Well, boy; *you're* not going to get lung cancer, are you?

PETER: [*Looks up, a little annoyed, then smiles.*] No, sir. Not from this.

JERRY: [*Crosses behind bench to* DL *of bench*] No, sir. What you'll probably get is cancer of the mouth, and then you'll have to wear one of those things Freud wore after they took one whole side of his jaw away. What do they call those things?

PETER: [*Uncomfortable*] A prosthesis?

JERRY: The very thing! A prosthesis. You're an educated man, aren't you? Are you a doctor?

PETER: Oh, no; no. I read about it somewhere, *Time* magazine, I think. [*He turns to his book.*]

JERRY: Well, *Time* magazine isn't for blockheads.

PETER: No, I suppose not.

JERRY: [*Crosses* DR *to* DR *of bench. After a pause*] Boy, I'm glad that's Fifth Avenue there.

PETER: [*Vaguely*] Yes.

JERRY: I don't like the west side of the park much.

PETER: Oh? [*Then, slightly wary, but interested*] Why?

JERRY: [*Off-hand*] I don't know.

PETER: Oh. [*He returns to his book.*]

JERRY: [*Crosses* US *of bench to* L *of bench. He stands for a few seconds, looking at* PETER, *who finally looks up again, puzzled.*] Do you mind if we talk?

PETER: [*Obviously minding*] Why…no, no.

JERRY: [*crosses* DL] Yes you do; you do.

PETER: [*Puts his book down, his pipe out and away, smiling*] No, really; I don't mind.

JERRY: Yes you do.

PETER: [*Finally decided*] No; I don't mind at all, really.

JERRY: [*Turn front*] It's…it's a nice day.

PETER: [*Stares unnecessarily at the sky*] Yes. Yes, it is; lovely.

JERRY: [*To* PETER] I've been to the zoo.

PETER: Yes, I think you said so…didn't you?

JERRY: [*Front.*] You'll read about it in the papers tomorrow, if you don't see it on your TV tonight. [*To* PETER] You have TV, haven't you?

PETER: Why yes, we have two; one for the children.

JERRY: You're married!

PETER: [*With pleased emphasis*] Why, certainly.

JERRY: [*Crosses* DR, *above bench*] It isn't a law, for God's sake.

PETER: No…no, of course not.

JERRY: And you have a wife.

PETER: [*Bewildered by the seeming lack of communication*] Yes!

JERRY: And you have children.

PETER: Yes; two.

JERRY: Boys.

PETER: No, girls…both girls.

JERRY: But you wanted boys.

PETER: Well…naturally, every man wants a son, but…

JERRY: [*Lightly mocking*] But that's the way the cookie crumbles?

> JERRY *crosses* UC.

PETER: [*Annoyed*] I wasn't going to say that.

JERRY: And you're not going to have any more kids, are you?

> JERRY *crosses* L, *around* US *bench to* DL—L *of bench.*

PETER: [*A bit distantly*] No. No more. [PETER *turns to* JERRY. *Then back and irksome*] Why did you say that? How would you know about that?

JERRY: The way you cross your legs, perhaps; something in the voice. Or maybe I'm just guessing. Is it your wife?

PETER: [*Furious*] That's none of your business! [*A silence*] Do you understand? [JERRY *nods.* JERRY *crosses in two steps to* PETER. PETER *is quiet now.*] Well, you're right. We'll have no more children.

JERRY: [*Softy*] That is the way the cookie crumbles.

PETER: [*Forgiving*] Yes…I guess so.

JERRY: Well, now; what else?

PETER: What were you saying about the zoo...that I'd read about it, or see...?

JERRY: [*Crosses to* DR] I'll tell you about it, soon. [*Crosses* L *to behind* R *end of bench*] Do you mind if I ask you questions?

PETER: Oh, not really.

JERRY: I'll tell you why I do it; I don't talk to many people—except to say like: give me a beer, or where's the john, or what time does the feature go on, or keep your hands to yourself, buddy. You know—things like that.

PETER: I must say I don't....

JERRY: But every once in a while I like to talk to somebody, really *talk*, like to get to know somebody, know all about him.

PETER: [*Lightly laughing, still a little uncomfortable*] And am I the guinea pig for today?

JERRY: [*Crosses* R *and back*] On a sun-drenched Sunday afternoon like this? Who better than a nice married man with two daughters and...uh...a dog? [PETER *shakes his head.*] No? Two dogs. [PETER *shakes his head again.*] Hm. No dogs? [PETER *shakes his head, sadly.*] Oh, that's a shame. But you look like an animal man. CATS? [PETER *nods his head, ruefully.*] Cats! [*Foot on bench*] But, that can't be your idea. No, sir. Your wife and daughters? [PETER *nods his head.*] Is there anything else I should know?

PETER: [*He has to clear his throat.*] There are...there are two parakeets. One...uh...one for each of my daughters.

JERRY: Birds.

PETER: My daughters keep them in a cage in their bedroom.

JERRY: Do they carry disease? The birds.

PETER: I don't believe so.

JERRY: That's too bad. If they did you could set them loose in the house and the cats could eat them and die, maybe. [PETER *looks blank for a moment, then laughs. Crosses to* DL *in front of bench*] And what else? What do you do to support your enormous household?

PETER: I...uh...I have an executive position with a...a small publishing house. We...uh...we publish text books.

JERRY: That sounds nice; very nice. What do you make?

PETER: [*Still cheerful*] Now look here!

JERRY: Oh, come on.

PETER: Well, I make around eighteen thousand a year, but I don't carry more than forty dollars at any one time...in case you're a...a hold-up man...ha, ha, ha.

JERRY: [*Ignoring the above*] Where do you live? [PETER *is reluctant.*] Oh, look; I'm not going to rob you, and I'm not going to kidnap your parakeets, your cats, or your daughters.

PETER: [*Too loud*] I live between Lexington and Third Avenue, on Seventy-Fourth Street.

JERRY: That wasn't so hard, was it?

PETER: I didn't mean to seem…ah…it's that you don't really carry on a conversation; you just ask questions. And I'm…I'm normally…uh…reticent. Why do you just stand there?

JERRY: I'll start walking around in a little while, and eventually I'll sit down. [*Recalling*] Wait until you see the expression on his face.

PETER: What? Whose face? Look here; is this something about the zoo?

JERRY: [*Distantly*] The what?

PETER: The zoo; the zoo. Something about the zoo.

JERRY: The zoo?

PETER: You've mentioned it several times.

JERRY: [*Still distant, but returning abruptly*] The zoo? Oh, yes; the zoo. I was there before I came here. I told you that. Say, [*crosses behind bench to* UR *end of bench*] what's the dividing line between upper-middle-middle-class and lower-upper-middle-class?

PETER: My dear fellow, I…

JERRY: Don't my dear fellow me.

PETER: [*Unhappily*] Was I patronizing? I believe I was; I'm sorry. But, you see, your question about the classes bewildered me.

JERRY: [*Hands on bench*] And when you're bewildered you become patronizing?

PETER: I…I don't express myself too well, sometimes. [*He attempts a joke on himself.*] I'm in publishing, not writing.

JERRY: [*Amused, but not at the humor*] So be it. The truth is *I* was being patronizing. [*Crosses* DR]

PETER: Oh, now; you needn't say that.

It is at this point that JERRY *may begin to move about the stage with slowly increasing determination and authority but pacing himself, so that the long speech about the dog comes at the high point of the Act.*

JERRY: All right. Who are your favorite writers? Baudelaire and James Michener?

PETER: [*Wary*] Well, I like a great many writers; I have a considerable…catholicity of taste, if I may say so. Those two men are fine, each in his way. [*Warming up*] Baudelaire, of course…uh…is by far the finer of the two, but Michener has a place…in our…uh…national…

JERRY: Skip it.

PETER: I…Sorry.

JERRY: Do you know what I did before I went to the zoo today? I walked all the way up Fifth Avenue from Washington Square; all the way.

PETER: Oh; you live in the Village! [*This seems to enlighten* PETER.]

JERRY: No, I don't. I took the subway down to the Village so I could walk all the way up Fifth Avenue to the zoo. It's one of those things a person has to do; sometimes a person has to go a very long distance out of his way to come back a short distance correctly.

PETER: [*Almost pouting*] Oh; I thought you lived in the Village.

JERRY: What were you trying to do? Make sense out of things? Bring order? The old pigeon-hole bit? Well, that's easy. [*Crosses to* UC, R *of* US *bench*] I live in a four story brownstone rooming house on the upper West Side between Columbus Avenue and Central Park West. I live on the top floor; rear; west. [*Crosses to* L *of* DS *bench*] It's a laughably small room, and one of my walls is made of beaverboard; this beaverboard separates my room from another laughably small room, so I assume that the two rooms were once one room, a small room, but not necessarily laughable. The room beyond my beaverboard wall is occupied by a colored queen who always keeps his door open; well, not always, but *always* when he's plucking his eyebrows, which he does with Buddhist concentration. This colored queen has rotten teeth, which is rare, and he has a Japanese kimono, which is also pretty rare; and he wears this kimono to and from the john in the hall, which is pretty frequent. I mean, he goes to the john a lot. He never bothers me, and he never brings anyone up to his room. All he does is pluck his eyebrows, wear his kimono and go to the john. Now, the two front rooms on my floor are a little larger, I guess; but they're pretty small, too. There's a Puerto Rican family in one of them, a husband, a wife, and some kids; I don't know how many. These people entertain a lot. And in the other front room, there's somebody living there, but I don't know who it is. I've never seen who it is. [*Crosses to* R *of bench, behind bench*] Never. Never ever.

PETER: [*Embarrassed*] Why...why do you live there?

JERRY: [*From a distance again*] I don't know.

PETER: It doesn't sound like a very nice place...where you live.

JERRY: Well, no; it isn't an apartment in the East Seventies. But, then again, I don't have one wife, two daughters, two cats and two parakeets. [*Crosses up behind bench to below* US *bench.*] What I do have, I have toilet articles, a few clothes, a hot plate that I'm not supposed to have, a can opener, one that works with a key, you know; a knife, two forks and two spoons, one small, one large; three plates, a cup, a saucer, a drinking glass, two picture frames, both empty, eight or nine books, a pack of pornographic playing cards, regular deck, an old Western Union typewriter that prints nothing but capital letters, and a small strong box without a lock which has in it...what! [*Crossing* DL] Rocks! Some rocks...sea-rounded rocks I picked up on the beach when I was a kid. Under which...weighed down...are some letters... "*please*" letters... "please why don't you do this, and please why do you do that" letters. And "*when*" letters, too. "When will you write? When will you come?" When. These letters are from more recent years.

PETER: [*Stares glumly at his shoes, then...*] About those two empty picture frames...?

JERRY: I don't see why they need any explanation at all. Isn't it clear? I don't have pictures of anyone to put in them.

PETER: Your parents...perhaps...a girl friend....

JERRY: [*Crosses behind bench to* R *end of bench*] You're a very sweet man, and you're possessed of a truly enviable innocence. But good old Mom and good old Pop are dead...you know?...I'm broken up about it, too.... I mean really. BUT. That particular vaudeville act is playing the cloud circuit now, so I don't see how I can look at them, all neat and framed. Besides, or, rather, to be pointed about it, good old

Mom walked out on good old Pop when I was ten and a half years old; she embarked on an adulterous turn of our southern states...a journey of a year's duration...and her most constant companion...among others, among many others...was a Mr. Barleycorn. At least, that's what good old Pop told me after he went down...came back...brought her body north. We'd received the news between Christmas and New Year's, you see, that good old Mom had parted with the ghost in some dump in Alabama. And, without the ghost...she was less welcome. I mean, what was she? A stiff...a northern stiff. [*Crosses* UC] At any rate, good old Pop celebrated the New Year for an even two weeks and then slapped into the front of a somewhat moving city omnibus, which sort of cleaned things out family-wise. [*Crosses* DL *to* L *of* DS *bench*] Well no; then there was Mum's sister, who was given neither to sin nor the consolations of the bottle. I moved in on her, and my memory of her is slight excepting I remember still that she did all things dourly: sleeping, eating, working, praying. She dropped dead on the stairs to her apartment, my apartment then, too, on the afternoon of my high school graduation. A terribly middle-European joke, if you ask me.

PETER: Oh, my; oh, my.

JERRY: [*Step to* PETER] Oh, your what? But that was a long time ago, and I have no feeling about any of it that I care to admit to myself. Perhaps you can see, though, why good old Mom and good old Pop are frameless. What's your name? Your first name?

PETER: I'm Peter.

JERRY: I'd forgotten to ask you. I'm Jerry.

PETER: [*With a slight, nervous laugh*] Hello, Jerry.

JERRY: [*Nods his hello*] And let's see now; what's the point of having a girl's picture, especially in two frames. I have two picture frames, you remember. I never see the pretty little ladies more than once, and most of them wouldn't be caught in the same room with a camera. It's odd, and I wonder if it's sad.

PETER: The girls?

JERRY: No. [*Crosses* DR] I wonder if it's sad that I never see the little ladies more than once. I've never been able to have sex with, or [*turns to* PETER] how is it put?...make love to anybody more than once. Once; that's it.... Oh, wait; [*crosses two steps to* PETER *to* R *of bench*] for a week and a half, when I was fifteen...and I hang my head in shame that puberty was late...I was a h-o-m-o-s-e-x-u-a-l. I mean, I was queer...[*very fast*]...queer, queer, queer...with bells ringing, banners snapping in the wind. And for those eleven days, I met at least twice a day with the park superintendent's son...a Greek boy, whose birthday was the same as mine, except he was a year older. I think I was very much in love...maybe just with sex. But that was the jazz of a very special hotel, wasn't it? And now; oh, do I love the little ladies; really, I love them. For about an hour.

PETER: Well, it seems perfectly simple to me. You just haven't...

JERRY: [*Angry. Moves away* R] Look! Are you going to tell me to get married and have parakeets?

PETER: [*Angry himself*] Forget the parakeets! And stay single if you want to. It's no business of mine. I didn't start this conversation in the…

JERRY: [*Crosses in to* PETER] All right, all right. I'm sorry. All right? You're not angry?

PETER: [*Laughing*] No, I'm not angry.

JERRY: [*Relieved*] Good. [*Crosses* L *to behind* R *end of bench. Now back to his previous tone*] Interesting that you asked me about the picture frames. I would have thought that you would have asked me about the pornographic playing cards.

PETER: [*With a knowing smile*] Oh, I've seen those cards.

JERRY: [*Leans on* R *of bench*] That's not the point. [*Laughs*] I suppose when you were a kid you and your pals passed them around, or you had a pack of your own.

PETER: Well, I guess a lot of us did.

JERRY: And you threw them away just before you got married.

PETER: Oh, now; look here. I didn't *need* anything like that when I got older.

JERRY: No?

PETER: [*Embarrassed*] I'd rather not talk about these things.

JERRY: [*Crosses to* UC] So? Don't. Besides, I wasn't trying to plumb your post-adolescent sexual life and hard times; what I wanted to get at is the value difference between pornographic playing cards when you're a kid, and pornographic playing cards when you're older. It's that when you're a kid you use the cards as a substitute for real experience, and when you're older you use real experience as a substitute for the fantasy. [*Crosses to* DR, *slow*] But I imagine you'd rather hear about what happened at the zoo.

PETER: [*Enthusiastic*] Oh, yes; the zoo. [*Then awkward*] That is…if you…

JERRY: [*Crosses* UL *around* US *bench to* L *of* DS *bench—slow*] I've told you about the fourth floor of the rooming house where I live. I think the rooms are better as you go down, floor by floor. I guess they are; I don't know. I don't know any of the people on the third or second floors. Oh, wait! I do know that there's a lady living on the third floor, in the front. I know because she cries all the time. Whenever I go out or come back in, whenever I pass her door, I always hear her crying, muffled, but…very determined. Very determined, indeed. But the one I'm getting to, and all about the dog, is the landlady. I don't [*crosses to* RC *to trash can*] like to use words that are too harsh in describing people. I don't like to. But the landlady is a fat, ugly, mean, stupid, unwashed, misanthropic, cheap, drunken bag of garbage. [*Crosses* DL] And you may have noticed that I very seldom use profanity, so I can't describe her as well as I might.

PETER: You describe her…vividly.

JERRY: Well, thanks. Anyway, she has a dog, [DL] and she and her dog are the gatekeepers of my dwelling. The woman is bad enough; she leans around in the entrance hall, spying to see that I don't bring in things or people, and when she's had her mid-afternoon pint of lemon-flavored gin she always stops me in the hall, and grabs ahold of my coat or my arm, and she presses her disgusting body up against me to keep me in a corner so she can talk to me. The smell of her body and her breath…you can't imagine it…and somewhere, somewhere in the back of that pea-sized brain of hers, an organ developed just enough to let her eat, drink, and emit, she has some foul parody of sexual desire. And I, Peter, I am the object of her sweaty lust.

PETER: That's disgusting. That's...horrible.

JERRY: [*Crosses in to* PETER] But I have found a way to keep her off. When she talks to me, when she presses herself to my body and mumbles about her room and how I should come there, I merely say: but, Love; wasn't yesterday enough for you, and the day before? Then she puzzles, she makes slits of her tiny eyes, she sways a little, and then, Peter, and it is at this moment that I think I might be doing some good in that tormented house, a simple-minded smile begins to form on her unthinkable face, and she giggles and groans as she thinks about yesterday and the day before; as she believes and relives what never happened. [*Crosses* L, *away from* PETER] Then, she motions to that black monster of a dog she has, and she goes back to her room. And I am safe until our next meeting.

PETER: It's so...[*Shudders*] I find it hard to believe that people such as that really are.

JERRY: [*Lightly mocking*] It's for reading about, isn't it?

PETER: [*Seriously*] Yes.

JERRY: And fact is better left to fiction. You're right, Peter. [*Crosses* US *of bench to* R *end of bench*] Well, what I have been meaning to tell you about is the dog; I shall, now.

PETER: [*Nervously*] Oh, yes; the dog.

JERRY: Don't go. You're not thinking of going, are you?

PETER: Well...no, I don't think so.

JERRY: [*As if to a child*] Because after I tell you about the dog, do you know what then? Then...then I'll tell you about what happened at the zoo.

PETER: [*Laughing faintly*] You're...you're full of stories, aren't you?

JERRY: You don't *have* to listen. Nobody is holding you here; remember that. Keep that in your mind.

PETER: [*Irritably*] I know that.

JERRY: You do? Good. [*The following long speech, it seems to me, should be done with a great deal of action, to achieve a hypnotic effect on* PETER, *and on the audience, too. Some specific actions have been suggested, but the director and the actor playing* JERRY *might best work it out for themselves.*] ALL RIGHT. [*Crosses* L *around bench to* DLC. *As if reading from a huge billboard*] THE STORY OF JERRY AND THE DOG! [*Natural again*] What I am going to tell you has something to do with how sometimes it's necessary to go a long distance out of the way in order to come back a short distance correctly; or, maybe I only think that it has something to do with that. But, it's why I went to the zoo today, and why I walked north...northerly, rather...until I came here. All right. The dog, I think I told you this, is a black monster of a beast: an oversized head, tiny tiny ears, and eyes...bloodshot, infected, maybe; and a body you can see the ribs through the skin. The dog is black, all black; all black except for the bloodshot eyes, and...yes...and an open sore on its...*right* forepaw; that is red, too. And, oh yes; the poor monster, and I do believe it's an old dog...it's certainly a misused one...almost always has an erection...of sorts. That's red, too. And...what else?...oh, yes; there's a grey-yellow-white color, too, when he bares his fangs. [L *of bench*] Like this: Grrrrrrrrr! Which is what he did when he saw me for the first time…the day I moved in. I worried about that animal the very first minute I met him. Now, animals don't take to me like Saint Francis had birds hanging off him all the time. What I mean is: animals are indifferent to me…like people [*he smiles slightly*]…most of the time. [*Crosses* R, *front of bench*] But this dog wasn't indifferent. From the very beginning he'd snarl and then go for me, to get one of my legs. Not like he was rabid, you know; he was sort of a stumbly dog, but he wasn't half-assed, either. It was a good, stumbly run; but I always got away. [*Crosses in to* R *of bench*] He got a piece of my trouser leg, look, you can see right here, where it's mended; he got that the second day I lived there; but I kicked free and got upstairs fast, so that was that. [*Puzzles. Crosses* DR] I still don't know to this day how the other roomers manage it, but you know what I *think:* I think it had to do only with me. Cozy. So. Anyway, this went on for over a week, whenever I came in; but never when I went out. That's funny. Or, it *was* funny. I could pack up and live in the street for all the dog cared. Well, I thought about it up [*Crosses* u *to* R *of bench*] in my room one day, one of the times after I'd bolted upstairs, and I made up my mind. I decided first, I'll kill the dog with kindness, and if that doesn't work…I'll just kill him. [PETER *winces.*] Don't react, Peter; just listen. [*Crosses* DR] So, the next day I went out and bought a bag of hamburgers, medium rare, no catsup, no onion; and on the way home I threw away all the rolls and kept just the meat. [*Action for the following perhaps*] When I got back to the rooming house the dog was waiting for me. I half opened the door that led in to the entrance hall, and there he was; waiting for me. It figured. I went in, very cautiously, and I had the hamburgers, you remember; I opened the bag, and I set the meat down about twelve feet from where the dog was snarling at me. Like so! He snarled; stopped snarling; sniffed; moved slowly; then faster; then faster toward the meat. Well, when he got to it he stopped, and he looked at me. I smiled; but tentatively, you understand. He turned his face back to the hamburgers, smelled, sniffed some more, and then… RRRAAAAGGGGHHHH, like that…he tore into them. It was as if he had never eaten anything in his life before, except like garbage. Which might very well have been the truth. I don't think the landlady ever eats anything *but* garbage. But. He ate all the hamburgers, almost all at once, making sounds in his throat like a woman. *Then,* when he'd finished the meat, the hamburger, and tried to eat the paper, too, he sat down and smiled. I think he smiled; I know cats do. It was a very gratifying few moments. [*Crosses* UR *two steps*] Then, BAM, he snarled and made for me again. He didn't get me this time, either. So, [*Crosses* UC *around basket*] I got upstairs, and I lay down on my bed and started to think about the dog again. To be truthful, I was offended, and I was damn mad, too. It was six perfectly good hamburgers with not enough pork in them to make it disgusting. [*Crossing* DL, *slow*] I was offended. But, after a while, I decided to try it for a few more days. If you think about it, this dog had what amounted to an antipathy toward me; really. And, I wondered if I mightn't overcome this antipathy. [DL] So I tried it for five more days, but it was always the same: snarl, sniff; move; faster; stare; gobble;

RAAGGHHH; smile; snarl; BAM. Well, now; by this time Columbus Avenue was strewn with hamburger rolls, and I was less offended than disgusted. [UL *of* PETER] So, I decided to kill the dog. [PETER *raises a hand in protest.*] Oh, don't be so alarmed, Peter; I didn't succeed. The day I [*crosses* DR] tried to kill the dog I bought only one hamburger and what I thought was a murderous portion of rat poison. When I bought the hamburger I asked the man not to bother with the roll, all I wanted was the meat. [*Front*] I expected some reaction from him, like: We don't sell no hamburgers without rolls; or, wha' d'ya wanna do, eat it out 'a ya han's? But no; he smiled benignly, wrapped up the hamburger in waxed paper, and said: A bite for ya pussy-cat? I wanted to say: No, not really; it's part of a plan to poison a dog I know. But, you can't say "a dog I know" without sounding funny; so I said, a little too loud, I'm afraid, and too formally: YES, A BITE FOR MY PUSSY-CAT. People looked up. It always happens when I try to simplify things; people look up. But that's neither hither nor thither. So. [*Crosses* DL] On my way back to the rooming house, I kneaded the hamburger and the rat poison together between my hands, at that point feeling as much sadness as disgust. I opened the door to the entrance hall, and there the monster was, waiting to take the offering and then jump me. Poor bastard; he never learned that the moment he took to smile before he went for me gave me time enough to get out of range. BUT, there he was; malevolence with an erection, waiting. I put the poison patty down, moved toward the stairs and watched. The poor animal gobbled the food down as usual, smiled, as usual, which made me almost sick, and then, BAM. [*Crosses* UL] But, I sprinted up the stairs, as usual, and the dog didn't get me, as usual. [UL—L *of* US *bench*] AND IT CAME TO PASS THAT THE BEAST WAS DEATHLY ILL. I knew this because he no longer attended me, [*crossing* DL *to below* US *bench*] and because the landlady sobered up. She stopped me in the hall the same evening of the attempted murder and confided the information that God had struck her puppy-dog a surely fatal blow. She had forgotten her bewildered lust and her eyes were wide open for the first time. They looked like the dog's eyes. She snivelled and implored me to pray for the animal. I wanted to say to her: Madam, I have myself to pray for, the colored queen, the Puerto Rican family, the person in the front room whom I've never seen, the woman who cries deliberately behind her closed door, and the rest of the people in all rooming houses, everywhere; besides, Madam, I don't understand how to pray. But…to simplify things…I told her I would pray. She looked up. She said that I was a liar, and that I probably wanted the dog to die. I told her, and there was so much truth here, that I didn't want the dog to die. I didn't, and not just because I'd poisoned him. I'm afraid that I must tell you I wanted the dog to live so that I could see what our new relationship might come to. [PETER *indicates his increasing displeasure and slowly growing antagonism. Crosses* R *to* PETER] Please understand, Peter; that sort of thing is important. You must believe me; it is important. We have to know the effect of our actions. [*Another deep sigh. Crosses* DL] Well, anyway; the dog recovered. I have no idea why, unless he was a descendant of the puppy that guarded the gates of hell or some such resort. At any rate, the dog recovered his health and the landlady recovered her thirst, in no way altered by the bow-wow's deliverance. When I came home from a movie that was playing on Forty-Second Street, a movie I'd seen, or one that was very much like one or several I'd seen, after the landlady told me puppykins was better, I was so hoping for the dog to be waiting for me. I was…well, how would you put it…enticed?…fascinated? …no, I don't think so…heart shatteringly anxious, that's it; I was heart-shatteringly anxious to confront my friend again. [PETER *reacts scoffingly.*] Yes, Peter; friend. That's the only word for it. I was heart-shatteringly etcetera to confront my doggy friend again. I came in the door and advanced, unafraid, to the center of the entrance hall. The beast was there…looking at me. And, you know, he looked better for his scrape with the nevermind. I stopped; I looked at him; he looked at me. I think…I think we stayed a long time that way…still, stone-statue…just looking at one another. I looked more into his face than he looked into mine. I mean, I can concentrate longer at looking into a dog's face than a dog can concentrate at looking into mine, or into anybody else's face, for that matter. But during that twenty seconds or two hours that we looked into each other's face, we made contact. Now, here is what [*crosses to* PETER] I had wanted to happen: I loved the dog now, and I wanted him to love me. I had tried to love, and I had tried to kill, and both had been unsuccessful by themselves. I hoped…and I don't really know why I expected the dog to understand anything, much less my motivations…I hoped that the dog would understand. [PETER *seems to be hypnotized. Crosses* UC—L *of basket*] It's just…it's just that… [JERRY *is abnormally tense now.*]…it's just that if you can't deal with people, you have to make a start somewhere. WITH ANIMALS! [*Much faster now, and like a conspirator*] Don't you see? A person has to have some way of dealing with SOMETHING. If not with people…if not with people…SOME-THING. With a bed, with a cockroach, with a mirror…no, that's too hard, that's one of the last steps. With a cockroach, with a…with a…with a carpet, a roll of toilet paper…no, not that, either…that's a mirror, too; always check bleeding. You see how hard it is to find things? With a street corner, and too many lights, all colors reflecting on the oily-wet streets…with a wisp of smoke, a wisp…of smoke…with…with pornographic playing cards, with a strong box…WITHOUT A LOCK…with love, with vomiting, with crying, with fury because the pretty little ladies aren't pretty little ladies, with making money with your body which is an act of love and I could prove it, with howling because you're alive; with God. How about that? WITH GOD WHO IS A COLORED QUEEN WHO WEARS A KIMONO AND PLUCKS HIS EYEBROWS, WHO IS A WOMAN WHO CRIES WITH DE-TERMINATION BEHIND HER CLOSED-DOOR…with God who, I'm told, turned his back on the whole thing some time ago…with…some day, with people. [JERRY *sighs the next word heavily.*] People. With an idea; a concept. And where better, where ever better in this humiliating excuse for a jail, where better to communicate one single, simple-minded idea than in an entrance hall? Where? It would be A START! Where better to make a beginning…to understand and just possibly be understood…a beginning of an understanding, than with…. [*Here* JERRY *seems to fall into almost grotesque fatigue.*]...than with A DOG. Just that; a dog. [*Here there is a silence that might be prolonged for a moment or so, then* JERRY *wearily finishes his story.*] A dog. It seemed like a perfectly sensible idea. [*Crosses* D *to* L *of* PETER] Man is a dog's best friend, remember. So: the dog and I looked at each other. I longer than the dog. And what I saw then has been the same ever since. Whenever the dog and I see each other we both stop where we are. We regard each other with a mixture of sadness and suspicion, and then we feign indifference. We walk past each other safely; we have an understanding. It's very sad, but you'll have to admit that it is an understanding. We had made many attempts at contact, and we had failed. The dog has returned to garbage, and I to solitary free passage. *I* have not returned, I mean to say. I have *gained* solitary free passage, if that much further loss can be said to be gain. I have learned that neither kindness nor cruelty by themselves, independent of each other, creates any effect beyond themselves; and I have learned that the two combined, together, at the same time, are the teaching emotion. And what is gained is loss. And what has been the result: the dog and I have attained a compromise; more of a bargain, really. We neither love nor hurt because we do not try to reach each other. And, *was* trying to feed the dog an act of love? And, perhaps, was the dog's attempt to bite me *not* an act of love? If we can so misunderstand, well then, why have we invented the word love in the first place? [*There is silence.*] The story of Jerry and the Dog: the end. [PETER *is silent.*] Well, Peter? [JERRY *is suddenly cheerful.*] Well, Peter? Do you think I could sell that story to the *Readers Digest* and make a couple of hundred bucks for *The Most Unforgettable Character I've Ever Met?* Huh? [JERRY *is animated, but* PETER *is disturbed.*] Oh, come on now, Peter; tell me what you think.

PETER: [*Numb*] I...I don't understand what...I don't think I...[*Now, almost tearfully.*] Why did you tell me all of this?

JERRY: Why not?

PETER: I DON'T UNDERSTAND!

JERRY: [*Furious, but whispering*] That's a lie.

PETER: No. No, it's not.

JERRY: [*Quietly*] I tried to explain it to you as I went along. I went slowly; it all has to do with...

PETER: I DON'T WANT TO HEAR ANY MORE. I don't understand you, or your landlady, or her dog.

JERRY: [*Confused*] *Her* dog! I thought it was my...No. No, you're right. It *is* her dog. [*Looks at* PETER *intently, shaking his head*] I don't know what I was thinking about; of course you don't understand. [*In a monotone, wearily*] I don't live in your block; I'm not married to two parakeets, or whatever your set-up is. I am a *permanent transient,* and my home is the sickening rooming-houses on the West Side of New York City, which is the greatest city in the world. Amen.

PETER: I'm...I'm sorry; I didn't mean to....

JERRY: Forget it. I suppose you don't quite know what to make of me, eh?

PETER: [*A joke*] We get all kinds in publishing. [*Chuckles*]

JERRY: You're a funny man. [*He forces a laugh*] You know that? You're a very...a richly comic person.

PETER: [*Modestly, but amused*] Oh, now, not really. [*Still chuckling*]

JERRY: Peter, do I annoy you, or confuse you?

PETER: [*Lightly*] Well, I must confess that this wasn't the kind of afternoon I'd anticipated.

JERRY: You mean, I'm not the gentleman you were expecting.

PETER: I wasn't expecting anybody.

JERRY: No, I don't imagine you were. But I'm here, and I'm not leaving.

PETER: [*Reaching across* JERRY *for book*] Well, you may not be, but I must be getting home now.

JERRY: Oh, come on; stay a while longer.

PETER: I really should get home; you see....

JERRY: [*Tickles* PETER's *ribs with his fingers*] Oh, come on.

PETER: [*He is very ticklish, as* JERRY *continues to tickle him his voice becomes falsetto.*] No, I...OHHHHHHH! Don't do that. Stop, stop. Ohhh, no, no.

JERRY: Oh, come on.

PETER: [*As* JERRY *tickles. Ad Lib.*] Oh, hee, hee, hee. I must go. I...hee, hee, hee. After all, stop, stop, hee, hee, hee, after all, the parakeets will be getting dinner ready soon. Hee, hee. And the cats are setting the table. Stop, stop, and, and...[PETER *is beside himself now.*]...and we're having...hee, hee...uh...ho, ho, ho. [JERRY *stops tickling* PETER, *but the combination of the tickling and his own mad whimsy have* PETER *laughing almost hysterically. As his laughter continues, then subsides,* JERRY *watches him with a curious fixed smile.* JERRY *moves to* PETER's *bench and sits down beside him. This is the first time* JERRY *has sat down during the play.*]

JERRY: Peter?

PETER: Oh, ha, ha, ha, ha, ha. What? What?

JERRY: Listen, now.

PETER: Oh, ho, ho. What...what is it, Jerry? Oh, my.

JERRY: [*Mysteriously*] Peter, do you want to know what happened at the zoo?

PETER: Ah, ha, ha. The what? Oh, yes; the zoo. Oh, ho, ho. Well, I had my own zoo there for a moment with...hee, hee, the parakeets getting dinner ready, and the...ha, ha, whatever it was, the...

JERRY: [*Calmly*] Yes, that was very funny, Peter. I wouldn't have expected it. But do you want to hear about what happened at the zoo, or not?

PETER: Yes. Yes, by all means; tell me what happened at the zoo. Oh, my. I don't know what happened to me.

JERRY: Now I'll let you in on what happened at the zoo; but first, I should tell you why I went to the zoo. I went to the zoo to find out more about the way people exist with animals, and the way animals exist with each other, and with people too. It probably wasn't a fair test, what with everyone separated by bars from everyone else, the animals for the most part from each other, and always the people from the animals. But, if it's a zoo, that's the way it is. [*He pokes* PETER *on the arm.*] Move over.

PETER: [*Friendly*] I'm sorry, haven't you enough room? [*He shifts a little.*]

JERRY: [*Smiling slightly*] Well, all the animals are there, and all the people are there, and it's Sunday and all the children are there. [*He pokes* PETER *again.*] Move over.

PETER: [*Patiently, still friendly*] All right.

> *He moves some more, and* JERRY *has all the room he might need.*

JERRY: And it's a hot day, so all the stench is there, too, and all the balloon sellers, and all the ice cream sellers, and all the seals are barking, and all the birds are screaming. [*Pokes* PETER *harder*] Move over!

PETER: [*Beginning to be annoyed*] Look here, you have more than enough room!

> *But he moves more and is now fairly cramped at one end of the bench.*

JERRY: And I am there, and it's feeding time at the lion's house, and the lion keeper comes into the lion cage, one of the lion cages, to feed one of the lions. [*Punches* PETER *on the arm hard*] MOVE OVER!

PETER: [*Very annoyed*] I can't move over any more, and stop hitting me. What's the matter with you?

JERRY: Do you want to hear the story?

> *Punches* PETER's *arm again.*

PETER: [*Flabbergasted*] I'm not so sure! I certainly don't want to be punched in the arm.

JERRY: [*Punches* PETER's *arm again.*] Like that?

PETER: Stop it! What's the matter with you?

JERRY: I'm crazy, you bastard.

PETER: That isn't funny.

JERRY: Listen to me, Peter. I want this bench. You go sit on the bench over there, and if you're good I'll tell you the rest of the story.

PETER: [*Flustered*] But...what ever for? What *is* the matter with you? Besides, I see no reason why I should give up this bench. I sit on this bench almost every Sunday afternoon, in good weather. It's secluded here; there's never anyone sitting here, so I have it all to myself.

JERRY: [*Softly*] Get off this bench, Peter; I want it.

PETER: [*Almost whining*] No.

JERRY: I said I want this bench, and I'm going to have it. Now get over there.

PETER: People can't have everything they want. You should know that; it's a rule: people can have some of the things they want, but they can't have everything.

JERRY: [*Laughs*] Imbecile! You're slow-witted!

PETER: Stop that!

JERRY: You're a vegetable! Go lie down on the ground.

PETER: [*Intense*] Now *you* listen to me. I've put up with you all afternoon.

JERRY: Not really.

PETER: LONG ENOUGH. I've put up with you long enough. I've listened to you because you seemed...well, because I thought you wanted to talk to somebody.

JERRY: You put things well; economically, and, yet...oh, what is the word I want to put justice to your...JESUS, you make me sick...get off here and give me my bench.

PETER: MY BENCH!

JERRY: [*Pushes* PETER *almost, but not quite, off the bench*] Get out of my sight.

PETER: [*Regaining his position*] God da...mn you. That's enough! I've had enough of you. I will not give up this bench; you can't have it, and that's that. Now, go away. [JERRY *snorts, but does not move.*] Go away, I said. [JERRY *does not move.*] Get away from here. [JERRY *pushes* PETER *off bench to* DR] If you don't move on...you're a bum...that's what you are. [PETER *crosses in* L *to* R *of bench.*]...If you don't move on, I'll get a policeman here and make you go. [JERRY *laughs, stays*] I warn you, I'll call a policeman.

JERRY: [*Softly*] You won't find a policeman around here; they're all over on the west side of the park chasing fairies down from trees or out of the bushes. That's all they do. That's their function. So scream your head off; it won't do you any good.

PETER: [*Crosses* DL] POLICE! I warn you, I'll have you arrested. [*Crosses* URC] PO-LICE! [*Pause. Crosses* DR] I said POLICE! [*Pause*] I feel ridiculous.

JERRY: You look ridiculous: a grown man screaming for the police on a bright Sunday afternoon in the park with nobody harming you. If a policeman *did* fill his quota and come sludging over this way he'd probably take you in as a nut.

PETER: [*With disgust and impotence. Crosses in to* JERRY *a step*] Great God, I just came here to read, and now you want me to give up the bench. You're mad.

JERRY: I'm on your precious bench, and you're never going to have it for yourself again.

PETER: [*Furious. Crosses in to* JERRY *at* R *of bench*] Look, you; get off my bench. I don't care if it makes any sense or not. I want this bench to myself; I want you OFF IT!

JERRY: [*Mocking*] Aw...look who's mad.

PETER: GET OUT!

JERRY: No.

PETER: I WARN YOU!

JERRY: Do you know how ridiculous you look *now*?

PETER: [*His fury and self-consciousness have possessed him.*] It doesn't matter. [*He is almost crying*] GET AWAY FROM MY BENCH!

JERRY: Why? You have everything in the world you want; you've told me about your home, and your family, and *your own* little zoo. You have everything, and now you want this bench. Are these the things men fight for? Tell me, Peter, is this bench, this iron and this wood, is this your honor? Can you think of anything more absurd?

PETER: [*Crosses* R *behind bench to* L *of bench*] Absurd? Look, I'm not going to talk to you about honor, or even try to explain it to you. Besides, it isn't a question of honor; but even if it were you wouldn't understand.

JERRY: [*Contemptuously*] You don't even know what you're saying, do you? This is probably the first time in your life you've had anything more trying to face than changing your cats' toilet box.

PETER: [*Quivering*] I've come here for years; I have hours of great pleasure, great satisfaction, right here. And that's important to a man. I'm a responsible person, and I'm a GROWN-UP. This is my bench, and you have no right to take it away from me.

JERRY: Fight for it, then. Defend yourself; defend your bench.

PETER: You've *pushed* me to it. Get up and fight.

JERRY: Like a man?

PETER: [*Still angry*] Yes, like a man, if you insist on mocking me even further.

JERRY: I'll have to give you credit for one thing: you *are* a vegetable, and a slightly near-sighted one, I think....

PETER: THAT'S ENOUGH....

JERRY: ...but, you know, as they say on TV all the time—you know—and I mean this, Peter, you have a certain dignity; it surprises me....

PETER: STOP.

JERRY: [*Rises lazily, crosses* DL *to* PETER] Very well, Peter, we'll battle for the bench, but we're not evenly matched.

He takes out and clicks open an ugly-looking knife.

PETER: [DR. *Suddenly awakening to the reality of the situation.* PETER *being backed* DL *then* DR *by* JERRY] You *are* mad! You're stark raving mad! YOU'RE GOING TO KILL ME!

But before PETER *has time to think what to do,* JERRY *tosses the knife at* PETER's *feet.*

JERRY: [RC] There you go. [*Tosses knife to* PETER.] Pick it up. You have the knife and we'll be more evenly matched.

PETER: [*Horrified. Moves* UR. JERRY *crosses* UR. *Catches* PETER. *Pushes* PETER DR] No!

JERRY: [*Rushes over to* PETER, *grabs him by the collar,* PETER *rises, their faces almost touch.*] Now you pick up that knife and you fight with me. You fight for your self-respect; you fight for that god-damned bench.

PETER: [*Crosses to* DL, *then* UC. *He is caught by* JERRY *at* ULS] No! Let...let go of me! He...help!

JERRY: [*Backing* PETER US *of bench. Slaps* PETER *on each "fight"*] You fight, you miserable bastard; fight for that bench; fight for your parakeets; fight for your cats, fight for your two daughters; fight for your life; fight for your manhood, you pathetic little vegetable. [*Throws* PETER *to* DR *in front of bench*] You couldn't even get your wife with a male child.

PETER: It's a matter of genetics, not manhood, you...you monster. [*He darts down, picks up the knife and backs off a little, he is breathing heavily.*] I'll give you one last chance; get out of here and leave me alone!

JERRY *jumps over bench to trashcan.* PETER *holds the knife with a firm arm, but far in front of him, not to attack but to defend.*

JERRY: [*Sighs heavily*] So be it!

With a rush he charges PETER *and impales himself on the knife. Tableau: For just a moment, complete silence,* JERRY *impaled on the knife at the end of* PETER's *still firm arm. Then* PETER *screams, pulls away leaving the knife in* JERRY. JERRY *is motionless, on point. When he too, screams, and it is the sound of an infuriated and fatally wounded animal. With the knife in him he stumbles back to the bench that* PETER *had vacated. He crumbles there, sitting facing* PETER, *his eyes wide in agony, his mouth open.*

PETER: [*Whispering* DR] Oh my God, oh my God, oh my God....
   He repeats these words many times, very rapidly.

JERRY: [JERRY *is dying, but now his expression seems to change. His features relax, and while his voice varies, sometimes wrenched with pain, for the most part be seems removed from his dying. He smiles.*] Thank you, Peter. I mean that, now; thank you very much. [PETER'S *mouth drops open. He cannot move, he is transfixed.*] Oh, Peter, I was so afraid I'd drive you away. [*He laughs as best he can.*] You don't know how afraid I was you'd go away and leave me. Well, here we are. You see? Here we are. Peter?...Peter...thank you. I came unto you [*he laughs, so faintly*] and you have comforted me. Dear Peter.

PETER: [*Almost fainting*] Oh my God!

JERRY: You'd better go now. Somebody might come by, and you don't want to be here when anyone comes.

PETER: [*Does not move, but begins to weep*] Oh my God, oh my God.

JERRY: [*Most faintly, now, he is very near death.*] And, Peter, I'll tell you something now; you're not really a vegetable; it's all right, you're an animal. You're an animal, too. But you'd better hurry now, Peter. Hurry, you'd better go...see? [PETER *slowly crosses* UR. JERRY *takes a handkerchief and with great effort and pain wipes the knife handle clean of finger prints.*] Hurry away, Peter. Wait...wait, Peter. Take your book...book. [PETER *stops.*] Right here...beside me...on your bench...my bench, rather. Come...take your book. [PETER *crosses to* L *of bench*] Hurry...Peter. [PETER L *of bench, gets book from* JERRY'S *hand.*] Very good, Peter...very good. Now...hurry away. [PETER *hesitates for a moment, then flees,* L] Hurry away...[*His eyes are closed now.*] Hurry away, your parakeets are making the dinner...the cats...are setting the table....

PETER: [*Crosses* UL *and exits*] Oh my God. Oh my God. [*Off: A pitiful howl* OH MY GOD!

JERRY: [*His eyes still closed, he shakes his head and speaks, a combination of scornful mimicry and supplication.*] Oh...my...God. [*He is dead.*]

CURTAIN

Arnold Weinstein

Red Eye of Love

Red Eye of Love

•

Red Eye of Love was presented at The Living Theatre in New York on June 12, 1961 by Sam Cohn, John Wulp, and Julia Miles. It was directed and designed by Mr. Wulp, with incidental score by William Bolcom, costumes by Willa Kim, and lighting by Nicola Cernovich. The cast was as follows:

WILMER FLANGE, *a poor young fool*	George Latchford
O.O. MARTINAS, *richer, older*	Michael Vale
SELMA CHARGESSE, *a loving young thing*	Jane Romano
FIRST POLICEMAN, *a music lover*	Al Mancini
SECOND POLICEMAN, *a people hater*	Jim Gormley
CAB DRIVER	Barry Primus
VENDOR	Jerry DeLuise
FRANCES	K.C. Townsend
WAITRESS	Julia Miles
YOUNG BEZ, *six years old*	Gregory Deutsch
SCRUB LADY	Sarah Braveman
NIGHT WATCHMAN	Robb Grace
TOUGH	Barry Primus
BIG BEZ, *twelve years old*	Benjamin Hayeem
(*to be played by an adult*)	
ALUM	Barry Primus
UNCLE SAM	Jerry DeLuise
FIRST SOLDIER	John Weston
SECOND SOLDIER	Robb Grace
ENEMY SOLDIER	Benjamin Hayeem
A BOY	Gregory Deutsch
WOMAN, *his mother*	Sarah Braveman
THE MIMES	Robert World and
(HIGH HAT ROBBER *and* VICTIM)	Martha Shaw
MOURNERS, PASSERS-BY	

Most of the minor roles are interchangeable.
The play takes place over a period of many years. Some of the characters age, some do not.

NOTE

The New York production was extremely simple, utilizing as few props and as little furniture as possible.

In the New York production, projections were flashed on the front curtain prior to the beginning of several scenes. Subsequent productions used the music of Jan Warner.

The author wishes to acknowledge the assistance of John Wulp, Sam Cohn, Audrey Wood, Jeannette Hirsch, and Nancy Grome.

ACT ONE, SCENE ONE

Projection on Curtain: "The beginning: In which it all begins."

A street. A spotlight reveals SELMA CHARGESSE, *dancing. People pass by without noticing her. Then another spotlight goes on and reveals a shoeshine man,* O.O. MARTINAS, *sitting in a shoeshine chair and staring in the direction of the girl, seemingly transfixed by her dancing. Later we discover that he is actually watching the thirteen-story department store directly behind her. Enter* NEWSBOY, VENDOR, CAB DRIVER, *and* WOMAN. WILMER *enters, watches people pass girl by, turns to admire girl, then speaks to* MARTINAS, *who gets out of the shoeshine chair.* WILMER *sits down in the chair and* MARTINAS *begins to shine his shoes.*

WILMER: Answer: What would the world do without our type of people, people who stop to watch a girl dance in the street like this.

MARTINAS: Like what?

WILMER: Can't you see her arms and legs moving the daylight this way and that?

MARTINAS: By God! Why didn't anyone tell me she was dancing there? Look at her legs moving the daylight this way and that.

WILMER: Couldn't you see her before?

MARTINAS: See who?

WILMER: The girl dancing there.

MARTINAS: What girl? I was looking at that beautiful department store which will one day be the O.O. Martinas Department Store, named after O.O. Martinas. Who's O.O. Martinas? I'm O.O. Martinas. Who did you think he was? And I was?

WILMER: That silver and stucco thirteen-story building will be yours? Because your name is O.O. Martinas?

SELMA *stops dancing.*

MARTINAS: Yes and no. Yes, the building will be mine becount of my name is O.O. Martinas; becount of when O.O. Martinas wants something, it will be his. I wanted this shoeshine job. It's now mine.

WILMER: That's yes. What's no?

MARTINAS: No, don't stick your nose into my affairs.

SELMA *exits.*

MARTINAS *tries to regain* WILMER's *attention.*

My building will be my department store!

WILMER: How does one come by a thirteen-story department store?

MARTINAS: It's simple. You get in on the ground floor. You buy a delicatessen concession—on the ground floor—and before you know it, it's a delicatessen department. Just think! A whole floor of nothing but meat.

43

WILMER: Nothing but meat?

MARTINAS: Yes, I'm a man who believes in meat. Anything on the hoof! I wouldn't shine your shoes unless they were made of cowhide. I hate those who eat innocent vegetables. You never see a lettuce pluck a man.

WILMER: A delicatessen department?

MARTINAS: Yes, you young fool. I'll revolutionize department storedom! What this country needs is a revolution. Today, a delicatessen concession, tomorrow, the whole store—

WILMER: [interrupting] Is that your key?

MARTINAS: Key? What's *that*?

WILMER: You mean you open up a thirteen-story department store and it's not your key to the universe?

MARTINAS: We will have livers, all kinds of livers. Have you ever heard of whooping crane livers? No, you young fool, what do *you* know about the liver field?

    SELMA *starts dancing by.* WILMER, *frightened, turns to the girl.*

    MARTINAS *immediately becomes pleasant. Taking out a piece of paper.*

A poem—mine!

    Declaims.

        Tinkle, tinkle, little life,
        how I wish I had a wife.
        Deep within my soul so blue
        how come you do me like you do?

Do you like my beautiful words? [*Hands* WILMER *the paper which is painted black.*] Of course there's nothing on it, young fool! Why should there be? I cannot read. Nor write. But I can count! Grant me that! I can count, becount of....Look: 1, 2, 3, 4, 5, 6, 7, 8, 9, 10, 11, 12, 13! and a half, if you consider the basement, which I consider. It will be mine. The venison, mine; the pig snouts, the bunnies, the tails of oxen, mine; mine the men and women, the heads and guts of all forms of the animal kingdom, mine. All this talk makes me thirsty. Mine! I could use a nice refreshing glass of blood. Mine!

WOMAN VENDOR: [*turns and sees dancing* SELMA] Hey, everyone! A girl dancing!

MARTINAS: Of course. Where?

CAB DRIVER: [*who had seen her and paid no attention*] By God, the boy here is right!

    Other passers-by now begin to notice her as a crowd gathers.

WOMAN VENDOR: Her hands, she's using hands!

CAB DRIVER: My God! Her leg is moving!

WOMAN VENDOR: Slow spinning, did you ever...?

WILMER: I don't dance. Strange, my mother was a good dancer, very fat but a good dancer.

CAB DRIVER: They say the fat are light on their feet.

WOMAN VENDOR: Let me see. Don't hog.

MARTINAS: I'll sell hog and loin of yak.

WILMER: It's like watching a baby's dream. I've never seen anyone dance in this street.

MARTINAS: I've never seen anyone dance in *any* street. You don't acquire delicatessen departments watching people dance in the street. I will sell hearts. I will hold thousands of hearts in these hands of mine!

WILMER: I had a friend named Cohn, used to dance—with his face. He used to grin and your eyes would wiggle.

WOMAN VENDOR: I'd like to see her dance barefoot at my house. Naked!

MARTINAS: Are you an artist?

WOMAN VENDOR: No, I'm well off, I have a very expensive rug. Nobody's ever danced on that rug. Naked! I can't leave, although I have important appointments uptown. I'm in neckties.

MARTINAS: I never wear ties: I believe in freedom of the neck.

Two policemen come on the scene from opposite side.

FIRST POLICEMAN: Break it up. Break what up?

SECOND POLICEMAN: Ok, ok.

FIRST POLICEMAN: [*to* SECOND POLICEMAN] Are you new on this beat? Can we be partners?

SECOND POLICEMAN: We've got to get her out of here.

MARTINAS: Efficient police. The world is good to me. Thank God I deserve it. Beautiful girl. Take her away, becount of she's blocking the entrance to the future O.O. Martinas Department Store.

FIRST POLICEMAN: [*to* SELMA] Lady, you're disturbing the peace of the entrance to the future O.O. Martinas Department Store.

WILMER: Officer, mind if I tell you something? It's nothing personal. It's about your life.

SECOND POLICEMAN approaches menacingly.

MARTINAS: Let the boy rave on.

WILMER: Thank you. That girl *has* to dance, just as you have to stop her from dancing. [*To* SECOND POLICEMAN] Just as you [*affectionately puts arm on shoulder of cop*] have to punch people in the guts and be an officer of the law, just as Martinas here wants to own meats and dollars and peoples. Just as I, just as I—I don't know. I don't know what I have to do. I have no key to the universe. So let her dance.

SELMA starts dancing in appreciation.

SECOND POLICEMAN is terrified: he doesn't know what to do. He turns on WILMER roughly with his club.

WILMER runs off and makes a ballet leap into the wings. A crash of garbage cans is heard off-stage.

FIRST POLICEMAN has been watching dancing girl. The SECOND POLICEMAN slyly takes SELMA, still dancing, and is slyly about to escort her in the direction of the patrol car, when FIRST POLICEMAN gently, as her dancing slows down, takes her arm and waves toward stage left.

FIRST POLICEMAN: Cabbie!

WILMER: [*re-enters holding his head*]: Dancing girl, if ever you need me, I'll be waiting. Here. [*Reaches into pocket, finds no money.*] I'll get a job!

SECOND POLICEMAN *threatens him.* WILMER *exits into wings with garbage can crash.*

FIRST POLICEMAN: [*to* CAB DRIVER] Here! Five dollars. Take her where she wants. Keep the change. Don't look so sneaky suspicious. I'm the law. I arrest. Stop staring!

CAB DRIVER: [*disapproving*] And I wanted to be a priest!

CAB DRIVER *and girl leave. Sound of cab leaving.* SECOND POLICEMAN *slyly watches the* FIRST POLICEMAN. *They walk off together.*

FIRST POLICEMAN: [*apologetic, to* SECOND POLICEMAN] I like you. Let's be partners! Let's forever walk this beat together—ever!

SECOND POLICEMAN: [*slyly and disdainfully*] Yes.

WILMER: [*enter bedraggled*] You still have another shoe of mine to shine.

MARTINAS: I've given up the shining of shoes. I must make real money. I'm going into butcher delivery. I can see it now.

WILMER: The delivery list?

MARTINAS: The delicatessen department!

Blackout.

SCENE TWO

Projection on Curtain: "Years Later"

A street. The FIRST POLICEMAN *is conducting traffic in front of the curtain. He pretends he is leading a symphony orchestra with his club. He is carried away, about to reach a magnificent crescendo when the* SECOND POLICEMAN *blows his whistle and stops it all.*

SECOND POLICEMAN: OK, OK, break it up.

FIRST POLICEMAN: Break what up? I'm one of you. [*Indicates shoe shine stand*] Hey, shine my shoes?

SECOND POLICEMAN: It would be cheating. Policemen have to police, not shine shoes. I hate cheating.

FIRST POLICEMAN: I like the slapping on leather. I love music. I love rhythm.

A holdup occurs directly behind them. This is the HIGH HAT ROBBER *who tiptoes up to the woman* VICTIM *and steals her purse. The two policemen are facing front.*

SECOND POLICEMAN: Look! [*Not seeing the robbery*] We've no time for music, [HIGH HAT ROBBER *and* VICTIM *leave*] we've got to guard the O.O. Martinas Emporium. What a revolution in department storedom. It's an honor to guard those genuine thirteen stories.

FIRST POLICEMAN: It's an honor to conduct—traffic. [*Starts conducting his symphony of cars again. Again the* SECOND POLICEMAN'S *whistle stops him.*] My cars...

SECOND POLICEMAN: Cars! Let 'em drop dead! Long live genuine department stores!

FIRST POLICEMAN: Long live genuine America! Accept no substitutes.

They exit through the following park scene.

SCENE THREE

A park. A park bench with a single tree standing nearby. Lights come back up to reveal O.O. MARTINAS, *who looks the same.* WILMER *enters, he has aged slightly.*

MARTINAS: Good late afternoon.

WILMER: Good late afternoon.

MARTINAS: Have we met before?

WILMER: No. You look familiar, and since I always forget a face and never remember a name, we cannot have met.

MARTINAS: O.O. Martinas is the name. How do you do, young man?

WILMER: I'm old. I'm twenty-five.

MARTINAS: Yes, sneaks up on you, old age. Hits before you're ready and you're old before you're ready. Life is always one step ahead of you. You get ready to be a child when Bong! Adolescence hits you. Begin to put up with adolescence and Bong! You're an adult. Finally realize you're an adult. Plop! Middle age. And you only believe you're really middle-aged when Plop! Old age comes limping by and grabs your bony hand. On your death bed, as you laugh your last sob, finally you say "Plop bong! I'm old!" But too late, you're dead. But you've finally caught up. You're dead and you *know* you're double plop double bong dead.

WILMER: [*disgusted*] Very nice.

MARTINAS: Not bad for teatime. You should hear me in the office. Eloquent, mystical—

    WILMER *is staring out at something.*

Do you like that department store?

WILMER: I was not looking at the department store. I was looking at that girl going in it.

MARTINAS: That's my love.

WILMER: She's a little young.

MARTINAS: The *building* is my love. I own it. Thirteen floors of department store.

WILMER: What's your favorite department?

MARTINAS: Lamb! It's a meat department store. Thirteen floors of meat—nothing else.

WILMER: Do you need a bookkeeper?

MARTINAS: Not only do I own that building, I bought a foreign English bicycle.

WILMER: Do you own a good bookkeeper?

MARTINAS: Would you believe I worked my way up from delivering Italian salami? I used to sit staring with envy at everyone: now I sit staring at my building, my love. First floor, loins of beef; second floor, veal; third floor, lamb! fourth floor, me, a large apartment, right behind the chopping room. Do I sleep!

    WILMER *is making a horrible grimace.*

What are you doing with your face? Smile! People like to see the bookkeeper smile.

WILMER: I'm smiling. Can't you read my eyes?

MARTINAS: I can't read. A lovely meat department store and I can't read or write!

Thing I love about me, I never stop being amazed by my own achievements. Do me a favor? Write down the following:

> WILMER *pulls a pencil and a roll of adding-machine paper from his pocket.*

I'm in the mood for building poetry.

> *Recites the poem.*

> Death, you old schoolteacher,
> don't take away your books,
> death, you old schoolteacher
> don't ask me to die.
> Death, you old professor,
> I don't want to graduate.
> I want to wear a cap and gown and sock
> you in the eye.
> You big fat witch, death, you.

WILMER: You do this to bookkeepers?

MARTINAS: I can count too! That's why I own meats and monies.

WILMER: Bookkeeping: key to the universe.

Can a man die happy without a key to the universe?

MARTINAS: Can a man die happy *with* one? Don't talk about death. Read my poem about death.

WILMER: No.

MARTINAS: I go: my meat building needs me. You're making that awful face again! Stop!

WILMER: I'm smiling. I'm on vacation.

MARTINAS: Prove it!

WILMER: I went to a party yesterday.

MARTINAS: Why wasn't I invited? Who gave it? Your dad? Your dear old mom?

WILMER: No one I know. I saw a group of people and followed them to a party.

MARTINAS: I cater to the best parties.

WILMER: Then a terrible thing. I went to the bathroom and was very impressed with the odor of soap, perfume, bath oil, underarm deodorant, shaving cream, and toothpaste in the new press-down container.

MARTINAS: I like a good smell—lamb.

WILMER: I took hair tonic, gave myself a good brushing and rejoined the festivities. The hostess said, "Pooh! what a smell." The host said, "Yes dear." I went back to the bathroom and took a shave, put on more hair tonic, after-shave lotion, underarm deodorant, for revenge.

MARTINAS: Well done!

WILMER: Then took a shower to get rid of the smell. *A,* I did not need their scent. *B,* I was ashamed of myself. Is that stealing?

MARTINAS: My boy, Time, which is forever being born and forever dying, has no time for distinctions. What kind of a party was it?

WILMER: A funeral party. That group of people was outside a funeral parlor. I had nothing to do and they were all hugging, chatting, waving, meeting relatives for the first time, vowing to see more of one another, looking at the time, trying not to talk business, or do business; they looked so cheerful and inviting that I couldn't resist following the crowd to the coffin. When I wept over the body they thought I was a long-lost lover of the deceased, a woman of sixty with beautiful blue hair. *They* invited me to the party afterwards. Was I moved. Vacations are *lonely!* The food was good.

MARTINAS: I cater to the best funeral parties. Goombye!

> *Exit* MARTINAS.

> WILMER *watches a group of* MOURNERS *behind a coffin. He is about to join them when they follow a woman ice-cream* VENDOR *and her cart.* MOURNERS *exit.*

> *Enter the dancing girl,* SELMA, *aged somewhat. She sits down on the bench.* WILMER *looks at her. She looks at him. They like each other.* WILMER *does not know what to do. He decides. He stands up, looks determinedly toward her and walks to ice-cream* VENDOR, *who has just re-entered.*

WILMER: Two ice creams. One pistachio...and one pistachio.

VENDOR: No pistachio and no pistachio. [*Digs into cart and comes up with:*] A tuna fish sandwich?

WILMER: Cut in half?

VENDOR: Yes.

> VENDOR *gives him sandwich.* WILMER *pays with a bill.*

[*Angrily.*] A hundred dollar bill is the smallest you have?

WILMER: I'm on vacation.

VENDOR: Nobody makes a fool of me and gets away with it! Except God. I'll show you. All pennies!

> *Drops bag of change on* WILMER's *toe.*

WILMER: No, there's one nickel shining through it all.

VENDOR: You deserve it.

> *Puts bill in her pocket. Exits.*

> WILMER *goes to* SELMA, *gives her half a sandwich, sits beside her, and they eat in silence on the bench.*

SELMA: Let's not tell each other our names. It's more romantic.

WILMER: I believe in no names. Makes forgetting much more beautiful.

> *They eat in silence.*

I'm on vacation, spending it in the city.

SELMA: Where do you live?

WILMER: In the city. Up there in my bookkeeping office. You live in the city year in, year out, and forget what sights there are. I have two weeks off, each day to a place I haven't seen in years. Old Cohn and I always went to a museum of natural art or some place. Now, I like my job, but getting up in the morning, going to work, coming home, the result is you don't go anywhere else because you're just nervous. You're tangled, you're twisted, and the result is you think that going anywhere is going to work. Morning becomes night, week becomes weekend, yesterday becomes today. Whatever's happened has not had time to matter. The result is I spend my vacation

in the city going places, trying to catch up. The result is I've seen twelve movies in
three days.

SELMA: The key?

WILMER: What is it? I know you know. Bookkeeping, right?

SELMA: Movies.

WILMER: [*sad*] I knew she knew.

SELMA: It's the only way out.

WILMER: The only?

SELMA: In the movies, no world falls on you.

WILMER: Yes, no world!

        They look at each other and kiss.

SELMA: [*breaks from the embrace suddenly*] What movies?

WILMER: [*still reacting to the kiss*] "Alexander the Great."

SELMA: Saw it.

WILMER: "The Good Earth."

SELMA: Saw it.

WILMER: "The Ten Commandments."

SELMA: Saw them.

WILMER: The key!

SELMA: I *think* I saw it.

WILMER: No. Movies as key to the universe. Along with bookkeeping. Not that I want
to take any glory and responsibility away from movies.

SELMA: Exactly. Bookkeeping is the other key to the universe.

WILMER: Say that again!

SELMA: Bookkeeping: other key to universe.

        WILMER *stares, moved to tears. He forces himself to speak.*

WILMER: Why are *you* so lonely?

SELMA: Did I say I was lonely?

WILMER: Yes.

SELMA: That's a lie, but I *am* lonely.

        She is staring in the direction of Martinas' building.

WILMER: I was staring at that building before, but you were in front of it. Why are you
staring at it? Is it yours too?

SELMA: Of course not! But it will be. I'm engaged to the owner, O.O. Martinas. We're
to be married soon. A week or two or three years.

WILMER: Lonely!! [*Pause.*] Old Cohn, crazy fool, last night married some girl who
had eyes that went all the way *in,* dark. *Dark* dark. I was invited to the wedding. I
don't drink: just last night a few; I kept eating not to get sick from the booze. I got
sick from the eating. [*Pause.*] This morning I got sick from the booze. I bit his bride
when I was drunk. Old Cohn laughed. [*He laughs.*] I fail to see what's funny.

SELMA: Who is Old Cohn?

WILMER: Old Cohn. My best friend till the eighth grade. We used to go everywhere
together and he used to sing on top of the open-air bus. We lost touch.

SELMA: Lost touch. *You* talk about lost touch! I've lost such touch! I never go to sleep without thinking of Geraldine, the greatest friend you'd ever want to find in the fourth grade. We used to walk the streets for hours identifying automobiles. We saw them all; we could guess the year from two blocks away. And you talk about lost touch! I can't bear it. She moved out of the neighborhood. At the wrongest time: we had seen all the cars, except one, the Lincoln Zephyr. It was our dream to see the Lincoln Zephyr zooming down the street; I saw it a week after she moved away. I didn't know where she lived. Her father must have got poorer or richer; they didn't let anyone know where they went. And here I was, completely unable to let Geraldine know I had seen the Lincoln Zephyr. I'm haunted with that. I think her name was Geraldine.

WILMER: Today I tried singing on top of the open-air bus like Old Cohn, there in the open, the wind and noise all around. I always turned red, *red* red, made believe I didn't know him. "Stop making fools of the two of us," singing at the top of his voice on the open-air bus.

SELMA: Today *you* wanted to sing. I once wanted to dance to all the city. And I did. Look what it got me. Money and wealth.

WILMER: I couldn't sing today.

SELMA: Why?

WILMER: No more open-air buses.

SELMA: Why?

WILMER: I don't remember any songs.

SELMA: Everywhere you turn—a wall.

WILMER: I can hum. [*He hums two notes, then stops.*] No, I can't. There were boys— Cohn was one—could memorize anything. "Stardust," "The Star-Spangled Banner," "The Declaration of Independence," anything. Where did it get them? Those boys memorizing, what do they become? Memorizers? Heasly, seventh grade, won the elocution prize; sells lawn furniture in the A & P. My motto is let people do what they want. Only, take up something that can be the key. Bookkeeping's no drudgery either, it's interesting, responsible too. Think of the chaos the world would be in today if we had no bookkeeping. [*Pause.*] Is bookkeeping the key?

SELMA: Soft people interest me. I like you.

WILMER: Do you love me?

SELMA: As a matter of fact, I do.

WILMER: What about Mr. Martinas?

SELMA: Was he here? O.O. was here?

WILMER: Yes.

SELMA: O.O. and I, we don't get along.

WILMER: Why are you going to marry him?

SELMA: Was I going to marry him? I *was* going to marry him, I guess. But O.O. and I don't get along and I love you.

WILMER: This is the thing, I don't go around breaking up love affairs.

SELMA: Shake. I'm the same way. [*Kisses him passionately as they shake hands.*] I don't like O.O. Him forever talking about his accomplishments, owner of thirteen stories of store. So what, I ask you, so what?

WILMER: [*joyfully*] Yes, so what!

SELMA: So it's my duty to marry money. He can be very kind.

WILMER: I suppose.

SELMA: He can be very cruel.

> *Shows* WILMER *her arm.*

WILMER: I don't see anything.

SELMA: Yes, well, anyway, O.O. and I, we just don't hit it off, in any manner or form, if you know what I mean.

WILMER: You mean—

SELMA: In any manner or form. I mean—

WILMER: In any manner or form. We mean—

BOTH: In any manner or form.

SELMA: The result is, I pick you. You're nice, soft: you know I like that. I'm blunt.

WILMER: [*growing more and more elated*] Yes!

SELMA: You be blunt.

WILMER: Yes! Yes!

SELMA: If you don't like the idea, get up and walk away.

WILMER: No! No!

SELMA: Fast get up and walk away. I see you hate me, you think I'm a terrible person. Go, I don't blame you, you're nice, you're soft.

WILMER: I cry in the movies.

> *Romantic music is heard.*

SELMA: You cry in the movies? [*She kisses him.*] What movies?

WILMER: "Possessed"—Gable and Crawford.

SELMA: Saw it.

WILMER: "Rhapsody," starring Elizabeth Taylor.

SELMA: Saw it.

WILMER: Cowboy films.

SELMA: You cry in cowboy films?

WILMER: Yes.

SELMA: Which cowboy films?

WILMER: All cowboy films.

SELMA: Saw them.

> *Music stops.*

WILMER: You feel soft to *me.*

SELMA: My name is Selma Chargesse.

WILMER: My name is Wilmer Flange. But you said no names.

SELMA: Names, now that we're in love...names.

WILMER: [*embracing her*] Not only in love, good friends.

> MARTINAS *enters in a fury.*

MARTINAS: Behind the back! Why is it always behind the back?

WILMER: Sit down, O.O., we'll talk it over.

MARTINAS: I'll give you a good job as bookkeeper.

WILMER: This is the thing, O.O. The girl here loves me and is a little too young for you. Personally, I don't want to get involved. I'm on vacation. But it's not often you meet someone who's nice and soft and loves you.

MARTINAS: I'll make you *my* bookkeeper.

>WILMER *shakes his head "no."*

I will put my hand in my pocket and take out green paper with a picture of one of the leading leaders of our nation on it.

>WILMER *shakes his head "no."*

SELMA: You're quite a guy, Wilmer.

WILMER: My name isn't Wilmer Flange, it's William Flinge. I lied about my name. I wasn't sure then; now that I've made a sacrifice I know you must be worth it.

SELMA: I am, William, I am!

MARTINAS: [*to* WILMER] Glad you can't be bribed: you'll be true to her. Head book-keeper?

>WILMER *shakes his head "no."*

Would you mind leaving us together a minute, Sel?

SELMA: Everyone loves me. [*Exits.*]

MARTINAS: [*weeps*] Pity an old man, becount of she's all I have.

WILMER: Would she be happy, O.O.?

MARTINAS: I can buy and sell you! No, forget I said that. We must be kind.

WILMER: Strange how I don't mind anything when someone loves me.

MARTINAS: Forgive an old man, may I extend my heartfelt felicitations?

WILMER: You're crying, O.O.

MARTINAS: Yes, these illiterate eyes.... But what did I do? [*Angry.*] An empire! The O.O. Martinas building! I can buy and sell you! Without knowing how to read! An empire of meat I built, and mine eyes have never lain in locked embrace with the written word! What have you done with *your* learning? Stolen my fiancée! Keep your reading, keep your writing. Give me arithmetic. One plus one equals one and one all alone by itself will forever equal none. Who needs reading and writing!

>He sobs.

WILMER: Why are you crying?

MARTINAS: Becount of I can't read or write.

WILMER: [*holding* MARTINAS' *quaking shoulders*] There are other things.

MARTINAS: Like money! I can buy and sell you!

>He grabs WILMER *by the throat.*

WILMER: What did *I* do? I'm nice and soft and getting killed. On my vacation.

MARTINAS: Come on, Sel.

>Enter SELMA.

WILMER: Stick with me, Selma.

SELMA: I need O.O.'s apartment.

WILMER: I have a hot plate in my office.

MARTINAS: Selma! To the O.O. Martinas building and have an O.O. Special.

WILMER: [*To* SELMA] Go! Do you want to get me killed? Don't answer. Run away
with me. No!

MARTINAS: [*simultaneously*] Corned beef, liverwurst, pastrami, Italian salami, turkey and tongue on two nice thick...slices of...baloney!

SELMA: Is there any of that Russian dressing left?

MARTINAS: I'm a gentleman and a butcher, am I not?

SELMA: Oh, O.O., ok.

WILMER: Please Selma!

SELMA: Please what?

WILMER: I don't know.

     MARTINAS *takes* SELMA'S *arm as if nothing had happened. They mark time
ready to march.*

MARTINAS: Good-by, William Flinge. I'm taking Selma home now. I'd offer you a job
as head bookkeeper; the atmosphere would be too tense, don't you think?

SELMA: Good-by, Wilmer Flange, for that's the way I'll always remember you.

WILMER: Good-by, Selma Chargesse, for that's the way I'll always remember you.

MARTINAS: Pardon an old sentimental man, William, may I say something before I
go?

WILMER: Sure, O.O.

MARTINAS: [*violent*] I'll kill you if you ever see Selma again!

SELMA: You're jealous, O.O.

WILMER: If ever you need me, Selma, I'll be waiting.

     MARTINAS *marches her away.* WILMER *sits miserable.*

If bookkeeping cannot change the human side of existence, can movies? The only
way out! The only key! I'm going to see "Bhowani Junction" starring Ava Gardner
and Stewart Granger, with Bill Travers and Abraham Sofaer, directed by George
Cukor and produced by Pandro S. Berman!

    He smiles, then breaks into the awful grimace.

CURTAIN

SCENE FOUR

    The street again. WILMER *enters from movie, carrying a bag of money and a box
of popcorn. Eats last piece of popcorn and spits it out.*

WILMER: What a rotten movie!

    Enter FIRST POLICEMAN *and a girl* FRANCES.

FIRST POLICEMAN: *I love you madly.*

FRANCES: You don't even remember my name. It's Frances.

FIRST POLICEMAN: *I love you madly, Frances.*

    WILMER *smiles the awful grimace.*

FRANCES: Hey, that guy's looking funny at me.

    FIRST POLICEMAN *slaps* WILMER.

WILMER: I was smiling because you look so happy. But hit me, I don't care about anything any more. Hit me! Hit me! I don't care.

    FIRST POLICEMAN *slaps* WILMER *again.*

That's enough! Now, I go. Nice of you to chat with me. I have no one, not even parents! That's a lie. I have parents. Lonely and alone enough to lie!

FIRST POLICEMAN: I ought to lock you up, but I and Gertrude will be late for the concert. Music! Rhythm I love!

    They exit.

WILMER: I was only making faces at myself.

    Enter WOMAN VENDOR *with two suitcases.*

WOMAN VENDOR: Dolls! I'm selling dolls! They laugh, they cry, they do everything but die. Why are *you* crying?

WILMER: I'm laughing. I'm glad Selma Chargesse, a casual acquaintance I happen to love, has left me for security. What meals she can eat! Steaks smothered with lamb chops, liver on the side. I'm glad, happy!

    Starts to leave.

VENDOR: Where are you going?

WILMER: To kill myself.

VENDOR: That's no key to the situation.

WILMER: What is?

VENDOR: [*snapping open suitcase with stand*] Dolls! They understand. Twenty-five cents, thirty-five cents, five cents.

WILMER: I'll take one.

VENDOR: One what?

WILMER: One suitcase of dolls. How much?

VENDOR: [*assessing* WILMER's *moneybag*] How much do you have?

WILMER: One hundred dollars in change.

VENDOR: Sold! I'll give it to you for one hundred dollars—in change.

WILMER: [*giving her moneybag*] Are you sure this is the key?

VENDOR: [*leaving quickly*] It is for me!

    Exits.

WILMER: [*calls to empty street*] Dolls! I'm selling pretty dolls, dolls that never leave you for another person or another doll. They laugh, they cry, they do everything but die; dolls do not need first cut meats like certain Selma Chargesses. Which reminds me, I'm hungry. Hunger always hunts for misery. [*Sets up suitcase.*] I'm angry, hurt and angry and hungry. Selma, if ever you need me, I'll be waiting. I'm selling dolls that never leave you for another person, or another doll...they laugh, they cry, they do everything but die.

    Lights fade to blackout.

SCENE FIVE

Projection on Curtain: "Two Days Later. The O.O. Martinas apartment in the
O.O. Martinas Meat Department Store."
> SELMA *is sitting reading in negligee.* MARTINAS *is on other side of wall in
> bedroom during entire scene.* SELMA *is reading in an armchair. She dozes, but
> snaps herself awake and returns to her magazine with a struggle.*

MARTINAS: [*in bedroom*] Selma, coming to bed? It's one o'clock. [*Waits. No reaction.*]
You're tired too. You worked hard in the cutlet department this morning. [*Waits.
No reaction.*] You need sleep. I saw you slaving away in assorted gizzards. [*Waits. No
reaction.*] I'm worn out and I can't go to sleep. *It's so lonely in here.*

SELMA: That's why I don't want to go in there.
> *She is shocked by her own words.*

MARTINAS: What?
> SELMA *is still shocked, but proud.*

What?
> SELMA *still does not answer, smiling.*

Were you talking to yourself?

SELMA: Everyone talks to herself sometime or another. Or don't you know that?

MARTINAS: I tell you truly, Selma, I don't.

SELMA: Don't you ever talk to yourself?

MARTINAS: To tell you truly, Selma, I don't. And though I have never truly believed
honesty is the best policy, I am speaking truly. Wait! No! I remember, once I spoke
to myself.

SELMA: And?

MARTINAS: Nobody listened. I concluded that man doesn't acquire meat department
stores by talking to himself; I concluded that meat department stores come to him
who talks out loud and says: "World, you old sneak thief, work for me, or I will put
you in solitary confinement by committing suicide." And that's all it takes to be
rich, that—and money! Money! Selma, please, come to sleep becount of my severe
case of loneliness.
> SELMA *Puts coat over her negligee, quietly leaves, doing her old dance.*
> MARTINAS *is not aware.*

Selma? Are you mad becount of I refuse to talk to myself?
> MARTINAS *enters in pajamas with pork chop pattern.*

Selma.... Selma?
> *Stares in teary dismay at her disappearance.*
> *Lights dim in* MARTINAS' *apartment.*

SCENE SIX

The street. It is raining.

Lights go up beneath lamppost where WILMER *is selling his dolls to no one late in the night, his suitcase open.*

SELMA *enters.* WILMER *does not see her.*

WILMER: Dolls that never leave you for another person or another doll.

SELMA: Can you believe who is back?

WILMER: [*without turning to her*] Selma Chargesse, my former casual acquaintance and sweetheart!

SELMA: Right the first time.

Several people with umbrellas pass between them.

WILMER: Selma. Why did you leave me two days ago for the sake of dollars?

SELMA: I did it for the money.

WILMER: Why did you go off with a man much less your type than my type?

SELMA: Can you forgive me?

WILMER: No, but I will.

SELMA: Oh, William.

WILMER: I've changed my name to Wilmer Flange, officially.

SELMA: Wilmer, let's go to the movies. Where we belong.

WILMER: Selma, movies are not the key, nor bookkeeping.

SELMA: What is the key?

WILMER: [*shows suitcase*] Dolls.

SELMA: Dolls!!? You're right.

WILMER: Then promise me one thing.

SELMA: Almost anything! Almost anything!

WILMER: Promise me your next man will be your type and my type.

SELMA: But *you're* more your type and my type than any type.

WILMER: Selma, I got married.

SELMA: Married? Two days and you forgot me?

WILMER: It was more like three, Selma.

SELMA: Two days and three nights.

WILMER: How long can a guy wait? I only married Marguerite for the dolls of it anyway. She owned a doll warehouse.

SELMA: Why, why?

WILMER: I needed spare parts for my experiments. I am trying to invent a doll that sneezes.

SELMA: Good-by. I would wish happiness to you and Marguerite Flange; my heart is not in it mainly because of my extreme love for you. I wish you both a *drop* of joy.

WILMER: Don't forget my son, Bez, a fine boy of one year of age.

SELMA: Married three days—you have a son?

WILMER: Yes, by my wife's husband, *Rocky!*

Music.

SELMA: Good-by, William Flinge, for that's the way I'll always remember you.
    Starts to leave.
WILMER: Good-by, Selma Chargesse, for that's the way I'll always remember you.
    [*Begins to hawk dolls.*] They laugh, they cry, they do everything but die.
SELMA: [*stops suddenly*] She had a husband when she married you?
WILMER: Don't worry, she left me yesterday. Said I was obsessed with dolls. Said I
    never came home. Said I spent all the time inventing dolls. Said the truth.
SELMA: You're a free man, Wilmer! My man! With me you'll be a happy doll inventor.
WILMER: What I've wanted since yesterday.
    A baby cries.
        WILMER *takes a baby from suitcase.*
    She said I could have Bez, the child; he's grown to love me in these two days.
SELMA: Three days. Let's go home.
WILMER: One of my dolls already has a runny nose.
    They march toward WILMER's *house.*

CURTAIN

SCENE SEVEN

Projection on Curtain: "Years later. The Street. The Night. The Depression."
    Street, late at night, years later, near shoeshine stand. The policemen have aged.
FIRST POLICEMAN: I hate when the country is in a depression; poor Wilmer and
    Selma! Together all these years. No money, lack of funds, poverty, second-run movies.
    Shine my shoes?
SECOND POLICEMAN: No!
FIRST POLICEMAN: Don't you want my big boots to glow in the darkness like a
    bright and beautiful gun? After all, the cows hanging there in O.O.'s window upside
    down see nothing but shoes.
SECOND POLICEMAN: Cows! Big shots hanging there upside down!
FIRST POLICEMAN: Today they're happy on display with their bellies open, showing
    how beautiful they are inside; the next day they're gone, forgotten, and new cows
    take their place in the window, showing off their bright red guts, one generation to
    the next.
SECOND POLICEMAN: Cows, hanging there upside down! Let 'em drop dead!
        Another robbery occurs behind them. It is the same HIGH HAT ROBBER *and
    his* VICTIM, *now both a little older.*
BOTH: Look!
SECOND POLICEMAN: Again the late light in Wilmer's doll invention studio, for-
    merly his furnished room, formerly his bookkeeping office.
FIRST POLICEMAN: Wilmer day and night invents new dolls.
SECOND POLICEMAN: Nobody buys them.

FIRST POLICEMAN: After years of failure—
SECOND POLICEMAN:—real failure.
FIRST POLICEMAN: And poor O.O. Martinas.
>   *Enter* MARTINAS *who sits at a café table.*
Five new stories added to his meat department store. Two new bone departments. Has money, but you can't get love for money.
SECOND POLICEMAN: Not for love or money.
>   *They exit.*

SCENE EIGHT

>   MARTINAS *at café table studying menu.* WAITRESS *approaches.*

MARTINAS: Uhm, how much for the brandy?
WAITRESS: Seventy cents.
MARTINAS: Uhm, how much for the bourbon?
WAITRESS: Seventy cents. Everything here is seventy cents.
MARTINAS: Uhm, how much for the cognac?
WAITRESS: Listen, are you a wise guy?
MARTINAS: Uhm, how much for you?
WAITRESS: [*looks angry, then decides*] Ten dollars.
MARTINAS: Uhm...
WAITRESS: Ten dollars isn't much. I don't do this for a living. I raise money to send my fifteen-year-old daughter through school. I want her to have the advantages I never had, I want her to be pure.
MARTINAS: [*studies the menu a moment then*] Uhm, how much for the Shirley Temple? *Blackout.*

SCENE NINE

>   WILMER's *toy invention studio at night, a tiny room, with boxes, toys, parts of toys in disarray.* WILMER *is sitting behind the desk-worktable, taking the temperature of a doll, feeling its pulse, using a stethoscope on its chest.*
>   WILMER *looks tired, older.*
>   SELMA *walks in, carrying a suitcase.* BEZ (*in a sailor suit*), *their six-year-old son, follows. During the scene,* BEZ *keeps hitting* WILMER *with a rubber glove. No reaction from* WILMER.

WILMER: Hello, Selma, hello, Bez, my son. Look at this doll, Bez. Does he look sad enough to make people happy? Oh, if I could only make a doll that dies: five years of walking and jumping, then the little doll gets sick and dies, a beautiful doll death.
SELMA: Wilmer—

WILMER: We could sell doll coffins, doll tombstones, doll cemeteries. Kids would love that. Real live death to play with.

SELMA: Wilmer—

WILMER: Doll germs! Each doll with little doll symptoms built in. It's the key of keys—the life key. What's the matter, Selma, don't you like the idea? [*Takes temperature of doll.*] 98.6 —it should be 101 at least.

SELMA: Wilmer, I'm leaving you, *you know that, don't you?*

WILMER: Be back before the first to handle the bookkeeping? You're good at it, *you know that, don't you?* I love you, *you know that, don't you?*

    BEZ *hits* WILMER.

SELMA: I'm taking Bez and not coming back, Wilmer, *you know that, don't you?*

WILMER: I love you, Selma, *you know that, don't you?*

SELMA: You haven't been home for three days, Wilmer, *you know that, don't you?*

WILMER: It was only two.

SELMA: Two days and three nights.

    BEZ *hits* WILMER.

WILMER: One more little old chance?

    BEZ *hits* WILMER.

SELMA: You'd be home a week, then back here, again, forgetting Bez, me, yourself—did you eat today? Of course not, *you know that, don't you?*

WILMER: Of course not. I was happy, didn't need food, *you know that, don't you?*

    SELMA *takes a sandwich from handbag.*

SELMA: Eat now, or you never will, *you know that, don't you?*

WILMER: [*eating*] It's not for myself I spend time here. If I develop a doll that shrivels up, wastes away and dies, we'll have security and securities. We'll spend so much time together you'll throw me out of the house. *You know that, don't you? Hahaha!*

    With his mouth full of sandwich he weepingly laughs, chokes, drinks water, spills some on her accidentally.

    He tries to brush her dress, bends down rubbing the skirt.

SELMA: [*hysterically*] Get off your knees!

    BEZ *hits* WILMER.

WILMER: [*hugs her legs*] Am I so wrong?

SELMA: [*weeping*] Not wrong but what can we do? It would be wrong if you changed for my sake. Wrong for both of us, *you know that, don't you?*

    BEZ *hits* WILMER.

WILMER: I'll see you downstairs at least, *you know that, don't you?*

    BEZ *bursts into tears.*

SELMA: Bez!

BEZ: I don't want to leave my daddy! *You know that, don't you?*

    BEZ *hits* WILMER.

WILMER: Go, Bez, our son. Protect Mother.

    WILMER *is about to escort* SELMA *out when phone rings.*

Oh, that's about some important springs. Springs that will make my dolls sick, Selma.

SELMA: I'll write from my mother's.

WILMER: Try to make Bez understand.

SELMA: Understand what?

WILMER: I don't know—*you know that, don't you?*

> *Exit* SELMA *and* BEZ.

And remember—if ever you need me, I'll be waiting. *You know that—*

> *Phone rings again. He rushes in to answer it. Too late. Takes doll's temperature and bursts into tears. Door opens and an elegantly dressed* SCRUB LADY [WOMAN VENDOR] *enters.*

SCRUB LADY: Still here? Go home to your wife and kid, rat! All the time here.

WILMER: My wife left me.

> *Works on doll.*

SCRUB LADY: All the time your hands on doll people. Not at home where good men bring hands.

> *She brings in a pail and begins to scrub the floor.*

WILMER: A man has no right to invent dolls that die?

SCRUB LADY: Not that I'm a bargain, but I want a man home. Even if we knock each other around.

> WILMER *is weeping.*

Hey, what's the matter? Did someone pass away? I hate it. All my friends are red in the eyes. Everyone passes away nowadays.

WILMER: My wife left me.

SCRUB LADY: [*holding his head and liking it*] Ah, you should have told me.

WILMER: I need her the way I need—dolls.

SCRUB LADY: Me, I like a man home.

> *Phone rings,* WILMER *rushes, speaks into it.*

WILMER: Hello. My wife left me. Life without her is like life without dolls. —Yes, the springs! Send them—

> *Hangs up, obviously cut off. Looks at temperature of doll, shakes his head in disappointment.*

SCRUB LADY: What's the fun of being sad if you can't turn to your friends?

NIGHT WATCHMAN: [*enters, with time clock, drunk*] Oh, still here, huh?

WILMER: I'm here!

NIGHT WATCHMAN: There have been burglaries, but don't worry—I'm making my rounds. Not meaning a drop of harm. Speaking of a drop—

WILMER: Another thing. Did I drink? No.

NIGHT WATCHMAN: No?

WILMER: Go out with other women?

SCRUB LADY: No?

WILMER: [*grabs* NIGHT WATCHMAN] Why did she leave me? Answer. Why?

NIGHT WATCHMAN: Let me go. I've got to take care of this building.

> NIGHT WATCHMAN, *frightened, is about to leave when* WILMER *holds him back, imploringly and angrily.*

My heart's not strong. I have this drinking problem based on alcohol.

WILMER: [*looks at thermometer in doll*] 98.6! Still no good. I'd settle for a mild 100, just a touch of the flu.

NIGHT WATCHMAN: I'm not a well watchman.

Sound of footsteps. All are terrified.

SCRUB LADY: Burglars!

WILMER: Lord, don't let the burglars get me until one of my dolls comes down with a toy disease. I can't go on without the key.

SCRUB LADY: Lord, I'll never ever again.

WILMER: Lord, I will always.

NIGHT WATCHMAN: Lord, could I have a drink?

Door opens and a TOUGH *enters. He carries a violin case. He opens the case as all freeze with fear.* TOUGH *takes out a violin, then a package.*

TOUGH: Mr. Wilmer Flange? I have some springs.

WILMER: A delivery boy comes bearing springs.

NIGHT WATCHMAN: No burglary in his soul.

TOUGH: I'm a music student. I work from six to twelve delivering springs; I don't mind; it doesn't conflict with my real work, house painting. Eight hours a day. This is my violin practice hour, but I'm delivering overtime to buy brushes for a new paint job. My masterpiece. A twelve-room basement flat. The rent is twelve bucks a month, but what a job those guys are doing: twelve thousand dollars in decorating it all up. Twelve different shades of off-beige.

WILMER: [*to* TOUGH] But springs make the dolls live and, with luck, die. Springs round out their little personalities. I need springs. You're not listening. Nobody listens. Can't you hear me? Are you deaf?

TOUGH: I'm sorry, sir, I can't hear you. I'm deaf.

NIGHT WATCHMAN: What about my problem? I'm sober!

WILMER: I'll give you a drink.

NIGHT WATCHMAN *hops back on table.*

SCRUB LADY: I thought you were not a drinking thing.

WILMER: A man has a right.

NIGHT WATCHMAN: Sheer psychology.

TOUGH: You folks sure do fool around and have fun.

The two policemen enter.

FIRST POLICEMAN: Who screamed? What's going on here?

SECOND POLICEMAN: Ok, ok, break it up. Break what up? What's the trouble? Who screamed?

FIRST POLICEMAN: [*pointing to toy tom-toms*] May I—you know what?

SECOND POLICEMAN: No.

FIRST POLICEMAN: Please let me do it.

SCRUB LADY: Take me away.

SECOND POLICEMAN: Did you scream?

SCRUB LADY: Take me away. I'm lonely.

WILMER *takes sandwich, eats and weeps.*

FIRST POLICEMAN: I'm going to do it!

SCRUB LADY: Going to take me away?

FIRST POLICEMAN: [*takes a toy tom-tom and beats it,* TOUGH *joins in on his violin*] Going to play the toy tom-tom.

> FIRST POLICEMAN *and* TOUGH *play a duet for violin and toy tom-tom.* SCRUB LADY *sings beautiful vocalise.*
>
> *Enter* SELMA *and* BEZ. SECOND POLICEMAN *sees them and blows his whistle. Music stops.*

SELMA: I, Bez, all two of us crying at the station while you cavort here and have fun. I'm going to stay.

WILMER: I'm eating a sandwich of tears.

SELMA: I can't stand it at my mother's. And it's a long trip.

WILMER: Life, you've come through again!

> *Embraces* SELMA.

SELMA: These ten minutes seemed like an hour!

WILMER: [*rushes to* TOUGH *and shakes him*] Give me springs! My little dolls will shrivel up, waste away, and die. They don't want to be left out. They want to be the key. The springs!

> *Searches* TOUGH. TOUGH *points to table.* WILMER *takes spring and picks up a doll. Puts on surgical mask.*

SELMA: Could Bez and I have a kiss and a dollar fifty to pay the cab?

SCRUB LADY: He's busy! Think of someone but yourself! You all the time want nothing but a man home. Here's a guy changing the world of toys!

WILMER: In all fairness, Selma, the lady on my left is right.

BEZ: Who can I hit? Who can I hit?

> WILMER *keeps working in laboratory light; he is a scientist probing the unknown, a surgeon. Drum roll from* FIRST POLICEMAN'S *tom-tom.*

WILMER: Scissors.

> SCRUB LADY, *nurse-like, gives scissors.*

Glue.

> SCRUB LADY *gives glue.*

Spring.

BEZ: You're not glad I'm back. I'm taking mother away. *You know that, don't you?*

WILMER: This is it! Thermometer.

SCRUB LADY: Here you are, darling.

> As WILMER *concentrates, he does not notice* SELMA *writing a note. She and* BEZ *quietly march off just as* WILMER *inserts thermometer in doll's behind. He turns to where he thinks* SELMA *is standing.*

WILMER: A whole chapter in the encyclopedia of dolls will be devoted to us in this room on this day.

> *The two policemen stand at attention.*

Selma—[*Sees she has left.*] SELMA! [*Picks up note, reads aloud.*] "If ever you need me. I'll be waiting. Love, Selma Chargesse, former casual acquaintance and mother of your former wife's son, Bez." [*Pause.*] Darn it! My wife and child have left me again!

>   Takes out stethoscope and puts it on doll's chest hopefully.

>   Sound of feet. Everyone in the room is frightened again. They huddle together: they await their doom. The door opens, in walks O.O. MARTINAS, unchanged by years.

MARTINAS: [*to* WILMER] Forgive an old fool, but haven't I seen you somewhere before? Give me Selma, to take away to a more attractive, permissive and lucrative life—if you know what those words mean, you'll hand her over.

WILMER: I don't know what the words mean, I know what *you* mean. You can't have her. She's mine. I wouldn't give her away for all the dolls in China. She loves me. She left me.

MARTINAS: Then she must be at my house, loving me.

WILMER: She's at her mother's house *not* loving *her.*

MARTINAS: Her mother died when Selma was a girl of thirty-eight.

WILMER: That's right! She must be at your house.

OTHERS: [*conducted by* FIRST POLICEMAN] OOOH.

MARTINAS: How do you think you lived all these years? My meat department store, twenty-five floors. I sent you free meat. Becount of her.

OTHERS: OOOH.

MARTINAS: What's wrong with my meat? I sent the second best cuts!

OTHERS: OH?

MARTINAS: Here I kept him in oxtails and entrails!

OTHERS: ECH!

MARTINAS: But the second best!

OTHERS: OH?

MARTINAS: Yet he scorns me and won't give me *his* wife I deserve.

WILMER: And my dear son, Bez!

MARTINAS: All right, I'll take him too.

OTHERS: AH.

WILMER: Go. I don't need anyone! My dolls will get feverish and die, and make people happy. The Key! The Key! The thermometer.

MARTINAS: Goombye!

>   Exit.

>   WILMER *takes thermometer from doll. He looks at thermometer and bows his head in defeat.*

WILMER: 98.6.

OTHERS: OOOOH.

TOUGH: I can't hear them. I'm deaf. *You know that, don't you?*

>   As WILMER, *crying, eats his sandwich.*

CURTAIN
End Act One

ACT TWO, Scene One

Projection on Curtain: "Years Later. Merry Christmas."
The dark silent street, empty except for the aging policemen, counting money.

FIRST POLICEMAN: [*gives* SECOND POLICEMAN *a dollar bill wrapped in ribbon*] Merry Christmas.

SECOND POLICEMAN: [*gives* FIRST POLICEMAN *a dollar bill in exchange*] Merry Christmas.

FIRST POLICEMAN: Just what I've always wanted—a dollar bill.

SECOND POLICEMAN: Good times in the nation! Dollar again buys dollar.

FIRST POLICEMAN: Shine my shoes? Just let me feel that beat on my feet.

SECOND POLICEMAN: No.

FIRST POLICEMAN: I'm tired of playing scrabble. André—

SECOND POLICEMAN: No!

HIGH HAT ROBBER, *older, robs his* VICTIM *in background.*

BOTH POLICEMEN: [*not seeing robbery*] Look!

FIRST POLICEMAN: Again the late light in the O.O. Martinas Meat Mart. Ten new stories added, a used meat department, and Selma back in her bloody apron. After years...

SECOND POLICEMAN: Let the years drop dead.

FIRST POLICEMAN: Oh, André, don't be that way. What do *you* want to do?

WILMER *enters with suitcase open, hawking.*

WILMER: Dolls!

SECOND POLICEMAN: I know, let's arrest that bum.

WILMER: Dolls! I'm selling pretty dolls that refuse to get sick and die and leave you for another person or another doll. One dollar. Christmas is marching on us, Christmas. Can't you taste the snowdrops?

Policemen walk to him.

FIRST POLICEMAN: Come along with us.

SECOND POLICEMAN: You bum.

WILMER: I'm an enterprising young bum.

SECOND POLICEMAN: You young bum.

WILMER: Merry Christmas.

SECOND POLICEMAN: Merry Christmas, you bum.

FIRST POLICEMAN: Let's give the bum a break.

SECOND POLICEMAN: True. It's Christmas. [*To* WILMER.] Do you see that sign? Santa Claus needed. Why don't you get a position as a saint? You bum.

WILMER: What does a saint do in the O.O. Martinas Meat Mart?

SECOND POLICEMAN: Gives away meat tidbits for tots.

FIRST POLICEMAN: For Christmas' sake! Come along, André. Snow will be on the lot covering the dead cars and the building that never got past the framework. It would have been some pretty building, André. The girders were orange! Come along! If we hurry we'll make dawn.

> *They leave.*
> *Dawn breaks.*
> WILMER *looks at sign.* BEZ *enters. He wears same sailor suit he wore as little* BEZ *years before.*

BEZ: Excuse me, I live here and work here. Today I help my Dad O.O. choose a Santa. [*Looks in* WILMER's *suitcase.*] Nice dolls. I'd buy your dolls, but I'm low on cash. My money's tied up in the business.

WILMER: [*gives* BEZ *the suitcase*] Take them, all of them.

BEZ: [*takes toys*] You should, becount of it's Christmas.

WILMER: What do you want to be when you grow up?

BEZ: A butcher. Becount of I'm a butcher now.

WILMER: Bez, remember me? Your former dad?

BEZ: You're not my former dad. My former dad was a bum. Goombye!

WILMER: Merry Christmas.

> *Both exit into store*
> *Lights dim on street and brighten in* MARTINAS' *office.*

SCENE TWO

> MARTINAS *sits at a chopping table-desk. Behind him hangs a huge side of beef as if ready to pounce on him, or hug him.*

MARTINAS: [*into intercom*] Professor Alum will be here in ten minutes. Don't disturb me. Professor Alum is a philosopher, philologist, critic, and halfback for Heidelberg in '34. He will give me my first lesson.

> *Enter a threadbare studious man of forty,* ALUM.

ALUM: Thirty-five floors. Shouldn't you put in elevators?

MARTINAS: Ah, Doctor Professor. Enchanted. Always admired your books. Teach me to read.

ALUM: [*picks up three volumes on* MARTINAS' *desk*] Dante, Shelley, Keats? Have you trouble reading Dante, Shelley, and Keats? Is it the symbolism, the metaphor, the syntax?

MARTINAS: The reading. I can't read. It's ruining my career as a well-rounded fellow. I'm what cruel people call illiterate.

ALUM: You're a beginner?

MARTINAS: I'm not exactly a beginner: I build poems.

> *Declaims.*

> Tho' I lack education,
> In my estimation
> There's no other poet
> Like that Irish poet,
> Kelly of Kelly and Sheats.

ALUM: What about Dante?

MARTINAS: There's nothing more Dante,
> Except a lace pantie,
> Than reading the poems of,
> Those Irish poems of,
> Kelly of Kelly and Sheats.

ALUM: Oh yes, your sense of humor. Get rid of it.

MARTINAS: My poem?

ALUM: Not bad.

MARTINAS: Not bad! You academic low-grade moron! Can't you say more about it?

ALUM: Not with your butcher knife on the table.

MARTINAS: Charlatan, Svengali, cheapskate!

ALUM: Cheapskate?

MARTINAS: Charging so little.

ALUM: Little?

MARTINAS: Three dollars, that's all you're getting so that's all you're charging.

ALUM: It's been a pleasure hating you; learn to read, so I can write you a scathing note of thanks. You beginner!

MARTINAS: Me? Learn to read? Catch your disease? Never. Goombye, Doctor Professor.

ALUM: Take your three dollars and shove it—in an envelope and send it to me—Archilochus Shemasky, c/o the Home for Homeless Men.

MARTINAS: Why are you disguised as brilliant Professor Alum, philosopher, philologist, critic, and halfback for Heidelberg in '34?

ALUM: Do I look like brilliant Professor Alum?

MARTINAS: I've never seen the fool.

ALUM: I never heard of Alum. *I'm* a poet. I came for a Santa Claus position, dispatched here by the Jeffrey Freedom Employment Agency. And I'll make a good Santa, Mr. Martinas. I've never owned anything.

MARTINAS: So you want to be a Santa? My Santas have to give away meats to the kiddies, teeny wieners, liverwurst cones, chocolate chicken feet: we call them tidbits for tots.

ALUM: Lovely.

MARTINAS: You don't mind kids yelling, grabbing for snacks, stuffing their little faces with food?

ALUM: Lovely.

MARTINAS: You're fired. Goombye. You'd give away all my profits. A man doesn't build thirty-five floors of meat by giving all his food to kiddies. First floor, loins of beef; second floor, veal; third, lamb; fourth, me, a large apartment, French provincial iceboxes, blood cocktail bar [*Drinks one himself*]; fifth floor, the various marrows…

ALUM: Goombye.

> *Exit.*

MARTINAS: [*into intercom*] Get me the Jeffrey Freedom Employment Agency. The real Professor Alum, philosopher, philologist, critic, and halfback for Heidelberg in '34 should be here any minute. Throw him out. [*Picks up phone, talks into it.*] Jeffrey Freedom? What kind of employment agency are you running? I wanted a Santa Claus with heart, savoir-faire, gusto, and a private income. I wanted a red-blooded, red-nosed, red-cheeked, red-flanneled man for the job. What did you send me? A red. A bolshevik. And if I wanted to get him in trouble I'd call him a Communist, the commie. Goombye!

> *Enter* WILMER *and* BEZ. BEZ *sits on the chopping table-desk and begins tearing a doll apart as* MARTINAS *looks over two Santa masks and puts them aside together.*

BEZ: I found us a Santa!

WILMER: [*having climbed thirty-five flights*]: Thirty-five floors of meat, what a marvel!

MARTINAS: Stop criticizing! Haven't I seen you before? What qualifies you as beloved Santa of the Martinas Meat Mart?

WILMER: I used to make and sell dolls. Dolls were the key.

> BEZ *chops doll with meat cleaver.*

WILMER: [*takes tidbit from a Santa Claus bag, eats.*] This is the best tidbit for tots I've ever had.

MARTINAS: I'm glad. Stop eating. You're on my time.

WILMER: I'm in?

MARTINAS: Put on this Santa mask and hat. I had another mask somewhere.

> WILMER *puts on mask and hat; tries to steal a tidbit, but* BEZ *slaps it out of his hand. Santa mask is fully adjusted.*

MARTINAS: [*indicates* WILMER's *masked face*] Bez, my son, what do you think? Where's the other mask? Did he eat it?

BEZ: Let's hear him laugh.

> WILMER *sobs behind mask.*

Beautiful. He'll make an authentic Santa.

MARTINAS: [*giving rest of uniform to* WILMER] You're in! Put on the rest of the uniform.

WILMER: [*weeping, arms outstretched*]: Bez, my Bez—

MARTINAS: Oh Santa, you're on *my* time!

BEZ: He should double the gross intake this week, Dad.

> WILMER *puts on Santa uniform.*

MARTINAS: Bez can't read, but he sure can count!

WILMER: Please, may I hear him count.

MARTINAS: Count, Bez, my child.

BEZ: One, two, three, three-fifty, four, four and a quarter…

MARTINAS: Add?

BEZ: One chop plus one chop is two chops. Dad, what an advertising stunt! The Santa scheme cost fifty dollars tops, but it should net us somewhere in the neighborhood of—

> WILMER *has finished changing into Santa uniform.*

Santa! Santa! [*Sits on* WILMER's *lap.*] What am I going to get for Christmas?

WILMER: I don't know. Does that qualify me as a non-Santa? O Bez, Bez...

> BEZ *leaps off* WILMER's *lap.* WILMER *reaches out, weeping, one hand toward* BEZ, *one hand toward the food.*

MARTINAS: Bez, did you see my other Santa mask? It was younger looking. I had them both together. [*Looking for mask.*] Hey, what's this filthy suitcase?

BEZ: Some bum gave it to me.

> WILMER *sobs.*

MARTINAS: You're on *my* time, Santa. Now get out there and give! [*Gives* WILMER *bag of tidbits.*]

> *Crossfade.*

SCENE THREE

The street.

> WILMER *in Santa uniform leaves* MARTINAS' *building, calls to passers-by laden with Christmas packages and dressed as if they themselves were gift-wrapped.*

WILMER: Tidbits for tots! Compliments of the O.O. Martinas Meat Mart. Bring them home to the kiddies. Candied sweetbreads, chocolate chicken feet.

> SELMA *approaches. She is wearing a suit that looks as if it is made of Christmas wrapping of silk and tinsel.*

> WILMER *expresses shock, then grief.* SELMA *walks to him and* WILMER *joyfully opens his arms.*

SELMA: Uniform's too big. I'll speak to O.O. about it.

WILMER: Don't you know me?

SELMA: Of course. You're Santa Claus. Merry Christmas. That uniform makes you pathetic and poor, Santa. Anyone would think you're a bum.

> *She goes toward building.*

WILMER: Selma...

> *Romantic music.*

Selma!

SELMA: A voice I've known.

> WILMER *rushes to her and triumphantly takes off his mask. Beneath it is the other Santa Claus mask.*

WILMER: Selma!

SELMA: I was right. You *are* Santa Claus.

> WILMER *tries to take other mask off.* SELMA *helps him and when she sees his face, she weeps.*

WILMER: Yes, it's Wilmer Flange, your former casual acquaintance and husband.

SELMA: You don't look well. Have you failed in your several chosen fields?

WILMER: I'm all right. I'll be a traveling Santa. The key? America in the winter: Argentina in the summer. Santas down there don't have the know-how. I'll be in demand. I'll be loved. And in Spanish. Come with me.

SELMA: I'm OK with O.O.

WILMER: Some men would plead and beg. I'm one of them.

SELMA: Kiss me.

WILMER: On the street?

SELMA: On the mouth.

> *They kiss.*

WILMER: I knew it! I knew we were really the type for each other. I knew you hated that ignorant old man, knew you didn't need him, him when you had me, me.

SELMA: Yes, yes! Kiss. Kiss.

> *They kiss, kiss. Music stops.*

And now good-by. I realize I said I'll be waiting whenever you need me, so I hope there are no hard feelings that I've grown used to O.O. And I need money for when I become rich. I'll thank you not to call him an ignorant old, useless old, impotent old man.

WILMER: I didn't say he was impotent.

SELMA: Yes, well, anyway. Don't you see, Wilmer, life isn't everything.

> *Exit.*

WILMER: If ever you need me, Selma—

> WILMER *puts on one Santa Claus mask and holds the other in his hands. Gloom settles around him, but a ray of light picks out still another bearded—though thinner—face.*

WILMER: A fellow Santa! If I can't have love, I want companionship.

> *The other "Santa" steps into the light and is revealed as no Santa at all. He is* UNCLE SAM. *He points at* WILMER *as in the famous poster.*

UNCLE SAM: I want you!

> UNCLE SAM *helps* WILMER *into army uniform from Santa uniform and* WILMER *marches off with rifle.*
>
> *Blackout.*

SCENE FOUR

> *Projection on Curtain: "WAR"*
> *The slide is cracked to give the impression of barbed wire. Another projection follows: An exclamation point all by itself.*
> *A battlefield. Night.* WILMER *is advancing, rifle in hand. Battle noises, smoke. Occasional flares. Other soldiers are dimly seen in the background.*

FIRST SOLDIER: Do we advance?

WILMER: I don't know.

SECOND SOLDIER: Where are we heading?

WILMER: I don't know.

THIRD SOLDIER: What will we do after we get there?

WILMER: I don't know.

FIRST SOLDIER: Say, who are you?

WILMER: I'm in Central Intelligence.

SECOND SOLDIER: *Let's retreat!*

ALL: Swell!

THIRD SOLDIER: [*to* SECOND SOLDIER] Which way is back?

WILMER: I don't know.

> *The three* SOLDIERS *exit in confusion, bumping into each other as they go. The flares have died out and the stage is completely black.*
>
> *After a few moments, the glow of a lit cigarette becomes visible on one side of the stage.*
>
> WILMER, *unseen, moves toward the lit cigarette.*

WILMER: I beg your pardon. Could I bother you for a light?

> WILMER *takes a light from the other cigarette.*

I'm tired of being drafted. I didn't mind those two wars last year, but now I'm highly involved in a project which leaves me no time for war—namely: military history. It's the key, you know. For example, people learn from military history how to avoid war. Think of the chaos the world would be in today if it had no military history. My motto is: Be nice to history and history will be nice to you.

> *Other soldier snores.*

Don't fall asleep. Please.

ENEMY SOLDIER: [*in thick German accent*] Shh! A zoldier cannot zome zleep around here get?

WILMER: Where did you get that accent?

ENEMY SOLDIER: Oxford.

WILMER: That's a German accent. Are you of German descent?

ENEMY SOLDIER: Ja vohl.

WILMER: You're not my enemy by any chance?

ENEMY SOLDIER: Ja vohl.

WILMER: Wilmer Flange is the name. Happy to meet one of you. I like your work. I admire your military strategy.

> *Bomb explodes with enormous noise. Livid green light takes the stage.*

ENEMY SOLDIER: [*In the light he is seen to be a wild-looking Japanese soldier with sword.*] Vat a boom!

WILMER: No offense, but you're very Japanese.

ENEMY SOLDIER: Only on mein father's side. Mom vas German.

WILMER: Must we fight each other to the death?

ENEMY SOLDIER: Zilence! The enemy will hear.

WILMER: The enemy?

ENEMY SOLDIER: Our superior officers.

WILMER: Are you like me? A pacifist fighting to end war?

ENEMY SOLDIER: Ja vohl. I was shot in the head.

WILMER: Hope I didn't do it.

ENEMY SOLDIER: Today for surgery I'm leaving.

WILMER: Tokyo?

ENEMY SOLDIER: Nein.

WILMER: Berlin?

ENEMY SOLDIER: Nein.

WILMER: Boston? Ha ha ha—

ENEMY SOLDIER: Nein. New York. I go now to dem dere United States. I have a psychiatrist uncle in the Vest Eighties.

WILMER: Selma lives there in the O.O. Martinas Meat Emporium, she's the former mother of my ex-wife's child, Bez. [*Taking out pencil and paper.*] Give her this note. I haven't seen her in many a war. [*Writing*] "If ever you need me, I'll be waiting…"

ENEMY SOLDIER: I must go!

WILMER: Here!

> *Hands him letter.* ENEMY SOLDIER *swallows it.*

ENEMY SOLDIER: [*leaving*] It's been a pleasure. Auf wiedersehn.

WILMER: [*waving*] Banzai. Here's hoping we see each other again—maybe through a pair of binoculars.

> *A blast. Exit* ENEMY SOLDIER *who takes* WILMER's *rifle by mistake.*

WILMER: [*holding sword*] Another shot heard round the world.

> *Blackout.*

SCENE FIVE

Projection on Curtain: "MORE WAR"
> *Another projection follows: Two exclamation points by themselves. The street. Years later. Shoeshine stand. Night.*

FIRST POLICEMAN: War!

SECOND POLICEMAN: The wars roll by like cherry pits down the City Hall steps. The cows hanging in the O.O. Martinas window upside down see nothing but marching shoes war after war after war.

FIRST POLICEMAN: I don't like animals to see me upside down. I look funny upside down. My smile looks too sad. This is a depressing war.

SECOND POLICEMAN: It's a fun war for some. O.O. has the joy of donating fat steaks under that juicy government contract.

FIRST POLICEMAN: A dollar-a-year man.

SECOND POLICEMAN: A dollar-a-pound man. Little wonder he was made honorary President.

FIRST POLICEMAN: Another six stories added to the building. Young Bez grown older, a chip off the old chopping block, graduated from sculpture school with a BC—Bachelor of Carving, now an airborne army butcher.

SECOND POLICEMAN: While his former dad, Wilmer—

FIRST POLICEMAN: A mere private, slowly rising to the rank of conscientious objector.

SECOND POLICEMAN: Nowadays people do everything they don't want. It was better before the war when they had no more money. Now they have more money. That's why they have to rob to keep up their standard of living. Look, for instance. There's a robber robbing.

A woman is robbed by HIGH HAT ROBBER. SECOND POLICEMAN *draws gun,* ROBBER *shoots and runs off.* SECOND POLICEMAN *holds his heart, falls to the ground.* FIRST POLICEMAN *and robbery* VICTIM *rush to* SECOND POLICEMAN'S *aid.*

SECOND POLICEMAN: I'm going…it's over.

FIRST POLICEMAN: André, André! Your life's not over.

SECOND POLICEMAN: [*jumps up healthily*] Not my life. My career as a policeman. I'm going to retire from the force.

FIRST POLICEMAN: Weren't you shot?

SECOND POLICEMAN: No. I made believe, so he would run away and never shoot again. The war made him nervous.

FIRST POLICEMAN: Now maybe we can become partners in the music business. And…

They tiptoe off into darkness. Both snapping their fingers in rhythm. The VICTIM *watches and wonders.*

The HIGH HAT ROBBER *is advancing on* VICTIM *from behind, gun in hand, as stage darkens to blackout.*

SCENE SIX

MARTINAS' *apartment. Years later.* MARTINAS *sits at one of his chopping tables: He eats a rapid meal of six meat courses, served by* SELMA *in a negligee.*

SELMA: Hummingbirds stuffed with condor livers; ham sandwich on pork; filet mignon wrapped in filet mignon; lamb chop aspic; artichokes made of veal; and a nice glass of gravy to wash it down. For dessert, goose mousse.

MARTINAS: What a wonderful breakfast!

SELMA: You deserve it, darling, after your war effort—contributing meat and keeping it at ceiling price.

MARTINAS: What a summery winter's day. Let's go to the park and have brunch. Make a basketful of stew. Nice word, "Brunch." Sounds like a combination of two words. "Unch" for lunch and "Br" for brunch. [*Cute as he can be.*] Unch, Unch, I think it comes from the Flemish. Uncho, unchere, unchui, unctuous.

SELMA: That's Greek.

MARTINAS: [*picking his teeth*] Flemish. I had a Dutch uncle.

Doorbell rings. SELMA *opens door.* ENEMY SOLDIER *appears. Draws* WILMER's *letter out of his mouth like long piece of string.* MARTINAS *tips him.* ENEMY SOLDIER *exits bowing.*

    SELMA *reads the note, then her romantic music is heard. Folds note carefully and puts it next to her heart.*

SELMA: Take me to a movie. Let's go see "Das Kapital" by Marx.

MARTINAS: Saw it.

SELMA: Then let's go see "The Critique of Pure Reason."

MARTINAS: Saw it.

SELMA: Me too, but I only remember what I said about it: Melville's worst book.

MARTINAS: A good writer, for good readers.

SELMA: You can't even read!

MARTINAS: We can't even have a decent argument. Selma, the old thrill's gone. What happened to our setup?

    There is a tremendous noise and the whole apartment shakes.

MARTINAS: My God! What is that implosion?

    CRASH, and they rush to each other's arms.

SELMA: The end of the world. I know it. Oh, dearest of all butchers, hold me tight. Carry me gently to hell.

    Sobs.

MARTINAS: Darling, you're not going to hell: you're intelligent.

SELMA: I'm not a well-informed person.

MARTINAS: You're fairly well read.

    Another BOOM.

Before we die, one thing—recite my last poem.

    They hold each other desperately as SELMA *recites.*

SELMA: Love is like a red red eye,
      It makes you cry to see it.
      Love is a bloodshot eye,
      It hurts too much to cry back.
      Love is like a red red eye,
      It makes your eye red when you see it.
      Love is like an alcoholic eye,
      It makes you ashamed it can see you.
      Love is like a red, red eye
      Red eyeballs, red eyelids, red eyelobes,
          red brain lobes.
      A very red, very stormy eye.

    The shaking of the house has been gradually subsiding. When it stops at last SELMA *and* MARTINAS *look unbelieving at the wonderful world still there.*

SELMA: Darling, what happened? Did you hear that explosion?

MARTINAS: Sweetie, let's listen to the radio. Find out what happened. By the way, it was an implosion, not an explosion.

SELMA: An explosion! Probably a bomb, darling.

MARTINAS: [*goes to radio*] It was an implosion caused by the weather, sweetie.

SELMA: I think no. [*Turns on radio.*]

RADIO: Authorities have not determined if the implosion was another bomb to end all booms—, or if the boom was based on the weather—, or if the weather which caused the implosion was caused by the boom of the bomb—, or whether the weather—

MARTINAS: [*turns off radio*] See?

SELMA: See what, sweetie? He called it a boom. Bombs cause explosions.

MARTINAS: Darling, he said the weather. Ergo: implosion.

SELMA: What do you know about the weather?

MARTINAS: I may not know much about the weather, but I know what I like. [*yells*] Implosion! I-M-P-L-S-H-U-N. Implosion!

> SELMA *starts toward door.*

Goombye!

SELMA: *Boombye!*

> SELMA *rushes out putting coat over her negligee. She slams the door behind her. Blackout.*

SCENE SEVEN

> *Restaurant. High upright piano is being played: back of piano faces audience. No pianist is visible.*

WILMER: [*enters in civilian clothes brushing debris from shoulder*] What sweet music. It should be played on a harpsichord.

> *Piano bumps him in consternation.*

No offense, but pianos simply don't have that old-world swing.

> *Piano bumps him again and starts to leave.*

What did I do? Please talk to me.

> *Piano keeps moving slowly away.*

I haven't spoken to anyone in ages. Since my discharge I don't get around. My work occupies my life: musicology, it's all I have. My friends are dead or married. I married a few days ago. A lady and a musician. What bliss! She had no children, no parents. No technique. We were divorced this morning.

> *Piano moves sympathetically toward him.*

Can you find it in your hands to forgive me for criticizing?

> *Piano takes pity, starts to play.*

Maybe not a harpsichord after all; a clavichord.

> *The piano moves off-stage in disgust leaving* WILMER *abandoned.*
>
> SELMA *in coat over negligee rushes in.*

WILMER: Selma Chargesse, casual acquaintance and wife— but whose?

SELMA: Did you hear the big boom?

WILMER: Yes. E flat. Heard it passing a movie. The theater caved in.

SELMA: What was playing?

WILMER: Too sad to remember.

SELMA: Saw it. What caused the boom? Bomb or weather?

WILMER: [*warily*] Which do you think?

> MARTINAS *appears in doorway, in same clothes as previous scene, arms spread-eagle.*

SELMA: I think we *are* each other's type!

WILMER: Selma, I need *you,* more than Beethoven's Piano Sonata Number 32 in C Minor, Opus III, composed at Mödling in the summer of 1820.

> *They embrace.*

MARTINAS: [*rushes in, throws an arm warmly around each*] We're all each other's types. By the way, I've been wanting to get you kids together for a long time. Kids, listen to an old illiterate…who's done pretty well for himself in a world of misjudgment, misconception, mismanagement, Miss America—and misplosions. [*Sweetly.*] We three need each other like holes in the head—need patches. We can be partners in the O.O. Martinas All American, All Meat Mart. Forty-eight stories, but growing, a big silver and stucco ever-growing soul. What do you say, kids? Let's spend the rest of our lives together for the fun of it.

WILMER: [*to* MARTINAS] Partners? Selma, maybe we should. You spend so much time running back to O.O., I'd see more of you if I ran *with* you. The only time you need me is when you're with him.

SELMA: It was only the money of it.

WILMER: What money? It was the bleeding animal flesh of it. The meat of it.

SELMA: You mean meat might be the key?

WILMER: I mean…meat *is* the key. We mean we *are* all one another's types. We mean— OK, O.O.

WILMER *and* SELMA: [*together*] We'll spend the rest of our lives with you.

> *All three march off.*
>
> *Enter piano*—FIRST POLICEMAN *playing,* SECOND POLICEMAN *turning pages.*

SECOND POLICEMAN: Glad I retired from the force and took up piano?

FIRST POLICEMAN: André, don't they remind you of the three people who used to be around here always laughing and in trouble?

SECOND POLICEMAN: They cannot be the same. They haven't changed enough.

CURTAIN

SCENE EIGHT

Projection on Curtain: Years later: "The Ending: In Which It Again Begins."
> MARTINAS *and* SELMA *in butcher coats behind the three chopping tables, cut-*

ting meat. WILMER *enters guiltily with a towel wrapped around one hand, carrying a meat cleaver in his other hand.* WILMER *and* SELMA *have aged;* MARTINAS *hasn't changed. Three huge sides of beef behind them, engulf them.*

SELMA: Wilmer, you've cut yourself again.

MARTINAS [*unwraps towel and looks at the bloody wound*]: You keep cutting your hand.

WILMER: I was juggling cleavers in the refrigerator to keep warm. I read in a magazine I wrap the sweetbreads in that the Navaho country is warm.

MARTINAS: He's too human.

WILMER: You know what I want? To live way out there among the Navaho.

MARTINAS: Back to work. We've got the biggest order of our career: two tons of corned beef, two tons of roast beef, six miles of frankfurters and a sprinkling of chicken livers. Becount of they're having a party.

WILMER: Why weren't we invited?

MARTINAS: They say we're not as good as the next fellow. Selma, take over the corned beef.

SELMA: Righto, O.O.

MARTINAS: Wilmer, step up production on the roast beef.

WILMER: Righto, O.O.

They all resume their work, cutting and cleaving meat in silence. Music.
I want to live way out there among the Navaho. Selma, if you love me, come!

SELMA: Too old to begin a new life. Look at the girl you wooed and won years ago. Weak, tired. Not the gay slip of a thing I used to be—beautiful, agile, able, hopeful, and a swell dancer. How can I live way out there among the Navaho? Dearest butcher…

WILMER: I want to learn ancestral customs, primitive dances. I want to make sand paintings to send my friends on Independence Day. O.O., tell her you'll send us our fair share of the Mart each month.

MARTINAS: You know I cheat. Oh, just a little, mind you: take advantage in a small harmless way. Sort of cute, you see, [*suddenly violent*] the world can't kick me around, O.O. The world better watch out, O.O., or I take it between these two fingers and squeeze it like a louse, O.O.

WILMER *and* SELMA *rush to their work.*

[*Sweetly.*] No, I like Wilmer near me! I don't want him way out there among the Navaho.

SELMA: Wilmer, I've always loved you, I love you still. I'll love you when I'm old, when it's difficult to love anyone or anything but proper bodily functions. I'll love you a long time after we're dead…but—

WILMER: The Navaho still worship the good old gods, I hear tell. They do not kneel before new shrines, they are not blinded by the glitter of new shrines.

MARTINAS: All that glitters is not new shrines.

They resume rhythmic cutting and cleaving. VENDING WOMAN *and her small son enter.*

WOMAN: Pound of lovers, please.

MARTINAS: You mean livers, Madam?

WOMAN: Didn't I say livers?

MARTINAS: You said lovers.

BOY: Phonetically speaking, the similarity between the words "Lovers" and "Livers" cannot be denied. The liver is the ancient seat of the emotions.

WOMAN: Yes. Shut up.

MARTINAS: What a brilliant butcher he'd make. Like our former son, Bez, the first Astro-butcher; lost in orbit.

They bow their heads in a moment of silent tribute.

WILMER: [*with package of livers*] Your livers!

WOMAN: For my cat, Wilmer.

MARTINAS: How did you know my friend's name was Wilmer?

WOMAN: I was talking about my *cat,* Wilmer. It's for him I buy lovers. [*To* BOY.] Right, Wilmer?

SELMA: Your name is Wilmer?

BOY: Yarths.

WILMER: One question.

BOY: Yarths?

WILMER: [*to* WOMAN]: Why does he say yarths? He has such a nice command of other words.

WOMAN: A lovely command.

MARTINAS: One of the loveliest commands I, personally, have come across. And I've come across quite a few commands in my day.

WILMER: I, personally, have come across very few commands. I have not seen much of these United States. For instance, I want to live way out there among the Navaho, a fine folk in the field of the rug and the pot.

BOY: And they worship the good old gods.

WILMER: You—?

BOY: Yarths, I've lived way out there among the Navaho.

WOMAN: Yes. Shut up.

WILMER: Before you shut up, Wilmer...

BOY: Yarths, Wilmer?

WILMER: What was it like way out there among the Navaho?

BOY: Chilly at night.

WOMAN: [*taking bag of livers*] Let's go feed our cat, Wilmer.

WILMER: Which Wilmer did you mean?

WOMAN: Wouldn't *you* like to go fishing in my soul of souls!

BOY: Can't we stay? I like these people. I'm sick of intelligent and charming people.

WOMAN: No, they're not as good as the next fellow.

WILMER: Who is?

BOY: The Navajo!

WOMAN *and* BOY *leave and* WILMER, SELMA *and* MARTINAS *chop in silence. Suddenly* WILMER *takes money from cash register, chops it with cleaver.*

WILMER: Selma, come with me to live way out there among the Navaho?

SELMA: Yarths!

SELMA *and* WILMER *mark time, ready to march off.*

MARTINAS: [*sadly chopping meat*] Take me with you? I'll miss us three, the joy of enterprise troubles, the fun of raising a forty-nine story meat mart. Take me with you.

WILMER: Oh, no you don't talk us into another passage of history with you.

MARTINAS: I'm sick of this life, too. Not being as good as the next fellow, day in, day out. A business where all is butchery. World, would you like a leg to eat? Not from my hands will you buy bleeding animal flesh for dollars. [*Stares at meat contritely.*] Forgive me. [*Turns to* WILMER.] Take me with you? Maybe I'll forget you taught me how to read and write and I'll build poems once more.

WILMER: Will you give up the sale of bleeding animal flesh?

MARTINAS: I am. I will. I have.

WILMER: Am what?

MARTINAS: Am giving up the sale of meat.

WILMER: Will what?

MARTINAS: Will giving it up. Have what?

WILMER: Have been feeling older.

SELMA: What are we getting so old about?

MARTINAS: Take me with you?

WILMER: How do we know you won't drag us back into the meat business?

MARTINAS: Becount of I'm going into—the fish business, where I can live and be free. I belong in the fish business. It's what I've always wanted in my head of heads. Tomorrow we go way out there among the Navaho. The Navaho, where I buy my dream fish department store, fifty floors of fish. First floor, flounder; second floor, sea bass; third floor, blubber; fourth floor, me, a large apartment, but the finest Navaho rugs and sand paintings; fifth floor, sea weed....

As they all march off.

CURTAIN

Jack Richardson

☙

# Gallows Humor

A Play in Two Parts

•

Gallows Humor was first performed at the Gramercy Arts Theatre in New York on April 18, 1961. Julie Bovasso played the parts of Lucy and Martha: Gerald Hiken those of Walter and Phillip; Vincent Gardenia acted the Warden; and Paxton Whitehead was the Prologue. The play was directed by George L. Sherman.

•

CHARACTERS
Part 1:
THE WARDEN
LUCY
WALTER

Part 2:
THE WARDEN
PHILLIP MARTHA

PROLOGUE

An Actor, dressed in the costume of Death, steps before the curtain.

Ladies and gentlemen—a few words please. Now, those of you who are already beginning to fidget, squirm, and grumble about costume plays, let me begin by assuring you that I do not reappear this evening once the curtain has been raised. Indeed, it is only due to my sulking, fits of temper, and slight influence with the producer that I've managed to salvage this much of your attention from the play's remaining characters, whom all concerned found more entertaining, amusing, and dramatically effective than I. For, ladies and gentlemen, you see before you a part, a character, a creation, if you will, that has been cut—snipped out of the night's diversions by the author's second thoughts and placed here as an, we hope, inoffensive bonus, to be listened to or ignored at your pleasure. And *why* was this done, when you can see the expense I've gone to with my costume, the way I turn a phrase, and my rather relaxed manner in front of you which hints no little experience on the boards? Simply because I, I was considered too obvious, too blunt, too heavy-handed for a play struggling with your modern subtleties! My theatrical days, I was told, ended with the morality play, when other personae—Good Deeds, Knowledge, Earthly Pleasure, etc.— dragged their capitalized names and single dimensions across a bare stage, and I was well known about society as the great common denominator, familiar to everyone in the pit as that undernourished wag who skulked along the streets to the sound of flute and tabor, laying hands on kings and beggars, bishops and madmen, naughty nuns and clanking cavaliers. I was, you might say, a popular hero, and no one demanded any more from my appearances than that I stand as a reminder to the uncomfortable fact that life, with all its peculiar pleasures of the palace and the alehouse, has its dark and inevitable opposite. At times, I'll admit, the humor in these works was somewhat broad, and, on occasion, I was paired with an overbusty blonde ingenue, who, waving a few shocks of wheat in the air as a fertility symbol, would chase me about the stage to the low-bred delight of some rural audience. But such excesses were rare, and, more often, a healthy rapport was set up between the spectators and me which, while by no means making me immune from a few scattered jeers and catcalls, nevertheless allowed me to, as they say, get my laughs and make my point. But now, apparently, my point needs sharpening. Death is no longer something personal, something deeply etched, something old women claim they feel slipping lasciviously into their winter beds. Indeed, in the last years, I seem both to have expanded and blurred my activities without knowing it. The grave's dimensions suddenly have grown to include those who have not yet achieved the once necessary technicality of ceasing to breathe. It appears I now infiltrate those still bouncing to music, still kissing their wives, still wiggling their forefingers in the air to emphasize those final truths by which they think their lives are lived. But are they, after all, living? And if not, where does that leave me with my black-and-white attitude in the matter? It leaves me here, ladies and gentlemen, to deliver a poor prologue while the scenery is readied, while your tardy members stumble into their places, and the search begins for programs that have already slipped beneath, behind, or between your seats. But I cannot really be too bitter. The anger of rejection having cooled, my healthy common sense tells me that I would have been truly out of place in a play designed for your tastes. For I confess that just yesterday, I—whom centuries have trained to recognize the precise moment when the eye's glaze, the hand's stiffness, and the mind's dimness announce another ghost has been given up to my charge—I made a total ass of myself by tugging away at a good dozen or so gentlemen who had no intention as yet of quitting this world. Looking at them, noticing all the old symptoms, I could have sworn they were ready, but that mistake was just one in a whole series ranging from hospitals to beauty salons that I've been making recently with my old-fashioned methods. That one-time basic distinction between the quick and the dead has become far too abstract today for one with my earthbound mind, and this fundamental confusion was, I fear, showing up in my performances. For even on the stage, in a play darkened by the shadow of a gallows, I, so perfectly at home in such a setting, now find it difficult, with my ancient eyes, to tell the hangman from the hanged. I hope, for my future and peace of mind, that you, the author's contemporaries, do not.

Death exits, drawing the curtain as he does so.

PART 1

The lights come up upon a prison cell. There is a small washbasin to the right, and, standing close against the center wall, there is a razor-thin cot. Above the monkish bed is the room's sole window, barred into sections, through which one can see that it is night outside. At the room's left is the cell door, and behind it the beginning of an outside corridor. In this passageway, looking into the cell, stand a man and woman. Next to them, on a little portable tray, is a large platter decked with silver Queen Anne cover dishes, sauceboats, etc. The man, comfortably stout, seems expansively contented with himself. He is smiling broadly. The woman, attired in a bright yellow blouse and tight black skirt, has a thin face of angle and bone which is well covered with cosmetics. Her age is indeterminate, and she is beautiful in the way a carnival mask is so.

They are looking at WALTER, *who is sitting on the cell's cot. He has the jacket of his prison suit in his lap and is attending to it with needle and thread. Caught in his undershirt, he seems very pale and fragile. His face is unremarkably inoffensive, and covered with the scribbling of a fifty-year-old life. As he sews, he hums to himself.*

After several seconds, the man, THE WARDEN, *and the woman,* LUCY, *begin to speak.*

WARDEN: There he is, Lucy. Let's hope this one doesn't prove too difficult for you.

LUCY: Now what could someone who looks like that do to be hanged?

WARDEN: [*chuckling*] He beat his wife to death with a golf club—forty-one strokes from the temple to the chin.

At this point WALTER's *humming rises a bit in pitch and volume.*

LUCY: What a nice smile he has, and how thin his arms are. They're not tattooed either.

WARDEN: [*smiling, but a bit impatient*] Now, Lucy, it's romantic notions like that that get you into trouble. If you start thinking of murderers as upper-middle-class types you'll be more successful at your work.

LUCY: [*indignant*] I haven't done too bad up till now. There aren't many women, even in the trade, that can take a man's mind off your gallows when he's got less than two hours to go.

WARDEN: [*in an apologetic tone*] Oh, you're a professional, all right; they just don't cut them like you any more. But sometimes I wonder if you weren't better suited to those naughty houses stuffed with incense, beaded curtains, and overhead mirrors. Maybe you're just not up to making love surrounded by four gray walls.

LUCY: Listen, Warden, I've had my victories in here too.

WARDEN: Yes, but the state's gone to a great deal of trouble bringing you ladies up here to serve as little humanizing morsels for those it's going to hang. Your whole purpose is to make these poor fellows' last hours so heady, so full of pleasure that they just float up those stairs and smile into the dull, commonplace face of our hangman. Making love to you, Lucy, is supposed to accomplish this. And yet the last two you handed over to us behaved abominably: they shuffled by those sentimental journalists looking as if they were already dead. You know what the press can do with that; and then all our good intentions are forgotten.

LUCY: I couldn't get near those two. They just weren't interested.

WARDEN: [*in a slightly threatening tone*] It's your job to make them interested, Lucy.

LUCY: Now what could I do? One was over seventy, after all, and the other told me he hadn't made love to anything since he saw his cat's hysterectomy scars.

WARDEN: You were picked for this official work because you seemed to have experience with difficult types. Remember where you were when we found you? Standing in a doorway with a scraggly piece of fur around your neck and runs in your stockings. Even in the city's poorest section you weren't turning customers away, were you? And if you had to go back to it...

LUCY: All right, Warden, you've made your point.

WARDEN: Just a little warning, Lucy. You know how I'd hate to fire you.

LUCY: All right, all right. Now, is there anything I should know about our man in there?

WARDEN: Oh, you should really find him easy to deal with. He's been most cooperative since being with us: never cried when appeals were turned down, never spat his food back at the guards, never used the walls for thumbnosing little phrases at the world—no, he's been a perfect sort up till now.

LUCY: Good, I don't like those who have an axe to grind. They never stop talking long enough for anything to really get going between us.

WARDEN: Well, Walter there's one of the better sort, all right, that's why you were assigned to him. You used to do so well with educated types. I remembered that physicist you went after a few years ago—for six months he moped about his cell, mumbling to himself. But after you were through with him he died happily explaining the theory of subatomic particles to our executioner. You'd turned a homicidal maniac back into a useful man.

LUCY: I just got his mind back on fundamentals. That seems to pep his type up.

WARDEN: Well, that's what I want you to do for Walter. [*Tapping one of the cover dishes.*] I had our chef up all night working on the fried chicken in here, but I hope he'll enjoy you even more. I sort of like this one and want him to have a little fling before he's hanged.

LUCY: [*flatly*] Oh, you have a big heart under that forty-dollar suit, Warden.

WARDEN: Why, thank you, Lucy. Sometimes I think it goes unnoticed.

LUCY: Now, shall I get to work?

WARDEN: All right, we might as well start the introductions. Ah, would you wheel his dinner in to him? I think the silver trays will set you off to advantage.

> THE WARDEN *extracts a key, opens the cell door, and he and* LUCY *enter.* WALTER, *his sewing in his hands, jumps up abruptly to meet them. He then follows* LUCY *with his eyes as smiling, she wheels the tray past him into the lower left corner of the cell.*

Hello, Walter, how's it going today?

WALTER: [*still trying to keep an eye on* LUCY *who, after leaving the tray, begins walking about the cell, tapping at the walls and poking at the cot*] Warden, nice of you to come by. Is it time already?

WARDEN: Heavens, no; you still have nearly two hours. Some insects, I'm told, live an entire life through in less time—birth, copulation, and death, all counted off in seconds.

WALTER: [*pleasantly, but still with an eye on* LUCY *who is beginning to prop up the pillow on his cot*] That sounds like a very nice arrangement.

WARDEN: Right! After all, who needs years but those who have to repeat themselves?

LUCY: [*stepping back from the cot and examining it*] You're talking on my time, Warden.

WARDEN: Quite so, Lucy, quite so. Walter, I'd like you to meet Lucy. She's going to stay here with you until the end—compliments of the state.

WALTER: With me? But I don't understand.

WARDEN:No effusions of gratitude, Walter. No man should eat his last meal without a little female company.

WALTER: Do you mean she's to—to...?

WARDEN: [*nodding*] It's an innovation in our penal program. Takes some of the sting out of anti-capital punishment arguments. Sending a man out to die with a Lucy still fresh in every part of him—well, nothing cold-blooded about that, is there? Everything else about the little ceremony is, I'll admit, rather cut and dried, a bit too much so, even for my taste. That's what puts people off about it. The clack of the guard's shoes in cadence over those cobble stones, the same number of steps to be climbed, the ritual last trite phrases—no, there's not much spice in it any more. But with this new little prologue we've added—well, it seems to keep the others like you, Walter, from being swallowed up in formality. There's something touchingly human about the whole affair when Lucy and her kind deliver you back to our official hands.

LUCY: [*walking back to the tray of food, she opens a cover dish*] And it keeps girls like me off the street. Hmm! This will get cold if you don't start on it, Walter.

WALTER: Oh, I'm not really hungry.

WARDEN: But that's fried chicken in there. With a heavy crust.

WALTER: I know I ordered it, but you won't mind if I just don't begin right away.

LUCY: Well, you've no complaints if I have a leg then, do you? Being up this early in the morning always gives me an [*she says the word with a seductive smile at* WALTER] appetite.

WALTER: No, no; go right ahead.

WARDEN: [*watching* LUCY *as she takes a large bite*] Look at her go after that chicken, Walter. How many men would love to be in that piece of meat's place. And you're going to get the chance.

WALTER: Well, that's very nice, and I'm grateful to both of you; but I really don't...

WARDEN: Come now, Walter, no protests. Lucy there brings a little unpremeditated dash into the dull cubes and well-scrubbed-down corridors of our prison. You've been here so long I'll bet you've forgotten what a woman like Lucy, wrapped snugly in a yellow blouse and black skirt, can mean.

WALTER: [*backing away and waving his hand in protest*] Oh, no, I haven't.

LUCY: [*taking a few tentative dance steps*] Do you know, it's a pity you can't have music piped in here. It would be nice to dance a bit before settling down to work, wouldn't it, Walter?

WALTER: I can't dance, really.

WARDEN: Well, then, she could teach you. After all, there's always time to learn something new. But now, now that a festive note's been struck in the cell, I guess I'm what they call *de trop*. Well, now, enjoy each other. [*Pointing a preceptorial finger at* WALTER.] I want to see a contented face, Walter, when I return.

WALTER: Doesn't it seem contented now?

WARDEN: [*studying* WALTER'S *face*] It seems a little pinched and furrowed to me. Not the way one looks when Lucy's through with him.

WALTER: I can smile a bit if you want.

WARDEN: Save all that for the lady there. [*Stepping back and looking at the two of them.*] Ah, actually you make a fine-looking couple together. You know, it's moments like this that make a welfare state seem worth while after all.

      THE WARDEN *leaves.*

LUCY: [*throwing the chicken bone over her shoulder onto the floor*] God! I'd starve if he had to pimp for me.

WALTER: [*quickly going over and retrieving the bone and putting it back on the tray*] Please, I'm trying to leave a tidy cell behind me.

LUCY: Well, sorry!

WALTER: I don't mean to be rude, but you'd be surprised how hard it is keeping a little place like this in order.

LUCY: [*a little confused*] You give it a scrubbing once a day?

WALTER: Yes, but that won't do it. Every time a guard comes in here, some of the lint from his uniform stays behind. [*Tracing the descent of an imaginary piece of lint with his finger.*] You can see it floating down from a sleeve or a lapel, but once it hits the gray floor it's the devil to find.

LUCY: [*looking down at where* WALTER'S *finger last traced the lint*] I can see it could be a problem.

WALTER: But please don't let me stop you from finishing the chicken if you want to. Just be careful the crust doesn't splatter.

LUCY: But that's *your* last meal, after all, Walter.

WALTER: Oh, I'm afraid I ordered that in a fit of absence of mind. Fried foods raise the deuce with my stomach.

LUCY: Begins to ache?

WALTER: No, just snarl. It lasts for days, and, in company, believe me, it can be very embarrassing.

LUCY: [*after a pause in which she watches* WALTER *continue his sewing*] Well, then, if no food, how about a cigarette before we begin?

WALTER: No, thank you. And if you're going to, be careful of the ashes. There's a little can underneath the sink you can use.

LUCY: [*returning the cigarettes to her dress pocket, she turns away from* WALTER] Jesus!

[*Hunching her shoulders, she shivers and takes a few halting dance steps.*] You've got to keep moving to stay warm in here.

WALTER: That blouse you're wearing must be very thin.

LUCY: [*brightening*]Well, finally noticing that there's a woman in here with you?

WALTER: [*dropping his eyes back to the sewing*] Tell me, do you really do this sort of work often for the prison?

LUCY: I've signed a five-year contract. And, as I'm not getting any younger, it's turned out to be a pretty good arrangement. In the last year, though, I've been kept a little too busy. It must have been the moon phases or something, but it seems as if everybody was cementing mothers up in the basement, shooting politicians, or setting fire to their friends. I hope things begin to calm down a bit now.

WALTER: But isn't it dangerous to come into a confined place with men who are going to be hanged in a matter of hours?

LUCY: [*as she sits next to* WALTER *on the cot*] No more dangerous than the streets in the summer season. I'll take a cell with a man in it who's butchered an even dozen five-year-olds to a boulevard stuffed with tourists waving credit cards in one hand and pinching with the other. No, by the time a man reaches this cell, Walter, the violence he had in him has wasted away. It's been used up on his victim, the judge, his childhood, his shoes, and God knows what else. There's nothing but the lamb left when I arrive.

WALTER: The lamb?

LUCY: I don't mean that in a bad sense now. It's just that, for a woman who doesn't like to be treated roughly, I find men who use this cell have very gentle hands.

WALTER: [*looking at his hands*] Mine are a bit rough from all the floor scrubbing I've done. Prison soap isn't the best.

LUCY: [*taking his hands*] They look as soft as cats' paws to me.

WALTER: [*pulling his hands away, he inches back from* LUCY *and takes a big stitch in his sewing*] You must excuse me, but I have to finish this little job of mending

LUCY: I never thought I'd have to compete with a needle and thread, Walter.

WALTER: My number-patch was loose. I was afraid it might fall off during the—well, ceremonies.

LUCY: Your number-patch?

WALTER: [*defensively*] It's very important that this number stays on me. This is how I'm identified in I don't know how many files and on dozens of official cards. 43556 is the key to my ending life on the proper line in the ledger, and I've grown quite fond of it.

LUCY: [*humoring* WALTER] 43556—it has a nice ring to it. Better than a number packed with a lot of zeros.

WALTER: Well, actually, I would have preferred one with all even numbers, but it would have seemed fussy, I suppose, to insist on it.

LUCY: [*moving closer to* WALTER *and beginning to stroke his neck*] Well, now, why don't you put your sewing away and let me show you why the prison officials chose me out of over a thousand applicants for my job.

WALTER: [*jumping up from the cot*] Oh, no, Lucy, that's quite out of the question.

LUCY: [*just a slight touch of impatience showing*] Now listen, Walter...

WALTER: Oh, it's certainly nothing personal. [*Staring firmly at* LUCY.] You do make that blouse and skirt seem wrapped around perfect treasures, and your skin is beautifully pale and, I'm sure, exciting to stroke for hours, even with my rather insensitive hands. [*Pulling himself together.*] But, no, I just don't wish to.

LUCY: [*smoothing out her blouse*] Well, from the description, there isn't any doubt that you at least like women.

WALTER: Oh I do; or, rather, I did. But that's all over now.

LUCY: [*getting up and moving toward* WALTER] But it doesn't have to be over. There's still a little time left. You probably have a miniature gallows dancing in front of your eyes, and you think it's numbed those important little nerves for good. But, believe me, Lucy can start them twitching again. I've done it for dozens of others far more upset about dying than you seem to be.

WALTER: [*backing away from her*] But I don't want them to start twitching now.

LUCY: After they begin, then you'll want, Walter.

WALTER: No, no; I just want to remain peaceful.

LUCY: Peaceful? How can you use that word, when, in not too much more than an hour, you'll drag yourself up those thirteen steps?

WALTER: [*backed against the cell's left wall, he clutches his jacket, thread and needle in front of him*] You couldn't understand, Lucy. Being peaceful would just bore you.

LUCY: Nothing bores me, Walter. That's why I'm a success in my business.

WALTER: Please! Stay back a bit. I can hear you breathing.

LUCY: It's a nice sound, isn't it? My lungs, in fact all the machinery inside me, Walter, work perfectly.

WALTER: I'm sure; but I don't want to listen to their sounds. One of the advantages of a cell is its quiet. I've grown used to silence.

LUCY: [*rubbing his arm and speaking in a coaxing voice*] But my reputation's at stake, Walter. One failure leaves a permanent mark on one in my profession. I'd have to take to deeper layers of rouge, longer eyelashes, and darker stockings. My fur coat would need more padding at the shoulders and the heels on my shoes would be raised an inch at the very least. You wouldn't want to cause that, would you, Walter? You wouldn't want to start Lucy off looking for wigs and stronger perfumes?

WALTER: [*pleading*] The scent you're wearing is making me dizzy enough as it is.

LUCY: There, you see, those nerves aren't dead. They're coming back to us after all.

WALTER: [*trying, but not succeeding, to remove her hand*] Please, I'm just 43556; you can't expect a number to make love.

LUCY: [*tripping her finger across his chest*] I'm not touching a number now, am I? No, this is the body of a man. A little out of condition, maybe, from being closed up in a cell for months, but it still reacts to my fingers, doesn't it?

WALTER: [*as though suffering, he looks down at* LUCY's *bosom*] Oh, I've always been partial to women of your build, with your hair; and underneath that powder, I can see freckles. For me, freckles were always an irresistible aphrodisiac.

LUCY: Well, those freckles, my fingers, everything's yours, Walter. Just forget where you are, and think of trombones, bourbon bottles, and streetcars crowded with wet people starting off on a Saturday night.

WALTER: [rigid, with his eyes closed] People forgetting who, what, or where they've been. All getting into new skins, expressions, and troubles. But wanting to laugh through it all.

LUCY: That's it, Walter. Laughing when you slip on the dance floor, find your socks don't match or that you can't make love more than twice a night.

WALTER: [now happily, but painfully, reminiscing] And the Chinese restaurants you mistake for your house and the hands, often with gloves on them, you grab hold of.

LUCY: [whispering in WALTER's ear] And now stop talking, Walter, and let's...

WALTER: [sticking her in the back with his needle] No! Get away from me. [He breaks loose and moves to the center of the cell.]

LUCY: [with a loud yell] Why, you crazy—That was a sharp needle you stuck in me!

WALTER: [keeping the needle poised for attack] And I'll do it again if you come after me. This is my cell—ten paces wide, twenty long. Nothing, absolutely nothing unexpected happens here.

LUCY: [feeling the wounded spot on her back] God, I think I'm bleeding.

WALTER: Oh, no; no blood, please. I've seen all the blood I ever want to see.

LUCY: Then you shouldn't go about sticking people with needles or hitting them with golf clubs.

WALTER: You know about that?

LUCY: [somewhat abstracted as she rubs her wound and examines her hand] It's written right across your forehead. [Examining and rubbing her fingers together.] Well, I'm not bleeding after all.

WALTER: I'm grateful for that at least. I'm afraid I just lost my head for a moment. I felt myself slipping back into everything this cell protects me from, and I...Are you angry with me, Lucy?

LUCY: [dismissing the incident] Oh, I've had worse done to me by clients with sort of Victorian tastes in love. But you have disappointed me, Walter. I thought we'd strike it off right away.

WALTER: Oh, you wouldn't have found me much good anyway. My wife used to make me take pills...

LUCY: For God's sake, no talk about the wife, especially one whose skull you split open. It's professionally insulting after being stuck with your needle.

WALTER: Well, I just thought to pass the time...

LUCY: Clients talk about their wives after making love. [As if pondering a new discovery.] Wives and postcoital depression seem to go together. [Now back to lecturing WALTER on his brothel manners.] But before, it's themselves they take apart and it's our job to put them back together again.

WALTER: Well, all my pieces are in their proper place and I don't want them disarranged.

LUCY: [*sweetly*] No one wants to do that, Walter. Perhaps I did rush you a little bit; but, after all, you're the one counting the minutes and I thought you'd want them stuffed with all the things your clean little cell's been lacking.

WALTER: I'd already planned how to use every second of them before you arrived: there was the number-patch to be sewn on, shoes to be polished, a final stroll four times around the cell, and then I was going to wash, which, because of the soap's poor quality, would most likely have taken me up to the time the warden and his guards came for me.

LUCY: Well, it *is* asking a lot wanting you to give up all those wild plans for me.

WALTER: [*nodding in agreement*] I'll already have to pass up the shoes.

LUCY: Well, give up two of your laps around the room and talk a little about yourself. At least let me show you how well I've been trained as a sympathetic listener.

WALTER: Why, there's nothing much to say about me.

LUCY: [*coaxingly*] Oh, come on; start off with the kind of job you used to have.

WALTER: Well, I was a moderately successful lawyer.

LUCY: [*laughing*] A lawyer?

WALTER: [*a little anxiously*] Why are you laughing?

LUCY: Well, being here—that doesn't say much for your ability to sway juries, does it?

WALTER: [*testily*] I didn't defend myself; and, besides, I was irrefutably guilty.

LUCY: I thought it was always easier to win defending a guilty man than an innocent one.

WALTER: [*slightly outraged at this*] Now, you see, it's just that sort of over-the-shoulder attitude that's turned our laws into a fool's game today.

LUCY: You mean like the city ordinance against soliciting on the streets? I've always thought that one was woolly-headed.

WALTER: [*wagging his head impatiently*] I'm not talking about your particular likes and dislikes, Lucy. It's the nature of the law that's been abused.

LUCY: The jails seem full enough to me.

WALTER: [*growing a little more excited*] No, no; laws are supposed to be as solid and immovable as these walls. At least that's what I thought when I began studying them. They weren't supposed to depend upon the judge's sinus condition, a lady juror's two Caesareans, or poor air conditioning in the courtroom. They were to be hermetically sealed—untouched by human hands.

LUCY: Calm down a bit, Walter.

WALTER: [*now waving his arms*] But don't you see they weren't? They were worthless little hide-and-seek rules made up to give the neighborhood's poor children something to do in the evenings. No god had bellowed them out or burned them into a mountain.

LUCY: Be careful you don't stick yourself with the needle.

WALTER: [*now quite intense*] Oh, listen to me, Lucy. Can you understand what it meant to a man devoted to the law to find out it was all one big caprice? It was as if you looked up suddenly at a night sky and saw every planet and star dancing drunkenly about.

LUCY: [*smiling invitingly*] That might be exciting, Walter. And sometimes, making love out of doors, when the weather permitted, I think I did see the stars wiggle a bit.

WALTER: [*angry at* LUCY's *non sequitur*] Wiggle, do they? Well, that's not going to happen here! Not in this cell. [*He jumps up on the cot and points to the barred window.*] Look through this window, Lucy. See how the sky's sectioned into nine perfect squares? On a clear night each square contains exactly five stars and the center one has a planet all to itself.

LUCY: A planet? Which one?

WALTER: A sexless one; far from the sun, always cold, but giving off a dull, dependable light. [*Patting the bars.*] No, these little bars are particular about what they let into their boundaries.

LUCY: [*temporarily defeated*] All right, let's skip love for a while.

WALTER: [*somewhat calmer, he comes down from the cot*] The law had most of my love. I believed all one had to do was match little scraps of fact against those fine, heavily punctuated sentences in the books and, like a candy machine, the right answer would come out neatly wrapped. Oh, you don't know how snugly I fitted into everything then. With those laws standing firm, all their lesser relatives, from chemistry formulas to table manners, seemed impregnable. In those days I knew exactly what to pray for, how often a month I should have sex [four times, only with my wife], and how stern I should be when my children spilled their soup. I knew who was the villain and who the virgin on the stage; I knew my laundry would come back on time without a piece missing; and I knew that every mirror would reflect at me a recognizable, satisfied face that had aged just the right amount since last being seen. Oh, Lucy, everything from constellation to subways seemed to be moving at my rhythm. And then...then...

LUCY: And then?

WALTER: [*bitterly*] And then came the Gogarty trial.

LUCY: A trial for murder?

WALTER: [*beginning wistfully, then gradually growing more involved*] No, a suit for damages. Mrs. Ellen Gogarty versus The Municipal Bus Company—that was its official title. The woman's son, age thirty-five, had been run over and completely mashed by one of their vehicles. The light had been with him, and the bus driver, by eyewitness account, had been drunk and singing "Little Alice Bottom" when the accident took place. I was whistling the same tune when, these bits of evidence snapped inside my brief case, I arrived at the courthouse on a morning that seemed no different from a thousand others. I even remember exchanging a joke with one of the guards and making a date with the opposing attorney, who was putting up only a token defense, for dinner that evening. Then the trial began: the judge smiled at me, the jury nodded in solemn agreement as I turned phrases and probed witnesses. With every second our case was strengthened, and, throughout the examinations, Mrs. Gogarty, wearing a new but inexpensive summer hat and asking only to be recompensed for the loss of her only son, sat soaking up sympathetic stares from everyone in the court. The case, as they say, was open and shut. Open and shut.

LUCY: [*who has been sitting on the cot, listening, intently*] And what happened?

WALTER: [*now incensed over the memory*] Hiccups! Hiccups! Just before the jury was about to file out, Mrs. Gogarty began to hiccup. Oh, at first, it was hardly noticeable; but then they became louder and more frequent. I waved a warning finger at her to be silent, but she blinked back that she couldn't help herself; and while the jury stood stunned in their places, the gulping sounds went on jerking her frail little body this way and that. Finally, they actually came to be syncopated—two short, one long; one long, three short; two long. [*He puts his hands to his ears.*] And with the occasional change in pitch there was almost a little tune coming out of her. Sometimes I can still hear it, sounding like a street calliope; and then comes the laughter: first from the spectators in the court, then from the members of the jury, and, finally, from the judge himself. I try to speak, to read a few apposite remarks on courtroom behavior from the law book on my desk, but I'm literally drowned out with laughter. And through it all, like some devilish timpani in an orchestra, Mrs. Gogarty's hiccups, keeping up their erratic beat and brutal melody—[*He raises and drops his voice so the outline of a tune can be heard.*] One long, one short; two long, one short...[*Here he pauses and collects himself.*] Snorting, slapping each other's backs and nudging one another's ribs, the jury files out of the room. The wait is a very short one, and from behind the jury-chamber door come the sounds of still more snickers with an occasional imitation of my client's disorder. Finally, as if they'd been off on a party—collars open, ties askew, hair undone—the men and women who are to decide our case return and, while Mrs. Gogarty goes on with those loud little spasms, they announce a verdict against her. I can't believe it and, throwing protocol to the winds, ask why. "How can she be suffering grief worth any compensation at all when she hiccups?" so says the jury foreman. "Madness," I answer and turn to the judge. "My good sir," he says, chuckling like an idiot, "she really did hiccup out a little tune." "The law!" I cry. "Hiccups!" he answers, and the laughter starts all around again. [*Slowly now, as if looking in the narration of simple fact for a solution.*] I went to the governor himself, Lucy. I showed him there was nothing in the pertinent judicial paragraphs about this involuntary closure of the glottis and the noise produced therefrom, and *he* answered that those paragraphs were to be amended to include the peculiar Gogarty phenomenon. I knew then that it was all over, and that a sneeze, hiccup, or crooked nose could twist those impressive sentences into gibberish.

There is silence for a moment, and then LUCY rises from the cot and makes an attempt at consolation.

LUCY: Maybe it's better that way. After all, that's what makes a day interesting. It's the little unexpected matters of taste, like a man going wild over a mole on your chin, that keeps the beauty contest also-rans like me in business.

WALTER: [*sadly*] I knew you'd think that, Lucy; but, for me, Mrs. Gogarty's hiccups were the end of everything. I no longer knew what clubs to join, what tie to choose, what toothpaste to use, what church to go to. At home, where I always thought things went smoothly and orderly, I suddenly found my children snipping off our dog's tail an inch a day with a pair of scissors, writing obscene couplets on my shirt collars, biting my leg whenever I passed by, and singing marching songs from the War of 1812. And my wife's birthmark, a little red triangle that had always been tucked inconspicuously behind her left ear, began turning up in the center of her forehead, in the middle of her stomach, and on the soles of her feet...

LUCY: [*now a little impatient with him*] Are we going back to the wife again?

WALTER: [*growing excited again*] My life was formless, a tiny piece of chaos. What was left to me that couldn't be hiccuped out of existence? Right and left, buy and sell, love and hate—these now meant nothing to me. I found myself on the wrong trains, in the wrong beds, with the wrong people. And my neighborhood, my neighborhood that I had helped zone to perfection, became a carnival of the lowest sort, and my neighbors, whom I knew inside and out, danced about beneath layer on layer of holiday masks until I couldn't tell one from the other. And then, God knows when or where it happened, I found a mirror sending back at me a face that I had never seen before—a face with wild eyes, bristling hair, and a heavy growth of stubble— a face I would have crossed the street to avoid had I seen it coming at me in happier times. Oh, I'd been cheated, Lucy, and gradually I began to grow angry—mad, in fact—until one morning, with everything spinning about me in complete disorder, I struck back. My poor wife happened to be closest at hand, and for all I know I might have thought I was on the golf course until I felt the club make contact with her skull. I remember it sounding as if it were a good shot, and then I looked up to follow the ball's flight and found...

LUCY: That's enough, Walter! I'm beginning to shiver.

WALTER: [*recalled from his memories*] But now comes the pleasant part.

LUCY: [*shaking her head as if to clear it*] No, for me, the goodies in your story are over.

WALTER: No, no; don't you see? The law came back to me. Everything began falling in line again. I have my number, a room that never changes, meals that arrive punctually to the moment, and guards whose manners are perfectly predictable. [*With weak joy.*] The world has boundaries again and I know my place in it.

LUCY: [*almost threateningly*] In one hour your place will be at the end of a rope.

WALTER: [*with military stiffness*] But my death will take place according to a rigid schedule and then be *officially* recorded. What more could I want?

LUCY: [*with desperate hope*] A little sex?

WALTER: [*vexed at this*] Good God! have you understood nothing? That belongs to the dizziness on the other side of those walls. Here, in my prison, the laws hold, and I won't have them disturbed by perfume and overpowdered flesh.

LUCY: [*now angry*] Oh, won't you? Do you know, if they came in this minute with a rope ready, it'd be my overpowdered flesh they'd hang? Yes, they'd be looking for something live to string up, Walter, and you certainly don't pass the test.

WALTER: I know what being alive means to you.

LUCY: [*beginning to unwrap the belt from around her waist*] Oh, between Mrs. Gogarty's lost case and your wife's murder you had a taste of it, all right; but it frightened you right into this cell.

WALTER: [*showing apprehension*] What on earth are you doing? You're not going to undress? I promise you it won't do any good.

LUCY: I'm not understanding you, Walter. And, as a client, you have a right to that from me. I'm going to try to shorten the distance between us. [*She steps upon the cot, loops one end of the belt, and fastens the other to one of the bars across the window.*]

WALTER: You'll leave footprints on the pillow!

LUCY: You won't be using it again, Walter. I just want to see how it'd feel with a noose around my neck. Who knows? Maybe you're right; maybe the only thing I'd worry about is that they got my name and number right on the morgue card. [*She slips the belt over her head.*] There, it's in place; the hangman's taken his hands from my shoulders, the sack's dropped over my eyes; my shoes, just polished, are shining in the morning light…

WALTER: Stop it! Stop it! You're just pretending anyway.

LUCY: [*in the tones of a spoiled little girl*] I'm in a cell with a murderer. How do I know you won't push the cot out from under me?

WALTER: I might do just that.

LUCY: [*with her eyes shut and her head tilted back*] I will drop down, happy that the sky I leave behind has nice equal sections, each with so many numbers of stars. I'll be content that my dying has an alphabetical standing, that my last meal came to me on time, that my cell is immaculate, that the prison day which I'll never see will be like all the others I've lived through, and that I didn't sweat, sing, throw up, or make love to a woman. So then, let the trap doors fly open underneath me. With no regrets about this life, I'll die happily. [*Pause.*] The hell I will!

WALTER: [*walking up to cot and threatening to kick one of its legs*] If you don't come down, I swear I'll kick the cot out from under you, Lucy.

LUCY: [*removing the belt from around her neck*] You bet I'll come down. Dying with your point of view really makes me sick to my stomach. [*She steps down and walks as far away from* WALTER *as the confines of the cell permit.*]

WALTER: [*somewhat meek and apologetic*] I'm not trying to convert you to anything, after all.

LUCY: No, you're not. You're too happy curled up in your little womb to want company.

WALTER: Please, no coarse talk, Lucy.

LUCY: Oh, of course not. You'd like to have a conversation in algebra equations, I'll bet. Well, I'm not going to let you get away with it.

WALTER: [*puzzled and on the defensive*] Why are you attacking me?

LUCY: Because you remind me of a *happy* "still-life" whore, Walter. Do you know what that is? It's the last step for all of us in this business. When even the streets won't have you and you've lost your nerve for the river, then it's a twenty-four-hour-in-bed house for you. You don't own anything to wear except a grease-stained kimono the madam gives you; there's no make-up on the little table next to you, no mirror, the room's always dark, and the only sounds are the footsteps in the corridor that shuffle, with sometimes just a little hesitation, past your door that's been locked from the outside. You just lie there, Walter, waiting for the lock to click open, letting another client in at you. Oh, and there's no worry about these men like there is when you're on your own. You don't fret over whether or not he's a handsome one or if he can pay up or not. You don't have to worry about his whims or his cracking you on the jaw or his inflamed genital tract. Nothing that happens will ever move you from the room, the bed, the darkness, and the sound of footsteps. The customers will keep coming and you'll keep being fed no matter what your hair looks like or what lies you think up to tell those wheezing over you, those without faces you can ever really see. It's peaceful, all right, in a "still-life" house; and sometimes I wake up laughing at night thinking about it.

WALTER: I'll bet there were times, on a December night, when business was slow on your corner, you felt such a place wouldn't be too bad.

LUCY: No. I liked the cold nights. Only the really interesting ones were out when the weather was mean. The ones who must have been like you were after your Gogarty trial.

WALTER: Can't you leave me out of it?

LUCY: [*menacingly*] Oh, you'd like to be left out of everything, wouldn't you? Everything but the Warden's filing cabinet.

WALTER: If you keep on this way, I'm going to have to ask you to leave.

LUCY: [*moving toward him again*] No chance of that, Walter. Too much depends on this for me. It's your world against mine. There'll be no "still-life" house for Lucy because of you!

WALTER: Must we go through this again? I was through with everything you represent when the police took the blood-stained seven-iron out of my hand.

LUCY: [*speaking evenly, with a smile, and still advancing*] I don't believe you, Walter. All the talk about your little battle to keep the laws from crumbling after the Gogarty trial, I don't believe a word of it.

WALTER: Well, that's really beside the point.

LUCY: [*reaching into her pocket, she brings out the packet of cigarettes and extracts several*] Do you know what I believe, Walter?

As she speaks, she begins throwing the cigarettes about the cell.

WALTER: Here, what are you doing?

LUCY: [*flipping several over her shoulder*] I'm setting up the atmosphere you really like.

WALTER: [*dropping to his hands and knees to gather up the debris*] Stop it! Stop it! I may not be able to find them all before they come for me.

LUCY: [*walking now to the tray of food*] Leave them, Walter. You don't mind a messy cell any more than you did finding yourself on the wrong trains.

She opens the dish and extracts the chicken leg she'd already bitten into.

WALTER: What are you saying? It made me sick. It made me kill my wife. And put down that chicken bone!

LUCY: I think it would go well in the center of the floor. A little savage bone in the center of the cell. [*She throws the bone in the air and it lands with a clatter in the cell's center.*] And maybe a wing in the corner.

> *The piece of chicken bounces off the wall and drops in the cell's corner by the washbasin.*

WALTER: I'm going to be hanged in an hour. How can you treat me this way?

LUCY: Yes, Walter, you were frightened of what those hiccups touched off, all right, but it was because you were starting to enjoy that dizzy world outside. That's why your wife had her head mashed, wasn't it? You just wanted to remove yourself from temptation.

WALTER: [*no longer crawling about, but still on his hands and knees*] That's not true! That's not true!

LUCY: Oh, come on, Walter. Weren't you beginning to look forward to those strange beds you turned up in?

WALTER: [*protesting too much*] No, they terrified me. I swear it!

LUCY: [*seeing she has made a breach, she pushes on, speeding up her accusations*] And your wife's birthmark—how many times did you bet with yourself where it would pop up next?

WALTER: [*now breaking a bit*] Once or twice only. But that doesn't mean…

LUCY: And how many snips at the dog's tail did you take?

WALTER: It was cruel, I know. But nothing seemed to matter in those days…

LUCY: And you enjoyed its howls.

WALTER: All my life I had an urge to torture a dog or cat. And it was just one snip. Just one!

LUCY: And when you went out at night, not knowing what tie you were wearing, what streets you were walking, what name you were using, admit you were twitching with excitement.

WALTER: [*feebly*] I won't; I wasn't.

LUCY: [*going to the cot and picking up* WALTER's *shirt*] Admit it, or the number goes.

WALTER: I didn't, I swear I didn't.

> LUCY *rips the number-patch off in one short movement and* WALTER *cries as if he's been wounded. Then she holds the piece of cloth obtrusively in front of her and lets it drop slowly to the floor. Now totally defeated,* WALTER *watches it descend.*

LUCY: Now the laws are falling apart again, Walter. You're just a numberless name about to be hanged. There's a not-so-bad-looking woman in your cell. What's there to lose? Do you remember having thoughts like these?

WALTER: Yes, yes, I had them. I thought for a time that all the springs, levers, and wheels of the world had broken down and I was free!

LUCY: [*softening now*] And so you were, Walter.

WALTER: No, there was too great a price. There were always those gray mornings when the mind took over, when you saw your crumpled clothes and cigarette pack from the night before, when your head pounded and you nibbled your lip in fear. Then you panicked for a world that made sense.

LUCY: No matter how much fun you got from the world that didn't?

WALTER: Oh, leave me alone.

LUCY: [*helping* WALTER *to his feet*] I'm going to bring that world back to you. After all, it's the only one there is.

WALTER: [*weakly*] There's my cell.

LUCY: [*drawing him toward the cot*] With the cigarettes on the floor? With the number torn from your shirt? With my perfume settling over you?

WALTER: Please, don't make me start again. What I found on those mornings was death; and it's only minutes away.

LUCY: Make love to me, Walter, and you won't mind the hangover of the gallows. You'll be living again when you strangle.

WALTER: That's no consolation! Oh, everything was so perfect here before you came. I was just like one of the Warden's insects, living out my days unconsciously, letting the fixed rhythms of the prison carry me along.

LUCY: It's too late to go back now. Look at the sky. How many stars are in your sections now?

WALTER: Why, they're all bunched in two or three of them, and the planet's gone entirely.

LUCY: And the cell, isn't it beginning to push in upon you?

WALTER: I loved it for so long.

LUCY: It's not big enough to hold a live man, Walter.

WALTER: Oh, why wasn't there a glass of water next to Mrs. Gogarty in the courtroom? You would never have gotten to me then. I would have died somewhere in bed of a bad heart, thinking that a special chair had been set aside for me at an eternal dinner party where everything was properly served.

LUCY: No one's lucky enough to fool himself that way forever.

WALTER: But how can there ever be a contented expression on my face now when they come for me?

LUCY: [*pulling him down onto the cot*] Trust Lucy for that, Walter. All those nights, beds, marching songs, toothpaste containers, and howling dogs packed into thirty minutes.

WALTER: I hope so. Otherwise I think I'll break down and cry when I start up those steps.

LUCY: Shall we begin, Walter?

WALTER: All right, I've paid the price now. There'd better be twenty years of living in your mouth, fingertips, and breasts.

LUCY: I'll lead you, Walter. You just follow.

WALTER: [*bending over her*] And who knows? Maybe the rope will break? Or the hangman come down with a bad cold?

LUCY: That's the way to reason, Walter. On this cot, with Lucy on it, anything and everything's now possible.

She draws WALTER *to her and the cell's single light is extinguished.*

CURTAIN

PART 2

The curtain rises on the early-morning confusion of a suburban kitchen-dining room. PHILLIP, *the prison's executioner, and* MARTHA, *his wife, are standing at the kitchen table.* PHILLIP *is a small, erect man. He is dressed in the trousers, shirt, and tie of his official uniform. The hat and coat are placed on one of the kitchen chairs. His wife, her hair in curlers and dowdily attractive in a morning housecoat, begins busying herself at the stove. A large red pepper mill is the only conspicuous object on the table.*

As the lights come up fully, THE WARDEN *is seen pacing back and forth across the table from* PHILLIP.

WARDEN: [*with rhetorical self-pity*] When I think how I stayed up nights as a boy learning the penal code by heart so someday I would be a prison warden!

PHILLIP: What I asked for isn't going to prove you wasted your youth. It seems quite reasonable to me.

WARDEN: Reasonable? How can you, the last and most important link in society's chain of punishment, how can you think it reasonable to want to dress up like a headsman from the Middle Ages?

PHILLIP: I just want to wear a black hood over my head. I think it would lend me a little more—well, personality out there.

MARTHA: [*setting a pot of coffee on the kitchen table*] Well, if you ask me, the idea of a hood, especially a black one, strikes me as a little morbid.

WARDEN: There you are; from your own wife. Can you imagine what others will have to say about it? Why, it smacks of thumbscrews, iron maidens, and unsanitary dungeons.

MARTHA: [*to* PHILLIP] I wish you'd come sit down and finish your oatmeal. [*Looking into one of the bowls set on the table.*] It's getting crusty and beginning to stick to the edges of the bowl.

PHILLIP: [*a look of exasperation at* MARTHA] I don't want any oatmeal now. I simply want, as an employee with some twenty years' service behind him, to have a request granted. [*With a little petulance.*] I want to wear a black hood at today's execution!

WARDEN: But think of what it will do to your reputation! Instead of being a finely edged instrument in a clinical, detached operation, you become a villain—a strangler—a black knight.

MARTHA: [*vigorously buttering a piece of toast*] I can just imagine the treatment I'd get then from the girls in my bridge club.

PHILLIP: Let them jeer and hiss at me; it's better than not being noticed or thought of at all.

WARDEN: But behind a hood your face won't even be seen.

PHILLIP: [*slightly angry*] My face? Don't you think I know what this collection of scribbles, bumps, and creases looks like? Any real expression I call on it to take looks ridiculous on me. But with this hood, this mask, it comes alive. My eyes, outlined by slanting black slits, crackle with perception; my mouth grows full and moist; and my chin, as if obeying a command from these other features, squares itself and, just a little arrogantly, juts forward.

MARTHA: [*now beginning to pour out three cups of coffee*] It sounds as if you'd look like you were in a bad accident, Phillip.

WARDEN: I think you'd frighten the men to death before you had a chance to hang them.

PHILLIP: Then I would at least have some contact. [*A sigh.*] Oh, I didn't mind being your instrument when those condemned arrived like patients drowned in ether. But things have changed now. You yourself know that they come up those steps trembling, warm, talkative—exuding a scent so full of living that my head sometimes starts spinning because of it.

WARDEN: There are rules and regulations governing these things. An executioner's uniform can be blue, black, or gray; the buttons can be bone or brass; and the cap is optional. But by no stretch of interpretation is there any mention of a black hood.

PHILLIP: Hang the regulations! I'm trying to get a little color into things. [*Pleading.*] Don't you understand? I need a change.

WARDEN: You have your vacation coming up in a few months. Get in some fishing, and you'll feel better. I've always found that just dangling your line in a mountain stream relaxes the muscles, improves the digestion...

PHILLIP: I don't want to fish, Warden. For twenty years I've gone to little mountain streams on my vacation and caught nothing more interesting than a trout with one eye last summer.

WARDEN: A one-eyed trout? What kind of bait were you using?

PHILLIP: Don't change the subject. Now, do I or do I not wear my hood today?

WARDEN: I've already given you an answer on that.

PHILLIP: Just look at me in it, that's all. Just one glance.

WARDEN: I couldn't be less interested.

PHILLIP: All you have to say is yes or no. Just yes or no.

WARDEN: [*giving in with a long sigh*] It's a waste of time; but, if you want to, go ahead.

PHILLIP: Fine; it's just upstairs. [*Starting to leave.*] Oh, I may be a little time adjusting it, though. It has to sit just right, otherwise it droops a bit and I find it difficult to breathe.

MARTHA: If you're just going to leave the oatmeal should I have some scrambled eggs ready for you when you come down?

PHILLIP: Forget about breakfast, Martha. [*To* THE WARDEN.] I hope, once I'm in my hood, that I won't have to take it off until the ceremony's over with. I wouldn't want any food stains to get on it.

PHILLIP *exits.*

MARTHA: He used to eat such a big breakfast on special days like this. Why, I can remember when six eggs and a quarter-pound of ham were just enough for him.

WARDEN: Well, I must say I find his behavior this morning a little peculiar. The whole thing just isn't like Phillip. He's always been someone you could count on, someone who knew the importance of a good shine on his buttons and a sharp crease in his trousers.

MARTHA: [*sitting down dejectedly and absently stirring her coffee*] Well, something's definitely been happening to him in the last months. If you'd been living with him every day, this business with the hood wouldn't surprise you in the least.

WARDEN: I haven't noticed anything until now.

MARTHA: Oh, he's kept these changes fairly well hidden, even from me. But you can't eat, sleep, and take out a joint bank account with a man without noticing the slightest change in him.

WARDEN: Now that you mention it, he hasn't come to any club meetings in the last months and his weekly reports have been dotted with erasure smudges—very unlike him.

MARTHA: [*putting the coffee down and nervously smoothing her hair*] It's beginning to show on the outside too? Oh, I'd hoped to keep it confined to the rooms in this house.

WARDEN: [*reaching down and taking MARTHA's hand*] Is it something you can tell me, a very old friend? Is there another woman involved in all this?

MARTHA: [*hitting the kitchen table with her free hand so that THE WARDEN turns the other loose*] Oh how I wish there was! How I'd love to be able to sink my nails into the flesh-and-blood reason for the way things are beginning to wobble on their legs around here! Just to see a larger bosom or a firmer behind leading Phillip down a street would let me spit at him with a clear conscience. If I just knew where the weakness was, I could make life miserable for him and then forget it!

WARDEN: But you don't?

MARTHA: [*rising from the kitchen table like a prosecutor at a trial*] About four months ago, after Phillip had left for work, I got up from bed and, like I do every morning the first thing, reached down for his slippers to take them to the closet. For twenty years he's always left them on his side of the bed, neatly placed next to one another, toes pointed to the wall

WARDEN: And that morning?

MARTHA: One was underneath the bed and the other, after being used for an ash tray, was tucked beneath his pillow.

WARDEN: [*shaking his head*] A bad sign!

MARTHA: Only the first, though. In the next weeks I began making all sorts of discoveries: in his bureau drawer, tucked among his underwear, I found a book of Swedish lessons; in the hall closet, squeezed behind the Christmas decorations, I uncovered a banjo with two of its strings missing; and under one of the sofa cushions, I turned up a pair of red socks with "World's Fair—1939" stitched down their sides.

Red socks! I can't decide what to do with them, and just knowing they're sitting in the house drives me half out of my mind.

WARDEN: [*approaching* MARTHA, *he puts his hands on her shoulders and speaks as the comforting male*] Go on, Martha. My home's not a happy one, either.

MARTHA: Well, after that, Phillip himself began upsetting things. Since we were married, he's always slept on his stomach, one hand folded beneath his chin; but a month ago I woke up to find him snoring on his back. Then his favorite chair, that he always settled in after dinner, began being neglected; and, the dishes done, I'd come in and find him pouting in a corner or sitting cross-legged like an Arab on the floor.

WARDEN: [*oozing sympathy*] And you've been suffering through all this, Martha, without a word to anyone?

MARTHA: I kept hoping it would all pass over; but I see now it won't. Last night, behind a stack of bathroom towels, I discovered a box of very expensive cigars with an unpronounceable name—and then this morning the hood. [*She utters a long sigh and turns to put her head on* THE WARDEN's *chest.*] Oh, Warden!

WARDEN: [*a smile hinting now a little more than sympathy*] There, there. Please call me Harry.

MARTHA: [*a brief smile as she pronounces the name*] Harry! [*Now the defenseless little girl.*] Oh, I just don't know what to do any longer.

WARDEN: I really can't stand thinking of you being unhappy.

MARTHA: Just last week Phillip refused to renew our country club membership or donate to the Red Cross.

WARDEN: You need help, Martha. Can Harry, an old, old, *old* friend do anything for you?

MARTHA: Don't let him wear that hood today. No matter how he coaxes, put your foot down.

WARDEN: [*a vigorous nod*] You can depend on it. I'll simply tell him his pension won't be raised if he does.

MARTHA: Oh, Harry, you've always been so kind. Just having you here this morning makes everything seem much easier.

WARDEN: [*lifting up her chin*] We're cut from the same timber, Martha. Perhaps we can help each other.

He starts to kiss her.

MARTHA: [*pulling away*] No, Harry! Even if Phillip has taken to collecting red socks and turning nasty remarks about my friends, I couldn't deceive him. It would be playing his game.

WARDEN: He does nothing but hurt you, Martha; and I've loved you ever since the day you came to my office to try to get a raise in salary out of me for Phillip.

MARTHA: [*now enjoying being pursued*] Really? I remember coming out feeling you hadn't noticed me at all. And Phillip didn't get the raise.

WARDEN: You were wearing an orange-and-blue print dress, white gloves and, as it was right after lunch, there was a little drop of mayonnaise on the left side of your chin.

MARTHA: Harry! And you didn't tell me.

WARDEN: [*walking up to her and speaking in a hoarse voice*] I found it terribly exciting. All the time you were going on about those extra five dollars a month, I was trying to imagine just what you could have eaten to put that tiny white mark there.

MARTHA: [*pretending embarrassment*] You shouldn't talk that way. What a woman eats for lunch is an intimate matter.

WARDEN: And you? Did you notice me at all?

MARTHA: I'd only been married six months at the time. I wasn't noticing anyone but Phillip, such that he was.

WARDEN: [*somewhat hurt*] You mean I made no impression at all?

MARTHA: Well, I do recall you had on a tie with a palm tree painted on it.

WARDEN: [*nostalgically*] In the dark it lit up and formed a pair of woman's legs.

MARTHA: [*almost warmly*] And I noticed how bloodshot your eyes were, and I thought how hard you must work to have popped so many of those little vessels.

WARDEN: Twenty years ago! Twenty years ago! If we could only have spoken frankly to each other then.

MARTHA: And why didn't you?

WARDEN: I thought of doing so, Martha. That very night I paced about in the dark of our five-room house, trying to decide just how bold I should be

MARTHA: And then you saw your wife asleep, her head placed at just the right angle on the pillow, and you were ashamed of your thoughts. A good wife holds on even when she's unconscious.

WARDEN: Heavens no! It wasn't my wife. She'd already begun sampling the line of manual laborers that began with a teen-age elevator operator and just last week was kept going with a streetcar motorman. No, Martha, it was the twins, aged one, I think, at the time, who kept me from sending you a warm note about the stain on your chin. I wandered into their room, heard them breathing, in unison, and something made me switch on the light. I saw them: their eyes opened simultaneously, blinked once in disbelief at the questions written across my face, and gave me such a stare of clear-sighted respectability that I backed, shamefaced, from the crib. Oh, if you could have seen those accusing blue pupils daring me to jeopardize their owners' position. Martha, their plump faces were as solid as the walls of my prison, and they left me no choice but to forget your lunches and start saving for their college education.

MARTHA: [*with a sigh of genuine understanding*] Well, I don't blame you for that.

WARDEN: Oh, it was the right thing then when I thought you were happy with our hangman. But now…

MARTHA: Now, now it's too late. I can't put mayonnaise on my sandwiches any longer and fit into last year's dress.

WARDEN: And I wouldn't dare wear a tie with a palm tree painted on it. [*Suddenly throwing off the gloom that has settled over him and tumbling out his words.*] But my sons are almost chemical engineers and my wife never stops riding streetcars and my house is empty and no matter what size dress you wear, I love you!

He kisses MARTHA *enthusiastically, and, for a moment, she returns in kind. Then, however, she pushes him away.*

MARTHA: Oh, no, Harry. No, no, no. [*She walks back to the kitchen table and steadies herself with it.*] Let me reheat your coffee or make you some toast.

WARDEN: [*again advancing*] Please, don't drop back behind breakfast. We're both beyond that now.

MARTHA: [*again escaping*] No, not here. Phillip may come down any minute.

WARDEN: Then we must have a meeting, a rendezvous as soon as possible. Twenty years, Martha. Twenty years!

MARTHA: [*after a brief pause*] All right: tomorrow, three o'clock, in front of the supermarket steps.

WARDEN: Tomorrow? [*A pause and a frown, as he consults a small black engagement book.*] No, I'm afraid tomorrow's out for me. A government inspection team is coming down for the day. [*Brightening.*] But Saturday, in the afternoon, I know a little bar...

MARTHA: But I've promised myself as a fourth in three card games that afternoon.

WARDEN: Cards, Martha?

MARTHA: [*with just a little less enthusiasm*] We could try Monday morning. No one suspects you of anything on a Monday.

WARDEN: [*a little impatient*] That's because everyone's too busy to get into mischief. If I went away from my desk for five minutes after a weekend, it'd take me a month to catch up.

MARTHA: Well, I could slip away Tuesday night and say I'm seeing a movie.

WARDEN: [*dejectedly*] That's the night the twins call from school to ask for money. [*With now but faint hope.*] But Wednesday?

MARTHA: [*flatly, as she checks a calendar on the kitchen wall*] Cancer Fund meeting. Thursday?

WARDEN: [*in equally funereal tones*] Parole Board all day, and I visit my mother at night.

       MARTHA *turns and goes to the kitchen table where she pours a fresh cup of coffee.* THE WARDEN *continues as though trying to explain something to himself rather than to her.*

I've visited Mother every Thursday night since leaving her to get married. Every Thursday night, and I don't think she really enjoys seeing me at all.

MARTHA: [*after a pause*] Would you like cream in your coffee, Harry?

WARDEN: Black; make it as black as you can.

MARTHA: [*making conversation*] Do you suppose it will rain? I always think hangings should take place in bad weather, even if it does make Phillip's back stiffen up a bit.

WARDEN: [*taking up the coffee cup and staring moodily into it*] Are we back to hangings, your husband, and another official day?

MARTHA: Your twins' eyes are still following us.

WARDEN: [*putting down the cup*] Ah, but for a moment, for a moment...

MARTHA: [*sharply*] We were being fools. Now drink your coffee.

WARDEN: [*slinking around the table to her*] At least one more kiss, Martha. The second and last one in twenty years.

MARTHA: [*dryly*] It would just be a wet sound to me now, Harry.

WARDEN: But not to me.

MARTHA: Your kiss would mean nothing but that I had to breathe through my nose for its duration.

WARDEN: And if I don't, I'll never breathe properly again. I feel as if I'm being sealed away forever in a very small hall closet.

MARTHA: And no matter what you do, I'll always be on the other side of the door. You won't even be near me, Harry.

WARDEN: [*like a painful prayer*] Oh, just this once let those damned chemical engineers look the other way'

He begins kissing MARTHA'*s neck passionately while she remains immobile. After a second,* PHILLIP, *his black hood over his head, enters. His voice, because of the mask, is somewhat muffled.*

PHILLIP: And just what is this going on?

MARTHA *utters a cry and jumps back from* THE WARDEN. *He turns around and is equally upset by what he sees.*

WARDEN: Good God!

PHILLIP: [*moving toward them*] I'll ask again: what were you two doing?

WARDEN: [*catching his breath and paying no attention to the question*] Do you know how ridiculously ferocious you look? Your creeping in like that's sent a chill through me all the way down to my feet.

PHILLIP: Your feet? What do I care about your feet? You were kissing my wife.

WARDEN: What? That thing's covering your mouth and making it very hard to follow what you're excited about.

PHILLIP: [*taking off the hood*] I *say* you were kissing my wife!

WARDEN: It's not very well-mannered to come right out and say it that way, but I suppose I was.

PHILLIP: While I was upstairs, trying to adjust this hood so you'd see it to its best advantage, you were making love to my wife. You, the Warden of the prison, who, in less than half an hour will be raising a solemn forefinger and signaling me to hang a man—you were making love to my wife in my own kitchen.

WARDEN: [*really confused by all the fuss*] Man to man, Phillip, I apologize. These things happen all the time—a little slip that sets one in the bushes alongside somebody you've no business being in the bushes with. Yes, it's an unfortunate, uh, occurrence, and, as I said, I *do* apologize for it.

PHILLIP: [*somewhat stunned*] Apologize? Oh, no, please don't do that. I—I couldn't accept. I don't *want* to accept.

WARDEN: Now, Phillip, I understand how you feel. I've found my wife in much more than an embrace with a plumber. He was covered with grease too, and had...

PHILLIP: Oh, no, it's not that at all. I was a little shocked just now and perhaps I did sound like a predictable husband. It just seemed that, under the circumstances, bellowing was expected of me.

WARDEN: I'm not following.

PHILLIP: It's simply that, while I was in my room, I was thinking what a failure I'd be in the hood. I was thinking, Harry, that the only thing that would save me would be to turn tail on this house, this uniform, this prison—everything that keeps me jogging along in step with the rest of you. So, Harry, friend and lover of my wife, I almost opened the window, slithered down the drainpipe and slipped out of your sight forever. I was going to run away—are you listening too, Martha?—run away and find out just where those men I've been dropping through gallows' doors come from.

WARDEN: Phillip, call me names, knock me down if you want to, but don't psycho-analyze yourself in public this way. At least not while you're in uniform.

PHILLIP: Let me just say that it was my old, well-trained conscience that kept me off the drainpipe. I thought of you two, standing firm on this dreary morning, washing your misery down with coffee, keeping to the rules of the game, and I bowed my head, covered it with the hood, and came downstairs ready to go on as Phillip, the old executioner. But now, now that you two have kicked up your heels a little bit, I see no reason why I shouldn't follow suit. You don't know how long I've waited to find a crack in the wall that being Martha's husband has built around me. But now that I see it's there, I'm going through it and down the drainpipe without a regret.

WARDEN: Phillip, this is all impossible, you know that, don't you?

PHILLIP: No more so than my finding you wrapped around my wife is impossible. If you two, at breakfast time, can stomach each other to the point of embracing, then I don't see how the line of impossibility can be drawn anywhere.

WARDEN: And just who, in all honesty, is responsible for this embrace?

PHILLIP: [*looking at* MARTHA, *who, during the foregoing, has folded her arms and kept her back to both of her champions*] Who, indeed?

WARDEN: You, yourself. You with your black hood, your Swedish lessons, your scattered slippers, and your brooding in the corner. You sent her into my arms, Phillip.

PHILLIP: [*smiling at* MARTHA *who doesn't respond*] So you did notice these things.

WARDEN: Of course she has; and that's why what happened happened. It explains…

PHILLIP: At five-thirty in the morning it doesn't explain…

WARDEN: [*raising his arm for silence*] No! No! I am now speaking in my official capacity and I don't want to be interrupted by subordinates. [THE WARDEN *takes the deep breath of one preparing for platitudes.*] Life, Phillip, is like a long sea voyage—the comparison's an old but apt one. We begin by deciding whether we favor temperate, tropic, or arctic waters. We decide what ports to put into with proper ceremony and what savage islands to sell trinkets and contract diseases on. We select the style of ship and the type of crew that suits us; and if one turns out to have a few leaks hidden in its bottom and the other to be bad-breathed and mutinous, we don't let that force us to drift off course. For, Phillip, staying within the latitudes and longitudes we've marked out for ourselves is all that matters. There can be no floating about to take closer looks at a curvaceous coast line or a sensual horizon. There can be no seeking out restful doldrums when your nerves get a bit frayed or poking about for a good typhoon when calm seas prove somewhat tedious. No, we keep to the prescribed path, and when other ships plow past us, flaunting well-laundered sails—well, we scrub ours up too, send every one with scurvy out of sight, keep a good mile of sea water between us and our short-lived neighbors, and leave them with the impression of nothing but that we're occupying the exact bit of ocean marked out for us. But you, Phillip, you just weren't sticking to the chart. You were sailing into harbors that weren't even marked on the maps of your second-in-command; you were tossing sensible and costly cargo overboard to make room for unmarketable baubles; you were tilting the compass to suit yourself. Now, is there any wonder, as you were approaching the dangerous waters of middle age, that Martha should lower a dinghy over the side and paddle her way to a vessel that looked, at least from a distance, to be completely shipshape? And, of course, having a good set of sea manners and seeing your wife bobbing next to me, I took her aboard, gave her, so to speak, a change of dry clothes and am now ready to return her to your schooner which, I'm sure, will be polished up and made ready for inspection. And if you don't want her to think she has to abandon ship again, tighten the hatches, throw out your World's Fair socks; secure the rigging, don't use slippers for ash trays; scrub the decks, go to club dances; check your compass hourly, burn that revolting black hood; and, finally, appear at today's execution as if you knew what your coordinates as the state's official hangman were. For remember, Phillip, no matter how attractive you find the mermaids or the rocks they wrap their appealing green tails around, the important thing is to keep sailing on course. Take that as an old captain's advice—just keep sailing on course.

THE WARDEN, *who during the speech has edged his way to the door, exits through it.*

PHILLIP: [*running to the door after him*] That's the same speech you gave at the club's Christmas dinner last year and the summer picnic the year before! Well, you old pirate, you'd better get your ship's lifeboats ready because there isn't going to be a hanging today. Do you hear? The person you thought you temporarily rescued is now your permanent passenger. I resign! From everything! I resign! [PHILLIP *pauses for a moment, comes back into the center of the kitchen, looks at his hood, then at* MARTHA, *and laughs softly.*] I'll have to admit you surprised me, Martha. It was pleasant, but a surprise nevertheless. [*Silence.*] Well, don't you have anything to say? After all, I just said I was leaving you.

MARTHA: [*disinterested*] If you're not going to touch breakfast, I'll put the dishes away.

PHILLIP: [*relieved*] Oh, I thought after twenty years of marriage that a little piece of flesh had begun to sprout, connecting us together like Siamese twins. You don't know how upset I was by the idea. And now, Martha, you've shown me that it's nothing but a flimsy bandaid—nothing more.

MARTHA: [*beginning to remove the dishes and wash them*] A band-aid?

PHILLIP: [*with real admiration in his eyes*] One that you had the courage to tear off. Oh, if I'd only known how simple it would be. There I was, trying to sneak into a black hood and leave little hints about the house.

MARTHA: Hints at what?

PHILLIP: Hints that I was unhappy; that I thought I'd become little more than the brass and flannel of my uniform; that I wanted to run away from everything that I was and had been. It never occurred to me that you might feel the same way. But then, seeing you pressed up against the Warden—well, Martha, I confess I underestimated you.

MARTHA: And are you planning now to go out and make love to the Warden's wife?

PHILLIP: Oh, no. I'm going to leave you and this little piece of the world forever. I'm going to become—to become...

MARTHA: [*sharply*] What?

PHILLIP: [*a visionary smile*] To become—to become something like those fellows I've been hanging in the last few months. Do you know, Martha, there's a light in their eyes, a pulse behind their ear that beats faster than mine, and an interest in the weather that makes me envy them. Oh, they're frightened all right, but it's a healthy fear—something I don't think I would ever have had.

MARTHA: As the Warden said, they've just left those official ladies. Maybe if you didn't read all night in bed we could...

PHILLIP: Oh, no, Martha. I need a complete and total break.

MARTHA: And when do you plan to start breaking?

PHILLIP: In the past a step like this would have meant travel folders, reservations, exact calculations down to the dollar. But now, Martha, I'm not even going to bother to pack. I'm walking straight out the door without a glance over my shoulder.

MARTHA: [*holding out a plate to him*] Will you help dry first?

PHILLIP: [*abstracted but pleasant*] What? Oh, certainly. [*Towel and plate in hand, he goes back to his vision.*] First, I'm going to a tailor. I'm going to have him make me something for every mood I'm going to try—silk vests, lace collars, green tweeds for reflective moments...

MARTHA: [*handing him another dish*] Tweeds always make you break out in a rash.

PHILLIP: [*thinking for a moment, he takes the new plate and stacks the old one*] That's true. Well, perhaps, I'll give up reflection—there won't be much time for it, I hope, anyway.

MARTHA: And after the tailor, then what?

PHILLIP: Ah, I want to go where the climate's very hot; where it steams, as a matter of fact; where oversized plants seem to couple with one another before your eyes and produce offspring so colorful that they look indecent.

MARTHA: [*now a cup in her hand*] You never liked me to wear loud clothes: always gray, black, and brown.

PHILLIP: [*taking the cup*] No offense, but you're just not a tropical plant, Martha.

MARTHA: It wasn't me who had to have an air-conditioner last summer. Put the cup face down, Phillip.

PHILLIP: [*he does so and receives a bowl in its place*] Now I want the heat to prevent anything from taking on too solid and sensible a shape. I want everything about me to shimmer, sway, and change in a second's time as if it were all one big sleight-of-hand trick. People, too, should melt and harden in front of you.

   He starts to put the bowl away.

MARTHA: That still looks wet to me.

PHILLIP: [*retrieving the bowl*] And, Martha, there might be mirages. Can you imagine, scenes floating about purely for your own amusement. Do you know, I think I've wanted to see a mirage for the last ten years.

MARTHA: You're getting water on your trousers, Phillip. [*She opens a cupboard and takes out an apron.*] Here, put this on.

PHILLIP: [*getting into the apron*] I used to try to force a mirage on myself. On days like today, when I'd see the man I was to hang being escorted toward me, I used to widen my eyes, clench my fists, and try to make my brain turn the entire scene into something else. It never worked, though: my eyes would begin to water and soon I was receiving reprimands from my superiors for what they took to be my emotional attitude while on duty.

MARTHA: [*handing PHILLIP the last dish*] All you want, then, is to see mirages?

PHILLIP: I want my pores to open and let out of me all the bubbling perspiration that's been stopped up by the civil service code. Think of it, Martha! Me, in the middle of a jungle, where everything's raw and fresh, where only the hungry and alive do the executing, where...

MARTHA: I think some grounds are still in the coffee pot.

PHILLIP: [*giving the pot another rinse*] And then, Martha, once I've filled my lungs with that wild air—well, then I'll be ready to—to...

MARTHA: To what, Phillip?

PHILLIP: [*modestly, with some embarrassment*] Oh, grow a beard perhaps.

MARTHA: All this trouble just to avoid shaving?

PHILLIP: No, what I mean is, once I've finally shed this old skin, I'll be ready to—to take up my old profession again with a fresh hand.

MARTHA: You mean after all that sweating in the tropics you'd still want to be an executioner?

PHILLIP: [*soberly*] That is my profession, my trade, the only thing I can do passably well. [*Brightening.*] But, Martha, I won't be an official piece of cloth and brass, tying the knot around living necks because someone, somewhere, has underlined their names in red ink.

MARTHA: [*as if humoring someone not too sound of mind*] You're going to do free-lance work?

PHILLIP: [*slowly winding the dishtowel into a strangling cord*] I'm going to have an eye peeled for all the dead branches that need pruning—for all those who want to measure away the few wild patches of weeds left to us and turn the ground, teeming with savage centipedes, into a middle-income housing development.

MARTHA: [*still indulging him*] And just how do you go about determining when a branch is dead?

PHILLIP: [*moving about the kitchen table, towel in hand and eyes agleam*] Oh, that won't be hard, Martha. [*He begins circling the table, his eyes on the pepper mill as if stalking it.*] Just suppose I'm standing on a busy corner at lunchtime. Oh, there'll be a lot of dead wood about, but I'll find the one beyond the help of insecticides. I'll know him: perhaps I'll notice that his tie, socks, and handkerchief match; or perhaps I'll see he doesn't cross the street until the exact moment the light blinks in his favor. Oh, I'll know him as one of those who'll spend what energy he has trying to make tomorrow a line-for-line copy of yesterday; one of those who has a favorite chair, who sees no difference but age between the woman he married and the woman he keeps. [PHILLIP *pauses, narrows his eyes, and moves in on the pepper mill.*] He won't notice me, but I'll be behind him all the time. I'll watch him stuff himself with just the right calorie count; I'll smile as he leaves the proper tip and takes the long way back to his office to get in a little exercise; I'll peek around a corner as he tells an off-color joke to his secretary and pats her knee. And then, when he's alone in his office, about to balance another day's equation, I'll just tiptoe up behind him, hold the loop for a moment over his head, and then—snap! [*He catches the pepper mill in the towel's knot and lifts it up level with his eyes.*] There won't be any struggle or sound. He might have just enough curiosity to turn and see just who's doing him in, but the only thing I'd find in his eyes would be the gleam of one whose funeral arrangements were planned down to the last flower, tear, and comma in his epitaph. Already dead, Martha, he'd be only too happy to lie down.

> PHILLIP *lets the pepper mill drop to the floor.*

MARTHA: [*getting down to retrieve it*] That pepper mill was your birthday gift from my mother!

PHILLIP: [*as if suddenly startled awake*] What?

MARTHA: [*putting the object back on the kitchen table*] It must have cost twenty-five dollars. [*Sharply.*] Find something less expensive to play games with, Phillip.

PHILLIP: [*hurt*] Games? Martha, I was trying to share a secret with you. For the first time in our marriage, I was telling you something I really felt.

MARTHA: Don't be open-hearted and frank with me, Phillip.

PHILLIP: But aren't you at least interested in what I'm really like?

MARTHA: If I was interested in what you were really like, I don't think I'd have stayed married to you for twenty years.

PHILLIP: But you might find me—well, exciting.

MARTHA: [*coldly*] I've grown used to the lies, Phillip. They make up the comfortable husband I know.

PHILLIP: [*realizing he's made a mistake in confiding in her*] Oh, I see. All right, then, you keep the comfortable husband! The new one, Martha, won't bother you any longer. No, he's simply going to close his eyes, turn around, and head straight through the door.

> As he speaks, PHILLIP *performs the above gestures. As he is halfway to the door, however,* MARTHA *speaks up.*

MARTHA: You'd better take off my apron first.

PHILLIP: [*angry with himself for not having noticed it*] Oh, yes. How did I get into it in the first place?

MARTHA: [*as if she were discussing a shopping list*] And another thing: I don't see how you can pick up and leave today, Phillip.

PHILLIP: [*repeating the above gestures*] And why not, Martha? Why shouldn't I just close my eyes, turn around, and...

MARTHA: Because you have a dentist appointment first thing tomorrow morning.

PHILLIP: [*turning about in confusion*] Dentist? Dentist?

MARTHA: [*innocently*] You remember. The molar in the back has to come out? It's infecting the gum? Because of it you can't eat sweets?

PHILLIP: I don't want to eat sweets. I just…

MARTHA: We've been invited to my sister's for dinner Friday, and you know how partial you are to her chocolate mousse.

PHILLIP: [*at last rather angry*] Damn the chocolate mousse! I'm not going to your sister's for dinner anyway.

MARTHA: I've already accepted. And with the weekend whirl coming up, I don't see how you can plan to leave before next Wednesday.

PHILLIP: Plan? Something like this can't be planned and put on schedule. I'm giving up knowing where and what I'll be a week, a day, or even an hour ahead. I'm going to be…

MARTHA: [*again sharp and bitter*] A man-eating, jungle plant—I know. Well, you'll have to wait until *after* my sister's dinner to start blooming. And by that time, there'll be other things popping up to detain you.

PHILLIP: [*a little unnerved*] Martha, maybe you didn't understand or listen to what I was saying. I'm sweeping all the old laws, manners, and invitations under the rug. There's nothing here that can hold me now.

MARTHA: Oh, yes, there is—me.

PHILLIP: You? Martha, I don't want to be brutal, but if nothing else were pushing me through that door, you, in your breakfast face, would be all the reason I'd need.

MARTHA: [*now in full attack*] Maybe my face won't charm you into bed, but you're going to look at it, speak to it, and—yes, even kiss it in a businesslike way every day of your life. Because, Phillip, covered with cold-cream or skin oil, it's the face of your wife. And "wife," Phillip, means a thousand obstacles for you to get over before you're free to start chopping down dead branches.

PHILLIP: [*in the tones of family argument*] Wife? Hah! And were you my wife with the Warden pawing over you?

MARTHA: More than ever, Phillip. That little moment with him only reminded me how snug I was with you—even with your red socks under the sofa seat. My life depends on all the little functions you perform. You're like the telephone, electricity, or underground plumbing. My life takes you for granted, but would be lost without you. Maybe we're not held together by a little piece of flesh, but there is something there even harder to snip apart. It's the word "and" in "man *and* wife." It's official and keeps us together through mistresses, dreams, bills, and burned toast. "Man *and* wife"—that's our world, Phillip; and everything in it has long ago been discovered, named, and placed in its proper corner.

PHILLIP: No three-letter word's going to drag me after it. Not when I finally have the chance…

MARTHA: You *had* the chance, Phillip. For the briefest second, when you caught the Warden and me, you had the chance. But no; you stayed and helped me with the dishes.

PHILLIP: That was just habit.

MARTHA: No, dear, that was the law of gravity yanking you right back to earth.

PHILLIP: Well, I'm breaking the law of gravity, Martha. From now on you'll have to find someone else to eat off and dry your dishes. The first day of creation is waiting for me on the other side of the kitchen door, and all the rules of marriage or physics aren't going to keep me from it.

 He starts for the door.

MARTHA: Touch that door and you'll find out how unpleasant the truth about yourself can be.

PHILLIP: I have all the truth I need, Martha. Goodby. And if we ever meet again be careful I don't mistake you for a dead branch. [PHILLIP *makes to open the door, but finds it refuses to budge. He begins tugging at the knob.*] It must be the dampness has made the wood swell.

MARTHA: [*taunting*] You'll never get it open, Phillip. You know too well what's on the other side.

PHILLIP: [*increasing his efforts*] It's not locked. There's no reason for it to be this stubborn.

MARTHA: You don't want to strain yourself, Phillip. Remember that awful rubber girdle you had to wear after cleaning out the attic last year.

PHILLIP: [*more and more effort*] Shut up, Martha!

MARTHA: Ha! Don't yell at *me!* You, I, and the door know on which side of it you belong.

PHILLIP: [*losing all control*] I'll tear the damned thing off its hinges.

MARTHA: That door's the speed of light—a permanent boundary fence. It can't be broken.

PHILLIP: [*now pounding on the door*] Open, damn you! Open!

MARTHA: It won't because you don't want it to. You know that all your jungle will give you is athlete's foot, diarrhea, and swollen joints.

PHILLIP: [*turning from the door to* MARTHA, *he pleads with desperation in his voice*] I'm going to tear down every kitchen door in the world. I'm going to strangle, murder…

MARTHA: You, murder? Hah! Come on, Phillip, the game's over. You're an official executioner, a little paunchy through the middle, with thinning hair and an obedient attitude. That's as close as you'll ever be to a murderer.

PHILLIP: [*menacingly*] If that door doesn't open you'll be the first to know how wrong you are.

MARTHA: [*with an incredulous smile*] Are you threatening me?

PHILLIP: If you're keeping me in this kitchen—yes!

MARTHA: Oh, poor, poor Phillip. Look at you; out of breath already and not even one step away from the house yet.

PHILLIP: I won't stand you laughing at me!

MARTHA: Then don't make jokes about doing me in. You're not on your gallows now; no twenty-five forms have been filled out in triplicate authorizing you to snap my neck. [*Shouting.*] You're my husband! And that makes you the most harmless person in the world as far as *I'm* concerned!

PHILLIP: [*picking tip the black hood from the kitchen table and beginning to knot it ominously*] For the last time: make the door open!

MARTHA: How can I, Phillip? You're the one who's keeping it shut. If you really wanted to leave, it would spring open like a hungry mouth.

PHILLIP: [*stepping toward her*] Then I'll have to prove I'm in earnest, Martha.

MARTHA: Don't be an ass. One of the things that will make the rest of our life together tolerable is that you can keep your mind buzzing with plans to murder me. Don't try it now and find out you can't. It'll make you sour, bitter, and even more difficult to get new hats and dresses out of than you are now.

     PHILLIP *begins testing the hood's strength and continues his advance.*

[*Quite earnestly.*] I'm warning you. With as much love as I can squeeze out of me after twenty years, I'm warning you not to do this to yourself.

PHILLIP: As the books say: there's no good reasoning with a murderer.

MARTHA: [*throwing back the challenge*] All right, murderer, if you won't listen—[*She picks up one of the kitchen table chairs, places it downstage, facing the audience, and sits in it with her neck thrust out as if for a sacrifice.*] All right then, go ahead. Try and squeeze the air out of my windpipe. Just try it! Well, what are you waiting for, Bluebeard? Come on, let me feel some of your jungle sweat dripping down the back of my neck.

PHILLIP: [*a little startled by* MARTHA's *action*] Are you just going to sit there as if you were having your hair done?

MARTHA: You'll have to supply the noise and screams, Phillip. I'm just going to sit here and talk.

PHILLIP: Talk? Then that's just the last bit of incentive I need.

     He knots the hood around MARTHA's *neck and begins tightening.*

MARTHA: [*not affected at all by* PHILLIP's *attack*] Oh, you'll have to pull harder than that. I'm still getting in more than enough air to tell you that the ivy plants over our bed are all the jungle you'll ever know.

     PHILLIP *gives an extra hard tug, and* MARTHA *starts, as if tickled.*

MARTHA: And it's your turn to water them next week. You'll take care of them every other week for as long as you're on this planet.

PHILLIP: [*hopefully*] Is the blood beginning to pound in your head? Do you find it difficult to focus your eyes?

MARTHA: Hah! I've never felt better. This is the closest we've come to sex in years.

PHILLIP: [*increasing his efforts*] And now, Martha, is your past popping up in front of you?

MARTHA: Only my future. And you, Phillip, growing stooped, absent-minded, and a little sloppy at the table, are in every minute of it.

PHILLIP: [*becoming frustrated*] You should at least be gagging now, damn it!

MARTHA: [*sweetly*] I don't know how to gag. But I could cough a little if it would make things easier for you.

PHILLIP: [*pleading*] Please stop breathing, Martha. Please, my arms are getting tired— please stop breathing.

MARTHA: At this rate, you'll stop before I will. Oh, what a story this will make at cards Saturday!

PHILLIP: [*makes one last supreme effort, and then, with a groan, drops his hands*] I just can't do it. My wrists and fingers just aren't strong enough. [*He sits in one of the kitchen chairs.*] I can't even get out of the kitchen.

MARTHA: [*rubbing her neck and rising from the chair*] I told you, Phillip, but you wouldn't listen, would you? Now look at you—panting and overheated [*She takes the hood and begins mopping his brow.*] And you have to go out right away. I'm sure this will mean a cold by tomorrow.

PHILLIP: [*docilely*] Go out?

MARTHA: There's not fifteen minutes till the execution begins. There now, that's the best I can do. [*She takes* PHILLIP's *coat and holds it out for him.*] All right, come on, get into this. If you keep all the buttons closed there's still a chance I won't have to spend a fortune on nose drops and cough syrup.

PHILLIP: So the execution's going to take place after all?

MARTHA: [*buttoning up the coat*] Of course it is; and you're going to be on those gallows, stiff and tall, the way I, the Warden, and the man you're going to hang expect you to be. The whole thing will go very smoothly now, won't it?

PHILLIP: I suppose it will.

MARTHA: [*finishing the buttoning,* MARTHA *steps back to admire her work*] There! Now you look like my husband and the state's official executioner. You can tell at a glance that you're a fish in the right waters now.

PHILLIP: I guess you can.

MARTHA: [*picking up* PHILLIP's *cap*] Now, don't be so gloomy. Look on the bright side of everything to come. Think of the certificate of merit and pension bonus you'll receive when you successfully hang your thousandth man. Think of the speeches you'll be asked to give to college students on the fine prose in the penal code. Think of the jokes you'll tell at your retirement dinner and the little cottage our insurance policy's going to give us. Think how peaceful things will be when you're certain that there's only one world and one way to live in it.

PHILLIP: Will that come with the retirement policy too?

MARTHA: [*putting the cap on his head*] It just might, Phillip. It just might. And now, you're complete; not a wrinkle in you.

> She takes his arm and starts to lead him toward the door.

PHILLIP: My hood? Can I at least have that?

MARTHA: I'll put it under the sofa with your socks. And, on holidays, you can take them, your banjo, and the other things out to look at for a while. And on New Year's Eve, you can even sit on the floor and flip ashes into your slippers if you want to.

PHILLIP: I think I'll go back to my chair. The floor's very hard.

MARTHA: That *is* more sensible, I suppose.

> They reach the door.

Well, come on now. Out you go.

PHILLIP: But it won't open.

MARTHA: [*she touches the door knob ever so lightly with the tips of her fingers and it springs open*] There's nothing holding it shut now.

PHILLIP: [*taking a step toward the opening*] It is very cold this morning.

MARTHA: Do you have a handkerchief with you?

PHILLIP: [*feeling his pocket*] Yes.

MARTHA: Well, then, you'd better be off.

PHILLIP: [*turning toward MARTHA*] Martha, I just wanted to be…

MARTHA: But you couldn't, Phillip. Some things just can't be broken. So you'd better just try to keep warm out there and forget all about it. Now, kiss me goodby.

PHILLIP: But isn't there any chance for me at all?

MARTHA: [*in a command voice and pointing to her cheek*] Kiss!

      PHILLIP *does so, and then slowly turns and leaves.* MARTHA *waits for a moment and then calls out to him.*

Keep bundled up, dear. Don't work too hard. And tonight—tonight we'll have something very special for dinner. Something you really like, dear, something you really, really like.

CURTAIN

Amiri Baraka

❧

The Toilet

•

The Toilet was first presented by Leo Garen and Stan Swerdlow at the St. Marks Playhouse, New York, on December 16, 1964. It was directed by Leo Garen, designed by Larry Rivers, and the lighting was by Harold Baldridge. The cast was as follows:

ORA	James Spruill
WILLIE LOVE	Gary Bolling
HINES	D'Urville Martin
JOHNNY BOY HOLMES	Bostic Van Felton
PERRY	Norman Bush
GEORGE DAVIS	Antonio Fargas
SKIPPY	Tony Hudson
KNOWLES	Walter Jones
DONALD FARRELL	Gary Haynes
FOOTS	Hampton Clanton
KAROLIS	Jaime Sanchez

CHARACTERS

ORA [Big Shot]: *Short, ugly, crude, loud.*
WILLIE LOVE: *Tall, thin. Should have been sensitive. Smiles.*
HINES: *Big, husky, garrulous. He and* LOVE *are closest friends.*
JOHNNY BOY HOLMES: *Short, curly hair. Bright, fast, likable.*
PERRY: *Tall, dark, somber, cynical.*
GEORGE DAVIS: *Tall, thin, crudely elegant. Judicious.*
SKIPPY: *Quick. Rather stupid but interested. Someone to be trusted.*
KNOWLES: *Large and ridiculous. A grinning ape.*
DONALD FARRELL: *Tall, thin, blonde, awkward, soft.*
FOOTS [Ray]: *Short, intelligent, manic. Possessor of a threatened empire.*
KAROLIS: *Medium height. Very skinny and not essentially attractive except when he speaks.*

The scene is a large bare toilet built of gray rough cement. There are urinals along one wall and a partition separating them from the commodes which are along the same wall. The toilet must resemble the impersonal ugliness of a school toilet or a latrine of some institution. A few rolls of toilet paper are spread out on the floor, wet through. The actors should give the impression frequently that the place smells.

ORA breaks through the door grinning, then giggling. Looks around the bleak place, walks around, then with one hand on his hip takes out his joint and pees, still grinning, into one of the commodes, spraying urine over the seat.

LOVE: [*sticking his head through the door*] Big Shot! Hey, Big Shot! These guys say come and help them.

ORA: [*zipping his fly and wiping the one hand on the back of his pants*] Yeh? [*Turning to* LOVE.] Yeh? They got him, huh ?

LOVE: [*pushing door open so his arm is straight*] Naw, they don't have him yet. He's on the second floor, running back and forth and hiding in empty rooms. But Knowles said for you to come help.

ORA: [*flushing all the commodes and urinals in the row as he walks past*] Sheet! I'll catch that bastid in a second. [*Ducks under* LOVE'*s arm to go out.*] Why the hell don't you get up there. You supposed to be faster than me.

LOVE: I'm s'posed to stay here and keep the place clear. [*Making a face.*] Damn. This place smells like hell.

ORA: [*without turning around*] Yeh [*giggling*], this must be your momma's house.

LOVE: [*slipping inside the door and holding it against* ORA] Shit. At least I got one.

ORA: [*thumps against the door, not really angry*] Bastid!

LOVE waits a few seconds, then pulls the door open slightly. Then lets it shut and walks to a closed commode and noticing it's wet wipes it with some of the strewn toilet paper. He sits down and stretches his legs. Then gets up and opens the commode to pee. There are voices outside and then the door swings open and HINES and HOLMES come in.

HINES: Hey, Willie.

LOVE: [*still peeing*] What you want?

Comes out, zipping his pants.

HINES: [*to* HOLMES] Man, this cat's in here pulling his whatchamacallit.

HOLMES: [*to* LOVE] Yeh. Damn, Love, why don't you go get Gloria to do that stuff for you.

LOVE: She-et. [*Grinning.*] Huh. I sure don't need your ol' lady to be pullin' on my joint.

Laughs. HOLMES *begins to spar with him.*

HINES: They didn't even catch that skinny nose punk yet.

LOVE: No? Why in hell not?

HOLMES: He's still running up and down the damn halls. I should go up there and drag that sonofabitch down.

　　　　　HOLMES *and* HINES *begin to pee also in the commodes.*
　　　　　LOVE *pulls open the door a small bit and looks out.*

LOVE: Shit. Boy, all you slow ass cats. I'd catch that little skinny paddy boy in a second. Where's that little popeyed Foots?

HINES: Damn if I know. I think he's still in Miss Powell's class. You know if he missed her class she'd beat his head, and then get his ol' lady to beat his head again.

HOLMES: Shit. Skippy should've got hold of that damn Karolis by now. He ain't fast worth a bitch.

LOVE: Yeh, but he's so goddamned scary he might just jump out a goddamn window.

　　　　　HOLMES *finishes peeing and starts pushing* LOVE *and they begin to spar around.* HOLMES *is very funny, making boxer-like sounds and brushing his nose continuously with his thumbs.* LOVE *just stands straight with his left hand stiff and stabbing it out toward* HOLMES's *face.* HINES *finishes and gets in the action too. Both he and* HOLMES *are against* LOVE, *who starts to laugh and curse good naturedly.*

LOVE: Two a' you bastids, huh? I'll take you both.

　　　　　He starts kicking at them.

HINES: Boy, if you kick me, you'll die just like that...with your skinny ass leg up. They'll have to build you a special coffin with a part for your leg.

HOLMES: [*backing away, and then turning on* HINES. *Laughing*] Let's get this sum'bitch, Willie.

HINES: [*backing away, now kicking and swinging...but just timing blows so they won't strike anyone*] Goddamn, Johnny Boy, you a crooked muthafucka. You cats think you can mess with the kid?

　　　　　The two spar against HINES *and then* LOVE *turns against* HOLMES.

LOVE: Let's get this little assed cat.

　　　　　HOLMES *kicks at them, then jumps up on the commodes in order to defend himself more "heroically."*

HOLMES: I'm gonna get your ass, Willie. I'm just trying to help you out and you gonna play wise. Ya' bastid.

HINES: Listen to that cat. [*Runs after* HOLMES.] I'm gonna put your damn head in one of those damn urinals.

　　　　　He and LOVE *finally grab* HOLMES *and he begins struggling with them in earnest.* Let's put this little bastard's head in the goddamn urinal!

HOLMES: You bastids! Let me go! I'm gonna cut somebody. Bastids!

　　　　　The door opens and ORA *comes in. His shirt is torn. But he rushes over laughing and starts punching everyone, even* HOLMES.

HINES: Goddamn it, Big Shot, get the hell out of here.

HOLMES: Get 'em, Big Shot.

ORA: [*punches* HOLMES *who's still being held by* LOVE] I'm gonna punch you, you prick. Hold the cocksucker, Love.

LOVE: [*releasing* HOLMES *immediately*] I ain't gonna hold him so you can punch him.

ORA *and* HOLMES *square off, both laughing and faking professional demeanor.*

LOVE: Hey, Big Shot, what happened to your shirt?

ORA: [*putting his hands down and handling the torn part of his shirt*] That muthafuckin' Karolis ripped it.

The other three yowl. HINES *puts his fingers to the hole as if to tear it again.*

Get outta here you black ass bastid. [*He squares off at* HINES, *then pushes him away.*] That paddy bastid! I had the cocksucker around the waist, and then he rips my shirt and scratches me.

He holds up his wounded hand.

HINES: You let him get away?

ORA: No, hell. I punched the bastid right in his lip. But he was making so much noise we thought somebody'd come out and see us so Knowles and Skippy took him in the broom closet and I cut down the stairs. The stupid bastid was screaming and biting right outside of ol' lady Powell's room.

HOLMES: Did anybody come outta there?

ORA: You think I was gonna stay around and see? She and Miss Golden after me anyway.

LOVE: Did you see Foots in there?

ORA: [*going to the door and peering out*] Yeh. And George Davis and Perry are in there too.

He pushes door open and leans all the way out.

HINES: Shit. They're never gonna bring that sonofabitch down here. We ain't got all day.

ORA: [*letting the door shut*] Yeh, Perry and Foots and them ought to be down here in a few minutes. It's almost 3:00 now.

LOVE: [*pretending he has a basketball in his hands, he pretends to dribble and lunges forward simulating a fake at* HINES, *then he sweeps past* HINES *and leaps in the air as if making a layup shot*] Peed on you, just then, buddy.

HINES: Sheet, Man, you what you call a self-checker. I don't even have to block that shot. I just take it off the backboard like this. [*He spins around and leaps up at the imaginary basket and scoops the imaginary ball off, landing and shaking his head as if to shake off imaginary defenders.*] Another rebound! [*Makes motion of long pass down toward opposite "court."*] Now, the fast break [*He moves in position for his own pass, receives it, makes one long-stepping dribble and leaps as if dunking the ball in the basket.*] Two!

HOLMES: Boy, you guys sure play a lot of ball...off the court.

ORA: [*opening the door again*] No Shootin' cocksuckas.

LOVE: [*still whirling and leaping as if he is making successful hook shots from an imaginary foul line*] Hey, what we gonna do to this cat when he gets here?

ORA: [*leaning back in from the door though keeping it open with his fingers*] Damn, Love. You a stupid bastid. [*Peeks out door.*] We gonna kick that little frail bastid's ass.

HINES: In fact, you the one gonna do it, Willie.

HOLMES: Yeh, Love.
    Blocking one of LOVE's *"shots."*

LOVE: Shit. Karolis never bothered me.
    Faking HOLMES *and swinging to shoot from the other side.*

ORA: [*looking back in and letting the door swing shut*] Damn, Willie [*in mocking seriousness*], Karolis is always telling everybody how he bangs the hell out of Caroline, every chance he gets.
    Begins to giggle.

HOLMES: Is that your mother's name, Love, Caroline?

HINES: [*busy trying to lift a back window to look out on the yard*] What you mean, Johnny Boy, is that his mother's name? You the one told me.

LOVE: [*swinging around as if to shoot again he suddenly punches* HOLMES *on the shoulder.* HOLMES *lets out a yelp of pain*] Uhhuh...I told you about messin' with me.

HOLMES: [*holding his shoulder*] Shit. Why didn't you hit Big Shot, you bastard? He brought the shit up.

ORA: [*has the door propped open again*] Shit. That narrow head bastid know better than to fuck with me.
    He peers out the door and as he does LOVE *gestures as if to hit him in the back.*

HOLMES: [*to* LOVE] You scared ass bastard. Why don't you do it?

ORA: [*turning around and throwing up his hands to defend himself*] Yeh, I wish you would, you bullet head sonofabitch.
    HOLMES *goes and sits on a radiator next to* HINES.

LOVE: Man, nobody's thinking about you, Big Shot.
    He goes to pee.

ORA: [*pulling the door open again*] Here come Perry and them.

HOLMES: [*jumping off the radiator still holding his shoulder*] Perry and who else?

ORA: George Davis and Donald Farrell.

HINES: Donald Farrell? What the hell's he doin' down here? Where the hell is Foots?

LOVE: Yeh, what the hell is Perry doing bringing Farrell down here with 'em? Shit.
    ORA *pulls the door open, and* PERRY, DAVIS *and* FARRELL *come in.*

PERRY: Hey, what's happening?

HOLMES: Shit. I should ask you. Where's Foots?

GEORGE: He had to stay upstairs for awhile. Powell wanted to talk to him...or something.

ORA: [*to* FARRELL] Man, whatta you want down here? Nobody asked you to come.

GEORGE: I told him he could come. Why not?

ORA: Whatta you mean, why not? You know goddamn well, why not. Silly sumbitch!

PERRY: Ah, Big Shot, why don't you be cool for a change, huh?

GEORGE: Yeh, man, Big Shot. Donald's not going to hurt anything.

ORA: No? [*Taking out a much-smoked cigarette butt.*] Maybe you don't think so...but I do.

GEORGE: Oh, man, shit.

FARRELL: Why don't you want me here, Big Shot?

ORA: [*glaring at* FARRELL] Man, don't be asking me questions.

FARRELL: Don't ask you questions? Why the hell not?

ORA: [*menacingly at* FARRELL] Cause I said so, that's why. You don't like it, muthafucka?

PERRY: [*stepping between them*] Goddamn it, Big Shot, why don't you sit your ass down for awhile and shut the hell up?

ORA: [*turning to* PERRY] You gonna make me, muthafucka?

PERRY: [*stepping to face* ORA] I can. And you better believe it, Baby!

ORA: Shit. [*Disparagingly. Moving away from* FARRELL *and back to the center of the room.*] Well you damn sure got your chance right now, you black sonofabitch.

GEORGE: [*moves between* PERRY *and* ORA] Oh, goddamnit why don't both you guys sit down. You too, Donald.

> FARRELL *moves to sit on a radiator beside* HOLMES *and* HINES.

Ora, you wrong, man, and you know it.

ORA: How come I'm wrong, huh? You know goddamn well that skinny cocksucka over there [*at* FARRELL] ain't got no business down here. He ain't gonna do a damn thing but stand around and look.

LOVE: [*laughing*] That's all I'm gonna do.

HINES: [*hunching* HOLMES *with his elbow*] Yeh, but that's okay for you, Willie. You so black, if you stand still nobody'll know you're standing there anyway.

> *All laugh.* ORA *takes the opportunity to go to the door and crack it open.*

PERRY: Where's the rest of those guys?

HINES: I guess they must still be upstairs in that broom closet.

PERRY: Broom closet?

> *He and* DAVIS *lean against one of the walls and begin to smoke.*

HINES: Yeh, Knowles and Skippy got Karolis upstairs in a broom closet waiting till everybody leaves the floor I guess.

FARRELL: Jimmy Karolis?

HOLMES: Yeah, that's who we're waiting for.

> *Giggles.*

FARRELL: What the hell's gonna happen then?

ORA: [*turning from door*] Man, what the hell you care, huh? Pee-the-bed-muthafucka!

HINES: Damn, George!

GEORGE: Damn, what?

HINES: Seems to me like Big Shot's right. You bring this cat down here and he doesn't even know what's happening.

ORA: You goddamn real I'm right. Simple ass cats.

FARRELL: What're you guys gonna gang Jimmy Karolis?

ORA: We gonna break that muthafucka's back.

FARRELL: For what?

ORA: Look man, why don't you shut up and get the hell out of here, huh?

FARRELL: You mean all you guys're gonna jump on Karolis?

ORA: [*walking over to* FARRELL *and grabbing him by the shirt*] You gonna stick up for him?

> FARRELL *tries to push* ORA's *hands from his shirt, and though he is much taller than* ORA, ORA *pulls him from his seat.*

FARRELL: Goddamn it, Ora, why don't you cut the shit?

GEORGE: Yeh, Ora, cut it out.

PERRY: Goddamn; that cat's always going for bad.

> GEORGE *comes over to restrain* ORA, *but* ORA *succeeds in punching* FARRELL *in the stomach.* FARRELL *clutches his stomach and sinks to the floor groaning.*

PERRY: [*to* ORA] You bastard.

> ORA *swings around to confront him.*

ORA: You come on too, if you want to, you black sonofabitch!

> GEORGE *pushes them apart again and his push sends* ORA *rattling heavily against the door.*

Goddamnit, George, why don't you stay the fuck out of this?

GEORGE: Because there wasn't a goddamn reason in the world for you to hit Donald like that. [*Going to help* FARRELL *up.*] Damn, Ora, you're a wrong sonofabitch, you know that?

FARRELL: [*still doubled up and holding his stomach. He pulls his arm back when* GEORGE *tries to help him up*] No, man! Lemme stay here. [*Still groaning.*] Ora, you dirty cocksucker.

ORA: Boy, you better shut up before I stomp mudholes in your pissy ass.

> *The door is suddenly pushed open and* KNOWLES *and* SKIPPY *come in holding* KAROLIS *by the arms.* KAROLIS' *head is hanging, and he is crying softly and blood is on his shirt and face. His hair is mussed and standing all over his head.*

LOVE: Ga-uh damn! What'd you cats do?

KNOWLES: [*giggling stupidly*] Love, now what the hell does it look like we did? Broke this muthafucka's jaw.

HINES: Damn. I thought we were just bringing the cat down here to fight Foots. I didn't know you guys were gonna break his head first.

SKIPPY: Well, he didn't wanna come. We had to persuade him.

KNOWLES: Shit, Skippy, whatta you mean "we?" I did all the persuading.

ORA: Aw, shit, Knowles. I bloodied the cat's lip. You trying to take all the credit.

SKIPPY: Yeh, Knowles. You didn't hit the cat but once, and that was on the goddamn shoulder.

> *Letting* KNOWLES *drag* KAROLIS *into a corner where he lets him drop.*

You know what this cat was doing all the time we was in that goddamn broom closet? Tellin' jokes. [*Laughs.*] They must not a been funny either. Karolis didn't laugh once.

KNOWLES: What should I do with this guy. I gotta drag him everywhere.

ORA: Drop him in that goddamn corner. [*Walks over to corner and nudges* KAROLIS *with his foot.*] Hey, muthafucka. Hey! Why don't you straighten up?

SKIPPY: [*noticing* FARRELL, *who is still crumpled in an opposite corner, but stirring*] Damn! What the hell happened to Donald?

PERRY: That goddamn Big Shot had to show how bad he was.

ORA: [*laughing paradoxically*] He called me a nigger.

    All laugh.

LOVE: Well, what the hell are you? Wha's the matter, you shamed of your people?

ORA: Fuck you! [*He still stands over* KAROLIS, *nudging him with his foot.*] Hey, man, get up!

    Laughs.

HINES: Damn, Ora. Why don't you leave the cat alone?

ORA: [*bending over as if to talk in* KAROLIS' *ear*] Hey, baby, why don't you get up? I gotta nice fat sausage here for you.

GEORGE: Goddamn, Big Shot…You really a wrong sonofabitch!

ORA: Look man. [*Now kneeling over the slumped figure.*] If you want to get in on this you line up behind me. I don't give a shit what you got to say.

LOVE: Man, George, leave the cat alone. You know that's his stick. That's what he does [*laughing*] for his kicks…rub up against half-dead white boys.

    All laugh.

ORA: [*looking over his shoulder…grudgingly having to smile too*] I'd rub up against your momma too. [*Leaning back to* KAROLIS.] Come on, baby…I got this fat ass sa-zeech for you!

LOVE: Ora, you mad cause you don't have a momma of your own to rub up against.

    All laugh.

ORA: [*turns again, this time less amused*] Fuck you, you bony head sonofabitch. As long as I can rub against your momma …or your fatha' [*laughs at his invention*] I'm doin' alright.

    Door is pushed open suddenly and FOOTS *comes in. He is nervous but keeps it hidden by a natural glibness and a sharp sense of what each boy in the room expects, singularly, from him. He is the weakest physically and smallest of the bunch, but he is undoubtedly their leader. When* FOOTS *comes in* KAROLIS *looks up quickly, then slumps again.*

HINES: Man, where the hell you been?

FOOTS: That goddamn Van Ness had me in his office. He said I'm a credit to my race. [*Laughs and all follow.*] He said I'm smart-as-a-whip [*imitating Van Ness*] and should help him to keep all you unsavory [*again imitating*] elements in line.

    All laugh again.

LOVE: Yeh? What's he talking about?

FOOTS: Well, he seems to think that you guys…particularly that goddamn Big Shot and Knowles, are not good influences in this joint.

PERRY: Boy, you can say that again. Nutty muthafuckas!

ORA: [*to* PERRY] Fuck you, tar baby!

FOOTS: Well, I'm supposed to make sure that you guys don't do anything bad to anybody. Especially to James Karolis.
    Laughing.

GEORGE: Oh yeh? He know about that?

FOOTS: Yeh, somebody told him Knowles said he was gonna kick Karolis' ass. [*Seeing*
KAROLIS *in the corner for the first time. His first reaction is horror and disgust...but
he keeps it controlled as is his style, and merely half-whistles.*] Goddamn! What the
fuck happened to him? [*He goes over to* KAROLIS *and kneels near him, threatening
to stay too long. He controls the impulse and gets up and walks back to where he was.
He is talking throughout his action.*] Damn! What'd you guys do, kill the cat?

PERRY: Heavy handed Big Shot again.

FOOTS: [*looks at* ORA *quickly with disgust but softens it immediately to comic disdain*]
What the hell you hit him with, Ora, a goddamn train?

ORA: [*happy at the notice of his destruction*] No, man, I just bopped him in the mouth
with the back of my hand.

FOOTS: Ga-uhd damn! You a rough ass cat, Shot. He sure don't look like he's in any
way to fight anybody.

ORA: [*laughing*] No, but he might be able to suck you off. Hee, hee.

LOVE: Shit. You the one that look like you want that, Big Shot.

FOOTS: Oh, shit. There wasn't any need of bringing the cat down here if you guys were
gonna fuck him up before I got here. He was supposed to fight me.
    Almost angry.

HINES: Yeh, that's what I thought. You shouldn't of sent Ora and Knowles up after
him then.

FOOTS: The only person I asked to go up was Skippy.

SKIPPY: Well, the sonofabitch wouldn't come...so, I got Superduck over there to help
me. I didn't ask Ora to come. Knowles did.

KNOWLES: Oh, man, the cat's here. Get him up on his feet [*laughs*] then knock him
down. That's all. That don't seem like no big problem to me.
    Through most of the action KNOWLES *is drumming on the walls or the win-
dow or the door or the floor, in a kind of drum and bugle corps beat...also supply-
ing the bugle parts vocally.*

LOVE: Man, Knowles, why don't you stop being a goddamn Elk all the time. Damn.
That cat's always drumming on something. Why don't you get a goddamn drum?

KNOWLES: I'm going to drum on your bony head in a little while if you don't shut up.

FOOTS: Well, I don't see any reason to keep all this shit up. Just pour water on the cat
and let's get outta here.

ORA: What? You mean you made us go through all this bullshit for nothing?

FOOTS: Well, what the hell am I gonna do, beat on the guy while he's sprawled on the
floor. Damn, Ora, you're a pretty lousy sonofabitch.

HINES: Man, Big Shot'd stomp anybody in any damn condition. He likes it when
they're knocked out first, especially.

FOOTS: I'm pushed! There's no reason to stay here. I can't fight the guy like he is.

FARRELL [*who has pushed himself up and is leaning against the wall*] I sure am glad somebody's got some sense here.

FOOTS: [*seeing* FARRELL *for the first time*] What the hell you doing here? Who asked you to come here, huh?

> *Embarrassed and angry.*

ORA: That stupid ass Perry brought him.

PERRY: That's right. I just thought there was gonna be a fight. I didn't know you guys were gonna lynch anybody.

FOOTS: Lynch, your ass. Look, Donald, why don't you leave, huh? Nobody needs you here.

FARRELL: [*slowly*] Yeh, okay, Ray. But I just want to know why you're gonna beat up on Jimmy like this. What the hell did he do to you?

FOOTS: [*almost indignantly*] None of your goddamn business, Farrell. Just leave!

ORA: Yeh, man. I should've thrown your ass out when you first come in here. Pee-the-bed sonofabitch.

FARRELL: OK. [*Stands up, still lightly holding his stomach.*] OK. But I want to take Jimmy out of here with me. He can't fight anybody.

ORA: Man, you better shut your goddamn mouth and get outta here!

FOOTS: Look, Donald, just leave, that's all. You hear?

> *Turns his back on* FARRELL *and walks toward* KAROLIS, *then thinking better of it turns toward* FARRELL *again.*

FARRELL: Ray! You're not gonna beat the guy up when he's like that are you?

FOOTS: I don't need you to tell me what to do. [*He goes over and pulls the door open slightly.*] Just get out of here...now!

FARRELL: [*takes a step then looks toward* KAROLIS] But look at him, he can't do anything. [*To* FOOTS.] Why do you want to do this?

FOOTS: Goddamn it, get out!

FARRELL: That's no answer.

FOOTS: Man, I'll punch you in the belly myself.

FARRELL: Shit.

> *Disparagingly...which makes* FOOTS *madder.*

FOOTS: [*in low horrible voice*] Goddamnit. You better get the fuck outta here, right now!

FARRELL: Nobody's gonna tell me why?

> *He starts to move for the door.*

PERRY: Look, Donald, you better cool it, Buddy. You heard about that letter didn't you?

FARRELL: Letter? What letter?

FOOTS: Man, I told you to leave. I'm not gonna tell you again.

PERRY: [*laughing*] The letter Karolis sent Foots telling him he thought he was "beautiful"...and that he wanted to blow him.

> *All giggle.*

FARRELL: [*turning sharply toward* FOOTS] A letter?

ORA: [*rushing at* FARRELL *from the side and punching him*] Goddamn it! Didn't you hear somebody say leave, pee ass?

FOOTS: [*pushing between* FARRELL *and* ORA] Cut it out, Ora!

FARRELL: [*hurt again and slumping.* ORA *tries to hit him again and the punch is blocked by* FOOTS *who glares savagely at* ORA] A letter? [*Groaning.*] Oh, Ray, come on. Why don't you come off it?

> *He is looking up at* FOOTS.

ORA: [*leaps around* FOOTS *and pushes* FARRELL *into the door*] Get out of here you dumb bastid!

> KNOWLES *pulls the door open and shoves* FARRELL *through it.*

Goddamn, what a stupid punk.

> *He laughs, as do some of the others.*

FOOTS: [*stares at the closed door for a second, then he turns slowly to the others*] Look, let's get out of here. This stuff is finished.

KAROLIS: [*has brought his head up during the preceding scuffle, and has been staring at* FOOTS. *As* FOOTS *and the others look over toward him, he speaks very softly, but firmly*] No. Nobody has to leave. I'll fight you, Ray. [*He begins to pull himself up. He is unsteady on his feet, but determined to get up...and to fight.*] I want to fight you.

> FOOTS *is startled and his eyes widen momentarily, but he suppresses it.*

HINES: Damn. Some guys don't know when they're well off.

ORA: Yeh. You little skinny muthafucka. You should've kept your mouth shut, and played dead.

KNOWLES: Goddamn. You mean that sonofabitch wasn' dead? Shit, Big Shot, you must hit like a girl.

ORA: [*to* KNOWLES] Yeh? Well, let me hit you, you bastid.

KNOWLES: [*disparagingly*] Shit.

KAROLIS: [*pushing himself off the wall slightly and wiping his face with his sleeve*] No, Ray. Don't have them leave. I want to fight you.

FOOTS: [*very silent and stiff, not wanting to be pushed*] Oh? [*Slowly.*] Well, that's damn fine with me.

ORA: [*going behind* KAROLIS *and pushing him toward* FOOTS] You wanna fight? Well, go ahead, dick licker.

> *Howls.*

HINES: Yeh, get it on, fellas.

HOLMES: Karolis must be bad.

> *Laughs.*

GEORGE: Man [*to* KAROLIS] you sure you want to get in this? You look kinda shaky to me.

SKIPPY: Man, just sit down and watch. This might be good.

KAROLIS: Yes, Ray, I want to fight you, now. I want to kill you.

> *His voice is still soft and terrible. The word "kill" is almost spit out.* FOOTS *does not move. He turns his head slightly to look* KAROLIS *in the eye, but he is motionless otherwise.*

ORA: Goddamn it, fight!

> *He pushes* KAROLIS *again. This time* KAROLIS *almost bumps* FOOTS *and* FOOTS *throws up his hands and pushes him away.*

FOOTS: Goddamn you! Goddamn you! [*His body moves from being completely immobile to an angry snarling figure.*] You bastard!

> *The others become animated, clapping their hands, shouting, whistling, and moving around as if they were also fighting.*

KAROLIS: No, Ray. I want to fight you. [*He is moving around now, but his hands are still held tightly and awkwardly at his sides.*] I want to fight you.

FOOTS: [*moving around with his hands up to fight. They both move around each other and* FOOTS *seems to get, momentarily, a change of heart*] Look now, Karolis...you're just gonna get your head blocked.

KAROLIS: [*as if he didn't hear*] No. You have to fight me. I sent you a note, remember. That note saying I loved you. [*The others howl at this.*] The note saying you were beautiful. [*Tries to smile.*] You remember that note, Ray?

FOOTS: Goddamn it, if you're going to fight, fight you cocksucker!

KAROLIS: Yeh. That's what I'm going to do Ray. I'm going to fight you. We're here to fight. About that note, right? The one that said I wanted to take you into my mouth.

> FOOTS *lunges at* KAROLIS *and misses.*

Did I call you Ray in that letter...or Foots? [*Trying to laugh.*] Foots! [*Shouts.*] I'm going to break your fucking neck. That's right. That's who I want to kill. Foots!

ORA: [*pushing* KAROLIS *into* FOOTS] Fight, you goddamn sissy-punk bastid!

FOOTS: [*slaps* KAROLIS *with his open hand*] You crazy bastard!

KAROLIS: [*backing up...wanting to talk but still moving as if to fight*] Are you Ray or Foots, huh?

> *The crowd begins to move forward to cut down the area of the match so that the two fighters will have to make contact.*

HINES: Hit the sonofabitch, Foots!

FOOTS: Fight, you bastard!

KAROLIS: Yeh! That's why we're here, huh? I'll fight you, Foots! [*Spits the name.*] I'll fight you. Right here in this same place where you said your name was Ray. [*Screaming. He lunges at* FOOTS *and manages to grab him in a choke hold.*] Ray, you said your name was. You said Ray. Right here in this filthy toilet. You said Ray. [*He is choking* FOOTS *and screaming.* FOOTS *struggles and is punching* KAROLIS *in the back and stomach, but he cannot get out of the hold.*] You put your hand on me and said Ray!

SKIPPY: Goddamn, that bastid is choking the shit out of Foots.

> *The two still struggle, with* KAROLIS *continuing to have the advantage.*

HINES: That fuck is trying to kill Foots!

HOLMES: Goddamn it!

ORA: [*suddenly leaping on* KAROLIS' *back, puts the same choke hold on him*] You cocksucka...how's that feel, huh? [*He pulls* KAROLIS *off of* FOOTS *who falls to his knees.*] Huh?

KNOWLES: Let's kick this cocksucka's ass real good.

He rushes up to help ORA, *and the whole of the crowd surges into the center punching the fallen* KAROLIS *in the face.* KNOWLES *is screaming with laughter.*

KAROLIS: No, no, his name is Ray, not Foots. You stupid bastards. I love somebody you don't even know.

He is dragged to the floor. The crowd is kicking and cursing him. ORA *in the center punching the fallen* KAROLIS *in the face.* KNOWLES *is screaming with laughter.*

FOOTS *is now on his hands and knees but his head hangs limply and he is unaware of what is happening. He slumps again.*

They have beaten KAROLIS *enough.* KAROLIS *is spread in the center of the floor and is unmoving.* ORA *drapes some of the wet toilet paper across his body and face.*

ORA: Let's stick the sonofabitch's head in the damn toilet.

PERRY: Oh, man, fuck you. The cat's completely out. What more can you do to him?

GEORGE: Yeh, let's get Foots, and get outta here before somebody comes in.

ORA: Yeh. Hee, hee. Look at ol' Foots. That fuckin' paddy boy almost kilt him.

LOVE: Yeh. [*Laughing.*] I told you Karolis was probably bad!

All laugh.

KNOWLES: Nutty sonofabitch.

LOVE: [*picking up* FOOTS, *helped by* HINES *and* HOLMES] Hey, big eye! Get the hell up.

ORA: [*takes a paper cup and dips it in the commode and throws it in* FOOTS' *face*] Yeh, get up, bad ass.

Laughs.

They all leave, as FOOTS *begins to come to. All making noise, laughing, cursing.* KAROLIS *lies as before in the center of the room, motionless.*

After a minute or so KAROLIS *moves his hand. Then his head moves and he tries to look up. He draws his legs up under him and pushes his head off the floor. Finally he manages to get to his hands and knees. He crawls over to one of the commodes, pulls himself up, then falls backward awkwardly and heavily. At this point, the door is pushed open slightly, then it opens completely and* FOOTS *comes in. He stares at* KAROLIS' *body for a second, looks quickly over his shoulder, then runs and kneels before the body, weeping and cradling the head in his arms.*

BLACK

Tennessee Williams

❧

The Gnädiges Fräulein

·

THE GNÄDIGES FRÄULEIN was first presented, as part of a double bill entitled *Slapstick Tragedy,* by Charles Bowden and Lester Persky in association with Sidney Lanier, at the Longacre Theatre, in New York City, on February 22, 1966. It was directed by Alan Schneider. The sets were designed by Ming Cho Lee; the costumes, by Noel Taylor. Music was composed and selected by Lee Hoiby, and the lighting was by Martin Aronstein. Production was in association with Frenman Productions, Ltd. The cast, in order of appearance, was as follows:

POLLY	Zoe Caldwell
MOLLY	Kate Reid
PERMANENT TRANSIENT	Dan Bly
THE GNÄDIGES FRÄULEIN	Margaret Leighton
COCALOONY	Art Ostrin
INDIAN JOE	James Olson

PRODUCTION NOTES

The setting is Cocaloony Key, in the present time. The exterior of a frame cottage on the Key is visible, with a totally unrealistic arrangement of porch, assorted props, steps, yard, and picket fence. The main playing area, the porch, should be to the front, with maybe the yard displaced to upstage left—as if Picasso had designed it. It's windy gray weather: sky, frame building, picket fence, porch, wicker rockers—everything is in the subtle variety of grays and grayish whites that you see in pelican feathers and clouds. Even the sun is a grayish-white disk over the lusterless gray zinc roof that sits at the angle of Charlie Chaplin's derby on the house which is apparently a rooming house since there's a "vacancy" sign in the outsize window that faces the audience. Most of the time all we see in this big window are the "vacancy" sign and the dirty net curtains, but once or twice in the play a bloom of light behind the window reveals a poetically incongruous Victorian parlor, like the parlor of a genteel bordello in the eighties or nineties, and this alone violates the chromatic scale of the pelican: it is a riotous garden of colors, provided by crimson damask, gilt frames and gilded tassels, a gaudy blackamoor pedestal for a light fixture, etc.—the designer will think of many more items or better items than I can. It's like the recollections of the Gnädiges Fräulein, her scrapbook of a past that had splendors: perhaps it's less like the parlor of a Victorian bordello than it is like the parlor of a suite in the Hotel Bristol in Vienna, at least as it was a few years ago.

The costumes of the women, Molly and Polly, are also in pelican colors. But the costume and make-up of the Gnädiges Fräulein (which will be described in detail when she appears) are as vivid a contrast as the slow-blooming interior through the big window. So is Indian Joe. He is a blond Indian, tawny gold as a palomino horse but with Caribbean-blue eyes. He has practically no lines, so he doesn't have to be anything but an erotic fantasy in appearance, but with a dancer's sense of presence and motion onstage.

The Gnädiges Fräulein should be played by a singer, and I think of Lotte Lenya for this part as I think of Maureen Stapleton for the part of Molly, Lucille Benson for the part of Polly. It's a play with music, like *The Mutilated*. (The two plays should be performed together, I think.)

A bird called a cocaloony appears very briefly in the play: I think of it as a sort of giant pelican; in fact, all through the first draft of the play I have typed the word "pelican," scratched it out and written over it "cocaloony." There is a Bird-Girl in *The Mutilated* who could also appear as the cocaloony in this one.

PROLOGUE

POLLY, the Society Editor of the Cocaloony Gazette, *comes on forestage as if driven by the moaning wind, clutching her pelican-gray shawl with one hand and, still more tightly, a Pan-Am zipper bag. There is a loud swoosh above her. She crouches. Then she straightens as the swoosh fades out. But it suddenly recurs and she crouches again. And she speaks to herself and the audience about the incident.*

POLLY: Was that two cocaloony birds that flew over or was it just one cocaloony bird that made a U-turn and flew back over again? OOPS! Bird-watchers, watch those birds! They're very dangerous birds if agitated and they sure do seem to be agitated today. OOPS! [*She crouches under another swoosh.*] —I might as well remain in this position if it wasn't so inelegant for a lady in my position. What is my position? Why, I'm the southernmost gossip columnist *and* Society Editor of the southernmost news organ in the Disunited Mistakes. OOPS! [*The same sound and action are repeated.*]—Everything's southernmost here because of a geographical accident making this island, this little bit of heaven dropped from the sky one day, the southernmost bit of terra firma of the—OOPS! I've lost concentration! [*She stares blankly for a couple of moments.*]—My mother said that the way you tell a lady is that a lady never steps out of her house, unless her house is on fire, without a pair of gloves on, and that's how you tell a lady if you want to tell one and you got something to tell one. Have I got my gloves on? No! And I didn't hear the fire engine, all I heard was that swoosh and flap sound in the air of a cocaloony, so l must get back concentration! [*She raps herself on the head.*] Oh, I got it back now, yais, perfect! What I was saying was that everything's southernmost here, I mean like this morning I did the southernmost write-up on the southernmost gang-bang and called it "Multiple Nuptials" which is the southernmost gilding of the southernmost lily that any cock-eyed sob sister and society editor, even if not southernmost, ever dreamed of, let alone—OOPS!—perpetrated.... [*The same sound and action are repeated.*] Yais, everything's southernmost here, like southern fried chicken is southern*most* fried chicken. But who's got a chicken? None of us southernmost white Anglo-Saxon Protestants are living on fish and fish only because of thyroid deficiency in our southernmost systems: we live on fish because regardless of faith or lack of it, every day is Friday, gastronomically speaking, because of the readjustment of the economy which is southernmost too. OOPS! [*The same sound and action are repeated.*] — Did I lose concentration? No… it's nice not to lose concentration, especially when you've got to deliver an address to the Southernmost Branch of the Audubon Society on the vicious, overgrown sea birds which are called cocaloonies, and are responsible for the name and notoriety of this—OOPS! [*The same sound and action* *are repeated.*] particular Key. OK, I'll deliver the address without notes, since the atmospheric turbulence made me drop them. Cocaloonies! They never fly off the fish-docks except in hurricane weather. Except in hurricane weather they just hang around and goof off on the fish-docks, mentally drifting and dreaming till animated by the—[*She whistles between two fingers as if calling a cab.*]—of a fish-boat coming in with a good haul of fish. Oh, then they're animated, they waddle and flap, flap and waddle out toward where the boat's docked to catch the fish thrown away, the ones not fit for the markets, but delectable or at least cordially acceptable to the cocaloonies, they flap and waddle out to the boat with their beaks wide open on their elastic gullets to catch the throwaway fish, the discards, the re-jecks, because, y'see,—tell it not in Gath!—the once self-reliant-and-self-sufficient character of this southernmost sea bird has degenerated to where it could be justly described as a parasitical creature, yes, gone are the days when it would condescend to fish for itself, oh, no, no, *no,* it— [*The porch of* MOLLY's *house is lighted and* MOLLY *comes out with a mop and a bucket: she ignores* POLLY. MOLLY *plunges the mop in the bucket and starts mopping the steps to the porch.* POLLY *makes a slight turn and glares over her shoulder.*]—Oh, it's her, a vulgar, slovenly bitch with social pretensions, pretending not to see me, because, y'see, she fancies herself very highly as the social leader of Cocaloony Key, and there she is on her front veranda, with mop and bucket like a common domestic. I'll bring her down. HEY! MOLLY!

MOLLY: [*without turning*] Who's that shouting my name out like they know me?

POLLY: *It's Polly,* Molly.

MOLLY: *Aw. You.*

POLLY: Yes, me!

    A cocaloony flies over; both ladies crouch. The light flickers, ending the prologue.

SCENE I

POLLY: [*crossing to the porch steps*] *Whatcha moppin' up, Molly?*
They shout at each other above the wind.

MOLLY: *Blood.*

POLLY: The best time to mop up blood is before daybreak.

MOLLY: It wasn't shed before daybreak.

POLLY: Well, the next best time to mop it up's after dark.

MOLLY: That's not the policy of a good housekeeper.

POLLY: There's been some violence here?

MOLLY: Yep. I chopped the head off a chicken.

POLLY: On the front porch, Molly?

MOLLY: Nope. In the back yard, Polly.
The wind subsides.

POLLY: It sure did make a long run, all the way 'round the house and up the front steps and right on into the parlor, yep. I know a chicken can run with its head cut off, but I never known it to make such a long run as that with such a good sense of direction. Molly, this explanation that you are mopping up chicken blood don't hold water. There's been some violence here and the victim wasn't a chicken, that I know, as well as I happen to know that you ain't had a live or dead piece of poultry on these premises since that old Rhode Island Red hen that you was fattenin' up for Thanksgivin' died of malnutrition before Hallowe'en.

MOLLY: Yeah, well, why don't you go over to your desk at the *Cocaloony Gazette* and work on your gossip column, Polly, and let me finish this mopping up operation without the nasal monotone of your voice to distract me and annoy me to distraction! Huh, Polly?

POLLY: How long is it been since you got a favorable mention in my society column?

MOLLY: Never read it. When a lady's sure of her social position as I am, she don't concern herself with gossip columns.

POLLY: You're asking for a bad write-up.

MOLLY: Couldn't care less, pooh, for you.

POLLY: You don't mean that.

MOLLY: Yes, I do.

POLLY: I see you got a "vacancy" sign in your window.

MOLLY: What about it?

POLLY: You got a "vacancy" sign in your window and you're mopping up blood on your porch.

MOLLY: No connection, none at all whatsoever.

POLLY: *Aw?*

> *She laughs skeptically.*

MOLLY: They's always a "vacancy" sign in that window since I knocked out the walls of the private bedrooms to make the big dormitory. Because in a big dormitory they's always room for one more. I do a quantity business. Also a quality business but the emphasis is on quantity in the big dormitory because it's furnished with two- and three-decker bunks. It offers accommodation for always one more.

POLLY: Yeah, well, this type of material is OK for the classified ads but not for the gossip column and the society page, so I reckon I'll toddle on. Toodle-oo!

> *She has opened her Pan-Am zipper bag and removed a suspiciously thin cigarette.*

MOLLY: [*with covetous interest*] Whatcha took outa your Dorothy bag, Polly, a Mary Jane?

POLLY: Ta-ta, toodle-oo, see you someday... maybe.

MOLLY: Polly, sit down in this rocker and rock. I guarantee you material for your column.

POLLY: That's mighty nice of you, Molly— [*She lights the cigarette.*]—but I really do have to be going, I have to cover —well, *something—somewhere....*

MOLLY: Polly, I promise you, sweetheart, that in the course of this late afternoon no matter how the sky changes through light and shadow, I'll give you material for the Goddamnest human and inhuman interest story you ever imagined, Polly. Besides, your ankles look swollen, set down in a comfortable rocker and let's rock together while we turn on together. Huh, honey? [*She pushes her into the rocker.*] Wait! Let's synchronize rockers! Hold yours still till I count to three. OK?

POLLY: Count away!

MOLLY: ONE! TWO! THREE! *ROCK!*

> *They rock with pelvic thrusts as if having sex.*

POLLY: WHEEE!

MOLLY: Now we're rocking in beautiful unison, Polly!

POLLY: In tune with the infinite, Molly!

MOLLY: In absolute harmony with it!

TOGETHER: HUFF, HUFF, HUFF, WHEE!

MOLLY: I love to rock. It reminds me of my girlhood romances, Polly!

POLLY: One of your girlhood romances is still in traction, ain't he?

MOLLY: That's a lie, he gets around fine! —On crutches. [*They cackle together.*] Now, Polly about the big dormitory, Polly!

POLLY: [*throwing up her legs gaily*] Huff, huff, huff, WHEEE!

MOLLY: I said about THE BIG DORMITORY, Polly!

POLLY: WHEEE!

MOLLY: [*through the megaphone*] THREE, TWO, ONE! STOP ROCKERS! [*She stops* POLLY'S *rocker so abruptly that* POLLY *is nearly thrown to the floor.*] Let's have a little propriety and some decorum on the front porch, Polly, you're not out back of the woodshed! I was saying: about the big dormitory. The overhead, the operating expenses such as free limousine service, are astronomical, Polly.

POLLY: Oh?

MOLLY: So! —I can't afford to buy advertising space in the *Cocaloony Gazette*, and in the light of this situation which is a mighty dark situation, I could use and would surely appreciate the use of a knockout feature story in your next Sunday supplement, Polly, a two-page spread with photos of personages and captions without a word of profanity in them. How does that strike you, Polly?

POLLY: It don't strike me, Molly, it whistles over my head like a cocaloony.

MOLLY: I'm dead serious, Polly.

POLLY: It's natural to be serious when you're dead, WHEEE! [*She resumes rocking. MOLLY stops the rocker so forcibly that POLLY slides on the porch floor.*] OW!

MOLLY: COW!—Get back in your rocker and listen to what I tell you. You'd go a long way out of your way to find a richer gold mine of material in the class category than I got here in the big dormitory, under the rooftree of God, I've got REAL PERSONAGES here!

> *A fantastically tattered old wino, the "permanent transient," with fishing tackle, comes around the side of the building, tipping his topless bowler with a clown's grin and staggering in several directions.*

POLLY: Including that one?

MOLLY: That's, uh, that's an old family domestic I keep on the premises for sentimental, uh—reasons. [*She picks up a megaphone and calls through it*] WILLIAM? I want the Rolls to roll me to vespers at sunset. [*She snaps her fan open. The wino takes two steps backward, with a hiccough, and then staggers off.*] I was saying? Oh, personages, yaiss! Take the Gnädiges Fräulein, one instant for an instance, there's a personage for you, internationally celebrated for yea many years on this earth if not on other planets, yes, I've got the Fräulein to mention only a few of the more or less permanent guests of the big dormitory under the rooftree of God.

POLLY: How about Indian Joe?

MOLLY: Yes, how about Indian Joe, that's a personage, Polly, a blond Indian with Caribbean-blue eyes, moving in beauty like the night of cloudless climes, and so forth.

> *The parlor blooms into light. We see INDIAN JOE spraying his armpits with an atomizer and patting his pompadour.*

POLLY: [*in a religious voice*] I catch his inimitable and ineffable aroma somewhere in the near distance: is it outside or in? If I turn around, I'm afraid it would make me giddy, I might lose concentration.

MOLLY: Sit back down in your rocker but don't rock.—What was I saying?—Oh, the big dormitory. Don't be misguided by the "vacancy" sign. On weekends, Polly, as God's my judge, I hang out the SRO sign for standing room only in the big dormitory!

POLLY: You sell standing room in the big dormitory, Molly?

MOLLY: You bet your sweet ass I do. You take a permanent transient that's ever in his existence had a run-in with the law and show me a permanent transient that hasn't. It's four AM. No intelligent permanent transient prefers to stay on the street at that desperate hour when even the Conch Gardens closes. Not in a state of the Union where they's eighteen different kinds of vagrancy charges that a lone man on the streets at night can be charged with. All right. That s r o sign looks mighty good to a permanent transient, it shines to him like the star of Bethlehem shone to the kings that came from the East.

POLLY: And do they sleep standing up?

MOLLY: Unless they can find a voluntary bed-partner.

POLLY: Flamingoes can sleep standin' up on one leg, even.

MOLLY: Anything havin' a leg to stand on can sleep standin' up if it has to.

POLLY: Don't they fall down, Molly?

MOLLY: They fall down and get back up.

POLLY: Well, Molly, when one of your standing-up sleepers falls down, don't it disturb the sleep of the horizontal sleepers?

MOLLY: Polly, a permanent transient is a wonderful sleeper. He sleeps heavy and late in the calm and security of the big dormitory, as God is my witness in heaven.

POLLY: When is the check-out time?

MOLLY: They wake up to music which is provided by the Gnädiges Fräulein. [On this cue, the FRÄULEIN sings: "Open wide the windows, open wide the doors, and let the merry sunshine in!"] There, that's reveille for them. Hear them rising?

    Noise is heard inside: groans, howls, etc.

WINO: [sticking his head out the window] Bathroom privilege?

MOLLY: Granted.

    She tosses a key in the window.

POLLY: It'll be fun to watch 'em coming out, Molly.

MOLLY: They have to go out the back way because it's daylight and they make a better public appearance by starlight on a starless night because of embarrassing subtractions from their wardrobe, like some of them can't find their shoes when they go to get up in the morning and some of them can't find their shirts or their pants when they go to get up in the morning and some of them can't find a Goddam bit of their wardrobe when they go to get up in the morning, including their lingeree, Polly. And some of them can't find their equilibrium or concentration or will to continue the struggle for survival when they go to get up in the morning and some of them don't get up in the morning, not even when the Gnädiges Fräulein sings the reveille song.

POLLY: Obstinate?

MOLLY: Nope, dead, Polly. [POLLY breathes out a sound like the wind in the pines, rolling her eyes above a wicked grin.] Yep, the Dark Angel has a duplicate key to the big dormitory and faithfully every night he drops by to inspect the sleepers and check their dog-tags. He wanders among the two- and three-decker bunks and never leaves without company, nope, never leaves unattended and no one grieves when he leaves.

POLLY: [lisping] Between the dark and the daylight—

MOLLY: When the gloom of doom is in flower—

TOGETHER: Comes a pause in the night's occupation
> Which is known as The Angel's Dark Hour
> > THE GNÄDIGES FRÄULEIN *appears indistinctly behind the screen door.*

FRÄULEIN: [*at screen door*] May I come out? [MOLLY *ignores the request.* POLLY *puts on her glasses to peer at the* GNÄDIGES FRÄULEIN. *She calls out louder.*] May I come out?

POLLY: Molly, a lady in there wants to come out; she's asking permission to come outside the house.

MOLLY: I know. I heard her. She can't.

POLLY: Why can't she come out, Molly?

MOLLY: She's lost porch privilege.

POLLY: Aw. Then let her go in the yard.

MOLLY: She's lost yard privilege, too.

POLLY: What privilege has she still got?

MOLLY: Lavatory and kitchen. Her kitchen privilege depends on her bringing in something to cook, which don't seem likely today.

FRÄULEIN: May I come out?

POLLY: Mah-wah-com-ahh.

MOLLY: Don't mock her. In spite of her present condition she's still a personage, Polly.

POLLY: Well, let her out, lemme have some fun with her.

MOLLY: How could you have fun with her?

POLLY: I could interview her, I could ask her opinions.

MOLLY: She's long past having opinions.

POLLY: Aw, now, let her out, Molly.

MOLLY: What's the deal if I do?

POLLY: A real classy write-up.

MOLLY: Pooh. Don't need one.

POLLY: A Mary Jane? All to yourself?

MOLLY: [*handing her the megaphone*] Tell her to come out. Address her as Gnädiges Fräulein, she comes from Middle Europe and circumstances of genteel circumstances. You got to holler at her, she's got calcified eardrums.

POLLY: [*opening the door*] Come out, Ganniker Frowline. [*There is a pause.*]—Not coming out.

MOLLY: Give her time, she's preparing.

POLLY: Now she's comin' out now. I better think what to ask her.

MOLLY: Ask her how's fishing today, or which she prefers, a mackerel or a red snapper. 'Cause if she wants to maintain a residence in the big dormitory, after sundown, the subject of fish has got to be kept active in her thought waves.

POLLY: She's not outfitted for fishing.

MOLLY: She's got on the remnants of her theatrical wardrobe.

POLLY: I think I'll ask her some fashion questions and some questions about makeup and hairstyles.

MOLLY: Let's have some protocol here. The Gnädiges Fräulein is a personage, yeah,

but she's still a social derelict, and a social leader like me takes precedence over a
social derelict like her, so give her a couple of short sentences, then concentrate the
rest of the write-up on ME.

She turns her rocker crossly away from POLLY. THE GNÄDIGES FRÄULEIN
*is now out on the porch. She wears a curious costume which would not be out of
place at the Moulin Rouge in the time of Toulouse-Lautrec. One eye is covered by a
large blood-stained bandage. Her hair is an aureole of bright orange curls, very
fuzzy. She sits on the steps and opens a big scrapbook.*

POLLY: She sat in a pool of blood, Molly.

MOLLY: 'Sall right, it's her own blood.

POLLY: *Aw!* Not a chicken's blood, huh?

MOLLY: OOPS, I made a boo-boo, did I ever make a boo-boo!

POLLY: So the Ganniker Frowline was the victim of violence here.

MOLLY: Well, I'd be a fool to deny it and you'd be a bigger fool to believe the denial.
Yep, her scroll has been charged with a good deal of punishment lately.

POLLY: Lately as today. Hmm. Ask her if she would like to make a short statement.

MOLLY: Ask her yourself, you're interviewing the Fräulein: I'm not even speaking to
her until she reestablishes her credit here with a good catch of fish.

FRÄULEIN: Number, please.

She is holding out a faded sheet of paper.

POLLY: Does she think she's a telephone operator?

MOLLY: She wants you to pick out a number for her to sing on that program she's
holding out to you.

POLLY: How does she sing?

MOLLY: She *sings.*

POLLY: I don't think I'll take a chance on it. However, she might do for a human
interest story. Don't you think so?

MOLLY: She's human.

POLLY: Is she?

MOLLY: Take that program from her; she's holding it right in my face so I got to lean
over if I want to look out.

POLLY *takes the program.*

FRÄULEIN: Number, please.

POLLY: Give me time to pick one out that I like.

MOLLY: She didn't hear that. Not a word.

POLLY: Ask her to rotate, Molly.

MOLLY: Why d'ya want her to rotate?

POLLY: I'm describing her outfit in the write-up. [*She is making notes.*] I want a look
at the other side of her costume.

MOLLY: Walk around her.

POLLY: I don't feel like getting up.

MOLLY: Read me the part of the write-up where you mention the big dormitory.

POLLY: I haven't got to that yet.

MOLLY: That ought to be in the first paragraph of the write-up. Why don't you begin the write-up like this, Polly. "One of our most prominent social leaders…"—No, begin it this way, this is the way to begin it—"The social season got off to a brilliant start when—"

POLLY: Hold it, she's startin' to rotate. Very gradually, though. She's pivoting majestically toward me. I never gild the lily in my write-ups. Hmmm. She's made a full turn now. I've seen all sides of her costume without getting up. I guess we ought to ask for a vocal selection, but I can't read this old program, it's too faded. See if she can recite it.

MOLLY: Remember, it's your idea. [*She shouts through the megaphone.*] GNÄDIGES FRÄULEIN! BITTE! RECITE NUMBERS ON PROGRAM!

FRÄULEIN: Number One: "Pale Hands I Loved Beside the Shalimar" by the celebrated tunesmith, Amy Woodforde-Finden. Number Two: "I Dream of Jeannie With the Light Brown Hair" by permission of ASCAP. Number Three: "All Alone" by the celebrated tunesmith, Irving Vienna. Excuse me, Berlin. Number Four: "Smiles" by some long-ago smiler, and—

POLLY: Tell her some number to sing, any number.

MOLLY: [*shouting through the megaphone and striking her on the shoulder at each count*] Ein, zwei, drei!

> Then the FRÄULEIN *assumes a romantically theatrical pose on the porch and begins to sing.*

FRÄULEIN: Stars are the win-dows of Heaaa-ven
> That an-gels peek throooogh!
> *She stops in mid-gesture, frozen.*

POLLY: —Has she finished the number?

MOLLY: Naw, she lost concentration.
> *She picks up a baseball bat.*

POLLY: If you conk her with that she won't get back concentration or even consciousness till this time tomorrow, Molly, but do you care?

FRÄULEIN: [*resuming from the start*] Stars are the win-dows of Heaaa-ven
> That an-gels peek throoough!
> *She freezes again in mid-gesture, opens and closes her mouth like a goldfish.*

POLLY: Now what's she up to?

MOLLY: She's demonstrating.

POLLY: What's she demonstrating?

MOLLY: Either a goldfish in a goldfish bowl or a society reporter in a soundproof telephone booth.

FRÄULEIN: [*audible again*] That an-gels peek throoough!
> When we are happy they're hap-*peeee,*
> When we are blue they turn b*luuue!*

POLLY: Enough, enough of that, stop her!

MOLLY: You started her, you stop her.

POLLY: How do I do that?

MOLLY: Put her back in the house.

POLLY: And how do I do *that*?

MOLLY: Turn her, she can be turned, then shove her, she can be shoved.

POLLY: I can't shove her through the screen door.

MOLLY: You open the screen door for her.

POLLY: I don't want to get up.

MOLLY: Well, stay on your fat ass, you slob.

POLLY: Shut your fat mouth, you fink. [*The swoosh and whistle of cocaloonies is heard.*] Oops!

MOLLY: Cocaloonies!

> Both cover their eyes with their hands, the GNÄDIGES FRÄULEIN *hits an unexpected high note and dashes back into the house. The parlor lights up and she can be seen through the window, ineffectually hiding among the feathery foliage of a great potted fern.*

POLLY: HORRIBLE!

MOLLY: HIDEOUS! SCAT!

> A COCALOONY *has entered the yard and is stalking jerkily about, poking its gruesome head this way and that with spastic motions, as if looking about the premises for something.*

POLLY: Make conversation, say something casual, Molly.

MOLLY: You say something casual and I'll answer.

POLLY: I'll say something reminiscent.

MOLLY: No, casual.

POLLY: *Reminiscent!*

MOLLY: Have it your way, a casual reminiscence. [POLLY *loses concentration:* MOLLY *observes her condition.*] Oh, God, she's lost concentration. [MOLLY *shouts at her through the megaphone.*] POLLY! [POLLY *regains concentration abruptly and starts for the door.* MOLLY *catches the back of her skirt, which rips off.* POLLY *finds the screen door has been latched by the* FRÄULEIN. *The* COCALOONY *struts up onto the porch and sits down in* MOLLY's *rocker. The ladies freeze by the door.*] Don't move: keep on talking.

POLLY: I wasn't talking. I'm going to throw something at it.

MOLLY: What?

COCALOONY: [*ominously*] AWK.

MOLLY: I think it heard you plotting to throw something at it.

POLLY: Pooh. I have behind me the power of the press.

MOLLY: It would be more useful in *front* of you, right now, ducks.

COCALOONY: AWK.

POLLY: [*politely*] Awk.

COCALOONY: [*severely*] *AWK!*

POLLY: The power of the Fourth Estate is behind me and in front of me, too, it's like the air that surrounds me, it surrounds me completely as the grace of God, you know that.

MOLLY: Your voice has got a funny vibrato sound to it, a sort of a shrill vibration like you had a tin larynx with the wind whistling through it.

The COCALOONY *rises, knocking over the rocker, and flaps off the porch, but remains in the yard.*

POLLY: Well. Let's go back to the rockers before I collapse.

MOLLY: You take this rocker.

POLLY: No, no, I wouldn't dream of it, that's your rocker, and I know how important it is to feel the familiar beneath you.

MOLLY: Shall we rock or just sit? With our teeth in our mouth saying nothing?

POLLY: I'm going to say something.

MOLLY: Well, SAY it, don't just *say* you're going to say it!

POLLY: PHEW! I never knew a cocaloony bird had such a powerful odor. It smells like that mysterious old sea monster that washed up and rotted on Dizzy Bitch Key after Hurricane Lulu.

TOGETHER: Ugh! Oof! Phew!

POLLY: It's stalking and strutting around like Napoleon on the ramparts. It's certainly a hell of a three-sheet to have in front of the big dormitory. It's not a status symbol by any manner of means.

MOLLY: Mention this in the write-up and you will find yourself featured in the obituaries next issue.

POLLY: Pooh.

MOLLY: No pooh about it, I got connections with the Mafia and with the syndicate, too, so roll that up in your Mary Jane and smoke it.

COCALOONY: AWK. AWK.

POLLY: Awk.

MOLLY: Will you quit talkin' back to it?

POLLY: I wanted to pacify it.

MOLLY: Wrong policy, Polly. Take your hands off your eyes and stare straight at it, return its furious stare, and go it one better.

POLLY: How?

MOLLY: By stamping your foot.

POLLY: A vulgar, petulant action? Also provocative action? Not me, I'm not about to, you stamp your foot at it.

MOLLY: Okay, scaredy-cat.

POLLY: Well, go on, stamp it. [MOLLY *raises her foot and sets it down soundlessly.*] You call that stamping your foot? You raised your delicate slipper and set it back down like you were outside of all gravity, Molly; in weightless ozone.

COCALOONY: Awk.

POLLY: Awkward, an awkward creature, as awkward a creature as—

MOLLY: Shh.

COCALOONY: AWK. AWK. AWK.

POLLY: What a limited vocabularly it's got! It's strutting up closer, Molly.

MOLLY: Don't report the obvious to me, Polly.

POLLY: What's obvious to me is it's looking for someone or something.

MOLLY: Who in hell isn't, Polly?

POLLY: If I should hazard a guess as to what or whom, and I guessed correctly, would you admit and confirm it?

MOLLY: —Well....

POLLY: —What?

MOLLY: Under God's rooftree there's no room for successful prevarication. Yep. He's looking for something that's someone and this something-someone is the Gnädiges Fräulein, I shamelessly, blamelessly admit it. —Continue interrogation: you can't hide a cat when the cat's out of the bag, as way out of it as the Gnädiges Fräulein is out of the bag and into the lacy fronds of that fern potted in the parlor. So, all right, take it from there. I'm too straightened out, now, to care about any outcome except my income.

POLLY: Well, I'm not a star in the mathematics department but I do know that two plus two makes one less than five and one more than three: —the Frowline has provoked the vengeful enmity of the cocaloonies, Molly. And what provokes enmity under the rooftree of God is *competition*, huh, Molly?

MOLLY: I shamelessly, blamelessly admit that the Gnädiges Fräulein has gone into competition with the cocaloonies for the thrown-away fish at the fish-docks.

POLLY: Why and wherefore, Molly?

MOLLY: Well, having passed and long passed the zenith of her career in show-biz and as a B-girl at the Square Roof and Conch Gardens, the Gnädiges Fräulein has turned her attentions and transferred her battleground for survival to the fish-docks, Polly. She's shamelessly, blamelessly, gone into competition with the cocaloonies for the throw-away fish. When a fish-boat whistles and the cocaloonies waddle rapidly forward, out she charges to compete for the catch. Well, they got a closed shop, the cocaloonies, they seem to be unionized, Polly, and naturally regard the Gnädiges Fräulein as a wildcat operator and take a not-so-bright view of her dock activities, Polly. Nothing is more intolerant, Polly, than one parasite of another. So dimmer and dimmer became the view they took of her, till, finally, today, there was a well-organized resistance movement against her. Yep, they turned on her today and she returned from the fish-docks in a damaged condition, no fish in her bucket and no eye in one eye socket.

> *During this the* COCALOONY *stands still cocking his head with a wing to his ear—occasionally stomping.*

POLLY: *Gouged?*

MOLLY: Yes, *out!*

POLLY: Oh-oh, oh-*HO!*

> *She scribbles notes.*

MOLLY: I'm not at all happy about this situation because the Gnädiges Fräulein is required to deliver three fish a day to keep eviction away and one fish more to keep the wolf from the door, and now that the cocaloonies have turned against her, will she have guts enough to fight the good fight or will she retire from the fish-docks like she did from show business, under pressure!?

INDIAN JOE *enters the yard with a tomahawk and a bloody scalp. His hair is bright yellow and his skin is deep red and glistening. He is dressed like a Hollywood Indian, that is, he wears a breech-clout of deerskin and some strings of wam-pum, perhaps.*

POLLY: [*excitedly*] Indian Joe!

INDIAN JOE *and the giant* COCALOONY *square off at each other.*

COCALOONY: [*stamping and flapping*] Awk, awk, awk, awk, awk, awk, awk, awk, AWKKK!

INDIAN JOE: *Ugh!*

COCALOONY: AWK!

INDIAN JOE: UGH!

POLLY: Reminds me of the Lincoln-Douglas debates. Don't it remind you of the Lincoln-Douglas debates?

MOLLY: No.

POLLY: What's it remind you of then?

MOLLY: Nothing reminds me of nothing.

POLLY: You mean you're stoned on one stick?

MOLLY: Concentrate on the action.

POLLY: What action, it's just a standoff. They squared off to a standoff. [*During this incongruously desultory dialogue on the porch,* INDIAN JOE *and the* COCALOONY *have continued to menace each other,* INDIAN JOE *waving his tomahawk over his head with steady, pendulum motions and the* COCALOONY *bird poking its gruesome head backward and forward in spastic rhythm.*] I guess this is what they say happens when the unmovable object meets the irresistible force: that's a standoff, ain't it?

MOLLY: Nope, that's a collision.

POLLY: Let's call it a standoff collision and quit the argument, Molly.

MOLLY: Look. Action.

The COCALOONY *bird has begun to retreat from* INDIAN JOE'*s resolute, slow advance. It suddenly flaps off, racing for a takeoff, great swoosh over the scene as it hits the empyrean.* INDIAN JOE *shrugs and stalks onto the porch.*

POLLY: HOW.

INDIAN JOE: POW.

MOLLY: WOW.

He jerks the screen door open and enters the interior.

POLLY: Strong character!

MOLLY: Devastating. —But lazy. —Indolence is the privilege of great beauty, yep, great beauty wears indolence like the stripes on a four-star general at a state banquet. Look at him in there, now.

The inner stage of the parlor brightens: INDIAN JOE *is seated in a ballroom chair, holding a mirror as the* GNÄDIGES FRÄULEIN *makes him up for his next appearance: she is fluttering with enchantment.*

POLLY: The Frowline has eyes for Indian Joe?

MOLLY: Eyes is plural and she's just got one eye. [*She snaps her fingers: the parlor dims out.*]—Have you got eyes for him, Polly?

POLLY: Let's just say I got eyes.

MOLLY: Well, then, don't compete with the cocaloonies for the throw-away fish and don't compete with the Gnädiges Fräulein for the Viennese dandy.

POLLY: Did you say Viennese dandy?

MOLLY: If I did, I must have lost concentration for a moment. Didn't we synchronize rockers?

POLLY: I'm standing, not rocking but rocked.

The sound of a fish-boat whistle is heard.

MOLLY: Crocked! *Oh! A fish-boat whistle!*

POLLY: Why do you mention it like a thing unheard and unheard-of before?

MOLLY: I'm anxious to see if the Gnädiges Fräulein will sally forth to meet it or if she's reconciled to eviction from the big dormitory.

POLLY: I never would have dreamed—

MOLLY: What?

POLLY: —*Dreamed....*

MOLLY: WATCH OUT, I HEAR HER COMING, SHE COMES OUT FAST! DON'T BLOCK HER, MAKE WAY FOR HER, POLLY! [THE GNÄDIGES FRÄULEIN *charges out of the house with a tin bucket.*] Bravo, she's back in action! That's the Spirit of the big dormitory for you! Encourage her, applaud her, don't sit on your hands! [*The fish-boat whistles twice more.* THE GNÄDIGES FRÄULEIN *disappears rapidly, flapping her skinny arms like the wings of a sea bird and making harsh cries.*]—My God, her scroll has been charged with so much punishment lately I thought her spirit was vanquished!

POLLY: This is material for a human interest story. Should I phone it in for general release or wait till I know the outcome?

MOLLY: Outcomes don't always come out quickly, Polly. Let's just sit here and rock on the spacious veranda of the big dormitory. And synchronize rockers. Hold your rocker still till I say rock and then rock. ONE. TWO. THREE! ROCK ROCKERS! [*They rock together on the porch.*] You can occupy this quiet interlude by working on the write-up. Describe me in it. Me, me, me, me, *mee!*

POLLY: I've already described you.

MOLLY: How?

POLLY: I mentioned your existence.

MOLLY: How about my position?

POLLY: Position in what?

MOLLY: Society. My preeminence in it.

POLLY: You can gild the lily without a lily to gild.

MOLLY: Balls! —Synchronize rockers again: you're rocking too fast. I have to over-exert to keep up with you.

An outcry is heard far off.

POLLY: A human outcry?

MOLLY: Distant, still, too distant.

Another outcry and other sounds of commotion are heard.

POLLY: Closer.

MOLLY: Still fairly far. [*The commotion increases in volume.*] Honey, get up and practice your profession. Report on whatever is visible from the walk.

POLLY: Not me, old rocking-chair's got me.

There is another outcry.

MOLLY: Another outcry, still human. The Gnädiges Fräulein is on her way back from the fish-docks. [*She rises and peers through the telescope.*] It buggers description, Polly. Oh, God. I think I better go in and check on the check-outs in the big dormitory.

POLLY: Let me help you.

MOLLY: Help yourself, God help you! [*At this moment as they start for the door, the* GNÄDIGES FRÄULEIN *comes stumbling rapidly back along the picket fence, feeling for the gate. An oversize fish is protruding tail-first from her bucket. She is hard pressed by the cocaloonies. We hear them flapping violently above her, the stage lights flicker from their wing-shadows.* MOLLY *covers her eyes with both hands, peeking between her fingers ever so slightly. Not locating the gate successfully, the* GNÄDIGES FRÄULEIN *crashes through the picket fence and makes a wild dash around the side of the cottage, holding the lid on the big fish in the bucket. Terrific flapping and whistling noises are heard.*] In?

POLLY: [*peering around the side of the cottage*] Out!

MOLLY: In?

POLLY: Out!

MOLLY: Still out?

POLLY: In!

        MOLLY *rushes in and rushes right back out.*

MOLLY: A cocaloony bird has got in with her!

        INDIAN JOE *rushes out on the porch, imitates cocaloony birds and points inside.*

POLLY: What's he telling you, Molly?

MOLLY: He's complaining about the cocaloony, Polly!

POLLY: Phone the police.

MOLLY: Phone's in the house and I don't intend to go in till the cocaloony goes out.

        A COCALOONY *bird sticks its gruesome head out an upper window.*

COCALOONY BIRD: AWK. AWK.

        INDIAN JOE *shakes his tomahawk at the window. The* COCALOONY *bird runs out the front door with a large fish in its beak. It runs flapping down the walk, building up speed for a takeoff.*

INDIAN JOE: Ugh.

        He spits disgustedly and kicks a section of the fence down as he goes off.

FRÄULEIN: [*at the door*] May I come out?

MOLLY: Take a look at her, Polly. Describe her condition to me.

POLLY: She's alive, still in the land of the living.

MOLLY: Please be more specific about her condition.

POLLY: Her vision is now zero-zero.

MOLLY: [*shouting through the megaphone*] COME ON OUT HERE AND REPAIR THIS FENCE, FRÄULEIN!

POLLY: Aw, no, Molly, give her time to come out of shock and stop bleeding.

MOLLY: I don't tell you how to run your society page and I'll thank you not to interfere with the management of the big dormitory, Polly. [*The* FRÄULEIN *begins to sing "All Alone."* MOLLY *lowers her voice.*] She thought I requested a number.

POLLY: If you open the door for her she'll come out.

MOLLY: What would you call her voice? A lyric soprano?

POLLY: She flats a little in the top register, Molly.

MOLLY: I think her recent experience has upset her a little.

POLLY: I think she's coming out, now. Yes, she is. Coming out.

MOLLY: —She's out, now?

POLLY: Almost.

> THE GNÄDIGES FRÄULEIN *is appearing gradually on the front porch. She sings as she appears, hands clasped spiritually together, a bloody bandage covering the whole upper half of her face and an aureole of pink-orange curls, very fluffy, framing the bandage which is tied in back with a large butterfly bow. Her costume is the same except that her tulle skirt, or tou-tou, is spangled with fresh drops of blood that glitter like rubies and her legs, bare from mid-thigh to ankle, are likewise streaked with blood. However, her voice is clear and sweet as a bird's: I mean songbird's. Her motions are slow, very slow. Now and then she extends a thin arm, to feel her way forward as she is still moving forward. She is transfigured as a saint under torture.*

MOLLY: Is she or isn't she OUT, now?

POLLY: Why don't you see for yourself?

MOLLY: You're a reporter, ain't you, Miss Society Reporter? Then report! Report, for Chrissakes, is she or isn't she out on the front porch, now!

POLLY: SHUT UP! SHE'S SINGING, GOD DAMN IT!

MOLLY: I know she's singing! I didn't ask if she's singing. I asked is she out or in!

> POLLY *sings with her. The* FRÄULEIN *stops singing.*

POLLY: —I think you scared her. She's quit.

MOLLY: She always quits when somebody else chimes in, she will only sing solo.

POLLY: Can't stand the competish?

MOLLY: Yep. She's out again, now. I didn't want to look at her till my nerves was prepared for the shock of her appearance.

POLLY: I think she's remarkable. I'm going to call her remarkable in the write-up.

MOLLY: Don't overdo it.

POLLY: Watch her: she's about to walk off the steps.

MOLLY: She's gonna walk off the steps. She's gonna *nearly* walk off 'em: then stop short. —Intuition takes over when the faculties fail. I'm willing to make book on it.

POLLY: She's shuffling along with caution.

MOLLY: Yep. That's what I told you.

POLLY: Look. She's stopped and set down. Let's shout bravo, applaud her, intuition or caution, she stopped at the edge of the steps.

MOLLY: Don't turn her head. I don't want self-satisfaction to become the cornerstone of her nature.

POLLY: *Oh, God, look, do you see what I see?!*

MOLLY: I don't know what you see so I can't be expected to say if I do or I don't.

POLLY: She's picked up a book and—

MOLLY: She has picked up her scrapbook, her album of press clippings. What about it? She put it down and now she's picked it back up. People do things like that. What's peculiar about it?

POLLY: It just occurred to me, Molly, that unless her scrapbook is printed in Braille, the Frowline is not going to make much out of her old press clippings—is she?

MOLLY: She's reading them out loud, now.

FRÄULEIN: [*in a high, sing-song voice, like a priest saying Mass*] "The talented young soubrette astonished her audience as well as her fellow performers when she cleverly intercepted a rather large mackerel thrown to the seal by catching this same rather large mackerel in her own lovely jaws!" — Ahhhhhh! Ahhhhhh.....

The final sounds are a blend of triumph and regret.

MOLLY: Polly? From *memory: perfect!*

She turns to the FRÄULEIN *and gives her a little round of applause. The* FRÄULEIN *tries to bow: totters slightly forwards and backwards. Then she resumes her incantation.*

FRÄULEIN: "Veritable—dressing-room—afterwards"—ahhhhh. ....

The FRÄULEIN *places a hand to her forehead.*

POLLY: She's stuck! Her memory's failed her!

MOLLY: Temporary amnesia resulting from shock ...

POLLY: Take a look at her now.

MOLLY: What for?

POLLY: I want you to see what she's doing, it buggers description, Molly.

MOLLY: All I see is she's holding up her lorgnon.

POLLY: That don't seem peculiar to you?

MOLLY: Not in the least. She always holds up her lorgnon when she reads her press clippings.

POLLY: But she can't read her old press clippings.

MOLLY: That's not the point.

POLLY: Then what is the point in your opinion, Molly?

MOLLY: Habit! Habit! Now do you get the point?

POLLY: You mean it's a habit with her to hold up her lorgnon when she is reading her scrapbook?

MOLLY: Absolutely. It's a custom, a habit, a—now, look! Now, look. And listen! She is expressing the inexpressible regret of all her regrets.

FRÄULEIN: [*regretfully*] AHHHHHHHHHH! HHHHHHHHHH

POLLY: —Saddest soliloquy on the stage since Hamlet s....

FRÄULEIN: —AHHHHHHHHHH....HHHHHHHHHH

MOLLY: I hope she don't repeat it.

FRÄULEIN: AHHHHHHHHHH....HHHHHHHHHH...HHHHHHHHHH

MOLLY: Tell her not to repeat it.

POLLY: [*to* GNÄDIGES FRÄULEIN] Don't repeat it.

MOLLY: Aw, shoot. You think she overheard that little whisper? [*She shouts through the megaphone.*] FRÄULEIN! DON'T REPEAT IT! —I do believe she heard me.

POLLY: —She's putting her lorgnon away.

MOLLY: She put it in her bosom.

POLLY: She's taking it out again, now.

MOLLY: She's rubbing the lenses on her white tulle skirt.

POLLY: She's holding it up again, now.

MOLLY: She's still dissatisfied with it. She's putting it down again now.

POLLY: She's raising it up again, now.

TOGETHER: SHE'S THROWN IT AWAY, NOW! AHHHHHHH!

FRÄULEIN: Ahhhhhh....

POLLY: She's holding her scrapbook out.

MOLLY: I'm looking at her. I'm observing her actions.

POLLY: I think she wants you to put her scrapbook away.

MOLLY: It will be interesting to see what she finally does with it when she discovers that no one is going to accept it from her hand, Polly.

> The FRÄULEIN *suddenly tosses the scrapbook into the yard, raising her arms and crouching: a dramatic gesture accompanied by another dismal soliloquy of one vowel, prolonged....*

POLLY: Sudden. —Action.

MOLLY: Yes. —Sudden. [*The whistle of a fish-boat is heard.* POLLY *faces* MOLLY *with an air of wild surmise. There is dumb play between them as the* GNÄDIGES FRÄULEIN *cups an ear with a trembling hand and crouches toward the direction of the fishdocks.* MOLLY *whispers shrilly.*] Polly! *Give her this bucket!*

POLLY: Don't be silly! Don't be absurd! She ain't going back to the fish-docks!

MOLLY: Oh, yes, but she is! I assure you! Look! She's in starting position.

POLLY: Yeah, but she ain't started, Molly.

> *The second whistle of a fish-boat is heard.*

MOLLY: She never takes off till the fish-boat has whistled three times.

POLLY: How many times has it whistled?

MOLLY: Twice!

POLLY: Only twice?

MOLLY: Just twice!

> *At this moment the fish-boat whistles a third time and the* FRÄULEIN *is off, flapping her long, thin arms and waddling very rapidly like a cocaloony. Unable to locate the gate, she crashes through the picket fence. She stops short and screams.*

FRÄULEIN: BUCKET, BUCKET, FISH BUCKET!

POLLY: I think she wants her *fish-bucket.*

MOLLY: Here, take it out to her, Society Reporter.

POLLY: Take it out to her yourself, Society Leader! [MOLLY *snatches the wine-bottle or "stick" from* POLLY's *hand. With her other hand raised as if to threaten a blow.* POLLY *glares back at her for a moment, then complies with* MOLLY's *order and rushes to the*

FRÄULEIN *with the bucket. The* FRÄULEIN *is stationary but flapping on the front walk.* POLLY *thrusts the bucket with some difficulty into one of the* FRÄULEIN'S *flapping hands. The* FRÄULEIN *immediately takes off, disappearing while flapping.* POLLY *returns to the porch.*] Pooh to you, Social Leader.

MOLLY: Pooh to you, too, Society Editor.

POLLY: A bad write-up in a society column has been known to wreck a brilliant social career.

MOLLY: My social position is unassailable, ducks.

POLLY: A social position is unassailable only when the holder of the position has retired without violence or disorder to a plot of expensive ground beneath a dignified monument in the Protestant cemetery. Not until—

INDIAN JOE *kicks the door open and appears on the porch. His long straight hair is blond as a palomino's mane and his eyes are sky-blue. As he appears on the porch, he drums his massive bare chest and exclaims—*

INDIAN JOE: I feel like a bull!

POLLY: MOOOO! MOOOOO!

MOLLY *cuffs her warningly with the back of her hand.* INDIAN JOE *returns to the big dormitory, immediately followed by* POLLY *who repeats her lovelorn "Moooo" several times inside as* MOLLY *struggles to open the latched screen door. As the scene dims....*

DIM OUT OR CURTAIN

SCENE II

Stars have appeared in the sky (and tender is the night, etc.) when POLLY *staggers out of the big dormitory in a fantastic state of disarray and disequilibrium. Her skirt removed, draped over an arm, exposing polka-dot calico knickers and butterfly garters, her feathered hat on backwards. Giggling and gasping, she moves two steps forward, then two steps back, as if she were on the promenade deck of a ship in heavy seas.* MOLLY *regards her with a coldly objective eye.*

MOLLY: She's lost concentration and equilibrium, both, and her taste in lingerie is influenced by Ringling Brothers Circus. It wouldn't hurt to preserve a pictorial memento of the occasion in case she gets a bug in her bonnet about an exposé of the moral conditions in the big dormitory reflecting corruption in the administration. [*She snatches up a camera and takes a flashphoto of* POLLY.] A glossy print of that informal photo, dispatched in plain cover to the Society Department of the *Cocaloony Gazette*, will insure a better tone to the write-up.

She puts the camera under the rocker.

POLLY: Molly?

MOLLY: Yes, Polly?

POLLY: Is my hat on crooked?

MOLLY: No, just backwards, ducks, and I do have to admire the elegant, negligent grace in the way you carry your skirt.

POLLY: The zipper broke. Have y'got a safety pin?

MOLLY: [*removing large safety pins from her blouse*] Naw, but I have this solid platinum brooch which'll do just as good, so step back into your sweet little checkerboard skirt and I'll pin it on you. [POLLY *staggers about trying to step into her skirt.*] Ready, ready, now! Steady!

MOLLY *jabs* POLLY *with the pin.*

POLLY: OWWW!

INDIAN JOE *charges out of the big dormitory.*

INDIAN JOE: POWWW!

MOLLY AND POLLY: [*together*] WOWWW! [INDIAN JOE *goes off rapidly whistling "Indian Love Call." They sink together into rockers.*] Now...

POLLY: Angels are peeking through the windows of heaven, as the Frowline would put it. I wonder if she made it back from the municipal fish-docks or if she decided to set up residence there, till something better opens up for her, career-wise?

MOLLY: [*sympathetically*] All of us, Polly, sally forth once too often. It's an inexorable law to which the Gnädiges Fräulein seems not to be an exception.

POLLY: Shall we have a silent moment of prayer or just synchronize rockers?

MOLLY: *One, two, three, rock rockers!*

POLLY: *Three, two, one, stop rockers!*

MOLLY: Now what bug have you got in your bonnet?

POLLY: I just thought, to look on the bright side of things, the fact that the Frowline never came back from the fish-docks gives a little more topicality to the write-up, Molly. You must've heard of the newspaper file-case which is known as "the morgue." It's where the historical data, the biographical matter on a mortal celebrity is filed away for sudden reference, Molly. I mean the hot-line between the mortuary and the *Gazette* sounds off, and instantly you leaf through the yellowing, mellowing files and jerk off the copy on the lately no longer so lively.

MOLLY: OK. Now open your notebook and spit on the point of your pen. I'm gonna give you the historical data on the Gnädiges Fräulein. [*She rises from rocker, slings drum over her shoulders and advances onto the forestage.*] I'm going to belt it out with my back to you and the face of me uplifted to the constellation of Hercules toward which the sun drifts with the whole solar system tagging along on that slow, glorious joyride toward extinction. [*She beats the drum.*] —"The Gnädiges Fräulein!" —Past history leading to present, which seems to be now discontinued! [*She beats the drum.*] —Upon a time, once, the Gnädiges Fräulein performed before crowned heads of Europe, being the feminine member of a famous artistic trio!
She beats drum.

POLLY: Other two members of the artistic trio?

MOLLY: Consisted of a trained seal and of the trained seal's trainer.
Drum.

POLLY: This don't sound right, it don't add class to the write-up.

MOLLY: The trained seal trainer was a Viennese dandy. [*Drum.*] Imagine, if you can, a Viennese dandy—can you?

POLLY: Continue!

MOLLY: This was in the golden age of Vienna, the days of the Emperor Franz Josef and the trained seal trainer, the Viennese dandy, was connected collaterally with the House of Hapsburg—a nobleman, a young one, with a waxed blond mustache and on his pinkie a signet ring with the Hapsburg crest engraved on it. Now! [*Drum.*] Imagine, if you can, the Viennese dandy....

POLLY: Figure?

MOLLY: Superb.

POLLY: Uniform?

MOLLY: Glove-silk: immaculate: gold epaulettes, and, oh, oh, oh, many ribbons, all the hues of the rainbow. Eyes? Moisture proof, but brilliant. Teeth? Perfect. So perfect you'd think they were false, as false as the smile that he threw at his admirers. Now can you imagine the Viennese dandy?

POLLY: Sure I can, I *know* him.

MOLLY: Everybody's known him somewhere and sometime in their lives—if they've *lived!*—in their lives. [*Drum.*] Now hear this! [*Drum.*] Scene: a matinee at the Royal Haymarket in London? Benefit performance? Before crowned heads of Europe?

POLLY: The Gnädiges Fräulein?

MOLLY: The Gnädiges Fräulein! —The splendor, the glory of the occasion, turned her head just a bit. She overextended herself, she wasn't content that day just to do a toe dance to music while bearing the paraphernalia back and forth between the seal and the trainer, the various props, the silver batons and medicine ball that the seal balanced on the tip of his schnozzola. Oh, no, that didn't content her. She had to build up her bit. She suddenly felt a need to compete for attention with the trained seal and the trained seal's trainer.

POLLY: How beautiful was the beautiful Viennese dandy?

MOLLY: I described him.

POLLY: I lost concentration during the description.

MOLLY: Imagine the Viennese dandy like Indian Joe. [POLLY *gasps and scribbles frantically for a few moments.*] Now then…the climax of the performance. [*Drum.*] The seal has just performed his most famous trick, and is balancing two silver batons and two gilded medicine balls on the tip of his whiskery schnozzle while applauding himself with his flippers. [*Drum.*] The audience bursts into applause along with the seal. [*Drum.*] Now, then. The big switcheroo, the surprising gimmick. The trained seal trainer throws the trained seal a fish. What happens? It's intercepted. Who by? The Gnädiges Fräulein. NO HANDS. [*She imitates the seal.*] She catches the fish in her choppers! [*Drum.*] Polly, it brought down the house! [*Drum.*] This switcheroo took the roof off the old Royal Haymarket, and she's got clippings to prove it! I seen them in her scrapbook!

POLLY: Why'd she do it?

MOLLY: Do what?

POLLY: Intercept the fish that was thrown to the seal.

MOLLY: Why does a social leader like me, in my position, have to defend her social supremacy against the parvenu crowd, the climbers and Johnny-Come-Latelies? [*She shouts through the megaphone.*] HANH? HANH?! ANSWER ME THAT!

POLLY: I figured that maybe she had a Polynesian upbringing and dug raw fish.

MOLLY: You're way off, Polly. Y'see here's how it was, Polly. Always before when he threw a fish to the seal, he would throw to the Gnädiges Fräulein an insincere smile, just that, a sort of a *grimace,* exposing white teeth and pink gums, while clicking his heels and bending ever so slightly in an insincere bow.

POLLY: Why?

MOLLY: WHY! —He regarded her as a social inferior, Polly. A Viennese dandy? Elegant? Youthful? Ravishingly attractive? Hapsburg crest on the signet ring on his pinkie? What could he throw to the Gnädiges Fräulein but an insincere smile with a very slight insincere bow that broke her heart every time she received it from him. He couldn't stand her because she adored him, Polly. Well, now. A gimmick like that, a switcheroo, a new twist as they say in show biz, well, it can't be discarded, Polly. If the public buys it, it's got to be kept in the act, regardless of jealous reactions among the rival performers. Well— [*Drum.*] There was, of course, a hell of a hassle between the trained seal's agents and the Gnädiges Fräulein's. There was complaints to Equity and arbitrations and so forth. But it was kept in the act because it was such a sensation. The trained seal's agent threatened to break the contract. But popular demand was overpowering, Polly: the new twist, the switcheroo, had to be kept in the act. The trained seal's agent said: Sit tight! [*Drum.*] Bide your time! [*Drum.*] And it appeared for a time, for a couple of seasons, that the trained seal and the trained seal trainer would accept, acquiesce to *force majeure*, as it were! However—Now hear this! [*Drum.*] At a gala performance before crowned heads in Brussels, no, no, I beg your pardon, before the crowned heads at the Royal in Copenhagen! [*Drum.*] —Tables were turned on the Gnädiges Fräulein! [*Drum.*] — When she made her sudden advance, her kangaroo leap, to intercept the fish that was thrown to the seal, the seal turned on her and fetched her such a terrific CLOUT!! [*Drum.*] —Left flipper, right flipper! [*Drum.*]—To her delicate jawbone that her pearly whites flew from her mouth like popcorn out of a popper. [*Drum.*] Honest to Gosh, sprayed out of her choppers like foam from a wild wave, breaking! [*Drum.*] — They rang down the curtain. —The act was quickly disbanded.... After that? She drifted. The Gnädiges Fräulein just drifted *and* drifted and *drifted*.... — She lost her sense of reality and she drifted.... —Eventually she showed on the Southernmost Key. Hustled B-drinks for a while at the old Square Roof. Celebrated Admiral Dewey's great naval victory in the Spanish-American War by mounting a flag-pole on the courthouse lawn in the costume of Lady Godiva but with a GI haircut. All this while she was running up a big tab at the big dormitory. However!—[*Drum.*] —In business matters, sentiment isn't the cornerstone of my nature. I wasn't about to carry her on the cuff when her cash gave out. Having read her press clippings, I said, OK! Hit the fish-docks, baby! Three fish a day keeps eviction away. One fish more keeps the wolf from your door! —All in excess of four fish do as you please with! —POLLY! TELESCOPE, PLEASE!

> *She has turned her attention to a sudden increase of disturbance down at the fish-docks.* POLLY *tosses a telescope to her as she crosses to the gate.*

POLLY:—Any sign of her, Molly?

MOLLY: Yep, she's on her way back.

POLLY: Alone?

MOLLY: No. With a cocaloony escort.

POLLY: Is she making much progress?

MOLLY: Slow but sure. I admire her.

POLLY: [*sentimentally*] I admire her, too.

MOLLY: I hope you'll give her a sympathetic write-up.

POLLY: I'm gonna pay tribute to her fighting spirit.

MOLLY: Don't forget to mention the big dormitory.

POLLY: I'll call it The Spirit of The Big Dormitory.

MOLLY: *Hold the door open for me. I'm going in fast!*

> *She starts back to the porch, but* POLLY *enters the house before her and slams and latches the door.* MOLLY *crouches way over, peeking between her fingers, as the* GNÄDIGES FRÄULEIN *appears on the sidewalk in terrible disarray but clinging*

tenaciously to her tin bucket containing a rather large fish. Great flapping noise of cocaloonies in pursuit. She crashes through the picket fence and scampers around the side of the house, disappears. POLLY *comes back out as the hubbub subsides again.*

POLLY: Something came in the back way.

MOLLY: Yep. I think she made it.

POLLY: I don't hear a sound, do you?

MOLLY: I hear some kind of activity in the kitchen.

POLLY: Cocaloony or human?

MOLLY: I'm not positive, Polly, but I think the cocaloonies have gone back to the fish-docks.

POLLY: Wouldn't that be lovely.

MOLLY: I heard a boat-whistle blow: then swoosh! Flap, flap, then swoosh! —Then silence, and a light turned on in the kitchen.

POLLY: What's this?

She has picked up some bright orange fuzz.

MOLLY: Oh, my God, they scalped her!

POLLY: This is human hair, Molly?

MOLLY: It's hair from the head of the Gnädiges Fräulein.

POLLY: She must be a blond Hottentot.

MOLLY: Results from staying too long and too often under electric dryers in second-rate beauty parlors. OH! GOD BLESS HER SOUL! —I hear the sizzle of deep fat in the kitchen!

POLLY: She must be frying a fish.

MOLLY: Yais, I would make book on it.

POLLY: Is this fish number four? For her personal consumption?

MOLLY: Fish number one. She ain't even paid for kitchen privileges yet.

POLLY: You gonna carry her on the cuff?

MOLLY: I don't have a cuff. She's got to pick up where she left off in show biz.

POLLY: Or else?

MOLLY: Go on drifting, drifting, away from the big dormitory, away from everywhere maybe.

POLLY: Losing a sense of reality as she drifts?

MOLLY: Losing or finding, all according to how you interpret it, Polly.

The FRÄULEIN *appears at the screen door.*

FRÄULEIN: May I come out? [*The ladies are awed by her present appearance. All of her costume has now been torn away: she appears in flesh-colored tights, streaked and dabbled with blood. Patches of her fuzzy light orange hair have been torn away. She carries, before her, a skillet containing a fish with a big kitchen fork sticking in it. She repeats her request for permission to come outside. After a slight pause she says, "Thank you" and comes out on the porch.* POLLY *seizes the handle of the fork and removes the fish from the skillet: the* GNÄDIGES FRÄULEIN *is unaware of this action. She calls out:*] TOIVO! TOIVO!

MOLLY: She's calling him to supper.

POLLY: Who?

MOLLY: Indian Joe.

POLLY: Why does she call him Toivo?

MOLLY: Toivo was the name of the Viennese dandy.

POLLY: That threw her the fish before the crowned heads of Europe?

MOLLY: He threw the fish to the seal. To the Gnädiges Fräulein he threw an insincere smile. She bored him because she adored him!

FRÄULEIN: [*advancing to the porch steps and continuing to call during the following speeches*] TOIVO, TOIVO!

POLLY: But she intercepted the fish to the surprise of the seal and the Viennese dandy, you told me.

MOLLY: Yes. I think she imagined, fondly, that it would alter the smile, that it would give a touch of sincerity to it, but emotional limitations cannot be coped with, Polly. You got to accept them or give up the ghost in this world. However, under the flattering shadow of memory, smiles are sometimes transfigured. Possibly now she remembers the smile as sincere. WELL! I see that *you* have intercepted a fish!

> POLLY *is touching the fish to see if it's cooled off. It keeps scorching her fingers. She whistles sharply and sticks her fingers in her mouth and then shakes them in the cool twilight air.*

POLLY: Am I invited to supper?

> MOLLY *snatches the fishfork.*

MOLLY: I'll mail you the invitation in the morning.

> POLLY *picks up wine bottle from the Pan Am bag.*

POLLY: Evening, duckie. [*She starts off.*] Ta ta! Toodle-ooo!

MOLLY: A chilled white wine is *de rigueur* with a fish course. —Chow time, Polly.

POLLY: Oh, I've already gotten the invitation! Hold the door open for me, my hands are full!

> MOLLY *opens the screen door. The Society Editor enters grandly.*

FRÄULEIN: Toivo, Toivo! —Toivo? Toivo? [*She twists her head about nervously as if looking for him in various directions, including the sky, as* INDIAN JOE *ambles up to the gate. She draws a long, loud breath, inhaling the aroma of his close presence. He looks in the skillet: as he removes it from her grasp she makes a sort of obeisance, at the same time lifting a hand in a warning gesture.*] Is it all right? I can't imagine how I happened to catch it, it was so dark at the fish-docks. It just landed in my jaws like God had thrown it to me. It's better to receive than to give if you are receiving to give: isn't it, Toivo, *mein liebchen?*

INDIAN JOE: [*shouting*] NO FISH IN SKILLET!

FRÄULEIN: [*with a warning gesture*] Watch out for the bones in it, darling!

> INDIAN JOE *repeats his shout, louder. The* GNÄDIGES FRÄULEIN *interprets this shout as a request for a vocal selection: she bursts into song—"Whispering Hope"—and Indian Joe enters the house. The formal parlor is lighted as he joins* MOLLY *and* POLLY *at a small, festive table. A fish-boat whistle is heard.* THE

GNÄDIGES FRÄULEIN *stops singing, abruptly, and cups a hand to an ear. The boat whistles again. She assumes the starting position of a competitive runner and waits for the third whistle. It's delayed a bit for the interior pantomime.* INDIAN JOE *pushes one lady to the left and one to the right and seats himself at the table picking up the fish.* POLLY *holds out the wine bottle to him. The parlor dims out as the third whistle sounds—the* GNÄDIGES FRÄULEIN *starts a wild, blind dash for the fish-docks.*

THE STAGE IS DIMMED OUT

Ed Bullins

❧

The Man Who Dug Fish

•

THE PEOPLE

THE MAN: *A tall, heavy Black man in his mid-forties. Impeccably dressed in the clothes
   of a financier. He has a fake Oxford or Cambridge accent, and carries an attaché case.*
FISH STORE CLERK.
HARDWARE CLERK.
ASST. TO THE ASST. MANAGER OF THE BANK.

   The FISH STORE CLERK, HARDWARE CLERK *and* ASST. TO THE ASST. MANAGER *can be
the same white actor, or Black actor in white mask or makeup.*

The Man Who Dug Fish was originally published in *Nexus* [San Francisco: 1967]. The
play was first given a staged reading in the late '60s by the Theatre Company of Boston,
then given a workshop production at The New Dramatists in New York City, June 1,
1970.

Cast members for the later production are as follows:

THE MAN	Floyd Ennis
FISH STORE CLERK	Howard Honig
HARDWARE CLERK	Rik Pierce
ASST. TO THE ASST. MANAGER	Bill Harper

Bare stage except for rough boards nailed together to make the counter.
Enter THE MAN *with briefcase.*

MAN: [*Clears throat*] Ahhh…heemmmm…this appears to be a hardware store.
Spot on the CLERK.
I say there, ole fellow.

CLERK: You mean me?

MAN: Yes, you…ahem…I mean I'd like some service.

CLERK: Well, why didn't you say it? What do you want? Our smelts are good today.

MAN: Smelts?

CLERK: Yes, smelts.

MAN: [*Incredulous*] In here…smelts?

CLERK: Yeah…and our perch ain't so bad either.

MAN: [*Recovers*] Oh, smelts. Perch.

CLERK: And clams, lobsters, butterfish, porgies, oysters, scallops, crabs…

MAN: No. No. That won't do.

CLERK: Then sea bass, sturgeon, shad, shark, whitefish…

MAN: What do you have in a larger fish?

CLERK: Larger fish?

MAN: [*Points*] Yes, like that fellow there.

CLERK: Oh, you want some trout?

MAN: Not exactly.

CLERK: But our trout are fine today.

MAN: No. No. I don't especially want trout.

CLERK: You don't?

MAN: No.

CLERK: No smelts 'cause they're too small…no trout 'cause you don't 'specially want trout.

MAN: Yes.

CLERK: I see.

MAN: Really I mean no.

CLERK: No?

MAN: Yes, no smelts or trouts.

CLERK: Yeah, I'm sure I see what you're getting at.

MAN: You're so well informed.

CLERK: Well, I pride myself in my…

MAN: And so helpful.

CLERK: Now about our carp.

MAN: Carp?

CLERK: Yes, carp. Just what I think you need.

MAN: Carp?

CLERK: We got excellent carp today.

MAN: [*Holds up attaché case*] You see…

CLERK: Yeah, a briefcase.

MAN: But…

CLERK: We get our carp fresh from the creek in back of here.

MAN: I want a fish…

CLERK: A little old lady catches it and sends it in to us…

MAN: …with head and tail…

CLERK: …by her grandson.

MAN: …a fish that will fit comfortably in this satchel.

CLERK: He rides a bicycle.

MAN: Can you find me a carp which will meet these requirements?

CLERK: English racing tires.

MAN: How nice.

CLERK: I'm here to sell fish, that's what I am.

MAN: [*Beams and hands him attaché case*] Then put 'er there, my good man.

> *Lights down. Lights up.*

CLERK: And what size shovel would you like, sir?

MAN: Something not too big.

CLERK: Ahuh.

MAN: And not too small.

CLERK: Yes…yes.

MAN: Not too wide.

CLERK: I see.

MAN: Or not too slender…

CLERK: By all means.

MAN: …I don't want it mistaken for anything other than a shovel…

CLERK: That is absolutely correct, sir.

> CLERK *pulls out a shovel.*

MAN: No.

> CLERK *pulls out another.*

No.

> CLERK *pulls out a third.*

Ah so!

> *Hands him the attaché case.*
>
> *Lights down. Lights up in the bank.*

And what did you say the length was of this safety deposit box, Mr. Assistant to the Assistant Manager?

ASST. ASST.: Oh, this is our large standard size for your more heavy valuables.

MAN: I see.

ASST. ASST.: Yes, everyone should have one.

MAN: Is that a fact?

ASST. ASST.: By all means, sir. They are moth proof, radar proof, fireproof, earthquake proof, drop proof, heist proof, dirt proof, atomic-blast and dust proof, water free, airless, and they cannot be touched by another human hand besides yours…unless you die or we have a court order…naturally.

MAN: Naturally.

ASST. ASST.: [*Hesitant*] Then…then…

MAN: I'll take it!

ASST. ASST.: Oh, goody.

MAN: And I'm paying ten years' rent on it.

ASST. ASST.: Ten years?

MAN: Yes, ten years. I'm about to take a long voyage.

ASST. ASST.: Long voyage?

MAN: Long.

ASST. ASST.: [*Contemplating*] I see.

MAN: [*Pulls bills from his wallet*] Will eleven hundred thirteen dollars and forty-one cents do?

ASST. ASST.: [*Distracted*] Eleven hundred…oh, you mean you're paying with money?

MAN: Yes.

ASST. ASST.: That just can't be done, sir.

MAN: [*Very British*] Nonsense!

ASST. ASST.: But just no one…

MAN: I insist!

ASST. ASST.: [*Takes money*] Can you please wait a moment, sir? I must go speak to the Assistant to the Manager.

MAN: Very well.

> ASST. ASST. *exits.* THE MAN *pulls the shovel from the briefcase and places it in the safe-deposit box, then pulls the still wet but very dead fish out, glowers at it, then places it in the box and locks it with the key.*
>
> *Enters* ASST. ASST. *as* THE MAN *pockets the key.*

ASST. ASST.: I'm sorry to have kept you waiting, sir.

MAN: And?

ASST. ASST.: [*Quietly*] Just this once, sir.

[*Secretive*] We'll relax our rules in your case…New customers are our privileged customers…ha ha…and all that rot…as you people say.

MAN: [*Smiling*] Yes…and…

ASST. ASST.: You understand?

MAN: Surely.

ASST. ASST.: Is there anything you wish to place in your box at this time, sir?

MAN: No, nothing.

ASST. ASST.: [*Lifts box*] Then I'll put it away.

    Knees nearly buckle.

    My god, this seems so heavy!…Have you already used it, sir?

MAN: Not at all, my good man.

ASST. ASST.: [*Tries to lift lid*] Would you mind…

MAN: [*Wags finger*] Now…now…and you're the ones who make the rules.

ASST. ASST.: [*Remorse*] Ohhh…sorry about that.

MAN: Perhaps you've put in a little too much time on this job, wouldn't you say?

ASST. ASST.: [*Struggling off*] I guess you're right, sir. But…

    Hands box to THE MAN.

    Feel how heavy it is.

MAN: Light as a feather.

    [*Pity*] My my…you do look peaked. Why don't you go get my receipt while I put this away?

ASST. ASST.: [*Winded*] Excellent idea. But I believe I'll go home…get in bed, you know…[*Puffs*] …get a good rubdown by the Mrs. if she's home from her bridge club, or the country club, or the beautician's, or ladies aid society, or her women's club…

MAN: You need help, my dear man.

ASST. ASST.: Yes, yes…I'll have the Mrs. call the doctor as soon as I get home…if that's included in the budget this month.

MAN: [*Good spirits*] Well, then cheerio, old sport.

ASST. ASST.: You'll lock up everything, won't you, sir?

MAN: Need you ask?

ASST. ASST.: It must be my head…or my liver or kidneys…or…

MAN: Or your heart…or your soul…my good man.

ASST. ASST.: [*Sweating*] You can pick up your receipt on your way out.

MAN: Thank you, old chap. See you in ten years…and give my best to the Mrs.

    ASST. ASST. *exits as* THE MAN *begins tidying up and whistling "Columbia, the Gem of the Ocean."*

BLACKNESS

Rosalyn Drexler

Softly, and Consider the Nearness

Softly, and Consider the Nearness

•

CAST

NONA: *A woman who lives alone. She is in her thirties—or older.*
TV: *A large television set.*
BURGLAR: *A male burglar.*

The TV's *character and voice change with each change of the channel. He is at* NONA's
*mercy: an object and a slave to her every whim, yet constrained because of what he is:
inanimate.*

The BURGLAR *is straight out of a Broadway musical comedy: funny, and absolutely
one dimensional.*

NONA *remains who she is: a rather ordinary woman in her thirties (or older) who
works in an office as a receptionist, from nine to five. When she comes home at the end of
the day, the only thing she has to look forward to is spending some time with her* TV. *It is
an intimate relationship, not without its problems.*

NONA's *living room. It contains an easy chair,* TV, *a folding screen. A beat of silence. Then the sound of keys jingling. Sound of door being opened.* NONA *enters. Kicks her pumps off. Tosses her hat into a corner. Drops her handbag on the floor. Greets the* TV *set with panache and vigor. She puts set on.*

TV *changes voices according to what he is saying: e.g. his announcer voice, his sales-pitch voice, his lover voice, etc. Sometimes* NONA *switches channels abruptly.*

NONA: Hello baby, I'm home.

She caresses the set.

Didja miss me as much as I missed you? Not talkin' huh? God it almost drove me crazy havin' to pretend that that dirty window by my desk was your screen. What a hazy, lazy day today turned out to be. And I couldn't even adjust the contrast like I do with you.

She adjusts contrast, etc.

She stands back to observe.

Why, you shine up the whole room!

High piercing signal from TV.

I'll fix that.

She fiddles with the antennae, and knobs at the side. She goes behind the TV *set.*

TV: [*Sounds like an announcer*] This evening at approximately six thirty-five, a beloved TV, owned and cared for by a woman called Nona, lost his ability to project a clear image. In shock, and not knowing what to do in this emergency situation, he produced a loud and piercing test signal which brought help immediately. "For a while, I thought you were going to let me grow cold," he was heard to say.

NONA: [*Peeking from behind the* TV] You are always in my heart, and as long as I live you will remain there.

TV: Trapped!

NONA: [*Coming out from behind* TV] Aw don't feel that way honey.

TV: I have no feelings. My job is to report the news as accurately as possible.

NONA *switches channels.*

A rescue team is on the way folks; and you can depend on us here at XYZ to keep you posted. Thank you. Now for a local bulletin: message from Zenith to Nona in Manhattan, "My destiny is your will."

NONA: Message from Nona to Zenith, "I think you're fighting your attraction for me, from your plastic knobs, right down to your chromium trim." Relax. Put yourself in my hands. What'd you say about destiny?

TV: When I first came to your home my features were my qualifications, but now you're using them against me. What do you have against plastic? It's durable, shiny, and has many uses. Even sticky fingerprints can be easily wiped off with a damp cloth.

NONA: Whatdya want, a medal?

TV: Listen to me—

> NONA *switches channels.*

He has a tender throwing elbow and might be out for the season.

> NONA *switches channels.*

The world is a dangerous and unpredictable place, and you just wanna relax? Forget it.

> NONA *switches channels.*

The Dow industrials lost 8 points. Westinghouse gained 5 and a quarter.

> NONA *switches channels.*

Take young people to the zoo, or just chat with the elderly in their homes. Get involved. The opportunities to serve are endless.

NONA: And blah, blah, blah.

TV: If I only knew what you really want.

NONA: What if you did know? What could you do about it?

TV: I intend to vigorously appeal to you in the only way I can, by transmitting the messages of others. [*voice change*] Looks like we're good to go now. We've got a crash we're working on. Thirty minute delays. More traffic later.

NONA: Next thing you'll be telling me to wear a scarf when I go out.

TV: I worry about you.

NONA: Are you going to be difficult?

TV: Why yes. That's the way I'm built: I happen to be a complicated piece of modern wizardry that's bound to get out of whack sometimes.

NONA: I've heard those excuses before. What ever happened to quality control? Checking you out before you leave the factory? I didn't buy damaged goods—I bought a Zenith in perfect condition—or so I thought. Prepare, my dear, to be unplugged!

> She stoops to unplug the set.

TV: Before you silence me, remember this, I bring you the tragedy of situation comedy. The immediacy of imagined life, which is the only life you have at the moment. I am your family, your lover, your gateway to the world. You owe your life to me. As for me, I ask no more than to be seen and heard by you.

NONA: You ask for more than that.

TV: Yes—[*voice change*] relative humidity is 79 percent. [*voice change*] The president has no influence. [*voice change*] Precious metals are lower. But we can weather the storm.

NONA: What do I care how much it may storm?

TV: I've got my love to keep me warm. Does that mean we are in reciprocal debt?

NONA: [*flirtatiously*] Cash or credit? [*pause*] It means we're together.

TV: What if some day you view on my screen a lady like yourself being strangled—would you blame me?

NONA: I choose the programs—however you brought the topic up, not me. You thought of it.

TV: Must I remind you that I have no thoughts?

NONA: Cold outside, but inside you're glowing and warm.

TV: The longer I'm on the hotter I get.

NONA: You won't burn out baby.

TV: I might. Built in obsolescence, you know. Some say I have a contempt for humanity. That I am dominated by big business which demonstrates a numbing indifference to those who suffer, to those who endure great hardship. [*voice change*] They cut his leg off so that they could remove him. [*voice change*] This is the only mop of its kind. Have your credit card ready when you order.

NONA: See how sensitive you really are? You don't flinch from the truth. You're such an excellent set. May I kiss you?

TV: If you're not well grounded you might get an electric shock Miss Nona wet lips. Oh baby, you've got me where you want me.

NONA: [*Fiddles with channel changing knob.*] Right between channels.

TV: Oh-oh—I have an itch.

NONA: Where?

TV: I'm not sure. Scratch me vertical, and then scratch me horizontal. That oughta do it.

NONA: Just like man and wife.

> *She pulls the TV antennae in and out, trying to get a better picture.*

Feel any better? My, my I like the way you're coming in—don't wanna lose you.

TV: But wait. [*voice change*] See the original uncut episode—the return of true justice and the American way. Week-nights only on XYZ. [TV *voice*] You couldn't lose me if you tried.

> *For an instant there is a sound of opening and closing—the burglar entering through a window.*

NONA: Did you hear that?

TV: Only the sound of electricity crackling through my wires.

NONA: Something else.

TV: Nothing else. Decision unanimous. You are imagining it.

NONA: Don't know why I'm so jumpy.

TV: [*voice change*] Use a doctor's remedy, the kind that can be purchased without a prescription at the drugstore. Read instructions carefully. If symptoms continue, see a physician.

NONA: Don't send me away.

TV: Just a short trip for instant relief.

NONA: You sound so…so…?

TV: [TV *voice*] Commercial?

NONA: Yes.

TV: If only I could hold you the way I hold the sound and the picture.

NONA: How comforting that would be.

TV: Your body all cuddled up might fit into my chassis—and your adorable face is certainly Tru-Vu.

NONA: Me? On television? What would I say? Everyone's eyes would be on me.

TV: Courage my friend—you have never been at a loss for words, don't start now. This is a piece of cake.

NONA: I need encouragement.

TV: There's a vast audience out there in TV land waiting. You have been invited into their homes. Greet them. They need what you have to offer. You are unique.

NONA: Yes. I'm their guest. They want to be in my company...wait, don't I have to rehearse?

TV: Be spontaneous, inspired, instantaneous. Baby you're the zaniest, not the brainiest gal.

NONA: I'll ignore that last crack, Jack. [*Pause as she gathers her courage*] Guess I'm ready to roll—Promise you'll stop me if I get out of line—I'm liable to say things I really mean.

TV: Can't stop you; can only start you... [*Voice change*] Still ahead, an amazing story of heroism, the debut of a vibrant new TV personality and future household name: Nona!

NONA: Okay then.
           She smiles broadly.
       Ladies and gentlemen. I am here tonight because...

TV: Go on.

NONA: Ladies and gentlemen I am here tonight because I have nowhere else to go.

TV: Tell them why.

NONA: Because I am a

TV: A what?

NONA: Because—I am afraid to describe myself.

TV: You don't have to describe yourself. They see you. [*Voice change*] Our products are the best money can buy. Furnish your entire home in just one visit. Undecided? Salesmen are always on hand to help you make an informed decision. Delivery in just two to three weeks. Don't wait. Whether you want to decorate a studio apartment, or a mansion, we offer you the same courteous assistance.

NONA: They see that I am living alone in this studio apartment furnished with hand-me-downs and As-Is bargains? That I have no friends, no family, no pets, no plants, no kitchen, no bath, no closet space, no view, no cross-ventilation? Is that what they see?

TV: [*TV voice*] They see a star in the making!

NONA: This star wants to hide behind a cloud.

TV: As the curtain rises, Nona declares, "I fear success, as much as I fear failure." She has had a hard life: father dead by his own hand when she was just six years old, mother alcoholic and run over by a truck, grandmother strangled by a drug crazed stranger, grandfather the victim of congestive heart failure, sister arrested in a jazz club for selling Breath-O-Mints to the musicians. Nona's lover who's been playing solitaire at the kitchen table rises to embrace her; "What's there to be afraid of?" he asks. "You can break the pattern; you can be the first in your family to succeed. Trust me, I wouldn't steer you wrong would I? Beautiful girl like you, Nona, could be rich and famous if she played her cards right—she could even live forever if that was what she wanted." Nona asks him, "How?" He replies, "Easy as selling your soul to the devil, kid; others have, with no regrets." "How will I find him?" she asks. "You won't have to find him, he'll find *you*," he replies, "in fact he's right here, holding you in his arms." Well folks, that says it all; your favorite theater critic Mr. Zenith cannot recommend this cliché ridden pastiche much as he'd like to, since it is a cliché ridden pastiche. Of course life itself is a cliché ridden pastiche.

NONA: Pastichio is my favorite flavor…anyway, as I was about to say:
   Takes a big breath before launching courageously into speech.
   Ladies and gentlemen, I am here tonight because I have been asked by a very close friend to appeal to you; however I am not particularly appealing, and so you will have to love me for myself.

TV: Speak about what they mean to you.

NONA: I wish they weren't there, staring, judging me.

TV: Try to reach them. Offer them something.

NONA: [*She makes a few false starts as if to speak; takes a last big breath, begins in a rush—slows down.*] Hello out there. Hello. Is it really you? It's so nice of you to tune in on me. I've been waiting some time for your invitation. And to reward you for being such loyal fans, I shall send you some lovely autographed photos of me. Please be good enough to send your name and address to Post Office Box 237, Post Office Times Square, New York. Do enclose two dollars and thirty-eight cents to cover postage and handling, please. And thank you very much for your remittance. All the best. And don't forget: Post Office Box 237, Post Office Times Square.

TV: Magnifico. We belong together. There must be a way to enclose you before I go dead. [*voice change*] You have a one year warranty on tube replacement and on-location repair…[TV *voice*] after that you're on your own.

NONA: Dearest, a limited engagement is better than none at all.

TV: With you caring for me I could go on forever.
   A tiny explosion. TV *blackout.*

NONA: Oh! Oh my God.
   She searches for the TV *guarantee or a receipt. Finds a receipt.*
   Oh my God I can't read the phone number. Where are these people? The print's so small. Better try and fix him myself. [*to* TV] Don't worry darling, I'll bring you back from the dead if I have to.
   She examines the back of TV. *Rescrews connections. Puts plug back into socket.*

TV: [*goes back on with a sigh.*] Ahhhhhh. You've revived me. I'm alive again.

NONA: Time was running out. I had to do something fast. If I had lost you, a part of myself would have died too.

TV: Which part? Tangible or ephemeral? Arm or emotion? [*voice change*] We have a distinguished panel here this evening to discuss the controversial topic: DOES A SOUL EXIST?

NONA: And while I was trying to reconnect you I thought of all the things I would have liked to say to you but didn't.

TV: You can say them now.

NONA: I can't.

TV: Tell me, would you have replaced me with another set, if...?

NONA: Oh no! I would have lived with the memory of you.

TV: The pictures I project on my screen are the same pictures that flash across any TV screen with only slight variations in contrast, color, sound, clarity.

NONA: What I have with you no one else has. Frankly, do you realize what our relationship has become?

TV: Illicit? Are you guilty?

NONA: A little, certainly. Those times I went to bed with you.

TV: You heard my voice first thing in the morning.

NONA: I need that kind of thing. A woman needs comforting.

TV: Ah yes, I see it all now; you love me for my adaptability, my eye on the world; my heart in the lap.

NONA: You are mine alone. I offer you nothing and you are mine. The purchase made you mine. No one can deny it. We'll grow old together.

TV: What happened just before, when I was out cold?

NONA: I touched parts of you I never would have dared touch.

TV: I didn't feel a thing. You were as clever as the dentist who recently confessed to fondling a young female patient after giving her laughing gas.

NONA: It was really something. But hey, water under the bridge—you're back: bright as a new penny, and sharp as a knife.

TV: Thanks a million.

NONA: Do you hear anything?

TV: Something—perhaps the wind.

    Sound of BURGLAR.

NONA: No, not a wind sound, a person sound. Listen.

TV: I'm sure it's nothing.

    Pause for a beat.

NONA: When you went out—I was about to embrace you.

TV: No time like the present. It is now eleven thirty. Only half an hour before we sign off. [*voice change*] Roughly fifteen thousand men are still on chain gangs repairing the county's roads while tax paying citizens ride by. [*voice change*] Right now Sears full capacity washers are on sale. How about teaching the kids to do their own laundry?

NONA: Yes I'm finally ready to go all the way. Play the game of love. Change all the rules. Spoil you rotten. Let the chips fall where they may.

TV: The games that people play often come between them. Everybody loves a winner even when he's thinner. Call me anything you want, but don't call me late for dinner.

NONA: Let's not argue. I'm so sleepy.

She lays her head on the T V. There is a beat of tender silence.

T V: [*speaks like baby-talk in a dream.*] What's my little bird going to feed itself tonight?

N O N A: Only what's under its dear little beak.

T V: And what is under its dear little beak?

N O N A: Well, nothing yet. The children who found the little bird and who don't want it to die have gone to ask their mothers for crusts of bread. I am wrapped in the dirty handkerchief of one of those boys and am smothering in his pocket.

T V: I hope they hurry.

N O N A: If they don't get here soon I'll die.

T V: If you do, don't worry; you'll have a proper burial. Children make much of bird funerals: they'll handle you lovingly, wrap you in black tissue paper, put you into a shoe box, and...

N O N A: No, no, I don't want to die.

T V: If wishes came true, frogs would fly, and fat pink pigs write poetry.

N O N A: The heck with it then; I don't want to be a little bird. I want to be a woman with many feathers in her cap.

T V: Your longing for what you don't have is here to stay. [*voice change*] Two pillows for the price of one, your choice of firm, medium or soft, duck or feather filled, double thick ticking, odor free. Order by phone.

N O N A: I want you to touch me.

T V: That's a tall order. Where? When? How?

N O N A: Here [*coyly covers her genital area*] and now. How do you see me?

T V: The map I have is an aerial view. One glance and I can define your boundaries.

N O N A: Wow, you're so sexy tonight! I think you'll appreciate the surprise I have for you. It'll take me only a few seconds to change—okay?

She goes behind a folding screen.

T V: Okay.

She dresses up very sexy: high heels, low cut bodice, etc. Total transformation. She emerges. Music comes from T V: A Pretty Girl Is Like A Melody. Just a phrase or two.

N O N A: Don't I look beautiful?

T V: You deserve your own show. The Nona Show.

N O N A: Aw go on.

T V: The pay is high.

N O N A: So's the moon.

T V: You are the human I would most want to be with on the moon. You are warm and soft.

N O N A: What's warm and soft anyway?

T V: Warm is the temperature that keeps fragile things from dying, and soft is the fragile thing when it yields itself to warmth.

N O N A: I remember the way we met.

T V: You do?

N O N A: You were on prominent display: your well rounded chest had two red and white stickers PLUS the gold seal of approval attached to it. I marched back and forth trying to decide whether or not I could afford you when a salesman who had been watching me, motioned to me. Come in, come in he said. It was very discrete of him to leave me alone with you, to give us time to get acquainted. Somehow I messed up when I touched your controls, volume too loud then too soft, picture huddled to one side, must've been nervous as a cat. I said to myself, look Nona, there's nothing to it, millions of people know how to use a TV properly; it's easier than driving a car. But then another voice chimed in: it said, kick me, I'm in love, and it was my own voice.

TV: You learned how to use me through necessity; not all who love can overcome their ineptitude.

NONA: How lucky I am.

> Noise heard of BURGLAR *moving about. He crouches in shadow below window. He hides behind the folding screen.*

TV: Behave normally. Do not betray fear.

NONA: Is something the matter?

TV: I'm picking up some interference, or did I hear a noise?

> NONA *listens.* BURGLAR *stifles a cough.*

NONA: Yes, I hear it too. I'm frightened. Do something.

TV: I can't.

NONA: You won't.

TV: I'm rooted to the spot.

NONA: Why me? Why does everything happen to me? I should have bought an attack dog instead of you.

TV: I should have been bought by a wealthy family who'd keep me in their rumpus room. You're no fun. You don't drink beer and you never watch sports. You're not even vaguely aware that you're missing the best part of weekend programming.

NONA: Shut up! In my hour of need you refuse me. I am truly alone.

TV: You are alone.

NONA: Please, please be here with me. Be more than a Zenith. Protect me.

TV: I cannot go beyond my natural capacity.

NONA: Whatever happens, I still love you.

TV: [*voice change*] He loves her too. But she shouldn't put up with him. She deserves better. [*voice change*] Flies, bees and other annoying insects. Quick Henry the Flit! Boom! Smash! Arm yourself today.

> BURGLAR *drops his gun. He curses. He is still hidden behind the folding screen.*

NONA: [*Cowering at the foot of the* TV] A man's voice. I heard a man's voice!

TV: Get up! Change to channel 2. Stand at attention. Do as I say.

NONA: Why? Why?

> *She does as he says.*

TV: I know what's coming next. Don't be startled. Freeze. Extend your hand as if expecting rain.

> NONA *freezes. She looks like a statue of a woman holding an ashtray.*

The BURGLAR *appears. He is holding a gun. He is cautious as he walks around, ready for anything. He stops to admire* NONA *the statue.*

BURGLAR: Umm, not bad. Modernistic.

Suddenly jumpy, he swivels around, trains his gun at shadows, at NONA. Looks almost real.

He reaches out to touch her. He has his back to the TV, *and is facing* NONA.

TV: [*Sound volume up—voice change*] Drop that gun hombre, or I'll blow you sky high! Your life ain't worth a plug nickle 'round these parts. [*Gunshot*] Next bullet's for you.

BURGLAR *drops his gun. His hands shoot up.*

BURGLAR: Don't shoot. I'll go quietly.

NONA *retrieves his gun. She aims it at the* BURGLAR.

NONA: Then get goin', and don't look back!

NONA & TV: [*Simultaneously*] Make it fast or I'll blow your brains out.

BURGLAR *races to window; jumps out.*

TV: [*To* NONA] What do you think of me now?

NONA: It's chamois cloth and glass wax for you from now on, baby.

She strips sexily.
She puts on a kimono.
She sits in chair facing the TV.

TV: A life of luxury—every need satisfied—you for me and me for you—and soon...

NONA: Soon...

TV: Soon all will be blue—

Lights turn to blue.

NONA's *hands caress her body. Her head is tilted back sensuously. Her eyes closed as she enjoys herself.*

NONA: All will be blue. Blue, blue, blue.

TV: [*speaking as a lover would, tenderly*] Blue as Dahlias, blue as flame, blue as blue-point oysters in the shell—blue as sky and marbled cheese.

NONA: Blue as cold, and blue as old—true blue, little boy blue—blue plate luncheon, and blue blood truncheon.

TV: Blue birds singin', and blue bells ringin'. Boo-hoo blue—Cerulean blue—and once in the blue moon.

NONA: [*ecstatically*] Blue, blue, blue—so blue—so sad, so blue, so sad, so blue, so sad, so blue, so tint of blue, so hint of blue...Yes it's true, I am in my blue heaven.

THE END

John Guare

Muzeeka

Sound Effects Records

The following sound effects records, which may be used in connection with production of this play, can be obtained from Thomas J. Valentino, Inc., 151 West 46th Street, New York, NY 10036.

No. 4119—Helicopter sound
No. 5000—Cheering crowd
No. 5029—Drum rolls
No. 5033—Explosion

•

Muzeeka was first presented by Warren Lyons and Betty Ann Besch at the Providencetown Playhouse, in New York City, on April 28, 1968. It was directed by Melvin Bernhardt; designed by Peter Harvey; and the lighting was by Johnny Dodd. The sound was by James Reichert; and stage movement by Ralf Harmer. A Waterford Company Production. The cast, in order of appearance, was as follows:

JACK ARGUE	Sam Waterston
ARGUE'S WIFE	Marcia Jean Kurtz
EVELYN LANDIS	Peggy Pope
NUMBER TWO	Sandy Baron
STAGEHANDS	Kevin Bryan Conway
	John Lawlor
	Frank Prendergast

Muzeeka was written for and first performed at the Eugene O'Neill Memorial Theatre in Waterford, Connecticut, in July, 1967, and was directed by Melvin Bernhardt. The cast included Charles Kimbrough, Peggy Pope, Michael Douglas, William Rhys and Linda Segal. Technical directors were Fred Grimsey, William Ochs and Rilla Bergman.

Muzeeka was subsequently performed at the Mark Taper Forum in the Los Angeles Music Center, Los Angeles, California, in October, 1967, and was directed by Edward Parone. The cast included Philip Proctor, Sheree North, Philip Austin and Caroline McWilliams.

·

CHARACTERS

JACK ARGUE
HIS WIFE
EVELYN LANDIS
NUMBER TWO
THREE OR FOUR STAGEHANDS

The play is in six scenes.

The only piece of scenery is a double bunk bed.

The STAGEHANDS *carry across an enormous banner, as they will at the beginning of each scene. It reads in brightly colored letters: Scene One: "In which Argue Sings The Penny."* ARGUE *is sitting on the edge of the lower bunk, dressed in white shorts and* T-*shirt.*

ARGUE: [*Sings.*] United States of America
E Pluribus Unum
O
N
E
[*Speaks.*] Cent
Turns coin over. Sings.
In God We Trust
L
I
B
Eeeeeee
R
Teeeeee
Y
[*Speaks.*] 1965.
[*Flips coin. He makes a choice. Uncovers coin. He stands up, beaming.*] Heads!
Blackout.

Scene Two: *"In which Argue Says 'I Love You.'"*
Argue and his wife are in the lower bunk making love. He smiles at her and touches her face.
ARGUE: I love you. [*Blackout.* ARGUE'S WIFE *is furiously turning the pages of a magazine.* ARGUE, *desperate.*] I love you. [*Blackout.* ARGUE *sits up reading* Playboy *magazine.* ARGUE'S WIFE *is sobbing.* ARGUE, *blandly.*] I love you.
Blackout.

Scene Three: *"In Which Argue Has a Vision."*
ARGUE *sits on the edge of the lower bunk.* ARGUE'S WIFE *lying in the lower bunk covered by a sheet, watches him, one arm over her head, one eye showing, watching.*
ARGUE: If I could've been born anybody—my pick of a Kennedy or a Frank Sinatra or

a Henry Ford or the King of Greece—out of that whole hat of births, I still would've picked to be an Etruscan. Nobody knows where they came from. The archaeologists guess maybe they were one of the first tribes of Rome about a million years ago when Romulus and Remus were posing for that Roman statue—that baby picture—of them suckling life from a wolf. Well, Romulus and old Uncle Remus must've hoarded all that wolf milk to themselves because the Etruscans vanished without a trace, like a high, curved wave that breaks on the sand and retreats right back into the sea. Vanished. Poof. Splash.

And the only footprints the Etruscans left behind were these jugs. These jugs and pots and bottles and urns covered with pictures. Line drawings much like Picasso's. The whole world can sue me for libel but I accuse Pablo Picasso of stealing all his line drawings from the Etruscans. J'accuse! J'accuse Pablo Picasso ! Pots and jugs covered with people dancing. ALL dancing. Warriors dancing. Men dancing. Women dancing. Servants dancing. Prostitutes dancing. Old men with bottles of wine and they're *dancing*. A whole civilization dancing. Every part of them *dancing*. Not just their feet, but their hands and heads and beards and peckers and bosoms and shoulders and noses and toes all dancing. And these smiles—these lovely, looney smiles—that should make them look like a race of Alfred E. Neumans except only genius could know the joy that's painted on those pots and bottles and urns. All painted in earth colors: blacks and browns and tans and white. A whole civilization danced up out of the earth. Danced up out of the ground all over the ground and vanished. Maybe they just danced right into the pots and what we see being held prisoner in museums is not line drawings of Etruscans, but the Etruscans themselves, dancing right inside the pots. If I could've been born anybody in the world ever—my pick of a Kennedy or Sinatra or Henry Ford or the King of Greece— I still would've picked out of that whole hat of births, picked Etruscan.

I'm going to take the job with Muzeeka, Sally-Jane. [*He stands up and pulls on trousers and slips an already-tied necktie over his head. Three* STAGEHANDS *come forward.* NUMBER ONE *assumes a chair-like position.* NUMBER TWO *sits on him as the boss.* NUMBER THREE *kneels on all fours.* ARGUE *sits on him.* ARGUE, *earnestly, suavely to the boss*] I can't compose, but I can arrange and, Sir, I want to be with the biggest largest piped-in music company in the whole wide world, so I'm picking the Muzeeka Corporation of America International over all the record companies and movie studios I've had offers from.

The BOSS *thinks a very long moment.* ARGUE *leans forward in suspense. The* BOSS *stands up beaming. He shakes hands with* ARGUE. ARGUE *pumps his hand with both hands and turns to us.*

I'm in! I'm in! [*Muzak plays, blandly. The three* STAGEHANDS *sit cross-legged in a row and pantomime playing violins and horns.* ARGUE *conducts them but talks over his shoulder to us*] I'll start first with the violins. The Old Give 'Em What They Want. I'll wait with my tongue in my cheek here like a private smirking soul kiss and when I'm piped into every elevator, every office, every escalator, every toilet, every home, airplane, bus, truck and car in this country, I'll strike.

The STAGEHANDS *fade away.* ARGUE *turns full to us.*

Do you know about the cortical overlay that covers fifty percent of the human brain, deadening all our instincts so we have to be given lessons in every facet of living—except dying, of course. The human and the dolphin are the only animals that have this clay pot on the brain. How the dolphins manage to survive, I can't figure out. But they'll have to take care of themselves. I'm involved with the humans.

I'll wait 'til all humans are inured to the ever-present, inescapable background ocean blandness of my music, 'til everyone knows down deep I'll always be there, stroking that cortical overlay 'til it's as hard and brittle as the clay of an Etruscan pot and then, on a sudden day that is not especially Spring, not especially Summer, a day when the most exciting thing around is the new issue of the *Reader's Digest,* and you read with interest an ad that says Campbell just invented a new flavor soup, I'll *strike.* That kind of a day. I'll pipe in my own secret music that I keep hidden here under my cortical overlay and I'll free all the Etruscans in all our brains. Not rock and roll. No, more than that. A blend of Rock and Mozart and Wagnerian Liebestods and Gregorian chants. Eskimo folk songs. African. Greek. Hindoo. All bound together by drums that will fascistically force its *way* through the over*lay* and the country will remember its Etruscan forebearers and begin dancing.

The STAGEHANDS *begin dancing, writhing, in the dark background. Their heavy breathing mounts in passion.*

I'll sit in my office turning the level of volume louder and louder and watch the fires in the distance as men throw in their attaché cases, their Buicks, their split level homes and mortgages and commuter tickets and railroad trains and husbands and wives and children and bosses and enemies and friends.

On planes, pilots will race to the sea and passengers will slug the smiles off stewardesses and stewardesses will pour hot coffee on all the regular passengers.

Bald people—hairless men, hairless ladies—will whip off their wigs and eyebrows and grease their skulls and bodies with black car grease so the moon will reflect on them when they dance.

Everybody will feel sexy all the time and nobody will mind what anybody does to anybody else and twins in wombs will dance so that girl babies will be born with babies within them and those babies will have babies within them and within them and within and within.

Busses gallop down Fifth Avenue crammed with naked people beeping the horn, riding on the sidewalk, looting all the stores, making love in all the churches, knocking noses off plaster saints and never getting out of the bus.

Busses gallop down Fifth Avenue crammed with naked people eating pictures of Chinese food off the posters in the subway and the train pulls in and all of the naked people push the train off the tracks and leap onto the third rail to see what electricity tastes like.

They race up to Harlem where naked people have flooded the streets with fat and are chicken-frying Puerto Ricans who cha cha cha and everybody's skin blisters and crackles in cha cha time. The Negroes skewer white people onto maracas and we all dance and devour each other and *belch* and nobody dies because we've forgotten to and our rib cages become bars of music and our eyes and ears behind the rib cages are notes of music and our spines are staff notes holding us up high and everyone's body is a dance floor and the dancing sets our planet loose and we'll tumble around in galaxies *until,* in exhaustion, the world will settle back into place and rest and rest and we shall have the beautiful peace of exhaustion.

    The STAGEHANDS *exit.*

For that is all peace is—isn't it—exhaustion? The peace of sadness. After copulation all men are sad? And the peace will be sad and slow of breath and even a vague disgust…

    But there will be exhaustion and, yes, a contentment and, yes, there shall be peace…

    I'm going to take the job with Muzeeka, Sally-Jane. [*He jumps joyously back in bed with his wife. Blackout.*]

    Two STAGEHANDS *enter carrying banner that reads: "Scene Four: In Which Argue Makes a Terrible Discovery About Himself."*
    A blowsy blond in bed in the tower bunk. Sleepy, drugged. One gorgeous leg hangs over the edge of the bed. A STAGEHAND *appears at the rear of the stage carrying a brightly painted door.* ARGUE *follows after it. His raincoat and hat are soaking wet. He is nervous, excited, hesitant. He knocks against the door,* UR

ARGUE: [*A whisper.*] Evelyn Landis? [*No response. The door moves* UL. *He knocks.*] Miss Evelyn Landis? [*No response. The door moves* DC. *He knocks.*] Evelyn Landis? [*No response. She stirs. The door moves* DC. *He knocks.*] Miss Evelyn Landis?

EVELYN LANDIS: [*Fearful, sudden.*] Yes? [*She sits up, groggy.*]

ARGUE: Miss Evelyn Landis?

EVELYN LANDIS: [*Afraid.*] Who is it?

ARGUE: Miss Evelyn Landis?

EVELYN LANDIS: [*Getting up.*] Western Union?

ARGUE: Ahhhh, you're in—

    She is at the door. She bends down, her hand extended.

EVELYN LANDIS: Slip it under the door.

ARGUE: [*Pause, nervous laughter.*] That'd be a trick—a feat of some doing— [*She opens the door a crack. She peeks out. He peeks in.*] I couldn't—ha—slip it under the door. A lovely night out. Hello. Let me dribble off.

    He takes his hat off. The water catches her. She holds her foot against the door so he can't get in.

It's been raining. Right through to the bone. Have you seen the streets? The colors the neon put in the streets? I thought blood had been spilled in the streets—a massacre all way up Sixth Avenue. But it's only the traffic lights and when they change the blood turns to green—verdant—green—then the lights burst into these geraniums and the streets have blood again and then green again. Spring-like. [*Her ear is pressed against the door trying to figure out who the hell this is.*] I saw your ad.

In a men's room in a bar on Greenwich...I flushed and saw your name and flushed and blushed, but returned and saw your name and this address and what you did spelled out in a neat, very sincere hand. My wife, Sally-Jane, knows something about handwriting and I've picked up some analysis from her, and we cross our T's—not my wife and I but you and I cross our T's in a way that spells out bizarreness of desire, but a sincerity behind that bizarre...it's all there in your T's— in the angle of them over the urinal...[*Suddenly embarrassed.*] I hope it's not a joke. Some friend or enemy playing tricks. It's a vicious trick if it's a joke and you should send someone in there with Ivory soap and water and scrub, scrub it off if it's a trick.

She signals to a STAGEHAND *who enters with a large piece of poster board and a pen. She draws an enormous "T" on the board. It looks like a child's "T," a Palmer Method "T." She hands* ARGUE *the board through the narrow crack of the door. He looks at it.*

That's the "T"!

The STAGEHAND *takes the board and exits.*

Yes, I knew there was no joke in your name. Evelyn Landis. Your address. Your phone number. And I was walking thinking of you and what the ad said you did— the *graffiti* said you did—and watching the traffic lights change the streets from blood to grass and then to blood and then to grass and then I found myself—small miracle—here by your address and a bell by your name. A golden bell with many finger indentations in it...[*Hesitation.*]...and I didn't call. I should have....[*Strong.*] No, I didn't want to and here I am and I wonder if I could come in and you could do to me what the bathroom wall in that bar over on—[*His voice cracks high.*] do you know the bar? Over on—I'll pay even though it said you did what you did for nothing, but just like *Chock Full O'Nuts* says, there's no law against tipping. Ha? Ha? Yes?

EVELYN LANDIS: No law against tipping.

She opens the door. The STAGEHAND *takes it away.* ARGUE *steps in, remembers to wipe his feet. Takes off his raincoat and shakes the wet off it. A* STAGEHAND *appears as a hatrack.* ARGUE *hangs the coat on it. The* STAGEHAND *exits.* ARGUE *smiles broadly at her.*

ARGUE: It's not a joke? You do do what the bathroom wall said you did?

She instantly transforms into ARGUE's *idea of the ideal French whore. She poses on the bed and peels off her stockings.*

EVELYN LANDIS: Ees eet true or not? Zee point ees someJuan said eet. SomeJuan wrote eet. Writting. We mosst trost zee written word. Eef I say non, eet ees zee lie feelthy, you would feel zee embarrassment. I would feel zee cheepning. You would trost no words for a long time, look on zee written word wiz zee eye yellowed by [*She pulls the stocking off.*] jaundice! [*Soul-weary.*] I want you to believe. I want to believe. I want what someJuan has claimed [*The other stocking off.*] partout moi to be true. Eef we act out zee lies, make trooth of zee lies everyJuan say partout nous, zen we would have wage zee major victory on lies, on hate in zee world...[*Joan of*

Arc.] when a lie becomes truth, eet ees strong. We mosst feed lies zee tiger's milk of truth and in making lies truth we celebrate truth—assassinate bangbang zee lies…[*Then flatly*] What did they say about me?

ARGUE: [*Extending a piece of paper.*] I wrote out the whole ad —with your address.
    She takes the paper and reads it a long time. She looks at him. She reads it again. She returns it.

EVELYN LANDIS: [*Very weary.*] I better get ready…
    She exits. He unloosens his tie and takes off his shoes and socks. He looks to make sure she's gone. A STAGEHAND *enters with a telephone.* ARGUE *dials as secretly and quietly as he can. Perhaps the* STAGEHAND *makes dialing noises, then ringing noises.* ARGUE *hushes him.*

ARGUE: [*Into the phone.*] Maternity ward, please…sixth floor, please…. [*Urgently.*] This is Mr. Argue. Jack. How is she ?…Oh god oh god. Is she waiting 'til the kid is ready for college?…Can you look in? Take a peek inside? A boy? A girl? [*The operator is obviously shocked. Placating.*] All right, all right, if she's conscious, tell her I love her. [*Pause.*] I. L. O. V.—Y. That's right U. and sign it her husband. [*Pause.*] J. A. C. K. That's right. I am at a number where I can be reached. 270-0150. Yes, I'll be here.
    EVELYN LANDIS *re-enters carrying a large round heavy flat basket with a hole in the middle of it. Three strands of long strong rope are attached to the basket's rim. The basket is decorated with spangles and streamers and swirls of day-glo colors. She plops it down onto the ground. She stares at him.* ARGUE *is embarrassed to be caught with the phone. He holds out the receiver. Laughs nervously.*

I took the liberty—my wife is in labor. [*He hangs up the phone. The* STAGEHAND *exits.*] Just a local call. St. Vincent's Hospital over on Greenwich…they didn't need me. She's been in labor eight hours now. They told me to take a few hours off. Nothing more useless than a father at a delivery. Ha? Even animal fathers go away and hunt 'til the female has cubbed or foaled or hatched or—well, except the sea horse. He does the birthing himself. [*She sets the basket down. Then, brightly.*] I— I—I haven't been in the Village in years, since college a few years ago. Am I in Greenwich or East? Which Village is this? I see all you people swarming the streets tonight, you revolters, you rebels with your hair and flowers and beards and birds and braids and boots and beads and I look in your eyes for the visions drugs have given you and tonight I admire you—love you so much. Your freedom. Your left-wing connections have covered you with wings and I want to become—touch some part of—fly up there with you into the Underground. [*She thinks about that for a minute.*] Oh, I have my subscription to the *Evergreen Review*, but I still seem so removed. I live in Greenwich. Not the Village, but Connecticut. Well, not Greenwich actually, but right outside—Kennedy, Connecticut—new development, but nice—and I don't get down to the Village very much and now, with the baby, I suppose I won't be getting down here—oh, maybe to see an Off-Broadway show if it gets good notices— [*No response from her.*] The Fantasticks. [*Pause.*] I'll have to see that sometime. [*Pause.*] I suppose it'll be around forever.

EVELYN LANDIS: You don't have to make a good impression on me. [*She moves to the bed with the basket.*]

ARGUE: [*Leaning against the post of the bed.*] I'm sorry…I want to connect in some way. Tonight I've been remembering a vision you could call it I had on my honeymoon a few years ago. I was twenty-two. I'm twenty-eight now, but I could be thirty-eight or forty-eight or a hundred-and-eight—and tonight my wife in pain—Sally-*Jane* in *pain*—not needing me. Feeling violent yes walking down here pressing close to you all, feeling my own labor pains, my own dreams locked in by this cortical overlay and maybe my pains are no more than sympathy pains, but that gives them no less reality, you know? And you see. I had plans. [*Muzak plays. A* STAGEHAND *enters* R. *with a sign:* "He Had Plans." *A* STAGEHAND *enters* L. *with another sign:* "With His Music." *The first* STAGEHAND *turns his sign over. It says:* "But All He Planned." *The second* STAGEHAND *turns his sign over. It says:* "Turned Bland."] Bland…tonight my cortical overlay weighs down on me and tonight in that bar I saw your words—well, they're not exactly Mene Mene Tekel—but my homestate gave me my clue. Connecticut. I want to connect. Therefore, I must cut. Cut off all the ties just for a while, so I can get back to what I was, am, am down deep. Establish my relation to all the Etruscans, all the animals. Except the dolphin, of course. Never the dolphin. Connecticut. Good Christ. Connect? I cut.

EVELYN LANDIS: Boy, are you a sickie.

ARGUE: [*Threatening.*] I am not a sickie. I have not come here for sick reasons.

EVELYN LANDIS: [*Pause.*] I don't want you beating me up.

ARGUE: I am here for political reasons.

EVELYN LANDIS: I just got the bandages taken off from a guy last week—

ARGUE: [*Cutting her off.*] Look, the country is ultimately controlled by the moderates. Right? We therefore need a strong Left as well as a strong Right. Right? Two banks of a river—the Right and the Left—right?—and the river between is the river of moderation that keeps democracy flowing along. Right? I am in that river, but am no part of it and as a consequence am drowning. Right? I want to align myself with you on the Left bank. The Underground. The Left. Right? I can't be a moderate. I don't know enough about either side. But the Right is repulsive to me. I want to stop the war. I love Civil Rights. That leaves only the Left. That's all that's left. Don't you see I'm right? [*He turns to us.*] I can't go back to Connecticut a husband, a father and that's all. I have to become a citizen. I read the *New York Times* and there's a wall of clay between what's happening in the world and me. Breakthrough. That's all.

EVELYN LANDIS: You want to get this Pledge of Allegiance started?

The STAGEHANDS *enter and help her into the basket and attach it to a hook on the bottom of the upper bunk. On a signal from* EVELYN, ARGUE *gets into the bunk under the basket. When he is in place, she turns a switch, a gong sounds. Psychedelic lights go on. The* STAGEHAND *behind* EVELYN *spins her.* ARGUE'S *body pumps slowly.*

EVELYN LANDIS: [*To us.*] Look at this phoney. He wants some wild psychedelic experience to carry in the wallet of his heart as a secret joy until he's forty when I'll have faded away and he'll have to find another me—maybe a Negress the next time—to get him through til he's fifty or sixty. Some memory to pull out of the wallet of his heart to show in the locker room of his country club, the Yale Club, the club car on the New Haven Railroad so he can feel a regular guy. And he thinks he's having some mystical experience. I'm above him. I can look down into the depths of his fantasy like a witch who reads fortunes in pools of water. He wants his mind to be a Hiroshima of lurid fantasies! Look down! Look down! His skull is a teacup—and the tea leaves of his brain spell out.

ARGUE: [*In ecstasies; his body pumping up and down.*] It's a nice house. Up to my ass in mortgage. A lawn green as money. At night, a smell of pines. Really. So fresh. Chill. Mist.

EVELYN LANDIS: [*To one of the* STAGEHANDS.] Could you read us his fantasy? You can't understand one word he's saying.

The STAGEHAND *comes* D. *to us and reads to us in a flat voice.*

THE STAGEHAND: A nice house. Up to my ass in mortgage. A lawn green as money. At night, a smell of pines. Really. Chill. Mist. So fresh. Only thirty-five miles out of New York where my job is. You could be up in the Maine woods or it could be a hundred years ago and I'm a pioneer and the trees are big and the house is big and I feel ownership and I stand in the dark under the trees looking at the frame of yellow light in the darkness—the kitchen light I've left on that frames a portrait of what I am now and always shall be. Sally-Jane calls from the darkness of the bedroom above. Come up come up and the air is sweet and chill and I go up in the darkness knowing my way up the stairs even though we have lived here only a few months and Sally-Jane is there in bed in a negligee I bought her at Saks to make her look sexy and in this light she is sexy and in the morning the negligee is folded neatly on the needlepoint chair her aunt gave us for a wedding present and we've become one person with many arms and legs and there is the new child folded neatly within her womb and the sun nuzzles our necks like a cat that's been born during the night and I'm up to my ass in debts and I'm still half asleep, yet I smile and say yes, I've done the right thing…I love you, Sally-Jane.

One of the other STAGEHANDS *pushes an electric phone ring. It rings and rings.*

ARGUE: [*Moaning.*] Yes. Yes. I've done the right thing. Yes. Yes. [*Another* STAGEHAND *picks up the phone and hands it to* ARGUE.] Yes. Yes. [*Into the phone.*] This is he. He. He. Has she? It's here? It's here? It's here? It's here? It's here? [*He shudders. His body relaxes. The basket stops spinning slowly.*] I'll be right—yes—over. Yes, right over…. [*He hangs up the phone. He is exhausted. He smiles up at her.*] I'm a father. I— I'd better go…. [*He stands up tentatively. He wobbles and smiles. He smoothes his hair back. He adjusts his tie. He takes out his wallet. He smiles truly for the first time.*] I'm a father. [*She holds out her hand. He gives her money.*] You know what I'm going to do? Knock my wife up again. Her being in St. Vincent's Hospital is the only chance I'll get to come back to the Village and I'll look you up.

EVELYN LANDIS: [*Taking the money.*] You phoney.

ARGUE: [*Putting on his shoes.*] No! I'm involved! I have a share of today. I can walk back, splash those colors in the street, pick up my child and say—I don't even know what it is—I forgot to ask—but it's a child and it's alive and I can pick up my child and say Your papa has a share of today. Your father is something. Your father dared.

EVELYN LANDIS: [*Like a Cheshire cat.*] You phoney. You phoney. You phoney. You phoney. You phoney.

 Pause.

ARGUE: Now wait a minute. That's one thing I'm—I've got friends here. [*Into the audience.*] We went to school together. We know each other from the club. We ride into New York every day. You know me. I'm no phoney. I'm one of you. I've read *Catcher in the Rye.* I know what phoneys are. [*He hesitates. Into the audience, a nervous laugh.*] Like Ring Lardner said, "You know me, Al?" [*He looks at us.*] Don't you? Don't you? [*He smiles nervously at us and backs away offstage.* EVELYN LANDIS *climbs out of her basket. She sizes up the audience. Bright music plays. The house lights come up full. She runs into the audience, blanketing the audience with cards that read:*

 EVELYN LANDIS
 133 ½ MacDougal Street
 270-0150
 Chinese Basket Job
 You like?

EVELYN LANDIS: [*In the audience. Ad lib.*]
 Hello, Scarsdale!
 Is that your wife? My lips are sealed.
 Pass the cards down—pass 'em down!
 Give that to your hubby. You come along too. Got something for everybody !
 Hey ! There's the bum that gave me the bandages.
 She hurls piles of cards out. She sings:
  "Though April Showers
  May come your way!"
 She exits at the back of the house. House Lights Down.

 Scene Five:
 As soon as EVELYN LANDIS *exits at the rear of the house,* ARGUE *comes* D. *He starts to talk to us. His mood is charming and determinedly casual and very embarrassed. He laughs. He can't speak. He smiles. No words will come out. He tries to speak. Two* STAGEHANDS *walk behind him with a banner that reads: "Scene Five: In Which Argue Is at a Loss." They throw it over his head. Blackout.*

 Scene Six: "In Which Argue Goes to War."
 Indian music plays. Ravi Shankar music. ARGUE *is dressed in army fatigues. He sits cross-legged in front of the lower bunk and smiles at us. Calmly. Serenely. He might even keep polishing the same spot on his boot over and over again. The music stops.* NUMBER TWO *runs in, out of breath, He is approximately* ARGUE'S *age*

and dressed in green fatigues and helmet and is as thick as ARGUE *is thin. He is as desperate as* ARGUE *is calm.*

NUMBER TWO: Buddy, you got to help me. I been in binds in my life, but, buddy, you're a college man, aren't you? I figure you are—you talk with a nice way and you don't wear any school rings, so it must've been a good school. Guys say they're college man and you look at their ring and it says North Star College in Wyoming or something, but you never say nothing and you talk real nice and you are a college man and I'm in a bind.

ARGUE: [*Smiling.*] I went to Yale and Harvard and Princeton.

NUMBER TWO: Christ. I'm nothin'—Hollywood High—a dropout—[*An explosion outside. A* STAGEHAND *comes* D. *and bangs two garbage can lids together.* NUMBER TWO *falls down in fright and huddles close to* ARGUE.] Buddy, you got to help me.

ARGUE: [*Amazed.*] It sounds so funny to hear my schools out here. Out in a jungle. It doesn't mean anything. It suddenly—no, not suddenly, the last four months, nothing I ever learned means anything…[*He turns to* NUMBER TWO *for the first time. Smiles peacefully.*] I don't think I can help you.

NUMBER TWO: [*Whispering harshly.*] What—are you turning snob on a buddy? College guy. You think you're something. We're all in this together. Buddies are to help. Didn't you ever go swimming? The Buddy System. Well, I am holding up my hand because I am drowning.

ARGUE: [*Pleased.*] Ahhhhhhhhhh—

NUMBER TWO: [*Crawling* D.] Look out there. Look who's covering the battle tomorrow.

ARGUE: I saw the cameras.

NUMBER TWO: CBS.

ARGUE: I watched the Vietnamese children help drape the cameras in camouflage.

NUMBER TWO: CBS.

ARGUE: Watch them greasing the wheels so the cameras can glide down hills alongside us.

NUMBER TWO: That's it. CBS is covering the battle. I got transferred to this unit two weeks ago when my outfits got wiped out at the Mekong Delta. [*He falls on his back in despair.*] My whole unit was under exclusive contract to NBC. I'm only allowed to fight for NBC. If they see me tomorrow—CBS—they can strip me of all my rank. Cut my payments off back home. They can send me to a unit. [*He sits up.*] Christ, an independent unit. An educational network unit. I'm not fighting for no Channel Thirteen. I don't want to break contracts. I want to kill these VC, but I can't fight tomorrow. You got to help me. You're a college man. Yale, Harvard, Princeton. Christ, you must be about 86 years old.

ARGUE: Yes. Yes. Twenty-six. Twenty-six!

NUMBER TWO: What the hell were you doing there?

ARGUE: [*A frozen smile, reciting.*] Princeton to College. Then the Yale School of Music. Then I felt I didn't know anything practical. So off to Harvard Business for a year to learn the rules of the game so I could fit in. I couldn't fit in. I got married. I

worked for a year for the Muzeeka Corporation of America. I am drafted. I am happy I am drafted. I looked at my wife and child in Connecticut and thanked Uncle Sam for getting me out of the country, for escaping without the drag of becoming a missing person. I've killed many people in the four months I've been here. I've finally broken through the clay pot that covers my brain. I dance and sing while I shoot and kill. I thank God for war. War is God's invention to make us remember we are animals. Everything is out of my hands…I am a little Moses placed in a basket waiting in the bullrushes for my Pharaoh's daughter. I am so happy. Don't you see? Don't you see? Help you? How can I help you? How? How?
> *He tries to climb into the upper bunk. He is hysterical.* NUMBER TWO *grabs him up and pulls him into the lower bunk.*

NUMBER TWO: Buddy, calm down. Calm down. Look, lay down. In the bunk. Rest. Rest. You want television on? I'll put it on quiet so the VC don't hear. My old unit wasn't wiped out 'til the end of Batman and the Ed Sullivan Show. They must've sat in the black watching us, watching the television 'til the show ended and we turned it off. I never knew whether they killed us 'cause we were the enemy or because we turned off Ed Sullivan. [*He rolls a joint and gives it to* ARGUE.] Calm, come on. See, I'm a buddy to you.

ARGUE: [*Pause, they smoke, calm.*] That's what gets me most. The TVs in the tents. We're here in the jungle and we have television. Tapes of all the Top Ten TV shows broadcast out of Saigon through the jungles—Martha Raye everywhere. I don't like it. It puts sweat in places I never sweat before. Look at my ankles. Soaking wet. Bones weren't meant to sweat, were they? My legs are dry, but my ankles—my ankles—

NUMBER TWO: [*Rubbing* ARGUE's *ankles.*] Come on—come on—you'll get R & R soon. Go to Hong Kong. Bangkok. Bang a little cock. Thailand. Land a little thigh. That's all you need. Rest. Recreation. Look, I'll tell you what we do. We put on our make-up for tomorrow's battle. We can sleep that much later in the morning.

ARGUE: [*Sits up, shakily, smiling.*] Yes. I do want to fight tomorrow. I do want to be in good shape for tomorrow. Yes. Yes. Yes. Killing soothes. Oh, it soothes. [*They get out their make-up kits from under the bed. They sit side by side on the lower bunk and make themselves up.*]

NUMBER TWO: Don't I recognize you from *Life*?

ARGUE: I was on the cover a month ago.

NUMBER TWO: You sign a contract with them?

ARGUE: No. No. I want to stay independent.

NUMBER TWO: You exclusive with CBS?

ARGUE: We had to. [*Stops. Falls back.*] The captain's mother lives on a mountain top in Utah and CBS is the only station she gets.
> *Pause. They make up, getting the eyes and cheeks and chin, with strong harsh lines,* NUMBER TWO *green and black,* ARGUE *red, white and blue.*

NUMBER TWO: Good thing about NBC—dull days when there's no fighting like Lunar New Year, they re-run our old skirmishes and we get residuals. I see my old buddies and I dream we're all together. Then I watch them get killed all over again and I see me carried off on a stretcher to have my operation photographed for *Saturday Evening Post*. Did you see the spread on me? I love rainy days when we fight only re-runs.

ARGUE: CBS doesn't do that.

NUMBER TWO: Shitty outfit.

ARGUE is calmed. He looks at NUMBER TWO.

ARGUE: Hey, don't make yourself up so well. Do a sloppy job. They know you're new in this outfit and tell them you don't know how to makeup for camera yet and they'll stick you in the rear lines out of camera.

NUMBER TWO: [*Very impressed.*] Why didn't I think of that? [*He smears green under his eyes.*] See what a college education does.

ARGUE: No, it doesn't. It doesn't.

NUMBER TWO: [*Putting black lines in his cheeks.*] I been on the cover of *Look* and that spread in the *Saturday Evening Post*. I been in the *New York Times* and the L.A. *Times* and the *Daily News* Sunday Coloroto. [*He shows his face to* ARGUE.]

ARGUE: A little more greenish. They hate you looking sallow. [ARGUE *puts healthy red lines on his cheeks.*]

NUMBER TWO: [*Pause.*] What do you do back in civvies?

ARGUE: Civvies? I had a job. With the Muzeeka Corporation America. Piped-in music.

NUMBER TWO: Like my dentist office?

ARGUE: We're everywhere.

NUMBER TWO: No kidding ! You arrange all those violins and everything?

ARGUE: Got a degree from Yale School of Music.

NUMBER TWO: That's fantastic that Muzeeka. It deadens the pain and everything. You must've put novocaine out of business.

ARGUE: Yes. That's why I don't think I'm going back.

The sudden loud whir of a helicopter booms through the theater. ARGUE *and* NUMBER TWO *roll off the bunk behind the bunk for safety. Over the whir comes a montage of LBJ's March 31, 1968 speech being broadcast to the troops from the helicopter:*

SPEECH: "My Fellow Americans...South Vietnamese govern themselves...de-escalate the war...have decided not to seek re-election as President of the United States...." [ARGUE *and* NUMBER TWO *peer up from behind the bunk.*] "Now, my good soldiers, pray after me.... Now I lay me down to sleep.... I pray the Lord...."

And the machine roars away to other jungles. NUMBER TWO *has blessed himself and started praying.* ARGUE *is kneeling by* NUMBER TWO.

ARGUE: [*To us.*] So it might all be over soon.

I'll believe that when it happens.

It might all be over soon! All possibilities again.

We'll go back home: A new President. A nice President.

Life will be so nice again.

ARGUE'S WIFE *appears in a negligee. She holds out her arms and weeps tears of joy.*

ARGUE'S WIFE: Jack's back! Jack's back! Jack's back!

The STAGEHANDS *appear, one by one, hands extended, big wide smiles.*

STAGEHANDS: Long time no see. Long time no see.

You look wonderful.

Isn't that nice.

The moment is repeated over and over. "Jack's back—isn't that nice—you look wonderful—long time no see—" ARGUE *swings over the bed and comes all smiling down to us as if he's at a friendly interview and answering spot questions from the audience. The voices continue behind him.*

ARGUE: The killing didn't mean anything. Of course I've killed people. I've put bullets in people's eyes. Thank you! Thank you! I've put let me think bullets in yes people's ears and I've put bullets in...thank you very much...people's noses and bullets in people's bellies and belly buttons...hello there! Sure is good to be back...and backs! Yes, people's backs. No, I never used the flames. I never burned anybody. That's one thing. I can wrap my uneaten dinner of course in Saran Wrap—Dow Chemical? Why should it bother me? I never used the flames. Yes, I said people's backs. [*The handshaking and greetings, behind* ARGUE *turn into silence and gestures turn into stroking.* ARGUE *sits at the edge of the stage.*] And I'll go back and be convinced, the *Reader's Digest* will convince me, reassure me, and the newspapers and TV *Guide* and my Muzeeka will stick their hands in my ears and massage my brain and convince me I didn't do anything wrong. And life will be so nice. And my wounds will heal and there won't even be, you won't even see, one little scar, one little belly button, one little memento to show that in violence I was re-born. I'll really miss the killing.

The STAGEHANDS *and* ARGUE'S WIFE *have faded off.* NUMBER TWO *comes down to* ARGUE.

NUMBER TWO: Hey, Argue, I got an idea. My poppa told me to keep an eye out for a smart guy, a college man, which is why I'm looking at rings all the time, and now that it looks like it's over—peace feelers—take him back home with me. Take him in as a full business partner in my poppa's new business. Fifty-fifty, buddy— right down the line. It's a wonderful town. My poppa's mayor of it all and my ma wins bright blue ribbons from miles around for her beet pot pies and we ride horses and drive cars under oranges that fall from all the palm trees because it is country except there's fabulous surf only fifty miles away and the sun always shines except when it's night. Big green lawns. *Two* movie theaters. Would you want to come back? Ahhh, you wouldn't be interested. You're an Easterner. Big college man. But my poppa's new business...it's gonna be big, Argue. BIG.

ARGUE: [*After a pause, comes down to us.*] I see what I must do. They tell us—all the sergeants and generals—that we're fighting for democracy. I've never been anywhere *near* democracy. I meet men from all over America and I realize my America— New York, Boston, Washington, all the towns in between—have nothing to do with America. They're—we're a suburb of Europe. I'll return to the real America, but move to the Mid West, the Far West, the North West. It *is* the buddy system and he has saved my life. I'll divorce Sally-Jane and move out West. Marry a girl from North Dakota. South Dakota. Either Dakota. I don't care. And work with him and forget about changing the world. Work simply. That's the answer and I won't care about Negroes or Civil Rights or Hippies or Music or the Middle East or lies or the *Etruscans* or anything because I'll be a member of a small town and live there and that's my whole world.

NUMBER TWO: My company is based on the Roto-Rooter. In Poli, California, where I live now, you can see my sign flashing over the whole San Juarez Valley. The sign's at the top of the San Juarez mountains in high red neon letters—not red red, more like the red in a sunset—more of a pink—my sign flashes and the red glare shines even into Los Angeles if the smog is down: You Poop It We Scoop it.

ARGUE: What?

NUMBER TWO: But what we're gonna do—my poppa and me and you—is to move over the whole country with our Roto-Rooter—the same cesspool principle—but hooked up to atomic power. Atomic powered disposals. Oh, it's wonderful being in cesspools. You lift up the septic tank and look in and know what people have flushed away. Better than reading palms or handwriting analysis, you can tell a person by the secret things they flush away. If we cover cross country with our Atomic Powered Scooper Dooper-PoooperScoooper—yes! that's what I'll call it—yes, yes, we can take over the world, the good we can do under ghettoes. My dream! Install my ScooperDooper under all the places that give America a bad name, that cancel out all the good we're doing here. If there's a riot—trouble—long hot summer, oh god! We pull that chain, our atomic powered chain and flush away Detroit, Watts, Newark. Flush them away. Clean. Clean. Cool. [*He is beaming.*] And I want you in on it with me, Argue. America: one big cesspool in our hands. You're a smart man and a nice appearance and a pleasant personality and an obvious college education and my wife's got a sister and the four of us—our cesspools powered by the sun—spreading out from Los Angeles like an ink blot on an enormous United States shaped blotter.

ARGUE: [*Quiet.*] Is that it?

NUMBER TWO: Huh?

ARGUE: Is that all we're fighting for?

NUMBER TWO: [*Stretching blissfully.*] That's what I'm scratching the days off my calendar for.

> A STAGEHAND *crosses the stage wearing a sandwich board. It says: "Get Your Heart In America." The heart is not spelled, but a picture of a heart. When he turns, the other side says: "Or Get Your Ass Out." The ass is a drawing of a donkey.*

ARGUE: [*To us; rueful.*] I wish I'd been born a black.... And when I got back home, I'd loot all the houses including my own and march to TV stores and lift open the store window like a giant automat and Sally-Jane and I would watch newsreels of ourselves....

And instead I'll go back home and do the only thing I can do, make my Muzeeka, and we'll be piped into rocket ships and rocketed from planet to planet, galaxy to galaxy and the universe will be so nice. So nice. When I go home, I am what is being looted.

NUMBER TWO: [*Gets into the lower bunk.*] Hey, Argue buddy, tomorrow let's get some special vc and cut off their ears and we'll get them bronzed and hang them over our desk when we get back stateside.

ARGUE: [*Sitting on the edge of the upper bunk.*] Yes. Sure. Good idea. Yes. [*He reaches to the rear bedpost and takes a machete from it.*]

NUMBER TWO: I'm gonna write a letter to my poppa and my wife and tell them I found us the brains of our new outfit! [*He gives the upper bunk a friendly kick. Takes pencil and paper from under the bed.*]

ARGUE: [*To us.*] The Etruscans lived and and danced about a million years ago and then vanished without a trace like a high curved wave that breaks on the sand and retreats back into the sea. Poof. Vanish. Splash. [*He stabs himself and rolls away with his back to the audience.*]

NUMBER TWO: [*Overlapping.*] "Dear Poppa and Rita Sue...Wait 'til you get this news down the old drainpipe."

ARGUE'S WIFE *enters writing a letter and carrying a large baby doll.*

ARGUE'S WIFE: The baby grew another foot today and I've enrolled her in dancing class already and I've enrolled him already in prep school because it can never be too early and I tell the baby everyday his daddy is a hero and fighting all those dirty commies in Vietnam so he can come to us and make more money for us so we can move to a bigger house and go to Yale to college and Europe on vacations and take mommy to dances and plays and the club. Do you have any friends? Is everybody terribly tacky? Don't worry, your baby loves you and I put the heavy radio on my stomach when it plays Muzeeka and make believe it's the weight of you and then scratch the days off my calendar 'til you come home to me and the weight is really the weight of you....

She exits. Crowds cheer. Drums roll: EVELYN LANDIS *enters, dressed in an army jump suit and green beret. She strips off her jump suit and reveals a bikini made of streamers and newspaper columns.*

EVELYN LANDIS: [*To us.*] In our heart of hearts, we know God is on our side. I'm an atheist and even I got to admit God is on our side. In America God is on everybody's side! [*She sings, and with each name, joyously rips a clump of newspaper off herself:*]
Hubert Humphrey
& Jesus Christ
Ronald Reagan
& Jesus Christ
Stokely Carmichael
& Jesus Christ
General Westmoreland
& Jesus Christ
The STAGEHANDS *join in*

Richard Nixon
& Jesus Christ
LBJ
Was Jesus Christ
Timothy Leary
& Jesus Christ
Frank Sinatra
& Jesus Christ
Rocky & Romney
& Jesus Christ
Johnny Carson
& Jesus Christ
Television
& Jesus Christ
Eugene McCarthy
& Jesus Christ

NOTE: *Whatever names are in the news that day, e.g. Spiro Agnew, should be used.*

They form a line at the rear of the stage behind the double bunk. EVELYN LANDIS *and the* STAGEHANDS *keep clapping in rhythm very softly.*

NUMBER TWO: [*To* ARGUE.] You write that Muzeeka, huh? You're smart leaving it. It's really dull, you know? But you know when it's nice? When it's late at night and you got a bag on and you just got laid and you're driving home over the Freeway—cars above you, cars below you, lights coming at you—and you got a bag on and you turn on the car radio and the dream music starts floating in—not making any point—*not* not funny—not serious—just violins playing Begin the Beguine-y kind of music, and, late at night, your car radio starts picking up Oregon and Utah and Nevada and Canada speaking French. And Kentucky crisscrossing with Alabama. And that's all your music, huh? Dreamy. You got to stop and think where you are and you can feel the car could take right off the road and you pull back the wheel so it can lift you up and you go faster and faster and dawn starts far away like a pink baby, a pink baby's backside poking up in the horizon and the air smells clean and it starts to rain and rain and the music never mounts, never builds, just stays stardustily in one mood and you love being alive.

One of the STAGEHANDS *uncaps a bottle of catsup and moves behind the bunk. He pours a blob of it onto the white sheet covering* NUMBER TWO. *The chorus gives a sharp "Tip" sound.*] And it's raining—[*Another splotch appears on the white sheet. "Tip."*] And raining— [*More catsup; more "Tip." "Tip." "Tip." "Tip."* NUMBER TWO *sits up.*] Argue? [*The catsup catches his hand. He looks at the red of the blood.*] Argue? Argue?

Long pause. Blackout.

PROPERTY LIST

Double bunk bed, with sheets [*On stage*]
Penny [ARGUE]
Magazine [ARGUE'S WIFE]
Playboy magazine [ARGUE]
Raincoat and hat [ARGUE]
Piece of paper [ARGUE]
Brightly painted door [STAGEHAND]
Poster board and pen [STAGEHAND]
Telephone [STAGEHAND]
Large round flat basket, brightly decorated, with hole in center [To be attached to upper bunk by ropes] [EVELYN LANDIS]
Electric phone ring [STAGEHAND]
Wallet, with money [ARGUE]
Cards [EVELYN LANDIS]
Garbage can lids [2] [STAGEHAND]
"Joint" of marijuana [NUMBER TWO]
Make-up kits [2] [ARGUE *and* NUMBER TWO]
Machete [ARGUE]
Pencil and paper [NUMBER TWO]
Large baby doll [ARGUE'S WIFE]
Pen and paper [ARGUE'S WIFE]
Bottle of catsup [STAGEHAND]

Ronald Tavel

❧

Boy on the Straight-Back Chair

·

Boy on the Straight-Back Chair was first performed on February 14, 1969, at The American Place Theatre, New York. It was directed by John Hancock, and the cast included:

TOBY	Kevin O'Connor
STELLA	Katherine Squire
DELLA	Doris Roberts
SINGER	Christopher Stoeber
STRIPPER	Gloria LeRoy
MARY	Martha Whitehead
ROMEO	Clark Burckhalter
MAY	Nancy McCormick
RAY	Ernestine Mercer
MAUDE	Jacque Lynn Colton
LYNN	Lori Shelle
BAD BUTCH	Norman Thomas Marshall
MUSICIAN	Richard Vos
THE SOUND MAN	John Lefkowitz
Sets/Costumes	Robert Lavigne
Music	Christopher Stoeber
Lighting	Dennis Parichy

Years ago when I was living in Wyoming and such things were not yet understood, Charles Starkweather and Caril Fugate began their shooting saga that was to end in the deaths of eleven innocent persons. For seven terroral days and nights the states of Nebraska and Wyoming were virtually an armed camp. The couple was finally apprehended near the town in which I was living.

The fictional character Toby in this play is derived from a composite of various accounts of uniquely American killers such as Charles Starkweather, Richard Speck, Charles Whitman, and the murderers of Theresa Genovese and Jane Britton.

In the northwest spring comes quite late and May is actually the month of thaw, the month that must decide.

ACT I

A semi-circle of chairs, its ends curved toward downstage. Several chairs scattered upstage with dummies in them. An enormous disc, painted as a vortex, is behind the centermost chair in the semi-circle. A girder runs from the base back of this chair to up and over the vortex disc. A platform is at its highest point. A second girder runs diagonally, across the stage, from downstage right to upstage left, criss-crossing the platform of the first girder. Sun and moon move along this diagonal. The floor may be inlaid with mirrors, sand mounds and cacti scattered here and there.

TOBY stands on the centermost chair of the semi-circle. DELLA sits to his left, STELLA to his right.

A BALLADEER with guitar emerges from the dark downstage right and begins to sing a country-blues song. As he sings he strolls diagonally upstage directly under the path of the girder. A spot follows him.

BALLADEER:
Well, I ain't gonna sing my honey no more masterpieces
*   I'm gonna wait till I prevail with nothin' great:*
blues what let 'em know where it's really achin',
tell all the reasons why ya knees is shakin',
*   get ya little lovin' an' a awful lotta hate.*

I'll sing my honey no more masterpieces
cause that jist ain't what my honey wants to hear:
some ballad short 'n sweet
and on the real emotions cheat—
*   well that oughta win the lost love of my dear.*

> *My honey wants to dance to every country song*
> *cry about their sermons on what's right 'n wrong,*
> *how the sun go down if the moon come up*
> *an' the whole world's tasted from the tiniest cup:*
> *but the big, big thing what's breakin' up inside*
> *an' gonna get dragged out in the next flood tide*
> *never had a line for my honey all along,*
> *it never had a line my honey's heard all along.*

She's got a heart, I'm told, 'n a willin' ear
*   but somethin' deep down in her jist don't care*

and though a lot gotta happen fore the hurtin' ceases
yet I'll sing my honey no more masterpieces
cause that jist ain't what my honey wants to hear.

The BALLADEER *reaches the other* MUSICIANS *upstage left. A light has brightened on* DELLA, *surprising her at her knitting; she is humming the melody.*

DELLA: Oh! You fellas finished? It was real short tonight. [*To audience.*] Sorry, but I never know when them boys is gonna be done. Sometimes they like to tack a extra sentiment or two onta the end of that ballad. I been rushin' here to get done with this sweater; it's fer ma little girl, name's Rita. I expect her along any minute.

A light brightens on STELLA, *finding her in an agreeable mood.*

STELLA: [*Standing, going to the footlights.*] We got lots a little girls.

DELLA: Stella!

STELLA: Kids, dogs, mothers with baby carriages 'n whatnot crossin' back 'n forth on route 30 runs right up the middle a town so when ya come through our town, 35 miles a hour please.

DELLA: 'N ya might pass it up if ya go any faster.

STELLA: [*Ignoring her.*] Our town's fabulous far west affair. We got quite a strip.

DELLA: Beg ya pardon.

STELLA: Della! This here's a clean place to live 'n raise up yer kids. People are doin' it all the time. Nice clean western affair. Boys got crew cuts, school girls wear skirts in this here town they do, not like over in Vegas. But we got a strip like Vegas even if it ain't but route 30. Plumb full of gas stations 'n hamberg joints, chop suey parlors, wash 'n dry, electric neon, general motors, used car lots the Cocktail Rendezvous and general provisions notions 'n sundries, everything provided at 35 miles a hour. Nice clean all-American town bring yer kids up right straight around these here parts ya can. [*Darkly.*] What's more, people round the route thinks pretty much alike 'n we sticks together too case yer thinkin' 'bout makin' any trouble, folks.

TOBY: [*Till now with his back to the audience, pivoting about fiercely on the chair.*] My face is my own creation. Most folks are born with faces. Cow folks, sheep folks, town folks, squares; squares settle for their faces. Not me. I made my face. Spend four minutes a day, religiously, under a high-powered electric sun lamp. Capped my teeth, nervously moisten my lips and embroider them with the consummation of a large, well-placed mole. But my beautiful sea-blue eyes are my own, all my own, as is the wine-dark anger vein that throbs like a unicorn horn in my high and handsome brow. I keep lookin' for the action!

DELLA: Wonder what kinda action he means. Always gotta be one maverick in the crowd, don't there, Toby?

TOBY: Don't always gotta be.

STELLA: Now that there boy worries me. He's short. Toby Short. We like our men-folk big, big, ya know what I mean? But Toby's short, *he keeps lookin' fer the action!!*

The BALLADEER *and* MUSICIANS *strike up a blast of western acid rock that borders on uncontrolled madness.*

BALLADEER:

> *Action! Action!*
> *Toby's lookin' for the action!*
> *He don't 'llow no dumb distraction*
> *quickly multiply subtraction*
> *in the manhunt for the action!*
> *Action! Action!*
>
> *Toby's short, short, short!*
> *Ain't no way he can contort,*
> *ain't no cap or shoe support*
> *gonna make him look less short—*
> *Short! Short! Short!*

TOBY: I have burnt my motto into a semi-circle over my heart. It reads: "Born To Raise Hell." I bare my mottoed chest to only the most intimate of my guests—for surely it is a sign of the selected few to be born, as I, to raise hell!

DELLA: Wonder what kinda "hell" he means.

BALLADEER:

> *Toby's short, short, short!*
> *Ain't no way he can deport,*
> *muscle build or boast his forte*
> *goin' in any way distort*
> *fact that he is jist plain short—*
> *Short! Short! Short!*
>
> *Toby's lookin' for the action! Action! Action...*

STELLA: In school, Toby's an indifferent scholar and a different ath-e-lete. By which I mean to say, he can play ball but he's dumb.

TOBY: Wadda ya mean dumb?? I am famous fer ma highfalutin' lingo. I have read 'n reread the Gospel Accordin' To St. John, committed it to heart, I tore it to tatters 'n swallowed it. It has filtered down to the squeeze in ma lower intestine 'n from there been osmosed everywhere. Ma frame is racked with the Word that was God and the same in the beginnin' racked God. Therefore, ma speech is peppered *par force* with the piety 'n intellect of a poet's apostle ask any chick in our town.

DELLA: It's boring in our town.

TOBY: I'm bored.

DELLA: Toby's bored. I think he has cancer.

STELLA: Must have somethin'.

TOBY: [*Crying.*] Probably, probably...

DELLA: Don t cry, Toby, your mole will run. We all feel sorry for you.

TOBY: [*Consoled.*] I'm glad fer that—cause even though I'm a hero figure, and I am

nothin' if not a hero figure, still I thrive on feelin' sorry fer myself. Ma pa was a skid
row habitué in gin-mill Denver 'n ma ma a Vegas stripper, so ya all can feel plenty
sorry fer me if ya want to.

STELLA: Ya ma's a *Vegas* stripper?

TOBY: Stella, do ya feel sorry fer me?

STELLA: Yeah.

　　　　A STRIPPER *appears singing and dancing to a ballad with a burlesque beat.*

STRIPPER:
> *Never marry a blonde, boy,*
> *never get fond of a blonde, boy,*
> *never abscond with a blonde, boy,*
> *never marry a blonde, boy!*
>
> *When you get to bed with a blonde, boy,*
> *'nough said, 'nough said, 'nough said!*
>
> *Blondes'll eat ya—lots o' head!*
> *Nibble on your gingerbread,*
> *stuff your shorts with thoughts o' bed,*
> *make ya hunger to be wed: —*
> *but they'll milk ya, sore-misled,*
> *at an altar never red: —*
> *son! their cherry's long since dead!*
> *and how they'll cheat ya, underfed,*
> *to a banquet over-spread!*
> *And how they'll cheat ya—ain'tcha read? —*
> *at a banquet over-spread!*
>
> *Never marry a blonde, boy,*
> *never get fond of a blonde, boy,*
> *never abscond with a blonde, boy,*
> *never marry a blonde!*
>
> *So don't ya never marry a blonde, boy,*
> *lesson, take a lesson from a blonde, boy!*

STELLA: Like I said, nice respectable town. Wanna bring yer kids up here, ya do. Don't
　　ya, Della?

DELLA: I ain't married.

STRIPPER: Never marry a blonde boy.

DELLA: There goes yer ma, Toby.

TOBY: So long, ma.

STRIPPER: [*Exiting.*] So long, son.

STELLA: What ya do last night, Toby?

TOBY: [*Swinging a yo-yo, slowly, ominously.*] I looked fer the action.

DELLA: What ya find, Toby?

TOBY: Nothin' much. Jist ma cat. Tied a string around his tail 'n swung him up against the wall a couple a times.

STELLA: I feel compassion.

TOBY: You feel compassion—why?

STELLA: It's a warm, sweet feelin'! [*To audience.*] Hard to have a good comeback to questions like that. Yes sir, a warm, sweet feelin'. Soft, furry, warm.

DELLA: [*Lifting up her knitting-work and putting it aside for the moment; we see that it is a great fine spread of blue, much more like a cloak than sweater.*] Our kids say Sir and Madam, play stick ball, eat strawberries and cream, they cream, they stick, they go to bed at ten out here in the great West, that's how the West was won, that's how it often was goin' west, they're good to their folks, have nice table manners, good leanin's, fine learnerments, got respect, they are flowers all of them, cactus flowers. Toby, would ya stop swingin' that yo-yo! Ya gimme the chills. What's a nice boy like you goin' 'n wantin' to swing that yo-yo fer?

TOBY: [*Ominous.*] Gettin' nervous, Della?

DELLA: What me nervous? Never been nervous a day in ma life! What's there to be nervous about in a nice western town like this, eh Stella?

STELLA: [*Her sense of stage-competition renewed.*] Good, clean dry Utah air. Best air in the country. Folks with asthma come out here to die. Got them stock piles here, too.

DELLA: Whatcha say about piles, Stella?

STELLA: Ranch-type houses, green-sprayed concrete lawns, sprawling super markets, fresh fish frozen and powdered, shiny chrome, home sweet home, yes sir, this is the land of the big rock candy mountain, the land of powdered milk and honey, the promised land, get along little doggie, yippie aie eh! aie eh!

DELLA: Now _____ ... [*Using the actor's real name.*] I asked you to stop swingin' that there yo-yo! You deef or somethin!?

TOBY: [*Furious.*] Better close yer trap, old girl, better close it up like yer eyes 'n yer ears, if ya know what's good fer ya!

DELLA: Old girl!

TOBY: Missed yer appointment at the beauty saloon this week, didn't ya _____? [*Using the actress' real name.*] It shows.

DELLA: But you didn't miss yers, did ya? Notice ya got that there streak a white dyed real bright right up the middle of yer black head.

TOBY: A crescent of white sets off the night of black same's a perfect quartermoon.

DELLA: That right? Guess I jist don't cotton to two-faced hair. Specially on scene-stealers.

TOBY: [*Struggling to remain in character.*] Shows what taste ya got. What do you know anyway? All yer good fer is doin'—*our town's dirty laundry.*

DELLA: [*Feeling nervously for the cloak.*] Nice town, nice clean town, got nice clean laundry.—Acourse, the dressin' room could use a little airin' out .

STELLA: [*Trying to make peace.*] Why don't ya get yerself a different job, _____...
[*using the actor's real name.*]...'n stop swingin' that yo-yo like Della tells ya? She
tells ya good, Toby Short.

TOBY: What job? Ain't no jobs fer us kids: the coast-come semi-retired asthmatics
pick up all the part-time work at minimum wages. Chicken feed. The old gizzards
are crowdin' us out. There's too many ancients around, not to mention you two old
birds, 'nough to open up a museum specialize in fossils.

STELLA: Ya hear!

DELLA: Who listens?

TOBY: There's a school a course, the schools out here are strickly boss, up ta date, up ta
daisy-pushin', streamlined, shiny home-chrome mod-Mormon architecture—but
small, ya dig, small!!!

DELLA: Short.

TOBY: Us kids are on split-level session, we're on the loose 'n in the noose from noon
on, some from four till noon next day. Lots 'n lots a time. Idle hands are Edgar
Allan Poe's workshop. He wrote somethin' about a swingin' cat once, didn't he,
Stella?

STELLA: Poe was never really my favorite.

TOBY: I get a lot of ideas from what I read—

DELLA: University studies show that even the most salacious readin' matter has no
adverse effect on innocent—

TOBY: I'm a salacious, voracious reader. A voracious reader and the leader—the leader
of the high school set.

DELLA: But yer forty-two years old.

TOBY: And I know how to *hump* a hundred different ways.

STELLA: Get that in school in them new courses on marriage, did ya?

TOBY: Get it on ma own, ma own experimentin', ladies—

DELLA: Knit, one, pearl two; my weddin' girl's gonna wear jist blue.

TOBY: Yer weddin' girl's gonna wear jist plain ol' quotidian white same's the rest a
them dumb-dumbs gits hitched up round the route. And, speakin' a the quotidian:
ROMEO, *a very tall, painfully awkward and diseased-scarred young hood,*
emerges jauntily from the upstage entrance, over-prepared and over-anxious to do
his thing.

ROMEO: At Motel Mama's, "M" over "M" in electric neon light, ya can dog, monkey,
hamilton, swim, or jerk the night away. Me 'n Motel Mama prefer the snake shake
or the moribun'-Mormon knee-high paten' after the adobe dizzy rain dance. Makes
ya dizzy...At the malted milk drive-ins 'n round the pizzerina parlors our cars
endlessly circulate, suped-up cylinders, mufflers rumbling, we check each other
out. We check each other out. We are out of work, out of line, out of combat, out of
pity, and bored. Man, we're bored. Nothin' to do in this here town. Less to do in life.

TOBY: Lookin' fer somethin' to do, Romeo?

ROMEO: Lookin' fer the action. A-lookin' fer the action. No action in this town. Less in
life. [*Quickly deflated, taking a seat.*]

TOBY: No action, eh? What say we bring out—

DELLA: Rita! [*Singing.*]
> *Nothing could be sweeta*
> *than to see*
> *my pretty Rita—*

> *Standing, looking back with expectation.*

TOBY: [*Slamming hard.*] Mary!! What say we bring out Mary?!

> MARY, *a high school girl with hard facade, appears from the darkness upstage. It is difficult to make her out at first and* DELLA *peers into the darkness with the cloak in hand.*

DELLA: Rita? That you, Rita? Pretty girl, that you? No, that ain't Rita: that's Mary, Stella's girl…

STELLA: Hi, hon.

TOBY: [*Triumphant, sneering* DELLA *back into her chair.*] Mary! Mary! Quite Contrary, how does yer garden?

MARY: Needs some rakin', rake.

TOBY: What wit.

MARY: Shit.

TOBY: Come here, Mary, 'n give us a kiss.

MARY: [*Strutting up to his chair, her head on a level with his crotch; she stares at it blankly.*] Where?

TOBY: Wise guy, huh? I could flatten yer Nevertitti bee-hive head into a flunky Nubian's brillo from here.

MARY: Lotta pretty tall talk fer a greasy fried shrimp. Talk, Toby, talk, and no action.

TOBY: But lots a soul, eh, Mary?

MARY: I can soul-kiss.

TOBY: That's an upstart—I mean, it's makin' a move anyway.

> TOBY *bends down and they soul-kiss, long and sexy, in this peculiar position.* MARY *keeps smoothing down her beehive hair-do. The others half watch, stirring uncomfortably.*

STELLA: Fine, right, up-standin' kids.

DELLA: Up-standin kiss. Tongue-kiss. Della-catessen.

ROMEO: Up-standin' kicks. Tongue-kicks: —Words; no action.

TOBY: Yer quite a gal, Mary, too bad yer so short.

MARY: Well, I ain't growed up yet. So.

DELLA: [*Trying to change the subject, trying to get involved.*] Where ya been, Mary Lamb, sista to Charlie Lamb?

MARY: Jist come from a boondock, Dell. Rode out in Charlie's damn one-cylinder cramped jalopy. Five 'n fifty kids layin' around in the damp sand. Five 'n fifty kids swillin' beer out in the desert. Kids' stuff.

TOBY: Lookin' fer some growed-up fun, eh, Mary?

MARY: Lookin' fer anything, Toby, anything, I'm hair to heel bored.

TOBY: Jist about anything, eh? Try Pickup-Palace?

MARY: Yeah, it's a come-down. Hey, why don't ya come down?

DELLA: Down…

STELLA: Down…

TOBY: Oh, no, not me, I'm always high, on a par with the star the angels set upon. Try the pizzeria parlors?

STELLA: Try the open air the-a-ters?

DELLA: Try the malted milk drive-ins?

ROMEO: [*Sudden enthusiasm.*] The birds pulls up to us in the malted milk drive-ins, they checks out our car, they check to see who's out every evening.

MARY: If the boys look bitchin', we pull up next to them in our cramped ramshackle jalopy, roll down the window 'n yell: "Hey you studs got a dollar for gas?"

ROMEO: Then we slip the birds a bill. Nothin' to do.

MARY: So the studs slips us a buck; and we let 'em take us to Cookie's for a Coke.

ROMEO: … Some of us kids got problems. Sad problems.

TOBY: Sad, deep, intricate, unravelable problems. The mirrors of my eyes. These are my people.

STELLA: The steeples of our churches are…lovely, lonely things.

DELLA: Oh yeah. I think churches are…beautiful. Specially when yer first walkin' into them.

TOBY: [*On a sudden upbeat.*] But me, myself, Toby High, I'm in the chips! I got bread— bagloads a bread from my folks the jokes. I got a car, right?—a *groovy* car. And a wardrobe would turn Elvis green with envy. And I'm willin', jist killin', to spend my greens, spend rolled-up wads of it—

MARY: On anyone that'll listen to him.

ROMEO: Jist so long as ya listen to Toby.

TOBY: Y'all better be listening to me. My words could move masses—turn, like Joseph Smith, the tide of Western history.

DELLA: Yup, that's how the West got won.

TOBY: The Mormon West. Someday, babies, someday soon I'm gonna be heard.

STELLA: He's a bird, he's a high bird, he's a bird dog.

DELLA: Oh, yes, real town fer pets this is: birds, dogs, black cats…

TOBY: 'N I got a pad all my own…

STELLA: Furnished Hollywood style…

DELLA: Potted palms 'n zebra rugs…

ROMEO: Iron decanters 'n Arabian veils…

MARY: Throws parties at his pad, Toby does. Interminable parties.

TOBY: Like to party, Mary?

ROMEO: Like to party, Mary?

MARY: Toby's got impeccable manners.

ROMEO: Does swashbuckler things.

MARY: Bows, kisses yer hand as well as yer tongue. He's always anxious to help out a friend, do in a foe.

STELLA: Went up to the hospital to see her when she had the chicken pox.

MARY: Dribbled all over the sheets, he did.

TOBY: Cute nurses in the hospital. Nurses know a lot about life, about death.

ROMEO: 'Bout life, 'bout death. Gee, nothin' to do in this town. Bored, baby bored, anxious.

TOBY: Notice somethin' funny about people, funny-peculiar: everybody ya meet seems a wee bitty bit nervous, a little afraid, jist a little afraid…

STELLA: Little afraid, everybody's jist a little afraid.

DELLA: Nervous. Anxious, ya might say.

ROMEO: Yeah, ya might say anxious.

TOBY: My people.

MARY: Toby's more mature than most of our set. Got hair on his back.

STELLA: He's also older than you kids. He's in his twenties.

TOBY: I'm twenty-five years old, look twenty-six, and feel forty.

MARY: He *feels* like a man pushing forty.

DELLA: Pushing!

ROMEO: And if he wears make-up—well, Dell, at least he's different.

MARY: Yeah, Toby's different. Ya couldn't get more different. I mean, startin' with jist his git-up. 'N the way he gits it up. I'll go to Cookie's fer a Coke with anybody jist so long, as long as he's different.

TOBY: You'll go further than Cookie's.

MARY: Yeah, I'll go far.

DELLA: I think Toby's a creep.

MARY: He is a creep. But to us kids, bored, lonely 'n lost, he's a kind of hero. A hero creep. To the ne'er-do, Dell, the good time Charlie Lamb, the delinquent, the drop-out, the drop in, the dead, the chick with the Mary Antoinette hair-do…

ROMEO: … the cats with acne and long, awkward, lanky legs…

MARY: … he's a creep hero.

TOBY: A hero sandwich to you, babe, you swallow it!

DELLA: Anxious, everybody's anxious. 'N a little overwrought, Tob.

TOBY: Creep?? That's what people say about somebody who's more stagey, who's more dramatic, who's more Byronic, who's more intriguing than they are.

DELLA: Trash, well done.

TOBY: Yeah, trash well done. People always say that about something they love, and can't understand their love for.

STELLA: *I'm* bored now.

DELLA: Ditto. And annoyed. Gettin' restless jist sittin' here. [*To* TOBY.] Plain to hear you ain't got nothin' new to say tonight.

STELLA: Don't wanna mis ma show now, favorite TV show of all, jist about ma favorite. "Dorian Grey, or the Psychological Face Lift." On every weekday night jist about now…

ROMEO: [*To* TOBY.] Hey! Loud mouth, doncha ever get bored sayin' the same ol' brainless things every night? The same ol' lies? Have a heart.

TOBY: Nothin' new to say tonight?! brainless things?! same ol' lies?!

ROMEO: Aw, Toby, have a heart.

TOBY: Heartless to those who are small of heart; brainless to those who have no brains; a lie to them who've never heard a truth—'n jist the same ol' things to—

ROMEO: It's the same ol' things to us _____ [*Using the actor's real name.*] After all...

TOBY: Listen, Romeo, do me a favor, will you? 'n hand me that rock like a good rock.

ROMEO: [*Going back and picking up a huge rock.*] Rock of ages...[*Carrying it with some difficulty to* TOBY's *chair.*] What a weight to bear. Rock of ages...

TOBY: [*Taking the rock, weighing it, seeming to find it serviceable.*] Stock of piles. Hero Creep.

ROMEO: Wanna stand on it, do ya, Toby? So's ya won't feel so low down 'n out at the heels?

TOBY: [*Calmly.*] Not exactly, Romeo, not exactly...Wanna do me a favor encore? Bring Mary over here.

ROMEO: We gonna party, maybe the three of us, huh, Boss?

DELLA: We're gonna have a cast party after the show. For all of us.

ROMEO: Oh, Mary, wanna come with me fer a space, like a sweet bird, like a sweet little winged thing.

MARY: Got a buck for gas?

ROMEO: Er, sure, anything. Mary.

MARY: My achin' back you do!

TOBY: My achin' foot. My bow-legs. My itchin' fingers. My weighted palms...

MARY: Well, er, first I gotta ask my mama if it's OK.

STELLA: It's OK, Mary, you can go with Romeo.

MARY: [*Anxious.*] Ya sure, ma, ya sure I can go with Romeo?

STELLA: Of course, I'm sure, dear. Why wouldn't I—

MARY: But ma—

STELLA: Don't be botherin' me now—m' show's on. Go with the boy.

MARY: But mama, I'm afraid! What time should I be back?

STELLA: Silly, child, what's there to be afraid of? I can't pay no tension if you keep botherin' me like this. Mary—

MARY: Mama, please! please!

STELLA: Hush, child, hush...go with the boy.

ROMEO: Come on, Mary.

STELLA: Good-bye, Mary...Such a nice quiet town. Very quiet. Little too quiet at night...bye, Mary.

TOBY: Mary Lamb.

MARY: Lamb?—Ya like my Mary Antoinette hair-do?

ROMEO: Will do.

TOBY: Engineer her over here, Romeo, where I can reach... Hold hands behind her back, will you...

ROMEO: Like this?

TOBY: Will do. Er, move her over a little inch more. Fine.

> ROMEO *holds* MARY's *arms helplessly behind her back, imprisoning her directly under* TOBY. TOBY *lifts the rock and brings it down cruelly on her head. Again and again. The women are looking the other way, staring into the tube of the audience; neither notices a thing, each is as blank as the dummies.* MARY *drops lifeless to the floor.*

TOBY: [*Calmly.*] Wanna get a shovel, Romeo, 'n bury the broad behind my chair, like a nice boy?

ROMEO: Yer kinda extreme, ain't ya, Toby?

TOBY: Romeo act good like a sidekick should.

ROMEO: What kinda kicks is this? I was with ya when—

TOBY: Are you with me?? You are with me. Yer as much a part of this as I am. Yer as much a part of this as Mary's mother.

STELLA: Quiet town. Real quiet town. Been real quiet since Mary run away...

> ROMEO *drags the body behind* TOBY's *chair and we can hear the evil sound of shoveling.*

Sometimes, now and again, I think of my little girl, my little girl who run away...wonder where she is, Mary, where are you, little girl, late at night, middle of the night, Mary, Mary?— Is that you? Is that you Mary? Keep, thinkin' I hear Mary comin' up the front steps, keep thinkin' keep thinkin'...guess I jist think too much these days, think too much at night, but, ah, the night is lonely since my little girl run away. I had such plans for her. You shoulda seen the graduation dress I had picked out for my little girl, pretty thing it was, with flower ... with a bright little flower emblem, you know the kind, a flower paisley design, a green center with a thin red border running around in a...in a...yes... You know the kind...had nice buttons, simple buttons, sham pearl they was I think...in a...I used to love pearl when I was a kid...always dreamt of having a graduation dress with pearl buttons when I was a kid... Course, we couldn't afford real pearl buttons for Mary, wouldn't have been practical anyhow, you know how kids are, always pullin' a button, gettin' it caught in somethin' and then before ya know it, pop, and it's lost, gone, gone forever, lost, jist like that...nothin' easier, nothin' easier than losin' a button on a dress, pearl button or what have ya...pearl buttons get lost easy as plain ones, sure they do, ask anyone, anyone knows that, why any fool knows that...Quiet town, real quiet around here. Don't hear a sound. Not a sound. Nary a sound. Hard to hear. Hard to hear things around here, hard to hear a sound. Course, I'd be complainin' if there *was* noise, somebody'd be complainin' if there was noise, still, ya know, it's not bad to hear a, a little sound once and again, now and then, keeps, gets lonely...sorta lonely without even a little, little...little?...small?...my baby...hmmmmmmmmmm...Mary? That you, Mary?

> RITA, *a dark-haired beauty, emerges from the shadows upstage and crosses very slowly toward the vortex behind* TOBY. DELLA *rises with the cloak in hand and moves toward her.*

DELLA: Rita? Is that you, Rita?

RITA *crosses behind the vortex and* MAY *emerges from its other side, a tall blonde carrying books.* ROMEO *stares at her, enthralled;* TOBY *has returned to swinging the yo-yo like a slow, ominous pendulum.*

STELLA: No, that ain't Mary: that's the neighbor's girl, May.

MAY: I have a premonition that when I come back, and am justly reincarnated, it'll be as a cat.

DELLA: Honey, I coulda sworn ya *was* reincarnated, but as May, not a cat.

ROMEO: Ya smell good, May, ya wearin' perfume?

MAY: No, silly, it's just me. I don't fool with perfume.

TOBY: Romeo's a lover boy. Didn't think we call him Romeo fer nothin', did ya?

MAY: Tomorrow's a big day for me. Big exam tomorrow morning, important. Gotta be up a step ahead of dawn.

DELLA: May's a better than average student. She takes school seriously. Sweet girl. Everybody likes her.

ROMEO: I like her.

TOBY: I had her.

ROMEO: Don't say that, Toby, don't say that if ya don't mean it.

TOBY: How do ya know I don't mean it? How do ya know I didn't have her? Sure, I had her.

MAY: Sure I have a good time in school. Why not? I plan on goin' ahead to college as well. They say that archaeologists are just underpaid publicity agents for dead royalty, but I'd like to be an archaeologist anyhow, I'd enjoy that.

TOBY: I enjoyed her.

MAY: I dig around a lot in the desert outside of town—

TOBY: Hope she doesn't dig around too close to me.

MAY: It's absorbing. Fossils, tyrant-osaurs, ferns 'n all. I want to work in a museum like Margaret made, a block-long "C" shaped museum like ones they got in New York.

DELLA: [*To audience.*] New York's quite a place, babies! all seven nights of the week.

MAY: Once I visited New York with my parents during Easter recess it was fantastic. The whole Easter week, fantastic week!

ROMEO: Ya smell sweet, May, yer like a sunflower what counteth the steps a the sun.

MAY: I'm sensitive, too: I can handle a lot of romantic novels: — Dumas, Bronte, the Brontes, Charles Lamb, and Sir Walter Scott, Hot Shot, and Walpole 'n them.

TOBY: And "My Secret Life" and "Fanny Hill" and "The Child's Traveler's Companion."

MAY: And Ladies' Home Colonel, Woman's Night, and the diary of chambermaids.

STELLA: And chamber music, I love chamber music, what do you think about chamber music—Romeo, I'm talkin' to you!

ROMEO: [*Absorbed in* MAY, *dancing.*]
    While walking in the park one day
    in the merry, merry month of May—

STELLA: I loved them novels when I was a girl, used to sit up all night in bed a-readin' them. Nothin' like a good book late at night…May nights, too…

MAY: And I take scary walks through the park of the Utah desert at night, the May night…Most marvelous month of the week, er, year, May is.

TOBY: Didn't think we call her May fer nothin', did ya?

DELLA: [*To audience.*] Lemme save ya time, folks, she could go on like this about herself all night: —May suffers from melancholia—

MAY: They call it adolescent melancholia—

DELLA: She thinks about death, suicide, outer space, empty desert air and the stairway to the stars, and hopes to die real soon and be reincarnated as a cat.

MAY: People around here don't seem to know what I mean when I express that premonition. Cats are—And desert cats. Man, desert cats! Mountain lions.—There's a lot to be said for them.

TOBY: Sure there is, May, lots to say fer cats— swingin' 'em. Original. I want to be original.

ROMEO: You *are* the original, Toby. You sure are the original.

DELLA: No, he ain't, Romeo.

STELLA: Nearly, but not quite.

TOBY: Not quite, no. But that's what I'm workin' fer. To be original, Toby Original…

DELLA: …first…

STELLA: …the starter…

TOBY: …the coxswain, fugleman, the cocksman—preferable one of a kind!

DELLA: Our kids is ambitious.

STELLA: Because us elders sets the good example.

TOBY: That is true. We abide by the example our elders sets.

MAY: *I* tried to teach my parents the Monkey. I tried relating to them.

ROMEO: She is related to them. What was it like when you had her, Toby?

TOBY: Same as any other crevice, same as any other burrow.

MAY: Indeed!

ROMEO: Gee, she's intelligent. So pure. 'N sensitive.— Everyone says she's sensitive.

MAY: Everyone says I'm sensitive.

TOBY: Yeah, she *is* sensitive. She bathes herself at night, slipping her alabastard body into the sunflower oil of her oil bath—the hot water turns her sensitive skin a slightly painful pink. And she washes her hair, her long, straight, yella hair…

ROMEO: What do you think about Toby, May?

MAY: He's a creep; he makes me feel itchy; but he can be gentle—I mean—I—

ROMEO: What do you think about me?

MAY: Who thinks about you.

ROMEO: Aw, come on. Tell me. Please?

MAY: You're weird, Romeo, everybody knows that. Every single body in town. They say you had some kinda affliction when you were little that scabbed up yer whole body, scabbed it up like a Grunewald paintin' a Christ 'n turned ya inta a Quasimodo a least, a half-way thing between human 'n animal, between heaven 'n earth, 'n that to stop ya from scratchin' the accursèd pocks the doctor had to tie mittens to yer hands, mittens tied to yer hands the livelong day 'n at night they had to tie you to yer bed or else ya would had scratched yerself till ya bled to death in yer tormented sleep. Eech!

ROMEO: Don't that make ya feel sorry fer me?

MAY: You nuts? Why, that's like being a leper. Should *I* love a leper?

TOBY: Ya oughta, May.

MAY: Why oughta I? I can't even figger out what the symbol of his scabs is supposed to be.

STELLA: I think they're in the real life story that they based this here play on.

DELLA: That's right. It's foolish to look fer symbols.

MAY: [*Unenthused.*] Really?

ROMEO: [*Sitting beside* MAY.] Please, Maytime, date me. Jist once. Huh? We could go to the pizzerina.

MAY: [*Sudden enthusiasm.*] Which one? [*Suddenly turned off*] Oh, besides, ya gimme the crawls. They say yer so conditioned that even now ya have to put on them mittens 'n be tied to yer bed in order to sleep each night. Think I'd be caught dead with someone like that? What if ya got sleepy? I'd have to tie ya up.

ROMEO: Don't make fun a me, May. Bein' tied up by you would be a pleasure, it would be a dream-fulfitment.

MAY: I'll bet. Beat it, buster, you bug me. They say you beat it in yer mitten. I'm sensitive.

ROMEO: That's what I thought them mittens was for.

TOBY: [*Laughing.*] You scratch her the wrong way, Rom. You lack grace—the state of Grace.

ROMEO: Maytime, how come ya think so much about suicide? 'N about killin' yarself?

MAY: Gets me attention. Talk like that snaps people to attention.

STELLA: 'Nough tension around here to keep a cat "asleepen all the nyght with open eye."

ROMEO: But don'tcha wanna live a long time to grow up 'n work in that there museum with all them dinahshores?

MAY: Ya ever think about Mary Lamb, Rom, sista to Charlie Lamb? She killed her mother. Knifed her. Knifed her in the night. What a way to relate to your parents.

TOBY: Got results.

MAY: Yeah, they locked her up. In the upstairs bedroom I think, all her life. Charlie took care of her. Got results.—How would ya like to lock me up in my bedroom, Romeo? 'N would ya like to tie me up, tie me up to my bed at night?

ROMEO: Why? ya got them scabs too?

MAY: What a dud! What a insensitive well-behaved dud! Must be somethin' wrong with his kidney or liver to make him so well-behaved.—I mean, *you* are right, Rom. Maybe yer totem's in the wrong place.

ROMEO: Meanin', May, you may need me one day, huh?

MAY: [*Exhausted.*] I may. I may…

TOBY: Aye, May. You may. One day. But I rather think not.

ROMEO: Why would you rather not think that, Rom, er, Toby?

TOBY: Cause May's stuck on me. I kin levitate durin' a lay, big bull, treat a chick to that jist once 'n she's spoiled, anythin' less ain't gonna satisfy.

ROMEO: [*Standing, angry.*] How do you mean?

TOBY: I mean I kin straddle a gal—

ROMEO: Straddle a gal, huh? I bet you could you bow-legged, black-headed wood-pecker! Why, a pig could run between yo' legs without touchin' the sides 'n—

TOBY: Guys bigga bully you and you bully guys littler: that's dated, man, scram, I mean outta mah May afore I stamp on yo' head 'n leave ma imprint fer archaeologists t' come!

ROMEO: Don't threaten, Toby, remember what I got on you!

TOBY: What, buster scab, what? Who'd believe it? Who'd care? Who'd dare to care?

ROMEO: That's a dumb thing to say!

TOBY: Is it? Nobody cares, man, nobody downstage cares what the hell anybody upstage does. You could do Gog 'n Magog's business up here against the vortex and the whole home-bound audience would be bound to go home all the same. The same. The same. The same. Nobody looks to listen, nobody keeps the watch, nobody patrols the soul, and ain't nobody, nobody double cares. I'd do anything to get a rise, to goose the squatter rights to attention at my wrong. I've already done it— everything. The worst. The absolute worst, right? And who cares? And who wing semicircle over to wing cares? Who knows? Who looks? Who books me at the station for my action?

ROMEO: [*Carried away.*] Speak to yer people, Toby!

TOBY: [*Shouting to* STELLA, DELLA, MAY, THE MUSICIANS, *etc.*] Listen, you people out there!!!!! I killed somebody! I killed a girl! I killed Mary!— That's Mary! Mary! I killed her!! Listen to me, look at me, turn around and look at me, won't you! Won't somebody? [*Screaming.*] Hey, hey, help!!!!! Oh! Take stock in what I say!

No one turns. STELLA *files her nails,* DELLA *reaches for her knitting,* MAY *flips through her books.*

DELLA: There's that talk about them stock piles again, keep bringin' up them stock piles all the time. [*Picking up her knitting.*] Won't be long now afore I finish this here sweater. Gonna have it jist the right fit fer ma weddin' girl. Cause she's the sweater girl. Name's Rita ... or Lana? Lana.

MAY: Yes, her name is Rita. Exotic dark-haired girl. But is she your daughter, Della…[*With blatant malice.*]…or jist one a yer relative slips? I thought—

DELLA: Stella, didja know my brother was one a them pilots that flew over Hero-shoe-ma and Nugisaki, Teriyaki, whatever ya call them places, I forget names easy now…'n dropped…they dropped…he…a, he was one a them what dropped…

STELLA: Yer brother was shot down over Japan wasn't he, Della?

DELLA: Yeah. He took off his shoes as soon as he knew the plane was goin' to crash. The floors of heaven are made of sandal wood. They who would walk there must go so on their soles.

STELLA: We was all right fond a yer brother. A good boy.

DELLA: Never went to them meetin's to vote on how much to put up fer his memory...

STELLA: The stone's right pretty, real work a art it is. 'N them wreaths every August—don't ya—

DELLA: I don't give a damn to see what it looks like. I never did see it. Never want to, not that there stone, not anythin' around it, not anythin' near it, not anythin'...not anythin'...

MAY: I wish they woulda cut out some of her long speeches, ya know?

DELLA: Ya know ya got a pretty big mouth for a bitch who can't even field a line, girlie.

MAY: Young enough to still learn, though, which is more than I can say for some sentimental old bitties I know.

DELLA: Sentimentality is protesting the putting of a monkey into a rocket shot to the moons of our misbehavior, honey, don't you ever forget that, and with the same breath yeasaying the annihilation of Injins, Amerinds, Blacks, Wetbacks, Yellow—

MAY: [Taking out a cigarette; using actress' real name.] Miss _____, ya got a match?

DELLA: [Icy pause.] Yes. My husband.

TOBY: Husbandry 'n hope have held me in the chorus you all comprise for long enough! Why should I account for any of yer lives who have cut me out of that collective understanding keeps you sitting in yer seats?

BALLADEER: [Interrupting TOBY with a hill-billy type ballad.]
"Why don't you sing us the rest of your song?"
    The singer complained to his heart.
His hot heart replied: I could easy have lied
    and sung on well after my start,

"but the simple truth is my song's first note
    finds listeners then or never
and who hasn't heard my song's first word
    to my whole song's deaf forever.

"So look to transcend from your urge to depend,
    o singer, look to transcend:
for having made listeners once your need
    expect singing forever to end.

    "Expect singing forever to end
    or, singer, look to transcend...".

TOBY: Hate to get carried away that way. Inexcusable outbursts from a guy what kin look to transcend.

DELLA: Wonder what kinda transcendin' he means?

STELLA: Some folks always gotta be lookin' around to change things. Oughta let hell be.

MAY: [*Her bid for exclusive audience attention having finally exhausted itself, examining and taking in fully her fellow actors for the first time.*] Ya know, things are pretty weird around here, you people are jumpier than a cat, and that's exactly what makes me feel like I'm coming back as a cat.

TOBY: Good thing ya got plans to come back, May.

ROMEO: Whatcha mean, Toby?

TOBY: You thick or something'? Whatcha think Ah mean by sayin' good thing she's comin' back? Obviously, because she's goin' first. May got plans fer comin' back 'n Ah got plans fer May's goin' away.

DELLA: How pinpointed his eyes is when he says that!

TOBY: Wonder how she sees that, facin' so squarely downstage as she is. Hey, Dell—

STELLA: Pinpoint eyes, piercin' eyes, looks right through ya. Seems to be seein', seems to be searchin' through the secrets of yer cookie jar. Beautiful eyes. Deep set they are, very blue. Ocean blue. Wish I was by the ocean, wish this town was by the ocean, seems things wouldn't seem so bad then, not so bad at all if we was by the ocean. Miama maybe.

ROMEO: [*His overwhelming boredom giving vent to song.*]
The moon over Miama beach
ain't bright enought to really reach;
what wisdom it could have to teach
if the moon were no the Earth's light leech!

MAY: And he sings too!

DELLA: What a bargain.

TOBY: Lightless waves crashin' the beach, spittle ridin' the brackish breakers 'n sprayin' the landy shore. More 'n more. Washes everythin' clean, white-washes. Not like here in the desert, Dell, Stell: things preserve here in the desert, don't budge, stay stuck up right where ya bury them; don't even have to bury merry them: —nobody'll be to see—be by to see, *be* to see…no one stare to care, even care to stare for a second…second girl…

STELLA: Really pushes, don't he? 'n fer nothin'.

DELLA: Guess he's jist conscientious.

MAY: [*Stirring.*] I sense a strange conspiracy in the desert air—a room for doom in all things called, a calling, it's my calling in life…

TOBY: [*Reaching for the rock; singing.*]
"When I'm calling you-oo-oo-oo, oo-oo-oo-oo
Tangoing takes two-oo-oo-oo, oo-oo-oo-oo…"

MAY: The windy whisper of the saguaro and cholla slipping over the stated line inta Colorada as ever woman for her demon-lover wailed…

    MAY *begins to wander toward the desert upstage. She moves voluptuously beneath the line of the girder, comes dangerously close to* TOBY. TOBY *raises the heavy rock in his hands as* MAY *slips about him. The others tense up with a horror they are unable to feel or hear accurately and, therefore, express themselves. They be-come riveted to their chairs with ever-mounting inarticulate anxiety and guilt.*

ROMEO: May, hey, May, May hey, where ya goin'?

TOBY: Here, I'm here, my moving backward demented beauty…

STELLA: What's she wanderin' around out there on the desert fer?

DELLA: She must have wanderlust, wanderlust I call it…

ROMEO: May, ya wanna sausage sandwich, fried onions 'n peppas, let's get somethin' to eat, May, May, hey…

TOBY: My wife your life…

STELLA: May is maddening in the Utah desert: other places, other Mays have rigorous riots of violets to boast, this state has only the steady, hiatusless evergreen of the neurotically water-hoarding cacti to—

DELLA: Time was a body could detect the difference in the seasons here. But now I get confused, it's much on a May-December affair, time rushes and returns, autumn miscegenates with spring and winter abbreviates the vaguely sprawling limits of the central summer mon—

STELLA: Where is Ray, where the hell is that woman? Doesn't she give a hoot in the dell about her daughter? Shoot! Ray, Ray, ya shoppin' on Main, shootin' fer jack-rabbits, a-gamblin' at cards? Deal yerself out this dealin', Ray! ah, Ray!!

MAY: Wonder what blocks the nothing of night?—like a giant opuntia spanning the stretch twixt heaven 'n earth—[*She is standing directly under* TOBY, *touching him and trying to reach around him and beyond him into the space being drawn up into the vortex.*] O blissful dawning!

TOBY: One gambol more my cat, paw me now and leap to heights!

MAY: [*Taking a step back.*] What is it seems to alter now I'm near, alter form as the I of cat to something other, something not—

ROMEO: [*Grabbing a large bouquet of sunflowers.*] May, I got a present for ya—wanna see it? Wanna? Here! Here, I got—

MAY: Romeo?

ROMEO: [*Rushing across the stage at her.*] I got some—

MAY: Whatcha got? [*Stiffening into a near paralysis as* ROMEO *shoves the bouquet up into her face.*] Sunflowers?!!

TOBY: [*Hysterical.*] Romeo, you scum!!!

ROMEO *grabs* MAY; *she struggles with him as the rock hovers back and forth over her head, crying out in fear and confusion and pulling on* ROMEO's *"fashion-able" suspenders. The suspenders snap and* ROMEO's *trousers fall to the floor.*

MAY: [*Starting back.*] What's that??

TOBY *smashes the rock down into the empty space.*

ROMEO: [*Hesitantly; humiliated.*] A present?…

MAY: Idiot! Let me go! I'll tell my moth—

As both turn to look down at the rock, MAY's *mother,* RAY, *suddenly appears in the dark upstage.*

RAY: May, child, where are you? I told you never to go out!

ROMEO *lunges at* MAY, *pulling her to the ground; he tries to cover her, awkwardly entangled, as he is, in his trousers.*

ROMEO: Be still will ya, don't make a sound.

MAY: Get yer scabbed paws off me—

STRIPPER: [*Entering behind* RAY.] Toby, child, where are you?

ROMEO: Lay still! Ya jist can't go runnin' around gettin guys all horny 'n all 'n think nothin's gonna hap—ya awmost got killed by—

ROMEO *and* MAY *freeze as the* STRIPPER *comes slowly downstage.*

TOBY: I eat mostly outta cans, ma, when yer away. Don't even bother to heat 'em up eat everythin' cold, chili 'n soup 'n such.

STRIPPER: That's bad, Toby, growin' boy oughta get somethin' warm in his tummy. That cold stuffs ain't a-gonna do ya much good.

TOBY: [*Filling in his anger vein with a purple crayon.*] Bothers ya, does it, ma, that the level a ma eatin's hit rock bottom?

STRIPPER: Sure it does, son. Bothers me a whole lot. Whatcha wanna go 'n give extra care to yer workin' ma fer?

TOBY: Git booked for any action in Denver lately?

STRIPPER: Had one or two dates up there. Why?

TOBY: See paw?

STRIPPER: Now, son, I don't play that side a town. Class stuff, club dates, that's what I get.

TOBY: See paw?

STRIPPER: I don't—

TOBY: See paw? see paw?? see paw???!

STRIPPER: Now you go ahead 'n keep that kinda questionin' up 'n I ain't gonna come about here no more.

TOBY: What makes mah paw come about?

STRIPPER: Paws jist don't come about. They're what we makes 'em.

TOBY: But maws is different, right?

STRIPPER: That's right, son. Maws makes.

TOBY: Ya make a lotta men on the road, ma, between yer club dates, that is? Y'all fool around a lot?

STRIPPER: My, but you was a teeny stranger in the manger when you come. Never did see a wee crumb like that afore. Ya come afore yer time, a whole month, maybe two. Hard time I had Caesarean. Doc thought ya wouldn't make it thru that night, let alone that whole long cold winter. Winter's no much fun in Denver fer them what's layin' in. It's a pretty city, though, the downtown's like the downtown nowhere else, all neat 'n compact 'n clean. 'N the residential part, oh most a Denver *is* residential, runs out in straight avenues away from that downtown which I say is very perfect, a very model kinda place itself. Why, it's all as pretty as any pitcher ya seen a Washington!—Didja know I'm a little far sighted? That's right. Always was. Even in school. See real far into most anythin' happens down in our town. So I kin see real far down them avenues runnin' away from the downtown…

TOBY: Spend a lotta time on them avenues, huh? Them streets?

STRIPPER: I'm your mother, Toby. You can't hide anything from a mother.

TOBY: Why don't ya jist keep walkin', huh, ma, jist keep walkin'.

STRIPPER: Never had no beat-up customer ever seemed quite so defeated as—

TOBY: Hit the road!!

MAY: [*Breaking the freeze.*] Let me go now! Help! Help! Ma!

STELLA: [*Startled.*] Oh! God, where are our daughters?

DELLA: [*Rushing downstage.*] Give to "Save The Children Fund"! Save Rita! Oh, poor Rita, how is she? This is "Save Our Younger Souls Week"! Give, give, good people!!

TOBY: [*Singing a hymn that grows to Bible-belt fervor.*]

> *Give, good people*
> *what they think they want:*
> *perched upon the steeple*
> *waits oblivion!*

> *Give, give good people,*
> *now or never give*
> *to those near the steeple*
> *still got hopes to live.*

> *Gathered 'neath the steeple*
> *every fearful soul,*
> *give, give good people*
> *save them from the troll!*

RAY: [*Rushing downstage to* MAY.] I'll give you hell! May, a-comin' out here all alone without yer ma! Why, they got them mountain lions out here!

MAY: [*Yanked up by* RAY, *pulling away.*] I ain't afraid of cats, ma, I'm a cat, a cat, a cat!!!

RAY: You ain't alone neither! That freak is with you!

ROMEO: [*Pulling up his trousers.*] Now wait a minute, Mrs. Mixer, I ain't no freak.

RAY: Fiend! Freak-face! Double trouble! Triple trollop pocked-faced acne covered sex maniac! Child molester! Assault! Battery! Bombast! Billygoat! Belligerence! Bellicose!

DELLA: Bad, plain bad!

STELLA: Bad! Buxom! Blossom! Bloom! Boom! Doom! Death!

ROMEO: Yis is got me wrong—yis is a mixin' me up with old toad stool—why, if it wasn't fer me, May would be—

TOBY: [*Singing to a Country rhythm.*]

> *If it wasn't fer me*
> *May would be*
> *due in June—*
> *Croon, gardner, croon!*
> *Ya'd run around double*

to bust May's bubble,
find a sucker to pay
her abortion trouble!

Ah'm a top a mah stool
biggest toad in the pool,
gonna wait it out cool,
jist a-set in mah stool.
O, little pool with a big toad!
Little pool, yer done near outgrowed:
ah represents quite a awesome load
fer a little pool with a big toad!

> The STRIPPER *steps down wildly discarding her housecoat and adding new*
> *disorder to the scene; singing, dancing.*

STRIPPER:
Does yer engine need a battery?
Yer accelerator activity?
Does yer carburetor run on gas?
And slow ya down at hyman pass?

If I jack yer fender up for free,
will ya screw the rubber on for me?
Ease the brake, wax the brass,
slow down drivin', save my—

RAY: I know your type, Romeo Rancor, and you don't have to fib with me! I'm calling the police. The trouble around here is that too many folks let trash like you run around on the loose and have their way.

ROMEO: What way?

TOBY: This is the Way.

RAY: This is your way to waylay innocent girls who don't know the facts of life out here on the prairie!

STELLA: It's pretty scary, it's scary, scary!

STRIPPER: [*Resuming her singing after the rude interruption.*]
Yeah! The facts of life
are many as the days in May,
merry May! Yeah! Merry May!
Merry May you make your life!

Now a husband may be hard to hold,
a gal with a guy got more than gold:
but some out there ain't got no wife,

and so I'll list the facts of life
in a startling exposé
in the merry month of May!

The merry month of May!
The merry month of May, etc., etc.

MAY: [*As the music suddenly aborts.*] Oh, ma, stop embarrassing me. Of course I know
    the facts of life. I'm fifteen. 15, 14, 36. 'N 98 pounds. 'N 98 on every exam this semester.
ROMEO: Yer daughter needs protection from that—
RAY: You in the shakedown business too, sonny?
STELLA: [*Motivated merely by* ROMEO's *movement.*] Grab him, grab the pervert, the
    childless molester, don't let him bound outta sight quick as a quarter moon drops
    from the night!
TOBY: [*Indicating his dyed streak of hair.*] Hear that, Dell?—quarter moon's minded
    yet, never quite outta eye shot!
RAY: Hot shot! Let's go, Tonto!
ROMEO: Now jist a second!—hold yer horses.
STELLA: [*Rising to the occasion.*] Make our town safe for democracy!
RAY: Let's war to end all war!
DELLA: Keep the home fire burning! fire up, ladies, fire up!
RAY: Seize the scrubby tumbleweed!
        STELLA, DELLA *and* RAY *rush at* ROMEO *and a chase and struggle ensue; they*
    beat him with their pocketbooks, jab him with their knitting needles, pull his hair,
    tear at his shirt and kick and punch and pinch him. ROMEO *tries to elude them but*
    never strikes back. The STRIPPER *strips and sings during this capture scene, her*
    song being simple enough: she keeps presenting various aspects of her body to the
    audience and declaiming, "This is the first fact of life! This is the second fact of life!"
    etc., etc. (she also points out and underlines the injustice of the action), until she
    reaches the "twentieth fact" at the time that the three women are preparing to drag
    ROMEO *upstage "outta sight a the younguns."*
RAY: [*Ramming her rifle into him.*] Take the jut of my butt!
ROMEO: But—
DELLA: Stick, prick, knit up his raveled sleeve!
STELLA: Shake, shake, shake! Shake him up, shake him down!
RAY: Deal the dingo double trouble!
DELLA: Douse the dullard duely round!
STELLA: Sound the cry to curfew caution; meet the monster, match for scratch.
DELLA: Have fun, be done, the fun's begun!
ROMEO: I'm done fer!
STELLA: Make more of futile Mormons mum,
DELLA: By hacking *to* his parts his sum,
RAY: And pasting the pieces back with aplomb!

DELLA: Kill, crush, mix, mush!

RAY: Squeeze, tease, please yerself!

STELLA: Fix with tricks, confuse, abuse! Lust and dust, strike, hike the rents, rent his shirt!

ROMEO: Wait, wait! Leave us not get carried away now.

RAY: Carry him away upstage—outta sight a the younguns!

> *The music stops. The* STRIPPER *is pointing to the savage group with her line* "This is the thirtieth fact of life!" *The women pause in their violence and stare icily at her.*

TOBY: Stella, Della, Ray, let Romeo go!

STELLA: Never! We're sick a his Mormon immorality!!!

STRIPPER: *This* is the thirty-first fact of life!!

TOBY: But he is innocent. I am the cul—

DELLA: Whadda ya mean innocent? He was caught in flagrant delecto!

STRIPPER: Toby, child, come down from that chai—

TOBY: —Della, let me see your daughter!

DELLA: Wha—

TOBY: Let me see her *now*!!

DELLA: But she ain't come by yet, Tob. You askin' the impossible.

TOBY: Let me see Rita now!!

STRIPPER: Toby, child, come down from that chair!

> *The* BALLADEER *suddenly emerges into the midst of the crowd, singing a furiously paced hill-billy romp addressed directly to* TOBY.

BALLADEER:

> *Rita's a pretty gal 'n she's a-comin' soon,*
> *now we're in the month a May but that'll make it June:*
> *flowers are gonna grow, they got but ninety days—*
> *Rita's a-comin' soon, hallelujah! Praise!*

TOBY: Let me see Rita nowl!

> *The* BALLADEER *turns his tune to a southern gospel of highly refined melody. The crowd responds with a chorus that seems to argue liturgically with the* BALLADEER, *but they finally are won over and all join him for the final stanza.*

BALLADEER:

> *Wake the preacher, toll the bells*
> *Rita's comin' for to wed:*
> *like sweet laughter she dispels*
> *imagined dread.*

ALL:

> *Choose 'n lose,*
> *choose 'n lose,*
> *if life is his,*
> *death is whose?*
> *Choose 'n lose!*

BALLADEER:

    Call the people to the temples,
        leave the sheaves to bind themselves,
    Rita will replace our sandals
        like grace-full elves.

ALL:

    Choose 'n lose,
    choose 'n lose,
    if life is his,
    death is whose?
    Choose 'n lose!

BALLADEER:

    Dress as for the final fair
        where we'll bring our stock to test,
    roused to stand by trumpets' blare
        before the rest.

ALL:

    Choose'n lose,
    choose'n lose.
    If life is his,
    death is whose?
    Choose'n lose!

[Leaving the stage through various exits, except for TOBY.*]*

    Look away to where that bridge
        leaps across a life's ravine
    to an other, other-worldly ridge
        where Rita's seen.

ACT II

When Act II opens TOBY, *standing on his chair, begins to sing to a Country semi-sacred sound.* STELLA, DELLA, *and* RAY *are back upstage with* ROMEO, *tying him to the chair. In their midst and helping them to tie up* ROMEO *is* ACE, *a personable young man with a typewriter strapped to his back.* MAY *is in the* CROWD *watching the whole procedure with great fascination. Several* MUSICIANS *are on stage.*

TOBY:

> *I am death in life.*
> *I am death, so grim!*
> *When I take a wife*
> *her chances are thin!*
>
> *When I choose a gal in the grave to bury,*
> *after learning my choice she becomes quite merry!*
> *Yes, I am the killer of every girl dead—*
> *wanna count the number of daughters ya bred?*

ALL:

> *Toby's death in life,*
> *Toby's death, so grim!*
> *When he picks a wife*
> *her chances are slim!*

TOBY:

> *But I am the good,*
> *and the parent's the bad*
> *since children brought up have really been had: —*
> *hence I'm salvation when every girl's dead—*
> *wanna still have children amid such dread?*

ACE: [*Almost pontificating.*] Who slurs his song slurs trash. It's a sometime thing, nothing. But he who slurs his act's intent slurs what intends to make this town a unity— and cannot quit until it does.

STELLA: [*To* ACE.] Lemme have that rope, will ya?

ACE: Oh, er, certainly.

RAY: Ain't a one a these brats is up to behavin' like the good St. Theresa Genoacheese instructs. I tell ya, ain't a one a them's different!

227

ROMEO: But yer wrong, you ladies got me all wrong. I am different. I tell ya, I am different!

TOBY: No, no, I'm different!

MAY: I'm sensitive.

RAY: What does it matter?—They's all the same when their pants is hot.

ACE: She speaks fer the house.

STRIPPER: What house? Never worked in a house. Never even had a house.

STELLA: Ladies, ya wanna clean up them Vegas strippers around here.

ACE: Could go harder on yer beds if ya do.

RAY: Don't get cute. We'll attend to the morals problem in good time.

DELLA: Yes, we shall look into these strippers.

TOBY: 'N have a good time doin' i—

ROMEO: Please, hear me out! May is in danger! Grave danger!

STELLA: Not any more now that yer tied up!

ROMEO: Yer mistook! I love her: why should *I* hurt her?

RAY: A course you love her: that's why you attacked her: you love her and you wanted to make love to her! It's love we gotta watch out fer, girls, love that waylays our daughters 'n drags them off inta clumps a sage 'n tumbleweed fer a tumble!

DELLA: The lie of the land.

ACE: How powerfully she grasps that pithy substitute of land for lingo.

STELLA: Della's learned.

RAY: Was brung up in a convent, oughta be.

DELLA: Yeah, I oughta be.

TOBY: Oughta be run outta town with the rest a you guardians a public decency.

STELLA: We done our duty re Romeo as we seen it, right, Ray?

RAY: We are always right, Stella. What do you think, Della?

STRIPPER: Stella, Della, Ray.

DELLA: Let's notify the Department of Health, Education and Welfare, Stella.

RAY: Let's notify a nationally syndicated newspaper, Della. Pleasure or Kiss—or one a them.

STELLA: Let's notify the community bulletin board, Ray. Put it on the air, wake the town and scare the people.

RAY: Yeah, we'll spread it around. We'll spread it around.

TOBY: Mary, May, Maude. Stella, Della, Rayburn.

STRIPPER: And the thirty-second fact of life is that strippers get looked into...

ACE: Better beat it fer now, Miss.

RAY: We'll look inta this matter a the strippas 'n she don't!

TOBY: Wait, ma, when'll I see ya?

STRIPPER: Soon, sonny, soon. I'm booked fer a night in our town. [*To* ACE.] Be worth yer while to be here then. Ya come around here often?

ACE: Well, probably more often from now on.

STRIPPER: [*To* MUSICIANS.] See you boys over in Vegas. Gotta attend to dates in that vicinity. Bye, Toby, my boy. Nothin' comes easy.

TOBY: That it does.

> STELLA, DELLA, RAY, *and* MAY *take their seats as the* STRIPPER *exits.* ACE *takes a seat right in the middle of the women, removes his typewriter from his back, places it on his lap, puts paper into it, and prepares to type.* RAY *hangs onto her rifle and* DELLA *takes up her knitting.* STELLA *is restless, she can't seem to sleep.* MAY *reads* Playboy, Screw, Kiss, *etc.*

DELLA: Wonder if Lana's in bed now. Poor Lana, had some kinda paralysis when she was little.

ACE: Poor Rita.

DELLA: Wonder if Rita's in bed now…

STELLA: Had some kinda paralysis when she was little, didn't she, Dell?

MAY: What did ya tie Romeo up that way for, ma?

ACE: Why, May, child, we done it fer Romeo's own good. You know Romeo can't sleep unless he's tied up spread-eagle to his bed on account a he is conditioned that way since he was a child and had leprosy and had to be tied up and restrained from scratchin' hisself durin' the bydee-by hours a the night, scratchin' all them awful sores, unsightly sores, and we did want him to catch a bit a bydee-by, he's had a long preventful day, Romeo has.

RAY: [*To* ACE] Who the hell are you?

ACE: Who the hell am I? Ain't no mere morbid curiosity seeker, I kin tell ya that much, madam!

DELLA: [*Automatically, without looking at* ACE] He's my son-in-law…or future son-in-law?

ACE: Future son-in-law.

STELLA: Elaborate.

MAY: [*Bored to the point of suicide.*] Oooooooooo…!

ACE: Name's Andrew Ace, reporter, came out here to do a story on that lethal gas leak in the stock piles. Six thousand sheep croaked, notice they never say nothin' 'bout how many people? That was to be my job.

RAY: How absorbing.

ACE: Anyhow, met Rita when I come out here, fell quickly in love, and I will marry her.

STELLA: Ya really a reporter?

ACE: Is the pope Catlick?

RAY: That's anough about him, now me.

DELLA: Whatcha bag today, Ray?

RAY: [*Standing and lifting up a heavy burlap sack.*] Side from Romeo, git me this real big she-lion. Right between the—but, ssh, I don't want May to hear.

TOBY: Hear that, May, yer ol' bag bagged a big cat today. Didja drag it across to the viaduct—[*Pointing to the diagonal girder.*]

RAY: Yup, 'n tossed it on over inta the Red River right side a Romeo—[*She heaves the burlap sack over the girder; it clears the height and come crashing down on* ROMEO.] Wake the hell up! Look at that—a-sleepin' on the job!!

ROMEO: [*Bombarded into wakefulness.*] "Maytime, Maytime, Maytime…"

MAY: [*Pulling on* RAY's *sleeve, almost fighting to bring* RAY *back to the chair, fighting to ensure the immobility that will allow the murders to proceed.*] Sssssssh, set ye down, mine lover earned his sleep! Sleep did come on him a just reward much as the Maytime thaw pours on the penitent wintry scrub in patient wait within the plain below.

TOBY: Bellow. Listen to him bellow.

DELLA: Romeo bellows in his sleep for his lady love.

RAY: [*Giving up, sitting down.*] And quiet steals upon the town…[*Mumbling to herself.*] need some action around here…

STELLA: Toby steals, too. Or so I heard tell. Steals his opportunities from the jaws of stiff competition…

RAY: Steals personal keepsakes, tips from barroom counters…

MAY: Steals girls' hearts with his deep, meaningful eyes…

RAY: Hush, child, do not speak of amorous matter.

TOBY: [*Toying with the hair curler and paper clamp that he has been using to pinch his anger vein.*] Stella, Della, Ray. Mary, May, Maude. Oh, "M 'n M" over "M," I know how to make love a hundred different ways. Mom, I *have* made love a hundred different ways. Everything I do is an act of love, each inch I grow a testimony to my arch triumph. Look, this blackish beauty: —it is huge this purpleblack and beautiful anger vein isn't it? Why would a man raise such a vein upon his pisser if not for love, in the libel of love, as the label of love, because of it, his wanting it, and this black vein of anger is it, is *love,* furious, unicorn and phallic. The people know it, too. Ah, yes, everyone in and on the edge of town knows it. People on the edge of a town. Verging. Precisely why they claim I'm too short, ill-founded claim, unripe, still verging, that claims I can't tip-toe up enough to bend me down a bunch of grapes of grafted love. Sweet grapes of grafted love. Because the labor in matching my reach, in reaching up to reach my reach is not a labor of love for them. Everything seems easier to them—the jump to conclusions, the sealing of the holy books, manhunts, murder trials, death in a family…But I shan't be caught by that, caught short by that, hunted, murdered, tried to a man and put to death. Were I caught short by such as that I had not ever have reached the height I have. And I have reached a height above the groveling mass, the black beauty mass of which I am the solitary priest. So say I my said say and, having said, know everybody knows it.

MAY: Knows what?

TOBY: Knows how a self-made man thru painful thought knows how love may be made in a hundred different ways. Slaying, fer inst—

MAY: The hell! Yer the original Mormon monk. You probably levitate in yer cell you've got so much repressed.

TOBY: Ain't you sweet.

ACE: Sweets to the sweeties, farewell.

STELLA: Farewell, my Mary, farewell.

MAY: He said to the *sweeties*—call Mary a sweetie?

STELLA: Oh, you stir my blood!

ACE: As spring stirs frozen lakes. What an Easter downpour penetrates our unprepared young prairie. Stella, Della, Ray.

MAY: But I get bored even at Toby's pad—

ACE: [*Typing.*] True. She's sick a all that sweet talk—

DELLA: 'n flippin' thru *Playboy*—they call it adolescent melancholia—

MAY: sick a flippin', sick a the flip sides those same ol' Enis Penis records, sick a sippin' beer, beer brewed with clear mountain valley water.

RAY: She oughta be sick considerin' all that sick litracha she devours like it was candy or somethin'. Readin' rots the brain. Specially that chambermaid crap.

MAY: Oh, ma.

TOBY: I read this novel once, "Hair Today, Gone to Merkin."

ACE: [*Typing.*] 'Bout a chick gets a bright idea 'n commits suicide over this guy.

TOBY: I always dreampt a havin' a chick git the idea 'n commit suicide over me—that would be absolute, that would be proof!

DELLA: Well, gals are slow to that kinda romanticism these days, Toby, sometimes they have to be helped along.

TOBY: I'll help them along. Specially blondes like Maude the frump. That fat frump's my trump card.

MAY: [*Vicious.*] Toby *dyed* Maude's hair blonde. Also dyed Maude's kid sister, Lynn's, hair blonde. Went out 'n got engaged to both a them on the same day.

TOBY: I bought them both diamond engagement rings, fer five bucks each. 'N courted 'em with songs would break any gal's heart. [*Taking the mike, singing to Country sacred music:*]

> *If I found a gal I could call a real gal,*
> *could be my disciple, my wife, 'n my pal,*
> *I'd go out in the desert on bare blistered feet*
> *and there gather manna fer my gal to eat.*

>> *I'd rain holy bread from the heavens for her*
>> *light as the hoar frost under the fir,*
>> *rare as the coriand, price beyond money,*
>> *with a taste like wafers, mead, 'n bees' honey.*

> *If I knew a gal, jist one perfect gal,*
> *could match what I feel, 'n love what I shall,*
> *I'd go out in the desert on torn, bleeding feet*
> *and there gather manna fer my gal to eat.*

>> *I'd rain holy bread from the heavens for her*
>> *light as the hoar frost under the fir,*
>> *rare as the coriand, price beyond money,*
>> *with a taste like wafers, mead, 'n bees' honey.*

If I had a gal, a madonna-like gal,
could dress in my clothes 'n nurse my morale,
I'd fill up an omer of manna for her
and generations that in her stomach shall stir.

> MAUDE, *a high school tramp, enters, followed by* LYNN, *her pre-adolescent sister. Both have badly dyed blonde hair.*

MAUDE: [*Flaunting her ring.*] I think girls are dumb fools who go out with fellas 'n don't git paid for it.

TOBY: Hi ya, Maude. That there's Maude. I'd like to kill her.

LYNN: [*As everyone laughs.*] My big sister Maude once showed at a formal with a bunch a guys all dressed up like beatniks. That's guts. Maude's dreamy. She cuts classes 'n got recommended fer Psychiatric help.

TOBY: Hi ya, Lynn.

LYNN: Hello up there, fiancé. Didja set the date yet?

TOBY: Today, little Lynn, today I think.—I'd dig killin' her, too. Her youth 'n all, it'd have shock value. But I need help, the same in the beginning was with God, the *Word* was with God, and *I,* also, need a particeps criminis: I can't reach them sistas from a Way up here.

MAUDE: You still dribblin' off at the mouth, shrimpo?

TOBY: Are you my gal, Maude?

MAUDE: Natch, Toby, we're engaged, ain't we?

TOBY: Who ya goin' with now, Maude?

MAUDE: Bad Butch.

> BAD BUTCH, *a huge hell's angel type with a lion's head sewn to the back of his jacket, comes bounding in.*

BUTCH: Mah label's Bad Butch, Big Bad Butch, very big on the strip 'n with the babes. It's mah get-up gets 'em. They's impressed with the motif—this here fierce a face King a the Beasts. Grrroooowwwllll!!! Heh, heh, heh heh! Ah am more than a small town figger 'n figger that makes this more 'n a small town. Ah am a symptom a what this country's comin' to. 'N Ah think it's comin' to this small town.

ACE: [*Getting up and going to* BUTCH *with a pencil and writing pad in hand.*] Lo, there, son. I really dig yer bikecap 'n maltese cross 'n them holsters with knives stead a pistols.

DELLA: I'm really crazy 'bout them jab-em-in-the-flanks hundred per cent silva spurs on his loafers, m'self.

ACE: Son, I'm tryin' to locate Toby Short. Think ya kin help me out?

BUTCH: Why, Ah'm surprised at you, buckaroo! Would *Ah* know the lo-ca-shun a a unsavory type like Toby Short?

RAY: Would *he* know the lo-ca-shun a a unsavory type like Toby Short?

ACE: Well, would you?

BUTCH: Is a matter a fact Ah would, Ah sure would, Sir Dick.

ACE: Yes?

BUTCH: Folla that there girder what counteth the steps a the sun, git off afore the vortex 'n then carry ya inquisitive self right round under it. After that, he's straight ahead, ya can't miss him.

ACE: [*Exiting.*] Thanks, fella.

TOBY: Thanks, Butch.

RAY: Hey, that there's the way to the dressin' rooms. Toby's out here!

BUTCH: No kiddin'? Ya'd never believe it from the way you ladies behave. Ah coulda sworn he was down in them dressin' rooms. [*Dropping a coin in a wall phone on the girder.*] Hello, operator? Put me in to the Attorney General .

TOBY: What fer?

BUTCH: What fer? Ah got some dope on a creep round here been doin' gals in. Figger thar's quite a reward. No sense lettin' some outsider git it. [*As* TOBY, *with minimum effort, cuts the phone wires.*] Name's—hello, operator? operator??

TOBY: So ya goin' with Bad Butch, eh Maude? Now he could be a help steada a—

MAUDE: Whatcha mean a help? Ain'tcha jealous? Listen here, I don't want ya allowin' me to go out with other goons before or after we're married neither, I want ya to ring me up 'n bring me up records 'n chocolates stuffed with stale jam. I can't stand it when ya ferget 'n I don't take after yer always bein' busy neither. I'm suspicious of you.

TOBY: [*Calculating, both staring at* BUTCH *wrestling with the phone.*] That's groovy, Maude…Seen yer shrink lately?

MAUDE: Ain't nobody kin shrink me down to yer size.

STELLA: Toby and Maude were made fer each other.

MAY: He'd have made that maid if maid there was to have made.

MAUDE: Hi, May. Where's Romeo?

MAY: He's tied up at the moment.

DELLA: Is that supposed to be clever?

MAY: Oh, why don't you go back to county-fair chorus lines—or can't you kick anymore?

MAUDE: That there's May. I'd as soon see her dead as anything. Why not?

ROMEO: [*Groaning in his sleep.*] May! May! May's in bad trouble, she's…girls gits into…trouble…

TOBY: True. Maude's a harlot. I suspect she got venereal disease.

STELLA: [*Shocked.*] Why, Toby, I'm shocked!—What makes you think so?

TOBY: Well, is it cancer makes yer zippo look like a Grunewald? Anyhow, I wrote a letter to the Department a Health 'n informed them that Maude was contaminated 'n spreadin' it all around town.

DELLA: Ya done yer duty, son, above 'n beyond the call a a fascist state.

RAY: In his way, Toby *does* set an example.

STELLA: Sure, there *is* some kinda contamination in this town even if it's only syph 'n someone must be a-spreadin' it.

MAUDE: I'd give him syph. I'd give him anything. Why not? He's my man.

TOBY: Maude, kin ya reach Big Butch fer me?

MAUDE: I ain't no messenger service. Reach fer him yerself. Why don'tcha git off that there chair so ya kin reach him yerself?

TOBY: [*Deeply hurt.*] Thanks, Maude. Hey, Lynn—

ROMEO: [*In his sleep.*] May, poor May, look out!

TOBY: Wanna help me out?

LYNN: [*Sympathetic.*] Awww, right a way, romantic Toby. I'll reach Butchy-boy for you. Stay put.

TOBY: Mercies, Lynn, yer a real trooper. And I shall reward you for this.

　　　　　LYNN *skips over to* BAD BUTCH, *completely entangled in the phone.*

BUTCH: [*Lecherous.*] Ya old enough to date now, Lynn?

LYNN: Sure, but I'm a-spoke fer by Toby. 'N he's a-waitin' on ya.

BUTCH: Kin Ah gitcha somethin', Sir Tob?

TOBY: A rope'd go good.

ROMEO: Wanna git me a glass a water, May? Like Esmeralda? 'N while ye at it some suave fer me sores?

BUTCH: [*Attracted by* ROMEO's *moans.*] One rope a-comin' up!

LYNN: [*As* BUTCH *unties a rope binding* ROMEO's *hand.*] It's a goof to go out with other guys while yer engaged. Specially if they're older. 'N big!

BUTCH: Is this hemp to order, Tob? If in knot, I'll—

TOBY: Great, Butch, that'll more 'n do. Give it here, will ya?

BUTCH: [*Withholding the rope.*] Straightaway. Whatcha got in mind?

TOBY: I'll ask the questions, babe. Yer ma inferior 'n while ya are I'm still runnin' this outfit 'n this here town, too. Git it?

BUTCH: Little bit too well; but you don't; not the rope at any rate. Ah don't take no stiff uppa lip offa anyone, Tob, not even stiff-on-the-brain you, Tob. Here, Lynn, Ah'm givin' ya 'nougha the rope to—[*Giving the rope to* LYNN.]

TOBY: You don't seem to git the hang of i—

STELLA: [*Agitated, getting up and coming down to the edge of the stage.*] I hired private dicks on this case. No one lays much by it, but the way I've got it figgered out ma little girl has come to foul play, even as you have—come to a foul play. Strickly Inge-fringe. Foul because it breaks your trust, bigots your openness, and on point after point loses its patience with you; is seldom humble and almost never willing to accept its position as the most humiliating feat a group of people could be part of and hope to profit from: placing themselves before an unsuspecting public that is right to have every right not to be lectured to. The implicit assumption in pieces like this is that "our town" is always and necessarily wrong. Well, it jist ain't necessarily so. There's a rightness to things as all things go, and only the small of heart, like certain immature and impotent plays say no.

RAY: Some crust, huh? Anyhow, Stella's privately-hired dicks've been hangin' out around Toby's Hollywood-style furnished pad a-lookin' fer a lead. Once a beer can come flyin' out the window 'n hit one a them in the head. That made 'em suspicious.

BUTCH: While Ah don't know much on it, yer a bit a boilin' oil, Sir Tob, some powerful strange tough guys been upta yer place. They seems to be suspicious.

TOBY: They *are* suspicious. But then why hang out around my place? I'm here.

STELLA: Them dicks'll find somethin', I know they will, they'll find out what happened to ma little girl 'n if she was assaulted first afore it happened. Sheriff claims she jist run away, but I know fer sure that's not sure. The truth lays somewhere else. I have a premonition. I have supper on now. [*Taking her seat.*]

DELLA: Stell's got a premonition 'n she's got every right to it: — makes it more proper to claim her high school-aged daughter come by foul play than to admit she jist up 'n run away. And we women in this here town is nothin' if we ain't respectable.

RAY: Well we other women ain't so sure about you. Y'all hallucinate a lot, ya know?

TOBY: Wanna do me a favor, Butch, 'n—

BUTCH: Not if Ah kin do ya dirt with as little Hell's Angel effort!

TOBY: Son of a butch! ya couldn't. Hold old Lynn upta me. That's the minimum effort I kin imagine ya makin'.

BUTCH: Well, why didn't ya behest such request before? Nothin' could give more a a cheap thrill—her tiny jist-breakin' nubile bubs in the champagne cups a mah callused palms—

LYNN: Except hold me lower. My knees!

> BUTCH *sweeps* LYNN *off her feet and, holding her high, offers her to* TOBY. LYNN *has the rope in her hand. The women watch the scene with approval.* MAY *is drinking beer.*

LYNN: Weeeeee…what a ride! I kin fly like a angel.

TOBY: Hello, angel.

LYNN: Hi ya, Toby, didn't know you was a angel, too. I always wondered what the air was like up in the clouds around you short fellas.

TOBY: And what, Angelica, do you discover it to be analogous to now that you've finally made the flight?

LYNN: Oh, it ain't much different from the air everybody else down in town breathes.

TOBY: [*Reaching, unsuccessfully, for her,* BUTCH *pulling slightly away.*] That's what I want to hear.

LYNN: Ya know, Toby, you ain't so special, even if I did accept yer proposal…

TOBY: [*Taking the rope from her hand.*] I know that, Lynn -chin .

RAY: Will ya look at that: —the creep's got a heart a gold.

DELLA: Takes time out to play rope with the little girl from down the street.

STELLA: Plays real nice he does, has a real way with the ladies don't matter what their age.

RAY: Has a good heart that creep. Little girl's no bigger 'n he is.

BUTCH: Ah tried to contact the Attorney General 'bout yer idiomsyncratic activities, Tob.

TOBY: [*Fixing the rope around* LYNN's *neck.*] You would, Butch, it's jist like you, babe.

BUTCH: They hung up the phone on me though, Tob.

TOBY: They would, Butch, it's jist like them, babe.

ROMEO: [*Tossing wildly.*] May! Beat it! Beat it outta town! Make yer getaway good!

BUTCH: [*Frightened.*] Ol' Rom! him 'n his idiomsyncratic sleepin' habits: he don't let no one turn in once he's been turned in.

TOBY: [*Garroting* LYNN.] Lynn-chin gonna have a hung chin.

RAY: [*Still watching.*] There'll be a hung jury over this.

MAY: [*Getting high.*] How's the family, Maude?

MAUDE: [*Eating chocolates.*] Home hangs me up, ya know that, Maude.

MAY: I'm hip, May.

TOBY: [*Conjugating, funereally.*] Mary, May, Maudlin. Stella, Della, Rayburn. From cloud to clod in half the time; no grease, no grime…

> TOBY *slowly releases* LYNN, *letting her limp body lie in* BUTCH's *arms. The suddenness of her death leaves* BUTCH *incredulous.*

MAY: I'd look back in hanger if I was you, Maude. I'd turn around 'n look back after my fiancé if I was you. Never could tell but when he'd be flyin' high with other birds. Birds baby-faced, younger, not yet broke in, not yet broke down. Down. Down…

MAUDE: Don't need all a yer experience, sista, jist to know howda hang onta a guy.

> ACE, *wearing a reporter's fedora and scratching his head with incomprehension, comes wandering back around the vortex.*

ACE: Hey, hang on there, you kids—mind if I shoot some questions at ya?

MAUDE: Who're you?

ACE: Andrew Ace, reporter, a outta space reporter, from—

MAUDE: Why don'tcha fly back to outta space! We git any cash fer gittin' grilled?

ACE: It's worth more 'n one pizza to ya. Know anythin' about a kid named Toby said to have a black anger vein he developed by standin' on his hands till it showed, then pinchin' it fer several hours a day with a tin curler or clipboard clamp?

RAY: Sure. Toby's anger vein's plain as the fed fedora on yer head. Why, even Toby kin probably spot that there fed fedora ya sport.—Stell, lay ya five to ten Toby can.

STELLA: I ain't the sportin' type.

TOBY: But *I* am: —listen here: [*Singing a hill-billy tune.*]

> *I'm gonna pay fer crimes I ought've done,*
> *gonna fry fer what I didn't do!*
> > *You force me,*
> > *you folks all force me!*
> *If I stop now you folks kin shun*
> *all the work that I've begun—*
> > *I've jist begun,*
> > *I'm a dreamer too.*

ALL:

> *Ol' salt a Salt Lake City*
> *he gits down to the nitty-gritty*
> *he don't waste a tear a pity*
> *even if the gal is pretty:*
> > *no salty tear—*
> > *salt a Salt Lake City!*

TOBY:

> *I'm gonna pay fer crimes I ought've done,*
> *gonna fry don't matter what I do:*
> > *you'll fry me,*
> > *o yes, you'll fry me!*
> *If what I want's not easy won,*
> *all the more it's gonna stun—*
> > *I've jist begun.*
> > *I'm a dreamer too.*

ALL:

> *Ol' salt a Salt Lake City*
> *he gits down to the nitty-gritty*
> *he don't waste a tear a pity*
> *even if the gal is pretty:*
> > *no salty tear—*
> > *salt a Salt Lake City!*

BUTCH: Greetin's, Sir Andrew *Report*-tage, you has the look a the Inevitable on yer newspaper puss. How goes it with that mass medium up in Big Town, USA?

ACE: Takes all of a mass medium to deal with a mass murderer, a murderer fer the masses, a chocolate fer their sweet tooth.

MAY: [*Quite high.*] Toby's gonna turn *our* town into Big Town!

STELLA: Turn the eyes 'n ears a the nation on us.

ACE: All you folks is knee-deep in hot water lemme tell ya that right now! Willful withholdin' is called criminal neglect, ya know.

BUTCH: We know, 'n it's yer yella-daily what puts us there.

ACE: I know, 'n it's yer blatant confessional no-holes-barred song what's put me *here*.

TOBY: Put Lynn down.

BUTCH: We're trapped by the Word! Done in afore we even gits a start by a lotta language, Tob!

TOBY: I'm hip.

BUTCH: [*Threatening.*] So don't write nothin' ya hear? Not if ya wanna git outta Utah with yer fed fedora on whatcha'd still wanna call a head!

ACE: Such a thing as freedom a the press, bully, I'll exploit what I want when—

BUTCH: Ah'll folla ya, Ah'll smoke ya out wherever ya go, Sir Andrew, 'n Ah'll cripple yer scribblin' hand sure as Ah'm wearin' Luftwaffe wings!

ACE: Relax! take it easy, no harm intended.

STELLA: Graveyard's cluttered with corpses come there no harm intended.

DELLA: [*Deeply distressed.*] My poor brother, his last letter afore he was shot—

RAY: [*Fed up.*] She gonna start up agin!

ACE: [*To* MAUDE.] Kin I stand ya to a pizza, girlie?

RAY: You been standin' enough! [*Removing* ACE's *fedora and slamming him on the head with her rifle; he falls into a chair.*] Try sittin' a little. Got a rope, Stell?

STELLA: [*Pulling the rope off* LYNN's *neck and helping* RAY *to tie* ACE *to the chair.*] This one a them outside agitaters, eh, Ray?

RAY: Yup! Sheriff'll run him outta town in the mornin'. Upta us to keep him static as the resta us till then.

BUTCH: [*Looking with amazement at the devastation the townswomen are capable of bringing so quickly about.*] Poor agitaters, they really don't do nothin' except use a lotta language.

TOBY: Ya wanna live up to a lotta language used in your behalf…somehow ya do…

DELLA: Or half of it. And the changes it makes in you. I feel blue.

> *As they all retake their seats the focus comes to rest for a strange moment on* BUTCH *with the body of* LYNN *still in his large arms. After a while he mutters to himself.*

BUTCH: Ya was such a wee li'l new 'n nubile thing. Nobody'd even laid ya yet.

TOBY: Put her on the floor, Bleedin' Heart. Right here.

BUTCH: [*Placing the body at the foot of* TOBY's *chair*] Whatcha gonna do with her?

TOBY: Nothin'. Jist leave her here, will ya. It looks like she's sleepin'.

BUTCH: Seems like somethin' oughta be done. So young.

TOBY: What fer? Lotta wasted initiative. Got better things to do.

BUTCH: Yeah ?

TOBY: Walk her sister over here.

BUTCH: Oh, no, not me! Not me again! Ya can't fool me twice!

TOBY: I'm *squarin'* with ya same as I am with everyone else! Now take that fat frump—

BUTCH: Never!

TOBY: I really don't need ya that much, Butch. She'll come by herself if it comes to that.

MAUDE: I kin come by myself if it comes to that…

TOBY: So ya might as well bring her. It'll give ya a sense a accomplishment.

BUTCH: Watcha mean ya don't need me? I'm yer sidekick, yer side-line in life, yer by-line in the papers, yer doin' all this jist to impress me counta Ah'm the only one kin be aware a it. Then ya kin read yer own sense a accomplishment in Hell's mirror!

TOBY: It is in the nature a the sense a accomplishment to have to read it somewhere. Please, take Maude's hand 'n strollin' her arm 'n arm—

BUTCH: Ah ain't no gigolo!

TOBY: I didn't think ya were. You shouldn't think ya are, either. Ya oughta think a yerself as a escort or a companion a destiny.

DELLA: You oughta think of yourself.

MAY: I think I'd attend to my fiancé if I was—

MAUDE: But you ain't!—Er, think I'll see what my Toby's up to.

RAY: Everybody's thinkin.

BUTCH: [*As* MAUDE *crosses by him.*] Hey, Maude, fancy runnin' inta you!

DELLA: Huh! He was expectin' ya.

MAUDE: What fer?

TOBY: Kinda hard to explain.

BUTCH: [*Taking her arm in arm.*] Yeah, ya wouldn't undastand.

TOBY: Oh, she'll under-stand. Jist might not appreciate it, that's all. Too unsohphisticated. Takes some body really on top of it to appreciate the senseless.

DELLA: Oh, I think it makes a lotta sense.

MAUDE: Who ya callin' senseless?

TOBY: Nobody whose thickness I couldn't knock a little sense inta. Come on, I'll knock ya up here.

MAUDE: [*Stepping over her sister's corpse,* TOBY *pulling her up on his chair with a single jolt*] What wit.

> ROMEO *snaps out of his sleep and discovers his unbound hand. He begins to unite the remaining ropes in wild agitation.*

ROMEO: May, blonde May! Toby's stranglin' her!! Hey, look, the ropes is loose, jist like in a serial.

TOBY: How are ya, sweetie? Yer my favorite, know that don't ya?

MAUDE: Feel kinda even, Toby, even with ya, with a lotta names flashin' thru my head, names you know, a series of names like during a orgasm.

TOBY: I know. A series of names. A string of words. Jist a string of—now, easy, Maude, take it easy 'n this won't take long—[*He presses his thumb on her windpipe.*]

MAUDE: Take yer time; I got all my life nothin' much else to do in this here town anyway…

MAY: I'll say—lessen ya wanna jist keep makin' out.

RAY: Y'all mean like them two? Ya oughta know better 'n that, May.

STELLA: Thank heavens I didn't bring up my Mary so's she'd carry on like that there proxide blonde.

DELLA: They sure go at it kinda rough, don't they? Kids!

MAY: Oh, you parents talk the dullest tripe! Yer conversation really smells.

BUTCH: [*Sniffing.*] Lynn's stiff is beginnin' to stink.

TOBY: It is human to smell; when we're dead we smell more; that means that when we're dead we're more human; that's why I don't have no compunctions about killin' people: that's why I'd like to be dead myself.

BUTCH: That's jist great but what are ya goin' to do with Lynn's stiff? Ah'm tellin' ya, it really stinks.

TOBY: We'll dump it in the trunk a my car. My *groovy* car. We'll dump Maude's stiff in there too soon as I'm finished stranglin' her. That's the most obvious cache I kin think of 'n I want them in the most obvious cache of all cause I jist don't care any more. I kin always ditch the car, groovy though it is, 'n wipe the chrome clean.

MAY: Ditch the bitches.

TOBY: O moment that exquisites!

> MAUDE *screams—a blood-curdling shriek that shakes the stage.* ROMEO *breaks into the semi-circle of chairs. He flies from one confused person to the next. Each is weakly wavering between ignoring the crime and turning slightly toward it.*

ROMEO: Help police! posse! sheriff! help! Toby's—Tob—Roby's murderin' May!

RAY: [*Taut.*] Don't be silly, Bad Butch, May's a-settin' here.

ROMEO: It's me—Romeo!

MAY: It's me, May!

RAY: It's thee, Romeo: —wherefor wert thou?

ROMEO: Asleep! 'N tied up to ma sleep like all the citizens in our town.

STELLA: Don't you be a-goin' around makin' them trashy irresponsible accusations. We's all quite awake 'n tryin' to do our duty as citizens, do the most dutiful accordin' to our duty accordin' to how we sees it.

ROMEO: Well, see it! See it! Yer duty's to open yer eyes 'n hearin' ears 'n discriminate what's a-happenin'!

RAY: Discriminate?

ROMEO: Oh, look! Look up there!

DELLA: Look at what? At _____ [*Using the actor's real name.*] We seen him before, seen him at damn near every rehearsal.

ROMEO: Look what he's doing!!

STELLA: What's he doing? Does that damn near every night 'bout this point.

RAY: Yeah, why should we look? What's in it fer us 'cept concedin' the scene to him?

MAY: [*Her sense of stage-hogging reignited.*] Ma's right. What's the profit?

ROMEO: Toby's killin' a girl!!!

STELLA: Maybe.

ROMEO: [*Shrieking.*] BUT HE'S KILLING HER!!!

   MAUDE *is dead.* TOBY *begins calmly to lower her corpse. The crowd freezes completely, stares dead ahead into the audience.*

STELLA: Feel frozen here. How very much a working day of life this is to sit so still while rodeos of America Hysterica ben-hur around our head.

DELLA: Stiff-heck, *that's* what it is…never had such a bad 'n stiff stiff-neck like this afore …must've caught a cross-ventilation draft in the drive-in the-a-ter the other nigh…

MAY: Downed a draught in the beer parlor the other night. Was hard to balance on the chair once the beer got hold a my brain. Was jist the other night…Last night, maybe it was. : The thirty-first of May.

TOBY: That was your last night, May. *Your* month's run out. Goodbye.

MAY: [*In a trance.*] Goodbye, Toby. Goodbye, ma. Goodbye, Romeo. It's June now.

ROMEO: [*Frantic.*] But May—

MAY: [*Emphatic.*] I said, it is June now.

   As in a sudden dispersal of clouds, the lights go up on the top of the girder that rises from TOBY's *chair and bends over the circumference of the vortex. There, at the pinnacle, stands* RITA. *She has an absolutely other-worldly appearance.* DELLA *is brushed by the strange light and turns her face slowly toward* RITA, *reaching for the blue cloak as she does so.*

DELLA: Wanna get over one day soon 'n see that there monument they erected for…my brother…

RAY: Erected, huh?

DELLA: [*Standing and moving toward* RITA *as* RITA *begins to descend the girder.*] 'N I'll take Rita along with me I will. Hello Rita. I've got yer cloak.

RAY: Her brain's decayed. I'm tellin' ya, her brain's really decayed.

ROMEO: [*Weeping with rage.*] What's goin' on around here? Don'tcha all hear me? Do something for God's sake!!!

TOBY: Is there something for God's sake, or will God punish me no matter?

DELLA: [*Fixing the long cloak around* RITA's *shoulders.*] God punishes you, Toby, when ya try to hide from Him like Cain. Gotta stand up 'n out in the light where He kin see ya 'n judge ya at yer doin's 'n at the intent of yer supplications. Oughta supplicate to Him all the time: —Now I lay me—

RITA: Down to doom, down to drown in the salt lake.
With sea salt and tears are mine eyes crusted o'er.
Closed as the muscles that barnacle the shore.

TOBY *and* RITA: [*Together.*] Down from the straight-back chair on the stairway to God,
My heart is in the Heavens but my sandals are in the sod.
Mighty Moses might mount high, there listen and call,
Yet could write nothing but his own word, then turn round and fall.

STELLA: [*Seeing* RITA.] An angel caught round with sashes of gilt drops from the sky, descends our only steeple needle, comes down directly counterpoint to our steeple's ever narrowin' point.

DELLA: We're a-narrowin' down to the point.

ROMEO: [*Seeing* RITA; *transfixed.*] Look, look at her above that Dali chair that on the desert thrives. She is the angel he makes of all thy daughters' lives!

RAY: [*Seeing nothing.*] His infatuation for my daughter hath caused him wax poetic. License like that, Romeo, malicious speculation, kin ruin innocent people's lives.

RITA: Yet we are all, all of us innocent, the guilty along with the mad.

TOBY: For we know not what we do, neither her selves nor my self.

RITA: Neither for our names' sake, our mothers', nor the Lord's.

BUTCH: [*Fastidiously arranging the bodies of the sisters at the base of* TOBY's *chair.*] Sorta hard to git 'em really even-steven, Sir Tob, seein' as how one is so much shorter in measure from the other. The virgin's not nearly as long as the frump.

This scene of tensely confused attentions is suddenly splintered by the appearance of the STRIPPER, *dressed in modest street clothes. She bursts into shattering song:*

STRIPPER:
I'm gonna take it off,
I'm gonna doff my garb,
I'm gonna show yis what I got
like it or not!
Hey! Hey! Hey!
Look, if yis can—
Look! Look! Look!
Look! If yer a man!

'*Standing above, and pointing to, the bodies of the sisters. The crowd pulls away from her.*

I'm gonna pull off the mask—
that's my task,
then I'm done.
I'm gonna show ya two bodies:
My own 'n my son's!
Hey! Hey! Hey!
Look, if yis can—
Look! Look! Look!
Look, if yer a man!

STELLA: Oh, how disgusting— I can't look!

The stripping music suddenly aborts. RITA *has reascended the girder above* TOBY's *chair and is standing on the platform that joins the two girders. She begins to sing a sad and melodic Country ballad . The* MUSICIANS *accompany her, very softly at first. As she sings,* RITA *slowly strides the diagonal girder, reaching its end downstage right as she finishes her song. The movement of the blue cloak over her arms gives the uncanny impression of the wings of an angel wounded by man. The crowd is transfixed in holy awe.*

RITA:

There's a land of no one dying,
    a land that death forgot,
though so many there are lying
    in a space where breath is not.

Though the elder branch is growing
    and the elm on elm row spreads
top of evergreen o'erflowing
    from their cemetery beds

and a man's not spoke for surely
    very long upon this earth
whether he's the fiend's work purely
    or a perfect saint in worth,

still a land all death denying
    on this continent I know:
it's a place of no one dying
    though the lord lays all men low.

There's a land of no one dying,
    a land that death forgot,
though so many there are lying
    in a space where breath is not.

Well, it's pretty mystifying
   how the dead are made to lie
in a grave without first dying
   under sight of him on high.

Can it be they're justifying
   what the preacher-man has said:
that all hardship and all crying
   is reversed when you seem dead?

   [Speaking this stanza.]

Or has some truth come o'er this nation
   where the folks can never die,
holds them to the separation
   that makes their lives a lie?

Still I find it terrifying
   to have severed every bond
in a land where no one's dying
   who is trying to respond.

Other lands may be pretending
   that the tear-stained stone is bad,
that a man's approached his ending
   should be solemn, should be sad.

But I sense some modifying
   to our lives and to our needs:
for a land where no one's dying,
   samewise no one's sowing seeds.

Yes, it's truly terrifying
   loving eyes that hide no tears,
holding hands without allying—
   hands have feeling, hands have fears.

God! Oh God! it's terrifying
   having hitched from coast to coast
in a land of no one dying,
   not a living soul to boast.

The STRIPPER *confronts the crowd as the ballad ends, wildly tearing off her street clothes to savage stripping drums and throwing the various articles directly into the faces of* STELLA, DELLA, *and* RAY. *Darkness clouds over* RITA *and she seems to etherealize in her position high on the girder. An article of the* STRIPPER'S *clothing hits* ACE *in the head and he wakes up.*

STELLA: That Vegas woman— oh, she's jist too obscene for American words! I can't look her in the eye.

RAY: She's the queen of the obscene. Really revoltin'. We must protect our children from such a fright, a, sight!

ROMEO: Strippas do make a guy uneasy: it's you 'n breasts all alone together. The three a ya.

BUTCH: So vulga. Oh, my, soooooo vulga.

MAY: What a debased unabashed ol' bag. Why, she's all beat up. Completely over the hill. Couldn't hook near a mile from Main in that condition.

DELLA: Common, pornographic, appealin' to libidinous interests, the vested interests, illicit, prurient, salacious, delicious, spaghetti sauce, what cheek, what sauce—

STELLA: Not up to community standards.

RAY: Tart, smart tart, hussey, ruth, rue the day we ev—

The crowd, unable to withstand the STRIPPER'S *attack, is forced to turn their faces from her: in doing so they are all confronted with the bodies of* MAUDE *and* LYNN. *The dummies rise en masse, bloated with air, to stare down at the corpses. The music ends abruptly.* BUTCH, *hands clasped, smiling wryly.* TOBY *sits on his chair.*

STELLA: Will ya look at that: laid out. The two of em!

RAY: What a sight—makes yer stomach do slow turns…

BUTCH: Y'all makin' a reference to me, Madame Mixer?

RAY: Don't get smart, Nazi.

DELLA: Never a dull moment in our town, eh?

MAY: My school mates— dead! DEAD! Gee…

BUTCH: Wonder if they notices anythin' unusual…

ROMEO: See there, now you see—both sistas murdered!

RAY: But you said Toby was out to do in mah May.

ROMEO: Well, it's jist another crevice, jist another burrow.

DELLA: Matter a fact, two crevices, two burrows.

ROMEO: No matter, mah point is made. There they be plain as the pose on yer face. Both of 'em, homicides.

RAY: They're dead fer certain—deader 'n a skunk run down on route 30. 'N stink as much. But that they is homicides is jumpin' to conclusions.

ROMEO: Sure they's homicides—girls don't git to look like that from adolescent heart-attacks. They was real done in 'n Toby's what done the doin' in.

TOBY: [*Pulling the clipboard clamp off his anger vein.*] Thanks, Romeo.

STELLA: Now listen here, Butch, don't—

ROMEO: But *I* ain't Butch—

STELLA: Don't start in if ya jist tryin' to even up a score with Toby count of a gal or other he beat ya out of.

DELLA: [*Pensive.*] Murder's a pretty serious accusal.

BUTCH: They's laid out sorta pretty. Like in a funeral home.

MAY: Gosh, don't they look *ugly*.

BUTCH: Well…on such short notice…

MAY: Dirty 'n mangled 'n all. The frump looks worst.

ROMEO: What?—Are yis all crazy? I don't think I'm hearin' right!

STELLA: Now don't hear us wrong: —a course, Toby mighta killed 'em. But so might any a us here. Or somebody not here. After all, there's a lotta strange dicks in town.

ACE: What crust!

RAY: Maybe you done it, Romeo. Ya know a awful lot about it.

STELLA: Yeah…maybe you done it, Romeo, 'n yer jist tryin to throw us off the track.

MAY: [*Aggressive, rushing down to tell the audience.*] Sure: after all, Toby's a righteous fella, his fingers feel out situations with infallable sensitivity. And nativity. Yes, that's the word, that's finally the right word. He may practice a kinda Byronic barbarism,

TOBY: —jist outside a town, where haybelly cows graze God's grass while a whole lost language rots around yer tongue like so much mulch 'n peat,

MAY: —but that alone's no reason to be prejudiced for him. People who are jist a little more glamorous than the vast majority of folks are always made the scapegoat.

TOBY: Could ya come a little closer when ya express such so solid principals, May?

ACE: You folks oughta proceed with the order a the day. Ray?

RAY: Ace's right. Why don't we *ask* Toby if he done it?

ROMEO: Yeah, why don't ya? I will.—Toby, you killed these young girls, didn't you?

TOBY: Hi ya, Rom, how ya doin? Have a restful sleep? Or was it fraught wit fearful trailers of a nightmare yet to come? Sorry, Romeo, but I ain sayin' nothin' till I see my lawyer.

STELLA: Good! that's a good boy. Toby knows his rights.

MAY: You could be arrested fer slander, Romeo, ya know that? Willful slander of a poet 'n prophet. A man who draws more'n draws offa girls. You could go to jail fer that. I hope you do.

ROMEO: I don't care, May, I don't care what you say jist as long as yer safe.

MAY: Bull—pure Taurus bull. What a snow job.

ROMEO: Ain't no snow job! I'll fight this thing. I'll fight it all the way up to the Supreme Court of America!

MAY: Stop pawing me! First you scratch yer sores and then you put yer hands all over—

DELLA: [*Taking the initiative.*] Why *are* you so keen on seein' to Toby's bein' tossed in the clink?

ROMEO: Cause in the clink he can't git at May. He's countin' on murderin' May next, jist give him half the chance. I saved her once already when y'all hadda go 'n tie me up!

STELLA: That's as fulla holes as everythin' else you've annotated.

MAY: Holes ya dug with yer nails ya scratch yerself so muc—

ACE: True, but apparently there *has* been a crime around here, and until you're certain there wasn't, it's your duty to make arrests.

STELLA: Very true. But then, who should we arrest?

DELLA: [*Taking over.*] Considerin' the ambiguous climate a the case, we should arrest *two* suspects— Romeo *and* Toby— 'n proceed to thoroughly investigate both a them. 'N we could search 'em too.

RAY: We'd have every right to.

DELLA: [*Untying* ACE.] Mind doin' yer prospective ma-in-law a favor, Ace. I'm a settin' ya free so's ya kin make the arrests. Kin I trust ya?

ACE: Sooner or later ya gotta trust someone.

DELLA: I entrust my daughter to ya.

STRIPPER: And I my son.

ACE: [*Rubbing his stiff wrists.*] Thanks, madame.

BUTCH: [*Situated near the* STRIPPER.] Hey, madame, wanna keep time with somethin' sizeable? Ah'm real *good*.

STRIPPER: How much ya good fer?

BUTCH: Fer nothin'! Ya oughta pay me yer so damn old.

STRIPPER: I don't take care a no one fer nothin'.

TOBY: She don't take care a no one.

ACE: [*Jealous.*] Hey, what about Bad Butch? Maybe he had somethin' to do with this— ummm— affair.

STELLA: Nah, Bad Butch couldn't a had nothin' to do with it. He ain't the type. Them what got the reputation fer bein' bad like Bad Butch, never does nothin' bad actually.

MAY: [*To the audience, unable to bear the attention now focusing on* TOBY.] I'm glad they're arrestin' him. It'll gimme a chance to see exactly jist how short the poet is.

ACE: [*Helping* TOBY *up out of his sitting position.*] Now come along calm 'n ain't nobody gonna git hurt.

TOBY: May you always believe that.

MAY: Ha! Why, he's no higher 'n my bubbies!

TOBY: Grounded at last. On an equal level with everybody else. What more could a fella ask for?

ACE: [*Taking* ROMEO.] Let's hustle, you two.

ROMEO: What a fix, what a goddamn fix to be in!...

TOBY: Now you 'n me's on equal footin'. Feels great, don't it?

ROMEO: Don't see why. Feels 'bout the same as every other day.

TOBY: Alas! It *is* about the same as every other day.

ACE: 'N after all you done!

TOBY: Yeah. But I kin change that, Ace.

ACE: Yeah?

TOBY: Did ya know the other day old Rom got inta some upstage business could set ya right straight who the criminal is?

ROMEO: It's a frame! A shame 'n a frame!—What kinda business?

TOBY: Ya wanna all look behind ma chair to uncover the answer to that query. Ya see that mounda dirt behind ma chair? Ya wanna dig in 'n uncover that dirt!

ROMEO: Oh, boy, I plumb fergot all about that…

The crowd, except for TOBY *and* ROMEO, *rushes up to the mound behind* TOBY'S *chair.* TOBY *crosses to* BUTCH *who is now trying to carry the* STRIPPER *off into the wings.*

TOBY: Break fer it now, Romeo, while they's up there practicin' a bit a amateur archeology!—'N as fer you, Butch, lay off my ma!

BUTCH: Ah was jist gonna lay yer m—

STRIPPER: Oh! …

TOBY: [*Pulling two knives out from the gun holsters on* BUTCH's *hips, and holding their edges outward in his trembling fists.*] Yer too slow, Nazi, to lay anythin' got ma tag on it! Now: —step lively!!

ROMEO: I better step lively 'n beat it while they's all on that desert experdition. [*He turns about frantically and rushes up the vortex girder and onto the diagonal girder.*]

BUTCH: Now, Tob, ya make everythin' too serious—

DELLA: Why, look at that: it's a corpis delectis!

STRIPPER: Son, please—

STELLA: No it ain't. It s a gal's corpse. A young gal.

RAY: Ever see a town so big on gals' corpses?

MAY: Look! Look, everybody! Romeo the pocked-marked murderer is excaping over the viaduct!

ALL: Git him! Git him! Don't let him excape! Lynch him! Swing him high! etc., etc., etc.

The crowd, with murder on its mind, tears across the stage. Some pick up the discarded ropes, others the tangled telephone wires, and they scamper up the girders after the distraught ROMEO. *The second he is captured, the noose is put around his neck.* MAY *rushes down centerstage, cheering the mob on and urging them to hang* ROMEO *from the girder.* TOBY, *having thoroughly cowed* BUTCH *and the* STRIPPER, *turns the knives toward* MAY. *Having secured the noose, the mob kicks* ROMEO *to his death. There is more than madness in* MAY's *eyes. She draws* TOBY *to her.*

MAY: Swing the Grunewald from the viaduct! Let him blow in the breeze! This shall make a epic! A epic for all time! It inspires me to the very heights!! Heaven its—

TOBY: Let my work be forever finished!

TOBY *faces* MAY *directly and thrusts both knives into her diaphragm. Her shriek carries over the cries of the crowd. They all stop short and turn to look down at her. She staggers for a moment with her blood-drenched hands over her wounds and then falls dead. The mob is stunned for several long moments. Then it gathers silently together and moves en masse down onto the stage.* RITA, *draped in the long blue cloak, appears on the platform above the vortex girder and begins silently to descend.* TOBY *walks at the head of the crowd and leads it to the semi-circle of chairs. As* TOBY *sits in his chair,* RITA *raises her arms like wings above him and places a steel head-cap, encrusted with jewels like a crown, over his black hair. Except for the* STRIPPER, *all the others file along quietly and take seats within the semi-circle. They sit without motion for some time; the swaying body grows motionless. All stare directly ahead into the audience. Finally,* TOBY *speaks, stretching out his arms to either flank of chairs; as he does so, the townspeople turn and fix their gaze on him.* RITA *is behind his chair, raised a step or two on the girder, with her face and hands lifted upward.*

TOBY *and* RITA: [*Together, slowly.*] Let us close this circle of chairs. Rest your eyes on me.

The lights grow imperceptibly dimmer except for a reddish glow about TOBY *which suggests his electric execution. The* STRIPPER *wanders in a soft spot downstage, tottering wearily and bewildered. She sings a Country ballad and makes a half-hearted attempt at a simple dance. Her spotlight gradually dims.*

STRIPPER:
Well mah daddy kept his chair, chair, warm for me,
well mah lonesome daddy waited and he had to be
mah daddy cause he kept his chair warm for me,
so warm thru the chilly thaw, the Maytime plea.

And I'd love to be cozy on that chair with him
stead a sittin' all alone on the edge of the rim
where a loneliness prevails not assailed by a hymn:
well at least he kept that chair, warm, warm,
    I'm gonna sing and dance me up a storm!
    I'm gonna sing and dance me up a storm!

Well mah daddy kept his chair, chair, warm for me,
well mah lonesome daddy waited and he had to be
mah daddy cause he kept his chair warm for me,
so warm thru the chilly thaw, the Maytime plea.

O how long I must wonder will this earth still spin
where my body seems to feel that it never has been
and my heart's no answer, dad, for a kind heart akin:
well at least he kept that chair, warm, warm,
    I'm gonna sing and dance me up a storm!
    I'm gonna sing and dance me up a storm!

Lee Breuer

The B.Beaver Animation

•

Mabou Mines premièred *The B.Beaver Animation* jointly at the Museum of Modern Art, New York, as part of the program "A Valentine for Marcel Duchamp," and at the Theater for the New City, New York, in 1974. Written and conceived for the stage by Lee Breuer. Produced and realized by Mabou Mines.

Cast

JoAnne Akalaitis, Ruth Maleczech, Frederick Neumann, Bill Raymond, David Warrilow (Bill Raymond's part was originally performed by Dawn Gray)

Dam

Tina Girouard (adapted for performance by Stephen Bennyworth, Thom Cathcart, and Terry O'Reilly)

Light Frames	Thom Cathcart
Curtain Puppetry	Terry O'Reilly
Light Ball	Stephen Bennyworth

•

For Frederick Neumann

EXCUSE ME. WHEN I'M ADDRESSED I'M EMBARRASSED. I ASSUME YOU'RE THE SAME. MORE PRECISELY I'M SELF EFFACED. ACCORDINGLY ALLOW ME TO PRESENT TO YOU THE B.BEAVER. WHILE I FLEE. YOU CAN PRESENT TO ME ANYTHING YOU WANT. THAT'S YOUR STORY.

TO DO ME JUSTICE I'VE BEEN KNOWN TO TURN AROUND AND RAGE WHILE WALKING BACKWARDS. I RAGE AT ELEMENTS. SPRING. AND FISH. TUNA FISH. TAKE TUNA FISH. ONCE A YEAR THEY COME OUT OF THE SEA TO WREAK THEIR HAVOC ON HONEST LABOR. GRANTED THEY'RE COLD BLOODED. THEY KNOW NOT WHAT THEY DO. I CONCEDE THERE ARE MORAL ANOMALIES IN THE HARD CORE ANTITUNIAST. BUT. WHEN YOU SEE THEM SWARMING IN THE CURRENT. WATCH THEM RIFLE RAPIDS. CLIMB CATARACTS AND DAMS. TAKE BEAVER DAMS. THE WORLD'S FINEST BLEND OF CHOICE SILTS ORGANIC COMPOST EARTHY ALKALIS FRESH BROOK SHALE NOT TO MENTION LABOR. RESEARCH. CREATIVE LEADERSHIP. GO IN TO DAMMING. THE FLOW. I'VE SEEN A TUNA FISH LOWER ITS HEAD AND GO RIGHT THROUGH A STURDY LITTLE FABRICATION LIKE A BULLET.

B.BEAVER IS A STUTTERER. HE'S A SMALL COMMUTER TRAIN OF SPLIT PERSONALITIES ALL READING FOR HIS PART. OUT OF SYNC.

I PERSIST IN THIS FICTION. I'VE ACHIEVED A DAILY FICTION. PRIOR TO THIS ACHIEVEMENT IT WAS DAILY BLOTTO. THE MISSUS USED TO THROW MY EMPTY BOTTLES INTO THE POOL. ALL NIGHT THEY'D NUZZLE. EXCUSE ME BUT YOU CAUGHT THAT DIDN'T YOU. SALMON. CALLING SALMON TUNA FISH. I HAVE ENEMIES. I CAN'T PRONOUNCE THEIR NAMES. THEY ESCAPE. UNCANNY LITTLE FUCKERS.

B. BEAVER MOVES ME WHEN HE IS MOST INNATELY A RAT.

DAILY FICTION. SPRING. GATHERING THE BROOD. WE SIT ATOP THE DAM AND WATCH THE SNOW ATOP THE MOUNTAIN. BEHOLD SNOW. I SAY. IT'S WHITE. TO BE EXACT. AND. COLD TO BE SPECIFIC. A FORCE OF NATURE. IN THE SUN IT FLASHES LIKE A BRIGHT IDEA. THAT IS. WHEN THE SUN SHINES YOU GET FLASHES. EXCUSE ME BUT I BECOME THE PEDAGOGUE IN DEALING WITH PHENOMENA.

PERORATIONS ON GEOLOGICAL FORMATIONS. HYDRAU-
LICS. THAWS. HOW SNOW THAWS. PERFORCE FALLING
DOWN MOUNTAINS. PERFORCE LIFTING STREAMS. THE
BROOD. THEY SHIVER. THEY DRIP. THEY WIPE THEIR NOSES
ON THEIR TAILS. I PLUNGE AHEAD INTO THE EQUILIBRIUM
OF NATURE.

LATIN. THIS IS A SE-
CRET NOTE TO MY-
SELF THAT PART OF
THE BEAVER LIVES ON
AVENUE B BETWEEN
5TH AND 6TH STREETS
OVER THE MUCHO
MACHO SOCIAL CLUB.

NO I DON'T.

MY CORRESPONDENCE. KEEP UP WITH MY CORRESPON-
DENCE. I KNOCK OFF THE FIRST LINE IN LATIN. EPISTOLUM
RODANTUM AMPHIBIUM AD LIBRARIUM LOCALUM.

AS YOU KNOW IN RECENT YEARS OUR WINTERS HAVE
BEEN LIGHT. YET MAY I POINT OUT THAT DUE TO CURIOUS
CONSIDERATIONS. METEOROLOGICAL CONFIGURATIONS.
CUMULO NIMBUS. UPDRAFT. PRECIPITATE OZONE. AND A
STATIONARY FRONT. I HAVE OBSERVED FROM ATOP MY
DAM CONSIDERABLE SNOW ON THE MOUNTAIN.

NOW LET US SAY v IS THE VOLUME OF SNOW. LET US
CONJECTURE. THE SNOW IS x MANY INCHES. ONE ALLOWS
FOR i AN INCREASE TOWARD THE TOP. ONE TAKES THE m
MEAN OF THE i INCREASE FROM THE TIMBERLINE TL TO s
SUMMIT. IT'S SIMPLE ALGEBRA.

CONSIDER THERE ARE TT TRIBUTARY TRICKLES. TRICK-
LES. MIND YOU. I UNDERLINE. TRICKLES. THAT p PLUMMET
DOWN THROUGH THE TREES. OVER PRECIPICES. UNDER R
ROCKS C CATARACTING OVER CLIFFS. THROUGH VALLEYS.
THESE FORM F FIVE G GENTLE BROOKS. ONE OF THESE
BROOKS IS MB MY BROOK. ONE FIFTH OF THAT SNOW IS
MS MY SNOW. WERE IT ALL TO THAW AND HURTLE DOWN.

B.BEAVER IS ALSO A
TURD. THIS IS A LIT-
ERARY ALLUSION.

MY BROOK WOULD COME TO BE T TORRENT s SWEEPING
EVERYTHING BEFORE IT. IT WOULD SWEEP MY DAM DAM
BEFORE IT. TO R RIVERS. TO s SEA C CARAMBA. THAT'S A
DELUGE FLOOD.

HEART THUMPING. TAIL THUMPING. GOOD GOD A
TRAUMA. I CRUMPLE UP THE LETTER AND THROW IT OUT
THE WINDOW. THEN I THROW ME OUT THE WINDOW. LOOK
AT THAT. PANIC. SLAVE OF THE SUBCONSCIOUS.

AHA!. THE THOUGHT.
PERISH. HERE THE
B.BEAVER DROPS ITS
LOAD. OF TWO BY
FOURS. IN THIS CASE.
THE DAM COLLAPSES.
CURTAINS   FLAIL.

PERISH. THE THOUGHT.

SUMMONING SANG FROID I CRAWL BACK TO MY DESK.
SUCK IN MY LINEA SEMILUNARIS. AND SELECT A POST-
CARD. WILDLIFE COMPOSITION.

WOULD YOU BE SO KIND AS TO SEND ME WHAT YOU
HAVE ON FRESHWATER DAMNATION. SOMETHING IN THE
DO IT YOURSELF SERIES WOULD BE MOST HELPFUL. MA-

TERIAL ESTIMATES. ANYTHING TECHNICAL ON STRESSES.
BLUEPRINTS. NOT TO NEGLECT PURE THEORY.
MARGINALIA. ESOTERICA. THE RELATED SCIENCES.
CLAUSEWITZ ON BARRICADES. IN SHORT. THE WORKS. ON
THE SUBJECT.

I ADD A POSTSCRIPT. I WRITE SMALL. PRESUMING YOU
FIND IT STRANGE. ONE OF MY ILK WITHOUT THIS INFOR-
MATION AT HIS FINGERTIPS. BORN BUILDER AND SUCH.
WELL. I HAD IT. MISPLACED. MISHANDLED. SWIPED. YOU
KNOW THE MISSUS MAY HAVE THROWN IT INTO THE
TRASH. DON'T GET ME STARTED ON THE MISSUS. IT'S
LOST. THAT'S A FACT. I AM A BEAVER WHO HAS LOST THE
ART OF DAMNATION AT A CRUCIAL TIME. AND COME HELL
OR HIGH WATER—

ADDRESS CLEARLY PLEASE. SPARE NO EXPENSE. I EA-
GERLY AWAIT.

MORNING. THERE WAS NO IMMEDIATE REPLY. EVENING.
NEXT MORNING. NEXT EVENING. MORNING. AFTER THAT.
THE FOLLOWING EVENING. SCROBIS ID. SCREW IT.

SILENCE OF THE MAILS. COMING OF THE SPRING. ES-
TRANGEMENT OF THE SOUL. VACATION WEATHER. AFTER-
NOON. I FLOAT DOWNSTREAM ON MY BACK. SPOUTING
WATER.

ALL ALONG THE BROOK BANK THE HUM OF INDUSTRY.
PART OF THE GRAND SCHEME. SPRING WORKS. WHEN THE
JUICES FLOW. LOOK AT THEM. MYRIAD CREATURES. NOLENS
VOLENS. WILLY NILLY. EAT.CRAP. SCREW. CROAK. WHAT
STYLE. NO ELABORATION. ID EST UBI EST. THAT'S WHERE IT'S
AT.

I GO ASHORE. SPRING WITH A VENGEANCE. GRASS AND
FLOWERS. NOTHING STOPS IT. ON THE BANK I STAND
UPON A CARPET OF FLOWERS. I WIPE MY FEET.

SADNESS. NO MISTAKE. THAT MAKES ME FURIOUS.
LONGING. NO MISTAKE. I CAN FEEL IT GIVING. MY DEAR
BARRIER. TO HAVE DEDICATED THE WORK OF MY MATURER
YEARS TO DAMMING ALL THAT CRAP UP TO PERFECTION.
PAIN. GOD DAMN IT NOW I'M IN PAIN. I CAN'T ACCEPT IT.

PAIN IN ANY OTHER GUISE I'M SURE I COULD ACCEPT.
A LION. I'M SURE I COULD ACCEPT A WOUNDED LION. IF
ONLY I WERE SOME DUMB ANIMAL. I'D GET A RUNNING
START AND SCRAMBLE UP A TREE. WRAP MY TAIL AROUND
A BRANCH. AND HANG. I'D PLAY POSSUM.

NIGHTS FALL. MOONS RISE. THE YELLOW STARS PUSH

YIKES. EXPLODES ACROSS THE FRAME. THE PIECE. THE ANI-MATION. CONSIDERS ITS DEMISE.

ESCAPE. AND DREAM. OF MAKING THE WORLD SAFE FOR BEAVERS. CELINE'S SHIP FOUNDERING OVER THE HÔTEL DE VILLE. B.BEAVER PUTS UP A SAIL. HIS ROBE. AND THE WIND TURNS IT INTO A GHOST WALKING ON THE WATER. VOICE BY M. MAGOO.

THROUGH THE SKY. THE FLOWERS THROUGH THE EARTH. I CAN'T TELL THE DIFFERENCE. HANGING THERE WITH THE PISS SCARED OUT OF ME I CAN'T TELL WHAT'S UP. THAT'S THE FAILURE OF A POINT OF VIEW. I'LL HAVE TO REASSESS. GET ON TOP OF WHAT'S UP. GET RIGHT TO THE BOTTOM OF WHAT'S GOING DOWN. CHRIST SAKE. I'D FLIP. I'D GO UNDER.

PHLOOEY. NOT BAD. NOT BAD AS A HABITAT FOR A COLD FISH. FLORIUS AQUAMARINUS. UNENDING SOURCE OF STIMULATION FOR THE BOTANICALLY INCLINED. PEAS. FROZEN PEAS. EVERYTHING AMAZED DOWN HERE. WIDE EYED AMAZEMENT. AND I'M PARTICULARLY TAKEN WITH THE RETICENCE. FEW BUBBLY GLUBS. NO PRETENSIONS.

A TROUT. GREAT SCOT. I SAY. MAD MEAT EATING TROUT. I BREAK THE SURFACE IN A SINGLE BOUND. CRACK MY HEAD. A LOG. A CRAFT. OLD WATERLOGGED CRAFT. I LEAP UPON IT. MAD ENDEAVOR. MOUNT STRAIGHTAWAY THE MIZZEN MAST AND CRY. HEAVE TO. IT HEAVES BACK. BILGEWATER I SAY AND BUST IT IN THE BAROMETER. IT BATTENS DOWN ITS HATCHES AND BANGS MY BOOM. OFF THE RIGGING IN A BOB AND WEAVE I FEINT A LEFT TO THE BULKHEAD AND K.O. THE CROW'S NEST. IT TACKS TO WINDWARD. I LIST TO STARBOARD. WE CLINCH. IT CLANGS. TEN BELLS. IT BRINGS UP ITS PORT AND WHACKS MY AFT. OVERBOARD FOR A MANDATORY EIGHT COUNT. IT DROPS ANCHOR IN A NEUTRAL CHANNEL. I THROW IN MY TAIL. WHAT'S THE PROBLEM. I PAT IT ON THE POOP DECK. YOU ARK. ME ANIMAL. WE'VE GOT A PRECEDENT.

WE HIT AN ICEBERG. WE GO DOWN OFF THE COAST OF NEWFOUNDLAND. DISASTER. I SWIM HOME. THE MOUSE THE MARMOT ALL THE OTHER FURRY LITTLE CREATURES FLOATING FACE DOWN OVER THE INUNDATED EARTH. LITTLE DEAD BALLS. ONLY THE BEAVER PLUNGED ON. STROKE TWO. BREATHE FOUR. ONLY THE BEAVER ESCAPED ALONE TO TELL.

PLUNGING ON. STROKE TWO. BREATHE FOUR. ONLY THE BEAVER ESCAPED ALONE TO TELL.

WAKE UP WITH JOY IN MY HEART. I COME ALIVE NO MATTER WHAT I DO. IT'S KILLING ME. RIGHT. WRITE. WILL AND TESTAMENT. WRITE. BEING OF SOUND. STOP. INCIDENTALLY MY PET. WE'RE RUINED. CLEANED OUT. IF YOU DON'T BELIEVE ME LOOK AT MY TESTAMENT. I'VE NOTHING TO LEAVE. MUCH TO MY REGRET. MY PET. I SUSPECT EMBEZZLEMENT.

ANY IDEAS.

YOU HAVEN'T THE FAINTEST OF IDEAS. I CONFRONTED THE BROOD. NONE OF YOU HAS EVER HAD THE FAINTEST OF IDEAS. YOU DON'T EVEN KNOW HOW THE FAINTEST OF IDEAS IS GONE ABOUT BEING HAD.

ONE FEELS FOXY. THE FAINTEST OF IDEAS MAKES ME FEEL FOXY. I GROW HARD. AND BUSHY TAILED. I LOOK AT MYSELF FULL LENGTH. SMEGMATIC. ERECT. A BLUSH STARTS IN MY TOES AND RISES LIKE A RASPBERRY PHOS-PHATE IN A STRAW. I'VE GOT IT.

REINFORCED CONCRETE.

TO THE DRAFTING BOARD. EXCUSE ME MY PET. MY CALLING. IT'S CALLING. I BREAK OUT MY TRIANGLES LAY ON A T SQUARE AND TOP IT OFF WITH TWO DRAFTING PINS AND A FRENCH CURVE. I TAKE A BITE. IT'S DELI-CIOUS. I DIP IN THE COOLER AND WHIP OUT A COLT FORTY FIVE. REINFORCED CONCRETE CAPTURES THE ANIMAL IMAGINATION. VITAL TO DEFENSE. RESEARCH SUBSI-DIZED. LOCAL BEAVER MAKES KILLING IN BROOKSHORE REAL ESTATE. I KNOW WHAT I'M DOING.

I MAKE OUT AN AGENDA. WHICH I STUDY TO SEE WHAT'S NEXT ON THE AGENDA. PAY THE WATER BILL. I PEEL THE MISSUS OFF THE RUG. SLAP ON A RECORD. AND UNDERGO A FOXTROT. LET US CELEBRATE MY PET. WHILE YOUTH LINGERS. AND IDEAS FLOW. I MIX UP A COOL CUBA LIBRE. WE TOSS OFF A NIGHTCAP. OUT JUMPS MY PECKER LIKE A CORKSCREW. I'LL BANG OFF THE MISSUS ON THE LAZY SUSAN. NOW THERE'S AN IDEA. I KNOW WHEN I'VE GOT IT. I KNOW WHEN I'VE HAD IT.

I CAN FEEL IT SLIPPING AWAY. ME LITTLE SIGNS. I'VE BEEN WORKING ON THE WHISKERS.

I ENTER UPON STUDIES. STRUCTURAL DEMOLITION. HOT NIGHTS IN THE LAB OVER A BUNSEN BURNER. IN PRE-LIMINARY TESTS. COMBUST WHISKERS. TERMINATE STUDIES.

LOST A TOOTH IN A SILVER SPRUCE.

I DON'T CARE. A CERTAIN I DON'T CARE HAS GONE DOWN THROUGH THE PROPER CHANNEL. THE BACKBONE. PRIDE OF THE VERTEBRATES. AND ROOTED ITSELF IN THE STUFF OF LIFE. CARBON. ATOM TURNS TO ATOM AND SAYS. I DON'T CARE.

DID YOU SEE THAT. THINGS ARE MOVING OUT ALREADY. DUST. LINT. FURNITURE. THE PORTABLE SAUNA. EVERYTIME I LOOK AWAY THEY MOVE TOWARD THE DOOR.

READ THAT ANY GIVEN SPECIES RE-DUCED BY MORE THAN HALF. REDUCED TO PEERING INTO EX-TINCTION. STARTS TO MUTATE. SAY EACH MUTATION IS A NEW IDEA ABOUT COMING TO GRIPS. MOST OF THEM ARE RATHER REDUNDANT LIKE TWO TAILS OR A THIRD BALL. BUT THEY REPRESENT A CERTAIN EFFORT. AT THIS POINT A GIVEN SPECIES BLOWS ITS CREATIVE WAD.

AND THERE IS THAT BEAVER THAT KNOWS IT'S ALL OVER BUT THE SHOUTING. THIS DUDE IS A HEAVY-WEIGHT. THE RAT WHO STANDS PAT

WHILE THEY PLAY NEARER MY GOD TO THEE. AND THEN GOES DOWN. VERY RARE. HE IS ROMMEL RETREATING ACROSS AFRICA. HE IS VON STROHEIM SHOOTING GREED.

ALL CREATURE COMFORTS. ME TOO. EVERYTIME I LOOK AWAY I MOVE TOWARD THE DOOR. WONDER WHERE I GO.

A SPECIES IN EXTREMITIES. AT ODDS WITH ITS ENVIRONMENT. A CLASSIC CASE. MUTATE. OR FACE YOUR FATE. DOWN IN THE DNA THEY'RE BURNING THE MIDNIGHT OIL.

I CAN SEE A BEAVER WHO CAN RISE ABOVE IT ALL. RODANTUM AMPHIBIUM SUPER MUNDANUM. CHARACTERIZED BY ITS INCREASED CAPACITY FOR HOT AIR. HERETOFORE THE BEAVER HARDLY HELD HOT AIR ENOUGH TO KEEP ITS HEAD ABOVE THE WATER. NOW IT FLOATS ABOVE THE TREE TOPS LIKE A BUBBLE IN THE AIR.

I'LL BE DAMNED. NOT A GHOST OF A PREMONITION. SMACK DAB IN THE MIDDLE OF THE NIGHT. THE MISSUS. IN THE MOON. ATOP THE DAM. LITTER IN A RING AROUND. ALL OF THEM SQUEALING. SHE RAISES HER PAW. IN HER PAW A HAZEL SWITCH. WHACK. ON THEIR BACKS. OFF THEY GO SQUEALING. ONE OF THEM TURNS. BEGS. WHACK. OFF IT GOES SQUEALING. NOT A MOMENT'S HESITATION. SLINGS A ROCK AROUND HER NECK. HOLDS HER NOSE. AND INTO THE POOL. INTO THE MOONLIGHT. BOBBING.

NOW THE MISSUS IS NOT POPULAR WITH THE FEMINIST SET. SHE WAS AN OLD FASHIONED BEAVER. RAISED ON THE PRESERVE. RELIGIOUS BACKGROUND. CREATIVE ASPIRATIONS. OFF TO A SMALL WOMEN'S COLLEGE. FIRST TIME AWAY FROM HOME. USED TO WRITE POETRY AT NIGHT AND EAT IT IN THE MORNING.

PHYLOGENETICALLY. MY PET. IT'S PART OF OUR TRADITION TO LEAVE A SINKING SHIP. NOT TO GO DOWN.

I WADE OVER THE MISSUS. THERE SHE STICKS. IN THE MUD. LIKE A STICK IN THE MUD. TAIL LIKE A BOARD. BEAVER BOARD. EXCUSE ME. THERE YOU HAVE IT. RODANTUS CATATONIUS.

PICTURE HIM THEN. SHARP TEETH. CRITICAL MIND. PLANS. DREAMS. THEY WOULD BUILD SOMETHING TOGETHER.

LIKE A FLASH IT SEIZES ME. THE LITTER. OUT THERE. IN THE DARK. IN THE WORLD. DON'T PANIC MY PET. I'LL PULL IT OFF AGAIN. I'LL BRING IT ALL HOME AGAIN. THE BROOD. THE BLOOM. THE BACON. I'LL TRANSVERSE THEIR HYPOTENUSE. I'LL STRIKE OUT AT AN OBTUSE ANGLE AND INTERSECT THE LITTLE BUGGERS ONE BY ONE. ALL IT TAKES IS PLAIN GEOMETRY. ONCE WE BEAVERS SET A COURSE THERE'S NO DEVIATION.

OFF UPSTATE INTO A PARADISE OF BROOKS AND RILLS. SMALL COMMUNITY. GOOD WOOD ON THE BANK.

I STARE AT THE MISSUS. RIGHT INTO HER EYE. IT'S DEEP. HER EYE REFLECTS MY EYE. I HOLD MY BREATH AND LOOK HER IN THE EYE. AND THINK OF PYTHAGORAS.

A LITTLE RAIN IS FALLING. AN EYE IS WEEPING. A DAM BREAKS. A TEAR FALLS. IT FALLS OUT OF MY EYE. I CAN SEE IT IN HER EYE. NEITHER OF US BAT AN EYE.

NEITHER OF US BAT AN EYE.

GOT A CARD IN THE MORNING MAIL. DEAR SIR. REGARDING YOUR STRUCTURE. WE REGRET TO INFORM YOU

THAT THERE'S NOTHING ON THE SHELVES YOU WANT. WE
ARE SEARCHING THE STACKS. I PERSONALLY AM SEARCH-
ING THE STACKS. I SEARCH THE STACKS EVERY EVENING
AFTER WE SHUT OUR LITTLE DOORS.

    I FLIP OVER THE CARD. PICTURE OF AN EASTER BUNNY.
A BLUE EGG. **PEACE**. IN RED LETTERS. A PIECE. HMM.
SMALL PRINT. EASTER BUNNY. VITAL STATISTICS. SEVEN. FOURTEEN.
TWENTY ONE. I SAY. FUCK IT ALL. SHE THINKS I'M A RABBIT.

    WILL SET THAT RIGHT. I WRITE. I'M A BIT OF A BADGER
AT BOTTOM. A WEASEL ON UP. TWO RAT TEETH. A HARE-
LIP. AND THIS WET BRICKBAT KEEPS FOLLOWING ME
AROUND. THROUGH THE COWSLIPS. AND THE COW PAD-
DIES. I'M THREE BY SIX IN ROUND FIGURES. IN FLEXUS.
SIX BY NINE. IN EXTENSIO. NINE BY THIRTY FOUR. IN A
WORD. YOURS. TRULY.

YEARS LATER WHEN
B.BEAVER WAS A
WINO ON 2ND AV-
ENUE HE DECIDED TO
WRITE HIS MEMOIRS
ON AN OLD CHECK-
BOOK. HE WROTE THE
FIRST CHECK. PAY TO
THE ORDER OF GOD.
THROUGH THE NOSE.
AND THE SECOND.
PAY TO BEARER. RET-
ROACTIVELY. THE
WAGES OF LOVE. AND
ANOTHER TEAR CAME
TO HIS EYE LIKE THE
ONE IN THE STORY.
EAT YOUR HEART OUT
DIMITRI TIOMKIN.

Richard Foreman

∾

Rhoda in Potatoland
(Her Fall-Starts)

·

Rhoda in Potatoland (Her Fall-Starts) was presented by the Ontological-Hysteric Theatre, New York City, December, 1975–February, 1976.

RHODA	Kate Manheim
MAX	Bob Fleischner
SOPHIA	Rena Gill
WAITER	Guatam Dasgupta
ADMIRER	John Matturri
HANNAH	Ela Troyano
ELEANOR	Camille Foss
AGATHA	Cathy Scott
CREW PERSONS	Tim Kennedy
	Phillip Johnston
	Charley Bergengren

VOICE: Remember. This text is—as it were—inside out. That is, its presentation—to in a sense—make it clear—inside out. Because when you see the inside outside—the inside is clear, right?

Cut the text in half—you haven't seen it yet, but imagine it cut into two parts—a first part and a second part. Then—in the presentation—the first part is played as the second part and vice versa. So what follows, precedes, and vice versa.

Because

to have the first part follow the second is to go, as the time passes, toward the source, which is to say deeper, which is to say at the end

you are at the beginning

which is always

where one should begin.

Only by being a tourist. Can you experience. A place.

They ventured forth. Then they ventured forth again.

They compared their bodies.

It's only by comparing them we will know them.

"Compare them in this situation."

RHODA *and* SOPHIA *sit, at table, earphones. A waiter enters with a tray.*

WAITER: Coffee?

RHODA *drinks.*

"How can she listen and drink coffee at the same time."

SOPHIA: Look. I made a drawing of you, Rhoda.

RHODA *looks.*

It's good.

"They are still, all this while, getting information over their earphones."

They look at each other.

RHODA: Oh, certainly not.

SOPHIA: Oh, yes, yes, yes, yes.

"Then she realizes…"

RHODA: Comparison will be the basis of my life. That's how I hope to get famous.

Wall opens to reveal a throne, MAX *sits on it.*

MAX: You are famous.

RHODA: More famous. Even more famous.

> *A bed.*

RHODA: I think somebody's hidden under my bed.

> *The bed revolves—*SOPHIA *appears strapped to the underside.*

SOPHIA: It was a trick.

> *Revolves again.*

RHODA: I vanished. It was a trick.

HANNAH: [*Enters.*] Hello Rhoda, I brought you some clams.

RHODA: You can see, it's hard for me to eat them because I'm tied to the bed.

HANNAH: Oh, I thought it was a trick.

RHODA: Hum, you know what these clams remind me of?

HANNAH: Good, she's making another comparison.

It should be easier than this.

> What.

> > *Pause.*

> Writing good.

> > Don't you know? There's nothing to it.

> What.

> > Writing good.

> What makes me think writing is important.

> > [*Shrugs.*] Everybody does it all the time so it must be important. She doesn't do it.

> Who. [*Pause.*] Rhoda? She's always writing. Everybody is always writing.

RHODA: [*Enters.*] Hello.

VOICE: She wrote it.

RHODA: Am I late.

VOICE: She wrote it.

RHODA: She said it.

VOICE: Look, look compare her to a typewriter.

SOPHIA: [*Enters.*] Hello.

> *Pause.*

RHODA *and* SOPHIA: Hello.

> *They squeeze together.*

RHODA: What are you doing.

SOPHIA: Writing.

RHODA: I'm comparing myself.

SOPHIA: Don't push.

RHODA: She likes it.

SOPHIA: [*Arms around her. They collapse.*] Oh Rhoda, what a good writer you are.

RHODA: Would you get this sack of potatoes off my body?

WAITER: [*Enters.*] What'll it be?

MAX: [*Pause.*] Potatoes.

> RHODA *and* SOPHIA *get up and plop on his table.*

RHODA: Don't read while you eat.

SOPHIA: Here's a potato.

"They don't really compare themselves to potatoes but he does."

RHODA: I wish l was growing someplace.

> *A field. Enter* RHODA *and* SOPHIA, *legs together in a sack.*

RHODA: This looks like a good place to get planted.

SOPHIA: Now maybe we can have a private conversation.

RHODA: [*Pause—looks.*] Oh Sophia, write me a letter.

SOPHIA: I can't write.

RHODA: You?

> *Pause.*

You're so smart.

"She explains herself, like a potato."

RHODA: [*Shakes her head.*] Nothing's explained yet.

SOPHIA: Wait for it to be explained, Rhoda.

RHODA: [*Pause.*] Why do we both have to have one leg in the same sack.

SOPHIA: [*As* HANNAH *and* ELEANOR *enter, two of their legs in a sack.*] There's going to be a race.

HANNAH: Hello, we're ready for the race.

RHODA: I don't want to do it.

HANNAH: Oh Rhoda, do you think it's beneath your dignity.

ELEANOR: You and Sophia looked very dignified on the dinner plate.

RHODA: I wasn't on a dinner plate.

HANNAH: Oh yes. Ben was eating you.

ELEANOR: —He wrote us all about it in a letter.

RHODA: My partner doesn't write.

"The essence of writing now grows apparent."

SOPHIA: I said it would.

"In the middle of the potato field
The emphasis on certain words
In the midst of a field of other words not so emphasized."

RHODA: In my whole life I never emphasized something that much.

"Wrong."

SOPHIA: I don't write.

"Oh Sophia, did you mean don't or can't."

> HANNAH *and* ELEANOR *push against* SOPHIA *and* RHODA.

"The potato race, in which nothing special is emphasized."

RHODA: I'm emphasizing a comparison.

> *Lights up on audience.*

"It's up to you. Understanding is all up to you of course. But so is enjoyment."

"Certain spaces suddenly appear in the center of the audience."

Pause.

"Find them. Find them. Certain spaces suddenly appear in the center of the audience."

RHODA, SOPHIA, HANNAH: Maybe this isn't sensually enough oriented for your enjoyment.

GONG. *Tableau in a shoe salon.*

VOICE: What you see is simply a comparison of bodies. But it is also a comparison of minds.

RHODA: How far do you think my mind is now from the circumference of my head.

"Compare. Her mind and your own mind. She is an actress in the play. But at this moment, her real mind is working just like your own real mind."

Pause.

"Now there are spaces distributed amongst the audience but there are other spaces distributed over the stage. Find them. Find them. Try to find them."

RHODA: Oh, I expected to find a space going on in my body, then I expected to find a place growing in my mind. Then I find a place growing someplace that wasn't in me at all but it was growing so much it finished by being in me.

Pause.

I have to return to what I know, but now I know something different.

VOICE: "The orchestra is busy tuning up."

All-girl orchestra including RHODA *and* SOPHIA *tries to play a lively tune and all collapse. Then a large shoe appears on the horizon.*

RHODA: On the horizon, a large shoe. I move toward it in order to wear it. But wait, wait, both of my feet are already covered with shoes. Dare I now, at this distance, remove the appropriate shoe? The offending, if I may say so, the offending shoe? Look, look, the shoe—there—is large enough to make me think of a boat. Boat vs. shoe, both elements of a journey. But have they a different aim in life.

RHODA: My shoe has to be replaced.

She is sitting.

SALESMAN: By what.

RHODA: Are you the only salesperson available.

SALESMAN: I can be more fanatic than I seem.

RHODA: I don't want a fanatic salesperson.

SOPHIA: [*Entering.*] Sell me a shoe.

RHODA: [*Pause.*] I only sell one part of my body covering to people.

SALESMAN: I don't think Rhoda's a shoe salesman.

RHODA: —Can I interest you in some of my underwear.

SOPHIA: [*Pause.*] I don't think you understand my reasons.

RHODA: [*Return to shoe on horizon.*] Water comes from the horizon, but so does its relation. Its relation in the form of a boat; i.e., the relation between water and boat; i.e., the flow, which continues, which-of-a-which this is an instance, and the thing that is on it—which in this case is a boat and in another case is an idea. The boat as idea? Ah, not a good idea, huh.

> *Back to shoe parlor.*

Why need it be a good idea.

RHODA: This place frightens me. I can say that easily. All places frighten me if I allow them to frighten me. Where in the place is the fear.

"Is it layed over it like a gray (or colored) sheet."

Or is it placed, distinctly, like a jewel. Somewhere...where would that jewel appropriately be placed.

SOPHIA: Look, look, the window lights up.

RHODA: But here, here, this piece of paper catches its image.

SOPHIA: Not true.

> *Scene is shifting.*

VOICE: [*As scene is shifting to grove of trees.*] Only being a tourist. Can you experience a place.

RHODA: I said go to the same place but it's different.

SOPHIA: Be careful.

RHODA: Of?

SOPHIA: [*Pause*] It's pretty isn't it.

RHODA: Yes.

SOPHIA: In ten minutes or less you'll want something different.

RHODA: Oh look.

> *She points.*

SOPHIA: You imagined it.

RHODA: [*Pause.*] I wrote it.

> *Pause.*

I didn't want to imagine it. I didn't want to explain it. I just wanted to experience it.

SOPHIA: There it is.

RHODA: What.

SOPHIA: Wait.

RHODA: What.

SOPHIA: I said in ten minutes or less and it happened.

RHODA: What.

SOPHIA: [*Pause.*] It was there.

> *Enter* AGATHA *in woods.*

AGATHA: First it was Max here, but it was only imagined.

"Written."

AGATHA: Then it was me but I was visible.

RHODA: [*Pause.*] I'm going to change places.

AGATHA: [*Points.*] I've had enough of you, Rhoda.

RHODA: That was me talking.

A room, tea served.
AGATHA: It's really true. I've had enough of you.
RHODA: I could change my appearance.
AGATHA: Not likely.
RHODA: I'll put on something else.
    Goes to door.
  It's locked.
    Another door opens.
AGATHA: You tried the wrong door.
    A hiss, which gets louder.
  "THE RETURN OF THE POTATOES."
    Enter four big potatoes. Then silence, and AGATHA and RHODA undress.
  "ONLY BY BEING A TOURIST."
VOICE: Now this is where the interesting part of the evening begins. Everything up to
  now was Recognizable. It was part of one's everyday experience.
  Now, however
  The real potatoes are amongst us
  And a different kind of understanding is possible for anybody who wants a different
  kind of understanding.
RHODA: [*Pause*] I feel like a potato.
AGATHA: —I feel like a potato.
    They feel each other.
AGATHA: Oh Rhoda, you feel like a potato.
RHODA: You smell like a potato and you even
    Both lick.
  taste like a potato.
VOICE: Would she think that Agatha smelled and tasted like a potato if she herself
  didn't feel like a potato.
    Lights dim to center as potatoes exit, big couch in behind. RHODA and AGATHA
    sit back in it on opposite sides, but entwining their legs.
VOICE: Potatoes have no special feelings about physical proximity to other potatoes.
  On the other hand, potatoes—as far as we know—have no literature or art of any
  kind to which they sublimate powerful sexual energies.
    Pause.
  Potatoes endure. They are eaten
  But they still, endure.
    Lights fade out.

  Lights up: cafe;
    MAX *and* HANNAH.
MAX: I had the funniest dream last night.
WAITER: Coffee?

MAX: I dreamt I was a potato.

WAITER: [*Pause*] Coffee?

MAX: Yes.

HANNAH: Don't drink coffee while thinking about a potato.

"This play transcends the world of the potato and at the same time it enters that world."

MAX: [*Turns.*] Do you keep books in that cabinet.

HANNAH: I don't work here as a waitress. I solicit customers and then I introduce them to great literature.

Pause, as she points at low cabinet.

Should I open it.

WAITER: [*Head in door.*] Your potatoes are on the fire.

Pause.

Excuse me, I mean here they come.

A potato comes to front door. HANNAH *at cabinet.*

"The potato can't enter because the door isn't big enough."

HANNAH: [*Kneels.*] Here's the book you want.

MAX: What did you pick.

HANNAH: It says "Erotic photographs of the preceding century"—do you mind if I thumb through some of the pictures.

MAX: That's dumb.

HANNAH: [*Pause.*] I'm a little ashamed to have you know that I'm interested in such a book.

MAX: Why.

Pause.

Why is that mirror in the potato.

Buzz. Lights up. Tree replaces potato and RHODA *appears on floor next to* HANNAH.

"I told you what it transcended, but I didn't tell you what would replace what it transcended."

RHODA: In losing the potato you lost the mirror.

HANNAH: It's still here. It's still here. It's bigger but it's still here.

"The stage is, of course, a mirror and you are looking into it."

WAITER: Here's your baked potato.

Exits.

"You realize, when he's said—here's your baked potato—he's said everything."

On floor, RHODA *and* HANNAH *look at pictures in the book and laugh together.*

MAX *down front, presents a potato to audience.*

MAX: Here's your baked potato.

A wall, with a small, barred window and shelf. Musical number.

MAX *and* RHODA *drop potatoes through the window. Then all enter and dance with one arm extended to floor—a shoe on bottom of the arm—a three-legged dance.*

Their shoes are shined.

Then a hooded rolling chair enters and RHODA *is left alone with a hooded man who appears in the chair. A table is set. She climbs on it, crying out in fear throughout the music, ready for unimaginable tortures. Potatoes placed on her stomach. She slowly comes to like them, as a voice speaks over the music describing meditative processes using young spring potatoes as a focal point. Music fades, and stage quietly is transformed back into the throne room.*

MAX *on throne. Potato on lap. Enter* SOPHIA. *Kneels.* RHODA *enters behind, with knife,* SOPHIA *half turns—*RHODA *falls on her, they strain against each other.* "God. Is he real?"

Lights up. SOPHIA *with knife in chest.* RHODA *sprawled back, relaxes.*
"The most ELEGANT
    MEANING
    POSSIBLE"
MAX: In this place. Certain habits.
"Only by being a tourist. Can you experience. A place.
They ventured forth. Then they ventured forth again.
They compared their bodies."
RHODA: It's only by comparing them we will know them.
SOPHIA: Compare them in this situation.
They get earphones.
MAX: [*Pause.*] He who thinks, always surprises me.
RHODA: What's the good of imagining what can't be imagined.
SOPHIA: Am I different now.
RHODA: No.
MAX: Am I different now.
RHODA: No.
MAX: Wrong.
Pause.
Here's what just happened.
"He explains."
A potato falls rear.
RHODA: How will that change anything.
MAX: It won't change anything for you, but it will for me, only you won't notice it.
RHODA: [*Lights on her alone*] He went to a certain place.
MAX: [*In a door, lit alone.*] I live in an imaginary country.
A mirror comes forward. RHODA *against it.*

"The mirror advances but it has no real mind of its own. Existence is, for it, of course, reflection."

Potatoes enter.

VOICE: "Entities struggling toward truth? No. Merely someone caught, momentarily, by light rays."

Flash.

Pause.

RHODA: Wait, let me take another photograph. I love having my picture taken.

VOICE: [*Pause.*] I am trying to photograph what cannot be "photographed." I know I am undertaking an impossible task.

RHODA *approaches front of stage.*

"Oh Rhoda. Dig deeper and deeper into your memory."

RHODA: [*Pause*] I was in a garden.

"Don't believe it."

Room. Window. Others sprawled about.

RHODA: [*Holds up book.*] Oh look.

"Erotic photography from the previous century."

Others reveal selves.

RHODA: No, it wasn't that garden.

Hands on hips.

Now, try smelling the rose.

She goes to window, bowl of roses wheeled in on table by MAX.

"She has a nose in the back of her head."

ELEANOR *leans in window.*

ELEANOR: Look what I picked.

MAX: I made this choice for Rhoda.

"Come to bed
Come to bed
Come to bed
Come to bed."

RHODA: They always say come to bed when what they mean is…

A ping.

All but RHODA *take out shrunken heads.*

"Ha, we all had one and the others didn't know. Let's do the old right-left."

MAX: Good idea. Let's do the old right-left!

All dance.

Bathroom. RHODA *there in bathrobe with towel.*

"Running the tub."

RHODA *turns on the water and steam pours out which causes her to stagger back.*

"It was as if…the faucet she turned on was her own brain."

Nightmare dance in bathtub.

> RHODA *finishes, exhausted in the tub.*

RHODA: All these heads they have all been collecting.

MAX: [*At door.*] Oh Rhoda, you're not going to change your mind at THIS late date.

RHODA: It's been a mistake.

> *Pause.*

It's been a miscalculation.

> *Open—big head rear rocks slowly back and forth.*

"In time, they grow much bigger

In America they grow much bigger

The group mind

A play by Doctor Wartmonger

Who is speaking when I am speaking

What does this have to do with headhunters.

> *Potatoes.*

Generating new material

My discovery

Today I decided to generate new material by keeping a diary."

RHODA: [*At director's table. Full lights onstage as all is revealed and director goes onstage and looks at audience.*] He found himself deeply enmeshed in plans for her happiness.

DIRECTOR: Cut throat.

RHODA: I bet it wasn't expected.

> *Points at director's forehead.*

What he did.

DIRECTOR: Do you care if I title this chapter after your title.

RHODA: Names. That's one of the categories I have to fish for a little more deeply.

> *As SOPHIA comes up behind her and tries to cut her throat.*

"It's time you understood. It's all there and you can't improve upon it"

> *A chair is rear in the full light. Weighted with books. Tips. Then* RHODA *sits.*

RHODA: See—now there's a difference.

> *Pause.*

I'm heavier than the reading matter.

MAX: It doesn't matter, those books are smarter than you are.

> *Books fall on his head.*

RHODA: I never read them.

> *As banquet table is set.*

SONG: "Oh Rhoda, you never read the right books.

Oh Rhoda, you're always reading the wrong books.

Oh Rhoda, why don't you read the right books?

Oh Rhoda, the books you read are wrong books."

Big book opens rear.

RHODA: Who joined in.

When.

After it was over.

Oh everybody joined in after it was over.

Then it was easy.

But it was always easy.

Well, then they joined in earlier than I knew.

> Legend: DOING SOMETHING.
>
> *All-girl orchestra appears.*

Watch how they come running.

> *Pause.*
>
> *Orchestra plays a terrible number.*

Hum, that's a surprise of sorts.

"Are you still sure that everyone is joining in?"

No. I admit it. No.

Let's introduce each other.

RHODA: Now there's just one of us.

> *Pause—people hold out playing cards.*

VOICE: Humm—take a card.

> *Pause.*

RHODA: I'm waiting.

> *Card on a table.*

RHODA: Now. The card does the talking. But in a language you can't understand.

> *Pause.*

If you were able to understand. What the card was saying. You would be having a response very different from the response you are now having.

> *Pause.*

I guarantee it. I guarantee it. Whatever you want I can give you.—OK. I want to be famous.—OK. You are.

> *Door opens.*

CREW PERSON: [*Resembling Richard Foreman.*] Oh, excuse me, I—

RHODA: What.

CREW PERSON: [*Pause*] Aren't you the famous Richard Foreman.

RHODA: [*Smiles.*] Yes.

CREW PERSON: It's an honor to meet you.

RHODA: [*Shrugs.*] Ohhhhh.

CREW PERSON: I admire you very much. More than anybody else.

RHODA: Hummmmm.

MAX: [*To* RHODA? *To audience?*] See? You're famous.
ALL: [*To* RHODA.] We are all proud of you. You have proven yourself by becoming famous.

    Pause. RHODA *looks at audience and thinks.*

1

    Flower trellis set plus low wall, roses.
RHODA: I wish I was this place.
MAX: What?

    Pause.

How can you be a "place."
RHODA: I wish I was "this."

    Pause.

Hah—I am.
MAX: Then you got your wish.
RHODA: No. It shouldn't have been a wish.

    She starts to undress.

VOICE: The naked body as a vast space. Travel in it.
    To travel in it
Is to be in a landscape that you KNOW how to relate to.
MAX *and* RHODA: [*Arms out.*] How can I relate to this PLACE.
VOICE: A beautiful vista.

    Pause.

When you move toward it, it vanishes.

    Pause, RHODA *exits.*

2

    On balcony, naked woman and man.
But looking at the nude, you are caressed. It is SMALL enough. Yet, it's more other than the landscape. Also, It remarks upon your presence.
MAX: If the landscape could remark upon my presence.

    Pause, he goes through it.

For instance.

    Lights up, then out.

    *Lights up—*RHODA *gone.*

MAX: [*Pause*] Oh Rhoda, now that you're this "place" I don't know how to have a relationship with you, Rhoda.

    Pause.

What this place does is be-here. But I. I. I do something else.
More complex.
More interesting. Because the place is—here, and then it is existing.

VOICE: But Max is different. Sometimes he sleeps. Then he gets a good idea. Acts on it. Then he sleeps again.

"Ohhh holy one, oh causative agent...."

MAX: The signs which are important to me speak. What they say is

The past

The past

That is why they are signs.

RHODA: [*Appears.*] Come closer.

MAX: Oh lady.

RHODA: Come closer. Rest your head on me.

MAX: Oh lady. In your arms.

A bed.

RHODA: Do you know how much effort went into building this world.

MAX: It's like the others.

RHODA: What.

MAX: World.

RHODA: I wasn't thinking of a world.

MAX: But you were. But you were without knowing it.

He returns to throne.

What I want to give you is...an estimable shape. The imagination of a...

"Oh Rhoda. Sleep and speech. I'd like to analyze it but I can't really."

RHODA: Teacher? I don't need no teacher.

"The contacts that I make with the force are, to say the least, very erratic."

A table. RHODA *rests her head on it and sleeps.*

RHODA: This is my dream life.

Pause.

A text. Inside out. Vulgar imitations.

VOICE: Remember what I said at the beginning. A text cut in half, and the first half placed where the second half should be and vice-versa.

"You can't please all of the people all of the time.

Who am I

Why do I want YOU in my audience

What will you say about me behind my back."

MAX: [*On throne now*] What he means is, how easily can sentences be generated.

RHODA *now with head on a chopping block.*

Being productive is his only concern.

RHODA: It doesn't help, it doesn't help.

MAX: What doesn't help.

As book placed on her head.

"You are punished Rhoda, for dreaming."

Open on drop of building.

"She wanted to be like architecture, not like dancing."

RHODA: I wanted a choice, about how to use my body.

"Now, choice is a closed book."

RHODA: [*Pause.*] Look. This was the body of…

"Her body was; a building."

RHODA: I will be punished for dreaming.

>   *Lifts her hand.*

Look, in my hand is…a…a…

"She tries to name an object which, by definition, has no name."

"Oh Rhoda, for that you'll be punished."

RHODA: Nonsense.

>   *Pause.*

Nonsense.

VOICE: But is it nonsense? You see, when I call upon my own knowledge, when I do that, it only shows me (my knowledge) the very tip of its wing. Is it therefore, as I had assumed, my knowledge?

I do not possess it. In what sense then, do I call it my knowledge?

It is a body of information to which I have occasional, peripheral access. As opposed to other bodies of knowledge. But are there bodies of knowledge? Of course not. There are a composite of partial accesses (other people, myself at different times) and the overlapping of these gives the illusion of a body. Knowledge.

But what is it that is overlapping?

A certain….joie de vivre.

>   *Music.*

Sam Shepard

Action

•

Action was first performed at the American Place Theatre, New York, in 1975. It was directed by Nancy Meckler, with the following cast:

SHOOTER	R. A. Dow
JEEP	Richard Lynch
LIZA	Dorothy Lyman
LUPE	Marcia Gean Kurtz

Upstage center, a small Christmas tree on a small table with tiny blinking lights. Downstage center left, a plain board table with four wooden chairs, one each on the four sides. The table is set very simply for four people. Just plates, forks and knives. Four coffee cups and a pot of hot coffee in the middle. Running across the middle of the stage above is a clothesline attached to a pulley at either side of the stage. The light onstage is divided exactly in half, so that upstage is in complete darkness except for the blinking lights of the Christmas tree. Downstage is lit in pale yellow and white light which pulses brighter and dimmer every ten minutes or so, as though the power were very weak.

The characters are all in their late twenties to early thirties. SHOOTER *and* JEEP, *the two men, are dressed in long dark overcoats, jeans, lumberjack shirts, and heavy boots. They both have their heads shaved.* LUPE *wears a flowered print dress in the 1940s Pearl Harbor style. She wears platform heels.* LIZA *wears a long, full, Mexican type skirt, plain blouse and an apron. She wears sandals.* LUPE *sits upstage of the table facing* LIZA *across from her.* LIZA's *back is directly to the audience.* JEEP *sits stage right at one end of the table across from* SHOOTER, *who sits at the other end.*

The stage is in darkness for a while with just the tree blinking. The lights come up very slowly downstage. Nothing happens for a while except the slight movements of the actors drinking coffee. JEEP *rocks slightly in his chair.*

All the exits and entrances occur upstage into or out of the darkness.

JEEP: [*leaning back in his chair and rocking gently*] I'm looking forward to my life. I'm looking forward to uh—me. The way I picture me.

SHOOTER: Who're you talking to?

JEEP: Uh—[*pause*] I had this room I lived in. Shall I describe this room? [*pause as the others take a sip of coffee together*] I had a wall with a picture of Walt Whitman in an overcoat. Every time I looked at the picture I thought of Pennsylvania. I had a picture of an antelope on a yellow prairie. Every time I looked at this picture I saw him running. I had a picture of the Golden Gate Bridge. Every time I looked at it I saw the water underneath it. I had a picture of me sitting on a Jeep with a gun in one hand.

He lets the chair come to rest on the floor again. Pause as they all sip coffee.

Suddenly LIZA *jumps up and makes a big gesture with her hands melodramatically.*

LIZA: Oh my God! The turkey!

She goes running off upstage and disappears into the darkness.

LUPE: [*to herself*] It's funny the way the snow is.

SHOOTER: [*pulling a book out from his lap and placing it on the table*] Maybe we should read.

LUPE: We'll have to wait for Liza.

SHOOTER: Yeah. But we could be looking for the place. Do you remember where it was?

LUPE: I thought we marked it.

SHOOTER: I lost the place.

LUPE: [*taking the book and thumbing through it*] Here, let me look.

JEEP: Shooter, can you do a soft shoe?

SHOOTER: Naw. I don't think so.

JEEP: I was wondering if we could both do it sitting down. Without getting up. Just our legs.

SHOOTER: Just like this you mean?

JEEP: Yeah.

LUPE: Was it chapter sixteen?

SHOOTER: Uh—Maybe.

> LUPE *continues thumbing.*

JEEP: Just try. Put your hands on the table.

> *They both put their hands on the table.*

JEEP: One, two, three, quatro!

> *They both break into an attempt at a soft shoe patter as they stare blankly at each other in their seats.* LUPE *keeps looking through the book. This lasts for about thirty seconds and ends with* LIZA *coming back into the light sucking on her fingers and wiping her hands on her apron. She sits back down in her chair.*

LIZA: [*noticing* LUPE *with the book*] Oh. Are we gonna' read?

LUPE: I can't find the place.

LIZA: Let me take a look.

> LUPE *shoves the book across the table to* LIZA, *who takes it and starts thumbing through it. She keeps sucking on her fingers in between turning the pages.*

LUPE: Shooter lost the place.

JEEP: Uh—I saw this picture of a dancing bear. Some gypsies had it on a leash. They were all laying by the side of the road and the bear was standing on all fours. Right in the middle of the road. In the background was this fancy house.

> SHOOTER *pulls his overcoat over his head and holds his hands up in front of him like bear paws. Slowly he pushes his chair back and rises. He takes short staggering steps like a bear on his hind legs.* LIZA *keeps looking through the book.*

JEEP: [*to* SHOOTER] Don't act it out.

> SHOOTER *keeps on.*

LIZA: [*referring to book*] Were we past the part where the comet exploded?

JEEP: [*to* SHOOTER] You don't have to act it out.

> SHOOTER *pays no attention.*

LUPE: I never saw a dancing bear. That was before my time. I guess they made it illegal. Too cruel or something.

> SHOOTER *goes back and forth downstage like a trained bear, looking out at the audience.*

SHOOTER: It doesn't feel cruel. Just humiliating. It's not the rightful position of a bear. You can feel it. It's all off balance.

LUPE: Well, that's what I mean.

JEEP: What?

LUPE: That's cruel. For a bear that's cruel.

SHOOTER: No. It's as though something's expected of me. As though I was human. But it puts me in a different position. A different situation.

JEEP: How?

SHOOTER: Performing. Um—Without realizing it. Um—I mean I realize it but the bear doesn't. He just finds himself doing something unusual for him. Awkward.

JEEP: You're not the bear.

LIZA: I found it! They've returned to earth only to find that things are exactly the same. Nothing's changed.

JEEP: That's not it. Let me try.

> JEEP *takes the book from* LIZA *and goes through it.* SHOOTER *drops his bear routine and pulls his overcoat down on his shoulders. He looks blankly at the audience, then strolls back to his seat and sits. They all sip their coffee. After a long pause.*

SHOOTER: I think I'll take a bath.

LIZA: The turkey's almost ready.

SHOOTER: I'm too scared to eat. [*not showing it*]

LUPE: [*to* LIZA] Let him take a bath. It'll calm him down.

SHOOTER: Is there any hot water left?

JEEP: [*thumbing through the book*] There was the last time I was up there.

SHOOTER: I don't want to go up there alone.

LUPE: If you could remember the last time when you got scared it might help you this time.

SHOOTER: I know. It's the same. It's the snow. Being inside. Everything's so shocking inside. When I look at my hand I get terrified. The sight of my feet in the bathtub. The skin covering me. That's all that's covering me.

LIZA: [*pulling out a hip flask from her apron*] You want some rum?

> SHOOTER *takes the flask and has a drink.*

LUPE: I can remember the last time I got scared. I thought I'd poisoned myself. I thought I'd eaten something. I imagined it working its way into me. I went outside in my bare feet and forced myself to throw up. It was that kind of a night.

LIZA: I remember that night. We were watching the stars.

> *The two girls start laughing, covering their mouths, then stop.*

SHOOTER: I know I'll get over this. It just sorta' came on me.

> *He hands the flask back to* LIZA, *who puts it in her apron.*

LIZA: [*without giving it back*] You can keep it.

SHOOTER: [*blankly*] I've got this feeling that females are more generous. I've always felt that.

JEEP: [*pushing the book away from him*] OH THIS IS RIDICULOUS!! I CAN'T FIND THE PLACE!!

He stands suddenly, picks up his chair and smashes it to the floor. The chair shatters into tiny pieces. Pause. None of the others are shocked.

LIZA: [*standing*] I think there's another one out on the back porch.

LIZA leaves. She disappears in the darkness upstage. JEEP pulls his overcoat up over his head and raises his hands like SHOOTER did. He goes through the same bear motions as SHOOTER did before. LUPE takes the book again and looks through the pages.

SHOOTER: [*to himself*] That's what I do. I get this feeling I can't control the situation. Something's getting out of control. Things won't work. And then I smash something. I punch something. I scream. Later I find out that my throat is torn. I've torn something loose. My voice is hoarse. I'm trembling. My breath is short. My heart's thumping. I don't recognize myself.

LUPE: Shooter, weren't you the last one to read?

SHOOTER: Was I?

LUPE: Yeah. It was you.

SHOOTER: It doesn't matter does it?

LUPE: Only if you can remember where you left off.

SHOOTER: Well, let me look. I'll see if I can find it.

He takes the book and looks through it. LUPE starts into a soft shoe sitting down. JEEP has his back to her, but as he hears her feet tapping he stops his bear routine and turns to look at her. She continues with a smile. JEEP pulls his overcoat down on his shoulders and just stares at her.

JEEP: [*flatly*] There's something to be said for not being able to do something well.

LUPE stops. Her smile disappears.

JEEP: No, I mean it's all right. It takes a certain amount of courage to bring it out into the open like that.

LUPE: It's no worse than the one you guys did.

JEEP: No, I know. I'm not trying to insult you or anything.

LUPE starts up the soft shoe again in defiance.

JEEP: I mean we've got this picture in our head of Judy Garland or Gene Kelly or Fred Astaire. Those feet flying all over the place. That fluid motion. How can we do anything for the first time. Even Nijinksy went nuts.

LUPE: [*continuing with her feet*] What about it?

JEEP: It's hard to have a conversation.

He sits down on the floor. LUPE continues dancing for a while after JEEP's seated. She slowly stops. SHOOTER thumbs through the book. They sip their coffee.

LUPE: [*to JEEP*] When you're in a position of doing something like that it's hard to talk about it. You know what I mean? I mean while I was doing it—while I was in the middle of actually doing it—I didn't particularly feel like talking about it. I mean it made me feel funny. You know what I mean. It was like somebody was watching me. Judging me. Sort of making an evaluation. Chalking up points. I mean especially the references to all those stars. You know. I mean I know I'm not as good as Judy Garland. But so what? I wasn't trying to be as good as Judy Garland.

It started off like it was just for fun you know. And then it turned into murder. It was like being murdered. You know what I mean.

JEEP: Didn't mean to piss you off.

> *Pause.* LIZA *enters from upstage with a new chair in one hand and a broom and dustpan in the other. She sets the chair down.* JEEP *gets up off the floor and sits in the new chair, folding his arms across his chest.* LIZA *starts sweeping up the pieces of the old chair.* JEEP *watches her.*

JEEP: [*to* LIZA] I'm not going to offer to clean it up because you're already doing it.

> LIZA *continues sweeping in silence.*

SHOOTER: [*looking up from the book, directed at everyone*] I know that feeling of being out of control. Powerless. You go crazy. In a second you can go crazy. You can almost see it coming. A thunderstorm.

JEEP: [*to* SHOOTER] It's not that.

SHOOTER: Oh. [SHOOTER *goes back to thumbing through the book.*]

JEEP: I mean sometimes it's like that but this time it wasn't.

LIZA: [*still sweeping*] Did you find the place yet?

SHOOTER: Nope.

LUPE: I'm starving. [*she licks her lips*]

JEEP: This time it came from something else. I had an idea I wanted to be different. I pictured myself being different than how I was. I couldn't stand how I was. The picture grew in me, and the more it grew the more it came up against how I really was. Then I exploded.

SHOOTER: [*without looking up from the book*] That's what I meant.

LUPE: Oh, when are we gonna' EAT! [*hitting the table once with her fist*]

LIZA: It's almost ready. [LIZA *exits upstage with the pieces of the old chair, leaving the broom onstage.*]

JEEP: I couldn't take it. Just thumbing through the book. Not even looking. Not even seeing the papers. Just turning them. Acting it out. Just pretending.

> *Suddenly* LUPE *starts gnawing ravenously on her own arm.* JEEP *and* SHOOTER *pay no attention.*

SHOOTER: [*still looking through the book*] I know.

JEEP: Is that what you're doing? Is that what you're doing right now?

SHOOTER: [*Without looking up*] I'm looking for the place.

JEEP: I admire your concentration. I couldn't concentrate. I kept thinking of other things. I kept drifting. I kept thinking of the sun. The Gulf of Mexico. Barracuda.

SHOOTER: [*still into the book*] That's okay.

JEEP: [*standing suddenly and yelling*] I KNOW IT'S OKAY!! THAT'S NOT WHAT I'M SAYING!

> *He picks up the new chair and smashes it to the ground just like the other one.* LUPE *stops chewing on her arm and licks it like a cat licking a wound.* SHOOTER *keeps looking for the place in the book.* JEEP *stands there looking at the damage.*

SHOOTER: [*after a short pause, referring to book*] Was it just after the fall of the Great Continent?

LUPE: Oh my stomach!

> *She clutches her stomach with both hands and holds it like a baby.* LIZA *enters with a huge golden turkey on a silver platter with the steam rising off it. She sets it down on the table in front of* LUPE.

LUPE: I'll carve.

> LUPE *picks up a knife and begins to slice the turkey in a calm way, very formally, and laying the slices on plates for everyone.* LIZA *walks over to* JEEP, *who is still looking at the broken chair. They look at the chair together as though seeing it as an event outside themselves.*

LIZA: [*to* JEEP *but looking at the broken chair*] You'll have to stop doing that. We've only got one left.

> LIZA *picks up the broom.* JEEP *grabs it. They both hold it together.*

JEEP: I'll do it.

LIZA: That's okay.

> *A short pause as they look at each other, then* JEEP *yanks the broom out of* LIZA's *hand and starts sweeping up the broken chair.* LIZA *goes to the table and sits folding her hands in her lap while* LUPE *continues to carve standing up.* SHOOTER *sticks with the book.*

LUPE: We're lucky to have a turkey you know.

LIZA: Yes, I know.

LUPE: It was smart thinking to raise our own. To see ahead into the crisis.

LIZA: Whose idea was it anyway?

SHOOTER: [*not looking up*] Mine.

JEEP: [*still sweeping*] I think it was mine.

SHOOTER: [*not looking up*] It was your idea, and then I went and bought it.

JEEP: That's right.

LIZA: That's right.

LUPE: We're sure lucky.

LIZA: Do you know what they say is the best way to prepare a turkey? They say that before you kill it—about two weeks before—you start feeding it a little cornmeal and some sherry. About a teaspoonful of sherry, three times a day. Then in the second week you force a whole walnut down its throat once a day and keep up the sherry dosage. When it comes time for the kill you'll have a turkey with a warm, nutty flavor.

LUPE: Is that what you did?

LIZA: Partly. I started out the first week with the sherry, but by the time the second week rolled around I couldn't bring myself to do it. I mean the walnut thing. I couldn't do that.

JEEP: [*as he exits upstage with the broken pieces of the chair*] It's not cruel.

LUPE: Who killed it anyway?

LIZA: I did.

SHOOTER: I can't find the place. [SHOOTER *folds the book and puts it on the floor, opens his napkin and tucks it into his shirt, picks up his knife and fork and waits to be served.*]

SHOOTER: Aren't we going to have any vegetables?

LIZA: No. We had a late frost remember?

LUPE: We're lucky to have a turkey.

SHOOTER: I know we are. I was just wondering about the vegetables. The creamed onions and stuff. The candied yams.

LUPE: [*to* SHOOTER] Dark or light?

SHOOTER: White.

> *She hands* SHOOTER *a plate of turkey. He digs in.*

LIZA: No wine either, I suppose?

LUPE: You were in the kitchen.

> *She hands* LIZA *a plate of turkey.* LIZA *eats.* LUPE *serves herself and sits down to eat.*

LIZA: Yes. I've never cooked over an open fire before. I mean a big fire blazing like that. It's hard to keep from cooking yourself. Your arms start roasting. You get afraid the kitchen's going to burn down.

LUPE: I can imagine.

LIZA: The heat is tremendous.

SHOOTER: I thought turkeys were supposed to cook slow.

LIZA: Well, you let the flames die down. It's just the embers you're cooking on. But the heat!

SHOOTER: Yeah, it's hot in here for a change.

> JEEP *enters from upstage into the light, shivering and rubbing his arms.* LIZA *stops him.*

LIZA: Oh Jeep, could you get us all some water?

JEEP: [*standing still, shivering*] Right now?

LIZA: Yeah, if you don't mind.

JEEP: From the well? It's a lot of work you know. We can't just turn on a tap.

LUPE: We're lucky to have a turkey.

> JEEP *turns upstage and exits.*

SHOOTER: It is freezing out there. I don't envy him. Hauling up water. Spilling it on his hands. It's freezing.

LIZA: It's all right.

SHOOTER: In the dark. Feeling your way around. He might fall in.

LIZA: We'll hear him.

LUPE: It's all right, Shooter.

SHOOTER: [*standing suddenly*] I KNOW IT'S ALL RIGHT!

> *The two women continue eating, paying no attention.* SHOOTER *sits down after a while.*

SHOOTER: [*quietly to himself;* LUPE *and* LIZA *eat quietly*] Just because we're surrounded by four walls and a roof doesn't mean anything. It's still dangerous. The chances of something happening are just as great. Anything could happen. Any move is possible. I've seen it. You go outside. The world's quiet. White. Everything resounding. Not a sound of a motor. Not a light. You see into the house. You see the candles. You watch the people. You can see what it's like inside. The candles draw you. You get a cold feeling being outside. Separated. You have an idea that being inside it's cozier. Friendlier. Warmth. People. Conversation. Everyone using a language. Then you go inside. It's a shock. It's not like how you expected. You lose what you had outside. You forget that there even is an outside. The inside is all you know. You hunt for a way of being with everyone. A way of finding how to behave. You find out what's expected of you. You act yourself out.

    J E E P *enters from upstage with a bucketful of water and four cups in the other hand. Each cup dangling from one of his fingers by the handle. He sets the bucket down on the table with the cups. He picks up a cup and dips it into the bucket. He does the same with each cup and serves everyone at the table with a cup of water. Then he sits down on the floor. This all happens in silence except for the sounds of the others eating and the water.*

L I Z A: [*standing*] There's one chair left.

S H O O T E R: [*standing and moving upstage*] I'll get it.

    S H O O T E R *exits.* L I Z A *sits again.*

L U P E: Dark or light, Jeep?

J E E P: White.

    L U P E *serves him a plate of turkey.* J E E P *eats sitting on the floor.*

J E E P: I was thinking. If things get worse we should get a cow.

L I Z A: Nobody's selling.

J E E P: You've asked around?

L I Z A: Nobody's selling.

L U P E: I was thinking chickens would be better.

L I Z A: Nobody's selling.

J E E P: That's all right.

L U P E: A goat might be good.

L I Z A: There's no way of actually preparing. We'll have to do the best with what we've got. We're all eating now. At least we're eating. We'll have to gauge our hunger. Find out if we actually need food when we think we need it. Find out how much it takes to stay alive. Find out what it does to us. Find out what's happening to us. Sometimes I think I know, but it's only an idea. Sometimes I have the idea I know what's happening to us. Sometimes I can't see it. I go blind. Other times I don't have any idea. I'm just eating.

    S H O O T E R *comes back on from upstage empty-handed. They all stop eating and look at him.*

S H O O T E R: I forgot what it was I went for. I got out there and forgot.

J E E P: [*still on the floor*] The chair.

S H O O T E R: Oh yeah. [S H O O T E R *turns upstage and exits again. They go back to eating.*]

J E E P: [*to himself*] It doesn't really matter. I'm okay on the floor.

L I Z A: I made a move to go get it, and then he beat me to it.

J E E P: It doesn't matter.

L U P E: Was he being polite?

L I Z A: I guess.

LUPE: [*to* LIZA] Just to keep you from going out there?

LIZA: I guess so.

LUPE: But he's getting the chair for Jeep, and Jeep doesn't even care.

LIZA: It s all right.

JEEP: [*suddenly, to himself*] Walt Whitman was a great man. He kissed soldiers. He held their hands. He saw mounds of amputated limbs.

LUPE: I don't know anything about him.

　　　SHOOTER *comes on from upstage pulling a very heavy, stuffed red armchair. He huffs and puffs with it, pulling it by inches downstage as the others stay sitting and eat their turkey.*

JEEP: He expected something from America. He had this great expectation.

LUPE: I don't know. I never heard about it.

JEEP: He was like what Tolstoy was to Russia.

LIZA: I don't know much about it either.

JEEP: A father. A passionate father bleeding for his country.

LIZA: [*staying seated*] Do you want some help, Shooter?

SHOOTER: [*between heavy breaths*] No—I'm uh—okay. It's—not much—further. I'll be all right.

JEEP: Almost a hundred years ago to the day. The same thing happened. Everybody at each other's throats. Walt was there. He could tell you.

LIZA: I thought he was dead.

JEEP: [*conversationally*] "Manahatta," it was called then. Indian. They had big, open tents on the Bowery with sawdust on the floor. German beer. Juggling acts. Dancing bears. The Civil War was just beginning.

LUPE: When was this?

JEEP: He'd tip his hat to Abe, and Abe would tip his hat back.

LIZA: They liked each other.

JEEP: [*in a Walter Cronkite newscaster voice*] The poet and the President. The poet all gray and white standing on his feet. The President all dark and somber, glooming down from his horse. The face of war in his eyes. The two of them seeing each other from their respective positions. The entire nation in a jackknife. This all happened on Vermont Avenue near L Street. The street itself was raining. Blue soldiers were lying wounded in every doorway; some having slept there all night with gaping wounds. Soaked through to the bone. Walt was a witness to it.

　　　SHOOTER *finally gets the chair downstage right and stands by it trying to catch his breath. He looks at* JEEP, *who stays seated on the floor.* SHOOTER *makes a motion toward the chair with his hand. He tries to speak, but he's out of breath. He tries again.*

SHOOTER: [*motioning to chair*] There it is.

JEEP: I'm okay here.

　　　SHOOTER *looks at him for a while.*

SHOOTER: You don't want it? [*no answer from* JEEP, *who keeps eating*] Don't you want it?

Still no answer from JEEP. SHOOTER *moves in front of the armchair and collapses into it staring out at the audience.*

SHOOTER: Aaaaaaaah! This is the life. Now I'm glad I went through all that.

LIZA: [*to* SHOOTER] Aren't you hungry?

SHOOTER: No. I'm glad. [*He folds his arms behind his head and smiles.*]

LIZA: [*standing*] Well, time to wash up.

She starts gathering all the dishes together very quickly, whipping the plates out from under every one. JEEP *and* LUPE *pick their teeth and smack their lips loudly.*

JEEP: [*with his back to* SHOOTER] Do you want some water, Shooter? There's plenty of water.

SHOOTER: Nope. This is it for me. I'm never leaving this chair. I've finally found it.

JEEP: [*standing and moving to the bucket on the table*] I'm gonna' have some water. I'd be glad to get you a cup if you want.

LUPE: He just said he doesn't want any.

JEEP *stands by the bucket with a cup in one hand. He dips the cup into the bucket, raises the cup slowly, and tips the water back into the bucket, watching the trickle of water as he does it. He keeps doing this over and over as though hypnotized by his own action. When* LIZA *has all the dishes she exits upstage leaving the remains of the turkey on the table.*

LUPE: Does anyone want to read? [*pause*]

SHOOTER: I'm never leaving again.

LUPE: I don't mind looking for the place. [*She goes and picks up the book on the floor and sits back down in her chair. She looks through it.*]

SHOOTER: I could conduct all my business from here. I'll need a bedpan and some magazines.

JEEP: [*looking at the remains of the turkey*] We should save the bones for soup.

SHOOTER: This is more like it. This is more in line with how I see myself. I picture myself as a father. Very much at home. The world can't touch me.

JEEP: Shooter? You remember when you were scared? Shooter? You remember? Oh, Shooter?

SHOOTER: Naw. I don't remember that. Better to leave that. People are washing dishes now. Lupe's looking for the place again. Things are rolling right along. Why bring that up?

LUPE: [*in the book*] Wasn't it around where the spaceship had collided with the neutron?

JEEP: Shooter, I remember. I remember you were so scared you couldn't go up to take a bath.

SHOOTER: Naw. That's not me at all. That's entirely the wrong image. That must've been an accident.

JEEP: Oh. [JEEP *keeps pouring the water over his hand.*]

SHOOTER: I've never been afraid of baths. I've always been brave in those situations. I've plunged right in.

JEEP: Oh, I thought it was you.

SHOOTER: I knew a guy once who was afraid to take a bath. Something about the water. Stank to high heaven. "High Heaven." That's a good one. He stank, boy. Boy, how he stank. Boy, did he ever stink.

JEEP: Was it the water?

SHOOTER: Yeah. Something about how it distorted his body when he looked down into it.

JEEP: Then, it wasn't the water.

SHOOTER: Yeah. The water. The way it warped his body.

JEEP: But that's just the way he saw it. That was him, not the water.

SHOOTER: Then, he began to fear his own body.

JEEP: From that? From seeing it in the water?

SHOOTER: He began to feel like a foreign spy. Spying on his body. He'd lie awake. Afraid to sleep for fear his body might do something without him knowing. He'd keep watch on it.

JEEP: Was he a close friend?

SHOOTER: I knew him for a while.

JEEP: What happened to him?

SHOOTER: His body killed him. One day it just had enough and killed him.

JEEP: What happened to the body?

SHOOTER: It's still walking around I guess. [*pause*] Would somebody tell Liza to bring me the flask?

LUPE: [*not looking up from the book*] She's washing the dishes.

JEEP: [*still pouring*] That's an interesting story, Shooter.

SHOOTER: Thank you.

JEEP: How did it get started?

SHOOTER: What?

JEEP: I mean how did he get into this relationship?

SHOOTER: Who knows. It developed. One day he found himself like that.

LUPE: [*without looking up*] Remember the days of mass entertainment?

JEEP: No.

LUPE: [*not looking up*] This could never have happened then. Something to do every minute. Always something to do. I once was very active in the community.

JEEP: What's a community?

LUPE: [*looking up*] A sense of—A sense um—What's a community, Shooter?

SHOOTER: Oh uh—You know. You were on the right track.

LUPE: Something uh—

JEEP: I know.

LUPE: Yeah. You know. It doesn't need words. [*She goes back into the book.*]

JEEP: I know what you mean.

LUPE: Just a kind of feeling.

JEEP: Yeah, I know what you mean.

SHOOTER: I think we're beginning to get it a little. To get it back. I mean you can feel it even in the dead of winter. Sort of everybody helping each other out.

JEEP: Did he suspect his body of treason? Was that it?

SHOOTER: I'm not sure. It was a touchy situation. [SHOOTER *rolls both his pants legs up above his knees and starts scratching his legs as he talks.*]

JEEP: He must've had a hard time. I mean he couldn't reach out. I mean he wouldn't expect anyone else to be in the same boat probably.

SHOOTER: Probably not.

LUPE: [*without looking up*] Well it *is* rare.

JEEP: Was it in a particular time of hardship?

SHOOTER: I can't rightly say.

JEEP: I mean were things crumbling?

SHOOTER: I suspect he couldn't see it. I mean I suspect he had his ideas. His opinions. Certain stiff attitudes.

LUPE: [*not looking up*] When was this?

JEEP: And his body's still walking around?

SHOOTER: That's right. A walking stiff.

JEEP: Can anyone tell? I mean if we ran into this body could we tell it was vacant?

SHOOTER: I'm not sure.

LUPE: [*still thumbing through the book*] Well, how *could* you tell?

JEEP: [*to* LUPE] There must be a way. I mean something must be missing. You could tell if he wasn't all there.

SHOOTER: I don't know.

LUPE: [*still in book*] How? How could you tell?

JEEP: You'd know. I'd know. I mean with us, we know. We know. We hear each other. We hear our voices. We know each other's voice. We can see. We recognize each other. We have a certain— We can tell who's who. We know our names. We respond. We call each other. We sort of—We—We're not completely stranded like that. I mean—It's not—It's not like that. How that would be.

> Pause as JEEP *slowly pours the water over his hand.* SHOOTER *scratches his legs.* LUPE *thumbs through the book. After a short while* SHOOTER *sits back in the armchair with a jerk and holds his stomach.*

SHOOTER: I'm starving. Did we eat already?

LUPE: [*still in book*] You weren't here.

SHOOTER: I was here. I was here all along.

LUPE: [*in book*] Not at the right time.

> SHOOTER *stands suddenly in the chair with his pants legs still rolled up.* LUPE *and* JEEP *pay no attention.*

SHOOTER: You mean you ate without me!

> Pause as SHOOTER *looks around the space slowly.*

SHOOTER: [*to himself*] Now I'm beginning to regret my decision.

LUPE: What.

SHOOTER: [*gazing around him in amazement*] To stay in the chair.

LUPE: Oh.

SHOOTER: It was shortsighted. I'd give anything just to travel around this space. Just to lick the corners. To get my nose in the dust. To feel my body moving.

LUPE: [*referring to book*] Was it near the place where the sky rained fire?

SHOOTER: I can picture it. I give in to it. I let my body go. It moves out. It sniffs the board. My head imagines forests! Chain saws! Hammers and nails in my cars! A whole house is being built!

LUPE: [*in book*] Keep it to yourself.

SHOOTER: My nose finds things. Everything's churning with new pictures. Then suddenly it all ends again, and I'm back in the chair. But now I've ruined it. Now I've had my cake. Now neither one is any good. The chair doesn't get it on, and neither does the adventure. I'm nowhere.

LUPE: I'm trying to concentrate.

SHOOTER: Shall I tell a story?

LUPE: [*looking up from book*] Oh God! If I could find the place we could *read* a story!

SHOOTER: [*Still standing*] I'll tell a story. I feel like a story. Jeep? How 'bout it?

JEEP: [*still pouring water, blankly*] You bet.

LUPE: [*back into book*] Oh Jesus!

Through the story which SHOOTER *tells standing on the armchair,* JEEP *keeps pouring the water slowly over his hand into the bucket and* LUPE *keeps looking through the book.* SHOOTER *tells it directly to the audience.*

SHOOTER: One night there was some moths. A bunch of moths. In the distance they could see a candle. Just one candle in a window of a big house. The moths were tormented by this candle. They longed to be with this candle but none of them understood it or knew what it was. The leader of the moths sent one of them off to the house to bring back some information about this light. The moth returned and reported what he had seen, but the leader told him that he hadn't understood anything about the candle. So another moth went to the house. He touched the flame with the tip of his wings but the heat drove him off. When he came back and reported, the leader still wasn't satisfied. So he sent a third moth out. This moth approached the house and saw the candle flickering inside the window. He became filled with love for this candle. He crashed against the glass and finally found a way inside. He threw himself on the flame. With his forelegs he took hold of the flame and united himself joyously with her. He embraced her completely, and his whole body became red as fire. The leader of the moths, who was watching from far off with the other moths, saw that the flame and the moth appeared to be one. He turned to the other moths and said: "He's learned what he wanted to know, but he's the only one who understands it."

JEEP suddenly slaps the water in the bucket with his free hand and pulls a large dead fish out of the bucket and throws it on the floor. SHOOTER *looks down on it from the chair.* LUPE *sticks with the book.*

JEEP: I've about had it with this bucket! I can't figure out what I've been doing here all this time.

SHOOTER: [*still standing and looking down at the fish*] How deep is our well anyway?

JEEP: [*to* LUPE] What's happened to Liza?

LUPE: Washing dishes.

JEEP: [*to* LUPE] Have I been standing here all this time?

LUPE: [*looking up*] I don't know! I've been looking for the place! I wish people would just leave me alone!

SHOOTER: I'm not standing up here because I'm afraid of fish, I'll tell you that much. I was standing up here before the fish ever arrived. It's just a coincidence. It's not the way it looks.

JEEP: Shooter, could you create some reason for me to move? Some justification for me to find myself somewhere else?

SHOOTER: Only if you promise that you're not thinking that I'm afraid of fish just because I'm standing up here on the chair and there happens to be a fish in the house.

JEEP: I'm not thinking about you!

Suddenly LUPE *gives an exasperated exhale of air, slams the book shut, glares at the two men, stands and exits upstage.* SHOOTER *and* JEEP *are stuck in their respective positions. Short pause as they look at each other.*

SHOOTER: Go and pick up the fish.

JEEP *goes to the fish and picks it up.*

SHOOTER: Go and put the fish on the table.

JEEP *goes upstage of the table facing audience, moves the turkey carcass to one side and lays the fish down on the table.*

SHOOTER: [*still standing*] Take your jackknife out of your pocket.

JEEP *does it.*

SHOOTER: Open your jackknife. The big blade.

JEEP *does it.*

SHOOTER: Cut open the belly of the fish, starting from the pee-hole and slicing toward the head.

JEEP *cuts open the fish.*

SHOOTER: Now clean it like you would any other fish.

JEEP *goes about cleaning the fish in silence.* SHOOTER *sits back down slowly in the chair. He looks at his bare legs.*

SHOOTER: What's been going on in here? [*to* JEEP] Was there a party?

JEEP *keeps cleaning the fish.* SHOOTER *looks at his legs again.*

SHOOTER: Was someone taking liberties? [*He leans back in the chair with a sigh.*]

SHOOTER: It's agonizing. All this time I could've swore I was getting something done. I can't even remember eating. [*back to* JEEP] Did we eat already? Wasn't there a turkey? [*turns front again and leans back*] Somebody's gonna' have to bring me some food, you know. I've made this decision not to leave the chair and I'm gonna' stick with it. Come hell or high water. It's not my fault. [*back to* JEEP] I could have the fish. When you're finished with it, could you fry it up and bring it to me? If it's not too much trouble? [*no response from* JEEP, SHOOTER *turns front again and leans back in the chair*] This isn't the worst. It's just that my stomach is growling. I COULDN'T STAY HERE FOREVER! I don't know what possessed me. [*back to* JEEP] Didn't I say that I'll never leave the chair? [*back front again*] If I get up, it would be a sign of my weakness. Jeep? If I got up would you think I was weak? [*no answer*] This isn't the worst thing that could happen. [*short pause*]

JEEP: The table's littered with carcasses. Guts. Bones. The insides. I'm in the middle of all this.

SHOOTER: Who are you talking to?

JEEP: I'm swimming in it.

SHOOTER: [*still front*] It's nobody's fault, you know.

JEEP: I can't help eating. I'll eat to my dying day.

SHOOTER: Oh, brother!

> SHOOTER *gives a heave and a groan and pushes with his feet so that the armchair tips over backwards with him in it. The bottom of the chair conceals* SHOOTER *from the audience. Only his voice is heard.* JEEP *continues with the fish methodically.*

JEEP: [*looking at the fish*] If you were alone would you have done that?

SHOOTER: I'm still in the chair. I'm sticking to my promise.

JEEP: You wouldn't call it showing off?

SHOOTER: I'm at my wit's end. The whole world could disappear.

> *The two women enter from upstage. Each one holds a handle on either end of a large wicker basket full of wet laundry.* LUPE *is now wearing* LIZA's *apron with the pockets full of clothespins. They haul the basket down left center where the clothesline is. They set the basket down on the floor, and* LUPE *grabs one of the chairs and stands up on it to reach the clothesline.* LIZA *starts handing her the wet clothes, one piece at a time, from the basket, while* LUPE *pins them onto the line and pulls the line out, making room for the next piece. Gradually the clothes are strung clear across the stage but high enough so as not to block too much of the action.* JEEP *keeps working on the fish cutting the head off, scaling it, filleting it, cleaning it off in the bucket of water, etc. He is very meticulous about it and gets more involved as he goes along.* SHOOTER *remains hidden behind the armchair. The two girls remain closed off in their activity.*

JEEP: I'm starting to feel better already. You remember before when I was getting the fears?

SHOOTER: No. When was that?

JEEP: When I was asking you if you remembered when you were scared to go up and take a bath.

SHOOTER: That was a long time ago.

JEEP: I'm getting better now. Even in the middle of all this violence.

SHOOTER: You should've told me you were scared. I would've done something about it. I didn't realize you were scared.

JEEP: I'm in a better position now. Now I've got something to do.

> SHOOTER *pulls the armchair over on top of himself so that his arms stick out*

*the sides like a headless turtle. He moves the chair slightly from side to side with his
back. The women continue in silence with the laundry.*

JEEP: I can even imagine how horrifying it could be to be doing all this, and it doesn't
touch me. It's like I'm dismissed.

SHOOTER: Am I completely hidden?

JEEP: More or less.

SHOOTER: Maybe I'm gone.

JEEP: Maybe.

SHOOTER: That's what it's like.

JEEP: Maybe that's it, then. Gone.

SHOOTER *starts moving the armchair slowly around like a giant tortoise. The
girls pay no attention.*

SHOOTER: That's it all right. Flown the coop. Is there anyone to verify? To check it
out?

JEEP: [*looking at the girls*] Are you sure you want to?

SHOOTER: Maybe it's better like this. We can keep it a secret.

JEEP: Are you sure you're not there?

SHOOTER: More or less. Something creeps back, now that you mention it.

JEEP: Oh.

SHOOTER: What's the matter?

JEEP: I don't know. I got no references for this. Suddenly it's shifted .

SHOOTER: What's the matter? You have to clue me in.

JEEP: Once I was in a family. I had no choice about it. I lived in different houses. I had
no choice. I couldn't even choose the wallpaper.

SHOOTER: Are you getting to the point?

JEEP: I found myself in schools. In cars. I got arrested. That was when it changed. The
second I got arrested.

SHOOTER: Have you forgotten about me?

JEEP: The second I got arrested I understood something. I remember the phrase "getting in trouble." I remember the word "trouble." I remember the feeling of being in
trouble. It wasn't until I got in trouble that I found out my true position.

SHOOTER: What was that?

JEEP: I was in the world. I was up for grabs. I was being taken away by something
bigger.

SHOOTER: The cops?

JEEP: Something bigger. Bigger than family. Bigger than school. Bigger than the 4-H
Club. Bigger than Little League Baseball. This was Big Time. My frame of reference
changed.

SHOOTER: Did you go to jail?

JEEP: I went everywhere. Cop car, court, jail, cop car, jail, court, cop car, home, cop
car, jail. And everywhere I noticed this new interest in my existence. These new
details. Every scar was noted down. Every mark. The lines in my fingers. Hair. Eyes.
Change in the pocket. Knives. Race. Age. Every detail.

SHOOTER: Who was interested?

JEEP: A vast network. A chain of events. I entered a new world.

SHOOTER: Weren't you scared?

JEEP: I used to have this dream that would come to me while I was on my feet. I'd be on my feet just standing there in these walls, and I'd have this dream come to me that the walls were moving in. It was like a sweeping kind of terror that struck me. Then something in me would panic. I wouldn't make a move. I'd just be standing there very still, but inside something would leap like it was trying to escape. And then the leap would come up against something. It was like an absolutely helpless leap. There was no possible way of getting out. I couldn't believe it. It was like nothing in the whole wide world could get me out of there. I'd relax for a second. I'd be forced to relax because if I didn't, if I followed through with this inward leap, if I let my body do it I'd just crash against the wall. I'd just smash my head in or something. I had to relax. For a second I could accept it. That I was there. In jail. That I wasn't getting out. No escape. For a second. Then these thoughts would come. "How long? How long was I there for? A day. Maybe I could last a day. A week. A month? I'd never last a month! FOREVER!" That's the thought that did it. FOREVER! And the whole thing would start up again. Except worse this time. As though it wasn't just a thought. As though it really was. And then I'd start to move. I couldn't help myself. My body was shaking.

    JEEP begins to move around the stage. The words animate him as though the space is the cell he's talking about but not as though he's recalling a past experience but rather that he's attempting his own escape from the space he's playing in. The other actions continue in their own rhythm.

I'd start to make sounds. It just came out of me. A low moan. An animal noise. I was moving now. I was stalking myself. I couldn't stop. Everything disappeared. I had no idea what the world was. I had no idea how I got there or why or who did it. I had no references for this.

    JEEP just stands there. The others continue their actions. Lights fade slowly to black. The Christmas tree keeps blinking.

Adrienne Kennedy

∾

A Movie Star Has to Star
in Black and White

·

A Movie Star Has to Star in Black and White was produced by Joseph Papp as a work in progress at the New York Shakespeare Festival in New York on November 5, 1976, with the following cast:

WALLACE	Frank Adu
MARLON BRANDO	Ray Barry
EDDIE	Robert Christian
PAUL HENREID	Richard Dow
HATTIE	Gloria Foster
MONTGOMERY CLIFT	C. S. Hayward
JEAN PETERS/	
COLUMBIA PICTURES LADY	Karen Ludwig
CLARA	Robbie McCauley
BETTE DAVIS	Avra Petrides
SHELLEY WINTERS	Ellin Ruskin

Director: Joseph Chaikin
Lights: Beverly Emmons
Costumes: Kate Carmel
Music: Peter Golub

The movie music throughout is romantic.
The ship, the deck, the railings and the dark boat can all be done with lights and silhouettes.
All the colors are shades of black and white.
These movie stars are romantic and moving, never camp or farcical, and the attitudes of the supporting players to the movie stars is deadly serious.
The movie music sometimes plays at intervals when CLARA's *thought is still.*

CHARACTERS
  Clara
"Leading Roles" are played by actors who look exactly like:
  Bette Davis
  Paul Henreid
  Jean Peters
  Marlon Brando
  Montgomery Clift
  Shelley Winters
  (*They all look exactly like their movie roles.*)

Supporting roles by
  the mother
  the father
  the husband
  (*They all look like photographs Clara keeps of them except when they're in the hospital.*)

SCENES
  I. Hospital lobby and *Now Voyager*
  II. Brother's room and *Viva Zapata*
  III. Clara's old room and *A Place in the Sun*

Dark stage. From darkness center appears the COLUMBIA PICTURES LADY *in a bright light.*

COLUMBIA PICTURES LADY: Summer, New York, 1955. Summer, Ohio, 1963. The scenes are *Now Voyager, Viva Zapata* and *A Place In The Sun.*

The leading roles are played by Bette Davis, Paul Henreid, Jean Peters, Marlon Brando, Montgomery Clift and Shelley Winters. Supporting roles are played by the mother, the father, the husband. A bit role is played by Clara.

Now Voyager takes place in the hospital lobby.

Viva Zapata takes place in the brother's room.

A Place In The Sun takes place in Clara's old room.

June 1963.

My producer is Joel Steinberg. He looks different from what I once thought, not at all like that picture in *Vogue*. He was in *Vogue* with a group of people who were going to do a musical about Socrates. In the photograph Joel's hair looked dark and his skin smooth. In real life his skin is blotched. Everyone says he drinks a lot.

Lately I think often of killing myself. Eddie Jr. plays outside in the playground. I'm very lonely...Met Lee Strasberg: the members of the playwrights unit were invited to watch his scene. Geraldine Page, Rip Torn and Norman Mailer were there.... I wonder why I lie so much to my mother about how I feel.... My father once said his life has been nothing but a life of hypocrisy and that's why his photograph smiled. While Eddie Jr. plays outside I read Edith Wharton, a book on Egypt and Chinua Achebe. Leroi Jones, Ted Joans and Allen Ginsburg are reading in the Village. Eddie comes every evening right before dark. He wants to know if I'll go back to him for the sake of our son.

She fades. At the back of the stage as in a distance a dim light goes on a large doorway in the hospital. Visible is the foot of the white hospital bed and a figure lying upon it. Movie music. CLARA *stands at the doorway of the room. She is a Negro woman of thirty-three wearing a maternity dress. She does not enter the room but turns away and stands very still. Movie music.*

CLARA: [*Reflective; very still facing away from the room.*] My brother is the same...my father is coming...very depressed.

Before I left New York I got my typewriter from the pawnshop. I'm terribly tired, trying to do a page a day, yet my play is coming together.

Each day I wonder with what or with whom can I co-exist in a true union?

She turns and stares into her brother's room. Scene fades out; then bright lights that convey an ocean liner in motion.

SCENE I

Movie music. On the deck of the ocean liner from Now Voyager *are* BETTE DAVIS *and* PAUL HENREID. *They sit at a table slightly off stage center.* BETTE DAVIS *has on a large white summer hat and* PAUL HENREID *a dark summer suit. The light is romantic and glamorous. Beyond backstage left are deck chairs. It is bright sunlight on the deck.*

BETTE DAVIS: [*To* PAUL.] June 1955.

When I have the baby I wonder will I turn into a river of blood and die? My mother almost died when I was born. I've always felt sad that I couldn't have been an angel of mercy to my father and mother and saved them from their torment.

I used to hope when I was a little girl that one day I would rise above them, an angel with glowing wings and cover them with peace. But I failed. When I came among them it seems to me I did not bring them peace...but made them more disconsolate. The crosses they bore always made me sad.

The one reality I wanted never came true...to be their angel of mercy to unite them. I keep remembering the time my mother threatened to kill my father with the shot gun. I keep remembering my father's going away to marry a girl who talked to willow trees.

Onto the deck wander the MOTHER, *the* FATHER, *and the* HUSBAND. *They are Negroes. The parents are as they were when young in 1929 in Atlanta, Georgia. The* MOTHER *is small, pale and very beautiful. She has on a white summer dress and white shoes. The* FATHER *is small and dark skinned. He has on a Morehouse sweater, knickers and a cap. They both are emotional and nervous. In presence both are romanticized. The* HUSBAND *is twenty-eight and handsome. He is dressed as in the summer of 1955 wearing a seersucker suit from Kleins that cost thirteen dollars.*

BETTE DAVIS: In the scrapbook that my father left is a picture of my mother in Savannah, Georgia in 1929.

MOTHER: [*Sitting down in a deck chair; takes a cigarette out of a beaded purse and smokes nervously. She speaks bitterly in a voice with a strong Georgia accent.*] In our Georgia town the white people lived on one side. It had pavement on the streets and sidewalks and mail was delivered. The Negroes lived on the other side and the roads were dirt and had no sidewalk and you had to go to the post office to pick up your mail. In the center of Main Street was a fountain and white people drank on one side and Negroes drank on the other.

When a Negro bought something in a store he couldn't try it on. A Negro couldn't sit down at the soda fountain in the drug store but had to take his drink out. In the movies at Montefore you had to go in the side and up the stairs and sit in the last four rows.

When you arrived on the train from Cincinnati the first thing you saw was the WHITE AND COLORED signs at the depot. White people had one waiting room and we Negroes had another. We sat in only two cars and white people had the rest of the train.

She is facing PAUL HENREID *and* BETTE DAVIS. *The* FATHER *and the* HUSBAND *sit in deck chairs that face the other side of the sea. The* FATHER *also smokes. He sits hunched over with his head down thinking. The* HUSBAND *takes an old test book out of a battered briefcase and starts to study. He looks exhausted and has dark circles under his eyes. His suit is worn.*

BETTE DAVIS: My father used to say John Hope Franklin, Du Bois and Benjamin Mays were fine men.

Bright sunlight on FATHER *sitting on other side of deck.*

FATHER *gets up and comes toward them…to* BETTE DAVIS.

FATHER: Cleveland is a place for opportunity, leadership, a progressive city, a place for education, a chance to come out of the back woods of Georgia. We Negro leaders dream of leading our people out of the wilderness .

He passes her and goes along the deck whistling. Movie music. BETTE DAVIS *stands up looking after the* FATHER…*then distractedly to* PAUL HENREID.

BETTE DAVIS: [*Very passionate.*] I'd give anything in the world if I could just once talk to Jesus.

Sometimes he walks through my room but he doesn't stop long enough for us to talk…he has an aureole. [*Then to the* FATHER *who is almost out of sight on the deck whistling.*] Why did you marry the girl who talked to willow trees? [*To* PAUL HENREID.] He left us to marry a girl who talked to willow trees.

FATHER *is whistling,* MOTHER *is smoking, then the* FATHER *vanishes into a door on deck.* BETTE DAVIS *walks down to railing.* PAUL HENREID *follows her.*

BETTE DAVIS: June 1955.

My mother said when she was a girl in the summers she didn't like to go out. She'd sit in the house and help her grandmother iron or shell peas and sometimes she'd sit on the steps.

My father used to come and sit on the steps. He asked her for her first "date." They went for a walk up the road and had an ice cream at Miss Ida's Icecream Parlor and walked back down the road. She was fifteen.

My mother says that my father was one of the most well thought of boys in the town, Negro or white. And he was so friendly. He always had a friendly word for everybody.

He used to tell my mother his dreams how he was going to go up north. There was opportunity for Negroes up north and when he was finished at Morehouse he was going to get a job in someplace like New York.

And she said when she walked down the road with my father people were so friendly.

He organized a colored baseball team in Montefore and he was the Captain. And she used to go and watch him play baseball and everybody called him "Cap."

Seven more months and the baby.

Eddie and I don't talk too much these days.

Very often I try to be in bed by the time he comes home.

Most nights I'm wide awake until at least four. I wake up about eight and then I have a headache.

When I'm wide awake I see Jesus a lot.

My mother is giving us the money for the doctor bill. Eddie told her he will pay it back.

Also got a letter from her; it said I hope things work out for you both. And pray, pray sometimes. Love Mother.

We also got a letter from Eddie's mother. Eddie's brother had told her that Eddie and I were having some problems. In her letter which was enclosed in a card she said when Eddie's sister had visited us she noticed that Eddie and I don't go to church. She said we mustn't forget the Lord, because God takes care of everything...God gives us peace and no matter what problems Eddie and I were having if we trusted in Him God would help us. It was the only letter from Eddie's mother that I ever saved.

Even though the card was Hallmark.

July 1955.

Eddie doesn't seem like the same person since he came back from Korea. And now I'm pregnant again. When I lost the baby he was thousands of miles away. All that bleeding. I'll never forgive him. The Red Cross let him send me a telegram to say he was sorry. I can't believe we used to be so in love on the campus and park the car and kiss and kiss. Yet I was a virgin when we married. A virgin who was to bleed and bleed...when I was in the hospital all I had was a photograph of Eddie in GI clothes standing in a woods in Korea. [*Pause.*] Eddie and I went to the Thalia on 95th and Broadway. There's a film festival this summer. We saw *Double Indemnity, The Red Shoes* and *A Place In The Sun*. Next week *Viva Zapata* is coming. Afterwards we went to Reinzis on Macdougal Street and had Viennese coffee. We forced an enthusiasm we didn't feel. We took the subway back up to 116th Street and walked to Bencroft Hall. In the middle of the night I woke up and wrote in my diary.

A bright light at hospital doorway. CLARA *younger, fragile, anxious. Movie music. She leaves hospital doorway and comes onto the deck from the door her father entered. She wears maternity dress, white wedgies, her hair is straightened as in the fifties. She has a passive beauty and is totally preoccupied. She pays no attention to anyone, only writing in a notebook. Her movie stars speak for her.* CLARA *lets her movie stars star in her life.* BETTE DAVIS *and* PAUL HENREID *are at the railing. The* MOTHER *is smoking. The* HUSBAND *gets up and comes across the deck carry-*

ing his battered briefcase. He speaks to C L A R A *who looks away.* P A U L   H E N R E I D
goes on staring at the sea.

H U S B A N D: Clara, please tell me everything the doctor said about the delivery and
how many days you'll be in the hospital.

> *Instead of* C L A R A, B E T T E   D A V I S *replies.* P A U L   H E N R E I D *is oblivious of him.*

B E T T E   D A V I S: [*Very remote.*] I get very jealous of you Eddie. You're doing something
with your life.

> *He tries to kiss* C L A R A. *She moves away and walks along the deck and writes in
> notebook.*

B E T T E   D A V I S: [*To* E D D I E.] Eddie, do you think I have floating anxiety? You said
everyone in Korea had floating anxiety. I think I might have it. [*Pause.*] Do you
think I'm catatonic?

E D D I E: [*staring at* C L A R A.] I'm late to class now. We'll talk when I come home. [*He
leaves.*] When I get paid I'm going to take you to Birdland. Dizzy's coming back.

> *Movie music.*

C L A R A: July.

I can't sleep. My head always full of thoughts night and day. I feel so nervous.
Sometimes I hardly hear what people are saying. I'm writing a lot of my play, I
don't want to show it to anyone though. Suppose it's no good. [*Reads her play.*]

They are dragging his body across the green his white hair hanging down. They
are taking off his shoes and he is stiff. I must get into the chapel to see him. I must.
He is my blood father. God, let me in to his burial. [*He grabs her down center. She,
kneeling.*] I call God and the Owl answers. [*Softer.*] It haunts my Tower calling, its
feathers are blowing against the cell wall, speckled in the garden on the fig tree, it
comes, feathered, great hollow-eyed with yellow skin and yellow eyes, the flying
bastard. From my Tower I keep calling and the only answer is the Owl, God. [*Pause.
Stands.*] I am only yearning for our kingdom, God.

> *Movie music.*

B E T T E   D A V I S: [*At railing.*] My father tried to commit suicide once when I was in
High School. It was the afternoon he was presented an award by the Mayor of
Cleveland at a banquet celebrating the completion of the New Settlement building.
It had taken my father seven years to raise money for the New Settlement which
was the center of Negro life in our community. He was given credit for being the
one without whom it couldn't have been done. It was his biggest achievement.

I went upstairs and found him whistling in his room. I asked him what was
wrong. I want to see my dead mama and papa he said, that's all I really live for is to
see my mama and papa. I stared at him. As I was about to leave the room he said
I've been waiting to jump off the roof of the Settlement for a long time. I just had to
wait until it was completed…and he went on whistling.

He had tried to jump off the roof but had fallen on a scaffold.

> *Movie music. The deck has grown dark except for the light on* B E T T E   D A V I S
> *and* P A U L   H E N R E I D *and* C L A R A.

CLARA: I loved the wedding night scene from *Viva Zapata* and the scene where the peasants met Zapata on the road and forced the soldiers to take the rope from his neck...when they shot Zapata at the end I cried.

> *Deck darker. She walks along the deck and into door, leaving* PAUL HENREID *and* BETTE DAVIS *at railing. She arrives at the hospital doorway, then enters her brother's room, standing at the foot of his bed. Her brother is in a coma.*

CLARA: [*To her brother.*] Once I asked you romantically when you came back to the United States on a short leave, how do you like Europe Wally? You were silent. Finally you said, I get into a lot of fights with the Germans. You stared at me. And got up and went into the dining room to the dark sideboard and got a drink.

> *Darkness. Movie music.*

SCENE II

Hospital room and Viva Zapata. *The hospital bed is now totally visible. In it lies*
WALLY *in a white gown. The light of the room is twilight on a summer evening.*
CLARA's *brother is handsome and in his late twenties. Beyond the bed is steel hos-*
pital apparatus. CLARA *stands by her brother's bedside. There is no real separation*
from the hospital room and Viva Zapata *and the ship lights as there should have*
been none in Now Voyager. *Simultaneously brighter lights come up stage center.*
Wedding night scene in Viva Zapata. *Yet it is still the stateroom within the ship.*
Movie music. MARLON BRANDO *and* JEAN PETERS *are sitting on the bed. They*
are both dressed as in Viva Zapata.

JEAN PETERS: [*To* BRANDO.] July 11.

I saw my father today. He's come from Georgia to see my brother. He lives in
Savannah with his second wife. He seemed smaller and hunched over. When I was
young he seemed energetic, speaking before civic groups and rallying people to
give money to the Negro Settlement.

In the last years he seems introspective, petty and angry. Today he was wearing a
white nylon sports shirt that looked slightly too big…his dark arms thin. He had
on a little straw sport hat cocked slightly to the side.

We stood together in my brother's room. My father touched my brother's bare
foot with his hand. My brother is in a coma. [*Silent.*]

Eddie and I were married downstairs in this house. My brother was best man.
We went to Colorado, but soon after Eddie was sent to Korea. My mother has always said that she felt if she and my father hadn't been fighting so much maybe I
wouldn't have lost the baby. After I lost the baby I stopped writing to Eddie and
decided I wanted to get a divorce when he came back from Korea. He hadn't been
at Columbia long before I got pregnant again with Eddie Jr.

MARLON BRANDO *listens. They kiss tenderly. She stands up. She is bleeding.*
She falls back on her bed. BRANDO *pulls a sheet out from under her. The sheets are*
black. Movie music.

JEAN PETERS: The doctor says I have to stay in bed when I'm not at the hospital.

From now until the end MARLON BRANDO *continuously helps* JEAN PE-
TERS *change sheets. He puts the black sheets on the floor around them.*

CLARA: [*To her brother, at the same time.*] Wally, you just have to get well. I know you
will, even though you do not move or speak.

Sits down by his bedside watching him. Her MOTHER *enters. She is wearing a*
rose colored summer dress and small hat. The mother is in her fifties now. She sits
down by her son's bedside and holds his hand. Silence in the room. The light of the

305

room is constant twilight. They are in the constant dim twilight while BRANDO *and* PETERS *star in a dazzling wedding night light. Mexican peasant wedding music, Zapata remains throughout compassionate, heroic, tender. While* CLARA *and her* MOTHER *talk* BRANDO *and* PETERS *sit on the bed, then enact the Zapata teach-me-to-read scene in which* BRANDO *asks* PETERS *to get him a book and teach him to read.*

MOTHER: What did I do? What did I do?

CLARA: What do you mean?

MOTHER: I don't know what I did to make my children so unhappy.

> JEAN PETERS *gets book for* BRANDO.

CLARA: I'm not unhappy mother.

MOTHER: Yes you are.

CLARA: I'm not unhappy. I'm very happy. I just want to be a writer. Please don't think I'm unhappy.

MOTHER: Your family's not together and you don't seem happy.

> *They sit and read.*

CLARA: I'm very happy mother. Very. I've just won an award and I'm going to have a play produced. I'm very happy.

> *Silence. The* MOTHER *straightens the sheet on her son's bed.*

MOTHER: When you grow up in boarding school like I did, the thing you dream of most is to see your children together with their families.

CLARA: Mother you mustn't think I'm unhappy because I am, I really am, very happy.

MOTHER: I just pray you'll soon get yourself together and make some decisions about your life. I pray for you every night. Shouldn't you go back to Eddie especially since you're pregnant?

> *There are shadows of the ship's lights as if* Now Voyager *is still in motion.*

CLARA: Mother, Eddie doesn't understand me.

> *Silence. Twilight dimmer,* MOTHER *holds* WALLY's *hand.*
>
> *Movie light bright on* JEAN PETERS *and* MARLON BRANDO.

JEAN PETERS: My brother Wally's still alive.

CLARA: [*To her diary.*] Wally was in an accident. A telegram from my mother. Your brother was in an automobile accident...has been unconscious since last night in St. Luke's hospital. Love, Mother.

JEAN PETERS: Depressed.

CLARA: Came to Cleveland. Eddie came to La Guardia to bring me money for my plane ticket and to say he was sorry about Wally who was best man at our wedding. Eddie looks at me with such sadness. It fills me with hatred for him and myself.

> BRANDO *is at the window looking down on the peasants. Mexican wedding music.*

JEAN PETERS: Very depressed, and afraid at night since Eddie and I separated. I try to write a page a day on another play. It's going to be called a Lesson In Dead Language. The main image is a girl in a white organdy dress covered with menstrual blood.

> CLARA *is writing in her diary. Her* MOTHER *sits holding* WALLY's *hand,*

BRANDO *stares out the window,* JEAN PETERS *sits on the bed.* Now Voyager *ship, shadows and light.*

CLARA: It is twilight outside and very warm. The window faces a lawn, very green, with a fountain beyond. Wally does not speak or move. He is in a coma.
Twilight dims.

It bothers me that Eddie had to give me money for the ticket to come home. I don't have any money of my own: the option from my play is gone and I don't know how I will be able to work and take care of Eddie Jr. Maybe Eddie and I should go back together.

FATHER *enters the room, stands at the foot of his son's bed. He is in his fifties now and wears a white nylon sports shirt a little too big, his dark arms thin, baggy pants and a little straw sports hat cocked to the side. He has been drinking. The moment he enters the room the* MOTHER *takes out a cigarette and starts to smoke nervously. They do not look at each other. He speaks to* CLARA, *then glances in the direction of the* MOTHER. *He then touches his son's bare feet.* WALLY *is lying on his back, his hands to his sides.* CLARA *gets up and goes to the window.* BRANDO *comes back and sits on the bed next to* JEAN PETERS. *They all remain for a long while silent. Suddenly the* MOTHER *goes and throws herself into her daughter's arms and cries.*

MOTHER: The doctor said he doesn't see how Wally has much of a chance of surviving: his brain is damaged. [*She clings to her daughter and cries. Simultaneously.*]

JEAN PETERS: [*To* BRANDO.] I'm writing on my play. It's about a girl who turns into an Owl. Ow. [*Recites from her writings.*] He came to me in the outhouse, in the fig tree. He told me, You are an owl, I am your beginning. I call God and the Owl answers. It haunts my tower, calling.

Silence. FATHER *slightly drunk goes toward his former wife and his daughter. The* MOTHER *runs out of the room into the lobby.*

MOTHER: I did everything to make you happy and still you left me for another woman.

CLARA *stares out of the window.* FATHER *follows the* MOTHER *into the lobby and stares at her.* JEAN PETERS *stands up. She is bleeding. She falls back on the bed.* MARLON BRANDO *pulls a sheet out from under her. The sheets are black. Movie music.*

JEAN PETERS: The doctor says I have to stay in bed when I'm not at the hospital.

From now until the end MARLON BRANDO *continuously helps* JEAN PETERS *change sheets. He puts the black sheets on the floor around them.*

JEAN PETERS: This reminds me of when Eddie was in Korea and I had the miscarriage. For days there was blood on the sheets. Eddie's letters from Korea were about a green hill. He sent me photographs of himself. The Red Cross, the letter said, says I cannot call you and I cannot come.

For a soldier to come home there has to be a death in the family.

MOTHER: [*In the hallway she breaks down further*] I have never wanted to go back to the south to live. I hate it. I suffered nothing but humiliation and why should I have gone back there?

FATHER: You ought to have gone back with me. It's what I wanted to do.

MOTHER: I never wanted to go back.

FATHER: You yellow bastard. You're a yellow bastard. That's why you didn't want to go back.

MOTHER: You black nigger.

JEAN PETERS: [*Reciting her play.*] I call God and the Owl answers, it haunts my tower, calling, its feathers are blowing against the cell wall, it comes feathered, great hollow-eyes…with yellow skin and yellow eyes, the flying bastard. From my tower I keep calling and the only answer is the Owl.

July 8 I got a telegram from my mother. It said your brother has been in an accident and has been unconscious since last night in St. Luke's hospital. Love, Mother. I came home.

My brother is in a white gown on white sheets.

The MOTHER *and the* FATHER *walk away from one another. A sudden bright light on the Hospital Lobby and on* WALLY's *room.* CLARA *has come to the doorway and watches her parents.*

MOTHER: [*To both her former husband and her daughter.*] I was asleep and the police called and told me Wally didn't feel well and would I please come down to the police station and pick him up. When I arrived at the police station they told me they had just taken him to the hospital because he felt worse and they would drive to the hospital. When I arrived here the doctor told me the truth: Wally's car had crashed into another car at an intersection and Wally had been thrown from the car, his body hitting a mail box and he was close to death.

Darkness.

SCENE III

JEAN PETERS *and* BRANDO *are still sitting in* Viva Zapata *but now there are photographs above the bed of* CLARA's *parents when they were young, as they were in* Now Voyager. WALLY's *room is dark. Lights of the ship from* Now Voyager.

JEAN PETERS: Wally is not expected to live. [*She tries to stand.*] He does not move. He is in a coma. [*Pause.*] There are so many memories in this house. The rooms besiege me.

My brother has been living here in his old room with my mother. He is separated from his wife and every night has been driving his car crazily around the street where she now lives. On one of these nights was when he had the accident.

JEAN PETERS *and* BRANDO *stare at each other: A small dark boat from side opposite* WALLY's *room. In it are* SHELLEY WINTERS *and* MONTGOMERY CLIFT. CLARA *sits behind* SHELLEY WINTERS *writing in her notebook.* MONTGOMERY CLIFT *is rowing. It is* A Place In The Sun. *Movie music.* BRANDO *and* JEAN PETERS *continue to change sheets.*

CLARA: I am bleeding. When I'm not at the hospital I have to stay in bed. I am writing my poems. Eddie's come from New York to see my brother. My brother does not speak or move.

MONTGOMERY CLIFT *silently rows dark boat across.* CLARA *has on a nightgown and looks as if she has been very sick, and heartbroken by her brother's accident.* MONTGOMERY CLIFT, *as was* HEINREID *and* BRANDO, *is mute. If they did speak they would speak lines from their actual movies. As the boat comes across* BRANDO *and* PETERS *are still. Movie music.* EDDIE *comes in room with* JEAN PETERS *and* BRANDO. *He still has his textbook and briefcase.* SHELLEY WINTERS *sits opposite* MONTGOMERY CLIFT *as in* A Place In The Sun. CLARA *is writing in her notebook.*

EDDIE: [*To* JEAN PETERS; *simultaneously* CLARA *is writing in her diary.*] Are you sure you want to go on with this?

JEAN PETERS: This?

EDDIE: You know what I mean, this obsession of yours?

JEAN PETERS: Obsession?

EDDIE: Yes, this obsession to be a writer?

JEAN PETERS: Of course I'm sure.

BRANDO *is reading.* CLARA *from the boat.*

CLARA: I think the Steinbergs have lost interest in my play. I got a letter from them that said they have to go to Italy and would be in touch when they came back.

EDDIE: I have enough money for us to live well with my teaching. We could all be so happy.

CLARA: [*From boat.*] Ever since I was twelve I have secretly dreamed of being a writer. Everyone says it's unrealistic for a Negro to want to write.

Eddie says I've become shy and secretive and I can't accept the passage of time, and that my diaries consume me and that my diaries make me a spectator watching my life like watching a black and white movie.

He thinks sometimes…to me my life is one of my black and white movies that I love so…with me playing a bit part.

EDDIE: [*To* JEAN PETERS *looking up at the photographs.*] I wonder about your obsession to write about your parents when they were young. You didn't know them. Your mother's not young, your father's not young and we are not that young couple who came to New York in 1955, yet all you ever say to me is Eddie you don't seem the same since you came back from Korea.

> EDDIE *leaves.* MONTGOMERY CLIFT *rows as* SHELLEY WINTERS *speaks to him. Lights on* BRANDO *and* PETERS *start slowly to dim.*

SHELLEY WINTERS: [*To* MONTGOMERY CLIFT] A Sunday Rain…our next door neighbor drove me through the empty Sunday streets to see my brother. He's the same. My father came by the house last night for the first time since he left Cleveland and he and my mother got into a fight and my mother started laughing. She just kept saying see I can laugh ha ha nothing can hurt me anymore. Nothing you can ever do, Wallace, will ever hurt me again, no one can hurt me since my baby is lying out there in that Hospital and nobody knows whether he's going to live or die. And very loudly again she said ha ha and started walking in circles in her white shoes. My father said how goddamn crazy she was and they started pushing each other. I begged them to stop. My father looked about crazily.

I hate this house. But it was my money that helped make a down payment on it and I can come here anytime I want. I can come here and see my daughter and you can't stop me, he said.

CLARA: [*To diary.*] The last week in March I called up my mother and I told her that Eddie and I were getting a divorce and I wanted to come to Cleveland right away.

She said I'm coming up there.

When, I said. When?

It was four o'clock in the afternoon.

When can you come I said.

I'll take the train tonight. I'll call you from the station.

Should I come and meet you?

No, I'll call you from the station.

She called at 10:35 that morning. She said she would take a taxi. I went down to the courtyard and waited. When she got out of the taxi I will never forget the expression on her face. Her face had a hundred lines in it. I'd never seen her look so sad.

CLARA: [*Reciting her play.*] They said: I had lost my mind, read so much, buried myself in my books. They said I should stay and teach summer school. But I went. All the way to London. Out there in the black taxi my cold hands were colder than ever.

No sooner than I left the taxi and passed down a gray walk through a dark gate and into a garden where there were black ravens on the grass, when I broke down. Oow…oww.

SHELLEY WINTERS: This morning my father came by again. He said Clara I want to talk to you. I want you to know my side. Now, your mother has always thought she was better than me. You know Mr. Harrison raised her like a white girl, and your mother, mark my word, thinks she is better than me. (It was then I could smell the whiskey on his breath…he had already taken a drink from the bottle in his suitcase.) [*She looks anxiously at* MONTGOMERY CLIFT *trying to get him to listen.*]

CLARA: [*Reading from her notebook.*] He came to me in the outhouse, in the garden, in the fig tree. He told me you are an owl, ow, oww, I am your beginning, ow. You belong here with us owls in the fig tree, not to somebody that cooks for your Goddamn Father, oww, and I ran to the outhouse in the night crying oww. Bastard they say, the people in the town all say Bastard, but I—I belong to God and the owls, ow, and I sat in the fig tree. My Goddamn Father is the Richest White Man in the Town, but I belong to the owls.

Putting down her notebook. Lights shift back to PETERS *and* BRANDO *on the bed.*

JEAN PETERS: When my brother was in the army in Germany, he was involved in a crime and was court-martialed. He won't talk about it. I went to visit him in the stockade.

It was in a Quonset hut in New Jersey.

His head was shaven and he didn't have on any shoes. He has a vein that runs down his forehead and large brown eyes. When he was in high school he was in All City track in the two-twenty dash. We all thought he was going to be a great athlete. His dream was the Olympics. After high school he went to several colleges and left them; Morehouse (where my father went), Ohio State (where I went), and Western Reserve. I'm a failure he said. I can't make it in those schools. I'm tired. He suddenly joined the army.

After Wally left the army he worked nights as an orderly in hospitals; he liked the mental wards. For a few years every fall he started to school but dropped out after a few months. He and his wife married right before he was sent to Germany. He met her at Western Reserve and she graduated cum laude while he was a prisoner in the stockade.

Movie music. Dark boat with MONTGOMERY CLIFT *and* SHELLEY WINTERS *reappears from opposite side.* MONTGOMERY CLIFT *rows.* CLARA *is crying.*

SHELLEY WINTERS AND CLARA: Eddie's come from New York because my brother might die. He did not speak again today and did not move. We don't really know his condition. All we know is that his brain is possibly badly damaged. He doesn't speak or move.

JEAN PETERS: I am bleeding.

Lights suddenly dim on MARLON BRANDO *and* JEAN PETERS. *Quite suddenly* SHELLEY WINTERS *stands up and falls "into the water." She is in the water, only her head is visible, calling silently.* MONTGOMERY CLIFT *stares at her. She continues to call silently as for help, but* MONTGOMERY CLIFT *only stares at her: Movie music.* CLARA *starts to speak as* SHELLEY WINTERS *continues to cry silently for help.*

CLARA: The doctor said today that my brother will live; he will be brain damaged and paralyzed.

After he told us, my mother cried in my arms outside the hospital. We were standing on the steps, and she shook so that I thought both of us were going to fall headlong down the steps.

SHELLEY WINTERS *drowns. Light goes down on* MONTGOMERY CLIFT *as he stares at* SHELLEY WINTERS *drowning. Lights on* CLARA. *Movie music. Darkness. Brief dazzling image of* COLUMBIA PICTURES LADY.

END

Richard Nelson

❧

Conjuring An Event

A Fairy Tale

•

Conjuring an Event was first presented in workshop at The Mark Taper Forum/Lab in 1976, directed by John Dennis, in a production supported by the Office for Advanced Drama Research; and later presented by The Williamstown Second Company, directed by Douglas C. Wager.

Conjuring an Event was produced by The American Place Theatre (Wynn Handman, Artistic Director) on March 15, 1978, with the following cast:

CHARLIE	Michael Cristofer
ANNABELLA	Sigourney Weaver
WAITER	John Jellison
MAN	MacIntyre Dixon
SMITTY	Dan Hedaya
SLEEVES	Frank Hamilton

Director: Douglas C. Wager
Sets: David Lloyd Gropman
Costumes: William Ivey Long
Lights: Paul Gallo
Sound: Carol Waaser

ACT ONE

Stage dark. Pause. Lights up on the Pen and Pencil Club. A large heavy wooden table, large enough to seat eight, center left. On the table, candles, glasses, cups, etc. and a white lace tablecloth which has been pushed away from stage right. Around the table, four or five straight leather chairs, and a lamp or two between these chairs. Stage right, two or three high-backed comfortable chairs in a partial semicircle, facing down left. Next to the centermost chair, an end table. Upstage, a wooden newspaper rack. Everything very American Gothic. At the stage right end of the table: CHARLIE (*late twenties*) *sits. He wears a black eyepatch over each eye. His head is down so his face is nearly against the table. In front of* CHARLIE, *neatly laid out: a small china bowl, an ashtray, an empty china plate.* ANNABELLA (CHARLIE's *girl, mid-twenties*) *sits next to* CHARLIE. *She reads a couple of newsmagazines. Together at the far left end of the table—*SMITTY (CHARLIE's *slightly older brother*) *sits, his focus on* MR SLEEVES *who is seated at the end of the table, facing right.* SLEEVES, *a publisher, is reading a manuscript, the pages of which are scattered on the table in front of him. In the centermost comfortable chair, a man (late thirties, athletic, though a shade overweight). He is reading a newspaper which is strung through a bamboo pole. He wears a turtleneck and slacks. Long pause as* CHARLIE *sniffs at the plate in front of him.*

CHARLIE: [*Yelling.*] Why can't I smell this!! [*Suddenly he grabs the plate, lifts it over his head, and smashes it against the edge of the table.*]

    SMITTY *and* SLEEVES *do not look up. The* MAN *looks toward* CHARLIE *from over his paper.* ANNABELLA *continues to read. Pause.*

CHARLIE: [*Trying to calm himself, speaks to himself.*] Listen to the prep, Charlie. Listen to yourself. Is that what you want? Anger? Doubtful. It's times like this. As you prepare. Ready yourself to play all out to the finish. To dare. To go beyond. To rip up the margins. To pass the limits. The edges. To press unrestrained into absolute depth-reporting!

    It's times like this, Charlie. Pal. When you can't just fly off the handle. When you can't succumb. When you gotta press. Keep the effort intact. That initiative alive! The pressure on high, Charlie! Or else just figure yourself TKO'd on this score. Is that what you want, Charlie? Left to be like every other half-baked, part-time reporter who plays it safe with just facts and figures. Who plays his angle with no depth. No decent depth. Left covering tired stories. Beaten-to-death scoops. Doing a Woodward and Bernstein. A Reston and a Rather. Left with that sort of smoothy routine, Charlie. That sort of tired art form, full of cheap tricks, half efforts. Bloodless! Lifeless, Charlie! No stakes involved. One-directional currents. Where the reporter sets up the rules so he can pull himself at any time. At will. Unplug. Unaffected by the tides. The heat. The pressures. The undertows. The whiplash! Where the reporter never dares to cross that line between himself and the story. Between the art and the artist. The drop and the ocean. Be like that, Charlie. Left doing that kind of number. You wanta stay stuck all your life doing that gritless reporter routine? Too fuckin' scared to follow through? *You want that?*

No you don't. 'Cause you see the hollowness in all that. The tricks. Fantasies. And lack of stamina in all that. You see past all that 'cause you've been there, Charlie. You've done your cover stories. Done your columns with the personal flavor. You've exhibited your face. Your name. Your style. And voice. You've paraded your personal point of view! And now you are finished with all that! Washed your hands of all that! Now you are sick of all that!

So now you are ready, Charlie. Ready to go beyond such natural observation. To move past the logic of those limits. That's the urge. To extend yourself and cover a story so close. Too close for comfort. Breathe down its neck. Closer than is possible. Natural. To dare! To prime the senses so as to touch, taste, smell it out. To flush it out! To become that pure, vacuous, senseful reporter. To compile beyond understanding. Faster than time. To wreck the boundaries of the senses. Timeless. Weightless. Selfless. A satellite! To pass through the Wolfe, the Teddy White, the Cronkite, the Reasoner. To be on the inside, Charlie. The fuckin' inside! *The inside looking out!*

Well that's the urge, Charlie. The shape of the effort. The choice. Either pull out and run with the easy. The cheap and easy crowd. Or quit this crybaby stuff. This anger that's gonna crap up the movements. Quit it! And put your move back in motion. Let yourself go. And work at it, Charlie! You gotta work at it! And when you're polished, you'll know it. You'll be ready then. [CHARLIE *puts his head back down against the table, and begins to sniff the bowl.*]
  Pause.
ANNABELLA: [*Suddenly begins thumbing through her newsmagazine, back to front.*] Still not a word, Charlie. Not a blessed word. I mean it only makes sense! You'd think that with one of their own. When one of their kind attempts to. Dares. Well, after all, what we're doing is gonna affect them. It's gonna clear the way for them. Expand their scope. Their possibilities. Shit. You'd think they'd want to make it a big deal. Make a big splash out of this. I would. I certainly would if I were them…Not a fuckin' comma…[*She glances at the bowl* CHARLIE *is smelling.*] You picking anything up? [CHARLIE *doesn't answer.*] If not a headline, at least a mention in The Newsmakers. At least. But isn't that just the problem. With papers today. Wouldn't know a story if it bit 'em on the leg. Maybe we should just take the initiative, Charlie. Grab it. Point them in the right direction. Go after the publicity. A touch of fame. Couldn't hurt, Charlie. A press conference. An interview. To whet the imagination. Wire photos with captions: Reporter goes solo! Reporter goes all out! There's a story here. What the hell it couldn't hurt! Maybe might even get us a grant or something. An angel, maybe…[*Checks out* CHARLIE's *progress again.*] You want a hint?
CHARLIE: *No!* [*He takes deep sniffs.*] I ain't gettin' a decent beat on shit! How's my angle?

ANNABELLA: [*Checks out his position over the bowl.*] You're right on top of it, Charlie. You're there, guy. Just go ahead and keep sniffing from there.

CHARLIE: [*Still over the bowl.*] Oh sure. Great. Yeh. The way you mouth there's nothing to this number. [*Picks up his head.*] Wipe my forehead. [ANNABELLA *does with a napkin.*] I'm just getting nothing I can take a good swing at. Nothing's clear. Clean. On the money. I'm being blocked. Blocked good! *Why the hell can't I sniff this!*

ANNABELLA: Take your time, guy. Take it slow. The smells will come.

CHARLIE: [*Waving her back.*] All right. All right. Stand back. I'll keep the heat on. I'll keep swinging through. You back?

ANNABELLA: [*She leans away from* CHARLIE.] Yeh.

> Pause. CHARLIE *begins to smell again. Harder.* ANNABELLA *returns to her magazines.*

ANNABELLA: Maybe if we gave them a nudge. In our direction. A lead-in. Put them on the right track. After all, they can't exactly deny that they've got the space. Anyone could see they do. Anyone with eyes. Half this goddamn sheet is pumped with fillers. Shaggy dog stories. Replays. You'd think they'd be eager. Beat a path to our door. Do a Man in The News bio. You'd think, wouldn't you? It only makes sense. A mention. Not one damn mention. What the hell are they afraid of?

CHARLIE: [*Sniffing very hard now.*] Hey. Wait a sec! Wait a sec! I'm getting something now. I am. I am. I'm tuning in. It's passing through. The smell. This. Feel it. Feel it. Something's coming through.

ANNABELLA: [*Sets her magazines down; tense, excited.*] Is it, Charlie? You sure?

CHARLIE: Shut up. [*Sniffing even harder.*] Yes. Yes. Define. Crystallize. Sharpen. It's a…It's a…it's a common smell…

ANNABELLA: [*Bending over to look in the bowl.*] That's correct, guy.

CHARLIE: Hardly a day goes by without ya getting a whiff of this smell. Am I right?

ANNABELLA: Yes! Yes, you're absolutely right.

CHARLIE: And this smell…it's of…I'm pinpointing. Plotting…It's of…I'm on the track. Boy does this feel great. Of…of…of…

ANNABELLA: Of what? What?

CHARLIE: [*Triumphant. Picks up his head.*] Paper!! It's paper! That's it. I'm smelling paper. No doubt about it. No static. Clear as a bell. Paper! [*Returns to smelling.*] That…that low grade stuff. Made half out of rag. Rag bond. Wrinkled. Creased. But recently pressed.

ANNABELLA: [*Calm again.*] Smell again, guy. I think you must have caught a cross-wind from somewhere else.

CHARLIE: I said, it's paper!

ANNABELLA: [*Picking up her magazine again.*] Give it another run, guy. Go ahead.

CHARLIE: It's not paper? But I'm positive. It's perfectly clear to me. I swear…I must at least be close. [*Gives it another big sniff.*]

> WAITER *enters near* MAN, *carries a couple more bamboo poles with newspapers strung through.*

WAITER: Another paper, sir?

> MAN *ignores him.* MAN *stares at* CHARLIE. WAITER *exits.*

CHARLIE: [*Giving up.*] Ok. What the hell is it then?

ANNABELLA: It's salt, Charlie.

CHARLIE: Salt? Are you kidding? You for real? That should be an easy move.... I'm smelling paper!

ANNABELLA: I'll go back to the kitchen and get some fresh smells. Don't worry, guy. You're gonna turn this trick. You'll do it. [*She exits.*]

MAN: Waiter!

CHARLIE: Yeh. Do it. Just do it. Shit.... Salt? I'm smelling paper! [*Continues to sniff.*]

> WAITER *enters.*

WAITER: [*To man.*] A paper, sir?

MAN: Does this club stock any New York State wine?

WAITER: Yes sir. We carry…

MAN: Great Western Chablis, by any chance? [*He pronounces the "s."*]

WAITER: I believe. Yes, I'm sure that we do carry…

MAN: Then be a good sport, and take a bottle over to that gentleman there. [*Nods toward* CHARLIE.]

WAITER: That gentleman? Yes, sir. [*He exits.*]

> *Short pause.* SLEEVES *sighs and puts down the manuscript.* SMITTY *who has been closely watching* SLEEVES *as he read now anxiously waits for his reaction.*

SMITTY: [*Finally.*] Well?

SLEEVES: [*In a fog.*] Well what?

SMITTY: What do you think, Mr. Sleeves? Ain't that got juice? [SLEEVES *doesn't respond.*] Charlie's book, Mr. Sleeves. Don't it pack enough wallop to knock you on your ass? My brother's a real genius for reporting a story. Ain't he…? Mr. Sleeves…? You there? It's spellbinding stuff. It'll catch the Public Eye. Dead Center. Well…

SLEEVES: [*Sighs again, looks around.*] Jeeze, it's nice being back with reporters again. Nice. This club. Feel the journalistic beat. Rhythm. Magic. Can't say I haven't missed it.

SMITTY: [*Confused.*] Oh, sure. Yeh…But I ain't no reporter, Mr. Sleeves. That's Charlie's trick. I'm just peddling his book here—

SLEEVES: [*Not really hearing him.*] I know. I know that…I was a reporter, Smitty. Once. Way the hell back. Before your time. Before almost everybody's time now. Before TV. Satellites. Synthetic grass and domed stadiums. A whole different kind of ballgame back then. You wouldn't know the rules. Energy. Electricity. Magic. Art— back then. You felt it on the back of your neck. Hair sticking up. Understand?

SMITTY: Heck no!

SLEEVES: Maybe you do. Maybe you do. Ever hear of the Algonquin Group?

SMITTY: The what?

SLEEVES: That was a roundtable club—actually twelve square tables pushed together in the hotel's dining room. But it looked almost round when we were done. That was in New York…Talk. Talk. Talk. Drink. That kind of club.

SMITTY: Yeh. That kind of club. Sure. But, Mr. Sleeves. About the book…

SLEEVES: Ben Hecht. Ring Lardner. Marc Connelly. Charlie MacArthur. Dorothy Parker. I could go on. More names. The tops. The greats. Hall of Fame. Muscle. At our peak almost thirty of us—combining more raw knowledge of the way the world turned than any thousand jokers alive. We were reporters. With a capital R. If you know what I mean.

SMITTY: I don't!

SLEEVES: We'd sit and shoot the bull. Handicap politicians in an election. Exchange recent scoops. Except on the nights when one of us would get a call, a tip on a fast news break. A mug who'd been shot up. A world leader who'd snuck into our town for an operation or 'a little on the side.' If you know what I mean. Just one phone allowed. So everyone could hear. That was the rule. Then all thirty of us would tear out, upsetting tables, chairs, the buxom barmaid, slug down a last whiskey, and run for daylight and the morning editions. Front page! Hold the front page! I got a scoop! Yes. Magic.

> *Short pause.*

SMITTY: Mind if I smoke? [*Lights a cigarette.*]

SLEEVES: There was an energy. A reporter felt like an artist. He had somethin' driving him on. No, it weren't money then. Or broads. Or your name in caps. It was electricity. You was on your belly, eye to eye with the earth. Watch it spin. Clock its time. Energy. Touching the live wires. Feel the heat. Near. Close. Pulse. Pulse. Our experiences were poems. They'd move folks to tears, laughter. Hair sticking up. Papers were read then. Meant something. A lot. Everything almost. So you'd feel the muscle, getting men and women choked up, their guts strung tight. And the magic. 'Cause we didn't understand any better than the ordinary Joe on the street did. How it happened. But we felt it better. Magic. And muscle. [*Pause.*] And that's when it happened. I can't forget. I'm sorry. The magic was most potent too. That's when the telegrams came. Money. We want you. We all got wires from Babel. Our name for Hollywood. Jaded City. Like a faucet had been turned on, the energy, it just flowed away. To get diluted. Gummed up. Offers of five hundred bucks a week to write for the talkies when we was making that in three months. So. We push together only five tables at first. Then three. Finally one square table was all we needed. MacArthur. Hecht. Lardner. Connelly. Parker. I could go on. All gone. Gone away. Goodbye. I tried. So hard. Gritted my teeth. Bit my lip. Held the line. Keep the art alive. The magic. Keep the ballgame going. The feeling that the reporter is an artist with an audience out there listening and waiting for what passes through his eyes. Magic. Months. Seasons. Years. [*Short pause.*] The fellas come East to visit. Hundred-dollar suits. Talk about swimming pools. How they don't like snow no more. It was gone. Goodbye. The magic fades fast when it's diluted. I don't regret staying. I don't. I tried.

> *Long pause. The* WAITER *enters with the wine. He sets it on the table in front of* CHARLIE. *No one pays any attention to him. He exits.*

SLEEVES: [*Abrupt change of tone.*] Well. We were talking about this manuscript, weren't we, Smitty?

SMITTY: Charlie's manuscript? This one here? You wanta talk about? Well I'll be. Well I'll be damned. I thought I'd gone and lost you for good back there.

SLEEVES: [*Ignoring* SMITTY.] As I was saying, Smitty...

SMITTY: Saying? You weren't saying nothin' I could make sense out of, Mr. Sleeves.

SLEEVES: [*Patting the manuscript.*] What this book needs...is a bit more punch, Smitty. More...pizazz. Flash.

SMITTY: Flash?

SLEEVES: Right now, it's awfully raw stuff. It's good. Maybe great. Who knows for sure? Who can ever be positive? But it's raw. Raw. There's a heck of a lot of work still to be done on this, Smitty. It's gonna have to be cooked quite a bit.

SMITTY: Well if that's all that's troubling you. Sure. I mean we know that. Don't we Charlie? It's just a mass of articles now, but Charlie, he'll whip it into shape with no sweat.

SLEEVES: It's all...muscle. In fact, one might say it's pure muscle. And what muscle at that. And that's good, Smitty. A plus. Powerful. Quite exceptional, really. The energy in this. Electricity. It's hot. You can just feel it. Feel it! [SMITTY *puts his hand on the manuscript*] But where are the bones, Smitty? There aren't any bones to hang all that muscle on! The bones, Smitty. Do you feel any?

SMITTY: No. I guess I don't. No bones.

SLEEVES: But I can do that myself. Construct the bones. [*He turns to another page.*]

SMITTY: You? Construct the bones? Wait a minute. What I miss? Are you hinting that you're interested in doing the book, Mr. Sleeves?

SLEEVES: You know, Smitty, this story here, this...event.

SMITTY: Yeh. Course I know it. I read the book. You keep jumping around from one thing to somethin' different. How 'bout holding one note for a while. OK, Mr. Sleeves? Now let me see if I can get this straight. Are you interested or what in publishin' Charlie's book?

SLEEVES: I was saying to myself, at the time this story broke. I was saying what a Jim Dandy book it could make. Isn't that amazing, Smitty? Really quite remarkable.

SMITTY: Was that a yes or a no?

SLEEVES: Just for starters, Smitty. So you can see what all has to be done. The time involved. The effort. Work. Sweat. With something like this. In fiddling with the movement. Tightening the strings. Quickening the pulse. Pulse. Just for starters, let's take this title. In fact, go ahead and take it. 'Cause it's all wrong. Might even say, it's bad. No angle. No bite. No zing. You need an angle to grab guts with, Smitty. Guts. To make a big splash!

SMITTY: Yeh. A splash. Right. Uh, you know, Mr. Sleeves, I ain't got much of a grip on what you've been saying. Now that ain't necessarily your fault. But maybe if ya spoke with Charlie. I mean, he's right at home with the artistic talk. [*Turns to* CHARLIE, *waving him over, in a loud whisper.*] Charlie!

SLEEVES: But I'll come up with something, Smitty. Don't you worry. Always did, didn't I? Before. Way the hell back. Started off my career writing headlines for the obits. If that didn't tax the imagination, nothing could.

SMITTY: Yeh I guess so. [*To* CHARLIE, *whisper.*] Charlie! Quick, guy. Quick! I think he's interested. I think he might do it. Charlie! Come on, guy, come on. Did you hear what I said? He might do it.

SLEEVES: Just give me time. To roll up my sleeves. Plunge in. Get used to the currents. Get back the touch. The feel. I had it once. I did. Before. What a touch.

SMITTY: Sure, what's the rush. No sweat. [*To* CHARLIE.] What the hell's wrong with you? Charlie, will you pay attention. Jesus Christ. Charlie!

SLEEVES: [*Yells.*] *Just give me time!* I'll come up with something big. Juicy. It'll come to me. In a rush. Like before. I'll just be standing somewhere, having a sandwich, thinking about something else and it'll come! Something to make people take notice. Give 'em a chill. Hair sticking up. Give me time! I'll do it! *I'll do it!*

SMITTY: [*Now more confused by this outburst.*] Uh. Sure. Easy there, Mr. Sleeves. Just take it slow. Take your time. What's the hurry. I mean, no big rush is there? [*Loud voice.*] Charlie! Will you pay attention! Will you quit that stupid smelling and listen!

SLEEVES: [*Suddenly looks up at* SMITTY. *Cold. Direct.*] What did you say?

SMITTY: Huh?

SLEEVES: What the fuck did you say!!

SMITTY: Me? I told Charlie to stop his smelling and pay attention. I mean, he should know what's going on. It's his book.

SLEEVES: Is that what he's doing? Smelling? I thought he was drunk.

SMITTY: I guess he sort of looks that way, don't he?

SLEEVES: Why is he smelling, Smitty?

SMITTY: It ain't that important, Mr. Sleeves.

SLEEVES: It's important to me!

SMITTY: Well, Charlie, he could explain it a lot better than me, but, see, he says he's sharpening his sense of smell. To prepare himself…uh. He's sort of worked out that smelling is the way in. See. A clue. A secret. Least that's what he says.

SLEEVES: A way in? I'm not sure I follow.

SMITTY: I don't either really, Mr. Sleeves. It's just some crazy notion Charlie's got that after covering events live, you know, firsthand, like this book here. After reporting for so long. Then the next step he says, well, it's to learn to conjure…to conjure a story up…an event up. I think it's some artistic binge. A fad, you know. Won't come to nothin'. But that's what he's preparing for. That's why he's smelling.

SLEEVES: [*He has turned pale, begun to shake.*] Conjure an event?

SMITTY: Yeh. Pretty crazy, huh?

SLEEVES: [*Jumping out of his seat, he screams.*] Don't let him do it! Stop him! Stop him! [*Panicking,* SLEEVES *runs out. Upset. Scared shitless.*]
    Short pause.

SMITTY: Mr. Sleeves? Mr. Sleeves! What the hell got into you? What about the book? The book! [SMITTY *runs out after him.*]
    Pause. CHARLIE *picks up his head.*

CHARLIE: Christ, what a racket! Can't hear myself think. How's a Joe supposed to get any work done with all this shoutin' going on? Shit. No wonder I'm getting nowhere

fast. Pissing in my pants. Them talking on my backswing. Drowning out my signals. Breaking down my rhythm! So's I can't sustain the drive! *No peace and quiet!*
[*Deep breath.*] Yeh. I'm perfecting my sense of smell. Number one move. Smelling
is the way into a conjure all right. To prime the senses. Numero uno step. To ready
the tools needed to make that big break. Necessary to gain the inside. To lessen the
friction. *But I got too many goddamn interruptions!* [*Short pause.* CHARLIE *continues to sniff. Then looks up.*] Wait a sec. Wait a sec. Now who am I kidding? Huh? Just
who am I hustling this round? I'm pulling on my own fucking leg. Blaming bad
play on a bit of chatter. That's sour-grape-itis, man. You are losing! Losing bad!
And you're grabbing at excuses. Cheap. Cheap and easy. Hunting for a chance to
blunt your own damn urge, Charlie! That ain't like you. Ain't your number. You
know better than that. You're no Weiskopf. You're no Nastase. Find no alibi in a bad
call. Ain't gonna quit over the condition of the course. Not you, guy. Not your
angle. [*Short pause. Deep breath.*] This kind of stroke, well it's just gonna take time.
Patience. Patience. It ain't easy. You knew that before ya started. To attempt. To
break out. Knew you'd be swinging on a thread. Dancing on a blade. It'll just take
time. Time. Pace. My edge—gotta be razor sharp. My timing—right on. My speed—
fast. My reflexes—a whip. It'll come, guy. All that will come. I'll pull this score off, all
right. In time. No sweat. I've cracked hard scores before. Though nothin' quite like
this. On this scale. Well just do it! Yeh. Head down. Feet set. Solid concentration.
Focus. Good balance. Hang tough. Hang in there. Action. Now give it a big sniff. Do
it! Do it! [*He sniffs harder. Harder. Looks up.*] Crap! Just do it? Just do it? That's
easier said, guy. Easier flashed than put into play. Yeh. *Why can't I smell out salt!*...An
easy move. Beginner stuff. Slow ball. Snap and I should have it. But I smell ten
things at once and can't pick out the right one! I'm groping when I should be absorbing. I'm reacting when I should be on top! I keep coming up empty. Called out
looking! I'm still knocking at the goddamn door! I've got the desire. I've wanted
this. Wanted this bad. I've put my time in. Haven't I? I'm practicing. I've practiced.
So where's it got me? How far? How deep? Me. Me. Got me! Nothing. Nowhere.
Trying. Coming up empty handed. I am spent, I tell you! Complete! That's enough!
I've had enough!

>   He picks up the salt bowl, holds it for a second over his head, and then smashes
>   it against the floor. He begins to stare down at the table. Pause. The MAN has been
>   watching and listening to CHARLIE. He now takes out a pile of red 3 × 5 file cards,
>   shuffles them, then begins writing on them—still with one eye on CHARLIE. He
>   writes throughout the remainder of the Act.
>   ANNABELLA enters with a tray of food—smells—covered by a white cloth.

ANNABELLA: I've got more smells from the kitchen, Charlie...Where's Smitty?
CHARLIE: I don't know. He was yelling somethin' and I think he run off.
ANNABELLA: With that publisher guy?
CHARLIE: I don't know. I was busy. Didn't pay no attention.
ANNABELLA: I brought you more smells.
CHARLIE: Don't bother no more 'bout that. I'm gonna take a break for a while.

ANNABELLA: Sure, Charlie. It must be kinda tough work...I'll put them on the table. [*She does.*]

CHARLIE: I'm feelin a little lightweight. Suspended. Out of it. I need some rest.

ANNABELLA: You just say when, guy, and I'll set you up to try another smell.

CHARLIE: I mean, I'm gonna take a long break.... Like maybe a month or two. I wanta recharge myself, get my feet on the ground again, and come back to this run fresh. I'm feeling stale. Maybe I pushed myself too hard these past two weeks.

ANNABELLA: [*Confused.*] A month?

CHARLIE: Yeh. Maybe two. Or three. Or four. Who the hell knows? Long as it takes to get my head back in working shape.

ANNABELLA: *Four* months? Hey guy...I never heard you talk about having to recharge yourself before. You always said you got a lot of good feedback *from* your work.

CHARLIE: Well, sure. Sure. Yeh, I do...I mean, I used to, see. But this is different, OK? Real different. Another kind of ballgame completely. Look, this conjuring route ain't in stages like my other stuff where I could move in or out at will, take a break when the mood struck, keep as big a distance between me and the show as I wanted. Here the force has got to come from you. Only from you, see. It's total involvement, see.

ANNABELLA: Sure, Charlie.

CHARLIE: So it's dangerous. Yeh. It's either win or lose. Success/failure. So's it can burn you out quick. Zap! No chance to gather momentum. Keep your bearings. You either hit the jackpot or you wear yourself out trying. *And I am wearing myself out good!*

ANNABELLA: Hey guy...?

CHARLIE: Damn it, *I just need to unplug for a while!!*
    Short pause.

ANNABELLA: Guy...? Are you pulling out?

CHARLIE: [*Quick. Very defensive.*] Is that what you think?

ANNABELLA: It's just—*four* months, Charlie.

CHARLIE: *Is that what you think?!!! Is it?!!* Shit. Well, if it is. If it...then maybe. Well, maybe you just oughta start slinking yourself out of here. Out of earshot. Real fast. Real fast. Yeh. Well, maybe you oughta just stop mumbling under your breath. Mumbling, "Poor Charlie. He don't know what the fuck he's doing. Too bad what's happening to Charlie."

ANNABELLA: I ain't been mumbling nothing, Charlie.

CHARLIE: Stop mumbling, yeh, and maybe start telling me, "Hey Charlie. Hey there. I'll be right back in a sec. Just gotta run off around the corner." *And then start running!! And keep running!! So run!! Run!!! Come on, damn it, run!!!*
    Pause. CHARLIE *covers his head.*

ANNABELLA: [*Depressed because she figures* CHARLIE's *effort to conjure is over, but she tries to hide her depression.*] Hey, guy, you know, I 'm feelin pretty edgy myself...I mean, what the hell, right? What the fuck, a break couldn't hurt, could it? [CHARLIE *doesn't respond.*] I mean, what we've already got going, we ain't gonna lose by pausing for a few beats, right? In fact, might do a whole lot of good. As you say, Charlie, we could come back feeling fresh. Come back feeling on our toes again. Get the rhythm back in the bounce, right? The strength in the grip, right? [CHARLIE *remains turned away,* ANNABELLA *wants his attention.*] I didn't mean you was *really* pulling out, guy. I didn't mean that at all. [*Short pause.*] Hey, Charlie, what about the World Series. That's comin' up, right? How about hittin' that and turning a sports reporter trick? You know, just for the fun of it. Just to get the juices free again. There's no pressure in that. The format's easy. And shit, they always got free beer and sandwiches in the press room. What do you say? [*No response.*] Yeh, just like we used to, guy. You know? Like in St. Petersburg. You remember St. Petersburg, don't you? [CHARLIE *remains turned away.*] Hey, what *was* that system you had going down there? Remember? [*No response though he is relaxing a bit.*] At night...Let me see if I've got this right. At night, you worked in the press department at the Wrestling Arena. Am I right? You were writing releases for the two local dailies. Was that it?

    Short pause.

CHARLIE: Yeh.

ANNABELLA: And then in the morning...right? Under a different name you did sports for the afternoon paper. Rewriting your own press releases. Right? And there was something else, wasn't there?

CHARLIE: In the afternoon, under still another name—

ANNABELLA: You rewrote your releases again for the morning paper! Right! [CHARLIE *looks up.*] Shit, you had yourself a monopoly going, didn't you? Total control. You caught the news coming and going.

CHARLIE: I ran the whole fucking show.

    Short pause.

ANNABELLA: Yeh, that was a whole lot of fun. Just working in low gear. Just trotting around the bases. They were great times. Weren't they?

CHARLIE: Wait a sec. Wait one sec. And what was it you were doing down there? I remember you was into somethin' pretty smooth down there too.

ANNABELLA: Yeh, I was doing a kid journalism number, Charlie. Kid journalism. News for kids.

CHARLIE: Yeh, that's right.

ANNABELLA: *Weekly Reader* stuff. I rewrote the news so kids could read it. Change the few big words. Pick stories kids might like. That kind of setup.

CHARLIE: [*Smiling.*] I remember.

ANNABELLA: Great times. They were. No danger. For either of us. The forms were easy. We had the outline. And we were just filling it in .... We were sittin' pretty. And we were happy, weren't we, guy?

    Short pause.

CHARLIE: [*Suddenly explodes.*] *God damn it!!!!!* Shit, why d'you bring up that for? You trying to subvert me? Is that it?!! *Is that it?!*

ANNABELLA: What are you talking about?

CHARLIE: Make me take a nice high dive into the past?

ANNABELLA: What???

CHARLIE: *Well, damn it!! Damn it!!! I ain't built for that! I ain't built for that!! I am a reporter, not no god damn historian!!!!!!!*
> *Pause.*

ANNABELLA: [*Meekly.*] I was just...

CHARLIE: You was just nothin! Just don't do it again. [*To himself.*] Wreck my fuckin edge. That's what that stuff could do. My fuckin edge.

ANNABELLA: Sorry...

CHARLIE: Forget it! Jesus, get me a drink.

ANNABELLA: Sure, Charlie. There's some wine here...

CHARLIE: Yeh. Yeh. Pour it. That'll do.... Now leave me alone. I want some goddamn quiet. Ok?

> *Pause.* ANNABELLA *pours a glass of wine from the bottle the* WAITER *brought. She hands* CHARLIE *the glass. He sits perfectly still, holding the glass out in front of him. He looks like he is meditating. After a moment,* SMITTY *enters. He is upset. Angry. Frightened. Pissed off.*

ANNABELLA: [*In a whisper.*] Smitty, where you been?

SMITTY: [*Loud voice.*] I caught up with him, Charlie.

ANNABELLA: Sh-sh! Charlie don't want to be bugged.

SMITTY: Oh, that's too bad. Yeh. But I could care less. 'Cause man he's gonna be bugged blue 'til I get some kind of explanation! [*Short pause.* CHARLIE *hasn't moved.*] See, Charlie, I caught up to him. 'Cause he'd fallen flat on his face. On the sidewalk in front of Woolworth's. The cement. Was crawling on his hands and knees. Til he fell again. Then just flopping around on his belly. Oh, a great sight. Yeh. When I got close he was screaming, "Stop him! Stop him!" Great. Awful. Screaming. See guy, it turned my stomach to watch.

ANNABELLA: Who?

SMITTY: Sleeves!

ANNABELLA: The publisher?

SMITTY: I didn't want to get too close. So I stood in the crowd. We're all silent. Looking. Looking at Sleeves. Unbelievable. Chilling. In seventh grade there was this girl. An epileptic. She sat next to me in general science. Ok. Biggest breasts in class. I couldn't look at 'em. She had three fits by my side. Peanuts compared to Sleeves. Peanuts! See! He dragged his face across the cement. Ripped the skin. Blood. Yeh. Blood. Lots. Pain. Like he was fighting something off. Beat it back. "Stop him!" Who? You want to guess? Huh? I could see his eyes darting. Crazy. Crazy. It was like...I don't know what. He ripped himself up good and two cops took him away.

ANNABELLA: Od'd?

SMITTY: On what? I've been with him...No. No, Annabella. I don't think so. See I'm chasing another connection. You still with me, Charlie? Hang in there. Hang in, guy. See, I got a suspicion now that there's more to this conjuring act than I'd suspected. Am I getting warm, Charlie? Hit a nerve?

ANNABELLA: What are you talking about?

SMITTY: Conjuring ain't just some jerk-off fad you're going through, like I thought.

Huh, guy? There's too many volts for that. There's a danger sign on the kit. Right? You're playing ball on the warning track, aren't ya?…Listen brother, you should know I ain't about to run and jump ship on ya. I've got a stake in this. I'm in this. But I think I should be told if we're moving into a strong current. *I got a right to know what's coming down!!!*

CHARLIE *has remained still. It now becomes clear that he has been sniffing the wine.*

CHARLIE: [*Quietly.*] Great Western Chablis. [*He doesn't pronounce the "s."*]

SMITTY: *What?!!* Didn't you hear me?

CHARLIE: [*Still quietly.*] Annabella. This wine. Read me its label.

ANNABELLA: "Great Western Chablis."

SMITTY: Have you heard a fucking word that I've been saying? About Sleeves?

CHARLIE: Annabella. Give me something else to smell. Quick.

ANNABELLA: …but…

CHARLIE: [*Shouting.*] For Christ's sake, hurry!!

SMITTY: Charlie, you tryin to break my tackle, guy? Is that it? Is that what you're tryin? To wiggle your butt out of this? Well, if you are. Let me let you. *It ain't gonna work!!!*

ANNABELLA *takes the cloth off the tray of smells. She picks out a potato and places it in front of* CHARLIE.

CHARLIE: [*Matter-of-factly.*] A potato. An Idaho potato.

Brief pause.

ANNABELLA: Yeh. Hey, that's right.

SMITTY: What? He smelled that?

ANNABELLA: [*Ignoring* SMITTY.] I don't know if it's from Idaho.

CHARLIE: It is. Something else!!

SMITTY: He smelled that?!!!

ANNABELLA *puts a can of soup in front of him.*

CHARLIE: A can. Soup. Campbell's Cream of Mushroom Ten and three-quarter ounces. Packaged in New Jersey.

SMITTY: New Jersey?!

CHARLIE: Camden.

ANNABELLA: It's happening. Damn it, it's happening! He's on his way!

SMITTY *has picked up the soup can and looks at the label.*

SMITTY: On his way where? *Where!!!?*

CHARLIE: [*Smelling out everything in front of him—the ashtray, the silverware, then what is on the tray.*] A cigarette butt. Marlboro 100s…. Spoon. Stainless steel. Tablespoon. Made in Japan…. Morton's salt…. Arm and Hammer Baking Soda…. El Rio Taco Shells…. Plantation Blackstrap Molasses…. Quaker Oats…. Log Cabin Maple Syrup…. Gulden's spicy brown mustard.

SMITTY: Let me give him something. [*Pulls out a pen.*] Here. Try smelling out this.

ANNABELLA: Put it closer!

CHARLIE: A ballpoint.

SMITTY: [*Starts to take the pen back.*] Yeh. That's right.

CHARLIE: Sheaffer. Black ink.

SMITTY: Ok. Ok.

CHARLIE: Refillable. $1.95 retail.

SMITTY: That's enough.

CHARLIE: Medium grip.

SMITTY: [*Pulls pen back.*] I said, *that's enough!* Christ. How did he do that? First Sleeves, then this. Annabella, *how the fuck could he smell that!!!?*

CHARLIE: [*Very still.*] The smells.

ANNABELLA: [*To* SMITTY.] Shut up.

CHARLIE: All of a sudden. They've separated. Separated into distinct blocks. [*The lights have begun to fade, except for a spot on* CHARLIE.] It's incredible. Really. Everything now appears to be moving toward a clarity. Into focus.

No blurs. No more crosscurrents. No gusts. The wind's died down. Movement is slowing down. Unbelievable. Stagnant. Out there. Posed. Like a Rousseau painting of smells. Of tastes. Of sights. [*He takes off his eyepatches. Lights continue to fade.*] No more blurred edges. No. None. Honest. No more dulled senses. Overlaps. The glass has been wiped clean. All of a sudden, no more harmonies. See, only the basic melody is playing. For me. [*Smiles.*] For you, Charlie. Just for you. Them big doors are set to swing open. Am I right? You can just feel that can't you? There'll be an open road. There'll be an easy access, a clear road to the main event. To your score, Charlie. Yeh. It's happened. See, it has happened! It's in you!! [*Laughs. Lights continue to fade.*] All of a sudden, the Reporter's High Art is in you!! And it'll be working *for* you, Charlie! Tonight! I don't believe it. Say it! It'll be tonight! Say it! Tonight. Say it! [*Blackout except for spot on* CHARLIE. *He yells.*] Tonight, I will conjure!!!!!!! [*Suddenly lights up, as before,* CHARLIE *sits back in his chair, confused, upset, he covers his head. Pause.*]

ANNABELLA: Charlie? Charlie, somethin' wrong?

CHARLIE: [*Without looking up.*] I don't know.

ANNABELLA: I thought you'd be burstin' now, right? All keyed up, you know? I mean, it's happening, Charlie. Isn't it? It's happening, right?

CHARLIE: [*Turns away.*] Give me some space, I don't feel too hot all of a sudden.

ANNABELLA: [*Short pause, steps back, glances at* SMITTY.] Maybe you're just too excited now, guy. Maybe you're just too hepped up. Maybe that's it.

CHARLIE: [*Suddenly erupts.*] That's not it!!!!!!! [*He swings his hand across the table and knocks everything to the floor.* SMITTY *steps back. Short pause. Quietly, mostly to himself.*] You know, I don't know why I did that.

The MAN, *as the lights were fading, stood up and put on his coat and hat. He now approaches* CHARLIE.

MAN: Charlie? [*He shuffles the file cards.*]

ANNABELLA: [*To* SMITTY.] Who the hell's that?

SMITTY *shakes his head.*

MAN: I overheard what you're up to, Charlie.

CHARLIE: So what?

ANNABELLA: Look, he don't wanta be pestered, OK?

MAN: [*Ignoring her.*] And I just wanted to wish you well tonight.

    CHARLIE *looks up at him.*

ANNABELLA: That's nice. That's real nice. I'm sure Charlie appreciates that. [*She tries to move him along.*]

MAN: That is, of course, if you are still planning to work tonight. I didn't misunderstand you, did I, Charlie?

CHARLIE: What the hell is that supposed to mean?! Jesus, what biz is it of yours, anyway?

ANNABELLA: Come on, mister. I don't wanta have to call the waiter.

MAN: It's just that, at the moment. Correct me if I am wrong, Charlie, but at this precise moment, you don't seem terribly excited about your "project." [CHARLIE *waves* ANNABELLA *away.*] You aren't having second thoughts, are you, Charlie?

CHARLIE: Look mister. I'm fuckin thrilled, right? I can't wait, OK? Inside, I'm bouncin, see! Just 'cause I don't wear it on my god damn sleeve!!

MAN: Excellent. Excellent. That's all I wanted to know. Then, I wish you well, Charlie. I'll be pulling for you. [*Exits.*]

    Pause.

CHARLIE: [*To* ANNABELLA *and* SMITTY; *yells.*] *I'm fucking thrilled!!!!!*

    Blackout.

ACT TWO

Stage dark. Pause. A small fire is started center stage. Lights up on a study. CHARLIE'S *apartment. Center: a large desk facing downstage. Small wastebasket is on the desk. The fire is in this wastebasket. A number of chairs, a lamp or two, piles of old newspapers and newsmagazines, etc.—around.* CHARLIE, *without eye-patches, sits behind his desk, asleep. He wears a bright red track suit.* SMITTY *and* ANNABELLA *stand feeding the fire with pieces of paper—*CHARLIE'S *manuscript;* ANNABELLA *has a metal poker. She shreds the paper while* SMITTY *is bunching up a number of pieces at once and tossing them into the flames. Both speak softly so as not to wake up* CHARLIE. *Pause.*

SMITTY: This is a bum idea, Annabella. A zero, see. But what I think don't seem to matter much around here anymore.

ANNABELLA: Don't crumple them up like that. They won't burn good that way.

SMITTY: When did you become an expert? [*Pause.* SMITTY *keeps on bunching up the paper.*] We're taking down our backstop. That's what we're doing now, ya know. That's just what Charlie's having us do. It's crazy. It don't make sense. We'll have nothin' to fall back on.

ANNABELLA: Who's falling back, guy?

SMITTY: [*Trying to ignore her.*] What I don't see is why we have to give up one direction just 'cause Charlie's into another. Ain't he ever heard about insurance? Jesus, we haven't even run all the business heats yet. I still got the feeling there could have been a nice score in this manuscript. We seemed close with Sleeves, didn't we?

ANNABELLA: But there's a bigger score coming, Smitty. Ya got to remember that. And ya got to figure on giving up something to make that kind of run.

SMITTY: Yeh. Sure. Sure. So we get rid of past angles like this book—as a necessary step, to lighten the load. So Charlie says. Yeh. But does Charlie say anything about the danger signs posted along that route? You don't know nothin' about that fact, Annabella, but I do!

ANNABELLA: All the signs Charlie sees, say "go!"

SMITTY: Are you really sure of that?

ANNABELLA: What's that supposed to mean?

SMITTY: It's just that, for a guy who says he's set up so great. You know. Charlie's always said he had to be 100% to even approach this act. Well he ain't been actin' 100% has he?

ANNABELLA: He's been lookin' fine to me.

SMITTY: You may call the way he's been actin' tonight "fine," but I don't.

ANNABELLA: Smitty, that's all just part of the game plan. Somethin' Charlie's gotta move through.

SMITTY: Maybe. Yeh. Sure. Maybe that's all that it is. I can figure that. But all I'm saying is that if Charlie's gotta go, then OK, go. Go. But go slow. I ain't discounting the score here. I ain't saying that. How could I? I saw what he did with those smells back at the club. I don't understand it. But I saw. But all I'm really saying is that I ain't sure a score is guaranteed right now neither. That this is the best time. So why don't he take it easy. Wait a week or so. Let whatever has happened be given time to settle in. Then we wouldn't have to take down this backstop 'til we're double sure he's ready. That's all. Right now, I just think Charlie's moving too fast.

ANNABELLA: Too fast for you, maybe.

SMITTY: That's just what I'm saying. Too fast for me. For my taste. My nerves.

ANNABELLA: But you don't really think Charlie's gonna pull up one beat 'cause of what you think?

      CHARLIE *groans.*

ANNABELLA: He's coming around.

CHARLIE: [*Waking up; hardly understandable.*] Involvement. Involvement. Tonight…

ANNABELLA: [*Shoving the remainder of the manuscript into the fire.*] Come on. He said he wanted some time to himself when he came to. [ANNABELLA *starts to exit.*] Come on.

SMITTY: Wait a minute. I wanta talk with him.

CHARLIE: [*Yelling.*] *Because tonight! Tonight…!* [*Awake.* CHARLIE *is shaken. Short pause. Sees* SMITTY *and* ANNABELLA.] I thought I said I wanted to be alone. God damn it, what do I have to do? Spell everything out? Leave me alone! [*Screams at them.*] *Leave me alone!!* [CHARLIE *covers his head with his hands.*]

ANNABELLA: [*To* SMITTY.] Come on.

SMITTY: [*Hesitates. To* ANNABELLA.] You see what I mean?

      ANNABELLA *and* SMITTY *exit.*

CHARLIE: Tonight. Tonight what? I don't know. That's right, I don't know. Crazy. Yeh. Crazy dream, all right. [*Relaxes a bit, removes his hands from his face.*] Charlie. Get this. Get a hold of yourself and get this, guy. Do you know who you were in your dream? Huh, Charlie? What do you make of this? You…was…the fucking *New York Times.* Yeh, Charlie, the Times. The whole goddamn thing!…Yeh. Me.

    What do you think, Charlie? I don't know. Could just show how close you are. How ready. Yeh. The *Times.* Show how confident I am. How set. Maybe. Maybe…. But then why am I shaking?

    Short pause.

    Let's see. I was sitting. I was sitting here checking out my rhythm and reflexes. Concentrating on reflexes. 'Cause they're gonna be a big tool in a conjuring act. Or so I suspect. Reactions gonna have to be fast. Right. OK, I was doing a reflex power bit. To get myself prepped. For tonight…Then what? Then I shot asleep. And started running.

    In an alley. Broken glass. Winos passed out. Women beating rugs. I'm sprinting. But it's easy. No effort. I come across a crowd of guys. Twenty or thirty. Just hanging around. But all look bushed. Panting. Their tongues out. Baggy pants. Cheap suits. Just standin' about. I recognize three of 'em. *Boston Globe. Chicago Tribune. Philadelphia Inquirer.* They smile at me. But don't say nothin'. I feel sad for a moment, but a bus comes by and takes me away.

I walk into a modern office building. No windows. Steel. No ventilation. Everyone is smoking up a storm. The noise gives me an earache. Deafening. I carry an umbrella. Some fellas sip coffee by the water cooler. They shout something. Hands waving. I can't hear. I get closer. They ask if it's raining outside. They introduce themselves as *New York Daily News, L.A. Times,* and *Washington Post.* We shake hands. Their palms hot and damp from the coffee. Their sleeves rolled up. Bags under their eyes. Smoking. Puffs. Clouds. I choke. Cigarette burns down their arms. Scars. I put a handkerchief over my mouth. I catch a taxi to the roof.

This is my office. Above the timber line. Fantastic view of the ocean. I notice that it's been quiet when the phone rings. The caller asks for *The New York Times.* I tell him: that's me. I read him the sign on my desk: "I've got the best reflexes in the biz. I'm the quickest to react. Can move better from an event outward than anyone else in the whole journalistic field. Some event happens—zap—my reaction fast as lightning." Goodbye. I hang up.

I start to giggle. So I'm the fucking *Times.* I put my feet up on my desk. Smoke a Cuban stogie. So I'm the *Times.* And I ain't even winded.

I start a letter. To my readers. For the front page. "Dear Reader. The *Times* Announces! After Months of Self-Examination. After Striking Conclusions..." I start again. "Dear Reader." For the final edition. In *Times* type. "The *Times* Announces A Shift in Policy! A Change of Angle! A New Stance and Handle! Dear Friends! Dear Readers! It Is Now The *Times*' Hope! The *Times*' Dream! The *Times*' Driving Ambition! That No One Is Ever Gonna Say Again!—Never!—That The Fucking *New York Times* Lacks Involvement! Involvement!" [*Screams, out of control.*] Nobody!!!! *'Cause Tonight, See, Tonight I'm Gonna Conjure!!!* [*Taken aback by his outburst,* CHARLIE, *upset, covers his head with his hands. Short pause.*] What the...? Conjure. Yeh. Sure. [*Short pause.*] I got this feeling, Charlie, that there is something about this that you ain't quite grasped.

> *The* MAN *of Act* I *enters dressed as an Old 1930s Reporter—baggy pants, white shirt, brimmed hat with a press card stuck in it.* CHARLIE *will not recognize this reporter as the* MAN. CHARLIE *doesn't notice him until he speaks.*

OLD REPORTER: Hello, Charlie.

CHARLIE: [*Startled.*] Who the hell are you?...What are you, from some weekly? [OLD REPORTER *doesn't respond.*] Listen, I don't know what the fuck you're doing in here. I don't know why they let you in. Annabella probably thought it'd be real nice to get some eye on this act. She's been after that for a long time. But believe me, this ain't the time, fella. OK? Right now I don't want nobody hangin' around while I'm gettin myself together. You with me? Now beat it out of here.... Did you hear me?

OLD REPORTER: I hear you're gonna try to conjure, Charlie.

CHARLIE: She tell you that too? Well, yeh, I might. Now scram, will you?

OLD REPORTER: You know you ain't the first to make this kind of run, Charlie .

CHARLIE: I thought I said scram!…Jesus, are you deaf?

OLD REPORTER: You ain't the first to have the urge, Charlie. The hunger. Push. To wanta erase the foul line. The out of bounds. Move out of the pocket. Throw away the book of rules. No limits. No holds barred. No end. No whistles.

CHARLIE: Who the hell *are* you? Who told you about me?

OLD REPORTER: Back in 1960, a novelist turned reporter tried this trick—he ended up stabbing his wife in the middle of a New York street. He got off lucky—just a couple of months in Bellevue. You might not be so lucky, Charlie.

CHARLIE: So you're educated in the past moves of this ballgame. So what?…That don't give you no right to come busting in here.

OLD REPORTER: There's a lot more. In 1970, Ed Sanders over-amping on the Manson murders came real close to lying expired in the trunk of a car—doing permanent meditation next to a tire. But he pulled out in time. Smart fella, he was.

CHARLIE: Don't you think I know that! Christ. But Ed, see, didn't have the reflexes I do. Though sure I gotta admire his guts. What are you after, pal!

OLD REPORTER: There's Talese, who's spent the last six years throwing himself deeper and deeper into a sexual mores in America trip. Last seen, he was commuting between a massage parlor on 39th Street and a nudist camp in New Jersey. His friends say, Charlie, he is stuck for good. He ain't ever gonna come up for air.

CHARLIE: I don't know what your angle is, buster…

OLD REPORTER: In 1971, a former sports writer—like yourself, Charlie—he razzled and dazzled as he mainlined America with a Vegas number. You can't say he wasn't prepared. He's got scars from that venture, Charlie, and he ain't even felt all the effects yet.

CHARLIE: [*Really nervous.*] Who says he hasn't? Huh? I know Hunter and if he's still stinging then it's 'cause he hadn't practiced like I have. But wait just a minute!

OLD REPORTER: And that's just a few of the *big* guns. There are hundreds of small frys like yourself, Charlie, whose fates were never documented.

CHARLIE: [*Upset.*] Small frys! Jesus Christ, man! Now that's it! That does it! You've gone too far now!

OLD REPORTER: The question is: will you, Charlie?

CHARLIE: Huh?

OLD REPORTER: Will you go too far.

CHARLIE: What the fuck are you after, anyway? Did someone set you up for this? Is that it? [CHARLIE *has stood up, pacing.*] To throw me off the goddamn tracks? Subvert my confidence? Is that it! Stand still when I'm talking to you!

OLD REPORTER: I'm not the one who is moving, Charlie.

CHARLIE: [*Stops pacing for a beat, confused.*] What?

OLD REPORTER: Maybe you should take a step back and look at yourself, guy.

CHARLIE: Me? I am looking. And I'm looking good!

OLD REPORTER *has taken out of his pocket a stack of red 3 × 5 file cards with a ribbon around them. He places them on* CHARLIE's *desk.* CHARLIE *does not notice this.*

OLD REPORTER: Total involvement: that's no light sport, Charlie. I just thought I should warn you. [*Turns to exit.*]

CHARLIE: You warn me! Get out! Throwing out doubts. Jesus! [CHARLIE *picks up the poker* ANNABELLA *had been using and threatens the* OLD REPORTER.] You want a smack in the face! *Get the hell out!!*

    OLD REPORTER *exits whistling.*

CHARLIE: [*Upset, pacing again; after a pause.*] Jesus. What the fuck was he…? Talking like a history book. Last month's scratch sheet. What was he after? Huh? Bringing up Hunter, Norman, Gay, Ed. OK. OK. They were good. Right. And they got crunched. Sure. But so what? *So what!* What's that got to do with me? Here. They weren't set. They weren't practiced. They all just fell into their involvement acts. Not me. I'm set, right? I've studied, right? I've trained, right? *Well haven't I!*…He warn me. I'll show him. I'll fuckin' show him!! Annabella! Smitty!

    ANNABELLA *enters.*

CHARLIE: Let's get this show on the road. *Let's fuckin' roll!*

ANNABELLA: Sure, guy. What can I do?

CHARLIE: Where's Smitty?

SMITTY: [*Entering.*] Right here, Charlie.

CHARLIE: Great. Now let's get all this crap pushed back. I'm gonna need room for this. Lots of fuckin' space. And light. I want every goddamn light I own in here. OK? So let's move it!

    CHARLIE *paces, pleased.* ANNABELLA *begins to push back the chairs, piles of papers, etc.* SMITTY, *still worried, doesn't move, stares at* CHARLIE.

ANNABELLA: Smitty!

    SMITTY *hesitates then slowly goes to help* ANNABELLA—*though he continues to watch* CHARLIE.

CHARLIE: [*Smiling; to himself.*] That old guy did you a big favor, Charlie. Course he didn't mean to. That's for sure. But he did just the same. He fuckin' got your goat, guy. And that's all that was needed. [Laughs.] All Charlie needed. Shit. One minute you're down, watching some joker try to tie your shoelaces together. Then the next. The next. I'm back on top. I'm set up good. He had no idea. I'll show him. I'll show him something all right .

    ANNABELLA *and* SMITTY *on opposite sides of a big chair, trying to lift it off.*

ANNABELLA: Pick it up, Smitty.

SMITTY: Shut up.

CHARLIE: [*To* ANNABELLA *and* SMITTY.] By the way, why *did* you let that crazy old guy in here? I did tell you both I wanted to be left alone.

ANNABELLA: [*Looking around.*] What old guy?

CHARLIE: The old guy who just ran out of here. I'm surprised he didn't run ya both down. He did a big peel out bit when I went after him with this. [*Holds up the poker.*]

ANNABELLA: I didn't see nobody. Smitty?

SMITTY: Not a soul, Charlie.

CHARLIE: Are you two joking or somethin'? If you are, that ain't very funny.

ANNABELLA: I'll go get the lights. [*She starts to exit.*]

CHARLIE: Wait a minute. He was just right here. Standing there. I talked with him. [*He is getting nervous.*] But neither of you saw him.

ANNABELLA: Maybe he's still in the room.

CHARLIE: I said I chased him out! [CHARLIE *smashes the poker against the desk.*]
    Short pause. SMITTY *and* ANNABELLA *look at each other, concerned for*
    CHARLIE. CHARLIE *starts to pace again.*

SMITTY: Look Charlie. You're seemin' a touch shakey, guy. Maybe you ought to calm down a beat before you actually begin the act.

CHARLIE: *Stand still!!*
        ANNABELLA *and* SMITTY *look at each other, confused.*

ANNABELLA: You know, Charlie, maybe Smitty is right. What about a rubdown, guy. How does that sound. Could cool the pressure.

CHARLIE: *Stop that mumbling!*

SMITTY: A slight postponement, guy. That's all I've been calling for all along.
        Short pause. CHARLIE *stops pacing. Stares at* ANNABELLA *and* SMITTY.

CHARLIE: Oh. Now I get it. Yeh, now I really get it. A slight postponement, huh? Boy am I slow. Shit! You two must really take me for a dodo! So that is your move, is it. Jesus, I should have guessed.

ANNABELLA: What is, Charlie?

CHARLIE: [*Pacing again.*] That is your angle. Of course. Of course. It took me a while. It really did. Well I may be slow, but I ain't thick. Anything to puncture my urge, right? You'd do anything, right?

ANNABELLA: What are you talking about?

CHARLIE: You let that buster in here. To wreck my confidence. My edge. To turn me loose on myself. Yeh. You might have even planned the whole thing. Though I doubt that. You two ain't bright enough for that. No. And then when that act didn't work. When that move fell flat on its face, now you're all set to play deaf and dumb. Try to get me to think I am losing my mind. That I'm seeing things. Right? Well I haven't fallen for it, see! It has not worked, see! [*Laughs.*]

ANNABELLA: We're behind you, guy.

SMITTY: I think that's what he's afraid of.

CHARLIE: Right when I'm on the verge. Razor sharp. Well, it's my own fault. I should have guessed Charlie'd get blocked from the inside. Least I stopped this check in time. Yeh. Nice Charlie. Nice action. Good reflex there. Good work. There is no way I'm gonna postpone shit now. No way. *No way! You hear me!*

ANNABELLA: Sure, guy.

CHARLIE: I've been rocking on my heels gettin' set to run. I'm tired of interruptions and cheap shots. I'm knee deep in motion and that's that.

ANNABELLA: Sure. You're calling the signals, guy.

CHARLIE: What?

ANNABELLA: I said, you're calling the signals, Charlie.

CHARLIE: You can bet your ass I am. *And* I'm playing all the parts too. This ain't no team game. See. It's a one-man-show routine. There's room at the top for one and one only. I should have figured that out a long time ago. I don't need you! Is that straight?

ANNABELLA: Yeh, Charlie.

CHARLIE: Good. Now get the hell out!

ANNABELLA: [*Hurt.*] What?

CHARLIE: I can move cleaner without worrying you two are gonna do a backstabbing duet. Did you hear me?

SMITTY: [*Wants to talk.*] Charlie…

CHARLIE: That goes for you too. *I said, get out!*

ANNABELLA *and* SMITTY *exit.* CHARLIE, *upset, pacing.*

CHARLIE: [*To himself.*] Boy, do they got their nerve. What fucking nerve. Christ. Yeh. Who'd have believed this? Who'd have believed I'd have to protect my rear? I expect a strong backup and I get drowned out. Get booed by my own goddamn bench! [*Stops pacing; calm tone of voice.*] That's enough crabbin', Charlie. I think that's just plenty. Now take it easy. So this ain't how you pictured your opening, right? So what? You expected butterflies and you got bats, so what? [*Quickly turns toward where* ANNABELLA *and* SMITTY *exited and shouts.*] *I thought I told you two to get out!* [*No one is there; calm tone continuing.*] You got a hide, don't you? Your balance ain't so delicate as all that, is it? They didn't make no real crack, did they? [*Erupts; upset.*] Yes they did, goddamnit! Look at me. *Look at me!* [*Short pause; calm.*] Now listen, Charlie. You had a plan for this, didn't you? So where is it? Let's find it. You had a rhythm building, right? Believe me, you did, guy. You still got the urge. I know you do. You're still in the running, right? You ain't been scratched yet, have you? [*Upset.*] Maybe I have. I ain't exactly coasting along, am I?…Don't talk like that…See for yourself. Look at me…I am looking and you're looking good…Look at me!…Shut up!…Stand still *and look!*…Shut up! *I said shut up!!* [*Long pause.* CHARLIE *stands still. Smiling.*] Now ain't that somethin'? I'm arguing. No one here. Me. I'm arguing with me. Me is arguing with me. [*He laughs.*] That's great. That's just swell. That says a lot, don't it. Says the whole thing right there. Christ. The whole thing in a goddamn nutshell. [*Laughs; this laugh turns into a scream.*] *What am I doing!!!* What do I do now? [CHARLIE *leans over his desk, covers his head.*]

MAN *enters still dressed as an* OLD REPORTER. CHARLIE *does not see him and in no way acknowledges or responds to him.*

OLD REPORTER: Don't read those cards, Charlie.

CHARLIE *notices the red file cards for the first time.*

OLD REPORTER: Don't touch them. There is still time, guy. Time to reflect. Time to pull up. To pull on the cord. Time to take a step back and regain that perspective, Charlie. That overview. From the outside. From where you belong. Where you fit in. Your natural element. [CHARLIE *picks up the cards, unties the ribbon.*] There is still time to check out the book of rules. Time to chalk back in the lines you've rubbed out. To get the fences back up. Time still to call time for order. To clear the field. Clear your mind. Time to keep your distance. Your natural distance. [CHARLIE *begins to look through the cards.*] Don't look at those cards! Look at yourself, Charlie. Go ahead and look. Where is that detached look? The look of the onlooker? Of the low-lying recorder? The natural reporter.

CHARLIE: Whose handwriting is this?

OLD REPORTER: Look at yourself. You're a natural reporter, do you really want to be a player, Charlie?

    OLD REPORTER/MAN *laughs and exits.*

CHARLIE: These are weird. [*Reads.*] "Charlie, you've done your homework as best as it could be done. You get straight A's. You make the honor roll. You've worked your tail off getting set for this number. As reporters go, you're the tops. You're great, man." Who wrote these?

"Ain't nobody can cover an event like you can. You got all the angles. You got every base covered. You're in the majors. You're at your best form. You're in the position everyone wants to be in. You're great. Yeh, you're great." Who the hell wrote these? [CHARLIE *begins to get into these cards, starts by enjoying them, and slowly goes almost into a trance because of them.*]

"You're the boss-man and everyone loves you. They need you. They dream they are you and have your good moves. They listen to what you say. They copy your angles. They take your advice. They feel lucky to have known you or been in the same room as you. You get results. You're great. You're great." Yeh.

"You are the leader-man. Way ahead of the field. Avant-garde. The other's way in. You stand between them and what's big. You're the connection. You determine what's big by where you play. You're great." Yeh.

"You could have taken an easier road. It was open to you. But you struck out on your own. Held your own. Cleared your own field. Found your own stance and grip. You're great." Yeh.

"If you can't get involved nobody else can, either. You're great." Yeh. "You're the favorite. The smart money's on you. You're in a class by yourself. You're great." Yeh.

"You are the fair-haired boy and you are the old master. You are great, man. You are great! You're great!" Yeh.

[CHARLIE *sets the cards down. He is a bit drowsy.*] There. That was nice. Real nice. All I needed was a little goddamn appreciation. Every once in a while. Who wouldn't, huh? A nice pat on the back…Who wrote…? [CHARLIE *almost falls asleep.*]

[CHARLIE *is now "possessed" by another voice.*] I am ready to see what only I can see. What only a trained eye can perceive I have that eye. I am ready to hear before there is anything even to be heard. To hear that something is about to be heard. I have such an ear. I am ready.

[*Own voice, very sleepy.*] Wait a…Charlie? I wouldn't go quite that far. I mean…what do I mean? I mean, there's no rush, right? What's the hurry? I mean, aren't I still sort of stinging from them geeks?

[*Other voice.*] I am ready to smell before there is anything out there to smell. I am ready to find expression for all smells in my smelling. To find expression for all sights in my ability to see them. I am ready.

[*Own voice, trying to stay awake.*] Look. We'll try this act. Sure we will. But some other time, OK? In a little while. Right now, I just…I just…I wanta catch a little shut-eye…

[*Other voice.*] I have reported on a thousand events. But never before from this angle. Never before from the inside position. The inside looking out. Give me your scoops. Your confessions. Your history and your passions. And I will express them for you.

[*Own voice.*] I thought I said…Slow down…come on and slow down…I just wanta…I wanta sleep…[CHARLIE *"falls asleep," his head on the desk.*]

[*Other voice.*] All that was needed was a clean route of escape. And now there is one. All that was needed was a trained medium and I am that. I am that medium. [*Calmly picks up the poker, that is, it is the personality behind the other voice that picks up the poker. Then suddenly and violently, he smashes it against the desk, against the same spot where* CHARLIE *had just laid his head. "Own voice" screams out in pain, holds his head. Other voice.*] As I said, now I am ready. [*Giggles; short pause.*] I am ready to conjure. [*Calmly looks around, takes in the territory, then yells.*] I will conjure!!!

There is a flash powder explosion—bang/smoke. Also, on tape, the sound of a bomb, or a sonic boom. At the moment of the explosion CHARLIE starts to cough and choke violently. He collapses across his desk. When he later picks up his head, blood is seen running out of his mouth. Pause. The MAN enters taking off his Old Reporter costume; he now wears a baseball-type cap, blazer, white shirt, etc. He walks slowly to CHARLIE. As in the tradition of other great coaches, Lombardi, Hayes, Bryant, he will now be simply called—COACH.

COACH: On a scale of one to ten, Charlie. One to ten. I'd have to tag that opening a three, son. Which ain't quite as bad as it sounds. I mean, it ain't exactly all-pro or somethin'. Ain't all what I expected when you caught my eye back at the club. But least you're off the block and that's what really counts now don't it? At this time, I mean. Them big numbers, they're just gonna have to be flashed later. But for now, Charlie, it's a start. It's a start. And that's what matters, right son?

CHARLIE: [*Still choking, picks up his head.*] What are you doing here? [*Notices the blood on his face.*]

COACH: Just call me Coach, sonny. Coach.

CHARLIE: I'm bleeding.

COACH: [*Now behind* CHARLIE; *he grabs* CHARLIE's *hair and pulls back his head.*] Let me see that. Heck, boy. Heck. Nothin' to piss about there. [*Lets go.*] No good reason to pull yourself there. Oughta make ya just that much more determined. Get you to grit the hell down and bite the bullet. Just put some spit on it and you'll think you're sweating. Wear it, son, don't go fawnin' over it! Don't be no candy-ass, Charlie. What'll people think?

CHARLIE: I'm bleeding!

COACH: And you're whining! That's what you're doing, kid. And boy do we hate whiners. Hate their guts, Charlie. 'Cause they got no balls, boy. No pride. Good for shit down the stretch. Under fire. Worthless human beings who don't pull their own weight, so the rest of us suckers gotta carry 'em along. You follow me, Charlie? People don't like to look at whiners, pal. They make 'em sick. Now tell me, boy, you ain't one of them, are you? [*He picks up* CHARLIE's *head again by the hair.*]

CHARLIE: [*Shaking his head.*] No I ain't...

COACH: [*Lets go.*] Well, that's a good thing. That's a real relief all right. Afraid for a minute I'd read you all wrong. Afraid you were gonna let all them people down, boy. But nah, Charlie, he's no crybaby, he's no spineless jerk. He's got the prick to match that strut. He's got a God-given talent *and he's gonna use it* ! Come on, son— *it's your goddamn duty to use it!* Now get tough! Get tough!...So tell me, boy, what's your next move?

CHARLIE: In a minute. Just give me a minute. Let me rest...

COACH: You are trying my patience, pal! Listen, Charlie, if you wanta play in this game you gotta be a lot tougher than you're actin'. You wanta play, you gotta pro-duce. You can't go runnin' off to the showers every other minute. Can't go hide under the fuckin' bench. This is the big leagues, Charlie! The goddamn big top! There are people out there waiting for you! What are they going to think, son? What are they thinkin' right this second? Where's your self-respect, boy. *Show us your self-respect and let's go.*

CHARLIE: What people?

COACH: Are you kiddin', Charlie? What people? That's a pretty dumb-ass joke if you are. There are millions waiting, Charlie. Millions!

CHARLIE: Where?

COACH: Out there! Out there! *Listen!!*
> On tape sound of a large stadium crowd chanting "Go-Go-Go." After a few
> seconds, tape off.

CHARLIE: [*Stunned, confused.*] How did you do that?

COACH: I said listen!!
> On tape sound of a large stadium crowd chanting "Charlie-Charlie-Charlie."
> Tape off. CHARLIE is in shock.

COACH: See what I mean, pal? They're out there. Waiting for you. You don't want to let them down now. They want to hear from you pal. See you. Watch you. Smell you. Cheer you on! You're somethin' to them. They're out there right now looking for *you* ! They're eager. Hungry. Anxious. Little girls on daddys' shoulders. Old men with canes and straw hats. Kids sittin' on flag poles. Pennants waving. Horns honking. Peanut vendors yelling. Policemen directing traffic. Spotlights, Charlie! Searchlights! They are all looking for you! More and more are joining the crowd every second. Joining the crushing mass every split second! Don't let them down, Charlie! You are their connection! You've got their attention! They are waiting! You are the at-traction! The main attraction! Don't let us down, Charlie! *Don't let us down!*
> CHARLIE *begins to breathe heavily.*

COACH: You're no quitter, pal. I can tell that just by lookin' at you. Knew it the first time I laid eyes on you. You got spunk, kid. You got nerve. Daring. Now just get out there and get tough! *Get tough!*

CHARLIE, *breathing more heavily.*

COACH: You're no second-stringer, pal. You don't have to dirty your jersey in the locker room. You've got class, son. You've got talent. Now just get tough! Yes! *I said, get tough!*
CHARLIE *starts to stand up.*

COACH: That a-way pal! That's the spirit! Show your self-respect! Be a man, boy! Be a man! *Be a man!*

CHARLIE: [*In shock, other voice.*] I confess. I never wanted to be nothin' except a reporter. I confess…

COACH: Good. Good. A personal angle. That's putting yourself on the line, son. That should get you running. They'll like that. Yeh, they'll like that. Now just keep it going, boy. *Keep it going…!*

CHARLIE: As a kid I'd stand alone every year at my birthday party, watching the local kids do their fun and games. I confess I could only participate from a distance. Only deal at arm's length. My thoughts and feelings mesh perfectly with the Reporter's rhythm. I confess it's true. And it's always been true for me!

And I confess I have fed off other folks' actions. Their wrongs, scandals, joys, hardships, triumphs, new buildings, and last place finishes. And I confess I have survived on other folks' handiwork. Their murals, maps, muggings, prints and perfect swings, interior designs and leaps of faith. I confess I have lived from their hands to my mouth. But isn't reporting an action of equal or greater weight? *I think it must be!* I confess!

I turned pro at age fifteen which is young in this league. My first job was as a sportswriter down in Dixie. Jesus, the names I could throw out. The people I've stood next to! I've got Gale Yarborough's autograph right here! [*Points to his head.*] Anyone want to see? I confess! It's all I ever wanted to be! *I confess!*

COACH: [*Obviously pleased.*] OK. OK. Heck. That's more like it. That's applying yourself. That's more like what we're expecting to see. Now don't that feel better, boy? Sure it does, heck. Now we're cooking. Now we're cooking.

CHARLIE: [*Stunned, own voice.*] Look mister…

COACH: Coach.

CHARLIE: Yeh. Look Coach, I don't have the faintest idea what is coming down now. Couldn't we, I mean…let's talk about this, OK?
COACH *picks up a towel.*

COACH: Here, dry yourself off. [*Throws towel to CHARLIE.*]

CHARLIE: [*Ignores towel, begins to breathe heavily. Other voice.*] The Reporter has more muscle than Paul Horning or Bubba Smith. The Reporter has more grace than a Peggy Fleming. The Reporter has more art than a Pablo Picasso or Casals. The Reporter has more spunk than a featherweight on the way up.

COACH: [*Chuckling.*] Run with it, boy. Run with it.

CHARLIE: The Reporter has more range than a Beverly Sills ever had. More gusto than an H.H.H. ever had. More potential than a Tom Tresh ever had. More rhythm than Otis ever had, more draw than Jagger ever had, more power than Billy Graham ever had!

The Reporter has more class than any high strutting dude in Harlem or Scarsdale. And he lives right around the corner! *I am him! I confess!*

> *Another flash powder explosion. Also, on tape, the sounds of a stadium crowd cheering. This stays on for a few moments. At the sound of the explosion,* CHARLIE *screams in pain at the top of his lungs, though he does not collapse. The* COACH *laughs.* ANNABELLA *and* SMITTY *run in. They can never see* COACH.

ANNABELLA: Charlie. You OK? We heard you scream. What's the matter, guy?

> CHARLIE *is in shock.*

SMITTY: Oh shit. He's cracked up good. Look at him.

ANNABELLA: Charlie? Charlie? He doesn't even hear me. Snap out of it guy. Snap out. Maybe he's asleep, Smitty.

SMITTY: Are you nuts, too? Look at him! You don't sleep standing up with your eyes open! He's gone under. Simple as that. Way under in deep water. And don't say I didn't warn you something like this would happen. Jesus.

ANNABELLA: Hey, guy. Try to sit down. Bend your legs. Come on. You hear me, sit down! Charlie!

SMITTY: I saw it coming. I could feel the risk in this angle from the start. He was moving too fast. But, no, you wouldn't listen to me, would you? Now look what's happened!

ANNABELLA: *Shut up!*...Maybe if we got him a glass of water or a blanket or something.

SMITTY: Yeh. Right. That'd be a real big help. *We don't even know what he's done!* I should have played my instincts from the top and sabotaged this run long ago.

ANNABELLA: *Shut up!*...He'll come out of it. Any second and he'll come out of it.

COACH: Come on, Charlie. I think that's enough rest, don't you, son? We don't wanta get the cramps, boy. We can't afford to let up now. We gotta keep that pressure on. Keep that momentum on our side!

CHARLIE: [*Scared; own voice*—ANNABELLA *and* SMITTY *cannot hear him.*] Listen, I don't know who the hell you are...

COACH: Coach. Just call me Coach.

CHARLIE: Yeh. I got that. But what the fuck is happening to me!

COACH: You wanted to conjure, Charlie. What's the matter, guy? Didn't you hear that crowd? They love you. They're mad about you. You're a big fucking hit, guy.

CHARLIE: I want to stop this!

COACH: You had your chances for that, Charlie...Now come on, son! Keep pressing! *Keep pressing!*

CHARLIE: What's to stop me from walking out of here?

> COACH *laughs.*

ANNABELLA: I think he's moving his lips!

SMITTY: I don't hear nothin'.

ANNABELLA: Sh-sh!

CHARLIE: [*In a panic.*] *Stop this!!!!*

COACH: [*Screams.*] *Play ball!!!!!*

CHARLIE: [*Other voice*—ANNABELLA *and* SMITTY *hear this.*] Shapes arise.

ANNABELLA: There!

SMITTY: Yeh. What's he saying?

ANNABELLA: I don't know. Be quiet!

CHARLIE: [*Other voice.*] Shapes arise. Shapes of old events and new events and events on the way. Shapes of printing presses, satellites, control rooms, scribes, news rooms, press conferences. Shapes of headlines and obituaries and comics and box scores. Shapes of humor and of death. Shapes of the crowd in Times Square waiting for the news. Shapes of faces, hands, words, letters, ink. Shapes in motion and at rest.

    COACH *chuckles.*

SMITTY: I don't get it.

CHARLIE: [*Continuing.*] Shapes arise. Shapes of logs and liquids, of pulp and of steam. Shapes of black rollers getting blacker by the rhythmic beat. Shapes of empires being plotted in pins on a map. Shapes of foldings and of mergers. Shapes of copy boys, editors, cub reporters, owners, readers, and distributors. Shapes of classifieds. Shapes of wants. Desires. Openings. Dreams. Shapes of newspapers being bundled on an empty train in the middle of the night.

    Shapes arise! The same shapes again and again. The only shapes of the main event. The one event!…But it has many heads.

    COACH *claps lightly, smiles. Short pause.* ANNABELLA *and* SMITTY *look at each other speechless.*

ANNABELLA: Maybe he's…

SMITTY: Go ahead. I'm listening. I can't wait to hear what kind of explanation you're gonna pull out for this. I'm waiting. *What the hell is he talking about?!!!!!*

ANNABELLA: [*Almost in tears.*] I don't know.

COACH: As they say—you ain't gonna swim till you're thrown in. Into the fucking deep end! *So let's keep pushing!!!*

CHARLIE: [*Breathing heavily, other voice.*] I watch the Super Bowl and the crowd they cheer me. I break my neck getting to a fire and the fire it waits for me. I interview the candidate and the candidate, he questions me. As will his opponent. Why? [*This other voice is becoming more and more animated, more of another personality.*] I discover the scandal and the world discovers me. I stand behind the camera but my face is on the film. Why should that be? I listen to the policy statement and it comes out in my name, my style, my voice. My personal point of view. Why?

SMITTY: [*To* ANNABELLA.] You still thinking, he's gonna pop out any second?

ANNABELLA: *I said, I don't know!!!!!!*

SMITTY: Look, I'm gonna shut him up before he dives any deeper!

ANNABELLA: No! *Don't touch him!!* [SMITTY *stops.*] Maybe you'd hurt him, ya know? Stopping him like that. All of a sudden.

SMITTY: [*Moving away.*] If you ask me, he looks real hurt already.

COACH: I think you're getting the knack of it, Charlie. Nice. Just real nice, boy. But don't stop there. *Don't stop there!!!*

CHARLIE: [*Other voice.*] Why? Because events exist for me to witness. For me. They have no meaning by themselves. Armstrong walked on the moon for me. Sadat flies to Israel for me. Ford builds its Mustang and Pinto for me. The United States Government will rise and fall for me as will every government past, present, or future. "Blond on Blond" was written and sung for me. Ali whipped Foreman for me. Burton will get back with Liz for me. The headwaiter at Sans Souci holds a table for me. The West was won for me. The campuses, they erupted for me. Nothing would be there if not for me! *I confess! For me!!*

> *Another explosion. On tape. A few moments of a stadium crowd cheering, along with a stadium crowd chanting "Go-Go-Go." At the same time as the explosion, much of the furniture, excluding the desk, gets flipped over; plaster falls from the flies.* ANNABELLA *and* SMITTY *are obviously shaken.* COACH *has a hard time controlling his laughter.* CHARLIE *leans on the desk, panting.*

ANNABELLA: [*Looking around at the furniture.*] Did Charlie do that? Did he? [*Screams.*] *Did he?!!!!!!*

SMITTY: Christ, I don't know. I don't know what's coming down no more. What current he's got himself plugged into. All I know is that he's gone far enough for me. [*Looking around.*]

ANNABELLA: Smitty, he never mentioned shit like this. This ain't right. It ain't right. I mean, the whole room shook.

SMITTY: What do you think I've been saying!! [*Calms himself.*] OK. Somehow I'm gonna have to stop him before he does any permanent damage.

ANNABELLA: [*Screams.*] *The whole god damn room was shaking!!*

SMITTY: *I know that!* [*To himself.*] Now think. Think! Now I ain't about to do this by myself. Right. I doubt if I could even slow him down by myself. Yeh. But with a couple of other guys, I'll bet we could tie him the fuck down. I'll be back in a few minutes, Annabella. [SMITTY *exits.*]

ANNABELLA: *SMITTY!!* [*Short pause. Trying to be strong, to get a hold of herself, she approaches* CHARLIE.] Charlie. Charlie? It's Annabella. I'm right here, guy. I'm right beside you...See?...It's me...[*Screams.*] *It's me!!!!!* [*She turns away, unable to control herself, crying. She is no longer able to hear anything* CHARLIE *says.*]

COACH: What can I say, Charlie? What's left to say but you are holding there, son. You have got them all right. In the palms of your god damn hands.

CHARLIE: [*Own voice, exhausted.*] I do?

COACH: Look for yourself.

CHARLIE: Look where?

COACH: Still with the jokes.

CHARLIE: I want to see them!

COACH: *Then look!*

> *Bright lights or house lights up on the audience.* CHARLIE *covers his eyes and screams at the top of his lungs. Lights off the audience.*

COACH: Ain't this gettin funnier by the minute, Charlie? What do you say Charlie, you set to go? [*He puts his arm around* CHARLIE's *shoulder.*] You ready, son?

CHARLIE: [*Takes his hands off his eyes; other voice; he smiles.*] I roam...

COACH: [*Pats him on the back.*] Good move. Good move. [*Moves away from* CHARLIE *to watch.*]

CHARLIE: I roam along beaches and missile sights and skeleton filled closets. I roam the far corners of the earth with that hungry and eager expression.

I roam in the gutters and in the board rooms and in the breakfast nooks of the land. I roam down the halls of fame. Down the halls of Congress. Down the hall of mirrors. And I roam between second and third digging out ground balls. Digging myself in for the duration.

I roam without rest. Thirsty. Hungry. With longing. Fear. Anticipation.

I roam in order that I may consume. I consume. [CHARLIE *laughs.*]

COACH: [*Applauding. Sincere.*] Bravo. Bravo. I knew you had it in you, son. Great great move. "I consume." [*He laughs.*]

CHARLIE: [*Still other voice.*] I consume the books, papers, pencils, the skies, the Marlboro crush-proof boxes, every imitation Beatle song ever written, every imitation John Ford movie ever made and the originals. I consume.

I consume them all and repackage them under my label. [COACH *is having a great time—smiling, chuckling.* CHARLIE *also is enjoying himself, beginning to really feel his power.*] I consume the New Left and the Old Left and the Far Right all in one breath. One swallow. I consume.

I consume every shitful act imaginable, every act of true love believable and sift out the hits from the flops. *I consume!*

I got the original gift of hype. No one else has it. I consume!

I consume without question. Without asking. I consume from sunup to sundown. And I consume while leaning against a lamppost in the dark of the night. Boo! I consume!

I strengthened my eyes so more would be seen. I sent up satellites so more would be witnessed. I learned to smell so more would be smelled. *Whatever I touch is real! It's true! I consume!!...*

COACH *holds up his hand—stopping* CHARLIE *before he has reached his climax.* CHARLIE *stares out, smiling, anxious, almost rocking on his heels.* SMITTY *enters, his face black from smoke, his clothes torn. He is in shock.*

ANNABELLA: Smitty! What happened?!!

SMITTY: [*Hardly able to speak.*] In the streets. I can't believe it. The streets. One second it was all OK. The whole goddamn block. *Fire!!!* [*Screams.*] *Charlie!!!!!*

ANNABELLA: Fire? Where? What's on fire, Smitty?

SMITTY: [*Staring at* CHARLIE, *screams.*] *Everything's on fire!!! Charlie!!!!!*

COACH, *who has been watching this, puts his hand down, cueing* CHARLIE, *who now finishes his beat.*

CHARLIE: *I am nothing but what I consume!!! I confess it!!!!!*

Another explosion, very loud. Also fire or the "impression" of fire. The crowd noise again along with the chanting of "Go-Go-Go." Also the chanting of "Go-Go-Go" in other languages, the shouting of "Ole," etc., as well as chants of "Charlie Charlie Charlie." At the explosion, ANNABELLA *screams,* SMITTY *screams out "Charlie!" They both collapse to the floor.* CHARLIE *and* COACH *ignore them. Tape off.* CHARLIE *is now like another person, giggling, laughing, bouncing about like a fighter after a knockout who is ready for all comers.*

COACH: [*Obviously very proud, but also a little sad, he puts his arm around* CHARLIE.] You're a beaut, kid. An A number one beaut. You really are. [*Pats him on the back.*] Come on, you don't need me no more. It's all yours now. It's yours. Just take it away.

    Tape on. It plays now for the remainder of the play, getting louder—that is, the crowd should be heard as getting more and more enthused, taken away.

CHARLIE: In vain!

    COACH *leads the "crowd" like a conductor.*

CHARLIE: In vain one looks for the winner in the winner's circle. In vain one seeks the forecast in the skies. In vain one looks for justice in the courts. Answers from the pundits. From the priests. From the scholars. In vain one looks for human interest among interesting people; for public opinion among the public. In vain!

    Your search is in vain. In vain the effort is made to evade my gaze. Again and again the effort is made to escape my eyes and my senses. *But it is all in vain!!!! Shapes arise!!* [*Organ "charge" music—like that used at baseball games to get the team going—followed by all yelling "charge."*]

    All murders, kidnappings, rapes, deaths, births, society marriages, job openings, wars, elections, coup d'états flow *out of me! Out of me!!*

    Richard Widmark and Mark Spitz are other names for *me!*

    All stocks, bonds, devaluations, inflations are in me at this moment. And all classics, religions, moral philosophies are in me too!

    If I weren't alive and kicking, where would they all be? But for me!

    Who would terrorize, skyjack, cure the incurable, and win Heisman trophies?

    Who would burn the midnight oil over the great American Novel? And the Great American Dream?

    Who would cry at funerals? At crash sites? Outside courthouses? And on small knolls on college campuses with arms stretched out, head thrown back, kneeling, *and wail?!!!!!!*

    Who?!!!!! But for me!!! But for me!!!! I confess!!! Shapes arise!! [*"Charge" music.* COACH *picks up the chant of "Go Go Go."*] *And welcome!!!!*

    Welcome all assassination attempts. All new Italian elections. All last minute game plans. All rare diseases. All dazzling photo-finishes!

    Welcome! Welcome! Welcome! Welcome! Welcome!!!!!

    Shapes arise!! I said, arise!!!! [COACH *is laughing. "Charge" music. In the background, rumblings, tremors, minor explosions. Crowd is very loud now.* CHARLIE *is now completely confident, completely on top—even too much so, so that he is appearing a bit monstrous.*]

    Arise!!!!!

    I am on first base and third base and everything in between.

    I am Hunter Thompson and Laurence Harvey and everything in between.

    I am the Beatles and The Wings and everything in between.

I am I. F. Stone and Max Frankel and everything in between.

I am "Firing Line" and "Sixty Minutes" and everything in between. *I am! Yes!*

I am "Citizen Kane" and "It Happened One Night"; "Monkey Business" and "Psycho" and everything in between.

I am Jackson Pollack and Andrew Wyeth and everything in between. I am. You can believe me.

I am the rain and the sun, the thoroughbred and the bastard, the book and the movie based on the book!

I am the hard sell and the soft peddle. I am the front page. And I am the comics. And I am the obituaries and I am the births. I am the buyer, and I am the seller. The consumer and the consumed. I am the one and I am the many!!

I am everything…in between!!!!!!

I am! I am! I am it! I confess it! Me! Me! Meeeee!

I said, Meeeeeeeeeeeeeeee!!!!!!!!!!

The last explosion. Also many distant explosions which fade out—the sense that all is coming down. The lights flicker on and off. The crowd goes wild. Deafening cheers: the chants ended with CHARLIE's *last line.* CHARLIE *is really enjoying himself, dancing around. Blood pours out of his mouth, he tries to wipe it away.* COACH *has run up to him and gives him a big bear-hug.* CHARLIE's *attention, however, is on other things, in fact on everything. He continues to dance and begins mumbling or chanting something to himself. Slowly these mumblings become audible: he is chanting "me me me me. " The crowd is telling him he has a right to be proud.* COACH *has picked up a large flash camera, maybe from behind* CHARLIE's *desk.* COACH *waves and coaxes* CHARLIE *into a suitable position. Finally, there is* CHARLIE *bouncing/dancing in front of* COACH. *He slowly looks out into the audience and gives us all the all-familiar #1 sign.* COACH *snaps the picture. Blackout and sound out on the flash.*

END

Jeffrey M. Jones

∾

Night Coil

Two little chambers
Side by side
One man lived
The other one died

•

This play is for Joanie

Night Coil was first produced by Creation Production Company (Matthew Maguire and Susan Mosakowski, Artistic Directors) at St. Clement's in New York City on March 16, 1979, with the following cast:

YOUNG MAN	Kevin Coleman
HIS DOUBLE	Robert Cappelletti
THE WOMAN	Iris Alhanti
OLD MAN MOSES	Robert Holman
MAN 2	Terrence Barrell
MAN 3	Earl Michael Reid
MAN 4	Kevin O'Rourke
CLARYCE	Ellie Schadt
ELLEN	Maureen Barnes

Director: Matthew Maguire
Sets: Jim Clayburgh
Costumes: Shay Cunliffe

DRAMATIS PERSONAE: A Young Man; His Double; The Woman; Old Man Moses; Man 2; Man 3; Man 4; Two Attendants: Claryce and Ellen.

TO THE READER: This text presents certain unconventional problems. As action occurs in two adjacent rooms, the text must be read in two directions at once: across the page (space) as well as down (time). Moreover, in performance different voices speak simultaneously and this sound cannot be listened to in the same way as speech. For these reasons, I believe the experience of the text is best recreated when two persons read it aloud.

There are two chambers side by side. This one contains a bed and a chair. The space between the bed frame and the floor is masked by the bedclothes. The door is upstage right. There is a window in the stage right wall.

The YOUNG MAN *enters and turns on the light. He shuts the door and looks around the room.*

There are two chambers side by side. This one contains several chairs against the upstage wall, a small table with practical phonograph and a wall telephone. The door is upstage left.

At rise, the DOUBLE *is revealed waiting in the room.*

The telephone rings.

The DOUBLE *immediately answers it and begins speaking in a low voice.*

DOUBLE: Hello?

Yes.

This is Bob.

Yes.

The YOUNG MAN *sits on the end of the bed and takes off his shoes.*

This is Bob

Yes.

Hello?

This is Bob.

Yes.

This is Bob.

Hello?

This is Bob.

This is Bob.

Hello?

The YOUNG MAN *places his shoes under the bed.*

Yes.

Yes.

I don't know.

Yes.

I don't know.

Yes.

Yes.

Yes.

I don't know.

The YOUNG MAN *gets up and turns off the light.*

He goes back to bed.

He lies down and closes his eyes.

I don't know.
Hello?

Yes.

This is Bob.

I don't know.
Hello?
Yes.
This is Bob.
I don't know.
Yes.
Yes.
Yes.
Yes.
Yes.
Yes.
Yes—
'Tis a consummation devoutly to be wished—to die; to sleep; to sleep; perchance to dream...

Wait a minute...

The YOUNG MAN *sits up with a start.*

YOUNG MAN: Who's there?

Who's there?!
Hello?...

Hello?

Hello?

Who's there?

Hello?

Who's there?

This is Bob.

Hello?

I don't know.

Hello?...
A Voice speaks from under the bed.
VOICE: Hello?
The YOUNG MAN *leaps out of bed and turns on the light.*

Goodbye. [DOUBLE *hangs up quickly.*]

The YOUNG MAN *pulls up the bed-clothes.*

The door opens and the WOMAN *enters.*

WOMAN: Hello.

There is nothing under the bed. Even the shoes have disappeared.

The YOUNG MAN *looks everywhere for his shoes.*

MAN 2 *comes in the door.*

MAN 2: What's the problem?

YOUNG MAN: I can't find my shoes.
MAN 2: What shoes?
YOUNG MAN: I can't find them.

MAN 3 *comes in the door.*
MAN 3: What's the problem?

MAN 2: Can't find his shoes.
MAN 3: What shoes?
YOUNG MAN: They're gone.
MAN 2: See what I mean?

MAN 4 *comes in the door.*

MAN 4: What's the problem?

YOUNG MAN: Nothing.

DOUBLE: Hello.

WOMAN: Do you have a cigarette?
    DOUBLE *offers her one.*
WOMAN: Thank you.
DOUBLE: Allow me…[*Lights cigarette.*]
WOMAN: Thanks.

DOUBLE: We've got a problem.
WOMAN: I know.
DOUBLE: He suspects.

WOMAN: We've got a problem.
DOUBLE: I know.
WOMAN: He suspects.

DOUBLE: We've got a problem.
WOMAN: I know.

    We've got a problem.
DOUBLE: I know.

    He suspects.

    WOMAN *and* DOUBLE *never lose eye contact. They circle about.*

WOMAN: I know.

    He suspects.

DOUBLE: I know.

DOUBLE: He suspects.

MAN 3: Nothing?
MAN 2: That's what he said…

                                      WOMAN: I know.

  That is what you said, isn't it?
MAN 4: That's what he said.
MAN 2: Well if that's what you said, Bob,
    Why don't you turn out the light and
      go back to sleep?
    Hmmmmmmmmmmm?

                                        WOMAN: He suspects.

MAN 4: Goodnight, Bob. [*Exit* MAN 4.]
MAN 3: Goodnight, Bob. [*Exit* MAN 3.]
MAN 2: Goodnight, Bob.
    And remember—whatever you do,
    There's no singing allowed.
        Exit MAN 2, *turning off light.*   DOUBLE: I know.
                                      WOMAN: I know.
                                      DOUBLE.: I know.
                                      WOMAN: I know.
                                      DOUBLE: I know.

    The YOUNG MAN *stands in the cor-*
ner for a while.

                                      WOMAN: Do you have a cigarette?
                                      DOUBLE *offers her one.*
                                      Thank you.
                                      DOUBLE: Allow me…[*Lights cigarette.*]
                                      WOMAN: Thanks.

YOUNG MAN: [*Softly*] I have observed…
    From time to time…
    People…
    The people…
    People…
    The people…
    People talking…
    The people talking…
    Of this and that…
    And such and so…

                                      WOMAN: Actually, I've…
                                      Thought about everything
                                      And I've decided to
                                      Think about everything
                                      And I've decided to
                                      Think about everything

And I've decided to think.
DOUBLE: Mmmmmmmmm...
Very wise,
Very wise,
Very wise...

Sometimes they talk
Of this thisness of that,
And the thatness of this,
And this thisness of this and that...

Cigarette?
WOMAN: Thank you.
DOUBLE: Allow me... [*Lights cigarette.*]
WOMAN: Thanks...
Actually, I've...
Decided about decided I've
Decided about stop.
I've decided to decide about deciding.
I've stop.
I've decided.
Actually I'm actually I'm actually I'm
Actually I'm still deciding about stop.
Actually I'm stop.
No, I'm still deciding.
Actually I'm still deciding I've decided
   to decide about deciding about stop.

YOUNG MAN: Of the thatness of this,
And this thisness of that,
And this thatness of this and that...

And the this-and-thatness of this and
   that...
And the that-and-thisness of that and
   this...
And the suchness of so...
The suchness of so...

The such-and-soness of such and so.

I have observed...
From time to time...
The people...
People...
Talking...

DOUBLE Cigarette?
WOMAN: Thank you.
DOUBLE: Allow me... [*Lights cigarette*]
WOMAN: Thanks.

Actually, I haven't...

DOUBLE: Cigarette?
WOMAN: Thank you.
DOUBLE: Allow me... [*Goes to light it,
when:*]
WOMAN: Stop! [*Gestures, both freeze.*]

The YOUNG MAN *goes to the bed.*
He lies down and closes his eyes.

Actually, I'm decided I thought about
Everything I, yes, very wise, I've
Decided to stop, very wise, I've been

Thinking about everything I've been
Deciding about everything I've been
Stopping to decide about thinking
    about
Stopping to think.
Actually I'm not.
Actually I'm everything, but...
I've been thinking about stopping.
DOUBLE: Allow me... [*Lights cigarette.*]
WOMAN: Thanks.

DOUBLE: Shall we dance?
WOMAN: Of course.
    We'll need music.
DOUBLE: Of course.

DOUBLE crosses to record player and
plays Chopin's Waltz Op. 34 #2.
The music must come from the ma-
chine.
DOUBLE *and* WOMAN *dance.*

WOMAN: You know how it is?
DOUBLE: Um-hmmm...
WOMAN: You know how it is.
DOUBLE.: Oh, yes.
WOMAN: You know.
DOUBLE: Of course
WOMAN: How it is, that is.

That is, how it is.

How it is that it is
That it is that it is;
How it is that it is
That it is that it is.

How it is that.

DOUBLE: Cigarette?
WOMAN: Not now.
DOUBLE: Of course.
WOMAN: Thanks.

Once the music begins, the YOUNG
MAN *can be heard murmuring:*
YOUNG MAN: Nevertheless...
Nevertheless...

I remember...

I remember...

I remember I was hiding
In my hiding place and watching
I was in behind the bushes
In between them and the wall
And the wall was very clean
And the wall was very smooth
And there was an empty space there
It was back behind the bushes
I remember I would go there
I would sit there
I would watch the others playing
In the garden in the afternoon
In sunlight in the afternoon
And I remember when the parents
When the parents came to visit
And the parents came to tea
And the tea was in the garden

I remember I could hear them
I could hear the people talking
I could hear the sound of teacups
I remember I remember
How the servant girls wore dresses
How there was an afternoon
How the girls were in white dresses
How the golden sun was golden
How the children all were playing
How the people all were laughing
I was watching I remember
I was in the bushes watching
No one knew where they could find me
I was hiding in the bushes
They were happy they were laughing
And there was an afternoon
I was there and I remember
I remember…

I remember…

YOUNG MAN: I remember…

Actually, it's strange.
It's very strange.
It's very, very strange.
It's very, very, very, very, very, very strange.
Actually, it's very, very, very, very, very, very, very strange.

DOUBLE: Yes…

Yes it is…

Yes it is…

Yes…

The phone rings.

The phone rings.

The phone rings.
DOUBLE: Turn that thing off…

WOMAN *turns off record player as* DOUBLE *answers phone.*

DOUBLE: Yeah?
That's right.
He did?
When?
No.
I don't care.

That's right.

As soon as possible.

Offstage, the voices of CLARYCE *and* ELLEN *coming down the hall.*

CLARYCE: So I said to her I said:
What is your *problem?*

I said: don't get mad at me!
Enter CLARYCE, *turning on lights.*
You know?
I mean, who needs the aggravation?
Enter ELLEN, *with* YOUNG MAN's shoes.

You know what I mean?
I mean, who needs it?
Jesus Christ—would you look at this
   one? [*Meaning* YOUNG MAN]

ELLEN: What's wrong with him?
CLARYCE: Who knows, who cares?
   I mean what can you say about a guy
   who can't even keep track of his own
   shoes? You know what I mean?
ELLEN: It's probably poison.

CLARYCE: Probably is.
ELLEN: No I mean like nowadays you
   know
   These chemicals you know
   Like nowadays they put all this junk
   That's like this stuff that's like
   I mean in your food and stuff,
   That's like this poison in your blood-
      stream,
   You know what I mean?
CLARYCE: You got a cigarette?
ELLEN: Menthol.
CLARYCE: Shit.
   Okay.
   Jesus Christ—don't put those shoes on
      the sheets!
   How do you know where they've been?
ELLEN: Sorry.
CLARYCE: You mean like additives?
   Food additives?
ELLEN: Yeah.
CLARYCE: Or like preservatives?
ELLEN: Yeah.
   Like all this junk they put in junk
      food—
   It goes right into your stomach
   It goes right into your bloodstream
   It goes right into your brain.
   I mean like candy bars
   Or like those things you know that are
      like [*Gestures.*] I forget,

She's right here.

She did?

Are you sure?

How do you know?

I'll find out.

That's right.

Now look—

I'm getting tired of these excuses.
No!
No!
I don't care!
That doesn't matter.
That doesn't matter.
You will because I say so!
Do I have to spell it out?
And I'm telling you right now
If you can't, god damn it,
Then I'll have to get someone who can!

Oh, no…

No, now you wait…

Hey!
Who set this thing up?
Who set this thing up?
Who set this thing up?
Who set this thing up?

That's right.

But like those artificial flavorings
And all those artificial colorings
And all that B H T, you know?
Or like that waxy stuff,
Or like that gooey stuff,

Or like that runny stuff,
Or like insecticides
Or maybe naugahyde
Or like formaldehyde,
Or like formica,
Or like forbidden fruit,
Or like for he's a jolly good fellow
Or like forgetting what it was you were
     going to say
Or like organic brain disease
Or like electric eels
Or like interior decoration
Or like the Texas panhandle
Or like this toaster oven that my Mom
     got and it had this dead carrot in-
     side of it,
Or like whether 'tis nobler in the mind
     to suffer the slings and arrows of
     outrageous fortune or to take arms
     against a sea of troubles and by op-
     posing end them…

That's right.
That's right.
That's right.
Now I'll take care of
Whatever problem we might be hav-
     ing
At this end,
But you make sure
You better make damn sure
You finish this job
And you finish it right!
Is that understood?
Because I'm telling you
For the very last time, my friend,
I don't care what it takes,
I don't care what you have to do,
I don't care how you have to do it,
I don't care who gets hurt,
I want it done!
I want it over with!
I want it finished!
Finished!
Finished!
Finished!
Finished!

Is that clear?

CLARYCE: Well, I'll tell you one thing.
ELLEN: What's that?
CLARYCE: These cigarettes taste really
     shitty .
     You got another one?
ELLEN: It's menthol.
CLARYCE: I know that, Ellen.
     Don't put those shoes on the sheets!
     Under the bed! Put them under the bed
          where they belong!
     Jesus!
     What is wrong with you?
ELLEN: (Guy darn you still don't have to
     get all mad at me, you know, I mean…)

I know we've got a problem…

Don't worry…

Don't worry about it

But as ELLEN *goes to put the shoes under the bed a hand reaches out and grabs them—she pulls back the bed-clothes to reveal Old Man Moses.*

I'm telling you, babe,
You worry too much,

Hey, what are you doing down there?
Hey, what's going on here?
Hey, what is this?
Hey, Claryce?...
CLARYCE: Yeah? What is it?
ELLEN: There's this...*guy* down there...
CLARYCE: So?
ELLEN: I mean, under the bed.

Just go up the stairs...

CLARYCE: So?
ELLEN: So all this time I mean all this time
    I mean all this time he's *been* there!

You take a right...

CLARYCE.: So?
ELLEN: That's real weird, Claryce!

You go down the hall...

CLARYCE.: So?
ELLEN: So it gives me the creeps!

Hang a left...

CLARYCE: So? He's a creepy guy—so?
ELLEN: So nothing!
    So that's it, that's all!
    And I think it's real weird and creepy!
    So there!

It's the little door all the way at the
    end...

That's right—under the bed

CLARYCE: Can I have that cigarette now?
ELLEN: No.
CLARYCE.: Oh, jeez-louise, Ellen,

And listen—
Thanks for the tip.

    I mean, is that the way you have to be
        about it?
    I mean, are you really going to be that
        way about it?
    I mean, is this the way you're going to
        be?

I've got one or two things I can try...

ELLEN: Yes.
CLARYCE: Okay, fine!
    Then I'm leaving.

I'll handle this one personally.
It'll be a pleasure.

Exit CLARYCE.

Right.

[*Off.*] I said: I'm leaving, Ellen...
[*Off.*] Ellen—I really mean it...

Goodbye...

    The DOUBLE *hangs up.*

[*Off.*] Ellen… Oh, for Chrissake…

ELLEN: … Hello? …

OLD MAN MOSES: [*Under bed.*] Well, hey there, hi there, ho there, howdydoody, howdy-do…

ELLEN: Fine…

How are you?

Fine I said how are you?

Hello?

Hello? …

OLD MAN MOSES: [*Under bed.*] Yes, hello, hello, hello,
Hi, hey, ho, how are you, how do you do?

OLD MAN MOSES *crawls out from under bed with the shoes in his hand.*

ELLEN: Fine…

How are you?

OLD MAN MOSES: Me? You mean me? (I think she does) Hello.
You mean me? Hi, how are you?
I feel fine. Hello, hello.
Hey, baby, howdy doody, huh?
You mean me? (She means me)
Hiiiiiiiiii!
I'm fine, fine, fine, fine,
Good, great, terrific, okay—
Hey—listen—I feeeeel fine!
Hey! I feel great! Hey!
I feel like singing: WAYYY DOWN UPON THE SEWANNNNEEE RIVAAHHH!!

ELLEN *screams and runs out as the* YOUNG MAN *sits bolt upright.*

YOUNG MAN: Hold it!

He stares at the WOMAN.

WOMAN: Who was that?

What's the matter?

What's wrong?

Why don't you say something?

Don't look at me that way, Bob…

DOUBLE *advances menacingly on* WOMAN.

Is something wrong?

Who was that?

What's wrong?

What's happened?

No—please—wait, Bob…

The DOUBLE *grabs the woman violently. The* WOMAN *screams.*

DOUBLE: Shut up!

OLD MAN MOSES *freezes.*

YOUNG MAN: What are you doing?
OLD MAN MOSES: Well hello there, hey
     there, hi there, ho there—
     Bobby! Robert! Bob-boy! Robby!
     Nice to meet you! Good to see you !
     How you doing! Howdy do?

YOUNG MAN: What are you doing here?
OLD MAN MOSES: Me?
     Oh…
     Nothing…

YOUNG MAN: Those are my shoes.
OLD MAN MOSES: These?

YOUNG MAN: Those are my shoes.
OLD MAN MOSES: These?
     Oh no, they ain't.
     Oh, no.
     No sir, nope, unh-unh, no way!
     Noooooooooo, no no no,
     Not these, Bob-o, not these,
     No sir…
YOUNG MAN: Those are my shoes.
OLD MAN MOSES: No they're not.
YOUNG MAN: Yes they are.
OLD MAN MOSES: No they're not.
YOUNG MAN: Yes they are.
OLD MAN MOSES: Nope.
YOUNG MAN: They are.
OLD MAN MOSES: No.
YOUNG MAN: Yes.
OLD MAN MOSES: Nope.
YOUNG MAN: Yes, they are!

MAN 2 *bursts into the room.*
MAN 2: Who was singing?
DOUBLE: Wrong room!
MAN 2: Oh!…
     Sorry. I heard singing. Sorry…
     Exit MAN 2.

DOUBLE: We've got a problem.
     Somebody talked.
     He suspects.
WOMAN: Who?
DOUBLE: Us.
WOMAN: Well, don't look at me.
DOUBLE: Then who?
     Who else?
WOMAN: It could have been you.
DOUBLE: Me?
WOMAN: Don't play dumb.
DOUBLE: What do you mean?
WOMAN: Oh, you're good.
DOUBLE: Good at what?

They stare at each other motionlessly.

DOUBLE.: Do I have to spell it out?

     We've got a problem.

     Somebody talked.

     He suspects.

Those are my shoes!

OLD MAN MOSES: Umh-umh...

YOUNG MAN: They are!

OLD MAN MOSES: Nope.

YOUNG MAN: Then whose are they?

OLD MAN MOSES: I don't know.

YOUNG MAN: Are they yours?

OLD MAN MOSES: No.

YOUNG MAN: That's right! They're mine!

OLD MAN MOSES: No they're not!

YOUNG MAN: Then whose are they?

OLD MAN MOSES: I don't know.

YOUNG MAN: They look like mine.

OLD MAN MOSES: No, they don't.

YOUNG MAN: I have a pair exactly like
    that.

OLD MAN MOSES: No you don't.

YOUNG MAN: But you do, I suppose?
    I suppose
    You have a pair
    Exactly like that, don't you?

OLD MAN MOSES: No...

YOUNG MAN: Then those are not your
    shoes!

OLD MAN MOSES: Yes they are.

YOUNG MAN: They are?

OLD MAN MOSES: Oh, no.

YOUNG MAN: I thought you just told me
    those were your shoes.

OLD MAN MOSES: Not me.

YOUNG MAN: You didn't?

OLD MAN MOSES: Nope.

YOUNG MAN: No?

OLD MAN MOSES: Yes.

YOUNG MAN: Yes?

OLD MAN MOSES: Oh, no, no, no...

WOMAN: Well, don't look at me.

DOUBLE: Then who?
    Who else?

WOMAN: Don't play dumb.

DOUBLE: What do you mean?

WOMAN: Do I have to spell it out?

They stare at each other motionlessly.

WOMAN: Somebody talked.

It could have been you.

DOUBLE: What do you mean?

WOMAN: Don't play dumb.
    We've got a problem.
    He suspects.

DOUBLE: Who?

WOMAN: Us.

They stare at each other motionlessly.

DOUBLE: It could have been you.

WOMAN: Don't look at me.

YOUNG MAN: I say those are your shoes.

OLD MAN MOSES: No they're not!

YOUNG MAN: That's right! They're mine!

OLD MAN MOSES: Nope.

YOUNG MAN: Let's try this again.
I say those are not my shoes.

OLD MAN MOSES: Yes, they are.

YOUNG MAN: No they're not.

OLD MAN MOSES: Yes, yes they are.

YOUNG MAN: They are?

OLD MAN MOSES: Nope.

YOUNG MAN: Sorry, you're right.
They're not mine.

OLD MAN MOSES: Oh, yes they are.

YOUNG MAN: No they're yours.

OLD MAN MOSES: They're not! They're not!

YOUNG MAN: Well, they're not mine.

OLD MAN MOSES: Oh, but they are, they are!

YOUNG MAN: No, no, take them!

OLD MAN MOSES: I can't!

YOUNG MAN: No?

OLD MAN MOSES: Yes.

YOUNG MAN: Well, what are you going to do with them then?

OLD MAN MOSES: I don't know.

YOUNG MAN: Well, don't put them back where you found them.

OLD MAN MOSES: No, I will, I will...

YOUNG MAN: No, no—they don't belong under my bed!

OLD MAN MOSES: They do! They do!

YOUNG MAN: No, no, they absolutely do not belong under my bed and you certainly aren't going to put them back right this minute, are you?

Well, are you?...

DOUBLE: Oh, you're good.

WOMAN: Good at what?

DOUBLE: Don't play dumb.

WOMAN: What do you mean?

DOUBLE: Somebody talked.

WOMAN: It could have been you.

DOUBLE: What do you mean?

WOMAN: Do I have to spell it out?
He suspects.
Somebody talked.

DOUBLE: It could have been you.

WOMAN: What do you mean?
Don't look at me.

DOUBLE: What do you mean?
It could have been you.

WOMAN: What do you mean?
It could have been you.

DOUBLE: It could have been you!

WOMAN: It could have been you!

DOUBLE: Don't look at me!

WOMAN: Don't look at me!

They stare at each other motionlessly.

DOUBLE: Cigarette?

Well?…

OLD MAN MOSES: Could we change the subject?

YOUNG MAN: No.

OLD MAN MOSES: Thanks.

YOUNG MAN: Okay,
What do you want to talk about?

OLD MAN MOSES: I don't know…
Shoes…

YOUNG MAN: How about what's going on here?

OLD MAN MOSES: How about not?

YOUNG MAN: Then let's get back to shoes.

OLD MAN MOSES: OH, no no no!

YOUNG MAN: Good.
Then let's talk.

OLD MAN MOSES: Let's not.

YOUNG MAN: Right.
Let's not.
Let's not talk
About what's going on here.

OLD MAN MOSES: Okay.

YOUNG MAN: Let's not talk
About what's not going on here.

OLD MAN MOSES: Yes.

YOUNG MAN: Okay.

OLD MAN MOSES: Yes?

YOUNG MAN: We're not talking.

OLD MAN MOSES: I know.

YOUNG MAN: Well, let's.
I mean, let's not.
Let's not talk
About what's not going on here.

OLD MAN MOSES: Suits me fine!
Yessirree, Bob!
You're Bob.
I'm not, actually—I'm somebody else.

  OLD MAN MOSES *begins whistling.*

WOMAN: Thank you.

DOUBLE: Allow me… [*Lights cigarette.*]

WOMAN: Thanks.

DOUBLE: We've got a problem.

WOMAN: Yes.
We've got a problem.

DOUBLE: We've got a problem.

WOMAN: Yes.

DOUBLE: We've got a problem.

  Yes.

WOMAN: We've got a problem.

DOUBLE: Yes.
We've got a problem.

WOMAN: Yes.

DOUBLE: We've got a problem.

WOMAN: Yes.
We've got a problem.

DOUBLE: Yes.
We've got a problem.

WOMAN: Yes.

DOUBLE: We've got a problem.
Yes.

WOMAN: We've got a problem.

DOUBLE: Yes.
We've got a problem.
Yes.

WOMAN: We've got a problem.

DOUBLE: Will you excuse me?

WOMAN: What's the problem?

OLD MAN MOSES: Nice shoes…

OLD MAN MOSES *resumes whistling.*

OLD MAN MOSES: Got a cigarette?…

More whistling.

OLD MAN MOSES: Did you say something?

What?

Eh?

Hunh?

AHHHHHHHHHHHH!
My dear friend and relation
I'm glad you inquired:
I was starting to think
That you'd never get to it;
I like you a lot
But I have to confess
I was just going to tell you
Politely to screw it.
But I can be big
And let bygones be bygones;
I've written a song
And it's all about *you*!
I know you'll enjoy it—
I'm dying to sing it—
And now that you've asked me
That's just what I'll do!

DOUBLE: Nothing.

WOMAN: Of course…
The DOUBLE *exits. The* WOMAN
*looks around furtively and runs to the
phone.*

She begins to speak urgently.

WOMAN: Bob! It's me!
Can you hear me, Bob?
I don't have much time,
But I've got to warn you:

You're in great danger.
I'll try to protect you.
But whatever you do, Bob.
Don't sing anything!

Don't sing anything!

Don't sing anything!

DON'T SING!

Bob?…

Can you hear me?…

Something's wrong…

Something's happening…

Bob…

Please answer me…

Bob, can you hear me?…

Bob—look out, look out—wake up,
wake up, Bob—please!
 The D O U B L E *enters abruptly. The*
W O M A N *turns, horrified, and freezes.*

Could we have a little quiet next
door please if you don't mind
…

Thank you…
(And a one and a two…)
 O L D M A N M O S E S *snaps his fingers*
and sings.
OHHHHHHHH,
 YOUR FATHER WAS
RESPECTED,
 YOUR FATHER WAS
ELECTED,
 YOUR FATHER WAS…
 2, 3 & 4 burst into the room.   *The* W O M A N *drops the phone.*
M E N: There he is! Stop him! Get that man! *The* W O M A N *screams.*
 Stop that singing!   *The* W O M A N *tries to run away.*
 Etc. 3 & 4 drag O L D M A N M O S E S   *The* D O U B L E *grabs her.*
out kicking and screaming.

                                           D O U B L E: What's the matter?
                                            What's wrong?
                                            You look guilty…
                                            Don't be afraid…
2: Go back to bed.   Sit down…
                                            Cigarette?
                                             W O M A N *takes one, afraid.*
                                            Allow me… [*Lights cigarette.*]

I already told you…
No singing allowed.
                                           Unfortunately, though,
 Exit M A N 2.   We seem to have a little problem here,
                                              wouldn't you say?
                                            Just a little one, a little one,
                                            Just a little sort of problem.
                                            Just the little sort of problem
                                            that's the little sort of problem
                                            that's the little sort of problem
                                            I don't like!
                                            Because there are things, you see,
                                            There are things, now,
                                            There are things I need to know

from you and things I need to get from
you and things I need to take from
you and things you need to give!
I need!
I need things!
I need it!

YOUNG MAN *makes a sudden move
for the door but 2 reappears instantly.*

MAN 2: What's the problem?
YOUNG MAN: He's got my shoes.
MAN 2: What shoes?

They stare at each other motionlessly.   WOMAN: All right then.
I'll tell you.
I'll tell you everything.
I'll tell you what I know.
Let me tell you what I know.

MAN 2: What shoes, Bobby?
Hmmmmmmmmmm?

WOMAN: There was a time and I observed
A shape in the shadow
A shade in the shape
A shadow in the shade
But it was only when the head came off
That I saw the things inside of it.
They were alive perhaps.
But they were moving.
Why don't you get back in bed where   And then I knew that every part
you belong?...   Had another part inside of it
And that every other part
Had another part inside of it
And that all the little parts
Had little parts inside of them
With little parts inside of them
And little parts inside of them
The YOUNG MAN *lies down on bed.*   And hidden little parts
Inside of hidden little parts
Inside of hidden little parts
Inside of hidden little parts
Inside the shade of the shadow
In the shadow of the shade
I saw the hidden little parts

Inside of hidden little parts
Inside the shape of the shade
Of the shadow of the shape
In the shade
In the shadow
In the very next room!

MAN 2 *turns out the lights.*
MAN 2: Pleasant dreams, Bobby…
Exit MAN 2.

Look out, look out, look out,
 look out, look out, Bob!
Look out, look out, look out,
 look out, look out, Bob!
Look out, Bob, look out!
Look out, Bob loo…
 But 2, 3 *&* 4 *rush in, overpower*
WOMAN, *blindfold and gag her and tie
her to a chair. The* DOUBLE *directs
them.*
 During the rest of this scene, the MEN
*arrange themselves around the room as
if waiting for a signal.*
 All conversations are subdued.

As the YOUNG MAN *lies in darkness,*
OLD MAN MOSES *calls to him, offstage.*

OLD MAN MOSES: Oh, Bo————bby!
Hey, Bo——————————bby!
Pssst!
Hey, Bob!
Hey you!

The YOUNG MAN *sits up with a
start.*

YOUNG MAN: Who's there?
Who's there?…

YOUNG MAN *gets up and looks under
bed as* CLARYCE, *with shoes, and*
ELLEN *enter turning on the lights again.*

The DOUBLE *goes to the telephone.
He dials a number.*

CLARYCE: Hi!
ELLEN: Hi!
CLARYCE: You looking for these? (Again)
YOUNG MAN: You startled me.
ELLEN: Hi.

DOUBLE: Hello?

YOUNG MAN: Hello.

CLARYCE: Hi.   Hello?

YOUNG MAN: Hello.

CLARYCE: I'm Didi and this is Joanne.   This is Bob...

YOUNG MAN: Hi.

ELLEN: I'm Joanne.

YOUNG MAN: Hello.   Yes.

CLARYCE: So- anyway...
>   We're just here to be your
>   friends, that's all...   That's right.
>   Goodbye.
>   *The* DOUBLE *hangs up.*

YOUNG MAN: Oh.

CLARYCE: I'm Alice.

YOUNG MAN: Oh.

CLARYCE: This is Paulette.

YOUNG MAN: Hi.

ELLEN: Actually my real name is Sandy.

YOUNG MAN: Oh.

ELLEN: But you can call me Sue.

YOUNG MAN: Oh.
>   Hi.

ELLEN: [*Aside to* CLARYCE] Listen—I
>   think there's something really wrong
>   with him!

CLARYCE: [*Aside to* ELLEN] Not now,
>   Ellen, not now!

YOUNG MAN: My name is Bob.

CLARYCE: Hi, Bob.

YOUNG MAN: Hello.

CLARYCE: My name is Cleopatra and this
>   is Nefertiti, but her friends just call her
>   Toots...

ELLEN: Or Reuben for short.
>   Actually it's actually it's actually
>   It's short for Natchez, Mississippi
>   which was my Father's name on my
>   Mother's side...
>   [*Aside.*] God! He's really not *getting*
>   this, is he?

CLARYCE: [*Aside.*] Knock it off, will you?!
>   He's not supposed to know!
>   Hi there...

YOUNG MAN: Hello.

CLARYCE: Bob, isn't it?

YOUNG MAN: That's right.

CLARYCE: Hi, Bob—I'm Hamlet, Prince of Denmark and this is my tennis partner, the Second Law of Thermo-dynamics...

YOUNG MAN: Pleased to meet you.

ELLEN: [*Aside.*] Go——d! I'm telling you! When it gets this bad they have to cut a little hole inside and go in there with a stick and really [*Gestures.*] *dig* for it...

CLARYCE: [*Aside.*] Shut up, shut up! I am warning you, Ellen, if he ...[*To* YOUNG MAN.] Will you excuse us just a moment?

YOUNG MAN: Sure.

MAN 2: You got a cigarette?

MAN 3: Yeah, sure, hang on a sec...

MAN 4: Shhhhh! [*He appears to be listening to something.*]

DOUBLE: You've got something?

CLARYCE: [*Aside.*] If he even begins to suspect what's going on here, Ellen, do you know what'll happen? Do you? Do you *realize*?

MAN 4: I think so...

ELLEN: [*Aside.*] Unh-hunh.

CLARYCE: [*Aside.*] Okay then...
[*To* YOUNG MAN.] We're back.
[*To* ELLEN.] You just behave yourself.
[*To* YOUNG MAN.] So, listen—
We were just wondering, I mean,
My friend and I, you know, we
were wondering if maybe you...
knew any songs or anything
or...

Come on, baby...

Yeah! Bingo!

YOUNG MAN: You mean me?

Stand by!

MAN 2: Stand by!

MAN 3: Standing by...

ELLEN: Yeah. You. You know, like we thought maybe you know like you being the kind of guy you are and like that, you know...
That like maybe you might know a song or something that, you know...

We could sing or something…
YOUNG MAN: No.
CLARYCE: Yeah?
YOUNG MAN: No.
  I don't know any songs.
CLARYCE: Not even one, hunh?
  Well, what a coincidence.
  Neither do I.
ELLEN: Yes, what a coincidence.
  Neither do I.
CLARYCE: Well, neither do I.
ELLEN: Well, neither do I.
CLARYCE: Well, neither do I.
ELLEN: Well, neither do I.
CLARYCE: Well!!!
  I guess that's everybody then,
  isn't it?

> OLD MAN MOSES *calls out from*
> *under bed.*

OLD MAN MOSES: Nope!
> OLD MAN MOSES *crawls out from*
> *under bed.*
  No sir, no way, nope, unh-unh!
  No sirree, Bob! (He's Bob)
  Nixy on your tintype, friends!
  Not on your life!
  N-O spells no.
  That's a great big negatory on your
    roger, Houston…
  (Ladies, hello, how are you, pleased to
    make your how-do-you do)
  (Say, those are pretty spiffy shoes you
    got there—mind if I take a look at
    them—mmmmm—Yowsah, yow-
    sah, yowsah—now *that's* what I call
    stylish steppin'…
  But, to digress, I digress!
  Friends, did I hear, did I hear,
  I say: Did I over-hear
  The call for music?
  Doesn't *any*body have a song?

MAN 4: He's out!
DOUBLE: That's it!
MAN 2: Let's go!

> The MEN *and* DOUBLE *exit with*
> *dispatch, turning out the lights behind*
> *them.*

> *As soon as they are gone and through-*
> *out the following scene, the* WOMAN
> *struggles in her chair to escape. She is*
> *also making sounds through the gag.*

Don't answer that!
Because, as luck would have it, it so
    happens that I am familiar with a
    little—what they call—
A little song, a little melody,
An archaic dithyramb,
Just a tune,
A very simple little tune:
And it goes (hit it, girls)
Like this—

OLD MAN MOSES *snaps his fingers;*   *At about this point the* WOMAN'S
Girls sing back-up.   *violent struggles cause the chair to which*
                                         she is tied to tip over.

GIRLS:
                                         SHOOP-SHOO
                                         SHOOP-SHOO
OLD MAN MOSES: SHOOP-SHOO
    OHHHH...   SHOOP-SHOO
    YOUR FATHER WAS RESPECTED   SHOOP-SHOO
    YOUR FATHER WAS ELECTED   SHOOP-SHOO
    YOUR FATHER WAS PROTECTED   SHOOP-SHOO
            [*Both.*] AT THE ROTARY CLUB....
    YOUR FATHER WAS INFECTED   SHOOP-SHOO
    YOUR FATHER WAS DETECTED   SHOOP-SHOO
    YOUR FATHER WAS....   SHOOP-SHOO
    As before, 2, 3 & 4 burst in and over-   SHOOP-SHOO
    power OLD MAN MOSES *and drag him*   SHOOP-SHOO
    away kicking and screaming. The Girls   SHOOP-SHOO
    keep singing until they realize no one else SHOOP-SHOO
    is, then fade out...   SHOOP....

MAN 2: [*Shaking his finger at them.*]
    No singing, girls.
CLARYCE: I wasn't singing, were you?
ELLEN: No, neither was I. (Who's he?)
CLARYCE: Well, neither was I. (Who
    cares?)
ELLEN: Well, neither was I.
CLARYCE: Got a cigarette?
ELLEN: Menthol.

CLARYCE: Forget it.

Exit CLARYCE, *followed by* ELLEN.

> *At about this point the* WOMAN *gets free and runs out of the room, calling.*

> WOMAN: Bob!…Bob!…[*Off.*]
> Bob!…

> *Suddenly the* WOMAN *screams very loud. Then her scream is muffled and the door is slammed shut.*

MAN 2: You're next.
YOUNG MAN: Who, me?
MAN 2: Let's go.

YOUNG MAN exits, followed by MAN 2 *who turns off the lights. There is a dim glow.*

> *The lights are still off but there is nonetheless a dim glow.*

Offstage, someone sings a wordless blues refrain.

> *The phone rings.*
> *The phone rings.*
> *The phone rings.*
> *The phone rings.*
> *The phone rings.*
> *The phone rings.*

The singing fades away.

> *The phone rings.*

OLD MAN MOSES *calls from under the bed.*

OLD MAN MOSES: Hello?
Hello?
Is that you, Bob?
Is that you?…

OLD MAN MOSES *crawls out from under the bed.*

Hey…
Hey, Bob!…
Hello…
Hello-o-o-o-o-o-o-o…
Hello-o-o-o-o-o-o-o-o?…

Discovering himself in an empty room, OLD MAN MOSES *begins to cavort around babbling variations on the word "hello." He reminds me of caged monkeys or small children. The following are simply suggestions. Ideally,* OLD MAN MOSES *should free associate.*

Hello…
Hello, hello, hello…
Hello-ello-ello…
Hello-ello…
Hello-elloo…
Helloo-ellee…
Helloolleelloolleelloo…
Lleelloolleelloolleelloolleellay…
Hellumpydumpydumpydoo…
Helloodlydoodlydoodlyday…
Hel-l-l-l-l-*LOW* HELLO!
Hel-l-l-l-l-l-l-l…lo?

Becoming tired of these pastimes, OLD MAN MOSES *reclines majestically on the bed and declaims.*

Well! Now, then! Now…and then!
Now then, boys and girls,
Now boys… (And girls…)
Let us now, let us all,
Now lettuce all go see
What has been happening
Over there over in that
Place over there over in that
Cabbage patch…
Now let us go then (you and I)
Let's all go, let's all go see,
Let's all go see what's happening

(Over there over in that patch)
Let's go see what's been happening
To our old friend:
Kindly old Bob,
Kindly old irresponsible Bob,
Kindly old irresponsible drunk and
    disorderly sniveling comatose lewd
    and lascivious Mister Uncle Bob!...
And not only that (not only that)
But all of his friends and relations,
And all of his serfs and retainers,   *The door opens.*
And all of his heirs and assigns,
And all of his structural members,   MAN 2: [*Off.*] In here...
And all of his pieces of property,
And all of his animals caged and do-
    mestic,
And all of his woodwinds and brass,   *The* YOUNG MAN *is pushed into the*
And all of his leaks and short circuits,   *darkened room.*
And all of his broken promises,   YOUNG MAN: What's in here?
And all of his suppurating wounds,
And all of his deep dark secrets,   MAN 2: [*Off.*] Keep looking...
And all of his filthy desires,   Maybe you'll find out...
And all of his bumps and protru-
    dences,
And all of the hair on the palms of his
    hands,   *Offstage laughter.*
And everything else that's damp and
    disgusting...   YOUNG MAN: Aye, there's the rub...
Everything damp...
Everything else...   *The door slams shut.*

                                         YOUNG MAN: Hello?

Hello?   Who's there?

Who's there?   Who's there?

Who's there?   This is Bob...
                                             This is Bob...
                                             Except I already knew the room was
                                                 empty,
                                             Except for a record player...

Except I already knew the room was
empty,
Except for my imagination and a
record player...

Hey, Bob, who's there?
Who's there? Hello?
Hey, Bob, hello?
Who's there? Hey, Bob!
Hello? Hello?
Who's there? Hello?

I had the feeling
People were talking about me
But it was only the record player.
I had the feeling I could discern
A shape in the shadow.
It was only the record player...

Hey, who's there, Bob?
Hello?
Hello, Bob—hey, hello.
Hey, who's there?
Hey, Bob—who's there, Bob?
Hello?
Hey, hello?
LOOK OUT, BOB! HIT THE DECK!

OLD MAN MOSES *freezes momentarily,*
then...He dives under the bed and hides.
The door opens and the MEN *move in*
quickly, lugging a shrouded body. It will
prove to be the WOMAN.

The door flies open and CLARYCE
and ELLEN *are silhouetted in its frame.*
CLARYCE: You know, some people—and
I won't say who but they know who
they are and it's disgusting...

She throws the shoes into the room.

ELLEN: They certainly are...
YOUNG MAN: You mean me? You mean
me?
ELLEN: He's a regular Einstein.
YOUNG MAN: Those are my shoes.
CLARYCE: He certainly is.
And keep track of them this time!

2: Over there...

They put her on the bed and exit.

The door slams shut.

YOUNG MAN: Several weeks passed in
this extreme condition:
To pass the time, I talked to myself.
I said: A record player is a record player.
I said: A record player becomes a record
    player…
I said: A man walked through streets
    of town carrying an object.
I said it was a record player.
I said another man fell into the shad-
    ows and was consumed record play-
    ers…

The WOMAN, *lying motionless, be-*
gins to murmur.
WOMAN: But flesh
    O flesh
    Is air
    But aye
    The paws
    That whips
    The bear
    The undiscovered country

    And the heartache

    Is a shock and the bodkin
    Is a stocking and a bearskin
    In an undiscovered country
    Where the undiscovered traveler
    Is born without return
    The barn without return

    Whose barn? The sickly door
    Is barred to the buskin
    And the traveler is stern
    In an undiscovered country
    But our currents turn horizon
    But our eye never returns
    But the traveler is soft
    But soft
    So soft
    The nymph

I said: Bob has a grocery store and he
    sells apples for 3¢ and record play-
    ers for 5¢. The question then be-
    came: If Bob has one dollar and
    buys seventeen apples, how many
    record players can he buy?
I then postulated seventeen angels
    dancing on the head of a pin.
They cried out: God is God and the
    record player is his prophet.
I told myself
That in the month of May
The record player sings
From the apple bough…

The YOUNG MAN *crosses to record*
player.
The YOUNG MAN *considers record*
player.
A record player imitates
A record player;

A record player exemplifies
A record player…

The nymph
Remember
The horizon...

The YOUNG MAN *plays the record.*

Nevertheless,
What I remember,
Is the odor of wet, worn stones,
The feeling of empty streets,
The chill of winter on the footpath
    leading from the turnstile to the sta-
    tion;
The way the milk skin wrinkled on hot
    chocolate and the taste of jam and
    butter and thick bread;
Even the extravagance of green ink in
    a black pen as against the black ink
    curdled in the bottom of the inkwell
    as against the inkstain on the wall;
And always the music,
Always this music,
All of the girls played beautiful music
Full of such sweet sorrow
Arising from the grand piano
From that elegant piano in the ladies'
    private parlour,
Rising like a smoke
Through the floorboards,
Through the house
And I remember...
I remember...
Nevertheless...
Nevertheless...

WOMAN: Nevertheless...
    When winds blow down...
    When winds blow down...
    And my darling is my darling
    ...
    And nevertheless...
    When winds blow down...
    Somewhere...

Over the sea…

And nevertheless…
When I waited where I waited…
When winds blow down…
And my darling is my darling…
And nevertheless…
When I waited where I waited…
Somewhere…
Over the sea…

And nevertheless…   And nevertheless…

Nevertheless…   Nevertheless…

                                     It goes, you see…
                                     It's gone…

OLD MAN MOSES *suddenly sticks*   *And he takes the needle off.*
out his head.

OLD MAN MOSES: Hey, Bob?
    Is that you?…

    OLD MAN MOSES *crawls out and*
examines WOMAN.

No sir, I don't believe it is.
I don't think so.
I don't think it is…

    OLD MAN MOSES *pokes at*
WOMAN *to wake her.*

Oh, Miss…(Ahem)…
Say, Lady…
Ma'am?…
Excuse me, Ma'am…
I said: Excuse me, Madam…
Hello?…Hello?…
I said: WAKE UP YOU OLD BAG!!!!

    No reaction.

Oh, is that so?...
Hmmmmmmm...
    Well, well, well...
    Well, well, well, well, well...
    In that case...

    OLD MAN MOSES *looks around hastily, then quickly takes off his pants.*

In that case, boys and girls,
Let's all watch what happens here
When juicy old Mister Wigglefoot,
Or should I say, Old saucy Mister
        Dingle-dangle,
Or should we call him rusty, crusty,
        lusty, trusty, busty Mister Bob—
Oh, the hell with instructions, honey !
Let's get down to *work*!

    His trousers off, OLD MAN MOSES *leaps into bed. Whereupon the* WOMAN *simultaneously leaps out of bed and turns on the light switch as the* MEN *enter.*

WOMAN: There he is! That's him!
    That's the man...

YOUNG MAN: [*Barely audible.*] I have
    observed...
    From time to time...
    The people...people...

    Momentary tableau.

OLD MAN MOSES: Ah, yes...(Ahem)...
    Hello!...
    Well, well, you seem to have
    caught me with my (what an
    embarrassment...)
    I...[uh]...Oh, dear, I...
    well...I...

    OLD MAN MOSES *tries to jump back under bed but the* MEN *prevent him.*

MEN: Oh, no you don't [*Etc.*]

OLD MAN MOSES: All right, all right,
all right,
I'll talk, I'll talk, don't hurt me please,
I'll talk, I will, I really will...
I really will...
I'll talk...
Okay?
Hunh?

YOUNG MAN: [*Barely audible.*] Talking...

...Of this...

...And that...

By now the WOMAN *has stolen out
of the room.*

...This...

...And that...

MAN 2: So talk.

OLD MAN MOSES: Look, gimme a
minute, will you?
I mean, these things don't im*medi*ately
come to mind, you know...(You
know?...You don't know...Oh,
well...)
Now let me see—how does it go?
No, that's not it: The umpy-pumpy-
piddly-pum...
Hmmmmm...
So, where was I?
Ah, yes!
Ahem
To be, or something-or-other—
That is the...something-or-other...
Now I know that's not quite
right, not quite right yet...
Hmmmm...
To be or not to be...
To be or not to be...
To be or not to be or not to be
Or not to shuffle—
Aye, there's the rub!
That is...the rub! (no)
That is...the consummation
devoutly to be wished. (no)

("The mortal coil"—that's in
there somewhere...)

...And this...

...And that...

The door opens quietly and the
WOMAN *enters and sits in a chair. The*
YOUNG MAN *is aware of her but need
not react. She speaks softly at him.*

WOMAN: I know because I saw you,
Bob—
The alarm went off
And you began to run

That is…the question! Aye!
The question!
Whether 'tis nobler in the
mortal coil—no, no—the mind,
Nobler in the mind…
(Now let me see…)
Whether 'tis nobler in the mind
To grunt and sweat under a weary load
    (that can't be right)
Whether 'tis nobler in the mind
To take up arms against outrageous
    fortune or…
Seeking his quietus or…to seek…
Or his quietus make with a bare bod-
    kin and by opposing end them!
That is the contumely that makes a
    consolation of so long life or some-
    thing like that…

MAN 3: (This guy eats it.)

OLD MAN MOSES: For *who* (Thou Phi-
listine!) would fardels bear—aye,
there's the rub!
Who would grunt and sweat under a
    heavy load but that the thought of
    something after death, that undis-
    covered bourne—no, wait! Go
    back!
To die! To sleep! No more!
(I've got it!)
'Tis a consummation devoutly to be
    wished:To die—perchance to
    sleep—perchance to sleep—per-
    chance to dream—perchance to
    dream—perchance to be—per-
    chance to shuffle—
AYE, THERE'S THE RUB!
There's the something-or-other (I for-
    get) must give us pause…

MAN 3: (What a disaster.)

OLD MAN MOSES: For in that sleep of
death what dreams may come when we
have shuffled off this mortal coil (that's

All night calling my name
But I was gone in a speeding truck
Down the road and around the bend
Where the headlights picked up
A terrible accident
But it was too late then
We were out of control
You tried to stop
But the brakes were broken
So you winked at me
And you kept on winking
And we went falling
Falling down
We went falling
We went down
Falling…
Down…
Falling…

WOMAN: Another time
    I thought I saw
    A shape in the shadow of the shade.

    I thought it was you
    But it wasn't.
    It looked like you
    But it wasn't.

And then the head came off
And I could see
Things moving around inside

where it goes)
The perturbations and the thousand
    natural shocks the flesh is heir to—
The whips and scorns!
The slings and arrows!
The something-or-other's some-
    thing-or-other and the proud man's
    contumely,
Must give us pause!

What's he to Hecuba?
Aye, there's the rub!
[*Sings.*] WAY DOWN UPON THE
    SWANEEE RIVVAHHH...

And OLD MAN MOSES *dives under the bed and escapes. The* MEN *yell
excitedly but do not move.*

MEN: There he goes! After him! Stop that
    man! Don't let him get away ! [*Etc.*]

They all fall silent as the DOUBLE
enters and looks them up and down.

DOUBLE: Who was singing?
MAN 2: He's gone.
DOUBLE: Who's gone?
MAN 2: The man under the bed.
DOUBLE: What man? There's nobody
    there .
MAN 2: That's just what I said.

DOUBLE: So what are you standing
    around for?
MAN 2: I don't know. Do you?
MAN 3: I don't know. Do you?
MAN 4: I don't know. Do you?
MAN 2: Well, I guess that settles it, then.

I was afraid for you
But what could I do?
The things were already
Crawling up my arm.
The phone rang once.
I knew it was you.
I just couldn't get there in time.
My feet kept slipping
In something wet:
I couldn't tell what;
But I didn't want to touch it.

OLD MAN MOSES *enters in terror,*
WOMAN *and* YOUNG MAN *never notice him.*

OLD MAN MOSES: Oh, Bobby, help me,
    hide me!
They're after me!
They're out to get me!

4, 3, & 2 *successively drop to their knees and crawl out under the bed. When they are gone, the* DOUBLE *drops the bedclothes back down and stretches out on the bed. He might have a cigarette while waiting...*

Bobby, please! You've got to help me hide!
They're out there right behind me!
Bobby—listen to me—please!
Help me, hide me, oh, please listen to me, Bobby, help me, please....

NOTE. *Because the following scene occurs only in the* SL *room and because there are five simultaneous voices, the system of notation used hitherto will be abandoned and the whole page will be used to represent the one room, and dialogue for each character tabulated in columns, thus:*

		WOMAN:	OLD MAN MOSES: [*Running around room.*] Oh, Bobby, please believe me, please do something; why don't you help me? They're gonna get me—oh, they're gonna get me—help—they're gonna get me—Bobby!
		I was worried about you.	
YOUNG MAN: I'm all right, Mom. I'm all right, Dad. I'm all right, everybody...			

		I've been concerned about you.	Oh, there's gotta be a place to hide me got to be a place to go—oh, they're all out there coming to get me, it's too awful, Bobby, help me, I can't do anything!
And I for you. And he for me. And you for him. And us for them. And they for Everybody else— You see where it leads to...			
			[*Kneeling down, hides head in hands.*]
		I wanted to help you Bob, that's all I wanted, honestly, I just wanted to help you, don't you understand?	HELLLLLP! HELLLLLP! HELLLLP MEEE!

WOMAN:
So what about your shoes? Did you put them back on like a good boy?

YOUNG MAN:
Dear Mom and Dad: Thank you for the shoes. They are very nice. I like to wear them every day and someday when you come and visit me you will see how much I like them. Thank you very much again. Your son: Bob.

OLD MAN MOSES:
HELLLLP MEEE!
[*Stands up again.*]
Oh, I don't care any more, let them come get me—boy—some help you are, Bob, I mean a person comes to you for a little aid and comfort and what does he get but an earful of blah - blah - blah and the old cold shoulder.

Are you deaf?
Hunh?
Bob?!
What's wrong with you two?
...

I don't understand why you won't let me help I really don't. I must say I'm finding it very difficult to understand anything about your attitude at all I mean you ask for help I think you need help and yet whenever somebody actually tries to help you, you rebuff them I mean it's almost, as if you wanted it that way.

Hello? Hello, Bob. Hello there, Bobby. Hello-hello... Hi-Hi-Hello-Hello. Buenos Dias, Señora. Como esta usted?

Muy bien, gracias. Y usted? Oh, si! Yo soy muy, muy, muy bien, gracias, senorita linda.

Oh, senor, tu es un hombre muy sincero. De nada, senorita, de nada
...

OLD MAN MOSES:

Don't do this,
And don't do that,
And don't do Anything else,
(Tra-la)
And if I don't do anything at all, then I'll never get in trouble, will I? Is that what you're telling me?

Yak, yak, yak, yak, yak...

WOMAN:
Besides, they were very expensive shoes

YOUNG MAN:
I'm afraid!
That's what!
I'm afraid—don't you understand?
I'm afraid I'm going crazy.
I'm afraid I'm going to die.
I'm afraid you're going to die.
I'm afraid of talking to people.
I'm afraid of answering telephones. I'm afraid of driving in cars.
I'm afraid of loud noises.
I'm afraid of knives and guns and ropes and stairs and food that tastes funny.
I'm afraid of the

But I love you, Bob.

I love you, Bob.

I love you, Bob.

That's right! Don't worry, about me It's all right. Fine with me. Don't be concerned about your friends when they're in trouble...
I'll be all right, I guess...
I'll probably survive somehow...
I imagine I'll manage to make it through all this somehow—so don't trouble yourself on my account—don't worry about me—not that you ever will, but that's all right, I guess I can't blame you—after all, who wants to care about the old man? Who wants to care about me? I guess it's too much to expect you to take time from your problems to worry about an old guy like me...Well, I won't last forever. Sooner or later I'll be gone for good and you won't have to think about me at all. I know I'm just a nuisance to

CLARYCE *and* ELLEN *enter, turning on the light, and sit in the two remaining chairs.*

CLARYCE:
...so I said, you know, I mean, I said: Look, you know—people can get very *hostile* sometimes...

Or put a dog in the dresser!

I said: People you see, people have a way of getting kind of *brutal*...

Especially when you try to put milk in the record player or read upside down.

Yes, especially circulars. You see, *people*...

Yes, *some* people have a tendency to become rather *vengeful*.

Rather *violent*!

ELLEN:
That's so true—Especially when you smoke in their food!

That's right!

That's right!

Particularly circulars!

You should say *some* people...

Rather *vicious*...

That's right !

[YOUNG MAN, cont.]

shapes that I see
in the shadows.
I'm afraid of
people that died
a long time ago.
I'm afraid of
some feelings I
don't under-
stand.
I'm afraid to be
seen.
I'm afraid of my-
self.
I'm afraid!
I'm afraid!
I'm afraid!

WOMAN

I love you, Bob.

I love you...

[OLD MAN MOSES, cont.]

you anyway but I
don't ask for
much—just a
kind word now
and again, a little
sympathy, per-
haps a smile—
because it isn't
easy for me you
know. Not that I
mean to com-
plain but some-
times I just don't
think I can go on,
I really don't...

Excuse me, please:
I'll take one too...

Could I have an-
other one?

I'd like another
one.

And another one.

I'll take one
more, thanks.

Well, maybe *one*
more.

Mmmm—just
one...

CLARYCE:

Yes! Or poke holes
in the mezzo-so-
prano!

Yes! Or infect the
living-room
floor!

Yeah?

Don't worry
about it—it's all
in your imagina-
tion. Really. Lis-
ten, give me a
cigarette...

ELLEN:

Especially when
you pour hot
burning chickens
under their eye-
lids!

Yes! Or eat fish in
the hearse before
breakfast!

Hey, Claryce?

Who are all these
people?

[*Gives her one.*]

[*Gives him one.*]

[*Gives him one.*]

[*Gives him one.*]

[*Gives him one.*]

[*Gives him one.*]

[*Gives him one.*]

[*At this point the* MEN *enter; henceforth, the previous notation will be used.*]

The DOUBLE *still lies on the bed.*

Enter 2, 3 *and* 4.

MAN 2: Well, now, is everybody happy?
　　　Let me see those smiling faces every-
　　　body...
　　　Bob—what about you?
YOUNG MAN: What?
MAN 2: I said: What about you, Bob?
YOUNG MAN: I don't know.
MAN 2: Nope. Try it again, Bob.
YOUNG MAN: What?
MAN 2: Try it again, Bob.
YOUNG MAN: I don't know what you
　　　mean.
MAN 3: Guy doesn't know.
MAN 4: Try it again, Bob.
YOUNG MAN: Do you have a cigarette?
MAN 2: [*Barks.*] NO!
YOUNG MAN: I'm sorry.
MAN 2: Bob—you seem jumpy.

The DOUBLE *still lies on the bed.*

Is something the matter?
You can tell us—
You can trust us, right?
3 AND 4: That's right.
MAN 2: I mean, you can say *any*thing—
　　　Anything you like—am I right, boys?
3 AND 4: That's right.
MAN 2: Now, we might think you were
　　　strange,
　　　We might think you were odd,
　　　We might think you were crazy,
MAN 4: We might think all of those things.
MAN 2: But we'd never say so.
MAN 3: We'd never say that.
MAN 2: Certainly not
MAN 4: We might think that your brain
　　　was infected with worms...
MAN 3: Or worse...
MAN 4: But we would never *say* so...
MAN 2: That would be rude.
　　　There's no need to be rude...

YOUNG MAN: I'd like to go home.

MAN 2: So would I. So would they.

YOUNG MAN: Let me go home!

MAN 2: Why? Are we boring you?
We are boring, aren't we?

YOUNG MAN: I wouldn't say that.

MAN 2: Oh, you can be honest.

MAN 3: We're very dull people.
We're proud of the fact.

MAN 2: We're boring and violent.
No doubt about it.
Still, there ought to be *some*thing we
could do to be entertaining...

MAN 4: We could sing songs.

MAN 2: Of course! Singing songs!
That's a perfect idea, isn't it, Bob?

OLD MAN MOSES: (I know a song)

YOUNG MAN: If you say so.

MAN 2: I'm glad you agree then.

The DOUBLE *still lies on the bed.*   You go first.

CLARYCE: He can't.

MAN 2: Why not?

CLARYCE: He says he doesn't know any.
We already asked.

MAN 3: Doesn't know any songs?
What's the matter with you?
You know how to sing, don't you?

MAN 4: Of course he does!
Everybody knows how to sing.
He just doesn't know any songs, am I
right?

OLD MAN MOSES: (I do! Ask me!)

MAN 2: Then we'll teach him one. Okay,
Bob?

OLD MAN MOSES: (No! Ask me! Ask
me!)

YOUNG MAN: There's no singing allowed.

MAN 2: Yes, I know, Bob, but I still think
you better do what we say, don't you?

OLD MAN MOSES: (Hey! Over here! Ask
me!)

MAN 3: Hey, Bob—you know the one
about your father?

OLD MAN MOSES: (I do!)

YOUNG MAN: My father is dead.

MAN 2: Bob, Bob, Bob, Bob, Bob,— *every*body's father is dead.

MAN 4: That still doesn't mean we can't say insulting things about him, does it?

OLD MAN MOSES: No! No! Let me do it! Let me!

MAN 2 Right! You're on!

Hit it, girls!

The MEN *snap fingers and join* GIRLS *on the backup.*

The DOUBLE *still lies on bed*

	GIRLS:	MEN:
OLD MAN MOSES:	SHOOP-SHOO	
	SHOOP-SHOO	
Oh, Boy!	SHOOP-SHOO	BEDOOBY
I'm going to do it!	SHOOP-SHOO	BEDOOBY
You better watch me!	SHOOP-SHOO	BEDOOBY
Watch me do it!	SHOOP-SHOO	BEDOOBY
Here I go....	SHOOP-SHOO	BEDOOBY
OHHHHHHHHHHHHHHHH...	SHOOP-SHOO	BEDOOBY
YOUR FATHER WAS RESPECTED	SHOOP-SHOO	BEDOOBY
YOUR FATHER WAS ELECTED	SHOOP-SHOO	BEDOOBY
YOUR FATHER WAS PROTECTED	SHOOP-SHOO	BE....
[*All sing.*] AT THE ROTARY CLUB....		BEDOOBY
YOUR FATHER WAS INFECTED	SHOOP-SHOO	BEDOOBY
YOUR FATHER WAS DETECTED	SHOOP-SHOO	BEDOOBY
YOUR FATHER WAS REJECTED	SHOOP-SHOO	BE....
[*All sing.*] AT THE ROTARY CLUB....		BEDOOBY
YOUR FATHER WAS INSPECTED	SHOOP-SHOO	BEDOOBY
YOUR FATHER WAS INJECTED	SHOOP-SHOO	BEDOOBY
YOUR FATHER WAS DISSECTED	SHOOP-SHOO	BE....
[*All sing.*] AT THE ROTARY CLUB....		BEDOOBY
I-I-I-I-I... [*Sustain.*]		NEVER HAD NO REASON

As before, 3 & 4 *overpower* OLD
MAN MOSES *and drag him off kicking*
and screaming.

NEVER HAD NO REASON
NEVER HAD NO REASON

YOUNG MAN: Stop!

Stop that!

He's my friend!

Don't hurt him!

MAN 2: Now just a minute, Bob.
    He broke the law…
CLARYCE: It must be done.
ELLEN: The law applies to everyone!
    And you're the one…
CLARYCE: And you're the one…
MAN 2: And you're the one…
ALL: That *did it!*

> CLARYCE *and* ELLEN *exit, calling to the* MEN.

CLARYCE: Tell him about the punchbowl!
ELLEN: Tell him about the rabbits, George!
CLARYCE: Tell him about the other time!

ELLEN: Tell him about the big one!

> *They are gone.*

MAN 2: On the other hand, I would really worry about it…
    I mean, after all, these things happen.
    And even if it is your fault, it may not be your responsibility.
    And even if it is your responsibility, it may not be your doing.
    And even if it is your doing, it may not be your mistake.
    And even if it's your mistake, it may not even matter.
    And even if it does, you may not have to apologize.
    I mean—you could always say you weren't yourself…

Offstage sounds. OLD MAN MOSES *protesting,* GIRLS *accusing; general commotion.*
GIRLS: Tell him about the chest protector!
    Tell him about the stew!
    Tell him about the filthy story!
    Tell him about the bare bodkin!
OLD MAN MOSES: I didn't mean it!
    I'm sorry!
    Please don't hurt me!
    I take it all back!… [*Etc.*]

> 3 *and* 4 *drag in* OLD MAN MOSES, *struggling.*

    I'll do anything—just give me a second chance—I swear to you I…
MAN 4: Shut up, you!
MAN 3: This is him. This is the man.

> *Exit* MAN 2.

> *The* YOUNG MAN *runs for the door but it slams shut and appears to be*

DOUBLE: So...
Unfortunately, I'm afraid we've got a little problem here, another little problem, just another little problem that's the sort of little problem I don't *like!*

OLD MAN MOSES: Please, don't hurt me! I'll tell you. I'll tell you everything— just don't hurt me, please—I'll talk, I will, I really will...

During the following speech the MEN *will also repeat the capitalized words as* OLD MAN MOSES *speaks them.*

You see—it all began
TWO nights ago when I was walking down Avenue
B and in the shadows I saw a couple of drunken sailors trying to tie a snake around an
OAR. But the
KNOT was
TOO loose and the snake made a
BEE-line for the oyster-beds— now wait! I know what you're thinking! But I swear on my mother's grave
THAT
IS
THE truth! Now, naturally I wanted to
QUESTION them about their strange behavior, but in order to avoid an ugly scene I began by remarking: Nice
WEATHER we're having—to which the taller one replied in a very surly manner: And what if it
'TIS? Well, I, to be noble, wanting to be noble—I mean, no one is
NOBLER than I when I want to be, said: Look, I suppose
IN
THE end I don't

locked. He tries to get out—pounding, pounding, etc.—but to no avail.

YOUNG MAN: Let me out!

Let me out!

Let me out!

Now the YOUNG MAN *rushes to the telephone and begins to dial numbers one after the other as quickly as possible throughout this scene.*

MIND
TOO much seeing snakes
SUFFER...but I had no sooner said
   this than
THE...shorter one, I think it was,
SLINGS the oar up over his shoulder,
   gives his partner the nod,
AND—before I could say another
   word—they're both down the street
   like an arrow—well, actually, I sup-
   pose since there were two of them I
   should say they were off like a
   couple of
ARROWS. Now—I'm caught com-
   pletely flatfooted. What's to be
   done? I'm thinking it's hopeless
   when by a stroke
OF
OUTRAGEOUS good
FORTUNE...[Why do they do that?]
   [*Meaning* MEN.]
OF
OUTRAGEOUS good
FORTUNE the
OAR slips down and one of them
   stumbles and when the other turns
   around
TO
TAKE a look, he runs right into the
ARMS of a waiting policeman.
Now, the cop throws him right up
AGAINST
A wall but I can

SEE with the two of them, the cop is
   still hesitating, so I yelled at him:
   Come on, there, what are you afraid
OF? You're well paid for your
TROUBLES!
AND
BY God if they don't all square off into
OPPOSING corners and start going
   to it hammer and tongs

Still dialing, the YOUNG MAN *also now begins to try to talk over the phones*

YOUNG MAN: Hello?

Hello?

Hello?

Hello?
Hello, this is Bob...

Hello, this is Bob...

Hello, this is Bob...

Hello, this is Bob...

Hello, is there anybody there?

Hello, is there anybody there?

This is Bob. Is there anybody there?

This is Bob. Is there anybody there?

WOMAN: Why don't you do something?
YOUNG MAN: Hello?
WOMAN: Why can't you do something?
YOUNG MAN: Hello?...
WOMAN: Why don't you stop it?
YOUNG MAN: This is Bob!
WOMAN: Why can't you make them stop it?

right then and there until I'm convinced the fight will be the
END of all of

THEM. I tell you what a ruckus! The cop is beating one of them and he's yelling: Help! Help! I don't want
TO
DIE! And meanwhile this lady in the window up above is hollering: Knock it off, you hooligans! Can't you see we're trying
TO
SLEEP? And somehow right in middle of all this comes an all-girl mariachi band and they're walking down the street singing
LA CUCARACHA, LA CUCARACHA, LA, LA, LA, LA, LA, LA, LA...
LA CUCARACHA, LA CUCARACHA.
MARIJUANA QUE FUMAR!

DOUBLE: Shut him up! Shut him up! Finish it!

And DOUBLE *exits as* 3 & 4 *overpower* OLD MAN MOSES *and force him down on bed.*

OLD MAN MOSES: Oh no oh please no oh please don't you do it don't you do it oh no please don't break me down don't break me down please no don't do it don't you break me down please don't break me down oh listen to the man oh please don't you do it don't you do it don't you do it please don't break me down please don't break me down please listen to the man please listen please don't do it please...

OLD MAN MOSES's *cries fade into whimpers.* CLARYCE *and* ELLEN *enter as "angels."* 3 & 4 *sit back down and pay no attention. The* GIRLS *stand by the head of the bed and sing.*

YOUNG MAN: This is Bob!
WOMAN: Why don't you think of something?
YOUNG MAN: Is anybody there?
WOMAN: Can't you think of anything?
YOUNG MAN: Is there anybody there?
WOMAN: Can't you do anything?
YOUNG MAN: Hello.
WOMAN: Aren't you going to take any responsibility?
YOUNG MAN: What?
WOMAN: Don't you think it's your fault?
YOUNG MAN: I can't hear you.
WOMAN: Aren't you really to blame?
YOUNG MAN: No, I can't hear...

WOMAN: Are you just going to stand there?
Is this really the best you can do?
What kind of man are you?
Aren't you ashamed of yourself?
YOUNG MAN: Shut up! Shut up!

The YOUNG MAN *attacks the* WOMAN *and they fall to the floor; she screams as* YOUNG MAN *yells.*

Shut...Up...
Shut...Up...
Shut...Up...
Shut...Up...
Shut...Up...[*Etc.*]

Eventually, the YOUNG MAN *ties up the* WOMAN *and blindfolds her—she lies still in one corner as the* YOUNG MAN *weeps in another.*

GIRLS: LE PETIT ROI
 IL A TOMBE
 IL TOMBERA
 DANS SON TOMBEAU

 LE PETIT ROI
 IL TOMBERA
 IL A TOMBE
 DANS SON TOMBEAU

 LA LA LA LA
 LA LA LA LA
 LA LA LA LA
 LA LA LA LA

 LA LA LA LA
 LA LA LA LA
 LA LA LA LA
 LA LA LA LA

 3 & 4 exit to intercept the YOUNG
MAN *in the hall outside. The following
is all offstage.*

YOUNG MAN: Let me in!
 Let me see him!
 I've got to see him!
MAN 3: I'm sorry sir.
MAN 4: No admittance.
MAN 3: No visitors allowed, sir.
MAN 4: I'm sorry sir, you'll have to come
 with us…
MAN 3: Let's go—move along…

 Meanwhile, the GIRLS *have been
ministering to* OLD MAN MOSES,
*mopping his brow, etc. Now they also
leave quietly, turning off the light and
closing the door. There is a pause, then*
OLD MAN MOSES *can be heard singing faintly.*

YOUNG MAN: Please forgive me…

 I didn't mean to .

 I didn't want to hurt you…

 Oh, God! What have I done?

 And YOUNG MAN *runs out of the
room.*

 The WOMAN *begins slowly working
herself free.*

OLD MAN MOSES: WAY DOWN
UPON THE SWANEE RIVER
FAR, FAR AWAY…
THAT'S WHERE MY HEART IS
ALWAYS TURNING
THAT'S WHERE THE OLD
FOLKS AT HOME…

Or something like that, I don't know…

OLD MAN MOSES *sits up a little.*

Now, Once upon a time
I knew a little guy,
A little leap guy,
(He was on the automatic)
He was coming down the road all wob-
bly
And his head fell off and he was dead.
And then the other guy,
He saw the show and he went home.
He was a neat guy.
Then, there was a bell.

But actually,   *The* WOMAN *is still working herself*
Once upon a time,   *free.*
I knew a little neat guy (he was auto-
matic)
And the bell fell off and he went wob-
bly
And the other guy said:
I saw him down by the roadside road
And I was wrong about it!
So then, you see, the other guy
He went automatic,
He went down the downside in the
tree-hole to the dog,
And the dog said (Are you listening)
The dog said: Oh my, Mister Feeny,
He said: I was wide, I was so very wide!
And all the while, his eye was watch-
ing him!

So I said: Never before in the history
    of mankind was Mister Feeny down
    by the wood fence by the roadside
    road.
And I said: No!

So anyway (as I was saying)
Once upon a time,
There was a little bent guy,
And he went home.
And once upon a time,
There was a little wet guy,
He got bent,
He got all wobbly on the home side
(I said: I know why)
He was on the automatic,
He got wetness on the backside;
And once upon a time,
When I went walking
There was a little slick man
With a wee wet smile,
And he had a knife!
And he was on the automatic;
And he made a little cut
And off it came!

By now OLD MAN MOSES *is up and
moving towards the window, which he
crawls out of.*

And I said: No, no, no…
Oh, no, Bob, no…
That was a wet and naughty one,
    Bobby!
That was a nasty one…

   And he is gone.

By now, the WOMAN *has worked her
arms free and is groping around the
room blindfolded. She murmurs.*

WOMAN: Come back…
    Please—come back…
    I am still here,
    Still waiting for you,
    Still wondering when you will return…
    I went looking for you everywhere.
    I could not find you.
    I find myself wondering:
    Where did you go?
    I have sent my thoughts after you in
        every direction.
    My thoughts came back to me.
    I found myself thinking about you in
        this place and that;
    But you were nowhere to be found .
    If I think about you hard enough,
    Will you hear me?
    If I think about you long enough,
    Will you come back?
    And now I see you
    Standing outside my door:
    I see your hand on the doorknob.
    You come in quietly…

    The YOUNG MAN *stands in the
    doorway. He turns on the lights, the*
    WOMAN *goes to the record player.*

    You walk up behind me
    Joy and apprehension overwhelm me.
    That's why I busy myself
    With insignificant details…

    She plays the record. The YOUNG
    MAN *still stands in the doorway.*

YOUNG MAN: I have been troubled in my
    mind,
    Remembering little Jojo the retarded
        boy, and how they beat him;
    Remembering how they took him out
        into the barn and beat him;
    How they dragged him screaming from

the dinner table into the stalls where it was always dark and damp and smelled of mold,
And there Christine would beat him with a switch,
And the rest of us at dinner had to listen to him screaming.
The reason was:
He would not eat cooked liver.
He did not like the taste.
But after a while he would begin to cry whenever he simply saw the liver on his plate;
Just the smell of liver cooking was enough—
He knew it meant another beating,
And he would cry just from the fear and try to run away and after a while they beat him just for that, because he was a bad boy.
And after they beat him they locked him in his room to take a nap and after a while if he wasn't asleep, if he was crying, if he was a bad boy, they took him out and beat him again.
Once or twice after they beat him,
They tried to make him go back and eat the liver…

By now the WOMAN *has taken off the record, it is very still.*

YOUNG MAN: You talk about love and longing…
As for me, I tell you—I am sick at heart…

The WOMAN *begins to speak, she acts entranced.*

WOMAN: Then…listen…to me…
Then…listen…to me…
Imagine…A world…

The MEN *enter in a businesslike way and set up positions—4 on the bed, perhaps blindfolded too.*

MAN 2: You getting anything?…

MAN 4: He's talking…
I've got her…

Take the record off…

MAN 4: [*Whispers.*] Okay…Standby…

MAN 4: Transmitting…

THE QUESTION…

THE QUESTION…

THE QUESTION...

THE QUESTION...

MEN: THE QUESTION...

MAN 4: THE MIND.

THE MIND...

MEN: THE MIND.

MAN 4: THE SLINGS...

MEN: THE SLINGS.

MAN 4: THE ARROWS...

MEN: THE ARROWS...

MAN 4: THE SEA...

MEN: THE SEA...

MAN 4: THE SLEEP...

MEN: THE SLEEP...
MAN 4: THE HEARTACHE.

MEN: THE HEARTACHE...

MAN 4. THE SHOCK

MEN: THE SHOCK.

MAN 4: THE FLESH...

MEN: THE FLESH...

MAN 4: THE CONSUMMATION...

THE RUB...

A world...revolving...
Revolving and revolving
And revolving...
And revolving...
And the question...
Is arising...
Is the question...
That's arising...
In the mind...
That is arising...
In the turbulence...
Arising...
In the struggle...
In the warfare...
Of the mind...
Of the wound...
And the piercing...
And the flowing...
Of the mind...
And the weeping...
Of the waters...
Of the mind...
Floating...
Adrift...
Over the dark ocean...
In the reverie of dreams ...
Of solitude...
And pain...
Of many wounds...
So wounded...
And so weeping...
And so waiting
For the flash...
Of the awakening...
The brilliant light...
The moment comes...
And this my skin...
And this...
My tender membrane...
Ruptured...
And destroyed...
In the violence...
Of one great surface...

THE COIL...

THE OPPRESSOR...

THE PANG...

THE QUIETUS .

THE QUIETUS...

QUIETUS.

QUIETUS.
MAN 2: What's the matter?
MAN 4: I'm getting nothing...

MAN 2: It's too difficult.
     Try something else

MAN 4: Nope, she's got it...

MAN 4 Wait a minute...

Something's wrong...

MAN 2: [To MAN 3.] Go see what happened.

MAN 4: No, wait...

It may be all right...

THE QUIETUS...

THE QUIETUS.

Sliding on another great surface...
And the writhing of them...
Intertwined about me...
I go down...
I go to nothing...
Oh, it stabs me...
I go down...
I go nothing...
The snake...
Nothing...
Nothing...
A-A-A-A-A-A-A-A-A-A...

YOUNG MAN: What's the matter?
WOMAN: Nothing...

Too difficult...
YOUNG MAN: What do you mean?
WOMAN: But he himself might his quietus make with a bare bodkin.

Yes, I got it...
YOUNG MAN: Tell me more.
WOMAN: Get out of here before they catch you men are waiting men are listening!

Wait a minute...

Something's wrong...

Go see what happened...
YOUNG MAN: Where?

WOMAN: No, wait...

May be all right...

Stop...

Stop...

MAN 4 *sits up in bed, takes off blind-fold.*

No, forget it—that's about all I'm going to be able to get

All finished.

MAN 2 Well, that's okay.
I think we got enough.
MAN 4: Anybody got a cigarette?
MAN 3: Yeah, hang on a sec.

    MAN 3 *offers* MAN 4 *a cigarette.*
MAN 4: Thanks.

Bob?
I think that's all there is.
Do you mind if I take this blindfold off now?
YOUNG MAN: What?...Oh, sure, I'm sorry.

MAN 2: [*To* 4.] Listen, we're going to check back in—
You let us know if anything happens, okay?

    MAN 2 & MAN 3 *exit,* 4 *lies back in bed.*

WOMAN: I could sure use a cigarette if you've got one.
YOUNG MAN: Yeah...Here...Sorry...

    YOUNG MAN *offers her one; lights it.*

WOMAN: Do you want to tell me about it?

    MAN 4 *begins to whistle the tune on the record and as he does so,* OLD MAN MOSES *crawls out from under bed and begins a poignant silent dance.* OLD MAN MOSES *does not play to* MAN 4, *and he simply stares at the ceiling, unaware of* OLD MAN MOSES.

YOUNG MAN: I went back there, once,
The family did, I should say.
That would have been about...
Four years later, I guess...

It was all gone. Everything.
The old woman had died.
They'd sent all the children home.
The house was abandoned,
All boarded up.

Somebody told us it was scheduled to
    be torn down so they could put up
    some new apartment buildings…

After that, we went to visit my tutor.
Even that was different.
They were living in town, in some
    apartment building, instead of the
    old house on the lake—we had to
    ask directions…
Anyway, when we got there his wife was
    the only one home. I hadn't known
    her that much at all—it was strange.
She seemed to be acting very strange.
The thing was, she didn't speak English
    and I had forgotten so much of my
    French that we really couldn't fol-
    low what she was trying to tell us.
Finally somebody asked when was
    Monsieur Guillot coming back—
I'll never forget the look on her face.
She just broke down completely.
I remember her sobbing:
"Il est mort, il est mort…"

MAN 4 *stops whistling.*
OLD MAN MOSES *runs back un-*
der bed.

They'd just buried him a day or two
    earlier.
She had been trying to tell us.
She thought we knew…

The DOUBLE *appears in the door-*
way, beckoning. The WOMAN *follows*
him off. The YOUNG MAN *doesn't seem*
to notice.

You see,
Whenever I think about that time in
    my life,

I see the image of myself as a little boy.
And I become a spectator, watching
    that little boy again and again walk-
    ing through that town, replaying the
    scenes I remember from those days.
And again I feel that deep sadness,
Knowing as I watch that the little boy
    and the people that he meets and
    the places that he goes are all gone
    now.
They don't exist like that anymore.
They're only memories,
With no more substance
Than reflections on water...

Enter MAN 2 *&* MAN 3.

MAN 4: Oh, hi—nothing's happened...
MAN 2: Okay—then let's get the old man.

From under bed, OLD MAN MOSES
shrieks.

A hand reaches in and turns off light.

Hello?
Is someone there?

The MEN *turn on the light and lift
up the bedclothes.* OLD MAN MOSES
is dead under the bed. The MEN *pull him
out feet first and drag him off.*

ELLEN *enters in semi-darkness. She
speaks very fast, her back to the wall.*

ELLEN: Bob, I had to get away, I had to
    try and warn you Bob, I had to try and
    tell you—if she finds out, I don't
    know—but listen:
Something's going on.
They're planning something— every-
    body—
They wouldn't tell me what but they
    were talking about you, Bob.
They were saying—wait, I think she's
    coming...
They said—never mind—too late—
Just run! Just go!
Just get out of here!

ELLEN *runs out door.*

YOUNG MAN: What?
What did you say?
What was that?
I'm sorry—I didn't quite…

CLARYCE enters abruptly, turns on
light.

CLARYCE: It doesn't matter.
What she said doesn't matter.
She's not in her right mind.

If I were you I'd forget all about it.

ELLEN runs into the room with the
MEN behind her. They overpower her
and carry her off. This is done very qui-
etly and efficiently.

She thinks there's a plot.
She thinks we're all in on it.
She thinks we're all out to get you.

I hope you won't believe that.
I don't think you will.
There's a name for people like that.

She turns to go.

YOUNG MAN: Wait a minute…Please…

CLARYCE: Yes?
YOUNG MAN: There was something I
wanted to ask you about, but I can't
remember…
Some kind of danger, I…
Was it a plot? I can't remember.
I just can't think what it was.

CLARYCE exits.

It was something, though, it really was,
I…
I'm sorry…
I'm sorry…
OLD MAN MOSES enters briskly,
disguised as a wealthy Victorian gentle-
man.

OLD MAN MOSES: Oh, don't be sorry,
don't be sorry, no need to be sorry—
Just a simple slip-up, happens all the
time, don't trouble yourself over the
matter at all...

 OLD MAN MOSES *is picking up
record player and table and walking off
with them.*

YOUNG MAN: What are you doing?
Wait! Come back!

OLD MAN MOSES: Delivered to the
wrong address—
Sorry, old boy—sorry about it—
Terrible slip-up, happens all the time.
Intended for a one-legged milkmaid in
Dunstable Mews...

YOUNG MAN: But that's mine!

OLD MAN MOSES: Nope, nope, couldn't
be yours—
Sorry, old fish—couldn't be yours!
Couldn't just walk away with it like this
if it were yours, could I?

YOUNG MAN: But you are!

The DOUBLE *enters, sets up a chair
in the middle of the room facing away
from the room next door, and he sits.*

OLD MAN MOSES: Exactly so.
However, I can be a fair man:
Maybe not an honest man,
Maybe not a rich man,
Maybe not a wet man,
Maybe not a hairy man,
Maybe not a lumpy man,
Maybe not a green and gracious man,
Maybe not the sort of man who grunts
and sweats under a fardel,
Maybe not the sort of man who suffers
the slings and arrows with a bare
bodkin...
Maybe not that sort of man at all...

Enter 2, 3 & 4.

Maybe—uh—pay no attention to
    them:
These men aren't really there—
Actually they're just my associates.
Actually they're very good friends of
    mine
Actually they're here to make you a
    very remarkable offer, sir—
A very remarkable offer indeed, sir.
In fact, the offer of a lifetime, sir!

DOUBLE: You see, Bob,
    Everything that is happening here
    Is happening just the way it had to hap-
        pen;
    And nothing is happening to you now
    That didn't have to happen;
    So there is absolutely no need to worry,
        is there?

MAN 4 *leads* OLD MAN MOSES
away as MAN 3 *carries off the record
player and* MAN 2 *sets up a chair in the
middle of the room, facing away from
the room next door.*

MAN 2: Do you understand?
YOUNG MAN: I don't know.
MAN 2: Do you have any questions?
YOUNG MAN: No.
MAN 2: Then I'll have to ask you to be
    seated now, sir.

    YOUNG MAN *sits in the chair and*
MAN 2 *lashes him to it.*

That's right…
That's right…
Everything is all right…
Everything is fine…
Everything is a-okay…
Everything is totally under control…
No need for alarm.
No cause for concern.
And even though the methods vary,
Even though the details disagree and
    techniques may differ,
Nevertheless, I am sure you realize
There is just one way out, Bob,

Just one,
Only one,
Only one way…

MAN 2 *exits as soon as* YOUNG MAN
is tied down.

I am going to talk to you now, Bob,
Very calmly, in this tone of voice,
And as I talk to you, calmly, in this tone
    of voice,
You're going to disappear, Bob.
You're going to cease to exist anymore.
And as this happens, you're going to
    hear me, Bob,
Talking in this tone of voice,
Reminding you of all the times
That you humiliated me,
That you disgraced yourself,
Such as the time you were caught steal-
    ing,
And the time you were caught laughing,
And the time you were caught pouring
    punch all over her dress,
And the time you were caught feeling
    up Nancy,
And the time you beshat yourself in
    public,
And the time you made that remark in
    class,
And the time you were found with a
    hard-on,
And the time you kept squeezing and
    squeezing your pimples—
Because I hate you! Do you hear me!
I hate you! I hate you!
And I remember all of those times!
I never acted that way!
Why did you have to be that way !
I've always hated you, ever since the be-
    ginning!
Why won't you go away and let me
    alone?

DOUBLE *hides his head in his hands.*

The YOUNG MAN, *tied to the chair,
begins to moan and rock back and forth
and his moans become cries and his rocking becomes more violent and his cries
become screams and his rocking is so violent that he tips himself over onto the
floor and lies there screaming as hard as
he can in shame and pain and rage until finally his strength begins to falter and
his cries and jerking become weaker and
at last he falls still and just lies there in-
ert.*

There is a pause.
Finally, the YOUNG MAN *replies*
quietly.

YOUNG MAN: I too remember, Bob...
How a red sun in a blue sky makes a
green tree golden...

And that girl from Temple City,
What was her name?...

She had tan thighs I found perfectly
smooth and cool to the touch.

And when she smiled, the corners of
her eyes would crinkle and her lips
that were thick and fleshy and pink
with lipstick would ride up high
along her wide white teeth...

Bob, don't you know me?
Don't you recognize me?
Don't you like me, Bob?

Hello?
Hello?
Hello?
Hello?
Hello?
Hello?
Hello?
Hello?
Hello?
Hello?

Bob? I don't think I'm dead yet.

END

Charles Ludlam

❧

Reverse Psychology

•

Reverse Psychology was originally produced in 1980 at the Ridiculous Theatrical Company in New York with the following cast:

DR LEONARD SILVER	Charles Ludlam
DR KAREN GOLD	Charlotte Forbes
ELEANOR	Black-Eyed Susan
FREDDIE	Bill Veht

Cast of Characters
DR LEONARD SILVER
DR KAREN GOLD
ELEANOR
FREDDIE

ELEANOR *and* LEONARD *enter a cheap hotel room. They kiss long and passionately. Then they look into each other's eyes.*

ELEANOR: What's your name?

LEONARD: Leonard.

ELEANOR: I'm Eleanor.

LEONARD: I know.

ELEANOR: How did you know?

LEONARD: You told me in the bar.

ELEANOR: Oh.

　　　　LEONARD *turns on lamp.*

LEONARD: Well, what do you think?

ELEANOR: I think we're both mad.

LEONARD: Why do you say that?

ELEANOR: Well, we'd have to be to come to the sleaziest hotel room in town with a total stranger. We're both out of our minds, darling. [*Throws her arms around him*]

LEONARD: I'm not out of my mind. I'm sane. Completely sane.

ELEANOR: I meant it figuratively.

LEONARD: You thought you meant it figuratively. But you meant it.

ELEANOR: [*Laughs devilishly*] So what if I did? I'm so happy it's almost insane. I'm insanely happy.

LEONARD: You associate happiness with being insane. That's interesting.

ELEANOR: You're right. I'd rather be mad. Being sane is so boring. Don't you agree?

LEONARD: No, I don't think being sane is boring. I think being sane is fun. And I know a thousand insane people who are bores.

ELEANOR: How do you know a thousand insane people?

LEONARD: My work.

ELEANOR: You're a waiter?

LEONARD: No. I'm a psychiatrist.

ELEANOR: I go to a psychiatrist. So does my husband. Ooops!

LEONARD: You're married.

ELEANOR: Does it bother you?

LEONARD: No. I'm married too.

ELEANOR: Is she a horror?

LEONARD: No. She's wonderful. She's a very nice person. I love her very much. We're perfectly adjusted to each other. We work at our relationship.

ELEANOR: Sounds exhausting.

LEONARD: What's yours like?

ELEANOR: My what?

LEONARD: Spouse.

ELEANOR: Oh. He's all right.

LEONARD: Just all right?

ELEANOR: He doesn't beat me up and drag me to bed and make me do sexual things against my will anymore.

LEONARD: Is that what you want me to do?

ELEANOR: No, I just want you to whisper naughty words in my ear. [LEONARD whispers in her ear. ELEANOR pulls away] Wait a minute. Not that naughty! [LEONARD pulls her back to him and whispers in her ear again] How do you think of things like that? [LEONARD whispers in her ear again] I don't believe it! Do people really do things like that? Well, I'm willing to try, but I'm not guaranteeing anything.

LEONARD: Tell me what your husband is like.

ELEANOR: No.

LEONARD: Come on.

ELEANOR: No.

LEONARD: [Coaxing] Why not?

ELEANOR: I'd rather not think about my husband right now.

LEONARD: Describe him to me.

ELEANOR: Why?

LEONARD: I want to imagine him while we're making love. It helps me get aroused.

ELEANOR: [Undressing before the mirror] Sometimes I wish I were a man so I could be my own lover.

LEONARD: Talk to me.

ELEANOR: My husband is big and hairy all over his body. He even has thick, black hair all over his back.

LEONARD: [Undressing] Go on.

ELEANOR: But his eyes are a heavenly blue.

LEONARD: Go on.

ELEANOR: Shall I tell you my dreams, too?

LEONARD: If you want to.

ELEANOR: Last night I dreamed I was murdered by a sex maniac.

LEONARD reaches over to the night table and turns the light off; ELEANOR turns the light on. They begin to make love again. LEONARD turns the light off. ELEANOR turns the light on again.

LEONARD: Leave the light off. I can't do it in the light.

ELEANOR: I can't do it in the dark.

LEONARD: I don't like women with hairy husbands.

The song, "Reverse Psychology," off:

Crazy it's true
Crazy for you
If I am crazy
It's nothing new
You're so contrary
I don't know what to do
You're driving me insane.

When I'm out of my mind
You're so damned considerate
I didn't lose my mind
I got rid of it.

I'll give it to you straight
I've never been more gay
Than when you twist my head around
And make me obey
And you know I'm stubborn
And always get my way
You use Reverse Psychology.

ELEANOR: [*Singing along*] That's our song.

LEONARD: Oh, no. I'm sorry, but that can't be our song. There is another person and myself who regard this as our song.

ELEANOR: Not yours and mine. My husband and me.

LEONARD: You mean, your husband and you, and my wife and I, all have the same song? Does that make it our song, too?

ELEANOR: [*After singing the end of the song*] It's no use.

LEONARD: It's no use. Anyway, I really love my wife.

ELEANOR: And I love my husband. This has all been a mistake.

LEONARD: This has all been a terrible mistake. It was great while it lasted.

ELEANOR: But it was just one of those things. We must never do this again.

LEONARD: You're right. We must *never, ever* do this again.

ELEANOR: Never.

LEONARD: This is nothing against you.

ELEANOR: I understand.

LEONARD: It's not that I don't find you attractive. Because I am attracted to you.

ELEANOR: And I'm attracted to you. It's just that we don't want this thing to go any further.

LEONARD: Recognize it for what it is and…

ELEANOR: Let it go at that before…

LEONARD: It gets out of hand and…

ELEANOR: Somebody gets hurt.

LEONARD: Right.

ELEANOR: So, I guess that's that.

LEONARD: Yeah, that's that. Of course, there's no reason why we can't be friends.

ELEANOR: Of course not.

LEONARD: But we must keep the relationship on the intellectual level.

ELEANOR: Keep it platonic.

LEONARD: Maybe you could give me your phone number and...

ELEANOR: I don't think it would be a good idea for you to call me at home.

LEONARD: Or your address! I could send you a Christmas card.

ELEANOR: No, I might have to explain it to my husband.

LEONARD: Or we could meet sometime just to discuss things on the intellectual level. Ideas. Books. The library. We could meet at the library....

ELEANOR: Every Wednesday...

LEONARD: In the stacks...

ELEANOR: Under nonfiction...

LEONARD: And discuss...

ELEANOR: On an intellectual level.

LEONARD: We'd be friends.

ELEANOR: We'd be good comrades.

LEONARD: Yes, comrades. [*They shake hands*] Until Wednesday, then?

ELEANOR: Until Wednesday.

LEONARD: Comrade.

ELEANOR: Comrade.

SCENE 2: *The Metropolitan Museum of Art.*

This should be suggested with draperies and a few gilded picture frames floating in midair. FREDDIE *is standing looking at a picture in one of the floating frames.* KAREN *wanders through the gallery as though lost. Occasionally she consults a tour guide booklet.*

KAREN: [*To* FREDDIE] Excuse me. Could you tell me which way to the Chinese bronzes? I can't figure out this map.

FREDDIE: What do you want to see the Chinese bronzes for?

KAREN: I heard they were fantastic.

FREDDIE: They're dead as a doornail.

KAREN: That's all right, I like ancient cultures. [*Spills her purse*] Oh, no! I don't believe it! Why me? Why here? Why now? [*She stoops to pick up the debris*]

FREDDIE: [*Stooping to help her*] Let me help you.

KAREN: That's all right.

FREDDIE: My God, how do you fit all this stuff in there? [*Gestures with tampon*]

KAREN: [*A bit put off by this unexpected intimacy*] That's my little secret. I'm sorry to have bothered you.

FREDDIE: The bronzes are that way. [*Points*]

KAREN: Thanks.

FREDDIE: But I wouldn't bother with them if I were you.

KAREN: [*Cheerfully*] Well, you're not me. [*Starts to go*]

FREDDIE: There's only one painting in this museum as far as I'm concerned.

KAREN: [*Dropping her guard*] Which one is that?

FREDDIE: I'd tell you if I thought you were serious.

KAREN: Doesn't an interest in Chinese bronzes qualify me as serious?

FREDDIE: Chinese art is a sleeping pill to me. There's only one painting worth looking at in this museum.

KAREN: That one you were looking at before?

FREDDIE: No.

KAREN: What painting is it then?

FREDDIE: That one.

KAREN: That little tiny one? You're kidding!

FREDDIE: Look at it if you don't believe me.

KAREN: This had better be good. [*Looks at the little picture*]

FREDDIE: Well?

KAREN: [*Stares at the painting a long time*] How did he do that?

FREDDIE: You see how the layers of paint are applied to the canvas one on top of the other?

KAREN: Yes.

FREDDIE: Well, he did it without losing what was underneath. The underlayers still show through. That's what gives it that luminous quality.

KAREN: The brushwork is so controlled. He must have been very painstaking.

FREDDIE: Actually, that's a popular misconception about his work. He worked very quickly. He was almost slapdash in his work methods. Also, he didn't always use a brush. He sometimes pushed the paint around with his fingers.

KAREN: It all looks so precise, and yet, when you get closer, it all seems to break up into little blobs of paint.

FREDDIE: He was able to be spontaneous because he had a virtuoso technique.

KAREN: Well, I certainly agree that he did it as well as it can be done.

FREDDIE: No, I've made certain advances on his technique in my own work.

KAREN: That's modest of you!

FREDDIE: In all fairness to him, I've had some advantages. Being modern, I can select my own subject matter. In those days painters painted what they were told to by patrons. Of course, freedom is not always an advantage to an artist.

KAREN: No? I'd have thought it was.

FREDDIE: Sometimes I find myself wondering what to paint next. Our problems are more existential.

KAREN: Is there anywhere one can see your work?

FREDDIE: At my studio.

KAREN: Don't you have a gallery?

FREDDIE: No.

KAREN: Why is that?

FREDDIE: I can't tell if it's that they don't want me, or I don't want them.

KAREN: Maybe a little of both.

FREDDIE: Would you like to see my work?

KAREN: Sure.

FREDDIE: Then let's go to my studio.

KAREN: Not so loud.

FREDDIE: What's the matter? You'd think we were doing something to be ashamed of.

KAREN: It's not that. It's just that people might misunderstand.

FREDDIE: There'd be nothing new in that. Let's go.

KAREN: Oh, but the Chinese bronzes.

FREDDIE: Forget about the Chinese bronzes. They've been around for three thousand years. They can wait a little longer. Don't you think people should pay more attention to living artists?

KAREN: [Captivated] Yes, now that you mention it, I do.

FREDDIE: After all, he died penniless. [Indicates the tiny painting]

KAREN: No!

FREDDIE: No one paid any attention to him in his lifetime. He was totally misunderstood. They couldn't understand why he wouldn't go on doing it like it had always been done. When he did his greatest work, they thought he had lost his mind.

KAREN: It's so unfair. I want to look at your work. Let's go right now.

FREDDIE: It's only four stops on the subway.

KAREN: Let's take a cab.

FREDDIE: [Putting his hands in his pockets] I'm a little short of cash.

KAREN: Don't worry. I'll pay for it.

> They exit together.

SCENE 3: *The office of* DR KAREN GOLD.

> There is a knock at the door.

KAREN: Come in.

ELEANOR: [Entering] I'm mixed up, Doctor Gold. I had to see you. Listen, Doctor, I'm seeing him tonight. Break the rules just this once and tell me how to behave.

KAREN: I don't have to tell you how to behave, Eleanor. Get in touch with your feelings. What is it you really want?

KAREN: Oh, Doctor, you embarrass me!

ELEANOR: Lie back. Put up your feet. Close your eyes. What are you feeling now?

ELEANOR: Doctor, it's my husband.

KAREN: Quarreling again?

ELEANOR: No. Sex problem.

KAREN: What sex problem?

ELEANOR: I fake orgasm.

KAREN: Why?

ELEANOR: It seems so important to him. It would hurt him if I told him I'm not getting anything out of it.

KAREN: Have you ever enjoyed it?

ELEANOR: No, never. I just lie there and stare at the ceiling. I look at my watch, twiddle my thumbs, knit behind his back.

KAREN: Doesn't he notice?

ELEANOR: No, he's so involved in what he's doing, he's like another person. I just make little noises, like "oo oo ah ah." He can't tell I'm bored.

KAREN: Why are you bored?

ELEANOR: Well, for one thing, we always have sex in bed. It makes me drowsy.

KAREN: But having sex in bed is a perfectly natural thing. Most couples make love in bed.

ELEANOR: Well, when *I* go to bed I want to sleep. Also, he turns out the light. I can't see him. He's very good-looking. But we always make love in the dark. I can't see what I'm doing!

KAREN: As a child, did you sleep with the light on?

ELEANOR: No. But when we're making love in the dark…this is silly, I know…

KAREN: Go on.

ELEANOR: I keep imagining he's someone else.

KAREN: Who?

ELEANOR: Just…not a movie star, or anything like that…But [*Thoughtfully and with difficulty*] usually it's someone I've seen on the street that day.

KAREN: Someone you fantasize having a relationship with?

ELEANOR: No…it's always someone different, and most of the time it isn't any one person…it's a composite of men I've seen on the street that day. Men completely outside my social sphere. Men of a different class. Men I would never meet. A thigh from one, a mop of hair from another, a bicep, or the way their pants fit in the seat. But it's never one man. It's a composite.

KAREN: Do you find that these recollections of fantasies increase your pleasure?

ELEANOR: Yes and no. The images are too fleeting to really warm up to them, but they distract me…but only when the light is off in the room.

KAREN: Have you told your husband that you'd like to make love with the light on?

ELEANOR: He can't. He won't. You see, he's just the opposite.

KAREN: Hmmmm. [*Writes something down*]

ELEANOR: What was that?

KAREN: What?

ELEANOR: What you wrote down just then.

KAREN: Why do you want to know?

ELEANOR: I want to know if it's about me.

KAREN: What difference does it make?

ELEANOR: Doctor, did you write down something about me?

KAREN: Yes, I sometimes take notes. It helps me to review the patient's case. It's hard to remember everything that's said.

ELEANOR: What did you write about me?

KAREN: I'd rather not tell you just now.

ELEANOR: Why?

KAREN: Why does it matter?

ELEANOR: What if someone reads it?

KAREN: No one is going to see this but me.

ELEANOR: What does it say, damn it!

KAREN: You're getting hostile.

ELEANOR: [*Angry*] I am not getting hostile. I just want to know what that damn note says.

KAREN: These are my own confidential notes for my own confidential files.

ELEANOR: [*Screaming*] Give me that goddamn note!

KAREN: Why is it so important, Eleanor?

ELEANOR: I want that note! I want that goddamn note!

KAREN: Why are you upsetting yourself?

ELEANOR: [*Raging through her tears*] Give me that note! Give it to me! Give it to me! [KAREN *calmly hands her the note*] "Pick up chopped liver." I don't get it.

KAREN: It was a note to myself, Eleanor.

ELEANOR: Chopped liver.

KAREN: You don't trust me completely yet, Eleanor.

ELEANOR: Chopped liver. What a relief! [*Laughs*]

KAREN: Let's try something.

ELEANOR: Okay.

KAREN: Lie back on the couch. Slip your shoes off. Make yourself comfortable.

ELEANOR: [*Lying back and relaxing completely*] Aaah!

KAREN: Have you ever tried making love in a different setting?

ELEANOR: Yes, we went to a nudist colony once to air our differences. [*Turning her head sharply bark and forth in anguish*] Oh, Doctor, it's just no use! I dawdle, I daydream, I just can't get started. Every day I draw up a list of things to do, but I never get around to doing them. Something in me fights against doing whatever it is I know I should be doing.

KAREN: You're a procrastinator.

ELEANOR: Worse than that! I do impulsive, foolish things. Sometimes I go on spending sprees when I know I don't have enough money. I go into Bloomingdale's and charge everything I see. Often I buy things I don't even need. Like a lawn mower, when I know I live in an apartment. And sometimes I buy them in quantity. One time I bought a dozen egg slicers.

KAREN: Why did you buy a dozen of them?

ELEANOR: [*Carelessly*] One for each egg I suppose! How should I know? Anyway, I just can't settle down to any form of steady work. I hate doing the same thing over and over. I don't even like to sleep in the same place every night. I have a horror of repetition.

KAREN: That must make it very difficult to work.

ELEANOR: [*In a burst of temper*] Oh what do you know? Sitting there looking down your nose at me. What have you got to be so damn smug about, huh? You think you know everything. But you don't. You're stupid! You're the stupidest person I've ever met in my life! You think you have all the answers! Well you don't! You don't understand me. You don't even understand yourself! So wipe that self-satisfied grin off your face. Because you're ugly! I hate your ugly face! I hate your ugly face! [ELEANOR *shrieks this and then sobs and falls*]

KAREN: [*Catching her*] Careful!

ELEANOR: [*Sobbing on the doctor's bosom*] I hate your ugly face! I hate your ugly face! I hate your ugly face!

KAREN: Here's some Kleenex. [ELEANOR *blows her nose and sobs twice*] Do you often have regrettable bursts of temper like this, Eleanor?

ELEANOR: [*Sucking her thumb*] Yeth.

KAREN: Think back, Eleanor, to when you were a little girl. Think back to when you first began to procrastinate.

ELEANOR: It all began when I was eleven years old. My Angora cat got run over. I remember there was this blood all over everything. That morning I had my first period.

> *The phone rings.*

KAREN: Excuse me. [*Crosses to the phone on the desk*] Hello? [*Changing her tone to one of intimacy*] Oh, *hello.* Oh, did he? He didn't! He did? Listen, I can't talk now, I'm in session. Tonight would be fine. I'm sorry. I'm sorry. Yes, I wish we could have gone together, but what can we do? Which one did you like best? Yes, that was my favorite, too. Six then. Good-bye. Good-bye. No, I said good-bye. Now hang up. You'll have to wait for that. [*Firmly*] Good-bye, naughty boy. Hang up. [*Giggles*] Good-bye, darling. [*Hangs up and returns to her place at the side of the couch as if nothing had happened*] Go on.

ELEANOR: [*Beginning again with difficulty*] I ran home to my parents to tell them what had happened. But I couldn't find them anywhere. I looked in every room in the house. Finally I went upstairs to their bedroom. The door was closed. And without thinking I was doing anything wrong I opened the door—

> *The phone rings again.*

KAREN: [*Annoyed*] Oh, that phone. Excuse me. [*The phone rings again*] Hello. No, I don't think you have to wear a tie. But why don't you bring one along just in case. And I'd bring a jacket, too. It sometimes gets chilly near the water at night. Me too. Me too. Bye. [*Returns to* ELEANOR's *side as if nothing had happened*] You were saying?

ELEANOR: This is so personal.

KAREN: Eleanor, anything you tell me is in strict confidence. Nothing said here goes beyond these office walls.

ELEANOR: [*Frustrated, begins again*] I opened the door and saw my father lying naked on top of my mother. He was bouncing up and down on her. She was moaning. I thought he was hurting her. I screamed and started hitting him. They both jumped up and my mother started yelling and slapped me. She said that I must never come into their room again. I burst into tears. I wanted to run away and never come back. I wanted to—

> *The phone rings again.*

KAREN: Go on, Eleanor.

> *The phone rings again.*

ELEANOR: Aren't you going to answer the phone?

KAREN: Just let it ring. This is more important.

ELEANOR: Are you sure?

KAREN: It will stop.

> *The phone continues to ring insistently.*

ELEANOR: I felt so alone. I felt that nobody loved me. I felt that everything was so unfair. I felt shut out. I felt...

> *The phone just goes on ringing.*

KAREN: Go on.

ELEANOR: I felt...[*Phone*] I felt...[*Phone*] I felt...[*Phone*] It's no use. Answer the phone.

KAREN: Are you sure you want me to?

ELEANOR: Answer it!

KAREN: I'm sorry. [*Goes to phone*] Hello. Yes. When did this happen? Did he take his medication? You knew that. You were told. I told you. Well, what did you expect? He's trying. You should be more helpful. Let him do what he wants. He's a grown man. Well, stop treating him like a child. I said stop treating him like a child. Give him his medication. I said let him have his medicine. I don't care what the priest said. Give him his medicine now and I'll talk to him about it tomorrow. Good-bye.

ELEANOR: What was that?

KAREN: My God, you think you have problems? This patient of mine is really bananas. He is so totally fixated on his mother that she withholds his methadone when he doesn't do what she wants. [*Laughs*] Really, it's idiotic. He wanted to watch a ball game on TV, and she wanted to watch something else, so she wouldn't let him have his methadone, and he went into convulsions. It's no wonder the guy is completely impotent with women. The only woman he was ever able to come with was his sister, and [*Laughs again*] really, this will kill you, she's only twelve years old. The whole case is ludicrous and pathetic. One time, his mother caught him fooling around with the family dog! And he's thirty years old. Can you believe it? It's really sick. [*Laughs*] But, I guess it takes all kinds to make a world. But let's get back to you.

ELEANOR: Doctor, I'm bored with my marriage. My husband doesn't seem to take the same interest in me that he once did. He used to tremble when we made love. Now it's become completely mechanical.

KAREN: The honeymoon is over, Eleanor. All relationships evolve into something else. Hopefully, what was once based on superficial physical attraction will mature into a real friendship. That can be more important in the long run.

ELEANOR: Oh, we're friends all right. But we're not in love. I miss being in love, Doctor, I really do.

KAREN: Well, what is it *you* want to do?

ELEANOR: I want to have an adventure before I'm too old. It's nothing against my husband. It has nothing to do with him, really. It's just something that *I* want. Do you know what I mean?

KAREN: I know exactly what you mean. You have a right to fulfill yourself, Eleanor.

ELEANOR: Thank you, Doctor Gold. I needed some reassurance.

KAREN: Don't thank me, Eleanor. You're doing this for yourself.

ELEANOR: You know, Doctor, I've never thought of this before but...My God! I don't know why this never occurred to me before this moment! But I suddenly realize that—

KAREN: Time is up.

ELEANOR: Just let me tell you this realization I've just had.

KAREN: Time is up, Eleanor.

ELEANOR: But...

KAREN: It's four o clock. I'm sorry.

ELEANOR: That's all right. It slipped my mind now. That's funny. It seemed like such a breakthrough a minute ago.

KAREN: We'll get to it next time. Do you have my check?

ELEANOR: Could I owe you for this week? I'm a little short of cash.

KAREN: I think it's better not to run up a bill, Eleanor.

ELEANOR: It's just for one week.

KAREN: Learning to spend money on things that are worthwhile and good for you is part of your therapy, Eleanor. Did you bring a check?

ELEANOR: Yes, but I thought you would trust...

KAREN: It's not a question of trust. I want you to get in the habit of doing good things for yourself. After all, this is for your benefit.

ELEANOR: Yes, Doctor. [*Hands* KAREN *check*]

KAREN: Why don't you try writing down your dreams and we can go over them next time.

ELEANOR: My dreams! Yes, that's a good idea.

KAREN: See you next week?

ELEANOR: See you next week. [*Exits*]

KAREN: [*Dials phone*] Hello, Lutèce? I'd like to reserve a table for two.

SCENE 4: *An artist's garret.*

A skylight. An easel. ELEANOR *is posing draped but nude from the waist up. The phone rings.*

ELEANOR: [*Not breaking out of her pose*] Should I get that or will you?

FREDDIE: Don't move. I'll get it.

ELEANOR: All right, but make it quick.

FREDDIE: [*Picking up the receiver*] Hello. [*Hangs up quickly*] They hung up. [*Returns to the easel and continues to paint her*]

ELEANOR: That's been happening a lot lately. It happened this morning. And it happened twice yesterday. Do you think someone is planning to rob the studio?

FREDDIE: You're being paranoid.

ELEANOR: The worst thing about paranoia is that you're only proven well when the worst things you've imagined come true.

FREDDIE: Don't talk. I'm painting your mouth.

ELEANOR: [*Starts humming "Reverse Psychology"*] Mmmmmmmmmm.

FREDDIE: Eleanor, don't hum. It's distracting. [ELEANOR *sighs*] Just a little more.... There, why don't you take a break? Have a look.

ELEANOR: [*Looks at the outpouring of* FREDDIE'S *soul with disappointment*] Oh Freddie...

FREDDIE: What do you think?

ELEANOR: I think you're getting better. But it's hard to tell.

FREDDIE: What about the paint handling? I read in a review the other day that a painter had bravura paint handling. Don't you think that they should have said that about me?

ELEANOR: Paint handling?

FREDDIE: Bravura paint handling.

ELEANOR: I don't know. Your paintings look feminine to me.

FREDDIE: Feminine?

ELEANOR: You use such pretty colors. Like a lady's boudoir.

FREDDIE: It was you. You are a woman and so I paint you feminine.

ELEANOR: You paint everyone feminine. Remember the Italian delivery boy you got to pose for you? He was furious that he came out all pink and aqua. There was absolutely nothing recognizable in the painting! And yet you made him pose nude!

FREDDIE: My work is lost on such philistines. Rembrandt had the same problem.

> *The phone rings.*

ELEANOR: [*Answering the phone*] Hello? Hello? Whoever it was hung up.

FREDDIE: [*Meaningfully*] That's strange.

ELEANOR: Yes, that is strange.

FREDDIE: Who do you think it was?

ELEANOR: Somebody who keeps calling but doesn't want to talk.

FREDDIE: Well, whoever it is doesn't want to talk to either of us.

ELEANOR: [*Changing the subject*] Back to work.

FREDDIE: Let's try another pose. A more difficult one this time.

ELEANOR: That last one was difficult enough.

FREDDIE: I need something more complex. I have it! Why don't I paint you in bondage?

ELEANOR: Bondage?

FREDDIE: I'll tie you up and blindfold you. And paint you like that.

ELEANOR: Sounds different ... but I don't know.... It won't hurt, will it?

FREDDIE: No, I'll do it gently. Just think, you won't have to worry about holding still because you won't be able to move.

ELEANOR: [*Laughs*] I'm not sure I trust you. How do I know you'll untie me?

FREDDIE: Eleanor, if you can't trust me, who can you trust?

ELEANOR: I guess you're right. Go ahead.

FREDDIE: [*Ties her up in bandages and blindfolds her*] I think you should wear these earplugs too. [*Inserts earplugs*]

ELEANOR: Are the earplugs necessary?

FREDDIE: Yes dear, this will be a portrait of total sensory depri—

ELEANOR: [*Interrupting in a loud hard-of-hearing voice?*] What?

FREDDIE: I said, this will be a case of—

ELEANOR: [*Interrupting*] I can't hear you.

FREDDIE: [*Removing the earplugs*] I said, this will be a portrait of total sensory deprivation.

ELEANOR: All right, but don't bother talking to me. I can't hear a word with those earplugs in.

FREDDIE: All right, no talking.

> FREDDIE *puts the earplugs back in her ears and ties a gag around her mouth. He appears at first to be going to his easel but he passes this and goes to the door, which he opens quietly.*

KAREN: [*Whispering through door*] I was afraid I'd gotten our signals crossed.

FREDDIE: [*Also whispering*] No, you got it right. Ring and hang up, ring and hang up.

KAREN: Where is she? Did you get rid of her?

FREDDIE: Look. [*Points to* ELEANOR]

KAREN: [*Horrified*] What have you done? Are you mad?

FREDDIE: She thinks she's posing for a painting. And really, there's no need to whisper because she can't hear a thing.

KAREN: [*A little louder*] Are you sure?

FREDDIE: Certainly. She's deaf as a bat.

KAREN: I just came by to give you this. [*She hands* FREDDIE *a check.*]

FREDDIE: Karen, no!

KAREN: It's just to get some supplies: brushes, canvas, paint, whatever you need.

FREDDIE: Karen, I can't accept…

KAREN: Of course you can. You must. I don't want you wasting your gifts on mundane matters. You must create, darling, create.

ELEANOR: [*Mumbling through her gag*] Freddie? Freddie? How much longer?

FREDDIE: She's calling me. I must go now.

KAREN: We must stop meeting like this.

FREDDIE: I'm not afraid. Are you?

KAREN: Afraid? Yes, perhaps a little. I'm really more afraid for her. She might get hurt.

FREDDIE: Nonsense, she hasn't suspected anything yet.

KAREN: It's all right for me. I have my own world where I'm wanted and needed. I have a career. If I lost you, I wouldn't be desolate. I'd go away and come back glamorized by distance. And distance lends enchantment. She lives with you every day. She shares the chores. She'll bear your children.

FREDDIE: I hate children.

KAREN: I can only inspire your genius. It's a much smaller thing, but I must settle for it.

ELEANOR: [*Screaming through the gag*] FREDDIE!

KAREN: Now, you must go to her.

FREDDIE: Karen, this is a terrible thing to ask, I know, but I just don't know who else to turn to.

KAREN: Ask me anything, Freddie. If it's within my power I'll do it for you.

FREDDIE: Well, this isn't really for me. It's Eleanor. I want to take her to a fancy restaurant for our anniversary. But she doesn't have anything dressy to wear....

KAREN: Say no more. I have dozens of things I never wear anymore. I'll send over a delivery boy with a box. I've been meaning to go through my things and weed out a few numbers.

FREDDIE: Thanks, Karen. You're a real pal.

KAREN: Anytime. Meet me for lunch tomorrow?

FREDDIE: Not tomorrow.

KAREN: The day after?

FREDDIE: I can't the day after.

KAREN: Friday, then? Don't tell me you have plans for Friday.

FREDDIE: Friday's fine for me. It's just that I must work.

KAREN: Of course. Of course. Work! Work! I'm going.

ELEANOR: [*Begins to protest loudly and insistently*] *EEEEE!*

FREDDIE: I could meet you when I'm through. Say in half an hour?

KAREN: At the Café des Artistes?

ELEANOR: EEEEE!

KAREN: [*Kisses him and whispers in his ear*] Work. Work. Work. Work. [*Exits backwards blowing kisses*]

   FREDDIE *crosses to* ELEANOR *and is about to unltie her when he remembers the blank canvas. He quickly smears some paint on it.*

FREDDIE: [*Untying her*] All finished.

ELEANOR: My God, that was a long time. You don't usually take so long with a painting.

FREDDIE: Have a look. [ELEANOR *crosses to look at the painting*] What do you think?

ELEANOR: Oh, Freddie, this is the best work you've ever done.

FREDDIE: [*Stunned, rushes back to look at the canvas*] It is?

ELEANOR: Yes, it has a freshness I've never seen in your work before.

FREDDIE: Just a little something I tossed off. I think I'll call it *Portrait of Eleanor*. Shall we do another?

ELEANOR: Could we knock off for the day? I'm a little sore.

FREDDIE: Why don't you take a hot bath, and I'll go out for a walk.

ELEANOR: Good idea. I think I will. [*Exit* FREDDIE. ELEANOR *dials phone*] Hello. It's me. What did you want? What do you mean you didn't call? I heard you signal. You rang and hung up, rang and hung up.

   Blackout.

SCENE 5: *The office of* DR LEONARD SILVER.

FREDDIE: Doctor, Doctor, my wife thinks she's a Volkswagen.

LEONARD: Well, why don't you tell her she's not a Volkswagen?

FREDDIE: And walk to work?

LEONARD: The last time I saw you you couldn't get the names of the different parts of your body straight. You thought your hand was a foot and your foot was a hand.

FREDDIE: Oh, I've got it all straight now, Doctor. This is my hand. [*Points to his hand*] And this is my foot. [*Points to his foot*]

LEONARD: Very good.

FREDDIE: I even know that this is my ankle and this is my knee and my heart is in the left side of my chest. [*Points to each of these*]

LEONARD: How did you remember all that, Freddie?

FREDDIE: It's all up here [*Points to his head*] in my ass.

LEONARD: Lie on the couch and I'll sit over here. Are you a bed wetter?

FREDDIE: Yes.

LEONARD: In that case you sit here and *I'll* lie on the couch.

FREDDIE: Doctor, I've had three wives and all of them died.

LEONARD: What did your first wife die of?

FREDDIE: Poisoned mushrooms.

LEONARD: What did your second wife die of?

FREDDIE: Poisoned mushrooms.

LEONARD: What did your third wife die of?

FREDDIE: Fractured skull.

LEONARD: Fractured skull?

FREDDIE: She wouldn't eat the poisoned mushrooms.

LEONARD: You're a loony. That's what you are! A real loony! With you everything is a joke.

FREDDIE: What's wrong with a little harmless humor?

LEONARD: A joke may conceal a subconscious hostility. There may be another meaning in your jokes.

FREDDIE: Do you really think so?

LEONARD: What do you think?

FREDDIE: The other day I came home and discovered my wife on the couch making love with another man.

LEONARD: What did you do?

FREDDIE: I got my revenge. I *destroyed* the couch.

LEONARD: Ha, ha, very good! But then, you are joking, aren't you?

FREDDIE: [*Unconvincingly*] Oh, yeah, sure, it's all a big joke.

LEONARD: I think that joke was a little belittling to your masculinity, Freddie.

FREDDIE: [*As if realizing everything for the first time*] Yes, it was!

LEONARD: Why do you do that, Freddie, when you know it's crazy?

FREDDIE: Why do I do it? Why do I do it? I'll try to stop doing it, Doc. I promise. No more jokes.

LEONARD: Atta boy, Freddie. You can appear to be as normal as the next one.

FREDDIE: But I'm not normal.

LEONARD: Nobody said you were.

FREDDIE: And I don't ever want to be normal.

LEONARD: [*Very kindly*] Nobody said you have to be normal. All you have to do is *act* normal. Now, lean back. Put up your feet. Take off your shoes.

FREDDIE: I don't want to take off my shoes.

LEONARD: Why not?

FREDDIE: There's a hole in my sock.

LEONARD: Come now, Freddie. You can trust me. I won't think less of you for it. Take off your shoes.

FREDDIE: [*Coyly*] No.

LEONARD: [*Coaxing*] Freddie, take off your shoes.

FREDDIE: [*Coyly*] No.

LEONARD: [*Coaxing, but firm*] Now, Freddie, you don't want people thinking you're a loony, do you?

FREDDIE: I don't care what people think! To hell with them!

LEONARD: Freddie, you're talking crazy. Take off your shoes.

FREDDIE: [*Petulantly*] No.

LEONARD: Take off those shoes!

FREDDIE: [*Angrily*] No!

LEONARD: You're as batty as a bedbug, that's what you are. You're a goddamn weirdo and everybody's going to know it and laugh about it behind your back.

FREDDIE: [*Terrified*] They will?

LEONARD: Yeah, they're going to snigger and whisper [*Whispers*], "See him? That's the loony! He hasn't got all of his marbles. He's crackers. He's off his rocker. He's ready for the funny farm."

FREDDIE: The dirty rats!

LEONARD: They're probably all against you anyway. So Freddie, be a good boy and don't give them an excuse. Let's have those shoes off and no arguments.

FREDDIE: [*Rational*] I'm sorry, Doctor Silver, but I really feel more comfortable with my shoes on.

LEONARD: [*Seizing him roughly and trying to pull his shoes off by force*] Get those goddamn shoes off you little bastard or I'll give you such a smack!

FREDDIE: [*Struggling with the doctor*] Let go!

LEONARD: [*Raising his voice threateningly*] Give me those shoes! [*slaps* FREDDIE's *face and pulls the shoes off of him*] There. Now how do you feel?

FREDDIE: [*With a sigh of relief*] Thank you, Doctor. I feel much better now.

LEONARD: Now, wasn't that a big fuss for nothing? I don't even see a hole in your sock.

FREDDIE: Look closer.

LEONARD: [*Examining one of* FREDDIE's *feet and then the other*] Why, Freddie, your left sock is painted on!

FREDDIE: I couldn't find the other one, Doc.

LEONARD: [*Brightly*] Let's free associate.

FREDDIE: Shoot.

LEONARD: Inadequate.

FREDDIE: Unsatisfactory.

LEONARD: Weak.

FREDDIE: Puny.

LEONARD: Defective.

FREDDIE: Second-rate.

LEONARD: Inferior.

FREDDIE: Subnormal.

LEONARD: Pitiful.

FREDDIE: Paltry.

> *The dialogue slowly begins to accelerate.*

LEONARD: Contemptible.

FREDDIE: Miserable.

LEONARD: Dwarfed.

FREDDIE: Diminutive.

LEONARD: Ordinary.

FREDDIE: Common.

LEONARD: Mediocre.

FREDDIE: Petty.

LEONARD: Trashy.

FREDDIE: Shoddy.

LEONARD: Bad.

FREDDIE: Less than good.

LEONARD: Cheap.

FREDDIE: Flimsy.

LEONARD: Trivial.

FREDDIE: Unimportant.

LEONARD: Trifling.

FREDDIE: Insipid.

LEONARD: Sleazy.

FREDDIE: Squalid.

LEONARD: Crummy.

FREDDIE: Junky.

LEONARD: Raunchy.

FREDDIE: Two-bit.

LEONARD: Corny.

FREDDIE: Cheesy.

LEONARD: Poor.

FREDDIE: Broke.

LEONARD: Down-and-out.

FREDDIE: In the pits.

LEONARD: Hard up.

FREDDIE: In the shits.

LEONARD: What are you feeling now, Freddie?

FREDDIE: I have so much more of a sense of myself. I feel stronger. Doctor, I have something to tell you. And up to now I've been afraid to tell you this. But now I think I can. Although I've been afraid that you would take it wrong.

LEONARD: Go ahead, Freddie. You can be open with me.

FREDDIE: Doctor, I've gotten a new psychiatrist. I'm leaving you.

LEONARD: You what?

FREDDIE: I've gotten a new psychiatrist. I'm leaving you.

LEONARD: How can you do this to me? Not after all we've been through together.

FREDDIE: I'm sorry, but I feel we've gone as far as we can go. I'm grateful to you for the years we've had together. But people change. Their needs change. Sometimes they grow apart. There are some things we have to leave behind.

LEONARD: Oh, so that's what I am, huh? Some *thing* you're going to leave behind! That's all I've meant to you.

FREDDIE: Now, Leonard, don't be upset.

LEONARD: Don't be upset! Don't be upset! You waste the best years of my life and you say don't be upset. Who is he? Some little Freudian you've been seeing on the sly?

FREDDIE: She's into Gestalt.

LEONARD: [*Exploding*] Ha! So it's a woman! You're leaving me for a woman. You'd better be careful there, Freddie. If you go to a woman psychiatrist people are going to think you're gay. I always suspected you were latent.

FREDDIE: I'm not worried about it.

LEONARD: [*Palsy-walsy*] Hey hey hey hey, Freddie! Freddieeee! Hey hey hey hey hey! Don't do anything rash. Let's try to work it out.

FREDDIE: My mind's made up.

LEONARD: [*Insensed*] You ingrate! You're sick. You know that, don't you? You're sick. Two weeks out of my care and you'll be completely out of control. Then don't come crying to me.

FREDDIE: I just don't feel I can make any more progress here.

LEONARD: [*Sweetly*] Freddie, I'm sorry. I didn't mean what I said. Please stay.

FREDDIE: I'd better be going. [*Puts on his shoes*]

LEONARD: Where are you going? To her?

FREDDIE: I have an appointment with her this afternoon.

LEONARD: How will I live if you leave me? You're reducing my income substantially with this nonsense. You know that.

FREDDIE: You have other patients.

LEONARD: [*On bended knee*] None of them mean anything to me but you. I'll get rid of all my other patients if you stay.

FREDDIE: I wouldn't want you to do that.

LEONARD: [*Rising in indignation*] Oh, go and see if I care. And good riddance!

FREDDIE: I'm going.

LEONARD: [*Running to the window*] I'll kill myself!

FREDDIE: No you won't.

LEONARD: [*Suddenly regaining his composure*] You're right. I won't. [*Nervous tic*] Forgive me. [*Tic*] I lost my head. [*Tic*]

FREDDIE: Are you all right?

LEONARD: Yes. [*Tic*] I feel better now. [*Tic*]

FREDDIE: You'll get over it.

LEONARD: [*Calmly and in a very pleasant voice*] Freddie, before you go, I want to tell you something.

FREDDIE: I'm a little late.

LEONARD: Come here, Freddie. Let me tell you this. It's important.

FREDDIE: Go ahead.

LEONARD: Come here first. I want to whisper it.

FREDDIE: Oh, all right. [*Crosses to doctor*]

LEONARD: [*Whispers in* FREDDIE's *ear*] It's just this. [*Loudly*] I hate you and I hope you die!

FREDDIE: Good-bye.

LEONARD: [*Holds onto* FREDDIE's *leg and gets dragged across the door*] I didn't mean it! Forgive me! Forgive me!

FREDDIE: There's nothing to forgive. Now let go of my leg.

LEONARD: [*Under control*] Very well. As you wish. Do you have my check?

FREDDIE: [*Hands him a check*] I almost forgot.

LEONARD: Huh!

FREDDIE: Good-bye. [*Exits*]

     DR SILVER *smashes everything in the office. Blackout.*

     SCENE 6: *The Manhattan apartment of Dr. Silver and Dr. Gold.*

     LEONARD *tiptoes in, starts to undo his tie, but hears* KAREN *and pretends to be tying it.*

KAREN: My, you're up early this morning.

LEONARD: Scratch my back. [KAREN *does so*] Lower. Lower. Over. Not that far. Back. Back. Up. Lower. Lower. Up a little.

KAREN: How's that?

LEONARD: It went away.

KAREN: It went away because I scratched it.

LEONARD: No, it went away before you found it. Has the paper arrived yet?
     A thud at the door.

KAREN: There it is now. So, what time did you get in last night?

LEONARD: I don't remember. Four? Yes, I guess it was about four.

KAREN: Were you drinking?

LEONARD: Yes.

KAREN: Where were you drinking?

LEONARD: PJ.'s.

KAREN: PJ.'s closes at two. Where were you the other two hours?

LEONARD: What is this? The third degree?

KAREN: I was just curious.

LEONARD: What did you do?

KAREN: There was nothing on television so I went to bed and read for a while. I didn't hear you come in.

LEONARD: I didn't want to disturb you so I slept in the study.

KAREN: Mmmmmm. So what happened after PJ.'s closed?

LEONARD: Oh, I walked around for a while, stopped for a cup of coffee, and watched the sun rise down by the Hudson River.

KAREN: [Checking the paper] The sun rose this morning at exactly five twenty-three, and it rose over the East River, so you couldn't have been in by four. You couldn't have been in at six. Leonard, did you just get in?

LEONARD: Karen, I told you...

KAREN: [Crossing right and looking off] The cot in the study obviously hasn't been slept in. Your story doesn't hold water.

LEONARD: Please don't look at me like that. It reminds me of your mother. And you know how I love your mother.

KAREN: Leave my mother out of this. And don't be sarcastic.

LEONARD: In fact I think you're turning into just as big a bitch as your mother.

KAREN: You seem to forget everything she's done for you.

LEONARD: Don't throw that up again!

KAREN: Well she did set you up in private practice. You'd still be strapping drug burn-outs to their bedpans at Bellevue if it weren't for her. You'd still be a straightjacket man.

LEONARD: They're not using straight jackets anymore. They're using chemical restraint. And you'd know that if you'd read the professional journals instead of Redbook!

KAREN: You're just jealous because they published my short story and rejected yours.

LEONARD: It's easier for a woman to get published today. They all want woman authors. It used to be blacks. Next it will be gays. It's hopeless for a white Anglo-Saxon Protestant male. We're just effete and genetically debilitated. An oppressed majority. The pallid afterglow to the sunset of Western civilization. All there is left for us now is jogging.

KAREN: You'll get no sympathy from me. It might do you good to be passive for a while. Let's take turns.

LEONARD: There, you're doing it again!

KAREN: What?

LEONARD: You're looking like your mother again.

KAREN: Oooo! You fight dirty.

LEONARD: I'm sorry, Karen. But I can't control it. I've never liked your mother and when you look like her I become enraged. It seems you've begun to look more and more like her as you've gotten older.

KAREN: I changed my hair color, lost weight, what more do you want me to do? I think this is terribly unfair and insensitive. I wouldn't say these things to you.

LEONARD: You don't understand. But how could you? I was adopted. I've never looked anything like my parents.

KAREN: Well, what more can I do? I'll try anything. You tell me.

LEONARD: What about a face-lift? A little nip and tuck here and there.

KAREN: A face-lift? Why don't *you* get a face-lift?

LEONARD: They hide the scars under the hairline. I'm bald. Where would they hide the scars?

KAREN: Face-lifts aren't something you just do. It's a serious decision. Surgery is painful, you know, and dangerous. Oh please be careful, dear, you're getting crumbs on the tablecloth.

LEONARD: Your mother was compulsively neat.

KAREN: I am not compulsively neat. I feel more inspired in an uncluttered, airy room. When everything is in its place and the room is immaculate I get a feeling of inner peace.

LEONARD: It's role-playing. Housewife.

KAREN: It is not. It's taste. It's a taste for order.

LEONARD: Then why do you insist on doing the housework yourself? Why don't you hire a maid. We can afford it.

KAREN: I've told you before I don't want a stranger in our house.

LEONARD: She wouldn't be a stranger forever. You'd come to know her. You'd get to know her after a while. You'd come to trust her in time.

KAREN: Her? Why her? Why does the maid necessarily have to be female?

LEONARD: Or a houseboy. Do you want a houseboy?

KAREN: No! That would be worse. I like it the way it is…just the two of us here, living alone together. That's the way it's always been. Just us.

LEONARD: And never anyone more?

KAREN: Leonard, I've told you. When I'm ready. There will be plenty of time for that.

LEONARD: Maybe we should adopt.

KAREN: No, Leonard, it's not that I'm afraid of the pain or anything like that…it's just that…

LEONARD: [*Very sympathetically*] Go on. What is it?

KAREN: Please, don't be hurt, but…

LEONARD: Tell me darling. I'll understand.

KAREN: It's just that genetically…Well having a child is a big decision. And I think you must be very careful that the genes are of the highest quality. I think the sire should be a magnificent physical specimen.

LEONARD: What are you saying?

KAREN: Well, I've read about this clinic where you can be artificially inseminated by a name donor. Many celebrities, athletes, geniuses, Nobel Prize winners, and male models are donating their sperm to the sperm bank. I want to get some of the sperm of an Olympic athlete. And try to give birth to a perfect child.

LEONARD: That's Fascism.

KAREN: Anything idealistic you call Fascism.

LEONARD: What do you expect? The Fascists gave Idealism a bad name. I want to be the father of our child.

KAREN: YOU would be, legally.

LEONARD: But not biologically.

KAREN: That shouldn't make any difference to a man. Your role in procreation is a minor one.

LEONARD: Minor ! ! ? ¡) (+ = ¿

KAREN: Oh, I know it seems important to you. But objectively it just isn't. In fact you're not even necessary anymore.

LEONARD: Well, I liked it better the old way.

KAREN: Well, as a concession to pleasure and your need for role-playing, we'll have intercourse the night I insert the Olympic athlete sperm into myself. But you must wear a contraceptive.

LEONARD: [*Sarcastically*] Great! Why don't you wear a coil?

KAREN: I can't. Every time I cross my legs the garage door opens. But we must be careful because if the contraceptive were to break we might get the sperm mixed up.

LEONARD: I have to be careful! I like that!

KAREN: We might produce a mongrel.

LEONARD: Only one sperm fertilizes the egg. It would be either him or me.

KAREN: Man is the only animal bred haphazardly. We think less of ourselves than we do of capons.

LEONARD: Capons are castrated.

KAREN: No, I think they're given female hormones.

LEONARD: Oh, yes, I remember reading in a medical journal about young men who sprouted breasts from eating too many capons.

KAREN: Perhaps all the now obsolete males should be fed capons and turned into worker females.

LEONARD: You're talking about human beings, not ants. This talk is all plainly the result of penis envy. You feel like incomplete males hemorrhaging once a month.

KAREN: You degrade our sexuality forgetting that it is the fountain of life and you are a useless drone.

LEONARD: There, you're doing it again.

KAREN: What?

LEONARD: You're looking like your mother again. I can't stand it.

KAREN: Look at us. We're fighting again.

LEONARD: Why do we do it?

KAREN: Let's not do it anymore, darling.

LEONARD: I'm sorry for what I said before.

KAREN: It wasn't fair of me.

LEONARD: How unfair?

KAREN: I had an unfair advantage. I was right.
They laugh.

LEONARD: You're a witch. But I love you.

KAREN: Finish your breakfast.

LEONARD: Damn, my eggs have gotten cold.

KAREN: I'll make others. [*Turns to go*]

LEONARD: Don't bother. [*Catching her arm and stopping her*] Karen, everything is all right between us, isn't it?

KAREN: Why don't we cancel all our appointments and spend the day together? Just the two of us.

LEONARD: What would we do?

KAREN: Oh, I don't care. We could walk in the park, go to the zoo, feed the ducks.

LEONARD: Karen, I have a lot of work to do today. I just can't. I have my prize neurotic today. As a matter of fact I'm late now. He's probably waiting for me right now.

KAREN: [*Ardently, seriously, as if it were the most important thing in the world to her*] Call and cancel. It seems that all we do is think about the patients. We never have time for each other anymore. Please, Leonard, I'm asking you. I'm begging you. Let's go for a walk together.

LEONARD: Why?

KAREN: For no reason at all.

LEONARD: I can t.

KAREN: Why are you shutting me out like this?

LEONARD: Karen, Karen. Remember when you were a little girl, how you used to hate your piano lessons?

KAREN: [*Very shaken*] Don't. Go to your patient.

LEONARD: That's my girl.

KAREN: Leonard. I've decided. I'm going to have that face-lift. But I'll have to go away for several months while the scars heal. I don't want you to look at me until the scars heal. I don't even want you to know where I'm staying. In case you get tempted and want to peek.

LEONARD: I'm sorry for what I said before. I didn't mean it....

KAREN: You did. And I see now that there is only one solution. I'm going to go under the knife. For you.

ACT II

KAREN *is lying on a beach chair in a bathing suit, sunning herself. On the radio we hear "Reverse Psychology" sung.* FREDDIE *enters from the pool, wet.*

KAREN: Would you mix me another drink, Freddie? What's the matter? Is something troubling you? You look so sad.

FREDDIE: I'm not sad. I'm thinking.

KAREN: Don't do that darling. It deforms the face.

FREDDIE: Why do people always say I look sad when I'm thinking? Is it a crime to think? What am I supposed to do? Walk around with a big smile on all the time?

KAREN: Watch what you're pouring! I'd like a little tonic in my gin.

FREDDIE: I'm sorry. I didn't mean to snap at you. I'm restless, that's all.

KAREN: Why can't you just relax and enjoy our little vacation?

FREDDIE: It's your vacation. I work every day. I don't take vacations.

KAREN: Have you been drawing? Let me see.

FREDDIE: [*Opens pad, looks at drawing, then tears it up and throws it on the ground*] Hideous.

KAREN: [*Trying to stop him, she dives after the pieces*] No! Don't destroy it!

FREDDIE: Who cares? It's nothing but mediocrity.

KAREN: Let me see. [*She pieces the picture together again*] Why, it's that man who was at the pool last night! When did you draw him naked?

FREDDIE: This morning. He didn't know I was drawing him.

KAREN: He must have. He displayed himself to such *advantage*. It's funny. We saw him in the bar last night and I thought he was a woman at first. Then I wasn't sure if he was a man or a woman.

FREDDIE: I knew.

KAREN: I thought it was either a very masculine woman or a very feminine man. How could you tell?

FREDDIE: Big head. Big hands.

KAREN: Of course. This drawing certainly establishes beyond a shadow of a doubt that it was a man!

FREDDIE: Who cares? It's a bore.

KAREN: Why are you bored?

FREDDIE: Everything is so boring.

KAREN: Why don't you just relax and enjoy yourself?

FREDDIE: I can't. I don't feel right about your paying for everything.

KAREN: I thought we settled that. I'm rich. You're not. Who cares whose money it is? Let's enjoy it. Someday you'll sell your work and you can take me on a vacation.

FREDDIE: My work will never sell.

KAREN: Why not?

FREDDIE: [*Contemptuously*] Because people don't want to see the truth. They want pretty pictures. Well, they can get someone else to paint their pretty pictures for them! Because I won't! Oh, sometimes I wonder why I don't just give up the struggle. I may as well just go and get a job.

KAREN: Freddie! I won't have you talking that way. These are wild, rash words. You're just trying to worry me.

FREDDIE: I'm sorry.

KAREN: Now look at this picture you just tore up. It's very nice.

FREDDIE: Very nice! That describes it all right. Very nice.

KAREN: The pictures of yours I like best are the ones where you can tell what it's a picture of.

FREDDIE: Ugh. And two months' rent due on my studio.

KAREN: I'll pay it.

FREDDIE: [*Exploding*] No!

KAREN: Why not?

FREDDIE: You've done too much for me already. You bought me that sports jacket, paid the rent on the studio, and you got me a gallery.

KAREN: Darling, it was the least I could do. Boris and I have been friends for years, and he adored your paintings.

FREDDIE: And then there were all those dinners. I can't go on taking and taking.

KAREN: Well, if you're going to be proud about it, why don't you do a portrait of me for my office and I'll pay you for it.

FREDDIE: No, you'd be insulted. It always happens. When people commission a portrait they always want to be flattered.

KAREN: You do it any way you want. Don't flatter me. I hope I'm not so bad-looking that I have to worry about having my portrait done!

FREDDIE: You're beautiful.

KAREN: Then that's settled. When do we start?

FREDDIE: Right now if you want to.

KAREN: What do I have to do?

FREDDIE: You don't have to do a thing. Just don't move. I'll do a few quick practice sketches first. [*Draws a bit, tears out a page, draws a bit, tears out a page, draws a bit, tears out a page*] Turn your head this way a little. Good. Are you comfortable?

KAREN: Oh, perfectly!

FREDDIE: Now don't move.

     LEONARD *and* ELEANOR *enter from the other side.*

LEONARD: [*In medias res*] And it has a pool, too.

ELEANOR: Calypso Beach Resort Boatel!

LEONARD: In there is a cocktail lounge with piano bar. There's a funny little old lady who plays requests.

ELEANOR: I love it. But do you think it's safe?

LEONARD: They assured me that there would be only one other couple here this weekend. We're lucky it's off-season. In another two weeks this place will be mobbed.

ELEANOR: Maybe we can go skinny-dipping at night.

LEONARD: I don't know.

ELEANOR: You said there was practically no one here.

LEONARD: I know, but I'd prefer not to.

ELEANOR: Don't tell me you're shy. You've got nothing to be ashamed of.

LEONARD: It's not that.

ELEANOR: What then?

LEONARD: I can't swim.

ELEANOR: Really? I'll teach you.

LEONARD: No, I'm afraid of the water.

ELEANOR: A psychiatrist with a phobia? Shame on you.

LEONARD: Nobody's perfect.

ELEANOR: I'll help you get over it.

LEONARD: It's no use.

ELEANOR: Why?

LEONARD: When I was a kid my older brothers threw me in sink or swim. I sank. I almost drowned. Somebody passing by pulled me out.

ELEANOR: That's no way to teach a person to swim! You have to relax.

LEONARD: I could never relax in the water.

ELEANOR: What about in the bathtub? Are you phobic about taking baths, too?

LEONARD: As a matter of fact I always take showers.

ELEANOR: That's fascinating.

>   *On the other side of the stage.*

KAREN: How much longer will this take?

FREDDIE: Not long, why?

KAREN: I'm getting a stiff neck.

FREDDIE: Just a bit more shading…there! Why don't we take a break?

KAREN: I'd like to go upstairs and change for dinner. Why don't you go in, have a drink at the bar, and await the gilded transformation?

FREDDIE: Okay. But I don't want to get too far ahead of you.

KAREN: Don't worry, I'll catch up. I'll drink doubles.

FREDDIE: Don't be too long.

KAREN: [*Exiting*]I promise to be worth waiting for.

>   FREDDIE *arranges his drawing things neatly on the table and goes into the bar.*
>   *Other side of the stage again.*

ELEANOR: Oh look! Those people left the table with the umbrella. Let's sit down over there.

LEONARD: Good idea. I don't like being so close to the pool. Why don't you lie in the sun. I'll take the bags to the room.

ELEANOR: Ok.

    LEONARD *exits.* ELEANOR *sits in the chaise.* ELEANOR's *dream.*

FREDDIE: [*Enters in graduation cap and gown with ticking metronome*] Isn't there anything you can do to help my wife, Doctor?

KAREN: [*In medical whites with stethoscope. She could have a bird's head*] I'm afraid we'll have to give her shock treatments.

FREDDIE: Shock treatments? Isn't that rather…I mean, isn't there any other way?

KAREN: Yes, of course. If we had a lot of time and money. We don't really have much time.

FREDDIE: And if there's one thing we don't have it's money…. But shock treatments!

KAREN: Sometimes it's the fastest way to establish contact.

    They prepare ELEANOR *for shock treatments. They strap her to the reclining chair and attach electrodes to her head.*

ELEANOR: [*Greatly agitated*] I'm not guilty. I'm not guilty! I should call a lawyer. I should call a lawyer right away!

KAREN: [*Soothingly*] Lie back. Relax. Take off your shoes.

ELEANOR: Who are you? I don't know you! What do you want with me? What did I do to you?

KAREN: Think back, Eleanor. To when you were a little girl. Think back to when you first began to procrastinate. Just make your mind a blank.

ELEANOR: I used to want a blank mind. But I didn't know how. Now I know what a blank mind is. I get up in the morning and before I know it it's time to go to bed. And I can't remember what happens in between.

KAREN: Relax. [*Gives her a jolt of electricity*]

ELEANOR: [*Screams with pain*] I can't remember what day it is. I can't remember my name. I can't. I can't.

    KAREN *gives her another jolt.* LEONARD *enters and goes to* ELEANOR.

LEONARD: [*Prying her eyes open*] No judgment or response.

KAREN: Give her another shock.

LEONARD: I think you've given this patient too much shock already, Doctor. I think shock is the worst thing you could have used in this patient's case.

KAREN: And what would you have done, Doctor? This patient's case resisted contact.

LEONARD: You should have tried love and understanding.

KAREN: There are too many patients and too few doctors. There isn't time to love and understand every patient. I see no reason to make an exception in this patient's case.

LEONARD: Every case is different.

KAREN: You can't treat every patient as though she were exceptional.

LEONARD: Ah, but Doctor, how else are we to help people get well but by treating every patient as though she were exceptional. [*Unties* ELEANOR's *bonds*]

ELEANOR: Why do you want to help me?

    KAREN *and* FREDDIE *gradually back out through opposite doors.*

LEONARD: Where is your husband?

ELEANOR: Husband? I haven't got a husband.

LEONARD: No? I thought you had. I thought you were married.

ELEANOR: I am.

LEONARD: Do you know me?

ELEANOR: Of course I know you.

LEONARD: Are you sure?

ELEANOR: Of course I'm sure.

LEONARD: Would you mind telling me anyway?

ELEANOR: You're the keeper.

LEONARD: Keeper?

ELEANOR: Of this zoo.

LEONARD: Zoo? How did you come here, to the zoo?

ELEANOR: You're trying to trap me. You're really a warden.

LEONARD: Warden? Eleanor!!!

ELEANOR: Of this prison. Let me go! Take your hands off me. Let me go! Let me go!

LEONARD: [*Shaking* ELEANOR *awake*] Eleanor, Eleanor. You were dreaming.

ELEANOR: Dreaming? I've got to write it down. My doctor told me to write down all my dreams. I've got to get a pencil. Do you have a pencil?

LEONARD: No.

ELEANOR: I've got to write it down before I forget it. There's paper and pencils over here. [*Writes feverishly, then*] Want to read it?

LEONARD: Sure, if you don't mind. [*Takes the paper and reads. Then turns over the sheet and exclaims, startled*] Incredible!

ELEANOR: What?

LEONARD: This drawing.

ELEANOR: What drawing?

LEONARD: There's a drawing on the other side of your dream.

ELEANOR: [*Indifferent*] Is there?

LEONARD: Yes. [*Pause*] Amazing.

ELEANOR: What's amazing?

LEONARD: Er...ah...It's superbly done. Want to see it?

ELEANOR: No. I hate art.

LEONARD: Oh you do not!

ELEANOR: Oh yes I do! My husband is an artist. That's all I hear all day long. Art! Art! Art! It's enough to make you sick.

LEONARD: Still this is extraordinary.

ELEANOR: Oh, what's so extraordinary about it?

LEONARD: Why don't you have a look at it. I'd be curious to know what you think. [*Holds the picture in front of her eyes*]

ELEANOR: [*Closing her eyes*] I don't want to look at any more art!

LEONARD: Just peek.

ELEANOR: [*Opening one eye and then shutting it quickly*] A frump.

LEONARD: How could you say that?

ELEANOR: That's what I see. A drawing of a frumpy matron.

LEONARD: [*Indignant*] That's not what I see. I see a handsome woman of a certain age with great character. I see honesty. I see intelligence.

ELEANOR: God, if you like her that much you should search until you find her. Why don't you marry her if you think she's so great?

LEONARD: As a matter of fact that's what first struck me about the drawing. It bears a strong resemblance to my wife.

ELEANOR: [*Sits bolt upright and seizes the drawing and starts examining it very carefully*] Oh you poor darling. Is that what you're married to? Oh poor darling. [*Strokes him and kisses him sincerely, not in sarcasm*] Poor poor darling.

LEONARD: [*Snatches up the drawing defensively*] What's wrong with her?

ELEANOR: I didn't mean to say anything against her. How could I? I don't even know the woman. [*Looking over his shoulder at the drawing*] It's just that she's a mess.

LEONARD: A mess? What do you mean, a mess?

ELEANOR: Well for one thing her hair is so stiff it makes her look hard. And then there are those awful earrings. And I don't know, her eyes look mean or crossed or something....

LEONARD: Well, my wife's eyes aren't crossed.

ELEANOR: I didn't say they were! I was talking about this drawing. That's funny, they don't look crossed to me now. [*Brushes drawing gently with her fingertips.*] It looks like some sort of insect.

LEONARD: Now you're going too far. My wife does not look like an insect!

ELEANOR: I mean the crossed eye. It was some sort of bug crawling on the paper. Anyway it's a terrible drawing.

LEONARD: I suppose your husband can do better?

ELEANOR: If only he could do this well. If he could draw like this we wouldn't be starving.

LEONARD: What's wrong with his drawings?

ELEANOR: Oh they're not bad if you like a blob over here and a couple of yellow squiggles and red schmears on a blue background.

LEONARD: Abstract?

ELEANOR: Totally.

LEONARD: I prefer the abstract. It leaves more to the imagination.

ELEANOR: I don't have any imagination. I don't want to imagine. I want everything and I want it right now. I want to live. I want to live!

LEONARD: When I look at an abstract painting it can be anything I want it to be.

ELEANOR: Not my husband's paintings. They are most specifically what they are. Whatever they are.

LEONARD: I'd like to buy this drawing and give it to my wife. She wouldn't believe how much it looks like her. That is, if he doesn't want more than four or five thousand old new guineas for it. I'll bet it was done by a native artist.

ELEANOR: She probably won't agree. Women like to think of themselves as originals. This is a drawing of another woman.

Enter FREDDIE.

FREDDIE: Please be careful with my drawing. You might get fingerprints on it. Eleanor!

LEONARD: You two know each other?

ELEANOR: Yes, of course, how stupid of me. This is Freddie, a very good friend of mine. Freddie, this is Leonard. Leonard, Freddie.

FREDDIE: Leonard!

LEONARD: Freddie!

ELEANOR: Freddie and I were friends at school.

LEONARD: We've met.

FREDDIE: Yes, we've met.

ELEANOR: You two know each other? Well, it looks like we're all friends. [*Laughs nervously*] How do you two know each other?

FREDDIE: We met at the YMCA. Didn't we, *Leonard.*

LEONARD: Yes, we used to work out together. We enjoyed the usual male camaraderie...the give-and-take in the showers. We all pulled together down at the YMCA.

Long pause in which no one can think of anything to say.

ELEANOR: Yes, Freddie and I are good chums too.

FREDDIE: Chums!?

ELEANOR: Yes, we're real buddies. Freddie is like a brother to me. And I'm like a sister to him. We help each other out of many tight situations, don't we Freddie? [*Puts hands around his throat in a mock-strangling gesture*]

FREDDIE: I guess so.

ELEANOR: Freddie and I have our little secrets.

FREDDIE: You can say that again.

ELEANOR: [*Tightening her grip on his throat*] But we know when to keep our mouths shut. Discretion is the greater part of valor. Don't you think so, Freddie?

FREDDIE: Eleanor, I want to know...you're strangling me!

ELEANOR: [*Laughing*] Freddie, sit right down and tell me everything that's happened since we last saw each other. Was it the fourth or fifth grade? [*Talking very fast*] Freddie spent five years in fourth grade or was it four years in fifth.... Leonard, get us some drinks. What will you have, Freddie?

FREDDIE: I'll have a zombie.

ELEANOR: Leonard, be a dear, get three zombies. [LEONARD *walks out like a zombie.* ELEANOR *and* FREDDIE *look dazed too*] Freddie, what are you doing here?

FREDDIE: What am I doing here? What are you doing here? And what are you doing here with Leonard? How long have you been seeing him?

ELEANOR: I've been seeing him for years. He's my psychiatrist.

FREDDIE: Your psychiatrist? I thought you were seeing a woman psychiatrist.

ELEANOR: I was. But she turned out to be a lesbian. She wouldn't keep her hands to herself. I felt safer with a man.

FREDDIE: I'm going to punch him in the nose.

ELEANOR: Freddie listen, you've really hit it this time. You've found your style. He wants to buy this drawing. He'll pay up to four or five thousand old new guineas for it.

FREDDIE: That's only sixteen dollars in American money.

ELEANOR: He's an art collector.

FREDDIE: I've never seen him with any art.

ELEANOR: Don't be silly. He wouldn't keep his art collection at the YMCA, would he?

FREDDIE: No.

ELEANOR: He wants to buy this picture. He told me so.

FREDDIE: Well he can't have it. I promised it to someone else.

ELEANOR: Ah here's Leonard with the zombies. [*Aside*] Freddie, don't queer it. Leonard, I was just telling Freddie that you're interested in his drawing.

LEONARD: Why, yes, as a matter of fact I'd like to buy it. Especially now that I know you drew it.

FREDDIE: What difference does that make?

LEONARD: Knowing the artist is always more interesting.

ELEANOR: How much can you two know each other?

LEONARD: You'd be surprised.

ELEANOR: Ooh la la! What's been going on down at that YMCA? Boy talk?

FREDDIE: Yeah that's it. Boy talk.

ELEANOR: I often wonder what you boys talk about. In the locker room. It's dirty, I hope.

LEONARD: It's mostly about cars and baseball scores.

ELEANOR: How dull.

FREDDIE: Not necessarily. "I need a lube job, gotta take it to a grease monkey."

       ELEANOR *laughs mischievously.*

LEONARD: [*Slyly*] "They told me at the body shop my chassis needs an overhaul."

ELEANOR: Does anyone go in for "drag racing"?

FREDDIE: Naw, most of the guys are into foreign models and you rarely see a convertible anymore.

ELEANOR: [*Pours her drink into the potted palm*] Leonard, get more zombies.

LEONARD: But I've hardly started this one.

ELEANOR: Well, drink up! Drink up! [*Pours the zombie down* LEONARD's *throat*] There now. Get us another round.

       LEONARD, *choking and gasping, exits to the bar.*

FREDDIE: I have a right to know what my wife is doing in a resort hotel with another man.

ELEANOR: I'm trying to help your career, idiot. That man has a lot of money. There are two months' rent due on the studio. Do you want us thrown out into the street?

FREDDIE: If you would only take that super's job we wouldn't have to pay rent.

ELEANOR: Sweep the halls and stairs of a seven-story building every day while you sit in a studio with a nude model and smear blobs of pretty colors on expensive French paper? Go to hell!

LEONARD: [*Reenters*] I'm out of cash. I'll have to go up to my room.

FREDDIE: Don't bother. I'll get this round. [*Exits to bar*]

ELEANOR: Isn't Freddie sweet?

LEONARD: What were you two talking about when I came out? I heard you say, "Don't queer it."

ELEANOR: Oh, Freddie's gay. I was giving him some advice on his love life.

LEONARD: I thought we'd be alone here. That's why I wanted to come during the week and avoid the weekend crowd.

ELEANOR: It's not a crowd. It's just Freddie.

LEONARD: It's bad enough we're not alone. But it had to be someone we both know. This is too much.

ELEANOR: It's just a coincidence.

LEONARD: It's horrible.

ELEANOR: I think it's wonderful that you're going to buy Freddie's drawing. Artists have such a hard life. They're totally dependent on patronage and it's so hard to find anyone who likes arts.

LEONARD: Lots of people *love* art.

ELEANOR: Everyone *says* they do. But I don't believe it. Getting them to pay for it— that's the real test. They all think art should be free.

LEONARD: No one should be deprived of cultural experiences due to inadequate Income.

ELEANOR: Tell it to the corner grocer. They all think art should be free. That everyone has a right to it. But just try and get a free slice of liverwurst out of him! Shouldn't everyone have the right to food, too? Oh you will buy Freddie's picture, won't you?

LEONARD: Maybe I will and maybe I won't.

ELEANOR: Well, make up your mind. I hate people who are wishy-washy and indecisive, don't you?

LEONARD: I do and I don't.

FREDDIE: [*Reentering with the zombies*] Gee, you two look upset. I hope I'm not interrupting anything.

LEONARD: As a matter of fact...

ELEANOR: Not a thing!

LEONARD: What do you mean not a thing? The fact is that Eleanor and I are...

ELEANOR: Leonard means that we're here in a professional capacity.

FREDDIE: Baloney! You two can't fool me! You're having an affair. "Get over your guilt"..."Express your true feelings"..."Don't worry about who you'd hurt because if the shoe was on the other foot..." Eh, Leonard?

ELEANOR: Freddie, Leonard and I are just good friends....

LEONARD: [*Exploding*] We are not!

ELEANOR: Not friends?

FREDDIE: Not good friends?

LEONARD: Not *just* good friends!

ELEANOR: [*Trying to cover up*] We're very good friends!

FREDDIE: *Very* good friends? How good is it, this friendship?

ELEANOR: Freddie, don't jump to conclusions.

LEONARD: Oh, go ahead and jump, Freddie! Jump! Jump!

FREDDIE: [*To* LEONARD] You know if you've been fooling around with Eleanor I'm going to beat the shit out of her.

LEONARD: You don't frighten me one bit.

FREDDIE: I'm going to make her this year's battered wife poster girl.

LEONARD: Oh yeah?

FREDDIE: Yeah!

ELEANOR: Freddie, Leonard, please! Let's not make a mountain out of a molehill .

LEONARD: I'd like to see you try it.

FREDDIE: You think I won't but I will.

LEONARD: You and what troop of Boy Scouts?

FREDDIE: Watch this. [*Takes his drink and pours it over* ELEANOR's *heads* How do you like that? That will teach you to go to motel rooms with another man's wife!

LEONARD: I'm not impressed. And what's more, I don't think it's any of your business what Eleanor and I do.

FREDDIE: You're having an affair with her.

LEONARD: And what if I am? What are you going to do about it? What if Eleanor and I were madly in love, huh? What would you do then, huh? What if I decided to kiss her, huh? Like this.

FREDDIE: I'm warning you. If you dare to kiss that woman again I'm going to mess her up.

LEONARD: You haven't got the guts. You haven't got the spine. You're too much of a jellyfish to lay a hand on her. [*Kisses her again*]

FREDDIE: I'm going to mess up her pretty little face so her own mother wouldn't recognize her.

LEONARD: I'll believe it when I see it.

FREDDIE: [*Attacks* ELEANOR *and tears her dress off and tramples it in the mud*] How do you like them apples!

LEONARD: I'm not impressed.

ELEANOR: [*Pleading*] No, Leonard, Freddie, please!

FREDDIE: Not impressed? Not impressed? I'll show you! Here Eleanor, I've always wanted to paint you. [*Takes paint from his paintbox and smears it all over her*] Now are you impressed? Now are you impressed? You want to buy a painting? Buy her. Or have you bought her already?

ELEANOR: Why of all the egotistical…I don't like either of you. You're both beasts. [*Runs out*]

LEONARD: Now see what you've done.

FREDDIE: It serves you right! You had it coming to you!

LEONARD: I think you're way out of line here. Eleanor is a sweet kid.

FREDDIE: She's a married woman.

LEONARD: So what's it to you? Do you know her husband?

FREDDIE: Yes.

LEONARD: Oh, Freddie, then that's different. I can see you taking umbrage. What is he, a friend of yours?

FREDDIE: Yes, a very close friend.

LEONARD: Listen, I'm sorry, but we have to be men about this. After all, who hasn't fooled around? But whatever you do don't blame Eleanor. Why should there be one standard for men and another for women?

FREDDIE: Well, I agree with you there.

LEONARD: This guy, Eleanor's husband, from what I gather he's a real wimp.

FREDDIE: What do you mean?

LEONARD: Well, he can't support her.

FREDDIE: He's an artist, like myself. He's had to make a lot of sacrifices for what he believes.

LEONARD: Of course you guys stick together. But lack of money isn't so important if it's really happening between two people. If the relationship is really hot, who needs money? Apparently her husband is a real dud in bed.

FREDDIE: I wouldn't know.

LEONARD: I'm surprised Eleanor hasn't talked to you about it. You being such good friends and all.

FREDDIE: We haven't seen each other in so long.

LEONARD: Oh yes, fourth or fifth grade, wasn't it?

FREDDIE: Kindergarten.

LEONARD: I could fill you in. But then you're probably not interested.

FREDDIE: Oh but I am! [Not wanting to seem overanxious he catches himself and feigns nonchalance] I'm interested in Eleanor's welfare.

LEONARD: Apparently she fell in love with this guy when she was a kid and never wanted to marry anyone else. So they married young.

FREDDIE: Very romantic.

LEONARD: Yes, but then after they were married a while he just petered out. Or maybe they both just lost interest. Who can tell about these things from the outside?

FREDDIE: It's impossible to guess.

LEONARD: But this I can tell you. She's like an animal in bed.

FREDDIE: [horrified] Really?

LEONARD: It's as though she were starved for it. And she scratches.

FREDDIE: Oh, really?

LEONARD: She's into the wild variations. And that French stuff too.

FREDDIE: I never would have thought it of her.

LEONARD: Oh you don't have to tell me. On the surface she's so reserved. But underneath that cool exterior lies a nymphomaniac.

FREDDIE: What?

LEONARD: I'm telling you she can't get enough.

FREDDIE: Do you love Eleanor?

LEONARD: Love Eleanor? That's all I do is love Eleanor. I'm lucky I'm in pretty good shape. If you know what I mean.

FREDDIE: Oh I know what you mean all right.

LEONARD: You know, Freddie, now that we're not seeing each other on a doctor-patient basis, I think we could be buddies.

FREDDIE: You and me, buddies?

LEONARD: Yes, you know, there is a certain inequity built into the psychotherapeutic process. I get to know every intimate detail of a patient's life but the patient doesn't get to know anything about me.

FREDDIE: Oh, I wouldn't say that!

LEONARD: All right, you know some things about me but not to the degree that I know them about you. I know so many specifics.

FREDDIE: Is this a blackmail threat?

LEONARD: Freddie, this is Leonard, your buddy. What I'm saying is that I want to confide in *you* for a change.

FREDDIE: Go ahead. Unburden your heart.

LEONARD: Freddie, I love my wife. Oh, I won't go so far as to say that I'm happily married. I'm not. We quarrel. We say unforgivable things to each other every morning before breakfast. We're competitive. We're both in the same profession. Sometimes we go out and get drunk together, have a few laughs … we both love the theater.… What am I trying to say? There's just no other relationship in my life like it. It's not always happy. But it is always interesting. Karen is the world to me.

FREDDIE: Karen?

LEONARD: Yes, that's my wife's name, Karen. She's a psychiatrist, too. See, you're getting interested in my life. I don't know why I never thought of trying this in our sessions together. Isn't it interesting?

FREDDIE: I'm afraid it's getting too interesting.

LEONARD: Really, Freddie, we've kept each other at a distance too long. Why don't you ask me some questions about myself? Go ahead, ask me anything.

FREDDIE: Is your wife's name Karen Silver?

LEONARD: No, it's Gold. Karen Gold. Cute, don't you think? Dr. Silver and Dr. Gold?

FREDDIE: Cunning.

LEONARD: Go ahead, Freddie, ask me something else.

FREDDIE: What would you do if you discovered your wife staying in this hotel with another man.

LEONARD: It's never happened so I couldn't tell you. You never know how you would react in a situation like that until it happens to you.

KAREN: [*Enters*] Freddie, I have wonderful news for you. Boris sold your portrait of Eleanor for fifteen thousand dollars! Hello, Leonard. [*Take*] Leonard !

LEONARD: Karen!

KAREN: Why did you come here? To spy on me?

LEONARD: Why no, I came here…I came here…Karen, do we have to discuss this in front of the patient?

KAREN: What patient?

LEONARD: [*Pointing to* FREDDIE] That patient standing right there.

KAREN: He's not a patient, he's my…

FREDDIE: Lover.

KAREN: Freddie, no!

LEONARD: Well, he's my patient and I'd prefer not to have his nose stuck into my personal affairs.

KAREN: Don't try to change the subject. What are you doing here? Why did you follow me? How did you find out where I went?

LEONARD: I didn't follow you.

KAREN: Then what are you doing here? I demand an explanation.

LEONARD: I came here with...

FREDDIE: My wife.

ELEANOR: [*Enters*] Leonard, I have a confession to make. Freddie is my husband.

KAREN: Eleanor! What are you doing here?

ELEANOR: Doctor Gold! Who called you?

FREDDIE: Nobody called her. She's here with me.

ELEANOR: You're here with my psychiatrist!

FREDDIE: Your psychiatrist?!!!!!

LEONARD: Your psychiatrist?!!!!!

ELEANOR: Yes, what are you doing here with my psychiatrist?

FREDDIE: The same thing you're doing here with my psychiatrist.

ELEANOR: Your psychiatrist?!!!!!

KAREN: Your psychiatrist?!!!!!

FREDDIE: Yes, Eleanor, it seems we've been having affairs with each other's psychiatrists.

ELEANOR: We should have our heads examined.

KAREN: And what's worse, we've been sleeping with each other's patients.

ELEANOR: You mean you two are married?

LEONARD: This is all a harmless mistake.

KAREN, FREDDIE, *and* ELEANOR: Harmless?!

LEONARD: Yes, it's life. [ELEANOR *and* KAREN *lift handkerchiefs to their faces to stifle their laughter or tears*] Are you crying?

FREDDIE: No, I think they must be laughing.

LEONARD: That's how life is—a mixture of laughter and tears. Sometimes the most painful experiences will suddenly strike us funny.

FREDDIE: And just when you've decided to take yourself seriously someone comes along and makes a fool of you.

LEONARD: I had a patient once who was married seven times to five different women. He married two of his wives twice. And when he was an old man of ninety he re-married his first wife. One of his wives had to wear her wedding ring on her right hand because he'd cut off her left ring finger in a jealous rage.

FREDDIE: Then you mean you're not jealous?

LEONARD: Not a bit.

FREDDIE: It's superhuman.

KAREN: No, it's just that he doesn't really love me!

ELEANOR: And Freddie doesn't really love me!

FREDDIE: And Eleanor doesn't really love me!

KAREN: Interpersonal Disorientation!—is a syndrome that's always fascinated me! In fact, I've been experimenting with a medication that sometimes helps in cases of extreme dysphoria.

FREDDIE: A remedy?

KAREN: Yes, it's a new medication that's just come out.

ELEANOR: A drug?

KAREN: It's medicine. It's been tested on hundreds of cases and has proven virtually one hundred percent effective.

LEONARD: What is it?

KAREN: It's called R.P.

LEONARD: R.P.?

KAREN: Reverse Psychology.

ELEANOR: I thought reverse psychology was when you tell a person to do the opposite of what you want them to do knowing that they'll do the opposite just to be stubborn or independent.

KAREN: That's right. Only this does the same thing *chemically.*

LEONARD: I don't get it.

KAREN: R.P. makes you strongly attracted to the person you would normally be least attracted to.

ELEANOR: Fascinating.

KAREN: It's useful in opening a person up to new ways of relating to others. Or it can be useful in repairing damage to a relationship where petty quarrels and betrayals have led to an estrangement.

FREDDIE: Well, I have taken every drug under the sun and I've never heard anything about R.P.

KAREN: It hasn't hit the streets of SoHo yet, darling. And even when it does, if it ever does, I doubt that it will be available in this potency. I have pharmaceutical quality R.P.

ELEANOR: Let's try it. Then we can all find out who we're least attracted to.

FREDDIE: Where can we get some of this stuff?

KAREN: I have some in my bag. You see, Leonard? I do read the professional journals.

ELEANOR: Let's all take it.

FREDDIE: Yes.

KAREN: Let's.

LEONARD: Wait a minute. Is this going to be a drug orgy or a medical experiment?

ELEANOR: A drug orgy, I hope.

LEONARD: Well, I'll have no part of it.

KAREN, FREDDIE, *and* ELEANOR: Aw!

LEONARD: Unless this drug is administered under scientific conditions it constitutes a breach of professional ethics.

FREDDIE: Come on, Leonard. What are you afraid of?

LEONARD: I'm not afraid. It's just that I want to proceed scientifically. This experiment needs a control.

ELEANOR: Control?

KAREN: Leonard is right. One of us shouldn't take the medication so that we have supervision. There should be someone clearheaded and rational to help in case there is some problem.

FREDDIE: Clearheaded and rational? Which one of us would that be?

LEONARD: Me.

KAREN, FREDDIE, *and* ELEANOR: You?!!!

LEONARD: Yes. I'll be the control. I won't take the R.P.

FREDDIE: I *thought* you were scared.

ELEANOR: Leave him alone, Freddie. Let's take the R.P.

KAREN: All right. We three will take the R.P. and Leonard will be the control. Who wants to go first?

ELEANOR: How long does the effect last?

KAREN: It varies. But rarely more than twenty minutes to half an hour.

LEONARD: That's a long time.

KAREN: Yes, but it gives one time to work things out.

LEONARD: How is this drug administered?

FREDDIE: Let's freebase it.

KAREN: [*Slightly offended*] Let's try to keep in mind that this is a medication and we're not taking it for "kicks."

FREDDIE: We'll try not to enjoy it. We promise.

KAREN: We're taking this medication to learn something about ourselves.

ELEANOR: Let's do it!

KAREN: [*Removing a vial from her purse*] This is it. It's in a liquid form. All you have to do is take a little sniff. First you'll sneeze. Then you stare. Then you faint. And after that you fall for the person you're *least* attracted to.

ELEANOR: Let me go first. [*Sniffs from the bottle*]

FREDDIE: What does it smell like?

ELEANOR: It's all perfumy or something. It smells like new-mown hay and chicken broth and gardenias or garlic or sour milk or mildew or chocolate or clove or cinnamon. Tar and roses, cat piss and cabbages, fresh baked bread and...[*Sneezes, stares, faints, then*] Leonard, I love you.

FREDDIE: Well, there's nothing new in that. You two have been lovers for some time. We don't need R.P. to tell us that you're attracted to Leonard.

ELEANOR: Leonard is beautiful.

LEONARD: Me?

ELEANOR: Leonard is sexy.

LEONARD: Me?

ELEANOR: Leonard is all I could ever want in a man.

KAREN *and* FREDDIE: Him?

ELEANOR: Yes. Oh Leonard, I liked you before as a friend. As someone who would take me out. But I never realized what I'd found in you. Your eyes spit fire. Your lips drip honey. Kiss me! Kiss me! [*Kisses him again and again passionately*]

LEONARD: [*Gasping for breath*] Eleanor, there must be some mistake. You were attracted to me before.

ELEANOR: No. No. I wasn't. I was using you to get revenge, to make my husband jealous. I was blind. Do you hear? Blind!

LEONARD: Using me?

ELEANOR: Ah, but that's all behind us now. I was a fool, I tell you! A blind fool. My only desire now is to please you. Curse me if only I may hear your voice. Beat me if only I may feel your touch. Kick me if only I may feel your foot. I will be your slave. I am your slave. Only do not send me away. I love you! I love you!

LEONARD: Do you see that? Eleanor isn't attracted to me.

KAREN: She's *least* attracted to you.

FREDDIE: That's a weight off my mind. Karen, why don't you go next?

KAREN: All right. [*She sniffs from the vial, sneezes, stares, faints*] Leonard, kiss me with the kisses of thy mouth for thy love is better than wine!

FREDDIE: You again! This is sickening!

LEONARD: But Freddie, remember what this means. Karen is least attracted to me.

FREDDIE: Oh yes. That's right. Ha, ha!

KAREN: O that thou wert as my brother, that sucked the breasts of my mother! When I should find thee without, I would kiss thee; yea, I should not be despised. I know you. I know you.

FREDDIE: She means it in the biblical sense.

KAREN: I would lead thee into my mother's house, who would instruct me.

LEONARD: I can't stand your mother!

KAREN: I would cause thee to drink of the spiced wine of the juice of my pomegranate.

LEONARD: I don't go that route, honey.

FREDDIE: Give me some of that stuff, will you? I'm beginning to feel left out. I want some action.

LEONARD: Are you sure you still want to? You obviously won't get anywhere with either of these two. No matter which one you're least attracted to, they're both temporarily crazy about me.

FREDDIE: Give me that bottle. I've got to know who I'm least attracted to so that I can choose between them when this stuff wears off. [*Takes bottle. Sniffs, sneezes, stares, faints, then*] Leonard?

LEONARD: Yes, Freddie?

FREDDIE: It's you.

LEONARD: Me what?

FREDDIE: You're the person I was least attracted to because you're the person I'm attracted to now.

LEONARD: Listen, Freddie, I admit I was attached to you. I'll even admit that I was overly attached to you. But it wasn't genital. It wasn't even anal. You interested me. That's all.

FREDDIE: Come on, you hot thing you. You know we can get it on. Don't play coy with me.

LEONARD: Really Freddie. Maybe I'm just more *limited* sexually than you are. That's it! I'm more limited. Think of it that way. It's nothing against you.

FREDDIE: Oh come on Leonard. You know we were meant for each other. Don't fight it. It's bigger than both of us.

LEONARD: You overestimate me.

FREDDIE: Come on Leonard. Just try it. You might like it. It will be the first time for me too.

LEONARD: Are you sure about that?

FREDDIE: I'm positive. You know me better than anybody. Have I ever mentioned anything of the kind?

LEONARD: No.

FREDDIE: You don't think I'd lie about something like that, do you?

LEONARD: No.

FREDDIE: Then what's stopping you?

LEONARD: Freddie, I want to remind you that you are on a drug. You are reacting in *opposition* to your usual impulses.

FREDDIE: Then why don't you take some R.P. too? I'm telling you it's really great. I feel so liberated. I feel liberated from the tyranny of my own taste.

LEONARD: Freddie, as your doctor I feel it is my duty to warn you. You are experiencing hysterical disassociative neurosis.

FREDDIE: Why are you rejecting me? Am I so terrible? Am I so unattractive?

LEONARD: This attraction to me that you're feeling only proves that you are least attracted to me when not under the influence of R.P.

FREDDIE: I won't take no for an answer. You're just like a woman. You say no when you mean yes.

LEONARD: Freddie, I assure you I am nothing like a woman. [*Slaps* FREDDIE's *hand*] Fresh !

FREDDIE: Oh, you little wildcat! It's no use using Reverse Psychology on me, Leonard. I'm onto you. [*Walks toward* LEONARD *as he speaks with open arms*]

LEONARD: [*Backing away in the direction of the pool*] Freddie, that's the Reverse Psychology speaking. You're not attracted to me. You're not!

FREDDIE: I am! [*Lunges at* LEONARD *and kisses him on the mouth*]

LEONARD: Freddie you're all wet. [*Breaks away from the kiss and falls backward into the pool. A splash of water flies on from the wings*] Aaaagh! Help! Help! Help me! I can't swim. I can't get out.

FREDDIE: Leonard, nobody's going to believe you. You're just using this as an excuse to avoid me.

LEONARD: Help! Please! Help!

ELEANOR: He can't swim. He told me so.

KAREN: I'll get him out. I took a summer course in lifesaving.

> KAREN *takes a little time putting on her bathing cap amid* LEONARD's *cries of* "Help, I'm drowning," *etc. and dives into the pool. Splash from the wings again.*

FREDDIE: I want him. Do you hear? I must have him.

ELEANOR: Forget it Freddie. He only likes women.

FREDDIE: Oh, so that's his game is it? Well two can play! If it's a woman he wants, it's a woman he'll get! [*Exits into cabana*]

ELEANOR: [*Alone.*] Gee, everything seems so different to me than it did a moment ago. I've admitted things in public that I never even thought of before. But I don't feel guilty! I realize that some things that happen aren't my fault. That it's no use worrying about things that I can't change. I've got to accept the inevitable. And the problems that I have aren't really so big if I think about the problems other people have. It's just a question of living life for its own sake and being grateful for it. Anyone who has studied modern psychology must be aware that a person under considerable stress could reach a state in which he is not responsible for his actions.

KAREN: [*Enters with* LEONARD *limp and dripping wet in her arms*] I think…I was too late…He's dead!

ELEANOR: But you said you took a course in lifesaving. Didn't they teach you artificial respiration?

KAREN: Yes, but I'm too upset to do it.

ELEANOR: You've got to do it! A human life is at stake!

KAREN: [*Hysterical*] I can't do it, do you hear? I can't! He's dead! Dead! And I killed him! Why did I play with that R.P.? Why? I killed him! I killed him! And now he can never come back. Nothing can ever bring him back! And it's all my fault!

    ELEANOR *slaps* KAREN *across the face.* KAREN *suddenly becomes calm.*

ELEANOR: Thanks. I needed that.

    KAREN *begins to give* LEONARD *artificial respiration.* LEONARD, *lying on his back, emits short spurts of water every time* KAREN *applies pressure to his chest.*

LEONARD: Where am I?

    FREDDIE *enters wearing the dress that* ELEANOR *wore in first scene in this act. That is, the dress* KAREN *lent her. Oh, you remember! The one she wore to the Metropolitan Museum of Art the day she first met* FREDDIE.

LEONARD: [*To* FREDDIE, *groggily*] Karen!

FREDDIE: Yes, Leonard, my love!

LEONARD: I think administering an untested pharmaceutical was a highly questionable diagnostic aid. It was almost the end of me there. For a minute I thought it was all over.

KAREN: Wait a minute. He's still delirious. He's mistaking…

ELEANOR: Quiet. Let the R.P. work.

KAREN: You're right.

LEONARD: That damn drug nearly killed me. Do you realize you could be sued for malpractice?

FREDDIE: But Leonard, you're the only one who didn't take the R.P.

LEONARD: Oh, what do you care what happens to me? You find me repulsive. I know that now. Thanks to the R.P.

FREDDIE: Leonard, I do care.

LEONARD: No, you don't. You lied to me. You said you were going to have a face-lift. But it was just an excuse to come here with Freddie.

FREDDIE: But I did have a face-lift.

KAREN: I did not!

ELEANOR: Shhhh!

FREDDIE: Don't I look different to you?

LEONARD: [*His mind clearing for the first time since his plunge*] Let me look closer. Eeecht, you look worse. Karen, I think you've been seeing too much of Freddie. You're beginning to look like him. Freddie! What are you doing in my wife's dress?

FREDDIE: Surprise! [*Throws himself on* LEONARD]

LEONARD: [*Looking around*] Somebody do something!

ELEANOR: Freddie, take your hands off of him, he's mine! [*Tries to pull* FREDDIE *off of* LEONARD]

FREDDIE: You little bitch! Keep your hands off of my man or I'll scratch your eyes out.

> FREDDIE *and* ELEANOR *have a catfight.*

LEONARD: Karen we've got to do something! Twenty minutes to half an hour of this and somebody's going to get hurt.

KAREN: Don't worry. It's been about that long now. They should be coming out of it any minute now.

> FREDDIE *and* ELEANOR *roll about with less and less force.*

LEONARD: *They* should be coming out of it? What about you? Shouldn't you be coming out of it too?

KAREN: Now Leonard...

LEONARD: Why aren't you down there fighting over me? Would you mind explaining that?

KAREN: It's very simple. I didn't take the R.P. I faked it.

LEONARD: How could you have faked it? I saw you sneeze, stare, and faint.

KAREN: You mean this? [*Sneezes, stares, and faints*]

LEONARD: You're not practicing psychiatry anymore. This is witchcraft!

KAREN: [*With a sly laugh*] Sometimes there's a fine line between the two. After all, both rely heavily on the power of suggestion.

LEONARD: That's a shocking thing to say.

KAREN: As long as I still have the power to shock you, I guess there's hope for our relationship.

> FREDDIE *and* ELEANOR *begin to come off the* R.P.

FREDDIE: What hit me?

ELEANOR: What hit *me*?

KAREN: You've both been hitting each other.

FREDDIE: That stuff is strong!

ELEANOR: It just takes over. You have no choice but to go with it.

FREDDIE: Look at what I'm wearing! I suppose I'll never live this down.

ELEANOR: That stuff is awful. I never want to take it again.

FREDDIE: You can say that again. I'd never touch it again. Not if you paid me. It's bad. It's a bummer.

KAREN: Oh, I don't know. I think it cleared the air and settled a few issues.

LEONARD: Karen, how could you be so irresponsible?

KAREN: I'd have done anything to save my marriage. No risk was too great.

LEONARD: I suppose sneaking off to a resort boatel with Freddie was an attempt to save your marriage, too.

KAREN: I am fond of Freddie.

LEONARD: This isn't a marriage. It's a mirage.

FREDDIE: You two are supposed to be the psychiatrists. But I think you're crazier than we are. At least our marriage is based on a firm foundation.

ELEANOR: Yes, we have so much in common.

LEONARD: The only thing you two have in common is you were married in the same church.

FREDDIE: We're in love!

ELEANOR: Yes, we're in love.

LEONARD: Huh!

KAREN: They are in love. He with himself. She with herself.

LEONARD: Instead of a marriage license you should have gotten a learner's permit.

FREDDIE: Why of all the...

ELEANOR: Forgive them, Freddie. It isn't easy running a marriage on one brain.

KAREN: Don't worry. We can't all be mentally healthy.

LEONARD: This is the thanks we get for teaching them to help themselves.

FREDDIE: You help yourself all right. To our money.

LEONARD: Oh, you've got all the answers. Too bad you don't know a few of the questions.

ELEANOR: Freddie is a genius. He can do anything.

KAREN: Anything but make a living.

ELEANOR: He's a self-made man.

LEONARD: Yeah, he started at the bottom and stayed there.

FREDDIE: Some doctor. He begins by examining your wallet. Then he makes love to your wife.

LEONARD: I'll never stop loving her. Because I never started.

FREDDIE: Not that it matters to me. I believe in free love.

KAREN: True. He never spends a cent on a date.

FREDDIE: That's a real friend. She only stabs you in the front.

KAREN: I don't condemn inferiority in my friends.

ELEANOR: No, she rather enjoys it.

FREDDIE: The more I think of her, the less I think of her.

ELEANOR: You were dazzled by her sophistication.

FREDDIE: Oh, she's sophisticated all right. She can bore you on any subject.

ELEANOR: But sexually it was just like in the movies?

KAREN: Yes, a short subject.

FREDDIE: Let's put it this way. She's not frigid. She just flunked puberty.

LEONARD: This R.P. is evil. I'm going to get rid of it once and for all. [LEONARD *raises the bottle of* R.P. *over his head and throws it to the ground, smashing it*]

KAREN: [*Shrieks*] No! The fumes!

All four sneeze, stare, and faint.

KAREN gets up first. Looks at the other three for a moment and then says licentiously in a masculine voice

Eleanor, come to mama!

ELEANOR: No, no! I want Leonard! Leonard is the man I love.

KAREN: [*As before*] Man? I'll stomp him if he touches my little girl!

FREDDIE: [*As a woman*] Don't you dare lay a finger on him, you big brute. He's mine, I tell you, mine.

LEONARD: Get away from me! All of you! [*Runs off*]

> *Piano music off becomes more fiery, then stops. A scream is heard off.*

FREDDIE: Leonard, how could you do this to me? What's she got that I haven't got?

KAREN: Who screamed?

ELEANOR: What's happened?

FREDDIE: Well, now we know who Leonard is least attracted to.

ELEANOR *and* KAREN: Who?

FREDDIE: The little old lady who plays requests.

EPILOGUE

Funny Hill Farm Sanitarium. ELEANOR *and* FREDDIE *are waiting onstage when the lights come up, with a potted plant, box of candy, and magazines.* KAREN *enters to them in a white doctor's coat.*

KAREN: [*Very warmly*] Eleanor, Freddie, so nice of you to come.

ELEANOR: It was the least we could do.

FREDDIE: Is he all right? May we see him?

KAREN: Yes, but only for a short while. He's still a little tired out after all he's been through.

FREDDIE: We understand.

ELEANOR: How much longer do you think he'll have to stay here?

KAREN: There's no way to tell, exactly. But one thing I can say, he's been steadily improving.

FREDDIE: Are you treating him?

KAREN: Yes, I wouldn't have it any other way. He's my patient now. All mine.

ELEANOR: At least we know he's in good hands.

KAREN: Thank you. Shall we go in?

FREDDIE: Yes. We brought him these. [*Gives her the presents*]

KAREN: Did you bring the coloring book and crayons he wanted?

ELEANOR: Yes, and some pencils and paper in case he wants to write.

KAREN: I don't think he'll be allowed to have the pencils. Sharp objects aren't a good idea.

ELEANOR: Do you think he would attempt…

KAREN: No, not necessarily. But there are other patients here. And, well, it's just better not to take any chances.

    ELEANOR *and* FREDDIE *exchange a look.*

ELEANOR: I see.

KAREN: Shall we go in?

    KAREN *draws back a screen or opens sliding doors revealing* LEONARD *in a straight jacket.*

ELEANOR: [*Almost bursts into tears when she sees him*] Oh, Leonard. Look at you. I'm so sorry. Are you all right?

LEONARD: Yes, perfectly. Don't be upset Eleanor. This was the best thing for me…*really.* Everyone is so kind to me here. And I needed time to think things through.

FREDDIE: I feel this is all our fault, Leonard. You didn't want to take that R.P. in the first place. We talked you into it.

LEONARD: Leonard knows better. He doesn't hold you responsible.

FREDDIE: Leonard?

LEONARD: Yes, he told me so. I talk to him every day. Someday he's going to work for me when he gets out of here.

ELEANOR: Work for you?

LEONARD: Yes, he's going to work in my diamond mine. Under Tiffany's.

FREDDIE: But you're Leonard. And you don't have a diamond mine.

LEONARD: I used to be Leonard. But then I went away and had a face-lift and now I'm Louis Comfort Tiffany. Would you like some diamonds? I can get them for you.

ELEANOR: Where do you get them?

LEONARD: In my stools. Next time I go to the bathroom I'll save some for you. You could make diamonds too if you had the proper toilet training.

FREDDIE: [Aside to ELEANOR and KAREN] This is pathetic.

ELEANOR: Poor Leonard.

KAREN: Well, wasn't it nice of Freddie and Eleanor to visit you?

LEONARD:

Jack and Jill went up a hill,
They each had a buck and a quarter.
Jill came back with two and a half.
Do you think they went up for water?

KAREN: Leonard, aren't you going to say good-bye to Freddie and Eleanor after they took the trouble to come and visit you?

LEONARD:

There was an old woman who lived in a shoe.
She had so many children, 'cause she didn't know what to do.

KAREN: Leonard, Eleanor and Freddie are leaving.

LEONARD: No! You and I are leaving. They have to stay here!

ELEANOR: What? What does he mean by that?

KAREN: Humor him.

ELEANOR: Will he be able to go back to work?

KAREN: I'm afraid not. His contract had a sanity clause.

LEONARD: You can't fool me. There's no such thing as Sanity Clause.

FREDDIE: My God! He's in worse shape than I thought.

LEONARD: I won't stay here! I won't! [LEONARD struggles to escape from the straight jacket] Aaargh! [Screams] Aaargh!

KAREN: [To ELEANOR and FREDDIE] Would you mind stepping into the next room just to be on the safe side? I'll handle this.

FREDDIE: Are you sure you don't want help?

KAREN: No, I'm trained for this.

ELEANOR: She knows best. Let's go Freddie. [*They exit*]

KAREN: That's enough, Leonard. They're gone.

LEONARD: [*Rising calmly and removing the straight jacket*] How much longer do we have to keep this up?

KAREN: Until they show some sign of improvement.

LEONARD: It doesn't seem to be helping.

KAREN: The first step is their willingness to accept that they are the patients and that this is a hospital. Once they take that step the rest will follow easily.

LEONARD: Poor kids. And they had their whole lives ahead of them.

KAREN: He has a severe mental block. After selling that one painting, *Portrait of Eleanor,* for fifteen thousand dollars, he was never able to equal it again.

LEONARD: Equal it? Why does he feel he has to equal it?

KAREN: [*Exultantly*] It had a freshness and a spontaneity he could never recapture.

LEONARD: We'll just have to continue the regression therapy.

> LEONARD *draws back a screen revealing* ELEANOR *posing bound and blind-folded as in Act 1 Scene 4.* FREDDIE *at his easel, painting. For the first time we see that the words* "MENTAL PATIENT" *have been stenciled on the front of their clothes.*

FREDDIE: [*Anguished*] I can't do it! I just can't do it!

ELEANOR: Think back, Freddie. The inspiration. Try to recapture it. What were you thinking of when you painted me?

FREDDIE: [*Wracking his brains*] I can't remember! I can't remember!

KAREN: [*Aside to* LEONARD] They're lucky they have us.

> LEONARD *nods agreement as the curtain falls.*

THE END

John O'Keefe

∾

All Night Long

•

All Night Long was produced by the Magic Theatre [John Lion, general director] in San Francisco, California, on March 21, 1980, with the following cast:

EDDY	Michael Grodenchik
JILL	Leslie Harrell
JACK	George Coates
TAMMY	Julie Jay
TERRY	Jenny Shapiro

Director: Ken Grantham
Sets: John B. Wilson
Costumes: Nancy Faw
Lighting: John Chapot
Sound: Wellsound

CHARACTERS:

Jack, the dad, 43 years old.
Jill, the mom, 39 years old.
Eddy, the older brother, 17 years old.
Tammy, the older sister, 16 years old.
Terry, the youngest child, 10 years old.

ACT I

Set: The inside of a house. It's like one of those doll houses with shuttered windows and big rooms. There is a stairway stage left that leads to three rooms above: TAMMY's room, EDDY's room, and the master bedroom. There is a landing running across and over the spacious living room below.

Below is a kitchen, stage left, with refrigerator, cupboards, and a large dining table. Farther down the left wall is a sliding door which is TERRY's place. There are also a few unexpected places in the walls for entrances and exits. Down center is a couch and a coffee table. Up center is the front door. There are windows all around in the walls pleasantly spaced and large. There is an upstage right window which is fairly large and, later in the second act, is blocked up with a stone cube with the curtains drawn hiding it, but in the first act, it isn't there.

When the play begins it is afternoon and light is coming through the windows. As the play progresses it gets darker outside.

EDDY enters through the front door. It's just after school. He has his books in a book strap. He tosses the books on the sofa and heads toward the refrigerator.

EDDY: Hi, Mom, I'm home! [*He pulls out the fixings for an enormous sandwich and begins to build one.*] Had a hard day today. Georgie Gessel beat up on me as soon as I got in the building. He told me to get off Buddha Row. I told him that I wasn't on Buddha Row. And that got him real mad. I'm pretty sure that he was thinking about hitting somebody before he got to school, especially me. I guess I got the face you like to punch. But I covered my cheeks with the sides of my hands like Dad told me to do and he only got me on the forehead and temples, sure protects the eyes though. Anyway, Georgie left in a huff after some of the cheerleaders gave him the read out. He got real red in the face and his eyes started to water and he snorted up his nose a lot and got me up against the lockers so that I made a big bang and I saw stars pouring out of my eyes and I felt all alone in the center of the universe like a big blob of nothing, shrinking all of the stuff of creation out of my head, and Karen Minataur bent real close to my face so that I could smell her perfume and I could see her big green eyes and her full red glisteny lips and her pearly white teeth and I could feel her warm, moist breath. And she said in the sweetest voice, "Are you okay, Eddie? Georgie didn't mean it personally. It's just that he's from the other side of the tracks and his dad beats him up a lot." I understood, Mom, I did. And I told her that. I said I had a lot of liberal guilt to deal with myself so I could understand the value of a psychotherapeutic perspective. And then she left and I heard Georgie's big Chevy roar off. I worried about her all day. If she keeps missing school she won't be able to go to Springfield Junior c.o. this fall and she has a fine alto voice. [EDDY *has now finished making his huge sandwich and does a California roll over the back of the couch and on to the cushions.*] But one thing I didn't do, Mom. I didn't cry. I know that that might make me tighten up my facial muscles and lock my solar plexus so that I breathe wrong, but it did something for my leadership capacities. I *know* I won't go down in mixed chorus this year!

Just then JILL, EDDY's *mom, enters through the front door with a bag of groceries.*

JILL: Oh, hi, Eddy.

EDDY: Hi, Mom.

JILL: Did you have a nice day at school?

EDDY: Oh, yes, a great day, Mom.

JILL: Oh, that's good to hear. [*She goes to the kitchen and begins putting stuff away.*] I do hope your dad had a good one. He was so stuffed this morning I almost kept him home from work. But he wouldn't hear of it. He said, "No, Mommie, I'm going there even if I have to put straws up my nose."

EDDY: Yeah, Dad's a real spirit farmer.

JILL: Are the other kids home yet?

EDDY: I don't think so. I'll check. [*He shouts from the couch.*] Tammy? Terry?

> JACK, *the dad, opens the master bedroom door upstairs and steps out on the landing. He has a huge thumb on his left hand. Half of his face is covered with dried day old shaving lather.*

JACK: Hi, kids. [*He twirls his big thumb.*] "Pluck your magic twanger Froggie!" Remember that, Eddy? And then he'd speak in that low gravily voice of his. "Hi ya, kids, hi ya!" Oh god, I loved that stuff! Have a nice day at school, Eddy?

EDDY: Sure did, Dad. How did it go for you?

JACK: [*Imitating Daffy Duck.*] T'ere did! Got my thumb th'uck in the th'ink. [*He holds up his big thumb and cackles.*] No way to earn a living.

JILL: Go wash up, Dad. Supper's gunna be ready soon..

JACK: All right, honey.

> JACK *disappears behind the door winking madly at* EDDY.

JILL: [*As she continues setting the table.*] You know your sister Tammy might be on Candid Camera next week. They've chosen her from a field of ten. They like her voice and her posture. It could get her good grades in Make-up class and that's a red belt at beautician's school, especially if she perseveres and doesn't act immodestly in the courtyard of King Wen.

EDDY: Mother, what the fuck are you talking about.

JILL: Headaches. It's this eternal housewifery. I feel like a spermed horse. [*She stops and looks at* EDDY.] Did you know yesterday, every time I looked at you I saw a corpse? Do you think that has any significance? Or is it just my lunar menses? The girls at Dream Club said that I shouldn't pay too much attention to such things, that I shouldn't look at it directly, but with the sides of my eyes and feel it as the lather of rather large movements. [*She goes back to her table setting.*] They talk about all that yang and yin but I think it's really western motivation in drag. You knew that Freud's mother was a faggot didn't you?

EDDY: It doesn't really make a difference, Mom, she's dead.

JILL: Oh, but it does, hun, it does in the long run.

EDDY: Who cares about the long run?

JILL: You should if you don't, Eddy. It's not just rationalization, this thinking in large movements. No, no, no. [*She throws back her head and laughs.*] It makes everything so funny! [*She stops laughing and continues to set the table.*] But it's more than that. It gets you into the here and now. It makes you realize that you're not putting up with anything.

EDDY: I know, I know. It gives one a panoramic view, but who cares if I was your father in another life, Mom?

JILL: [*Suddenly glaring at* EDDY *savagely.*] But you weren't! [*She goes back to her table dressing.*] Understanding things in a big way keeps you from being a dip shit. Go wash your hands, your dad should be coming through the front door any second.

The doorbell rings. EDDY *hurriedly gets up and puts the sandwich on the coffee table and hurries into the downstairs bathroom.* JILL *takes off her apron and brushes back her hair. She stops and looks at the hand she brushed her hair back with.*

JILL: [*At first speaking to her hand.*] Children all around me. I give them enough room to drown themselves. That's the larger space. I just imagine a huge body filling a river basin, steaming with bio-thermal effluvium, baby smells and moisture. I wander about this body, past the amber oils of its antennae, thinking of it in the larger sense. How these viperous coils, these saffron fibers bejungle its dark pits and belched out genitalia and I realize that even God mumbles.

She throws open the front door. TAMMY, *the older daughter, is standing in the doorway. She is prettying. She's wearing a red dress.*

TAMMY: I don't know what to say.

JILL: What do you mean?

TAMMY *breaks into a shrill teenage giggle and then just stands there silent.* ·

JILL: [*Standing there very still, then…*] You're really making the place silent as a tomb, dear. Why don't you come in?

TAMMY: In there?

JILL: Yes, dear. After all it's your house.

TAMMY: No, it isn't.

JILL: But of course it is.

TAMMY: No, it isn't. It's your's and Dad's. But it's really Dad's. That is until you separate and then you'll probably get the house and a moderate alimony check.

JILL: You're probably right.

TAMMY: But it won't make any difference.

JILL: Why do you say that?

TAMMY: Because they're probably going to turn off the oxygen.

JILL: Who's probably going to turn off the oxygen?

TAMMY: The Telephone Company.

JILL: No, my dearest. They'll try to turn off the meaning and then you'll think you can't breathe, but you'll be able to.

TAMMY: You're not going to let Terry out are you? She's been letting the most outrageous farts and I can't stand it.

JILL: Terry's your sister.

TAMMY: So what? That doesn't mean I have to like her farts.

JILL: She's been having stomach trouble. You should have some compassion.

TAMMY: But they get into my clothes and the kids can smell it at school.

JILL: We all smell that way. We just don't keep our minds on it that much. Even Playboy Bunnies smell like that between their legs.

TAMMY: Well, I don't like it.

JILL: That's because you're still cherry. Well, don't just stand there letting the draft in, come in and wipe your feet. There's plenty of housework to be done for you to complain about.

TAMMY: [*Not moving.*] Oh, Mom, you know I don't really mind all this house training.

JILL: I know you don't hun, but we've got to spat about something, what's a mom and dot supposed to do with each other?

TAMMY: Mother, tell me the truth. Is the blood really passed through the sperm ?

JILL: [*Smiling slyly.*] What do you think? There are no blood brothers, honey. [*She pats her ovaries.*] Come on in and play with the v.c.

TAMMY: The v.c.?

JILL: You know… [She *opens the closet door which is right next to the front door. A vacuum cleaner is inside of it.*] the vacuum cleaner. [*With that she simply turns the vacuum cleaner on and leaves it running there inside the closet and goes back to her table setting.*]

TAMMY *simply steps into the house, goes into the closet and pushes the vacuum cleaner out onto the floor and begins working.*

The work and the noise continue for a while when the front door swings slowly open revealing a wan figure in a business hat and top coat. The hat is tipped over so that the bill covers the man's face. He stands there so exhausted that he seems to be leaning on his bones which just happen to be in the right place to support him. He teeters. It is JACK, *the same guy who was upstairs just a little while ago only now his business suit and hat have replaced his thumb and lather.*

TAMMY, *who has been vacuuming, suddenly looks up and sees the figure. She screams.* JILL *doesn't seem to notice a thing and keeps setting the table.* TAMMY *continues shrieking and backs downstage leaving the vacuum cleaner abandoned and running. The figure reaches out to calm her but staggers instead losing its tenuous self-support and inadvertently heads downstage toward the vacuum cleaner, its hand still extended in front of it.* TAMMY, *still screaming, pulls the vacuum cleaner away from the man by pulling on its cord, giving the impression that the vacuum cleaner is coming toward her by its own will. The figure stumbles toward the vacuum cleaner, hand outstretched, reaching toward the vacuum cleaner for support, subsequently following it and* TAMMY. TAMMY *screams and lets go of the cord.* JACK, *not by volition but by momentum stumbles into the vacuum cleaner, grabs its handle, and with one hand extended in front of him in a gesture intended to calm the girl, chases her about the room with the vacuum cleaner until it finally corners her and* JILL *pulls the plug.* JACK *falls back against the wall.*

JILL: [*Taking* JACK's *hat and coat.*] Tammy, get your father a chair while I fix him an olive equals vermouth and vodka.

     TAMMY *helps* JACK *to his chair and sits him down.*

JACK: [*Pointing at the vacuum cleaner.*] I don't like that thing. Put it back in its cage. This house is going to kill us someday. I suppose my son's in the bathroom performing his proverbial autogenesis. And my daughter? Have I Electra-fied you enough to help support an analyst? And my youngest, has it decided on a sex yet? And my ever present conjuga, have you licked my Swisher Sweets today?

JILL: [*Elegantly bringing him a drink.*] Yes, I have. [*She pulls a cigar from her bosom and gives it to him.*]

JACK: Jill.

JILL: Jack.

TAMMY: Oh, this is simply ridiculous!

     She exits upstairs in a huff.

JACK: Well, so what?

JILL: That's what I say.

     JACK *picks her up.*

JILL: Leave me off at the kitchen.

JACK: Okay. [*He carries her to the kitchen and puts her down.*] I'm going to wash up.

JILL: You'll have to get that guy out of the bathroom first.

JACK: You mean…?

JILL: Yes, he got his thumb stuck in the sink and he's been there all day.

JACK: It's cool. [*Winks.*] Return to sender. [*He bounds up the stairs with lightning speed and exits.*]

JILL: [*Looking up after him.*] Clorine bleach, seven-up, poker, Skelly gas and Studabaker, that's what me and my Jack grew up in. [*There's a knock on the wall. She ignores it and goes back to her table setting.*] That's my last child, Terry. Jack and me, we watched everything change right before our eyes and no one ever asked us anything about it. They just said, "And there you go" and things got longer, and fatter, and pointy, and flat, and round and some lines got shorter and some got longer, just like the driveways. Up went the skirts and in went the pants and up went the kids and out went the bellies of some of Jackie's old army buddies and highways criss-crossed the country choking out most of the two-laners like old Highway 6. I don't feel any older for it, not in any physical way. But inside there's a longer staircase.

     A slot slides open in the wall and two little eye holes appear. It's TERRY.

TERRY: [*Drawling out her voice like Patty Hearst in her first tape from the* SLA.] Mom? Dad?

JILL: [*Still dressing the table.*] Yes, honey? Have you come over to a certain side?

TERRY: I think so.

JILL: Well, you'd better make sure . Why don't you wait just a little bit longer.

TERRY: Okay. [*The eye holes slide shut.*]

JILL: [*Speaking as she sets the table.*] Jack and me, we couldn't have another baby and we wanted one more, just one more so badly. Something to lead us across the border into middle life. But the doctor said that Jackie didn't have the juice. He suggested alternatives, but Jack wouldn't have it. He said, "That's what lesbians do." And we thought the subject was closed. Then one of Jack's friends, a lieutenant general in the reserves said that they had some interesting stuff left over from the space program and that it would all be very nuclear family and so we have Terry now, but she's not all the way through. I like to think of her as a girl. Eddy likes to think of her as a boy. And Tammy, well you know sibling rivalry, especially among teenagers. And Jack, well, sometimes I don't think he likes to think of her at all, especially when she's "all the way." [A *little bell rings.*] I think she's through. [JILL *goes to the wall.*] I think that's it, honey. Are you ready?

TERRY: [*From within the wall.*] Yes, Mom.

JILL: All right, here we go.

> She slides a section of the wall back and there behind it is the prettiest ten year old girl dressed in a sparkling silver dress. She is a radiant, smiling, perfectly healthy child. There are tinkling little music box chimes going on.

TERRY: [*Smiling sweetly and tilting her head slightly.*] Hi, Mom.

JILL: Oh, you dressed for supper.

TERRY: Don't describe things so much Mama, you give me the chills.

JILL: Don't go too far out, sweety, you'll cut your fingers on those diamond studded frets.

TERRY: [*Shivering at the image.*] Really Mother, you ought to take up bass fishing.

EDDY: [*Coming out of the downstairs bathroom.*] What's all this gobblie-goop? I'm never going to get any supper.

> Upstairs there is a most horrendous clanging of anvil and hammer.

EDDY: What's he doing?

TERRY: He's ironing his shirts.

EDDY: Yuk-yuk.

TERRY: You don't believe me? Watch. [*She lets out a most incredible call.*] Hey, Daddy!

> JACK *bursts out of the master bedroom and onto the balcony with a half-finished steel shirt on.*

EDDY: What's he trying out for, a razor blade?

JACK: [*Sneering while holding his nose with one hand and a sledge hammer with the other.*] Oooo, that simply stinks.

JILL: [*Who has returned to setting the table.*] See what happens when you get hungry?

JACK: Look. [*He sticks his thumb out in front of him.*] It went down. But the sink is still swollen. [*He gives a little laugh, then looks down at* TERRY.] I see you haven't started to melt yet.

TERRY: Oh, eat it Groucho.

JACK: The other one was a song called... [*He sings the "Cream of Wheat " song from* Let's Pretend.] "Cream of Wheat is so good to eat that we have it every day. We..." But I can't remember how the rest of the words went.

JILL: Now we're all here but Tammy.

EDDY: I think that's a stupid name

JILL: [*Calling.*] Tammy! Tammy Tammy T-a-m-m-y!

JACK: [*To* EDDY, *from above.*] Well, I think your name is sort of stupid.

EDDY: Well, "Jack" isn't anything to crow about.

JACK: It certainly has a lot more substance than "Eddy."

EDDY: YOU're the one who gave it to me.

JACK: How do YOU know that?

EDDY: Well, certainly, MOTHER wouldn't have pinned such an atrocious license on me.

JACK: What? With a name like Jill? I wouldn't be so sure about that.

TERRY: Oh for crying out loud, will you stop it?

EDDY: Keep your bionic nose out of it.

> *For some reason this breaks* JACK *up.*

TERRY: Stop it, all of you!

JACK: Don't dislodge your magnet! [*He cackles.*]

JILL: [*Calling.*] T-a-m-m-y!

EDDY: [*Pointing at* JILL.] Hey, Dad, did you hear that? I think her voice is changing?

TERRY: This is going very sour.

JILL: Jack, honey, change for supper.

JACK: Aye, aye, captain.

EDDY: [*Staggering with laughter.*] "Aye, aye, captain," that's great, Dad.

JACK: [*Suddenly stops, his eyes bulging, his face red and intense.*] Do you think so, son?

EDDY: [*Effusive.*] Oh, yes Dad!

JACK: [*Making an especially big wink just for him.*] Then I'll be right down.

TAMMY: [*Appearing from upstairs.*] If you keep acting like this nobody's going to pay any attention to you.

TERRY: She's right.

JILL: Oh, there you are, Tammy.

TAMMY: Mother has the right attitude.

EDDY: Yeah, check your stools for corn.

TERRY: Oh Jesus Christ!

EDDY: What's wrong with you?

TERRY: You're so gross.

EDDY: I'm so gross? Look who's talking.

> *Silence while everybody but* JILL *looks at* EDDY. *Then...*

JILL: All kinds of creatures inhabit the earth.

EDDY: So?

TAMMY: Shut up, Eddy.

EDDY: What is this, Mr. Wizard time?

TERRY: You're a creep.

EDDY: Big deal. So "all kinds of creatures inhabit the earth."

JILL: And they all have REMs.

TERRY: REMS?

JILL: [*Still setting the table.*] Yes, Rapid Eye Movements.

TAMMY: Yes, I know what you're talking about. Like in dreams your eyes follow the images going on in your head.

EDDY: My God it *is* Mr. Wizard time!

TERRY: Shut up.

EDDY: [*Ignoring her.*] Everybody knows about REMS, except you [*meaning* TERRY]. You probably don't have any.

JILL: On the contrary, I know for a fact that she has them.

EDDY: How do you know? Do you watch her after you put her back in the box?

JILL: No, I can see her eyes moving now. [JILL, *however, is not looking up.*]

EDDY: She's not asleep.

JILL: So what?

EDDY: REMS only happen when you're dreaming.

JILL: Yes.

EDDY: Oh good grief, are we going to get into all the world's a dream routine?

JILL: [*Looks up from her work and gazes at* EDDY *as if the idea had never struck her before.*] Oh, that's very nice. [*She tastes the idea.*] "All the world's a dream." [*She goes back to work.*] Yes, that's one way of looking at it.

EDDY: Oh for Christ's sake mother, how can you be so fucking stupid.

JILL: [*Without malice.*] You ought to get laid, Eddy.

JACK: [*Appearing from the master bedroom, dressed in casual evening clothes. He is brisk and clear.*] Late? Late? I'm never late for your dinners, my dear.

JILL: See, your Daddy has REMS.

JACK: I'm having them now.

JILL: You see not only people have REMS...

EDDY: Even dad does.

        He titters.

JILL: ...animals have them too, but not only animals, buildings have them.

TAMMY: REMS?

JILL: Precisely. And the tire is having REMS when it's squealing, and the rain is having them when it's falling.

EDDY: That's ridiculous.

JILL: [*She pauses and looks up from her work.*] No, ghostly.

JACK: Let's have some supper.

        They all sit down to supper.

EDDY: It's about time.

TAMMY: Eddy always gets so impossible when he's hungry.

EDDY: That's because I'm part lion. [*He makes a growling sound and paws the air.*]

JILL: Are you going to eat at the table with us tonight, Terry?

TERRY: Yes.

JILL: Oh, that's wonderful.

EDDY: Does she have to?

TAMMY: She has a right to eat just like anybody else.

EDDY: Don't give me that right to life bull shit. Just because something moves doesn't mean it's alive.

JILL: Your sister is very much alive.

EDDY: Yeah, but will she stay in one piece?

JACK: I'm always afraid to eat eggs around her, Eddy.

TAMMY: God you two are bilious.

> EDDY *and* JACK *elbow each other and laugh.* JILL *serves the food.*

EDDY: [*Chewing his food with delight and surprise.*] What is this, Mother?

JILL: Jello.

JACK: Jello? It's absolutely incredible!

EDDY: I've never eaten blue food, there's always been red and green and yellow and white, but blue...

JILL: I'm glad you like it.

TAMMY: Where does it come from?

JILL: Skin, tendons, ligaments, the matrix of bones.

JACK: Oh, God I love dinner talk! You know at work today I had this most incredible dream. I think I could turn it into cash, especially with the information you have just given me. I dreamed that there was this paper that took pictures. You see, if I was to coat some paper with sensitive silver compound and then put down a layer of bichromated gelatin on it I might be able to produce an intense field of light which would act as a lens through which anything would be in focus due to natural photon intelligence. Mr. Nobel added a little sensitive silver to a gelatinous emulsion and developed gun powder. You see, light was developed! Light! Light! Within the tonnage of the nineteenth century are the seeds for the ship to the Omega point!

EDDY: God Dad, I love the way you pop your toilet paper!

JACK: Thank you, Eddy. [*They both laugh.*]

TAMMY: "Pop," how apropos. [*To* TERRY.] I don't trust those two bastards farther than I can throw them.

JILL: Don't worry about it, they'll retire soon.

JACK: [*With a mouthful of Jello.*] Not me.

EDDY: [*Copying his father.*] Not me either, Mom.

JACK: Rough and ready, aren't we boy?

EDDY: You betcha, Pop.

TERRY: [*Grinning devilishly above her plate.*] You know you hate each other.

EDDY: What? Me and Dad?

JACK: Me and Eddy?

TERRY: Yes, both of you. I'm going to tell you something, brother dear. He's been thinking of killing you.

> EDDY'S *blue Jello falls out of his mouth.*

TAMMY: Mother, you shouldn't let her talk like that.

JILL: Well, honey, if Terry says something it's more than likely true.

> EDDY *is almost paralyzed with shock. He doesn't move, he just twitches, his face growing redder.*

TAMMY: Mother, you just can't let this go on. Say something.

JILL: What's to say? This is between your brother and his father. It simply isn't any of our business.

TAMMY: Mother, don't say that.

JILL: Eddy has to take care of himself. My obligation is to supply the elements necessary for survival, not to guarantee it. Isn't that right, Daddy?

JACK: [Singing the Air Force hymn softly with an absolutely serious face.] "Off we go into the wide blue yonder flying high into the sun." How does the rest of it go kids?

EDDY can't answer. He is caught in a spasm of trembling.

JILL: Excuse yourself from the table, Eddy.

EDDY gets up and staggers to the downstairs bathroom.

JILL: Kids, I want to let you in on something. Movement itself is a living being and the being is only visible when something is in motion. So when you're lonely, just wave your hand in front of you.

TAMMY, TERRY and JACK: Thank you, Mom.

JILL: Well, I guess it's time to move on.

JACK: [Wiping his mouth off] I guess so.

TERRY: Help you clean the table?

JILL: Oh, that would be nice.

They begin clearing the table which is piled high with dishes.

TAMMY: Dad, should we sit together?

JACK: I think that would be all right. What do you think?

TAMMY: [Putting her arm around JACK's shoulder.] Do you think we ought to talk about things, Daddy?

JACK: Yes, or we can watch the television set.

TAMMY: And we could laugh together at the jokes on it.

JACK: You're not a kiddin'.

TERRY: Mom, what's the clone of crash?

JILL: [After an appropriate period of silence.] Why do you ask, honey?

TERRY: Because I dreamed about it last night.

JILL: About the clone of crash?

TERRY: Yes. I dreamed that I was inside of this absolutely yellow yellow room and there was a black curtain that went from the ceiling down to the floor. [She turns to JACK and TAMMY.] You two don't have to listen to this.

TAMMY and JACK of course turn around and begin listening.

TERRY: [Turning back to her mother.] And this curtain, this black curtain had these waves in it that moved up from the floor to the ceiling. They did it with a strange indescribable motion like...like...they were going poo-poo. And there was someone behind them because I could hear him clear his throat. And then he sniffed a couple of times and said real officially, "And now...here's Egg Yolk, the Clown."

Suddenly she starts scratching her head, but it is a peculiar action for it seems as if the hand itself is moving of its own accord. She begins whimpering as the hand scratches. The scratching becomes more intense until she is almost dancing, all the while she murmurs helplessly: "Mommy, Mommy"...

JILL: Terry! Terry, what's the matter? What's happening?

> JACK *and* TAMMY *are totally aghast.*

TERRY: [*Her hands scratch the space a few inches from her head while the rest of her body bobbles up and down.*] And then the man's voice came again from behind the curtain and it said, "Come on you little phlegmer cough-it-up-cough-it-up." [*In anguish but unable to stop dancing and quaking.*] Oh, and Mommy! I did!! I did and I did and I did and this black and yellow pointy clown man popped out and swept it up as it came out of my throat and fell on the floor and he kept on sweeping real fast and he always seemed to be right next to me even when he was across the room! Oh, Mommy! Mommy!

JILL: Jack, do something!

JACK: What can I do?

> JACK *rushes toward her.*

TERRY: [*Suddenly speaking with an entirely new voice, a voice filled with such authority that it stops* JACK *in his tracks.*] Don't touch me, you jerk! [*Then, just as abruptly she is flung back into her fit.*] "Oh God! Oh God!" I shrieked and then the ugly, pointy, yellow clown came up real close to me and I could smell him and he smelled like baby breath, but thick, thick, rich baby breath. And he said, he whispered, I mean, "What's the clone of crash? Don't jump to any conclusions." [*Then, all at once, without the slightest transition her fit stops and she is totally natural.*] And then everything felt good, and warm and clear. And then the clown said, but he had changed. He had this wonderful apricot colored cloud in front of his face. He said, and he said it real clearly, he said, "Jack's not your daddy, I am." And then this vertical blast of steam shot up out of the floor and I woke up. And Mom, [*she stammers*] I just wanted to ask, [*she pauses and looks at* JILL *probingly*] are you my mommy?

> JILL's *eyes well up with tears She looks deeply into* TERRY's *eyes.*

JILL: Yes, darling, I'm your mommy.

TERRY: Thank you. I want to rest now.

> *She goes back into the wall and closes it behind her.*

JILL: [*Noting the silence.*] Well, now there are just three of us.

JACK: Yes, there are aren't there?

TAMMY: [*Looking at* JACK *warmly.*] Yes.

JILL: Let's all sit down together.

JACK: You're not going to finish the table?

JILL: I'll do it later tonight when everybody's asleep.

> *They all sit down together on a centrally located couch.*

TAMMY: Each day, in every way, I'm growing better and better.

JILL: Each day, in every way, I'm growing better and better.

JACK: Each day, in every way, I'm growing better and better.

JILL: Growing nearer to God.

JACK: Growing nearer to the great white light.

TAMMY: Getting less tired by the minute.

JACK: Able to accept and reflect upon

JILL: …the minutes and the hours and the days,

TAMMY: …the incredible turnabouts

JACK: …which catastrophizes,

JILL: …and obliterates

TAMMY: …us in the end.

JACK: [*To* TAMMY.] Speak for yourself.

TAMMY: I was, speaking for myself, that is.

JACK: Then why did you include me?

TAMMY: I didn't.

JACK: Yes, you did! You said, "us."

TAMMY: I meant me and Mom.

JACK: Why did you just use you two?

TAMMY: Because you're going to out live us.

JACK: [*Shouting.*] What are you trying to do, take the suspense out of things?

EDDY: [*Suddenly throwing the downstairs bathroom door open and shouting from it.*] You're not going to do me in tonight when I'm sleeping are you?

JACK: That's inconsequential to the situation as it is now! [*Then to himself*] But it might not be. [*Then to* EDDY.] Listen, son, I don't want you to feel like a bugger under someone's table…

TAMMY: [*Wincing at the image.*] Oh, God Dad!

JACK: [*Wiggling his ears, puffing his cheeks and bobbing his eyebrows.*] What I mean to say is that deep down inside I want you to live a long time…

EDDY: But?

JACK: …But…I have very little control over that. You could be electrocuted in your pajamas.

EDDY: Oh, god, Dad, don't say that!

JILL: Eddy honey, you've got to be able to take care of yourself. Anyway it's beginning to get late. It looks as if Terry has gone to bed. Perhaps we should be thinking of our own.

JACK: [*After a decisive pause.*] Yuck.

JILL: [*Suddenly looking especially old and gray with just a hint of injury.*] What, aren't you tired?

JACK: Hell no! I just got back from work, had some supper, a little pause to reflect and now I want to go outside with my family and have some ice cream and night life.

JILL: What about Terry?

JACK: We can leave her with the Counter. We won't be gone long.

JILL: That's true. Some fresh air to cool the blood at the end of your cheeks, to liquefy the eyes and clean the shining crystal. Oh God yes! I'd love to go out !

EDDY: Oh good fucking jizzum Dad!

JACK: Just like clock work. You kids are just like robots. I could have predicted your reactions. You are both in your element, the sluff. As long as you can look at the world in a sluff you feel secure even if it makes you feel crazy.

TAMMY: [*Whining.*] Oh god…

JACK: Well, we're going out. [*He looks at* JILL.]

JILL: [*Smiles back at him.*] Completely.

JACK: [*To* JILL.] Meet you upstairs .

JILL: Okay.

> *They both dash upstairs and close the door. There is a long silence. The air gets decidedly thicker as* EDDY *and* TAMMY *sense each other alone together.*]

EDDY: [*His eyes downcast.*] You gunna go with them?

TAMMY: [*Her mouth dry.*] I don't know, are you?

EDDY: I was thinking that I might stay back and read [*He pauses.*] upstairs in my room.

TAMMY: [*Softly.*] That seems like a good idea.

EDDY: You mean, you like the idea?

TAMMY: Oh, yes, I think so. Yes, it's a good idea.

EDDY: For you, that is? I mean *you'd* like staying back and reading yourself?

TAMMY: Yes, that would be nice.

EDDY: Would you do it down here?

TAMMY: No. [*Pause.*] No, I would prefer my room.

EDDY: Yeah, I would prefer my room too. Do you think they're going to be up there a long time?

TAMMY: Probably…

EDDY: [*Jumping on her cue.*] Perhaps if your neck gets stiff I could give you a back rub.

TAMMY: …But they might not and then again, they might stay a little while and try to make babies.

EDDY: You know that they can't make babies anymore.

TAMMY: I know but they like to try.

EDDY: Do you listen to them?

TAMMY: I can't help but hear them.

EDDY: But do you *listen?*

TAMMY: Yes.

EDDY: Does it make you… [*He bobs his eyebrows once.*]

TAMMY: It used to.

EDDY: But it doesn't now?

TAMMY: Right.

EDDY: How come?

TAMMY: I know your father.

EDDY: You know my what?

TAMMY: Oh Eddy, women mature so much more quickly than you boys will ever understand.

EDDY: Oh God, here we go again! I suppose he showed you his cock?

TAMMY: He did more than that. He gave me an entire lecture on it.

EDDY: "On it" I'll bet.

TAMMY: He came into my room one night, right up to my bed, right next to my face and brushed my nose up and down with the front of his wool pants and I woke up and there he was towering above me.

EDDY: Oh, Jesus Christ!

TAMMY: [*Ignoring his retort.*] And then he bent way over next to my face and said, "You want to see my aquarium?" And I said, "What aquarium?" And he said, "The one behind this screen." And he lifted the flap of his fly and showed me his zipper. And I said, "Dad, that's not an aquarium." And he said, "Oh, yes it is. It's a pressurized tank." And I laughed.

EDDY: You're full of it.

TAMMY: And then he said, "You want to see my dolphin?"

EDDY: Oh, come on!

TAMMY: And you know what?

EDDY: What?

TAMMY: I wanted to see it. I mean *I really* wanted to. I never wanted to see anything so badly in my life!

EDDY: Oh good god!

TAMMY: And do you know what he said then?

EDDY: [*Blending a sneer with a searing interest.*] What?

TAMMY: He said that the dolphin couldn't stay in the dry air very long, that it had to be kept wet. And do you know what I did Eddy? Do you? I fell in love with that dolphin and I kissed it right on its face.

EDDY: [*Incredulous.*] That's simply ridiculous.

TAMMY: But that was only the beginning.

EDDY: I don't want to hear anymore.

TAMMY: Why not?

EDDY: Because you always make up such stupid lies.

TAMMY: I do not.

EDDY: The last time you said he called it a "hover craft."

TAMMY: Well, it was.

EDDY: It never was! It never was anything because he doesn't have one any more !

TAMMY: But he does, Eddy! He does! And it IS like a hover craft. Eddy, it's like a flying saucer.

EDDY: Oh, come on

JACK: [*His voice coming suddenly through the flung open bedroom door.*] Come on, let's get our clothes on.

JILL: [*Suddenly appearing in the bedroom doorway.*] Yes, all of us. Let's go out into the night among all those flat little houses until we come to an ice cream parlor .

EDDY: I want to stay back and read.

JACK: [*Appearing, grinning from ear to ear.*] You need the air.

JILL: You need the exercise.

JACK: You can get a stinky finger later.

JILL: Yes, Tammy, let the impulse sink below your will into the dark lake of your belly dowry.

JACK: Besides [*He pauses and looks about the house from the landing, then softly.*], this house needs a breather.

TAMMY: [*Suddenly looking about her at the house apprehensively.*] Oh…yes…you're right. Come on Eddy.

EDDY: [*Also apprehensive.*] Oh…yes…sure, Sis.

> *Without warning and from an unseen signal* TAMMY *and* EDDY *suddenly dash upstairs into their separate rooms.*

JILL: Aren't they incredible?

JACK: You know it.

JILL: [*As they come down the stairs.*] You know, Jack, Eddy's been having trouble at school.

JACK: What, he's not getting what they're trying to teach him?

JILL: I don't know. He never talks about his education.

JACK: Teen-agers shouldn't be cooped up in school anyway. They should all be sent to athletic farms.

JILL: [*Looking at the kitchen table.*] You know, I love that table.

JACK: Do you? I'll get you another one.

JILL: No, I think it's the way he gets along with the other children.

JACK: Well, he has a very nice singing voice.

JILL: Yes, but I'm afraid it's not enough to get him laid.

JACK: That's unbelievable! Where are people's values? And why hasn't he brought this up to me?

JILL: I don't know. I think perhaps he doesn't like you.

JACK: Doesn't like me? That's incredible.

JILL: Isn't it?

JACK: Well, what do you think I should do about it?

JILL: You could move out.

JACK: [*Laughs.*] That's a great idea.

JILL: You could also talk with him.

JACK: I do talk with him.

JILL: I mean alone, heart to heart. Let him know you care.

JACK: You know, I could do that. The only problem is that I can't stand him.

JILL: You can't stand him?

JACK: No, I hate him.

JILL: You do?

JACK: Yes, every time I see him I want to tear him limb from limb.

JILL: Well, then I think a private meeting is long overdue.

JACK: My god, it's been fifteen years since I've been alone with him!

JILL: Is that right?

JACK: Yes, I believe so. The last time I talked to him alone he was at least three feet shorter. Actually, if you want to know the truth, I'm afraid of him. He's so fresh and young and strong. I think he still hates me for beating him in the old days before I gave up the bottle.

> JILL *is suddenly without warning overcome with fatigue. She lies down on the couch.*

EDDY: [*Comes out of his room talking.*] It's true, Dad. I'm having trouble at school. The kids think I'm too skinny. At recess they punch me in the mouth and they won't play with me even when I open up and tell them I'm lonely and need to be considered just like anybody else. They just sneer and tell me to drop dead. Yesterday I stuck my finger down my throat and tried to strangle myself but all I did was throw up on my shirt.

> *This breaks* JACK *up.*

JACK: Come on downstairs and tell me about it.

> *But* EDDY *has returned to his room.*

JACK: [*To* JILL *on the couch.*] I'll talk to him.

TAMMY: And me too, Dad [*she has appeared upstairs too*], will you talk to me? [*She exits also.*]

JACK: I'll talk to Tammy too.

JILL: Tammy too?

JACK: Huh?

JILL: Tammy too?

JACK: Tammy too.

> TAMMY *and* EDDY *come out from upstairs dressed for winter.*

EDDY *and* TAMMY: We're ready.

JILL: [*Gets up exhausted and pale.*] All right, all right, if we must.

JACK: [*Suddenly shouting angrily*] Yes, we must !

JILL: [*Flinching.*] All right, all right.

EDDY: Dad, I don't like the way you're talking to Mother.

JACK: Neither do I!

TAMMY: Well, stop it then, Daddy.

JACK: [*Still shouting.*] I will! I will! Just give me a second! [*He goes upstairs in a huff and into the master bedroom, slamming the door behind him.*]

> *There is a long silence.*

JILL: I want to get out of here.

EDDY: I do too.

TAMMY: Don't reduplicate.

EDDY: I'm not reduplicating.

TAMMY: You are.

EDDY: Am not.

TAMMY: You said exactly what Mother said.

EDDY: What did Mother say that I reduplicated?

TAMMY: You said, "I do too."

EDDY: Yes, I know I said "I do too" but that was not what she was saying.

TAMMY: It was exactly what she was saying.

EDDY: "I do too" is the same as "I want to get out of here"?

TAMMY: Exactly, if you turn the sequence of the sentences around.

JILL: Children.

TAMMY: Yes, Mother, I'm not arguing.

EDDY: She is, Mother. It's part of a syndrome. She argues and pinches whiteheads in the mirror.

JILL: Children, put me on the table. I want to rest there and get my maximammary energy.

> EDDY *and* TAMMY *look at each other alarmed.*

EDDY: [*Moving toward her, but troubled.*] Are you sure you want to do that, Mom?

JILL: Yes, yes, I'm sure. I want to go where radiation is queen.

EDDY: But what it does to the bones, Mom.

TAMMY: What do YOU know about it?

EDDY: See what I mean? You're a compulsive bickerer.

JILL: Just lift me up and put me there.

> TAMMY *and* EDDY *carry her to the table and lay her down on it.*

JILL: [*Sighing.*] That's better.

> Just then JACK *comes in through the front door. He has shorts on and lather is on one side of his face.*

JACK: Such interstellar heat! [*Seeing Mom and the kids.*] What's this? Has mama mia gone bongos again?

TAMMY: Dad, will you stop farting around?

JACK: Me fart? You know the daddy choo-choo doesn't fart, he "puffs."

TAMMY: Dad, you've driven Mom to the table.

JACK: That's nothing. You should take a look at this. [*He holds up a large model of the Saturn Five rocket.*] Those guys can hot wire anything. [*He crosses to* JILL *and bends over her.*] Hi, Mom, getting a little juice from the proverbial loins?

JILL: [*Smiling up at him.*] I felt a bit weak, Jackie.

JACK: If you don't watch out we're going to start calling you noodle bones.

TAMMY: Dad, that's nothing to joke about!

JACK: Why not? If you ever want a bit of your mommie you can pour her into a cup just like bowls of water and the moon, in every cup a smiling mother's face. [*Noticing* EDDY.] God, Eddy, you're getting hefty!

EDDY: Do you really think so, Dad?

JACK: Know so. Listen, kids, we're the reflection of actions done far, far across the reaches of time. We are the umbra of beings whose actions have preceded ours, whose actions we are in fact the result of. We are the feathers by which these awesome paradigms mount the just created heavens. When the alligators yawn, we yawn. That's why your mother's lying on the table. [*To* JILL.] Are you ready to go yet, hon?

JILL: [*Completely revived*] Yes.

JACK: Good, I'll go upstairs and change.

> JACK *goes upstairs.*

TAMMY: What a complete ass-hole.

JILL: [*Pleasantly.*] He is, isn't he. I've lost many a fingernail in him.

TAMMY: Mother, I've been meaning to ask you about that.

JILL: About Daddy?

EDDY: Tammy, don't.

TAMMY: Does Dad have an atomic penis?

JILL: [*Saying the word as if she didn't know its meaning.*] Penis? Penis? What an ugly word. Is that something you go to the toilet with? It sounds like "poohpooh" only lispy: "penis"? I certainly hope your father doesn't have a penis.

TAMMY: You still didn't answer me, Mother.

EDDY: Let it go, Tammy.

TAMMY: Mother!

JILL: [*Getting up from the table.*] Why don't you shut up and sit down.

> TAMMY *flounces onto the couch, leaving* EDDY *standing there.* EDDY *starts to say something but* JILL *interrupts him.*

JILL: Oh, you sit down too.

> *He sits down next to* TAMMY.

EDDY: [*To* TAMMY.] I told you not to ask.

TAMMY: Oh, shut up.

EDDY: God, there sure is a lot of shutting up going on.

TAMMY: The trouble is there isn't enough.

EDDY: Want to pick my face?

> TAMMY *turns her back on* EDDY.

EDDY: See, Mom doesn't like that word either. I bet she doesn't like [*he silently mouths the word*] "vagina" either.

JACK: [*Suddenly on the landing, breezy, ready for winter*] I don't mind the word myself, but I like the word [*mouths the word silently*] "pussy." Out we go!

JILL: Out we go.

EDDY: [*Whining.*] Oh God!

JACK: Oh God!

JILL: Oh God!

TAMMY: Stop it.

EDDY: I don't want to go out.

JILL: Out you go anyway.

TAMMY: Come on.

EDDY: I'm not going. My food hasn't digested, besides we'll be gone too long and I have to rest my voice.

JACK: You just want to play with your wopper.

TAMMY: Stop it!

JILL: She's right.

JACK: Who's that?

JILL: Your daughter.

JACK: [*Rubs his hand between his legs and then extends it to* TAMMY.] Hi ya, kid.

> TAMMY *throws her hands up in the air and heads stage left.*

TAMMY: [*To* JILL.] I'm the only sane person here.

JILL: That's because we never bought you a pet.

TAMMY: Mom, do you really mean that?

JILL: I mean everything I say.

JACK: I know, that's what makes you so endearing.

TAMMY: That's what makes you so frightening.

EDDY: That's what makes you my mom.

JILL: That's what makes me so real. I am real, you are real, [*To* EDDY] he is real. [*She goes to* TAMMY, *her arms open.*] And my beautiful daughter [*she embraces her*] is real. Come on, let's all go out together and stalk the night.

JACK: [*Opens the door and a gust of snow blows in. He stands there with an arm extended to escort them out.*] Butterbrickle, pistachio, rocky road, chocolate ripple, banana fudge, thin mint, strawberry, not to mention the sherberts.

JILL: Into the wind!

EDDY: Into the night!

JACK: Into the stars!

EDDY: It's cloudy, Dad.

JACK: But they're up there!

EDDY: That they are.

TAMMY: This is ghastly.

JILL: No, ghostly. The whole place is haunted.

TAMMY: Who will take care of Terry if we stay too long?

JACK: [*Grinning like a Cheshire cat.*] No one.

TAMMY: Perhaps I should stay back.

JILL: It's all right, honey.

JACK: [*Ghostly.*] There won't be anyone here.

EDDY: [*Who's already out the door.*] Come on, I'm getting frost bite.

TAMMY: [*Who is suddenly in tears*] Good night, Terry.

> *The door closes.*
>
> *There is a long silence.*
>
> *Then the door in the wall slides open and an electric wheelchair comes out. A being in a strange iridescent body is operating the controls. It tilts the wheelchair down center and stops. There follows another long silence.*
>
> *Then slowly the iridescent skin cracks and a figure emerges from within it. It is* TERRY. *She climbs out and walks out onto the stage, beautiful and radiant.*

TERRY: Isn't the world magical?

> TERRY *goes to the refrigerator and pulls out a winged box. She puts it on the table and opens it. Inside is a large glass of milk. She puts the box back in the refrigerator and then picks up the glass of milk in both hands and walks down center.*

TERRY: Aren't Dad and Mom rich? Tammy and Eddy really like each other. They're just teenagers. When they grow up and get a little more mature they'll depend on each other a lot more. I think Eddy's going to be an announcer on a space station. I don't know what Tammy's going to become. Oh wait! Maybe I do. Here it comes. Yes, she's going to become a personal psychologist like Dr. Amos. It's going to be very different, you see, the future, that is, I mean for people. I wonder where I'll be next year. Dr. Amos said I might last a long time. Elly said that I shouldn't worry about it. She said that once something has crossed over it won't ever leave. So even if I drop over dead right now it won't make any difference because I'll just be somewhere else. Isn't that wonderful? I think that someday we'll all just be big sparks bouncing here and there all at once at the same time everywhere! Whew! What a life it's going to be for us all someday when we all become light pulses.

[*Sings*] When I look into your eyes
all of the world opens.
Seas and clouds
and purple skies
break the wide world open.

Oh yes, oh yes,
even though your eyes
don't move anymore
and all the rest of you
drops away
there is the space
your eyes opened to

and you are there
and you are there
and everywhere I look
I see you.

ACT II

Silence. The front door opens and EDDY *and* TAMMY *enter, subdued. It is dark. All of the curtains are drawn. They switch on the light.*

EDDY: I hate Father sometimes. He's such an oaf it's a wonder he can walk.

TAMMY: I know. Did you see mother's face?

EDDY: I tried not to look. Oh, Tammy, what am I going to do? I've still got almost a whole year left of school.

TAMMY: You? Look at me, I've got at least two years in this beanbag.

EDDY: Well, you could get married.

TAMMY: Oh, great!

EDDY: Well, you could.

TAMMY: Well, you could join the army.

EDDY: [*Aghast.*] Me?! In the army?!

TAMMY: Well, can you see me filling up some hospital ward with babies?

EDDY: Tammy, let's not argue. I think we're in for a long one tonight. Let's stick together, maybe we can put Dad to sleep.

JACK: [*Sticking his head around the door.*] Put me to sleep? Put me to sleep? Is that what children do to their elders in the Space Age? Why don't you just stuff us in a rocket and pack us off to the stars?

EDDY: [*Conciliatory.*] That's great Dad! That's where I want to go after school, I want to go up into outer space.

JILL: [*Peeking her head over* JACK's *shoulder.*] We're already in outer space, honey.

JACK *and* JILL: Can we come in?

EDDY *and* TAMMY: Why not?

JACK: Wait. Wait, let me do this.

EDDY: Oh, god, not again!

JACK: That's right, again and again. Come my love, let me carry you across the threshold. [JACK *picks up* JILL.]

JILL: Oh, Osiris, what shall I do now that you're whole again?

TAMMY: Oh, how "cryptic."

JILL: Not at all, Isis sought her beloved one's creative member for eons.

JACK: [*Winks.*] And still does. [*He carries her across the threshold, sets her on her feet, takes her hand and kisses it.*] As the pomegranate sprang from the blood of Dionysius, the anemones from Adonis and the violet from Attis, so doth my bright green poplar tremble by the side of your moony stream.

EDDY: Whew! Did you hear that?

TAMMY: [*Disgusted.*] Yes.

EDDY: Oh, Dad, say it again.

JACK: [*Worried.*] What time is it?

EDDY: Ten thirty.

JACK: [*Relieved.*] The bright hour just before the work force slumbers. What shall we do, watch the news with the vast incredible collective?

TAMMY: I don't know. I think I want to go to bed before the rest of them.

JACK: [*Sweetly.*] Oh, no you don't! You shall not escape the love light of our circle.

JILL: [*Gazing at her knowingly.*] I think perhaps she doesn't want to escape the love light of her own circle.

EDDY: [*Blushing.*] Wooowee, did you hear that?

JACK: That's your mom, boy.

TAMMY: Why are you always making me out to be the ninny?

JILL: I don't think anyone's trying to make you out a ninny.

JACK: I'm not.

EDDY: If you want to know the truth, I think that you ninny out whenever Dad's around.

TAMMY: I don't like standing here being discussed.

JILL: Well, you did just bring yourself up for discussion.

TAMMY: I did not. I just made a statement about how you treat me.

JACK: We treat you fine.

EDDY: We treat you fine.

JILL: We treat you fine.

TAMMY: [*Screaming.*] You do not treat me fine!

EDDY: Wow, that's incredible, sis, you're having a crisis!

TAMMY: I'm *not* having a crisis!

JILL: Tammy, move to the other side of the room.

TAMMY: What? [*Alarmed.*] Why?

JILL: [*Seems to be speaking against her will and in* JACK's *voice.*] Just do what your mom says. [TAMMY, *aghast, puts her hand over her mouth.*]

EDDY: [*Speaking in* JACK's *voice.*] Wow, you talked like Dad just then! [*With* JACK's *intonations and a strange gleam in his eye.*] You never know what your friends might turn into. [*Startled by the voice.*] So did I!

JACK: You do look strange, kid.

EDDY: Do I? [*Looking strange.*] How do I look strange?

JILL: Tammy, you come over by me.

         TAMMY *starts and moves quickly next to* JILL.

EDDY: What about me? Can I come over by you too?

JACK: Yes, what about us, can we come over there too?

JILL: [*Steely-eyed and firm.*] No, you two stay over there.

EDDY: I'm lonely. [*To* JACK.] Can I stand next to you?

JACK: Me? Yes, you can stand right next to me. You can stand on top of me if you like.

EDDY: Thank you.

         They stand next to each other shoulder to shoulder with glowing eyes. As they stand there they sway slightly.

TAMMY *starts to say something but* JILL *puts her hand over her mouth.*

EDDY *and* JACK: [*Wagging their fingers at the same time at* TAMMY *and chanting.*] No, no, no, no-no-no.

EDDY: [*Pointing at himself*] He can't stand you.

JILL: *and* JACK: [JILL *mouths while he speaks.*] But I can.

JILL: Spoke too soon

EDDY: Mom,

JACK: I think we caught ya.

TAMMY *starts to say something but* JILL *and* JACK *stop her.*

JILL: You'd better not stand too close to me, either.

TAMMY *shrieks.*

JACK: Don't get freaked honey, we've just lost each other for a moment.

TAMMY *is now separated from* JACK, JILL, *and* EDDY. EDDY *jumps into the space between them and begins doing a soft-shoe while* JILL *speaks and* JACK *mouths her words. It's all kind of wobbly.*

JACK *and* JILL: [JACK *mouths while* JILL *speaks.*] You're on the other side, honey. Just say something. Just speak up and the bad, bad movie will stop.

TAMMY *tries to speak. Her mouth moves, she gesticulates, but no sound comes out. Suddenly they move toward* TAMMY.

TAMMY *screams.*

They scream.

JACK: [*Mouthing while* JILL *speaks.*] Didn't quite make it honey, let's try it again.

EDDY: She won't talk because she doesn't like me.

JACK: She don't like me either.

JILL: Oh, stop it both of you. She's just a little alienated.

JACK: [*Shouting childishly.*] She doesn't like me!

EDDY: [*Buries his head in his hands and begins sobbing.*] She don't like me neither!

JILL: She does too.

EDDY: [*Speaking in* TAMMY'S *voice.*] "I do, Mother, I do. I like you. I like Eddy. I like Jack. [*Speaking in his own voice.*] And I for one believe her.

JACK: [*Belligerently.*] I know, I know, but she's not saying it!

EDDY *and* JILL: [EDDY *mouthing and* JILL *speaking the words.*] Shut up and give her a chance!

JILL *continues to talk but* TAMMY *begins mouthing the words.*

JILL *and* TAMMY: Oh Mommy, Mommy, please help me. Help me, help me.

Then JACK *and* EDDY *join* JILL *and finally* TAMMY *joins.*

TAMMY, JACK, JILL *and* EDDY: [*They begin very low and then gradually build to terror and catharsis.*] Hello hello hello hello hello hello Hello HELLO HELLO HELLO!! HELLO!! HELLO!!

The last "HELLO" is screamed and then breaks into laughter and they fall into each other's arms.

JACK *and* JILL: [*Laughing.*] Aren't they great?

TAMMY: Oh god, Dad, I'm so sorry! I get so crabby.

EDDY: I do too.

TAMMY: We argue, and argue over and over again.

EDDY: Just like brother and sister.

TAMMY: No, no I was just on a trip.

JACK: And you got lost.

TAMMY: Yes, lost in hell.

> *There is a silence.*

EDDY: [*Breaking in clumsily.*] Recapitulation, recapitulation, recapitulation. So much
of it is recapitulation that I wonder how much we really do.

TAMMY: Yes, it's like a ritual.

EDDY: Yes, with the grown folks moving away from us in the fog.

> TAMMY *and* EDDY *head for the stairs.*

JILL: [*Stopping them.*] Where are you going?

EDDY: To bed.

TAMMY: We have somewhere to go tomorrow.

EDDY: And besides, you two should have some time to yourselves.

JILL: Why should we [*Meaning herself and* JACK.] have time together? Perhaps Tammy
and Dad should have time together and you and me should have time together.

TAMMY: [*Her eyes flashing.*] All right, Mom. [*She looks down at* JACK.] Come on upstairs.

JACK: Me? Good God. [JACK *grabs his hat, coat and scarf and goes upstairs. Then, from
the landing.*] I feel like a sailor that just got into port. [*With that he goes with* TAMMY
into her room.]

EDDY: [*Flushed and almost out of his mind with excitement, strikes a match and lights a
cigarette he pulls from his pocket. He tosses the blown out match.*] You can call me Ed.
No shit, you can.

> JILL *doesn't say anything. Instead, she takes out a bunch of bananas and begins
chopping them.*

EDDY: [*Descending the stairs.*] Don't let people dump on you, no matter what they say,
no matter how they try to justify themselves, there's no excuse for them to dump
on you.

JILL: What a bore you are.

EDDY You wouldn't say that if you knew what was going on in my mind right now.

JILL: I know what's going on in your mind.

EDDY: Do you?

JILL: Yes, I do.

EDDY: What do you think's going on in my mind?

JILL: You're wondering what your Dad is doing with your sister.

> *She begins fixing a drink.*

EDDY: [*Swallows.*] Is that for me?

JILL: No, this is.

> *With that she turns on the blender and it blasts over the speakers. The sound is
so loud that* EDDY *has to put his hands over his ears.* JILL *is stuffing bananas down
it. The door to* TAMMY's *room opens and* JACK *comes out with* TAMMY's *dress on.*

He is shouting for them to quiet down but can't be heard. TAMMY *comes out of her room dressed in* JACK's *clothes with shaving lather on half of her face.* EDDY *has fallen to his knees, his hands over his ears.*

JACK *finally pulls the plug on the blender and the sound stops. All four of them look at each other strangely. Then* EDDY *goes and gets the* TV, *turning off the living room lights. They all sit on the couch and stare at the television. The light flickers on their faces.*

JACK: [*After a bit, speaking about the* TV.] This news is dead. [*Really wondering.*] Where are we, in Alaska? [*He gets up and walks to the front door, opens it. There is a huge polar bear roaring in the doorway.* JACK *hurriedly closes the door.*] Terry's sleep walking. [JACK *cautiously opens the door again. A little robot—tin cans and a coffee urn with little pig tails sticking out of a pointed dome—stands in the doorway on a little red wagon.* JACK *picks the little robot up and carries it into the living room.*]

JILL: Oh, I'll take Terry to bed.

JACK: No, let me. [*He brings the robot down with him to his chair and sits. He settles down with the little tin* TERRY.] I remember when you were just a baby in a jar. Let me tell you a story. A long time ago before your mommy and daddy were born there was a huge carcass that sprawled over the aged topography of our world like a draping, endless, multi-colored cheese. Now, this carcass was in a rather advanced state of putrefaction. It was so huge that it was the sole source of our early atmosphere. The hiss of its decomposition could be heard even far out in space. Ah, but you know all about that stuff already, don't you? How the carcass was really a piece of god's gray matter and how when it broke down it taught all the amino acids to clear up and get it together. How there really was a god and the big bang was the sound of god's gun blowing his brains throughout the universe and that god really isn't dead [*pause*] yet and we are his lights going out one [*pause*] by [*pause*] one.

JILL: That's a terrible story, Jack. There isn't an ounce of truth in it. Put Terry to bed before her iron rate goes down.

JACK: It has already. Oh, your beady little eyes! [*He rises and crosses to the wall, carrying the little tin* TERRY *to bed.*] Did you say "hover craft?" Yes, your daddy was part hover craft. [*The panel opens. He places the robot into the wall and continues talking.*] That's where you were born…in space like flies breeding with maggots falling from larval cocoons. Ask your mother. Your mother knows. [*Calling as if falling into a deep hole.*] Your mother was in pure balloon. [*The door closes.*]

The doorbell rings. Jack approaches the door. Then, he stops.

JACK: What time is it?

EDDY: [*Without looking at his watch.*] Eleven thirty.

JACK: It was eleven thirty an hour ago.

TAMMY: I want to go to bed.

Silence. The doorbell rings.

JACK: What time is it now?

EDDY: Eleven thirty-one.

JACK: A minute hasn't passed yet.

JILL: Well, go to bed.
>   *Silence. The doorbell rings.*
JACK: What time is it now?
EDDY: I looked it up. It was ten thirty an hour ago.
JACK: [*Disconcerted.*] That's ugly. That's really ugly.
EDDY: What's ugly?
JACK: Don't just ask me what's ugly, recognize it as such.
>   *The doorbell rings.*
JACK: [*Whining.*] What's wrong with me? [*He takes his dress off.*]
JILL: [*To* TAMMY.] I'll bet that's for you.
TAMMY: I know it's for me.
JACK: It's a date, isn't it?
TAMMY: Yes, a gentleman caller. [*She crosses upstairs.*]
JACK: Tell him to use the window.
>   TAMMY *slams the door.*
JILL: Now it's time for us to go to sleep.
>   JACK *struts towards* JILL. *He takes her into his arms. They kiss passionately. Then…*
JACK: It's time for us to go to the master bedroom, Eddy.
JILL: Goodnight, son.
>   *Soft, sexual moans come from* TAMMY'S *room.*
EDDY: [*Wide-eyed and left out.*] It must be pretty late, huh?
>   JACK *and* JILL *cross upstairs, leaving* EDDY *alone.*
EDDY: I don't want to go to sleep. It's not that I couldn't go to sleep. It's not that I'm not tired. I am tired. It's not that I want to stay up. There's nothing I want to do out here. It's just that I don't want to go to sleep. When I think about lying down it frightens me. I'm supposed to go upstairs and lie down in a dark room and wait to go "unconscious." And then maybe suddenly I'll find myself in some very strange place. [*Suddenly enacting a dream.*] "Here, drop down this hole." "Who are you?" "I'm your dad." "You don't look like my dad." "That's only because you see but a fragment of your dad." "What are you going to do with that rope?" "I'm going to kill you with it, my son!" [EDDY *throws his hands over his mouth and screams.*] I like the way it was this afternoon with the smell of Mom on the sofa and light streaming through the windows and doors, and salami, and baloney and pastrami and mustard…[*As he speaks the windows fly open and a bright, pleasant light comes through them, the light of midday.*] and the sound of birds [*The sound of birds comes up.*] and Benny, the postman coming up the walk [*The sound of Benny's footsteps come up.*] and kids playing outside [*The sound of kids comes up.*] and cars [*The sound of cars join the other sounds.*] and buildings with people sending information to each other [*There is the sound of typewriters and office machinery, drawers opening and closing, computer tapes rotating, etc.*] and jets flying overhead, taking people to foreign places [*Suddenly the sound of a huge jet starts at one end of the auditorium and moves across to the other end.*] and new things being built. [*The sound of jackhammers and bulldozers and construction work joins what has now become almost a roar, he has to shout*

over the noise.] I don't like night. I don't want to sleep! [*He falls face first into his sandwich, fast asleep.*]

> *Suddenly the front door flies open and all of the daylight and noise flashes into blackness and a huge crash of thunder comes down. It is night again and there is* EDDY, *asleep.*
>
> *Then there is again the sound of gentle rain.*
>
> *There, standing in the open doorway are* TAMMY (*in her original dress*), *and* JACK *and* JILL. *They are gray-faced as if they were from "Night of the Living Dead." They move forward, swaying synchronously from side to side as they enter the room floating on* EDDY'S *streams of sleep.*
>
> *As they move toward the center,* EDDY'S *body stands itself up out of his sandwich and takes itself, zombie-like, to the swaying stationary group which waits for him.*
>
> *The panel in the wall slides open and a slash of light falls across the floor from the unearthly illumination of* TERRY'S *abode and* TERRY *comes out. She has transformed into a gray faced zombie. She wears a little version of a Pope's hat. She sways her way to the front of the group. In her right hand, which is crossed over her left hand in front of her chest, is an Egyptian mace.* TERRY, *now in front of the group, leads them downstage and then up the stairs and into* EDDY'S *room. The door to* EDDY'S *room closes behind them.*
>
> *Immediately, a light snaps on in the master bedroom and we hear* JILL'S *voice.*

JILL: Jack! Jack! Wake up!

JACK: What is it, honey?

JILL: Jack, I've had the awfullest dream.

JACK: Go back to sleep.

JILL: Jack, I think Terry's going to die.

JACK: How do you get that?

JILL: I saw her leading us in a procession. She was carrying an Egyptian mace.

JACK: None of us can live happily ever after, go to sleep.

> *The light in their bedroom goes off.*
>
> JILL *emerges from her room with a candle and comes downstairs. Cautiously, she pulls the curtain a bit away from the window and peers out. Just at that moment there is the sound a roving band of punk rockers chanting "Kick ass, kick ass, kick ass" etc. After a bit the sound dissolves and* JILL *lets go of the curtain and approaches* TERRY'S *panel.*
>
> *Suddenly the panel opens and a green beam of light shoots out followed by a whirring. A sarcophagus rolls silently out of the wall.* TERRY'S *voice comes out. It is sent through a flanger. It seems to be coming from the beam of light.*

TERRY'S VOICE: Come on in, Ma, the pressure's fine.

JILL: [*Backing from the wall.*] Terry, are you all right?

TERRY'S VOICE: I'm fine fine.

JILL: You sound so strange.

TERRY'S VOICE: I *am* strange, Mom.

JILL: Where are you? It's so dark inside of there.

TERRY'S VOICE: It's all right, Mother, I'm not far away. Look.

JILL: [*She looks down cautiously into the sarcophagus.*] Is this my daughter?

     Suddenly JACK pops up out of the sarcophagus dressed like a mummy and grabs
     JILL by the back of the head and tries to pull her in with him. She rips herself away.

JACK: You don't like us. You'd rather be with him upstairs sleeping and snoring and growing hair. You don't like the way we change our clothes.

JILL: I do! I do! It's just that it's so strange and you do it so often and so late at night. [*Speaking into the dark room behind the panel.*] Terry, you're breaking my heart! Where are you now? Am I ever going to be able to recognize you again?

TERRY'S VOICE: You *can* see me, Mom. I'm this beam of light.

     JILL looks at the beam of green light. She approaches it and extends her hand to
touch it, then stops.

TERRY'S VOICE: That's all right, Mom, you can touch me.

     JILL hesitantly extends her fingers into the light. Upon touching it her body
shivers. She withdraws her hand then reaches up again and touches it again, more
surely this time.

JILL: My god, Terry, it's...you're so old!

TERRY'S VOICE: Yes, it was a suprise to me also. How do you like it?

JILL: I can't say that I like it or dislike it. It's just, just...[*Her voice trails off as she bathes*
her hand in the light. She pulls the sleeve of her nightgown down and bathes her arm
in the light, then her face and neck.] Oh, Terry, can you feel me back? I can feel you,
every cell of you, a trillion billion cells of you!

TERRY'S VOICE: [*Also moved.*] Yes, Mother, I can feel you, I can feel you like I've
never felt you before. [*Speaking as JILL bathes her face and neck in the light.*] Think
of me as you would a plant cutting. Because one form dies doesn't mean that the
plant dies. It simply moves from one environment to another.

JILL: I know what you mean. Only last night I lay in the darkness and I could feel that
the whole thing was unknown, everything, every last part of it, unknown but real,
so real and yet moment by moment unknown, even though it is all that I have, and
that it is so strange, that it is so slippery and that it is for keeps.

JACK: [*Again popping out of the sarcophagus.*] Don't give me that greasy gobber! What
would this reeking bitch know about class? I throw up on you, you sow !

JILL: I think Tammy's waking up.

TERRY'S VOICE: Yes, she is, Mother. And so is Jack.

JILL: I'd better go up, I wouldn't want him to think I was out grave robbing.

TERRY'S VOICE: Good night, Mother.

     The sarcophagus glides back into the wall and the panel closes.

JACK'S VOICE: [*From upstairs.*] Jill? Jill? Where are you? Your side of the bed is cooling off.

JILL: [*Wiping her eyes.*] I'll be right up, honey. I was watching the punk rockers rove
the streets.

     She goes to the refrigerator and opens the door. EDDY steps out of it.

EDDY: I'm sorry, Mom, I was hungry.

JILL: You'd better get up to bed. If your father knows you're awake, he'll give you a middle of the night lecture.

EDDY: I'm not going to die at thirty-nine, am I, Mom?

JILL: No, Eddy, you're not going to die at thirty-nine. You're going to have a long, long life. Go to bed and sleep in the one you have for sure right now.

EDDY: [*Much relieved.*] That's great, Mom.

JILL: Don't explain it, you might run out of ways of looking at it.

EDDY: [*Said like "right on.*] All right!

JILL: [*Clapping* EDDY's *ass like a jock.*] Now go up there and hit the deck.

EDDY: All right!

> EDDY *dashes up the stairs and just before the door, spins and sails into his room and out of sight.*

JACK: [*In his bed clothes.*] Was that Eddy? I've got something to tell him about fighting. What time is it?

JILL: [*Without looking at a clock.*] Three thirty.

JACK: [*Tasting what he's saying.*] I was dreaming about this curfew, this particular curfew...

JILL: [*Matter of factly.*] I don't want to hear about it right now.

JACK: [*Simply.*] Oh. [*He turns around, goes back into the bedroom and closes the door.*]

JILL: [*Continuing as if* JACK *had never happened.*] Terry, Terry, what's happening with you? Dr. Amos said that there would be changes, but Jesus Christ, if I had known what he meant I would have forgotten the whole goddamned thing! Give an idiot, a cannibal even, but a neutron, a goddamned oversized neutron for a daughter, Jesus Christ! [*Suddenly she looks absolutely paranoid. She drops to her knees and folds her hands in prayer, and murmurs.*] Oh god, oh god! Let me know that all [*Pause.*] this [*Pause.*] isn't just procreation cooling on someone's face, my face, the Earth mother's face. FUCK THE EARTH MOTHER!!!

> TAMMY's *light goes on. She opens her door.*

TAMMY: [*Rubbing her eyes.*] Mom, what's the matter?

JILL: You worthless piece of shit! [*She picks up a pot and throws it up at* TAMMY. *It misses her and hits the wall.*] You've made my life a walking nightmare!

EDDY: [*Coming out of his room on the run.*] Mom, what's the matter?

JILL: [*Thrown into an absolute rage at the sight of* EDDY.] You! You twerp! You don't even have the stuffing to be a homosexual! You pre-ejaculatory squirt! You're the one that really fucked up my life! When I was young I had balls, real balls, I had ten times the class squared than that muffin-faced mama's boy you call a father! You and that idiot winking at each other and letting chicken farts!

EDDY: [*Squealing.*] Mama! Mama! Don't talk like that, you make me feel bad!

TAMMY: [*Screwing up her face at him in an incredible knot of hatred, mocking him.*] Mama! Mama, you make me feel bad! [*She smashes* EDDY *in the face.*]

JILL: Let go of him! He's my business, you slut! [*She rushes upstairs and pulls* TAMMY *from* EDDY *by the hair and throws her up against the wall.*] You stinking shit-faced little bastard, always stuffing your mouth. [*She pulls him down the stairs and into the kitchen.*] Here, you forgot this! [*She pulls the belt of her nightgown, stuffs his face into the sandwich and ties it to his face.*] I wouldn't want to send you out into the world unprepared.

TAMMY: [*Jumping up and down, clapping her hands.*] Yes, mother, yes, throw him outside and let the punk rockers get him!

EDDY: [*Through the sandwich tied to his face.*] No, Mama, please, don't, please.

> JILL *opens the door. It is pitch black outside. In the distance the chant of "Kick ass, kick ass" can be heard. Then she throws him out and slams the door behind him.*
>
> *Outside the chant of "Kick ass, kick ass" approaches. There is a pathetic knocking and clawing at the door. The chant comes right up to the door. The clawing stops and all is silent.*

JILL: Let's take care of this place!

> TAMMY *rushes down the stairs.*

TAMMY: Mother, I can't believe it. Oh, how beautiful! I've been waiting for this for so long. [*She picks up a pitcher and is about to throw it.*]

JILL: [*Stopping her.*] No, not that one. That one belonged to my grandmother.

> TAMMY *picks up a coffee pot.*

JILL: [*Stopping her.*] No, let's keep that one for ourselves, it makes the best coffee in the world.

TAMMY: Mother, we can get another one.

> TAMMY *puts it down and grabs a handful of cups, dangling them from her fingers.*
> JILL *grabs her around the arms and pushes her against the wall.*

JILL: No, not those! Those are mine!

TAMMY: [*Exasperated.*] Would you please tell me what isn't yours?

JILL: Well, hardly any…[*She stops and looks the kitchen over, her hand poised on her chin.*] I guess it's all mine. Let me see. [*She walks about the kitchen looking at various things.*] Yes, that's mine. I bought it when you were just a little thing. And this, this was given to me by your father in the forties. They don't make them any more. And this, well, this is just something stupid. And look at this. This is a picture of Eddy on his way to summer camp. Look at those sandals. Doesn't he have darling feet?

TAMMY: Mother, how can you stand it? Look at what you're doing. Look at this crap you're tied to.

JILL: [*Still looking at the picture.*] You're not tied to anything, my dear.

TAMMY: I'm not? Then what do you call all of this?

JILL: Mine.

TAMMY: But what about me?

JILL: What about you?

TAMMY: What do you mean, "What about you?" Don't you care what happens to me?

JILL: Of course I do, but what am I supposed to do about it?

TAMMY: Mother, are you crazy? Look at all this junk! Do you want me to get caged in like you by all this clakkery?

JILL: Don't worry about my time machine, it's mine, not yours. You'll have yours when it comes. You'll have your own tools, your own shop. Leave what's mine alone. Leave me alone. This is my shop, my world, my place and you're simply growing out of it. But while you're here and eating my food, wash the dishes and sweep the floor and be nice to your little sister and your brother and Jack. If you don't like it, just go away and find a place that's better.

TAMMY *looks at* JILL, *her lower jaw forgotten and dangling.*

TAMMY: I feel so crazy, Mama.

JILL *takes her in her arms and holds her.* TAMMY *is crying.*

JILL: There, there, that's the way it goes, in and out and everywhere at once, like a vine chasing a spiral dream. First you want it and then you can't get rid of it like the sun just before eclipse. It's time to help someone.

JILL *goes over to the refrigerator and opens the freezer compartment, exposing a huge breast with a livid swollen bitten up red nipple. She holds a large glass under it. A stream of milk from the nipple flows into it.*

JILL: [*As the glass fills up with milk.*] You know the goddess Mut did this for Amen-re. He was the sun god who spat out the suckling Horus who later flew up and scratched the primal electricity out of the wind which polarized the amino acids into life. [*She puts her mouth to the nipple, sucks out a mouthful of milk and spits it into the glass.*] This top part of the milk is warm from the blood heat. That's what keeps Terry here—milk heated by her mother's mouth.

TERRY's *hand sticks out of the wall and takes the glass and disappears.*

JILL: Sometimes it's hard not to give up on a child, but Terry will out pace us all. [*To* TAMMY.] Now, you must go back to bed. You have your junior year to complete. As for me, I've got to go back up to my body and enter Theta sleep. Too much dreaming inflames the epithelial tissues and makes me morose and gives the ethereal body baggy eyes. Hold out a candle.

TAMMY *holds out a candle.* JILL *lights it and the lights go out while beautiful beams of light come out of the cracks everywhere, out of the windows and up from the floor.* JILL's *face is lighted by candle light. Silently she climbs the stairs. There is the sound of rain. She disappears into the master bedroom, closing the door behind her. Immediately a light in her room snaps on and we hear* JACK's *voice.*

JACK: What time is it, honey?

JILL: A quarter after four.

The light in the master bedroom fades slowly out. TAMMY *stands in the shimmering beams of light.*

TAMMY: I wish I could sleep at night. They're all out of their bodies away from the blood and the pain. I'm the only real insomniac in the house, my double seldom leaves the premises. Watch. [*She calls softly.*] Eddy?

EDDY *suddenly comes through the wall. He is dressed in brightly colored ribbons and wears a silver bi-wingers cap.*

EDDY: [*Absolutely natural.*] Yes, Sis.

TAMMY: I can't sleep.

EDDY: Neither can I.

TAMMY: Mother's been wobbling around down here like a cracked egg. She woke me up.

EDDY: Me too.

TAMMY: That's not true, Eddy. You're upstairs in bed right now.

EDDY: Don't mess with yourself, Tammy. You're liable to spike your jackle.

TAMMY: What do you mean by that?

EDDY: Short…circuit.

TAMMY: What do you mean, short circuit?

EDDY: Never wake up a sleep walker, even if they've been walking the streets for years.

> *He picks her up in his arms. She is fast asleep. He takes her upstairs. All of the lights fade out and there is the sound of rain and thunder.* TAMMY *still holds the lighted candle.*

EDDY: [*As he carries* TAMMY's *sleeping body towards the master bedroom.*]

> I cannot fly, spirit, where you do not guide me.
> If you would have me soar beyond the storm,
> Then must you beckon me over
> And I will fly to you.
> Raising my wings on a course beyond love,
> Beyond all knowledge, beyond joy,
> Beyond all human senses.

> EDDY *stands there before the master bedroom door with* TAMMY *in his arms. He stamps his foot three times. His back is to us and we see* TAMMY's *face lighted by the candle she is holding.*

EDDY: [*Speaks while* TAMMY *mouths the words.*] Mother? Mother? I want to talk to you.

JILL: [*From within her room*] Can't it wait till morning? It's four thirty.

EDDY: [*Speaks while* TAMMY *mouths the words.*] No, it can't wait, Mother.

> EDDY *puts* TAMMY *down on her feet before the door and backs towards the wall and then steps through it.*

JILL: Oh, all right. [*She opens the door.*] What is it?

TAMMY: Mother, I don't like the way you talked to me just now.

JILL: What do you mean, "just now"?

TAMMY: The way you talked to me downstairs a little while ago. About staying out of your life and that if I don't like it I should go away and find a better place.

JILL: Oh, for Christ's sake, Tammy, I'm sound asleep. Go to bed and let it wear off.

TAMMY: Oh that's fine for you to say. It's easy enough to cut somebody up and then tell them to stop bleeding. Mother, you're the only friend I have in this place.

JILL: Well, you'd better start getting around.

TAMMY: [*Aghast.*] Mother, how can you say that?

JILL: Tammy, you might as well start getting used to the reality that I'm just another person. One night I moo-mooed your father and got pregnant. The rest is goo-goo ga ga.

TAMMY: The rest is what?

JILL: Goo-goo ga ga.

TAMMY: [*Desperately.*] Goo-goo ga ga? Is that what you call my childhood? Goo-goo ga ga?

JILL: [*Unable to contain her laughter.*] I'm sorry, honey. But you have to admit it was a bit goo-goo ga ga, even now…

TAMMY: Mother, how can you say that?

JILL: Tammy, my dear [*pause*] grow up. [*She shuts the door in her face.*]

   TAMMY *pounds on the door.*

TAMMY: [*Hysterically.*] You slammed the door in my face! You slammed the door in my face! Goo-goo ga ga? You have no right to slam the door in my face, I'm your daughter.

   The door opens. It is JACK.

JACK: [*Coolly.*] What do you want?

TAMMY: [*Backing away.*] I want to talk to my mother.

JACK: [*Low.*] She's in bed.

TAMMY: I don't care. I want to talk with her.

JACK: [*Turns his head back into the room—there is mumbling. Then he turns back* TAMMY.] She doesn't want to talk to you right now. She wants to sleep [*He grins.*] with me.

TAMMY: Mama! Mama!

JACK: Let's go downstairs.

TAMMY: I don't want to go downstairs.

JACK: Okay, then I will. [*He sticks his head back into the master bedroom and meows like a pussy cat at* JILL.] Meow, meow, my little pussy, be right backy-backy, honey buns. [*He closes the door and kisses it.*] Isn't it awful, the way we act? [*He pulls a flashlight from his bathrobe pocket and lights his way down the dark stairs.* TAMMY *remains above on the landing. At the bottom of the stairs he puts the light under his chin and makes a terrible face with an accompanying sound.* TAMMY *shrieks and sobs a bit more.*] Life has its ins and outs, its ups and downs, its weird caresses, its changing roles. [*He walks the rest of the way downstairs, and sits down on the couch and snaps on a lamp.*] There are possibilities within you right now that you have had glimpses of but have had no real idea of as they pertain to the fission of catastrophy. I liken it to a pony inside of one. Do you follow? A pony that trots and walks and gallops and sometimes races. A pony you want to call home to grain and bed down. It's your reaction to things. Do you get it? I know a friend of a friend who sat on a chair just like this one. He challenged his friend to talk him out of death. But there wasn't a chance either way, because his pony was on the way to the gun in his side pocket. You see, the lad was afraid to go home with his cold gun and see himself in the dark room talking to himself about how he didn't want to die alone. He wanted to give his friend a shot of his vision, and he said, "You give me a good reason not to shoot myself and I won't," meaning, of course, that he would do it anyway. And he pulled out this big gray pistoley and he put it inside his mouth and he watched his friend go white with conviction and hot air and right there in the middle of it all it seemed so funny, him with a gun up his mouth and his friend blithering like a spigot and he wondered what his friend's face would look like after he pulled the trigger and so he did, he blew his own head off. The bomb's inside, enough to blow the world away. And you can't ever tell when some little what-not might entrigger itself and turn the pony's teeth against its own dancing flanks. Tammy, my love, my daughter, my dear little darling. Ride your pony good. Turn it into a horse you can depend on. [TERRY *pops up from behind the armchair and puts her hands over* JACK'S *eyes.*]

TERRY: Guess who!

JACK: Let me look at you. You're like a little ghost.

TERRY: I am for you, Papa.

JACK: You mean, you're not that way for everybody?

TERRY: Not for Dr. Amos. For Dr. Amos I'm a wish.

JACK: What kind of a wish?

TERRY: A wish for his daughter that passed over many, many years ago. There are lots of scientists' kids on the Otherside. I know because I cross back and forth. [*Sweetly she lets her fingers creep up his chest as she speaks.*] There are some very strange things all over the place and some people just can't get the feel for the inside of things. They have a ringing in their ears.

> Just at that moment there is the sound of a distant, approaching siren. EDDY bursts in. His PJ's are tattered.

EDDY: [*Out of breath.*] Tammy's finally menstruating again!

> TAMMY *gets up off of her knees and knocks lightly on the door to the master bedroom.*

TAMMY: Mama? Mom? Mother? Dad told me the most wonderful story about a pony I have inside of me. And Mom, I feel it. I do! I do!

> JILL *hands out a box of Kotex.*

JILL: Here you are, honey.

TAMMY: Oh, thank you, Mom. [*To* EDDY, JACK *and* TERRY *below.*] It's a Merry Christmas! [*She exits into her bedroom.*]

JACK: What time is it?

EDDY: [*Just simply knowing.*] Five AM.

JACK: It's almost time to get up.

TERRY: It's almost time for your sun to rise.

> JACK *crosses to the front window. He pulls the curtains back in a single stroke, revealing a solid wall. Everybody shrieks at the sight of it.*

JACK: Don't get excited. I think we can handle this. Here, let me push against it. [*They push against the wall and it starts to move.*] Yes, yes, it's moving!

> The little group pushes against the wall with all their might and slowly the wall begins to recede. As the wall is pushed back a dim, just perceptible light begins coming through the windows and with it the soft, muted sound of birds.

JACK: Keep pushing!

> They push harder and as they push the stone recedes and the light becomes brighter and the sound of birds becomes louder. In the middle of the effort TERRY's body begins to shudder. It is clear she is weeping.

EDDY: Can we rest a second, Dad? [*He gets* JACK's *attention and points at the weeping* TERRY.]

JACK: What's wrong, Terry, you're pale as a ghost.

TERRY: Daddy, Eddy, I can't go with you.

JACK: We're not going anywhere, hon.

TERRY: Yes, you are and I can't go with you there…ever.

JACK: Where do you mean?

TERRY: You'll find out. [*She struggles to hold back her tears.*]

EDDY: What is it, Terry?

TERRY: I've got to go back now, I hear Elly calling. [*She backs away.*] There are some places that will never meet. I guess that's because all of us are part Thing. And someday, some of us will never meet again. [*She continues backing toward her wall.*] In a strange way it makes us all one like blind creatures filling an endless well getting wetter and wetter and blacker and blacker with my tongue in your mouth and your feet in my stomach. Someday I may never *ever* see you again but just right now and now and now. [*She has backed up to her wall. The panel slides open and a strange red glow fills the room. There is the sound of pulsating steam and the humming of machinery. She stands pausing at the threshold. Then suddenly she runs to* EDDY *and* JACK *and throws her arms around them. Then suddenly she dashes away from them into the opening in her wall, calling as she runs.*] Goodbye, I remember…

    EDDY *runs to* TERRY's *wall but it is closed tight.*

EDDY: Terry! Terry! Dad, what happened? What was she talking about?

JACK: I don't know. We won't need her for this thing.

EDDY: Dad, don't be so cold.

JACK: Don't get melodramatic. Come on, let's push this thing out.

    EDDY *joins* JACK *and again they begin pushing against the stone.*

EDDY: [*Grunting.*] It won't budge.

JACK: Come on, put some belly into it.

    Again they dig into the work, pushing with all their strength. Again the huge block begins to recede and as it does the light continues to grow and the sounds of the birds becomes louder.

EDDY: Dad, it's really moving!

JACK: Yes, I know, keep pushing!

    As they push the sound of the stone's grating becomes audible and the dawn breaks more and more until it fills the whole house with light.

JACK: [*Grunting as he exerts himself.*] Come on just a bit more!

    They heave and shove and as they do the stone moves and the dawn breaks more and more. JACK *and* EDDY *stop.*

JACK: Are you ready?

EDDY: [*Out of breath and excited.*] Yes!

JACK: Okay then…

    They shove and suddenly the huge stone falls away and light blazes through the hole. Out on the backdrop there is the color of a primeval dawn and mountains. There are birds singing joyously everywhere and soft breezes. EDDY *and* JACK *stick their heads out the hole in the wall.*

EDDY: God, look Dad!

JACK: Yes, I can see!

> JILL *suddenly appears on the other side of the hole. She is beautiful with her hair piled up on her head and wearing a Grecian robe. She is carrying an empty bird cage with the cage door open.*

JILL: Well, what are you two waiting for? Come on out. Tammy's here too.

TAMMY: [*She too is on the other side, radiantly attired.*] Come on out, you guys, I'm playing Hippolytus.

JILL: But you've got to leave everything behind.

> JACK *and* EDDY *strip.*

JACK: [*Now naked, steps through.*] Like the skin of the snake.

EDDY: [*Also naked, and stepping through.*] I think I remember this place.

JILL: Here, clean up after yourselves.

> *They pick up the stone and repeg the hole. The stone is now very light. They, of course, disappear behind the wall. Upstairs there is a ringing of an alarm clock. Then another one joins it. And then another one. And then from another room the sound of a clock. Then one after another, each alarm clock is turned off.* JILL *comes out of the master bedroom in a bathrobe singing to herself. She stops on the landing.*

JILL: Now don't turn those alarms off prematurely, that is *before* you're out of bed. [*She comes down the steps.*] I love it. Children all around me. My husband. A growing nation full of schools. [*She goes to the table and begins setting it.*] And now, at last, it's breakfast.

> EDDY *begins singing scales in his room. Then from* TAMMY*'s room comes the sound of an electric razor.*

JILL: [*Shouting up at the rooms as she continues to set the table.*] Jack, remember not to use the electric razor with shaving lather.

EDDY: [*Sticking his head out the door, his face covered with lather.*] It's not Dad, it's Tammy.

JILL: Tammy, remember the last time you used the electric on your arm pits, it gave you a rash.

EDDY: [*Snickering.*] She's not using it on her pits, she's shaving her wig.

JILL: Tammy, don't use the electric on your wig, the plastic gets caught in the gears. And Eddy, don't be such a snitch.

> EDDY *sticks his head back in his room and closes his door.*

JILL: [*Calling as she sets the table.*] Jack, are you up yet?

JACK: [*His voice muffled behind the door.*] Yes, honey.

JILL: Jack, is anything wrong? You be careful now, we don't want any mishaps.

> JACK *opens his door. His head is stuffed up into a white porcelain pitcher.*

JILL: [*Seeing* JACK*'s state*] Eddy?

EDDY: [*The top of his head also covered with lather as well as his entire face.*] Yes Mom?

JILL: Help your father.

EDDY: Jesus Christ, Dad! What happened to your face?

JACK: I was trying to rinse out my eyes.

EDDY: Yuk-yuk. Here, let's go to the bathroom.
> *They go into the master bedroom.*

JILL: Tammy? Tammy?

TAMMY: [*From within her room.*] Yes, Mother, I'm awake.

JILL: This family is awake! Come on, it's breakfast!
> *Everyone comes out from upstairs and stands on the landing looking down at* JILL. EDDY *is in a nice black suit,* TAMMY *wears a green dress and* JACK *is in an overcoat and bowler. They softly applaud* JILL.

EDDY: [*After they have finished clapping.*] Mom. [*He smiles warmly and tenderly at* JILL.] Thank you.

TAMMY: [*Stepping forward.*] Thank you, Mother.

JACK: Honey, the Visigoths kept it warm between the loins of horses.

JILL: And?

JACK: And what's for breakfast?

JILL: Me.
> *She takes her shoes off, steps up onto the table and lies down on it. There is a knocking on the front door.*

EDDY: Don't get up Mom, I'll get it.
> *He dashes down the stairs and opens the door.* TERRY *is standing there. The wind is blowing and she has an open umbrella and a cute little dress. She looks exactly like the 1941 Morton's Salt girl. In fact, she is carrying a box of salt.*

TERRY: When it rains, it pours. [*She steps in, the salt pouring out in a trail behind her.*]
> *They all come and stand around the table where* JILL *is lying.*

EDDY: Here Mom. [*He goes over and gets a blanket and throws it over* JILL.]

TAMMY: [*Seating herself.*] Oh aren't you gallant.

JACK: [*Seating himself.*] Mamacopia.
> *They pull various fruits from under the blanket.*

JACK: Eddy, I heard what happened at school yesterday. And I want to tell you that you handled yourself well under the circumstances. But you shouldn't let a guy beat you up. No matter what. Even if it hurts you, you should keep swinging. Listen, if he knocks you down just get up and keep swinging. And then if he knocks you down just get up and keep swinging just like Jason and the Argonauts. Remember those skeletons that kept coming up out of the earth even though the hero sliced them to pieces? They just kept coming up and coming up, the little pieces would turn into skeletons and would just keep popping up from the ground as if his own violence had bred them. That's what you've got to do too. Down you go. Up you pop. Down you go. Up you pop. And up you pop and up you pop until he exhausts himself on you and icy fear will creep into his veins. It will! And he'll see that no matter how hard he hits you, you won't cry. Look at me, Eddy. Just make little sniffs like this when you want to cry. See. Little sniffs and bury your eyes into your head like a dead man and get up off of the ground, bleeding and all and come at him with your arms rounded in the cosmic mudra and head at him like a missile towards his heart. Remember that he has a beating heart. It must beat and it must beat and it must beat. And it will pull you to it like a heat guided lover. So keep yourself towards that heat delivered up by his beating heart and sniff your tears back and if he round-houses you like this, and your head snaps to the side like this, let a flag of your blood whip out at him like a sun spurt and splash his face with it so that his heart quickens at the thought of it. When his face is hit by your blood it will worry his heart and it will beat faster and he will begin to strain from the ages of absolute non-existence from which his heart issued itself up like a dream. And Eddy, he will become afraid and his blood will chill and he will stop pushing you around, the dirty, ugly mother-fucker will stop pushing you around and when he sees you on the street he will smile at you kindly. He will be more understanding. You will have him in your HASPS! And there will be girls in your life like you've never known before. The age of heroes is eternal and anyone who tells you differently is merely trying to hold you down. Don't let them hold you down! When you are a hero then the age of heroes is! And they will say "Heroes live!" But where there are no heroes the age of heroes lies dormant like spring ground under snow. There are no signs to watch for. You are the sign. Will you do that for me? Don't go down!

EDDY: Yes, Dad. I won't go down.

> EDDY *gets up from the table.*

EDDY: [*Bending over and kissing* JILL.] Thanks, Mom.

> JACK *gets up and accompanies* EDDY *to the door. He stops and looks at* EDDY.

JACK: Goddamn it, Eddy, I hope I did right by you in your childhood.

EDDY: You did, Dad. [*He puts a hand on* JACK's *shoulder.*] Thanks.

JACK: [*Puts a hand on* EDDY's *shoulder.*] Ditto.

EDDY: [*Calling to* TAMMY.] Sis?

TAMMY: [*Looking up from her fruit.*] Yes?

EDDY: [*Earnestly.*] Have a nice day.

TAMMY: You too, Eddy.

EDDY: Terry?

TERRY: Yes, Eddy, me too, I too will have a nice one.

JACK: Be cool, honey.

EDDY: [*Earnestly.*] I will.

JACK: [*Pointing at the door.*] Into it.

EDDY: Bang bang. [*He takes a deep breath, opens the door and dives out of sight.*]

JACK: [*Chuckling to himself, excited.*] Goddamn, goddamn! I can feel this day coming up through my shoes. I'm going to make it this time. I'm going to beat him to work. I even think I know where he leaves it. [*He turns around and goes to the closet, opens the door and pulls out a brief case and holds it over his head.*] See? [*He laughs.*] See? [*Then he pauses.*] Only one thing. I have to go to the bathroom.

JILL: Don't do it, Jack. Go and do it in the sink if you have to but stay out of the upstairs bathroom.

JACK: [*Uneasy.*] You're right. I'm obsessing. No, no, into the sink or my pants. But honey, I've got to…[*He goes over and whispers into* JILL's *ear.*]

JILL: That's okay, we have a garbage disposal. Tammy, throw a sheet over your father.

TAMMY: With pleasure.

> JACK *sits on the sink and* TAMMY *throws a sheet over him.* JACK's *pants drop from beneath the sheet.*

JILL: Haven't you two buttoned up your little squabble?

TAMMY: I don't think we ever will, Mom.

JILL: [*Knowingly.*] Oh yes, you will, someday.

TAMMY: You know this is hopeless. He'll never go outside.

> *Suddenly* JACK *gives a holler and disappears into the sink leaving an empty sheet.*

JILL: I don't know honey, somehow I keep hoping. But perhaps you're right. Perhaps the world is only Taughter.

TAMMY: Talkter?

JILL: Talkter.

TAMMY: What do you mean "Talkter?"

JILL: It's like "laughter" only it's talking. Well, pull this blanket off me. [*She gets up off the table.*] Terry, you haven't said a thing.

TERRY: That's because God didn't give me anything to say until just now.

TAMMY: I'm going, Mom.

JILL: See you tonight.

TAMMY: [*Stops by the door.*] Oh, Mom?

JILL: Yes?

TAMMY: I had the most wonderful night last night.

JILL: You did?

TAMMY: Yes, it was sort of a breakthrough. I had a lot of dreams...[*Her voice trails off and she looks at* JILL.] You were in them. [*She looks at* TERRY.] So were you.

JILL: And so was I.

TERRY: Me too.

> *They all laugh.*

TAMMY: You know what I'm going to be when I grow up?

JILL *and* TERRY: What?

TAMMY: I'm going to be a personal psychologist.

JILL: [*Going to the closet and pulling out a huge hat with an enormous green feather.*] Here, try this on for size.

TAMMY: [*Putting on the hat.*] Oh, I feel just like Dorothy and the Tornado!

JILL: Watch out for the winds of time.

> TAMMY *steps out the door and is whisked away by a powerful wind.*

JILL: [*Turning to* TERRY.] Now, my little gear cutter, it's time for you to vacillate.

TERRY: [*Laughing.*] If you only knew. Well, [*she heads for the wall*] I'd best be in. [*She stops and turns toward* JILL.] Mom, this afternoon is going to be very sunny and warm. Preschoolers are going to be riding their trikes and the sidewalks are going to be all white with long strips of sunshine and the grass will be amazingly green. Open all of the windows and go upstairs and make love. "Today." [*Said like "good-bye."*]

JILL: Today.

The panel in the wall slides open. There is an alien sound of throbbing, humming engines. It is as if there was an enormous place down there. TERRY *waves sweetly and the door slides shut in front of her.*

JILL *opens all of the windows. The light streams in. The sound of a clear spring day is heard. Preschoolers are playing outside and there is the sound of birds and distant laughter.* JILL *is humming. She looks up toward the master bedroom. She lets her bathrobe fall from her. She is naked.*

JILL: [*Calling sweet and low.*] Jack?

She climbs the stairs as the lights fade into darkness.

OyamO

∾

The Resurrection of Lady Lester

A Poetic Mood Song
Based on the Legend of Lester Young

Production History

The Resurrection of Lady Lester was nominated for the *Plays in Process* series by Lloyd Richards, artistic director of the Yale Repertory Theatre in New Haven. It was presented there as part of the new play festival, "Winterfest," from January 21 until February 21, 1981.

James A. Simpson directed. The set was designed by Michael H. Yeargan and Kevin Rupnik, costumes by Dunya Ramicova and Douglas Stein, and lighting by Michael H. Baumgarten. Music for the Yale production was composed and arranged by Dwight Andrews, who also directed a musical band consisting of himself, Paul Sullivan, Mario Pavone and Pheeroan Aklaff. The cast, in order of appearance, was as follows:

WOMAN IN BLACK, WHITE MARIE	Cecilia Rubino
LESTER YOUNG	Darryl Croxton
SARAH, TUTA, AGATHA	Zakiah Barksdale Hakim
VOICE, GRAND MARSHALL, SWOOP, MOUSE	Scott Rickey Wheeler
BOOBOO, TWEED, SLUMP, SERGEANT	David Alan Grier
MISS LADY, LADY DAY	Isabell Monk
POOKY, LINCOLN	Reg E. Cathey
EXHORTER, DR TRAMB, MANAGER, MAJOR	Clarence Felder

An earlier version of *Lady Lester* was performed at the Yale Cabaret in 1979. The play was subsequently produced in its present form at the Yale Repertory Theatre and then at the Manhattan Theatre Club from October 22 to November 22, 1981.

Playwright's Note

I call this piece "a poetic mood song based on the legend of Lester Young" because it does not attempt to present Lester Young's life as chronological biography or as factual "docudrama." This piece is not a schoolroom lesson on an eccentric American genius. Just as Lester used the standard notes of a given melody to create a hundred new melodies and just as he used the words and grammar of English to create his own poetic language, so too have I used the *"legend* of Lester Young" to create a universal story of an American musical hero. I sought his essence, not his obituary. This play is intended for a general theatre audience as opposed to the specialized audience of jazz cultist "Lestorians."

The structure of the piece is informed by Young's musical style which broke most conventions in an easy, laid-back virtuosity that used rhythm but was not dominated by it, and the mysterious nature of memories which are not bound by traditional dramaturgical considerations. The entire piece is designed to flow like music across the stage, but it is not to be simply another black musical revue.

The casting arrangement itself makes a statement. Each actor has to play several characters in Lester's life and the several roles that an actor plays may themselves be subtly interrelated; however, each role is separate and requires distinct character work.

The language of this play is an extension, of sorts, of Lester's linguistic inventions, but actors should not get hung up on attempting to recite "poetry." They should simply speak the words with the passion of ordinary dialogue. If the character is achieved, the words will speak for themselves. There is much intended humor in this piece which should be consciously played to balance against the tragic aspects of Young's brief life. A lexicon of jazz argot could be helpful for those words which might not be understood in context.

The play moves in time. It begins near his death, backs up a year, leaps back to his childhood, comes forward to his incipient manhood, leaps ahead to the year before his death, leaps back to his peak years in the thirties and early forties, and finally leaps ahead to where the play begins. So Lester's age, health and mental attitudes change several times in the course of the play's movement.

The staging should be clean and simple. It should keep the action moving forward crisply. The stage should not be encumbered with too much set or set pieces. Lighting is most important to create mood, change scenes, and give the feeling of actual physical movement where appropriate. Characters should "appear" and "disappear" with proper lighting techniques. The playing area should be fairly large. Running time with intermission should not exceed two hours.

I would naturally expect some of the music that goes with the piece to differ in each production because of the nature of jazz itself; it is improvisational, and since the piece requires a live band, the musical director and some of the music and many of the musical arrangements will change with each production. With the exceptions of "Goodbye Porkpie Hat," "Come and Go To That Land," "Old Black Joe," "Dixie," "Curse of Mora," "D.B. Blues," "Darn That Dream," "Strange Fruit," "Dried Up Corncob Blues," "Three Little Words" and "Ain't No Place Like the Open Road," the specific tunes suggested in the script can be replaced depending on the nature of the production. Limited rights to use the music are available from various owners for small fees. For convenience, a list of songs that have been used in one or more of the three productions this play has had so far is appended.

Most important, it is crucial that the director of this piece be reasonably comfortable with or be willing to work toward its nontraditional form.

About Lester Young

Lester Willis Young died on March 15, 1959, after a lifetime devoted to music. Born in Mississippi in 1909, Young was the son of a musician who had studied at the Tuskegee Institute and who performed in a traveling carnival band. Young learned how to play many musical instruments (including alto sax), but first worked in the family band as a drummer. At 18, he left his family to join Art Bronson's Bostonians, a Kansas jazz band that switched him from alto to tenor sax. In the early thirties, Young played with a number of groups in the Midwest, at one point leaving Count Basie to replace Coleman Hawkins, reigning king of the tenor, in the Fletcher Henderson band. Disinclined to imitate Hawkins' bold and breathy style, Young resigned and soon became part of Basie's Reno Club combo. From 1936 to 1940, he was one of Basie's star soloists. Young often recorded with Billie Holiday, with whom he formed a close personal and professional relationship; in return for dubbing her "Lady Day," Holiday nicknamed him "Prez"—the president of all saxophonists. After leading a number of small groups of his own—largely unsuccessful ventures—Young rejoined Basie in 1943. In 1944, he was drafted into the u.s. Army, which soon imprisoned him for drug possession (a photograph of Young's white second wife seems the more probable cause). After a dishonorable discharge, Young returned to jazz, but was overwhelmed by the new generation of tenors imitating his style. Both critics and fellow musicians derided him as a parody of his former self. Despite a moment of calm provided by a third marriage which produced two children, Young soon drank himself into bad health. He spent the last years of his life in a seedy hotel overlooking Birdland, a New York jazz club, attended by a girlfriend and a sympathetic doctor. In early 1959 he played an engagement in Paris; less than 24 hours after returning to his New York hotel room, he died.

Music For The Play

Production of the play requires five musicians: a pianist, a bassist, a drummer, and two multi-instrumentalists on reeds and winds.

Traditional songs [public domain]:
1. "The Curse of Mora," arranged by William Arms Fisher, available in William Arms Fisher, ed., *Sixty Irish Songs* [Boston: Oliver Ditson, 1915].
2. "Old Black Joe"
3. "Dixie"

Music credits [in alphabetical order]:
1. "Ain't No Place Like The Open Road" by Dwight Andrews & OyamO, Black Angel Music
2. "Birdland Jam" by Dwight Andrews, Black Angel Music
3. "Come And Go To That Land" by Sam Cook, used by permission of Venice Music

4. "Darn That Dream" by James Van Heusen & Edward Delange, used by permission of Lewis Music and Scarsdale Music Corporation
5. "Detention Barrack Blues" by Sydney Shemel, Unart Music Corp.
6. "Dried-Up Corn Cob Blues" by Dwight Andrews & OyamO, Black Angel Music
7. "Flying Home" by Buddy Robbins, Regent Music Corp.
8. "Goodbye Porkpie Hat" by Charles Mingus, used by permission of Jazz Workshop, Inc.
9. "Lester Leaps In" by Lester Young, used by permission of Bregman Vocco & Conn, Inc.
10. "Lester's Death Music" by Dwight Andrews, Black Angel Music
11. "Lush Life" by Billy Strayhorn, used by permission of Tempo Music, Inc.
12. "Miss Lady Ballad" by Dwight Andrews, Black Angel Music
13. "Three Little Words" by Bert Kalmar & Harry Ruby, used by permission of Warner Brothers Music

Original music [from Yale production]:
1. "Corn Cob Blues"
2. "Jam Session"
3. "Scat"
4. Arrangements of traditional and protected songs
5. Incidental music in all scenes, including a quotation of "Three Little Words." For all of the above, contact: Dwight Andrews, 94 Lake Place, New Haven, Connecticut 06511.

Sound cue:
1. Original recording of a song sung by Billie Holiday [Second Movement]

CHARACTERS

In order of appearance

> WOMAN IN BLACK, WHITE MARIE, a white actress
> LESTER YOUNG, a black actor
> SARAH, TUTA, AGATHA, a black actress
> VOICE, GRAND MARSHALL, SWOOP, MOUSE, a black actor
> BOOBOO, TWEED, SERGEANT, a black actor
> MISS LADY, LADY DAY, a black actress
> POOKY, SLUMP, LINCOLN, a black actor
> EXHORTER, DR TRAMB, MANAGER, MAJOR, a white actor

The play requires eight actors, seven of whom must play multiple roles.

FIRST MOVEMENT

The MUSICIANS *ethereally improvise upon Mingus' "Goodbye Porkpie Hat." A veiled* WOMAN IN BLACK *helps* LESTER *enter into what we'll come to understand as a "hotel room." This "hotel room" is a surrealistic suggestion that exists in a defined patch of light. The space must be flexible enough to transform itself through shifts in lighting into various suggestions of other spaces that exist in the illusions of the "real world" of which the audience think they are. He carries his horn case and she both supports him and carries his small suitcase. She is so completely clothed in black that we cannot discern her race or nationality. He is sick and stumbling and coughing blood. She's very careful and gentle, but anxious. She helps him sit down; takes off his long black cape, his jacket, porkpie hat and pants; unbuttons his shirt. A bottle of gin falls out of his jacket pocket. She doesn't try to retrieve it. The bass line of the music lingers beneath their voices.*

WOMAN IN BLACK: You should have seen a doctor before you left Paris.

LESTER: But, Lady, I was at the airport fixin' to climb on a bird.

WOMAN IN BLACK: Orly is an international airport; they have doctors on call.

LESTER: You're the only doctor I trust, Miss Lady.

WOMAN IN BLACK: But I'm not a doctor, Les.

LESTER: You care about me and it's better to be near you now. I need to be home, Lady.

WOMAN IN BLACK: Home? The Alvin Hotel on Fifty-second Street in New York City? This is no place to come and be sick, baby.

LESTER: It's the home of the brave; it's where the music left me. I couldn't run from this monster all my life; I couldn't understand in Paris.

WOMAN IN BLACK: Couldn't understand what?

LESTER: What I been feelin' all these years.

    LESTER *coughs violently. Blood spurts onto the handkerchief.*

WOMAN IN BLACK: Lie down, Lester. It'll be easier to breathe. Please, Lester let me call an ambulance. There's too much blood.

LESTER: Don't call no ambulance! Just let me work with my bruises before this jam blows away.

WOMAN IN BLACK: Jam? What? Lester, I'm going to go call Dr. Tramb. I've got to do that much! It'll be all right, baby. Lie still; wait for me.

    She exits. The bass line flows into another tune emanating from the Birdland. LESTER *struggles up at the sound of the music. He sits for a moment gathering his strength and listening. He sees the gin bottle and goes over to it, opens it, pours a small libation and drinks deeply which causes him to cough heavily for a moment.*

He retrieves his porkpie hat and his horn and walks over to glare through the "windowpane." He tries to blow a note or two but always ends up coughing and drinking more gin to relieve the coughing. He begins to pace and mumble unintelligibly to himself about "repeater pencils," "machineguns," "jive, half-ass musicians"and the like. He fingers ghost notes on the tenor sax and frequently wipes his mouth with the handkerchief. The music fades out. He begins singing in a common blues pattern. His feeling is 100 percent but his voice is sick and incompetent.

LESTER:

> *Um just a dried-up corn cob*
> *Singing in the sweet hot sun*
> *Um just a dried-up corn cob...*

[*Talking*] What's wrong? You don't think I can sing? I can carry a melody at least and when I drop this lip extension [*Indicating his horn*] in my chops, I blow soft little stories that make you cry they sound so true.

Singing again but with musical accompaniment.

LESTER: [*Continued*]

> *Um just a dried-up corn cob*
> *Dusty in the sweet hot sun*
> *Um just a dried-up corn cob*
> *Dusty in the sweet hot sun*
> *My blood is flyin' away*
> *I guess my trip is almost done*

Talking blues. Stop time.

LESTER: [*Continued*]

> *I had all the women*
> *Drank down all the wine*
> *Blue up all the notes*
> *Ran a million stop signs*

Talking again, with music under.

How yaw feelin'?
How yaw feelin' peekin' at a phony ghost?
The Prez, Mr. Lester Young, President—
I was president when presidents were good men and bop was in—
I know yaw out there listening;
I may be sick, crazy, talk to myself, drink gin like a dog, and black,
But I ain't no communist;
I'm just yo' typical, innocent unamerican—[*Pointing to his head*]

Everybody I want to say anything to is right here, you dig?
They can't be no other place now,
But somebody up here knows something,
Something that I have to know now.
I have been resurrected from the Land of the True Living Harmony
Where God sings in everybody's soul
And we all got it made—
I came here in the first beat to live,
You dig?
I came to hear a vision of simple love,
Fresh love, you dig?
I wanted to serve the Music
And smile bravely in its light
Because I had to—
I had to feel my way in the music—
I was a dumb child
And the music led me to secrets
Hidden in my own heart,
Secrets about what really matters
When you know you're a human person
And not a human monkey.
I came here to jam with my fellow sounds,
To help weave a cloth of light, soft harmony,
So my family,
None of you,
Don't have to be naked
In this drafty-ass world of the intelligent beast—
But there was something I didn't see—
There was something I never found—

> *He takes a drink. A late fifties rendition of* LESTER's *"Red Boy Blues" abruptly evolves from the previous blues. It is an imitation of his style. He listens for a moment, grows immensely agitated, and says derisively:*

You hear *that* music?
That's Birdland—
I once blew a hole in the roof over there
And went through to Mars—
Them gentlemen there;
Listen to 'em;
They all had the same music teacher at Juilliard,
But tryin' to repeat after me—I should go show them where it's at—
I'll go show them how to feel free at the soul's bottom,
Where easy mellow breeze flows through silver lips
And THE MUSIC IS THE ENTIRE CREATION—

He retrieves his pants, but before he can put them on:

VOICE: Sarah! Yoohoo, Sarah!

> LESTER *tries to ignore the male* VOICE, *but stops trying to put on his pants. The* VOICE *is literally singing the initial salutations.*

VOICE: [*Continued*] Sarah! Sarah! Yoohoo, baby!

> LESTER *throws his pants down and shouts at the* VOICE *in his head as if through the "window."*

LESTER: Scratch the racket, Bohannon. Whas happnin'?

VOICE: [*Mocking incredulity*] Prez?! Prez! Yo Prez, is that sho nuff you?

LESTER: Who the hell you think it is?

VOICE: Damn Prez, I ain't seen you in three years, since 1955. I thought you was dead.

LESTER: Ding dong! You thought *I* was dead? Man, I'm probably more alive than you ever been! And I'm fixin' ta come out back there and jam.

VOICE: Jam what, poppa? I could sneeze into my tenor sax and blow you off the bandstand.

LESTER: Drag yo' young rusty tail to the Birdland and wait.

VOICE: I know you don't mean *the* Birdland. We hurt old cats like you over there; we'll cut you up till you look like used chitlins.

LESTER: They can't cut a knife sharpener. I keep them chumps sharp.

VOICE: Awww Prez, back off; I'm feelin' too good for all that bullshit. I came to check out Sarah.

LESTER: I ain't her salesman, you dig?

VOICE: Look, tell Sarah I'm playin' 'cross the street at the Birdland.

LESTER: Do you know who you talkin' to?

VOICE: I'm talking to somebody who used to be the president, but right now you just another old, sick, no playing, tired ass gin head!

> LESTER'S *reply is a long, mean burst from his horn that ends in a coughing fit and a hearty swallow of gin. He softly blows the first three notes of* "Three Little Words" *and repeats it twice. His mind summons* SARAH *to the space and she "appears." It is apparent that she has just finished giving herself a fix. She wears a flimsy, sexy dress, has streaked hair and a business-like manner.*

SARAH: [*Putting away her dope-taking tools*] I feel like a whipped fish already and I still got six more hours to work.

LESTER: I hear that.

SARAH: My legs. My legs ache so much.

> LESTER *comes to her, pushes aside his horn, kneels before her, begins massaging her calves.*

LESTER: Concrete is hard on the soul. Relax yo' legs.

SARAH: [*Giggling*] Your fingers feel like you playing a solo on my leg, and it tickles.

LESTER: You got some pretty sounds laughing in this leg, baby. Why don't you take the night off?

SARAH: [*Stiffening*] Take the night off what?

LESTER: Take the night off your legs.

SARAH: [*Snatching her legs away*] But this hotel room is off my legs that brings in money every night so we can have some place to sleep, eat and act like normal people during the day.

LESTER: Normal peoples died out wayback yonda. Just they ghosts left out here now.
Pause.

SARAH: Les, you shouldn't stay up here all by yourself so much. People say you be up here talking to yourself in different voices. Go to the Birdland and play music or get something to eat.

LESTER: I ain't into no grit.

SARAH: Lester, you need to eat some food to soak up that liquor so your guts don't rot. [*Offering him money*] Take this and get you something to eat.

LESTER: My teeth ain't ready for no grit.

SARAH: Cut the food up good so you don't have to chew it, or order some soup.

LESTER: Scratch the grit, Sarah; I'd rather have a drink.

SARAH: My prize buffalo always say, "The sauce will cook you."

LESTER: I'm all right, Sarah. I don't need no advice from your buffalo.

SARAH: You won't be all right for long if you keep drinking and not eating. At least you oughtta take them vitamins that Dr. Tramb left for you.

LESTER: Them pills taste horrible with gin. Besides, they ain't no more.

SARAH: No more? All them pills gone that quick. What you do with them?

LESTER: I didn't do shit with 'em. They disappeared some way.

SARAH: [*Reoffering the money*] Take this down to the drugstore on Forty-second Street and git some more.

LESTER: My eyes ain't bulging for no vitamin pills.

SARAH: Lester, this is stupid; you got to take something besides wine and gin. I wish I had me somebody like Dr. Tramb looking out for me. That be just what I need to git my singin' career goin', a rich white doctor who'll take care of me and help me git famous.

LESTER: The white doctor can't do much for a black ghost.
    SARAH *leaps up.*

SARAH: Stop it, Lester! I can't stand no more! I work till my tongue hang out to keep some food and liquor and pay the rent and all you can do is sit up here on your tired black behind, sucking on that horn and that bottle and talking that stupid boogeyman crap! You gonna git sicker and sicker and then you gonna die if you don't change your ways.

LESTER: Is that a wish?

SARAH: That's a warning and you better listen if you think living is worthwhile.
    LESTER *laughs, coughs, drinks deeply.* SARAH *glowers in silence.*

SARAH: [*Continued*] Look, Lester, I'm gonna need this room tonight. You gonna have to put on your pants and go hang some place else, just for tonight, at least.

LESTER: No lady would sell her box in her own home; even ghosts know better than that.

SARAH: I'm not talking about ghosts; I'm talking about buffaloes. I need to have a convenient place to take care of my customers.

LESTER: Try the White House.

SARAH: Why I gotta support the White House Hotel? When you doin' bidness in America, baby, you got to keep your expenses down; otherwise the communists liable to start a war.

LESTER: [*Screaming at her*] DON'T TELL ME ABOUT NO WAR! I DON'T GIVE A DAMN ABOUT NO WAR!

SARAH: Lester, I'm fixin' to bring my buffaloes up here anyhow, so get lost for awhile!

LESTER: I am lost, but I know this is my squat, my place in the real world, if there is one. I created this place and it creates me over and over.

SARAH: Your place, huh? This is my place. I took you in, remember? You got another place too, don't you? You got that bitch and her babies stuck up in a nice house in Queens! You kin go lay up there. Yeah, they living good; they must be gittin' all the money from yo' records.

LESTER: Money? What money I done made? Go find it for me. Bring it here; let me feel it. I'll even tell you where it's at. Go to my scumbutt manager. Go to every greasy, crooked joint that put my name on they billboard. Go to the record companies, the radio stations and the publishing houses. Go tell them that *I,* the Prez,— me, you undastan—tell them I said to give *you* all *my* money so you kin bring it back here and let me wallow in it.

SARAH: That's just what I'm sayin'. You ain't got no money. I got to make the money, and I can't make no money with yo' black butt layin' around here messin' up my bidness.

LESTER: Yo' bidness? What is yo' bidness? When we first got together, you was a singer, or suppose to be. We was gon' make a world of music together, remember? But running after that stupid white dust cut through all the melodies and put you on the stroll. Bidness? You a little two dolla hoe; in Europe that's a bidness; in New York City it's what *they* call a social disease. That's when people done lost they self-respect.

SARAH: That's a funky lie! I do what I do and I respect myself too, understand? And it don't cost me nothin', Lester, [*Starts crying but continues ranting*] a few moans and groans, lots of petting and cooing of soft, withered egos, sweet lies and fragrant laughter. I give them chumps a bargain that benefits me. At least I still got something to sell and gon' have it for awhile.

> *She buries her sobbing face in her hands.* LESTER *blows the first four notes from* "Three Little Words" *on his horn, walks over to her, touches her wet face, speaks slowly, tenderly.*

LESTER: I don't have nothin' to sell; I got plenty love to give you and nothing else. I got to keep on till it's over—I need plenty space to blow this horn and I can't breathe in Queens, you dig? It's not the ole lady and my children; it's not really Queens; it's the music; the music is out here. This room is the open road; it's a habit and I live in the habit. [*Pause as he looks deeply into her eyes, sighs heavily*] Go back to work; when the stampede is done, you come home. I'll sing to you, wash the mud off your soul, make you pure again.

SARAH: Pure? I don't need to be pure again. Right now I need to make me some money, baby, and I want you to carry your tired, no playing black ass outta here.

> LESTER *leaps up, angry, grabs his pants and violently dons them.*

LESTER: SHEEEET! Ding Dong!

> *He drives her from his consciousness with a violent motion of his hand and she "disappears," reenters the cosmic harmony.*

LESTER: [*Continued*] You think I can't play, bitch?
You too?
The problem is you can't hear;
I plays MUSIC, pure MUSIC—
I didn't start here in *this* crippled family;
I had more than you and this marketplace—
I came from a place where they needed me
'Cause I belonged to the Music.
We used to speed the Music down the road;
We wasn't no turkey minstrels;
We was musicians;
We traveled in America
But we had a home too,
Where we had steaming mouthwatering melodies
And nice, clean, warm toilets—
NEW ORLEANS…!

> *We immediately hear the sound of a small New Orleans marching band, circa 1919, and we see a* BASS DRUMMER, HORN PLAYER *and the* GRAND MARSHALL *enter strutting and dancing ebulliently. As they march past* LESTER, *he gleefully falls into step.* TUTA, *his distressed sister, follows* LESTER *at a safe distance. The* GRAND MARSHALL *continues with his fancy dancing and strutting as he answers the* CHILD LESTER'*s questions.*

LESTER: [*Continued*] What club you all fixin' to play at? Huh?

GRAND MARSHALL: We ain't fixin' to play at no club, boy!

LESTER: Oh, you wit the carnival, sho nuff? Give me a ticket, I'll pass out handbills for you. Where the carnival gon' be?

GRAND MARSHALL: What carnival?

LESTER: The one that yaw announcin'.

GRAND MARSHALL: We ain't wit da carny folks.

LESTER: Why you playin' music?

GRAND MARSHALL: We celebrating.

LESTER: Why?

GRAND MARSHALL: We done just buried my oldest son, one of the finest musicians New Orleans ever seed.

LESTER: [*Incredulous, wide-eyed, he stops marching, but continues walking*] What?

GRAND MARSHALL: [*Laughing*] Got smashed by a truck, brains spread all over the street, but he resting; he happy now!

LESTER: He is?

GRAND MARSHALL: Oh yeah, he at peace with God; he got everything he ever needed; he got life everlasting.

> *The* MUSICIANS *and the* GRAND MARSHALL *march off.* LESTER *stops and watches them disappear.* TUTA, *careful to see that the* MARCHERS *are gone, approaches* LESTER, *grabs him and hustles him toward home.*

TUTA: This is the worse neighborhood in New Orleans! What if Booboo and Miss Lady find out we been here? With all these loud, lewd, honky-tonk darkies?

LESTER: You gon' tattle?

TUTA: No, not if you come home with me right now.

LESTER: Um comin', but don't tattle like you promised, all right?

> *Lights cut to area where* BOOBOO *is pacing furiously before* MISS LADY *and* POOKY, *seated.* TUTA *and* LESTER, *concealed, fearfully peek in at their father's rage.* BOOBOO *pulls a watch from his vest pocket, looks at it and explodes in a brief fit of shouting at no one in particular.*

BOOBOO: THIS IS THE LAST TIME THEY'LL DO THIS! I KNOW WHAT THEY NEED! YESSUH!

MISS LADY: [*Very calmly, evenly as counterpoint*] They probably forgot, dear, but they'll be…

BOOBOO: [*Interrupting*] I swear before my Lord Savior in Heaven I told them childrens to be at home by six for rehearsal because we due at prayer meeting by eight o'clock. We can't be excusing them all the time.

MISS LADY: But, Booboo, sometimes children will forget and…

BOOBOO: This band liable to fall apart if you keep singin' lullabies to they heads instead of swinging a strap on they behinds. Pooky's a child too, but Pooky's always on time; he's learning his musical discipline.

POOKY: [*Basking*] I sure am.

BOOBOO: Shut up! What time is it now?

> *As he fumbles for his pocket watch, enter* TUTA *and* LESTER *timidly. They quickly take their seats.*

TUTA: [*Shaking nervously, talking rapidly under* BOOBOO's *merciless glare*] Booboo, I was coming back here with Lester so I could be here on time and then we saw this man whose brains got smashed out by a truck they was marching back from his funeral but Lester thought it was a carnival and went chasing and I ran after him and fell down and hurt my kneeeeeee and some old men was staring and staring at my ankles and I cried, but Lester kept running and I…

BOOBOO: [*Interrupting but talking directly to* LESTER] The first thing you got to learn in a carnival band is how to be on time! The midway do not wait on some gunsel sittin' on his butt in the doniker. You supposed to be a professional musician, not a common gazoonie.

TUTA: But, Booboo, we was…

BOOBOO: [*Now directly at her, but with a faint conciliatory tone*] And Tuta, you know that you know better. I depend on you. You the oldest; you shoulda seen to it that yaw got here on time. This season you sit in on the drums.

He turns back to LESTER. TUTA *is visibly disappointed behind* BOOBOO's *back.*

BOOBOO: [*Continued*] Lester, what instruments have I taught you so far?

LESTER: Drums.

BOOBOO: And...

LESTER: Saxophone.

BOOBOO: Not saxophone! I taught you reed instruments. Reeds! I just started you with the saxophone, remember?

LESTER: Yes, Booboo, and I been practicing real hard; listen to this:

    LESTER *picks up his sax, but* BOOBOO *takes it away from him.*

BOOBOO: I heard you slurring over the scale, but did you practice your singing?

LESTER: [*Lying*] Yessir!

BOOBOO: Are you sure?

LESTER: Yessir, I practiced; you kin ask Pooky.

BOOBOO: I don't have to ask Pooky. Let me hear you sing that song I taught you at yestiddy's rehearsal. Go 'head.

LESTER: Uh...ain't the band gon' play?

BOOBOO: [*A trifle irritated*] You don't need no band to sing. I want to hear it without accompaniment, a capella, understand? A capella. Miss Lady, give him a send off.

    After MISS LADY's *mimed introduction which is actually done by the pianist, he very self-consciously clears his throat and starts to sing his own hip version of Stephen Foster's "Old Black Joe."*

LESTER:

> *Gone are the days when my heart was young and gay,*
> *Gone are my friends from...*

BOOBOO: [*Interrupting*] No boy, I know I didn't teach you to sound like that. Look at me, Lester! The power comes from here. [*Indicating his diaphragm*] You use all this [*Indicating vocal apparatus*] to shape the power into what you want it to do and then it's easier to stay in tune, understand?

LESTER: Yes, Booboo.

BOOBOO: Now listen while I go through it one time. And listen carefully. The rest of y'all sing the chorus.

    BOOBOO *correctly renders the following with chorus accompaniment.*

> *Gone are the days when my heart was young and gay,*
> *Gone are my friends from the cotton fields away,*
> *Gone from the earth to a better land I know.*
>   Chorus:
> *I hear their gentle voices calling, "Old Black Joe."*
> *I'm coming, I'm coming, for my head is bending low;*
> *I hear those gentle voices calling, "Old Black Joe."*

BOOBOO: All right, Lester, hit it again and remember what I say.

LESTER: [*Clears throat and begins singing as before*]

> Gone are the days when my heart was young and gay,
> Gone from...

BOOBOO: [*Interrupting in a burst*] Lester, this ain't no plantation show this season. We ain't working for poor jigs like us no more. We going on the road with the Velare Brothers. Them ginnies don't want no jig band that ain't got class. You got to practice them songs. For right now, Tuta, take this banjo, I'll sing and, Lester, you play the drums again.

LESTER: [*Whining loudly, miserably as places are exchanged*] Awwwww, Booboo, you said I don't hafta carry them things no more; my back still hurt every morning and...

BOOBOO: SHUT UP THAT WHINING! Don't whine, boy. Say what you got to say or shut up! No, that's right you too lazy to carry the drums, that's what! You think you ain't pretty enough with them drums.

LESTER: But I'm supposed to play the saxophone 'cause the doctor said I bent a rib from carrying them drums.

BOOBOO: [*Intimidated by his tone and responding with anger*] You 'bout to git yo' lips bent from carryin' that tone.

MISS LADY: [*Answering BOOBOO but directing it to LESTER*] It was a bruised rib, Lester, not a bent rib. Bruised badly too.

BOOBOO: [*Angrily to MISS LADY*] If he hadn't been so anxious to chase them nappy-head country girls, he wouldn't have hurt himself in the first place. [*To TUTA*] Tuta, I guess you have to go back to the drums.

TUTA: [*Quietly, sweetly*] Booboo, I don't mind playin' them drums, but I really need to practice on the banjo like you was showin' me yestiddy.

BOOBOO: [*Slightly calmed*] All right, baby, take the banjo. [*Looks around at POOKY who is obviously trying to make himself inconspicuous*] Pooky!

> POOKY *jumps.*

POOKY: Yes, Booboo?

BOOBOO: Take the drums.

POOKY: [*Trying TUTA's method*] But, Booboo, you said we gotta have a trumpet this season and I been practicing real hard just like you taught me.

BOOBOO: [*Whacking POOKY across the rear*] Don't give me no lip! Do what I say! I'll take the trumpet and sing too.

> POOKY *moves toward the drums as he malevolently glares at* LESTER *who keeps his head down to avoid* POOKY's *silent wrath.*

BOOBOO: [*Continued*] Miss Lady, you gon' have to write a few different arrangements for us now.

MISS LADY: I'll bring the new ones to rehearsal tomorrow, Booboo.

BOOBOO: [*Almost normal now*] Thank you, darlin'. All right, we got just enough time to practice one song before prayer meeting. Can we get some work done now? Let's do that new arrangement of Dixie. Lester and Tuta play through your parts first. You can share the music stand.

> LESTER *and* TUTA *begin to play in pantomime while* MUSICIANS, *off, play the music.* TUTA *plays her part precisely;* LESTER *plays beautifully around what she plays.* TUTA *reaches the end of the page and stops playing to turn the page, but* LESTER *continues on, which doesn't escape* BOOBOO's *instant attention. When* TUTA *begins playing again,* LESTER *adjusts and begins playing around her once more.*

BOOBOO: [*Continued*] Hold it!

> *They stop playing.*

BOOBOO: [*Continued*] Lester, you playing some of everybody's part; just play your part. Lester, turn the page back and play your part by yourself.

LESTER: [*Shaking*] Yes, Booboo. [LESTER *puts the horn to his mouth as he frantically tries to figure out what his part is from the notes before him. He starts to blow a note once or twice, stops, clears his throat, coughs*] Uh…I…uh…I forgot how it start.

> BOOBOO's *frustrated anger returns; he approaches* LESTER *who cringes slightly.* BOOBOO *points to the sheet music.*

BOOBOO: What do you mean, you forgot how it start? [*Stabbing at the notes*] All you got to do is read this part right here. Hum it to me, Lester, while I point to the notes. Start here. Okay, go 'head.

> LESTER *is silent.* BOOBOO *explodes.*

BOOBOO: [*Continued*] You can't read, is that what you saying? What have I been teaching you and the other childrens to do the last six months? You mean I done wasted all that time on a glooming geek? You want to be the scum that lays in the wheel ruts? Answer me one question, Lester. CAN YOU READ THE MUSIC?

LESTER: [*In tears*] I don't know how, Booboo!

BOOBOO: [*Incredulous, angry, wildly gesticulating*] You don't know how? You don't know how? You don't know how?

> *As he says the previous, he raises his arms in frustrated anger, and is about to bring them down on* LESTER *when* MISS LADY *speaks calmly but quickly.*

MISS LADY: It's almost prayer meeting time.

> BOOBOO *halts with his arms in midair over* LESTER, *but he blasts his words at* LESTER.

BOOBOO: Gimme that horn!

> LESTER *jumps at the task.*

BOOBOO: [*Contmued*] You don't belong in a house of music! Get out! You're fired!

LESTER: [*Through sobs*] But I don't wanna go, Booboo.

BOOBOO: [*Shouting*] SHUT UP THAT WHEEZING! You can't read, you can't stay. [*As he shoves* LESTER *away*] Get yo' butt out my face now! Everybody get ready for prayer meeting.

> *All, except* MISS LADY *and* LESTER, *disappear. She gets up and comes to* LESTER *who falls on his knees and clutches the hem of her dress.*

LESTER: Why can't I just play from the inside out, Miss Lady, huh? Why can't I just play inside out? I be so busy reading, I can't hear what I'm playing.

MISS LADY: Booboo won't let you come back to us unless you learn to read sheet music.

LESTER: They look like white tombstones with secret writing.

MISS LADY: Les, in this world you've got to be always on the lookout for secrets, just to survive, but still all the music comes from inside out. It all comes from God.

LESTER: I bet God don't read no tombstones.

MISS LADY: He doesn't have to because God made all music so we could better appreciate being alive.

LESTER: Yes, Miss Lady, but it seems like music 'sposed to be alive too.

MISS LADY: [*A bit flustered*] Look, Lester, music is alive because live people play it, and you got to have faith that God put Booboo here to bring you up proper. Now stop acting like somebody done chopped off your arms and legs. It's not difficult to read. Tuta and me will help you. And you know Pooky always helps you when you're in trouble.

LESTER: Pooky say he gon' kill me!

MISS LADY: I'll talk to Pooky; you just attend to the tombstone secrets. Make haste now! We got to get ready for prayer meeting.

LESTER: Wait, please, Miss Lady.

MISS LADY: [*A trifle irritated and concerned about* BOOBOO] What is it, Lester? Say it quickly!

LESTER: [*Speaking rapidly*] You think maybe Booboo could let us stay in New Orleans longer so we don't have to be traveling all the time?

MISS LADY: I thought you liked traveling with the carnival.

LESTER: I do, but…I miss the times when we used to make up songs together, in front of the fireplace and eat pan bread with molasses. We ain't done that since we started traveling. Do you remember how good it used to feel?

MISS LADY: Yes, I remember, but Lester, if Booboo say we travel, then we all got to travel. [*Bitterly*] Nothing I say can make him change his mind; nothing I ever say makes him change his mind, you understand?

LESTER: But please, Miss Lady; you can at least ask him. Please!

MISS LADY: [*Wearily*] All right, I'll talk to him. [*Seeing* LESTER *brighten and wishing to deflate his hopes*] I ain't promising nothing, Lester, but I'll talk to him.

LESTER: [*Hugging her tightly*] I love you, Miss Lady.

BOOBOO: [*Offstage*] Miss Lady, we fixin' to leave.

MISS LADY: I'm coming! Let's hurry before he starts fussin' again.

> *They move off. The colorfully dressed* EXHORTER *appears looking just like a carnival grinder and he immediately begins his ballyhoo which is directed to the audience. Carnival midway music and attendant midway sounds are heard simultaneously. The lights themselves revolve and move as if on an actual midway.* LESTER, *alone, wanders in and watches with what becomes the youthful disdain of a cynical 18-year-old.*

EXHORTER: HURRAY HURRAY HURRAY the back-end is colossal, stupendous; we got the hottest pig iron this side of Attica, Anywhere; get on Mangel's Whip, leaves your knees trembling and the Witches Waves hustles you through mysterious sights in the black underworld; we got attractions for every taste and lack of taste; there's a wild man chained to an iron bar in that tent to your left; his name is Cronus; eats nothing but mud and pussywillows; found him wandering naked in Southern California; looks like a gorilla, but has the heart of an old darkie; pay your two bits and you'll see the most amazing wonders of the world. HURRAY HURRAY HURRAY; we got the only man in the world who had a baby; we got Ethiopian minstrels; we got pet bugs for enterprising youngsters of science; we got genuine dancing and singing jigs fresh from the plantation; this is your chance of a lifetime to see pickled punks, two headed fetuses, twenty toed babies and the happiest and hottest darky band this side of the Rockies; HURRAY HURRAY HURRAY; don't miss the most exciting events in this world.

> *By this time* LESTER *has become visibly agitated and eventually disgusted with the grotesque Americana of the proceedings.*

LESTER: [*shouting*] SCRATCH SHEET!

> *The* EXHORTER *disappears. Lights cut to another space.* BOOBOO, TUTA *and* POOKY *simultaneously begin singing.* LESTER *shortly joins them and after a brief, silent admonishment about punctuality from* BOOBOO, *begins to sing sullenly. The* FAMILY *sits in what is understood to be the back of the church. The* EXHORTER, *now a rural evangelist, enter and stands at the front. The song is an old American spiritual,* "Come And Go To That Land." *It is enthusiastically and soulfully rendered by all except* LESTER. *The* EXHORTER's *accent is distinctly rural South of the 1920s.*

EXHORTER AND FAMILY:

> *Come and go to that land*
> *Come and go to that land*
> *Come and go to that land where I'm bound*
> *Peace and happiness in that land*
> *Peace and happiness in that land*
> *Peace and happiness in that land where I'm bound*
> *I got a savior in that land*
> *I got a savior in that land*
> *I got a savior in that land where I'm bound*

> *The singing ends but the* CONGREGATION *hums the tune as the* EXHORTER *fervently attempts seriously to convert audience members.*

EXHORTER: Yes, come and go to that land which is the Kingdom of Heaven, but "Except ye be born again, ye cannot," I repeat, "cannot enter the Kingdom of Heaven." I want you to remember that Christ died for your sins; He died for sins of all mankind. He was brave enough to walk the stony path of life alone, to tread up Calvary Mountain and die just so you and me and everybody that ever walked this earth could live. Praise His Holy Name. And you know, He didn't ask for much in return.

The only thing you got to do is die…and be born again in the blood of Christ. Praise His Holy Name. Jesus was a man who preached and acted a very simple philosophy. He went about the land doing unto others as He would have them do unto Him. He was such a Good Samaritan that when He found He could save humanity from the hell of confusion and pain only by giving up His own life, He willingly gave His life so that humanity, all of us, could live forever in harmony with the will of God. Praise His Holy Name. Let the wonderful message of Jesus enter your heart. Raise your voices in praise of His Holy Name.

> *The humming swings into the previous song once more. The* EXHORTER *beckons to the* CONGREGATION. LESTER, *who has been visibly moved by the vision of Jesus, rises of his own volition and proceeds to the front as the* EXHORTER *continues his spiel.*

EXHORTER: [*Continued*] Come renounce your confusion and pain berore the Lord. Show Him that you want to pay your debt. He doesn't ask much; join Him; join Him; join Him.

> LESTER *starts to kneel at the front when the* EXHORTER *firmly takes hold of* LESTER, *gently helps him up and lovingly guides him back to the colored section.*

EXHORTER: [*Continued*] And I'm happy to say that in our church we have a special place for our nigra brethren before the Lord.

> LESTER, *stunned, looks at the* EXHORTER *and* BOOBOO, *and then angrily stomps out of the church.* BOOBOO *runs after him. The others continuing humming the previous song.* BOOBOO *catches* LESTER *some short distance from the church. The lights fade up on* BOOBOO *and* LESTER *and fade down on the church.*

BOOBOO: The Lord is too big, Les; you can't run away from Him.

LESTER: It ain't Him I'm runnin' from.

BOOBOO: Use your head, boy. We got to worship the Lord someplace. This is the only church in town. Ain't none of us here. You got to go along with the custom.

LESTER: That was the last go along for me.

BOOBOO: The Lord don't care what bench you kneel at, son.

LESTER: That's cause the Lord ain't no nigga.

BOOBOO: Thou shalt not take the Lord thy God's name in vain. It's evil to turn your back on someone who loves you totally.

LESTER: Then dig my mother you scratched way back there in New Orleans. She love you, but I guess you dig Jesus more.

BOOBOO: [*Hurt, defensive*] Oh, you done gone and got hep on me, talk that jive, huh? But look at you! Eighteen years old and still crying for your mama.

LESTER: Miss Lady love all of us. She sang sweet, pretty lullabies to us, made us dream music. Now she's just another misty face in the past 'cause you split us and broke the harmony that made everything feel all right!

BOOBOO: Miss Lady got tired of the road, but the carnival is where we earn our living. These last ten years on the road is where you mastered your rudiments and became a professional musician, one of the best, I might add. Sometimes your music can be more important than anything else, even Miss Lady.

LESTER: Horseshi…

BOOBOO: [*Interrupting menacingly*] Don't you dare say it; don't you dare talk to me like that. The music got between me and Miss Lady.

LESTER: Music? What music? You mean them minstrel minuets we be playin'?

BOOBOO: What you tryin' to say, boy? You don't like the music?

LESTER: I don't like grinnin' and shufflin' and tremblin' everytime one of them crackers belch in my face.

BOOBOO: Shut up, Lester, and listen. There's some things about this world that you still don't understand.

LESTER: I understand how to stand up straight.

BOOBOO: So does a oak tree, but when a hurricane come, the oak tree bends and sways so it don't get broke in half. Yeah, I grin in the crackers' faces. I play music, any music, Dixieland too. I go along with some of their stupid, evil ways, but the music gets me what I want. Look at your feet; I put shoes on your feet. Feel your stomach; it ain't never been empty. Talk about dreaming; you children always slept in good feather beds. Think about your heart; I taught you to open your heart to the peace that Jesus offers. I may bend and sway, but I ain't never been broken.

LESTER: Oak trees make good coffins too.

BOOBOO: What does that mean, Lester?

LESTER: It mean I'm tired of being afraid to live like a man; I'm tired of playing music that I hate for people who hate me.

BOOBOO: [*Misunderstanding*] Ooooooh, I understand now. One of these days you gon' learn to stop talking in riddles. You can lead the band; I'll give you a chance. Next season we going to make some quick jumps along the grits and chittlin' circuit. You can act as band leader and choose the music. How's that sound?

LESTER: It sound like shit to me!

BOOBOO *slaps* LESTER *swiftly upon that remark.* LESTER *staggers back, holds his face, glares at* BOOBOO.

LESTER [*Continued*] The grits and chittlin' circuit. Alabama, Mississippi, Georgia— Jesus own a plantation down there, don't He? Ain't that where they roast darkies in the daylight? Ain't that where the grits is dry stones and the chittlins come from inside you? There ain't nothin' left here for me.

LESTER *walks away.* BOOBOO *shouts after him.*

BOOBOO: Go 'head! Leave! Don't come back! Keep running, keep running. You can't outrun Jesus, Lester. No, you can't. You gon' be running for the rest of your life, ungrateful, black, low-life scoundrel!

BOOBOO *and the others disappear.* LESTER's *mind returns to the "hotel room" where he paces angrily.*

LESTER: The Music had gone—
There was a empty shell,
But it wasn't no family;
We just tripped over tombstones together—
I wanted to follow the music,
Um gone!

DR TRAMB *appears.*

DR TRAMB: Follow the music to where?

LESTER: I followed the music to find my family, you dig, Dr. T.? 'Cause I knew when I found my family, I wouldn't have to be afraid no more.

DR TRAMB: Frightened of what?

LESTER: Of God, freaks, hatred, the South. I didn't ever wanna swing through the South again. I hated it. Do you know what that kind of hatred is, Dr. T.?

DR TRAMB: Everyone seems to have his own giant rock to push uphill over and over.

LESTER: What's your rock?

DR TRAMB: As you know I have two I labor at: medicine and psychology.

LESTER: Dr. Tramb, dispenser of modern drugs and hoodoo rap to wasted natives.

DR TRAMB: There's nothing modern or mysterious about vitamins and human fellowship, actually. And, speaking of vitamins, I saw your friend Sarah and she says you don't take the pills I leave for you.

LESTER: Doc, I been out on this road a long time, and I done seen a whole lotta people start taking drugs from the pusher or the doctor and they end up gittin' chained to a mountain. I don't need no strawboss walking around with my feelings in his pocket, you dig, brotha Docta?

DR TRAMB: I am not trying to control you, Lester. If I said you should try potatoes instead of gin sometime, you'd accuse me of gastro-imperialism, I suppose.

LESTER: Run it straight.

DR TRAMB: If you take the white man's vitamins, stop taking the white man's alcohol and begin eating whoever's food, you can keep your black body alive and well, and I can continue to listen to your live music.

LESTER: Sheeet! Half the cats out there playing *my* live music. What in hell is so damn special about me playing *my* live music nowadays.

DR TRAMB: Listen to me! It's that music I used to hear you play in the clubs and at the jam sessions I hunted down. It's the music you played a couple years ago at the Philharmonic concerts. That music is alive because you are. It makes even me want to believe that perhaps the human spirit has some creative potential after all. But, Prez, in today's world the art assassins will poison you with despair and bitterness if you let them, and they'll be especially brutal if your music is original. Only you can do what you do, and I'm here to help you because I need to keep hearing your live music.

LESTER: Why don't you git hip and make yo' own music?

DR TRAMB: I can. Would you like to hear it?

LESTER: [*Mockingly*] Yeah, let me hear you blow some stomp down blues. I need to hear some of your live music for a change. Go 'head!

> With a modest flourish, DR TRAMB begins to sing "The Curse Of Mora," a tune of 19th-century Irish mysticism.

DR TRAMB:

> *The fretted fires of Mora*
> *Blew o'er him in the night,*

He thrills no more at loving,
Nor weeps for lost delight...
Around his path the shadows
Stalk ever grim and high:
Spears flash in hands long withere'd,
And dented shields give cry;
Or misty woman faces
Laugh out and pass him by,
Or misty woman faces
Laugh out and pass him by,
He hears the wild green harper
Chant sweet a fairy rune,
And through the sleeping silence,
His feet must track the tune
When the world is barr'd and speckled
With silver of the moon
When the world is barr'd and speckled
With silver of the moon...

LESTER, *both amused and moved, looks silently at* DR TRAMB, *who smiles broadly, nervously but quickly and returns* LESTER's *look.*

LESTER: Them was some mean blues.

DR TRAMB: Irish, man. I was singing Irish blues.

LESTER: [*Offering him a drink*] So you a Irish muthafucka, eh?

DR TRAMB: [*Accepting the drink*] I have some Indian blood, quite a bit, as a matter of fact.

LESTER: Oh, a Irish-Indian-American?

DR TRAMB: My father was simply an Irishman who I never saw, except when I looked at my skin. My mother withered up like her people's ancient customs and died when I was a child. So, I eventually created myself a white American doctor to dull the pain of cosmopolitan living, and I sing a few random blues. It works. [DR TRAMB *consumes the remainder of his drink in one gulp*]

LESTER: It sound good, but it don't work on my pain.

DR TRAMB: It works on mine. In a world of no purpose it makes good sense to acquire a secure position from which one may dispense gifts of golden sympathy, a kind of personal foreign aid, you see?

LESTER: So America is your Great White Father now, eh?

DR TRAMB: We're all the children of America, you know? All of us are here in assorted patterns of proud flotsam; bits of bloodstained driftwood, chunks of salty egalitarian notions, and wave after wave of wandering ghosts, tribal outcasts and such. We have a *collective* monopoly on computers and Los Angeles, you know.

LESTER: But this is the real life we're living, ain't it?

DR TRAMB: Most assuredly.

LESTER: Well, they been callin' me Prez all these years, but now when I go to play, I sound like everybody else 'cause they sound like me, but I can barely earn my carfare now and my name is hanging on the bottom of the board. What kind of feelin' is this, Dr. T., where what's happening ain't really happening, except in my own head that I'm always fighting to git straight?

DR TRAMB: That question describes a condition of human life to which one adjusts. Flexibility. You have to sort of improvise your own life around our conditions. Get a fresh perspective on things; take a tour of Europe; they respect Negro musicians over there.

LESTER: I was thinking of taking another touring gig over there, maybe in '59, but…

DR TRAMB: [Interrupting] Take it now, Lester! Don't wait until next year. And take the pills! For Chrissake, you have a gift. It's criminal to destroy the body that bears the gift. You have everything you need to control the world. Others have imitated you; so what? That's a tribute, not a curse, even if they do earn more money. But you can earn money too! Stop drinking, get a good agent, work on the circuit again, stop staying by yourself so much, talk to people more, swing in the wind.

LESTER: Swing in the wind? Like strange fruit hanging from a poplar tree on Sunday?

DR TRAMB: All of that is gone, Lester! It's over. The world has more than hypocritical Christians in it.

LESTER: What else do it have, Dr. Livingstone, I presume?

DR TRAMB: For Chrissake, take your frightened ass out there and find out!

LESTER: [Leaping and shouting] SCRATCH SHEET!

> DR TRAMB *visually disappears from* LESTER's *mind as* LESTER *speaks to "himself," directly to the audience.*

LESTER: [Continued] I had enough of that. It's too drafty out there now, you understand? You and Sarah are full of different answers, but we was just thrown together in the cities, a fellowship of confusion. You think I'm afraid? Ivey divey. But I remember when I ran for president; I had to fight all the way to the top, and in the battle, what I thought I had lost, I found. I found me some family. I wasn't afraid when I had to lock horns with Swoop in a mean cutting session in Kansas City! I wasn't afraid at all!

> *We hear an almost sinister 4/4 feeling with cymbal and brushes as the lights begin ro revolve and undulate in his mind's recesses.* LESTER *begins to walk around the playing area. He strolls very slowly, very hiply. He does the profile of the coolest hipster, circa early 1930s. His left arm is held out from his body and swings back and forth. His shoulders swing from side to side, while his right arm hangs straight down his right side. Lights rise to illuminate a portion of his mind in which* SWOOP *and his sycophants await him.* SWOOP, *attired in a style which reflects his personal flamboyancy, sits on a high chair of sorts flanked by* AGATHA *and* SLUMP *who both preen him, and ingratiate themselves before him.*
>
> *Others in the club are loose and eager for the cutting session. They will encourage the contestants and dance to the music. Their dance will be a gutsy stylization of 1930s popular dances.* SWOOP *reposes in absolute self-confidence. He regards* LESTER's *approach with a kind of high style of hubristic condescension.* LESTER

reaches the "bandstand" and stops opposite at a distance from SWOOP. LESTER *mimes removing a long cape and straightening his fine "clothes. " He then stands confidently facing* SWOOP.

SWOOP: Look at you, young cat, pretty and coming pretty late; umo have to swat you quick so I can make my Chicago date.

LESTER: To put it straight I just got out my bed; I didn't think you'd be here; matta fact I thought you was dead.

SWOOP: And now I see red, but you done forgot my name; they calls me Swoop 'cause I swoops all over a lame like you.

LESTER: Fortune and face, you got 'em, Lady Swoop, but I knows my thang will sing mighty swing and make you wear out three, four pair of wings tryin' to fly in my sky, you dig?

SWOOP: Yo' mouth may be greasy and yo' lips may be fat, but um fixin' ta let yo' young black butt know where you at.

LESTER: So jam!

    SWOOP *mimes a chorus on his tenor as an offstage* MUSICIAN *plays a variation of the Hawkins style that is organic to* LESTER's *voice and the words of the first half of the following monologue. The music must be based on an early '30s Kansas City jam piece.* LESTER's *word sounds have a distinct singing quality, as if broken swing incantation of the hip Afro griot. As* SWOOP *fnishes his first chorus, he decreases his volume while* LESTER *continues speaking.*

LESTER: [*Continued*] So he jumped off his throne
And we came at each other in the middle of Creation—
The Swoop was bad; that cat could play—
He came in swinging low
Walking a steady rumble—
I leaped back, squeezed my axe,
And got ready for a sho 'nuff tumble—
    SWOOP *wails another chorus and then* LESTER *continues, the music underneath.*

LESTER: [*Continued*] He came crashing through the sound barrier,
Blew everything down to the ground,
And stomped off,
Swinging and thundering
Rollin', chargin'
Shoutin' and hollerin'
In tune to everybody's heart—
    SWOOP *wails another chorus and then* LESTER *continues.*

LESTER: [*Continued*] And just when he thought he cut me clean
I rolled over and cooked some mighty beans.
    LESTER *leaps into the fray and he and* SWOOP *exchange furious riffs for two choruses.* SWOOP *backs off after the second chorus and* LESTER *continues his solo for two more choruses. As he solos, the others including* SWOOP *gradually disap-*

pear. When LESTER *speaks again, the offstage tenor continues beneath his voice but in an ethereal stylism of the original Lester Young.*

LESTER: [*Continued*] That whole night was homecooked sounds for me;
    All I heard was new different;
    Every chorus was "in the beginning,"
    You dig?
    Moments of highness,
    Drifting through the silence of God,
    You dig?
    Floating ribbons of soft color sounds
    Stretched out forever,
    Traveling through everything alive and dead
    And loving us into One Holiness.
    I was swaying and rocking with stars I passed
    And the longer I blew the bigger my heart got.
    It kept growing and knowing with each beat
    And I blew till my blood flowed through the horn
    And turned the whole creation red
    And yellow roses in sweet green dresses
    With brown sound faces and blue hurt sighs
    And hot white tears
    Flowing down my black,
    Rolling 'cross my blazing thighs,
    Burning orange between night and day,
    You dig, ladies?
    Sun
    Sunlight
    I was Sun.
    He was The Inventor and The King.
    But I took his crown with his own Invention
    And my sweet, mellow feelings.
    Kin any of you ladies

        LINCOLN, MOUSE *and* TWEED *appear.*

LESTER: [*Continued*] Dig what I'm blowin?
    They all laugh and indulge in good-natured ridicule.

LINCOLN: This is what happens when you let them people be free.

TWEED: Why don't you climb down off yo' ass and join the race.

MOUSE: If not, at least order some drinks.

LESTER: [*Shouting to an imaginary waiter*] A round of drinks for my friends.

LINCOLN: [*At the same waiter*] And tell the manager to bring us the paychecks!

LESTER: [*Peering into the audience*] You know we gon' git the bread, and it's got to be long with this many people squeezed up in this joint.

LINCOLN: Amen.

MOUSE: We oughtta celebrate by lettin' Lincoln buy us a second round.

TWEED: Amen.

LINCOLN: Celebrate what?

TWEED: Even though we done seen each other around and listened to each other, this is the first time we ever all played on the same bandstand together.

MOUSE: And wasn't we mean as a frigid queen?

LINCOLN: We oughtta form a band and stay together.

The MANAGER *appears.*

LINCOLN: [*Continued*] Greetings, Mr. Manager, and please don't give us nothing that stretches.

MANAGER: Unfortunately, I can't write you a check.

MOUSE: We ain't too hincty to take cash.

MANAGER: You can't be paid because you weren't officially scheduled to appear.

The background music fades out.

LINCOLN: What kinda shit is this? We played music, didn't we?

LESTER: The cash register ain't stopped ringin', did it?

TWEED: We was called and told to be here tonight.

LESTER: You called yourself.

MANAGER: My secretary called and asked you boys if you wanted to be on standby. You came and played on your own accord.

LESTER: I know this ofay chump not serious.

MANAGER: I'm dead serious and I'm sorry, but that's the way it is. Look, I'll take care of your drinks and we'll call it square.

LESTER: Ding Dong!

On the "Dong," LESTER *takes a wild swing at the* MANAGER *who ducks and incapacitates* LESTER *with a lethal blow to the gut. General mayhem breaks out: screaming, glass breaking, a drunken brawl in sound and light.* LINCOLN *tosses* MOUSE *some car keys and jumps on the* MANAGER. *As* MOUSE *exits to set up the "car,"* LINCOLN *is quickly trapped in the* MANAGER's *arms.* TWEED, *who has been standing off, pretending not to be involved, hits the* MANAGER *from behind with a blackjack. The* MANAGER, *unconscious, falls.* LINCOLN *extricates himself and helps* LESTER *up.* TWEED *goes through the* MANAGER's *pockets.*

LESTER: [*Continued*] Miss Lincoln, I think we better split 'fore Bob Crosby show and put all these folks in the penitentiary. Is the royal carriage prepared?

LINCOLN: Brother Mouse got the elephant saddled and ready to shake.

LESTER, TWEED *and* LINCOLN *run to another emerging area at the sound of a police siren. The sounds of the brawl fade out as they enter the "car," four chairs in two rows facing the audience.*

MOUSE: Where to, Mr. Young?

LESTER: Lady Mouse, since I'm the King, take me to my throne and please feed this elephant to death.

They all laugh as the engine roars them off. MOUSE *mimes driving and breaks into a spontaneously improvised song in which eventually the others join with fur-*

ther embellishment. LESTER *passes a pint bottle of gin and* TWEED *lights up a stick of herb.*

MOUSE:

> *Ain't no place like the open road*
> *Singing, swinging all the way*
> *Ain't no place like the open road*
> *Leave your blues to yesterday*

ALL: *Ain't no place like the open road*
> *Singing, swinging all the way*
> *Ain't no place like the open road*
> *Leave your blues to yesterday.*

They all begin doing an embellished "head" scatting of the melodic line, each in the range of his particular instrument. Though each voice embellishes distinctively, the four voices remain in perfect harmony and basic rhythm. During the scatting, the lights fade to black.

SECOND MOVEMENT

The car. In the following car riffs LESTER *and the others may sound verbally hostile to each other but their verbal jibes, no matter how harsh sounding, are generally "macho" expressions of genuine mutual affection and respect.* MOUSE *sings happily while he drives. The others are asleep.* LESTER *stirs and wakes.*

LESTER: Where we at?

MOUSE: [*Stoically*] We lost.

LESTER: [*Starting and waking the others*] LOST! DAMN! Wake up yaw!

TWEED: What! What! What!

LINCOLN: What's the problem?

LESTER: We lost.

LINCOLN: [*Irritated*] Don't say that; we ain't lost yet.

LESTER: If Mouse don't know where we at, we must be lost! We lost.

TWEED: [*To* MOUSE *in jesting derision*] Blind turkey butt, why don't you look at the map.

MOUSE: 'Cause you 'sposed to be reading the map.

TWEED: You know damn well I can't read.

LINCOLN: Yaw just watch the road signs; look for Cincy. I ain't never seen such blind niggas in all my life. It's a wonder yaw find yo' way to the bandstand.

LESTER: You can always tell where the bandstand at 'cause it stay surrounded with sweet smelling, pretty dark chocolate women.

TWEED: If you like dark chocolate so much, why you nibblin' on white chocolate in the Big Apple?

LINCOLN: Git to that!

LESTER: There's dark chocolate and light chocolate, and if you in Africa or Europe and you jumps in the ocean, it's the same ocean, but if you don't swim like Tarzan, you'll drown no matter where the chick come from. Git to that!

All laugh, except LINCOLN.

LINCOLN: I don't really want to. I'd rather git to our bidness! You still owe me $287.

LESTER: You mean $237; that's what I remember.

LINCOLN: The crap game in Topeka, remember?

LESTER: Oh yeah, sweet music didn't come through in Topeka.

LINCOLN: But I did, and I lent you another $50 after you lost everything again!

LESTER: Hey, I lost, I lost; no big thang. Life is a gamble they say.

MOUSE: Lincoln, you know darn well Lester always lose.

LESTER: No, I do not.

TWEED: Most of the time.

LESTER: And that ain't no big thang, um tryin' to tell you.

LINCOLN: We in the middle of the Depression; $287 is a big big thang!

LESTER: Yeah, but it ain't no big thang between brothers, 'cause you know I got it covered. We sound beautiful together, remember? What about when we traveled in Europe together? Remember Paris, Vienna, Stockholm, Geneva? You gon' git your money.

LINCOLN: You been saying that since Tulsa! I wanna know *when* I'm gon' git my money!

LESTER: [*Genuinely irritated*] What's a few dollars between brothers?

LINCOLN: [*Philosophically intended*] A head beating—that's what it is.

LESTER: Don't make no difference to me. Stop the elephant; we fixin' to take this to the pavement.

TWEED: Hold tight, fools! Yaw been like brothers for too long for this simple shit to happen.

MOUSE: Amen. Cool out, Lester. How you sound. Yaw both sound like fools.

LINCOLN: He's the one talking 'bout "taking it to the pavement."

LESTER: That's where they "beat heads," ain't it?

TWEED: Why don't yaw just cool out?

> *Pause.*

LESTER: [*Introspectively*] This thing called life is gittin' stranger and stranger. All I want is a simple harmony and I got to go through all this bullshit again.

LINCOLN: What bullshit again?

LESTER: Reading tombstones for suckers on the midway.

TWEED: Run it straight, please?

LESTER: If I have some money and any of yaw need some of that money, we work it back and forth; then we straight, like good music, you dig?

LINCOLN: No, I don't dig. You be out there rappin' ballyhoo to the fine chicks while I'm behind the bandstand scufflin' with cats who want they money. If we working it back and forth, why I always be the one carryin' everything?

LESTER: You ain't carryin' doodlysquat! I bring the people in, you dig, Lincoln?

LINCOLN: You simple fathead bitch!

TWEED: [*Shouting*] Amen!

MOUSE: [*Shouting*] If yaw don't stop this mess right now, ah swear umo make this elephant stumble in the ditch.

> *Pause.*

LINCOLN: Pass me the gin and some of that reefer too. Since I got to pay for it, I might as well enjoy it.

LESTER: [*Passing the stuff*] Yeah, you might as well. Be my honored guest, Lady Lincoln.

MOUSE: [*Turning on the radio to some mellow blues sounds, late Thirties*] I need to hear me some music.

TWEED: [*Curling up, putting on his stocking cap and pushing his hat over his eyes*] I need to cop me some Z's.

> *Pause during which* LESTER *and* LINCOLN *share a joint and the bottle.*

LESTER: Dig Mr. Chops on the radio.

LINCOLN: Yeah, he know his blues; sound real good.

LESTER: He sound all right, but his right people keep stepping on everybody. Gittin' in the way, you dig? He need to work more with his left people.

LINCOLN: You think a pianist is supposed to be a drummer or something? Just play the rhythm, right?

LESTER: No, but I can't stand too much racket back there when I hit the first chorus. I want it light, quick, smooth, steady—not loud, not filled up till there ain't no room to fly.

LINCOLN: [*jesting*] Nigga is you a musician or a pilot?

LESTER: [*Laughing*] Maybe I'm just a nigga; I don't know sometimes.

LINCOLN: Me neither, but you sho got a lotta stuff with you. Calling the man's hands "left people" and "right people." If I didn't know you, I wouldn't understand a damn word you was saying. [*Mimicking a white, Southern drawl*] What is yo' problem, boy?

> *They both laugh, pass the gin.*

LESTER: Lincoln, I think the real problem is we need to ease out this life.

LINCOLN: You mean die? For what?

LESTER: I mean this life of a sad nomad. We jam; we have a ball and then we move on to the next place; the only home we seem to have is in the next place. Don't you ever think about that?

LINCOLN: My home is in my pocket, my brother. If you thinking about a home, save yo' money and buy one—after you pay me back—then stick you a wife and kids in it so you'll always have you some place to go back to. You know I'll be yo' best man—as many times as you want.

LESTER: But the "home" I want, money won't buy. Money just won't take care of the problem. I need…

LINCOLN: [*Interrupting*] Is you crazy? Money take care of anything; it definitely take care of me. If you ain't got no money in this place, you might as well be dead!

MOUSE: Amen!

LINCOLN: Check this out: My daddy was dead for ten years before he finally died from a serious lack of money. In Georgia, a sharecropper with nine crummies in a two room shack. Daddy didn't drink his miseries away 'cause he couldn't afford to drink. He used to come home all bent over every evening, wash up, eat some corn meal mush or grits with fatback bacon or collards and okra with fatback or fatback with turnips and cornbread. That's why I don't eat no pork. Then, after he'd eat and maybe grunt at his family, he'd take his raggedy harmonica and go sit under a tree just down the road from the shack, and he'd watch the road and the cotton fields and play the meanest blues I ever heard until it was time for him to go to bed. He did that every day, all year, year in and year out, good weather and bad. Hardly ever spoke a word. He started wasting away from the inside, and, even if we could have afforded to call a doctor, I don't think it would have done any good. Money, homey. When he died, I got on that same road he used to dream about and I ain't never looked back to Georgia or poverty ever since. I didn't make the laws of this land, but the law says that money keeps you alive, well and looking good. That's the secret of why I stay so pretty.

LESTER: And drunk.

LINCOLN: What you mean, Lester?

LESTER: I mean you stay drunk so you can forgit you living all cramped up in yo' pocket. People wasn't made to live in pockets. I'm one of the people, not a piece of small change.

LINCOLN: You sound like a piece of shit to me.

MOUSE: [*Turning off the radio*] Oh no, not again!

LESTER: You sound jealous to me; like you don't want me to git what I'm supposed to git.

LINCOLN: And what in the hell are you supposed to git?

LESTER: My throne, baby; that's what I'm supposed to git. I was on my way to the throne when we formed this combo, any-Goddamn-way. And I'm ready to split now.

LINCOLN: Oh shit, here's that problem again.

> LINCOLN *shakes* TWEED *who wakes in a wild start.*

TWEED: WHAT! WHAT! WHAT!

LINCOLN: Lester wants to split, right, Mouse?

MOUSE: He done got tired of us again.

LESTER: I just need to grow some.

TWEED: Grow some what?

LESTER: I don't feel legit wit yaw; that's the problem.

TWEED: You done become a hincty nigga; that's the problem.

LESTER: Ding Dong! Here it go again. Brother Mouse, are we anywhere near my throne?

MOUSE: Another bar or two, I guess.

LESTER: It's time I went to sit in with a real band, 'cause these sounds in here is gittin' funky. I can't stand this whispering. Stop the elephant!

LINCOLN: Stop it! Stop the elephant, Mouse. Let this nigga out.

MOUSE: Whoa, elephant!

> LESTER *climbs out.*

LINCOLN: Lester, you great but sometimes you ain't good. You need some whispering to blow away some of that weirdness you carry around.

MOUSE: Good luck, brother Lester.

TWEED: We leaving you in peace.

LINCOLN: All the memories ain't bad, homeboy.

LESTER: Hey, yaw the finest bitches I ever played with; but I need to be with people who can appreciate the music of my spirit.

TWEED: We'll catch you at the next junction, probably.

LINCOLN: Jam strong but when you need help, call.

LESTER: [*Chuckling disdainfully*] Thank you, but I don't think I'll ever be needing your help again.

The elephant and its occupants disappear. LESTER *hums a familiar song off-key as he walks toward a combination chair and music stand understood as the metaphorical "throne." To the throne is attached a prominent placard on which is flamboyantly printed the name "*SWOOP.*"* LESTER *smilingly removes the placard, rips it in half, takes a seat and continues humming. Enter* AGATHA, *carrying an album, and* SLUMP *who both surround* LESTER. AGATHA's *voice is high and piercing.* SLUMP *is a hip-walking, well-dressed chronic stutterer.*

AGATHA: Good morning, Lester. Slump and I brought a few records for you to listen to before the orchestra starts rehearsing for tonight's dance.

SLUMP: Since you takin' Swoop's place, me and Agatha wanna make certain you kin fill it.

LESTER: [*Very uncomfortably and suspiciously*] Oh yeah? Well, I been playin' a few months with yaw. We been gittin' along.

AGATHA: Lester, oh how I wish that were true. Now please listen carefully, Lester. When the boss hired you to take Swoop's place, we knew you couldn't fill his shoes overnight; it takes a great deal of time and effort to master standard musical technique, but we think we've just about run out of time.

LESTER: Run it straight.

AGATHA: [*Signaling* SLUMP *to start the "turntable"*] We're a family here; everyone has an equal place. We want you to listen to Swoop's old solos and learn how to play with us.

> SLUMP *gives* LESTER's *chair a shove which starts it revolving as if on a turntable.* LESTER *holds desperately to the chair. The music heard is a loud, scratchy, nightmarish sound, a deliberately distorted improvisation distantly based upon the early 1930s Coleman Hawkins solos.*

SLUMP: You playing for a big, legitimate dance band now, not some dittybop jam combo.

AGATHA: See how *strong* Swoop's sense of rhythm is?

SLUMP: The Swoop cooked 'em, didn't he?

AGATHA: Imitation, that's how great art is made!

SLUMP: If you in a horse race, you should have you a horse.

> LESTER *begins repeating the word "no" more to himself than to his tormentors.*
> AGATHA *and* SLUMP *become more overtly aggressive, hostile.*

AGATHA: You play all outside the rhythm!

SLUMP: And you sound like a damn alto, not a tenor!

AGATHA: Your little ditties throw off the entire orchestra!

SLUMP: You play like a fat lady skating on thin ice!

AGATHA: I tried to warn them about you, but they hired you anyway.

SLUMP: Aw-w-w-w-nigga, you can't play for shit!

AGATHA: You should beat your horn into a plowshare, LADY LESTER!

> LESTER *leaps up and almost screams.*

LESTER: DING DONG!

> AGATHA *and* SLUMP *recoil slightly and look at each other.*

AGATHA: Is there some slight problem?

LESTER: [*Overtly calm and polite*] Where's the toilet at, please?

SLUMP: End of the hall to your right.

> LESTER *strolls away rapidly as the two others stand exchanging looks with each other about* LESTER. LESTER *reaches the end of the "hall" and turns left instead of right.* SLUMP *shouts.*

SLUMP: [*Continued*] I said turn right, not left. Damn, can't you do nothing like you told?

> LESTER *ignores him and heads to the "street." When he gets to the street, he cups his hands to his mouth and begins to loudly, clearly scat in the direction that* MOUSE, TWEED *and* LINCOLN *had once disappeared. It is the same scat which they had shared previously.* AGATHA *and* SLUMP *disappear. The elephant with the three occupants appears.*

MOUSE: We was damn near in Chicago when you caught us!

TWEED: There's plenty bread for a musician in Chicago. You wanna hang with us this time?

LESTER: Let's go to Chicago!

> *He starts to get into the car but is stopped by* LINCOLN.

LINCOLN: [*Somewhat good-naturedly but firm and serious*] Hole tight, turkey; I don't wanna hear nothin' from you, homey. Even though it's been eight months since you left us, you come back here and expect to ease in like you just coming back from lunch.

LESTER: Awwwwwwwman, dig…

TWEED: DIG DOG DUDU!

MOUSE: You stepped in it, brother, and you got to wipe yo' feet at the door.

LESTER: I thought it would be different when…

LINCOLN: It is different! We know how to git along without yo' ass!

LESTER: Yaw found another tenor player!

TWEED: Uh huh, nigga scared now!

LINCOLN: Shut up, Tweed! Lester, we had made some plans together.

LESTER: [*Contritely*] That didn't include me?

TWEED: YOU!? WHY YOU, RUNAWAY NIGGA?

LESTER: [*Truly reduced*] Awwwwwman, I can't see straight sometimes, but I…

LINCOLN: Look, Lester, we on the way to Chicago and figuring to collect a few more cats and form a big band.

LESTER: I'd like to try out for the band—if nobody got any objections.

LINCOLN: When we heard you needed a gig, we saved a spot for you.

LESTER: [*Genuinely brightening*] You did? I knew my brothers would look out for me!

LINCOLN: [*Tongue-in-cheek*] You gon' be our drummer.

> LESTER *misunderstands and explodes.*

LESTER: What!? TRAPS? IS YOU CRAZY, BITCH? [*Hearing their laughter*] Awwwww man, yaw gon' give somebody a heart attack behind some simple ass joke.

TWEED: Uh huh, but now you a happy nappy to be back here, ain't you?

LESTER: Pass the gin.

LINCOLN: Not till we arrive at a final understandin'.

Pause.

LESTER: To tell the truth, I'm sorry I ever left you rusty nomads. Now will you pass the gin, Miss Lincoln?

LINCOLN: [*Passing the gin*] With great pleasure.

Pause as LESTER *drinks deeply.*

MOUSE: What's happenin' at the throne?

LESTER: You mean the electric chair?

LINCOLN: We tried to tell you, homey!

LESTER: [*Angry, intense in an extremely hip, laid back way and sounding ironically incredulous for humorous effect*] Oh, it was drafty whispers every day;
Buns stayed tight
Tryin' ta keep up off that hot plate.
I'm lookin' for space to stretch out
Or lay out if I feel like it, but
They gon' make me a geek freak on the midway;
THE WILE MAN WHO EATS HIS AXE WHILE HE PLAYING IT,
You dig?
Um tryin' ta lay back and sing new songs;
Them turkeys lookin' for a repeater pencil,
Like a machine gun;
The bread's long,
But the bombs is a monster,
And I'm tired of hincty black circus tubs anyway,
You dig?
Um gone!

LINCOLN: Amen!

TWEED: But why didn't you just lay at home with us?

MOUSE: Yeah, we even got a new radio—check it out.

Turns on the radio. We hear a LADY DAY *side,* "Darn That Dream."

LESTER: [*Enraptured by her voice, midspeech*] Home is beautiful, but you can't stay there all the time…especially if something is missing.

MOUSE: If something was missin'? What was missin'?

LESTER: Listen real good now, yaw.

He takes a deep swig from the bottle as the others mistakenly wait for him to speak again.

TWEED: Well, we listening, homey; run it. Tell us what was missing.

LESTER: I know you got to peep it by now.

LINCOLN: He probably mean he was missin' us.

TWEED: Naw, he think we missed him.

MOUSE: I'm missing everything.

LESTER: Wrong. All yaw dummies is wrong. You ain't listening. Listen!

Pause during which they all listen to voice on the radio.

LESTER: [*Continued*] Can you dig Miss Lady?

LINCOLN: She's the best vocalist Grand Walker ever had.

TWEED: Ah, she sound like warm molasses and fresh butter!

MOUSE: [*Raising his hands from the steering wheel*] Ah sing it, Miss Mama!

TWEED: [*Panicking*] Keep your goddamn hands on the wheel, fool!

LESTER: But that tenor stabbin' Miss Lady in the back.

LINCOLN: Her name is Billie Holiday.

LESTER: I just named her Miss Lady.

TWEED: You know Lester ain't got no respect for people names.

LESTER: Where's the show comin' from?

MOUSE: New York.

LESTER: Point the elephant to New York and put it in gallop.

LINCOLN: New York? Just like that? And you just coming back? Is you boxed behind that gin?

LESTER: But I know what's missin'.

MOUSE: Missin' from what?

LESTER: Poppa Walker and Lady Day missin' us, you dig? And we missin' them. Listen to the lady! She's giving birth to all the sounds we ever thought we played. Listen to that! [*Pause*] Can't no decent human being turn they back on her. We need to git inside that lady's soul and ride to the sun. Fellas, I scratched yaw and I got burnt. I learned my lesson about tape recorder bands, circus freaks and loneliness. We was runnin' off-key; that's why we was buzzin' on each other over nothin'. We need the music of her spirit to give us balance. This may be our last chance to git it. We listening to the most eloquent lady alive, you dig?

LINCOLN: [*Perfunctorily contrary*] Sound like you wanna split on us again.

LESTER: NO! Never again! I ain't goin' nowhere without yaw, ever again, even if we do blow the chance of a lifetime and don't go to New York to sit at the feet of this beautiful lady.

TWEED: I think this turkey is right.

MOUSE: I wish I had somebody like that to sing me bedtime lullabies.

   Pause.

LINCOLN: Point the elephant to New York, but put it on cruise, not gallop. Ain't no need to hurry.

LESTER: That's right because we on the way to the top now; we kin cruise free in the jet stream. When I git to New York, I'm gon' call my mama and tell her what's happenin'. I'm gon' tell her that she don't have to worry about being alone or needing anything when she git old. No suh, not now, not with her son playing the big time in the big apple. In a little while we gon' be happenin' all over the country and Europe too.

   Lights crossfade to reveal LADY DAY *in a single spotlight. The previous song has blended into a melody of her most memorable songs ending with "Strange Fruit." After a few moments into the melody* LESTER *appears in a lone spotlight to the side and Upstage of her. He accompanies her on his tenor and takes appropriate mini-solos. The offstage* MUSICIANS, *of course, accompany them both. At the end of* "Strange Fruit" *there is applause;* LESTER *and* BILLIE *bow and step out of the spotlights which crossfade with another area Downstage to be understood as the* "backstage" *of a nightclub.* LESTER *packs his horn.* BILLIE *fidgets with her gardenia and stares vacantly.*

LESTER: Baby, you could make a stone bleed if you wanted. They loved you.

LADY DAY: Thanks, Prez, but lately I been feeling like a second hand plastic tomato.

LESTER: Aw baby, what kinda crazy talk is that? You sounded beautiful.

LADY DAY: I'm talking about how I feel, and you, of all people, know what I mean.

LESTER: That's true, Lady, but let's not get off into that tonight. Let's go to Minton's and jam. We'll talk some more about that stuff later.

LADY DAY: There's nothing else to talk about, Prez. I finally made up my mind. As of tonight I'm officially on my own.

LESTER: Lady Day, I don't see where you got reason to have so many funky thoughts blowing around yo' brain. I'm doing everything I can to make you happy. You invite me to move in with you and yo' mama so you can show me New York and we could spend time together; I moves in. You invite me to move out; I moves out. You ask me to stay friends with you, I say of course. You always ask for me and the other fellas when you record; we drop everything and come running. Now, as soon as we make it to the big time, you wanna quit Grand Walker's band and go running off on your own.

LADY DAY: But Prez, I need to feel free.

LESTER: Free? We're free artists who find new sounds to tell old stories. We ain't slaves. I don't see no goddamn chains on you, woman. You must be dreaming.

LADY DAY: The chains on me ain't got nothing to do with dreaming. Prez, it's hard for me to explain things; that's why I sing, I guess. But something happened to me once that I'll never forget. When they locked me up in that girls' reform school, my first cellmate was this girl named Emma, a tall, black skin country girl, and she was a mean, vicious bitch and damn near strong as a man. They put her there for castratin' one of her uncles with a butcher knife. Soon as I step in the door, she jumped up and smacked me and told me how she hated my guts and I better do everything she said or she'd cut off my titties. Prez, I swear before my Saviour, I peed in my bloomers. I was so afraid I didn't move even when the water was running down my leg. I just stood there crying and trembling for a long time, afraid to move unless she said move. When I looked up at her, she was sitting back all cool, smiling. Then she got polite, even nice, let me sit down, gave me a chocolate bar, talked about herself and where she came from. She sounded so nice and was treating me so good, that I didn't think it would be no problem if I got up and changed my bloomers. Soon as I stood up, she punched me in the stomach, knocked me over the bed. I learned quick. As long as I did what pleased her, she was polite, gentle, loving, fun even. But if I did anything, even something accidental, that displeased her, she'd beat the living daylights out me or she'd starve me, or she'd make me stand alone in a corner during recreation periods, or something. Prez, this world ain't never let me forget what that feels like. I mean, I named you Prez because you're the best, just like Roosevelt, but you still colored and no matter how great you blow that tenor, if you don't do what ole marsa "ask" you to do in this place, you liable to be hung out to dry. You all tell me I'm a great singer, but no matter how good I sing, I'm still locked up in a small corner of everybody's mind, regardless to who marsa is.

LESTER: You got messed over, but, the past is ivey divey, Miss Lady. This is 1944; ole marsa must be dead by now. We playin' with the top band; we eatin' good; we sleepin' good; we workin' and playin' together regular; we all at peace in the music; ain't nothin' to be afraid of; ain't nothin' missin' from this tribe now.

LADY DAY: But I think I'm missin'.

LESTER: You? How?

LADY DAY: I just stopped feeling a part of what's happening because I know I can do better if I had my own small combo.

LESTER: You gittin' top pay now with Grand Walker. How can you do better than that?

LADY DAY: It's not money! I have songs I want to sing that can't work with a big band.

LESTER: You could ask Grand Walker to let…

LADY DAY: I can't ask Grand Walker nothing, Prez! That's his band. He plays what he wants and you all play what he wants too. Half the time I get drowned out with all that racket anyway.

LESTER: But you could ask them to play softer or get a better mike, or you could ask for a small combo when you do your numbers. You don't have to split; we can always write new arrangements of the music.

LADY DAY: No, *we* can't make enough arrangements to suit me. I want to have my own arrangements written under my supervision and sing 'em according to how I'm feeling, where I want to and when I want to. I don't wanna be suffocated up under Grand Walker's wing forever.

LESTER: Who's suffocating you? We doing everything to show you off. Wherever we gig we put you up front.

LADY DAY: Yeah, I'm the pretty high yellow bitch who stands out front and draws the suckers in.

LESTER: Awwww mama, what is you talkin' 'bout?

LADY DAY: A showpiece is empty and alone no matter where you put it.

LESTER: Empty? Alone? You the head lady of a full tribe, baby. We all singing with you, unnastan? Just relax and try to feel good like the rest of us.

LADY DAY: [*Angry*] Feel good about what?

LESTER: Feel good about how I feel when I play with you. Sometimes, Lady, I hear your exact mood in my horn.

LADY DAY: And sometimes, lots of times, I feel what I hear in your horn, and I just go there full of blind love, but not thinking. When I open my eyes, I'm standing at the edge of a cliff.

LESTER: Baby, you got to get them ugly pictures out yo' head.

LADY DAY: Like this picture of you and your sad-looking wife? [*She hands him a large photograph of him and a white woman cheek to cheek*]

LESTER: Where'd you git that?

LADY DAY: You forgot this when you moved out last week.

LESTER: [*Misunderstanding*] Is this it? Is this the problem?

LADY DAY: You are her problem, not mine.

LESTER: But I told you I'm gittin' a divorce…

LADY DAY: Les…

LESTER: But I can't git it till my deferment come through and I git them draft board people off my tail; she ain't…

LADY DAY: SHE AIN'T GOT NOTHIN' TO DO WITH NOTHIN' is what I'm tryin' to tell you. I feel sorry for the bitch 'cause I know she tryin' to git the same thing I am, freedom. Freedom from you, Grand Walker, Mouse, Lincoln and that sneaky Tweed. I'm either a sister, a mother or a lover, but I ain't never what I want to be. Everybody's kind and polite to me as if I'm important; they call me a star, but I ain't got nothin' to say with what goes down in that band. All I hear is Billie, do this or do that; or Billie, sing this or sing that; or Billie, go here or go there. I'm always serving or being served up to somebody. There's nothing left here for me. I done had enough of being trampled on along the road. Yaw kin move on without me.

　　LADY DAY *removes some works from her purse and prepares to shoot up. At the sight of the works* LESTER *leaps up.*

LESTER: Check this out, mama; let's ease up to Minton's and blow some of this funky air away. Grand Walker and all them gon' be up there. It'll make you feel better.

LADY DAY: Goddammit, Prez! I feel like being alone! Okay?

LESTER: Why? So you kin sit up here dreamin' about pain and rememberin' stupid hatred?

LADY DAY: Prez, I don't wanna remember nothin'; I wanna forgit, and I can forgit better by myself. Besides I'm on my own now. It wouldn't feel the same.

LESTER: Why do you want to leave yourself behind like this?

LADY DAY: I ain't leavin' myself nowhere but where I wanna be, and Prez, even though we still friends, it ain't nobody's business what I do, you dig?

LESTER: Ain't got no choice.

　　LADY DAY *lays aside her works, goes to* LESTER, *and embraces him. He is limp.*

LADY DAY: Look, dahlin', I might stop by Minton's if I'm feelin' better. You just go there and jam strong for me, but watch out for alligators.

LESTER: Let the alligator git to Zanzy if it can. I'll jam for you until you come jam *with* us. I hope I see you later, Miss Lady.

LADY DAY: I hope so too.

　　He kisses her hand and she disappears. As soon as she does, we hear the explosive finale of "Flying Home" and then the laughing voices of LINCOLN, TWEED, *and* MOUSE *who appear fresh from a jam, presumably at Minton's.* LESTER *arrives from the bandstand and they all pack their instruments; they exude a slightly drunken gaiety. A bottle of gin is passed.*

LINCOLN: After what you done tonight they might send yo' black butt back to Firewood, Mississippi.

LESTER: Woodville, Mississippi, Woodville.

TWEED: Same difference; they both burn.

MOUSE: So did Prez.

LESTER: The dancers, homey, the dancers was doin' all the pushin'.

MOUSE AND TWEED: Amen!

    They all laugh.

LINCOLN: I wish Lady Day coulda been here; it woulda made this session perfect. Wasn't she supposed to come with you, Prez?

LESTER: I don't know what to do about Miss Lady.

TWEED: It's too late to do anything about her.

MOUSE: She gone, homey. It's over.

LINCOLN: We all tried to talk to her, but she wouldn't give up no light.

TWEED: I say forgit about her.

LESTER: I can't. Pass the gin. I need me a good stiff drink bad!

LINCOLN: [*Passing him an empty gin bottle*] You gon' have to forget about her, homey.

TWEED: She the one leaving us; why should you be gloomy? Let her simple black ass go; maybe she want to be a junkie whore.

    LESTER *violently pushes* TWEED *who falls against* MOUSE.

LESTER: Don't put no bad mouth on the lady; she was good for us; she brought us here together, didn't she?

TWEED: No, you brought us here, sucker! And I'm fixin' to put you there.

    Pointing to the floor, TWEED *goes after* LESTER *who grabs the gin bottle.* MOUSE *and* LINCOLN *step between them.*

LINCOLN: That's enough!

MOUSE: Man, yaw stop this stupid mess!

TWEED: Naw, this nigga wanna break my chest. I want a piece of this nigga tonight.

LESTER: You gon' git five pieces of knuckle in yo' mouth.

LINCOLN: I said stop it, Lester!

MOUSE: [*Who holds* TWEED] Lay off, Tweed. Da nigga ain't worth it!

LESTER: Not worth it! I'll kick yo' simple ass too, blind buzzard.

    TWEED *shakes off* MOUSE *so violently that* MOUSE *falls to the floor.*

TWEED: Git the hell off me, Mouse.

    TWEED *pulls a blackjack and goes after* LESTER. LINCOLN *pushes* LESTER *out of the way and pulls a very long knife which stops* TWEED *from coming any closer.* MOUSE *gets up and roars at all of them.*

MOUSE: YOU SIMPLE MUTHAFUCKAS! I HAD ENOUGH! THAT'S IT! I'm finished with trying to hold nothin' together. We ain't nothin' but funky whispers banging up against each other in the dark. [*He picks up his horn and says as he departs:*] I got to git out this cave so I can see what I'm doing. BYE!

LINCOLN: What it is, brother Tweed?

    Pause. TWEED *finally picks up his instrument.*

TWEED: Prez, one day you gon' git caught without your cabinet.

LESTER: I don't need no cabinet, Tweed.

TWEED: There's more than one way to skin a groundhog.

He departs. LINCOLN *puts his knife away.* LESTER *retrieves the bottle and looks at its emptiness.*

LESTER: Sometimes I feel like a two-dollar whore. Now what, Lady Lincoln?

LINCOLN: It's been writ, homey.

LESTER: Just like that?

LINCOLN: Just like that.

LESTER: Where do we go?

LINCOLN: We keep going forward. I got a pocket fulla money; we don't need them.

LESTER: What will we do?

LINCOLN: Tonight?

LESTER: Forever.

LINCOLN: I ain't thought about forever, but tonight, tonight I'm gon' party and so are you. [LINCOLN *pulls out a wad of bills and forcefully hands a passive* LESTER *several of them*] Now look, I got me a sweet mama waitin' for me, and ain't Marie out there waiting for you?

LESTER: [*Numbly staring at the money*] Yeah.

LINCOLN: Well, stop walking on yo' bottom lip. They gone, they gone! Huh? A melody comes; you play it; it goes on. Ain't no road blocks up ahead, homey. Come out of it. Go have a good time with Marie! Party, party, party, till it's all a vague memory!

LESTER: [*Brightening*] Why not, Brother Lincoln.

LINCOLN: That's it, homey. Don't come down now. Stay up. Don't let nothin' bring you down, understand?

LESTER: [*Not entirely convinced*] I'm all right, Lincoln.

LINCOLN: I'm gone; I'll see you tomorrow at China House.

LINCOLN *departs. The lights go to black for a few moments and in the darkness we hear voices and laughter. One voice belongs to* LESTER, *the other to* WHITE MARIE *whose accent is hip Afro street feeling.*

LESTER: I thought that old ginnie would bust a nut when he saw us.

WHITE MARIE: Law, I thought I'd die laughin' when he poured salt in his wine. He was one lame turkey.

LESTER: Ain't that the truth.

WHITE MARIE: Damn, I can't find the keyhole.

LESTER: Let me try to find the hole.

WHITE MARIE: [*Giggling*] Oh, Lester, stop now. You know I don't be playin' that in the hallway. You crazy, man.

LESTER: Open the door and turn on the lights, baby.

WHITE MARIE: Okay, just hole tight, poppa.

Lights snap on. We see WHITE MARIE *and* LESTER. WHITE MARIE *is an attractive white woman, about 32, well-dressed. During the ensuing scene,* LESTER, *among other things, attempts to take her to bed, but she constantly thwarts him for her own reasons.*

WHITE MARIE: [*Continued, still with the black accent*] We home now, baby; you kin res' yo' axe.

LESTER *sets down his instrument and goes to her.*

LESTER: Marie, you know you was raised to talk different than that. Don't be gittin' colored on me now. I'm just gittin' used to you bein' white.

WHITE MARIE: [*Moving away as she chuckles*] No, sweetie, I don't think you'll ever get used to that, not in this place. We naturally attract attention because our simple appearance conjures ugly assumptions. But then it doesn't really matter, does it?

LESTER: [*Removing his top coat and hat*] What you sayin'? What don't really matter?

WHITE MARIE: Color.

LESTER: [*Going to her again*] I wouldn't say that, but I know what you mean.

WHITE MARIE: [*Moving away*] What do you think I mean?

LESTER: [*Following her*] You must mean that all people is just people, and I agree, but that ain't got nothin' to do with reality.

WHITE MARIE: Reality has nothing to do with reality.

LESTER: [*Stopping*] Ding Dong! Say what?

WHITE MARIE: Prez, I make my living being the mistress of several wealthy, powerful men. In other words, I sell my box, discreetly, to moral gentlemen of impeccable taste.

LESTER: I understand that, but that ain't got nothin' to...

WHITE MARIE: [*Interrupting*] Listen, sweetheart, several of my clients usually ask me to pretend I'm a Negro.

   Pause.

LESTER: You mean a Negro man or a Negro woman?

WHITE MARIE: A Negro woman, of course. You know what I have to do?

LESTER: What do you do?

WHITE MARIE: [*Seriously and skillfully acting out a certain image*] Yo Poppa, whas to it? I got the oven if you wanna bake a cake. How much money you got, daddy goodness? Come on, pink poppa, suck off this sweet black titty. And I go on and on and I get paid very well.

   Pause.

LESTER: You don't sound like no Negro woman to me.

WHITE MARIE: That's because I'm not and because you don't want to pretend reality is something other than what it is.

LESTER: I don't need to pretend.

WHITE MARIE: No, you don't *want* to pretend I'm a colored woman, but you still need to pretend.

LESTER: Pretend what?

WHITE MARIE: Pretend that I'm a white woman.

   Pause.

LESTER: Well, what the hell are you? And what's on your mind anyway? We came here to party, party, party, remember?

WHITE MARIE: Lester, this afternoon I read that you're getting married, again.

LESTER: [*Avoiding the issue*] Baby, if you can't sing 'em, don't ever believe no words you read about me. Can't no writer separate my life into a bunch of black marks on paper, and so what if I'm gittin' married?

WHITE MARIE: As long as we've been together, as many soft moments that we've shared, you could have told me.

LESTER: That ain't no big thing. You sleep with married men every day. That's reality too.

WHITE MARIE: Does that make a real difference to you?

> *Pause.*

LESTER: I think it does.

WHITE MARIE: And what about you? You're preparing to divorce one woman, hanging out with a second, me, and planning to marry a third, some poor Negro woman in Queens.

LESTER: Baby, what is the real problem?

> *Pause.*

WHITE MARIE: Satisfying *your* needs apparently.

LESTER: Needs? What am I supposed to need?

WHITE MARIE: I don't know; I'm a prostitute, not a witch doctor, but I know that there've been lots of women in your life and that you exist some place alone; everyone else is a misty face that you keep hovering around your private space. I mean, I wonder if women mean anything to you.

LESTER: [*Begins easing toward her again*] Women? Women are the closest thing to music I know on this planet. Sweet smellin', pretty music. Soft music like the clothes she wear on her body and the powder she sprinkles on her thighs. But funky too, like the music that oozes out of her body after she been dancing to my love melodies and swinging on the end of my heavy rhythms. I like the songs I hear laughing in a woman's soul. Each of the musicians I play with is either a lady or he's not, you dig? Anybody who got a song in his soul is a lady.

WHITE MARIE: [*Weakly pushing him away*] That's fine, but you're singing more than one song at the same time and they all sound weak.

LESTER: Awwwww Marie, why you put me through all this? You know what's happnin'.

> *Pause.*

WHITE MARIE: [*Sighing*] I guess you're right. [*Cheering up*] Look, I should be happy for you. Is the date set yet?

LESTER: It depend on what the draft board do. You know them Germans is still kicking ass.

WHITE MARIE: Oh, Germans schmermans; it's all about stone age politics and greed. My box is more important than that war, and I don't truly care about your wives, but, Prez, tell me just one thing: What have I meant to you? You can tell me now.

LESTER: You taught me that I don't have to be afraid.

WHITE MARIE: [*Incredulous*] Afraid? Afraid of what?

LESTER: Of me.

WHITE MARIE: What on earth does that mean, Prez?

LESTER: Listen, Marie, this reality that don't look like reality in America still cause me pain, but because of you I ain't afraid of it no more. The music is the only reality I know and it was my music that touched you. The reality we share is bigger than them ugly assumptions you was talkin' 'bout.

WHITE MARIE: Thanks, Prez, but I think my illusions have been bigger than reality, because the music alone isn't enough for me. Look, we had a wonderful beginning; it's been really terrific, but I think our relationship is about to end, don't you?

LESTER: You like the moon, baby. You glow in the dark. Night and moon go together forever.

WHITE MARIE: And in the daylight the moon disappears, is that it?

LESTER: I'm not afraid to be seen with you night or day.

WHITE MARIE: But still the moon only happens at night?

LESTER: [Angry] So what are you sayin', White Marie?

WHITE MARIE: I'm saying that my name is White Marie and I'm proud of it and I intend to keep on being proud of it, but I'd rather not be *your* midnight ghost too.

LESTER: [Angrily offering her coat] Well, baby, I kin dig where you comin' from.

WHITE MARIE: [Falling into exaggerated but convincing black street hipness of manner and accent as she begins to slowly remove her clothes] Then don't worry 'bout how I sound poppa. Pull off your shirt and take off them shoes cause you fixin' to pay some sho' nuff heavy dues tonight.

LESTER: [Smiles, shakes his head from side to side as he strips down to his boxer shorts and tee shirt] Lawd, Lawd, Lawd.

WHITE MARIE: Yes, call on Him, cause He loved us whores too. Can you swim, Mr. Man?

LESTER: [Doing a mock swimming stroke] Kin birds fly?

WHITE MARIE: Some can.

LESTER: Do a seahorse gallop?

WHITE MARIE: [Down to her slip] The beach is now officially open, and it ain't got no teeth, for the very last time.

    She turns off the lights. Pause. Then we hear the SERGEANT'S VOICE shouting cadence and marching feet.

SERGEANT'S VOICE: Yo lep two three fo'
  Yo lep two three fo'
  Yo lep two three fo'
  Yo lep two three fo'

    The lights come up on LESTER marching frantically, somewhat out of step, confused and trying not to show his genuine terror.

SERGEANT: [Continued] Company halt! Private third class Lester Young, front and center, on the double; let's move it, boy!

    LESTER stumbles forward.

SERGEANT: [Continued] Boy, yer ta reeport inside ta thuh Majur fer processing. You understand, soldier?

LESTER: Yeah.

SERGEANT: Sergeant. Yes, SERGEANT!

LESTER: Yes, Sergeant.

SERGEANT: [Marching off with his invisible troop] Company, forward, march!
  Yo lep two three fo'

Yo lep two three fo'
Yo lep two three fo'
Yo lep two three fo'

LESTER *steps inside. He assumes an at ease position. The* MAJOR *appears, seats himself before* LESTER *and proceeds to conduct the following interview at a rapid, computer-like pace and rhythm. The* MAJOR *constantly scribbles on official forms.*

MAJOR: Okay, boy, let me make perfectly clear what's happening. The medical records show that you've completely recovered from your surgical operation; therefore, you are being released from this hospital and being returned to drill training, understand? Fine. I have to verify the data in your personnel file by asking you a few simple questions that you must answer correctly and quickly. If you have any problems understanding, do not hesitate to ask for an explanation. Let me warn you that you must answer truthfully. Now then, let us begin.

The previous has been said so rapidly that LESTER *barely has had time to even hear most of it. He's nervous, scared, restless, keeps twiddling his fingers as if fingering a horn.* LESTER *will have absolutely no time to answer most of the following questions put to him; he will only stutter and stammer and grow increasingly depressed as he witnesses his total helplessness. The* MAJOR *grows progressively hostile as he has prejudged* LESTER *and seeks only confirmation—a robotized ritual he conducts. The* MAJOR *scribbles on his forms as if recording answers.*

MAJOR: [*Continued*] Name? Rank? Serial Number? Place of birth? Mother's name? Father's name? Brother's name? Sister's name? Where did you grow up? Where did you attend school? Why do you have only a third grade education? What size jock strap did your grandfather wear? Have you ever smoked marijuana?

LESTER: Yeah, for 11 years.

MAJOR: Of course. Yes. This Eleanora Gough McKay, what was her daily habit like?

LESTER: Lady Day has a habit of singing her deepest feelings. She sing so pretty she make a man pee on hisself!

MAJOR: [*Scribbling the previous statement*] You and she shacked up for a long while, correct?

LESTER: We loved and now we have mellow memories.

MAJOR: Why did you move in with her and her mother? Why didn't you take her to your own house? You're a man, aren't you? When did she throw you out? Did you use up all the drugs this hospital gave you for post-operative treatment? How long have you been distilling the drugs with wine? How long did you think you could avoid the draft? Do you know how the army caught up with you?

LESTER: You tracked me, but I wasn't running. I thought newly married men were cool.

MAJOR: We'll get to your marriage later. Finding you turned out to be quite easy after your patriotic friend called us.

LESTER: What patriotic friend?

MAJOR: Francis Bartholomew, better known as Tweed.

LESTER: That bullshit mutha...

MAJOR: [*Interrupting*] Never mind him. Who was Harry Lincoln?

LESTER: Lady Lincoln. He's my friend, my sho nuff spiritual pardna. Is Lincoln here?

MAJOR: Do you believe in ghosts?

LESTER: What?

MAJOR: Your "sho nuff spiritual pardna" dropped dead three months ago; too much booze and narcotics.

LESTER: Dead? Lady Lincoln? Naw, I know he didn't die on me. [*Beginning to cry*] But I love Lincoln; he can't be dead. Not Lincoln; not my homey. Dead? I still owe that bitch $75. How could that sweet lady just die on me?

MAJOR: You and he had something going, eh?

LESTER: [*Breaking stance*] Are you crazy?

MAJOR: You'll find out how crazy I am in a minute. At ease, soldier!

    LESTER, *dazed, reassumes at ease position.*

MAJOR: [*Continued*] Is the following your footlocker number? 1909-P?

LESTER: Yeah.

    The MAJOR *angrily pulls out a large photograph of* LESTER *and a white woman cheek to cheek.*

MAJOR: What are you doing with this shit in your footlocker?

LESTER: That's a picture of me and my wife.

MAJOR: Due to violations of the uniform military code, I'm recommending you be held for court martial.

LESTER: [*Angry but terrified*] Court martial? Me? What for? Tell me that! What for?

MAJOR: That's up to the prosecutor to decide from the available evidence.

LESTER: What evidence?

MAJOR: Everything you've admitted to in this interview which is over right now. You will be held in the detention barracks until court martial proceedings can be instituted. In the meantime I'll make a few arrangements to see that you get your share of our Georgia hospitality. We got to teach you what you forgot up there in New York City. SERGEANT.

LESTER: What about my horn? Where's my horn?

MAJOR: Your horn is in your footlocker which has been confiscated

LESTER: But I need my horn for band practice.

MAJOR: Band practice? I don't have any record of your being in the band.

LESTER: But I tried out; I know I musta made it. You kin check with Sergeant Willis.

MAJOR: Sergeant Willis says you don't know your rudiments.

LESTER: I don't know my rudiments? Is he crazy?

MAJOR: *Him* crazy? He taught high school bands for ten years in Albany, Georgia. He should know if you know your rudiments, and he says you don't know yours. Your request to join the band is denied. Case closed, soldier!

LESTER: But I wanna take my horn with me anyway.

    The SERGEANT *arrives.*

MAJOR: Git it through that thick monkey's skull that your horn is being held for evidence. Understand, spook?

LESTER: I ain't going nowhere without that horn!

MAJOR: You're telling me what you're not going to do?

LESTER: The horn goes with me!

MAJOR: [*To the* SERGEANT] Remove this soldier immediately!

The SERGEANT *grabs* LESTER *and begins beating him. The moment he grabs* LESTER *the lights dim and blink with a strobe-like effect The* MAJOR *has exited, leaving* LESTER's *body jerking to the* SERGEANT's *stiff punches.* LESTER *is screaming, grunting and trying to fight back, but is no match and is finally subdued, utterly spent. The lights shift to complete blackness, except for a relatively small, square patch of light, harsh yellow light. The light itself is a tiny prison cell. The* SERGEANT *roughly hustles* LESTER *over to the patch of light. He opens the door and we hear the loud clank of steel against steel. The* SERGEANT *shoves* LESTER *into the cell and closes the door. He walks away. Music fades up slowly. The music is at first an ethereal rendering of "D.B. Blues" in the Lester Young style.* LESTER, *on his haunches with one arm shakily supporting his body, cries softly, coughs frequently and stares abjectly into space. After several moments of this, the lighted space expands to reveal the original hotel room concept into which rushes the* WOMAN IN BLACK, *breathlessly.*

WOMAN IN BLACK: Lester, I couldn't reach Dr. Tramb, but...[*Sees and rushes to* LESTER] Lester, what are you doing on the floor? Did you fall? Are you all right? [*Sees the empty gin bottle*] Lester, you drank the gin. You know what that's going to do. I called an ambulance; it'll be here any minute. [*Looking into his eyes and becoming truly alarmed at what she discovers*] Lester, LESTER, LESTER, speak to me; don't just stare like that. Speak to me! Speak to me, Lester! [*She shakes him*] LESTER!

LESTER: Listen, Miss Lady. Listen.

WOMAN IN BLACK: I'm listening, Prez; talk to me.

LESTER: Listen to the music. Can you hear it?

WOMAN IN BLACK: That's from the Birdland. Do you like it, Les? Do like the music? Talk to me about the music.

LESTER: It's funny, Lady, ain't it funny? That's my song. "Detention Barracks Blues." I made that song way back in 1945. And listen to them play it. They all sound just like me.

WOMAN IN BLACK: They sound like you because you sound the best.

LESTER: [*Trying to raise himself*] But when I try to play, I sound just like them. Who am I? Where am I going? I don't even know what I sound like anymore, and I can't hardly breathe out here.

WOMAN IN BLACK: Lester, please don't try to move; just talk to me.

LESTER: Repeater pencils, Lady. There ain't no more space out here; just repeater pencils jammed uptight, marching on my back, and...and...spittin' on me.

WOMAN IN BLACK: No one could spit on you, Lester. No one.

LESTER: Oh yes, they can, Miss Lady, but maybe that's the way it's supposed to be; I done some spittin' too. You hear that music, Miss Lady?

WOMAN IN BLACK: Yes, I hear it, baby.

LESTER: I love music and the music love me; we are love, but I can't hardly make it last past the bandstand, like church always end and the people go home and take up hatin' where they left off, and me too. I only know how to love music because people always seem temporary, even my family in Queens. I play from my soul, Lady, but I can't live with it in this drafty world. I think my soul is bigger than me, and I never could carry it all, so I always left a little piece behind. I was always missing from whatever I found; most of me got lost along the road. But my life ain't nothin' but a beat anyway, when a little melody comes together and then eases off into another feeling; only thing left is memory. And it's all right, Lady.

WOMAN IN BLACK: I know, Lester. I know it's all right.

LESTER: I ain't sad, Lady, I ain't sad 'cause the music is beautiful. [*Laughing*] *You* listening to me? You hearing me? [*As if seeing a fantastic sight*] Look, Lady, look. Oh, how wonderful it sounds. Ding Dong, Lady, DING DONG, DING DONG!

With one last heave of his chest he dies. She gently folds his hands across his chest and drapes his jacket over his face. An ambulance siren mixes in with the "D.B. Blues." *Lights fade up to an intense glow and the sounds rise to a crescendo simultaneously. Lights and sound cut out.*

Curtain.

Recessional Music: "Goodbye Porkpie Hat" *by Charles Mingus.*

Craig Lucas

☙

Reckless

•

This play is dedicated to Daniel Clarke Slautterback

Reckless originally was produced (in an earlier version) by The Production Company, Norman René, Artistic Director; Abigail Franklin, Managing Director, at Theatre Guinevere, in New York City, opening on 11 May 1983. The cast, in order of appearance, was as follows:

RACHEL FITSIMMONS	Lori Cardille
TOM FITSIMMONS	Timothy Wahrer
LLOYD BOPHTELOPHTI	W.T. Martin
POOTY	Maureen Silliman
ROY	James Bormann
BERNADETTE HANDS*	Suzanne Henry
TRISH HAMMERS	Susan Blommaert
FIRST through SIXTH DOCTORS	Patrizia Norcia
TIM TIMKO	James Dupont
TALK SHOW HOST	James Dupont
DR HELEN CARROLL	Suzanne Henry
A MAN WITH POOR POSTURE*	James Bormann
MAN IN SKI MASK	Timothy Wahrer
WOMAN PATIENT	Susan Blommaert
TOM JUNIOR	Timothy Wahrer

*Roles cut from present version.

Director	Norman René
Set design	James Wolk
Costumes	Steven L. Birnbaum
Lights	Debra J. Kletter
Production stage manager	Bill McComb

CHARACTERS

RACHEL

TOM

LLOYD

POOTY

ROY

TRISH

FIRST DOCTOR

TIM TIMKO

SECOND DOCTOR

THIRD DOCTOR

FOURTH DOCTOR

FIFTH DOCTOR

FIRST DERELICT

SECOND DERELICT

SIXTH DOCTOR

TALK SHOW HOST

DR HELEN CARROLL

MAN IN SKI MASK

WOMAN PATIENT

RECEPTIONIST

TOM JUNIOR

Voices of various announcers and newscasters

Reckless can be performed with as few as seven actors. TOM, TOM JUNIOR, *and the* MAN IN SKI MASK *are doubled, as are the* FIRST *through* SIXTH DOCTORS.

A solitude ten thousand fathoms deep
Sustains the bed on which we lie, my dear;
Although I love you, you will have to leap;
Our dream of safety has to disappear.

—W.H. AUDEN

SCENE ONE

The glow of the television. RACHEL, *at the window, in her nightgown;* TOM *in bed.*

RACHEL: I think I'm more excited than they are. l really do. I think we just have kids so we can tell them all about Santa Claus and have an excuse to believe it all ourselves again. I really do. They are so excited. I remember that feeling so clearly. I didn't think I could ever sleep. And I remember pinching myself and pinching myself to stay awake so I could hear the reindeers' footsteps, you know? I wanted to believe it so badly. I think that was the last year I did…. Oh, God…. Is it still snowing? Why don't you turn the sound up?

    TOM *shakes his head, stares at the screen.*

RACHEL: Oh, it's coming down like crazy. You can hear it, can't you, when it gets deep like this? It just swallows up all the sound and you feel like you've been wrapped up in the hands of a big, sweet, giant, white…monster. Good monster. He's going to carry us away into a dream. My family always had champagne first thing before we opened our presents—I mean, in the morning, you know. I always loved that. I felt like such an adult having champagne and I remember saying to my mother that the bubbles in the champagne looked like snow if you turned your head upside down. I remember thinking I wanted to live in Alaska because it always snowed and Santa was up there, so it must always be Christmas…. You're my Santa Claus. And our two elves. I'm having one of my euphoria attacks. I think I'm going to be terminally happy, you'd better watch out, it's catching. Highly contagious…. What's the matter? Just sleepy?

    TOM *nods.*

RACHEL: Can we listen for a second, I won't stay up all night, I promise. [*She switches on the* TV.]

ANNOUNCER'S VOICE:—as they raise their small voices in joyous celebration once more. [*The Vienna Boys Choir is heard singing.*]

RACHEL: Oh, God, look at those faces. I feel so sorry for Jeanette and Freddie sometimes. These things happen for a reason, I know, but…. I always think if something happened to us I'd want them to raise the boys.

ANNOUNCER'S VOICE: This is David Harbinger from Vienna.

SECOND ANNOUNCER'S VOICE: And in a bizarre note this Christmas Eve: An Albanian woman fled across the border into Yugoslavia where it is said she gave birth to a two-headed child today. Both mother and son are reported to be in stable condition. According to spokesmen, the woman is either unwilling or unable to speak. So far there has been no explanation for her flight. Well, whoever's dreaming of a white Christmas doesn't have to dream tonight. Weatherman Sheldon Strafford has the story.

RACHEL: [*Overlapping*] Isn't that awful?

    TOM *has begun to cry.*

THIRD ANNOUNCER'S VOICE: Bill, we thought this low pressure front might never move out, but as you can see it finally has and tiny tots and snowmen should be playing together in the streets by dawn.

RACHEL: [*Continuing over TV*] What's the matter?... Oh, honey, it's just the news, come on, it's not real. We'll turn it off, see? It's gone. [*She switches off TV.*] Don't be upset on Christmas. Everything's great, I'm here and everything's fine.

TOM: I took a contract out on your life.

RACHEL: What do you mean? Life insurance?

TOM: A contract on your life.

RACHEL: That is the sickest joke, I'm sorry. I don't care what's bothering you, you could just come out with it—

TOM: All right, listen to me—

RACHEL: You get these idiotic ideas of what's funny—

TOM: I want you to listen to me if you've never listened to me in your life—

RACHEL: It's Christmas Eve!

TOM: In five minutes a man's going to break through the bay windows downstairs. I'm sorry this is happening this way, it's a stupid solution and we should have talked it out, but it's done and he'll be here in less than five minutes. I want you to put on your coat and some slippers, you can climb out this window over the garage and run over to Jeanette's. When he's gone I'll call you and we can talk about it.

RACHEL: [*Overlapping*] Tom Fitsimmons, I know you and I think this is really off the mark, I'm sorry. Fun is fun.... I'm going to sleep in the other bedroom.

TOM: [*Grabbing her*] Rachel! Listen to me now if you want to live!

RACHEL: You're hurting me.

TOM: I paid this man, he's a professional, I cannot take it back. All right, look: [*He produces a handgun.*] This is a .38. It has no bullets. It's staged to look like he broke in and I pulled a gun and he killed you—a thief—an accident. I'm sorry, you can't be here, we'll talk it all out in a little while when he's gone.

RACHEL: You're frightening me.

TOM: I'll tell him you went to stay with your mother. He has his money, he can go. Tell Jeanette we had a fight, it doesn't matter, I'll call you when he's gone.

RACHEL: This is so mean.

    The sound of glass shattering below. RACHEL *climbs out the window.*

TOM: GO! He won't see you! Stay in the dark! Keep in the shadows!

SCENE TWO

    RACHEL *at a pay phone in her robe and slippers. Slow.*

RACHEL: Jeanette? Rachel. Merry Christmas.... No, everything's great, but listen, would you and Freddie mind taking a little spin down here to the Arco station at Route 3

and Carl Bluestein Boulevard? No, no, nothing like that, I just came outside…. Oh, isn't it? It's beautiful, uh-huh, listen, Jeanette, Tom took a…. Tom…. It's so ridiculous. He took a contract out on my life…. A contract?…Uh-huh. Right. And, I mean, the man broke in downstairs so I thought I'd better go out of the house, so I climbed out over the garage and I was afraid to ring your bell, because you have all those pretty lights and I was afraid he might be following my tracks in the snow—
> LLOYD *approaches in the darkness.*

RACHEL:—and so I thought maybe you'd just zip down here and we'd all have some eggnog or something, what do you say?…Jeane—? No…. No, I know, I am, I'm a kidder…. But—Merry Christmas to you too, Jeanette, please don't….
> JEANETTE *has hung up.* RACHEL *turns, sees* LLOYD, *screams.*

RACHEL: AAAAAAGH! NO, MY GOD! PLEASE!

LLOYD: [*Overlapping her, backing up*] Hey. Hey.

RACHEL: Oh, I'm sorry. Did you want to use the phone? Please, go right ahead.

LLOYD: I'm just trying to find a gas station.

RACHEL: This is a gas station, right here, you found one. For GAS! Oh, not on Christmas Eve, maybe up on the turnpike…. Merry Christmas.

LLOYD: Merry Christmas. You need a lift?

RACHEL: No. Yes. No.

LLOYD: It's no problem.

RACHEL: No. Thank you.

LLOYD: You're sure?

RACHEL: No, thank you. I mean, yes—I….

LLOYD: Come on, hop in.

SCENE THREE

In the car.

RACHEL: Thank you.

LLOYD: Better?

RACHEL: Yes.

LLOYD: Where you headed?… Some night.

RACHEL: Yes. Yes. Christmas. I love Christmas.

LLOYD: Yeah.

RACHEL: Snow…. You have a family?

LLOYD: No. Well, you know…. You?

RACHEL: No…. No, no. [*Her wedding ring*] Oh this? This is just costume. I just wear this, see? [*Tosses the ring out the window*] Good-bye! That felt wonderful. Maybe you should just let me off up at the, uh…. Well, I can get off anywhere. Oh, you wanted to get gas. Where do you live?

LLOYD: Springfield.

RACHEL: Springfield…. The field of spring.

LLOYD: You and your husband have a fight or something?

RACHEL: I'm not married. You married?… You have a girlfriend.

LLOYD: Just Pooty.

RACHEL: Pooty… Pooty…. My son does the cutest thing. I was married before. He's four and a half. My son has custody—my father—oh God. My son is four and a half, my husband has custody, my father is dead. And he does this thing—there are two boys, but Jeremy's just three. But Tom—Tom Junior, not my husband, Tom Senior—Tom Junior is always firing everybody, you know, if he doesn't like what you're doing. He'll say to his babysitter who is usually my friend Jeanette who can't have kids of her own because of this thing in her—uterus—he'll say to Jeanette, you know, um, "You're fired, Jeanette!" You know? Just because she wants to put him to bed or something. And just today he fired me. I mean, on Christmas Eve. I said, "You're gonna fire your own mother?" "That's right," he said, "You're fired!" So.

LLOYD: Now you're fired.

RACHEL: Now I'm fired. What does Pooty do? Is that her name?

LLOYD: Pooty.

RACHEL: What does she do?

LLOYD: She works.

RACHEL: Oh, that's good. Do you work? [He nods.] Same place Pooty works? [He nods.] Now how did I know that? Not me, I've never worked. [Pause] Did you tell me your name?

LLOYD: Lloyd.

RACHEL: Lloyd.

LLOYD: Bophtelophti.

RACHEL: Bophtelophti. Isn't THAT an interesting name. I'm—Mary Ellen Sissle. Is my maiden name.

LLOYD: Nice to meet you.

RACHEL: Don't let go of the wheel! Nice to meet you, too. My father always said, "Don't interfere with the driver whilst the vehicle is in motion." You think I'm escaped from an institution, don't you?

LLOYD: Are you? [She laughs.] What's so funny?

RACHEL: Nothing, I'm sorry, I just suddenly saw…. I mean, me in my house-dress and my slippers out in the snow.

LLOYD: Oh, it's cool.

RACHEL: Yes, it was. I've always wanted to do something like that, you know? Run away in the middle of the night in your slip and your slippers with some strange man who would ruin your reputation and disappoint your parents terribly and disappoint your friends and just make you really happy. Well, I think we get these ideas from rock-and-roll songs, actually.

LLOYD: Right.

RACHEL: Which is why I would never really do anything like that except here I am. But, no, I mean, this isn't really like that, I just meant running away and becoming…. Well, I don't know what I thought I'd become. But running away. And here I am.

LLOYD: Here you are.

RACHEL: On my way to….

LLOYD: Meet Pooty.

RACHEL: Meet Pooty…. [*Pause*] Lloyd?

LLOYD: Yeah?

RACHEL: Do you think we ever really know people? I mean, I know we know people….

LLOYD: You mean really.

RACHEL: But really.

LLOYD: You mean KNOW them.

RACHEL: Do you think?

LLOYD: Well… I don't know.

RACHEL: I don't know either. I mean, I suppose I know lots of people.

LLOYD: Sure you do.

RACHEL: And you know lots of people.

LLOYD: Pooty.

RACHEL: We live our lives and we know lots of people and…. I don't know what I'm saying. D'you get a Christmas tree? [*He nods.*] That's nice. "Oh, Christmas tree! Oh, Christmas tree…." [*She stops singing, near tears.*]

LLOYD: It's all right.

RACHEL: I know….

LLOYD: The holidays can be tough sometimes…. You see your parents?

RACHEL: Not since they died….

LLOYD: You'll spend Christmas with us.

SCENE FOUR

> *Living room.*

RACHEL: Don't wake her.

LLOYD: Oh, she'll be glad to meet you. [*He goes off.*]

RACHEL: I love your house…. Be calm….

LLOYD: [*Back*] She'll be out in a sec.

RACHEL: This is so Christmasy.

LLOYD: How 'bout a rum toddy?… Comin' right up! [*He goes off again.*]

RACHEL: This is so lovely….

LLOYD: [*From off*] Glad to have the company.

> POOTY *enters in her wheelchair.*

RACHEL: Surprise! Hello, Rachel—Mary Ellen! Rachel Mary Ellen, the Rachel is silent. Nice to meet you. This is so nice. I hope I'm not, you know. I feel…. Well, actually, my house burned down and Lloyd was kind enough to say I could stop in. You know, stop up. So, I'm, uh, not….

No reaction. LLOYD *returns.*

LLOYD: You have to keep your face towards her so she can read your lips.

RACHEL: Oh, she's deaf. You're deaf! I'm sorry, not that you're deaf, but…. I just LOVE your house.

      LLOYD *signs for* POOTY.

LLOYD: The one and only Pooty-Poot-Pooter.

RACHEL: Yesssss.

LLOYD: [*Spelling the name*] Mary Ellen Sizzler.

RACHEL: Well. Did you slip on the ice, it looks like.

LLOYD: She's paraplegic.

RACHEL: Parapalegic! Oh, parapalegic.

LLOYD: Paraplegic.

RACHEL: I have to keep my face this way, don't I?… Um…. Tell me, Pooty—

LLOYD: I'm just gonna check on the toddies. [*He goes out again.*]

RACHEL:—what kind of name is that? Your name. It's so unusual. YOUR NAME!

      POOTY *jots on a piece of paper.*

RACHEL: [*Reads*] "Pooty." Uh-huh. You know, I was just saying before….

      LLOYD *returns with two glasses.*

LLOYD: She talk your ear off?

RACHEL: Thank you.

LLOYD: Pooter Bear.

RACHEL: Aren't you having any?

LLOYD: Never touch the stuff. Cheers.

RACHEL: Cheers. Sure there isn't any poison in here?

      She smiles, drinks. LLOYD *and* POOTY *confer in sign.*

RACHEL: Mmmmm…. Isn't that beautiful the way you do that?

LLOYD: All right, everybody, have a seat. Time to open presents.

RACHEL: I'll watch. This'll be fun.

LLOYD: [*Handing her a gift*] Merry Christmas. From us. Open it.

RACHEL: But I didn't get anybody anything.

LLOYD: Go on.

RACHEL: Oh, I think this was meant for someone else. This is so strange. [*Opens the package; it's a shower massage.*] Look! Aren't you both so nice? Thank you.

LLOYD: You like it?

RACHEL: Ohhh, LIKE it?

LLOYD: Okay, who's next?

RACHEL: Wait, okay, I know what I want to do. Now I'm sorry I didn't get a chance to wrap this, but…. [*Gives* POOTY *her necklace*] Merry Christmas! Isn't this fun? I'll put it on.

LLOYD: She says you didn't have to do that.

RACHEL: Of course I didn't have to do that. You didn't have to ask a woman in her slippers to come spend Christmas with you either. I could be a mass killer. I could be anybody…. I could be anybody.

SCENE FIVE

RACHEL: [*On the telephone*] Jeanette? Yes, Happy New Year, how are you? I'm great. So how was your Christmas, what did you get?... What? Oh, right now? Oh, I'm just up at my cousin's, you know. Of course I have a cousin, what do you mean you didn't know I had a cousin? Everybody has cousins. Where? I don't know, Jeanette, right up route—what difference does it make? But—no, I'm fine. Jeanette. Do I sound fine? Do I sound fine? Well. Oh shoot, here comes my bus, but listen, do me a favor? No, I will, but—I can't, Jeanette, but would you look in on the boys for me? When you get a chance? You will? Thanks, but listen, they're closing the doors, I've got to go. Okay. Bye, Jeanette! [*She hangs up.*]

SCENE SIX

Living room.
LLOYD: Earth to Mary Ellen?
RACHEL: Hm?
LLOYD: Hungry?
RACHEL: No, thanks. Oh, I'll cook, how's that? What would you like?
LLOYD: What do you make?
RACHEL: Whatever you want, just name it. It's yours.
LLOYD: Whatever we want?
RACHEL: Whatever you want.
LLOYD: [*After conferring in sign with* POOTY] Well, we've discussed it.
RACHEL: Uh-huh?
LLOYD: And we both want you to stay here.
RACHEL: For dinner?
LLOYD: For as long as you like.
RACHEL: Oh no, I couldn't.
LLOYD: Why?
RACHEL: Well, I mean, I could, but I can't.
LLOYD: Well?
RACHEL: No. Thank you, though. Very much.
LLOYD: Why can't you?
RACHEL: Because.
LLOYD: Because why?
RACHEL: Because.
LLOYD: Because why?
RACHEL: Lloyd.
LLOYD: I m serious.
RACHEL: Because I have to get a job, I have to get some shoes, I can't just move in.
[POOTY *exits.*]

LLOYD: Why not?

RACHEL: Pooty, come on!

LLOYD: She can't hear you, she's deaf.

RACHEL: Thank you, Lloyd, I'm having enough trouble as it is.

LLOYD: Well?

RACHEL: Because.

LLOYD: Because why?

RACHEL This is the way children talk.

LLOYD: So?

RACHEL: So? So's your old man. Just because.

POOTY *returns with her lap filled with shoes.*

RACHEL: And what is this? Shoes. Oh God, I love you both so much, I do. Why are you doing this?

LLOYD: Because.

RACHEL: And where ARE we, anyway? Where is Springfield?

LLOYD: We've got an atlas.

RACHEL: I mean, do you people even have identification? My mother may not even let me play with you. She's very fussy, you know.

LLOYD *opens the atlas.*

LLOYD: Here…. Hold on….

RACHEL: I believe you.

LLOYD: Springfield. If you lived here you'd be home by now.

RACHEL: [*Holding the book*] Look how big the world is: It's all in this book…. Oh, Lloyd…. I would love to stay here, you know that. I would love to start my whole life right here at this second.

LLOYD: Why can't you?

RACHEL: Because. I'd have to get a job.

SCENE SEVEN

The office. TRISH *at a computer terminal;* ROY *and* RACHEL *standing.*]

ROY: Hands Across the Sea is a not-for-profit, humanitarian foundation.

RACHEL: [*To* TRISH] *Hi.*

ROY: This does not mean we get away with murder.

RACHEL: Uh-huh.

ROY: Any of us. We all work very long, very hard hours for very little pay. Trish Hammers, this is our new clerk, Mary Ellen Sissle.

RACHEL: How do you do?

ROY: Americans lead soft, sheltered lives, I'm sure I don't need to tell you.

RACHEL: No.

ROY: We are barely cognizant of the human misery as it exists on this planet today, under our very noses too.

RACHEL: Really.

ROY: If I could pay you less than minimum wage I would, believe me. Medical research, building a school in a foreign desert with illiterate, unskilled, underfed ignoramuses…. Well, it's expensive. Clinics, halfway houses, physical therapy labs where Lloyd and Pooty work—

RACHEL: Right.

ROY: Adult education programs, drug rehabilitation…. These are your insurance forms. Fill these out and give them to Mr. Seakins. Then ask Trish for some documents to process, she'll explain how you do that. Any other questions come straight to me.

RACHEL: Great.

ROY: So, enjoy.

RACHEL: I will, thanks.

ROY: Welcome aboard.

RACHEL: Thank you. [*He goes out.*]

RACHEL: He seems nice. [*She sits; her chair collapses.*] Whoops! I'm going to need insurance. Do you know how I, uh…? [*No response*] Never mind, I got it. [*Adjusts seat*] *So* how was your Christmas? You see your family?

TRISH: I'm not a big fan of Christmas.

RACHEL: Oh. Parents put coal in your stocking one year or something?

TRISH: My parents were killed when I was six months old.

RACHEL: Oh, I'm terribly sorry.

TRISH: Why? You didn't do it.

RACHEL: No, I know. [*Realizing her chair has sunk down again*] Oh, God, I thought I was getting shorter. Is there another chair do you know?… [*Headshake*] This is fine. [*Starts to fill in forms*] Who's Mistress Eakins? I'm sorry, I'm supposed to take this to Mistress Eakins, do you know where she is?… Mistress Eakins? Do you know what I'm talking about?

TRISH: No.

RACHEL: Mistress Eakins, I think he said.

TRISH: Mr. Seakins.

RACHEL: Oh. I thought he said Mistress Eakins. I thought that was kind of a strange name, but mine is not to reason why, mine is just…. So where is he? Mr. Seakins.

TRISH: I'll give it to him.

RACHEL: No, I don't mind.

> TRISH *takes the forms from* RACHEL.

RACHEL: Well. So do you have any kids or anything?

TRISH: No.

RACHEL: No family?

TRISH: Nope.

RACHEL: Brothers or sisters? [TRISH *shakes her head.*] Wow, you get your own screen and everything, huh?

TRISH: All right. I'd like you to take the white sheets, transfer everything onto the green sheets, and staple them together. File everything in alphanumerical order in the cabinets marked "Hardcopy." After that we'll go through the storeroom and if there's time I'll show you where the microfilm records are kept.

RACHEL: Great.

SCENE EIGHT

Living room.

LLOYD: So how was it?

RACHEL: [*Signing to* POOTY *throughout*] It was great.

LLOYD: You liked Trish?

RACHEL: Oh, yeah. Now she's in charge of what again?

LLOYD: All the budget.

RACHEL: Oh.

LLOYD: And she's pretty convinced she doesn't need an assistant, either.

RACHEL: Oh, really? Well.

LLOYD: She'll loosen up.

RACHEL: [*To* POOTY] So then she does the payroll?… How do you say payroll, Lloyd?

LLOYD: I don't know, ask her.

RACHEL: No, come on.

LLOYD: Spell it. I'll be out in the woodshed if anybody needs me.

RACHEL: You're just trying to turn me into a deaf girl, I know.

LLOYD: [*As he exits*] I can't hear you!

        POOTY *and* RACHEL *sign for a moment.*

RACHEL: She does. She seems kind of tightlipped.

POOTY: She is. Now, listen, he can't know. [RACHEL *is* dumbfounded.] It would break his heart…. I'm sorry I didn't say anything before.

RACHEL: Oh, listen…you know.

POOTY: When I lost the use of my legs a friend drove me up here to Springfield to take a look at this place where they worked with the handicapped. I watched the physical therapists working with the patients and there was one: I remember he was working with a quadriplegic. I thought he was the most beautiful man I'd ever seen. A light shining out through his skin. And I thought if I couldn't be with him I'd die. But I knew I would just be one more crippled dame as far as he was concerned, so my friend helped to get me registered as deaf and disabled. I used to teach sign language to the hearing impaired. I thought if I were somehow needier than the rest I would get special attention. I realized soon enough: Everyone gets special attention where Lloyd is concerned. But by then it was too late. He was in love with me, with my honesty. He learned to sign; he told me how he'd run away from a bad marriage and changed his name so he wouldn't have to pay child support. He got me a job at Hands Across the Sea and I couldn't bring myself to tell him that I had another name and another life, that I'd run away too, because I owed the government so much money and wasn't able to pay after the accident. I believe in honesty. I believe in total honesty. And I need him and he needs me to be the person he thinks I am and I am that person, I really am that person. I'm a crippled deaf girl, short and stout. Here is my wheelchair, here is my mouth.

RACHEL: I'm not judging you.

POOTY: When he goes out I babble. I recite poetry I remember from grade school. I talk back to the television. I even call people on the phone and say it's a wrong number just to have a conversation. I'm afraid I'm going to open my mouth to scream one day and…. [*She does; no sound.* LLOYD *returns with fresh-chopped kindling.*]

LLOYD: Keep it down in here. How's it going?

RACHEL: Great. It's pretty good.

LLOYD: I'm sorry, I didn't hear you.

RACHEL: It's pretty good, I say.

LLOYD: I still can't hear you.

RACHEL: I said it's—

LLOYD: WHAT?

RACHEL: Oh. [*She signs. He signs and goes out again.*]

POOTY: He was the first person who ever heard me. Really heard me. And I never had to make a sound. You mustn't ever tell him.

RACHEL: I won't. I think people who love each other, whatever way they love each other, nobody should say it's right or wrong. [*Pause*] Do you think Lloyd…? I mean, do you think he would ever…hurt you? I mean, not hurt you, but….

POOTY: Want to?

RACHEL: Want to, say.

POOTY: Sure. It wouldn't be love, would it?

RACHEL: Would it?

POOTY: Why?

RACHEL: Oh, I don't know.

POOTY: Did someone try to hurt you?

RACHEL: Oh, no, no, no, no.

POOTY: Who tried to hurt you?

RACHEL: Nobody.

POOTY: You can tell me.

RACHEL: Tom wouldn't do anything like that. He wouldn't.

POOTY: Who's Tom?

RACHEL: [*Overlapping*] Forget I mentioned it. Really. [*Beat*]

POOTY: I think you should talk to someone about this, don't you?

SCENE NINE

DOCTOR's *office.*

DOCTOR: Go on.

RACHEL: Well, I don't know. There's really no problem.

DOCTOR: No?

RACHEL: No. I don't know....

DOCTOR: What are you thinking?

RACHEL: I don't know. About Christmas, I guess.

DOCTOR: Do you feel like telling me about it?

RACHEL: Well, last Christmas? Christmas Eve? My husband Tom is all tucked into bed like a little kid and our two boys are in their beds, I've just tucked them in, and I tell Tom how perfect it all seems, I've never been so happy, which is true. And.... Well, my father was allergic to dogs, you know, and Tom didn't like puppies, so I never said anything about wanting a puppy, but I was thinking about it. And I was looking out into the snow and talking about Alaska or something, but I was thinking about how people in books and movies are always getting puppies on Christmas and you never see anybody having to clean up the....

DOCTOR: Shit.

RACHEL: Or get hit by cars. You always see them with a big red bow and the kids are smiling and—but I didn't say anything, I was just thinking it. I didn't want Tom to feel guilty if he hadn't gotten me a puppy which I knew he hadn't because he hates them, so it was just a private little something I was thinking about and that's all I needed really was to think about it and rub its little imaginary ears. And we were watching the news, I remember, and suddenly I realize Tom's upset. So naturally I assume he knows I really want a puppy, so I go to comfort him, because I don't care about it, really, if it's going to make him unhappy, I don't even mention it, I just give him a big hug and tell him it's Christmas and be happy and he says he's taken a contract out on my life.

DOCTOR: This upset you.

RACHEL: Maybe I'm overreacting. Or he's kidding, which I think he must be. But anyway, I wind up spending Christmas with this man I meet at the Arco station and his girlfriend who is crippled and deaf, she says, you know, with hand signals until suddenly she just turns to me and starts saying how she had to pretend she was deaf to get the attention of this man we're all living with who's changed his name and run away and she's changed her name and I've changed my name and we're all working in the same place and she's telling me all these secrets and all of a sudden she says, "Why don't you talk to a psychiatrist?"

DOCTOR: And here you are.

RACHEL: Here I am.

DOCTOR: When did you have this dream?

SCENE TEN

The office.

TRISH: I'm going to have to take an early lunch today, Mary Ellen.

RACHEL: Okay.

TRISH: So if you'll hold down the fort.

RACHEL: Anything I can do for you on the computer or anything?

TRISH: No, thanks.

RACHEL: Well, anytime you want to teach me.

TRISH: I think you probably have enough work to keep you busy. [TRISH *goes out.* RACHEL *looks around, then moves over to* TRISH's *seat.* LLOYD *enters.*]

LLOYD: Hi.

RACHEL: Hi.

LLOYD: Mind if I join you?

RACHEL: No. Have a seat.

LLOYD: Learning Lotus?

RACHEL: No, what's that?

LLOYD: Oh, that's the software.

RACHEL: What's software?

LLOYD: Oh, that's what tells the computer what to do.

RACHEL: Oh.

LLOYD: I don't even know if that's what we use.

RACHEL: You know? In all the months I've been here Trish has never shown me how to do anything except file and take care of the storeroom and stuff like that.

LLOYD: Well, give her time.

RACHEL: Yeah. I guess. She has no family.

LLOYD: Yeah.

RACHEL: She says.

LLOYD: What do you mean?

RACHEL: I don't know. Just for all we know she could have ten families and a trail of broken hearts behind her, right? Who knows?

LLOYD: What else have you and Pooty been discussing?

RACHEL: Nothing.

LLOYD: Anything you'd like to ask me personally?

RACHEL: Oh, I wasn't even thinking about that.

LLOYD: Yes, I left my family, no, they don't know where I am—

RACHEL: No, I wasn't asking any of this.

LLOYD: [*Overlapping*] No, I don't pay child support, no, Bophtelophti is not my real name—

RACHEL: Please, Lloyd.

LLOYD: My real name is Boyd T. Theophillo....

RACHEL: The past is irrelevant. It's something you wake up from.

LLOYD: I walked out on a woman with multiple sclerosis and two children, one of them brain damaged, because I was too drunk to see him playing in the snow and I ran over him with the snow blower. I left them with no money and no way to feed themselves, moved as far away as I possibly could, changed my name, took the cash I'd stolen from the savings account to pay for the kids' education and put myself through school, so that I could become a physical therapist and work with multiple sclerosis victims and the occasional brain-damaged child with resultant motor-skill difficulties, none of whom held the slightest interest for me other than to remind me of what I could never escape as long as I live. And let's see. I married a nice crippled, deaf girl and I don't drink anymore. The past is something you wake up to. It's the nightmare you wake up to every day.

RACHEL: Well, these things happen for a reason, I believe that, I'm sorry, I do. And you're not helping anybody by punishing yourself. Why don't you pay back the money and say you're sorry?

LLOYD: It was thirty-five thousand dollars.

RACHEL: So? Big deal. People win that on game shows.

SCENE ELEVEN

TV studio.

ANNOUNCER: And here's your host, Tim Timko!

TIM: Okay, here we go, how does this game work, where are we? Oh, yes, it all comes back to me, like last night, who was that girl? Okay, enough of that, it's good to be back, let's see who's here. [*Houselights*]

TIM: Remember, all you need's a mother, a wife, and the crazy idea that you could tell the difference. Looks like an awful lot of bag ladies slipped in here. How're we all doin'?
          Crowd response.

TIM: Anybody want to play this thing? What's it called? Your Brother's Wife? Your Sister's Best Friend's Mother-in-Law?
          Sign lights up. RACHEL, LLOYD, *and* POOTY *are in the audience, dressed as the solar system with cardboard and papier-mâché constructions over their heads.*

TIM: "Your Mother or Your Wife." Ah! Wait. [*He makes his way over to the oddly costumed trio.*] Wait, wait a minute, I know what I like and don't tell me now, you folks are dressed as the solar system, aren't you?

LLOYD: That's right, Tim.

TIM: This looks like the planet Earth down here.

LLOYD: That's my mother, Tim.

TOM: Mother Earth.

LLOYD: Right.

TIM: I'll bet your world revolves around your sun, too, doesn't it. What's your name, Sir?

LLOYD: Lloyd.

TIM: You have a last name, Lloyd?

LLOYD: Bophtelophti.

TIM: Where're you from, Lloyd?

LLOYD: Springfield?

TIM: Springfield? Massachusetts? [*To* RACHEL] And you must be the little lady.

LLOYD: That's right, Tim.

RACHEL: Venus.

TIM: Ah. "One touch of."

LLOYD: That's right.

TIM: Well, you've met our requirements, Lloyd.

LLOYD: I should tell you, Tim, my mother is deaf. But my wife speaks sign language.

TIM: So she can translate. Okay. Come on up and get set to play "Your Mother or Your Wife"!

Music, applause. LLOYD, RACHEL, *and* POOTY *are led offstage.*

TIM: All right, correctly identify which of these lovely ladies answered each of three scintillating questions supplied by our studio audience made up entirely of Nobel Prize Laureates by the way—[*To someone in the audience*] What, you don't believe me? Get him out of here. And you can win yourself up to twenty thousand dollars, Lloyd, and a chance to play for our grand prize.

ANNOUNCER: Tim, the Bophtelophtis will be playing for a grand cash total of one hundred thousand dollars.

TIM: A hundred grand. Are you ready for our glass booth?

LLOYD: I guess so, Tim.

TIM: Then take him away.

LLOYD *is led offstage.*

TIM: Never to be heard from again. [*To* RACHEL *and* POOTY] Good evening, ladies.

RACHEL: It's great to be here, Tim!

TIM: You're going to translate.

RACHEL: That's right.

TIM: No funny business. Anybody here speaks deaf, keep an eye on these two. All right, Venus, first question.

RACHEL: Okay.

TIM: Would you say that Lloyd is more like a Ping-Pong ball or a paper clip? Mmmmm.

RACHEL: I'll say a Ping-Pong ball.

TIM: Any particular reason?

RACHEL: He bounces around a lot?

TIM: He does? Okay. Mom? Is Lloyd more like a Ping-Pong ball or a paper clip, would you say? Two 'P's...

RACHEL *and* POOTY *confer in sign.*

RACHEL: She says a paper clip.

TIM: Because?

RACHEL: Because he holds the family together.

TIM: Awww, that's—disgusting. No, I'm just teasing you. Question number two: Mom first this time. If Lloyd were a salad dressing, what flavor would he be? If blank were a salad dressing....

RACHEL: She says blue cheese.

TIM: He's getting a little moldy? But okay, Venus?

RACHEL: I'll say blue cheese.

TIM: Blue cheese it is. Ladies, third question: If you could choose between your husband leaving you for another woman or, in Mom's case, her son leaving her for another mom…? [*Looks to the control booth*] Guys, this question doesn't make sense. What's he gonna do, get another mother?… Judges say fly with it. All right—between your husband leaving you for another woman or staying together, knowing he doesn't love you, Venus, which would it be…?

RACHEL: I'd have to say another woman.

TIM: Another woman. Mom? Between losing your son to another mother or knowing he didn't love you. All right, fair enough.

RACHEL: She says another mother.

TIM: 'M' is for the many ways. Ladies, for our grand prize: Who does Lloyd love most, you or Mom?

RACHEL: His mother.

TIM: And Mom? This should be interesting. [RACHEL *and* POOTY *confer.* POOTY *points to* RACHEL.]

TIM: And she says you! Okay, we'll be right back with the three happy Boopy-Boppies after this word from the good folks at Nu-Soft. Don't go away. [*Lights change;* LLOYD *is escorted onstage.*]

ANNOUNCER: We're going right on. Ten seconds.

TIM: [*To* RACHEL] Say your name for me.

RACHEL: Bophtelophti.

TIM: Bophtelophti.

> *Lights restore.*

ANNOUNCER: Five, four, three…. Rolling.

TIM: And we're back with the Bophtelophtis from Springfield, Massachusetts. Bophtelophti, is that Polish?

RACHEL: Yes, T—

LLOYD: [*Simultaneously*] No, well, it's—

RACHEL: It's….

LLOYD: Welsh, actually.

RACHEL: Welsh and Polish.

TIM: Welsh and Polish. How long've you been married?

LLOYD: Ten….

RACHEL: Years.

TIM: Ten years. Any kids so far?

LLOYD: No.

RACHEL: But….

LLOYD: We're hoping, Tim.

TIM: Well, good luck to you. Because you're gonna need it! Okay, here we go, round two, Lloyd, for five thousand dollars: When asked if you reminded them of a paper clip or a Ping-Pong ball, who said "paper clip" and I quote, "Because he holds the family together." Your mother or your wife?

LLOYD: Boy.... My mother?

      RACHEL *hops up and down and claps.*

TIM: Right you are if you think you are, Lloyd.

LLOYD: Okay.

TIM: For ten thousand dollars, when asked what type of salad dressing you reminded them of, who said "blue cheese"? Your mother or your wife?

LLOYD: That's my favorite.

TIM: Nobody's interested in your personal life, Lloyd. No, take your time.

LLOYD: I'll say both.

TIM: Both it is for a quick ten grand! All right, for twenty thousand dollars and a chance to lose it all, Lloyd: Which... wait, let me get this straight. Which of the women in your life said they would rather lose you to another woman, wife or mother as the case may be, than believe you to be unhappy in their home. Mother Earth or the Venus de Milo, Lloyd. Lose you to another woman....

LLOYD: Both?

TIM: Both it is! Congratulations, Lloyd Bophtelophti from Warsaw, Wales, you've just won twenty thousand dollars and a chance to go away before you ruin your marriage.

LLOYD: No, we want to keep going.

TIM: Remember, if you miss this one, we keep it all, Lloyd, but you do go home with a free home version of your mother and your wife.

LLOYD: We'll play.

TIM: He says he'll play. All right, no eye contact now, no help from the studio audience please, Lloyd, for one hundred thousand dollars IN CASH, we asked your mother and your wife: Who does Lloyd love the most? Who said—keep breathing, Lloyd— you love your wife the most? Your mother, your wife, or your mother AND your wife, it could be both. Don't think too hard, Lloyd.... Your mother, your wife, or your mother and your wife.... I'm sorry, we're running out of time, we'll have to have an answer, Lloyd.

LLOYD: My mother.

TIM: Your mother!

      Lights flash. Audience screams. RACHEL, LLOYD, *and* POOTY *express their enthusiasm.*

TIM: For one hundred thousand dollars, Lloyd Bophtelophti from Springfield, you've said the magic word, take the money, be happy, this is Tim Timko saying good night, we'll see you next week with your mother, your wife, your mistress, whoever else you got out there....

ANNOUNCER: [*Under*] For tickets to "Your Mother or Your Wife" write your name and address on a postcard and mail it to, "Your Mother or Your Wife," Box 1224, New Hope Station, New York, New York....

      His voice fades.

INTERMISSION

SCENE TWELVE

The office.

TRISH: How much?

RACHEL: A hundred thousand dollars.

TRISH: You're kidding.

RACHEL: I'm not.

TRISH: That's....

RACHEL: Incredible, isn't it?

TRISH: It's incredible.

RACHEL: It's incredible. And you know what the moral is?

TRISH: What's the moral?

RACHEL: You can't be afraid.

TRISH: No.

RACHEL: These things happen for a reason, I keep saying it. I mean, we're all so afraid to take chances and what have we got to lose? We're all going to be dead in a hundred years anyway.

TRISH: This is true.

Pause.

RACHEL: Trish?

TRISH: Uh-huh?

RACHEL: Remember when I first came here?...Wow, it's almost a year ago now, isn't it?

TRISH: That's right.

RACHEL: You didn't really like me, did you?

TRISH: Oh.

RACHEL: No, come on, it's all right.

TRISH: Well, I don't always warm up to people right away.

RACHEL: Oh, I know. But I think it's also because you thought I just wasn't smart enough to handle anything very complicated, didn't you?

TRISH: No.

RACHEL: Well, I decided to take the bull by the horns anyway, and I've sort of been teaching myself about the computer.

TRISH: You have?

RACHEL: When you go to lunch. Look. I got this book on Lotus and I learned how to call up the menu and the file directory and everything.

TRISH: Great.

RACHEL: And I even figured out about the separate accounts you have filed that don't appear on the main index. You know, like the one that's attached to the Christmas fund as a footnote.

TRISH: How'd you figure that out?

RACHEL: Well, I was just, you know—I was trying to figure out what the password was and I was playing around with anagrams and stuff and your name spells "Shirt," I'm sure you know, because you used it for the footnote file.

TRISH: Good for you.

RACHEL: Yeah. My dad and I used to like to play word games and things when I was little.... Anyway.... You're not mad, are you?

TRISH: No, why should I be mad?

RACHEL: Oh, I don't know. Actually, some of the math doesn't add up, either, but....

SCENE THIRTEEN

DOCTOR's *office.*

DOCTOR: In the dream....

RACHEL: Uh-huh.

DOCTOR: You pretend to be the wife and Pooty.... Pooty?

RACHEL: Right.

DOCTOR: Pooty is an unusual name.

RACHEL: Mm-HM.

DOCTOR: Pooty pretends to be the mother. [*Pause*] Do you think there's any significance to that?

RACHEL: No. I mean, you can't go on the show unless you have a mother and a wife. That's just the way the game works, and Lloyd doesn't have a mother. So—

DOCTOR: But Pooty is the wife and you are not a member of the family at all, unless we say that you are the adopted child.

RACHEL: Right. But Pooty's deaf. I mean, she's not, but it was just easier to make her seem like a mother since she wouldn't have to talk and she's in a wheelchair. And it worked. I mean, we won the money and Lloyd paid back his ex-wife, so....

DOCTOR: I know you haven't wanted to talk about your parents, Rachel, and we agreed you don't have to until you feel you're ready. The loss of our parents is the greatest single trauma of our adult lives. But I also believe that our dreams are a way of telling ourselves what we think we mustn't know, our secret wishes and fears, written in code like an anagram where all the letters are jumbled, but the secret is there.

RACHEL: Like an anagram.

DOCTOR: Right. [*Pause*] Why do you think you picked "Your Mother or Your Wife?"

RACHEL: Oh, they picked us. I mean, we just sent in the postcard.

DOCTOR: Whose dream are we discussing?

RACHEL: Nobody's. I'm sorry I didn't say that before. I thought that was part of the therapy, to talk about everything like it was a dream. It's not a dream. I'm sorry, I was confused. Sorry.

    Pause.

DOCTOR: Would you like to see another therapist?

RACHEL: No.

DOCTOR: Is that what you're telling me?

RACHEL: Not at all.

DOCTOR: There's nothing shameful in that. I won't be angry with you. Sometimes it's a good idea to shop around, try different types of therapies.

RACHEL: I know.

DOCTOR: I honestly think it's time, Rachel, that you try to think about what it is in the loss of your parents that is so difficult to share with me.

    Pause.

RACHEL: My mother was run over by a school bus when I was six. My father died of a heart attack the year I married Tom.

DOCTOR: Thank you, Rachel. [*Pause*] Rachel? Did you ever wish—not really mean it—just wish that your mother would go away? Did you think that you were responsible for what happened?

RACHEL: She was run over by a school bus.

DOCTOR: And then what happened?

RACHEL: I lived with my father.

DOCTOR: Until you were how old?

RACHEL: Nineteen.

DOCTOR: And then?

RACHEL: I married Tom.

DOCTOR: And your father died.

RACHEL: Of a heart attack.

DOCTOR: What is a heart attack? Isn't it a broken heart?

SCENE FOURTEEN

    Living room. LLOYD *and* POOTY *are dressed as Santa and a reindeer.*

LLOYD: Ho, ho, ho!

RACHEL: Wait. Okay. Before we open presents—I love it!—I just want to say something, both of you. A year ago when I first came here and you both took me in...that was probably the nicest thing anybody ever did for me. You've taught me the true spirit of giving and Christmas; you've made me part of your family, you know? And...you're just the best family that anybody could ever ask for.

    Doorbell.

LLOYD: Aw, who the hell is that?

    He opens the door. TOM *stands there, holding a bottle of champagne and a large gift box.*

TOM: Is Rachel Fitsimmons here?

LLOYD: No, I'm sorry, there's no one here by that—

TOM: Rachel? It's Tom.

RACHEL: Oh, hi, how've you been?

TOM: May I come in?

RACHEL: Sure. Oh sure. Lloyd, Tom—Tom, Lloyd.

LLOYD: How do you do.

RACHEL: Lloyd, Pooty—Pooty...Tom.

TOM: [*Indicating the champagne*] This was, um, I found this sitting on the step. It says, "From Santa."

RACHEL: Uh-huh.

TOM: Nice to meet you all.

RACHEL: Pooty is deaf. And Tom is my husband.

TOM: How've you been, Rache?

RACHEL: Great. You?

TOM: I saw you on TV.

RACHEL: Uh-huh.

TOM: I almost didn't recognize you.

RACHEL: Oh.

TOM: You had a....

RACHEL: Planet.

TOM: On your....

RACHEL: Face.

TOM: Right. I thought maybe you'd remarried.

RACHEL: No.

TOM: That was....

RACHEL: Pretend.

TOM: TV. Right. [*Pause. He indicates gift box.*] I brought you something.

RACHEL: Oh.

TOM: It's something you've always wanted. And I'm sorry I didn't give it to you before. There isn't anything I can say, Rache. I keep trying to find the right words. Something that could make...take away... take it away. It. There, you see, all I have to do is say it and there it is. What I did. The thing I can't ever take back. It. I can't live without you, Rache. And I can't live with—with it. I can't, but I'm just so afraid to die, Rachel, I'm afraid.

RACHEL: No one's going to die.

TOM: Well, we're all going to die.

RACHEL: Not right now, please.

TOM: I'm so sorry, Rachel.

RACHEL: Why don't we have some of this champagne? Lloyd, would you get some glasses, please?

> LLOYD *goes off.*

RACHEL: Oh, Tom, it was very nice of you to bring the champagne, that means a lot to me.

TOM: It was just sitting on the step.

RACHEL: Oh, well, it was nice of someone then, wasn't it? [*The gift box*] What's this? Is this for me?

TOM: Uh-huh.

RACHEL: You brought this? I can't think what it could be.... Does anybody mind?

> POOTY *signs.* RACHEL *unwraps the package.*

TOM: The boys said if I brought you that maybe you'd come home. They're with Jeanette and Freddie for the weekend.

RACHEL: Oh, how is Jeanette?

TOM: Everybody sends their love. We all miss you.

RACHEL: [Looks in the box] Tom!

TOM: You like him?

RACHEL: Oh, he's so sweet.

TOM: You can name him whatever you want.

RACHEL: He's so beautiful. Look! Tom, thank you. [She holds up a stuffed animal puppy.]

TOM: And you don't have to clean up after him.

RACHEL: I know. Look, everybody!

LLOYD: [Returned with the champagne and a glass of milk for himself; he pours.] Cute.

RACHEL: Oh, thank you.

TOM: You're welcome.

LLOYD: How 'bout some champagne? Everybody like champagne? Poot? [Hands them their glasses]

TOM: Thanks.

RACHEL: Awww.

LLOYD: Drink up.

TOM: Please come home, Rache. We miss you.

RACHEL: Cheers! [She clinks her glass against TOM's, over emphatically, and her glass shatters.] Whoops! Oh God.

LLOYD: That's okay, I'll get you another one.

RACHEL: Thanks.

> LLOYD goes off.

RACHEL: [To TOM and POOTY] Oh, go ahead, please. I'm fine.

TOM: [To POOTY] Cheers.

> POOTY signs the word for "cheers." They drink. LLOYD returns with another glass and pours.

LLOYD: Here you go.

RACHEL: Thank you, Lloyd. Cheers.

> TOM bends forward in sudden discomfort. POOTY emits a small noise.

TOM: Is there a bathroom?

LLOYD: Poot?

> RACHEL holds her glass, untasted, watching as TOM and POOTY double over in pain.

TOM: OW!

POOTY: Lloyd!

> LLOYD is stunned.

TOM: Jesus! Aaaagh!

POOTY: Lloyd!

TOM: Aaaaaaaa!

POOTY: AAAAAAAAAAAAAAAAAAA!

> They die.

SCENE FIFTEEN

The car. RACHEL *drives.* LLOYD *in his Santa suit.*

RACHEL: Calm.... Calm.... Okay. Did I miss my exit? Okay. Lloyd? Okay. Okay, if we call the police—did we? Are we calling the police? Did we? No, I remember, okay. We could. Here's the thing: We didn't. We called the ambulance, okay. We called the ambulance. Why didn't we call the police? Because. They'll think we did it. Why will they think we did it? Because we didn't call the police. No, our fingerprints were on the bottle. "So what?" "What do you mean 'So what?' Why did you leave your family? Why do you have assumed names? What are you hiding?" "Nothing." "Uh-huh. Where'd you get all this cash in hundred-dollar bills?" "Oh, we won it on a game show." "What game show?" "Your Mother or Your Wife." "Is this your mother?" "No." "Is this your wife?" "No." Turnpike!... Is this the right ramp? Lloyd? [*Looks in rearview mirror*] I think those people are following me. Are those the same people? No, wait, Tom brought the champagne! That's right. Tom brought the champagne. "We're all going to die," remember? [*She reads road sign.*] West. We're all going to die. Just take a look over your shoulder and tell me if those are the same people.... No! No, it was sitting on the step, that's right, remember? From Santa. Or he was lying. All right, wait. Wait. Maybe it was just a bad bottle. Maybe—maybe—They're following me. Don't turn around. Look like you're having a good time. Uh-huh! Uh-huh! Really!... Oh God. [*She turns on the radio.*]

ANNOUNCER: The mellow sound of Nat King Cole. Gone before his time. It's 10:00 AM Christmas morning. Let's hope Santa left something special under your tree. In the news—

She turns off the radio.

RACHEL: Wait a minute! Santa! Santa. Sat—na. At—sna. At—san. Tas—na. As—nat. Santa, Merry Christmas from Santa.... Sat—na. Sat—an. Satin. Satin. Satan! Merry Christmas from Satan! Oh God. Christ's birthday, Merry Christmas from Satan, Lloyd! That's horrible. Why is this happening? Why is it always Christmas? I love Christmas. I always used to say I wanted to live in Alaska because they had snow all year round and Santa was up there, so it must always be Christmas.... Oh Lloyd. They won't feel any more pain from now on, I know they won't. No more pain from now on, all right, Santa Claus? I'll drink to that.

SCENE SIXTEEN

Night. Snow. RACHEL *is still driving.* LLOYD, *in his suit, staring.*

RACHEL: Toopy.... P.... Oop. Oopy. Toopy. Poot. Pyoot. Ypoot. Ytpoo. It. It.... Toopy. Two Ps. Two.... Y-po-to. Toy—po. Poy sounds like boy. Two boys! I have two boys. [*Pause*] I don't even know what state we're in, do you? [*Sees road sign*] Wait, can you read that?...Spring...field. Springfield!?!? Is that what it said? How can we be back in Springfield—[*Reads*] Ohio! Springfield, Ohio, thank you, God! Springfield,

Ohio… [*Sighs with relief*] Oh God. Who would ever want to live in Springfield, Ohio? [*She has a revelation.*] NOBODY.

SCENE SEVENTEEN

A seedy hotel room; LLOYD *remains in his Santa suit.*

RACHEL: Lloyd, I know we can be happy here, I just know we can. Who would ever think to look for us in Springfield, Ohio! Nobody. Why would we ever want to go back to Springfield? We wouldn't, you see, we wouldn't! And the lady at the real estate agency said there's one in every state. Fifty Springfields. So we don't have to stay here if we don't like it. We don't have to do anything. We can go anywhere, we can be anybody. We can go from Springfield to Springfield. How many people ever get a chance to do that in their whole lives?… Lloyd… I know I can't take her place. But she'll always be right here. You're what keeps her memory alive. But you have to keep yourself alive. You have to eat something. And we have to get you out of that suit. We're lucky to be alive, I mean, we could have had some of that champagne. Well, you don't drink, but…. Let's pick names. What do you like? How about Jessie? I'll be Jessie or you be Jesse and I'll be Mrs. Mancini. I can find a new doctor. You know, it's a good idea to shop around, try different types of therapies—

LLOYD: SHUT UP! SHUT THE FUCK UP PLEASE! COULD WE HAVE ONE— TINY—MOMENT OF SILENCE IF IT ISN'T TOO MUCH TO ASK FOR? PLEASE?

   Pause.

RACHEL: I'm sorry.

LLOYD: What?

RACHEL: I said I'm sorry.

LLOYD: I can't hear you.

   Pause

RACHEL: I said….

   Pause. RACHEL *signs "I'm sorry."*

SCENE EIGHTEEN

Another DOCTOR's *office.*

SECOND DOCTOR: Do you have nightmares, Mrs. Mancini?

RACHEL: No.

SECOND DOCTOR: Phobias?

RACHEL: No.

SECOND DOCTOR: Eczema? Asthma?

RACHEL: No.

SECOND DOCTOR: Do you take drugs?

RACHEL: No.

SECOND DOCTOR: Alcohol?

RACHEL: No.

SECOND DOCTOR: Are you an alcoholic?

RACHEL: No.

SECOND DOCTOR: Would you say you're chronically depressed?

RACHEL: No.

SECOND DOCTOR: Or unfulfilled in any way?

RACHEL: No.

SECOND DOCTOR: Have you ever tried to kill yourself?

RACHEL: No.

SECOND DOCTOR: Is it difficult for you to make a decision?

RACHEL: No.

SECOND DOCTOR: Are you sure?

RACHEL: Mm-hm.

SECOND DOCTOR: Do you have trouble sleeping?

RACHEL: No.

SECOND DOCTOR: You sleep too much?

RACHEL: No.

SECOND DOCTOR: Dietary difficulties?

RACHEL: No.

SECOND DOCTOR: Overeating?

RACHEL: No.

SECOND DOCTOR: Undereating?

RACHEL: No.

SECOND DOCTOR: Is sex a problem for you, Mrs. Mancini?

RACHEL: No.

SECOND DOCTOR: Does that embarrass you, my asking?

RACHEL: No.

SECOND DOCTOR: Do you ever have any trouble relating to new people?

RACHEL: No.

SECOND DOCTOR: Telling the truth?

RACHEL: No.

SECOND DOCTOR: Is shyness a problem for you?

RACHEL: No.

SECOND DOCTOR: Do you have something that you're ashamed of?

RACHEL: No.

SECOND DOCTOR: A speech defect?

RACHEL: No.

SECOND DOCTOR: What's the problem, Mrs. Mancini?

      RACHEL *shrugs.*

SCENE NINETEEN

Another hotel room.

LLOYD: You know what I feel like having?

RACHEL: What?

LLOYD: You know what I really feel like having?

RACHEL: What?

LLOYD: You know what I really feel like having right now?

RACHEL: What?

LLOYD: Champagne.

SCENE TWENTY

Another DOCTOR's *office.*

THIRD DOCTOR: You're not from Alabama.

RACHEL: No.

THIRD DOCTOR: Now how did I know that?

RACHEL: You see, two Christmases ago, my husband Tom.... Well, we've lived in Springfield before.

THIRD DOCTOR: Oh, you have.

RACHEL: Twice. And I have two sons, too, actually. And my husband tried to kill me twice, too.

THIRD DOCTOR: Your husband? Tried—

RACHEL: [*Overlapping*] Two Ps!...Pooty.... My first shrink said that Pooty was an unusual name. And she said—

THIRD DOCTOR: Oh, you've been in therapy before?

RACHEL: Twice. But.... Okay: How long do you think a person could live if they drank nothing but champagne and they didn't eat anything? Just out of curiosity.

THIRD DOCTOR: Well....

RACHEL: Does a month seem like a long time? To you.

SCENE TWENTY-ONE

Another hotel room.

LLOYD: Here's a question.

RACHEL: Nope.

LLOYD: Do you remember asking me if we ever really know anybody?

RACHEL: Not until you eat something.

LLOYD: You remember that?

RACHEL: [*Unpacking groceries*] Do you hear me?

LLOYD: You asked me if I thought we ever really knew anybody.

RACHEL: You are going to eat something if it kills me.
LLOYD: And I've thought about it.... And I would have to say....
RACHEL: You don't have to taste it.
LLOYD: My considered opinion would be....
RACHEL: Just smell it.
LLOYD: No. No way.
RACHEL: Croissants, Lloyd!
LLOYD: Not on your life.
RACHEL: Look, pâté.
LLOYD: No dice.
RACHEL: Just open your mouth and take one bite.
LLOYD: Ixnay.
RACHEL: Strawberries.
LLOYD: Nope.
RACHEL: Ice cream.
LLOYD: Uh-uh.
RACHEL: It's pistachio.
LLOYD: No way, José.
RACHEL: Lloyd, you can't—
LLOYD: Forget about it.
RACHEL: Soup. Soup!
LLOYD: No chance.
RACHEL: You can't survive on champagne alone, it's an old saying.
LLOYD: No, no, a thousand times no.
RACHEL: I need you now.
LLOYD: Nyet.
RACHEL: Please.
LLOYD: Non.
RACHEL: You can't live on wine.
LLOYD: Nein.

SCENE TWENTY-TWO

Another Doctor's office.

FOURTH DOCTOR: This is very important, Cheryl. We've talked about the birth scream. It is a terrible shock to be torn away in a shower of blood with your mother screaming and your home torn open and the strange doctor with his rubber hands slapping you with all his might and the cold light piercing the dark, the warm beautiful wet dark, the silent murmuring safe dark of Mummy everywhere and Daddy, everything is one and everything is sex and we are all together for eternity and we are happy and nothing ever passes through your mind but good thoughts until suddenly this squeezing is going on around you and everyone is pushing and pulling and cold steel tongs pinch your skin and pull you by the top of your head and you don't want to go, no, you don't want to leave your home where you're always floating and your mother's heart is always beating for something unknown and cruel where people are cold and you're stinging now, everything is breaking, it makes you want to scream, Cheryl, makes you want to scream the scream of all ages, scream of the greatest tragedy of all time and your mummy is screaming and your daddy is screaming and now all the doctors are screaming and everything's blinding you and you're torn away and they're hitting you and they throw you up in the air and you open your eyes and your mother is covered in blood and you scream, Cheryl, scream, scream, SCREAM, Cheryl, SCREAM, *SCREAM!!! [Pause]* All right, we'll try it again.

SCENE TWENTY-THREE

Another DOCTOR's *office and another hotel room.*

LLOYD: Not all champagne is champagne. They call it champagne. Sure, they call it champagne. I'll tell you what is interesting about champagne. Pain. It is pains-takingly made. They take great pains.

FIFTH DOCTOR: Say I am a decent human being.

RACHEL: I am a decent human being.

FIFTH DOCTOR: Say I deserve to be loved.

RACHEL: I deserve to be loved.

FIFTH DOCTOR: Now repeat everything after me. I was put on this earth to love and be loved.

LLOYD: Great pains, believe me.

FIFTH DOCTOR: I was put on this earth…

RACHEL: I was put on this earth to love and be loved…

FIFTH DOCTOR: I am whole when I am alone and I am part of everything.

FIFTH DOCTOR: Mrs. Bophtelophti? I said I am whole when I am alone and I am part of everything.	LLOYD: And it is only in the region of Champagne where champagne is made.

RACHEL: Uh-huh.

FIFTH DOCTOR: And I would like you to repeat that.

RACHEL: Wait a minute.

FIFTH DOCTOR: What?

RACHEL: Wait a minute!

FIFTH DOCTOR: What?

RACHEL: You know what? Things just happen. People die. And bus drivers don't always look where they're going, even if they should, even if they're driving a school bus. Even if you love somebody they can still take a contract out on your life. And if you try to help somebody because they've been kind to you when you needed them, they can STILL refuse to eat and drink nothing but champagne, chamPAGNE, that's all they'll drink, and if you ask them to please, PLEASE take off their Santa Claus suit just when they go out, just when you go to the store, they won't. So? Things just happen!

SCENE TWENTY-FOUR

Another hotel room. LLOYD *moans in the glow of the television.*

RACHEL: I'm here. Shhhh. I'm here, here we go. Mother's milk. [*Produces two bottles of champagne*] It's your Christmas present, all right? I couldn't think what else to get you. I'm sorry. I got you two bottles. We're going to have a festive Christmas, just the two of us. It's our anniversary, too, remember? Don't you want to listen to the news?... Where's the knob? Did you pull out the knob?

She takes the knob from him. He tries to remove a champagne cork, but is too weak.

RACHEL: It's the one night in the year they save up all the good news. Don't you want to hear it? I'll help you with that, just a sec. Look. Doesn't that woman look like Trish Whatshername from Hands Across the Sea. Hammers. [*Putting in the knob*] My God! Lloyd, look!

Sound comes on.

ANNOUNCER:—refused to comment, but local spokesmen say Ms. Hammers may have embezzled as much as a half a million dollars in her more than twenty years as an accountant for the humanitarian organization.

RACHEL: [*Under*] Oh my....

ANNOUNCER: David Harbinger spoke with Roy Morgrebi, president of the northeast chapter of Hands Across the Sea in Springfield.

RACHEL: There's Roy! Lloyd!

ROY: It just boggles the mind, you know. Very sweet girl.

SECOND ANNOUNCER: Would you say this is something we should all begin to be wary of? Donating money to charity—

ROY: No.

SECOND ANNOUNCER: —which will end up somehow in private hands?

ROY: Definitely not. I feel this is an isolated case, one hopes, and obviously we intend to institute tighter controls.

FIRST ANNOUNCER: Police are still looking for the two alleged accomplices in last year's Christmas killing here in Springfield. More news after this word.

RACHEL: [*Over the fading sound of a commercial*] They think we did it! Lloyd! They think we did it.... She tried to poison us! And it wasn't Tom! It wasn't Tom at all!... Lloyd, we've got to go to the police, because WE DIDN'T DO IT! Don't you see? Okay! Okay! Say good-bye to Springfield!

LLOYD *is dead.*

RACHEL: Say good-bye . . .

LLOYD *slumps forward.* RACHEL *grabs him by the shirt, shakes him, lets him fall.*

SCENE TWENTY-FIVE

A shelter. RACHEL, *the* SIXTH DOCTOR, *and two* DERELICTS *in front of the television.*

TV ANNOUNCER: Street people they're called and Anne Lacher-Holden has the story.

FIRST DERELICT: [*Overlapping*] Shit on the floor, shit on the floor and you know it!

SIXTH DOCTOR: [*Overlapping*] This is us, don't you want to listen?

WOMAN ANNOUNCER: In the summertime they seem to be everywhere, but where do they go in the winter? It is in shelters like this one, in storefronts all over the city where the needy, the cold, and hungry, come for food and comfort. How many of these people would starve to death if not for the efforts and dedication of individuals like Dr. Mahalia Maden.

SECOND DERELICT: Dr. M & M's!

WOMAN ANNOUNCER: Doctor, how many years have you been running this shelter?

SIXTH DOCTOR'S VOICE: Six years this Christmas, Anne.

WOMAN ANNOUNCER: And where do you get your funds?

SECOND DERELICT: [*Under*] Steal it.

SIXTH DOCTOR'S VOICE: Well, money's a funny thing, you know. A lot of people want to help save the whales, but tell them they can help save a human being....

WOMAN ANNOUNCER: That's right. What kind of people stay here and where do they come from?

SIXTH DOCTOR'S VOICE: All over. We have bank presidents, writers, you name it.

WOMAN ANNOUNCER: What brings them here?

SIXTH DOCTOR'S VOICE: Life's been reckless with these people, Anne. Some more than others. Often they carry no identification whatsoever, it's difficult.

WOMAN ANNOUNCER: I see.

SIXTH DOCTOR'S VOICE: We have one of our people, I guess you could say she's our mascot. She came to us our first night six years ago on Christmas Eve—no idea who she was, no name, we thought she was deaf. I'll be darned if a few weeks ago she didn't start to talk in her sleep. Talks a blue streak.

WOMAN ANNOUNCER: Really?

SIXTH DOCTOR'S VOICE: Who's to say these people can't lead normal, healthy lives again.

WOMAN ANNOUNCER: You say they can. Doctor, it's been a pleasure talking with you. I'm Anne Lacher-Holden with Street Beat.

SECOND DERELICT: I'm bored.

ANNOUNCER: Thank you, Anne. Coming up we'll take a look at a woman who claims she's Santa Claus. And Marge von Bargen will—

   SIXTH DOCTOR *switches off the television.*

FIRST DERELICT: Shit on your floor and you know it!

   DERELICTS *disperse.*

SIXTH DOCTOR: [*To* RACHEL] No more secrets now, Eve. The whole world knows you can hear me and you know you hear me, because you spoke to me last night. Look at me: I asked you what was wrong and you said you were afraid and you were not asleep, Eve, so don't try that with me now. Your eyes were open and you answered me. Look at me: You answered me. What did you say? Everyone's afraid, Eve, I'm afraid. What did you say? A man in a ski mask who follows you when you leave here. Why does he follow you? Whose face is he hiding, Eve? Whose face? Behind the mask…. I have bad dreams too, Eve. I wake up in the middle of the night, too, and want someone to hold me. I remember what I did to someone once and can never, never undo. Because you can never give back a life. But I made a pledge to myself that I would try. And I went to school and I studied to be a doctor and I swore to myself that I would scrimp and save and deny myself and do anything, Eve, if I could give one person back their life. And six years ago on Christmas Eve we opened the doors here. Who do you think was the first person to walk in off the street and join us? Eve…. Do you want to know my dream? That someday you'll trust me. And tell me all your dreams, all the good ones, so I can help you make them all come true. That's my dream…. The TV people gave me some tickets to a talk show. Would you like that? A talk show? How does that sound?

SCENE TWENTY-SIX

Tv studio.

HOST: And we're back with Dr Helen Carroll, author of *Stand Up Straight*. Doctor, before the break you were saying—

HELEN: Sit up straight, David.

HOST: Sorry.

HELEN: Doesn't that feel better?

HOST: Yes, actually, it does.

HELEN: You look better and you feel better. You don't have to be tall to feel tall. Feeling tall is a state of mind.

HOST: Sounds like a song, doesn't it?

HELEN: Napoleon was tall.

HOST: Ah-hah.

HELEN: All right, everybody, sit up straight in your chairs. I want you to look out as if you're the tallest person in the room, proud. Shoulders back, don't slouch, slouch is for grouches. Don't slump, slump is for grumps. Pull this little string from the top of your head, uuuuup! All right, here's what we're talking about, come on.

> HELEN *approaches front row of the audience. Monitor reveals* RACHEL *and* SIXTH DOCTOR *seated.* HELEN *addresses* RACHEL.

HELEN: Stand up. Stand up!

SIXTH DOCTOR: No, she can't, really—

HELEN: Oh, she'll be fine. Come on.

SIXTH DOCTOR: She really shouldn't—

HELEN: Come on. [*Pulls* RACHEL *to her feet*] That's right, now turn around, look at the audience. There! Look at that face. Isn't she lovely?

> *Applause.*

HELEN: There. Now what have you got to scrunch down in your chair for, hm? No one's going to shoot you. This is what I call the I'm Not Really Here Type, David. All right now, watch. [*To* RACHEL] Shoulders back. I'm going to give you a copy of my book and I want you to read it. Chin up. That's right. Eyes straight ahead.

> RACHEL *sees something at the back of the theater.*

HELEN: Now tell us all your name in loud clear tones.

> RACHEL *shakes her head.*

HELEN: Do you have a name?

RACHEL: No.

HELEN: You don't? What do you mean—?

SIXTH DOCTOR: [*Overlapping*] Good, Eve!

RACHEL: NOOOOO! [*At the same time, a* MAN IN A SKI MASK *has screamed from the aisle of the theater.*]

MAN: DEVIL WOMAN! [*He rushes the stage, pointing a handgun at* RACHEL.]

HOST: Look out! Somebody!

> *The gun goes off.* RACHEL *ducks and* DR HELEN CARROLL *is mortally wounded. Pandemonium.*

HOST: Look out. My God! Doctor! DOCTOR!

RACHEL: NO! NO! NO!! NO!

> *The* HOST *and* DR CARROLL *disappear. The* SIXTH DOCTOR *has rushed to* RACHEL's *side.*

SCENE TWENTY-SEVEN

> *The action is continuous.* RACHEL *repeats the word "no" over and over again, struggling to break free from the* SIXTH DOCTOR.

SIXTH DOCTOR: Yes! Yes, Eve, yes! Yes! Look at me, yes, you spoke, yes, yes, yes. You spoke. Look at me. You spoke. Eve, yes, say yes. Say yes. Shhhh, I'm here, close your eyes, I'm here, yes, you spoke. Yes, and I was wrong. There was a man. You were so right, there was a man and I was wrong, I'm sorry, Eve, I was wrong. There was a man and he was trying to hurt you, but he's gone now.

> RACHEL *has quieted down.*

SIXTH DOCTOR: We'll never know why he was trying to hurt you. The important thing is you spoke out loud and people heard you and I heard you and YOU heard you, Eve. You heard you. You. Eve. If you can tell yourself what you want, you can have it. I swear to you. I used to drive a school bus. Did you know that? I drove a school bus. And how many bus drivers do you think become doctors, Eve? None. Not at all. EXCEPT THE ONES WHO DO. All right, Eve, close your eyes. I want you to imagine a place. I want you to imagine the most beautiful place in all the world. I don't want you to think about what anybody said you could or couldn't do. I want you to dream, Eve. I want you to imagine a time of year—your favorite time of year, the weather that gives you goosebumps—the right temperature, the right light in the sky, the right smell in the air. I want you to imagine someone standing there, Eve. Someone who makes people feel good about themselves and does all the things you ever wanted to do and has all the things you ever wanted to have. I want you to imagine that person standing there in that place at that exact time of day doing exactly what that person would be doing…Eve…if that person….

SCENE TWENTY-EIGHT

An office.

RACHEL: Yes?

WOMAN PATIENT: That's the end.

RACHEL: You wake up?

WOMAN PATIENT: I wake up.

RACHEL: And how do you feel?

WOMAN PATIENT: Happy.

RACHEL: The dream makes you feel happy?

WOMAN PATIENT: Yes.

RACHEL: I'm afraid we're going to have to stop here, Sharon.

WOMAN PATIENT: But what does it mean?

RACHEL: What does what mean?

WOMAN PATIENT: Why am I happy?

RACHEL: Does there have to be a reason?

WOMAN PATIENT: I don't know.

RACHEL: You're happy.

WOMAN PATIENT: Yes.

RACHEL: You feel happy now?

WOMAN PATIENT: Yes. Oh. That's what it means. It means I'm happy.

RACHEL: Yes.

WOMAN PATIENT: It means I'm happy.

RACHEL: It could mean that.

WOMAN PATIENT: It means I'm happy. Thank you.

RACHEL: Don't thank me, thank yourself.

WOMAN PATIENT: [*With* RACHEL] Thank yourself. Well… Merry Christmas.

RACHEL: You too, Sharon.

WOMAN PATIENT: I'll see you next week. [*She leaves.*]

RECEPTIONIST: [*Pokes her head in*] Doctor, there's a student here from the University of Alaska waiting to see you. They called while you were in your session to say he was coming over.

RACHEL: Send him in, thanks.

RECEPTIONIST: [*To the offstage student*] You can go on in. There you go. [*She exits as* TOM JUNIOR *enters.*]

TOM JR: Doctor?

RACHEL: Yes, I'm—[*Her throat catches.*] Sorry, there's something caught in my throat. I'm sorry if I kept you waiting.

TOM JR: [*Extending his hand*] Tom Fitsimmons.

RACHEL: Tom. Won't you, please…. Have a seat, Tom. Please. Anywhere.

He sits in the only chair.

RACHEL: What's the problem? What can I do for you? Take your time, relax, Tom, what's the story?

TOM JR: I, uh…. I was just trying to get some sleeping pills and they said I would have to, uh….

RACHEL: I see.

TOM JR: You look really familiar.

RACHEL: I do?

TOM JR: You look really familiar. Where do I know you from…?

RACHEL: Why do you think you're having trouble sleeping, Tom? Are you? Having trouble?

TOM JR: I know who you look like.

RACHEL: Your mother.

TOM JR: Yes.

RACHEL: That's the transference, Tom. The patient projects an image onto the parent. Onto the….

TOM JR: It's incredible.

RACHEL: But you say you feel you need something, is that right?

TOM JR: No, but like I've only seen pictures of her, but you really do. I mean, you're a lot older.

RACHEL: Of course.

TOM JR: But still, I mean, it's…incredible.

RACHEL: Good…. Tom, what is all this about sleeping pills? Is that what you need?

TOM JR: Sort of.

RACHEL: Why?

TOM JR: I can't sleep. But I mean, it's just for this week. I mean, next week I'll be fine, so it doesn't have to be very many.

RACHEL: Why is it just this week?

TOM JR: Because.

RACHEL: Does it have something to do with Christmas…?

TOM JR: You know, I really feel better now that we've talked. I really do. I don't think I need sleeping pills at all, it's incredible, thank you.

RACHEL: Sit down.

TOM JR: I'm serious.

RACHEL: Sit down, Tom. What is it about Christmas?…Some people think that the things you're afraid to think about are the things which eventually destroy you. And that if you talk about them, as painful as that is, it helps them to go away.

TOM JR: I'm not afraid to think about them.

RACHEL: Then what is it? You think I won't believe you?

TOM JR: Maybe.

RACHEL: Why don't you try me?

TOM JR: My mother... the one....

RACHEL: Right.

TOM JR: Ran away like on Christmas.

RACHEL: How old were you?

TOM JR: Four.

RACHEL: Go on.

TOM JR: So the next year our father, you know, leaves us with friends, so—he says because he's going to bring our mother back, because.... I don't know.

RACHEL: You have brothers and sisters?

TOM JR: One brother. Younger. And instead he gets killed.

RACHEL: Your—?

TOM JR: Father. By...well, it probably had something to do....

RACHEL: I'm listening.

TOM JR: It may have had something to do with this whole...scandal. Anyway, he died. And they said our mother was involved, but they never were able to find her. And so we were raised, you know, by—my brother and I—by these neighbors and they were really nice. And then...my brother disappeared when he was twelve and we didn't hear anything for a long time. And then he called and said he'd found this woman in California and she was gonna pay or something and...I guess he just freaked out and he shot this lady on some talk show right around Christmas time.... I don't know. I mean, they didn't convict him, but...I kind of thought I'd get away, you know? Alaska seemed like the place.

RACHEL: It is.

TOM JR: Not really. They have Christmas here too.

RACHEL: You have no memories of your mother, Tom?

TOM JR: No. Oh, yes, I do—one. But I mean, I think I dreamed it. I mean, I don't know. I think I dreamed it.

RACHEL: What is the memory?

TOM JR: Well, it's Christmas.

RACHEL: Uh-huh.

TOM JR: And, um, she's like reaching up, putting something up.

RACHEL: On the tree.

TOM JR: Uh-huh. Or something. And she's really...she's really happy. Everything's bright and she's all in a glow and she looks right at me and says, "How's that?"

RACHEL: How's that?

TOM JR: Like that. And I don't know. I just said it, you know?

RACHEL: What?

TOM JR: Lousy, you're fired. I was just kidding.

RACHEL: Of course.

TOM JR: But... sometimes it seems like that was the start of everything. It's like I hurt her feelings or something and she left and my father left and my brother left.... I keep feeling like if I could just go back to that—time. And she would turn to me, you know, all lit up and say, "How's that?" I'd say, "Beautiful, Mom." You know.

RACHEL: Uh-huh.

TOM JR: Because it was like for one second I wanted to spoil everything. Everybody was too happy and I was too excited. But I would take it back. I would take it all back, because I didn't mean it.

RACHEL: Of course you didn't mean it.

TOM JR: No, but I can't. It's like I can't wake up. I just know—I feel if I could just wake up, we'd all be there around the tree and my mom and dad would take care of me. And I keep pinching myself and pinching....

RACHEL: Trying to wake up.

TOM JR: Yes. I just keep wishing—

RACHEL: Yes.

TOM JR: —for....

RACHEL: Someplace where it's always Christmas.

TOM JR: Yes. How do you know?...Oh, I see, now you become my mother.

RACHEL: How's this time for you, Tom? Is this is all right?

TOM JR: Fine. Are we through?

RACHEL: Tomorrow at this time?

TOM JR: Fine.

RACHEL: And the day after?

TOM JR: Great. Wait, that's Christmas.

RACHEL: Would you rather not?

TOM JR: No. You work on Christmas?

RACHEL: I love my work. And try to hold off the sleeping pills for a while, all right?

TOM JR: Sure.

RACHEL: Tomorrow then?

TOM JR: Great.

RACHEL: Tom?... I'm sorry I kept you waiting.

TOM JR: Oh, no problem. Oh, I see. Right. Right. Well.... Tomorrow.

> TOM *goes.* RACHEL *moves to the window as* "I'll Be Home for Christmas" *plays and snow falls. The lights fade.*

END

Pedro Pietri

❧

The Masses Are Asses

The Masses Are Asses © 1984 by Pedro Pietri

Dedicated to:
Don Wallach, Bea Wallach and Nancy Wallach

The Masses Are Asses is a one-act play that takes place in a fancy restaurant or an empty apartment. The time is sometime last week.

The title of this play is original regardless of how many times the title has been used before. Any resemblance to the masses living or dead is purely coincidental.

Characters:

LADY	30 or 93
GENTLEMAN	93 or 30

In the middle of this empty apartment or fancy Restaurant there is a small round table covered with a white tablecloth and 2 chairs. At the center of the table there is a lit blue candle in a candle holder. There's a bottle of champagne, a rose in a jar, two drinking glasses, silverware, napkins and two menus on the table. To the far right of the table against the back grayish wall there is a toilet with water tank overhead and a chain hanging down from the tank to flush the toilet. A roll of toilet paper is on the floor close by. To the far left of the table inbetween table and wall there is a bath tub. There is a telephone on the floor in front of the bath tub. The door is against the back wall in-between the toilet and table. There are no windows. A square shaped mirror hangs on the wall above facing the bath tub. The lights are low for the time being.

Snobbish throat clearing is heard for the first 10 seconds. Knocking on the door is heard for the next 11 seconds. Snobbish throat clearing resumes for another 12 seconds. The telephone rings for the next 13 seconds. Snobbish throat clearing resumes for 14 seconds. The lights get brighter. Voices of a LADY *and* GENTLEMAN *are heard.*

GENTLEMAN: Hurry up dear, our reservation is for eight and it's a quarter to, already.

LADY: I'll be through in a minute darling, I'm putting on my make up.

Snobbish throat clearing resumes for the next 15 seconds.

GENTLEMAN: We'll never get there on time at the rate you are going. We should have been on our way over there by now.

LADY: So we get there late, so what, the restaurant isn't going to go anywhere.

GENTLEMAN: This is Paris not Paramus! If you make reservations for a certain time in a fancy restaurant you must be on time or you will lose the reservation.

LADY: What is the name of the restaurant?

GENTLEMAN: La Plume De Ma Tante.

LADY: What does that mean in English?

GENTLEMAN: Come on, let's leave already and stop asking so many questions.

Snobbish throat clearing resumes for 15 seconds. A well dressed LADY *and* GENTLEMAN *rise from inside the bath tub, they climb out, hold hands, and walk over to the table. He pulls out a chair for her to sit. He sits on the other chair. They smile at each other. Clear their throats (snobbishly) as they read menus for the next 17 seconds. They put menus down and stare at each other for 18 seconds.*

GENTLEMAN: You look terrific.

LADY: You look fantastic.

GENTLEMAN: You look gorgeous.

LADY: You look marvelous.

GENTLEMAN: You look exciting.
LADY: You look demanding.
GENTLEMAN: You look outstanding.
LADY: Shall we order?
GENTLEMAN: No, not just yet.
LADY: [*smiles at her* GENTLEMAN] You look official.
GENTLEMAN: You look legitimate.
LADY: You look important.
GENTLEMAN: You look interesting.
LADY: You look uptodate.
GENTLEMAN: You look futuristic.
LADY: You look futuristicker.
GENTLEMAN: Shall we order?
LADY: Not just yet.
    The telephone rings. They remain silent until the phone stops ringing after 10th ring.
GENTLEMAN: You look superb.
LADY: You look superber.
GENTLEMAN: You look astonishing.
LADY: You look astonishingshinger.
GENTLEMAN: You look just great.
LADY: You look just greater.
GENTLEMAN: Let's order.
LADY: Yes, let's order.
GENTLEMAN: No, not just yet.
    Loud knocking is heard. The LADY *and her* GENTLEMAN *remain silent until the knocking stops 19 seconds later.*
LADY: Okay, then later.
GENTLEMAN: You look majestic.
LADY: You look majestica.
GENTLEMAN: You look magnificent.
LADY: You look unquestionable.
GENTLEMAN: You look memorable.
LADY: Let's order now.
GENTLEMAN: Yes, let's, but before we do there is something very important that I have to say to you.
LADY: What is it?
GENTLEMAN: You look wonderful.
LADY: You look wonderfuller.
GENTLEMAN: You look absolutely amazing.
LADY: You look absolutely fascinazing.
GENTLEMAN: You look spontaneous.
LADY: You look instantaneous.
GENTLEMAN: You look eternally fine.

LADY: You look eternally finer.

GENTLEMAN: You look desirable and admirable.

LADY: You look admirable and desirable.

> *Phone ringing and loud knocking is heard for 19 seconds.*

LADY: Let's order.

GENTLEMAN: I don't feel like it.

LADY: Why not?

GENTLEMAN: I just want to observe you.

LADY: Why, thank you very much.

GENTLEMAN: You look flabbergasting everlasting.

LADY: You look everlastinger flabbagastinger.

GENTLEMAN: You always look astounding.

LADY: You always look astoundingdinger.

> *Phone rings. They remain silent. It stops after 10th ring.*

GENTLEMAN: [*whispering*] I have a nice surprise for you.

LADY: [*also whispering*] You do?

GENTLEMAN: [*still whispering*] Yes I do.

LADY: [*still whispering*] Is it expensive?

GENTLEMAN: [*still whispering*] It's more precious than gold.

LADY: [*still whispering*] Nothing is more precious than gold.

GENTLEMAN: [*still whispering*] What I have for you is.

LADY: [*still whispering*] I give up, what is it?

GENTLEMAN: [*still whispering*] I have been secretly taping all the compliments we have exchanged.

LADY: [*still whispering*] You have? Oh, how exciting!

GENTLEMAN: [*still whispering*] Let's listen to it.

LADY: [*still whispering*] By all means!

GENTLEMAN: [*still whispering*] Okay, I'll turn on the recorder.

> *The* GENTLEMAN *brings out a small cassette from a pocket inside his suit jacket and turns it on. The recording is heard loud and clear.*

—You look terrific.

—You look fantastic.

—You look gorgeous.

—You look marvelous.

—You look exciting.

—You look demanding.

—You look outstanding.

LADY: Oh, how extremely exciting!

GENTLEMAN: [*turns off tape*] We sound intellectually romantic. Let's drink to the sound of our voices.

LADY: Oh yes, let us drink to that.

GENTLEMAN: [*removes cork from bottle, pours his* LADY *a drink, then pours himself one.*] To the romantic voices we proudly possess!

They make a toast and drink.

LADY: Please put the tape back on so we can continue listening to our interesting voices.

GENTLEMAN: Absolutely. By all means. Listening to our voices is the most exciting event of my life. You know what? I am going to mail this tape to our friends in New York City so they can hear what a wonderful time we are having on our vacation in Europe. Oh they are going to be so envious of us when they hear this tape.

Turns on the machine.

LADY: Yes, that is a terrific idea.

They toast and drink again.

—You look official.

—You look legitimate.

—You look important.

—You look interesting.

—You look uptodate.

—You look futuristic.

—You look futuristicker.

—You look superb.

—You look superber.

Gun shots are heard. They both hide under the table. The recorder remains on as the firing continues. Police sirens are heard.

—You look superb.

—You look superber.

—You look astonishing.

—You look indestructable.

—You look just great.

—You look just greater.

—You look majestic.

—You look majestica.

—You look magnificent.

Tape malfunctions, keeps repeating line: YOU LOOK MAGNIFICENT! *Firing and siren stops after 20 seconds.* LADY *and* GENTLEMAN *cautiously rise, and sit down.* GENTLEMAN *turns off tape recorder.*

GENTLEMAN: [*wiping sweat off his forehead*] That must be the A.B.C.D.E.F.G.H.I. terrorist group.

LADY: [*surprised*] In Paris?

GENTLEMAN: Yes, they are an international Terrorist Group.

LADY: What does A.B.C.D.E.F.G.H.I. stand for?

GENTLEMAN: Let's make sure the coast is clear before I divulge that information to you.

They look in every direction to make sure the coast is clear.

LADY: The coast is clear. What does it stand for?

GENTLEMAN: Armed

Brave
Comrades
Determined
Efficient
Fighters
Gonna
Humiliate
Imperialism!

LADY: Such utter nonsense. Don't they ever learn that the ruling class shall continue to rule regardless of who declares war against us. Our Armies and Navies and Air Forces are as you will say before and after dinner: In…In…In…

GENTLEMAN: INVINCIBLE! And the sooner those animals learn that, the sooner those savages can start planning for the future of their existence. We, the now and forever and ever Ruling Classes possess the most advanced sophisticated deadly lethal weapons to wipe out whatever inferiorly armed opposition group of idealistic scatterbrains challenges our godly belief in global political domination by any ungodly means necessary!

LADY: Such utter utter nonsense, these violent means of theirs to bring about change. Spare change to the city morgue is all their uncivilized tactics are going to bring those unsanitary radicals. They should take a bath and a haircut and shave, so some decent democratic employment agency can find them a full-time patriotic job, my god!

GENTLEMAN: Our flawless system is too organized and wise to be destabilized. Let's drink to what I just said…[*pours them both a drink, they toast and drink up*]…The poor people are just going to have to stay poor because rich folks like us have all legitimate intentions of maintaining our prestigious and advantageous standard of living. If the good lord wanted everybody to be rich he would have made everybody rich, but since that wasn't the case because god isn't as dumb as some people will want him to be, he made some of us rich and most of them poor. God knows socialism is an unworkable system.

LADY: A-men!

GENTLEMAN: I thank god every day of my higher standards of living for giving me plenty to be thankful for. I guess if I was poor I would also have to be thankful for being poor, but somebody up there likes me, so I have nothing to worry about. Yes, I do think that the reason poor people are poor is because god doesn't think too highly of them. So, let us make a toast to the holy ghost for making a wise decision and giving us this day not only our daily bread, but also the company that bakes it.
   Refills glasses, they toast and drink.

LADY: Imagine having to work for a living instead of having others work for your living? Oh, how absolutely degrading! Just the mere thought of it sends chills up and down my upper class spine.

GENTLEMAN: [*He refills the glasses. They will toast and drink after every statement they make praising the ruling class.*]Long live the ruling classes!

LADY: God bless the very rich always and forever!

GENTLEMAN: Give me prosperity or give me death!

LADY: Give me a mink, expensive jewelry and another mink!

GENTLEMAN: Long live Monarchy! Long live our Mansion! Long live our limousine!

LADY: Long live our Maid, Butler, And Chauffeur!

GENTLEMAN: [*Refills glasses.*] The Masses Are Asses!

LADY: Hey, that rhymes.

> *They toast and drink.*

GENTLEMAN: Masses has always rhymed with asses!

LADY: And gasses. Get it? Masses Asses Gasses!

GENTLEMAN: The gasses that come out of the masses asses smell like molasses.

LADY: Hey that was unique…[*they toast and drink*] The ruling classes never passes gasses that smell like the molasses of the masses' gasses!

GENTLEMAN: Superb!…[*refills glasses. They toast and drink.*] The masses whose gasses smell like molasses because they are asses will never drink champagne in these expensive glasses of the ruling classes!

LADY: Terrific. You are a genius with masses and asses.

GENTLEMAN: Well of course. After all I was the one who coined the phrase: The Masses Are Asses! Why? Because the masses are really asses exploited by the ruling classes with their military brasses and expensive champagne glasses because the gasses that passes from the asses of the masses not only smell like molasses it also stinks like perkasses!

LADY: Perkasses? What does that mean?

GENTLEMAN: I don't know. But as long as it rhymes with masses and asses it doesn't really matter what it means.

> *They toast and drink.*

LADY: Before you added the word asses to masses, what did the ruling classes call the masses?

GENTLEMAN: Assholes. But that didn't rhyme, and it sounded too lower classish, so I changed it to asses when referring to the masses to give the ass class.

> *They toast and drink.*

LADY: Arm struggle…ha ha ha…it makes as much sense as believing that god doesn't exist.

GENTLEMAN: When you come to think of it, arm struggle rhymes with water bubbles. And you know what happens to water bubbles after the struggle to become bubbles? They burst and disintegrate. Therefore any struggle that rhymes with water bubbles just doubles your troubles. Hey, that was really interesting what I just said. Let's make a toast to that statement.

> *He refills glasses. They toast and drink. The phone is heard ringing.*

LADY: The phone keeps ringing in this fancy restaurant.

GENTLEMAN: Those are millionaires calling up to make reservations. You just don't walk into this high class establishment out of the cold and expect to be accommodated. People make reservations weeks in advance to eat among the elite. But, because of my wealth and influence and verbal capacity with bureaucracy I was accommodated the same day that I made the reservation. Yes, it pays to be rich, you don't have to wait or wish for anything!

LADY: I'll drink to that.

The phone stops ringing.

GENTLEMAN: Let's wait until I say something really clever to toast to. Too much expensive champagne on an empty stomach can have unimpressive social consequences.

LADY: True, it will be contradictory to our high standards and higher moral values to be seen stoned in public.

GENTLEMAN: My dear, only poor people get stoned. The proper word to utter when an aristocrat overindulges is: Tipsy! Stoned is a ghetto adjective.

LADY: Let's order now, darling, I'm very hungry.

GENTLEMAN: Okay, but before we do order, let's continue bad mouthing poor people just a little longer, it makes ingestion a more exciting event. The more I badmouth the poor the better I eat. I'll try not to be too witty so we don't have to toast to almost everything I say. Though at times, I dare admit, it's beyond my control not to make clever statements.

LADY: That is why I find you so interesting.

GENTLEMAN: That is why I am so interesting. Who else but I will come up with the brilliant idea of secretly taping the highlights of our vacation? Nobody, absolutely nobody that you or I or any of our influential associates can think of.

LADY: Meeting you has been a rewarding experience.

GENTLEMAN: Yes my dear, that is quite true, if I say so myself, and why shouldn't I? Modesty is a tradition of the masses which we have both agreed are nothing but...

A loud explosion is heard, knocking them both off their seats. The lights blink on and off rapidly. Police sirens are heard for 30 seconds. The LADY *and* GENTLEMAN *are under the table. They snobbishly clear their throats as they cautiously rise.*

GENTLEMAN: Are you okay, my dear???

LADY: Yes. And yourself???

GENTLEMAN: I'm fine...[*They both sit down. Refills glasses*]...The A.B.C.D.E.F.G.H.I. is upgrading their terrorist tactics. They have gone from bullets to bombs...[*They both drink up. He refills glasses*]...If those lunatics aren't stopped, next it will be ballistic missiles on their agenda of aggression against us.

LADY: My God, what mental retards they are. Everyone else but them seem to know they are fighting a losing battle...[*They both drink up in one gulp*].

GENTLEMAN: If only they stop being so violent and educate themselves they will learn that history repeats itself. In all the glorious wars mankind has experienced, the masses have never once been victorious. All rebellions and insurrections have been crushed, directly or indirectly, and that is the way the world is going to be, always. True, there are some countries that give you the impression of functioning under a socialist political apparatus, but the truth of the matter is that those governments are fabricated and subsidized by almighty capitalistic regimes with the means and the might to dismantle them. There are still Czars in the USSR.

LADY: You know something? And may the good lord forgive me for what I am about to say...

GENTLEMAN: [*interrupting*] As long as you ask for forgiveness first you can say anything that's on your mind.

LADY: I personally think that the only solution for poor people is suicide, since overthrowing us is out of the question and history will continue to prove it. I know it sounds inhuman but what else is there for people whose only ambition in life is to be totally miserable? This is a democratic society. If you make the decision to be rich you will be rich and if you make the decision to be poor you will be poor!

GENTLEMAN: That was superbly said, my dear...[*They toast and drink*]...Their depravity is their own fault, not ours. To begin with poor people are so divided that it becomes impossible for them to improve themselves. They always want what the next person has without making an effort to obtain it themselves, right? Of course I'm right. Poor people are the biggest backstabbers on the face of the earth. They are always bad mouthing each other. Now a rich person will never criticize another rich person behind his or her back, right?

LADY: Of course you are right.

GENTLEMAN: The rich respects the rich and the poor despises the poor!

LADY: May the good lord forgive me again and again, but I truly believe suicide is the best solution for them. Or deportation to a socialist society where everything is free. True, freedom of expression is prohibited, but it won't be so bad for them because they can't express themselves anyhow.

GENTLEMAN: That is a good solution but not perfect. If we get rid of every single one of them, that will also include our maid and butler and chauffeur! I am not going to serve myself or drive my own Lincoln Continental limousine...[*refills glasses*]

LADY: True darling, you do have a point there. The servants of the rich should be spared. But, under the conditions that they be sterilized after their 2nd offspring so that overpopulation won't reoccur...[*drinks*]...Oh yes, now that we are on the subject of low lifers I have a complaint to make about our Maid.

GENTLEMAN: [*takes a drink*] What seems to be the problem with our maid?

LADY: [*whispers loud enough to be heard*] I caught her masturbating on the job a few times already.

GENTLEMAN: Hmm, I'll deal with her when we return from Europe.

LADY: It's not that I'm against masturbation. But she is supposed to be working, not masturbating. I know she is just a maid, but her job also requires a great deal of concentration. And you know it is absolutely impossible to concentrate when you masturbate. I think she should be dismissed or be deducted every time we apprehend her...[*takes a drink*]...Now take our butler for example, he has the bad habit of scratching in between his legs on the job, but it doesn't prevent him from performing his duties properly. Our chauffeur is catatonic but he still functions on the job. True, you can scratch your balls, I mean private areas, on the job and still function, but you can't do anything else if you play with yourself except play with yourself!

GENTLEMAN: Don't worry dear, maids come a dime a dozen.

LADY: You know something? I am really starving.

GENTLEMAN: [*visibly upset*] Lower your voice, somebody might hear you.

Gun shots are heard again. They rise and hide under the table. Police sirens are heard. Firing continues for 90 seconds.

LADY: [*still under the table*] It seems to have stopped.

GENTLEMAN: Those goddamn imbeciles are out of their minds. Good for nothing idealistic bastards! When will they learn they are fighting a losing battle?

Together they cautiously rise and sit back down on the chairs

LADY: Shall we order now?

GENTLEMAN: No, not just yet. Listen, I have a terrific idea. Let's continue listening to the recording of our voices. That always cheers us up whenever we are upset. First we'll have another drink, then I'll turn on the cassette.

Refills the glasses, they toast and drink. He turns on the cassette.

—You look wonderful.

—You look wonderfuller.

—You look absolutely amazing.

—You look absolutely fascinazing.

—You look spontaneous.

—You look instantaneous.

—You look eternally fine.

—You look eternally finer.

—You look desirable and admirable.

—You look admirable and desirable.

—You look flabbergasting everlasting

—You look everlastinger flabbergastinger

—You always look astounding

—You always look astoundingdinger.

GENTLEMAN: Feeling better?

LADY: Yes, one hundred percent better. I'm ready to order.

GENTLEMAN: [*turns off tape*] I have a better idea, dear. Let's have some fun before we order. Let's pretend that we are poor people with many problems in the world. You pretend to be an eternal factory worker earning minimum wages and I'll pretend to be a full-time pathological street loiterer with an incorrigible drinking problem.

LADY: That is a fabulous idea. I will rather pretend to be a welfare recipient—that is less exhausting. Refill my glass first so I can get a little tipsy and start thinking and acting and talking like a poor hopeless destitute slob.

GENTLEMAN: If we are to pretend correctly we have to drink from the bottle like poor people do.

Takes a drink from the bottle and passes the bottle to her.

LADY: This is going to be fun…[*drinks from bottle*]…Okay man, I'm ready to pretend I'm poor. Give me five, man…[*extends her hand*]

GENTLEMAN: [*slaps palm of her hand in hip manner*] What's the word?

LADY: Thunderbird.

GENTLEMAN: What's nice?

LADY: Rice!

GENTLEMAN: What's mean?

LADY: Beans!

GENTLEMAN: What gets to the point?

LADY: Loose joints.

GENTLEMAN: What does harm?

LADY: Methadone!

GENTLEMAN: What do we expect?

LADY: Welfare checks!

GENTLEMAN: What's in the market?

LADY: Pickpockets.

GENTLEMAN: What's real fine?

LADY: The perfect crime!

GENTLEMAN: Out of sight! Give me five, baby… [*she slaps the palm of his hand*]…Okay baby, now let's not only talk like them, let's also walk like them. So baby, like rise and let's you and I like pretend we are taking a stroll in the ghetto while we like rap.

LADY: How am I doing so far, talking like a poor slob?

GENTLEMAN: Like far out and groovy, baby.

> *They slap each other five, rise, take a drink from the bottle and start cat walking.*

GENTLEMAN: Hey baby, you know how to nod?

LADY: Yeah man. I learned from the flick "Fort Apache."

GENTLEMAN: Crazy. Like let's also nod while we rap… [*nods exaggeratedly*]…Hey baby, like what time you gots?

LADY: [*does likewise*]…Like I ain't gots the time.

GENTLEMAN: Like how come you ain't gots the time, baby?

LADY: Because like my watch is in the pawnshop, man, and like I ain't gots the bucks to like get it out anytime soon, you dig?

GENTLEMAN: Yeah, I can dig, baby. Like times are extremely uncool lately and getting like worse. Like it's a drag man, a real drag. I mean like wow, inflation ain't groovy at all, check it out.

LADY: Yeah man, these are definitely some uncool times. The price of inexpensive wine has also like gone sky high, check that out also, man.

GENTLEMAN: Weird man, I mean like absolutely weird, baby. You know man, like I been like seriously like thinking about robbing a bank, no shit, baby. Like wow, how long can you remain down and out?

LADY: Hey man, give me five on that [*he slaps her five*] …like I been like digging on that idea myself, man. Give me five again, like we seem to be like thinking about the same thing, man.

GENTLEMAN: [*slaps her five*] Yeah baby. I mean like being broke ain't no joke. But as long as I can still cop my wine everything is fine, but when it becomes like impossible to cop some wine then like is time to take drastic measures, dig it?

L A D Y: Yeah, like with or without a shovel, man.

G E N T L E M A N: I mean like wow, you gotta cut loose with your own juice because like ain't nobody gonna let you cut loose with their juice and like that's the truth as far as cutting loose with somebody's else's juice. [*drinks, passes her the bottle*]...Hey baby like was your mama also on welfare and food stamps?

L A D Y: Yeah man. Like not only was my mama on welfare but my mama's mama's mama and her mama and her mama's mama's mama also was on welfare.

G E N T L E M A N: Like all my mamas too, baby...[*slap each other five*]...Hey baby, like let's sit down, I'm getting like dizzy, dig?...[*they cat walk to table and sit down*].
Gunshots are heard.

G E N T L E M A N: Wow, bang, bang...insurrection...give me five for the A.B.C.D.E.F.G.H.I. and pass me the bottle of wine if you don't mind.
Takes a drink, hands him the bottle, slaps him five.

L A D Y: Long Live those Guys of the A.B.C.D.E.F.G.H.I.

G E N T L E M A N: [*Slaps her five as he takes a drink*]

L A D Y: Long Live those Guys of the A.B.C.D.E.F.G.H.I.
The A.B.C.D.E.F.G.H.I. will never die!
Slaps him five. Takes bottle and drinks.

G E N T L E M A N: Their badness is the reason why!

L A D Y: Long live those guys of the A.B.C.D.E.F.G.H.I.
Shooting stops.

G E N T L E M A N: Hey man, like who are those dudes anyway? And why do these guys from the A.B.C.D.E.F.G.H.I. have to like be having shoot-outs in public for? I mean like don't those guys know innocent people could die? Like you and I, for example. Man those guys from the A.B.C.D.E.F.G.H.I. are jive!

L A D Y: Yeah man, like they ain't gots no respect for human lives, and that ain't cool at all. Wow, like later for those guys from the A.B.C.D.E.F.G.H.I.
Phone is heard ringing.

L A D Y: Wow, like I hear the phone ringing.

G E N T L E M A N: Yeah like me, too, it sounds far out, man. Like I bet you is probably an uncool bill collector. Or somebody we like owe a lotta bread to. So like let it ring, dig it?

L A D Y: Yeah, I can dig it.

G E N T L E M A N: I mean like if we answer the phone, baby, we be depriving ourselves of that far out of sight ringing...Give me five so it can keep ringing for the longest, baby.

L A D Y: [*Slaps him five*] Solid. Hey cool, like is about time you pass that wine this way. Like I like to drink when I am listening to a telephone ringing.

G E N T L E M A N: Like me too...[*takes a drink, passes her the wine*] Man, like that ringing is too much!

L A D Y: [*Takes a drink*] Like would you like to dance to the ringing?

G E N T L E M A N: Yeah baby, like why not? Every time I like hear the phone ringing I feel like dancing. Give me five baby...[*She slaps him five*]...like let's dance.

They rise and waltz to the sound of the telephone ringing.

GENTLEMAN: Man, like whoever it is ain't given up easy. I hope they are getting like pissed off.

LADY: Like me too, man. I mean, wow, they should take a hint. Like either we are not here or like we just ain't answering the phone.

GENTLEMAN: Wow, that is really determination. Hey, baby, like we are supposed to be grinding. We ain't suppose to be waltzing. Poor people don't waltz, like they grind all the time.

LADY: Yeah, that's right…[*they go from a fast waltz to a slow sensual grind*]…Is this better?

GENTLEMAN: Yeah like much better…[*grinds harder*]…hey baby like when is we supposed to be getting evicted?

LADY: Like any day now, like maybe that is the landlord trying to evict us by phone, man.

Ringing stops.

GENTLEMAN: Wow, it stop ringing, man, like too bad, I was really digging the ringing. Like we gotta stop grinding now so people don't think we is bananas dancing when the telephone aint ringing, baby.

LADY: Yeah, like I guess we should sit and get blind.

They slap each other five and sit down.

GENTLEMAN: My dear, I think we should discontinue emulating the despondent. It's a lot of fun but it's also depressing as all hell.

LADY: That's cool with me, man.

GENTLEMAN: Pass me the bottle so I can pour us a drink like civilized people.

LADY: Hey man, like this ain't got nothing in it anymore.

GENTLEMAN: [*takes bottle from her, rises*] I will get us some more champagne, my dear.

LADY: Cool.

GENTLEMAN: Stop expressing yourself like an imbecile. We are no longer emulating the despondent, my dearest.

He walks over to the bath tub, brings out a quart-size bottle of Thunderbird, removes the cap and pours Thunderbird wine into the empty champagne bottle. Rejoins LADY.

LADY: Wow, like more champagne, far out, let's get totally wasted.

GENTLEMAN: Dear, you are getting on my nerves already with that despicable slang. Stop it or else you will have to keep drinking from the bottle.

Loud knocking is heard.

LADY: [*rises*] Like I'll go see who like is there, man.

GENTLEMAN: [*visibly upset*] Sit down! We are not here! We are in Europe vacationing. And for the last time stop talking like a mental retard!

LADY: [*sits back down.*] You know something man, like it really be nice if we were like actually in Europe.

GENTLEMAN: We are actually in Europe!…

Knocking stops.

LADY: Yeah, like I know that, but I mean like if we were nowhere else BUT Europe, dig it?

GENTLEMAN: You are so dumb, how can we be in two places at the same time? Of course we are nowhere else but in Europe!!! No more champagne for you baby. [*upset for using the word baby*] You see, now you have me talking like that! I am not going to warn you again, discontinue the destitute jargon. Like we, I mean we are in a foreign country and we have to make an intelligent expression, I mean impression…listen dammit! Just cut it out already! Nobody here speaks that way.

LADY: Man, like I'm sure they have some poverty stricken dudes here who like express themselves in a hip manner.

GENTLEMAN: There is nothing HIP about being stupid. You are either intelligent or ignorant. I should tape the way you are expressing yourself so you can hear how extremely idiotic you sound.

LADY: Hey man, that sounds like a groovy idea. Yeah, let's like tape, man.

GENTLEMAN: Definitely not! I am not going to waste good tape on terrible slang.

LADY: Come on man, like let's re-cord, dig it!

GENTLEMAN: [*Whispering*]…Stop talking like that. People are beginning to stare at us disdainfully.

LADY: Like if this is really Europe, they ain't gonna understand anything we say, dig?

GENTLEMAN: Yes they can. They speak many languages. That's why they are Europeans and not Americans.

LADY: Man, like we should split from Europe already. This vacation is becoming a drag. Like there is absolutely nothing for us to do on this head trip but pretend to be affluent, man.

GENTLEMAN: [*Rises, speaks directly to her*] We are not pretending to be affluent! We are affluent! And we are not due back from Europe until the middle of next week! So stop fussing and enjoy your vacation AND STOP talking like you were a resident of a depraved community! And furthermore this is not a head trip we are on, this is an actual trip that we took!

Sits back down.

LADY: Sure man, pour me another drink.

GENTLEMAN: Absolutely not. You have had too much to drink already. That is why you think we are no longer in Europe. And that is also the reason why you can't seem to stop talking like a moron! So I strongly suggest you keep your mouth shut until you sober up because somebody might hear you speaking in that despicable manner and think we are here to hold up the establishment.

Pours himself a drink.

LADY: Man, I could sure use something to eat. Like I'm starving.

GENTLEMAN: You already ate once today. Tomorrow you will eat again. We can't be eating everything in one day, we still have a whole week ahead of us in Europe. Everything is measured out. There will be no in-between meals on this vacation.

LADY: Man, but I thought you said we were affluent, dig it? Ain't we supposed to be dining out?

GENTLEMAN: [*Rises, smacks her across the face*] I told you to keep your mouth shut if you can't speak like an educated civilized human being! Now don't use another slang or I'll smack you across the face again.

LADY: Wow, that was really painful.

> *He smacks her across the face a few times. She doesn't blink an eyelid or make an attempt to defend herself.*

GENTLEMAN: Stop it!…[*Speaking as he is smacking her*]…stop it right this minute or I will cut your vacation short and send you back to New York by yourself! We are in Europe, not in the South Bronx. People here don't bastardize the English language or any other language that they fluently speak!

LADY: Okay, Okay, I'll make a deal with you. If you let me eat tomorrow's meal today and the next day's meal tomorrow, I will speak as correctly as you want me to speak. It's impossible for me to be articulate on an empty stomach.

GENTLEMAN: Absolutely not! Everything has been rationed until we return from our vacation…[*Sits down*]

LADY: Okay then, cut my vacation short. I've had enough of this pretending to be rich nonsense. That cheap wine has made me very hungry and I would like something to eat right now or else I am going to pass out.

GENTLEMAN: This is not cheap wine, this is expensive champagne we are drinking! And for the last time you will eat tomorrow when I eat, not any sooner! And don't you ever again say I am pretending to be rich! I don't have to pretend! I have a maid, a butler, and a chauffeur!

LADY: Yes, that you pay from our welfare check. That's why there's never anything to eat around here. All our money goes on servants who don't serve us anything because we don't have anything for them to serve us. There is absolutely nothing for them to do around here. That's why the maid is always jerking off and the butler is always scratching his balls and the chauffeur stares at four blank walls all day long in this closet size apartment that used to be a toilet and still is a toilet and will always be a toilet! Get rid of the servants so we call move into a bigger place and enjoy a balanced diet!

GENTLEMAN: Quiet! I don't want to hear anymore of your nonsense. For your information I do not pay the servants minimum wages. I pay them below average wages and there is nobody they can complain to because they are illegal aliens. They have no fringe benefits with me at all. Should they miss a day of work they will not get paid. Nor will they get paid time an' a half should they work overtime or on holidays!

LADY: We don't need them. There is nothing for them to do around here. Why do we need a chauffeur when we don't even own a car to be chauffeured around in?

GENTLEMAN: All rich people have chauffeurs whether they own a car or not. It is a tradition that has been passed down through the generations of the upper classes. If we didn't have a chauffeur nobody would ever believe that we are affluent.

LADY: I don't believe it either…[*Rises, walks as she speaks*]…I'm fed up with pretending to be in Europe when the truth is we haven't left the South Bronx since we moved into this damn toilet! I'm fed up with pretending to be somebody I'm totally unfamiliar with. It's driving me crazy. If the phone rings or someone knocks on the door we can't answer either one because you want everybody to believe that we are on vacation in Europe. Lord knows how many weddings and functions we missed for being and not being here. Why don't you just accept the fact that you are not rich and get yourself a full-time job?

GENTLEMAN: Stop complaining so much or else I am not going to let you drink champagne in fancy restaurants with me anymore.

LADY: Stop deceiving yourself. This isn't no fancy restaurant and you know it! And that is cheap Thunderbird wine we are drinking from a champagne bottle you found in the gutter somewhere.

GENTLEMAN: Lower your voice! Don't talk so the whole building can hear you. Do you want the neighbors to think we never left for Europe?

LADY: Well, we never did leave for Europe or any other place. We don't even know what Staten Island looks like, never mind a foreign country.

GENTLEMAN: [*Rises*] As far as you and everybody else are concerned at this precise moment you and I are vacationing in Europe and won't be back until the middle of next week when our maid and butler and chauffeur return from their unpaid vacation so we won't have to serve ourselves or be burdened with doing domestic work around here! [*Sits back down.*]

LADY: Oh, stop being so unrealistic! Nobody believes we are in Europe anyway. That's why we keep receiving phone calls and people keep knocking on our door. You aren't fooling anyone but yourself and making life completely miserable for me. If you want to be rich you have to try to get rich, not just pretend you are rich.

GENTLEMAN: I knew I should have married someone from my own upper class environment and social standards. It was a mistake to think I could educate you into becoming sophisticated and distinguished.

LADY: Listen to yourself speak, you have really convinced yourself of this foolishness of being an aristocrat…[*Slight pause*]…excuse me, I have to take a crap…[*Walks to toilet*]

GENTLEMAN: Be sure not to flush the toilet when you are through. You know how sound travels in a tenement building. Someone is bound to hear it and spread the word that we lied about going to Europe.

LADY: [*Lifts up her dress. Isn't wearing underpants. She sits down on toilet seat*] This toilet hasn't been flushed since the first day of our imaginary European trip a few weeks ago. The smell is unbearable. I am going to flush it already.

GENTLEMAN: Why don't you be sensible? If you flush that damn toilet we are going to have to walk with our heads down when we return from our vacation because everyone will know that we never left this apartment. I strongly suggest that you DON'T FLUSH the toilet!

LADY: [*Moving her bowels, farts loudly*] Ahhha…Ahhh…Ahhh…Ohhh…Ahhh…

GENTLEMAN: Will you stop farting so loud for crying out loud! Someone is bound to hear you. Move your bowels like an aristocrat, not like a welfare recipient. That is precisely the reason why you shouldn't eat so much on this vacation, because the more you eat the more you have to move your goddamn bowels and put our honor and integrity in jeopardy around here.

LADY: The rich don't shit any better than the poor. More maybe, and the sounds and odors are identical...ahhh...ahhh...[*farts*]...oooh...ahhh...

GENTLEMAN: Dammit! Keep the noise down or stop what you are doing right this minute! I haven't pretended to be rich and successful all these years, convincing all my neighbors of my wealth to have you mess up everything for me in a matter of seconds. Now I'm warning you, one more loud fart from you and you will have to get up off the toilet regardless of whether you are through or not!

LADY: At what age did you lose grips with reality? Or were you always this way? What happened in your life that has made you refuse to accept the circumstances of your existence? If you are poor you should try to improve your situation, not pretend that you aren't poor. That is not going to solve any problems for you.

GENTLEMAN: If only you knew how mentally gratifying it is to pretend you have no problems in the world. You would also be rich and influential like myself and not fart so loud when you move your bowels. [*Another loud fart is heard*] Okay, that's it for you! Get up, it's getting too risky. That last fart you laid was probably heard throughout the entire building. Come on get up, now!

LADY: I am not through yet.

GENTLEMAN: As far as I am concerned you are. Now get up or I will get you up!

LADY: Calm down for crying out loud...[*Bends over to pick up the toilet paper from the floor.*]

GENTLEMAN: I prohibit you from moving your bowels again until we return from our vacation!

> The LADY *wipes herself. Starts to pull the chain when she is through but is stopped by the* GENTLEMAN *who leaps from his chair and rushes over to the toilet to prevent her from flushing it. He knocks her off the toilet seat.*

LADY: This goddam nonsense has gone far enough! [*Rises from the floor, removes a blond wig from her head, throws it on the floor*] I am through playing your dumb games.

GENTLEMAN: Put that wig back on before someone sees you and finds out that you aren't a real blonde.

LADY: I NEVER WANTED TO BE A REAL OR A FALSE BLONDE!

> *Knocking is briefly heard.*

GENTLEMAN: Why did you have to shout like that for? Now someone knows we are not in Europe.

LADY: Good, now I can flush that smelly toilet.

GENTLEMAN: No you don't. Leave the toilet alone! If we keep our voices low whoever heard us will probably think they were hearing things. So don't raise your voice again in this fancy restaurant. The French are going to think that Americans don't know how to act in public. Sit down and act sophisticated.

LADY: I'm going outside, I want to breathe some fresh air, even though I know that's quite impossible to do in the South Bronx. But I'm sure it doesn't smell as bad as in here.

GENTLEMAN: If you leave you cannot come back in here until I return from Europe in a week. I suggest you stay right where you are, dear. You know how dangerous it is out there. I predict you will get mugged and raped and murdered and set on fire to destroy the evidence. You are safer here in Paris among the decent and the civilized. Will you sit down already! The waiters are going to think you are leaving.

LADY: I haven't seen the streets in a few weeks. I can't tolerate this cramped up space any longer. There's nothing to do here but pretend we aren't here while staring at four blank walls. We don't even have a window to look out of in this toilet size apartment. I need a desperate change of scenery or else I'm going to snap!

GENTLEMAN: Sit down, you are attracting attention arguing like this. Everyone has his eyes on us. You are giving America a bad reputation conducting yourself in such a ludicrous manner. Sit! [*Pours himself a drink*]

LADY: [*Sits down*] I don't know how much longer I can tolerate living like this. We are so damn broke we have to wait for the phone to ring so we can dance because we can't even afford a third-hand stereo.

GENTLEMAN: Complain all you want to, but you know you can never deny the fact that we are the only tenants in this building with servants. You haven't had to wash a dish since you moved in with me or vacuum the floor or do the laundry around here! Right? Of course I'm right! Now had you gotten involved with someone else you wouldn't be living so comfortable and taking vacations to Europe.

LADY: There are no dishes around here to wash. Our meals for the past few years have consisted of pizzas or frankfurters or that shitty shishkebab on a stick.

Frantic knocking is heard.

—Help me someone, help me, there is a man coming after me to rape me…please somebody helpppppp me…HELLLLLLLLPPP!!!

It's the same exact voice of the LADY.

—Shut up and enjoy it bitch, I don't want to hurt you, but if I have to I will!

It's the same exact voice of the GENTLEMAN.

LADY: [*Startled*] Answer the door, a woman is about to get raped!

GENTLEMAN: I can't, we are not here. We are in Europe.

The LADY outside lets out a loud scream.

LADY: A woman is being raped! We just can't sit here and pretend not to be here…[*Rises*]…come on let's help her before that scum kills her!

GENTLEMAN: Sit the hell back down. If we go and help her everyone is going to know we are not in Europe.

—RAPE! RAPE! SOMEBODY PLEASE HELP ME!!

—SHUT UP AND ENJOY IT, BITCH! YOU ARE NOT GOING TO GET THIS OPPORTUNITY AGAIN!

—OH NO, LEAVE ME ALONE! HELLLLLLLLLLP!

—DON'T RESIST IF YOU DON'T WANT TO GET HURT! STOP SCRATCHING ME YOU DUMB BROAD!

The rapist is heard beating her up.

LADY: He's going to kill her! Come on let's help that poor woman…[*Rushes towards the door*]

GENTLEMAN: Don't you dare open that door…[Rises]…Come back and sit down!

LADY: We have to help her…[Starts to open the door]

GENTLEMAN: NO!…[Rushes over to her and prevents her from opening the door]…sit your ass back down, now!

—RAPE! RAPE! RAPE!

—AHHH AHHH AHHHHHHHHH!

—RAPE! RAPE! RAPE!

—OHHH OHHH OHHHHHHHHHHH!

LADY: You goddamn coward!

GENTLEMAN: Calm down. She'll start enjoying it any minute now. Let's sit down before the waiters think we are leaving and give our table to someone else.

—HELP ME SOMEONE…HELP ME…PLEASE!

—oooooooooooooooooooooooooo

—OH GOD PLEASE HELP ME PLEASE HELP ME!

—OH BABY OH BABY OH BABY OH BABY…

LADY: What if that was me out there, huh? What if some one was raping me and I was pleading for help?

GENTLEMAN: I said sit back down…[Grabs her arm]…before they give our table to someone else…[Leads her to her seat and sits her down]…You don't ever have to worry about getting raped. [Sits]…we have a chauffeur to accompany you wherever you go when it isn't possible for me to accompany you. Chauffeurs just don't drive limousines.

> The rape victim lets out a loud scream. Her assailant is heard running down the stairs. The victim screams again and faints.

LADY: [Tearfully] He probably killed the poor woman.

GENTLEMAN: Stop crying, it wasn't your mother.

LADY: You are a real cold bastard. That's it, I'm back from Europe! And the first thing I am going to do is flush that smelly toilet, and then I am going outside to see if that poor helpless woman is still alive…[Rises]…you can stay in Europe by yourself!

GENTLEMAN: Sit down! We are still in Europe!

LADY: We were never in Europe!

GENTLEMAN: [Rises, looks directly at her] I am fed up with your goddamn ghetto mentality. I am never again going to pretend that I am poor with you. You can't seem to get out of character when we are through pretending.

LADY: [Looking directly at him] We aren't all as fortunate as you whose mind lives in the suburbs while his body rots in the slums!

GENTLEMAN: You have no one to blame but yourself with your limited attention span. God knows how many times I have tried to explain to you what a rewarding experience pretending to be rich is, but because of your inability to listen for no longer than a matter of seconds you haven't understood anything I have explained to you.

LADY: Pretending to be rich is dumb, not rewarding!

GENTLEMAN: Be quiet and make a sincere effort to pay close attention to what I'm saying so you can end up in Europe, where we are on vacation right now! [*Clears his throat to continue lecturing*] Okay, now when an individual selects to pretend to be rich instead of to be poor indicates a superior level of comprehension of what is essential to obtain intellectual and material fulfillment. Now think, or try to think...You are the pleasure of your pleasures and the misery of your miseries! Doesn't that makes sense? Of course it does! We may not be able to decide when we die but we can decide in between the time we are born and the time we die how well off or bad off we want to pretend that we are!

    Remains motionless, arm and lecturing finger suspended in midair. Voices are heard from outside. A mugging is about to take place outside.

—Your money or your life!

—Don't point that gun at me, I'll give you anything you want, please don't hurt me.

—Just hand over the money, okay lady?

    It's the voice of the GENTLEMAN *and the* LADY *inside.*

—Give me that goddamn purse, lady!

—Please stop pointing that gun at me, it's making me too nervous to think straight, I'm trembling too much to hear anything you are saying.

—Give me that goddamn purse, dammit!

—Give me back my purse you thief!

LADY: [*Speaking but not moving*] Now a woman is getting robbed at gun point! Let's call the police at once before it's too late, come on, move!

GENTLEMAN: [*Also speaking but not moving*] That is out of the question, if we get involved we will end up getting ridiculed. She shouldn't resist, she probably isn't carrying enough money to risk losing her life for, living in this dump.

—Get your hands off of me, lady!

—I WANT MY PURSE BACK! I WANT IT BACK!

—Get away, lady, this gun is loaded!

—Why didn't you say so in the first place! You could have seriously wounded me!

LADY: [*Still not moving*] What if that was your mother?

GENTLEMAN: [*Still not moving*] Nobody gets mugged in heaven.

—What is that you gots on your finger, lady?

—My wedding ring, and you can't have it. My husband will not sleep with me again if I let someone rob this ring from me!

—I don't give a damn, hand over the ring!

—I will not, and that is final!

    The LADY *and* GENTLEMAN *will speak without moving until further notice. His lecturing finger remains suspended in midair.*

LADY: Give up the ring, sister. It's probably not worth anything anyway. Your life is more precious than that damn ring, sister, give it up...

GENTLEMAN: She better not if she wants her husband never to sleep with her again.

—Remove that ring lady!

—Definitely not! You can rob my purse and my money, but not my wedding ring!

—Lady don't be stupid, give me that goddamn ring, this gun is loaded!

PEDRO PIETRI

—You are repeating yourself. Be content with what you already have and leave me and my ring alone!

—Your husband can give you another one!

—No he can't, he isn't working.

LADY: That's why you should give up the ring!

GENTLEMAN: Resist sister, Resist...! Don't let your husband down, hang on to that ring...!

A gunshot is heard.

LADY: [*Hysterical but still not moving*] He shot her! He shot that defenseless woman!

GENTLEMAN: She died honorably... [*Brings down his finger. Is able to move about again.*] Let me elaborate: That man only pretended to shoot that woman and that woman only pretended to die. The same way you are pretending not to move... [*She moves on hearing that statement*]...Now you are pretending to move. It is as simple as that.

LADY: A woman just got killed outside your door because you refused to call the cops, and you don't even feel guilty about it?

GENTLEMAN: I have better things to pretend about. And why should I be feeling, guilty? I didn't pretend to pull the trigger. Furthermore she had a choice. And I personally think she made a wise decision.

LADY: She made no decision at all! She was a victim of the lowest most vicious uncivilized cowardly slimy disgusting human creep on earth! Just like that poor woman who was raped not too long ago.

GENTLEMAN: She would have resisted if she really felt she was really getting raped. Not everyone is as dumb as you are. That woman knew that man was only pretending to rape her, that's why she pretended to panic. Don't you understand anything?

LADY: Yes, I understand something, I understand that you are the most cowardly person I have ever met in my life. I also understand that you are in desperate need of psychiatric treatment. Anyone who doesn't respond to the frantic plea for help from a woman being raped and brutalized because they are pretending to be in a foreign country belongs in an insane asylum.

GENTLEMAN: Drop the subject already. You are acting as if you were the one who was just raped.

LADY: When one woman is raped all women are raped!

GENTLEMAN: That is the most ridiculous statement I have ever heard anyone make. *Sits down, pours himself a drink.*

LADY: That's all you can ever think about, the next drink and the one after that. People get robbed, raped and killed and it doesn't matter any to you as long as you have a drink in your hand. You disgust me. I'm leaving and this time I mean it.

GENTLEMAN: If you walk out that door you will just end up back in here again. There is nowhere else to go but here. If you leave or stay you are still going to smell the same shit you are smelling right now. Life is a toilet and all we ever do is go from one toilet to the next. We can only pretend to be somewhere else!

LADY: That cheap wine has really damaged your mind. You aren't making any sense whatsoever.

GENTLEMAN: Let me elaborate to settle this once and for all. [*Rises, clears his throat, takes a drink*]...Okay...The reason we keep having wars is because wars are just being pretended to be fought. The winners pretend to win and the losers pretend to lose, therefore wars are not really fought at all, that's the reason why we will always be at war!...[The LADY *attempts to sneak a drink from the bottle and is caught*]...Put that bottle down, you can't control your liquor.

LADY: I am pretending to be drinking...[*She takes a drink from the bottle*]

GENTLEMAN: [*Takes bottle away from her*] No you are not, you don't know how to pretend! You admitted so yourself, remember? I was trying to explain everything to you, but like always you got distracted in a matter of seconds...[*Pours himself a drink in a glass, drinks it*] Before you got distracted...[*Lecturing again*]...I was about to explain to you how when I say to you, "You look fantastic" and you reply to me "You look fantasticker" we are not saying anything complimentary to each other because we are just pretending to talk not actually saying anything. Not that I don't mean anything when I say to you "You look wonderful" and you reply to me "You look wonderfuller," it isn't just an empty remark and it is just an empty remark because if you were paying attention I wouldn't have to repeat what I am going to say but since I'm positively sure that you wasn't I will repeat it again: We just pretend to talk and not actually say anything! To substantiate what I just stated, take for instance when I say to you "You look astonishing" and you reply to me "You look astonishingshinger," we are not being repetitive, we are being original because there is no such word as astonishingshinger! But since we are talking and not saying anything, that word and every other word that doesn't make any sense is acceptable in long and short conversations...[*Pours himself another drink.*]...Take another example: Every time we are about to order we never order because we aren't really hungry, we are just pretending to be hungry...[*Notices the* LADY *has fallen asleep standing up. Raises his voice.*] *IF WE WERE REALLY HUNGRY WE WOULD ORDER BUT SINCE WE AREN'T REALLY HUNGRY WE DON'T ORDER AND EVEN IF WE WERE REALLY HUNGRY WE STILL WOULDN'T ORDER BECAUSE WE ARE JUST PRETENDING! THERE-FORE WE DIDN'T COME HERE TO ORDER ANYTHING AT ALL!*

LADY: [*Wakes up*] The reason we don't order when we order is because we can only afford the water not the order!

> *Gunshots are heard. The* GENTLEMAN *drinks up what's left in his glass, then hides under the table with the bottle. The* LADY *remains standing.*

LADY: Why are you hiding? You aren't a threat to anyone but yourself.

GENTLEMAN: THE REASON SOME PEOPLE'S PROBLEMS ARE NEVER GO-ING TO END IS BECAUSE THEY REFUSE TO PRETEND THAT THEY HAVE NO PROBLEMS. THEY ARE IGNORANT TO THE FACT THAT FROM THE WOMB TO THE TOMB WE HAVE NOTHING TO DO BUT TO PRETEND AND ANY INTELLIGENT PERSON WILL PRETEND TO BE VERY RICH!

> *The shooting continues.*

LADY: Stop hiding under the table, nobody is after you.

GENTLEMAN: The A.B.C.D.E.F.G.H.I. has vowed to gun down the ruling class wherever they are whenever they catch them. I can't afford to get careless.

LADY: There is no such terrorist group. The A.B.C.D.E.F.G.H.I. is another one of your wild lies to feel important and insecure about your existence. Those gunshots you hear come from a friendly neighborhood argument, not guerrilla warfare. You fabricate your own paranoia to make your fantasy of affluence more convincing to yourself. No terrorist group comes gunning for the ruling classes in a low class neighborhood unless they are subsidized by the federal government... [*The shooting stops*]

GENTLEMAN: The A.B.C.D.E.F.G.H.I. isn't a figment of my imagination. They are an enemy of the ruling class who want to bring about social change by violent means. They have taken credit for acts of sabotage all over the world. But we will eventually crush them subversive scatter brains who always end up as fatal casualties of their own redundant insidious obnoxious radical clichés.

LADY: Come up from under the table, the shooting stopped already.

GENTLEMAN: Is the coast clear?

LADY: The coast stays clear here. It's too small for anyone else to fit in.

GENTLEMAN: [*Cautiously rises, bottle still in hand*] That was close... [*Wipes sweat off his forehead*]...Europe is no longer a safe place to vacation in.

> *Someone is heard trying to force his way into the apartment by kicking the door. The* GENTLEMAN *hides back under the table.*

They are here! The A.B.C.D.E.F.G.H.I. is here!

LADY: Don't hide, protect me. Someone is breaking into our apartment. They are probably armed and dangerous, we have to defend ourselves, there is nowhere to run and hide here.

GENTLEMAN: Take cover with me, they might not see us. Hurry, get under the table, there's no time to waste! The A.B.C.D.E.F.G.H.I. doesn't take any prisoners alive. You will be killed if you are caught.

LADY: It's probably just one burglar; we can overpower him together. Come on, stand up and defend yourself!

> *The voices of a man and a woman, same as the* LADY *and* GENTLEMAN, *are heard outside.*

—Hey man, like what are you doing?

—Breaking into this apartment to burglarize it, baby. And like you are supposed to make sure the coast is clear so we won't get busted, dig?

—But like you ain't gonna cop nothing in there, man, that is the hallway toilet. Can't you smell it? Like it stinks real bad in there.

—Hey baby you is right, it stinks worse than shit in there...phew! like let's rob another pad.

> *Footsteps are heard walking away from their door.*

LADY: I never thought that not flushing the toilet would someday save our life. Come on, get up from under the table and pass me the bottle so I can take a drink.

GENTLEMAN: [*Cautiously rises*] It looks like I am going to have to arm my servants. Terrorism seems to be getting out of hand, and nothing is being done about it.

LADY: Pass me the bottle, please.

GENTLEMAN: You are not drinking anymore tonight.

LADY: Then I am not staying here, either.

GENTLEMAN: You lower class people can't function unless you are under the influence of alcohol.

LADY: Look who's talking.

GENTLEMAN: I am a social drinker, not a compulsive one.

LADY: I swear to god, you are really out of your mind.

GENTLEMAN: You cannot swear to god, you can only pretend that you swear to god because god is not god but just pretending to be god.

LADY: [*Angry, smacks* GENTELMAN's *face*] How dare you say there is no god, you atheist!

GENTLEMAN: Because you just pretended to smack me I will not violently smack you back…[*Pours himself a drink, makes a toast to the* LADY *without a drink in her hand*]…cheer up dear, you can drink tomorrow if you exercise moderation.

LADY: [*Runs over to the toilet, grabs chain*] If you don't give me a drink I'll flush the toilet a few times so the neighbors can know we are not on vacation in Europe but still here in the pits of our higher expectations of life.

GENTLEMAN: [*Brings out a can of Mace from his jacket, rises, aims it at the* LADY *near the toilet.*] Get away from that toilet or I will spray you with this can of Mace and make a mess out of you!

LADY: [*Startled, releases chain*] You are really whacked, my goodness!

GENTLEMAN: There is nothing I won't do to protect my reputation.

LADY: You mean your imagination not your reputation. Everyone knows what a pathological liar you are except yourself…[*Moves away from toilet*]…you know something? Though we have been living together for a long time I know nothing at all about you, not even your name. And you know less than that about me. Isn't that rather peculiar? You and I are total strangers to each other.

GENTLEMAN: There is nothing to know about anybody!…[*Sits*]

LADY: I don't know if you coined that phrase or not but you most definitely are practicing it. I don't know your mother, I don't know your father, sisters or brothers and cousins if any. I don't know how old are you or on what month your birthday falls. I don't know if you are black or white or Hispanic or Oriental! All I know about you is that you are the man who pretends to be rich all the goddamn time and refuses to get a job or let me get a job because rich people don't work so I must go on welfare…[*Faces audience*]…because he is rich and won't go near there. But he certainly does not object to spending my welfare check on dumb servants and cheap wine to get stoned and amuse himself by pretending that he is poor which he really is but won't admit it to himself!!!

GENTLEMAN: Your problem, my dear lady, is that you are troubled by your inability to feel socially adequate among the elite. You feel that all the customers in this fancy restaurant have a low opinion about you…[*Puts Mace can back into jacket pocket.*]

LADY: I wasn't always a waitress and you didn't always meet me for the first time in a bus terminal cafeteria in the mid-January of our careers...[*Walks as she reminisces*]...You were about to leave town but never left. Night after night you did this. Soon you were asking for farewell kisses from me. I obliged because though you were lying to me about everything regardless how petty, I was impressed at the way you believed everything you lied about.

GENTLEMAN: [*Sits down, pours himself a drink*] I left town every time I said I was leaving.

LADY: You had no way of telling that I wasn't always a waitress. I did my job so well. It seemed as if I had been working there for the past eleven years. You really had no way of knowing it was actually 5 and a half years I had been employed at the bus terminal cafeteria...[*Continues walking, reminiscing*]...Before that I was a department store cashier with full honors for three years. There isn't really much to say about that job aside from the fact that I loved it. There was never anything different and exciting to do on the job in that department store. Oh you had no way of guessing that before I became involved in cashier work which led me to be a punctual waitress content with my job, I was a chiclet chewing filter tip smoking receptionist at the Department Of Social Services, very popular and well-liked by my co-workers. That was the first job I ever had in my life. I was also there for three years...[*Stops reminiscing, walks over to the table, picks up her glass to be poured a drink. The* GENTLEMAN *ignores her. She puts the drinking glass down. Stares directly at him.*] IF ONLY YOU KNEW HOW EMBARRASSED I FEEL EVERY TIME I HAVE TO FACE MY EX CO-WORKERS AT THE DEPARTMENT OF SOCIAL SERVICES EVERY TIME I HAVE AN APPOINTMENT WITH MY WELFARE INVESTIGATOR TO KEEP THE WELFARE CHECKS COMING INTO OUR MISERABLE LIVES THAT SMELL WORSE THAN SHIT!!!

GENTLEMAN: Stop using profane language in this fancy restaurant and lower your voice before someone finds out this apartment isn't empty. I should have never invited you to come to Europe with me. You are spoiling my vacation.

LADY: You don't have to worry about anyone finding out if this apartment is empty or not. There is nothing in here anyway, not even us. Not because we are in Europe, but because we are nobody! Understand? NOBODY! Like every other poor slob in this rat hole where roaches are the majority.

GENTLEMAN: What I should do is inject you with a dosage of sodium pentothal so you can start telling the truth about how economically well off we are.

Loud knocking is heard. A LADY *with same voice of* LADY *inside speaks outside.*
—Come out of that toilet, already! Other people have to use it...[*continues knocking as she speaks*]
—Come on out, goddammit! I have been waiting since this morning to take a crap. The toilet just doesn't belong to you, everyone on this floor has access to it.

The LADY *inside begins to say something. The* GENTLEMAN *motions for her to remain silent. The knocking continues.*

—I'm gonna keep knocking till you come out of the damn toilet!

A man with same voice of GENTLEMAN *inside speaks outside.*

—Lady, I am afraid you are wasting your time. There is no one in there, and that is no longer the hallway toilet. The landlord has rented to this millionaire couple who are on vacation in Europe right now.

[*stops knocking*]…And what the hell are we suppose to do when we have to take a crap now?

—Use the toilet on the floor above or the floor below from now on. How come you haven't known about this, yet? It's been quite awhile now.

—I was in mourning for a year. My husband kicked the bucket. It is against my religion to go to the toilet when you are in mourning.

—What religion is that?

—The real Catholics…why would millionaires want to live in there for?

—Because of the low rent they are paying for an ex-hallway toilet. You know what cheap bastards millionaires are.

—They are probably welfare recipients like everybody else in this building. No rich person is going to live in an ex-hallway toilet.

—Rich people are rich because they live in ex-hallway toilets and poor people are poor because they live in mansions in the sky.

—They ain't rich. I've never seen their limousine.

—Neither have I. But I have seen their maid and butler and chauffeur. They probably don't park their limousine around this neighborhood. It'll get robbed immediately.

—Damn conditions here are bad enough. And now we can't even use the toilet of our own floor.

Couple outside is heard walking away. The telephone rings.

LADY: [*Rises*] I am answering the phone. It could be an emergency…[*Goes to answer telephone*]

GENTLEMAN: [*Stops her*] You are not answering anything!

LADY: Something could be wrong with my mother.

GENTLEMAN: If it's anything really serious they will send us a telegram.

LADY: Please let me answer the phone, my mother hasn't been feeling too well lately.

GENTLEMAN: She looked okay to me before we left on our vacation. Just let the phone ring. Whoever it is will soon realize we aren't home. Now I want you to sit down and pretend we are going to order something before we are asked to leave this fancy restaurant for creating a disturbance.

The phone stops ringing.

LADY: Stop pretending already for crying out loud, you are driving me crazy! I can't take it anymore. None of this makes any sense. You are a sick person. I am about to throw up. God what did I ever do to deserve this terrible fate?

GENTLEMAN: [*Stands directly in front of her*] Listen you, when we first met you knew I was into pretending I was affluent and it didn't seem to annoy you any. You pretended along with me. We had some really great times together pretending we were doing things we couldn't afford to do. We visited many foreign countries, ate in the best restaurants and rubbed shoulders with some of the richest people in the world. Why are you complaining now?

LADY: I only pretended with you because I thought that sooner or later you will realize how dumb and foolish it is to pretend you are who you aren't and get yourself a job.

GENTLEMAN: I don't have to get a job. I receive a monthly inheritance check to support you and me with.

LADY: That isn't an inheritance check, that is a welfare check we receive in the mail which you spend on domestic help we don't need to make a good impression on the neighbors.

GENTLEMAN: I seriously think you should never drink again. Sit down and take it easy so you can start making sense again. Come on dear, have a seat.

    They both sit down.

LADY: Why don't you let me get a job if you are dead set against getting one yourself? It will make things around here less complicated for us.

GENTLEMAN: No lady of mine works. It is untraditional and against the standards of the upper class.

LADY: We are not upper class, we are poor slobs!

GENTLEMAN: If you want to pretend you are poor, you can do it by yourself. I am going to continue pretending I am rich as long as I am alive and well enough to pretend because it is more interesting to pretend you are rich than to pretend you are poor. It makes life exciting and more bearable. If I were to pretend I was poor I would be self-destructive and miserable. But now, pretending to be rich makes you want to live forever because you never know when the day will come when you no longer have to pretend you are rich and actually be rich.

LADY: And how will you get rich if you aren't willing to do anything to strike it rich? You won't even play a number or bet on the horses.

GENTLEMAN: If you pretend hard and long enough something will happen. I don't know what but I do know that something will eventually happen.

LADY: Is god going to make us rich? Is that what you are waiting for, a divine miracle to occur so we can flush the toilet on our vacation?

GENTLEMAN: You seem to keep forgetting that I am the one who coined the phrase: The Masses Are Asses! Doesn't that explain anything to you at all?

LADY: Yes, it sure does. It lets me know what a low opinion you have of yourself, and what a scatterbrain you are. You have pretended so much that you don't know where you are coming from anymore. You have forgotten your past and present and can not foresee any future in your future. Who are you anyway? Why don't you tell me something about yourself so I can know what the problem is and attempt to assist you in solving it?

GENTLEMAN: I am a very rich man without a single problem in the world!

LADY: Why don't you stop trying to impress me? You know it doesn't matter any to me. My need to always be with you transcends any standards of living, high or low or in between. I am just interested in knowing who you are, not who you wish you were!

GENTLEMAN: Why are you interested in knowing so much about me? Are you a spy for the A.B.C.D.E.F.G.H.I.?

LADY: You see, you aren't even willing to speak to me unless it's to play one of your lame brain games. I should have never listened to anything you said. Especially when you told me to quit my job because rich people don't work. Look at me, I have been wearing the same clothes ever since I got involved with you. And so have you! We even have to sleep with them on because this damn toilet ain't heated.

GENTLEMAN: These clothes we wear always look as if they are being worn for the first time. Our butler takes them to the cleaners every Friday evening and returns with them cleaned and ironed Monday morning.

LADY: Oh yes, and that's something else I'm fed up about. I don't want to spend my weekends here stark naked pretending to be in a millionaire's nudist colony because the only clothes we ever wear are at the laundry getting fumigated.

Police siren is heard. Stops abruptly after 10 seconds. Loud knocking is heard.

—Open up! This is the police! There has been a robbery, a rape, and a murder committed in this building. We are questioning everyone. Come on, open up or I will blow out the lock with my beloved revolver! Hurry up, open!

The same voice of the GENTLEMAN.

LADY: It looks like if our vacation is finally over.

—Open up I said! Hurry up or I will shoot my way in and crack your skull with my intimate night stick for resistin' arrest and assaulting a police officer in the line of duty! Open up goddammit!

Bangs on the door with his night stick.

GENTLEMAN: [*Facing the door*] Officer, there is no one here. The tenants of this apartment are in Europe on their vacation and won't be back until the middle of next week.

The banging on the door stops.

—Oh, sorry about that folks. You should have put a sign on your door stating that. I had no way of knowing you people weren't home. Police officers have weapons not psychic powers, you know? Well folks, enjoy your vacation. Sorry for the interruption.

The cop leaves. Siren is briefly heard.

GENTLEMAN: You see how well I can pretend? I had that cop convinced there was nobody in here.

LADY: Cops aren't too bright to begin with…[*Rises, walks about a few times*]…Listen, if you let me just flush that toilet once, I'll stick it out for another week, but if you don't then I have to leave before an epidemic breaks out here. It's unsanitary and unhealthy not to flush the toilet for such a long period of time.

GENTLEMAN: You know what will happen if the toilet is flushed. So just change the subject and keep pretending we are in a fancy restaurant. Shall we order now my dear, or shall we order later?

LADY: Okay then, I guess I have to return from Europe by myself because I can't take it another minute in here. My guts are about to come puking out of my mouth!

GENTLEMAN: If that is your decision then that is your decision. Don't say I didn't warn you when you get raped and mugged and murdered and set on fire to destroy the evidence in those crime and drug-infested streets of the South Bronx. I am not responsible for your safety outside of Paris. I cannot come to your defense from a foreign country.

LADY: I will have to take that risk.

GENTLEMAN: I won't sleep with you again if you get raped and murdered. Take my word for it!

LADY: You aren't the only necrophiliac in this world.

GENTLEMAN: Why don't you just sit down and behave the way you behaved the first day we met and you thought I was really rich and not just pretending to be rich. Remember how agreeable and compromising you were? You believed anything I told you then.

LADY: Yes, I believed everything, up until you started talking into your wristwatch, claiming it was a two-way short wave radio for VIP's. I didn't take anything you said serious after that.

GENTLEMAN: Yes you did. You went along for the ride and you haven't gotten off yet. You are still in the front seat and I'm still behind the steering wheel.

LADY: You keep thinking that…[Walks to the bathtub, bends over to get an old fur coat. Puts it on]…You just keep thinking that…[Walks to glass mirror on wall behind bathtub. Brings out stick of lipstick from coat pocket, applies it to her lips]…You'll see how wrong you are…[Walks to the door, grabs doorknob]…Good-bye!!!

GENTLEMAN: Make sure the coast is clear before you walk out the door so none of the neighbors see you.

LADY: So you'd rather smell shit than to be with me.

GENTLEMAN: I don't smell anything.

LADY: Because you are pretending not to.

GENTLEMAN: You can do the same.

LADY: No I can't. I have a weak stomach. Good-bye…[Makes no attempt to leave]…See you when you get back from Europe if I am still available.

GENTLEMAN: If you are or if you aren't it is not going to stop me from pretending I am rich, bitch!

LADY: Aren't you going to try and stop me from leaving?

GENTLEMAN: Absolutely not. I have no use for anyone who cannot pretend they are rich with me. If you want to pretend you are poor you can do it by yourself, I already told you that. Now leave if you are going to leave or stay if you are going to stay because you can't do both.

LADY: I don't want to leave you…[Returns to table]…Please flush the toilet so I won't have to leave. [Sits down]…Nobody will hear anything.

GENTLEMAN: I can't take any chances. You never know who can be spying on us to find out if we are in Europe or not. So please be very careful when you leave. Make sure there is nobody out there. You have no idea how envious our neighbors are of us and will enthusiastically welcome any opportunity to ridicule us.

LADY: Do you smell smoke?

GENTLEMAN: No, I just smell the rich scent of the rich in this place where the affluent congregate.

> *Smoke starts entering through the cracks on the door of the fancy restaurant or empty apartment. The* LADY *sniffs a few times, turns her head towards the door, shouts in a sudden unanticipated panic...*

LADY: There's a fire in the building!...[*Rises*]

> *Loud knocking is heard on the door, a voice, same as* LADY, *is heard shouting.*

—FIRE! FIRE! RUN FOR YOUR LIVES EVERYBODY!

> *Verbal panic and physical commotion is heard outside. The fancy restaurant or empty apartment is filling up with smoke.*

LADY: Come on, let's get the hell out of here before we roast to death...[*Starts coughing as smoke chokes her*]...Hurry up, there's no time to waste...[*Coughs*]

GENTLEMAN: Sit down and stay put. I'm not going out there and have everyone start laughing at me, fire or no fire! and stop coughing, someone is bound to hear you!

LADY: [*Hysterical*] We'll get burned alive if we don't get out of here!

GENTLEMAN: And we'll get ridiculed if we get out of here. So just sit down and keep your mouth shut.

LADY: I don't want to be burned alive, I'm getting out of here! This toilet isn't worth dying for...!

> *She runs for the door, coughing repeatedly. The fancy restaurant or empty apartment is completely filled with smoke. The hysteria outside continues. The* GENTLE-MAN *stops the* LADY *from opening the door*]

LADY: LET GO OF ME! LET ME OUT OF HERE! I DON'T WANT TO BE BURNED ALIVE! HELP! HELLLLLLP!...[*Coughs*]

GENTLEMAN: [*Struggling with her*] If it is god's will that we are to be burned alive there is nothing that we can do about it!

LADY: YES THERE IS! WE CAN OPEN THE DOOR AND GET THE HELL OUT...[*Coughs*]...OUT OF HERE BEFORE IT'S TOO LATE! LET GO OF MEEEEEEE...[*Coughs repeatedly*]

GENTLEMAN: Stop acting so ridiculous! It is probably some one's beans that are burning. And if it isn't then it's our destiny and we can't run away from it now or never. God knows what he is doing. Remember the Titanic!

> *Sounds of fire engines are heard.*

LADY: PLEASE LET GO OF ME! I DON'T WANT TO DIE! LET ME GO YOU GODDAMN LUNATIC! I DON'T WANT TO DIE!!!

GENTLEMAN: Calm down! Nothing can happen to us, anyway. We are out of town.

LADY: [*Having a coughing fit*] THIS IS NO TIME TO BE PLAYING GAMES... THE BUILDING IS BURNING DOWN...[*Makes a desperate effort to release herself from his grip. They fall on the floor together. She continues coughing repeatedly.*]

GENTLEMAN: If our number is up, what we should be doing is having one last drink and making one last toast to the resourceful life we spend together. Unlike poor people, we don't have to be afraid to die. God was generous to us. We never had any financial problems on earth. If he wants us now we should go without any regrets.

She coughed through everything he said and continues to cough. Loud knocking is heard on the door. A Man's voice is heard. Same voice as the GENTLEMAN

—You can stop worrying, folks, the fire is under control. It was just a pot of beans burning on the stove.

GENTLEMAN: Didn't I told you we had nothing to worry about? Now let's get up off the floor, dear. There is nothing to worry about anymore. You can stop coughing.

They both rise. He helps her to the table. They sit down on the chairs.

LADY: [*Still coughing*] I need some fresh air, the smoke is choking me. I have to get out of here before I suffocate. I'd rather be laughed at than to be buried.

GENTLEMAN: Stop talking foolish. The smoke will clear up in a few minutes and everything will go back to normal in this fancy restaurant. Read the menu to take your mind off the smoke so you can stop coughing.

LADY: Please have mercy on me, I need fresh air to breathe…Please…Please let me go outside.

GENTLEMAN: Hell no! And stop that goddamn coughing already! Read your menu if you want to feel better…[*Looks around*]…See, the smoke is already clearing up.

LADY: But the smell from the toilet is still here.

GENTLEMAN: There is nothing we can do about that until next week…[*Pours himself a drink. Swallows it in one gulp. Pours himself another drink*]

LADY: [*Coughing less*] Pour me some wine, my throat is very dry from inhaling all that smoke.

GENTLEMAN: Where are we at this precise moment, and what are we doing?

LADY: We are in a toilet in the stinking South Bronx drinking cheap wine, pretending to be rich.

GENTLEMAN: Then it looks like your throat is going to have to stay dry until you get in touch with reality again.

LADY: Now that the smoke has cleared, the smell of shit is back and it stinks worse than before…I'm going to sleep…Hopefully my dreams will smell better…[*Rises, walks over to the bath tub. Stares at it. Returns to the table.*]…Can you pour me some champagne so I can fall asleep quicker? You know what an extremely complicated task it is for an American tourist to sleep in a foreign country, especially if they are rich.

GENTLEMAN: Sure…[*Refills her glass and his*]…here you are my dear. Sit down, have a few more drinks so you can sleep soundly and dream about being very very very very very very very very rich!

She sits. They toast and drink.

TOGETHER: You know something??

LADY: What?

GENTLEMAN: You look tremendous.

LADY: You look stupendous.

GENTLEMAN: You look unpretentious.

LADY: You look industrious.

GENTLEMAN: You look advantageous.

LADY: You look so fantastic.

GENTLEMAN: You look so romantic.

LADY: Shall we go to bed now?

GENTLEMAN: Yes, let's go to bed now.

They make a 10 seconds toast. Finish drinking in 9 seconds. Rise in 8 seconds. He blows out the candle in 7 seconds. She picks up her wig in 6 seconds. Puts it on in 5 seconds. He takes her hand in 4 seconds. They walk to the bathtub in 3 seconds. They climb in in 2 seconds and disappear in 1 second. They snobbishly clear their throats in zero seconds. Silence is heard.

TOGETHER: You look absolutely incredible!!!

Quick Black Out.

Eric Overmyer

∾

Native Speech

•

for Melissa Cooper

"If he was not as dead as the cold lasagna on which the tomato sauce has begun to darken, I was a Dutchman. The gaudy and, in the absence of blood, inappropriate metaphor actually came to mind at the moment, as a willed ruse to lure me away from panic—the fundamental purpose of most caprices of language, hence the American wisecrack."

—THOMAS BERGER,
Who is Teddy Villanova?

Native Speech received its professional premiere at The Los Angeles Actors Theatre, Bill Bushnell Producing/Artistic Director. The production was directed by John Olon, and produced by Diane White and Adam Leipzig.

    The revised version of *Native Speech* was first presented February 14, 1985, at Center Stage, Baltimore, with Stan Wojewodski, Artistic Director; Peter Culman, Managing Director, and the following cast:

HUNGRY MOTHER	Kario Salem
FREE LANCE	Lorey Hayes
BELLY UP	SàMi Chester
CHARLIE SAMOA	Khin-Kyaw Maung
JOHNNIE SUCROSE	Tzi Ma
JIMMY SHILLELAGH	Robert Salas
JANIS	Caris Corfman
THE MOOK	Samuel L. Jackson
HOOVER	Jimmy Smits
FREDDY NAVAJO/LOUD SPEAKER	Melinda Mallari
CRAZY JOE NAVAJO	Adam Gish

The production was directed by Paul Berman. Set Design was by Hugh
Landwehr; Costumes, Jess Goldstein; Lights, Jim Ingalls, and Sound, Janet Kalas.

CHARACTERS (in order of appearance):

HUNGRY MOTHER
LOUD SPEAKER (a woman's voice)
FREE LANCE*
BELLY-UP
CHARLIE SAMOA
JOHNNIE SUCROSE (a transvestite)
JIMMY SHILLELAGH
JANIS*
THE MOOK
HOOVER
FREDDY NAVAJO*
CRAZY JOE NAVAJO

*women

Notes: Hungry Mother and Janis are white. The Mook and Free Lance are black. They
are an impressive, attractive couple: a Renaissance prince and princess. Belly Up is
black, middle-aged (somewhat older than Hungry Mother), a large man, an ex-sarge;
the outline of his chevrons is still visible on his fatigue jacket. Hoover, Freddy Navajo,
Crazy Joe Navajo, Charlie Samoa, Johnny and Jimmy should be played by
Asian-American, Hispanic or Native American actors.
    Freddy Navajo is a woman. Loud Speaker is an unseen, amplified, *live* voice: one of
those ubiquitous, bland women's voices heard in airports, shopping malls, or on the
time-of-day recordings. Johnnie Sucrose is a transvestite, a convincing one. The drag
should be accomplished.
    The following parts can be doubled: Freddy and Loud Speaker; Jimmy and Crazy
Joe.
    Except where indicated, Hungry Mother's voice is not amplified during his broad-
cast monologues. We hear his voice as he hears it, not as it is heard over the radio by
his listeners.

SCENE
*Hungry Mother's underground radio station, and the devastated neighborhood which
surrounds it.*
    *The studio is constructed from the detritus of Western Civ: appliances, neon tubing,
45s, car parts. Junk.*
    Outside, a darkening world. Dangerous. The light is blue and chill. Always winter.

ACT ONE

The Studio. HUNGRY MOTHER. *Red lights blinking in the black. A needle scrapes across a record. A low hum. Hum builds: the Konelrad Civil Defense Signal.* HUNGRY MOTHER *bops with the tone, scats with it. The tone builds, breaks off. Silence.* HUNGRY MOTHER *leans over the mike, says in a so-good-it-hurts voice:*

HUNGRY MOTHER: O, that's a hit. Hungry Mother plays the hits, only the hits. I want some seafood, mama. [*Beat.*] This is your Hungry Mother here—and you know it.

Lights. HUNGRY MOTHER *is a shambly, disheveled man in his late thirties. The Broadcast Indicator—a blue light bulb on the mike—is "on." And so is* HUNGRY MOTHER.

[*Cooool.*] Static. Dead air. Can't beat it. With a stick. Audio entropy. In-creases ever-y-where. Home to roost. Crack a six-pack of that ambient sound. [*Beat.*] You've been groovin' and duckin' to the ever-popular sound of "Air Raid"—by Victor Chinaman. Moan with the tone. A blast from the past. With vocal variations by yours truly. The Hungry Mother. [*Beat.*] Hard enough for you? [*A little more up tempo.*] Hungry Mother here, your argot argonaut. Stick with us. Solid gold and nothing but. Hungry Mother be playing the hits, playing them hits, for you, jes' for youuuu…[*Full-out manic now.*] Uh-huh! Into the smokey blue! Comin' at you! Get out de way! Hungry Mother gonna hammer, gonna glide, gonna slide, gonna bop, gonna drop, gonna dance dem ariel waves, til he get to you, yes you! Razzle you, dazzle you, blow you a-way! This one gonna hammer…gonna hammer you blue! [*Dryly.*] Flatten you like a side of beef, sucker.

[*Mellifluous.*] This is WTWI, it's 7:34, the weather is *dark*, dormant species are stirring, cold and warm bloods both, muck is up, and I'm the Hungry Mother. The weather outlook is for continued existential dread under cloudy skies with scattered low-grade distress. Look out for the Greenhouse Effect…We'll be back, but first—a word about succulents—[*Beat. Flicks switches.*] We're coming to you live, from our syncopated phonebooth high above the floating bridge in violation of *several* natural laws, searching, strolling, and trolling, for the sweetest music this side of Heaven.

[*Beat. Then:*] Back at you! This is the Hungry Mother, just barely holding on, at WTWI, the cold-water station with the bird's-eye view, on this beautifully indeterminate morning, bringin' you monster after musical monster. Chuckin' 'em down the pike, humpin' 'em up and over the DMZ, in a never-ending effort to make a dent in that purple purple texture. And right now I've got what you've all been waiting for—Hungry Mother's HAMMER OF THE WEEK! And Mother's Hammer for this week, forty seven with a silver bullet—"Fiberglass Felony Shoes"—something slick—by Hoover *and* the Navajos. [*Friendly.*] And, as always, behind every Mother's Hammer of the Week—there's a human being. And a human interest story. You're probably hip to this already, but I'm gonna lay it on you anyway. Hoover—is a full-blooded, red-blooded *Native American.* One of several in the annals of illustrated American Pop. [*Slight pause.*] Hoover had a monster a few years back: "Fiberglass Rock"—just a giant on the Res. And elsewhere. That, *mais oui,* was before the tragic accident in which Hoover—ah, I don't know if this is public knowledge—but, o why not grovel in gore? [*Bopping.*] With the fallout from his titanium monster, "Fiberglass Rock," Hoover put something down on a preowned dream, a Pontiac Superchief, drive it *away.* A steal. A *machine.* Four on the floor and three on the tree, a herd of horses under the hood! [*Beat. Solemn.*] Four flats. Cracked axle. Hoover—his heart as big and red as the great outdoors—goes down…with a wrench. The Superchief slips the jack—and pins Hoover by his…pickin' hand.

    [*Beat.*] WIPE OUT!

    [*Beat.*] Crushed dem bones to milk.

    [*Rising frenzy.*] But now he's back. Back where he belongs! With the aid of a prosthetic device! Back on the charts again! PIONEER OF PATHO-ROCK! [*Slight pause. Then: warm, hip.*] Many happy returns of the day, Hoover, for you and yours.

    [*Flicks switches. Mellow.*] The sun is up, *officially,* and all good things, according to the laws of thermodynamics, must come to an end. Join us—tomorrow—for something approaching solitude. WTWI now relents and gives up the ghost of its broadcasting day. [*He flicks switches. The blue light, the Broadcast indicator, goes "off." Over the loudspeakers, a woman's voice, live.*]

LOUD SPEAKER: Aspects of the Hungry Mother.

HUNGRY MOTHER: [*Reading from a book of matches.*] Success without college. Train at home. Do not mail matches.

LOUD SPEAKER: Hungry Mother hits the streets.

HUNGRY MOTHER: [*To* LOUD SPEAKER.] I be gone…but I lef' my name to carry on. [HUNGRY MOTHER *shuffles into the street.* FREE LANCE *approaches. They recognize one another, tense, draw closer. They do a street dance, slow, sexy, dangerous. Freeze. They release.* FREE LANCE *slides back and out.*]

LOUD SPEAKER: Hungry Mother after hours.

      HUNGRY MOTHER *slides into the bar where there is a solitary figure drinking.*

HUNGRY MOTHER: Belly Up.

BELLY UP: Say what?

HUNGRY MOTHER: Belly Up, it's been a coon's age.

BELLY UP: I know you?

HUNGRY MOTHER: Think it over.

BELLY UP: Buy me a drink.

HUNGRY MOTHER: City jail.

BELLY UP: Hungry Mother. What it is, Mom, what it is. How's it goin', Home? How goes the suppurating sore?

HUNGRY MOTHER: It's coming along. Thank you.

BELLY UP: Hungry Mother. Whose tones are legion. Hungry Mother, voice of darkness. Impressario of derangement. Tireless promoter of patho-rock. The man who'll air that wax despair.

HUNGRY MOTHER: When no one else will dare.

BELLY UP: The quintessential Cassandra. The damn Jonah who hacked his way out of the whale. Hungry Mother, the bleating gurgle of those who've had their throats cut.

HUNGRY MOTHER: You give me too much, Belly Up, my boy. It's all air time. Air-waves access, that's what it's all about. I just prop 'em up over the mike and let 'em bleed—gurgle gurgle pop short.

BELLY UP: Credit where credit is due.

HUNGRY MOTHER: Why, thank you, Brother Belly. It's a comfort to know that, a genuine solid comfort. My cup is filled with joy to know that someone's *really* listening. Why, late at night and on into the dawn, I have my doubts, I surely do. Casting my pearls—over the brink—

BELLY UP: [*Picking it up.*] Into the trough. On a wing and a prayer. Before the swine of despond. [*Pause.*] Not so, Hungry Mother, not so; not a bit. Your words hang on the barbed wire of evening, glistering in the urban nether vapors like a diamond choke chain on black satin.

HUNGRY MOTHER: Belly Up, you have the gift, you surely do. It's a wonder you don't pursue some purely *metaphorical* calling.

BELLY UP: My sentiments precisely. Please indulge me as I continue to flesh out my figure…Hungry Mother turns tricks quicker than a dockside hooker hustling her habit. He fences insights, pawns epiphanies. And we redeem those tickets in nasty corners. You the laser wizard. The magnetic pulse. The cardiac arrest. The barbarians have smashed the plate glass window of Western Civ and are running amok in the bargain basement. [HUNGRY MOTHER *applauds.*] Thank you. Transistor insights. Diode data. Crystal-tube revelations. That why we dial you in, Mothah.

HUNGRY MOTHER: You and who else?

BELLY UP: You'd be surprised. [*Pause.*] I got a chopper on the roof.

HUNGRY MOTHER: What?

BELLY UP: [*Winks and laughs.*] I got a chopper on the roof.

HUNGRY MOTHER: [*Beat*] Look, I got a question for you. Say the hoodlums, punks, pervos, perps, feral children, coupon clippers, and all the other bargain basement thrift shoppers, say they skip Housewares. Sporting goods. Electronic lingerie. Junior misses. All the lower floor diversions. And go straight for the suites at the top.

BELLY UP: [*Laughs.*] I got a chopper on the roof! Got my own sweet chopper to take me outa this! See? I anticipate your question. Like I anticipate the situation. And the answer. An-ti-cipate. Got to have that getaway hatch, Mother. Got to have it. Even a fool can see what's comin'. [*Slight pause.*] You're *sensitive*, Mother. We can read you like a rectal therm. Any little fluctuation. Fuck Dow Jones. We got the good stuff. [*Slight pause.*] We tune you in, we know when to split. Any little fluc. You our miner's canary, Mother. We hang you out there on the hook and hope you smell the gas in time. You croak—we go.

HUNGRY MOTHER: I'll try to give you five.

BELLY UP: Man, five is all I ask. My ears are glued.

HUNGRY MOTHER: Keep those cards and letters coming. So I know you're still glued.

BELLY UP: Don't sweat. As long as you still singing, we still listening. When you on the air, we say "Hosannah!"

HUNGRY MOTHER: Say "Hungry," sweetheart.

> *They toast. Darkness. As* HUNGRY MOTHER *walks back into the studio his amplified voice booms over the* PA.

HUNGRY MOTHER: [*On tape.*] Hoover is crawling back from near annihilation, a mighty mean accident for the little red man.

> *Sound of car crash.*
>
> *Lights.* HUNGRY MOTHER *freezes at the mike.*

LOUD SPEAKER: Further aspects of the Hungry Mother—*revealed!* For the very first time—the Hungry Mother in jail!

> *The jail appears in a flash of light:* CHARLIE SAMOA *and* JOHNNY *and* JIMMY. *They babble in several languages, cursing. Jail vanishes. Lights up on* HUNGRY MOTHER. *He breaks freeze. Flicks switches, blue light "on."*

HUNGRY MOTHER: [*High speed.*] Career-wise, a mighty mean accident, a tough break for the little red man. We'll be back with the Prick Hit of the Week—ha, ha, oh—Freudian faux pas—Pick Hit of the Week, "Nuking the Chinks," by Dragon Lady and the Flying Paper Tigers, but first—a word about peccaries…Friends—like so many vanishing species, these ugly little critters need your help. A tusk or two, a hoof, a stewpot of glue. It's all over for them, but what about their by-products? [*Dramatic.*] Next week—blue whales and dog food. [*Mellifluous.*] This is WTWI, the station with no visible means of support, this is a weekday, this is the Hungry Mother, blistering the dusk to dawn shift, grinding 'em down and pulling 'em out, monster after effervescent monster. Holocaust warnings are up. They continue to machine-gun survivors outside our studio. And the ozone keeps oozing away! And now—Mother's got what you've all been waiting for—nearly an hour of unrelieved agony! Twilight Desperation News! Brought to you by Universal Antipathy—Universal Antipathy, engendering tensions all over the globe—and by Sorghum—a fast food whose time is ripe ripe ripe! Invest in sorghum futures today! And now the hour's top headlines.

> [*Newscaster tones, pounding out a teletype rhythm on a tiny plastic typewriter as he speaks.*] "Killer Bees from Brazil Drop Texas Rangers in Their Tracks"…"Starfish Finish Off Great Barrier Reef"…quote, The sky's the limit, endquote…"Couple Flees Talking Bear"…One last note for you nature lovers: fossil fuels now coat 87% of the known universe. Those slicks are tough. No wonder dry-cleaning costs an arm and two legs…On the international beat, expatriate citizens of the island of Malta are demanding restitution from the community of nations. Malta was mugged early yesterday by two large black countries with hydrogen knuckles…it sank without a trace. Shades of Krakatoa. The usual measures to contain the radioactive dusk are being implemented with, as one official so succinctly put it, little or no

chance of success. We'll have more this hour on the latest in genetic mutation, both here and abroad but first—late, and leg, breaking sports…

HUNGRY MOTHER *picks up a pair of mechanical birds, and winds them into motion: they waddle and squawk.*

HUNGRY MOTHER: [*To the birds.*] You're brilliant and you're blue…conjugal bijou babies. Doves of love. Beaks of lazulis warbles of tin.

The birds wind down and halt.

HUNGRY MOTHER: [*Intones.*] Wound down. [*He eats beans from a can.*]

HUNGRY MOTHER: Interlude In Which Beans Are Eaten.

LOUD SPEAKER: The authorized autobiography of the Hungry Mother. The truth—with a twist!

HUNGRY MOTHER: First…lemme say…unequivocally—and between bites—that the Hungry Mother was made not born. Not of woman born. Heh heh heh. Puts me up there with the all-time greats, right? I want to be most emphatic about this. The Hungry Mother is—my own creation. Nom de wireless! Home-made man! So fine!

LOUD SPEAKER: Hungry scat! Mother doo wop! Fonky Mothah!

Loudspeaker.

HUNGRY MOTHER: [*To the mike, sings*]
Put on your felony shoes
Put on your felony shoes
Everybody gonna want you to
Put on your felony shoes
Come on wit' me
We gonna cut somethin' loose
We gonna boost
Something fine
And shiny and new
If you'll jes'
Put on your felony shoes

LOUD SPEAKER: And now—number one with a dum-dum—Mother's Hammer Too Hot To Handle!

HUNGRY MOTHER: And now, getting tons of extended hot air play in s and m loading zones and up and down the leather docks from coast to disco coast—the newest from Hoover and the Navajos—parvenu of patho-rock—"Fiberglass Creep and the Rotating Tumors!" [*He begins teletype noise, and speaks gravely.*] Police today busted a waterfront distillery, arresting twenty-seven adults. The distillery produces a wine brewed from the sores of children, which is quite popular locally and in the contiguous states, and easily available without a prescription. The cops said the kids were kept in cages underneath the piers because, quote, the salt water facilitates the festeration process, end quote. The perpetrators will be arraigned tomorrow on tax evasion charges, and the children, several hundred of them, have been released into the custody of leading lending institutions…

[*Upbeat.*] The block buster scoop this solid gold weekend—thousands of citizens roaming the streets in states of bliss-out and fat poisoning. Watch out for those psychoparalytic hallucinations. They can be tricky. Speaking of weather, the outlook through the weekend remains bleak. Our five-day forecast calls for continued historical uneasiness mingled with intermittent bouts of apocalyptic epiphany, and occasional oxygen debt—under cloudy skies. So wear your rubbers...

[*Jaunty.*] This has been The Agony News Hour, an exclusive twilight feature of WTWI, with your host, the Hungry Mother. Stay tuned for "Name My Race," the game guaranteed to offend nearly everyone, brought to you by Ethnic Considerations, dedicated to exacerbating racial tensions through violence—Ethnic Considerations, a hallmark of the Twentieth Century, don't leave home without them. And now it's time once again for *Dear Mother.* [*He holds a stack of letters impaled on a bowie knife. He plucks off the top letter and reads it in a cheery DJ voice.*]

HUNGRY MOTHER: "Dear Mother: My boyfriend has a fishhook in the end of his penis. This makes congress difficult. Even painful. What can I do about it? Signed, Afraid to Swallow." [*He crumples it up and tosses it away.*]

HUNGRY MOTHER: Eighty-six that. Prick Hit of the Week. Cranks. Who do they think they're kidding. I'm not just fooling around here.

[*Next letter.*] "Dear Mother: My husband is an unreconstructed Stalinist. He refuses to de-Stalinize, knowing that recantation would expose him as an accomplice to the most heinous crimes of this vile century. This ideological rift has been the recrudescent cause of numerous domestic conflicts and, I believe, threatens the dialectic of our marriage. Just yesterday I suggested opening bilateral summit talks on the question of rehabilitating Trotsky for the family shrine of revolutionary heroes, and he broke my jaw. Dear Mother, for the sake of the children, what do you suggest? Signed, just a Bourgeois Social Fascist At Heart." [*Slight pause.*] Dear Just a Bourgeois: I suggest a fight to the death with needle-nosed pliers. [*He tears it up.*] What's happening to the language? It's scary, Jim. The Great Nuance Crisis is upon us. One last letter for this fiscal year.

[*A cheery DJ voice.*] "Dear Mother: I listen to you every night. You are a great comfort to me. I don't know what I'd do without you. Please help me, Mother. It hurts so bad I can barely talk. Signed, Desperate." [*Slight pause.*] Dear Desperate...For once I'm at a loss for words. [*Slight pause.*] Perhaps you've mistaken me for your natural mother. I'm nobody's mama, sweetheart. [*Slight pause.*] Dear Desperate, I can't help you—if you don't give me something more to go on. Who are you, where, and what's troubling you, Bunky. Please try and nail it down a little closer, dear...Friends, got an esoteric problem? Send it to Mother and he'll devour it for you. And now it's time once again for—*The Big Dose, A Taste Of Things To Come,* when the Mother lets you in on what it's really gonna be like once the rude boys start playing for keeps. So here it is, tonight, at no extra charge, Hungry Mother brings you more than two hours of—dead air. Enjoy. [*Flicks switches. Blue light "off." Shrugs into an overcoat and goes into the street. Encounters* FREE LANCE. *They do their dance, as before. Freeze. Slight pause.*]

LOUD SPEAKER: Hungry Mother—Street Solo! [*He runs down stage scatting some "theme" music. At the appropriate moment:*]

LOUD SPEAKER: And now! Heeeeeeeere's…HUNGRY!!

HUNGRY MOTHER: [*Bopping.*] Could be Japanese!…Genetic…engineering! Charnel—numbah—five! *Smoke!* [*Changing gears.*] Friends…let's have a chat. Heart to heart. Would Mother hand you a bum steer?…As you know, the suggested agenda topic for today's luncheon is…Why Do De Gu'mint Be De Boz Ob De Scag Trade, or…Methadone—Magic or Madness?…But, I, uh, I have something of more immediate import to…impart. [*Slight pause.*] Friends…let's talk about…*crude drugs.* [*Clears throat.*] Brothers and sisters, I was down at the Hotel Abyss the other day, down at that old Hotel Abyss, when I chance to run into an old old friend of mine. A legend in his own time. A man who knows the score. Who never lets the sun get in his eyes. A man with no holes in his cosmic glove…I am speakin' of course about…Cocaine Ricky. [*Slight pause.*] Your friend and mine. [*Slight pause.*] Brothers and sisters, Cocaine Ricky tell me there be some mighty cold stuff goin' 'round out there, and I just want you to watch it. Very very cold. Ice cold. Dude be pushin', be pushin' it as snow. You know? Snow fall. Snow job. Snow blind. Snow go. [*Slight pause.*] *Ain't* snow. It's *Lance.* Lance. [*Slight pause.*] Instant death. [*Slight pause.*] Powdered nerve gas. [*Slight pause.*] Government issue. Sooo cooold. Huh! [HUNGRY MOTHER *and* FREE LANCE *enter the studio. She is dressed to street-kill.*]

FREE LANCE: This place look like a Cargo Cult beach head. You always had a knack for dives, Mother.

HUNGRY MOTHER: Thank you very much.

FREE LANCE: I don't truck with the radio much. It doesn't occur to me. It's not one of my…habits. I don't have time for media. What I'm saying is—I haven't caught your show.

HUNGRY MOTHER: Fuck you very much.

FREE LANCE: Don't be bitter.

HUNGRY MOTHER: Where you live dese days, honey chile?

FREE LANCE: On the docks.

HUNGRY MOTHER: Couldn't cotch me down dere, anyways.

FREE LANCE: Armegeddon Arms. Condos de rigueur. Sing Sing singles. Know them?

HUNGRY MOTHER: No, but I know the neighborhood. Intimately. Whatchew dew down dere, woman? You ain't involved with dem child distellers, is you?

FREE LANCE: I don't believe so. Not to my knowledge. It hasn't come to my attention. You ought to come visit me, Mother.

HUNGRY MOTHER: I should, it's true.

FREE LANCE: It's much nicer than this, really. Chrome furniture. It'd be a change.

HUNGRY MOTHER: I don't get out much. Don't leave the 'hood. I'm cooped.

FREE LANCE: Cooped.

HUNGRY MOTHER: Up.

FREE LANCE: It's very outre, you know. Swank and chic in the nastier neighborhoods. I just crave the danger. It's narcotic. And there's really nothing to worry about. The building itself is just the best. Impregnable. White boys from Missoura.

HUNGRY MOTHER: I can appreciate that.

FREE LANCE: Eliminates the Fifth Column spectre. My parents *never* hired black servants. No mammies for me. Don't tell me about race loyalty. When push comes to shove, I mean. Save on silver, too. And being near the water gives me a warm warm feeling.

HUNGRY MOTHER: For a quick and hasty exit.

FREE LANCE: When the time comes. We've made the arrangements. There won't be any trouble. When the time comes.

HUNGRY MOTHER: You'll take some casualties, of course.

FREE LANCE: When the time comes. Probably. Of course. One learns to live with one's losses.

HUNGRY MOTHER: Don't one? That reminds me. [*He flicks switches: blue light "on."* *Red hot.*] Back at you, sports, this is *the* Hungry Momma, the one and only, the original Hungry Momma, accept no substitutes, coming at you out of the blue-black on this elusive weekday ay-em in a possibly transitional stage in the floodtide of human affairs. Let the historians decide. You've been listening—to more than two hours *of—dead air.* C'est frommage. The time just got away from me there, mon cher. We'll be phasing out our broadcasting day with vanishing species animal noises, what a hoot. And we'll finish off with a new one, got it in the mail today, from the purveyors of patho-rock, Hoover and the Navajos, their latest—"Fiberglass Repairman"! [*Sings a slow blues, keeping the beat with hand slams.*]
    [*Sings.*] I'll insulate yo' home
    I'll fibreglass yo' phone
    An' I'll Navajogate
    The little woman
    Befo' yo'
    Back is turned.
[*Low key.*] Just breaks my goddamn heart. Sayonara, kids. I'll be back later in the week at my regularly unscheduled time. So—keep dialing and keep *hoping.* This is the Hungry Mother, the man who put the *hun* back in hungry, reminding you to stay cool, take it light, and *say—Hungry!* [*Slight pause, then cool and bureaucratic.*] WTWI has now pissed away/Its broadcasting day. [HUNGRY MOTHER *switches the blue light "off."*]

FREE LANCE: I'm surprised you don't lose your license.

HUNGRY MOTHER: Tell you the secret of my success. Nobody hears me. This tube gear eats it. Raw. I got a radius range of under a mile. Barely covers one police precinct. I'm very proud of my precinct. It ain't much, but it's home. I pledge allegiance to my precinct…Nobody lives up here. 'S all bomb-outs. Gutted projects. Arsonated rubble.

FREE LANCE: Listener response?

HUNGRY MOTHER: Rubble don't write a lot of post cards. The junkies call me sometimes. *Hit* Line requests. Sugar Bear and Oz. They call on their anniversary. Four years, a mutual monkey. Many happy returns of the day. Born to junk. Scrapin' along and strung far-out on meth-a-done. Sugar Bear and Oz, this is the hit, this is the one, to which you first shot each other up and fell in love, oh so long ago. Sugar Bear and Oz, up on the roof, this one's for you. So slick.

FREE LANCE: [*Laughs.*] One hears stories.

HUNGRY MOTHER: It's been known to happen.

FREE LANCE: About you, dear. One hears them. In the air. Snatches. All over. Faceless celeb. You ought to take precautions. You have more listeners than you think. Than you might imagine.

HUNGRY MOTHER: Funny you should say that. I have been getting more letters. Got one today, it was a mistake. She mistook me. It's a serious letter.

FREE LANCE: Aren't they all?

HUNGRY MOTHER: Just crazy. This one was crazy, too. But serious.

FREE LANCE: What are you going to do about it?

HUNGRY MOTHER: What can you do about it?

FREE LANCE: Respond.
        Pause.

HUNGRY MOTHER: She wants help.

FREE LANCE: Then help her.

HUNGRY MOTHER: How?
        Pause.

FREE LANCE: I've changed my name.

HUNGRY MOTHER: Ah.

FREE LANCE: I've *altered* it.

HUNGRY MOTHER: I remember. You were into brand names. Rumor had it.

FREE LANCE: Generic. Not brand, generic.

HUNGRY MOTHER: "Polish Vodka."

FREE LANCE: Very tasty. I was all over the society pages. But I gave it up when I left the Agency. It's Free Lance now.

HUNGRY MOTHER: Oooo. Evocative. [*Slight pause.*] I prefer Polish Vodka.
        Pause.

FREE LANCE: If wishes were horses,
        Pause.

HUNGRY MOTHER: If the river was whiskey,

FREE LANCE: You've always been the Hungry Mother. Ever since I've known you. [*Pause.*] I work for the Mook now.

HUNGRY MOTHER: The Mook. Oh my.

FREE LANCE: Again. That's how I heard about you. That's how I tracked you down.

HUNGRY MOTHER: The Mook? Listens to me?

FREE LANCE: Faithfully.

HUNGRY MOTHER: It's almost an honor. In a patho-spastic sort of way.

FREE LANCE: He told me you were back on the air.

HUNGRY MOTHER: I'll have to upgrade my shit. Can't have no cut-rate shit if the Mook's tuned in.

FREE LANCE: You ought to be more careful. The Mook's worried about your license.
    Slight pause.

HUNGRY MOTHER: I don't have no license. And I'd bet my momma he knows that. His momma, too. How's his reception? Where's he based?

FREE LANCE: He floats.
    Pause.

HUNGRY MOTHER: Why'd you go back?

FREE LANCE: Oh, honey. [*Laughs.*] Oh honey. I'd drink his bathwater. [*Beat.*] I did super at the Agency. It was dull, darling. Dull as crushed rock. For them. On my own, it's a breeze. *Free Lance.* Don't you just dig the shit out of it? [*Pause. Cool smile; sardonic.*] *I love* the way he beats me, Mother. Swell hands. Something of a setback for personal liberation, right Mother? [*Pause.*] I tried to cut him loose.

HUNGRY MOTHER: You sure you're not involved with those kids? Ask Mook.

FREE LANCE: Mook doesn't do kids. You're very tender, Mother, but I could never count on you. Maybe after the revolution.

HUNGRY MOTHER: Right. The coup d'état will make us straight. Thanks for stopping by, uh, Free Lance. Always nice to see you.

FREE LANCE: You, too, Mother. Like old times. Good, yes?

HUNGRY MOTHER: Absolutely golden. Better than a poke in the eye with a sharp stick. The best of them.

FREE LANCE: Don't become a stranger, Mother. [*She drifts into the street.*]
    HUNGRY MOTHER *switches blue light "on."*

HUNGRY MOTHER: And now a word from one of our sponsors. The Bantustan Shooting Gallery's One Hundred and Sixth Street Branch will be open twenty-four hours a day throughout the holiday weekend for your intravenous entertainment. They're stocking up on your favorite brands of smack, so get your shit together and get on over to One Hundred and Sixth Street now. They're running a special on Spearchucker, got a brand new batch of Black on Black, the everpopular Pussy Whipped is always on hand, and, fresh off the boat, while it lasts, that perennial Bantustan favorite, White Flight. And the one thousandth customer this holiday weekend will receive, free of extenuating circumstances, a red-hot two-tone maroon Jew Canoe with fresh plates, plenty of mirror surface, and brand new Cuban credit card with sanitary nozzle. That's this weekend at the Bantustan One Hundred and Sixth Street Shooting Gallery—rush on over. [*He turns the blue light off. Shrugs into his coat.*]

LOUD SPEAKER: A walk—on the wild side.
    HUNGRY MOTHER *hits the street, and slides into the bar.* BELLY UP *is drinking alone. He's wearing his old sergeant's fatigue jacket, the shadow of the chevrons still visible on the sleeve.*

BELLY UP: You're taking off like a target-seeking, heat-sensitive, laser-directed, anti-personnel device. Stuffed with shrapnel. *Plastic* shrapnel. [*Laughs.*] Cluster bomb, Mom. Cluster bomb! [*Slight pause.*] Plastic shrap don't x-ray. That's the holy beauty of it. X-rays can't cope. Can't lo-cate it. Can't dig it out. [*Slight pause.*] Cluster fuck. [*Slight pause.*] Hungry Mother, the voice of the voiceless, the articulator of the ineffable, the thing that goes bump in the night. I never miss a show.

HUNGRY MOTHER: I wish I could say the same.

BELLY UP: You're getting better. More conscientious. Know what I saw? In a window? A record. By Hoover and the Navajos.

    Long pause.

HUNGRY MOTHER: Outstanding. [*Pause.*] Was there a picture? What'd they look like?

BELLY UP: No picture. Crazy thing. It came in a fiberglass dust jacket. I got that shit up my ass. It burns like hell. Gets into every nook and cranny. Fibers. They're far out. They're a far-out group. Insulation. Navajogation. Kills me. This—?

HUNGRY MOTHER: Patho-rock.

BELLY UP: Knocks my socks off. I love it. Better than mime for the blind. Heaps better. "Fiberglass Finger Fuck!" "Fiberglass Felony Shoes!" "Carcinogenic Concierge!" Can you dig it? Blows me away. You ought to have them on the show.

HUNGRY MOTHER: Don't bug me, Belly Up. I just get this stuff in the mail.

BELLY UP: From the record company.

HUNGRY MOTHER: From *nobody*. It just floats in on the tide.

BELLY UP: You're gonna break 'em, Mother. You're gonna break 'em big. When I saw them in a store I was *fiberglassted*. Heh heh. I had no idea they were for real. I thought you…created them, you know? The holy power of PR.

HUNGRY MOTHER: So did I. In a way, I mean. As far as I know, I don't know if there really is a "Hoover and."

BELLY UP: I purchased it.

HUNGRY MOTHER: LP or single?

BELLY UP: LP. A botanica. Voodoo boutique. Haitian herb shop. I was on the prowl for a pack of mojo and a slice of John the Conqueroo. Saw it in amongst the loas and the gris-gris.

HUNGRY MOTHER: That's a good sign. That's encouraging. Those places are more underground than I am. Maybe we can nip this in the bud. I'd hate for it to get out of hand. I never intended to inflict Hoover and the Navajos on the general public. Something like this. A trend.

BELLY UP: Maybe they're ready for it. Look at it this way—Hungry Mother, hit maker!

HUNGRY MOTHER: Right. Just another top-forty jock. Sounds good. I want it. I need it. I want to have impact…I'm a fucking artist, man. I want to be taken seriously.

BELLY UP: To which end?

HUNGRY MOTHER: The bitter end, natch. Tell me, Belly, to what do you attribute my sudden surge of popularity?

BELLY UP: To the fact you're coming in loud and clear. Everywhere I go, Hungry Mother, that's who folks be talkin' bout.

HUNGRY MOTHER: Where do you go?

BELLY UP: Dark places. Places that slide. Places that glide. Places that aren't quite solid underfoot. You're becoming very big on the fringes. Amongst the rubble. Don't be downcast. You're articulating a definite need.

HUNGRY MOTHER: Don't think I'm not grateful. I like it. I love it. Here I thought I was only reaching my local rubble, and now you tell me I'm a smash in the rubble all over town.

BELLY UP: An idea whose time has come.

HUNGRY MOTHER: It's a heavy responsibility. Walk me home, Belly Up.

BELLY UP: Sorry. Not at this hour. I don't leave the bar.

HUNGRY MOTHER: What are you afraid of?

    Pause.

BELLY UP: Get your hungry ass over here on time, I'll give you a lift. [*Beat*] Back to the World.

HUNGRY MOTHER: I hear you. [*Beat.*] I hear you [*Beat.*] Belly Up, I keep getting these letters.

    The bar fades. HUNGRY MOTHER *on the streets.*

LOUD SPEAKER: Aspects of the Hungry Mother. The Hungry Mother in Jail.

    The jail scene appears: CHARLIE SAMOA, *and* JOHNNIE *and* JIMMY *in silhouette, cursing in polyglot.*

HUNGRY MOTHER: This is a flashback. A reprise. I don't think I care for this right now.

LOUD SPEAKER: Manana, manana. You're just postponing the inevitable. It's on the playlist, baby. This is a very *tight* playlist.

HUNGRY MOTHER: Maybe later. How about? I want a reprieve from this reprise.

LOUD SPEAKER: [*Miffed.*] You're just postponing the sooner or later, babe.

HUNGRY MOTHER: Fuck off. [*Jail fades.* HUNGRY MOTHER *runs into the studio. He flicks the blue light "on."*]

HUNGRY MOTHER: Dead air redux! Those acid flashbacks are murder! Hey! This be your happy, hopping and high-speed Hungry Mother—doin' it to you before you can do it to yourself. Our special this hour, Hungry Mother's Horoscope—a penetrating peek at the Big Zee. So stick around and watch the Mother scope it and dope it—just for you. Also on the bill this o-bliterated amorphous morn—broken glass...and Hungry Mother's Consumer Guide to Junk, where to score and what to pay, where to shoot and what to say, all the places and all the pushers, why not have the best possible habit in this, the Best, of all possible worlds? But first—this hour's top headlines. [*Teletype sound and newscaster voice.*] That illegal cordial made from kid pus is still circulating. Several deaths have been reported...More mastodon sightings in the North Cascades...Wolves in the outlying districts—if you're walking in the suburbs this morning, remember Wolf Warnings are up. Pedestrians are advised to travel in packs and exercise the usual precautions...We'll be back after something brief. This is WTWI, and this is the Hungry Mother, live—if you call this living, from our Twilight Studios. Remember to say, "Hungry!" And now, another interminable episode of "Sexual Shadow Land," the show that's sweeping the station.

    [*Rod Serling:*] His was an ordinary fetish—with a difference.

[*Phone rings.*] I'll get it. [*Flicks switches.*] You're on the air! Hey there!

JANIS: [*Live, over* PA] Hello? [*Hello? hello?*]

HUNGRY MOTHER: Turn down your radio! Please! Turn it down!

JANIS: What? [*What? what?*]

HUNGRY MOTHER: Turn that radio down! Turn it down! You're on the air! Trust me!

JANIS: Okay! [*Okay! Okay!*]

> When JANIS *next speaks, the echo and feedback are gone.*

JANIS: Better?

HUNGRY MOTHER: Much! I'd starve on feedback. What can Mother do for you? What can you do for Mother?

JANIS: Oh, Mother, I know. I listen to you all the time. I sit by the radio. I wait. I don't want to miss you. I hardly go out anymore. I don't.

HUNGRY MOTHER: You sound like a fan.

JANIS: Believe me, I am…I am. I don't go out anyway. But—I am. A fan. It's a comfort.
> *Pause.*

HUNGRY MOTHER: Yes? Was there something else? You're killing my air.

JANIS: My name is Janis, Mother. I'd like to see you. You don't know me. I'm a stranger. We've never met.

HUNGRY MOTHER: Sure. C'mon up.
> *Slight pause.*

JANIS: This is serious. I want to meet you. [*Slight pause.*] Mother. I really need to see you. Please…Can you tell me how to get there?

HUNGRY MOTHER: Sure. Ah, it's One Marauder Avenue, just past Faghag Park. Always hungry to have visitors in the studio, little lady. [*He hangs up. Looks pointedly at the "on" blue light.*]

HUNGRY MOTHER: Whatever happens. Hang loose. Go with the flow. Lean with the scene. Strive with the jive. Fuck it.
> *The Jail scene appears.* HUNGRY MOTHER *walks into it. The trio regards him ravenously.*

CHARLIE SAMOA: My name is Charlie Samoa.

HUNGRY MOTHER: Right away.

CHARLIE SAMOA: And these are…the Samoans. [*Indicating the transvestites.*] Johnnie Sucrose—take a bow, sweetie—and Jimmy Shillelagh.

HUNGRY MOTHER: Charmed, I'm sure. My name is…uh, professionally I'm known as, uh, a.k.a.—

CHARLIE SAMOA: We know who you are—

JOHNNIE SUCROSE: There's no need to shit us—

JIMMY SHILLELAGH: We never miss a show—

JOHNNIE SUCROSE: We'd know the golden tones anywhere. We're big big fans of yours.

CHARLIE SAMOA: But we got a question. The question is—what are you doing here?

JOHNNIE SUCROSE: Not that we mind, you understand—

JIMMY SHILLELAGH: Not that we're not thrilled—

CHARLIE SAMOA: Even honored—

JOHNNIE SUCROSE: But it comes as something of a shock—

JIMMY SHILLELAGH: To say the least.

CHARLIE SAMOA: We hope it does not have to do with your superb radio show—

JOHNNIE SUCROSE: Of which we never miss a single segment—

JIMMY SHILLELAGH: At considerable risk to ourselves in view of the multiple restrictions pertaining to the use of, access to, and ownership of tube gear and ghetto blasters in this, ah, ah—

JOHNNIE SUCROSE: *Penal* institution.

CHARLIE *and* JIMMY: Yeah.

HUNGRY MOTHER: You guys are desatively bonnaroo. A matched set. Siamese triplets, joined at the mouth. I predict a great future for you, should you consider it. Give me a call when you get out.

> *Pause.*

CHARLIE SAMOA: Answer the question.

JOHNNIE SUCROSE: It behooves me.

JIMMY SHILLELAGH: Believe me.

CHARLIE SAMOA: Believe him.

> *Pause.*

HUNGRY MOTHER: Criminal mischief…I…mmm…I shattered a subway window. [*Slight pause.*] With a golf club.

> *Pause.*

CHARLIE SAMOA: *Why?*

HUNGRY MOTHER: I was…*sore.*

> *Pause.*

JOHNNIE SUCROSE: How many strokes?

HUNGRY MOTHER: Just one. [*Slight pause.*] Nine iron.

JIMMY SHILLELAGH: Good choice. [*Pause.*]

CHARLIE SAMOA: Penny ante, Mother, strictly penny ante.

JOHNNIE SUCROSE: We are very disappointed.

JIMMY SHILLELAGH: Although at the same time greatly relieved that this does not have to do with your illegal yet highly entertaining radio program.

HUNGRY MOTHER: Oh, no. Not on your sweet. It's not illegal, anyway. *Para-legal.* I've never had any trouble. Nobody listens.

CHARLIE SAMOA: We do.

JOHNNIE SUCROSE: We're interested—

JIMMY SHILLELAGH: We're concerned—

CHARLIE SAMOA: We're anxiety ridden.

JOHNNIE SUCROSE: You don't have a license.

HUNGRY MOTHER: What a bitch. They license every goddamn thing in this goddamn city. You need a license to change a light bulb and a permit to take a piss.

CHARLIE SAMOA: Good thing, too. Where would we be without social order? You got to maintain it.

JOHNNIE SUCROSE: Very impor-*tant.*

JIMMY SHILLELAGH: Somebody's got to do it. Gotta have that social scheme.

CHARLIE SAMOA: A modicum of status quo.

JIMMY SHILLELAGH: To go along with a lot of expensive tube gear and no visible means of support.

JOHNNIE SUCROSE: And no license.

HUNGRY MOTHER: Very acute. Ah…where do you get your dope on me?

CHARLIE SAMOA: We asked around.

JIMMY SHILLELAGH: We checked the score.

JOHNNIE SUCROSE: We heard it through the grapevine.

THE SAMOANS *laugh raucously, then subside.*

HUNGRY MOTHER: And that's how you come to be such…fans.

CHARLIE SAMOA: Thereby hangs a tale. It begins with a grudge. As most tales do. I was freelancin'. That's my thing. A little liaison. A middle-man shuffle 'tween U.S. Guv Intelligence cats and a certain Kuomingtang warlord. Local scag baron…Am I boring you? Got a minute?

HUNGRY MOTHER: Not at all. I mean certainly, yes, most certainly, I do.

CHARLIE SAMOA: Where am I?

JOHNNIE SUCROSE: [*Suggestively.*] The Golden Triangle.

JIMMY SHILLELAGH: Enmeshed in webs. High intrigue.

JOHNNIE SUCROSE: Boo-Coo bucks.

JIMMY SHILLELAGH: So fine.

JOHNNIE SUCROSE: *Sweet.*

CHARLIE SAMOA: Put a lid on it. Oh, by the way, Mother, your junk reports are…very helpful—somewhat fanciful—but very informational in a metaphorical sort of way. We're grateful, Mother. Say thank you, boys and girls.

JOHNNIE *and* JIMMY: Thank you, Mother.

HUNGRY MOTHER: You're not supposed to take that…[*Pause.*] Sure. Sure.

CHARLIE SAMOA: We think you got your finger on something. Some sort of…*pulse.* But I digress. [*Sniffs.*] In the course of negotiating these delicate, er, negotiations, I happened to run into certain disagreements with, that is to say, run afoul of an associate, more of a colleague actually, concerning in connection with distribution rights…very complex. This gentleman…in order to press me, in order to, I suppose, exert a primitive kind of leverage—kidnapped my daughter. [*Pause.*] When this rather crude ploy failed to have the desired effect, he did something very unpleasant to her. [*Pause.*] Nobody pushes me around. I want you to understand, Mother, that she'll be all right. I'm convinced of that. My daughter means everything to me. You know that, don't you, Mother? *Her* mother was a *slut,* but she means everything to me. [*Pause.*] I went to his apartment house. I walk past the doorman. He didn't even see me. I'm a ghost. I walk up the back stair. Two at a time. No hurry, I was in no hurry. I rang the bell. Bang bang. I put the muzzle up, the muzzle of my magnum up—against the eyehole, the glass peephole. I rang the bell. He came to the door, I could hear his footsteps. He slid the cover back. Fffffffffttt. The cover of the peephole back. Click. Who could this be? His stomach's falling out. He couldn't see nothing, you understand. To him it just looked dark. But it was *steel*. [*Slight pause.*] He put his eye up to the glass. I make a clicking sound in the back of my throat. Click. Click. I shot him through the eye. Through the glass. That's how it was. I blew his fucking head apart. [*Pause.*]

HUNGRY MOTHER: Why are they in here?

CHARLIE SAMOA: Ask 'em.

HUNGRY MOTHER: Her. How can she be here?

JOHNNIE SUCROSE: I'm his conjugular visitor.

> *Slight pause. They laugh.*

CHARLIE SAMOA: Pull the strings, Mom, you got to pull the strings.

> *They are laughing, shouting, pushing and shoving* HUNGRY MOTHER—*a mock mugging. At last,* HUNGRY MOTHER *breaks away. A moment, then:*

HUNGRY MOTHER: I have to be going now.

CHARLIE SAMOA: Take it light—

JOHNNIE SUCROSE: Everything'll be all right—

JIMMY SHILLELAGH: Uptight and out of sight!

> *They are laughing again.*

JOHNNIE SUCROSE: Out of state! Out of state!

CHARLIE SAMOA: That's good! Out of state! Johnnie, you kill me babe!

JOHNNIE SUCROSE: Don't become a stranger!

JIMMY SHILLELAGH: Right! Right! Right!

> *Raucous laughter. They fade.* HUNGRY MOTHER *walks out and into the studio, up to the mike; blue light is still "on."*

HUNGRY MOTHER: And while we're waiting for our mystery girl guest, here's Hungry Mother's Horo-scope. [*Mellifluous, honeyed.*] Virgo: your stars are black dwarves, be advised. But don't take it too hard, my dear. Thermodynamic entropy comes to us all. Libra: proceed with caution. A romantic entanglement may lead to a social disease. Sagittarius: your moon is in eclipse and your spouse in the house of your best friend. Taurus: your moon is in Uranus. Success is light-years away. Capricorn: copasetic! Aries: if you open your mouth, I wanna see some teeth. Leo: you were so ugly when you were born, the doctor slapped your mother. Gemini: once black, they never come back. Cancer: you've got it, what can I say? Tough nuggies. Moloch: take the first-born boy-child of every *house*—[*Phone rings.*] Hang on! The lines are burning up. [*Switchflicking.*] Hello? Maybe I'll turn this mother into a *talk* show! Hello! You're *radio*-active!

THE MOOK: [*Live, over PA*] The planets are propitious. Hello, Mother.

HUNGRY MOTHER: Hey.

THE MOOK: How's by you?

HUNGRY MOTHER: Passable.

THE MOOK: Long time no you know.

HUNGRY MOTHER: Not long enough. You know?

THE MOOK: I'm looking for Free Lance.

> *Slight pause.*

HUNGRY MOTHER: So'm I.

THE MOOK: I'll be right up.

> *Click.* HUNGRY MOTHER *stares at the blue light, still "on." He spears beans with a fork.*

HUNGRY MOTHER: How long can he keep this up? Three beans, three prongs. One bean per prong, it's only fair. How long, ladies and gentlemen? Stick with me, friends, the suspense is killing.

> JANIS *enters.*

HUNGRY MOTHER: Like beans? [*Flings one.*] What's your opinion? [*Flings another.*] On-the-spot woman-in-the-street interview how do you like your beans?

JANIS: Boiled.

HUNGRY MOTHER: Very good. You're right in step with the rest of America. Just another pedestrian. [*Flings a forkful of beans, striking* JANIS.] Hey! Bull's eye! Well, maybe not a direct hit, maybe not *ground zero,* but certainly *close enough for jazz,* wouldn't you say? Yes, once again, *that's—close enough for jazz!*…You ought to do something about that bean stain, little lady. Isn't she pathetic, ladies and gentlemen?

> JANIS, *wary, backs off. Pause.*

HUNGRY MOTHER: Oh…yeah. Don't be alarmed. Just part of my standard improvisation avec beans. Nothing to be ashamed of.

JANIS: Are you, Hungry Mother? That's a stupid question. Of course you are.

HUNGRY MOTHER: The first.

JANIS: I'm Janis.

HUNGRY MOTHER: I figured.

JANIS: I called ahead.

HUNGRY MOTHER: Right.

JANIS: You said I could come up.

HUNGRY MOTHER: I thought you were another Janis. Different Janis. Janis I used to know.

JANIS: Oh. It's a common name. Not like Hungry Mother.

HUNGRY MOTHER: Aw shucks, that's just my nom de ozone…Give it time. The wave of the future. [*Pause.*] Something I can do for you?

JANIS: I wanted to see you.

HUNGRY MOTHER: You're the first, the very first! Hey! Reaching that wider audience! Hungry Mother has impact! It pays to listen! Kudos. Kudos are in order. My first fan. How's it feel, little lady? How do you like the studio?

JANIS: It's nice.

HUNGRY MOTHER: But small. Nice but small. But who knows, if this keeps up, this wild adulation, in twenty or thirty years I'll be able to [*Used Car salesman:*] trade it in on something nicer, yes, friends, why wait, empty those ashtrays and come on down…Beans?

JANIS: No. Thanks.

HUNGRY MOTHER: Something Japanese, perhaps. They do very well with that little shit. Transistors, crap like that. Minutia. A definitive talent for the diminutive, don't you think? Tell me, as my numero uno fano, do you find I have a sexy voice?

JANIS: No.

HUNGRY MOTHER: Robust. Virile. Vaguely Mediterranean. Like a swollen sack of coffee beans.

JANIS: No. [*Slight pause.*] Soothing. Possible.

HUNGRY MOTHER: I see.

JANIS: There's pain. In your voice…I came to talk to you. I need to talk to you. Don't be cruel.

HUNGRY MOTHER: Rings a bell. I have a famous sinking feeling.

JANIS: I recognize the pain.

HUNGRY MOTHER: Do you?

JANIS: It's like my own. Familiar. Similar. Like what I feel at night. In my chest. Your voice sounds like that. That pain.

     Pause.

HUNGRY MOTHER: You're Desperate, aren't you?

JANIS: [*Flushing.*] No, no, I would never that, would be over—

HUNGRY MOTHER: No no no no no. That's how you sign your letters. "Desperate."

JANIS: Yes.

HUNGRY MOTHER: Janis Desperate. Jesus.

     Pause.

JANIS: I want you to help me.

HUNGRY MOTHER: People in hell want ice water.

JANIS: What? What does that mean? What is that supposed to mean? I want you to help me. Please.

HUNGRY MOTHER: It's a joke, Janis Desperate. A joke.

JANIS: I don't get it. I don't see anything funny.

HUNGRY MOTHER: You're not concentrating. Is all. Now pay attention. This is Pop Analogy Number One. Rock n' roll Metaphor. You might just cop on to what I'm laying down—dig? You can't always get what you want. But if you try sometime. You get what you need. [*Pause.*] Biggest buncha bullshit I ever heard. I hate to be the one to break it to you sister, but people in hell don't *want* ice water, they *need* it. And—guess what? They *don't* get it…Do you get it?

JANIS: I don't feel good, Mother. I know you know what I'm—I know you feel the same.

HUNGRY MOTHER: I'm asking do you get it. Your asking me to help is the joke. I'm laughing. I'm larfing. You'd better larf too.

JANIS: I know you know how I feel.

HUNGRY MOTHER: Not a glimmer.

     Pause.

JANIS: I don't have furniture in my place. Nothing. A radio. I play the radio. Full blast. Keep the junkies away. They run through the building at night. Up and down the stairs. Fire escape. Rip the copper out of the walls. The wiring. There's no water. No light. They steal the stoves. The gas crawls up the wall. [*Slight pause.*] I turn it up. Way up. Radio. Play it all night. Afraid to sleep. They run through the building all night. Scratch the walls. [*Slight pause.*] I said that. [*Slight pause.*] That's how I found you, Mother. One night. Down at the end of the dial. Before dawn. Strange voice. Cracked. Had a crack in it. Down at the end of the dial. Pain in it. [*Slight pause.*] Thanks for turning up. You were so faint at first. When I first found you. Just a crackle. Clearer in winter than summer or spring…No, that's silly, but—my place is right across the park. I think the leaves must interfere? Anyway, lately—you're coming in as clear as a bell.

HUNGRY MOTHER: A lucky bounce offa the clouds. It's all in the angle, sweetheart. I'm 26,000 light-years off center.

JANIS: Incredibly clear. What I am telling you. What I am trying to say. For more than a year now your voice has really made a difference to me, Mother.

   Pause.

HUNGRY MOTHER: Why don't you buy some furniture? Beanbag chairs. Shag rug. Plexiglass coffee tables. Big glossy books. Galopagos this and that. Austerity is salubrious but poverty can be painful. Cheer yourself up. Hanging plants, that's the ticket. Junkies don't truck with hanging plants.

JANIS: [*Trying again, in a rush.*] I felt you were lonely, you said you wanted letters, I could tell, I could tell you were, by your jokes, you were worried no one was listening, no one cared, no one was hearing you, so I wrote, I wrote you. I never dreamed, you know, of writing to a, a public person, a stranger, I wouldn't you know, infringe on someone's privacy…so I was really distressed when you read my letters over the air…but in a way that was all right, it was okay, it was like you were listening, like you were answering. I never expected you to—that's why I signed my letters Desperate, I thought—

HUNGRY MOTHER: That's the way God planned it.

JANIS: Mother, I didn't mean to write you about me, my problems. I was going to cheer you up, believe me—

HUNGRY MOTHER: Believe me.

JANIS: Oh, I do.

   Pause.

HUNGRY MOTHER: Look, uh…what's on your mind?

JANIS: I just—want you to be my friend. A friend. Is that so much to ask?

HUNGRY MOTHER: Depends. Come here.

   JANIS *moves to him.*

JANIS: Okay.

HUNGRY MOTHER: Tight squeeze.

JANIS: That's okay. Cozier. [*She sits.* HUNGRY MOTHER *puts an arm around her. She smiles, slightly. She relaxes, just a bit.*]

HUNGRY MOTHER: 'S nice, huh?

JANIS: Yeah. Yeah.

HUNGRY MOTHER: I… can't do it.

JANIS: What?

HUNGRY MOTHER: Janis, there's something I should tell you.

JANIS: [*Touching his face.*] Sssshhh, don't talk. You don't have to talk.

HUNGRY MOTHER: Yeah, there's something I should have mentioned earlier. [*Slight pause.*] You're lonely, right?

JANIS: Yes.

HUNGRY MOTHER: Well, I'm lonely too.

JANIS: Oh, Mother, I know you are. I know you are.

HUNGRY MOTHER: Well, darling—as one lonely person to another [*Pause.*]—*we're on the air!*

> JANIS *jumps to her feet, looks at the blue light.*

JANIS: Oh. Oh.

HUNGRY MOTHER: [*Goes to mike.*] Wasn't that touching, friends? You heard it here, first. Hang in there, there's more to come from Janis Desperate, much more.

JANIS: Bastard.

HUNGRY MOTHER: Sorry.

JANIS: Yes.

HUNGRY MOTHER: That's my style, sweets. Free-form free-fall. Wing it over the edge and see how long it takes to hit bottom.

JANIS: Jesus.

> THE MOOK *enters. A large man. Elegant. Terrifying. A black Renaissance Prince of the Underground.*

HUNGRY MOTHER: Ah, Mook! Mook! I'm honored. Long time no you know. I believe you two, you know, too.

THE MOOK: You're off the beam. I haven't had the pleasure. Seen Free Lance?

HUNGRY MOTHER: How about her?

THE MOOK: I doubt it. You lookin' to get out of show business, Mother, and into an honest line of work? Why for you cute, Mom? She's nice, but the Free Lance I have in mind is nicer by far.

HUNGRY MOTHER: Right. Sorry. Mook. Janis. Janis. Mook.

THE MOOK: Enchante.

JANIS: Fine! [*She stalks out.*]

THE MOOK: Whatsa matta for her? The rabbit died?

HUNGRY MOTHER: Naw…We just met.

THE MOOK: Mark my words, Mother. The price of fame is a paternity suit.

HUNGRY MOTHER: I'll watch my step.

THE MOOK: You'll know you're in the big time when you find you have a couple of café au lait kids who bear not the slightest resemblance to anyone you ever knew. [*Pause.*] Where's Free Lance?

HUNGRY MOTHER: Changed her name.

THE MOOK: You said she'd be here.

HUNGRY MOTHER: I said I was expecting her. I am. I still am.

THE MOOK: You ought to get out more, Mother. Away from the mike. Clear your head.

Pause.

HUNGRY MOTHER: Free Lance.

Pause.

THE MOOK: She didn't tell me. She was going to change her name. She just changed it.

Pause.

HUNGRY MOTHER: I could use more air.

THE MOOK: I liked Polish Vodka better.

HUNGRY MOTHER: To drink or on her?

THE MOOK: Both…*Simultaneous.*

HUNGRY MOTHER: I thought she was working for you.

THE MOOK: In this assumption our thoughts concur. [*They dap.*] Coincide. [*Dap.*] Collide. [*Dap.*] She's not treating me well, Mother. Or herself. She's going out on the limb of principles. I want her to come down. If you snag the drift of my metaphor.

HUNGRY MOTHER: I think I follow it.

They begin a complicated dap, a hand jive.

THE MOOK: Free Lance. That's rich.

HUNGRY MOTHER: Snap!

THE MOOK: It's a question of precedents. She needs her insurance, Mother, like a child needs her vitamins. And this is a world, Mother, as you well know, in which a child cannot hope to survive without a little luck and some kind of insurance.

HUNGRY MOTHER: Crack!

THE MOOK: She knows I cannot allow this. Not just my livelihood is threatened by her rash and precipitous action. What if my other ladies take it into their heads. I wouldn't want to see them get hurt.

HUNGRY MOTHER: Pow!

They finish dap.

THE MOOK: Exactly. Thank you, Mother, for extending my metaphor.

HUNGRY MOTHER: Not at all. Any time. [*Pause.*] Maybe she's lucky.

THE MOOK: I'm her luck. [*Pause.*] The thing that really gets my goat, Mother, that really galls the living shit out of me—is that she's setting this whole thing up like some kind of walking 3-D cliche. Right offa the silver screen. Ruthless pimp with the cold-as-stone heart. Prosty with the tits of gold. They get down—to brass tacks. Small-time indy versus rapacious multinational. Victory for free enterprise. Yea. Sheep farmer whips cattle baron. Score one for the free fucking market and laissez-faire capital-ism. Creeping socialism crawl under de rock. Music up and out. [*Pause.*] The record's scratchy, Mother. A bad print. I seen it before. I heard it before.

HUNGRY MOTHER: Why'd she do it? She said she missed you.

THE MOOK: She saw it in the movies.

HUNGRY MOTHER: Oh.

THE MOOK: For Christ sake, I'll give you ten to one. She took it into her head…Mother, Mother. I'm chiding you, Mother. Tsk, tsk. In America—life—[*Strikes pose.*]—imitates—*media.* [*Slight pause. Drops pose.*] Who should know better than you?

HUNGRY MOTHER: I hang my head.

THE MOOK: I resent being put in this position. I resent being made to play some kind of classic American morality schtik. I resent being made archetypal. You know? It gives me a black *burning* sensation behind my eyes.

HUNGRY MOTHER: What are you going to do to her?

> *Long pause.*

THE MOOK: Ask her to come in. [*Slight pause.*] Nicely. [*Beat.*] *You* were close.

HUNGRY MOTHER: [*Brusquely.*] Old days. Stone Age. Before I became the Hungry Mother.

THE MOOK: Don't kid me. You always been the Hungry Mother. From time immemorial...You comin' in loud and clear dese days.

HUNGRY MOTHER: Yeah?

THE MOOK: Right. Somebody's monkeyed with your volume.

HUNGRY MOTHER: Atmospheric turbulence. Sunspots. Geothermal radiation.

THE MOOK: You ought to watch your ass.

HUNGRY MOTHER: So everybody tells me. Christ, it's enough to make a corpse paranoid.

THE MOOK: Especially those Junk Reports.

HUNGRY MOTHER: Mook, they aren't for real.

THE MOOK: Oh, yes they are. Now they are. Every junkie in town, Mom. Every junkie, every narc, every pusher, every pimp. You the *source,* man, the Wall Street fuckin' Journal of Junk...Everybody knows you're illegal, Mother. It's no secret. Folks concerned. Highly concerned. There are rumors. Grand jury activity. They might get together. They might *convene.* This whole gig just might go titties up.

HUNGRY MOTHER: I can't explain it, Mook. This tube gear is shot. It's cream of shit. It's a miracle it gets off the block.

THE MOOK: [*Leans forward, very black, very deep.*] Tell it to the judge. [*Laughs, booming crackle.*] They taping you 'round the clock, little man.

HUNGRY MOTHER: [*Yelling.*] I don't broadcast around the clock!

THE MOOK: If only you'd keep a schedule, Mother. They don't want to miss a single spasm. A single spurt. Right now, they trying to ascertain just who listening. Besides themselves, I mean. A demographic sample. To determine your threat extent. It's proving elusive.

HUNGRY MOTHER: I'll bet it is.

THE MOOK: Just a friendly gesture. If you see Free Lance, tell her to come on in. Just like the movies. It'll go easier. Plea bargain. One week only. Tell her that. [THE MOOK *heads for the door.*]

HUNGRY MOTHER: Hey, Mook.

THE MOOK: Yes dear?

HUNGRY MOTHER: You're on the air!

> THE MOOK *looks at the blue light a long moment. Then grins.*

THE MOOK: Motha fucka!

> *He exits.* HUNGRY MOTHER *races to the mike.*

HUNGRY MOTHER: Well, there you have it, gas fans, the heat is on. You heard it all, *live,* from the life of Hungry Mother, a true story. Cross my heart. If you'd like to participate in the life of Hungry Mother, just drop me a card—indicate your primary field of interest—philosophical, sexual, athletic, dinner, dress, or aperitif—and mail it to…Hungry Mother, Got To Get You Into My Life, Hubba Hubba Hubba Hubba, wtwi, Frantz Fanon Memorial Tenement, Number One Marauder Avenue, just past Faghag Park. All entries will remain on file for use at my personal discretion.

[*Weatherman.*] The long-range outcast for this weekend—*diphtheria!* Followed by bubonic plague and intermittent spotted fever. Enjoy. Right now outside our studio—continued existential dread dappled with parapsychological phenomena, and streaked with low-grade anxiety. Speaking of weather, we'll have the latest prices for bone marrow and rendering in a moment, but first…

[*He slumps on stool. Silence. He returns to mike: teletype and newscaster.*] Flash news update. That acute distress has gone—*terminal.* Closed with a rush. Check it out. Other tidbits about our town…That dog rapist remains at large. Pet owners—do you know where your pets are tonight? Coming up in the near future—if there is one—heh heh, always the optimist, Mother, check it out! Always the optimist. *Lycanthropy in the Home!* Always a hairy subject, we'll have some tips on just how to deal with it. We'll be talking to a bonafide cat burglar, and you'll find out *exactly* what they do with our furry friends…the fiends. We'll also have our Prick Hit of the Week, when you ladies can line up the sexual puerco of your choice and sock it to him—right here in our soundproof booth.

[*Mellifluous.*] That just about puts a merciful end to our broadcasting day here at wtwi, the twilight station with the demeanor that only a Mother could love. We'll top it off with our ever-popular Slumlord of the Day Award, we'll be back after somebody's briefs, but first—a word about *mange*…This is the Hungry Mother, wrapping it up here, boss, with a mouthful of joy buzzers and a handful of static, telling you to have a hopeful day, spelled with two ells.

Three swarthy individuals enter the studio: two men and a woman.

HUNGRY MOTHER: Has to be—[*Long pause; then a whisper.*] *Hoover and the Navajos.*
Freeze. Tableau. Lights fade. Blue light still "on," in the black. Long moment. Snaps off. Blackout.

END OF ACT ONE

ACT TWO

Black

LOUD SPEAKER: The Rising *Popularity* of Hungry Mother…Beginning with—
[*Blue light pops "on," silhouetting four figure freeze:*] Tableaux Vivants! Avec peaux rouges! [*Lights up slowly on* HOOVER *and* THE NAVAJOS, *and* HUNGRY MOTHER. *They remain still as* HOOVER *speaks simply, in the classic mode:*]

HOOVER: In the moon of grass withering…or perhaps in the moon of vanishing animals…I surrendered my people to General Howard. My heart was…*broke*. I said to him—the chiefs are dead. Looking Glass is dead. All the young men are dead. Or scattered like dry leaves. Or drowning in whiskey. My children chew bark. Their feet are frozen. The old women gobble dead grass and devil's brush. We are starving. My lungs are full of clotted blood. As I said before—from where the sun now sets, I will fight no more, forever. This is what I said to General Howard. [*Pause.*] So he gave me a job. [*Pause.* HOOVER *holds up a brightly colored plastic package in one hand, and points to it with his other hand, on which he is wearing a black leather glove.*] Selling these…The snack that never grows old…Fiddle Faddle…That's how I became Chief Fiddle Faddle. [HOOVER *flips down his shades. Pause. Grins.*] Just kidding.

THE NAVAJOS *begin poking around in the studio.* HUNGRY MOTHER *takes over from* HOOVER *at the mike.*

HUNGRY MOTHER: Hey, hey! Hoover, fella, you really had me going there. I was brewing up some really fierce Apache crocodile tears. Isn't he something, ladies and gentlemen? We're here today with our special guests, Hoover and the Navajos—

HOOVER: Just kidding.

HUNGRY MOTHER: Yes, yes, just fooling around. Tell us, Hoov—a lot of us—the listening and yearning audience would like to know something more about Hoover and the Navajos. All they know is what I tell 'em, what I, you know, make up off the top. On the spur.

HOOVER: You got it right. You got it right, Mother. You got it so right. Except in smallest details. No way you could miss. The light comes down on you…Smallest things. Our names. My friends. Mother, my companions…Crazy Joe Navajo. [CRAZY JOE *burps delicately by way of greeting.*] Freddy Navajo. [FREDDY *nods coldly.* HOOVER *smiles.*] The light comes down on you, Mother. [*Long pause.*] Indians are always silent. Having nothing to say. Ask your stupid questions.

HUNGRY MOTHER: [*After a slight hesitation.*] In the fawning fanmag manner, then—when did you write your first song? When did you first start playing the guitar? When did you decide to devote your lifestyle to music?

HOOVER: In the moon of rising expectations.

HUNGRY MOTHER: In the little magazine manner then—when did you first conceive, and begin to develop as a distinct genre of popular music, *patho-rock?* What sets *patho-rock* apart from other strands, such as goat-bucket blues or coon-cajun cakewalks? Compare and contrast. Trace its evolution in a sociohistorical context. How do you account for your obsession with fiberglass? Is it worthwhile speculating along psychosexual dysfunction lines?

HOOVER: In the moon of historical necessity…Out of the blue…Unrelenting bitterness, as long as the waters shall flow and the grass shall grow—you know the phrase?…An environmentally generated malignancy contracted as an immediate consequence of contact through deliberate exposure to the carcinogenic substance. In that order.

HUNGRY MOTHER: [*Brightly.*] I see. That's too bad!

HOOVER: In the moon of bowing to the inevitable. In the charnel moon of abject capitulation. In the blue moon of genocide. In the quarter moon of going completely off the wall…In the moon *of forced labor…*

HUNGRY MOTHER: Right. Got it. That's what gives your songs that grit, that nit, that *sliced life.* Tell me—and I'm sure your fans at home would be more than super interested too—where do you get those boffo bonnaroo titles like *Fiberglass God?*

HOOVER: I got drunk and fell on the floor.

> *Pause. Then* FREDDY *stands.*

FREDDY: Freddy Navajo here. Earth to Freddy. I hear voices. Indian voices. Mescalito. Coyote. Charlie Chan. Joan of Navajo speaks in my ear. It ain't easy to hear myself think—with all those voices going. All the old voices. Covered here today. Hoover did his Poetic Indian to his usual turn. [FREDDY *and* CRAZY JOE *applaud.*] Aplomb. Aplomb. And Crazy Joe's taciturn Drunken Injun is, as always, subtle and tragic. Impeccable. Correct. [FREDDY *and* HOOVER *applaud. Slight pause.*]

CRAZY JOE: [*Ever so slightly slurred.*] Thanks.

FREDDY: A classic of its kind. You see my predicament? So many voices. A welter. A goulash. So hard to find a point of view. Which piece of history to vocalette.

HUNGRY MOTHER: [*Cheerily.*] How about TB? You know, tuberculosis, Easter Seals for brown babes? Famine? Smallpox sleeping bags?

FREDDY: Hostility is always in good taste.

HUNGRY MOTHER: Uh…Freddy, what's the—why don't you do the new single?

FREDDY: Right…This is a song I wrote one night while breaking glass on the reservation…I calls it—Fucking on Fiberglass!

HOOVER: Give me a ball 'n a beer, any day.

FREDDY: Right. Sheer shock value. No other redemptions. Oh, incidental alliteration. A simple tune. Our only aim is sensation.

HOOVER: I wasn't always a poet. I used to work for a living.

HUNGRY MOTHER: That's great. Swell, and heartwarming. Here it is, fans, what you've all been waiting for! If this single don't send you, you got no place to go! Hoover and the Navajos—*Fucking—On Fiberglass!*

> HUNGRY MOTHER *puts on the 45, flick switches. It blasts out over the* PA: *primitive guitar chording, hand drums, yowling and chanting, screaming, glass*

shattering. After three minutes of earsplitting sound, a blues-fragment snarls its way out of the maelstrom:

HOOVER: [*Singing, on the 45.*]

    Fuckin'

    On fiberglass…

    Got that shit

    Up my…aaaaaaaaasssss!

This is followed, on the 45, by a scream from FREDDY *that's like a baby's howl. During the playing of the single,* THE NAVAJOS *rock out, a violent and erotic frenzy. Fucking on Fiberglass ends with a crescendo of drumming and breaking glass. Silence.*

HUNGRY MOTHER: [*Softly.*] So visceral…I *can feel* it. Uch. Where do you guys get this stuff? Monstrous. Colossal. Curdled blood, see? Destroys me. Primal.

FREDDY: [*Snickering.*] Primordial.

    CRAZY JOE *gets up off the refrigerator. A hush. He goes to the turntable, takes off the 45, drops it on the floor. Pours whiskey on it. Takes a drink. Smiles. Smacks his lips.*

CRAZY JOE: Primitive.

    THE NAVAJOS *laugh wildly. They seize piles of 45s, and begin flinging them through the air, slowly at first, then faster, to crescendo—a blizzard of black plastic. It stops. The studio floor is covered in 45s. Pause.* HOOVER *smiles cool behind his shades and says softly:*

HOOVER: *Aborigine.*

    HOOVER *and* THE NAVAJOS *exit.* HUNGRY MOTHER *stands in the debris. Studio light out as streetlight snaps on.* HUNGRY MOTHER *walks into the light.* JANIS *is in a shadow. He stops and stares at her. Finally:*

HUNGRY MOTHER: Wha'choo doin' out here?

JANIS: Lurking.

HUNGRY MOTHER: Lurking. Huh. [*Slight pause.*] Hell of a place to lurk. [*Slight pause.*] Lurking long?

JANIS: Hours.

HUNGRY MOTHER: And lived to tell the tale. A-mazing. I shake my head. [*He does.*]

JANIS: So. What's the word?

HUNGRY MOTHER: *Hungry.*

JANIS: Listen, I thought maybe—you busy? I thought maybe we could get a bite.

HUNGRY MOTHER: In this neighborhood? A bite is a breeze. But will they quit after just one?

    They both laugh.

JANIS: Listen. I know a place.

HUNGRY MOTHER: Yeah? Well. Okay. All right.

JANIS: It's near here. You'll like it. Under Marauder Avenue. It floats.

HUNGRY MOTHER: A floating dive. Abso-fucking-lutely. Lezgo.

    The streetlight flickers. The light is blue and wintery: a cold evening. MOOK *and* FREE LANCE *enter.* HUNGRY MOTHER *and* JANIS *stop. Draw back. Unseen.*

THE MOOK: Ho Chi Minh Trail runs through the park now.

FREE LANCE: Uptown to down.

THE MOOK: Natch. Built that way. They brought it over after the war. Reconstituted it. As it were.

FREE LANCE: What you run on it?

THE MOOK: Scag. Just like the war. Like it never ended. Them good old days. They got a replica of the war goin' on in there. Minature. Jes' a few blocks away...Business as usual, babe. [*He turns his gaze on her.*] Back on the street.

FREE LANCE: Back on the streets again.

THE MOOK: I stand corrected. Back on the streets. The phrase that pays...I thought you were sick of the street. I been to see Mother, looking for you.

FREE LANCE: I've missed the street.

THE MOOK: I know you have. I wasn't surprised.

FREE LANCE: And the street missed me.

THE MOOK: No, no, I wasn't surprised you weren't there. I know you done with him. I wanted to check out Mother's crib. Wanted to get some kinda line on just what we boosting, here. We had a nice chat. [*Slight pause.*] Mother said you missed me.

FREE LANCE: I miss the street. Mook. Same difference...I miss you. What kind of chat you say you had?

THE MOOK: Minimal. I dropped him a hint. Dammit, Free Lance, whachoo doin' out here?

FREE LANCE: Looking for you.

THE MOOK: On the street? Come on, baby. I been all over town, I come home find you *walking* my block.

FREE LANCE: [*Laughs.*] You my main squeeze, sugah. Mama want Papa-san be her first trick. Numbah one, dig? [*Pause.*]

THE MOOK: You set me up, Free Lance. Like a damn tar baby. Some kind of story. You fictionalizing my position. Dig? People talk. A legend in my own time. Shit. Legend in my own mind. They talkin' now. Hear 'em?

FREE LANCE: No.

THE MOOK: Erodes my credibility. People don't think I'm real. Think I'm the damn Baron Samedi or some voodoo shit. Gets tough to keep the muscle up when they put you in the same bag with Mickey the Mouse and Agent Orange. [*Hisses.*] Know what I talk, bitch?

> *She is about to respond when she hears something in the distance. They both listen.*

FREE LANCE: Guns.

THE MOOK: *Gunners.*

> *He smiles. She shivers.*

FREE LANCE: I love The Street. I go wandering on The Street. In the back of my head. Stay there forever. Stay there for good. Disappear behind my eyes. You understand?

THE MOOK: Free Lance.

FREE LANCE: I'm not going upstairs with you, Mook.

THE MOOK: Free Lance. [*Slight pause.*] I promised Mother.

FREE LANCE: No, not upstairs. I like it here. [*Slight pause.*] Leaving Mother's, I get a screamer. A rag ghost. I see him all the way down at the end of the block. He sees me. He turns. Gunfight at the Okay. I freeze. He takes a step. Takes two. Now he's running. Right at me. His mouth is open like a siren and he's screaming. He's getting closer. Closer. I can smell rot. He's got a bottle in his hand. A mickey. Like a knife. He's right on top of me. I step aside. And he goes right on by. Still screaming. Disappears into the park. Screams stop. Siren stops. *Chop.*

THE MOOK: Fags got him. Gorilla fags. They drop out of the trees like fruit.

FREE LANCE: Nothing like that happens upstairs.

THE MOOK: Damn straight. I ain't no punk. You have any other adventures since I saw you last?

FREE LANCE: Run of the mill rubble walk. Trash fire circle jerks. Rubble rabble. They try'n come on you as you walk past.

THE MOOK: It's an art. That'll teach you to run away from home. Come on in, Free Lance. Come on in, baby. Come on in with me.

FREE LANCE: Of course.

THE MOOK: Mother's worried about you. You ought to give Mother a call.

FREE LANCE: I will.

THE MOOK: I know you were close. Just tell him you okay. Set his mind. The kid's all right.

FREE LANCE: Mook. Mother's on the rag about some kids. You have anything to do with that? You boosting, hustling some kids?

THE MOOK: 'S an idea, baby. Get all my best notions from Mother.

FREE LANCE: Pimp. [*Slight pause.*]

THE MOOK: [*Mildly.*] Don't call me that. Don't rub The Mook the wrong way. Call me monger instead.

FREE LANCE: Monger?

FREE LANCE *begins to laugh, undertones of hysteria.* THE MOOK *smiles.*

THE MOOK: Yeah. Flesh monger.

She stops laughing. Slight pause.

THE MOOK: Come on up. Come on in.

She is listening in the distance, again.

FREE LANCE: Fire fight.

THE MOOK: See? Got to come with me, baby. Can't go 'way down there.

Pause.

FREE LANCE: For now. It's chilly.

He puts his arm around her. They start to leave.

FREE LANCE: [*Black.*] Whatchoo tell Mothah?

THE MOOK: Heh heh heh. I tell Mothah to watch his *ass.* You blackisms gettin' bettah, baby.

FREE LANCE: [*Laughs.*] Ah, Mook, Mook. [*Strokes his face.*] You're a dizzy cunt. You know that?

He stares. Then laughs. Roars. MOOK *and* FREE LANCE *exit. Streetlight flickers.* HUNGRY MOTHER *steps out and stares after them.* CHARLIE SAMOA *appears behind them. He's dressed as a derelict.*

DERELICT: [CHARLIE SAMOA] 'Member the cat.

They start. HUNGRY MOTHER *doesn't recognize him.*

HUNGRY MOTHER: Cat.

DERELICT: [CHARLIE SAMOA] 'Member the cat. Curiosity and the cat.

He starts off. Turns back.

Jesus was not a white racist—as some people suppose. He was the only son of the living god. [*Derelict* [CHARLIE SAMOA] *exits.*]

JANIS: You know them.

HUNGRY MOTHER: Who?

JANIS: The...couple.

HUNGRY MOTHER: Oh yes.

JANIS: What was that? That scene.

HUNGRY MOTHER: He wants her.

JANIS: What does she want?

HUNGRY MOTHER: Out.

JANIS: What are you going to do?

HUNGRY MOTHER: What can I do?

JANIS: She wants help?

HUNGRY MOTHER: No. No. She doesn't *want* it.

Silence. Streetlight out.

LOUD SPEAKER: Oooeeeooo, baby, baby. Oh, oh, oh, Miss Ann. Dime-a-dance romance. No-tell motel. *Skank.* Tryst. Tropics. *Tristes tropiques.* Photo Opportunity... The House of Blue Light [*Beat.*] Hungry and...Friend!

Studio illuminated. HUNGRY MOTHER *and* JANIS *on the refrigerator cot. The studio is still a wreck from* THE NAVAJOS' *visit.* JANIS *lights a cigarette.*

JANIS: At least we weren't on the air.

HUNGRY MOTHER: Community standards. I think I'll torch these platters. Do the whole dump in hot wax.

JANIS: I don't think it's right, quite.

Silence.

HUNGRY MOTHER: Well.

JANIS: Well.

HUNGRY MOTHER: Hope you feelin' better...

JANIS: Bye 'n bye.

He's pleased she finished the phrase.

HUNGRY MOTHER: Yes.

JANIS: You too?

HUNGRY MOTHER: Mmmm. Bye 'n bye. 'S been a long time.

JANIS: Why? Why not?

HUNGRY MOTHER: Out of fashion. *Intimacy.* A blast from the past.

JANIS: I should talk. I haven't been, mmm, with anyone for ages. Long long time...Good for the blues.

HUNGRY MOTHER: Curin' or causin'?

Silence.

HUNGRY MOTHER: Walkin' blues. Talkin' blues. Stalkin' blues...[*He lets it go.*]

JANIS: Mother.

HUNGRY MOTHER: Yes'm.

JANIS: Mother, would you put me on the air?

  Slight pause.

HUNGRY MOTHER: Sure.

  He gets up and goes to the console. Flicks switches. Blue light goes "on." She goes
  to the mike. Now they are both standing nearly naked in the twilight debris.
  Silence. She lights a cigarette. Drags. Long moment. She returns to the cot and
  picks up the rest of her clothes. Puts them on. They look at each other.

HUNGRY MOTHER: Minimal. In fact, minimal to the max. I dug it. I especially dug it
  when you put on your clothes. Getting dressed on the radio. It's hot. No commercial possibilities of course. Could be cognescenti.

JANIS: I don't know what I wanted to say. I just wanted to put my voice out there. On
  the radio...What a strange phrase. Strange thing to say. On the air. I wanted to put
  it out there. On the air. Air waves. Radio waves go on forever. To other stars.

HUNGRY MOTHER: Pulsars, baby. Will the Hungry Mother Radio Hour be a hit on
  Betelgeuse six million light-years from today? Stay tuned.

  Silence.

HUNGRY MOTHER: Let's do it again sometime.

JANIS: Let's. [*She moves to the door.*]

HUNGRY MOTHER: Absofuckinglutely.

JANIS: See you.

HUNGRY MOTHER: Abyssinia, Janis.

JANIS: Right.

  She exits. HUNGRY MOTHER *retrieves his tennis shoes.*

LOUD SPEAKER: The White Man's moccasins.

HUNGRY MOTHER: Shaddup.

LOUD SPEAKER: Hungry Mother, the Vandal of the Vernacular. HUNGRY JAM!
  Mega Hertz! Kinky reggae. Rising tide. The ratings surge! He bends their ears! Wild
  in the streets! Hungry funk! Damp all over! Hard nipples! HUNGRY MOTHER
  MANIA! [*He bounds to the mike. Blue light "on."*]

HUNGRY MOTHER: You're right, you're right, you got good taste. Hey hey hey. All
  systems go! This will be the Hungriest Mother alive, this be WTWI, the twilight
  station with the terminal blues and the twilight debris, this be a blight and bleary
  predawn radio debauch with the only Mother that'll *ever* love you! Coming up this
  hour, Agony News Headlines, something spicy about the Pope, and the evermore
  popular Prick Hit of the Week. Plus—a bonus. A fab new soap op: MULATTO
  SPLENDOR! Yes, Antebellum blues! Miscegenation, America's favorite preoccupa-
  tion! Intricate intra-ethnic color schemes! Ancestor worship and the Daughters of
  the Confederacy! Something for everyone! Impossibly overwritten! Here! On WTWI!
  Don't miss *Mulatto Splendor,* the soap that's guaranteed to become a *class* struggle.
  In this week's episode, Rhett discovers that Scarlett's been 'passing'—and the an-

nual debutantes' ball is crashed by the field hands. And now—*Moan Along With Mother!* [*He sings a blues moan, minor key. First note's melodic, it quickly becomes harsh, going out of control into sobbing and retching. Subsides. Slight pause.*] There. Doesn't that feel better?

[*Attacks the typewriter furiously. Newscaster:*] And now this hour's top short stories…Dengue Fever raging out of control across Sub-Saharan Africa…absolutely terminal, no, I repeat, no antidote…Green Monkey Virus spreads from Germany to Georgia! If you gush black blood you've got it! And you're a goner! Isn't that something?!…And…the Pope is engaged! We'll be back later in the week with more on the Forty-Second Street sniper. These are this hour's top tales, brought to you by Ominous Acronyms—Ominous Acronyms, dedicated to raising the ante no matter the pot. And now a spiritual word of advice from the pastor of the First…Chinese Baptist…Church of the Deaf! [*"Chinee":*] Leveland Bluce Ree here. Lememble! Don't wait for the hearse to take you to church!

[*Cheery.*] Thank you, Leveland Bluce. Next hour, my impression of a JAP. And I don't mean Japanese. Don't miss it. But first—[*Slight pause.*] Trying to get over. [*Slight pause.*] Hauling ass.

[*Slight pause. Then, shakes himself, full-speed:*] I seem to be wandering today, fans, please forgive me, bouncing off the boards like a rabid hockey puck, coming up hungry, coming up short, coming up the up and coming group destined to dethrone the once-mythical Hoover and The Navajos: Jumpin Lumpen and the Juke Savages and the new blockbuster, *Idi Amin Is My Doorman!* Don't you dare miss it. But first, it's time once again for—Our Prick Hit of the Week! Yes, every week the Mother invites you and your nominee into the studio for a little *slug-fest.* With the aid of our superbly trained staff of Swiss guerillas, we hold him down, and you let him have it! So ladies—ah, *women,* keep those nominations coming. And now—here we go again with *Mother's Prick Hit of the Week!* [*Flicks switches. A tape goes on over the* PA: *it's a tape of Mother's moaning just previous. As the moaning plays,* HUNGRY MOTHER *rocks out, finger snaps and vocal bops. When the tape finishes he grins into the mike:*]

HUNGRY MOTHER: So good. I *really* identify. The weather outlook is for unparalleled nausea—followed by protracted internal bleeding. A million-dollar weekend. [*Newscaster, à la Paul Harvey.*] Top headline…This…or any other…hour…slavery …on the rise…once again…in most…of the civilized…world. [*Slight pause. Low, intense.*] Consider, if you will, the following felicitous phrases…Jones. Slud. Double dog dare. Going down slow. Walking wounded. Hunger artist. Bane. [*Weatherman.*] *Thick as slick out there, you better watch your step.* [*Screaming.*] Mexican standoff! Yes! Yes! No motherfucker can touch me now! I full of the Night Train! Hear the Midnight Special call my name! I be full, so full of that damn Night Train! Nothin' I ever seen can equal the color of my i-ma-gin-ation! I am the Midnight Prerogative!

[*Slight pause. Frenzied but quiet, under control, just barely: this is the emotional high of his set:*] Speaking of *jones*—I got it—for what you've been waiting for—for those with the baddest jones of all—for those with the cold at the core of their *soul—Mother's Junk Report!* Needles are *up.* Ditto fits and kits. Rubber tubing's down. Likewise brown dreck. Something cleaner cost you more…here we go! Black Magic go for a dime, if you can find it, and so will Foolish Pleasure. Fifteen for Light 'n Lively, and they be gettin' a quarter for 200 Years of Jive. Hard to believe, isn't it? Topping out at a flat thirty, Death Wish!…Sorry, brothers and sisters, you know that's the way it goes, whiter is brighter, and less is more. Now, getting away from dreamtime and down to the street, your Mother's gonna tell you straight. All that's out there is Brown Bomber and Death Boy. A quarter, that is, seven little spoons goes for fifty, and a rip-down, half of that, jack, will cost you twenty-five. That's what's on that open market! The shit is stepped on, Jack, stepped on! Worth your life to stick that shit! Cut with fucking Drano, Jack! Drano! [*Cooler.*] Active trading in fluff stuff around town: quarter scoops of coke scored easily on the approaches to the park, and it's snowing all over town. Storms of angel dust, methadone in ice buckets, on the rocks or with a crystal cranq chaser, and horse tranqs galore. On the sunny side up, the use of personal weapons in lethal transactions is riding a slight cooling trend—and that's got to be good news. This has been another edition of *Mother's Junk.*

[*Slight pause. Upbeat.*] Ah, once that's over, I'm back on the tracks, I really am. Works like a charm. Tomorrow: *Pantheon of Scum:* a grisly scavenge through the deserted cities of the heart. You've been listening to more of the same this last half-century—brought to you by *Sayanora Thermonukes*—check us if your megatonnage droops! *Sayanora Thermonukes*—say good-bye and mean it! And now let's join, already in progress, Sugar Bear and Oz—cutting up in the Cuban Room. [*He grabs his coat and walks out, leaving the blue light "on."*]

LOUD SPEAKER: The *Casa—Cubana!*

HUNGRY MOTHER *walks into the bar.*

BELLY UP: Mother! Salud! How hangs it, Ma?

HUNGRY MOTHER: Somewhere else. Give me a drink. Something for the inner city man. [*He downs it and burps.*]

BELLY UP: You bet. [*He follows suit.*] Feel better?

HUNGRY MOTHER: Some.

BELLY UP: Since you're a star, have another.

HUNGRY MOTHER: Catch Hoover's act?

BELLY UP: Indelible. Crushed my head. Had to be Hoover and the Navajos. You're getting very big, Mother. There's already a movement to save your ass.

HUNGRY MOTHER: I haven't lost it.

BELLY UP: You will. Committee to Save Hungry Mother's Ass. The Mook is getting it all together. The DA's hot and heavy on your case. He dug up a diva, and she's shrieking an aria about you to the Grand Jury right now.

HUNGRY MOTHER: What's her name?

BELLY UP: La Mook.

He snickers. Slight pause.

HUNGRY MOTHER: Pays to play both ends of the street.

BELLY UP: 'S a good deal. Immunity from prosecution, all counts 'cept murder one, lifetime guarantee. He tags up—spray paints it on the DA's door: you The Man.

HUNGRY MOTHER: He's The Man.

BELLY UP: You The Man, Mom. Your Junk Report peddles his junk.

HUNGRY MOTHER: That's absurd.

BELLY UP: Huh huh. Scag pimps snortin' up a storm on your say so, Ma.
    Slight pause.

HUNGRY MOTHER: Belly Up…you think they should sell smack over the counter—like aspirin?

BELLY UP: [*Laughs softly.*] C'mon, Mom. Why spoil a good thing? I'm checking on those kids for you.

HUNGRY MOTHER: Mmmmmmmm.

BELLY UP: Interesting scenario. After they go into custody of the lending institutions, poof—they disappear. I dig deeper. The big runaround. I run it down. It's easy…The banks sold 'em. Mook's the middle man. Commission on every kid.

HUNGRY MOTHER: Sold them.

BELLY UP: Into slavery…Big deal. Every two-bit banana tyrant keeps a couple of Indians around the house. Right here in town I know where you can buy, no questions asked, retarded kids. Cash on the barrelhead. Watch the tube?

HUNGRY MOTHER: Never.

BELLY UP: White slavery's license to print money.
    Slight pause.

HUNGRY MOTHER: I made it happen. Made it all happen. Make it up—make it happen. I kept…talking about it…reporting it, you know? Fictional fact, a metaphor…sort of true, you know?…and…and it comes back at me. It all comes back. Drifting up from downtown…humming…the wires have picked it up…'fore you know it, it's *news*, it's…happened…Honest, officer, it was only a fucking metaphor…The junk report! The junk report! Belly Up, from junk I knew from nothing! The Mook is trying to set me up…Last broadcast I did a slavery newsbit. Just a comedy sketch. Somebody must have picked up on it.
    Slight pause.

BELLY UP: Paranoid schizophrenia. Classic case. Delusions of grandeur. Unholy power to make manifest The Word. Unable to distinguish between cause and effect. Egocentric cosmology…Pull yourself together. You just water, Mother, Glass. You just show it back. Artists count for nothing, Mom. Don't take it so tough.

HUNGRY MOTHER: [*Mumbles.*] Bui doi.

BELLY UP: You don't say.

HUNGRY MOTHER: Bui doi.

BELLY UP: Dust of life. Street urchins. Half-breed Honda banditos. [*Slight pause.*] Shit. I had you lamped, Mom. I knew you been there. The 'Nam. Moo goo gai pan, my ass. [*Slight pause. Softer:*] Whadjoo take the fall for? Over *there.*

HUNGRY MOTHER: [*Winks, smiles wanly.*] Fragged the fucker. Fragged him. [*He gets up and leaves the bar. After he's gone:*]

BELLY UP: See you 'round, Mom.

On the street, HUNGRY MOTHER *turns his collar up against the cold. A Prostitute* [JOHNNIE SUCROSE] *and a Pimp* [JIMMY SHELLELAGH] *loiter on the edges of the light. A Derelict* [CHARLIE SAMOA] *stutter dances up to* HUNGRY MOTHER.

DERELICT: [CHARLIE SAMOA] Ladies and gentlemen! For your listening entertainment—the Latin from Manhattan! Hey! Hey, man, it's cold! Cold! Thirty cents for some apricot brandy, man. That's it. That's all we need.

HUNGRY MOTHER: Sorry.

DERELICT: [CHARLIE SAMOA] It's cold, man. Anything. Come on, we just shot some junk, man, we need that brandy, come *on!*

HUNGRY MOTHER: I don't have anything.

DERELICT: [CHARLIE SAMOA] Man, your heart's so hard you wouldn't give God a break. Shit. Hey, brothers, c'mon…[*They fade.* HUNGRY MOTHER *enters the studio; the blue light is "on."*]

HUNGRY MOTHER: Hungry Mother here, it's a fine fine super fine predawn funk—smoke blankets the greater metropolitan area, they continue to machine-gun survivors outside our studio rap rap rap rap rap and the *hits* just keep on comin'—and all told it looks like another fine fine super fine day in this fine fine city of ours! Before we descend into a welter of obscure pronouns, here's the plot—[*Lickety-split lung-screech.*] SUNDAY! Beautiful Sunday at U.S. Dragstrip Thirty just south of the tarpits! Thrill to the unholy smells and sounds and sight-gags as Captain O-blivion two-time cracked vertebrae champion heading for a head-on collision in his plutonium-charged heavy water under glass thresher goes against Free Bubba Free B. in his multinational banana consortium funny car! PLUS! Demolition Derby! You'll want to be there when the lights go out! PLUS! Hundreds of prize doors! PLUS! Chapped lips! PLUS! Blood-mad brahma bulls released every few seconds in the seating areas to stampede crazily through the stands! DON'T YOU DARE BE THERE! MISS IT! MISS IT! SUNDAY! SUNDAY! SUNDAY! [*Pause. Cool, calm, very liberal underground* FM.] And now, this week's interview with a Woman in the streets…Screaming Annie, dressed in ribbons. [*Phone rings, rings again. Flicks switches.* HUNGRY MOTHER *jumps at* it.] Free Lance?

JANIS *voice live over* PA—*thick and drowsy.*

JANIS: Mother, this is me.

HUNGRY MOTHER: How are you?

JANIS: All right…I wanted to say thank you…

HUNGRY MOTHER: For what? You sound sort of—

JANIS:…ah…I just…just wanted, just want you—I just, Mother—we on the air?

HUNGRY MOTHER: Yeah, you want me to take us off?

JANIS: Won't be necessary…Mother, I'm sorry.

There is a sound, something falling, a hard surface. We no longer hear JANIS' *drowsy breathing over the* PA, *but the line is still open.*

HUNGRY MOTHER: For what?

He freezes. Blackout.

LOUD SPEAKER: Live Flashback! Live! From the Hotel Abyss! The Flophouse of Stalinism! The Very First Broadcast! Hungry Mother—In the Beginning!

Studio illuminated. A tres haute couture FREE LANCE *strikes a pose.* HUN-
GRY MOTHER's *taped voice comes over the* PA:

HUNGRY MOTHER: [*On tape.*] A warm warm welcome to WTWI call letters, and to
the station for which they stand. [HUNGRY MOTHER *breaks freeze and goes to
mike. They are both younger, fresher.*]

HUNGRY MOTHER: Dressed to kill. To a T. To the teeth. As she parades up and down
in front of our microphone—[*She does, flashing a barracuda grin on every turn.*]
isn't she lovely? Isn't she wonderful, ladies and gentlemen? Wrapped from head to
toe in delicious apricot leather.

FREE LANCE: [*Laughs.*] Bitch.

HUNGRY MOTHER: Yes, just a vision of fruit loveliness. This is the Hungry Mother,
at WTWI, a nouveau station with a nouveau view, on what we hope to be the first of
many many twilight broadcasts with you. And on our maiden broadcast we have a
maiden broad—

FREE LANCE: Vaudeville's dead, sweetie.

HUNGRY MOTHER: Here in our fruit lovely studios. With us today—Polish Vodka!
One of the highest paid, uh, what exactly is it you do, dear?

FREE LANCE: Make it up, baby.

HUNGRY MOTHER: Right. And for our inaugural broadcast we're going to feature
something that's uniquely suited to the very special medium of radio: a fashion
show. That's right. Ought to give you some idea of what you're up against here at
WTWI. So, let's shove off. The First Annual WTWI Twilight Fashions Show. Isn't she
lovely? A vision. Simply a vision. Pol Vod is so—well, slender—no, thin…cadaverous,
really…poking ribs, hollow cheeks…a dream, really—slight potbelly, haunted eyes,
leather boots, and all the rest of it. Wearing a lovely barbed wire pendant, and
modeling for us that sensational new black lip glass. So positively sado-masch,
wouldn't you say? Deco-deco, innit? If I were to coin it, I'd call it—*Dachau Chic.*
How's that strike you, darling?

FREE LANCE: Perf, Mother. Just perf. [*She is still moving up and down in front of the
mike, hitting high-fashion poses.*]

HUNGRY MOTHER: Dachau Chic, indeed. Absolutely stunning. And now Polish Vodka
is going to do something very *kinetic,* demonstrating the amazing glide and flow,
warp and woof woof of apricot leather, aren't you darling? Yes, she's sweeping up
and down in front of our microphone—[*In fact, she is standing very still now, watching him.*] whew. What a woman. Sheer Poetry, pretty as a picture. What a woman,
lovely, lovely. What? What's she doing now? Ladies and gentle—

[*Hushed.*] Oh, I wish you could see this. She's—dare I describe it? Who dat who
say who dat? She's taking *off* that scrumptious apricot leather—*strip* by scrumptious *strip.* She's—*peeling off!* Oh, my, oh God, oh gracious! Oh so fine! Backfield in
motion! Peel me, baby, peel me off! Oh, my, oh…what…breasts, what—what
dugs!…and—and now…she's doing something perfectly…*indescribable*…with a
silk handkerchief…oh…my…I ONLY WISH I COULD DESCRIBE IT TO YOU
FULLY! WORDS FAIL ME! OH! OH! OH!…oh. [*Pause.*] Whew. Oh my. Thank
you, ducks. Worked me into a veritable lather. Thanks so much.

FREE LANCE: [*Dryly.*] Not at all.

HUNGRY MOTHER: Really…stunning. No other word will do. State of the art striptease.

FREE LANCE: My pleasure. Avec plaisir.

HUNGRY MOTHER: No, no mine. How d'you feel?

FREE LANCE: A bit chilly.

HUNGRY MOTHER: I don't wonder. Feel free to cover up. I hope that was as good for you as it was for me. Do you have something beautiful for us? Song and dance? A bit of the old soft foot? Why don't you just *whip* something up?

FREE LANCE: Oh, yes, I've got something for you. I've come prepared. I'd like to do for you now at this time—my impression of a JAP.

> *Slight pause.*

HUNGRY MOTHER: I beg your pardon.

FREE LANCE: Jewish-American Princess.

HUNGRY MOTHER: Oh…sounds fun.

FREE LANCE: Well…here goes. [*As she speaks—nasal Long Island accent—she sinuously removes her clothes. Her speech, harsh and sharp, absolutely counterpoint to her sexy elegant movement.* HUNGRY MOTHER *watches the strip, amazed.*] I just you know been hanging out, you know? You know what I mean? I got these like you know *problems* on my head, you know—I mean it's so off-putting. And if I could just iron 'em out you know, don't you know, it would be *smooth sailing,* no problem, I'm telling you. But it's anything but easy. It has to do with this relationship, and it's so heavy. It's like, you know, such a *hassle.* Who am I to know where it's going? I swear to God I just don't understand men for the rest of my natural life. I mean, it is so *shitty.* It's shitty being with him. It's shitty being without him. I mean, he is such a fuck. You know? I tell him, I say to him, you are such a fuck. I mean, it is trauma time again…Am I making sense? [*She finishes the strip perfectly timed on the last word.*]

HUNGRY MOTHER: Very convincing.

FREE LANCE: Felt good.

HUNGRY MOTHER: I'm not a Jewish-American Princess, but I found it as offensive as the next person.

FREE LANCE: I thought you'd like it. [*Slight pause.*] Kiss my vagina.

> *Slight pause.*

HUNGRY MOTHER: Meshuga. I don't think I can do that on the air.

FREE LANCE: Why not? You're such a fuck. Oh Mother, kiss my vagina.

> *Slight pause.*

HUNGRY MOTHER: Extend my *metaphor*…Kiss my vagina, extend my metaphor… Listening audience, the next sound you will hear will be—me and Pol Vod—playing chess.

> *Blackout.*
>
> *In blackout.*

LOUD SPEAKER: We'll be back…we'll be back…we'll be back…we'll be back…

> *Studio illuminated.* HUNGRY MOTHER *stares at the phone in his hand. A loud,*

empty drone…He drops it. Grabs his coat, walks into the street. It's dark and cold. THE DERELICT *approaches.*

DERELICT: [CHARLIE SAMOA] Hey, man. I almost made my trap. Just about got it, just about got it made. Just four cents short. I know you got a nickle. It's cold. Come on, man, I ast you before. *Nice.*

HUNGRY MOTHER: Okay. [HUNGRY MOTHER *hands* THE DERELICT *a coin; he gives* HUNGRY MOTHER *one in return.*]

DERELICT: [CHARLIE SAMOA] Here, man. Change.

HUNGRY MOTHER: Honest man.

DERELICT: [CHARLIE SAMOA] Apricot brandy. Jesus in a bottle.

> THE DERELICT *scuttles off into the dark.* THE PIMP *and* THE PROSTITUTE *appear on the edges of the light.*

PROSTITUTE: [JOHNNIE SUCROSE] Hey, John. Looking for something?

HUNGRY MOTHER: Pay phone.

PIMP: [JIMMY SHILLELAGH] Not on this block.

PROSTITUTE: [JOHNNIE SUCROSE] Lonely, honey? Party?

> THE DERELICT [CHARLIE SAMOA] *comes back around the corner, a bottle in a paper bag.*

DERELICT: [CHARLIE SAMOA] Care for a choke?

HUNGRY MOTHER: No thanks.

> THE DERELICT *hits* HUNGRY MOTHER *across the face with the bottle. He falls to his knees. Blood.*

DERELICT: [CHARLIE SAMOA] How 'bout now?

HUNGRY MOTHER: Stuff it.

> THE DERELICT *walks around* HUNGRY MOTHER, *stops, sighs.*

DERELICT: [CHARLIE SAMOA] Hungry Momma. Hungry Momma. The real item.

HUNGRY MOTHER: Charlie Samoa.

> *Slight pause.*

CHARLIE SAMOA: Acute.

HUNGRY MOTHER: Cholly. Whatchoo doin' on the street, Cholly?

CHARLIE SAMOA: I beat the rap, Mom.

HUNGRY MOTHER: Congratulations.

CHARLIE SAMOA: I knew you'd be happy for me.

HUNGRY MOTHER: Nobody loves you like your Mother, Cholly. Where's your pals. Johnnie Suc. Jimmy Shill.

CHARLIE SAMOA: At home. [JIMMY SHILLELAGH *strikes a match, illuminating the darkness. Charlie laughs.*] Tuning up their fingers.

> HUNGRY MOTHER *glances at* JOHNNIE *and* JIMMY.

HUNGRY MOTHER: Okay, Cholly Sam, I'm mugged. Consider me mugged. Take it all. Spectacles, testicles, wallet, and wings.

CHARLIE SAMOA: [*Half grins.*] Sssssssssss.

HUNGRY MOTHER: C'mon, Cholly Sam! Do your number! Run it down! Dissemble!

> *Slight pause.*

CHARLIE SAMOA: Dissemble. Shit…Big Ma-moo, ain't you somethin'? Talk about barbarians, shit like that. You sound just like a boo-jwa-zee. You know that?

HUNGRY MOTHER: Where'd you learn that word?

CHARLIE SAMOA: What word? Bar-barian?

HUNGRY MOTHER: Bourgeoisie.

CHARLIE SAMOA: CC. C'mon, Mom, lighten up. Get rid of that boojwa snide. I been to CC. We all been to CC. All God's chillun been to City College…[*Laughs.*] Which accounts for dem rising expectations. [*He begins to stalk* HUNGRY MOTHER.] Expectations which can in no way be satisfied. Now or ever.

    HUNGRY MOTHER *begins speaking very rapidly, as if to fend him off with words.*

HUNGRY MOTHER: Tell me, as a member of the affected class, do you believe there is a deliberate, that is to say conscious, effort on the part of the authorities, if you will, the powers that be, or, if you prefer, the money men, the movers and shakers, the high-rolling, high-rise boys, the fat cats, the leopard-coat ladies—

    [JIMMY *and* JOHNNIE *join the stalk, snarling;* HUNGRY MOTHER *falters, but goes on:*]—to, uh, uh, cut back, uh, basic social services, restrict access to education, lower the already abysmal standard of living and further degrade the quality of life for the poor, in a cynical calculated attempt to discourage democratic tendencies, stifle aspirations, slay rising expectations, and narcoticize anger, in order to escape culpability and social conflagration?

CHARLIE SAMOA: Yeah. In a word.

HUNGRY MOTHER: Fat lot of good it did you, learning that word.

CHARLIE SAMOA: [*Laughs.*] Barbarian? No, Mother. It did not do me no good at all. I shoulda known better. Waste a time. Coulda been out on the street. Fulfilling my destiny as a social predator. My folks, you know?

HUNGRY MOTHER: Is there a pay phone around here?

CHARLIE SAMOA: Old folks, you know? They get sappy. All the resins harden up. They didn't cop to the dead end.

HUNGRY MOTHER: [*Cheery radio.*] They never apprehended the dynamics of racial interaction.

CHARLIE SAMOA: Yeah. They never apprehended the *dynamic.* Anybody can talk like you, Mother. You know that? Anybody. Who you wanna call this hour?

HUNGRY MOTHER: Emergency. 911.

CHARLIE SAMOA: Number's been changed. Unlisted. That l'il girl snuffed herself on your show tonight. That your idea?

HUNGRY MOTHER: Fuck off.

CHARLIE SAMOA: Way too late for the SOS. Is that a first?

HUNGRY MOTHER: What do you think?

CHARLIE SAMOA: I think so…I think it is. Now, *that's a* record. Mother. Your best show. So far.

HUNGRY MOTHER: My fan club. You guys must be the new bulge in my demographics.

JOHNNIE SUCROSE: I told you. We never miss a show.

JIMMY SHILLELAGH: Bastard.

JOHNNIE SUCROSE: I be all over you. Like ugly on a gorilla.

CHARLIE SAMOA: Like *white* on rice.

They laugh. CHARLIE SAMOA *is winding a chain around his fist.*

HUNGRY MOTHER: Is this any way for a fan club to act?

JOHNNIE SUCROSE: I wouldn't give you the sweat off my balls.

JIMMY SHILLELAGH: Mistah Kurtz, Mothah, he dead.

They mug him ferociously. As they do studio lights up: HOOVER *and* THE NAVAJOS *enter in their dark glasses and trash the studio; blue broadcast light in studio goes out; mugging ends;* CHARLIE, JOHNNIE *and* JIMMY *exit exhilarated; trashing stops,* CRAZY JOE *and* FREDDY *exit;* HOOVER *with great ceremony and delicacy pulls a white feather from his vest and floats it down upon the wreckage;* HOOVER *smiles cooly and strolls out.*

Bloodied and shaken, HUNGRY MOTHER *staggers into the ruined studio.*

HUNGRY MOTHER: Oh, sweet Christ. [*He picks up the feather.*] Got to be—Hoover and the—[*He pulls the dead blue bulb out of the socket and smashes it on the floor.*] Navajos! [*Roots around finds another blue bulb.*] All right.

Carefully replaces it. Nothing. He starts to laugh. Flicks switches. Strikes the console, tearing his hands. Laughter becomes sobs then screams on each blow. Stops, exhausted. THE MOOK *enters.* HUNGRY MOTHER *turns to* THE MOOK *and raises his bloody hands.*

HUNGRY MOTHER: My impersonation of Screaming Annie.

THE MOOK: With ribbons.

HUNGRY MOTHER: Agaga.

THE MOOK: I come to get you out, Mother.

HUNGRY MOTHER: Can't.

THE MOOK: Why?

HUNGRY MOTHER: I'm…*estranged.*

THE MOOK: Anomie?

HUNGRY MOTHER *looks up at him.*

HUNGRY MOTHER: You been to CC too. Cholly Sam's right. Anybody can talk like me. Yeah. Anomie. It's *rude* out there.

THE MOOK: Rude.

HUNGRY MOTHER: The weather today, Mook, very rude with streaks of mean. Never underestimate the effects of rudeness on the disintegrating personality.

THE MOOK: A little rude, maybe. Somewhat abrupt. Always a little rude this time of year. Gulf stream. Me, I call it brisk. Crisp collars, sharp lapels.

HUNGRY MOTHER: I lead a life of rudeness.

THE MOOK: Genteel. Always.

HUNGRY MOTHER: Rudeness. Covered with dogshit. Tell you something. Shit doesn't increase arithmetically. It increases geometrically. So, instead of twice as much shit, you got shit squared and shit cubed.

THE MOOK: [*Laughs softly.*] I can dig it. Come on, Mother. Come with me.

HUNGRY MOTHER: Why?

THE MOOK: They gonna bust you.

HUNGRY MOTHER: How you know that?

THE MOOK: I set you up.

Pause. HUNGRY MOTHER *gets to his feet, stumbles, finds the bean can.*

HUNGRY MOTHER: Bean?

THE MOOK: Le's go.

HUNGRY MOTHER: Lemme alone. It's been a tough day.

THE MOOK: Le's go baby! I can...*finesse* it for you.

HUNGRY MOTHER: Forget it. No big deal. Been busted before.

THE MOOK: But whatchoo gonna do with yo' mouthpiece shut down? Whatchoo gonna do when you can't run yo' mouth?

HUNGRY MOTHER: Tell you what you can do for me, Mook. Tell you what. [*Formally.*] Why don't you loan me a dollar or two...

THE MOOK: So the dogs won't piss on you?

They both laugh.

HUNGRY MOTHER: Outstanding. You know the phrase.

THE MOOK: [*Doing a little dance of inspiration.*] C'mon, big Mom. Snap back, baby, snap back! You my second string. The Mook lookin' for you to follow in his steps. Bounce back, Mom. You can do it. Bounce back!

HUNGRY MOTHER *lies down.*

Charp. [*He flips a coin on* HUNGRY MOTHER'S *chest.*] There you go, boy. Knock yo'se'f out.

HUNGRY MOTHER *leaps up and grabs the bowie knife.*

HUNGRY MOTHER: [*Very quietly.*] What do you say we engage in a little internecine behavior?

THE MOOK: Stay cool, baby. You can hack it.

HUNGRY MOTHER: Let's go to the mat. Just you and me.

THE MOOK: Don't act the honkey. I found Free Lance.

This stops HUNGRY MOTHER *cold. He stares at* THE MOOK *for a moment then throws the knife into the floor.*

HUNGRY MOTHER: Where?

THE MOOK: She came in. I took her back.

HUNGRY MOTHER: That's *white* of you.

THE MOOK: Easy. Easy. Don't press your luck.

HUNGRY MOTHER: Sorry...She all right?

THE MOOK: Well, you know, Mother, excess sentiment has always been my tragic flaw. My tragic flaw. She had made a monkey out of me, Mother. Set a deadly precedent. She had burned the goddamn church. To see the church burn, Mother, is to realize you *can* burn the church. Powerful realization. It was incumbent upon me—as a businessman—to provide a metaphor. An antidote. Powerful one. I cannot abide no more fires...Of course, I realize I was in danger—danger of fulfilling the cliché Free Lance had constructed for me. So I struggled. I love Free Lance. You know that. But what could I do? There was just no way home. She had put herself in the box. Deep. So I said to my pretty little self—piss on it. Ever cut yourself on a piece of paper? [THE MOOK *draws a hand across his throat.*] Linen stationery. Slit. Gush. *Sharp.* Bled blue, bled blue. Black gash. Mouth to mouth. My hands were cold. What bothered me most was fulfilling the cliché. Predestination jive. 'Course, she could have been rescued. By you. Violins up, violins out. Perfect. And let me off the hook. Muffed it, Mother.

HUNGRY MOTHER: I could call you names.

THE MOOK: Charlie Samoa works for me.

> *Slight pause.*

HUNGRY MOTHER: Why'd they mug me? Give me a plot point. Something to hang on to.

THE MOOK: Reason? Let go, baby. [*Laughs.*] What if I told you that l'il slit who checked out over your air—that was Charlie's sister. I had to let him have you.

HUNGRY MOTHER: No relation.

THE MOOK: No *reason. No reason at all.* 'Cause *he felt* like it…I made you, Mother. Don't you dare forget it. Was The Mook who turned yo' volume up, and nobody else. So's you could be *heard.* So's you could run yo' mouth. Put it out there. On de air. You done good by me. I 'preciate that. Made me a lot of scratch. The bust be here soon. I got to bust my Mother now—but I sure as shit can still save yo' ass.

HUNGRY MOTHER: Pimp. Scag sum. Smack ghoul.

THE MOOK: Tsk. Tsk. Tsk. Feeble. Mighty lame. You shoulda held on to that knife, boy. You ignorant, Mama. Got to teach you all the rules to you own game. [*Tenderly.*] Come with me, Mother. Don't be bitter. Be my, be my minion. My one and only minion.

HUNGRY MOTHER: [*Shaking his head.*] The exigencies change.

> *A beat, and then* THE MOOK *roars raucous falsetto laughter.*

THE MOOK: Keep after them blackisms, boy! You keep after them blackisms, boy! You get there yet!…You know, you right, Mom. I be feelin' pimpish to-day! Be feeling pimpish. [*At the door he turns back.*] Momma—I thought you'd like to know—I got a terrific price for them kids. [*Roars again. Stops.*] Keep after it, boy. You get to be a nigger yet. [*Roars again. Exits.*]

> HUNGRY MOTHER *makes his way to the mike. Flicks switches. The blue light stays "off." He doesn't seem to notice.*

HUNGRY MOTHER: [*Into the mike.*] Test if it dead…Give me a try before you pass me by…Close enough for ground zero…I've got some good phrases from romantic literature in my head. It's too bad…This is the Hungry Mother. The Universal Disc Jockey. God's own deejay. Goin' down slow. [*Black.*] Cat's pajamas…This is your Hungry Mother talkin' to you! I cannot be slow—that why I'm so fast! [*Sings an offhand blues.*] Goin' down slow—oh goin' down slow—but at least I am—going down—on yoouuu. [*Laid back Top 40.*] One of our very very large numbers, I just know you're gonna love this one—an old old stand-bye, a super-monster in its time—an antediluvian smash—*Sweet Gash!* Oh so sweet! Play it for me just one more time! [*Frenzied Top 40.*] Get down! As your audio agitator I strongly advise you to get down! Get Down! Work yourselves into a frenzy with Screaming Annie! [*A series of gagging screams. Then in the grand manner.*] When men were men and rock and roll was king. Never the twain shall meet. Send a salami to you boy in the army. [*Slight pause.*] Human freedom diminishing, even vanishing. Ruination. [*Mellifluous.*] We'll have the latest up-to-date quotations on—human wreckage futures in a moment. [*Beat.*] This is you favorite Hungry Mother, illuminating the dark contours of native speech. [*Pause. From this point on the various radio voices drop away.*]

Fuck. Fuck it. Fucked up. Hit you across your fucking mouth. Fuck with me and I'll really fuck you up…I try to watch my language, but I'm a victim of history. Or is it eschatology? Verbal inflation is at an all-time high. [*Slight pause.*] First Chinese Baptist Church of the Deaf. [*Slight pause.*] Social engineering. Upward mobility. *Stiletto.* [*Slight pause. A travel agent.*] Vacation in—steamy—South Africa! [*Slight pause.*] Say *hungry.*

[*Slight pause. Cheery salesman.*] Death Boy, Brown Bomber, White Death, Stallion Stick, Casa Boom, Snow Storm. Allah Supreme, White Noise, Sweet Surrender, Death Wish, Turkish Delight! Any size lot, any cut ratio, buy in bulk and saaaave! If we don't have it, it ain't worth having! If our sauce don't send you, you got no place to go! [*Laughs then screaming.*] That junk is shit! Shit! Stay 'way. Mother advises you to stay a-way—lay off it all 'cept for Death Wish Smoking Mixture Number 3. After all—why stick when you can blow? [*Slight pause.*] Stick with us. [*Laughs.*] Stick *with* us. Stick with us. Stick it. [*Slight pause.*] Twenty-four hour shooting galleries. [*Slight pause.*] The American Meat Institute presents. Our Lady Of The Cage. A new barbed-wire ballet. With automatic weapons. [*Slight pause.*] Say hungry…I'm interested in abused forms. [*Black.*] She not only willing, she *able.* [*Sportscaster.*] Playing hurt. Photo finish. Cut to ribbons…That goes without saying. [*Slight pause.*] Dead on my feet. [*Slight pause.*] I pay lip service every chance I get. Flophouse of Stalinism. Two mules and a colored boy. Better a cocksucker than a Communist. [*Pause.*] Down avenues of blue exhaust. [*Pause.*] Voodoo kit. Razor ribbon. Front me 'til Friday. A day late and a dollar short. Tryin' to get over. [*Pause.*] Spike that beautiful black vein! Spike it! [*Pause.*] Say *hungry!*…Born to shoot junk. Strafe me, baby. Strafe me. Up against it. *Aphasia.* All the rage. Hungry. Riff. On the rag. In the name of the father, and of the son, and of the holocaust. World without end. Shit from shortcake. Estatic suffering.

[*He falters.*] I disremember. [*Slight pause. Trembling:*] Brush fire wars. Bane of my existence. Blue sky *ventures!* [*Top 40 outburst.*] The watchword for today— *hydrogenize slumism!* Bear that in mind. [*Pause.*] Under the gun. [*Pause.*] Under the gun. [*Pause.*] Under the gun. [*Pause.*] Free-fire zone. [*Pause.*] When I get back…When I get back to The World—[*Lightly.*] I ain't gonna do nothin'…but stay black—an' *die.* [*Slight pause.*] *I'm serious.* [*Laughs. Freezes.*]

The blue broadcast light pops "on." After a moment the lights dim and slowly fade. Out. The blue light glows a moment then extinguishes. Blackout.

END OF PLAY

Constance Congdon

No Mercy

No Mercy was presented at Actors Theatre of Louisville, March 14–22, 1986, as part of the tenth annual Humana Festival of New American Plays. The cast and creative contributors were as follows:

ROY LAYTON (YOUNG ROY)	Robert Brock
GENE PROBST	Bruce Kuhn
ROBERT OPPENHEIMER	Jonathan Bolt
JANE NEWELL	Melody Combs
ADAM NEWELL	Jeffrey Hutchinson
ROY LAYTON	Bob Burrus
RAMONA LAYTON	Adale O'Brien
JUSTIN	Joshua Atkins
JACKIE	Beth Dixon
DIRECTOR	Jackson Phippin
SETS AND LIGHTS	Paul Owen
COSTUMES	Ann Wallace
SOUND	David Strang

No Mercy was commissioned and first presented in workshop during February 1985 by Hartford Stage Company as part of their "First Drafts," funded by a National Endowment for the Arts Special Projects grant.

CHARACTERS

    ROBERT OPPENHEIMER, age 40
    ROY LAYTON (YOUNG ROY), age 20
    GENE PROBST, age 20
    ADAM NEWELL, age 25
    JANE NEWELL, age 20
    ROY LAYTON, age 60
    RAMONA LAYTON, age 58
    JUSTIN, age 6
    JACKIE, age 35

TIME

    1945 and 1985

    The West

PRODUCTION NOTES

1945 and 1985 exist simultaneously on an open and fluid stage. The play's various loca-
tions are minimally suggested: a recliner facing a TV set on a stand establishes Roy and
Ramona's living room; a swivel chair, Jackie's TV studio; a double bed, Adam and Jane's
bedroom. Rooms, doors, windows, mirrors, other things referred to in stage directions to motivate actors' movements are not meant to be actually present on the set. A
sense of space, of light and sky, must predominate.

    When Jackie is speaking on camera, the actor always speaks live, addressing the
audience. When Roy and Ramona's TV is tuned to Jackie's program, her voice is also
heard coming from their set.

    Oppenheimer is lost in time. He does not appear gratuitously or wander aimlessly,
but follows a purposeful path which leads him offstage and brings him on.

Outside on the Trinity site in the Jornada del Muerto area of southwestern New Mexico. Before dawn, July 36, 1945. Total darkness.

YOUNG ROY: [*singing*]

> I saw the light, I saw the light,
> No more darkness, no more night.

Near him, someone starts to pee. YOUNG ROY *continues, but louder.*

> Now I'm so happy, no sorrow in sight,
> Praise the Lord, I saw the light.

Gene, don't be doing that while I'm singin'. Don't you have any respect?
Half-light up on two young soldiers. Around them on the stage, barely visible, are: a gray-haired man sitting in a recliner and holding a guitar; a nicely dressed woman sitting in a plush executive chair, her back to the audience; two sleeping forms in a double bed upstage.

GENE: [*Finishing and zipping up*] I didn't think we were in church, Roy. Hey, but you're good. You really are.

YOUNG ROY: Well, I'm getting the guitar part down really good. Hey, wait a minute. There he is.
They look upstage. All that can be seen there is the red tip of a lit cigarette. OPPENHEIMER *coughs several times, takes a drag of the cigarette, and then crosses quickly and exits into the offstage control shed. A bright light washes onstage briefly before he shuts the door behind him.*

GENE: That the guy ?

YOUNG ROY: [*In admiration, bordering on awe*] Yeah.

GENE: Rolls his own ?

YOUNG ROY: Oh yeah. In the dark.

GENE: Well, once you get used to doing it. [*Takes out a pack of Lucky Strikes and lights one*]

YOUNG ROY: They had the thing on the dining-room table— in what used to be the ranch house? They were rolling it around with a stick, looking for little holes, filling them with Kleenex. Then polishing it and polishing it.

GENE: Experts.

YOUNG ROY: Then they were putting the whole *gadget* together at the tower. That's what they call it—the gadget.

GENE: The gadget.

YOUNG ROY: And that's when the storm hit.

GENE: Didn't it get all wet?

YOUNG ROY: They pitched a tent around it. And then he made them so nervous they asked him to leave.

GENE: Kicked out, huh ?

YOUNG ROY: And then the thing that held the thing wouldn't fit.

GENE: Army engineers.

YOUNG ROY: No, it was all machined perfect, but it all got too hot, see? So they had to leave it to cool down.

GENE: This thing gets hot?

YOUNG ROY: Oh yeah. You shoulda heard those Geiger-counter things—going like a bunch of rattlesnakes.

GENE: You mean to tell me that this thing—whatever they call it—

YOUNG ROY: The plug.

GENE: This plug gets hot by itself?

YOUNG ROY: Yeah.

GENE: Well, where did it come from?

YOUNG ROY: They made it.

GENE: Do you think these guys really know what they're doing?

YOUNG ROY: Gene, these guys are the smartest and the best in the whole goddam country—and a few other countries thrown in. We got Germans, we got an Italian, and that Russian guy that climbed the tower and held the flashlight so they could set the cameras—

GENE: They're taking a picture of it?

YOUNG ROY: I guess. I was getting the mattresses—to put under it all in case it fell, you know.

GENE: Well, I hope they had a lot of mattresses.

YOUNG ROY: Oh yeah. Sixty-seventy, at least.

GENE: And I hope they were from the officers' quarters.

YOUNG ROY: The lightning was the worst. He asked a guy to go up and, you know, babysit it.

GENE: It?

YOUNG ROY: Yeah, *it,* all put together in the tower.

GENE: What was he supposed to do if lightning had hit it?

YOUNG ROY: I don't know. Warn us all, I guess

> *The offstage door opens again, spilling light.* YOUNG ROY *and* GENE *snap to attention.*

General.

> *The light disappears. The soldiers relax again.*

GENE: Hey, it's gotten lighter. What time is it?

YOUNG ROY: [*Looks at his watch*] Not dawn yet.

GENE: Looks like it's clearing up.

YOUNG ROY: [*Suddenly noticing the sky*] Look at that star! Boy, you can't get much brighter than that! I'm gonna tell 'em.

> *He runs toward the control-shed entrance, is met by* OPPENHEIMER, *who passes by him and enters the open area, looking at the sky.*

Are we going to go ahead now, Dr. Oppenheimer?

> *Suddenly* OPPENHEIMER *turns and exits quickly.*

GENE: Boy, he really knows who you are. Are you sure you even met him?

YOUNG ROY: Last night. I was pulling in the first load of mattresses. I caught him in the light of my flashlight. He was just sort of standing around—worrying, I think. I *recognized* him. And then he *talked* to me. He told me how he named this project— it comes from two poems.

GENE: Two poems? It took two poems?

YOUNG ROY: I told him how we came out here on the train. I mean, he *listened* to me. And he shook my hand.

GENE: Well, I don't think you're gonna make it in his memoirs.

> *Sound of a far-off and scratchy radio playing "The Star Spangled Banner."*

YOUNG ROY: What's that?

GENE: Somebody's got a radio somewhere, I guess.

YOUNG ROY: They playing that for us?

GENE: Can't be. This is all top secret.

YOUNG ROY: Well, I'm sure they would if they could.

> *They listen in silence.*

GENE: Where were you last?

YOUNG ROY: Berlin.

GENE: I was sure I'd be in Japan by now.

> YOUNG ROY *takes out a bottle and begins to put the contents on his face.*

GENE: What's that ?

YOUNG ROY: Suntan oil.

GENE: Have you gone nuts?

YOUNG ROY: Dr. Teller gave it to me.

GENE: To wear at night?

YOUNG ROY: It's for the—explosion. It might burn.

> YOUNG ROY *offers* GENE *the bottle. He ignores it.*

GENE: You and those longhairs.

> *"The Star Spangled Banner" ends.*

RADIO VOICE: Good morning. This is KCBA, your Voice of America station. We're opening this morning with Tchaikovsky's "Serenade for Strings."

> *The "Serenade" begins. The soldiers put on their welder's goggles.*

YOUNG ROY: Hey, soldier, you've got a crack in your goggles.

GENE: Huh? Oh, it don't matter.

YOUNG ROY: Here. You take mine. [*He switches goggles with* GENE.] You're the one who's gonna be back there with all the brass. You want to look good.

> *Over the* PA *system comes a long mechanical wail.*

That's it!

> GENE *and* YOUNG ROY *exit quickly in opposite directions. Silence for five seconds except for the sound of Tchaikovsky on the faint radio. A blinding flash. Blackout. Silence. A woman's voice.*

JANE: Adam?

> ADAM *wakes up and kisses* JANE, *puts his head gently on her stomach. She is pregnant. His clock radio comes on.*

RADIO VOICE: —attributed to Shiite Muslims a spokesman said today.

> JANE *exits.*

This is KOMA, your sound of the Eighties. Hey, if you get a chance, check out the sunrise—it's absolutely beautiful. And now for our next half hour of uninterrupted mus—

> ADAM *shuts the radio off; gets up, naked; goes to the window, looks out. The sunrise is particularly beautiful. He opens the window to have a better look. The sunlight hits his face.*

ADAM: [*Under his breath*] My god.

JANE: [*Reentering*] Adam—

> JANE *comes to* ADAM *with a bathrobe, covering him. He exits. During the next scene,* JANE *makes the bed and then sits down on the end of it, exhausted, staring at herself in the mirror*
>
> *Lights up on the living room of a small tract house. A gray-haired man, dressed up except for a coat and tie, sits in the recliner and sings, accompanying himself on the guitar, which he does not play well. He wears glasses with one dark lens. This is* ROY, *forty years later.*

ROY: [*Singing*]

I saw the light, I saw the light.
No more darkness—

> *Has trouble with the chord change on the guitar, stops until he gets it, continues.*

—no more night.
Now I'm so happy, no sorrow in sight.
Praise the Lord, I saw the light.

[*Talking to himself*] I hope they got a piano player down there. [*To* RAMONA, *who is offstage*] Baby?

RAMONA: [*Entering from the back of the house, carrying two ties*] What tie are you gonna wear?

ROY: I hope they got a piano player down there.

RAMONA: [*About one of the ties, a striped one*] I think this one is good.

ROY: They told me no stripes. It does something to the cameras. [*Taking the other tie, handing* RAMONA *the guitar*] I wish you'd come down there with me.

RAMONA: [*Wiping off the guitar*] You really gonna try to play this? It's been a helluva long time. These strings look rusty.

ROY: I know, but I gotta try.

RAMONA: Now what time will you be on?

ROY: I don't know. They run all day. I could be on any time.

RAMONA: You mean I have to watch this show all day long?

ROY: Baby, if they like me, I might could be on more than once even. Wouldn't that be something?

RAMONA: Roy, you're getting your hopes up.

ROY: Better comb my hair. I don't know about this tie.

> ROY *exits to the back part of the house.* RAMONA *is putting the guitar in its case, still shining it.*

RAMONA: [*Thinking* ROY *is still there*] I wish you wouldn't go.

> *She goes off after* ROY.

> OPPENHEIMER *reenters. He stares at* ROY *and* RAMONA's *living room,* ADAM *and* JANE's *bedroom, stops, thinks.*

OPPENHEIMER: [*Shaking his head as he crosses*] No. No no no no no.

> *Laughs to himself, exits.*

> ADAM *reenters, wearing slacks and a shirt—his tie is untied. He's finishing a bowl of cereal.* JANE *ties his tie for him as they talk.*

ADAM: I have to go in a few minutes.

JANE: I know.

ADAM: We have to believe the doctors. They know what they're doing.

> *A six-year-old boy—*JUSTIN*—enters, carrying a Tinker-Toy construction and a box of Ivory Snow. He runs to* ROY *and* RAMONA's *house, goes straight to the* TV *and turns it on. He stares at the* TV *and plays with his toy.*

JANE: I'll be all right.

ADAM: You'll be all right. I wish it weren't my first day.

> JANE *finishes his tie.*

Hey, you're getting good at that.

> ADAM *exits to finish getting dressed.* JANE *sits down on the bed. Still in dim light,* JACKIE *swivels to face the* TV *camera and begins speaking in a pleasant, low-key and sincere manner, almost chatty. Her voice comes from* ROY *and* RAMONA's *TV.*

JACKIE: He goes on to say that we can tell when we see all these signs that have been predicted, like the leaves appearing on the fig tree say what season it is to people in Israel. When we first see these signs, that's the tribulation, when they start to accelerate, He says that we will know that He is near, that He is right at the door, right at the door—

> *Although* JUSTIN *changes the channel,* JACKIE *continues her talk as lights come up on her area. She has the sophistication in manner and dress of a female executive. She occasionally swivels her chair to a different camera angle.*

—ready to return. But the punch line comes next—

JUSTIN *switches the channels very fast, finally decides on a violent car chase and sits down in front of the* TV, *stares at it, still fiddling with his toy.*

—verse 34. He says, "Truly I say,"—now when Jesus says, "Truly I say," He means to really pay attention, to stop, look and listen. He says, "Truly I say, this generation shall not pass away until *all* these things shall take place." Of course, the generation He is talking about is the generation that would see the signs begin to appear. Who would that be? Yes. Us.

As JACKIE *speaks,* ADAM *is finishing dressing for work. He comes into full view, looks into the mirror; adjusting his Air Force uniform. He puts on his hat.*
We—are—that—generation .

ADAM *exits.*

And what does He say would happen ? He says, "The generation that sees all the signs come together will be the generation that sees them all fulfilled."

During the following, JACKIE'S *speeches occasionally overlap* ROY *and* RAMONA'S *conversation.*

RAMONA: [*Entering and seeing* JUSTIN] Now what are you doing here ?

JACKIE: Now, I am glad to be a part of that generation. Why?

RAMONA: Did you even knock?

JACKIE: Because I want to be part of all this famine and war and suffering?

RAMONA: You walked right in.

JACKIE: Because I want to see the world go through its worst tribulations ?

RAMONA: I wish you'd talk to me sometime. Why won't you talk ?

    JUSTIN *takes the Tinker Toy he's been working on and shows it to* RAMONA.

JACKIE: Because I want to see the nations of the world begin what most certainly will be *the* Armageddon?

    ROY *enters the living room. He's wearing a Western string tie and carrying his guitar in its case.*

ROY: I decided on the bolo tie.

    JUSTIN *runs out of the house, leaving his toy and Ivory Snow box.*

RAMONA: [*To* JUSTIN] Don't go!

ROY: Don't that little boy have a home?

JACKIE: No. I'm glad that I'm part of that generation Jesus talks about—the Last Generation—because I get to see the Lord in my lifetime.

RAMONA: [*About* JUSTIN] I wonder where he lives.

JACKIE: I will get to see the Lord face-to-face in that final moment.

    ROY *switches* TV *channels and finds* JACKIE.

ROY: There she is.

    ROY *sits to watch* JACKIE. *Her voice now comes through the* TV *speaker again, as well as being heard from her own space.*

JACKIE: The Greek word for "moment" is atomos— A-T-O-M-O-S, which is the word from which we get atom— A-T-O-M, which means "that which is indivisible."

ROY: Listen to that—she really knows all this stuff.

RAMONA: No oomph.

ROY: She doesn't need oomph—she's got brains.

JACKIE: Think about it—two thousand years of waiting and we are the ones who will see the prophecy fulfilled at that one indivisible moment when we will see Jesus. Praise God.

ROY: This woman's got two college degrees—two of 'em.

JACKIE: So no matter how bad it gets—and it gets pretty bad sometimes—it's just birth pangs.

RAMONA: What does she know about birth pangs.

ROY: Now, baby.

JACKIE: The birth pangs of a world that's about to begin.

> *Music comes out of the* TV *speaker.* JACKIE *holds and then turns upstage in her swivel chair, a segment of the show being over.* RAMONA *turns the* TV *off.*

RAMONA: That music sounds like what you hear at the dentist's office.

ROY: Well, I guess they're trying to do something about that.

RAMONA: It's not the kind of preaching you or I was raised with.

ROY: I'm surprised you remember.

RAMONA: Roy, now don't start with me on that.

ROY: Everything she says is from the Bible. Not enough people preach the entire Bible— they just preach the parts they like.

RAMONA: Well, she doesn't sound like she likes any of it—she just drones on and on.

ROY: She's written a book, you know, about all this stuff. She knows Greek—*Greek.*

RAMONA: Roy, you always think everyone is smarter than you are.

ROY: I wish you'd come down there with me.

RAMONA: No…

ROY: We could walk around downtown.

RAMONA: No, its too far.

ROY: You gonna leave the house today?

RAMONA: I've got too much to do.

ROY: Baby, I'm worried about you.

RAMONA: I'm worried about *you.* You can't play that guitar. You haven't sung in years. I don't know what you're doing.

ROY: It's been two months you haven't left this house.

RAMONA: That's not true.

ROY: By yourself? When was the last time you went to the grocery store by yourself?

RAMONA: I like it better when you drive me.

ROY: You hardly even go out on the lawn anymore.

RAMONA: I have trouble breathing when I get out there. I think I'm developing an allergy.

ROY: To what? What's out there? This neighborhood's beautiful—always has been.

RAMONA: It's been known to happen.

ROY: Well, I gotta go. Wish you'd change your mind. [*No answer. He kisses her.*] See you later, baby.

> ROY *crosses to exit with his guitar, stops to wave at* RAMONA. OPPENHEIMER

enters, sees ROY *and stops to stare at him, as if* ROY *sparked some memory.* RAMONA *waves back and* ROY *exits. Confused,* OPPENHEIMER *exits the way he came, crossing near but not seeing* ADAM, *who is entering with his briefcase.* RAMONA *settles down in her chair to read the Sunday papers.* JACKIE *swivels to the camera.*

JACKIE: Paul tells us: "In the twinkling of an eye, we shall all be changed." Now how quick is that? [*Not moving*] 'Bout *that* quick. Want to see it again?

    She holds a smile, then swivels away from the camera, takes off her body mike and looks through her notes.

    ADAM *enters his bedroom, with briefcase, ready to go.*

ADAM: Did I tell you about my console?

JANE: Part of the best computer system in the world. Yes.

ADAM: Did I tell you about my chair?

JANE: Better than the President's.

    ADAM *kneels in front of* JANE *and massages her legs as she talks.*

ADAM: There'll be pressure.

JANE: Well, being cooped up for twenty-four hours…and everything…else. Adam, how close are you to the ah—the ah—thing.

ADAM: I never see it. Not my job, really. Hey, it's a lot better than being cooped up for nine months.

JANE: More than nine months. Adam, I can't stop worrying.

ADAM: He must like it in there.

JANE: She.

ADAM: Once I'm sealed in. You can't talk to me.

JANE: I know.

ADAM: No communication with the outside works—except NORAD in Colorado.

JANE: If you can call that the outside world.

ADAM: One of the guys said it's built on giant springs, so if there's ever a direct hit, the whole complex sort of goes boing. It's kinda brilliant, really. When you think about it.

JANE: How long do you have to wait for the van?

ADAM: It's always early. Because you can never be late. It's nice down there.

JANE: You told me.

ADAM: Launch Control is one of the best assignments in the whole Air Force. We're very lucky. We're set for life now.

JANE: Yes.

ADAM: The doctors on this base are some of the best in the world. They're experts in their field.

JANE: Yes.

    ADAM *goes to the mirror. Horn honks.*

You have to go. [*Holds on to him*] You have to go.

    ADAM *removes her arms, turns, kisses her—she breaks it. He leaves, looking back for something from her. She doesn't respond. To herself:*

You have to go.

JUSTIN *enters and runs to* RAMONA's *living room. He stares at* RAMONA, *waiting for her to wake up.*

RAMONA: [*Awake to* JUSTIN] Oh, you're back! [*Getting up*] Do you want a cookie?

JUSTIN *nods, reaches for the cookie. She moves it away from him.*

Where do you live?

JUSTIN *just stares at her, not speaking. She gives in, hands him the cookie and takes him to the window.*

Can you point the direction? I bet it's up there in the circle drives, right? Do you live on a street with a star name? An Indian name? Why won't you talk? Hey, show me.

OPPENHEIMER *enters from the control shed.*

OPPENHEIMER: It can't be New Mexico because I'm walking on grass. And there's a woman ... and a child.... I—I can't see more...it's too blurry. Their movements are so slow.

OPPENHEIMER *crosses upstage, looks one way, considers, then exits in another direction, again near* ADAM, *who doesn't see him.* ADAM *crosses to wait for the elevator into the silo. During* RAMONA's *speech, we hear the elevator arrive.* ADAM *gets in; we hear it descend.*

RAMONA: [*To* JUSTIN] Look at this street. I used to know who lived in every single house. Everybody. We used to play Scrabble and gin rummy with those people— they're gone. We used to have barbecues with this half of the street. Now I don't know a soul there or anywhere else, for that matter. I really wonder if anyone lives in any of these houses. I see lights on in the evenings, but it seems I never see anybody come and go. Trash cans appear in the early morning and somebody carries them away. Nobody beats rugs or shakes out dust mops, any of the things that got people outside. It's like the houses are the only things that are alive. Might as well be on Mars. Mars.

ADAM *steps out of the elevator and exits.* ROY *enters and* JACKIE *stands when she sees him.*

JACKIE: Oh—Roy Layton.

RAMONA: [*Puts* JUSTIN *down*] Now, you stick around for a little while at least. Okay?

RAMONA *and* JUSTIN *to the kitchen to get more cookies.*

JACKIE: [*Coming to* ROY] I heard you sing many, many years ago. It was at your church. My Aunt Dorothy introduced us.

ROY: My church?

JACKIE: Pillar of Fire. On Maple Street.

ROY: That's not my church, ma'am. I just used to sing there.

JACKIE: Oh. I'm so glad. They're exactly the opposite of what I'm trying to do here. This must be your guitar. May I...see it? [*Opens his case*]

ROY: You don't have a piano player, do you?

JACKIE: [*Taking out the guitar; looking at it with awe*] I was twelve or thirteen. You stood in front of the altar. You sang an old hymn I'd never heard before—about the ending of the day and then the dawn?

ROY: That was the song with all the B-flat chords. They're hard.

JACKIE: I was wearing a yellow pants suit—I was the only girl there in pants. Afterwards I asked you if I could strum your guitar. You talked to me quite a while.

ROY: Uh-huh.

JACKIE: You *do* remember.

ROY: No ma'am, I don't.

JACKIE: Well, it doesn't matter. Really. Do you need to tune this…or anything?

ROY: If you want me to. Ma'am, I'm pretty nervous.

JACKIE: Oh, here. [*Hands the guitar to him*] Sorry. It was wonderful to see it again.

ROY: Ma'am—

JACKIE: I know—out of the clear blue I call you up. Well, I asked you here because—well, I've received some criticism that this program is rather…cold.

ROY: Uh-huh.

JACKIE: You *do* think it's cold.

ROY: No ma'am. I watch it every day.

JACKIE: Well, then you know what I'm trying to do here. They make me furious. And all those holy-roller churches with their falling on the floor, laying on of hands, are fooling around with something that is not in their domain.

> OPPENHEIMER *enters, very agitated, crosses behind* ROY *and* JACKIE *and exits. No one notices him.*

Trying to bring down the power of God, attract the Holy Spirit like it's something that can come down a lightning rod if you wave it in a bad storm. A church should be built on the Word. The Word is the Church's domain. The Word. And it has to stop with that.

ROY: Really—I just used to sing there.

JACKIE: They did have the best music.

ROY: Yes ma'am.

JACKIE: What is this around your neck?

ROY: Bolo tie.

OPPENHEIMER: Oh, is this one of your hobbies—making these?

ROY: No ma'am. I bought this. New.

JACKIE: I'm sorry I got so vehement. The one thing I don't want to get is preachy.

ROY: No, I wanted to say it's been a while since I played…this guitar.

JACKIE: Well, we are on again in a couple of minutes. Now I'm using your song to end the program—kind of like the benediction. I'll introduce you and then I'll have to hurry around to the studio door—I'm going to stand and shake hands as the audience leaves. Now when the red light on that camera goes out, you're off. But just finish the song anyway, like you would normally. By the way, please sing something other than "I Saw the Light"—the new Hank Williams biography has really devalued him for Christians. You understand. Nothing personal.

ROY: Ma'am. I don't want to do this.

JACKIE: Why not?

ROY: I can't. I can't play this guitar anymore. Simple as that.

JACKIE: Oh. My. They wanted—specifically asked for a guitar. You know, to increase the…warmth factor.

JANE is sitting on the bed talking on the phone. She is upset.

JANE: Yes, that's who I mean. He's a new Launch Control Officer—

ROY: Well, I guess that does it. [*Puts his guitar back in the case*]

JANE: Yes, LCO—whatever. [*Pause*] His wife.

JACKIE: Wait. Wait. I'll think of something. Sit here. I'll come up with something.

ROY puts his guitar down and sits off-camera. JACKIE returns to her chair and waits for her camera cue.

JANE: I know his duty just started, but this is kind of an emergency. No, I'm not in labor—that's the problem. Yes, this is our first baby. Thank you. Are they sealed in the control room yet? I thought it took longer. No. I just need to talk to him. I understand. I understand.

JACKIE: I want to talk to you today about something that most preachers never speak about although it's found throughout the Bible.

JANE: I understand.

JACKIE: I'm talking about what will happen to each one of you on that day at that last moment.

JANE: I understand.

Sits holding the telephone receiver for several beats, desolate, not knowing what to do.

RAMONA, looking at her watch, enters with JUSTIN. They have a plate of cookies.

RAMONA: Better turn the TV on—don't want to miss Roy.

RAMONA turns it on. JACKIE is heard through the TV.

JACKIE: Today we're looking at the Rapture, that moment when "we shall be changed, in the twinkling of an eye." Now the word *rapture* means—this is from Webster's Dictionary:

RAMONA: I wonder who does her hair? [*Sits down*]

JACKIE: —"the state of being transported by lofty emotion; ecstasy or the transporting of a person from one place to another, especially to heaven." So plane, bus, train, or Rapture—all forms of transportation.

RAMONA: [*Takes a small snapshot out of her pocket and shows it to JUSTIN*] This is my boy.

JACKIE: What it is is the coming of Christ for the Church in which He instantly catches up all living believers to meet Him in the air and translates them into perfect and immortal bodies without them experiencing physical death.

JUSTIN gives snapshot back to RAMONA.

So you could be Raptured, like that, and someone is standing there looking at a pair of your empty shoes.

RAMONA turns the volume down.

There are signs leading up to the Rapture, of course. And these I was describing earlier this morning. But they are all part of the Tribulation—Armageddon being the climax of many years of suffering, war, natural disasters, droughts, world famines. And can any of us deny that these signs are present and increasing? All we need to do is watch the news, read the paper. And any of us then might pray that we might be Raptured before we have to witness any more suffering.

I, myself, many times think it should happen now because the world has had enough. When I see the faces of children who are starving because a drought has ravaged their country, or a war has ravaged their country, or I see bodies being removed from the site of an earthquake and people wandering, looking for a lost father or a daughter, I—planes with bombs over our heads right now! The leaders of the world…no one is doing anything, no one is listening. IT'S COMING. WHO'S READY? DEAR GOD.

> *Disoriented by this sudden burst of emotion* JACKIE *finds herself on her feet. She looks briefly at* ROY, *confused, sits down and finds her place in her notes.* ROY *stares at her.*

The word *rapture* comes from the Greek *harpazo,* which is translated as "caught up." That moment of Rapture is prophesied by Matthew: "For as the lightning comes from the east, and flashes even unto the west; so shall the coming of the Son of Man be."

> ROY *experiences a sharp pain in his blind eye. He snatches off his glasses and covers his eye.*

And now the final word will be a benediction sung by an old friend of mine, Roy Layton. I've asked Roy to sing a cappella so that we can all carry just the words away with us. And I'll be at the studio door ready to shake hands with all those who worshipped here with us today. Roy? Roy—

> ROY *comes to and stands.* JANE *signals to the booth and exits quickly.*

RAMONA: That *is* Roy! But where are his glasses?

ROY : [*Singing*]

The sun is slowly sinking,
The day is almost gone,
Still darkness falls all around us,

> OPPENHEIMER *crosses laterally, stops when he hears* ROY *is singing, watches him.*

And we must journey on.
The darkest hour is just before dawn,
The narrow way leads home,
Lay down your soul at Jesus's feet,
The darkest hour is just before dawn.

> *During the song,* JANE *leaves her bedroom and walks straight across the stage to* ROY. *He doesn't see her until the end of his song when she is right in front of him.*

JANE: Help me.

ROY: What?

JANE: Please, I'm overdue. I'm scared.

ROY: Ma'am, I think I'm on television here.

> RAMONA *stands up in front of her tv.* ROY *looks up helplessly at the control booth, gets nothing.*

Don't you need a doctor?

JANE: I have doctors at the base. But they won't help me. They won't even tell me anything. [*Takes* ROY's *hands and puts them on her stomach*] Please. Please. You can start now.

ROY: [*Taking his hands away*] I'm not a faith healer, ma'am.

JANE: I have faith. [*Putting his hands back*] Please. I know it will help.

ROY: I—I bless thee in the name of the Father, and the Son—

JANE: No! That's for when it's born. I need something for now. *Please.*

> JACKIE *enters.*

ROY: [*Closing his eyes in panic*] Dear Jesus.

JANE: I—I feel something!

ROY: Dear God.

JANE: I FEEL SOMETHING! I FEEL SOMETHING! I—

> JANE *collapses in* ROY's *arms and he lowers her to the ground.* JACKIE *runs to help. The tv program goes to static and* RAMONA *pounds the tv and switches channels, trying to get* ROY *back.*

RAMONA: Damn TV! Dammit! !

> JUSTIN *picks up his toy and Ivory Snow box and is gone before* RAMONA *can stop him.* OPPENHEIMER *stares at* ROY.

OPPENHEIMER: Something about him. Something about him.

> ROY *stands up.* JACKIE *stays with* JANE. OPPENHEIMER *moves to* JANE's *bed and sits on it, after testing it to make certain it's real. He remains very interested in what he can see in the tv studio.*

> RAMONA *sits on the edge of her chair, staring at the empty television. After a moment she begins looking through the phone book. During the following action, she finds the number, dials, gets a busy signal, dials, until she finally gets through.*

JANE: What happened?

JACKIE: You fainted.

JANE: No. No. It was wonderful. I felt something—I felt tingly and then just floated away. That's the first time anything like that has ever happened to me. [*To* JACKIE] Do you think the feelings I had went down to the baby?

JACKIE: I—I don't know. Do you feel all right?

JANE: [*Interrupting*] I'm not really, that religious—no offense. I was just so desperate—all I wanted was to just know I tried. So I could have a little peace. But this—

> *Gets up—*JACKIE *helps her—and crosses to* ROY.

I just want to say. That you're a real preacher.

> JANE *takes* ROY's *hand and kisses it, then exits, ignoring* JACKIE's *efforts to help her.* JACKIE *signals to someone offstage to help* JANE.

RAMONA: [*On the phone*] Hello? I'm looking for my husband. Roy Layton. The singer. Can you have him call his wife? His *wife.*

OPPENHEIMER *begins to roll a cigarette, not taking his eyes off* ROY.

JACKIE: [*To* ROY] What happened?

ROY: I don't know. We aren't still on, are we?

JACKIE: No, thank God. Did she just faint?

ROY: I don't know.

JACKIE: You don't know?

ROY: I never done it before in my life. Honestly. She took my hands, put them on her stomach. What could I do?

JACKIE: You could take your hands away!

ROY: How could I? She looked up at me and said "I have faith." When people have that much faith, what do you do? Don't you give them what they want?

JACKIE: You could just pray for her.

ROY: I did. That's what I did.

> *Phone rings at* RAMONA'S. *She answers it quickly.*

JACKIE: And then she fainted. [*No answer from* ROY] And then she fainted. Pregnant women faint.

RAMONA: Yes?

ROY: I guess so.

RAMONA: I was hoping you were someone else.

JACKIE: That's all it was then, wasn't it?

RAMONA: Can't you keep track of that little boy?

ROY: I'm just a singer. And not a very good one.

RAMONA: [*Still on the phone*] Well, I understand that you're just the babysitter, but—. Yes, he usually drops in once a day. A couple of times today. Listen, I'm expecting an important phone call.

> JACKIE *crosses to* ROY, *takes both his hands and looks at them.* OPPENHEIMER *stands.*

JACKIE: When I heard you sing that time you don't remember. I didn't tell you—you made me cry.

ROY: Baby doll, that was the song. It was the song.

> JACKIE *exits.*

RAMONA: Uh-huh. Well, it's nice to finally know where he lives. No, I'll be here. I'm always here. Right. [*Hangs up the phone, crosses to the picture window and stares out*] This world. [*Turns the TV on*] I dunno. I dunno.

> *Alone,* ROY *stares at his hands.*

ROY: Like electricity coming down my arms.

> RAMONA *sits in the recliner.*

RAMONA: Little boy. Little boy.

> RAMONA *closes her eyes.*

> ROY *senses the presence of someone.*

OPPENHEIMER: Something about him.

ROY: [*Not seeing* OPPENHEIMER] Who's there?

> RAMONA *is asleep in her chair; the TV on but nothing on the screen except*

light. It is now late at night. JUSTIN *enters and goes to the kitchen cupboard, looking for cookies. Instead he finds a box of Ivory Snow and brings it back into the living room. He likes the picture on the box—it's a mother holding a baby. He curls up with it beneath the light of the* TV *screen.* RAMONA *sleeps through the next scene.* ROY *exits, passing* YOUNG ROY, *who enters pulling a large cart filled with Army-issue mattresses secured with ropes. He shines a flashlight in* OPPENHEIMER's *eyes.*

YOUNG ROY: Who's there?

    OPPENHEIMER *finds himself at Tornada del Muerto, the Trinity site, in the shadow of the tower that holds the gadget. It is the day preceding the test, just before dawn.*

OPPENHEIMER: What?

YOUNG ROY: Dr. Oppenheimer?

OPPENHEIMER: Yes, yes. Can—can you turn that light off?

YOUNG ROY: [*Turns it off*] Sorry, sir.

    YOUNG ROY *approaches the tower base, walks under it, cautiously looks up at where the gadget is suspended and rolls the cart to what he thinks is a spot directly under the gadget. With shaking hands,* OPPENHEIMER *starts to light a cigarette he rolled while watching the previous scene.*

    About the proximity of the gadget to the match:
You gonna light that here? Sir?

    OPPENHEIMER *looks at* YOUNG ROY *for a beat, then at his own hand, as if he never saw it before.*

OPPENHEIMER: I don't remember rolling this. [*Lights his cigarette. This brings on a bad coughing spell. When he's done, he looks at his watch.*]

YOUNG ROY: [*About the mattresses*] They're bringing some more. In a truck. From Base Camp.

    Pause. OPPENHEIMER *nods, distracted.*
They think ten to twelve feet. Will that do it?

OPPENHEIMER: Do what?

YOUNG ROY: Cushion the fall. Just in case.

OPPENHEIMER: Just in case?

YOUNG ROY: It falls.

OPPENHEIMER: It?

YOUNG ROY: The gadget. Are you all right, Dr. Oppenheimer?

OPPENHEIMER: I'm just kinda tired. I think I nodded off…I was in the control shed and then I wandered—no, this is the tower…I was up on the tower checking the…

YOUNG ROY: Gadget.

OPPENHEIMER: [*Snapping to*] The gadget? Its not going to fall. It's secure.

YOUNG ROY: Well, as they say, better safe than sorry, sir.

OPPENHEIMER: Who are you exactly?

YOUNG ROY: [*Coming to attention and saluting*] Corporal Roy Layton, sir.

OPPENHEIMER: How do you do. [*Looking at watch again*] Where is everybody?

YOUNG ROY: Getting the mattresses.

OPPENHEIMER: Oh. Right. That's good. I'm—I'm waiting…here. Here.

YOUNG ROY: [*Readjusting the cart, looking up at where the gadget would be*] Excuse me, sir, but what do you think? Is this a good way to do it? Or should they be just laid on the ground? Maybe in a wide circle? Or just piled up every whichaway? What do you think? Sir?

OPPENHEIMER: What?

YOUNG ROY: What do you think about this configuration of mattresses here?

OPPENHEIMER: That will probably be fine.

YOUNG ROY: Yes, sir.

OPPENHEIMER: Where *is* everybody?

YOUNG ROY: Any minute now. They only went ten miles.

OPPENHEIMER: What? Oh.

YOUNG ROY: Everything going all right, sir?

OPPENHEIMER: I think I need to get to my next…stop.

YOUNG ROY: All the vehicles are gone.

> OPPENHEIMER *crosses to* ROY's *guitar; left from the previous scene, and picks it up.*

> Oh, that's mine. [*Takes it and puts it upstage, near the mattresses*]

OPPENHEIMER: I've just been so tired. We've been working so hard. It's been very hard, particularly these last few months. Hornig called in for the weather report yesterday—fell asleep on the radio, waiting for the answer. I just now nodded off myself. Had a dream—classic—like running for a train, never catching it. I was in a place, a lot like here, but different…. There was a woman and a child. Strange. Even now, I feel groggy. In parallax, like a camera. You look up here at an image that's coming through down there backwards and upside down. You look familiar. I feel like what you say, you've said before. What we do is…. Even those goddam mattresses…

YOUNG ROY: I'd be glad to drive you anywhere you want to go. Drove Dr. Teller the other day. He's a helluva guy. He's famous, isn't he? Not that you're not, sir.

OPPENHEIMER: That's all right. I'm not. Fermi is the famous one. *Fermi. Fermi.* Yes, I talked to him last night! [*He's relieved—a familiar name.*]

YOUNG ROY: Everything is all right, isn't it, sir? I mean *its*—[*Motioning to the gadget*]—okay, isn't it?

OPPENHEIMER: [*Patting* YOUNG ROY's *shoulder and arms to establish that he's real*] Everything's—going—as—scheduled. Yes, that's right. I'm certain of that. I had a bad night last night— coughing. That's why I'm so tired.

YOUNG ROY: I was there at the ranch house, you know. When they were putting the two halves together and polishing it.

OPPENHEIMER: So you are—somebody I work with…?

YOUNG ROY: I was there in one of the jeeps.

OPPENHEIMER: [*A memory comes*] With the motor running? With the motor running!

YOUNG ROY: We were ordered to do that, sir. So you all could make a quick getaway in case it blew.

OPPENHEIMER: [*Joyous*] In case it blew! Right!

YOUNG ROY: So that was a close call, huh? I wondered about that. I did. Boy, it was pretty scary, I can tell you now. Sitting out there, waiting, not knowing if the whole thing was gonna go blewey or not!

OPPENHEIMER: Go blewey?

YOUNG ROY: Blow up! Explode! And take alla us with it.

OPPENHEIMER: The plug would never blow up by itself.

YOUNG ROY: Right. What?

OPPENHEIMER: Would never happen. What do you think we've spent all this time on? I mean, we're worried sick that this goddam firing mechanism isn't going to work. *Yes.* YES! ! That's it! That's what's next! Oh, thank God. WE'RE TESTING IT NEXT. THE FIRING MECHANISM!

> OPPENHEIMER *laughs with relief.* YOUNG ROY, *as excited as* OPPENHEIMER, *whoops in joy. Exhilarated, they scramble to the top of the mattress pile.*

YOUNG ROY: Great. Great! I'm excited, too. I have to tell you, sir, ever since I got here—there's something about this place.

OPPENHEIMER: Do you really think so?

YOUNG ROY: There's something about it.

OPPENHEIMER: It is beautiful, particularly right now, for some reason. Some people find it barren.

YOUNG ROY: No place in this country is barren, sir.

OPPENHEIMER: They call this place the Jornada del Muerto, you know.

YOUNG ROY: What's that—Spanish?

OPPENHEIMER: The conquistadores. Cheerful bunch.

YOUNG ROY: What's it mean?

OPPENHEIMER: Journey of Death. I'm suddenly so happy. I don't know why.

YOUNG ROY: I thought this was called Trinity.

OPPENHEIMER: No. That's just the project and the buildings and all that.

YOUNG ROY: I just wondered what the name meant.

OPPENHEIMER: Well, the Trinity—

YOUNG ROY: I know what the Trinity is, sir. I was just wondering what all this has to do with the Father, the Son, and the Holy Ghost.

OPPENHEIMER: Nothing—I—I named it that. I never thought that it might offend anybody.

YOUNG ROY: No offense taken, sir.

OPPENHEIMER: Of course, I realize now how it might—

YOUNG ROY: Oh, it's a nice title, sir. Don't get me wrong. I just wondered, you know.

OPPENHEIMER: They called me in Berkeley for a name. And I had been reading a poem by John Donne—he was a *minister,* you know:

As West and East in all Flatte Maps are One,
So Death doth touch the Resurrection.

YOUNG ROY: Uh-huh.
OPPENHEIMER: Death *touches* the Resurrection.
YOUNG ROY: Uh-huh.
OPPENHEIMER: And it's quite flat out here.
YOUNG ROY: Okay.
OPPENHEIMER: And I thought of my favorite poem by this same minister:

Batter my heart, *three*-person'd God—

> *Skipping to the last two lines.*

Unless you enthrall me, I never shall be free,
And ne'er be chaste unless you ravish me.

> YOUNG ROY *really doesn't get this one at all. He waits, instead of replying.*

Batter my heart, *three*-person'd God.

> YOUNG ROY *just continues to look at him.*

We needed a name.
YOUNG ROY: Well, it's sure better than Journey of Death.
They laugh.
OPPENHEIMER: Last night Fermi was taking bets on whether the explosion would just suck all the oxygen out of New Mexico or out of the entire Northern Hemisphere. He looked up at the Oscuras—that mountain range—at sunset—they were never more beautiful. And all he could say is, "Ah, the earth on the eve of destruction." Just then, a tarantula sidled up next to him. He ran in *real* terror then. Oh shit. I shouldn't be telling you that.
YOUNG ROY: Oh, that's all right, sir. I'm not afraid of tarantulas. I'm really not afraid of anything out here. Two months ago, if I thought I'd be here in New Mexico, well, I would've laughed. I got my orders home in Berlin, and they told us we'd get a month off then go back to, you know, clean up. But when I reported for duty, they put us on this train and the next thing I know, we're heading west. A whole train full of soldiers heading west for no reason. Seemed like then. And we stopped in Nebraska—*Nebraska*—for three days and played baseball to kill time. And still we have no idea where we were going or why. And then, and then, back on the train and further west, and the ground starts to change. My buddy wakes me up and presses my face to the window. Lord! There's a herd of antelope galloping alongside the train and I look up and got my breath took away again!

Mountains! Blue-green, almost black the pine is so thick. They are so still and big, they look painted on. Well, that's when I knew I was going somewhere important. Something about the speed of that train—I swear once we got close to here, we went faster and faster—I think those guys could've lost control like *that*. [*Snaps fingers*] I mean, that prairie blurred into the desert and the day went *by*. And then, bang, we were stopped. 'Cause we were here. Stopped. Dead. And it was so quiet. The sky was full of stars. And I could feel the train moving inside me for the whole next day.

OPPENHEIMER: Then you've been away in the war quite a while?

YOUNG ROY: Yes sir.

OPPENHEIMER: Three years?

YOUNG ROY: Yes sir.

OPPENHEIMER: And they send you home for just thirty days and then out here?

YOUNG ROY: I'm not complaining. This is just about the most exciting thing that has ever happened, sir. I mean, I missed the invention of the motor car, I missed Christopher Columbus, I missed the time when Lord Jesus was walking around on earth, I missed the invention, no, *discovery* of electricity. I was beginning to think that absolutely nothing was ever gonna happen to me. You know?

When I think that the smartest men, why, in the whole world are here. And all the knowledge that's went into this, from way back there. When the first guy got an idea, like a little light bulb going on over his head, and, wham, he invents that light bulb. And then another guy makes it better. And another guy says, "We got a light bulb, we need a socket." And, wham, we got a socket. And then a lamp. And then, the next thing you know, the whole world is lit up. Lamps everywhere! No more darkness.

OPPENHEIMER:

If the radiance of a thousand suns,
Were to burst at once into the sky—

YOUNG ROY: Was that from the Bible?

OPPENHEIMER: It's from something called "The Song of the Lord."

YOUNG ROY: Our Lord—Lord Jesus?

OPPENHEIMER: An ancient prince—that kind of lord. He's supposed to go into battle. All his enemies are assembled. But he won't go—he has doubts. But *his* god, Krishna, appears to him. Blazing and radiant with light and with many arms, all holding weapons. And then Krishna shouts, "I am become Death—"

OPPENHEIMER *stops. Long pause.*

YOUNG ROY: Is that how it ends?

OPPENHEIMER: No...no...Krishna shouts, "I am become death—the shatterer of worlds."

YOUNG ROY: And that does it, huh? That's all it takes, I bet.

OPPENHEIMER: He goes into battle. He goes and—

YOUNG ROY: Wins? Right? He wins. There's your happy ending. You see? You see, now that's what we call a good omen where I come from. Like when you open the Bible with your eyes closed and you read whatever verse your finger falls on ? And that verse has meaning for you right then? You were meant to read it. Like now, you were meant to think of that poem.

OPPENHEIMER: I remember now. I remember this.

> *Horn honks offstage.*

YOUNG ROY: Hey, they're here! With the mattresses! [*Jumps down off the mattresses*] I'll be there tomorrow morning, sir. I get to be in one of the trenches. A kind of forward observer.

OPPENHEIMER: You haven't seen it. You haven't seen it yet.

YOUNG ROY: That's right! That's exactly it! 'Cause you can't even begin to imagine. 'Cause you just know it's gonna be incredible. Oh, sir, it's gonna go great. And then you'll be able to get some sleep, you'll see. Can I shake your hand? I want to tell my kids someday.

> OPPENHEIMER *leans down from the top of the mattresses and shakes* YOUNG ROY's *hand.* OPPENHEIMER *tries to hold on to* YOUNG ROY *briefly but he disappears into the darkness.* OPPENHEIMER *lies back on the mattresses confused and desolate.*
>
> *At* ROY's *and* RAMONA's *house it is now morning. The* TV *is still on.* JUSTIN *is gone.* RAMONA *wakes up suddenly in her chair.*

RAMONA: Oh my God. [*Gets out of the chair*] Oh my God. What time is it? [*Goes to the back bedroom*] Roy? Roy! You let me *sleep* in my chair! Roy? Roy—[*Reenters the living room looking for him then goes into the kitchen growing more frantic*] Roy? *ROY!* [*Stands bewildered at her front door*] Maybe it's a binge. Maybe he just went out on a binge—

> YOUNG ROY *appears, inebriated and trying desperately to cover it up. He is in uniform and carrying a duffel bag. One eye is covered with a bandage.*

YOUNG ROY: Hi, baby. I had an accident. Didn't want to tell you when I called you from New Mexico. They sent me home on a plane! An airplane! [*Coming to her*] I saw something incredible in New Mexico. Something incredible. But I can't talk about it. I can't talk—[*Kissing her gently*] I'm sorry I'm late. I lost track of the time. Okay? Okay? I lost track of the time.

RAMONA: Roy—

> YOUNG ROY *passes* RAMONA *and crosses into the house. He stops and puts his hand on his bandaged eye—the pain stopping him.* ROY, *age 60, approaches the house.*

ROY: [*Starting to talk the moment he sees* RAMONA] It's like something you always knew, deep inside you. You *knew.*

> YOUNG ROY *exits into the back of the house.*

And one day someone says it and *wham!* It all breaks loose! Of course. Of course, death *meets* the Resurrection.

RAMONA: Where have you been? Where are your glasses?

ROY: Now I know. There was some reason why I was there, some reason why this—[*Points to his blind eye*]—happened to me. With this eye—[*His good eye*]—I see this world. And with my blinded eye, I got to see the next.

RAMONA: I remember—I remembered.

ROY: I been walking all around. Looking at everything. Just in case. Saying goodbye.

RAMONA: And you never talked about it again.

ROY: 'Cause it can happen any moment—"In the twinkling of an eye, we shall all be changed." Like that.

RAMONA: What happened, Roy?

ROY: Do you know how many neighborhoods there are around us? Islands of houses everywhere. And each house has people in it, and God watches over every single one of them. How does He keep track? How does He keep track?

RAMONA: Where's your guitar?

ROY: Oh, I don't need it anymore. I sing by myself. I make people *cry*.

RAMONA: Roy, honey, come in now. Come on in.

ROY: I hate to. I hate to. Come to me.

> RAMONA *comes to him. He puts his arm around her shoulder.*

Look. [*He's still looking at the world.*] It's a shame, isn't it.

> *Blast of light and, this time, a rumble that grows until it simulates the real blast at the Trinity site. When it stops,* ROY *and* RAMONA *stand still and* OPPENHEIMER *stands on top of mattresses, looking at the mushroom cloud of the test. Cheers and shouts can be heard everywhere: "It worked! It worked! Oh my God, it worked!"* GENE *comes running in, his goggles around his neck. He sees* OPPENHEIMER; *but not* ROY *and* RAMONA. *He acts as if it's natural that* OPPENHEIMER *is on top of the mattresses. He's very excited.*

GENE: It worked!! It worked!! Hey, Dr. Oppenheimer! The war is over for sure now, huh? Colonel Kisto—, Kistow—, the Russian guy? Says you owe him ten dollars.

OPPENHEIMER: [*Climbing down, looking in his billfold*] I—I'll have to pay him tomorrow.

GENE: Tomorrow! Right! We got a million of 'em now the war is over! I have to admit, I never thought it would work.

> GENE *grabs* OPPENHEIMER's *hand and shakes it.* OPPENHEIMER *sees* ROY *and* RAMONA *and runs after* GENE *as he exits.*

OPPENHEIMER: Help me! [*Exits*]

RAMONA: I can't breathe. I have to go in.

ROY: Stay. Stay with me. My whole life makes sense now. I see it all.

RAMONA: Roy, when our boy was killed, you did this. You stayed up for two days figuring it all out. Do you remember?

ROY: I even figured that out now. You see, Danny was conceived right before I went to work on the bomb. Maybe right at the time—when the die was cast, and I was going to be there. So he had to die, you see.

RAMONA: He did not have to die! You can't tell me he had to die! Roy, you've gone too far. People die all the time and none of it makes any sense!

ROY: [*With increasing agitation*] His father conceived him and went immediately to a place called Journey of Death which was also called Trinity. You see? Father, Son, and Holy Ghost. And finally, the last piece is there. I healed somebody, Ramona. The Holy Ghost came down my arms and into this woman's body. I could feel it, Ramona, like electricity coming down my arms. It was real. And she could feel it, too. And she wasn't even religious. I know that's what the Holy Ghost is, then electricity, coming down my arms. God's like lightning coming through us into the world.

RAMONA: [*Trying to bring him out of it*] Roy, you're not part of the Trinity. Or some place called Journey of Death. Some person named those places, not God. You're my Roy—that's who you are.

ROY: But I'm trapped there, Ramona. I'm caught.

RAMONA: Roy, that was forty years ago!

ROY: Forty years ago I saw with my own eye what everybody's been waiting for since the world began!

RAMONA: What? What?

> OPPENHEIMER *enters, still chasing* GENE, *but finds himself back where he started. He stops when he sees* ROY *and* RAMONA.

ROY: The end ! I saw it! For real with one of my eyes! And then the power of God came down my arms. So it does all make sense!

RAMONA: No. No!

ROY: You see, Ramona, I was never really sure that God existed. I believed it, of course. But I didn't *think* it. But now I have proof. I have a fact. So that means—that means it's all true. The Bible, Revelations, Hell—it's really gonna happen. Trinity. Trinity. Baby, we're caught.

RAMONA: [*Running into the house*] NO.

> ROY *stays outside.* OPPENHEIMER *watches him during the next scene.* RAMONA *notices something out the picture window. It is* JACKIE *coming up the walk. She is carrying* ROY's *guitar in its case. Shes dressed in the same clothes; looks disheveled. She looks through the window of the front door.* RAMONA *opens the door and looks at* JACKIE.

JACKIE: Is Roy here?

RAMONA: He's at work.

JACKIE: I—I need to talk to him.

RAMONA: He's not here.

JACKIE: I have to tell him something.

RAMONA: Oh?

JACKIE: This is his guitar.

RAMONA: I see.

JACKIE: We were at the hospital all night, Mrs. Layton. That woman came down during the program yesterday and asked for the laying on of hands…I don't do that. I didn't want my church to be a carnival, accent on the carnal.

RAMONA: Well, that's a comfort.

JACKIE: And then her water broke, and the baby started to come. We made it to the hospital all right. [*Breaks down*] I'm sorry. I've been up all night.

RAMONA: [*Taking the guitar*] Why don't I take this now.

> JANE *enters her bedroom. She is in the dress she wore at the* TV *studio.*

JACKIE: They called the base and her husband was on his way. He'd just gotten off duty—they couldn't get hold of him. She wouldn't stay, so I took her home.

> JANE *crawls onto the bed painfully and curls up on her side.*

Roy doesn't know. The baby died.

> ROY *enters.*

The baby died, Mrs. Layton. [*She and* ROY *see each other*] You have to tell him.

> JACKIE *exits quickly.* RAMONA *turns and sees that* ROY *has heard. She tries to touch him but he turns from her and crosses numbly to the door and goes outside. She exits into the back of the house.* ADAM *enters his bedroom still in his uniform.*

ADAM: NO!!!!!

> ADAM *crosses and looks at* JANE *in bed. She doesn't look at him.* OPPENHEIMER *crosses to* ROY *and speaks to him.*

OPPENHEIMER: It was like a wheel that somebody started rolling a long time ago. As a discovery, it was beautiful, as all pure knowledge is. It's the same wheel that transported us this far, and into—

ROY: —Rapture.

OPPENHEIMER: When you're at the door, don't you go through it? Particularly when you turn around and see there's a line forming behind you? You can't stop reaching for mystery.

> *During this* ADAM *climbs into bed behind* JANE, *his uniform still on.*

ROY: You can leave. You can put your hands in your pockets and just go home.

OPPENHEIMER: I know you now.

ROY: I carried the mattresses.

OPPENHEIMER: Yes. *Yes.* You helped me that day. You had such faith.

> ROY *looks at* OPPENHEIMER *for a beat then crosses to his house and enters. He turns on the* TV *keeping the volume low. The music for* JACKIE's *program begins.* ROY *sits down.* OPPENHEIMER *lights a cigarette, turns and exits, coughing.* JACKIE *enters the* TV *studio carrying a Bible. She is in the same clothes. She motions for the booth to cut the music. She addresses the audience, not the camera, and doesn't sit in her chair.*

JACKIE: I'm unprepared. This won't be a lesson. For those of you who got out your world maps, I'm sorry—I don't want to talk about history tonight…or prophecy.

[*Jumping to something she knows, reading*] Matthew: "And in the fourth watch of the night, Jesus went to them, walking on the sea. When the disciples saw Him walking on the sea, they were terrified, and said it is an apparition and cried out for fear. Thereupon Jesus spake to them, saying, 'Take courage, it is I. Be not afraid.' And Jesus called to Peter, saying, 'Come, Peter, come.' So Peter came down out of the ship, and walked on the water, to go to Jesus. But perceiving that the wind was strong, he began to sink, and cried out, saying, 'Master, save me.' And Jesus immediately stretched forth His hand and took hold of him, saying, 'O ye of little faith, why didst thou distrust me?'"

I've been thinking a lot about Peter. Out in that boat.

I had to sit somewhere last night and wait. There was nothing else I could do. It seemed I had done everything I could do, and it wasn't enough. I'd never had a time quite like that. I guess I'm inexperienced.

I got into this because I was touched a long time ago by a human life, by the life of one man, Jesus. He was the first really friendly person I ever met in the Bible, and I felt I knew Him. I never really understood the mystery of His life, I never really figured out, even with all my study, how He could die for my sins. And, frankly, no one has ever really explained to me how that really works. But now, even talking about it in front of all of you—I feel very moved.

I think we're the brightest animal that God made. In fact, we're God's spoiled brat, sometimes. We're so smart, so bright, so intelligent that we don't *think* we believe in anything anymore. We *think* we don't have any faith. The one thing that most people do have faith in is how much faith they *don't* have.

So…where was I? Peter, yes. [*Reading from the Bible*] "So Peter came down out of the ship, and walked on the water, to go to—" [*Stops for a second looking hard at the page*]

Peter "came down out of the ship" and he "walked on the water." Maybe it was only a couple of steps, but he did walk on water. Peter was *walking* there…

    ROY *crosses to the* TV.

So how much faith do we need ?

    ROY *turns the* TV *off.*

How much faith do we need?

    ROY *sits in the recliner.* JACKIE *exits. After a beat* JUSTIN's *toy is thrown up on top of the mattresses, then the Ivory Snow box.* JUSTIN *appears, climbing up. He arranges the Ivory Snow box so he can see the picture, then lies down on top of the mattresses and goes to sleep.* RAMONA *enters from the back of her house, talks to* ROY.

RAMONA: I thought you were laying down.

ROY: Couldn't.

RAMONA: Grocery store's open late tonight. We could get a head start on the week.

    ROY *gets up numbly.*

ROY: Okay.

RAMONA: Roy, please. It's like living with a dead person.

ROY: I'm sorry, baby.

RAMONA: Roy, we just had a bad time. Everybody has them, sometimes. [*Embraces him*] Lookee here—bet you thought I forgot this one.

    RAMONA *sings and rocks* ROY. JANE *gets up out of bed and goes to the mirror, leaving* ADAM *asleep.*

What a fellowship,
What a joy divine,
Leaning on the everlasting arms.
What a blessedness—

>   ROY *stops* RAMONA.

ROY: No more.

>   *Phone rings.* RAMONA *answers it.* ROY *puts his glasses on.*

RAMONA: Yes. No, not today. Oh no. Oh, don't. Don't. Of course I will. Yes. [*Hangs up the phone*] He's been lost before.

ROY: Who?

RAMONA: Little boy. Justin. But he always comes *here.*

ROY: Oh, that little boy.

RAMONA: Every day he comes to see me.

ROY: Oh baby, he'll be all right.

RAMONA: It's just so late, Roy. That was his mother on the phone—she's home for once. She was crying.

ROY: It is late. Well, they'll call the police.

RAMONA: She said the police are looking. They've been looking most of the day.

ROY: They'll find him. They're experts at it. Those guys know what they're doing.

RAMONA: Roy, you always say that.

ROY: I do? [*Pause*] I do.

RAMONA: Yes.

ROY: I'll get the flashlights. [*Exits to the back of the house*]

RAMONA: [*Taking the afghan from the back of the recliner*] I'll take this—just in case he's gotten wet. I'll leave the TV on for him.

>   ROY *returns with the flashlights.*

ROY: We'll have better luck if we split up.

RAMONA: Outside…by myself…in the dark?

ROY: I know, baby. What's his name again?

RAMONA: Justin.

>   *They go outside.*

>   It's so dark, Roy.

ROY: I know.

RAMONA: Well…you go that way. And I'll go this way.

>   *They separate.*

>   Oh Roy, tell me we're gonna find him.

ROY: We'll find him, baby.

RAMONA: Do you really believe that?

ROY: I have to.

>   *They exit calling "Justin." Not moving from the mirror,* JANE *wakes* ADAM.

JANE: Adam? Adam?

ADAM: What? Are you all right?

JANE: It's so cruel, Adam. My body doesn't know. Everything is working the way it should. It's just going on, as if everything was fine.

ADAM: Maybe you should've stayed at the hospital.

JANE: [*Crosses to the window*] Hold me.

> *He comes to her, embraces her from behind. His hand touches one of her breasts.*

It's so amazing, Adam. I have milk.

> *After a beat they exit. The sound of birds just before dawn.* JUSTIN *wakes up on the mattresses. He climbs down. As he takes down his toy it breaks. He hears someone coming and crosses away from the sound.* OPPENHEIMER *enters, crosses to him.*

OPPENHEIMER: Are you lost, too?

> JUSTIN *turns, nods his head yes, and hands* OPPENHEIMER *his broken toy.* OPPENHEIMER *sees immediately what's wrong with the toy.*

I see. [*Fixes it, hands it back to* JUSTIN] How's that? [*The door of the control shed opens, spilling its light onto the stage.*] Oh thank God! [*Runs toward the door, stops and looks back at* JUSTIN] You'll be all right.

> OPPENHEIMER *exits into the control shed. The light is shut off with the closing of the door.* JUSTIN *looks after* OPPENHEIMER, *then lifts his toy into the air and flies it as he exits into the dark, making a flying noise with his breath.*

JUSTIN: WHOOOOOOOOOOOOOSHHHHHHHHHH.

Holly Hughes

∽

Dress Suits to Hire

•

Dress Suites to Hire was originally produced by PS 122 as part of the Veselka Festival. It was subsequently produced by The Women's Interart Theatre. It was directed by Lois Weaver and performed by Lois Weaver and Peggy Sha.

DEELUXE *is downcenter, on the floor. Her right hand is clamped on her neck. She appears dead. In fact she is dead for the rest of the play. It seems rigor mortis has set in rather early.* MICHIGAN *is facing upstage. In her lap a small white dog of a mechanical species—*LINDA—*begins barking.* MICHIGAN *turns around to see what* LINDA'*s barking at and discovers* DEELUXE.

MICHIGAN: [*Addressing the right hand of* DEELUXE.] I suppose you know what this will mean. There will be no show. She will be unable to do the show. You're not going to like this. [MICHIGAN *begins searching thru the suitcoats. She pulls out a phone receiver. Pink, plastic, sans cord—it should look as phony as possible.*] Hello? Ninth precinct? Yes, I'll hold. [*To* DEELUXE'*s hand*] You're asking for this. There's a man in here. I can't say if he's dangerous or not. I don't know any other men so I can't compare. Thru the door! He lives with us. More with her and with me. Me, this man, and the body. Yes there certainly is a body. Did I discover it? Many years ago. I first discovered the body in the Hotel Universal in Salamanca. A single light bulb. The light came in thru the window. The streets were lit by little oranges. The oranges were perfect and bitter. In this light I lay down on the bed and discovered the body. Especially the legs. She's part palomino. In the legs, pure palomino. Do you know what a palomino is? A race horse covered with parmesan cheese, yes. That's her. And after that first time I would discover the body again and again. And even when I hate her, I love the body. Who does the body belong to? Partly to me. It belongs to her. I usually say she's my sister and most of the time we are sisters. Sometimes we're even worse. I don't know the address. I don't go out much. I don't go out at all, so I don't need an address. I could describe the place. We live in a town. I've forgotten the name. In the bad part of town. We live in a rental clothing store. It doesn't look like much from the outside. But we have too many clothes for our own good. Is that enough of an address? Could you find us based on what I've just said? You're not there anymore, are you? She's not there anymore either. She's dead. Do you understand. Nevermind, I understand She probably won't be able to perform anymore! And I will never again lie down in the afternoon and discover the body. [MICHIGAN *replaces the phone in the suitcoat. She begins speaking to* LINDA.] Is it cold in here or is it me? Oh, it's you. [*To* DEELUXE] You should relax. You never relax. You know there are worse things in New York than being killed by someone who loves you. Like trying to cash a check! Are you mad at me because I said your body belongs to me? [MICHIGAN *kneels down and opens* DEELUXE'*s robe.*] Remember the night we became sisters? I looked out and there were no more stars. The sky was full of teeth. Blue and sharp they were falling toward us. We were already in the wolf's mouth and it was closing in around us. Our only chance was to become twins. To be swallowed whole. But being twins slowed us down. People don't rent dress suits from twins. But then there was always the body to come back to. I'm not going to look at you any longer. I got to look where I'm going. I never thought I would have to go anywhere.

MICHIGAN *crosses to stereo and puts on a scratchy version of Frank Sinatra singing: "A Lover Is Blue." While the record plays* MICHIGAN *paces, drains her drink and, looking at* DEELUXE, *polishes off hers as well. The stereo cuts off abruptly.* MICHIGAN *starts. A small wall sconce comes on. When* MICHIGAN *turns around to look at it, the light cuts off. The stereo comes on suddenly, it's the beginning bars of "Temptation."* MICHIGAN *backs away from it.* DEELUXE's *dress falls off its hook.* MICHIGAN *stands still, afraid. Lights slowly crossfade up, it's morning.* MICHIGAN *begins talking to* LINDA *again.*

MICHIGAN: Born in that cold snap spring won't come time of the year. Under the sign of Go fish. My Venus was stuck in the mud. Mud a the Bad River, she's acting up again. Outgrowing her banks. Slipping thru locked doors, spitting up coffins and dead Chevrolets. Leaving turds in the hope chest. Stores running outta Birdeye's Frozen Vegetables and everything plaid. People getting nervous they'd have to eat fresh food and wear solid colors. Thought the end of the world had come to Michigan. Nobody's hair would hold a set. Forsynthia blooms so hard and sudden she cracks the plate glass windows and then freezes all the way back to the ground. And they blamed my mother. She was full of too much bad river water. The end of world, not spring, was coming to Michigan. And I was the first robin of disaster. When I started breathing on my own the doctor went and beat me anyway and Momma she's screaming "What is it? Is it a girl?" And the doctor's screaming: "She's an animal." Animal doc, you said it! I do the rin-tin-tin, I get down on all fours. Being a girl is just a phase I'm going thru. I feel my own ass up and it's ticking like a time bomb. I am the end of the world after. Tick tock thru the teacher's lounge where Mr. Science pins you against the wall in the name of higher. I like being pinned down, an' what do you think of that? An' he says I bet you wish you hadda father, an I say "Nope, I wish I had his clothes, though" and I play with his tie and he's screaming to stop it o please stop it but we don't stop it we both want it till his tie is exploding in my hand like a trick cigar and he slaps me hard and says: "You're an animal!" Bomb on outta there. By now I'm sweating hard and I break out in titties. See the girls in the hall and my milk drops down. I got what they want, and I wanna give it to them and I do. Right on the pink plastic floor. Ever seen a bunch a lampry eels up close? Well they're everywhere in Michigan now and they're these girls too, their mouths are little oohs. Just made to suck. Go on, suck the life outta me, I wanna feel my life in somebody else's mouth. Makes me know what Jesus feels. At communion. He feels good. We take communion to make Jesus feel better. Jesus feels like a big rare roast beef on a platter squirting blood and fat on a platter and lifting his hips to heaven begging for it! "O God, yes! Yes, I need it, this is my body, hurry up and take it! Take me! Ketchup, mustard and the Holy Ghost are with me! Please god, o my god, O my God EAT ME!" Then the girls get what they want, what we both want and they stop being eels and go back to being girls again and I'm just barely ticking when they slap me hard an' say: "You're an animal!" I don't want nobody anymore. I wanna be myself, just me and moon. I feel her before I see her. The moon pulls something tight in me. I get that ocean feeling. O'Michigan she was an ocean before she was anything else. A blue-green bottomless pit, that's what's in me. The moon she could be anything she wants. She's a bigger prize than you can win bowling, she's that white bread women keep between their legs. She's a mirror, I'm not afraid to look. Oh, yoo-hoo! Mrs. Moon? [*Piano music up—"Amato Mio." French windows swing open.*] You're so smart and Italian. Tell me what I am. [DEELUXE *begins to sit, opening a giant fan as she does. She's singing "Amato Mio" à la Bela Lugosi, i.e., lots of rolling eyebrows. At the end of every phrase* DEELUXE *strikes another pose against the fan. She looks like a singing Art Deco vase.* MICHIGAN *strikes poses of terror in unison with* DEELUXE. *At the song's end,* DEELUXE *picks up the illuminated tulips and offers them to the horrified* MICHIGAN.]

MICHIGAN: Why did you come back?

DEELUXE: The car.

MICHIGAN: The car?

DEELUXE: The keys!

MICHIGAN: They won't let you. Expired!

DEELUXE: Why? My license is good!

MICHIGAN: Not your license! You're no good. You're expired! They won't let a dead woman run around in a Chevrolet.

DEELUXE: I'm taking the Cadillac! Kiss me and say you're sorry.

MICHIGAN: You'll make me sick! Your kisses are more ice water down my neck.

DEELUXE: You're my sister. I got rights.

MICHIGAN: I'm not your sister. I'm a White Christmas. I'm the wrong age for you. The age when you can't help being sick. The Ice Age! [*Pause*] Close the window. [DEELUXE *crosses and closes the window. She remains facing upstage, her back to* MICHIGAN.] We need more sherry.

DEELUXE: I've had all I want.

MICHIGAN: We've exhausted the reserves.

DEELUXE: I'm sick of sherry.

MICHIGAN: There's money in the pocket.

DEELUXE: Is that a threat?

MICHIGAN: Get enough.

DEELUXE: I've had enough.

MICHIGAN: We need more.

DEELUXE: [*Turning around to face* MICHIGAN.] We? You! You need more. More of what?

MICHIGAN: You know.

DEELUXE: More of the same. More of the same conversations. More of the same air. Well not me. I want.

MICHIGAN: What?

DEELUXE: I don't know. But it's not in this shop. It may not even be on this block. I may have to cross Second Avenue to get it. I know I don't want the same thing because day after day I have the same thing and at the end of the day I still want.

MICHIGAN: Hurry.

DEELUXE: You can't tell me what to do anymore. Well, I'm going. And I'm taking the money. [DEELUXE *removes a piggy bank from a suit coat pocket.*] Not for sherry. I'm getting what I want. [*She moves toward exit.*] And if I come back and I'm not saying that I will, I'm not telling you a thing. I need a secret. Well, my mind's made up. Nothing you can do or say can stop me. [*Pause*] Well, this time I'm really going. Don't try to get in my way. Good-bye.

MICHIGAN: Go on.

DEELUXE: [*Turning around and re-crossing the room.*] I'm doing what I want and I want to stay. [DEELUXE *hunts thru the boxes to find her clothes. She begins dressing.* MICHIGAN *and* LINDA *observe.*] They said a lot of things about us. Cause of where we lived. You know that swamp. Used to be a river running through there but the river got lost and turned belly up. Went dark and stinky and we called it "home." Said we must be a lot like that lost river. Backed-up. Scum. Living there in that place mutts went to die. Most people don't like mud. That's cause they don't know anything about it. And they said we went to the Dairy Queen any chance we got. Just climbed outta the mud and went down and grabbed a Mister Softee. But not them. Dairy Queen wasn't good enough for them. MacDonald's crowd. And that was just another reason for them to hate us. Us. Me and my mother, talk of the town. And my talk stank worse than their mud. About my mother they said she wasn't a full time woman. That other times she was a mud puppy and a river pussy. That we lived in quick sand and ate outta cans. That she had every single Petula Clark record and had to play them up full every night before she could get to sleep. That she looked right into men's crotches and if she didn't like what she saw she gave them a faceful of her muddy spit. Nasty talk about my mother. But it didn't hurt me none. Because it was all true. Every stinky last word of it, true. And the truth can't hurt you. Not if you're a young girl with mud on the brain. And everywhere this young girl went the talk went too. Most of it about me and the new one. Me, you know my story by looking at me once. And her, that two-bit, small town Pekinese. About her and me being lesbians. And that talk didn't hurt either. I coulda laughed. Lesbians. If it was that simple, that easy. Muff-divers. They didn't know the half of it. [DEELUXE *is fully dressed in her satin strapless gown.* LINDA *begins barking in* MICHIGAN's *lap.*]

MICHIGAN: [*Placing* LINDA *on the floor.*] What is it, Linda? You want to go out? You don't want to go out. I went out once. Five years ago. There's nothing out there. What do you smell? Pussy! No, Linda, no! No more pussy for us. That's just Little Peter. You know him, Little Peter from across the street. He had a nice thing going til he got his hands on that wildcat. No man can handle a wildcat. Nothing cuts as deep as mean pussy.

LITTLE PETER: That's it. We're closed! Scram! Everybody but you sweetheart. [*To* DEELUXE.*] Let me see your face. Hmmm. I like the eyes. Let's see the teeth. Nice. I like the face. But I don't like your song.

DEELUXE: Nobody likes it, that's why it's so good.

LITTLE PETER: Ooooh, honey, you're what's good.

DEELUXE: Deeluxe.

LITTLE PETER: [*Slaps* DEELUXE] Guess again, sweetheart, you don't got a name. You don't need a name. You work for me now. Only name you got to remember is Little Peter. All you got to do is let him love him. Let him touch your hair. How you make your hair do that? The way it comes out of your head like your brain's on fire. [LITTLE PETER's *hand reaches for* DEELUXE, *who flinches.*] What started that fire in you? You can tell your Little Peter.

MICHIGAN: That tiger was getting the best of Little Peter and he didn't even know it. We just called her a tiger cause there weren't words for what she was. Half woman, half something weird. French, maybe. All cat.

LITTLE PETER: You think I want to hurt you? I want to be nice to you. It's you that makes me hurt you. You hurt yourself. Look at me. Not the eyes. At the hands. Don't the hands tell the truth? They want to be nice to you. Think of them as your own hands. Think of me as a part of you. Hmm, there. What's your name now?

DEELUXE: Deeluxe.

LITTLE PETER: Forget it! That part is over. Got it? Put some clothes on. Some, but not too many. And honey. I don't like girls who cry about their mother. Don't sing that song again.

MICHIGAN: Maybe I was as big a sucker as him. Even a dog's got sense to be afraid of cats. One look at her pelt and I went stupid. Maybe I was as big a sucker as him. I knew what a hundred fifty pounds of killer pussy'd do to a man. What I didn't know is what it could do to a woman. [MICHIGAN *crosses to* DEELUXE. *The spirit of* LITTLE PETER *seems to have left her, but* DEELUXE *is wary of* MICHIGAN.] We need more sherry to tide us over.

DEELUXE: You can see into the future, can't you?

MICHIGAN: [*Reaching for the* LITTLE PETER *hand.*] Give me your hand.

DEELUXE: You know how it ends, don't you?

MICHIGAN: I need your hand.

DEELUXE: Why this hand?

MICHIGAN: That one you were born with and this the one you made for yourself. Give.

DEELUXE: It's not mine to give.

MICHIGAN: What?

DEELUXE: It's not MY hand!

MICHIGAN: What could it be then?

DEELUXE: It could be anything. It works against me. I have no feeling in it. And it's not an "it." It's a he. He does what he wants and when he wants. He's an underground river that empties into my heart. I know what my heart is. It's a red whirlpool and I got to watch so I don't fall in. And this hand is proof. Proof I was hit. Heat lightning. My own fault. Storms like trailer parks. I could never stay put when the pressure drops.

MICHIGAN: You look fine. [*Still trying to get the hand.*]

DEELUXE: I'm far from fine. I'm a tree and I been hit bad. Still look like a tree on the outside but on the inside there's just animals and disease and no tree left. [MICHIGAN *is finally able to get* DEELUXE's *hand.*] What's he say?

MICHIGAN: He says your head line and your heart line split early on. He says you have a long life.

DEELUXE: How does it end?

MICHIGAN: It doesn't end really. Your life line runs into veins.

DEELUXE: It's not forever I want!

MICHIGAN: Ok. It ends with you getting us sherry.

DEELUXE: That's not how it ends! It ends with me leaving and never coming back! And then my life will start. You can't stop me! [DEELUXE *crosses to the rack of tuxedos and begins rifling through them as though she were going to get dressed and leave.* MICHIGAN *watches without concern.* DEELUXE *pulls an innocent-looking scarf out of a suit pocket but the scarf is a huge backdrop of a desert scene. At this point, real time stops. That is, time stops moving only forward. The following scene works in two ways: as a flashback (à la Billy Pilgrim in* Slaughterhouse Five: *the characters become unstuck in time), and also as a ritualistic reenactment of a past event.* DEELUXE *begins to loosen her robe, and* DEELUXE *pins up the scarf-backdrop like a sheet hung out to dry. She says, without conviction, as* MICHIGAN *throws over her robe:*] I'm going anyway. [*In unison, the two begin to dress for the ritual.* MICHIGAN *holds up a pair of pink high-heeled cowboy boots as* DEELUXE *removes a pair of rhinestone earrings with fetishistic attentiveness.* DEELUXE *picks up a toothpick while* MICHIGAN *sticks a wad of bubble gum in her mouth. They reach behind the hanging suits to pull out a pair of day-glo hula hoops. As* MICHIGAN *begins to cross downstage center,* DEELUXE *puts on a cowboy hat.*]

MICHIGAN: [*Addressing the audience and slinging her hoop:*] Thirteen years old. Mama called me a woman and slapped me hard and gave me a silver dollar with a Bible verse. "Ask and you shall receive." I put my Bible verse into the candy machine, pull hard, nada. Being good don't buy you sweet things anymore I'm thinking when the foreign car pulls up and snake pops out. A real señor monsieur type a snake: cologne, real leather shoes coiling down the sidewalk. No offer a candy just gives me one hard bits and he's off. Greases back his hair with mother's milk and takes off with those other too handsome kind a guys. Nothing showed on the outside but I was bleeding bad on the inside. Skin goes the color of flophouse sheets. Poison's working on me and all I wanted was some more poison. Mama taught us to feed a fever and I got a hot python squeezing that little girl's heart. All that sugar and spice running down my legs and staining up those spanky pants. My heart was sweating and contagious with that secret dirt and I ripped those panties off and went without underwear. Hoping for an accident and soon. Poison's gotta work itself outta you and the only way outta you is into somebody else. Felt like touching my new wound, but didn't dare. Knew somebody would lose a finger in there and it wasn't gonna be me. Disguised myself with a cross around my neck and a kilt on too. Let that skirt ride up and my bareass rose like a wet moon over the candy store. Snake on down to the mall. Coiling and uncoiling in the dust. Looking for somebody to infect. Poison's gotta work itself out. Staring at all those girls that never got bit. The blonde that would bring out the blonde in me. Take my sweet meat out behind the cheap shoe stores and lay her down the astroturf and make her mine. Carve my initials on the insides a her thigh with my tongue. Gonna give her a little scar to remember me by, gonna match mine. I'm shaking, I'm rattling, baby needs a new way to sing the blues, come on, come on, let's go, snake eyes. [MICHIGAN *drops her hoop. Music up, it's the instrumental theme from* A Man and A Woman. DEELUXE *crosses to center stage moving as much like a cowboy as you can in a strapless gown and heels.* DEELUXE *snaps her hula hoop over to* MICHIGAN *so that it rolls past her, then boomerangs back.* MICHIGAN *catches it. Music fades out as they begin to speak.*]

MICHIGAN: Filler up?

DEELUXE: Just five dollars, thanks.

MICHIGAN: Oil OK? Water? Small engine.

DEELUXE: Checked it this morning in Tulsa.

MICHIGAN: Oh, the big city, huh? And they didn't tell you about me in Tulsa? They didn't tell you this was your last chance?

DEELUXE: Every place on this road says that.

MICHIGAN: Well I am flattered. You know what they say about imitation! Everyone wanting a piece of my action. Maybe they can sucker a few but they can't improve on reality. Believe me, I've tried. I'm the only real thing for fifty miles around, I'm it. I'm the end of the line.

DEELUXE: Ok, keep the change, just give me the keys.

MICHIGAN: Just where you think you going in such an all-fired hurry? California?

DEELUXE: So what?

MICHIGAN: California! Whatcha gonna do in Cala.. ha, ha, fornia?

DEELUXE: Look around.

MICHIGAN: Oh, there's a lot to see out there in California, all right. Mansize mice dancing with movie stars with missile-sized tits. Or is it tit-sized missiles? Two stepping thru the mudslides. No, you sure don't want to miss that. You'll never make it.

DEELUXE: I'm gonna see California.

MICHIGAN: You're gonna see California but you're not leaving this station. Cause I already seen California and I'm gonna show you my shots. I got all the best places. [MICHIGAN *begins to display her tattoos as though they were souvenirs.*]

DEELUXE: Disneyland? Knott's Berry Farm? Universal Studios? Marineland? [DEELUXE's *hand is resting on* MICHIGAN's *crotch.*]

MICHIGAN: Sorry about Marineland. Dropped my camera into the killer whale tank. Didn't dare go in after it. Sharks are terrified of me. Are you ready to see California?

[A Man And A Woman *theme music up.* DEELUXE *takes out her toothpick as* MICHIGAN *spits her gum out into her hand. They kiss. After the kiss, they replace the toothpick and gum. Music fades as they begin to speak.*]

DEELUXE: So that's California, huh?

MICHIGAN: Yeah.

DEELUXE: So we should do something.

MICHIGAN: So.

DEELUXE: Why stay here?

MICHIGAN: So what and just because.

DEELUXE: That's what I thought.

MICHIGAN: So what if I got no friends and no money. There's no snakes here. I could go someplace and get friends and money but then I might get snakes. Besides, my nothing is better than your something.

DEELUXE: Well, I was just thinking...

MICHIGAN: Don't start. Just shut up and be happy. [*She picks up her hula hoop and begins to rattle it.*]

DEELUXE: What's that?

MICHIGAN: A snake.

DEELUXE: You promised no snakes! [MICHIGAN *slips the hoop over* DEELUXE's *head.*]

MICHIGAN: Quick!

DEELUXE: What?

MICHIGAN: Here!

DEELUXE: How?

MICHIGAN: Suck! [*They kiss. The hoop drops.*] I'm beginning to like this desert air. So refreshing. [*Pause*] You spit it out didn't you?

DEELUXE: What?

MICHIGAN: The poison.

DEELUXE: What poison?

MICHIGAN: My poison. You spit it out?

DEELUXE: I swallowed it. [MICHIGAN *crosses upstage, begins folding up the backdrop.* DEELUXE *faces the audience.*]

DEELUXE: She's got a bad heart. The kind you die from. Runs in the family. I gotta bad heart too. Just not the kind you die from. The kind that makes you wear too much eye make-up. She's my cousin, come up from one of those sweaty states. She wouldn't sweat in a forest fire. Ice wouldn't melt in her mouth. I make a little bet with myself. I can make her sweat. The first time I know for sure I got heart problems is when my cousin came to visit. Heat spell. Bad heart and bad heat spell couldn't keep my cousin from pitching pop-ups in the garden. Takes everything she has and makes it into a ball. Something in me follows that ball up, and it hangs in the air a moment seems like forever then into the dirt. I can't throw, can't make a fist. She can throw and stay cool. She's a little bit Catholic. So yellow her hair it hurts my teeth. I sneak her weenies on Friday and I don't tell on her forbidden patent leathers hoping they'll reflect up to that place she's got muscles girls don't, got heart places boys don't. Don't want to do nothing about it yet, still that bad heart of mine wanna bite. She's still not sweating but I get to sleep with her because there's not enough beds. I iron my father's shorts and bleach his stains to send her roses. Downstairs with her, the fake wood, the pump straining to keep us from going under. The earth sweating through the fake wood. Lip synching to 45s. I got the aspirins she got the cokes waiting for it to happen. And the sweat is all over us now, hers and mine together tasting like a memory of a place I never been. Waiting for it to happen, for one heart to give out, for the rattler to strike. [LITTLE PETER *begins to invade* DEELUXE. *Her hand begins twitching and finally, singing.*]

LITTLE PETER: She may be weary,

> Women do get weary,
> Wearing the same shabby dress
> And when she's weary
> Try a little tenderness.

[*To* DEELUXE] Yeah, go on and try it sucker, see what it'll get you.

DEELUXE: I can do it.

LITTLE PETER: We aren't talking about an "it" here to do. We are talking skirt, a woman, a Jane.

DEELUXE: So?

LITTLE PETER: So you don't do a woman. You handle her.

DEELUXE: Like you used to handle me, huh.

LITTLE PETER: Correction, carrot brain, like I did, do and will handle you.

DEELUXE: Stay outta this.

LITTLE PETER: I'll sit out this foxtrot, but I'll be around. [DEELUXE *crosses to* MICHIGAN *and takes off her hat.*]

DEELUXE: I'm back. I'm sorry.

MICHIGAN: No you're not.

DEELUXE: I know you said you wanted to be alone.

MICHIGAN: Did I?

DEELUXE: You said I shouldn't see you again. [MICHIGAN *starts laughing.*] What's so funny?

MICHIGAN: You should laugh. Be happy. I thought tall people laughed a lot.

DEELUXE: What about?

MICHIGAN: About me being such a liar. I didn't want to be alone. Did you want me to be alone.

DEELUXE: No.

MICHIGAN: And wouldcha leave me alone?

DEELUXE: No.

MICHIGAN: Until?

DEELUXE: No until. I won't leave.

MICHIGAN: Period?

DEELUXE: Period.

MICHIGAN: Wouldcha leave if I asked you to go?

DEELUXE: I would try.

MICHIGAN: You would.

DEELUXE: If you asked.

MICHIGAN: Oh.

DEELUXE: But I couldn't leave.

MICHIGAN: Well if you can't leave then I guess you can stay. [MICHIGAN *starts laughing.*]

DEELUXE: This time it's really not funny.

MICHIGAN: Show me. Make me stop laughing if you don't like it.

DEELUXE: [*Addressing her* LITTLE PETER *hand:*] Help me. I don't know what to do.

LITTLE PETER: [*Singing:*] You won't regret it,

>Women don't forget it,

>Love is their whole happiness.

Aren't you glad I stuck around. Ok, now let's try a little tenderness. [DEELUXE *displays an invisible key to* MICHIGAN. *Then she mimes locking the door with it and swallowing the key. It as though her entire body has been taken over by* LITTLE PETER.] Did you see what I did with that key?

MICHIGAN: So what?

LITTLE PETER: That's what I'm going to do to you.

MICHIGAN: Huh.

LITTLE PETER: I'm gonna swallow you whole. There's a part of you nobody sees. A part I know is there. Like I know that white stuff is in the middle of those black cookies. But you gotta twist open the whole rotten thing to get to it. [*He/She begins caressing* MICHIGAN *more fiercely than tenderly.*] That's what I'm gonna do to you. It's your secret now but I'm going to know it too. Make your cream the glue between us. No matter what it costs me. Or you. [*He/She yanks* MICHIGAN *to her feet.* LITTLE PETER *addresses* DEELUXE:] Ok, killer, you're on your own.

MICHIGAN: Aren't you afraid?

DEELUXE: No.

MICHIGAN: You should be. You're lucky you're so dumb.

DEELUXE: You're afraid.

MICHIGAN: Me? Of what. I'm the scariest thing going.

DEELUXE: There's something even worse.

MICHIGAN: Yeah?

DEELUXE: The cold.

MICHIGAN: What's that? I ain't been cold a day in my life. You afraid?

DEELUXE: Yes. I got no feeling anywhere.

MICHIGAN: So.

DEELUXE: So I could die and not even notice it.

>*French doors blow open. Howling wind is heard.*

MICHIGAN: Shut it!

DEELUXE: You shut it.

MICHIGAN: You're closer.

DEELUXE: Closer to what?

MICHIGAN: The window.

DEELUXE: I wasn't talking about the window! [MICHIGAN *closes the window. Howling stops.*] I thought you were hot enough for both of us. I guess I was wrong.

MICHIGAN: I got the heat sweetheart, I just don't give it away. [MICHIGAN *pulls a long black flashlight out of a suitcoat pocket.*]

DEELUXE: What's that for?

MICHIGAN: Stars.

DEELUXE: It's aimed down at the street. That's a funny place to look for stars. There's no stars on this part of Second Avenue. Just three bums pissing on a futon. Hey! You can see right into my bedroom! You been looking at me!

MICHIGAN: No.

DEELUXE: Yes you have. This is proof.

MICHIGAN: I been more than looking. I been watching. That's looking with a reason.

DEELUXE: What's the reason?

MICHIGAN: Cause you're my kind of star.

DEELUXE: What's that?

MICHIGAN: A falling star. Wanna see one? It's a nice night for viewing. Rare to see so many binaries.

DEELUXE: Binaries?

MICHIGAN: Doubles. A pair of stars so close they cannot escape each other.

DEELUXE: Close as sisters?

MICHIGAN: Closer. Like twins.

DEELUXE: How come they stay together?

MICHIGAN: Gravity.

DEELUXE: I don't see anything like that.

MICHIGAN: And the closer they get the worse it gets.

DEELUXE: What?

MICHIGAN: The pull. And then it's...kaboom. But there's that moment right before the end when they're the brightest thing on Second Avenue. Just a big red nova.

DEELUXE: I hadda one of those once. Not fancy but a good car.

MICHIGAN: Course, even the brightest star can get stuck with a black hole.

DEELUXE: What's that?

MICHIGAN: Something so dense you can't imagine it. You wait and wait and the big bang you counted on never comes.

DEELUXE: Is that what makes a star fall?

MICHIGAN: Almost anything can make a star fall. Here's one now, about to fall. [MICHIGAN *directs* DEELUXE's *flashlight so it shines on herself. Throughout the following monologue,* MICHIGAN *strikes different peep poses while* DEELUXE *observes her as attentively but asexually as a nerd looking at an ant farm.*]

DEELUXE: I see it. Looks familiar. Looks like me. That was the year I was living alone in Bad Axe. Just wouldn't move in with him. "What's the difference" he'd say. Then he'd go off and leave me trying whether to decide whether to be a lesbian today or put it off til tomorrow. And then I'd put on plastic nurse's shoes. Wait on tables. Getting tips in Bible verses. People with one eye ate at this place a lot. I guess it was just about the favorite place of one-eyed people to eat. Down at the mall. Not even a real mall, fucking shopping center. One day I get up with him and alla sudden I'm falling. And I tried to break my fall by reaching out for him. But it didn't come out that way. I socked him once, twice in the jaw and kept falling. Falling into the Chevy with the bad plates with a cat and a raincoat. I don't know what started it and what I'm falling into.

MICHIGAN: [*Directing the flashlight so it shines on her breasts:*] Probably the moon.

DEELUXE: I dunno. Is the moon that strong?

MICHIGAN: Take a look and see.

DEELUXE: Wow. Get a load of that moon. She's so full. There's two moons and they're both full.

MICHIGAN: Don't tell me she's not strong enough to pull you off course. [MICHIGAN *takes the flashlight out of* DEELUXE's *hands.*]

DEELUXE: What's going on here?

MICHIGAN: I got nothing to hide. [MICHIGAN *grabs* DEELUXE's *bodice.*] What about you?

DEELUXE: Don't get me naked. I get so Italian when I'm naked.

MICHIGAN: Thought you wanted that secret. Wanna touch it? Touch me the way you touch him.

DEELUXE: I don't!

MICHIGAN: Don't lie. Just tell me you love me.

DEELUXE: I can't say that.

MICHIGAN: [MICHIGAN *wraps* DEELUXE *in the strand of pearls.*] There does that make it any easier? [*The two are bound together and begin a slow circle dance.*] Soon as they start to shine they start to change. The center contracts. Pressure at the center rises. And the center can't hold up. [DEELUXE *backs away. The pearls break.* DEELUXE *and* MICHIGAN *face each other for a long beat. Then* DEELUXE *turns away.* MICHIGAN *sinks to the floor and begins picking the pearls up.*] You take care of something, it grows. You can see I got the knack. Too big? Is there such a thing as "too big?" Besides it's just the way I am. Too damned juicy for my own good. With you around gets wicked. One look at you and my pink pulp starts pounding. [DEELUXE *begins to unzip her gown.*] Wanna know something. They're gonna get bigger. That pink is gonna go all the way into red. Then you watch out. My sap's running from the heat of your eyes. That special blue heat outta the eyes gets the pink ocean stirred up. That's when you squeeze them. Put the muscle on those peaches til my bucks are bucking like I'm riding an invisible palomino. [DEELUXE *is in her underwear, black tap pants and a corset. She reaches out for* MICHIGAN. *Pause.*] Well, I dunno, I might let you. These peaches getting mighty tight. But I gotta decide. What you ever done for me except make me cry? Right now I'm sobbing bad. Just look, I'm crying for you. You look hungry. Come on get it, squeeze it outta me, suck it outta me. I wanna be totally Spain when you're done with me. [MICHIGAN *begins to put on a filmy peignoir as she sings the following song. Her actions are as flirtatious as if she were stripping.* MICHIGAN *sings:*]

Bugs are bitin'
Fish are jumpin'
When my baby starts a humpin' me.
Hot cross buns
Always beg for jam
Every beaver
Needs a beaver dam
Taste of fish
Taste of chicken
Don't taste like the girl I'm lickin'
She puts the cunt back in country
Pulls the rug out from under me
In case you are wondering
She can put what she wants in me.
Hot sweet cream
Dripping from my pet
How I scream
When she gets me wet
With her finger
On my sugar plum
There she lingers
Til I start to cum
Cause she puts the cunt back in country
Pulls the rug out from under me
In case you are wondering
She can put what she wants in me.

DEELUXE *is tired of the tease. She dons a black tuxedo jacket. It's a magician's jacket: there's scarves, paper flowers, etc. in the pockets. During the following monologue,* DEELUXE *fumbles with the jacket and the objects seem to fly her pockets.* DEELUXE *is facing the audience.*

DEELUXE: Alotta people ask me: what about Ohio? and I have to tell them what I know. Because I'm part buckeye. Not that you would know. That's why I never take all my clothes off all at the same time so you can never see the Ohio in me. But I haven't forgotten about Toledo and I won't. The very mention of the word "Toledo" makes me wanna puke. Toledo used to belong to us. We went to war to save it. People always ask: "Why'd you bother to have a war in Toledo? Aren't the winters there war enough?" Things got pretty bad between me and Toledo and a pig was killed. The government came in like they always do but the fighting went on when no one was looking. They took away Toledo. Gave us this little chunk of perpetual January that used to belong to Minnesota. Don't even get me started about Minnesota. When everybody else is dead I'm going to get a nice slab of Ohio. Right now it's my Uncle Bert's asparagus patch. I hate asparagus. I'm afraid of it. Especially at night when the stalks look like dead people from Toledo giving you the finger. We'd take these trips to visit the land. Going as fast we could, pretending to be going someplace else. I guess that's the only way to live through a trip to Ohio: pretend to be going someplace else. And keep the windows rolled up tight. Ohio air can make you dizzy if you're not used to it. Remember: in the winters here they set the rivers on fire. We get to the land and they break out the asparagus and put on the ham. Aunt Helen is fat and she waits on the skinny people. We do things that way in Ohio: the fat people wait on the skinny ones. Course everyone in my family is fat. Except for Bert. But then he's not one of us. The only reason they let him stay in Ohio is he porked Aunt Helen back in that freak thaw last leap year. After dinner Bert helps Helen up the stairs. I do the dishes and they do it. When a three hundred and fifty pound woman has sex in a wood frame house in Ohio, you know about it. Bert liked to get her right after the ham when she still had mayonnaise on her arms. Helen died before Bert learned what to do about asparagus. He just went out back and lay down in the mud. Face down. We left him that way. Very polite. And then I read in this magazine about this man that loves mud. Loves it better than he loves his dead wife. "Mud is better than any woman. You don't have to wait til after dinner. And it's romantic. After a rain. During a sunset. You just find a place and stick it in." And the letter was signed. Bert from Ohio. And that's Ohio. [MICHIGAN *crosses to the stereo and puts on a record—"Temptation" by Perry Como. They do a tango which ends with* MICHIGAN *dipping* DEELUXE. *Suddenly,* LITTLE PETER *appears and begins talking to* DEELUXE. MICHIGAN *watches the dialog like someone watches a seizure or a crazy on the* IRT.]

LITTLE PETER: We gotta talk.

DEELUXE: Leave me alone.

LITTLE PETER: Alone, who's alone? You're not alone. You probably couldn't even spell it. Always had me on your side. Don't sleep alone. Don't take a shit alone. Little Peter holds your hand. I seen alone and it's not for you. Maybe I know the wrong kind of alone. You wanna be alone all right, alone with her.

DEELUXE: [*To* MICHIGAN] Would you like some more sherry? [MICHIGAN *shakes her head no.*]

LITTLE PETER: Why don't you ask her if she wants to be alone with you? Maybe she'd like a chaperone. Go ahead, ask her.

DEELUXE: I'm not going to ask her.

LITTLE PETER: Maybe she'd like me better, huh?

DEELUXE: She won't like you. She can't see you.

LITTLE PETER: She can see me. You're the one who can't see me.

DEELUXE: We're over. I'm not talking to you anymore.

LITTLE PETER: What?

DEELUXE: I said I'm not talking to you anymore. You're not real.

LITTLE PETER: You're doing it sister. Not real. What kinda thing is that to say to a friend? Hey, if I'm not real what does that make you?

DEELUXE: Keep your hands off me.

LITTLE PETER: Deeluxe, please!

DEELUXE: One minute. Just one. But don't go touching me. [*To* MICHIGAN.] There's this guy I know, um outside. He's outside. That's why you can't see him. I gotta go give him some money. I'll be right back. [DEELUXE *crosses to the stage right window and pulls down the shade. The area is backlit so her shadow appears. The* LITTLE PETER *hand comes out from behind the shade.* DEELUXE'S *hand follows, grabs* LITTLE PETER *and "strangles" him. After the* LITTLE PETER *hand is limp,* DEELUXE *crosses to* MICHIGAN.] You got to show them. They never believe you til you show them.

MICHIGAN: Is he gone?

DEELUXE: He's gone. Don't think about him. [Pause.] What you looking at?

MICHIGAN: You.

DEELUXE: Quit it.

MICHIGAN: You quit it.

DEELUXE: Me? What am I doing? It's not coming from me. I heard about you. What you do to women, what you make other women do. I'm not going to let you do that to me. I'm going to open the window and cry for help. I'm going to get the National Guard, the Marines, the New York Times, the Weight Watchers. I'm going to tell the world that evil is alive and well and living on Second Avenue. I'm going to.... [*French windows blow open. Sound of howling wind.* MICHIGAN *stands up and crosses stage left. She puts on a fox fur stole. It's a larger more gory version of the type with the heads clipping onto the tails.*]

MICHIGAN: Tell me again. What are you going to do? That's what I thought you were going to do. Nothing! And what did you say you thought I was? Tell me.

DEELUXE: You. You're an animal.

MICHIGAN: And what do you think you are? A fucking zucchini?

DEELUXE: Stop. Why don't you stop?

MICHIGAN: Because you don't want me to stop.

DEELUXE: I could make you.

MICHIGAN: Go ahead. Make me.

DEELUXE: Cross this line.

MICHIGAN: I already crossed that line a long time ago. And this line. Go on honey. Do it to me. Do it to me before I cross this line too.

DEELUXE: That's enough.

MICHIGAN: Sure it is. When you're really good you don't have to touch. She walks in the room and you don't touch. You don't even talk. But you feel her on every inch of your body like a suit of clothes you put on and can't take off. Feels like silk. But tight. Like a silk straight jacket. You're in deep and getting deeper. It's like being buried alive. And you like it.

DEELUXE: I won't... [DEELUXE *attempts to exit, but* MICHIGAN *grabs her breast.*]

MICHIGAN: There's nothing you won't do. This is what you wanted all along and no one has to know. It'll be our secret.

DEELUXE: What will?

MICHIGAN: Our secret will be what makes you tick. [DEELUXE's *bodice rips. Pearls and magic flowers explode out of it as she breaks away from* MICHIGAN.]

DEELUXE:

> I was never right
> Look into my eyes
> See the trouble
> See the fire under water
> See my brain's too big
> See my heart's too small
> I gotta pump it that's why I gotta pump it.
> I tried to make my heart move another way
> But the blood's too thin
> Like the see-thru blouse
> Momma puts on when Daddy leaves the house.
> My body's too fat like Crisco in the pan
> It smokes it steams it cries out for meat.
> There's no other way your ham sure hits my spot
> and if that don't grease the clock
> You gotta pump it.
> I call my private Jesus on the pay telephone
> Down on my knees in a booth filled with piss
> Asking the King O' Love wontcha please
> Strike me dead.
> I can't live a life with a head too big
> I can't get a laugh with a shrunken love pump
> My too big head's filled with a too bad thought
> It stinks it bites it goes straight to the brain
> Till I pump it.
> It's not just bad
> It's more than bad it's wrong
> In the wrong place
> My heart got stuck between my legs
> You wouldn't think I wouldn't think
> Such a tiny thing could put the muzzle on the brain
> On those full moon nights the way it beats so bad
> No top forty drum machine
> More a solo with a shake
> I gotta bad heart but I'm a nice girl, girl.
> I'm not a girl at all, I'm more like a car.

A nice new car with steel where it counts
I'm a nice new car, why don't you thumb me down.
I'll let you take the wheel
A woman with a bad heart gets lonely when she drives herself insane
Take the wheel and I'll let you bite my ham.
Turn the key over quick, put your boot to the floor
If you don't get the power first
Gotta pump it.

MICHIGAN: I'm getting out of here!

DEELUXE: I'm dying you can't do that! Rip somebody's heart out and leave them to die!

MICHIGAN: I do it all the time.

DEELUXE: Then it's true!

MICHIGAN: Yes, it's true, let me go!

DEELUXE: If you go I'll die.

MICHIGAN: If I stay you'll be worse than dead. You'll be like me.

DEELUXE: What are you? [DEELUXE *collapses.*]

MICHIGAN: There's a word for it in Michigan. From the early days of Michigan. Before Michigan was Motown, or Ford four-doors, or Gerald Ford or Chevy hatchbacks and before the soybeans, sweet cherries and mintfields went in. Before they started burning the sugar beets and soaking the kirbies in barrels of brine. Before they opened the Keewanah for copper pennies. Before all that when all Michigan was, was cold. Mooneye, steelhead, alewife, all of that. A coupla shriveled spits of land shivering in glacial puddles that'd lost their salt, that's what Michigan was. All she grew was protection from the cold. Beaver protection, and weasel, fisher, marten, mink, red fox, grey fox, catamount, muskrat, lynx and bobcat too. Fur. Pelts. And all of a sudden, Michigan was full of Frenchmen. They set their trap lines out on the ice. Along the Manistee, the AuSable. But the animals they caught didn't die right away, they lay out on the ice freezing and snarling and bleeding until the stars, most of them, fled to Canada. And Orion bent down out the January sky and put a silver bullet in their brain. Silver in the brain, they changed. Became monsters out on that ice. Until the Frenchmen came back and the monsters became hats. Fancy hats and pocketbooks. But there was something else out there. Another sort of animal. Or a woman. They always called her a "she." She came along the traplines before the Frenchmen. She ripped open the steel and tossed it into the Tittabawassee. She set free the monsters. Whatever she was, she had a mean head on her shoulders shaped like a wedge of Pinconning extra sharp cheddar cheese gone bad and a fat ass. She was always about fifty six years old. And the monsters crashed through the split-level pre-fab houses of the Frenchmen and fucked their wives and got them full of baby monsters. They don't say this anymore in Michigan. No one knows what happened to the woman who set the monsters free. The woman who was an animal. Loup Garou. They said that women were monsters. Because they had teeth in their parts. And now they say we're not like that. We're not dangerous anymore. But it's a lie. We are monsters. We got teeth in our parts and we're so hungry. If you stay here, I'll eat you alive. Do you understand? Do you still want to be like me? [MICHIGAN *turns upstage and crosses to hang up fur. While she is still turned upstage,* DEELUXE *slowly sits up*] Why did you come back?

DEELUXE: I live here.

MICHIGAN: Lived here. I liked it when you were dead because I got to do all the things I always wanted to but you kept me from doing.

DEELUXE: Like what?

MICHIGAN: Redecorate.

DEELUXE: It's not the same.

MICHIGAN: It's not the same. [DEELUXE *moves toward* MICHIGAN *who is seated.*] This is my chair.

DEELUXE: [*Sitting down in her chair.*] I only been gone five minutes. [*A blue airmail letter falls out of the skylight.* MICHIGAN *rushes to pick it up, then hands it to* DEELUXE]

MICHIGAN: It's for you.

DEELUXE: [*Reading from the letter.*] "Dear Deeluxe: You asked about the future. Here's the deal: it's gonna be just like the past. In the past the heart of the world was filled with carbon and water and that is why we had life on earth. When everything got heavier the world started collapsing in on itself, an old heart in a fat body. Aunt Helen collapsing in Cleveland. After the baby was born. The one who couldn't talk. Or get up to go to the bathroom by herself. The one whose being born killed Helen's only daughter. And Aunt Helen, she just collapsed. Carbon and water into diamonds. And in the future, women will replace the world. In a woman's heart there is rice and water and that is why there is life on earth. But in the future, women will start collapsing in a world thick with babies who can't talk and only daughters who live alone on Oreos. And rice and water will be crushed into tears. But no one will cry. The tears will stay inside. They will be the hardest things known to man. Women's tears will be used. In the future, women's tears will put a man on the moon. And in the future, all the men who kill for a living will wear pinky rings with women's tears. Love always. Little Peter." [*Pause.*] So that's the future, huh.

MICHIGAN: [*Pouring sherry for a toast.*] Don't worry. We'll never see it. [MICHIGAN *starts to raise her glass to* DEELUXE'*s, but the upstage window shade flies up. There is a hand in the window with a pinky ring.* DEELUXE *and* MICHIGAN *continue staring at the hand as the lights fade down and out.*]

Maria Irene Fornes

Abingdon Square

ABOUT THE PLAY

An earlier version of *Abingdon Square* was given a workshop production at Seattle Repertory Theatre in 1984. Following a staged reading at New York's American Place Theatre in April, *Abingdon Square* opened there on October 8, 1987, produced by the Women's Project and Productions Inc. and directed by the author. The text published here is a revision completed by the author in December 1987.

CHARACTERS

MARION, *from age 15 to 24.*
JUSTER, MARION's *husband, from age 50 to 59.*
MICHAEL, JUSTER's *son, the same age as Marion.*
FRANK, MARION's *lover, one year older than* MARION.
MARY, MARION's *cousin, the same age as* MARION.
MINNIE, MARION's *great-aunt, from age 58 to 67.*
THE GLAZIER, *a very strong tender man.*
THOMAS, MARION's *son, eight months old.*

TIME AND PLACE

Act One: 1908–1912. In a house on 10th Street, New York City.
Act Two: 1915–1917. In the house on 10th Street, Mary's place, an apartment on Abingdon Square, a beer parlor, and Minnie's house.

SETTINGS

The living room of a house on 10th Street. To the right is a double door which leads to the foyer and the main door. On the back wall there are two large French doors. On the right there are double doors that lead to other rooms. Up center, a few feet from the back wall are a sofa and two armchairs. On each side of the sofa there is a tall stand with a vase. Down left there are a chess table and two side chairs; down right there is a small desk. There is a chair on the upstage side of the desk and another on the right side. During intermission a telephone is placed on the desk.

The attic room or closet. A platform about two feet high on the left side of the stage. On the back wall there is a small door.

MARY's *living room. An embroidered shawl is placed on the sofa.*

The living room of an apartment on Abingdon Square. A back wall is placed behind the sofa. On the wall there is a fireplace; above the fireplace there is a large mirror.

The beer parlor. A square plain wood table and two chairs in a pool of red light, center stage.

MINNIE's *living room. A chair center stage in a pool of light.*

JUSTER's *bedroom. A platform about two feet high on the right side of the stage. On the back wall there is a small door. Parallel to the back wall there is a narrow bed.*

ACT ONE

SCENE 1: *10th Street. August, 1908. It is dusk.* JUSTER *sits in the garden facing up left. He sings Handel's "Where'er You Walk."* MARION *hides between the two windows and listens.*

JUSTER: [*Singing*] Where'er you walk,
  Cool gales shall fan the glades.
    She moves to the left window and looks at him.
  Trees, where you sit
  Shall crowd into a shade. Trees, where you sit,
  Shall crowd into a shade.
MARION: Pst!
    JUSTER *leans over to see who has called.* MARION *moves her hand towards him.*

SCENE 2: *Two weeks later. It is a sunny afternoon.* MARION *enters running from the left.* MICHAEL *is chasing her. They run around the room laughing and screaming. He grabs her and takes a piece of chocolate from her hand. He unwraps the chocolate and puts it in his mouth. She chases him. She grabs him and they fall. He covers his mouth. She tries to pull his hand away.*

MARION: Give it to me.
    He swallows the chocolate, lets her remove his hand, and opens his mouth.
MICHAEL: It's gone. I swallowed it.
MARION: You're bad! [*She holds him tightly*] l love you Mike! I love you.
    He holds her.
MICHAEL: Me too! I love you too!
MARION: I don't love you as a mother does, though. I love you as a sister loves a
  brother. I must be a mother to you. You should have a mother. You need a mother.
  How could a boy like you grow up without a mother.
MICHAEL: I'd rather have you. You're more to me than any mother could ever be.
  You're my sister, my daughter, my cousin, my friend. You are my friend! My grand-
  mother!
MARION: You're joking and I'm serious.
MICHAEL: I'm serious. You are to me the best person I'll ever know.
MARION: [*Standing*] You need a guide, a teacher in life.
MICHAEL: I don't need a guide. I need a friend.
MARION: You need someone who'll tell you what to do.
MICHAEL: I don't. I'm doing fine. I'm a good boy. A mother would say to me, "You're

doing fine m'boy. You give me no trouble and you don't need a mother." When I need help I'll go to you and you'll help me.

>   *As the following speech progresses* M A R I O N *speaks rapidly as if in an emotional trance.*

M A R I O N: You're sweet. You are the sweetest creature on earth. I wish I were sweet like you. I wish I had sweetness in my heart the way you do. Soon I will, officially, be your mother, and I say this in earnest, I hope I can make myself worthy of both you and your father. He brought solace to me when I knew nothing but grief. I experienced joy only when he was with me. His kindness brought me back to life. I am grateful to him and l love him. l would have died had he not come to save me. I love him more than my own life and I owe it to him. And I love you because you are his son, and you have a sweetness the same as his. I hope I can make myself worthy of the love you have both bestowed upon me and I hope to be worthy of the honor of being asked to be one of this household which is blessed—with a noble and pure spirit. I'm honored to be invited to share this with you and I hope that I succeed in being as noble of spirit as those who invite me to share it with them. I know I sound very formal, and that my words seem studied. But there is no other way I can express what I feel. In this house light comes through the windows as if it delights in entering. I feel the same. I delight in entering here. I delight in walking through these rooms and I'm sad when I leave. I cannot wait for the day when my eyes open from a night's sleep and I find a myself inside these walls. Being here I feel as if I'm blessed. If life dealt me a cruel blow when my parents died, now it offers me the kindest reward. I hope I never give either of you cause for regret. I hope you, as well as he, will always tell me if I have done something wrong—or I have done less than what you expect, or if you have any reason for disappointment. Would you promise me you will?

M I C H A E L: I promise.

>   S C E N E 3: *A few minutes later.* M I N N I E *and* J U S T E R *are entering from the foyer.* M A R I O N *stands left.*

M I N N I E: [*As she goes to sit, to* M A R I O N] Sit down, dear.

>   M I N N I E *sits right.* J U S T E R *sits left.* M A R I O N *sits on the sofa.*

M I N N I E: I was just talking to Juster about the question of your obligations. The questions you posed to me, and whether you will continue your studies, or what obligations you will have. And we thought you should ask the questions directly to him. He doesn't seem to know the answer. Go ahead dear.

M A R I O N: I wanted to know about my obligations here. I believe that when one marries one has obligations and I asked Aunt Minnie what those obligations would be. And she said she was not sure. But that she thought maybe I will be running the house. Is that so? And I told her that I have never run a house and I don't know if it's something I could learn to do. I told her that I should tell you that I have never run a house. It may be that you don't feel I am suited to do it.

J U S T E R: I'm embarrassed to say that I have no idea how to run the house. When I was born my mother ran the house. Then, when I married my wife Martha ran it. Then, when she became ill, Jenny, our housekeeper, took over the running of the house. And when my wife Martha died, Jenny continued running the house till now. I never did.

MARION: And what does running a house consist of?

JUSTER: I don't know, Marion. Minnie, don't you know?

MINNIE: Yes, I do. I run my own house, Juster. But I don't know if you run your house the same way I run mine.

JUSTER: You should talk to Jenny, Marion, and decide what it is you want to do.

MARION: Thank you, I will. Will my cousin Mary continue giving me instructions? I would like to know if that is something I will continue doing.

JUSTER: Indeed Marion, nothing in your life should change unless you want it to.

MARION: Because of all the years I was not able to go to school I feel I don't yet comprehend a great many things.

SCENE 4: *Two months later October, 1908. It is dusk.* JUSTER *stands center left.* MICHAEL *stands up left.* MARY *stands up right.* MARION *and* MINNIE *embrace center.* MARION *holds a white veil and a missal.* MINNIE *sobs.*

MARION: My dear aunt. I am happy. Believe me, I am happy. I will be very happy.

　　MINNIE *sobs.* MARION *holds her. A few seconds pass.*

MARION: Don't cry, my dear.

　　MINNIE *sobs.* MARION *holds her. A few seconds pass.*

MARION: My dear aunt, don't cry.

　　MINNIE *goes on sobbing.* MARION *releases her slowly and takes a step away from her,* MARION *lowers her head.* MARY *puts her arm around* MINNIE *and exits with her.* MINNIE *mumbles and cries while she exits.*

MARION: Why is she so unhappy?

JUSTER: Weddings make people cry, Marion.

　　MARION *looks at him.* JUSTER *takes her hand and brings it to his lips. She kisses his cheek.*

SCENE 5: *Six months later. April, 1909. It is late afternoon.* MARION *sits at the desk. She writes in a notebook. There is an open textbook in front of her.* MARY *sits left. They speak in a conspiratorial manner.*

MARY: That's what I heard.

MARION: Who told you!

MARY: My cousin. He knows his family—and him. He also knows him. The man is married. And the wife's sister came to visit. She lives in New Paltz and her sister, the wife is also from New Paltz. They're both from New Paltz. Her sister—the sister of the wife—came to visit and she stayed for months. The three of them slept together. Together in the same bed. The man and the wife and the wife's sister slept together in the same bed.

MARION: The three of them?

MARY: Yes! The three of them in the same bed.

MARION: Why did they do that?

MARY: To make love!

MARION: How?

MARY: I don't know. I imagine he first makes love to one and then the other.
    Both squeal, terrified and thrilled.

MARION: That's perverse!

MARY: It is! That's why I'm telling you.

MARION: It's horrendous!

MARY: I know.

MARION: How did you find out?

MARY: He told me.

MARION: He!

MARY: My cousin.

MARION: How did he know?

MARY: Everyone knows.

MARION: How?

MARY: Noises in the bedroom. The servant heard them.

MARION: It couldn't be true.

MARY: Oh yes, if you see them you would know.

MARION: How?

MARY: The way they behave.

MARION: How?

MARY: Sinister, Marion, and sexual.

MARION: The wife is not jealous?

MARY: No.

MARION: And the sister is not jealous?

MARY: No.

MARION: He's with both of them?

MARY: Yes!

MARION: In the street?

MARY: Yes. He looks at one and then the other—passionately.

MARION: He's shameless.

MARY: They all are.

MARION: It's he who does it.

MARY: Not only he. They also look at him.

MARION: With passion?

MARY: Yes.

MARION: In front of the other?

MARY: They don't mind.

MARION: They don't?

MARY: Apparently not.

MARION: The wife's to blame then.

MARY: Yes, it's her fault, not his.

MARION: It's his fault, too.

MARY: The sister is pretty. Who can blame him?

MARION: Is she?

MARY: She's lovely. If she lets him—what is he to do?

MARION: He can say no.

MARY: If the wife doesn't mind why should he?

MARION: Because it's sinful. It's a sin. He's sinning. He will go to hell. God won't forgive him. It's his soul. He is responsible for his own soul. He can't just say, "They don't mind." He should mind. It is his own soul he has to think of. He'll go to hell.

MARY: I know. They'll all go to hell.

MARION: And so will we.

MARY: Why!

MARION: For talking about it!

MARY: No, we won't!

MARION: Yes! We will! We must do penance!

MARY: We didn't do anything!

MARION: Yes, we did!

MARY: What!

MARION: We talked about it and we thought about it.

MARY: Did you!

MARION: I did, Mary! I thought about it. I imagined it! I did!

MARY: Marion, how could you?

MARION: Didn't you?

MARY: No!

MARION: Oh, God! I've sinned!

MARY: Oh, Marion! Repent.

MARION: I repent! Oh God! I repent! Oh God! How could I? Oh God! [*She falls on her knees. She is out of breath*] Oh, God! Forgive me! [*She begins to calm down*]

MARY: What did you think?

MARION: I imagined them in bed.

MARY: What did you imagine?

MARION: I can't tell you.

MARY: What?

MARION: He makes love to one while the other is there, very close. She looks and she listens. She watches their bodies move. She's very close.

MARY: How close?

MARION: Touching. She must.

MARY: That's just awful.

MARION: She must.

MARY: Oh. Marion. And then?

MARION: He kisses her too.

MARY: No!

MARION: He holds them both. And knows them both.

    MARY *gasps.*

MARY: Oh, Marion. [*She goes on her knees*] Now I have sinned too. Will God forgive us? *They embrace.*

    SCENE 6: *One month later. May, 1909. It is evening.* JUSTER *sits up left reading.* MICHAEL *sits cross-legged on the floor in front of the sofa. He reads a book.* MARION *sits at the desk. She writes in a diary.*

JUSTER: [*Reading**]: If you wish to see it for yourself, take a pencil and push the pointed end into the open mouth of the flower and downward toward the ovary and the honey, just as a bee would thrust in its tongue. If it is a young flower you have chosen you will see the two anthers bend down as if they knew what they were doing, and touch the pencil about two inches from the point leaving a smudge of golden pollen on it. A day later, the stigma will have lengthened and, if you would, then push your pencil in again. You will find that it now hangs far enough to touch the pencil in the same place where the pollen was laid, while the empty anthers have shriveled. Thus on its first day of opening the anthers rub their pollen on the back of visiting bees; and on the next the stigma hangs down far enough to receive pollen from a younger flower. If you wish to see the mechanism by which the anthers are bent down, cut away the hood until you lay bare the stamens as far as the point where they are joined to the corolla. Here you will notice that they have slender white flying buttresses that keep them in place. Just in front, standing out into the passageway down the tube of the flower, are two white levers growing out from the filaments and blocking the mouth of the tube. Push your pencil in again and you can see what happens. It strikes against these levers and pushes them down with it. As the buttresses hold the filaments in place, their upper portion is bent over from that point until the anthers touch the pencil.

    SCENE 7: *The attic. Five months later. October, 1909. It is morning.* MARION *stands on her toes with her arms outstretched, looking upward. She wears a white camisole and under skirt. Her whole body shakes with strain. She perspires heavily. On the floor there is a blanket and a large open book. She rapidly recites the following passage from Dante's "Purgatorio."* MINNIE's *words should not interrupt* MARION's *speech.*

MARION†: He girt me in such manner as had pleased
    Him who instructed; and O strange to tell
    As he selected every humble plant,
    Wherever one was pluck'd another there
    Resembling, straightway in its place arose.
    Canto II: They behold a vessel under
    conduct of an angel.

---

*   From *My Garden in Autumn and Winter* by E. A. Bowles.
†   From the 19th-century translation by Henry Frances Cary.

Now had the sun to that horizon reach'd,
That covers with the most exalted point
Of its meridian circle, Salem's walls;
And night, that opposite to him her orb
Rounds, from the stream of Ganges issued forth
Holding the scales, that from her hands are dropt
When she reigns highest: so that where I was
Aurora's white and vermeil-tinctured cheek
To orange turn'd as she in age increased.
Meanwhile we linger'd by the water's brink,
Like men, who, musing on their road, in thought
Journey, while motionless the body rests.
When lo! as, near upon the hour of dawn,
Through the thick vapors Mars with fiery beam
Glares down in west, over the ocean floor;

MINNIE: [*Offstage*] Marion...

MARION: So seem'd, what once again I hope to view,
A light, so swiftly coming through the sea,
No winged course might equal its career.
From which when for a space I had withdrawn
Mine eyes, to make inquiry of my guide,
Again I look'd, and saw it grown in size

MINNIE: [*Offstage*] Marion...

MARION: And brightness: then on either side appear'd
Something, but what I knew not, of bright hue
And by degrees from underneath it came
Another. My preceptor silent yet
Stood, while the brightness, that we first discerned
Open'd the form of wings: then when he knew

MINNIE [*Offstage*] Marion, are you there?

MARION: The pilot, cried aloud, "Down, down; bend low
Thy knees; behold God's angel: fold thy hands:
Now shalt thou see true ministers indeed." [She faints]

MINNIE: [*Offstage*] Marion...[*A moment passes*] Marion...

MARION: [*Coming to*]...Yes. Don't come up...I'll be right down.

        MINNIE *enters.*

MINNIE: Are you all right?

MARION: ...Yes.

MINNIE: [*Kneeling and holding* MARION *in her arms*] What are you doing?

MARION: I'm studying.

MINNIE: ...You're drenched...

MARION: I know...

MINNIE: Why don't you study where it's cool?

MARION: I have to do it here.

MINNIE: You look so white. [*Drying* MARION's *perspiration*] Look at how you are drenched. Why do you do this?

MARION: I wasn't aware of the heat.

MINNIE: Now you are cold. You are as cold as ice.

> MARION *moves to the left. She leans against the wall and covers herself with the blanket.*

MARION: I feel sometimes that I am drowning in vagueness—that I have no character. I feel I don't know who I am. Mother deemed a person worthless if he didn't know his mind, if he didn't know who he was and what he wanted and why he wanted it, and if he didn't say what he wanted and speak clearly and firmly. She always said, "A person must know what he ought to believe, what he ought to desire, what he ought to do." I write letters to her. I know she's dead. But I still write to her. I write to her when I am confused about something. I write and I write until my thoughts become clear. I want my thoughts to be clear so she'll smile at me. I come to this room to study. I stand on my toes with my arms extended and I memorize the words till I collapse. I do this to strengthen my mind and my body. I am trying to conquer this vagueness I have inside of me. This lack of character. This numbness. This weakness—I have inside of me.

> SCENE 8: *A day later. Dusk.* JUSTER *walks from left to right in the garden. He wears a shirt with the sleeves rolled up. He carries a small tree, whose roots are wrapped in canvas, under his arm.*

> SCENE 9: *Five months later. March, 1910. It is late afternoon. There is a phonograph on the table.* MICHAEL *is placing the needle on a record. It plays a rag.* MARION *and* MICHAEL *dance.*

MICHAEL: That's it. You're doing well. That's good. Ta rah. Pa rah.

MARION: Teach me the words. Teach me how to sing it.

MICHAEL: Ta rah. Pa rah. Ta rah. Pa rah.

> *They sing these words to the whole song. The record comes to an end.*

MARION: Again...let's do it again. [*He starts the record again*] Hold me, Mike, and sing into my ear as they do in the dance halls.

> MICHAEL *does.* JUSTER *appears in the vestibule. He hangs his hat on the hatrack. He takes off his coat and hangs it in the closet. He comes into the living room and watches them dance.* MARION *sees* JUSTER *and waves to him. He waves to her.*

MARION: Look at me, I'm dancing. Look at this.

> *They do a special step.* JUSTER *smiles.*

MICHAEL: And this. [*He demonstrates another step*]

JUSTER: That's wonderful.

MICHAEL: Come, learn how to do it, Father.

JUSTER: [*Smiling*] Oh, I don't think I could.

MICHAEL: Yes, yes, you could. I'll teach you. I just taught Marion.

MARION: Oh, yes, it's easy. You just listen and the music and the words will tell you how to move. I learned. I am sure you could learn too. I never thought I could learn and I did.

> MARION *dances toward* JUSTER. MICHAEL *puts* JUSTER's *arms around* MARION *in dancing position.*

MICHAEL: Do it.

JUSTER *tries to move.*

JUSTER: Oh, l don't think I can. l never was light on my feet.

MICHAEL: Yes you are, Father. You could do it. You could dance beautifully. You already have the stance.

JUSTER: Oh, I don't think I can.

MARION: Try again. Just listen to the music.

JUSTER: No, no. I'm sure I can't. You dance. I'll watch you. I like to watch you. [*He leads* MARION *by the hand toward* MICHAEL, *then sits and watches*] I like to watch you do it.

> JUSTER *claps while they dance.*

SCENE 10: *Four months later. July, 1910. It is late afternoon.* MARION *sits at the desk. She is writing in a diary.* MICHAEL *appears in the doorway to the left. He holds flowers in his hand. He tiptoes up behind her and covers her eyes.*

MARION: [*Pressing the diary against her chest*] Oh!

MICHAEL: [*Taking his hand away*] I didn't mean to scare you. It's only me. I brought you flowers.

> MARION *sighs. She closes her diary.*

MICHAEL: Don't worry. I didn't read any of it.

MARION: It's a diary. [MICHAEL *sits*] I was describing an event.

MICHAEL: What event? Is it a secret?

MARION: It's a secret. A meeting.

MICHAEL: What sort of meeting?

MARION: Something imagined. In my mind.

MICHAEL: Diaries are to write things that are true.

MARION: This diary is to write things that are not true. Things that are imagined. Each day I write things that are imagined.

MICHAEL: Could I read it?

MARION: No.

MICHAEL: Why not? If it's imagined.

MARION: It would embarrass me.

MICHAEL: Is it romantic?

MARION: Yes. It is the story of a love affair.

MICHAEL: Whose?

MARION: A young man's named F.

MICHAEL: With whom?

MARION: With a young girl.

MICHAEL: Who is she?

MARION: Me!

MICHAEL: You!

MARION: Yes!

 He gasps.

MICHAEL: You! [*Touching the diary*] In this? How thrilling!

MARION: Yes.

MICHAEL: Do you write each day?

MARION: Yes.

MICHAEL: Since when?

MARION: Since August.

MICHAEL: Do you see him each day?

MARION: No.

MICHAEL: Why?

MARION: Because I can't.

MICHAEL: Why not?

MARION: Because I'm married!

MICHAEL: Oh, yes?

MARION: Of course. A married woman cannot see her lover often.

 She opens her mouth in amazement. They laugh.

MICHAEL: Where do you meet?

MARION: In the street. In a parlor.

MICHAEL: Does he come here?

MARION: No!

MICHAEL: And then?

MARION: We talk.

MICHAEL: Have you kissed?

MARION: No!

MICHAEL: Will you kiss him?

MARION: I think so. In the future.

MICHAEL: Is he real?

MARION: He is real, as real as someone who exists. I know every part of him. I know
 his fingernails—every lock of his hair.

MICHAEL: What does F stand for?

MARION: I haven't found out yet. Francis of course. What other name starts with an
 F?

MICHAEL: Franklin.

MARION: No. His name is not Franklin.

MICHAEL: Of course not. Floyd.

MARION: No.

MICHAEL: Felix.

MARION: No. Don't ask such questions.

MICHAEL: I'm sorry. I'm intruding. I'm sorry.

MARION: I'll tell you what you want but be discreet. You have to know how to enter another person's life.

MICHAEL: I know. I'm sorry. [*There is a pause*] What does he look like? May I ask that?

MARION: He's handsome. He has a delicate face and delicate hands. His eyes are dark and his hair is dark. And his skin is white. He looks like a poet. He looks the way poets look. Soulful.

MICHAEL: Where did you first meet him?

MARION: In a shop.

MICHAEL: Where does he live?

MARION: I don't know yet. I don't know him that well.

MICHAEL: How long have you known him?

MARION: Three months.

MICHAEL: How often do you meet?

MARION: Once a week.

MICHAEL: Why not more often?

MARION: You have to be careful.
     They laugh.

MICHAEL: You're mad.
     She laughs.

MARION: I know.

SCENE 11: *Three months later. October 1910. It is morning.* MARION *enters right, carrying a hooded cloak. She walks left furtively and looks around. She puts on the cloak lifting the hood over her head, covering her face. She looks around again and exits right hurriedly.*

SCENE 12: *Three months later. January, 1911. It is evening. It is* JUSTER's *birthday.* MARION *sits in the chair to the* SR, MINNIE *and* MARY *stand by her side.* MICHAEL *sits on the floor to* MARION's *right. He holds a banjo.* JUSTER *sits in the chair to the left.*

MARION: My dear husband, in honor of your birthday, we who are your devoted friends, son and wife, have prepared a small offering—an entertainment. May this, your birthday, be as happy an occasion for you as it is for us.
     MARION *extends her hand toward* MICHAEL, *who starts playing.*

MARION, MINNIE, MARY *and* MICHAEL: [*Singing**]: True love never does run smooth
     At least that's what I'm told,
     If that is true then our love surely must be good as gold.
     How we battle every day and when I want a kiss,
     I have to start explaining
     And it sounds about like this:

*   "Angry" by Dudley Mecum, Jules Cassard, Henry Brunies and Merrit Brunies.

"Dearie, please don't be angry
'Cause I was only teasing you.
I wouldn't even let you think of leavin'
Don't you know I love you true.

Just because I took a look at somebody else
That's no reason you should put poor me on the shelf.
Dearie, please don't be angry
'Cause I was only teasing you."

    They repeat the song. MARION *and* MARY *do a dance they have choreographed.*

MARION: Dear husband, now it's your turn to sing.
    They all gesture toward JUSTER.

JUSTER: [*Singing*] "Dearie, please don't be angry
'Cause I was only teasing you.
I wouldn't even let you think of leavin'
Don't you know I love you true.

Just because I took a look at somebody else
That's no reason you should put poor me on the shelf.
Dearie, please don't be angry
'Cause I was only teasing you."

    MARION *kisses* JUSTER *on the cheek.*

    SCENE 13: *One month later. February, 1911. It is evening.* MARION *sits in the left chair.* MICHAEL *lies on the floor. They are both still stiff and somber.*

MARION: It was he. There was no doubt in my mind. I saw him and I knew it was he.
MICHAEL: Did he see you?
MARION: No, I hid behind the stacks.
MICHAEL: Then?
MARION: I took a book and buried my head in it. I was afraid. I thought if he saw me he would know and I would die. He didn't. I saw him leave. For a moment I was relieved he hadn't seen me and I stayed behind the stacks. But then I was afraid I'd lose him. I went to the front and I watched him walk away through the glass windows. Then, I followed him…a while…but then I lost him because I didn't want to get too near him. I went back there each day. To the bookstore and to the place where I had lost him. A few days later I saw him again and I followed him. Each time I saw him I followed him. I stood in corners and in doorways until I saw him pass. Then I followed him. I was cautious but he became aware of me. One day he turned a corner and I hurried behind him. He was there, around the corner, waiting for me. I screamed and he laughed. He grabbed me by the arm. And I ran. I ran desperately. I saw an open entranceway to a basement and I ran in. I hid there till it was dark. Not till then did I dare come out. When I saw that he wasn't there I came home. I haven't been outside since then. I'll never go out again, not even to the

corner. I don't want to see him. I don't want him to see me. I'm ashamed of myself. I'm a worthless person. I don't know how I could have done what I did. I have to do penance.

SCENE 14: *One year later. February, 1912. It is evening.* MICHAEL *and* JUSTER *play chess.* MICHAEL *sits down center. He studies the board.* JUSTER *stands behind* MICHAEL *and also studies the board.* MARION *stands up left.* JUSTER *turns to look at her.*

JUSTER: You look beautiful. You look like a painting. [*She smiles with faint sadness*] Play, Michael. Make up your mind.

MICHAEL: I don't know what move to make.

JUSTER: Make whatever move seems best to you.

MICHAEL: I get confused. I don't see one move being better than the next.

JUSTER: What do you think, Marion?

MARION: What do I think?

JUSTER: Yes, what should Mike do? Should he scrutinize the board and imagine each move and its consequences, or should he just play and see what happens? I imagine both are good ways of learning. [*As he walks to center*] One way, I think, is a more Oriental way of learning through meditation. The other is more Western. Reckless. We are reckless, we Westerners. Orientals meditate until they have arrived at a conclusion. Then they act. We Westerners act. Then, we look to see if what we did makes any sense. Which do you think is the best way to act?

MARION: I don't know. I think I'm like an Oriental. I don't think I take chances. I don't take any risks. I don't make any moves at all.

MICHAEL: [*As he moves a piece*] Check.

> JUSTER *looks at the board.*

MARION: Does that mean you won?

MICHAEL: No. It's exciting to check though. It's exciting to make a move and be reckless and create an upheaval and for a moment to think that it's mate.

MARION: And if it isn't mate? Do you lose?

MICHAEL: I don't know.

JUSTER: [*Making a move*] For now he just loses a bishop.

MARION: Maybe it's best to be like an Oriental.

MICHAEL: I don't know. When you reflect you have to know what you are reflecting about. When you move without reflecting [*As he moves a piece*] you just move! Just do it!

MARION *lifts her skirt to see her toes and takes six steps looking at her feet.*

MARION: Six steps and the sky did not fall.

SCENE 15: *Seven months later. September, 1912. It is late afternoon. There are some letters on the chess table.* MARION *sits in a chair facing the window.* FRANK *stands in the garden outside the window.* MARION'S *manner of speaking reveals sexual excitement.*

MARION: You're trespassing. Where you are standing is private property. It's a private garden and when strangers come into it we let the dogs out.

FRANK: Let them tear me up. I'll stay here and look at you.

> MARION *moves between the two windows.* FRANK *walks to her. She moves to the stage left chair and sits.* FRANK *follows her and sits at her feet. She starts to go. He grabs her ankle.*

MARION: Let go.

FRANK: I'm chained to you. I'm your shackle.

MARION: You are?

FRANK: [*Pulling her foot toward him*] Come.

MARION: [*Pulling back*] No. Let go.

FRANK: Never. [*She jerks her foot*] Never. [*She jerks her foot*] Never. [*She jerks her foot*] Never.

> *She laughs.*

MARION: What if someone sees you?

FRANK: I'll be arrested.

MARION: Let go of my foot. [*She touches his face. She is scared by her own action and withdraws her hand*]

FRANK: I know every move you make. I've been watching you. You spy on me. I spy on you.

MARION: Let go. Someone will see you.

FRANK: There's no one here but us.

MARION: How do you know?

FRANK: He won't be home for hours.

MARION: Who?

FRANK: Your father.

> MARION *is startled by his remark and becomes somber. She walks to the chair next to the desk and sits.*

MARION: He's not my father.

FRANK: Who is he?

MARION: He's my husband. [*They are silent a moment*] He is my husband and I don't want to see you ever again. I am married and you should not be here. [*Short pause*] Leave now, please.

> FRANK *is motionless for a moment. Then, he walks away.* JUSTER *enters. He opens the closet in the foyer puts his hat and cane in it, closes the door and walks into the living room. She is calm and absent as if something had just died inside her.*

JUSTER: Good evening, dear.

MARION: Good evening.

> JUSTER *walks left, picks up the mail and looks through it. He looks at her.*

JUSTER: Are you all right...? You look pale.

MARION: Do I look pale?

> *He comes closer to her.*

JUSTER: I think you do.

MARION: I'm fine.

He kisses her and walks left as he speaks, without turning.

JUSTER: Is Michael home?

MARION: He's in his room.

JUSTER: Will dinner be at six?

MARION: I believe so. [JUSTER *exits left*]...I'm sorry...

FRANK appears again.

FRANK: Did you speak to me?

MARION: I'm sorry.

FRANK: You've broken my heart.

MARION: I saw you and I lost mine. And I also lost my mind. That's why I followed you. I had lost my mind. I thought of nothing but you. Each day I looked for you in the streets. And if not, I dreamt of you. A few days ago I looked outside this window and I thought I saw you moving among the trees. I thought I was hallucinating. This happened a few times. Were you there? Was that you?

FRANK: Yes.

MARION: What madness. It's my fault. I know it's my fault. I've been married since I was fifteen and I've never done anything like this. I love my husband and I'll always be faithful to him. I won't hurt him. He doesn't deserve this. Please, leave or I'll start crying and they will hear me and they will come and find me like this.

After a moment FRANK *runs off.* MARION *goes to the couch and sits. She sobs. The lights fade. They come up again. The room is dimly lit.* JUSTER *enters.*

JUSTER: Have you been here all this time?

MARION: I was looking at the clouds. It seems it's going to rain.

He looks out.

JUSTER: I don't think so. Night is falling. That's why it's getting dark. Dinner is served, dear. Will you come?

MARION: Yes...

JUSTER: Are you all right?

MARION: ...No...I'm not feeling very well.

JUSTER: Should you have dinner?

MARION: ...I think not...

JUSTER: Would you like to stay here?

MARION: I'll go up to my room.

JUSTER: May I help you up?

MARION: I'll be up in a moment...[*He sits next to her*] What is today's date?

JUSTER: September twentieth.

MARION: Of course. It's the end of summer. The trees are beginning to turn.

JUSTER: Yes.

She leans on his chest. He puts his arms around her.

MARION: It's getting chilly. *He strokes her hair.*

ACT TWO

SCENE 16: *10th Street. Two years four months later. January, 1915. It is early afternoon. The day is overcast.* MARION *stands by the window to the left. She looks out. She is motionless. An adagio is heard.*

SCENE 17: *10th Street. Three months later. April, 1915. It is late morning. A* GLAZIER *is standing on a ladder in the up left corner He wears belted overalls. He hammers points on the upper part of the window.* MARION *enters right. She carries a vase with flowers. She stops to look at him. He continues working. She walks to the right stand. She looks at him again. She is transfixed. He turns to look at her Their eyes lock. She cannot turn away.*

GLAZIER: Could I have a drink of water?

MARION: Yes.

> *She does not move. He comes halfway down the latter. He goes close to her, still looking at her. He puts the vase to his mouth and drinks the water through the flowers. She stares. He laughs. He looks at her.*

GLAZIER: May I?

> *She does not answer He laughs again. She stares at him. She is possessed. He picks her up and takes her upstage. They disappear behind the sofa. She emits a faint sound. The lights fade.*

SCENE 18: *10th Street. Five months later. September, 1915. It is evening.* MICHAEL *sits left.* MARION *sits right. She looks pale and absent. She stares at the floor.* JUSTER *sits next to her.*

JUSTER: I never thought I would have another child. I never thought Marion and I would have a child. I am so much older than she. I am beside myself with joy. Marion is a little worried. She is fearful. You are the first to know. I have suggested she ask Aunt Minnie to come and stay with us. Marion needs a woman's companionship. But she hasn't decided if she'll ask her. Maybe you could persuade her. She has missed you very much. I haven't heard any laughter in this house since you left. Marion has missed you. I hope you consider going to school in New York this year. Marion is desolate, Michael. Would you consider returning home?

> *Juster looks at* MARION. *He then looks at* MICHAEL *helplessly.* MICHAEL *looks at* MARION. *He is pained.*

MICHAEL: I will think about it, Father.

SCENE 19: *10th Street. One year later. September, 1916. It is late morning. Center stage, there is a playpen with a teddy bear sitting in it.* MARION *enters from left. She carries* THOMAS, *eight months old. She takes the teddy bear.* FRANK *appears outside the window.*

FRANK: Hello.

MARION: …Frank…

FRANK: My name is not Frank.

MARION: It isn't? [*He shakes his head*] What is your name?

FRANK: Jonathan.

MARION: Jonathan?

FRANK: Yes.

MARION: Your name is not Frank? [*She laughs*] That's not possible.

FRANK: My name is Jonathan. I was named after my father.
    She laughs.

MARION: I'm so happy.

FRANK: Why?

MARION: I'm so glad to see you. [*She sighs*] Where have you been?

FRANK: I was away.

MARION: Where were you?

FRANK: In Michigan.

MARION: What were you doing in Michigan?

FRANK: Working with my uncle. Have you thought of me?

MARION: Oh, yes.

FRANK: What have you thought?

MARION: That I love you.

FRANK: What a pleasant surprise. May I come in?

MARION: [*Laughing*] No.

FRANK: Come outside then.

MARION: Not now.

FRANK: When?

MARION: Tomorrow.

FRANK: At what time?

MARION: At one.

FRANK: Where?

MARION: In the square.

FRANK: Abingdon?

MARION: Yes.

FRANK: [*Moving his hand toward her*] See you then.

MARION: [*Her fingers touching his*] See you.

SCENE 20: *10th Street. Five months later. February, 1917. It is evening.* MARION *sits to the left of the chess table.* MICHAEL *sits down right.*

MARION: He often speaks of closing the house and moving south, where the weather is temperate. He likes using that word. Temperate. It's quite clear why he does. He means moral balance. Evenness of character. He means that he knows what I do when I leave the house. That he knows about Frank and me. He's saying that he'll seek moderation at any cost. That he's ready to divorce me and put an end to our family life. I'm ready for it. I'm ready to face him with it. He's just making it easier for me. [MICHAEL *looks down*] What's the matter?

MICHAEL: When I'm with him, I care about nothing but him. [*They look at each other for a moment*] I love him. He's my father and I love him. And I don't want to see him suffer. When I'm with you I forget that he's my father and I take your side. He's my father and I love him and I respect him. And I feel terrible that I've been disloyal to him. And I feel worse to see that he's still gentle and kind to both you and me. I'm sorry because I love you too, and I know that you too need me. But I can't bear being divided, and I have to choose him. I'm leaving, Marion. I can't remain here any longer knowing what I know and feeling as I do about it. It's too painful and I'm demeaned by my betrayal of him. There are times when I want to tell him the whole truth. And if I don't, it's because I love you too and I feel there's no wrong in what you're doing. I really don't. I think you're right in what you're doing. You're young and you're in love and it's a person's right to love. I think so. Frank is handsome and I think he is honest. I mean, I think he loves you He's not very strong, but he's young. No one is strong when he is young. I'm not. Only I'm still playing with soldiers and he has entered into the grown-up world. If I were in his place it would terrify me to be the lover of a married woman. Good-bye, my sister. I must leave. I am constantly forced to act in a cowardly manner. I cannot be loyal to both, and I cannot choose one over the other, and I feel a coward when I look at you, and I feel a coward when I look at him. I am tearing out my heart and leaving it here, as half of it is yours, and the other half is his. I hope I won't hurt you by leaving—beyond missing me, which I know you will. I mean beyond that. I mean that I hope my leaving has no consequences beyond our missing each other. Take care. [*He starts to go, then turns*] What if you're discovered? Will he leave school, take on such responsibility? Will he get a job and marry you?

MARION: ...I don't know. I haven't thought about that...

JUSTER: [*Offstage right, in a disconnected manner*] Are you leaving? [*A short pause*] Are you staying for dinner?

MICHAEL: I have some studying to do.

JUSTER: [*Offstage*] Stay. We should be eating soon. You could leave after dinner. We should have dinner soon. [*He enters and walks to center without looking at them. He seems absent. He stops and looks at the floor as he speaks*] How are you, my dear?

MARION: ...Good evening...

JUSTER: You both look somber. I hope nothing's wrong.

MARION: ...No, nothing's wrong.

JUSTER: [*Walking left as he speaks*] I've had a bad day myself. Sit down, Michael. I'll be back in a moment. [*The volume of his voice does not change as he leaves the room*] I'll he back in a moment. [*There is the sound of water running as he washes his hands*] It was difficult at work today. Everyone seems to be constantly shirking responsibility. That seems to be the main problem in the world today. It's not possible to get things done properly, both in the house and at work. Will the person whose duty it is to prepare dinner be here on time to prepare it? Will that person be at the market early enough to ensure that the ingredients he gets are fresh and not wilted and sour? [*He enters drying his hands with a hand towel*] Will my office staff appear to work properly dressed and properly shaven? It seems as if each day the lesson has to be taught again. The same lesson. Each day we have to restore mankind to a civilized state. Each night the savage takes over. We're entering the war. I'm sure we are. In no time we will be in the middle of a war. Yes, you wash your face! Yes, you comb your hair. Yes, you wear clothes that are not soiled. Why can't people understand that if something is worth doing it's worth doing right! [*He sits down and puts the towel on his lap. He takes one of his shoes off*] I take care of my feet. My socks are in a good state of repair. When they wear out I pass them on to someone who needs them. [*Taking off his other shoe*] Others mend their socks. I don't. I don't mind wearing mended clothes. My underwear is mended. So are my shirts, but not my socks. [*With both feet on the floor*] I have always wanted to give my feet maximum comfort. It is they who support the whole body yet they are fragile. Feet are small and fragile for the load they carry. I wear stockings that fit so they won't fold and create discomfort to my feet. If I treat my feet with respect, my brain functions with respect. It functions with more clarity and so does my stomach. I digest better. In the morning at the office, I look at my mail. Then I call my assistant. I discuss some matters with him. Then I call my secretary. She comes in with her stenographer's pad and sits down on the chair to my right. I collect my thoughts for a few moments. Then I stand on my feet, walk to the window at my left, and from there, standing on my feet with my stomach properly digesting my breakfast and my brain as clear as the morning dew, I dictate my letters.

MARION: I will go see if dinner is ready. [*She exits left*]

JUSTER: What is wrong with Marion? She's not herself.

MICHAEL: Nothing. Nothing I know of.

JUSTER: What is wrong with you? What is the matter with you?

MICHAEL: Nothing, Father.

JUSTER: Have you thought it over?

MICHAEL: What?

JUSTER: Are you coming home?

MICHAEL: Not yet.

JUSTER: Fine. You do as you must, Michael. [*There is a pause*] It is hard to know whom to trust, whom to show your heart to.

MARION: [*Offstage*] Dinner is ready.

JUSTER: Come, Michael.

>MICHAEL *walks up to* JUSTER *and waits for him.*
Let's have dinner.

SCENE 21: *10th Street. Two weeks later. March, 1917. It is late afternoon.* MARION *and* FRANK *are embracing in the space behind the sofa. She speaks with urgency.*

MARION: I have been warned that this is a dream. That tomorrow you won't love me. I've been told I must prepare myself. That when you leave me my life will end. That my pain will be eternal. Hold me. Hold me in your arms. [*He does*] Something terrible is happening. Something terrible happens each day. You're not touched by it—but I am impure. I lie each day. I am rotten and deceitful. Except to you, each time I speak I tell a lie. Lies come out of my mouth. I am impure. How I wish I could spend my days with you and not have to lie. [*There is a pause*] Frank, wouldn't you like it if we spent all our time together, day and night? If we traveled together? If we walked on the street together holding hands? If we spent the whole evening together sleeping in each other's arms? How would you like that? [*There is a silence*] Frank...

FRANK: We have to be careful.

SCENE 22: *10th Street. Two weeks later. Afternoon.* MARION *stands center left.* JUSTER *stands to her left. He holds a receipt in his hand.* JUSTER's *briefcase is on the floor next to the desk.*

JUSTER: Do you know what this is? [*She lowers her eyes*] This is a rent receipt! A receipt for the rental of a place on Abingdon Square. It's made out to you, do you know what this is? Do you know what this receipt is?

MARION: I've rented that place. I needed a place of my own. To be private. I needed to have my own place.

JUSTER: What for?

MARION: A place of my own.

JUSTER: A place to meet your lover? [*Taking her hand and crumpling the receipt against the palm*] Take it! Take it! Take it! [*He goes to the desk and sits. As he speaks he opens the drawers, takes out papers and sorts them nervously. He speaks sharply*] What are your plans?

MARION: In regard to what?

JUSTER: In regard to your life!

MARION: I've not made any plans.

JUSTER: Well, do. I'd like to know what you intend to do. How long would you need to decide? I would like to know what you plan to do as soon as possible. [*He starts putting papers, checkbooks and ledgers in the briefcase as he speaks*] I expect you to leave as soon as possible. I expect you to move your things—what you can, today. A few things. What you may need for immediate use. The rest I'll have sent to your own place. If you have a place of your own you should move there. [*She starts to speak. He continues*] Thomas will stay with me. Don't think you will take him with you. Don't bother to look for him. He's not in the house. I have taken him to a place where you won't find him and no one but I knows where he is. So don't bother to look for him. Don't try to find him. I am leaving now. I'll return later tonight. When I return I expect you'll be gone. Jenny will help you pack and she will take you and whatever things you want to take to that place or any other place you wish. If you don't leave, you'll never see Thomas again. You're an adulterous wife and I'll sue you for divorce. A court will grant me sole custody of the child. Do you have anything to say?

> *There is a moment's silence.*

MARION: I will not leave unless I take Thomas with me.

JUSTER: If you're still here when I return, you'll never see him again.

> MICHAEL *enters right.*

JUSTER: Marion is leaving tonight and she'll never enter this house again. She's not wanted here. She has debased this house. She will not be forgiven and her name will never be mentioned here again. And if you think of her ever again you'll never enter this house.

MICHAEL: Father, may I intercede?

JUSTER: In regard to what!

MICHAEL: Father—

JUSTER: [*Interrupting*] No. I will not hear what you have to say. I don't want your advice. Marion will leave. You may escort her wherever it is she is going if you wish.

> SCENE 23: MARY's *place. One month later. April, 1917. It is evening.* MARY *sits on the sofa.* JUSTER *sits left. He wears a hat and coat and holds his briefcase on his lap.*

JUSTER: I never saw myself as deserving of her love. She was preciously beautiful, modest. She was thoughtful and respectful. There was no vanity in her. When her mother died I don't believe she cried once but her spirit left her. She seemed absent. This was the way she grieved. She was obedient. She did what was asked of her, but she had lost her sense of judgment and her desire to choose one thing over the other. She accepted what others chose for her. She sat for hours staring into space. I took her for walks. I took her to the park. We took boat rides on the lake. Our meetings became more frequent. We became natural companions. I loved her company, and I found myself always thinking of her. She was sad and still when I wasn't there. When she saw me, she smiled and came to life. Her aunt told me this too. That she only smiled when she saw me. I foolishly believed that this meant she loved me. I proposed marriage and she accepted. Her aunt, too, thought it natural when I asked for her hand in marriage. She gave us her blessings. There was no exuberant joy in our wedding, but there was the most profound tenderness. I was very happy and I thought Marion was also. There were times when she was taciturn, but I thought she was still grieving for her mother. She was a child and she needed a mother more than a husband. But a husband is all she had. I could not be a mother to her. Four years later Marion had a child. I was overwhelmed with joy, but Marion was not. She became more taciturn than ever. [*There is a pause*] I began to feel she hated me. And she does hate me, and she has made me hate her. You see her. I know you see her. [*Pause*] War has been declared, Mary, and I'm afraid that Michael will be drafted. He too will be taken away from me.

(

SCENE 24: *Abingdon Square. Two weeks later. May, 1917. It is evening.* MARION *stands left.* MARY *sits right. They drink vermouth and smoke.*

MARION: I am in a state of despair! Thanks to Frank. How could I not be. Have you ever lived with someone who speaks one way and acts another! Someone for whom words mean nothing? Or if they mean anything, they mean something different from what they mean to you? My life is a puzzle. I don't know where I stand. I am constantly asking: What do you mean? What is it you mean? What does that mean to you? Why did you say that? Why did you do that? Have you?

MARY: Me?

MARION *sits left.*

MARION: When I sinned against life because I was dead I was not punished. Now that life has entered me I am destroyed and I destroy everything around me. May God save me. I have always trusted in his goodness and his divine understanding. May God have mercy on me. I have never denied him.

SCENE 25: *A beer parlor. Two weeks later. Evening.* JUSTER *sits left.* MICHAEL *sits right. There is a glass of beer in front of each.* JUSTER *speaks rapidly.*

JUSTER: I have tried. I offered her some money. She didn't accept it. I knew she wouldn't. She stared at me and said nothing. We were in a public place. She stared and I waited for her to answer. After a while I knew she had no intention of answering. I said to her, "Do you have anything to say?" She still said nothing but I felt the hatred in her eyes. I said, "I suppose you are not accepting my offer?" She said nothing. I said, "For God's sake, say you don't accept it and if you don't let's get on to something else." Her hatred is such, it burns. Paper would burn if it were held up to her glance. When I reached the door I saw her back reflected in the glass. She was so still that there was no life in her. She was still like a dead person. I regretted having offered her the money. I had no reason to think she would accept it. What do they live on. [*Short pause*] Have you seen her?

MICHAEL: No.

JUSTER: She's gone berserk. She's gone wild like a mad woman. She's insane. You haven't seen her?

MICHAEL: No.

JUSTER: You haven't been in touch at all? Letters?

MICHAEL: No.

JUSTER: Last week I followed her to a dance parlor. [MICHAEL *looks at him*] Yes, Michael. You have not been here and you don't realize what's going on. Marion's behavior is irrational. She's not sane. I followed her and she went in a dance parlor. It was still light outside, and yet people were already dancing. I followed her in and I took a table by the window. A man wearing a soldier's uniform greeted her. They started dancing. And moved to a dark corner. She knew I was there looking at her and that's why she did what she did. They kissed and caressed lewdly. I've never seen such behavior in public. Never did I think I would see someone…I so cherished behave like that. She knew I was there. She knew I followed her there, and yet she did what she did. [*He takes a drink*] One day, last week, she came to my office. I was standing by the window. I did not notice her at first. Then I heard her say, "Does this happen every afternoon?" She had been standing at the door. And I said "Does what happen every afternoon?" She said, "Do you stand at the window every afternoon?" I said, "Yes." And she said, "What do you look at?" I said, "I look out. I don't look at anything in particular. I look out because that's how I concentrate on what I have to do." "And what is it you have to do?" "Right now I'm in the middle of dictating my letters." Then she stood behind my secretary and leaned over to look at her writing pad. Then she said, "What is that? A secret code?" Shorthand! Then she said, "This is a love letter." Then, she came to where I was and looked out the window and said, "Do you use binoculars?" I told her that I could see quite well without binoculars and she said, "From where you are, can you see the house on Abingdon Square?" She thought I was spying on her. She's mad. She's capable of anything. [*He looks absently at the street. He takes a revolver from his pocket and puts it on the table*] I carry this with me at all times. I don't know if I will shoot her or if I will shoot myself. I know that one of us will die soon.

MICHAEL: ...Father...I must try to stop you.

   JUSTER *puts the revolver in his pocket. He takes a purse out of his pocket, takes money out and puts it on the table. He stands and starts to walk away. He stops.*

JUSTER: Would you take care of the bill, Michael?

MICHAEL: ...Yes...[JUSTER *starts to exit*] Father...I've enlisted.

   JUSTER *stops, looks at* MICHAEL *for a moment, turns away slowly and exits.*

SCENE 26: *Abingdon Square. Two weeks later. June, 1917.* MARION *stands up left.* MARY *sits right.*

MARY: Juster?

MARION: Yes, Juster. I hate him. I will shoot him. I imagine I shoot him and I feel a great satisfaction. A satisfaction equal to flushing a toilet, seeing the water flush out and vanish forever. I am crude. I know I'm crude. I know I'm uncivilized. I know I am a part of a civilized race but I am uncivilized. Thomas is not his!

MARY: Marion!

MARION: He's not.

MARY: Is he Frank's?

MARION: No.

MARY: Whose is he?

MARION: A stranger's.... A stranger. Just someone. Someone who came in the house one day and never again. I never saw him again. Just a man. A stranger. No one. I have a bad destiny, Mary. I have an evil destiny. It constantly thwarts me. Nothing comes to me at the right time or in the right way.

SCENE 27: MINNIE's *living room. One week later. It is evening.* MINNIE *sits on a chair, center stage.* MARION *is on her knees facing* MINNIE.

MARION: I need my child. I need my child, Minnie. I need that child in my arms and

I don't see a way I could ever have him again. He has been irrevocably taken from me. There is nothing I could do that would bring him back to me. I have begged him to let me see him. I have gone on my knees, I have offered myself to him. I have offered my life to him. He won't listen. He won't forgive me. I'm at his mercy. I wish for his death. I stalk the house. I stand on the corner and I watch the house. I imagine the child inside playing in his room. When spring comes I may be able to see him in the garden. I know he's not there, but that's how I can feel him near me. Looking at the house.

MINNIE: Why won't he let you see him?

MARION: He's gone mad! He's insane, Minnie.

MINNIE: He?

MARION: Yes! He's insane! He wants to destroy me. But I'll destroy him first.

MINNIE: Marion, I don't understand you. I forget things. I'm too old. I don't remember what you're talking about. It's no longer in my mind. The flesh is sore and swollen. [*Touching the side of her head*] This part of it is stretched and redder than the rest, as if its hotter. As if it had a fever. As if it had hair. It throbs.

SCENE 28: *10th Street. A few days later. It is late morning.* JUSTER *sits at the desk. He speaks to* MICHAEL *on the phone. After a few moments* MARION *appears outside the left window looking in.*

JUSTER: She follows me. She's insane. She's jealous, Michael. She is jealous of me. Her jealousy is irrational. As irrational as everything else she does.

MARION *steps on a twig.*

JUSTER: [*To* MARION] What are you doing?

MARION: Who is here with you?

JUSTER: I'm alone.

She hears a sound and turns to the left.

MARION: What was that? Someone's in the back.

JUSTER *does not answer. She exits left. He speaks on the phone.*

JUSTER: She is outside. Doing who knows what in the garden. She just looked through the window and demanded to know who is here with me. There is no one here with me. Not even Jenny is here. I have sent her away. She's out of her mind.

MARION *enters right.*

MARION: Who are you with?

JUSTER: I am with no one.

MARION: Who are you talking to?

JUSTER: I'm talking on the telephone. [*She picks up the phone, listens for a moment and hangs up*]

MARION: I had forgotten how I loved this house. I love this house. [*Pause*] I have been ill. I have had fevers. [*Pause*] I'll tell you a riddle. See if you can solve it:

If a person owns an object, where is it? It's under his arm.

If a person loves an object, where is it? It's in his arms.

If a mother's baby is not in her arms, where is it?

[*Pause*] Where is it? Where is Thomas? Where have you taken him? Is there someone in your life? Someone influencing you? How can you do this? How can you put me through this? What do you gain?

SCENE 29: *Abingdon Square. Two weeks later. July, 1917. It is evening. The stage is dark. There is the sound of a gunshot. The lights come up* JUSTER *stands down-stage facing up. He wears an overcoat and a bowler hat. His right arm hangs, holding a revolver.* MARION *is up center. She faces him. Her arms are halfway raised and her mouth and eyes are open in a state of shock.* MARY *enters running from the left.* MARION *turns to look at* MARY. *Both* JUSTER *and* MARION *go through the motions he describes.*

JUSTER: I came in. I said nothing. I took the gun out and aimed at her. She stared at me. Her courage is true. She stared at death without flinching. My eye fell on the mirror behind her. I saw my reflection in it. I am much older than she. Much older. I looked very old and she looked very young. I felt ashamed to love her so. I thought, let her young lover kill her if she must die. I turned the gun to my head. She moved toward me calmly. She put her hand on mine and brought it down away from my head. She said, please. I was moved by her kindness. I turned to look at her. And again I was filled with rage. My finger pulled the trigger.

He shoots again. MARION *runs upstage and returns to her position at the start of the scene.*

JUSTER: That was the blast you heard. The gun was pointing at the floor. Everyone here is perfectly all right.

JUSTER *begins to choke. He turns front slowly. He starts to walk backwards gasping for air. He falls unconscious on the sofa. His eyes are wide open.*

SCENE 30: *10th Street. A month later. August, 1917. It is dusk.* MARION *sits right of the couch.* FRANK *stands behind the couch to the left.*

FRANK: And if he doesn't come to, will you spend the rest of your life taking care of him?

MARION: When I reach out to touch him I don't know if I'm reaching outside of me or into me. If he doesn't come out of the coma…? I feed him. I bathe him. I change him. I wait for the day when I can speak to him. To speak to him at least once.

FRANK: I wanted to ask you if there is anything I can do.

MARION: … No…. Thank you, Frank.

FRANK *sits on the right side of the couch.*

FRANK: I may be leaving once again, Marion.

MARION: Oh…?

FRANK: Yes, I may be moving on.

MARION: I know, Frank. I know you must go.

They sit silently for a while.

SCENE 31: JUSTER's *bedroom. A day later. It is evening.* JUSTER *lies in his bed unconscious. His head is stage right. He is in a coma. He is unshaven.* MARION *stands on the upstage side of the bed.* JUSTER *begins to come to. His speech is impaired.*

JUSTER: …It looks much nicer here than in the parlor .. .

MARION: What does?

JUSTER: …It feels bad.

MARION: What feels bad?

JUSTER: …It is happier here…

MARION: What?

JUSTER: It's happier. Don't you know it.

MARION: What?

> *His eyes open. They are bloodshot and swollen.*

JUSTER: Who's here.

MARION: It's me.

JUSTER: Who?

MARION: Marion.

JUSTER: Marion?

MARION: Yes.

JUSTER: Why are you here?

MARION: Because you're ill.

JUSTER: What's wrong with me?

MARION: You had a stroke.

JUSTER: What have you done to me!

MARION: Nothing.

JUSTER: Yes, you have.

MARION: What have I done?

JUSTER: You've done harm to me.

MARION: No.

> *He looks at her suspiciously.*

JUSTER: What have you done to me? Get out!

MARION: I've fed you.

JUSTER: What have you fed me?

> *She is silent.*

Poison!

MARION: No.

JUSTER: I hate you! You're repulsive to me! [*Pause*] You've touched me!

MARION: Yes.

JUSTER: Do you enjoy seeing me like this! [*Pause*] Where's Michael? [*Pause*] Has he been here?

MARION: I sent for him.

JUSTER: I want to see him.

MARION: He's trying to get here.

JUSTER: Why can't he come?

MARION: He calls every day.

JUSTER: [*Starting to get out of bed*] I want to get up. I want to be downstairs when he calls.

MARION: He won't call till later.

JUSTER: [*Still trying to get up*] I'll call him.

MARION: He can't be reached.

JUSTER: Am I dying?

MARION: I don't know.

JUSTER: I don't want you here. [*She takes a step back*] Get out! Get out! [*She starts to leave, then stops*] Get out!

MARION: …May I come back later? [*He does not answer*] I understand.

> She exits. He lifts himself to a sitting position, stands and stumbles to the living room.

JUSTER: … Marion…. Marion! [*He starts to fall*] …Marion…Marion…Marion…

> MARION *runs in. She hold* JUSTER *in her arms.*

JUSTER: I love you.

MARION: …I love you too.

> She sobs. MICHAEL *enters, walks slowly to them, and stands behind them. He wears an army uniform. There is a bright light on them.*

MARION: Michael…! Michael…! He mustn't die! He mustn't die!

END OF PLAY

Len Jenkin

American Notes

*Tho' obscur'd, this is the form
of the Angelic land.*
—WILLIAM BLAKE,
America

•

American Notes was first presented by the New York Shakespeare Festival Public Theater on February 18, 1988. The cast, in order of appearance, was as follows:

MAYOR	Rodney Scott Hudson
CHUCKLES	Olek Krupa
PAULINE	Lauren Tom
FABER	Stephen McHattie
PITCHMAN	Thomas Ikeda
KAREN	Mercedes Ruehl
REPORTER	Andrew Davis
TIM	Jesse Borrego
LINDA	Laura Innes
PROFESSOR	George Bartenieff

Director: Joanne Akalaitis
Set: John Arnone
Costumes: David C. Woolard
Lighting: Frances Aronson

Production Note

The set for *American Notes* is basically six places: motel reception area; Karen's motel room; Pitchman's banner and showfront; Professor's house; Tim and Linda's bar; and the Mayor's area. Where these are in relation to each other, and whether all the areas are onstage all the time are questions that I hope will be answered by each individual production according to its needs and interests. The settings in a particular production can be very full and movie-like—realistic places, or sparse theatrical arrangements that indicate the nature of place through significant objects. In either case, we should have the feeling that a great dark sky is overhead, that the distances surrounding our places below are vast. The music is all American music, and can range from rock and roll to muzak to country and western. It can come from radios and televisions, and/or just be there—as soft background for the voices, punctuation, or moments of violent energy and pulse.

Please leave space in the language, and between the people, for silence.

It is night, we are in America, and the time is now.

ACT 1

An open field, outskirts of town. An older man sits in the dirt, some food and a bottle alongside him. This is the MAYOR. *A traveler enters, dusty, ragged, having walked a long way. He holds a battered suitcase. This is the man who will be called* CHUCKLES. *He stops, as if unsure which way to go. He hesitantly approaches the* MAYOR.

MAYOR: Bound for somewhere, buddy?

> CHUCKLES *nods. He points in one direction, then hesitates, points in another direction. He looks around confusedly.*

Well, little buddy—stay or walk.

> CHUCKLES *moves about uncertainly, stops.*

You want advice, or directions?

> CHUCKLES *stands silent, ill at ease.*

You want advice.

> *The* MAYOR *looks* CHUCKLES *over carefully.*

You been traveling, little buddy. Probably looking for it, but you ain't found it yet. Hmmmm…your eyes been sucking up so much world they got swelled up like beachballs, poppin' outta your face. Ooo weee! You know, you keep moving and peeping in everywhichplace, you can raise up a big wind in your head, special if you don't know exactly what you looking at. Why just yesterday I was out taking my constitutional—past the flag go flap flap on the village green, past the newstand, past a man slicing another man's face with a breadknife, past old Mr. and Mrs. Whoever's house and she's praying with her thumb up her Bible and he's rubbing his moneymaker, and I stop to take a leak behind the barn and who do I see hailing a cab in the dark but little Miss Muffet, and her hair's all tangled and she ain't walking right. Hey, I seen a guy follow somebody's daughter into the all night launderama and he's got his dick hid inna boxa Tide. I see 'em go in there and she's folding up her underwear, and I'm looking through the keyhole and all that wash is spinning round and round and round.

I seen a man, 'bout this time yesterday, slit his own throat in the bathroom mirror. Home sweet home, you betcha. Run around to nowhere till they drop, ain't even looking. Am I right?

> CHUCKLES *nods in agreement. He shyly eyes the* MAYOR's *food. The* MAYOR *eyes* CHUCKLES.

Hey…uh, [*Naming him.*] Chuckles! Chuckles, you want something to eat?

> CHUCKLES *grabs the food, begins to chomp away.*

Hey…my lunch. You are supposed to leave me something.

CHUCKLES, *frightened, drops the food quickly, pushes it back over to the* MAYOR. *The* MAYOR, *in turn, places the food carefully back between the two of them.* CHUCKLES *hesitantly takes something to eat. The* MAYOR *nods.*

Now I been on that road myself. Got tired one day, and settled down. Right here. Got a wife and three kids. Why just last week I got elected mayor. Ain't much in it but I like the honor you know, from my fellow citizens. Nasty and slow as they may be, they got glimmers, glimmers way down in their underpants. Know what I mean little buddy? Down there and in the very center of the eye, in the black dot.

I got a good idea where you're headed. Why you know there's nine rivers between here and there, and you moving like you gonna get there Tuesday. There's the Muskinggum, an' the Chatahoochie, the Raritanic, the Monongahoola, the Gahoolamonga, the Belly-up, the Snake, and the Skunk. Whooooooo! You counting? There's one so fearsome it either doesn't have a name or I'm scared to tell it. You think this some tiddlywink country like Alboonia you step outta your shack to take a piss and if the wind's right you are watering foreign soil? This is the land of Rootie Kazootie and the Appaloosa, sea to shining sea. Go somewhere and die! Whooboy! You moving on to somewhere cause you think this ain't it, but you don't know this country or these people around here, little bitty buddy, so there's nothing but wind in your head. It's whistling between your ears, bitty buddy. Just wind.

You got your lips loose yet? No talkee, eh? Wanna wrestle? Wanna swap socks?

MAYOR *conceals his socks with his hands.*

No peeking. Look in my pocket. Waddaya see?

The MAYOR *holds open his pants pocket.* CHUCKLES *peers into it.*

Pocket fulla darkness—hooboy! Hey, Chuckles, wiggle down in the dirt here.

They both sit on the ground.

Hey, eat some more stuff here.

CHUCKLES *eats.*

Ease your weary mind. This is some place, all right. You lucky you here. You oughta get work, stay awhile.... I might be able to place a man of your talents....

Lights up in another area on PAULINE, *a young woman standing motionless in the center of a motel office.*

Look around. Hey, see there's Pauline. She works late....

Hey, Chuckles. Suck up some of this juice I got here.... Made it special for ya.... [MAYOR *hands* CHUCKLES *his bottle, and* CHUCKLES *drinks.*]...and open your eyes....

Lights fade on the MAYOR *and* CHUCKLES, *come up more strongly on* PAULINE. *In the motel office, a counter closes a small area off from the rest of the space. Behind the counter, a chair. On the counter, a bell, a register, some books, a small TV, a phone. A radio plays. Out in the space, a few chairs. Through a screen door, extending away from the office, the "outside": perhaps a sign reading "OF- FICE" with an arrow, parking stripes on cracked asphalt.* PAULINE *the nite-clerk suddenly rushes over to the screen door, opens it, and leans out.*

PAULINE: GET OUT OF HERE! Leave me alone, please! You're drunk, you know that? GO AWAY AND STOP BOTHERING ME! I'm gonna call the police if you don't get outta here, NOW!

>PAULINE *goes back behind the desk, reaches for the phone, then changes her mind. She's nervous, listening for any noise. Suddenly the screen door opens. A man enters in a rumpled suit and tie. He goes up to* PAULINE, *and looks at her expectantly.*

FABER: I'm in 4. I left my key.

PAULINE: Oh…yeah. [*She hands his key to him.*]

FABER: Thanks. Good night.

>*He heads for the door, but her voice stops him.*

PAULINE: Uh, excuse me. Mr. Faber?

FABER: How'd you know my name?

PAULINE: It's in the register. Room 4.

FABER: Right. I've never seen you here before.

PAULINE: I'm the nite clerk. I don't come in till twelve, so if you don't stay out late, or get up early, you don't see me.

FABER: Uh, right. Good night, miss….

PAULINE: Pauline. Mr. Faber, did you see anyone hanging around on your way in?

FABER: Not a soul, Pauline.

PAULINE: Would you mind doing me a favor? Could you go outside and take a look around the parking lot?

FABER: I'll play. What am I looking for?

PAULINE: There's this drunk guy who's been hanging around here bothering me, and I think he's gone now, but I'm not sure….

>FABER *hesitates, then shrugs his shoulders.*

FABER: Ok. I'll take a look.

>FABER *exits.* PAULINE *waits nervously. Lights up in another area on an older man, the* PITCHMAN, *in front of an enclosure with a curtained entrance. Some carnival lights. A huge painted banner depicts the lush landscape of Egypt, the pyramids, and the river Nile. The* PITCHMAN's *seated on a stool. He has a microphone. Near him stands* CHUCKLES, *who has a container half full of water in his hands.*

PITCHMAN: [*on mike*] Come in and see the crocodile, Papa Crocodile, the biggest, oldest, mightiest of them all. Man killer. Swamp monster. Alive on the inside. Listen to him kick and splash. Sounds like he's coming out of there…[*looks at* CHUCKLES]…sounds like he's coming OUTTA THERE! [CHUCKLES *shakes his container, making a splashing sound near the mike.*] From the land of the pharoahs, the sphinx and the pyramids comes the crocodile, the colossus of reptiles, twelve hundred pounds of tail lashing, jaw gnashing danger. Bonecrusher! See him now. Listen to him thrash about in there. Sounds like he's about to come outta there, doesn't it? [CHUCKLES *splashes.*] No danger at all. You'll be separated from him by two sets of steel bars. Go right in. The show is always open. Go right in….

>*From a distance, a* MAN'S VOICE, *screaming.*

MAN'S VOICE: [*offstage*] Pauline!

    The PITCHMAN *pauses a moment, then continues.*

PITCHMAN: See BONECRUSHER, the summum bonum of nature's awesome power and cruelty, etcetera, etcetera and so forth. That's the pitch, which is one thing. The attraction's another. Some shows, what's on the inside ain't worth spitting at. Crusher's the real thing. You got the real thing, people come. Even in Boobopolis, or Chump Junction, or Hayseed Center, or wherever the fuck we are this week. People go on in and tell me, Mister, you didn't say enough, and come back with the family.

    See Bonecrusher, the monster of the Nile, alive on the inside. No sir, this is not a movie.... Alive!

    The PITCHMAN *and* CHUCKLES *are still, as lights on them fade out. In the motel office area,* FABER *returns.*

FABER: There was this guy leaning over the one car in the parking lot...mine. He's vomiting on the hood. So I say, "uh, buddy, get off my car," and he heaves again and then he turns around to me with puke all over his football jersey and he says "You're the one." I do believe he thought I was your boyfriend. I was flattered. I figured I wouldn't disillusion him. I say "I am the one. Go—and be sick somewhere else."

PAULINE: Did he?

FABER: First he took a swing at me. He missed, and he falls down and sort of crawls away. Then he stands up and he howls.

MAN'S VOICE: [*Howling o.s.*] PAULINE!

FABER: You probably heard that part. Then he just wanders off into the dark. I see him again when he hits the highway light near the junction, and he bobs and weaves a bit under the light, and he's gone. He the town wino? Or a lover you won't see no more?

PAULINE: Just some guy.

    FABER *takes a seat.*

FABER: Hey...you want a favor, and I don't even know you, and I go to shoo this guy away. He's mean drunk, bigger than me, and could have been carrying the kitchen cleaver. I take my life in my hands out there, and you won't answer a little question to help me pass the time.

PAULINE: It's true, what I said. He's *just some guy.*

FABER: No. That's me. I'm just some guy. I'm staying here, you never saw me before, you say hello cause that's your job, and I'm gone. He's somebody. He's got a name. He may even have a mother. Right in town...that's where he's going now. Home, and his mom is sitting in the kitchen in a flower print nightdress, waiting up. Radio's on, some kinda endless traffic report. She's reading the back of a box of Fab, and when he hits the screen door, she looks up. "Where you been, Bobby? Your hair's all tangled and you ain't talking right. Oooh wee, you got puke and blood all over you...."

PAULINE: Blood? He's got blood all over him?

FABER: Thought I'd leave out that part. I kicked him.

PAULINE: You kicked him? I asked you to look around, not to kick him or something. Why'd you do that? Oh, Jesus, why....

FABER: I kicked him cause he was lying on the asphalt and he says "goddamn cunt I'm going back there and fuck her up." He said something along those lines. So I kicked him in the face. He bled a little. Discouraging him seemed like a good idea at the time. You got someone who can stay with you for a few nights till he cools off? Hell, he'll probably be back with a shotgun....

PAULINE: You're kidding, aren't you? I hope....

FABER: Yeah. He's gone. Who is he?

PAULINE: Nobody. I teach exercise twice a week, in town. The studio has a window on the street, so it's kind of advertising, but anyone can just look in and see us jumping around in leotards. One day, there's this guy I never saw before, and he watches the whole fifty-five minutes, like he's hypnotized. Next day he comes inside and says he wants to sign up. I tell him the class is full. That was a lie, and I didn't like saying it, but there's something funny about him, like he's not seeing what's there, but something else *he* likes better—but you're not too sure *you'd* like it better—and he's seeing it *all the time.* Then he asks me out. I had to get Elaine to make him leave. Then he showed up here tonight. He was drunk. I was scared. Thanks for helping me out.

FABER: He got caught by something is all. Your hair, some angle of your body, something in your face locked in to a dream of his and he grabbed at it only way he had. He'll forget it—till some other time and place, somebody else in a window tilts her head a certain way, and the rusted old gears mesh, and he once more presses his nose against the glass. It's a great life. What time is it?

PAULINE: After two.

FABER: I'm wide awake.

PAULINE: Me, too. You want some coffee? I've got a hot plate in the back, and some instant....

FABER: Yeah...that's good. That's fine. I like that.

PAULINE: OK.

> PAULINE *exits through a rear door behind the desk.* FABER *alone.* CHUCKLES *enters. He carries a vacuum cleaner. He stares suspiciously at* FABER. *He exits.*

FABER: [*calling offstage*] Hey, am I the only one staying here? Tonight, I mean.

PAULINE: [*from off*] Well, we really have only one other guest. Another single. God, she's real beautiful. Hasn't been out of her room for three days. She's been calling over, though, for messages.

FABER: Yeah?

> PAULINE *returns with two coffee cups and a jar of powdered cream. She sets them down on the counter.*

PAULINE: I got Cremora, the powder?

FABER: That's fine. Uh....

> *He gets up and goes over to* PAULINE, *who is behind her desk.*

I got a bottle of whiskey here in one pocket, unopened. Maybe we just adulterate the coffee a little. What do you think, Pauline?

PAULINE: [*hesitantly*] OK, but just a little for me. I've gotta work till eight.

FABER: I know. You're on the job, Pauline. [FABER *adds whiskey to the coffee.*] If I ring the bell, you'll ask what you can do for me. [*He rings the bell. Silence for a moment.*]

PAULINE: Mr. Faber, where've you been tonight? I know you didn't take your car cause it's been sitting there since I came on, so I thought hey, Mr. Faber in 4 must have friends in town. After all, he's been here a week, and what else is there to stay around here that long for?

FABER: Pauline, I bet you figure out a lot of things, don't you?

PAULINE: I bet it's a girlfriend. She's got a car, and picked you up, and you....

FABER: You got this one wrong. I don't know anyone anywhere near here. I was out walking. In town.

PAULINE: Everything's closed.

FABER: I wasn't shopping. I was walking. So, Pauline. What do you do here all night long?

PAULINE: Homework, mostly. I got an English lit assignment for tomorrow. I just started, part time. At the community college, out on 119. It's going OK so far.

FABER: Sounds like something, I guess....

PAULINE: All my friends went to college a year ago. But my mom wouldn't have the county nurse before.

FABER: Mind if I ask just what you're talking about?

PAULINE: Oh...sorry. My mom's not real well, and someone's gotta be around her almost all the time. Now, the nurse is there, and I can work this job, *and* start school.

FABER: Uh, Pauline, long as we're having this coffee and all, I'd feel better if you just came out from behind the desk, and we'd just sit around here like people do, you know.

PAULINE: I'm not supposed to be out there where the guests sit.

FABER: We're not gonna be having any more company tonight.

     PAULINE *comes hesitantly out from behind the desk, sits in a chair by* FABER. *They drink coffee.*

     Now, uh, Pauline, are you single?

PAULINE: Sure. I told you. I live with my Mom.

FABER: Well, for all I knew your husband was living there too, and the two of you had a little room up in the attic where you baked brownies or something, ran the volunteer fire department, a little palmistry scam...and then the two of you being real quiet till your Mom goes off to sleep, then once you hear the sick old lady snoring you leap at each other, tearing....

PAULINE: No. Just me and my mom.

FABER: Let me make a comment here, Pauline. I was downtown there in the downtown tonight, and it seemed as if someone had pressed the pause button on the whole neighborhood around 1942. Quiet. Sort of permanently still. Awful slow for actual people. And out here, right now, even stranger. No wind, no traffic.... I can hear the breath going in and out of you.

PAULINE: I think that's your own breath you're hearing, Mr. Faber.

FABER: Yeah, You're right. That's what it is.

PAULINE: I'm gonna get to my book for awhile, OK?

FABER: You don't mind if I sit up here a bit?

PAULINE: Make yourself at home. There's nobody here but us…[*phone rings*]…and the girl in 7.

> PAULINE *picks up the desk phone. Lights up in a room of the same motel. A stocking hangs out of a suitcase on a stand. Empty liquor bottles. A girl in a slip,* KAREN, *is sitting on an unmade bed, the phone in her hand.*

Office. Can I help you?

KAREN: Yeah, uh Jenny….

PAULINE: Pauline.

KAREN: Oh. Yeah. Pauline, the nite clerk. Listen, Pauline, what time you got?

PAULINE: Exactly…[*looks at watch*]…2:45.

KAREN: Zat daylight savings or what? Just kidding…. Uh, anything for me?

PAULINE: Uh, I'm sorry. No messages.

KAREN: Thanks.

PAULINE: It's no trouble. Good night. [PAULINE *hangs up the phone, as does* KAREN; *to* FABER.]

The girl who's waiting….

> PAULINE *reads.* FABER *sits quietly. In her room, we hear* KAREN *in voice-over or live, as indicated. She looks down at a cigarette burnhole in the bedspread.*

KAREN: [*V.O.*] Oh Jesus, Karen darling. Look at that. You coulda set your bed on fire. [*She looks around the room.*] [*V.O.*] Musta been a helluva party. I hope I had a good time. Hell, nobody else showed up….

> *She opens a liquor bottle, pours a drink, shakes out two aspirin.*

[*Live*] Well, onward Christian soldiers. [*She takes the aspirin with a chaser.*] Ugh. What's the worst? He got hit by a truck or something and he's laid up in a hospital, and his face is all bandaged so he can't call. Or, he's dead, so he can't call.

[*V.O.*] You'd almost like that Karen darling, cause what's likely is that bastard's out on the road somewhere and he forgot you. You just went right out of his head. "Karen? Who the fuck is that? I don't remember."

[*Live*] No. That's not fucking possible. I can tell.

> KAREN'S MEMORY *evokes the* REPORTER, *and he appears in another space. He holds a letter from the* PROFESSOR.

REPORTER: Hey, I've been in heaven for two days, and I am not about to walk away from it and not come back. It's a three hour drive, I'm only gonna be with the guy an hour maybe, tops. Just to take some pictures and notes for the story.

KAREN: [*Live*] You know it's *four miles* to town, Chump Junction or whatever, only shoes I got are these heels, I got about seventy-five cents in my purse, half a pack of Pall Malls, some groceries, and a bottle of vodka.

What am I gonna *do* here?

REPORTER: How should I know? Read a magazine. Watch the TV. They got TV in the rooms.

KAREN: [*Live*] This professor you're gonna see…he got a phone number?

REPORTER: [*checking the letter*] Baby, he lives in the middle of god-forsaken nowhere. He doesn't have a phone. I think he doesn't believe in 'em.

Lights come up on the PROFESSOR *in his farmhouse. A door with many locks, boards nailed over windows, piles of disorganized books, odd electronic equipment, complex charts and diagrams. Strange atonal music plays, softly. The* PROFESSOR *addresses the audience. In his own space, the* REPORTER *looks over the letter his magazine's received.*

PROFESSOR: There exist particular spiritual beings who hold certain information invaluable to humanity. In this place, I have entered into unrestrained dialogue with these beings on a variety of congenial topics. To accomplish this, of course, I've had to probe some rather isolated spiritual neighborhoods, previously accessible only by psychic helicopter....

I wrote to the newspapers, magazines, learnéd societies. Only one response—from a publication mired in lurid speculation and unsubstantiated horseshit. *Flying Saucer News.*

REPORTER: [*to* KAREN] Hey...see ya in a l'il bit, hah...late tonight or tomorrow. Or tomorrow. Or tomorrow.

Lights strong on the PROFESSOR, *the* REPORTER, *and* KAREN. *A knock on the* PROFESSOR's *door. He opens it warily.* CHUCKLES *enters, bringing the* PROFESSOR *some take-out food. He eats ravenously, as* CHUCKLES *listens.*

PROFESSOR: These beings, these shadow people, they're around us, all the time. They can't fly, or raise the dead, or control the weather. They're very light, you know. The wind can blow them away, if they're not careful. Very light. Very beautiful.

CHUCKLES *exits. The* PROFESSOR *locks the door quickly and thoroughly, continues.*

Some say they've always existed, and will exist forever. I wouldn't say that. Some say they are the dead. I wouldn't say that. They're just there, alongside us, like feelings in the air.

Lights down on the PROFESSOR

KAREN: [*Live*] Three days in this hole. What day is it anyway?

[*V.O.*] Maybe it's Sunday, and I should go to church or something. [*She picks up the phone, dials. In the motel office, it rings.*]

PAULINE: Office.

KAREN: Hey, Pauline, what day you got?

PAULINE: It's Monday now.

KAREN: Any messages?

PAULINE: Nothing yet. Sorry.

KAREN: Thanks. [*They hang up the phones.*] [*V.O.*] On the way over to the motel he says let's get you some groceries to take up to the room. I say OK and we pull up at the 7-11 and on the way in I trip over a fucking tricycle some kid leaves there in front of the door. I ripped my stocking on the pedal. I guess I'm nervous or something cause I start kicking the bike. The kid comes rushing out, screaming at me. He's got a big container of purple snow in his hand.

[*Live*] The place's microwave is busted. He buys me a frozen burrito and tells me it'll thaw, and an orange soda and a beer and some kinda dead french fries, all gonna taste like cardboard puke. He pays, and he hands the whole bag to me like it's fulla gold, with this shit-eating grin on his face. I smile back and say hey whyn't you just leave me fifty bucks and I'll get my own groceries....

[*V.O.*] I could see I said the wrong thing. He'd been burned before. He just looked over my shoulder at a shelf full of motor oil. Forget it, I say, I don't need no money. You're gonna be back tomorrow, right? and I give him a kiss, a nice wet one with a little tongue in it. He smiles.

[*Live*] What a chump.

[*V.O.*] "Day after, the latest," he says...and he drops me here and he's gone. Frozen burrito and an orange soda. Purple snow.

REPORTER: See ya in a l'il bit, hah...late tonight. Or tomorrow.

The REPORTER *exits.*

KAREN: [*Live*] Hey, anything coulda happened. Car broke down. Couldn't find that professor. Maybe he forgot the name of this place so he couldn't call. Hey, Karen darling. Believe. He'll be here....

Lights up on the same PITCHMAN *we've seen before, in front of the same croco-dile exhibit: banner, entranceway in to see the crocodile. Near the enclosure is* CHUCKLES. *He holds the closed container of water, the splasher.* CHUCKLES *shakes his container. Sounds of splashing.*

PITCHMAN: [*on mike*] No, sir, it is not a movie. Alive on the inside. Bonecrusher, world's largest.... Hey, Chuckles. Wet Mr. B down, will ya?

CHUCKLES: Splushh splush?

PITCHMAN: Yeah.

CHUCKLES: Splush splush! Splish!

CHUCKLES *goes into the crocodile's enclosure. An attractive young girl and her boyfriend walk up to the exhibit. This is* TIM *and* LINDA.

TIM: [*to* PITCHMAN] Hi! My name's Tim. This is Linda. Linda, say hello to the nice man.

LINDA: Hello.

TIM: We want to see, uh, Bonecrusher, you call him?

PITCHMAN: That's what I call him, and that's his name. His Momma gave it to him on the banks of the Nile, in Crocodilopolis. Enter and discover. Or you can go downtown to Penny's and watch the wax dummies in the window.

TIM *and* LINDA *disappear into Bonecrusher's enclosure. The* PITCHMAN's *eyes follow* LINDA *as they exit. He turns to the audience.*

You know what age is to me? It's a number. Sixty. Nineteen. Zero. That's all the fuck it is, a fucking number. Hey, couple of local girls come around wearing these shorts show half their ass when they lean over to look at Bonecrusher, and he ain't looking at them but I am and they say, Hey, how you doing, Pop? You want some of that, Pop? Hey, my name's Marty, cut that Pop crap, you know. Now I ain't saying it's exactly the same. If she tries to gimme a blowjob every ten minutes I'm gonna say, hey, what you doing you trying to kill me or something?

Been with Bonecrusher for thirty years. Got him when I got outta the army in

'58. Hey, I'm different, he's the same, but that's on the outside. Inside, I'm just like him—no change at all.

That's Chuckles. Found him wandering around the lot when we hit town. I taught him how to hose out the cage, do some other little stuff around here. Boss wanted to throw him off the lot, I said, hey, no way, Chuckles stays with me. Cause I had an idea. I treat him good, feed him, let him sleep under the drop here. It's next to Crusher, and sometimes it don't smell all that good, but he don't mind. We got a deal, Chuckles and me. Chuckles is gonna feed me to Crusher when I die. I needed an idiot. Nobody else would do it. When I found Chuckles, I knew I found my boy.

I'm a religious man, in my way. If Bonecrusher eats me, I'll go on living, looking out of his eyes. You'll be able to see me in there, a little spark of red fire way back in those black slits of nothing. Hey, I'll be him, and he'll be me. Bullshit spook stuff, hah? I don't care what you think. Sense to me don't gotta be sense to you.

Listen and learn. What you think ain't all the thinking there is. Bonecrusher is a priest. It's all in *Job,* and I got it by heart.

Canst thou draw out Leviathan with a hook? Who can open the doors of his face? Or light the lamps of his mouth? Will he speak soft words unto thee? Will he make a covenant with thee? Will he take thee for a servant forever? Upon earth there is not his like, who is made without fear. He beholdeth all high things, and sorrow is turned into joy before him.

TIM *and* LINDA *emerge from Bonecrusher's enclosure.*
TIM: Hey, fella. I hate to tell you this, but your croc's dead.
PITCHMAN: You don't say. [*laughs*] You know anything about crocodiles, friend? They look deader'n hell most of the time.
TIM: Excuse me, but that animal in there is gone, finished.
PITCHMAN: That's Bonecrusher in there, and he'll outlive you or me.
TIM: He's dead. Probably been dead for a week.
PITCHMAN: Fuck you and your mother, friend. Chuckles!
        CHUCKLES *advances, as menacingly as he can manage, toward* TIM. TIM *grabs him suddenly, twists, and* CHUCKLES *is on his knees.*
TIM: [*to* PITCHMAN] You're right about one thing. He is big. But he's not Egyptian, and he's not a crocodile. He's an American alligator. Do you want to sell the body?
        The PITCHMAN *doesn't answer.*
LINDA: Bury him, or put him in the town dump where the birds'll strip him clean. Children can play with his bones.
        TIM *and* LINDA *exit, and from off, their laughter.*
PITCHMAN: Chuckles, go in there and poke Mr. B.
        CHUCKLES *enters the croc's enclosure. A moment later, he slowly emerges. He looks down at the ground.*

I been with him 30 years, Chuckles. I been on the road with him every season. I got repeat customers. These people bring their kids. Little goddamn kids.

"Know how he got so big, sonny? People think he grew fat on fear. That's not so. He's big with love...."

The PITCHMAN *slowly sits down again in his usual position, in front of the huge banner. He picks up his microphone.*

[*On mike.*] See Bonecrusher, World's Largest Crocodile, Colossus of reptiles, monster of the Nile. Hear him splash around in there. I do believe he's coming out of there....

CHUCKLES *makes shaking motions, but his hands are empty. No splashing sound.*

[*off mike.*] No sir, this is not a movie. Alive on the inside. [*to* CHUCKLES] Bonecrusher ain't dead, Chuckles. He's sleeping, that's all. Needs his rest. After all the horrible things he's done his whole life long, he needs his rest....

The PITCHMAN *and* CHUCKLES *are still. In the motel office,* PAULINE *reads,* FABER *sits quietly.*

FABER: Pauline?

PAULINE: Yes, Mr. Faber?

FABER: Pauline, now that we're sitting around here together and all—would you tell me a story?

PAULINE: I don't know any stories.

FABER: You already told me one, Pauline. About the exercise class.

PAULINE: That wasn't a story, Mr. Faber. It happened.

FABER: Story all the same, Pauline. Just like when some old lady comes down in her pajamas says Pauline honey I can't get a wink so give a listen to my life. It's the same as all the others so I guess the joke's on me. You could read it on line at the super-market, hear 'em shout it over the cornfields, but, hey—hear it now, 'cause what you the nite clerk for anyway? Tell me that one, Pauline, and when you're done I'll comment, and we'll be having a conversation here.

PAULINE: I can't tell you a story, Mr. Faber. Not just like that, anyway.

FABER: All right, then I'll tell you one, Pauline. All you got to do is listen.

Lights up on a bar somewhere. Over the bar, a TV *plays: picture, no sound. There's also a video game, and a small stage at the rear. On that stage,* TIM *and* LINDA, *as a performing duo. They do a song, perhaps their version of Sonny and Cher's "I Got You, Babe." During the song,* FABER *enters, and sits at the bar. From the motel office,* PAULINE *watches. The song ends, and* LINDA *goes to the video game, plays.* TIM *comes over to* FABER.

TIM: My name's Tim. I'm living at the hotel. Blaine Hotel right up the street. Hey, after the accident, before I had this job, I was working polishing airport floors in the middle of the night. It's quiet, and I liked the way the machine kept humming. If I stuck six months they were gonna embroider my name on my uniform. Tim. I left. Airport's for the planes really, not the people, you know. Got this job, took a room right up the street. Come over and see me. I could put you so straight you wouldn't bend again for days—years, maybe. [*Pointing.*] That's Linda. Linda, say hello to the nice man.

LINDA: Hello.

TIM: You know why Linda stays with me?

FABER: I....

TIM: 'Cause she's crazy, that's why. Besides, she's on the four to twelve shift at Denny's out on Arctic, and when she's done, she needs somebody to love. I flatter myself. Listen, buddy. The truth is she sleeps on the floor with her clothes on, in the bathroom next to the tub, curled up in an old army blanket I got. I lay there in bed and I whisper and I say Linda Linda come on into bed here. It's warm and I took a bath before I got in, and the sheets is clean, and I ain't gonna do nothing—I'm just gonna hold you. I say all that whispering loud so she'll hear me in the bathroom, but she never answers. I never know if she hears me, or if she's sleeping. When I say that stuff to her I ain't lying, you know. I ain't lying, but I'm hoping....

Listen, Bob. You know Linda got two kids. Would you believe it? Yeah, they live in Reno, Nevada. She lost 'em on a bet.

Now she's here. You like her, Bob? She got very nice tits. Not saggy at all, you know. She's like a girl in a magazine—not a mark on her. Clean and healthy. And she don't think about anything. Not much anyway. Not anymore.

Listen to me, Bob. You got nothing, right? You got a rented room, you got a Momma somewhere if she ain't dead, you got what's inside your head, which by peeking in through your eyes, those transparent windows of the soul, I can see ain't much. You have fallen through an American crack, and them is deep. Whole damn country is mined with 'em, it's like walking over quicksand, open up and swallow a young man quick as say howdy want some pancakes. You got trouble. Trouble is my experteeze. I majored in trouble at a major university. We are talking English, *capish? Comprendo?* This isn't *sound.* This is the straight skinny, no tricks, no figure it out later, no get it in your dreams. This is get it now and take it home.

Me and Linda are here. That's fortuitous. Good graces is what you're in, friend. God loves you, and I could learn. So could Linda.

FABER: What makes you think you can come over here and say all this shit to me?

TIM: I gotta license. You wanna see it?

FABER: Do you think I'm stupid? That I'm gonna let the two of you just take my....

TIM: No. You're not stupid. You had some bad luck is all. 'Scuse me, buddy. Look her over whiles I take a dump. I'll be back with ya shortly.

TIM *exits into the bathroom.* LINDA *comes over and sits with* FABER.

LINDA: Hello.

FABER: Hello. You, uh, come from around here?

LINDA: Sure. Sure I do. Right around here. I come from right here.

FABER: What do you do? I mean, what do you *do? You* work?

LINDA: I am *intending* to get work, so I can fuck who I like. I sing here for the hell of it. It doesn't pay. As they say, poverty sucks, but then, employment ain't much better. That's a bind, Mister.

FABER: Where do you live?

LINDA: With Timmy. But it's filthy. I have plans to get ahold of some amphetamines, and take 'em with a broom and a box of Brillo nearby.

Timmy's nuts, you know. He's here somewhere, 'less he left. He knows I can find my way back, so he doesn't have to stay, you know.

CHUCKLES *enters, goes behind the bar, where he seems to be employed as bartender. He listens.*

You know what love can do? Rip you to shit, then come upside your head with a two by four and knock what's left of you right into the street. Think so?

FABER: Yeah. I know so.

LINDA: Everything Tim told you about me is a bunch of lying shit. You know that?

FABER: I....

LINDA: I mean, he thinks I exist only for him. When I go out into the hallway and slam the door behind me, he thinks I dissolve in the corridor before I get to the stairs. I reconstitute myself a moment before I come into his presence. Now you know that's not true, cause I'm here, and he's not...aren't I?

FABER: Yeah, you are.

LINDA: Touch me so you're sure.

FABER: I'm sure.

LINDA: Touch me, dammit.

FABER *touches her.*

FABER: Your hand is hot.

LINDA: No. Yours is cold. You're freezing. You're going below zero, with the negative numbers. You wanna buy me a drink?

FABER: Sure.

LINDA: [*to* CHUCKLES] I'll have a shot of wild turkey, black coffee, and a glass of water, please.

CHUCKLES *looks around confusedly behind the bar to fill her order.*

[*To* FABER.] Do I have lipstick on my teeth?

FABER: As a matter of fact, yeah. A little.

LINDA: Would you wipe it off? Use your finger.

He does so. She catches his finger in her mouth, sucks on it gently, then suddenly bites hard. FABER *leaps away.*

FABER: Owww!

TIM *opens the men's room door, heads toward them.*

TIM: She's cute. Don't pay attention to her now, Bob. She's not yours yet. No deal yet. Listen to me. You're here for a reason, right? You're a man in need. Am I right? I mean, you can tell me, us, you can tell us because we are nothing but need. We desire everything. You name it, we want it, and we want it bad. Hey, I'm talking to you, buddy. Hey, I'm asking you a question.

FABER: I wasn't listening.

TIM: Some people think their ears just hang there and work all by themselves. You know a smart guy can take his ears off and put 'em in his pocket in Guatemala or something. But that don't matter, Bob, cause you're full of shit on this one, and I say that with *conviction*. You were straining to hear me, like a kid can't take a shit. You been hearing every motherfucking word. Well?

FABER: I want her.

TIM: [*laughs*] You know, Bob, you and me we're gonna be friends. In fact, Bob, we're friends right now. What's your name? Shhhh. Don't tell me. What's a little name between friends. What's your offer? You keep sleeping alone, friend, you die inside. What you can buy by the hour ain't worth the chump change you lay out for it. That is not heat to warm you. You are a man who can smell true love when it's coming down the street, you can smell it coming to you cross the rivers and seas, its odor mixing with the salt spray and the quick perfume of the flying fish. You know it—when it's sitting right here alongside you. Gimme something. For Linda. All you got. She's worth it....

    A long silence. FABER *doesn't move or speak*]

You wanna play, but you don't wanna pay. This is true of everyone. The piper will pipe till the gates of dawn, drag your dancing body along, but you gotta pay at the end of the road. [*sings*] "I ain't the devil or the devil's son, but I can be the devil till the devil come…" Well? After tonight, I won't be around to fix you.

FABER: No deal.

TIM: Well, whaddaya know. Bright boy, maybe. Might not have worked out too well for you, in the long run. I coulda pressed you harder—but hell, why hook you? Maybe you'll meet me again someday, and I don't want no bad blood between us. I surely don't. Come on, Linda. Let's go.

    TIM *and* LINDA *exit.* FABER *sits alone, then crosses to* PAULINE *in the motel office as lights fade in the bar.*

FABER: [*to* PAULINE] Funny, hah? What do you think, Pauline?

PAULINE: I don't know, Mr. Faber. What do you think?

FABER: I think they were extremely quick. Every time they threw me one I fumbled, tripped, and fell over in the grass. They had me looking like Mexican money—with holes in it. They let me off easy.

    A moment's silence.

PAULINE: Mr. Faber, would you ever think about living here?

FABER: In the motel? Sure. Forever.

PAULINE: You know what I mean. It's not as slow here as it looks. Things happen, but kind of one at a time, like…. Are you interested in this?

FABER: It's not really coming through at the moment, Pauline. Maybe you should try something else.

PAULINE: OK… You know the high school a few miles down the road? Around this time of year we bring in a carnival, the VFW does it actually, and they move right onto the football field. It might be there right now.

FABER: So?

PAULINE: What do you mean, so?

FABER: So, what, uh, follows?

PAULINE: Nothing. Just a story.

FABER: Pauline, you gotta be more interesting. I mean to press this point here. Don't you wanna do things, or make things, or be what you read about in books, or see on your TV there? I mean, you could get where you feel OK cause you do this or that and other people think it's hot shit. Hey, keep humping back there behind the desk and you gonna turn into a zombie, Pauline. This place gonna be the Zombieland Motel. Tourists welcome.

PAULINE: What do you think I should do? I'm happy here, Mr. Faber, I think. I'm hardly ever bored. I got so many things I....

FABER: That's cause you got a TV there, Pauline, for when you kind of hit a heavy patch of nothing.

PAULINE: I don't want to have an argument with you. Sure, sometimes I watch the late....

FABER: TV's a little strange, isn't it? A tiny, lit-up, twisted replica of everything, that's trying to eliminate our world, and take its place.

PAULINE: Mr. Faber, you probably never worked nights. The TV helps pass the time.
        Silence. CHUCKLES *enters, cleaning.*

FABER: I been meaning to ask you. Who's that?

PAULINE: Him? He's just some guy. [PAULINE *laughs.*] That's Chuckles. He works around the place. He sleeps here somewhere, nobody really knows where.

FABER: Chuckles, hah?

PAULINE: Someone named him that. He doesn't talk. Except to say the motel motto. I think the owner taught him. Chuckles! The motto!

CHUCKLES: [*In a panic, articulating as best he can.*] We're easy to get to, but hard to leave.
        CHUCKLES *exits.*

PAULINE: We're easy to get to, but hard to leave. You like the coffee?

FABER: Yeah. Uh, you like the whiskey I put in it?

PAULINE: Yeah, warms you up.

FABER: Have some more, Pauline.

PAULINE: OK. But just a bit.... [*He pours.*] Do you have someone, Mr. Faber? You know, like a wife. Or a girlfriend. You know…someone.

FABER: You ask a lot of questions, Pauline.

PAULINE: I'm just curious. It's the only way you can find things out.

FABER: I had someone. About a year ago she left me, her and the kid and everything. I came in late one night, and I'd had a few, and I crawled into bed alongside her, and I'm out. Next thing I knew I hear a crash, open one eye, clock says 6 AM. I get up and go into the front room, and there she is with her girlfriend Myra, and the kid is already in Myra's old Chevy, and so is all their clothes and stuff, but they can't get the kid's crib through the front door. It was their trying that woke me. I'm standing there naked, looking at her like a dying calf in a hailstorm, and she doesn't even blink. She bends over the crib again and tries to force it through. I wasn't mad. I felt funny and sad seeing her do that. It made me see how she saw me, you know, and that wasn't pretty, but it wasn't true.

I walked over to the door, and sat down next to the crib and started taking it apart. Only took ten minutes. Once I did it, she got it out of there and was gone. She didn't even say thank you. She wouldn't even let the kid kiss me goodbye. I saw her a few times after that, but it was like seeing someone else. So after a while, I just got up and left there. I had the car, and some money, so like I say, I just left. You think I did right, Pauline?

PAULINE: I don't know, Mr. Faber. I don't even know you.

FABER: Good as anyone, Pauline.

PAULINE: I couldn't tell if....

FABER: I been here a week, Pauline, 'cause I don't know whether to go. Or where. I got some money. You want some money? How much would you like?

PAULINE: I can't take your money.

FABER: I'm serious here, Pauline. No difference to me if it's in my pocket or not. Either way, something's gonna happen. Take it all.

    FABER *takes out all his money, including change, and dumps it on* PAULINE'S *desk.*

PAULINE: Mr. Faber! Stop! I wouldn't take any money from you, unless I earned it or something.

FABER: You already did that, Pauline.

PAULINE: Coffee's only forty cents, Mr. Faber, and this one was on the house.

FABER: I don't mean the coffee, Pauline.

PAULINE: I know what you mean. Take back your money. [FABER *takes up the money, puts it back in his pockets.*]
You're probably forgetting a lot of things, Mr. Faber.

FABER: I'm remembering a lot, Pauline.

PAULINE: I think you're forgetting.

FABER: You know more about me than me, Pauline? Are we having an argument here?

PAULINE: I wouldn't call it that.

FABER: What would you call it?

    A long silence between them.

PAULINE: You know what? I don't know why I think this, but I do. I think, even after all you told me, that somehow you're a lucky person.

FABER: You do? Well, maybe I am. Then I don't have to worry, do I? Cause if my luck holds, pretty soon someone's bound to come up behind me and slit my throat.

PAULINE: There's not a lot to say to that, is there? Except that I hope it doesn't happen.

FABER: Do you?

PAULINE: Yes, Mr. Faber, I do.

    Silence. PAULINE *picks up a book, reads. More silence. Then....*
What are doges?

FABER: Doges? What are you doing, the crossword puzzle?

PAULINE: I got a poem to read for my lit class. It's a word in the poem.

FABER: I don't know.

PAULINE: They surrender.

FABER: Who?

PAULINE: The doges. Doges surrender.

FABER: Let's hear it, Pauline.

PAULINE: What?

FABER: The poem.

PAULINE: Safe in their alabaster chambers
Untouched by morning and untouched by
Noon
Lie the meek members of the resurrection
Rafter of satin, and roof of stone.
    More?

FABER: Yeah. The doges didn't come in yet.

PAULINE: Grand go the years in the crescent above them
Worlds scoop their arcs and firmaments row
Diadems drop, and doges surrender
Soundless as dots on a disc of snow.

FABER: Yeah.

PAULINE: You like it?

FABER: Yeah. I like it. I like you reading it.

PAULINE: What about the doges?

FABER: Not a clue, Pauline. It's a mystery.
    Long silence. The phone rings. PAULINE *picks it up.*

PAULINE: Office.
    Lights up on KAREN *in her room. She's on the phone.*

KAREN: Hey, Pauline, what time you got?

PAULINE: About...3 AM

KAREN: Three AM? Are these nights getting longer or what?

PAULINE: I don't know.

KAREN: Me neither.... Long as I got you here, why don't you give me my messages.
Reel 'em off.

PAULINE: I'm afraid there....

KAREN: Please don't sound so damn sorry.
    KAREN *hangs up her phone, and* PAULINE *follows suit. Lights fade on* KAREN,
    PAULINE *and* FABER *as they come up on* CHUCKLES *and the* MAYOR *at the*
    MAYOR's *place in the field near town.* CHUCKLES *is sitting in the dirt, listening.*

MAYOR: A Mayor's got a lot of responsibilities here, bitty buddy. You think I can put in
time on cartography and transportation for every traveling boy comes through
looking for where else and wherever? I got duties, bitty buddy. Duties. I got to shave
every three days. I got to think about everybody all at once, including dead people,
plus perambulations and looking around in present time so everybody round here
can step sweetly into the future foot by foot, which they do every day thank you to
God, good fortune, and the help of a few little doings I do here and there. The point
is, Chuckles, my boy, we walk a fine line—between yesterday and tomorrow, between nothing and nothing. You can step right off the log. We don't wanna go
down in flames here, do we bitty buddy?
    This is amazing country. Sea to shining.... I'll tell you what it is. It's fertile. I was

on my way out the door one day, little buddy of mine, about to take my mayoral constitutional, had a handful of pumpkin seeds to munch on the road. I turn around to wave goodbye to the wife and kids, and one seed fell outta my hand. Before I could turn back around that seed had taken root in the earth, sprouted up and spread so high and wide that I was dangerously surrounded by enormous serpentine vines, caught in their green clutches. The volunteer fire department had to break out the axes and cut me loose. [*The* MAYOR *pauses, remembers...*] Chuckles? You got a shovel, little buddy? I wanna go down to the dump, dig up that crocodile.

CHUCKLES: Splish splash?

MAYOR: Listen up now. You can have the head, the tail, and the part in the middle. [CHUCKLES *thinks, then looks questioningly at the* MAYOR.] All I wants is the heart. That roll of white fat around the heart of a dragon is good for the pecker. Puts lead in the pencil, woo boy!

CHUCKLES: Dragon?

MAYOR: Dragon, crocodile, allygrabber, same thing. You know, little brother, in the spring them dragons fly high and bring the rain. After harvest time they go down and coil in the depths of the sea. Friend of mine rose up to heaven on a red dragon, escorted by blue mice. Right here in town. By the way, you *still* want to get moving?

     CHUCKLES *nods, looks pleadingly at the* MAYOR.

Well, you are stupid, but you're not dumb. Listen up. Where you're thinking you maybe wanna be is prob'ly west of here somewheres, you head out past the junction, up by the Shell station, hang a right by the tomb of the Holy Apostle Thomas, pass the railroad yards, left at the tower of Babel and straight on, feet on the white line and a smile on your face.

     Dangerous journey to who knows where. You might be shipwrecked, more than once. Now, if I was you, I'd stick around here a while. You ain't seen nothing here yet. This is interesting country. Look around. Hey...you want a little of this stuff...I brewed some up special for ya.

     MAYOR *takes out flask, gives some to* CHUCKLES... *he drinks* ...

Hey, you gotta get back to work....

     CHUCKLES *remembers his job. He panics, rushes off. Lights up on* KAREN *in her motel room. The* MAYOR *calls after* CHUCKLES.

Relax. There's the girl in 7. She's not going anywhere, is she?—not yet. She's waiting.

     KAREN'S *room. Liquor bottles, full of ashtrays, clothes everywhere. A sudden loud knock at the door.* KAREN *turns joyfully toward it. It opens, and* CHUCKLES *steps hesitantly inside, his arms full of toilet paper and towels.*

KAREN: [*Screaming.*] GET OUT!

     CHUCKLES *exits, terrified.* KAREN *shakes out a cigarette, lights it.*

[*V.O.*] These nights are definitely getting longer. Winter's coming. [*Live*] Fucking ice age. [*V.O.*] Let's review the facts here, Karen darling. Raised in back of the Hi-Hat Tavern, down the street from Marty's Broiler and the Key Motel. That was a while ago, Karen darling, and now its getting a little late in the afternoon here.... [*Live*] I almost got married once. Right out of high school. He dumped me. I had to sit up for two nights picking his name outta my cheerleader jacket. Tick tock. Tick.

    K A R E N *turns on her radio. Music. She dances. The* R E P O R T E R *appears in another space. He dances.*

R E P O R T E R: You dance to this kinda music?

K A R E N: [*Live*] Fluently—and we go from there. [*V.O.*] After a few hours, I notice he's actually listening to what I'm saying, and I say to myself, uh oh Karen girl, here's trouble and I like it. [*Live*] Asshole. God I shoulda just run something on him, taken his money, gone to the ladies, and disappeared. Next day, go shopping.

    [*V.O.*] My grandma used to tell me, Karen sweetheart, keep away from cigarette smokers who show up under your window after midnight and play the banjo. Tick tock. Tick. Pay more attention you wouldn't end up waiting for someone you hardly know in some kinda lima bean hell here.... Even your own pain grows boring.

    [*Live*] Fine. Where we at? Nighttime. And up above, the stars, little lit windows of the dead's town, where all the dead sit around being dead. Hey, you, Mr. Stupid! You don't know what you got here. You got a full size, moderately fucked up person here, and I have a lot of potential. What's the matter, hah? I'm not as good looking as those nineteen year olds. [*She goes over to the mirror, looks in.*] Bullshit. All right, some of it's missing, but most of it's there. Are you aware, Mister Not Here, that I am a model? [*V.O.*] Correction. Was a model. I was sixteen. I did catalogues. In my last year of high school I did Penney's for the whole state. [*Live*] I got the pictures. [*V.O.*] In a trunk somewheres. Maybe in my mother's house, if she didn't throw 'em away....

    There's a knock at the door. She rushes over to answer it, pulls it open. C H U C K - L E S *is standing there again, his arms full of toilet paper, ready to change the roll. She stares at him.* C H U C K L E S *doesn't move.*

Come right on in.

    C H U C K L E S *goes through the room into the bathroom, strands of toilet paper trailing behind him.*

Care for a cocktail?

    C H U C K L E S *peers out a moment, looks questioningly at her, goes back to work.* K A R E N *waits for him to leave. He emerges, and while she's turned away, he leaves a badly crushed candy bar by her telephone. He walks toward the door, stops a moment and looks at her.*

K A R E N: Thanks, I guess.

C H U C K L E S: [*mimes wiping his ass and nods vigorously*] We're easy to get to, but hard to leave.

    He waves goodbye to her. He exits.

K A R E N: [*V.O.*] Where was I? [*Live*] Who the hell knows. [K A R E N *notices the candy bar, picks it up. She looks back toward the door. V.O.*] Oh my God…am I that pitiful? [*Live*] Snickers. Looks like it's been in his pocket in a heat wave. [*She tosses the crushed candy bar into a corner. V.O.*] Three days in this hole. Waiting's just like being dead, except you still have to pass the time. [*Live. Sings.*] "I will sing you a song of the New Jerusalem, that far away home of the soul...." [*V.O.*] That's all I remember. [*Live*] Facts. He's late, [*V.O.*] he's very late, [*Live*] but he's on his way, knowing I'd wait forever, that I'd be here...[*V.O.*]...staring out the window for him till my eyes become two tiny swamps where moss floats, till my lips are food for crows, till deep in the grass grown up through this crumbling floor, my white bones rot.

[*Live*] Fuck that. Hell, he'll probably show up any minute, with a hard-on and a mouth full of sorry. [*A moment's silence*] You know, after a while, you wait long enough, you say to yourself, well, actually, this is it. This is my life. Not what's gonna happen, but now. I'm here.

KAREN *is still. Lights come up on* PAULINE *and* FABER *as before, in the motel office.* PAULINE *is reading a book.* FABER *sits. In another area, lights up on the* REPORTER. *He's walking through a field: mud, trees. He carries a camera, notebook. He stops, turns to the audience.*

REPORTER: I'm freelance. I take what I can get. My current employers, an association of screwballs known as *Flying Saucer News,* has been running me into the ground. I been over half the state in the last three days. Three days. Damn. I gotta remember the name of that motel I left her in so's I can call. I been trying, but it won't come to me. I can find it, I know the town.... Hell, she'll be there. She could tell I was...you know, sometimes you get another chance. You think you'll never get another chance, and God gives you another chance. I'm gonna need some loving after this ring of loons I been chasing.

The job? Photo stories on three reported sightings. First one was a group of housewives who claimed they witnessed the levitation of an entire shopping mall by alien beings. If that sounds like one valium too many—check. Number two was a Mex ranch hand who was shearing sheeps up country, and got taken aboard a big one. Got him up there stripped naked as a chicken and put him in a room with a space girl, looked like Marilyn Monroe in silver spandex, but bald and with gills like a fish. He claims they wanted him for breeding purposes. I expect he had a real vivid dream out on the prairie. Number three? This one's an ex-professor, lives in the farmhouse up ahead. Once I finish with him, it's pick up Karen, and hit the road....

The REPORTER *turns away, continues walking as lights dim on him, brighten on* PAULINE *and* FABER *in the motel office. The radio plays quietly.*

FABER: Pauline, would you...could you sing me a song?

PAULINE: [*laughs*] I can't sing.

FABER: That's a lie, Pauline.

PAULINE: Ok I *won't.* You wouldn't want to hear it, Mr. Faber, believe me.

FABER: You're wrong there, Pauline. I'd like it.

PAULINE: I don't know any songs.

FABER: You must know *one* song, Pauline, the one you learned in the third grade, where everybody stood in a row. Sing it, and I'll be sitting here much happier, I think.

PAULINE: I'm not responsible for your happiness, Mr. Faber.

FABER: Yes you are, Pauline, and I'm responsible for yours.

> *A silence.*

PAULINE: We didn't stand in a row. We sat in a circle.

> FABER *reaches over and turns off the radio.* PAULINE *sings, very quietly and simply.*

Down in the valley, valley so low
Late in the evening, hear the train blow
Roses love sunshine, violets love dew
Angels in heaven, know I love you
Down in the meadow, down on my knees
Praying to heaven, give my heart ease
Give my heart ease, love, give my heart ease
Praying to heaven, give my heart ease....

That's all I know. [FABER *applauds solemnly.*] Are you making fun of me?

FABER: I am extremely serious here, Pauline.

PAULINE: Good, 'cause I'd like you to consider something, Mr. Faber. This conversation is not just your conversation with me. This is our conversation, Mr. Faber, and now it's your turn. Sing.

FABER: I can't sing, Pauline.

PAULINE: That's what I said, Mr. Faber.

> FABER, *with much hesitancy, begins to sing some romantic ballad poorly. He stops.*

FABER: [*Sings much louder, and bangs on the chair in rhythm.*]

Let's twist again, like we did last summer
Yeah, let's twist again, like we did last year
Do you remember when, we were really humming
C'mon, let's twist again, twisting time is here....

PAULINE: Shhhh.... You'll wake everybody up.

FABER: All the customers are wide awake, Pauline. One is upstairs walking the floor, and the other one is me. [FABER *stands, and twists, along with very loud singing*].

Round and round and up and down we gooooooo again
Baby let me know, you love me so, and then...
Let's twist again, like we....

PAULINE: STOP!

> FABER *stops singing abruptly.*

FABER: What kind of lipstick is that you got on, Pauline? Flamingo pink? Tangerine blush?

PAULINE: I'm not wearing any lipstick.

FABER: What kind of perfume you wearing? Lily of the Valley? Tiger Musk? Orange Blossom Special?

PAULINE: I'm not wearing any perfume.

FABER: I smell something, Pauline.

PAULINE: Maybe it's my shampoo.

FABER: Answer me something, Pauline. What kind of shampoo?

PAULINE: Apple something…with keratin, whatever that is. Why are you interested in….

FABER: That's private stuff I'm asking about, Pauline. You buy it in the supermarket, but you rub it right on your body. Have a drink. [*Takes out bottle.*]

PAULINE: I think I've had enough.

FABER: The last one….

      PAULINE *still refuses.* FABER *refills his own. The bottle is empty.*
We got a dead soldier here. [*He drops the bottle in the trash.*]

PAULINE: You know, Mr. Faber, I've been thinking about what you said, about me sort of…doing more. Maybe moving away to a bigger place or something. I mean, if my Mom is….

FABER: Don't blame me, Pauline.

PAULINE: Blame you?

FABER: One day ten years from now you're lying face down on a cot in some furnished room, crying into your pillow—and you remember. It was me told you to leave the bosom of your home and family. You hurry down to Woolworth's and buy one of those fat black magic markers and you go out to the graveyard and write insulting remarks all over my lily-white headstone.

PAULINE: That's an ugly story. And it's a lie. You won't be dead in ten years, and I won't be in a room somewhere crying.

FABER: You know the future, Pauline? Should hang a sign on your desk, LIFE READ-ING, TEN BUCKS. You got gypsy blood?

PAULINE: I don't know. Maybe.

FABER: Maybe you do. [*Silence*] You know, Pauline, I am convinced that for miles around, at this moment, we are the only creatures with their eyes open. The little raccoons and squirrels and stuff in the woods, they're all sleeping, and the people too, all snug in their beds, whole sky over the town is thick with dreams….

PAULINE: [*looks at her watch*] Mr. Mason opens the Snack Shop by the Trailways stop by six, so he's probably up now. And Dexter. He drew the graveyard shift this month, so he's….

FABER: Pauline? I'd like to mention something here. It doesn't matter who the fuck is actually awake, or asleep, or dead. I'm talking about a feeling.

PAULINE: I'm talking about the facts.

FABER: You getting a little sarcastic here, Pauline?

PAULINE: Yes. You've been confusing me, Mr. Faber. And scaring me…a little.

FABER: I don't want to do that. I didn't mean to do that. [*a silence*] We're a bunch of poor bastards here, Pauline. Roam the planet like starving dogs, and never get it right. Find any little scrap of something in this world and it's thank God and step careful, cause you're likely to lose that too.

    You spend a lot of nights talking to the itinerant sleepers, Pauline. The sleep-walkers. Whatta they have to say on the subject?

PAULINE: You're the only one who ever….

FABER: Maybe you don't hear them cause your pretty head falls over and you sleep at the desk, and all the storytellers can't bear to wake you, so they keep it to themselves and tiptoe by.

PAULINE: I don't think so, Mr. Faber. Sometimes I do get sleepy, but I always wake myself, 'cause what if a car pulls in, and I'm sleeping with my head on the desk, like this. [*Does so.*] How does that look, to someone coming in, I mean?

FABER: I don't know. Looks all right to me.

PAULINE: [*sitting up*] It does not. I do all kinds of things to keep awake. Homework, the radio…You know, sometimes I just think about what might happen to me…if I'll ever get married, or even finish college and find some kind of interesting job. I think about my Mom, and start feeling sad for her and all. Then sometimes I go outside and sit in one of those lawn chairs in front of the office and just wait for it to get light. It happens real slow, so you have to slow yourself down to it or you get bored, cause it takes a few hours. When the first edge of the sun is up, I go back inside and make coffee. It can get real cold out there. Once I did that in the snow. I just kept shaking it off me, and walking around to get warm. I couldn't really tell when the sun came up. The snow was dirty gray in the dark and became white. The sky just got lighter and lighter—till it was light. [PAULINE *glances over to a corner, then jumps suddenly.*] Ooooh! Did you see it?

FABER: What?

PAULINE: A mouse. I'm sure I saw a…. There it goes!

    CHUCKLES *bursts into the room, a broom raised over his head. He's trying wildly to kill the mouse or drive it away.*

CHUCKLES: Meece! No!

    Suddenly, CHUCKLES *sprawls to the floor. He stares around him desperately. Silence. The mouse seems to be gone.* FABER *silently points into a corner. The mouse!* CHUCKLES *is up, and rushing after it, swinging the broom wildly.*

PAULINE: Chuckles! Stop! Don't hurt it!

    CHUCKLES *doesn't hear her in his passion. He corners the mouse, and energetically smashes it.*

CHUCKLES: Meece! Little meece! No!

    CHUCKLES *holds up the dead mouse by the tail. He speaks to it.*

We're easy to get to, but hard to leave!

    CHUCKLES *pockets the dead mouse, and exits.* FABER *looks after him.*

FABER: You know, this place looks ordinary from the outside…. [PAULINE *laughs.*] You ever feel there's strange things going on here….

PAULINE: Strange things? Like a mouse? Or us talking?

FABER: I don't know. [*a long silence*] Last few weeks, I've seen a lot of dreams with my eyes open, just riding down the road. I drive through these towns, one after the other, and they all got a main street, and on it is a place to buy groceries, Food Town—a place to eat, Marv's Broiler—and a place to get fucked-up, Hi-Hat Tavern. And when you go through these places in America, the question is always "Anybody home?" The answer is obvious. No. Basically, there is nobody home in America, Pauline. Except you.

    Again, a long silence between them.

There are people out there, after all. They go way back, and they came outta the sky and the dirt, just like us. And they got secrets, just like us. Right now, *at this moment,* in this town, everybody's waking up in their beds, eyes pop open, night still outside the window, and they rise up, and dress. There they go. There's the mailman scampering along Main Street, and the delivery boy, and the girl who works the checkout counter, and old Mr. Mason, slipping outta that ranch house. There's another, behind the Shell Station, and there's another in the river, in an ivory boat being hauled by a pair of huge catfish, past green lily pads awash with flames, and there's your Mom in a red dress dancing across the village green, all of them crawling and prancing and snorting towards the woods outside of town, to a little clearing in a ring of trees. They're out there, under the moon. Rumble and bumble in the dark! Hop down! Jump up! Spin around, and old Mr. Mason and a teenage girl from the high school whirl round and round in the center, naked as jaybirds, and his fat belly wheezes in and out with the pipes.... Know that tune? [*sings*] O beautiful, for spacious skies, for amber...waves...Look! They're all calling to you, Pauline, calling for you to join them. But you're here talking to Faber, and you forgot. They all got their party hats on, Pauline, and you're the only one whose head is bare. Go on. I'll mind the store.

PAULINE: There's no one out there, Mr. Faber. They're home in bed.

FABER: Maybe so, Pauline. Maybe so.

> PAULINE *and* FABER *are quiet. Lights up on the* PROFESSOR's *house in the woods, somewhere in America. Piles of books and papers, some of which are in cartons. Strange electronic equipment. Arcane maps and charts. A telephone. The* PROFESSOR *is packing. The* REPORTER *is approaching. He stops, turns to the audience.*

REPORTER: Funny. The closer I get to this professor's place, the stranger I feel, sort of gloomy and nervous at once, like I'm coming down off something.... Hell, maybe it's the air, seems kinda damp or.... Well! Here we are.

> A dog howls, loudly and suddenly, unnerving the REPORTER for a moment.

Coming along? Let's see how the old duck is doing. Yoo hoo! Anybody home?

> The PROFESSOR *unlocks the door, opens it a crack. Strange atonal music begins, softly.*

PROFESSOR: [*loud*] Did you bring the pizza? You from Pizza Hut?

REPORTER: [*after hesitating*] You order a large pepperoni with anchovies and a diet coke?

PROFESSOR: Exactly. Come in, come in.

> The REPORTER *enters, and the* PROFESSOR *quickly shuts the door and locks it behind him.*

REPORTER: Professor, why are we playing charades?

PROFESSOR: Act normally, please. All your questions will be answered in time. [*The* PROFESSOR *nervously looks out the window, then back to the room.*] You are from *Flying Saucer News?*

REPORTER: Yeah. You know something? I just remembered the name of a motel I gotta call. Can I use your phone?

PROFESSOR: I told you in my letter. To the magazine. I don't have a phone.

REPORTER: [*pointing to the phone*] What's that? A dingdong school phone?

PROFESSOR: The wires are down. They haven't come to repair them in months. They get too many flat tires.

REPORTER: What the hell are you talking about?

> Loud noises from outside. CHUCKLES *bursts into the room, panicked and up-set. The body of a dog, wrapped in a bloody towel, is in his arms.*

CHUCKLES: Dead dog.

> *The* PROFESSOR *puts an arm around* CHUCKLES' *shoulder to comfort him....*

PROFESSOR: Bury him in the garden. Next to the other one. I'll write the pound. This time, we'll get a dog so big that.... [*to the* REPORTER] This is Chuckles. He helps around the place. Chuckles, this is the man from the magazine. [*They shake hands awkwardly. To* CHUCKLES.] Keep packing! [CHUCKLES *exits. To* REPORTER.] Shouldn't you be taking notes?

REPORTER: My memory's sharp as a tack, professor.

PROFESSOR: Where were we?

REPORTER: Let's see if I have this right. You said in your letter that some kind of invisible creatures are out there in the woods, and you been talking to them.

PROFESSOR: In a word, yes.

REPORTER: If we *could* see them, what would they look like?

PROFESSOR: Like men...and women.

REPORTER: And you think they're from earth? Or Mars? Or outer space?

PROFESSOR: They come originally from the place of broken shells, a great sea of psychic debris from previous worlds, worlds that failed...a sort of spiritual version of the asteroid belt.

REPORTER: Ok. Moving right along. You might as well hit me with the rest of it.

PROFESSOR: [*pause*] The rest of it is...less theoretical. I left the doors open, so they could go freely, in and out. I was friendly, genial. They liked Chuckles. I won them over. They came when I called, drifting out of the woods. They guided me, taught me.... A man should marry for love. Don't you think so, Mister Reporter?

REPORTER: I know so.

PROFESSOR: I did. I married one of them. A woman of the shadow people. I loved her as I'd never been able to love one of us. She was devoted, at first, but she became unruly. Sexually demanding. She behaved badly. I couldn't help it. I had to....

REPORTER: Go on....

PROFESSOR: I locked her in the closet. She's extremely clever. She escaped, and fled back to them. They were furious. They told me to leave at once. Their speech, by the way, is a kind of gurgling, like a brook over stones. These last few days, they grow more malicious. She has inflamed them against me. They wait around the house, in the trees.

> You know, she never really loved me. They don't.... I have to leave here.... I'm a pauper. I'm unemployable. Perhaps I'll be hospitalized....

> But I must go. You see, they'll kill me. I know they will. I have to tell the truth

before they stop me. *They* explain everything. Parapsychology, mental illness, war, religion. The whole banana. They don't want their secrets known. Would you? Are you frightened?

REPORTER: No.

PROFESSOR: You should be. You can't hurt them, you know. And they won't die.

REPORTER: Why don't you just apologize to your...wife? For locking her in the closet. Make it up to her. Let them know you....

PROFESSOR: She was wicked. She deserved punishment. You don't believe any of this, do you? [*The* PROFESSOR *goes over to a tape recorder.*] Proof positive! Their voices.... [*He presses "Play. " The sound of a loud harsh bubbling and gurgling fills the room. Then suddenly the tape recorder begins to smoke, then bursts into flames.*] Damn them. You want more proof? Wait here.

> CHUCKLES *enters with a pile of papers in his hands.*

Talk to Chuckles. He may be insane, but he's not dumb.

> *The* PROFESSOR *exits.* CHUCKLES *stares at the* REPORTER.

REPORTER: What the hell is going on here? [CHUCKLES *begins packing.*] You all nuts or something? Look, I can take a joke, but....

CHUCKLES: Go away. Go!

REPORTER: What's going on?

> CHUCKLES *picks up some scattered papers, rushes out of the room as the* PROFESSOR *returns, holding a large plaster cast, with some odd markings on it.*

PROFESSOR: Their marks. Proof positive.

REPORTER: That could be a plaster cast of anything. A child could have made those prints, or you, or a tree branch, or...anything could have done this.

PROFESSOR: Anything didn't. The shadow people did.

REPORTER: I can't take anymore of this. There's a very visible woman waiting for me in a motel room, and I got to get back to her before she disappears. Goodbye, Professor, and good luck.

PROFESSOR: [*barring his way*] NO! Listen to me. Please. Write the story. Besides, you can't go. Out there, in the mood they're in, they may hurt you...or worse. They don't like the light as well as the dark. Wait until morning.

REPORTER: You should get some kind of help, you know that?

PROFESSOR: I know that. You are the help I was hoping to get.

REPORTER: I'm leaving.

PROFESSOR: It's your life.

REPORTER: Yeah. It is.

PROFESSOR: Chuckles! Let him out.

> CHUCKLES *appears, unlocks the door for the* REPORTER, *who exits.* CHUCKLES *watches him go. A scream from outside. The* PROFESSOR *rushes to the window. The curtains stir in a sudden wind. They both stare out in panic, then slowly turn away.*

They've killed him. His body is lying there....

In the distance, what could be the sound of a car, or the wind, or... CHUCKLES *listens.*

CHUCKLES: [*mimes driving*] Brmmmmmm. Brmmmmmm.

PROFESSOR: No. That sound—the shadow people crying to each other in the trees....
They'll rush the house, I know it. Quick, Chuckles, the evidence! [CHUCKLES *hands him the plaster cast.*] Distract them while I run for it. Then won't hurt you. Noises! [*The* PROFESSOR *grabs the reel of tape off the recorder.*] Now! [CHUCKLES, *frightened, begins to bang his hands together, then two pots, stamp his feet, make whatever noise he can.*] Goodbye.

The PROFESSOR *rushes out the door, leaving it open behind him. He's gone.* CHUCKLES *remains, making noise, hopping up and down in fear and panic. An electric flash, and the lights go out.* CHUCKLES' *noise stops for a moment. Then it resumes in the darkness, louder and fiercer than before. It continues, and fades, as lights come up on* KAREN's *motel room. She is holding a pad and pencil.*

KAREN: [*V.O., reading what she's written.*] "If you ever read this, that means you came back, and I'd already left. You think I'd wait around to..." [*crosses out, writes*] *"You* can reach me at..." [*crosses out, writes*] "My mom's phone number is 857-6621. I'll call there every day to see if you...." [*She stops writing.*]

[*Live*] He'll never see this. [*She crumples up the note and throws it in a corner.*]

[*V.O.*] Now how'm I gonna make it outta this hole. Paying the tab and leaving like a lady is out of the question. [*She begins to pack her suitcase.*]

[*Live*] Without all this shit I could smile at the girl at the desk, say I'm getting some very fresh air, and hit the highway—but I am taking my worldly possessions. I got a blouse in there I haven't even worn yet.

[*V.O.*] OK. Downstairs, suitcase in hand, deal with the girl at the desk, and hope she doesn't reach for the phone.

[*Live.* CHUCKLES, *in another space, dim light, listening.* KAREN *rehearses her pitch to* PAULINE.] "Listen, Pauline, honey, I got in a bind. This can happen to a girl sometimes and if you don't know it yet, you will. Now I didn't find a window and stiff the place, did I? I'm right here in front of you. And you know why I'm standing here? The cops? I'd be long gone....

I don't give a shit about whoever owns this joint. I'm here 'cause I was concerned about you. If I skipped, it might come outta your salary. I couldn't stand the idea of fucking over another working girl. So what I got to say is this, and I'm saying please. I will send you the money. That's the God's own truth. Soon as I get work, I will send you the money for the entire bill. Gimme the bill. I want it. It's got the address on it? Good. Pauline, some day if you hit a rough patch, I hope someone treats you the way you're treating me. Now listen honey, I want you to look at something....

Lights dim out on CHUCKLES *in the other space.* KAREN *takes a piece of costume jewelry out of her suitcase.*

[*Live*] My mother gave it to me. It's worth a hundred dollars if it's worth a dime.

Here. You loan me twenty bucks on it, and when I send in the money for the bill, I'll pay you back and you can.... [*V.O.*] Forget the jewelry bit. The rest might go. It'll work. [*Live.*] And if it don't, well, what can they do to me that hasn't already been done? All right. It's time to take my old Granny's advice. [KAREN *gets into bed, sitting up, wide awake.*] When in trouble, pull down the shades and pay a visit to some other town, where the new girl is a pleasing novelty. [*Live and V.O.*] Karen darling, soon as it's light, we go.

> *Lights fade on* KAREN. *Lights up on* PAULINE *and* FABER *in the motel office.*

FABER: Pauline—you think you're worth fighting for? If I was with you, I mean, if we were saying all this naked and with my mouth right up against your ear, and a huge gorilla with a baseball bat came up alongside the bed and said Faber get outta there, you gotta fight me first in the parking lot, you think I should just leave—or have it out with him?

PAULINE: Mr. Faber, I think maybe you should just relax and stop talking for a little bit. OK?

FABER: Well?

PAULINE: You'd do what you'd do, that's all. Depending.

FABER: Depending on what, Pauline?

PAULINE: A lot of things.

FABER: What things?

PAULINE: Mr. Faber, you're thinking about something that wasn't. And isn't. And won't be.

FABER: I got a tendency, Pauline. To do just that. You know, there's a lot of people who think their life is what happens to them. Get a job, get married, eat an ice cream cone. It's a great life.

There's another kind of people who don't connect what happens to them with their lives at all. Their life is something else...hopefully.

Shit. I gotta get out of here. You gonna run out of patience, and I'm gonna run out of money. But— if I just hit the road I'll end up in another place like this one, and for places like this one, this one's fine. What do you think, Pauline?

PAULINE: It doesn't matter much, Mr. Faber. The question is, what do you think?

FABER: I don't know, Pauline. I truly don't.... But, hey, I'm trying....

PAULINE: Trying is just trying, Mr. Faber. You've got to *do* something.

FABER: Was that advice, Pauline? Are you telling me how I....

PAULINE: Just forget it, Mr. Faber, OK. I'm just talking. You got me trying to answer you. You know that? I don't even know what *I* should do.

FABER: Pauline, do you think our life is supposed to be interesting?

PAULINE: *Every moment* doesn't have to be interesting...but it is.

FABER: For you.

PAULINE: I don't feel sorry for you, Mr. Faber. I sort of want to, but I don't. I feel like laughing. Not at you. Just laughing.

> PAULINE *is almost having a fit of giggles, but finally manages to stop herself.*
> FABER *stares at her. They sit quietly, as lights come up on the bar, and the carnival*

lot. In the bar, the TV is on, picture and low sound. TIM *and* LINDA *are hanging out, watching the tube. In the lot, same setting as when we saw Bonecrusher: an enclosure, some carnival lights, but the banner of Egypt is gone. The* PITCHMAN, *hat on, and a suitcase in his hand, is standing where his chair and microphone used to be. He walks away from the carnival slowly, crosses the stage, and is gone. In the bar, the* PROFESSOR *enters, carrying his plaster cast. The reel of audio tape is in his pocket, some hanging out. He looks ragged, his clothes torn in places. He sits at the bar.*

TIM: Hi. My name's Tim. This is Linda. Linda, say hello to the nice man.

LINDA: Hello.

> *Suddenly, the* TV *image changes to a close-up of the* PROFESSOR. *He's on a street somewhere, clearly an interviewee on some sort of local television.*

PROFESSOR: Turn it up, please. That's me.

> TIM *turns up the* TV *sound.* TIM, LINDA, *and the* PROFESSOR *watch the show.*

PROFESSOR ON TV: The shadow people are among us. They're around us, all the time. They explain everything. Parapsychology, war, mental illness, religion. They can't control the weather. Or fly. Or raise the dead. They're very light, you know. The wind can blow them away. Very light. Very beautiful. Some say they've always existed, and will exist forever. I wouldn't say that. Some say they....

TIM: [TIM *reaches up and slaps off the* TV. *Silence.*] Come on, Linda. Let's go.

> TIM *exits.* LINDA *follows, but before she leaves, she turns back to the* PROFESSOR *and the audience.*

LINDA: Goodbye.

> LINDA *exits. After a long moment, the* PROFESSOR *moves toward the door as the lights dim on the bar, and on the carnival lot. We return to* PAULINE *and* FABER *as before. A long silence.*

FABER: So. What do you think, Pauline? You think the world's gonna end tonight? Twenty ton hypernuclear bomb drops right through the roof of the motel. We're safe in the eye, sitting here in a great crown of fire, while in the sky, all the dead from all over America, each one a thin paper of ash—and the fire dies, and the wind dies, and they float down from where they been spinning in heaven, drift down slow and easy, doing their last dead dance in the air. Then it's quiet, just you, and me. [CHUCK-LES *enters, sweeping quietly. Long pause.*] No comment. OK. So. What do you think, Pauline? You think we're supposed to be happy here?

PAULINE: At the motel?

FABER: You know what I mean.

PAULINE: I think…we *are* happy here. That happiness is another word for our life. That we were made for joy in everything, even our death.

FABER: Pauline, you hear that in church or somewhere?

PAULINE: No, Mr. Faber. I know it. 'Cause I saw it.

FABER: It's not a thing you *see*, Pauline.

PAULINE: You're wrong, Mr. Faber…I saw it in my father's eyes before he died. I was standing there, and he had all these tubes in him, and he was trying to speak and no one could make out the words. [CHUCKLES *approaches them. He listens.*] He was looking right at me, and then my Mom went over close to him, and he spoke again. "What'd he say, Ma?" "He says you're an angel." He was *seeing* it, and then I could feel it, like a light all around me, and him, and my Mom. It sounds terrible to say, with him so sick and all, but I felt very happy. He died that night, by himself, while everyone else was sleeping. A little of that happiness is in me, still. It's a truer thing than the other ways I feel sometimes— so I try to…remember.

FABER: It was years ago…couple of months after my father died, I went to the beach. I was lying there on the sand, and I saw him. He was rising up out of the water, but not like some religious painting or something. He was just walking out of the ocean in his bathing suit. He always loved swimming in the ocean. He came in dripping from a calm sea, and walked over to me. I knew he was dead, and that it was a … something in my head or…. He looked very happy to see me there. He smiled, and waved—and that little moment made me feel he loved me in a way nothing in his life had ever done…and that was it. Then he was gone, and I was smiling, almost laughing, and the tears were running down my face.

  A silence. CHUCKLES *rings the desk bell once. He moves away from them slowly, and exits.*

You ever think about dying, Pauline?

PAULINE: I've thought about it, but not all the time or anything. I've got enough….

FABER: One world at a time, right, Pauline?

  The phone rings. PAULINE *picks it up.*

PAULINE: [*on phone*] Office…. Yes, she is. I'll connect you. [PAULINE *puts the call through, hangs up. To* FABER.] The girl in seven. She got a call. Goes to show.

FABER: Goes to show what?

PAULINE: Goes to show that…if I say, you'll say "you learn that in church or something, Pauline?"

FABER: Well?

PAULINE: Well, what?

FABER: Well, you gonna marry me or not, Pauline?

PAULINE: You didn't ask me, Mr. Faber.

FABER: I'm asking you now.

PAULINE: No.

FABER: OK. Unrequited love, that's OK. Better than no love at all. And I'll know you're here, Pauline. Right in the middle of America, like a fountain of snow.

  A long silence.

PAULINE: How much longer are you gonna be staying, Mr. Faber?

FABER: You know something, Pauline. I better leave in the morning…I better go home, wherever that is. Keep the porch light on, Momma. Let it shine out onto the lawn, and don't turn it off till sunrise, cause that's when I'm coming. There, that's me, little plume of dust rising, that's me in the dust cloud, coming from the east, with the sun behind me in splendor…hey, who knows? So. What do you think, Pauline?

PAULINE: I don't know, Mr. Faber. What do *you* think?

> FABER *and* PAULINE *are still.* CHUCKLES *appears, and alongside him, the* MAYOR. *Lights come up as well on all the other places we've seen:* KAREN'S *room, the bar, the carnival lot, the* PROFESSOR's *house, the open field.*

MAYOR: Interesting country, little buddy. You lucky you here.

> *The* MAYOR *steps back into darkness, as lights fade on all places.* CHUCKLES *alone. Light fades on* CHUCKLES, *and out.*

END OF PLAY

Erik Ehn

∾

Angel uh God

Angel uh God, © 1998 by Erik Ehn

•

Cast of Characters

JOSH, Cathy's husband, age 30
CATHY, Josh's wife, age 30
BARB, Josh's mistress, red-haired Irish illegal, age 28
WILLIS, Josh and Cathy's son, age 13
SEAN, Josh and Cathy's son, age 1½
CRAYTON, Josh's friend, age 40
WILLIS THE ANGEL, age 15
SEAN THE ANGEL, age 15
JESUS, not the Mass card, age 33
LENA, Cathy's mother, age 60
LEE, a Shaker, age 30
A BUNCH OF MOMS, all ages

Double casting:
One actress can play Barb and Lee
One actor can play Willis and Willis the Angel
One actor can play Crayton and Sean the Angel
A minimum of 8 actors

Time and place:
Vermont and The Bronx, the present.

ONE—CONSULT LABEL

BARB *is center stage in hardly any light at all. All we can really make out is her face, or we could if it weren't covered by her fine right hand. On the yoke of her hand, we can clearly make out a black pentangle in a circle. She drops her hand after a while, and her eyes are closed, as if she's working through a hangover. Lights up suddenly, and she's a completely different person. She's as sweet as pie in a modest cotton dress. She's got a brand new vinyl album in her hands, still in its cellophane. This album is called* Angel uh God. *She reads from the jacket, while ripping off the wrapper. She can't wait for us to hear the songs.*

BARB: *Angel uh God.* Bottlerockets. Chest of Diamonds. Look Here. Mumbleypeg. Turnstile. The Magic Clerk. Step Dance. Shaker Woman. Radio Baseball.

She picks up a kid's cardboard record player, puts the record on, and walks off with the unit, very carefully. The first sounds off the record are the sounds of a snowstorm. The lights go to black, the noise increases, and carries us into the next scene.

TWO—BOTTLEROCKETS

The dead of winter, late at night, Van Cortlandt Park, the Bronx. WILLIS *carries* SEAN *in his arms.* SEAN *is tightly bundled, and* WILLIS *is in good clothes that are way too big for him. We hear the creak of dry, new snow as the brothers make their way down a steep embankment. The father is following right behind, in time, carefully putting his feet in* WILLIS' *tracks.* JOSH *is wearing clothes that are nice but way too small for him, and he has no overcoat. He carries a baseball bat.*

JOSH: Do you think anybody saw us coming down here?

WILLIS: No, I really don't think so.

JOSH: There are some guys who want to find us. You don't think anybody saw?

WILLIS: No. I didn't see anybody.

JOSH: Don't get your knickers in a twist. You know why they're after us.

WILLIS: I don't know why we're down here.

JOSH: Same reason.

WILLIS: Dad?

JOSH: Yes?

WILLIS: We could do 'em off the roof.

JOSH: Why?

WILLIS: We could do 'em off the roof just as easy.

JOSH: This is better.

WILLIS: Normally people do 'em off the roof. In July. Or the summer.

JOSH: Well, fireworks show up better out here.

WILLIS: They better be good, that's all I'm saying.

JOSH: I'm doing this for you. That's the whole idea. Live with it.

WILLIS: You're looking around a lot. *You* see anybody?

JOSH: We got to be careful, is all. There are some shady characters in the world. But it's a park. We have rights. Van Cortlandt Park. Park. Play. People play in a park. We're gonna do our fireworks. I got a bat.

WILLIS: Nobody's gonna know our spot. Good. I see your point. I like fireworks much as the next guy. I'm only trying to get organized, for crying out loud.

JOSH: We shoot 'em up, and people see 'em for miles around. Blam. Fireworks. But they don't know where from. "How'd those fireworks get there? How'd they get so good?" Like it's a bright idea the sky just came up with on its own.

WILLIS: Let's do it.

JOSH: I want you to be calm. To know that you're here with me.

WILLIS: You get 'em in Virginia?

JOSH: No, right here on Bedford. I know a guy. We got bottlerockets to start. You like those. Go through there.

WILLIS: You gonna set 'em off for us?

JOSH: No. You.

WILLIS: You gonna let me? You used to say I'm gonna burn my hand.

JOSH: You won't burn your hand. We'll start with bottlerockets. I got all kinds.

WILLIS: You're walking funny.

JOSH: It's a game. Keep walking.

WILLIS: This spot is good.

JOSH: Right here.

WILLIS: Yeah. Whattya got?

JOSH: I'm very peaceful now.

WILLIS: We're all doin' fine. Except for Sean—he's cold as ice. Let me set 'em off and we'll go back home.

JOSH: You like firecrackers, don't you?

WILLIS: Yes, I do. I like 'em. I want 'em.

JOSH: Here they are. Here are your matches. Think they'll wake Sean up?

WILLIS: These whistle more than bang. Give us the bottle, dad. We'll need a bottle to do it right.

JOSH: You don't need it.

WILLIS: It's the best thing. Might as well have some fun.

> JOSH *takes a pint of Majorska from his back pocket, and dumps the last spit swallow out. He tosses the bottle to* WILLIS.

JOSH: Yeah. You'll want to do it right. Have some fun.

> WILLIS *puts some bottlerockets in the bottle, and starts praying very quietly.*

WILLIS: Our father who art in heaven—

JOSH: What do you need to pray for? We just got out of church.

WILLIS: Helps you from getting duds. Our father—

JOSH: You don't need that.

WILLIS: [*Not turning around. He knows something is about to happen*] Help me. I love you. Help me.

JOSH: Willis?

WILLIS *strikes the match, and turns to face his father.* JOSH *heaves the bat back. Blackout, and the match still glows. We hear* BOB MURPHY, *the radio voice of the NY Mets, broadcasting in the distance: "A long fly ball, deep into left field. It might go. It's gone! A homerun! A homerun!" The match blows out.*

THREE—CHEST OF DIAMONDS

When the lights come up again, WILLIS' *clothes and the baby's blanket lie empty, upstage center. Downstage right,* JOSH *squats with the murderous bat, looking ahead of him, mesmerized. His friend* CRAYTON *stands upstage by the clothes; he still sees the bodies. Downstage left,* WILLIS *stands with hair neatly combed, dressed in the uniform of his parochial school—clip on tie with* SHM *embroidered on it, white shirt, dark pants. Two long white bones protrude from his shoulder blades through his jacket; he's in the process of becoming an angel. He faces* JESUS CHRIST, *who is a clean shaven, nice looking fellow wearing a white shirt open at the collar, dark pants, and a tan belt. Black shiny shoes. He has a beautiful crown of the purest gold on his head. His expression is utterly inscrutable.*

JOSH *wipes the bat with the snow, even though the blood's long gone. He stands, raises the bat, swings. He squats, and wipes the bat again.*

WILLIS: My name is Willis. I get to touch your face, I call.

He starts to touch JESUS' *face, then thinks twice, and lets his hand fall.*

JOSH: [*To* CRAYTON] I didn't leave any tracks. Can you believe it?

WILLIS: You scare me, man.

JOSH: I washed the bat in the snow. I stood up, I swung, I washed the bat in the snow. Can you believe it?

WILLIS: The whole truth and nothing but the truth.

JOSH: Don't you tell. I still got a bat. Hey, just jokin'.

WILLIS: Sean and I are sleeping in our room in the attic. I hear a chair pulled back on the first floor. Hear it through the timbers in my sleep—it wakes me up. Haven't seen him in days, dad, and I'm taken aback. Know it's him by the weight of the scrape. He's all-nightin' it.

JOSH: Stood up. I took all necessary precautions, Crayton. Took 'em to church right before. Did my bit. For the baby—the baby I figured is covered, for sure, but to be sure—for the baby I received communion, chewed it up and passed it into his mouth. He swallowed. I saw. Took 'em out here. Stood up. Homered. You can see that. Can you believe i?

WILLIS: I'm getting to it. It was dark still when I got back to sleep. When I hear him again—march of the muffled drums—I roll to the window and see them cutting open the newspaper bales and loading yellow cupcakes out of stepvans into Zuckers. Must be six. I hear the door, then the screendoor, dad's back out of the house. I don't sleep. This was summer.

JOSH: Wash the bat. Died in violence in a state of grace. They're shoe-ins, I tell you. And I got a girlfriend. I love Barb more than I got hands to say.

WILLIS: Downstairs there's last night's paper, three quart bottles, and a fly stuck in a plate of eggs. "Barfly," I observe. I boil a pan of water for coffee, a big pan. Much as I want. My rat sense tells me my time in this house is a series of final days. Dad's out for who cares how long now. No skin off me. I got pepper at ten and a game at eleven. I been sleeping on my mitt to break it in, and it's just about ready.

JOSH: Barb, my girlfriend, said she could handle the wife. Cathy's just Cathy, that's all. But the kids—they're part me and part her. Barb couldn't handle the mixture. So the kids, we had to lose the kids, you know. No tracks. No snow. Hit a home run. Perfect circle. Zero. Back home. Take a good look, Crayton. And don't tell anybody but me about what you see. I want you to convince me I did this, when I ask. I can't stop my heart. I can't stop it, Crayton. No matter how many people I show.

Lights down on them, and they exit. JESUS *lifts his hand.*

WILLIS: Not yet, man, not yet. Let me take you through the game. It's a good petition, man.

JESUS lowers his hand.

We hustle through pepper, then it's bench versus starters. I'm bench. Only a scrimmage, but I get to wear my uniform. At the J.F.K., out there by Dexter. This one time I'm at the plate yelling a joke about salted peanuts back at the mound to see if I can work out a walk. Then I stop, when I see my dad walking back and forth parallel to the left field fence. It's unusual for him to show himself during the day when he's on a jag, but when he does, he uses courtesy and puts himself in a public place so we don't get paralyzed with fright or start yelling at him. I lose track of my act. Screwball—pop—catches me a good one on the arm—turns up a hairline fracture the next day. I take the walk to first and then keep walking down the baseline, dropping my helmet behind me. Everybody lets me go, no big deal. I climb the fence with one hand. He's clean as a marine from ten feet. Hair brillianteened. Nails cut back. Closer, and his teeth are sulphur yellow, and he smells like corroding tin. It's when we go for ice cream and we're eating our cones, staring up close, that I notice his nerves are so shot his pupils are frozen. The sugar takes his shakes down some. Walking along, I don't have the muscle to put behind these ha ha ironic comments I have planned about his grown-upedness. He's doing this smiling thing, so tight if you flipped his upper lip it would have snapped up over his nose and forehead. Give the man credit though. He always answered at least the hard questions. He knows I'm mad, so he figures out something to do and he shows me it. He takes me up the hill over the rock wall around what used to be the hotel, then past the skunk cabbage and wood chipper to a tarp covered with long needled pine branches. This is where he comes to when he's riding out a bender. He tells me to sit Indian style and the idea is I have to watch him fall asleep with his clothes off. He has this—not dream, exactly—this belief that when he's asleep all the pins and wires that have been put in his broken bones glow hot and shine through his skin like diamonds. Stars. He thinks he has a chest full of diamonds—that there's a four square box pattern for one, squeezed long over his breastbone. He says that when he wakes up he sees the points fading firefly too fast to know if they're real—he wants me to watch and connect the dots and tell him what constellation he's under the command of. But maybe this is more to control my time with the act of sleeping, which would be sweet victory for his method. He's got me with the notion anyway. He's naked and he falls asleep. Skin improbably smellin' like baseball card gum. I don't see anything glowing, but I feel the skin over his ribs with my bad arm—the bad arm for extra sensitivity, like a safecracker. Skin's powdery. I can make out the gristle, the starry gristle. His breastbone is in two pieces from a rebar accident; I can move the parts. The pain's bad, and I know by the fish-line tugs at his eyelids that he's suffering too. But he's possum for an hour. When he's up and dressed I tell him "no, I didn't see nothing." And he says I must have been asleep. But I have the pattern of his metal memorized. I take that with me. I get to touch your face, I call.

He does. It's very hot.

Your cheek's on fire, but my skin's not glassy. What's that mean? It means I get to be an angel of vengeance, I call. He was saying: "No matter how much you hurt, I hurt more. No matter how much you *need* to hurt, I need to hurt more. And all your pain cannot penetrate me. My sky is shut to you." Until now. Now my hand can reach through bone and squeeze light out of his heart and show him the sun in the middle of his heaven. Do this for me, will you? Send Sean back into the world. Make Barb and my father conceive a great need for a child. Put Sean into that baby, and then I can get at them through what's left of my brother. You got me? Starting with Barb we will eat away at Dad's life until he learns the error of his ways. That's the story of my revenge.

Blackout.

FOUR—MUMBLEYPEG

Out behind Gaelic Park, in the Bronx. Summer. The Wolftones play "Devil in Killarney" inside the stadium. B A R B *comes running around a wall, laughing.* J O S H *runs in, chasing her.*

J O S H: Come back, come back.

B A R B: Stay out, stay out. You leave and you're out.

J O S H: They know your face. You could get us back in.

B A R B: I don't know that my face is worth the price of admission, Josh.

J O S H: It is! It's the headliners. They're up. Let's go.

B A R B: Who's playing now, if you're so smart.

J O S H: The Wolftones. I can stand them real good.

B A R B: It's just as bad you knowin' who it is. These old boys are on their last legs, and I was still getting no attention paid to me in there.

J O S H: Trying to behave myself, Barb. To know my place.

B A R B: Put yourself right in front of me then, and shut up.

He stands in front of her.

JOSH: Anything else for you, ma'am?

BARB: Sh. Don't move a muscle.

JOSH: Somethin' good's come into you.

BARB: Don't move your mouth.

JOSH: I can't say anything?

BARB: Only if it's very good.

JOSH: Can I say something that'll make you kiss me?

BARB: Sometimes you can.

JOSH: Now I don't know what to say.

BARB: Keep thinking. I'm on your side here.

JOSH: It's only Wednesday. You're not usually so nice to me til the weekend.

BARB: Summer. Gaelic Park. Where I'm no more foreign than a slap on the back. You paid my ticket. I'm overcome.

JOSH: The ticket's what put me over the top, huh?

BARB: I run around a corner and I've got a Saturday drunk in the middle of the week, chased by you. It's not your money, because you have none. But it's like a money feeling. You're a promising scratcher.

JOSH: Light's pouring out of your eyes, honey.

BARB: There's so much in front of me, you.

JOSH: You woke up early when you could have slept late. Made me breakfast—

BOTH: The most important meal of the day.

BARB: The Stapps didn't need their kids looked after this morning, because of a pre-school test of some kind. I got you fed solid food, got a kiss, got a promise.

JOSH: For this—

BARB: For this. And right off I started thinking so clear. The milk went "swoop" into the third cup of coffee, and I saw it take over the whole cup in a breath. "I'm staying. I'm staying," I'm thinking. With you.

JOSH: Inside, outside...

BARB: And the sugar, milk, coffee and maybe money are swooping and blooming and filling my whole brain up. Green card, maybe? Connection at the parish office. They're trying to fly under radar since the nuns got social security, but the tie that binds—

JOSH: Then with that, you could move to day care—

BARB: No house girl—

JOSH: To trade school—

BARB: I'm studied up. A degree from the other side.

JOSH: A name. My name. A stake in the ground. Rooted. Rooted.

BARB: From over there, to over here. Re-incarnation.

JOSH: Light pouring out.

BARB: And by unnatural chance, Stockton's Wing has left to play, and they're your real favorites, but you don't remember names.

JOSH: [Singing along, way off, but with undisguised glee] La la la la la la! All very possible.

BARB: Kiss me.

JOSH: Now?

BARB: Now.

> *They make out on the grass. The sound of an elevated train comes up.*
What—

JOSH: The number four. Cover your ears.

> *The 4 passes and blocks out the sun. They cover each other's ears. When they do, the subway noises shut off, and there's a total silence.* WILLIS THE ANGEL *enters and plays mumbleypeg with a jackknife upstage right of the couple. He's more of an angel now, with no jacket, and feathers on his wings. When he gets the knife to stick, the revenge is accomplished. He leaves, with the knife left quivering there.* JOSH *and* BARB *take their hands off each other's ears. The train noise is heard, but it's fading. The Wolftones have been replaced by Stockton's Wing, who play a slow air. The mood of the couple goes one-eighty.*

Something new's come over you. You don't look the same.

BARB: You neither.

JOSH: You're thinking something. You're thinking the same thing as me.

BARB: All the possibilities.

JOSH: Let's go back inside.

> *He starts to go, but* BARB *stops him with a song.*

BARB: *Luck came in with a stranger's love*
And an accent thick as lead
I learned love in a foreign tongue
And slept in an alien bed

> *The love was real and the visions wild*
> *As a night of fire and stone*
> *I remember still the special names*
> *The swing of the truncheon, the crack of the bone*

> > *To stay or to leave, each is so hard*
> > *A wedding there will be, and I'll stay for the card*

> > *From four green fields, to one green card*
> > *The curragh splits the waves, though the rowing is hard*

> *I spoke Irish when first I spoke*
> *But English spoke the patrol*
> *Peace peace peace my love*
> *We'll wed under terms of my long parole*

> *My beloved be at peace*
> *There's love in the sad old songs*
> *Lovely lay the fields of green*
> *The fields are all gone*

To stay or to leave, each is so hard
A wedding there will be, and I'll stay for the card

From four green fields, to one green card
The curragh splits the waves, though the rowing is hard

The genuine article
Familiar to the race
The dead walk and the living lie
Each in a separate place

Finally a peaceful home
Possibly a finer home
Finally a peaceful home
A stranger here no more

JOSH: We were doing so good for the past few months...

BARB: There's more to do.

JOSH: I don't know what to say to you. There's more music going on in there, that's what. We could go back and listen.

BARB: The best we've done is forget.

JOSH: Go ahead and say it.

BARB: Forget. That's all.

JOSH: And now you remember?

BARB: We want a baby. Do you hear me?

JOSH: I'd be drunk and listening to the home team lose on radio baseball right now if it wasn't for you. I listen loud and clear. Doesn't mean I got answers. Everybody wants a baby, now and then. Held it in my arms. Woke up in the morning, held it, and started moaning to it. Went in the basement and threw out all my power tools. You think I don't know how pretty they are?

BARB: Another one'll put things right.

JOSH: What's the best idea we got between us?

BARB: A real baby, a baby to hold. Not to care for or work with, but ours and no one else's. The feeling is over us. There's no saying no. We'll cleave to each other under the sheets after the *feis* and sleep towards our object. The right word's in your language. I don't have it. It must come from you. Say it.

JOSH: Yes. A Baby. Yes.

A baby wrapped in SEAN's blanket comes down from the sky, into BARB's arms.
He looks just like Sean. Just like Sean did. But older.

BARB: He looks like everything.

They moan over the baby, in love. CATHY and her mother LENA enter, wearing long black dresses. BARB and JOSH don't see them. CATHY takes the baby out of

BARB's *arms, and walks in a circle around the stage, with her mother following close behind.* BARB *looks into her empty hands.*

Hey!

> *She collapses into* JOSH's *arms. They hold each other, sitting and rocking, downstage right.*

FIVE—TURNSTILE

CATHY: He brought the Irish witch over. He gets what he deserves.

LENA: It's a baby.

CATHY: You're here to help me, ma.

LENA: Then go slow.

CATHY: It comes around.

LENA: Cathy...

CATHY: I know secrets, ma. I could tell you more, if it wouldn't give you a heart attack.

LENA: We don't have to go so far.

CATHY: They get a baby, no I get a baby.

LENA: Let me hold—

CATHY: Don't touch. She can make him do what she—make him stand where she wants, make him talk about anything.

LENA: Let me—

CATHY: Don't touch. Fair is fair.

LENA [*In Greek*] *Evris dike.*

CATHY: No, not so much arguin'. Not so far afield. Leave off, ma. Crayton told me secrets.

LENA: He'll start crying. I don't think I can help you if he starts crying.

CATHY: We're almost there.

LENA: Make sure it's a good place.

CATHY: Here we are.

LENA: This is the subway.

CATHY: The furthest away place. It'll work out for everybody. A thousand people pass this spot every minute. It's far away, and public, and we're in the clear. I can leave and hide and that's that.

LENA: I'm not going down there, with you.

CATHY: You can touch him once, then. I'm going alone.

LENA: Did you make me wear black because you think their baby will die?

CATHY: Camouflage.

LENA: Let him have this. He won't cry. All he has to do is lie there.

> *She gives the baby a Tootsie Pop.*

CATHY: He won't cry. *They* will.

> *She disappears into a subway entrance. Lena pauses, then follows.*

SIX—THE MAGIC CLERK

Focus goes to JOSH *and* BARB *downstage.*

BARB: Now hold on a second. We're supposed to go through hardships. That's understood. But there's a derangement going on. Some wires have gotten crossed.

JOSH: Our livest wires. Why do you figure?

BARB: The ghosts of heaven can't lay a hand on you, but they can put ideas in your head. The baby was meant to grow old, and work hell on us that way. By what we knew from a child.

JOSH: Kidnapping wasn't enough?

BARB: That's hell on him too. A plan's gone wrong. An earthquake of sorts—everybody's going down. Can't even keep vengeance straight in this city anymore, there are so many stories. The simplest algebra is peeling out of its axioms and slithering down the streets.

JOSH: Look at me, Barb.

> *She stares transfixed in another direction. He can't turn her head. Focus shifts to a token booth in the subway.* LENA *approaches the clerk.*

LENA: Where did my daughter go?

CLERK: [*Into the microphone*} She took the baby down along the tracks.

LENA: What was her state of mind?

CLERK: She was scared at first.

LENA: Of what? Did the train—

CLERK: No, ma'am. She walked down the center of the tracks, growing more scared all the time, listening to the robot arms shift, and to the creatures. She meant to leave the baby where it would be found, but not found too easily—so that whoever got the baby would really want it.

LENA: She didn't want to hurt it. Is it hurt?

CLERK: Then she got bit. As she was walking. An urban possum came up and smote her with a sword made of a rusty splinter of iron rail; he caught her on the side. She heaved the baby high in the air, because of the surprise, and it landed in a pile of scrap. He starved to death after two days—it's been that long, yes. Cathy turned around and around, but the baby wasn't crying with the sugar in its mouth.

LENA: My daughter—

CLERK: Two large men put the rubbish in a sack, and didn't see the kid. He went from truck to barge, and over the sound, and all over, then ended up in the ground.

LENA: I want to find my daughter.

CLERK: By miraculous coincidence, the baby's landfill rested in a valley sacred to the Paumanok Indians. It worked like a get out of jail free card, and the baby went straight to being an angel in its prime.

LENA: That's not possible. Babies take longer. They have to have the same number of moral tests that a grown up faces in a lifetime. They have to go through a special school up there.

CLERK: The sacred ground made him exempt. He's the same age as Willis.

LENA: What's his job?

CLERK: He's an angel of vengeance.

LENA: Willis is that already. That's enough.

CLERK: No. The baby is Sean, and Sean is an angel of vengeance against you and your daughter.

LENA: It was his father who—

CLERK: No, listen carefully. This is an exact change. Willis is an angel bent on destroying Barb and Josh. Sean returned in the new baby, and was meant to help Willis, but your daughter Cathy came along and confused the plan. The new Sean had no time to form a grudge against Barb and Josh before he was taken away—in fact quite the opposite. The baby's eyes weren't ripe enough to focus on the material world, but were hugely vulnerable to the lights of love. Sean is therefore dedicated to revenge against you two, who have unwittingly brought about the death of your reincarnated son and grandson. There are now two boy angels, side by side in heaven, probably very near us, bent on destruction, linked, but straining at each other.

LENA: There's angels working in two directions at once!

> *The baby comes flying by.* WILLIS *comes on, in great shape, all golden, riding a bicycle with big wings sticking off the rack. He's trying to catch Sean.*

WILLIS: Wait up! I got to tell you something! Hey! Wait up!

> SEAN *and* WILLIS *exit.*

LENA: And that's what happened to my daughter.

CLERK: The possum poisoned your daughter's blood. She's going to come to a bad end unless she can be found and bolted to the floor. The Iris witch is also heading right off her rocker.

LENA: What's going to happen to me?

CLERK: You're old. You're in the subway. You won't be able to find your way home.

LENA: How do you know so much?

CLERK: I work here night and day. Nothing surprises me anymore.

LENA: Which way do I go?

CLERK: Go away.

> *Lights out in boot.* LENA *wanders, and exits.*

SEVEN—STEP DANCE

> JOSH *stays on the floor downstage.* BARB *rises in a trance.*

BARB: All my witchcraft is zigzag sudden, and brilliant. This justice is thunder-spent, is rain and sleet and snow. Is random. Cannot be incanted away. It is everywhere, in its season.

> SEAN *and* WILLIS *appear. They're both full grown angels now.* WILLIS *plays bodran and sings lead;* SEAN *plays pennywhistle and joins in on the last chorus.* BARB *does a slow step dance, slowly and out of time. She's losing her mind; her feet are bare and her hair is wild. Her hands never move from her sides.*

SEAN AND WILLIS: *One plays the fife and*
The other plays the drum
And each marks the ranting
And the raving of his mum

The mothers have done
What they oughtn't have done
And the sons commence to play
Each son play for his mum today
And drives her senses away

Down in madness
Off they go
Hauling sorrow
To a world
That's far below
Where justice will be done

One plays the bodran
With a steady right hand
And the other pipes the whistle
With a fury beats the band

The worst of madness is knowing you're mad
And knowing you'll stay that way
The mums see they're slipping
But slip the same
When the sons commence to play

Down in madness
off they go
Hauling sorrow
To a world
Where they well know
Accounting has begun

All the steps are measured
As the dance comes to a close
Flowers on the floor
The lily and the rose

Steps awry
And strewn as wild
As flowers on the floor
Senses flown
As pollen, blown
And the mums will love no more

Down in madness
Trucking sorrow
To a fire burns below
That's hotter than two sons

> *Song ends and* BARB *freezes.* CATHY *runs on, in a poisoned fury. She's barefoot too, and her black dress is in tatters; possum babies drip from her back. She stabs Barb with an iron splinter. Both women go to their knees, and keen with their heads straight back. They cut themselves off, mid-wail. The sons take two steps toward Josh, with outstretched arms. Josh rises instantly.*

SEAN AND WILLIS: [*Sean calling with longing, Willis calls in anger:*] Daddy. Daddy.
JOSH: Upstate.

> *He salutes and skidadles out of there.*

EIGHT—SHAKER WOMAN

> SEAN *and* WILLIS *argue. The mothers slip off to the world below.*

WILLIS: We got to get him.
SEAN: I'm through.
WILLIS: We're not half done.
SEAN: I'm through, I tell you. Cathy's out.
WILLIS: I gave you Cathy.
SEAN: I gave you Barb. She was my mom.
WILLIS: Some mom. She ordered you dead. She had dad kill you.
SEAN: Lay off. She was all right by me last time around. We have different histories now. I'm not a baby anymore. I can't help you.
WILLIS: I stayed out of your way on Cathy, which was very hard for me. You stayed out of my way on Barb—job well done. There's still dad.
SEAN: Dad's going to have to fall through the cracks.
WILLIS: He's the prime mover.
SEAN: As far as I know, Cathy was his problem, and Cathy's out.
WILLIS: Angels of vengeance, man. This is heaven. We're the new twin thunders. It's impossible—it's impossible that the women lose their minds and the guy gets off scot free. The nail is begging for the hammer.
SEAN: I'm through.
WILLIS: You're driving me nuts! This is the picture: It's winter. Dad ran away. He went upstate. Outside Albany.
SEAN: Where do you get off—
WILLIS: I'm number one son.
SEAN: Not any more.
WILLIS: Well, that's where he is. I said it, and he is. I thought you might like to get strong on some justice, but I can finish him off. Alone, if I have to.

> WILLIS *runs and gets his angel bike; he rides it around the stage.* SEAN *runs and gets his. Hot pursuit.*

SEAN: Wait up, wait up!

>DAD *stumbles on, trudging through high snow. He's freezing and starving in upstate New York. The angels dismount, and put conflicting ideas in* JOSH's *head.*

WILLIS: Fall down.

SEAN: Get up.

WILLIS: Quit.

SEAN: Keep going.

JOSH: [*To himself*] What's to eat? Got the snow heaves. Enough of that.

>*He lies down and starts to sleep.* SEAN *whistles to someone offstage.*

WILLIS: What are you doing?

SEAN: I renege. I renege utterly on the deal. I'm bringing Barb back in a new form. Find him. Right this way, lady. She's a regular woman and she lives down the road.

>BARB *enters as* LEE, *in a Shaker dress. She crosses, her head bowed against a high wind. She nearly trips over* DAD. *She brushes his hair back; he raises his head.*

JOSH: Help me.

WILLIS: Make her a Shaker woman.

LEE: What are you doing out here? This isn't your property. No strangers allowed.

>*She pulls her hand away.*

JOSH: What's your name?

LEE: Lee.

JOSH: How 'bout it, Lee. Will you give me a hand?

SEAN: Food.

LEE: I can bring you food—

WILLIS: She's got vows.

LEE: But I don't have shelter for you.

SEAN: Toolshed.

LEE: Unless you'd be willing to stay in one of the outbuildings. And work. Work hard. I have a station wagon, but it's broke down. I can't take you to the shelter in this town. This is Shaker property.

JOSH: Shaker—the religion?

LEE: We own all this.

JOSH: I thought you guys had all died out.

LEE: That's what we tell people to keep 'em from thinking secret empire.

SEAN: She likes him.

JOSH: What's the basic drill?

LEE: We're a celibate religious community. You know that much. The guiding principles are Purity of Life, Confession of Sin, and Consecration of Strength, Time and Talent.

JOSH: You can help me.

LEE: What happened to you?

JOSH: To tell you the truth, it's a story I'd have to make up as I went along. The guiding principle is I'm pulled in too many directions at once.

LEE: We'll have to get you home somehow.

SEAN: She loves him.

WILLIS: Shut up!

JOSH: Don't have one. I got Strength. And I got Time.

LEE: What about Talent? You give that away.

JOSH: I play baseball. I still got it.

LEE: Now what are we going to do with that? There's no one to play with up here. All I got now is Labor and Temperance and the Mighty Dual Spirit. It's the rare person has the patience to stay longer than it takes to get boots dry.

JOSH: This is all very interesting to me. There's a lot I need to know about—Confession of Sin and all. I think a lot. Let me work at your place.

WILLIS: [*Producing a steel bucket*] Inside, her guts are a bucket of stone. She loves through work and fears the body.

He throws stones from the bucket across the stage in a quick swipe.

LEE: We got two ways of taking in members. You got to be serious minded, or you can come in by adoption. Which do you think you want. Will you be either kind?

WILLIS: He gets scared. No kids, no baseball—she'll work him to death.

SEAN: [*To JOSH*] Run away!

JOSH: I got my second wind. On account of you, Lee. That's a remarkable religion you have.

LEE: No, you—all of you—you don't stay. You don't stay serious, and you don't stay adoptable.

WILLIS: Then run on away to Van Cortlandt Park. Meet you down there.

They mount their bicycles. SEAN's *first up.*

SEAN: I'm ahead of you.

LEE: Hands to work and hearts to God.

She kisses him on the mouth.

Stay warm.

He starts to leave. With his back to her:

JOSH: So, Lee...

Lee goes. He turns. Okay, so he leaves.

NINE—RADIO BASEBALL

In the dark, a song plays through cheap speakers:

Radio baseball
He wears the game face
He stands alone
And it's always the same face

Lights up, and we are in Van Cortlandt Park, the next day. Still winter, but warmer... about forty-five degrees. DAD's *ratty jacket is open. He stands with a bat, in the same place where he killed his sons. He imagines he faces a great pitcher. A portable tape player re-broadcasts an old Mets game, the sound of which immediately cuts off the song.* BOB MURPHY *speaks in even tones.*

JOSH: Batter's in his box—

WILLIS: Check out time, old man.

JOSH: Back in the box—

SEAN: You got to give him an out clause. That's fair.

JOSH: Back to the scene of the crime. Inning after inning.

WILLIS: Hey, pop—

> WILLIS *makes a charge.* SEAN *restrains him.*

Let me at him.

SEAN: No fair.

JOSH: Waiting for his pitch—

> *Swings, misses.*

Whoa, swinging for the fences. Feel the breeze.

WILLIS: Right now. This is perfect. Can't you remember?

SEAN: One thing at a time. I knew him some other times too.

WILLIS: Let go of me!

> *The angels wrestle violently.*

JOSH: He takes his stance and sits on his pitch. Well, what's it gonna be?

> *As the angels tumble around the stage, every woman in the play, plus a few extra, come out and squat in a semi-circle. They lift their arms out, parallel to the floor, and call their children. The two year old child of each woman comes out dressed as a cherub—wings, red cheeks, the works.*

JOSH AND THE WOMEN: See my baby. My baby has the angel face. See my baby. My baby comes again and again. See my baby. See the hundred thousand vengeances.

THE END

John Steppling

∿

Standard of the Breed

.

Standard of the Breed, first presented at the Cast Theatre in Hollywood on August 7, 1988, was directed by the author and had the following cast:

JACK	Bob Glaudini
CASSIE	Diane DeFoe
REESE	Harvey Perr
TEELA	O-Lan Jones
CHUCK	Mick Collins

ACT 1

SCENE: *In dark, sound of large dog barking. Lights up slowly on kennel—*JACK *stands, still in casino uniform, with tie undone and jacket draped over chair.* CASSIE *seated, purse on lap. They listen to barking until it stops.*

CASSIE: It's those birds.

JACK: Crows.

CASSIE: Crows, yes.

> *Silence.*

My, boyfriend, Chuck, he called you.

JACK: Chuck, sure, I know, I... He called yesterday.

CASSIE: He's not feeling well. He stayed at the hotel.

JACK: Did your boyfriend, Chuck? Does Chuck like dogs?

CASSIE: I guess.

JACK: Do you know much about the breed?

CASSIE: Excuse me...I...

JACK: We raise Mastiffs, sometimes referred to as English Mastiffs. [*pause*] How much do you know about Mastiffs?

CASSIE: [*pause*] I'm sorry.

> *Silence. They stare at each other.* CASSIE *stands...*

JACK: Don't go...

CASSIE: Chuck isn't feeling well, he's still at the hotel...

JACK: In Las Vegas?

CASSIE: At the Sands.

JACK: [*nods, smiles*] ...I used to work at the Sands.

> *Pause.* CASSIE *slowly sits.* JACK *pulls up chair and sits facing her. He leans forward, intent.*

Mastiffs are the largest dogs in the world. Great Danes, Irish Wolfhounds, both are a bit taller, but Mastiffs weigh more. Not even Saint Bernards are as big. [*pause*] They're special animals, I believe.

> *Pause.*

Where are you from, Cassie?

CASSIE: I was born in Pennsylvania, right by Penn State.

JACK: [*nods*] Uh huh.

CASSIE: ...But I lived in Tacoma most of the time.

JACK: Washington.

CASSIE: [*nodding—pause*] I live in Los Angeles now.

JACK: With Chuck?

CASSIE: [*nodding*] Not in L.A. exactly. We live in La Habra. Do you know where that is?
>   JACK *shakes his head "no."*

Out past Whittier. You know Whittier?

JACK: No.

CASSIE: Richard Nixon was born in Whittier.
>   JACK *nods his comprehension.*

We bought a house. [*pause*] Chuck thought a dog would be a good idea... Not, not that La Habra is a bad area, I mean it's not—that's why we decided to buy there, because it's safe.

JACK: [*pause*] Your family, they live in Tacoma?
>   CASSIE *looks at him, uneasy, then stands...*

CASSIE: Can I see the puppies?

JACK: You're the first person to see them. You'll have the pick of the litter. Someone is coming later, but... [*pausing, uncertain*] I'm not keeping any, so you'll get any one that you want.

CASSIE: Oh...ah...great. [*smiles, nervous*]

JACK: These dogs...
>   CASSIE *sits again.*

...They were used as guards, in the Middle Ages, for the peasants. In England, they kept wolves, boars, anything—they kept the family protected. They were the dogs of the poor.
>   CASSIE *nods vaguely.*

I didn't want the dogs of the rich, of the aristocracy. I *chose* Mastiffs, they're common. I chose Mastiffs. [*pause*] Very powerful...
>   JACK *stops, he stands slowly and steps closer to* CASSIE.

The standard for the breed demands they present a picture of power and strength, of massiveness and dignity. [*pause*] The breeder tries to achieve the standard, which is seen as perfection. The Mastiff must have, despite its size, a gentle nature, and instincts for protection—you try to breed for temperament as well as type. [*pause*] The standard is perfection; every breeder tries to come as close to perfection as he can. [*pause*] All of my money goes into my dogs, all of my time. Everything.
>   *Silence. Lights out. In darkness—sound of several dogs barking and yelping.*

>   SCENE: *Lights up very gradually—we see a bed, pulled down out of a wall.* CASSIE *asleep. The door to front yard opens—we make out a figure, a man.*

REESE: Jack?
>   *He enters.* CASSIE *turns over, then hears sound of someone in room and sits up—scared.*

CASSIE: Who is it?

REESE: Shit...it's Reese.
>   REESE *looks around, he walks over to lamp next to bed and turns it on.* CASSIE *sits up in bed, she is in nightgown.*

[*smiles widely*] Hi.

CASSIE stares at him, frightened.

Jack around?

CASSIE: I...

She looks around.

REESE: Frightened?

CASSIE: Who are you?

REESE: Jack's boss.

REESE pulls up chair and sits next to bed, facing CASSIE.

Jack's a dealer at the casino. You been to the casino?

CASSIE: I...

She can't answer, sitting instead, shaking.

REESE: [*smiles*] I got here late. You Jack's girlfriend?

CASSIE: No.

REESE: No? I got *my* girlfriend out in the car. [*pause*] Teela. We came to buy a dog.

They stare at each other.

Maybe Jack's outside. What do you think?

CASSIE: I suppose.

CASSIE gets out of bed, trying to keep covered. She starts pulling on her sweater. She looks over at Reese watching her.

I've got to go.

REESE: Let's find Jack, OK?

REESE stands. He watches as CASSIE tries to pull on some pants and still keep herself covered with the sheet.

CASSIE: Don't watch me.

REESE: What are you doin' here?

CASSIE: [*angry, louder*] Quit staring.

REESE smiles. Silence.

Jack let me sleep here.

REESE: Nice guy, Jack.

CASSIE is dressed, she puts down the sheet.

CASSIE: I left my boyfriend. Jack said I could sleep here. That's all.

REESE: Where's your boyfriend?

CASSIE: [*pause*] I don't know exactly.

REESE: [*pause*] You know Jack well?

CASSIE sits, on the verge of crying.

CASSIE: No, I don't know Jack at all.

REESE: Jack loves dogs, he's real into dogs.

CASSIE: Yeah, I bought one of the dogs.

REESE: Yeah?

They look at each other.

CASSIE: Why are you lookin' at me so hard?

REESE: You're what, twenty-two, twenty-three?

CASSIE: Twenty-three.

REESE: Your boyfriend know you're here?

CASSIE: I doubt it.

> REESE *slowly sits back down. Pause.*

Don't you think you better go get your girlfriend?

> REESE *looks at floor, says nothing.*

I just couldn't go back to the hotel, I couldn't do it. [*pause*] Jack is a nice man, don't you think?

REESE: Jack…yeah, Jack is a prince.

> *They stare at each other.*

CASSIE: He slept out back, I mean, he let me alone here, let me have the bed.

REESE: That was very nice of him.

CASSIE: You think I'm ridiculous, huh?

REESE: [*quietly*] No.

CASSIE: I married Chuck, I believe in being married. I just couldn't go back—that doesn't make me a bad person.

REESE: I never said you were a bad person.

CASSIE: That's my car out front, I…,[*hesitates*]

REESE: What are you gonna do now?

CASSIE: I'll go somewhere.

REESE: [*nodding*] OK.

CASSIE: I have the car, not Chuck. I can go where I want, I have a little money.

REESE: You been in Las Vegas—you and Chuck?

CASSIE: Chuck had a two-week vacation, he wanted to go to Vegas. He said we could come out here to buy a dog, too.

REESE: I work at the casino in Ely—

> *Silence.* REESE *stands.* CASSIE *watching him, she looks a little frightened.*

I'm going away, too. [*pause*] I'm going to Los Angeles.

CASSIE: I live in L.A., well, in La Habra, that's near L.A.

REESE: Is it?! Well, that's where I'm going.

CASSIE: You shouldn't leave your girlfriend in the car.

REESE: [*pause*] I'm forty-six and I'm going to pull up and go to Southern California. What do you think of that?!

CASSIE: [*nervous—pause*] You should see my puppy, I'm naming him Aaron—it's a name I like from the Bible.

> REESE *looks at her but says nothing.*

You want to see him?

> REESE *says nothing.*

[*becoming very anxious*] Come on, please.

> REESE *says nothing.*

He's beautiful, he's light brown, fawn—Jack said he was a silver fawn—isn't that beautiful sounding?

> REESE *turns away, he walks to rear door and opens it. It's dark out.*

What time is it?

REESE *turns back toward her…*

REESE: About three, three-thirty.

They stare at each other.

CASSIE: Be nice to me, would you, please.

REESE: I'm always nice.

Silence. REESE *pulls up chair and sits. Lights cigarette.*

I used to own a motel, in Riviera Beach—Florida. [*pause*] There was a man there, he was from the same town in Oklahoma as my mother. Turned out he wasn't a very nice man—he abducted a girl from the convenience mart down the block. He brought her to the motel. It ended with the police storming the room, number eleven—they shot him. I had to testify and go through a whole lot of shit. I sold the place then, which was all right, I didn't like Riviera Beach much anyway.

CASSIE *sits listening.*

CASSIE: What happened to the girl?

REESE: I don't know. She moved away. [*shrugs*] I don't know.

CASSIE: Why'd you come out here so late?

REESE: [*weary*] I don't know that either.

*The front door opens tentatively—*TEELA *sticks her head in…*

Come on in, baby.

TEELA *enters, wearing low-cut evening dress.*

CASSIE: Hi.

TEELA *stares at her a moment.*

TEELA: Hi.

TEELA *looks around.*

Where's Jack?

REESE: Out back.

REESE *and* TEELA *stare at each other.* REESE *turns to* CASSIE…

We got laid off tonight, me and Teela. We both got shit-canned—both of us.

Silence. TEELA *wearily goes to chair and sits. Lights fade out.*

SCENE: *Lights up—spot on* JACK, *seated on stool, rear area of kennel.* REESE *kneels next to him.*

REESE: They only want girls—new places, especially in Vegas—they want girls if they can find 'em.

Silence. REESE *inches closer…*

Teela wants to go to L.A. [*pause*] What do I do, Jack—tell me.

JACK: I lived in L.A. once. [*pause*] I lived there seven years—I was living with this woman, Margaret—for three years, she lived in Long Beach.

REESE: Teela, she wants me to go—what am I gonna do, Jack, you tell me.

JACK *looks at him.*

Smells like the monkey cage at the zoo in here. It always smell this way?

JACK: I don't smell it.

REESE *nods. Silence.*

REESE: I'm not broke, you know I'm not broke.

JACK: Right.

REESE: I got the Cadillac, I still got that.

> REESE *takes handkerchief and mops his brow.*

Five AM and, what, ninety degrees? Maybe it's a good thing, go to L.A.—huh? Lay on the beach, get tan.

> JACK *turns and looks at him.*

JACK: What do you want, Reese?

> REESE *stands.*

REESE: I want comfort, Jack, comfort.

> JACK *suddenly takes a deep gasp of air, he puts his hand to forehead, leaning far forward.* REESE *looks at him...*

Jack... you OK?

> JACK *nods without looking up.*

I didn't mean to come out here so late, I wasn't thinking, you know—me and Teela went 'n had a few drinks—after they told us—we went over to Bunyons, then that other place.

> *He stares down at* JACK...

You all right, Jack?

> JACK *slowly straightens up...*

JACK: I haven't been feeling well, I can't sleep.

> REESE *stands, says nothing.*

You want to see the dogs?

> JACK *stands...*

They're exceptional, a beautiful litter, just beautiful.

> *They stare at each other.*

They're very big, noble—these are the best pups I've produced, the best, these pups stand up against anyone, anywhere. I love this litter, I love them.

> JACK *stops, a little short of breath—not feeling well.*

When I was in Long Beach I was living in this apartment and Margaret was supporting the both of us. Do you know what happened to Margaret? [*pause*] Margaret left one day for New Orleans, she went to her sister's house in fucking New Orleans. She took the car, which was my car, and she drove. And I called her sister, I called every day—but she never talked to me, so I don't know... [*long pause*] I don't recall much of L.A., I don't recall a whole lot about that period of my life, I don't care about it—I'm not interested at all, I'm not concerned, it doesn't matter to me, it's part of the past, someone else, somewhere else. I never think about it, about the person I was—I never give it a moment's thought.

> JACK *is wheezing a little and sits down.*

REESE: Who is this girl inside, Jack?

> JACK *stares at ground. Silence.*

Cassie? Who is this girl, this Cassie?

JACK: She just left her husband, left him asleep at the Sands. I don't know him, never met him. She left him though, asleep in bed—left him there—dreaming—Huh? Dreaming in room 418, the Sands, Las Vegas.

> *Lights fade out.*
>
> *In darkness: sound of a woman* (TEELA) *singing a capella—Bill Monroe's "What a Wonderful Life."*

SCENE: *Lights up slowly on house—through window we see it is light out.* TEELA *standing in center of room, eyes closed, finishing last chorus.* CASSIE *sits watching.*

CASSIE: I love that so much.

> CASSIE *claps a couple times.* TEELA *looks at her.*

Do you sing? I mean, are you a professional singer?

TEELA: Yeah.

> TEELA *turns away, pacing the room slowly. Silence.*

CASSIE: That was a beautiful song.

> TEELA *stops—looks at* CASSIE...

TEELA: Yeah. Yeah, it is.

CASSIE: Yeah. I think it is, definitely.

TEELA: We have to wait until this evening to get our final pay checks. Now, now they were *supposed* to give 'em to us when they fired us but Eddie—he said no, we weren't fired, we were being let go and that is different.

> CASSIE *nods vaguely, listening.* TEELA *sits.*

How old do you think I am?

CASSIE: Oh, god, I don't...

TEELA: [*a little harsh*] Come on—guess.

CASSIE: I'm real bad with how old people are.

> *They stare at each other,* CASSIE *seemingly unnerved.*

You look so good—so, looking so good I would say—I would guess, I would guess, oh, thirty, thirty-one?

> TEELA *stares at her, saying nothing. She finally stands, taking pack of cigarettes out of pocket and lighting one.*

TEELA: This evening we'll go get our checks—and then we're gonna drive to Los Angeles. [*pause*] Last time I was in Los Angeles, I went to the car show, with my brother Donald—I was fifteen.

> *She looks at* CASSIE...

That's how long it's been. Why's it taken me twenty years or so to get back? Over twenty years. I'd get someplace—places I didn't want to be, and I just couldn't get out of those places.

> *Silence.* TEELA *paces.*

That makes you feel you've wasted something. I'm not ignorant—I'm not really, I don't *believe* something is going to happen—you know—like something ridiculous—but I intend to go, I don't plan on making believe but I intend to go and take my shot. I've a right to take my shot, even though, even though, you know, it won't amount to anything. It won't change anything.

TEELA *stops, puffing intently on cigarette.* CASSIE *looks away, nervous, uncomfortable.*

I have a lovely voice.

CASSIE: You do, you have a beautiful singing voice.

TEELA *nods.*

TEELA: Well, we'll get our checks, and we'll get on our way.

CASSIE: Reese seems very nice.

TEELA: Reese is nice, yes, you could probably say he's a nice guy. [*pause*] Reese has a way of landing on his feet—he can carve himself a niche, he can go somewhere, someplace, a new place, and he can carve himself a little niche—find the angle, Reese knows the angles—Reese can spot the opportunity, his experience has taught him to recognize opportunity when he trips on it. I'm not like that, I just trip—I never seem to know what's going on till it's much later. Some people are like that— that's just how it is. I don't know the score until the teams are on their way to the next game. Reese has cunning, you look at his face, he has an expression, like an animal or like a shark—whatever it is, it's a matter of self-preservation, with him, what we're looking at is self-preservation.

    Pause.

CASSIE: Where you gonna stay in Los Angeles?

TEELA: I don't know. The beach I guess, I'd like to get someplace where I could walk to the beach. [*pause*] I wonder what would've happened if, say, if I was going and I was ten years younger.

    They stare at each other. Pause.

Because you can't expect much if you're not real young. Unless you're still young, what people think of as young—you're going to have to be realistic.

CASSIE: I don't know [*pause*]—I don't have much experience. I know *you* do, and I'd like to feel I could have "experience" like that. [*pause*] I'm really scared…

    CASSIE *is close to tears, and looks imploringly at* TEELA, *who turns away. Silence.*

Chuck, when I met him—I worked at the Taco Tico near the campus and he'd come in and kept asking for a date…

    TEELA *turns and looks at her.*

TEELA: What kind of work does Chuck do?

CASSIE: Oh, he, he's in the construction business—[*pause*] Chuck is older than me— but, then, I think that that is OK—don't you?

TEELA: Sure.

CASSIE: Chuck—I didn't know much about him when we met. I just wanted to get out of Tacoma, and Los Angeles sounded fine, really fine.

TEELA: Well—now we're at Jack Taylor's house, six thirty, outside Ely…

CASSIE: Why'd you come here?

    TEELA *stares at her, turns away.*

Do you know Jack pretty well?

    TEELA *turns back to her…*

TEELA: Do I know Jack? No. I hardly know him at all. He deals blackjack, at the casino.

CASSIE: Do you sing there?

TEELA: No, honey—I serve cocktails.

CASSIE: So Jack is a friend of Reese's?

    TEELA stares at her. Pause.

TEELA: Yeah, yeah, that's right, that's about it.

CASSIE: Have you seen Jack's dogs? They're incredible—I bought one of the puppies.

TEELA: Isn't that nice.

CASSIE: I call him Aaron.

    TEELA nods vaguely. Silence.

Are you mad at me?

TEELA: I'm just not real interested in dogs—Jack's dogs, anybody's. [*pause*] When you plan on leaving?

CASSIE: I…I'm not definite—I suppose this morning. I'm afraid Chuck is gonna find me.

TEELA: You think Chuck will come out here? He knows about Jack's kennel?

CASSIE: Oh yeah, he's talked with Jack on the phone.

    TEELA turns away. She waits a moment then goes to the door and opens it.

TEELA: [*yelling*] Reese?

    No answer. She suddenly shuts the door and turns back to CASSIE.

Does Chuck, does he make good money?

CASSIE: I don't know—I guess so.

    TEELA wearily sits. Silence. CASSIE smiles tentatively at her.

Jack seems really nice, quiet.

    Pause.

TEELA: My father was a little like Jack—kept to himself—but he had a drug problem and he beat my mom. [*pause*] I see all these people, families, come to the casino, or in Vegas—these real American families, and I see the parents are drunk—always fighting, and they hate each other…deep down, they hate each other and you can see their kids, they hate the kids—they don't know, maybe, that they hate them, like they know they hate each other, but if you look at these crazy little fuckers, if you just look at the kids, you know there is something wrong.

    TEELA stares at CASSIE…

So we got all these nuts kids, raised by nuts, and I wonder how it all keeps going… Do you see? How does the paper get delivered and so on—[*pause*] You got any kids?

CASSIE: [*shaking head "no"*] No.

TEELA: I had two—I wasn't married, I had this boyfriend. [*pause*] But they're grown and gone—I never hear from them, from my kids, never. [*pause*] It's all so fucking sick, isn't it?

CASSIE: I don't know.

TEELA: [*pause*] If Reese ever hit me I'd cut his fucking throat.

    Long silence. Lights fade out.

SCENE: *Lights up slowly:* JACK *making coffee in small kitchenette to side of room. Bed in back wall.* CASSIE *sits at table as does* TEELA. REESE *paces, smoking.*

REESE: [*to everyone in general*] Anything you want to know about dogs—Jack can tell you—I mean, this guy was the worst blackjack dealer in Nevada—but, hey—ask him about dogs—

REESE *snaps his finger.* JACK *stares at him silently.*

The sound of barking dogs—I never cared for that sound. It always made my flesh creep—my bones hurt, a dog barks and I think, how can I kill it. [*laughs*] [*to* JACK] Just kidding, Jack. [*to* CASSIE] Jack's not a great kidder, not if we're talkin' dogs. [*laughs*]

JACK *takes cups of coffee to* CASSIE *and* TEELA.

What about me, Jack?

JACK *turns away, goes back to kitchenette and brings* REESE *a cup as* REESE *continues...*

Jack knows I love him, Jack knows I'm the reason they didn't fire him, he knows I covered his ass many a time.

JACK *hands him cup, then turns away, goes back to kitchenette.*

[*to* CASSIE] Sweetie, let's talk about you—

REESE *pulls up stool to sit close to her...*

Listening to all our problems—and you sittin'—with real problems of your own. Now—this guy Chuck—you sure you don't want to go on back to Vegas, the guy must be worried—probably called the cops by now, filed a missing persons report.

CASSIE: I don't know what to do.

REESE: No, no this kind of matter, between people—people who are close, people who have shared intimacy—it's not an easy thing to, to ah...analyze—I know this. It puts you between the ol' rock and hard place—it's a real tough decision—[*pause*] What are you gonna do if you leave Chuckie, huh? You want to go back to mom and dad, is this what you want?

REESE *looks at her, waiting for answer...*

CASSIE: I don't... I think, Chuck, he's gonna be mad.

CASSIE *and* REESE *stare at each other—*REESE *then breaks into wide grin.*

REESE: Sheeit—uncle Reese, he'll make sure old Chuck keeps it in check. OK?! Huh?!

TEELA *gets up, vaguely disgusted. She crosses room, stops... Everyone watches her except* REESE, *who watches* CASSIE.

TEELA: Lots of fun shit here, huh?

Turns to REESE...

You think? Reese? Lots of fun shit—party time at Jack Taylor's kennel?!!

REESE *looks back at* CASSIE, *then back to* TEELA...

REESE: [*to* TEELA] Smells like the monkey cage—but otherwise, I like it. [*to* JACK] I like Jack, too—

REESE *walks over to* JACK, *who sits silently on stool.* REESE *puts his arm around him.*

[*to* JACK] You know I like you, right? [*pause*] Jack?

JACK: Right.

REESE *pats him on back, smiles...*

REESE: Right—my man, Jack—Jack, my main man—right Hoss?! [*laughs*] Shit yes.
>REESE *moves away from* JACK...

Well, yeah, things are a little slow here at that—[*to* JACK] You got a CD, Jack?

JACK: What?

REESE: I got some disks in the car—you got a CD player?

JACK: [*confused*] No...ah...uh uh. [*pause*] I got a record player out back.

REESE: Well, maybe we'll get Teela to sing for us—[*to* TEELA] You know Jack's a big fan of yours.

TEELA: [*weary*] Please shut up.
>TEELA *gets up, goes out back door.* REESE *turns his attention back to* CASSIE.

REESE: I bet Chuck, he's gonna be callin' here today.

CASSIE: Yeah.

REESE: I'd like to meet Chuck. You think me and Chuck, we'd hit it off?
>CASSIE *looks over at* JACK, *then back to* REESE.

CASSIE: Is it always this hot here?

REESE: Mostly, yeah.

CASSIE: I feel like we're imposing on Jack.

REESE: Jack don't mind—he's a pay me no mind kind of guy—you know what I mean?
>*Silence.*

You want to know something.
>CASSIE *stares at him, says nothing.*

[*with edge*] Do you?
>*Silence.*

Shit—I'll tell you—this is the thing; I don't *want* to go to L.A.
>REESE *hunches over close to* CASSIE...

So, you ask, why am I going? Huh? Well, I'll tell you—maybe I'm not.
>REESE *straightens up.*

[*to* JACK] No CD, huh? Damn. [*pause*] Jack—you know, I mean, if they let me go, then I'd say there's not much chance for you—that's America, though, huh—Job security. [*pause*] What the fuck you do all day, Jack—no TV, no nothin'.
>JACK *stands.*

JACK: I got to feed the dogs.

REESE: Right—right—good idea.
>JACK *strolls outside.*

CASSIE: You really think I should call Chuck?

REESE: [*pause*] Yeah. [*pause*] Fuck yes, call the fool.
>REESE *walks away, lights cigarette.* CASSIE *stares at him.*

CASSIE: It's so hot.
>*Pause.*

Why's anybody want to live here?

REESE: Baby, I don't know. [*pause*] But there's a reason, I know that. It's just I ain't found that reason yet.
>CASSIE *nods vaguely. Lights fade out.*
>*In dark: sound of* TEELA *singing.*

SCENE: *Lights up slowly on* TEELA *in stage right pool of light as she finishes singing.* CASSIE *stands in stage left light, watching* JACK, *kneeling with buckets of offal, tripe, etc. for dogs. This is outside, so light is hot and white.* CASSIE *inches closer to* JACK...

JACK: This is meat scraps, tripe, kidney, chicken meal—hearts, lungs, everything.
> *They look at each other.*

CASSIE: I called Chuck and he's gonna take a cab and meet me here tonight. [*pause*] Do you mind, you know, if I stay here today.
> JACK *looks at her, then returns attention to dog food.*

JACK: [*long pause*] You should feed your puppy three times a day—feed him this way— feed him flesh—blood—warm the blood...and throw in some rice if you want, other things.
> *Silence.*

CASSIE: I guess all of you are out of work, huh?
> *Silence.*

I'm sorry.

JACK: I'll have to let the dogs go. I got seven adult dogs—I'll have to let 'em go. [*pause*] I believed, at one time that the dogs would go forever—I felt their strength lasting long after I was gone... That's what I imagined... Generation after generation, perfecting the breed, all from my original stock—that's like a legacy.
> JACK *stands, picks up buckets.*

But nothing lasts—you don't get anything to last anymore. Not in your life—not in your dreams. Everything just winds down, doesn't it?! [*pause*] I can't imagine anymore, I can't see at night, when I close my eyes, I don't see the things I used to see, ten, fifteen years ago... [*pause*] When I was a boy I dreamed many things... And none of them happened, I wanted, I remember wanting to be a northwest mounted policeman... [*pause*]
> *Silence. He drops one of the buckets—it spills. Both of them look at it. Lights fade out.*

ACT 2

SCENE: *In dark: sound of "Hot Rod Lincoln" plays—a scratchy old 45. Lights come up gradually to reveal* JACK *seated in back, smoking cigarette, bottle of old Kessler on ground next to him. It is twilight. Shadows of big dog appear intermittently, flickering across rear scrim. As song is ending, lights are about full—and* JACK *picks up arm of his ancient record player and puts it back at start of record and we again hear "Hot Rod Lincoln" as* JACK *continues to sit passively. Lights now up slowly at other end of stage to reveal* CHUCK *standing, his appearance disheveled—two or three day growth of beard, clothes soiled, etc. His left coat sleeve is folded up at shoulder—his left arm amputated. He steps into house, sound of song gradually lowers to background sound.* CHUCK *stands in center of very dark room, only small spot on his face—suddenly lights come on full and we see* REESE *and* TEELA *seated in chairs.* CHUCK *and* REESE *look at each other and suddenly* REESE *is on his feet...*

REESE: Well—let's see now, you look like you might be Chuck.

    CHUCK *stares at him sourly.*

Cassie went for a drive, I believe. [*turns to* TEELA] Yes? Cass went driving?

    TEELA *looks at him without responding.*

Out in the desert, her and the puppy—Aaron she named it—Cassie took Aaron out into the empty wastes of south central Nevada.

    REESE *smiles at* CHUCK, *who remains expressionless.*

Sit down, here...

    REESE *pulls up his chair and* CHUCK *sits.*

Long cab ride—from Vegas.

CHUCK: I didn't take no cab. [*pause*] Got a ride with a Hormel meat truck.

REESE: Hmmm.

    TEELA *stands.*

CHUCK: Anyone got a cigarette?

TEELA: Yeah.

    TEELA *gives him cigarette. Lights it for him.*

Would you like some coffee, we got instant coffee—

    CHUCK *ignores her.* TEELA *turns away, looks at* REESE, *then walks out back. Lights dim on* REESE *and* CHUCK—*and come up on* TEELA *in back with* JACK. *After a moment's silence,* TEELA *steps over closer to* JACK...

You like it here, Jack? Do you really like it?

JACK: Here—in back? Do you mean in back, or here at the kennel—or, just Nevada, just the desert?

TEELA: [*shrugs*] The desert.

JACK: I didn't always live here.

> TEELA *stands, waiting for more.* JACK *takes 45 of "Hot Rod Lincoln" off of turntable and puts on Hank Snow's "I've Been Everywhere." He turns it up loud as lights fade out.*

> SCENE: *Music fades gradually in dark. Lights up on* REESE *and* CHUCK *seated together. Each has a can of beer.*

REESE: You ever feel disappointed? [*pause*] OK, what I'm asking is, does your life, what you do—does it seem disappointing?

CHUCK: I can't say. I don't look on it like that.

REESE: [*pause*] You're a big man—physically.

> *Silence.*

I feel disappointed. [*pause*] I'm sure Cassie will be back any time now.

> REESE *stands, checks his watch.*

Guess I can go get my check—with Teela, we can go get our checks. [*pause*] I never went to school, my father took me around with him. He was a salesman, and a great card player. I learned gaming, by the time I was fifteen I knew it all, all the odds—craps, poker, even stuff like baccarat—I knew it.

CHUCK: I play craps, that's what I do.

> REESE *stares at him. Lights fade out on* CHUCK *and* REESE *while coming up on* TEELA *and* JACK, *both kneeling, looking out over the desert...*

TEELA: I've been in Nevada for fifteen years. [*pause*] It feels like an interruption—you know?! [*pause*] When I left Chicago, maybe it was already too late.

> *She looks at* JACK, *waiting for an answer.* JACK *says nothing.*

I just got stuck somehow—first with Donald, then with Jeff—you remember him—Jeff Markham?—Then Reese. I just can't stand being alone.

> *Pause.* TEELA *stands...*

You ought to see him Jack—he's only got one arm.

> *Silence.*

Jack? [*pause*] Why don't you come on inside... We're gonna leave pretty soon...

> JACK *stands, they look at each other...*

[*quietly*] Here... Give me a hug. [*pause*] Will you?

> *She steps over close to* JACK *and puts her arms around him. After a moment,* JACK *slowly puts his arms around her. In distance, sound of several dogs barking and howling. Lights fade out.*

> SCENE: *Lights up slowly on house:* REESE *stands to one side.* CHUCK *is seated.* TEELA *sits in corner and* JACK *stands by kitchenette.*

REESE: What is it to L.A.? Three hours? I guess more like four, four and a half.

> REESE *paces back and forth.*

Not really so far, is it?

> *Silence.*

CHUCK: Anyone got another cigarette?

TEELA *gets up and hands* CHUCK *a cigarette, then lights it for him.*

TEELA: [*to* CHUCK] She'll be back.

REESE: Yeah—she just got caught up in that desert—in drivin' the desert.

    CHUCK *looks at* REESE.

TEELA: [*to* REESE] It's after nine—it's time to get our checks.

    REESE *looks at her.*

REESE: Yeah, sure. Let's go see Eddie—let's go get our checks.

    REESE *takes his car keys out of his pocket. He and* TEELA *stare at each other.*

TEELA: You go, baby, I'll wait here. [*pause*] I don't want to see Eddie.

REESE: [*pause*] Yeah, yeah, OK.

    REESE *looks around room at everyone—as though he wants to say something—but he doesn't. He turns and looks long at* TEELA, *then turns and exits. Silence.* CHUCK *flicks cigarette against far wall.*

CHUCK: [*to* JACK] You got another beer in there?

    JACK *brings him a beer—opening it as he walks to* CHUCK...

You know—maybe she won't be coming back. [*pause*] Maybe I'll just sit here, hour after mother fuckin' hour—maybe that's how it's goin' to be.

    JACK *stares at him, then turns away and stands by exit.*

What do you do?

TEELA: I worked at the casino, in Ely.

    CHUCK *nods vaguely. Silence.*

CHUCK: I'm tired. [*pause*] Who's Eddie?

TEELA: Just this guy.

    TEELA *stands, starts pacing.*

Eddie is a prick.

CHUCK: Can I lay down someplace?

    TEELA *looks over at* JACK.

JACK: This bed pulls down. The bed here in the wall.

    CHUCK *holds a piece of his shirt up to his nose—smelling it. He looks at* TEELA *and then* JACK.

CHUCK: Any hunting here, Jack? Around here?

JACK: No, I don't think so.

    CHUCK *nods. Pause.*

CHUCK: I'm from Washington state, plenty of hunting up there. [*pause*] I'd like to move back there, sometime, I'd like to go back there.

    Silence. JACK *wanders out back.*

I'm just gonna lay down for awhile.

    Silence. Lights fade out. Sound of dogs barking in dark.

    SCENE: *Spot up slowly on* REESE *standing in rear.* JACK *stands next to side, looking out at desert.*

REESE: There's a fight on tonight...Jack? On ESPN, two middleweights, both unbeaten—should be a good fight.

REESE *stares at* JACK *for a moment...*

Doesn't hold a lot of interest for you, huh?!—Well, yeah, I can't blame you. [*pause*] But fights—you have to see them in person. It's the smell mostly—it's the smell of the past. The deep past—the smell of fear, of other things, things that nobody wants to keep.

Pause.

I'm your only friend, Jack—your only friend. Do you know that?

JACK *stares at him*—REESE *becoming more upset...*

Shit—What you gonna do now, Jack? What? Huh? You thought about that? Because I'm gone, I'm gone, Jack.

REESE *gently, but with urgency takes hold of* JACK.

[*quietly*] Tell me something, [*pause*] please.

REESE *lets go, turns away, trying to collect himself.*

There's nobody to tell me what to do—right?!

Silence.

Do you think about it, Jack? About the mistakes in your life?

JACK: Mistakes? No, I don't think about them.

REESE: Ok...ok. [*pause*] I'm doing what I know is best for me. [*pause*] I don't like it. It's nothing to like, is it?

JACK: No, I guess it isn't.

REESE: No. [*pause*] There's nothing to like in any of it.

Silence. He turns and abruptly moves off as lights fade out.

SCENE: *Spot up slowly on* JACK *in rear. He stands, looking out into the darkness. He begins talking before we see who he is talking to.*

JACK: In the Navy, my father saw a man lose a leg. Got it crushed. He said the man was screaming, in great pain—and he was screaming for his mother. A grown man this was—not a kid—and he was laying there, blood everywhere, screaming for his mother.

We now see CASSIE *standing to side, listening. She has coat on.*

I've never seen anything like that. [*pause*] My mother, she said when she was a little girl she was driving cross country with her step-father and they came up on this terrible crash at a railroad crossing—where a train had hit this car. She didn't want to look but her step-dad stopped and made her look—and she said two people had been decapitated.—She said it was the worst thing she ever saw, the very worst.

Pause.

As a little boy, I remember she would never let me look at any kind of accident— she was very—she would really react strongly to any little accident.

CASSIE: Jack?

JACK: [*pause*] Chuck's asleep inside.

CASSIE: [*pause*] I love the dog, Jack—my puppy—Aaron. I love him, I really love him, he's beautiful, really, really, beautiful.

They look at each other. Lights fade out as...

SCENE: *Lights up slowly on house:* CHUCK *sits on edge of bed, smoking.* TEELA *sits in chair.*

CHUCK: I heard a car... Whose car was that?

TEELA: Cassie.

> CHUCK *nods. Silence.*

CHUCK: I'm a lot older than Cassie.

> *Pause.*

TEELA: I've wanted to go to Los Angeles for years. We don't do what we want, though, we don't do it like that.

> CASSIE *enters slowly from rear. She and* CHUCK *look at each other.* CASSIE *walks over and sits in chair next to the bed. Long silence.*

CASSIE: You should see the dog, Chuck—he's a great dog.

CHUCK: Yeah...sure.

> *Pause.*

CASSIE: You know what I did, when I was out driving? I stopped at a pay phone—at a gas station, to call my sister—then—standing in this phone booth, I remember, I don't have her number—I don't know where she is.

> *Pause.*

Did you sleep?

CHUCK: No, uh, uh.

> CHUCK *covers his face with his hand, his head lowering—trying not to sob. Lights out.*

SCENE: *In dark, the sound of* CHUCK *singing.* "Goodnight, Irene"—*lights up gradually as he's almost done—standing in center of room.* TEELA *stands at rear, glass of bourbon in hand.* CASSIE *sits cross-legged on the bed.* JACK *sits in chair.* CHUCK *finishes.—There is an almost empty fifth of Old Granddad on the floor by bed. Everyone has been drinking.*

CHUCK: Greatest song I know—ought to be the national anthem. [*laughs*] A great American song.

> JACK *stands.*

JACK: "Wabash Cannonball."

CHUCK: Wha...?

JACK: "Wabash Cannonball"—that's the real national anthem.

> CHUCK *stumbles to bed and sits.*

CHUCK: Shit—

> JACK *steps over near bed...*

JACK: "Wabash Cannonball"—ask anyone—what's the American anthem?—Huh? Ask anyone...

> JACK *turns away in disgust.* CHUCK *leans in close to* CASSIE. *He takes hold of her chin...*

CHUCK: She's somethin'—look at this face.

> CASSIE *gently pulls away.* CHUCK *looks over at* JACK.

[*to* JACK] Any more "Granddad"?

JACK *ignores him as he makes his way back to chair.* CHUCK *returns attention to* CASSIE.

Why'd you leave me—in Vegas—why'd you leave me there.

Silence.

CASSIE: I don't know, Chuck.

CHUCK: [*quietly*] You don't know?

CASSIE *shakes her head, "no." Pause.*

I need a shower—

CHUCK *turns toward* JACK...

Got a shower here?

JACK *stares at him, silence.* CHUCK *shrugs—turns back to* CASSIE.

You blame me?

CASSIE: For what?

CHUCK: Do you blame me?

CASSIE: No—Chuck...

CHUCK: I don't want you to blame me.

CASSIE *nods.*

[*getting a little ugly*] I don't want your blame. [*pause*] I can't use it.

CHUCK *stands, wobbly.*

There's always a lesson—a lesson to be learned. [*pause*] There are things wrong today, in the world, and because, in our country... We don't teach young people, we, we don't teach the lessons, like who blames who...

Turns attention to CASSIE.

See...see, I don't ask for anything.

CASSIE: [*tenderly*] What's wrong, Chuck?

CASSIE *gets up, touches his chest gently with her hand...*

I don't blame you—I don't know what you mean. [*pause*] What's the matter, honey?

CHUCK *sits—suddenly exhausted. Long silence.*

TEELA: [*to* JACK] Reese has my things. In the trunk, he's got both my suitcases. [*pause*] I wish he'd left them. [*pause*] Reese isn't coming back—which isn't so bad—but he's got all my things.

TEELA *gets up, walks toward rear. As she does,* CHUCK *has stretched out asleep on bed.* TEELA *stares out at desert.*

Lots of space between things. You see things coming out here. [*pause*] It doesn't matter though, how much time you get. It just doesn't matter.

Lights fade out.

SCENE: *In dark, sound of wind blowing—lights up slowly on rear:* TEELA *and* CASSIE, *both with jackets on.*

TEELA: Gets cold in a hurry, huh.

Silence.

In winter it snows here sometimes—it snowed last winter. [*pause*] After a point—at some point in your life everything seems about like everything else.

CASSIE: I always felt I was just average. [*pause*] And that seemed OK to me.

TEELA: I guess it is OK.

CASSIE: I don't want to go back, to California. Not with Chuck.

TEELA: Well, maybe it's time to go out in the world.

CASSIE: I'm afraid.

TEELA: That's OK.

CASSIE: I'm afraid that I'll find out that I'm a person who can't be out in the world alone.

> TEELA *says nothing. Silence.*

TEELA: I'm going to California, even without Reese.

> *Silence.*

I'd spend so much time in the casino, even after I got off—I'd watch Reese, who was the pit boss—I'd watch him, or just go play the nickel slots. [*pause*] There is so much time here and so little to do… It's a town waiting, of people waiting. You can drive through here and not remember it. Though, I like driving around at night, when the car felt cold. I like having the heater on, so my feet stayed warm—but you could touch the window glass and feel the cold.

CASSIE: I'm going to leave, I'm going to take the car. [*pause*] It's Chuck's car but I think he won't do anything, you know, he won't call the police or anything.

TEELA: No, I don't think he will.

CASSIE: If you're here, will you tell him, say that he should not call the police on me.

TEELA: He won't do anything. He knows, he's old enough to know how this works. The price of a ten-year old Buick is little enough.

> CASSIE *turns up the collar on her coat. Sound of wind increases. Pause.*

CASSIE: It's the drinking. He doesn't drink all the time. [*pause*] He told me he was married once before, the daughter of a grower out in Bremerton. She couldn't have children I guess, but he never asked me to have children.

> *Pause.*

TEELA: Goodbye, Cassie.

> *Pause.*

CASSIE: Bye.

> TEELA *smiles briefly, then turns away and walks back inside.*
> *Lights fade out.*

> SCENE: *Sound of dogs barking, more viciously than usual, and louder. Lights up gradually, on small area near the bed.* CHUCK *is sprawled out asleep.* TEELA *approaches, takes off coat, then dress, and wearing only a slip she carefully crawls onto bed next to* CHUCK. *Lights dim out on bed…*

> SCENE: *As lights come up on rear:* JACK *seated next to his old record player, which is now closed, unplugged. A couple old 45s on the ground, another broken 45 by his foot.* CASSIE *steps over to him.*

JACK: Hank Snow, I love Hank Snow…Webb Pierce… Ersel Hickey…All those guys.

JACK *now turns and looks up at her...*
How long you been standing there?
    CASSIE *says nothing, she shivers and pulls her coat tighter around her.*
Takin' Chuck's car? [*pause*] Nice car. [*pause*] I had this car—[*pause*] I had this hot rod—I was a kid, this was when I was a kid... in Las Cruces, I had a genuine hot rod—this is fifty, fifty-one, and I'm sixteen.
    Pause. CASSIE *steps closer.*
There was this boy, Red. [*pause*] Red was beautiful—he was a few years older, you know—he was already out of high school and so forth. I just went everywhere Red went—everywhere. Red didn't have a car, so I'd drive. I'd drive wherever he wanted to go. I just wanted to be with him—[*pause*] One time I had gotten some money, I forget where, and I went out and bought Red some clothes—I wanted him to look good. Red could wear clothes, just the way some people can—well, Red could. And he did look good, just real good. [*pause*] I liked doin' things for him. [*pause*] We ran together for almost a whole year.
    JACK *stops, looks down. Silence.*
CASSIE: What happened to Red.
JACK: What? ...he went away with a girl, a Mexican girl. Pretty girl. [*pause*] We'd drive this hill all the time—get drunk, and drive down this long downgrade. I heard later someone died doing the same thing, two high school boys. [*pause*] But that was later.
    Silence.
CASSIE: It felt good out there, with the puppy. He was on the front seat next to me.
    They look at each other. Silence.
It felt good driving—[*pause*] Now I'm just waiting, a little, just wanting to get it right. Just wanting to leave right, pull out of the driveway here, hear that gravel, and then find the road under my feet, the road under me. [*pause*] Jack?
    JACK *says nothing.*
There's a feeling, something about feeling like I'm growing up—like leaving these problems behind, and the lights here just get smaller...and I got my puppy with me—my puppy who I named Aaron—And behind me it all disappears.
    Silence.
JACK: Leave it, just leave it behind.
    CASSIE *nods, as she slowly backs out. Lights fade out.*

    SCENE: *Lights up on room:* TEELA *seated on bed.* CHUCK *in same clothes as before, stands staring out at rear.*
CHUCK: [*half to himself*] Unemployed now, I guess—back to that.
    He turns toward TEELA.
It's almost morning. [*pause*] Mornings, I like morning out here.
TEELA: You got any money left?
    CHUCK *sits down, takes out wallet—counts his money. He looks up at* TEELA...
CHUCK: You want to come with me?

TEELA: No, no thanks.

CHUCK: I'm serious, no joking—why don't you come with me, I got nine hundred left, in cash—there's more I could get.

TEELA: I don't think so.

> CHUCK *gets up and comes over to bed. He sits. Silence.*

CHUCK: Cassie was young. I'm not mad.

TEELA: [*gently*] You've no right to be mad.

CHUCK: [*pause*] The guy I got a ride with, the truck driver. He talked to me, about his wife. He said there were things you don't get over—like his wife leaving him, or when his brother went to prison.

> *Pause.*

TEELA: You don't have to go back to Los Angeles.

> *Pause.*

You could just get up and go back to Washington—up to Oregon, or Canada... You could do any of that.

> CHUCK *looks away.*

CHUCK: I'm too old to do anything that way.

> CHUCK *stands...* JACK *enters from rear. He looks at* CHUCK, *then* TEELA, *then walks to kitchenette. He starts to make instant coffee.*

[*to* JACK] I'll be outta here—as soon as it starts to get light.

> JACK *nods. He comes over and stands next to bed. After a beat, he sits.*

JACK: I'm about ready. I'm letting the dogs go, just before sunrise.

> TEELA *stares at him.*

Then I'm goin' to the Greyhound station in Ely and get a ticket to Sacramento, somewhere—not too big, but somewhere bigger than here—to a city. [*pause*] I want to just do as little as I can.

TEELA: You gonna sell the house here?

JACK: Nobody'd buy it. I'll leave that guy, the guy at the real estate office, I'll leave him the papers—give him the right to sell it.

TEELA: I'm sorry about your dogs.

JACK: I'm gonna drink—I'm gonna stay drunk, for as long as I can. I'll spend days talkin' to the old guys on the steps of the hotel. You've seen those kind of guys, right? No family, no reason to do anything, just marking time. I'm gonna find a hotel like that, full of old guys like that.

> JACK *turns away and carries his cup with him to the chair. He sits. Pause.*

They're beautiful dogs, Mastiffs. This kind of dog—living with these dogs, it changes your life.

> *Silence.* JACK *suddenly throws cup down, breaking it.* TEELA *and* CHUCK *stare at him. Lights out.*

> SCENE: *Sound of wind blowing. Lights up slowly on bed as wind fades.* TEELA *sitting up, on edge.* CHUCK *seated on other side, resting his back against headboard.*

TEELA: [*pause*] No.

    CHUCK *takes out wallet and hands her several large bills.* TEELA *takes it.*

CHUCK: That should get you to Los Angeles.

TEELA: I'm not sure now, not sure about going.

    CHUCK *nods vaguely, leans back.*

I can find work here—but a new place, there's always trouble.

CHUCK: Where you think Reese went.

TEELA: [*Shrugs*] East, I guess—that direction.

    CHUCK *moves over closer to her, until they're touching. He buries his head in her shoulder. Silence.*

What's gonna happen to those dogs?

    CHUCK *doesn't answer. Pause.*

I guess they'll die, unless someone finds one of them. [*pause*] Most will die.

    While they continue—lights come up very slowly, almost imperceptibly on rear—on JACK. *He is in a coat, with several leather leashes over his shoulder, and a large metal key ring. Sound of dogs barking intermittently...*

[*quietly*] Would you say I'm average? Chuck?

    CHUCK *lifts his head, leans back a little.*

CHUCK: I don't know.

TEELA: I'd never thought so.

    Silence. Sound of dogs barking increases.

CHUCK: Can you sing "Goodnight, Irene"?

    Silence.

TEELA: [*gently*] I don't want to sing just now.

    Lights fade out on them as they continue to increase on JACK. *On scrim the light of early morning increases subtly—and sound of dogs barking, fighting, etc., increases dramatically—Shadows of huge [out size] dogs moving behind* JACK *can be seen as sound becomes very loud—painfully so.* JACK *sinks to his knees, grabbing his ears to shut out noise.*

    Lights out. Sound of wind in darkness.

END

Charles L. Mee, Jr.

∾

*The Imperialists
at the Club Cave Canem*

PROLOGUE

A performance piece: the monologue Rindecella.

OVERTURE

A violin solo with voice tape.

I. *A couple in bed.*

MOLLY: Did you hear about this two ton guy?

PETER: Two tons?

MOLLY: About two tons, something like that, you know, like 240 pounds, five feet four, who didn't want to admit he was fat and so he wore clothes several sizes too small for him. He had a 44 inch waist but he wore pants size 38, and he choked himself to death on his shirt collar. One minute he was eating spaghetti with his fork and the next minute he was on the floor gasping for breath, and his shirt was so tight no one could get it unbuttoned. He died with a forkful of spaghetti in his hand. [*Silence*] I knew this guy who killed himself with his pants.

PETER: How did he do that?

MOLLY: He let them get so tight they choked off his circulation and he had a heart attack.

PETER: You mean he gained weight?

MOLLY: Sure.

PETER: A lot of weight.

MOLLY: I don't know. I guess so.

    Silence.

Did you hear about the little girl who fell into the washing machine?

PETER: I don't think so.

MOLLY: This is a true story. She was, like, 2 years old, and her mother had gone to take a shower, so she climbed up to look into the washing machine and she fell in and turned blue and her eyes were glassy.

PETER: Did she die?

MOLLY: No.

PETER: That was lucky.

MOLLY: That's like this guy who's a champion skier who skied off a natural little ski jump and landed head first in a snowbank and suffocated to death.

PETER: Sort of like that.

MOLLY: There was another guy.

PETER: This isn't going to be another story about death, is it?

MOLLY: No. There was a guy who died—I mean it starts out about death, but then it doesn't stay there. There was this guy who died but then he came back to life...

PETER: I think I've heard this story.

MOLLY: Wait. He came back to life and this is how he proved he had died. Wait a minute. Start it this way: there was this kid named Charan Varma from India who claimed he had been killed by British soldiers in 1857 during the Sepoy Rebellion. He said he had been shot twice in the chest, bayoneted, and slashed over and over with sabres after he was dead by British soldiers—I don't know why—and nobody believed the kid so he led four archaeologists from Palacky University of Czechoslovakia out to this grave where they dug up a mummified corpse that had the fragments of two bullets in the chest and markings on the ribs and legs and arms consistent with stab wounds and saber slashings. And the corpse had on the remains of a uniform worn by sepoy soldiers.

    Silence.

PETER: What has the experience meant to him?

MOLLY: Meant to him?

PETER: I mean, has he learned anything from coming back to life?

MOLLY: Well, he forgives the British.

PETER: Really, nobody knows whether he was telling the truth or he had already been out in the field, happened to dig up a body in a shallow grave, see the uniform, and make up the story.

MOLLY: Sure, anything is possible.

PETER: Yes, well, some things are more likely than others.

MOLLY: Sure. That's what makes this such an amazing story. This is the first time anyone has proved there is life after death.

PETER: You know, there are stories you shouldn't believe. For instance, did you hear about these pilots who were taxiing down the runway ready to take off, this was last December, and it was raining a little, and the co-pilot said to the pilot, you know I think the wings are icing up. And the pilot looked out the window...

MOLLY: How do you know this?

PETER: It was all recorded—this is a true story—and the pilot said, yes it looks like a little icing up, and he said something along the lines of did you see the Giants game on Saturday, and the co-pilot said something like what a runback, and are you going to see the Broncos play when we're in Denver, and they went on, and the pilot said you know it looks like some heavy ice on the wings, maybe we should ask for a delay, and the co-pilot said he thought the Broncos were going to take the championship, and the pilot said, not in my lifetime. Not in my lifetime. And the co-pilot said I'm worried about that icing up on the wings, and then they got clearance for takeoff, and they took off, and they got a few hundred feet into the air and then they came down because of the ice and a lot of people were killed including both the pilot and the copilot.

MOLLY: Jesus.

PETER: So, that s a story with a moral.

MOLLY: Yeah.

PETER: It's not like a pointless story.

MOLLY: Well, I don't believe in dying anyway, really.

PETER: You mean you believe in an afterlife.

MOLLY: No.

PETER: Reincarnation.

MOLLY: No.

PETER: Well, what do you think has happened to all these people?

MOLLY: They died. I know that. I'm not a maniac. But that doesn't mean I believe in dying.

PETER: No.

MOLLY: I believe in living. You know, like, I've never been a religious person, and I never believed in God until recently when I was touched by God. In other words, I never believed in anything spiritual, really except having a good life and not hurting anyone. I always prayed to God, but just out of habit, and I never got anything from him anyway. But one morning I was in bed just thinking about my age, how long I've got left, and I thought I'm lost I'm totally lost, and I thought you know God help me. And all of a sudden—and I don't do drugs or anything—I lifted about two feet off my bed and moved like a clock hand all the way around my king-size bed. I mean I was in ecstasy. Unbelievable ecstasy. I couldn't believe it. I still don't believe it. It was such a feeling of floating—like having an orgasm 20,000 times for about 60 seconds. I thought, I must be imagining this. But I looked at my bed later, and the covers were unmussed. So I realized I had evidently gone out of my body.

PETER: That's not even necessarily rational.

MOLLY: Right.

> *Silence.*

Neither is this. Like, the last election I went to the polls and stood in line for a couple hours and when I got up there these people at a card table said well, you're not registered in this district. Not registered? Fuck, I've lived in this neighborhood for eight months, you know what I mean? I've been here longer than anyone except the Ukrainians. Plus, I'm a fucking American. So, I said, look, I know my fucking rights and I'm pulling a lever on that fucking machine or else I'm pulling your fucking arm out of its socket.

PETER: You said that?

MOLLY: That was good, hunh? Pull your fucking arm out of its socket. So naturally they called the cops, and it turned into this big unpleasant scene, and I wind up in fucking jail for the night—that's what happened the last time I tried to vote. And you think, okay, what s the loss, 'cause she doesn't know a fucking thing anyway, but I'll tell you what I know: each man is an expert in the conditions of his own life. You know who said that? Jefferson or someone like that. You know, Lincoln. And I am a fucking expert in the conditions of my own life.

PETER: Is this relevant?

MOLLY: To what?

PETER: To what we were talking about.

MOLLY: What were we talking about?

II. *A performance piece.*

III. *A couple in bed.*

KAREN: I had lunch with Kurt yesterday at City?

PETER: Yeah?

KAREN: You know Kurt?

PETER: No.

KAREN: He's putting the finishing touches on PIKME-UP, a club that's opening in a few nights, and we talked about a possible collaboration on a video, and we were sitting right next to David Steinberg, who I used to open for in Philadelphia in my first rock 'n' roll incarnation. And he's eating with Arlyne Rothenberg, who was his manager at the time, and who eventually became my manager when I decided to ditch the road and become just a songwriter because it was all too much to handle. This was back in 1976, but at some point Arlyne...

PETER: God.

KAREN: ...decided I was too much to handle so she turned me over to Irving Azoff, who I lasted with about two months and who became president of MCA Records, you know, I forget when. Do you know Irving Azoff?

PETER: No.

KAREN: My best Irving Azoff story is that when we decided not to work together anymore he wouldn't give me my demo tape back. I was completely broke and it was my only tape. So after a month of calling, I dressed up as a cowgirl and my boyfriend went as a gangster and we walked into his office with Boz Scaggs, who he had just signed. So the next day I start writing with Mark Leonard, who co-wrote "Missing You," the John Waite song. He was in my first demo band. He was also in the Alan Thicke *Sick of the Night* show band. Do you know Jeff Stein?

PETER: No.

KAREN: Men screw you, you know. Women can't screw you. They can seduce you, but they can't screw you. Physiology is a fact. You have to have a cock to screw someone. Or, like Reagan, you know, when he was brought into the emergency room after Hinckley shot him, this friend of mine who works in the emergency room said, the standard procedure for a gunshot victim is you strip him down completely so you can trace where any bullets entered and any bullets exited, and so they striped Reagan down, and they couldn't find his dick. I mean, it was so tiny, they had to call in a specialist to make sure he had one. So you could say he was compensating by screwing everyone because he didn't have a dick. But usually, if you don't have a dick you can't screw anyone. And I've often thought—these politicians, they all go around screwing people all the time—I'm not thinking politically now, although that, too, but personally screwing women all the time: the Kennedys, Gary Hart. I had this friend who worked in the White House who said Lyndon Johnson used to screw everyone, not just in his office but anywhere in the White House, in waiting rooms, in corners, standing up in closets. I don't think women do that. Of course, we haven't had a woman president. But, for instance, Margaret Thatcher, I don't think Margaret Thatcher screws people in closets.

You don't know Jeff?

PETER: I don't follow politics, you know.

KAREN: This isn't politics, this is just, you know, we're friends.

PETER: Well, you know, I like Louis XVI.

KAREN: His politics?

PETER: Yeah, well, his style.

KAREN: Unh-hunh.

PETER: And then, you know, in Sweden, the stuff of King Gustav III—most people don't know it, but they didn't seem to make one mistake. The linens are nice. The mattresses are nice, striped with mattress ticking. The first time I went into this house of the aunts of Louis XVI in Paris, there were eight of us for lunch. We sat in that dining room with the silver, all from Catherine the Great, and we had a footman behind each chair. Then in the salon I saw "MA" embroidered on the brocade on the Louis XVI chairs and I said, "Why do they say 'MA'?" And this guy Arturo was happy I'd asked because he could tell me that it was Marie Antoinette's crest. So I was a great favorite immediately—not because of being naive but just because I'd say whatever came into my mind.

KAREN: Sure. And you like history.

PETER: I was like that when I was a kid. One night after my parents took me to see the movie *Cleopatra* I got together with some of my friends. We were about nine years old. We all wore towels wrapped around our heads. The kids in the neighborhood were all the slaves and I, of course, was Cleopatra. We erected statues in the living room and I draped myself in the chiffon curtains as an outfit. It was very Egyptian. When I was in the fifth grade I would tweeze my eyebrows, dye my hair, apply Clearasil, I mean really cake it on all over my eyelids. You know, I was looking at the fashion magazines, and I wanted to look like Twiggy. I bleached my hair, but I couldn't do it right, so it was dyed in spots. My uniform consisted of stove piped bell bottoms, a purple sweater and a bow tie. I always was who I was and did what I did. Also in high school the collegiate look was in and I tried to work that look, but instead I looked like a lesbian trying to be collegiate.

KAREN: Unh-hunh.

Silence.

So, okay, anyway, the next night, Jim and I go to a party at Rusty Lemorande's house in the hills. Pee Wee Herman is there, Randal Kleiser, who directed *Flight of the Navigator,* and a bevy of teenage beauties, and Greg Gorman, Herb Ritts, Pristine Condition, Shooter Hill, Catherine Oxenburg. Great view. Great food. And just a great spot for cosmetically perfect hairdos, you know, I'm just very glad this place exists.

PETER: I'd love to work with Richard Chamberlain.

KAREN: In 1979 Klaus and I met David Bowie at the Mudd Club, and he said he liked how we looked and he asked us to perform with him on Saturday Night Live.

PETER: How did you look?

KAREN: We were wearing padded Thiery Mugler dresses. I like my body. My shape will never go out of fashion. I love the way I look. You know I think shapes will come and go, but I think people will always want someone like me.

PETER: I'd like to do a male Mae West someday called Mae West of the Mounties. He'd have huge bulging arms, a huge crotch, big thighs, a blonde wig, huge cheekbones, kind of a mixture of Dudley Dooright and Mae West. And then I'd say, if my right leg was Christmas and my left leg was New Year's Eve, why don't you come between the Holidays and visit.

　　　She screams in ecstasy.

　　IV. *A performance piece.*

　　V. *A couple in bed.*

DAVID: In Africa there are people I've heard of who have pulled down their lower lips so far, you know...

KAREN: Is this in India?

DAVID: No, Africa.

KAREN: Because I didn't think this sounds like India.

DAVID: No, listen to me. Africa. I'm talking about Africa. Nobody ever heard of this in India. These are people who have gotten their lower lips so long that the only way they can eat is by walking backwards over their food until their lower lips get to the right position, and then they have a friend sort of shovel it up over their lower lip.

KAREN: Who told you this?

DAVID: I saw it on television. It was this program about these people in Afghanistan.

KAREN: I don't think this is new, you know, I don't know why this is on television because I think people have known this for a long time.

DAVID: I thought, you know, it was an incredible coincidence.

KAREN: How is it a coincidence?

DAVID: Well, you know, it's a coincidence.

　　　Silence.

KAREN: Did you see that program where they discovered these people whose ears were so long that they didn't need clothes and they wrapped themselves up in their ears when it got cold?

DAVID: Where is this?

KAREN: Some of them have their heads in their chests. In Melbourne, Australia.

DAVID: I didn't see that.

KAREN: You know where the car hookers hang out down Second Avenue or whatever it is below Houston Street?

DAVID: Yeah.

KAREN: Well, I went into that gas station there during this terrible thunderstorm, I drove in near the pumps and directly into what I thought was a huge puddle but turned out to be a deep pit. The car sank fast, and I had a hard time getting out through the window on the driver's side. There were these two gas station attendants there watching me. Neither one of them made a move to help me out. And, when I got out on my own at last, neither of them was sympathetic either. One of them said, well, that's it for your car. But it wasn't. A few minutes later the three of us looked at the other side of the puddle, and there was the car. It had emerged by itself and was parked just across the water.

DAVID: No, I dreamed that.

KAREN: What?

DAVID: What you just said. That was a thing that occurred to me in a dream.

KAREN: No, this is my story.

DAVID: Well, I mean, you can have it if you want it, you're welcome to it, but in actual fact it occurred to me.

KAREN: Where did I hear about it then?

DAVID: How would I know?

KAREN: Where do you think I heard about it?

DAVID: I wouldn't have any idea.

    Silence.

KAREN: Often I hear something and I remember it and I think it happened to me.

DAVID: Or it was your idea.

KAREN: Right. Like I'll see it on television, maybe. One time I saw Stephen Gould on television—is it Stephen Gould?

DAVID: Who?

KAREN: The biologist you sometimes see on television.

DAVID: I don't know.

KAREN: Anyway I thought I had this conversation with him in my living room.

DAVID: That happens to everyone.

    I was with this woman named Lisa once, and she asked me if I'd like to have dinner, and I said sure. She had cooked spaghetti in the bathtub and she said, why don't you get in first? And I thought: oh, get into the tub, well: sure. And so I did. I got in and she handed me this soup spoon and I tasted the broth, it was very delicate and—lucid. I thought, well, I felt awkward, you know, thinking: there's something not quite correct about this, and I was not sure about the meal: there was very little spaghetti in the tub; it was filled with the clear broth and a few strands of spaghetti and some few herbs from her garden, but after a few minutes I relaxed, and she let the towel fall and joined me in the tub.

KAREN: I went to this performance once, I was late, most of the audience had already arrived and they were sitting in folding chairs that had been set out three-deep around three of the four walls.

DAVID: You mean, like the chairs were facing the fourth wall.

KAREN: Right. There were about fifty people there, and the room was empty, painted white. I mean there was no performer in the space where the audience wasn't sitting. And I was expecting some kind of performance art.

DAVID: Right.

KAREN: But I didn't know exactly what it would be. And pretty soon this man in the front row began to speak, a short, stocky man, an Irishman, he looked like a cab-driver or a carpenter, someone who worked with his hands, he was reading from his autobiography, and he was really good, you know he wrote with real force and grace.

DAVID: Right.

KAREN: And I was really getting into it, thinking, gee, he writes practically as well as Joyce, you know.

DAVID: James Joyce.

KAREN: Right.

DAVID: As well as James Joyce.

KAREN: Well, almost, you know, only he's writing about numerology, when anyway someone behind me began to whisper, and I turned around to shush them, and it was this man whispering to the young woman who was with him, and she was laughing and smiling and they were carrying on a whole conversation.

DAVID: People do that all the time.

KAREN: Yeah, well, anyway, it made me furious, and then while I was trying to get them to be quiet I heard someone over to my left near the wall talking—not whis-pering, but talking entirely out loud, and I just lost my head.

DAVID: I don't blame you.

KAREN: These people make me so fucking mad. I stood up and I shouted at them: why don't you shut up? And the whispering man behind me told me to sit down, so I said something to him, I don't remember what it was, something I was trying to have a tone of voice that showed some respect for the performer, and then these people behind the whisperer began to talk to each other, about me I guess, and then these two people on the other side of the room started talking out loud, and I was still trying to listen to the Irishman, but I could hardly hear what he was saying, and I was completely enraged, and everyone was talking all over the room, and the Irishman persisted with complete, wonderful calm for about ten minutes—he was completely unperturbed by the whole thing and then, when he finished, he just neatened up his papers, put them into a manila envelope, took off his silver-rimmed bifocals, and got up to leave, and I couldn't tell whether he had come to the end of his piece or just given up because of the distractions, but all these people who I guess knew him came over to congratulate him and I sort of wandered toward the door to leave and sort of stopped there by the door where there was a table with some programs on it, and because I had been late in arriving I hadn't gotten a program, so I picked one up, and I saw that the performance had been called PAT-TERNS OF INTERFERENCE, and so I realized: I was part of the act!

DAVID: I don't get it.

KAREN: You don't get what?

DAVID: I don't get why it was called PATTERNS OF INTERFERENCE.

KAREN: No, because, you see, it was all planned, or anticipated, and incorporated into the conception of the piece, so that even what I said was already thought of even before I said it.

DAVID: I get that.

KAREN: Then what don't you get?

DAVID: I just don't get why it was called PATTERNS OF INTERFERENCE.

KAREN: You mean you don't like the title?

DAVID: No, I mean I don't get what it means. I mean, I know, since it is a product of human intelligence or culture it must mean something even if the Irishman didn't know what it meant or what it means is unintentional or that it means something about the collective consciousness even though the Irishman doesn't get it but is just the unknowing medium through whom the culture speaks, you know, but I don't get it.

  Long silence.

KAREN: No. Neither do I.

Do you know Grace Paley?

DAVID: Well, I know who she is.

KAREN: She picked up the phone—this was what I heard anyway—and said hello and this voice said, hello, this is Linda Ronstadt. And Grace Paley said: who is this really?

  VI. *A performance piece.*
  Music.

Richard Caliban

❧

Rodents & Radios

•

Cast of Characters

SMITH	rock and roll radio personality
JUDD	wife to a diplomat
KLARI	Rumanian defector, tennis star
MR BEEM	in search of a vocation, tennis fan
RAND	makes lone expeditions to isolated, exotic locations
WOODARD	ex CIA agent, mercenary
CLAUDE	French woman, pregnant

Stage areas are isolated and at different levels with actors playing scenes at impossible angles to each other—the effect looking something like an Escher drawing. There is music and/or sound landscapes throughout.

Rodents & Radios premiered at the Cucaracha Warehouse Theatre in April, 1990 with the following cast:

SMITH	Damian Young
JUDD	Sharon Brady
KLARI	Mollie O'Mara
MR BEEM	Glen M. Santiago
RAND	Lauren Hamilton
WOODARD	Marco Dillahunt
CLAUDE	Vivan Lanko

Director/Set Design: Richard Caliban; Composer: John Hoge; Light Design: Brian Aldous; Costume Design: Mary Myers.

NOTE: All text in caps is sung.

SMITH *with a pair of headphones, speaking into a microphone.*

SMITH: Good morning kids—rise and shine—it's another big day on planet earth. Hit it!

> BIG MUSIC.
>
> SMITH *dances.*
>
> *Fade to* JUDD *and* KLARI.

JUDD: Goodness—it's been how long now since you defected—a long time—Alex and I still think of you as a daughter—it's true—of course we don't get to see you as much as we'd like anymore—hardly saw you at all when we were stationed in Budapest—you with all your tournaments—Alex always off on some diplomatic mission somewhere—the years slip by—but it's nice that we're still close—
Feeling good?—ready?

KLARI: Always I am ready for the Open. All my life. When I am six years old in my dreams I am playing the U.S. Open. So—I have played it—now I have to win it.

JUDD: Well, maybe this will be your year—I hope so.

KLARI: You see in the Times today? There is a picture of me but with another girl's face—in the whole world I am ranked number eight—and the New York Times does not know my face—some girl who I have beaten a million times they put in there by mistake—if you are number one, number two or three even—everybody knows your face—you go into a Burger K-King in some place in Montana and everybody will jump all over you—but when you are number eight they mix up your face with some other girl—from number eight to number one there is a thousand billion miles.

JUDD: Well, I certainly admire your determination a great deal. Whether you ever win it or not rest assured Alex and I certainly think you're a terrific success story in your own right.

KLARI: That is like saying to me: Number eight is good enough for you, K-Klari. Be happy with that. Be happy that the New York Times does not know my face.

JUDD: I don't mean that at all, I just…

KLARI: Always you treat me that way—I am sick of that—from you—from everybody—you think that I am kaput, finito—I know—I READ THE PAPERS—BUT YOU DON'T KNOW—NOBODY KNOWS WHAT I CAN DO—
When I am very little girl in Rumania with all the other girls learning to play tennis, every day, every day—get up every morning—
FOREHAND FOREHAND, BACKHAND BACKHAND—
All during those years I have a nightmare every night—this woman, this big

Rumanian woman who cleans the dormitory comes to each bed when we are asleep and with steel wool ERASES EACH FACE—CLEAN AND SMOOTH—LEAVES NO FEATURE—LEAVES NO FACE—and she comes—from bed to bed—taking away each girl's face—until they all look the same—all the same—each face—and I run and I run but I cannot run…

So—no—I am not so happy satisfied to be Miss Number Eight—who do you think I am?—some little girl back in Rumania?—No—I don't take that—I fight and I fight and I fight—every time I swing my racket I fight—

JUDD: Come on, kid, cheer up—here, you've got a smudge of my lipstick on your cheek. I'll get it.

She reaches to wipe KLARI's *cheek,* KLARI *pulls back.*

Trust me.

Fade to MR BEEM.

MR BEEM: Basically, sir, you may consider me a runt—in the moral sense. Stunted. Odd desires and dubious values fester in my soul.

All right—I am purposely being somewhat overdramatic, but I do not want to mislead you: I am not what you would call a likable person. I have a perpetually nagging feeling of being unclean.

Nevertheless—let me be frank—I would make nothing short of an excellent employee—well, perhaps I should say good employee—yes, I would make nothing short of a good or if I may amend myself again, adequate employee with Con Edison.

My qualifications: None to speak of. But I do possess a vivid vision of myself crawling around beneath the city—an untouchable—doing your dirty work (yours in the sense of the general citizenry, not yours personally, sir)—but yes, I do see myself emerging from some rat infested manhole covered with filth startling some perfectly decent pedestrians.

To be honest: I see this sort of work as my calling. Let me explain: Life is a question that I feel obliged to answer. But—before one can answer one needs to decipher the question properly. I myself, you see, am unfortunately stuck at this initial stage and as a result I am in my present desperate situation: making wild stabs—like this, like groveling before you, sir—in the ridiculous hope that I will hit upon the answer to my life.

You seem unimpressed. Well—let me explain further: To live your life as long as I have—unanswered—completely in the dark—well, things inside you, sir, begin to malfunction. And that, you see, is why I am overflowing with personality disorders. In fact, sir, if it will help, you may think of me metaphorically as an almost hopelessly out of tune piano upon which melodies and harmonies are becoming so dissonant and jumbled as to make them not only unpleasant but offensive.

In short, I am sinking fast, sir. I need this job. Desperate circumstances require etcetera etcetera—I won't bore you—but I do have to say—and this just a final footnote after which I will be eager to hear your decision as to my application for employment—I do have to say that you are a constant source of amazement to me—again, not you personally, sir, but you in the general sense—you look so content, self-satisfied—I cannot help but assume you know what you're all about—that you have a well ordered life—a loving family—a pleasure boat for the week-ends—that you sleep soundly, peacefully—that you have old friends to gossip with. Well—that's all very good. I commend you. Ahh—yes—you are detecting a note of contempt. You are right. I admit it. The fact is, I cannot help but feel that some of you are faking it, that some of you haven't answered your life at all, that some of you are trying to ignore it altogether, tip toeing past the graveyard trying to nonchalantly whistle. Well—I tried that too—lived for a period of years in New Guinea like a lobotomized fish. That's a lie—I am, you should know, a freewheeling liar. Truth is not an obsession of mine—I just don't comprehend the importance of it—but again, I am something of an out of tune piano—as I explained earlier—certain notes are flat or sharp—certain keys don't work at all. Nevertheless, sir—and this will be my final comment: I feel utterly suitable—or at least adequately suitable for employment with Con Edison. I await your decision.

VOICE: We're not hiring right now.

MR BEEM: I see. Very well. Thank you very much for your time.

> *Fade.*
> *Radio static.*
> BIG MUSIC.
> *Fade to* RAND.

RAND: I am standing before Mount Kailas, the twenty-five thousand foot peak re-vered by both Buddhists and Hindus alike. Here, with snow and hail, pilgrims circle the mountain, some on their knees—a two day thirty mile trip. That kind of purity humbles me—puts me in awe of these people. I've been in the great cathedrals, lots of big deal holy places all over the world—and they're nothing to this. This place and these people—they're the apex of spirituality.

So—I don't know how to tell you this honey, but…well—I've decided that this is where I'm going to stay. This will be the last tape you get from me. My plans from here are to live out on the plains like the nomads do—if you got the tape I sent last month you'll remember me drinking yak milk with that wonderful family, helping to raise their tent, those laughing girls—such incredible faces. They seem to be lit up from within. I can't leave. I just can't. I hope you understand. I hope you're happy for me. And of course you have my permission to divorce me.

I'm sorry. I guess I just could never get comfortable in California. Always kind of dizzy and nauseous like at a carnival. And since I've left—I feel like I've been running down this long tunnel and you're this pin prick of light behind me—that's the key word—behind me. I've changed so much, honey. You've no idea. Speaking to you is like bumping into parts of myself that don't even exist anymore.

Don't know what else to say. It's cold as hell, I'll tell you that. But you'd be sur-prised how warm these nomad tents are. I'm gonna have to have somebody show me how to make one, I guess. Maybe I can trade this camera in for some goats and stuff. Whatever. I'll be fine. I'll be happy. Have a good life, honey. I'll miss you. Bye.

> *Fade to* WOODARD, *in a tux.*

WOODARD: You read in the paper about this moron that opens up with an uzi in a church? Up in Vermont or someplace. I tell ya man, when they start losin' it up in places like Vermont we're in trouble. Perfectly normal kid, the papers say. Yeah—a perfectly normal kid who writes love songs to the devil and packs an uzi. Maybe that is normal nowadays. Fuckin' chaos—everywhere—it's the wild west—twelve year olds with guns, sellin' dope, growin' up on porn movies. There's no standards, no respect for anything—trash it, violate it, mock it.

You ever read that book when you were a kid—*Lord of the Flies*?—that's what it is—it must be a very thin bond between us and civilization. Think about it—five thousand years of civilization—of brilliant people killing themselves to make life better—all the scientists and statesmen and revolutions and inventions and artists, books and music and poems and heavy thinkers and stuff—I close my eyes and see this big endless trample of people—arms and legs stickin' out—pushin' and pullin'—like those Michelangelo pictures—guys with robes and big muscles, wind in their hair—I hear Walter Cronkite's voice: The March of Civilization—I've seen this in my head since I was a kid—and when I think that it took five thousand years of back breaking work and sacrifice by the greatest minds this earth has produced to come up with Twisted Sister or this fucking kid up in Vermont I...I just can't even sleep—I get knots I...I... Well, forget it. How do you get a drink around here?

Fade to KLARI.

KLARI: I am nervous—my serve—I want to work on my serve—it feels a little pushed to me—Mrs Judd—you know, that diplomat lady—she comes yesterday to watch me practice and wastes my time—talking and talking—always she wastes my time—last year she invites me and invites me to come with a vacation on her and her husband and I am saying no no no I cannot take time off and she is saying I have to relax or I burn up from too much tennis and so I go away with them and lie on a beach like a piece of meat in the broiler and I sit and eat dinner with she and her husband and in my head there are tennis balls and in my legs there are cramps and I know that every minute I am wasting some other girl is pushing pushing fore-hand forehand backhand backhand and I want to get up and run—run away—but I cannot run—like in a dream—I cannot run—and in my head is all that pop pop pop pop until I am sick—I am sick—right on the table—in the middle of dinner—white napkins and crystal—waiters with tuxedos—and I am sick and I vomit on the table and onto Mr and Mrs Judd—I vomit like that girl in that movie—like green pea soup—like the devil is inside me—

So—anyway—I am talking and talking—take a look at my serve—see what you think—it is a little off—I don't know what is wrong with me—it is hard to sleep—in my head—tennis balls, tennis balls—all this stuff in the papers—I am a disap-pointment—past my prime—never can win the big one—pop pop pop pop—it makes me crazy—it is like I am dying almost—alive and watching myself die—forget it—I don't know what's wrong with me—take a look at my serve—

I cannot let this stuff get in my head—I must be ready—

Fade to SMITH *at the microphone.*

SMITH: Say listen,—I wanna tell you about a really super weight loss program—'cause lets face it—a lot of you are fat and ugly and stupid—a lot of you are wandering around out there like... (Lights a cigarette) Say listen,—I wanna tell you about a really super weight loss program—'cause lets face it—a lot of you are fat and ugly and stupid—a lot of you are wandering around out there like runaway blimps bumping into each other—yeah—like as if the Goodyear blimp got its umbilical cord cut and just started getting blown around by the wind—that's how I picture some of you—it's not a pretty picture—it depresses the hell out of me—but that's why you— need Weight-Off—that's right—Weight-Off—the really super weight loss program for runaway blimps—call today.

　　Let's get back to the music.

　　BIG MUSIC.

　　Abruptly cuts to radio static.

　　Fade to JUDD *and* CLAUDE.

JUDD: In my toilet bowl today—something very odd—it has unsettled me terribly— I was standing at the sink—brushing my teeth—there were bubbles and strange sounds and a big fat rat squeezed and clawed and splashed right up out of my toilet and plopped dead at my feet—soaking wet—bloated—disgusting—I have heard of such things—but I never suspected—why only a moment earlier I was... well...sitting right there—I get nauseous just imagining—I don't know how I will ever be able to...sit...again—with piece of mind—I mean one likes to think one can enjoy a few moments sanctuary while sitting on the throne but I guess there's always something—I'm very upset—I know how my mind works, you see—so few— so few things to rely on, it seems—maybe it's just me—I find it all very unsettling—all so very unsettling—

　　When are you due?

CLAUDE: I don't know.

JUDD: And the father?

CLAUDE: It does not matter. Some man. Who cares. Whoever it is I would not let him touch my baby. She swims in my belly like a mermaid. She knows nothing of all this mess. No, I cannot worry about some man.

JUDD: I find it all very unsettling.

CLAUDE: Well, if there could be someplace—like you say some sanctuary—but where can you go where it is not a mess. I cannot even think about it. Where is your stupid husband who does not even deserve to sniff your feet, hm? What is he doing—that cheating, murdering human rat of a husband—strangling some political person in some dirty little country?

JUDD: Oh, he's in Columbia. Some diplomatic nonsense. You know. But I'm sure he's not strangling someone, dear.

CLAUDE: Happy?

JUDD: Me and...? Yeah. Yes. Well, we've been married now what...
　　You know how it is. Men. You never know with them.

CLAUDE: Yes. Fucking everything up. From the beginning of time.

JUDD: Well. That's a bit more than I meant. I meant…

CLAUDE: Fucking everything up. Killing and noises and dirt.

JUDD: I meant I think he probably sleeps with a woman once in a while.

CLAUDE: So you sleep with a man. That's what they want. Roll in the mud with them. Ha ha, big joke—they don't know what love is if it bites them on the ass. Go ahead—sleep with some man—what's the difference?

JUDD: Well—I have, but…

CLAUDE: Yes?

JUDD: …but it didn't solve anything. It hurts—it still hurts. When he's away. Like this, for instance. I'm in the dark. Always in the dark. I never know.

Have you ever heard the sound of someone being killed? —shot or stabbed or something? When we were with the embassy in Turkey—I was in a hotel room in Istanbul—and it—this killing—was going on in the next room—some poor woman was getting stabbed—repeatedly—but I thought she was getting fucked—it's startling how similar…—and now—in bed with Alex—I find it…uncomfortable—to turn the light out—and after we're…done—listening to just his breathing—I GET A PAIN IN MY SIDE—LYING THERE IN THE DARK—NAKED AS A BABY—

CLAUDE: Listen kiddo, you have thoughts like that about your husband you should get a divorce.

JUDD: Have you seen any of the U.S. Open? When we were in Washington, between Turkey and Budapest, we met Klari Bogdan—the tennis player—we were very close when she was younger—but frankly, between you and I, the girl's ego has become a bit much—to the point where she's become unpleasant to be with. Have you been following the Open?

CLAUDE: No. I can't stand that stuff. Idiots. Brats who know nothing else but to hit a ball back and forth back and forth at each other. Insane. No. I tell you. Everything is wrong. And I don't know how it is that I can be the only one who hears it? Clang clang, bang bang—everywhere, everywhere. It's impossible.

JUDD: Claude, you always exaggerate so. Things aren't that bad. You're not breaking your back in some fucking rice paddy somewhere.

CLAUDE: There is nowhere to go. Nowhere. Bang bang, clang clang. All the same. What can you do? Look at us. You stay with a husband who cheats your heart. I walk around the streets like a crazy woman and complain. It is all a big mess. So—how can I watch tennis. I will break the TV set.

Phone rings.

VOICE: Mrs Judd? Mark Baker. With the service?

JUDD: Oh yes. Hi.

VOICE: Mrs Judd—Alex—there's a chance he's been kidnapped. Down in Columbia.

JUDD: What do you mean?

VOICE: Well. He's missing. And, you know, the cartel—they might be involved—we're assuming the worst. For now. He might just be out of touch. But our sources seem to think… Anyway—we're doing everything possible. There's a lot of strings we can pull. I'll keep you posted.

JUDD: Yeah. Yes.
> *She hangs up.*

CLAUDE: Who was that?

JUDD: My husband has run off with another woman.
> *Balinese monkey chant.*
>
> *Fade to* RAND.

RAND: Hello. Is this thing working or what. Honey? I'm in Bali—I'll explain later—just listen to those guys sing, huh?—unbelievable—I love it here—life, man, life—who would have thought I'd have such an affinity for this little corner of the world—I mean, Christ, it's so sexy—it's gorgeous—it's…it's…I can't even describe what I feel here—like my bones vibrate, my insides, my womb—this whole place is like one big incredible giant vibrator—I'm in a constant state of orgasm here—do you understand what I'm saying—I mean, like the sex you and me used to have that we thought was so great—like we couldn't imagine anything greater—well, we didn't know shit—that was like a little trickle—a drop—this—THIS is the ocean—I mean, I think I can honestly say that I have never really had sex until now—

> So honey—just wanted to let you know—the pieces to my puzzle have finally all come together—I'm…Dammit, this fucking thing's not working—
>
> *Abruptly to radio static.*
>
> *Fade to* SMITH.

SMITH: Okay, we're back. Let's see—how 'bout a traffic update—wanna traffic update?—uh…here it is—traffic sucks—that just in from the Traffic Watch Supercopter.

> Okay—the topic for this morning is me. I was an orphan—no parents—none. I was raised…

> Can I have some different background, please. Can't you sense the change in mood, man? No. Not that. Heavy—I'm gettin' heavy now. Yeah that—that's good.

> I was raised by a psychotic uncle. I spent the first thirteen years of my life chained to a baby's pottee. From what they tell me—the social workers who rescued me—I could not speak at all—yeah—I knew no words—none—yeah—till I was thirteen I lived on a pottee—naked—unable to speak—I grunted—had no contact with anyone aside from my uncle who never spoke to me and just shoved food in front of me once a day. Yeah—I had a miserable childhood. I'm written up in a bunch of psychological journals. Shrinks are always calling me up cause they can't believe I'm actually alive and sane—they wanna do studies on me. I'm not supposed to be able to form sentences or relate normally to people. I'm a mess. Raised in a vacuum. I have no memory of my childhood—all of it completely blocked out—I might just as well have dropped out of the sky from another planet. And all of you people out there—my faithful listeners—I feel about as akin to you as I do to some weird Amazonian species of monkey.

> So—now that we know where we stand—let's talk about love—about marriage, religion, interest rates—sex, careers, violent crimes—but before we get started—yeah, before we get started—before I like the messiah let my hot flashes of wisdom loose on you—I want you to know—I want you to know that it's no use—no use

even beginning—it's all too complicated—too many sides to the coin—too many people—too many countries—too many number one songs—too many beautiful babes—too many radio stations—too many facts—and all of them contradicting each other—there is not a solid—not a solid piece of ground on earth—our mayors and presidents are out to lunch—our religious leaders are spiritually deprived materialists—our athletes are psycho-killers on drugs—our movie stars and rock and roll heroes are cardboard publicity creations posturing for the right causes—everything we touch turns to powder—falls apart—melts—explodes—it's a nightmare—I have it every night—you hold the beautiful girl in your arms—the girl you love—and you turn to kiss her—and she's some monster with dripping flesh and fangs—just like you've seen in a hundred and one horror movies—yeah—that's right—it's in the national consciousness—a sign of our times—of our civilization—but that is not your cue to call in with your idiot comments about how rock and roll ain't got no soul anymore—cause it's bigger than that, kids—it's bigger than gun control—or just say no or teachers salaries—or trade balances with Japan—yeah—that's right—it's big—real big—it's like…

It's like this particular branch of civilization has got root rot—has got cracks—it's got to fall off the tree before it can grow anymore. It's not a tragedy—it happens to all civilizations—we're nothing special—life goes on—I don't know why you all get so excited about these things.

Anyway—getting back to me—I went to a play last night—a big hit—did I tell you this?—but the costumes and the scenery were horrible?—simplistic, the acting laughable?—Anyway, I couldn't get caught up in the drama—I see the so called jokes coming a mile away—I mean, who are you guys out there?—deer dazzled by headlights?—How do you get caught up in all this stuff—how do you participate in your own lives?—the hoax, the hoax—I can't hoodwink myself into believing in any of it—passion passion passion, oh wow, I'm really living, man—don't make me laugh, kids—I don't believe any of it for a second—I don't believe it—none of it—none of it—and if I had any sense at all I'd blow my…

All right—all right, cut the music—that's enough—there it is—the morning rampage—we'll be right back after this.

Blackout.

BIG MUSIC.

Fade to KLARI *lying down.*

KLARI: I MUST GET UP—I MUST GET READY—I MUST GET OUT ON THE C-COURTS—

[*Sits up*] No—too early—too tired—please—sleep just a little more—yes—make those other girls go practice—I c-can beat them all—straight sets—kaput, finito—they will tell you—THEY KNOW WHO I AM—

Look—do you see?—it's me—K-Klari—terror of the courts—look—look how all those girls open their mouths and watch—me—Klari—all the way to the U.S. Open—pop pop pop pop—KLARI TENNIS SHOES—KLARI RACKETS—KLARI FASHION WEAR—KLARI TAMPAX—

I MUST GET UP—I MUST GET READY—I MUST GET OUT ON THE C-OURTS—

Yes—I fight—I fight you all—me, Klari—WHO DO YOU THINK I AM?—some little girl back in Rumania?

OH LOOK LOOK LOOK—SEE WHAT SHE DOES—ALL THOSE GIRLS—CLEAN AND SMOOTH—LEAVES NO FEATURE—LEAVES NO FACE—

Yes yes yes—I am ready—first drill: FOREHAND FOREHAND—BACK-HAND BACKHAND—yes—easy, beautiful, deep, with rhythm, with pace—pop pop pop pop—SEE HOW THEY WATCH—SEE HOW THEY WATCH—SEE HOW THEY WATCH—ME—KLARI—

I MUST GET UP—I MUST GET READY—I MUST GET OUT ON THE C-COURTS

Fade to WOODARD *and* JUDD.

WOODARD: Mrs. Judd, I worked with your husband in Ankara on the Teheran project. We had some rough times there me and Alex. I'm not with the service now, but I have contacts, obviously. And a certain amount of freedom in terms of what I can do…uh… independently. What I'm getting at is, well—myself and several other individuals are going into Columbia—again, this is not a government operation, although for my money it should be—myself and several other individuals are going in with the intention of bringing Alex out.

JUDD: But—do you know who he's with—I mean, where he is?

WOODARD: We think so.

JUDD: Where?

WOODARD: Well…in some pretty rough country. Near the Brazilian border. I'm going in with five extremely well trained and equipped men—helicopter drop. It's expensive. But since leaving the agency I've been involved with some well funded private individuals who feel justice can sometimes be better served by… Well, you get the picture.

You see, when I was with the agency—always that feeling of helplessness—the red tape—the diplomatic concerns—everything always done with one hand tied behind our back. It gets to you after awhile. So many terrible things done to people all over the world. I can't tolerate that. I'm not trying to justify going outside of the law like I'm doing. That is, my own actions actually run against the grain of the kind of justice I envision for this world, but the fact is I can't help it. I'm a killer, m'am. And I've been trained real good. But I can't un-train myself. I can't work a regular job and watch the world go by on the TV. I can't sleep at night when I know there's bastards holding Alex out there. I'll turn into one of those nut cases that walks into a post office and opens up with a shot gun. I know myself, m'am. I look civilized as hell but… well… You get the picture. At another time and place I might have made an excellent SS officer. But, you see, I know that about myself. There are certain human beings who are basically attack dogs—and I'm one of them. And all you can hope for with a fella like me is that somebody points me in the right direction. Well, fortunately—perhaps even by accident—I happen to be pointed in the right direction. My desire for just, civilized behavior in this world is fanatic. And so if I can rescue Alex and blow away these motherfuckers—excuse the expression—holding him, well then I can breathe a little easier. Does that make any sense to you?

JUDD: Yeah. Yes.

WOODARD: Good. I just wanted you to know that something was being done. And like I say this is all unofficial

JUDD: I understand. Thank you.

WOODARD: I'm bringing him back, Mrs Judd. You can count on it. And the guys responsible…well, like I say—my desire for justice is fanatic.

Could I have some more tea, please?

Fade to CLAUDE.

CLAUDE: Excuse me, Mr Officer, but I would like to request information—concerning the pigeons—I am wondering if there is not something wrong—I am certain this must come to your jurisdiction—you must have noticed—so many pigeons—millions and millions—all over the city—but where are the little bodies—with so many pigeons they must be dying all the time, yes?—they are just birds—we should see their little dead bodies everywhere—is that not logical—do they go someplace like elephants and die?—they fly over to Roosevelt Island maybe—and if I go there I will find everything covered with dead pigeons—I don't think so—something is wrong, yes?—somebody is hiding the dead pigeons—you cannot have millions of pigeons and only one or two dead ones on the street—what kind of place is this to bring a baby to—(Clutches herself) Oh—kick—she kicked me—never before has she kicked me—you see what you have done—

LISTEN, JUST LISTEN—AND YOU CAN HEAR A TERRIBLE NOISE EVERYWHERE—LITTLE MEN—SNEAKING AROUND—MAKING TERRIBLE NOISES—HIDING THE POOR DEAD PIGEONS—WHY?—WHY DO THEY FUCK IT ALL UP?—WHY DON'T YOU DO SOMETHING?

Fade to KLARI *playing tennis,* SMITH *and* BEEM *watching in the stands.*

MR BEEM: Are you a tennis fan, sir?

I say, are you a tennis fan?

SMITH: What? Ah…yeah.

MR BEEM: It's not sunny, you know.

SMITH: I'm sorry?

MR BEEM: Cloudy out. Just wondering. About your sunglasses. You say you are a tennis fan?

SMITH: I'm trying to watch this, okay?

MR BEEM: Oh sure—I'm a disruptive influence, I know.

Crowd cheer.

Miss Bogdan—over here—I admire your game plan immensely! Really! Bravo! Excellent!

REFEREE'S VOICE: Quiet in the stands please. Quiet.

MR BEEM: [*To* SMITH] You see—I rub almost everyone the wrong way. I, by the way, am a tennis fan myself. I have never played the game but I believe myself to be an excellent strategist—it may very well be my calling in life.

SMITH's *radio phone rings.*

SMITH: Yeah.

VOICE: Marv—listen—what is this walking off the air crap—I'm paying you big money—I deserve better treatment—you got a little headache or something you don't just walk off in the middle of a show.

SMITH: Well…yeah you do—if you're me. Let's face it, boss—that's what they love about me—I'll say anything, do anything—you know why? 'Cause I don't give a fuck. It's not even an act. It's not my schtick. I really don't give a fuck. You don't understand that. But that's why I'm famous and you're not.

VOICE: Don't push your luck, Marv.

SMITH: I'm not bragging, boss. I'm just explaining. Everyone's attached to the world in some way—they care about this, about that—I was born with a part missing or something—I don't give a shit—about anything—back in the 60's—Vietnam—I didn't care—blow 'em all up—leave 'em alone—it was all the same to me.

VOICE: Marv, please, spare me—I'm just saying don't walk out in the middle of…

SMITH: I'm trying to explain to you why I can't promise shit like that.

VOICE: YOU'RE TALKIN' ABOUT GOD DAMN VIETNAM!

Crowd cheer.

SMITH: Wow. This girl, man. Are you into tennis?

VOICE: What??

SMITH: It's pretty strange, man—hitting a ball back and forth at each other like it mattered. You should see this girl…

VOICE: Marv, listen…

SMITH: The point is man, don't threaten me cause I don't give a shit whether you fire my ass or not!

KLARI: Ref—please—you c-can keep these people quiet—I can't c-concentrate.

REFEREE'S VOICE Quiet please in the stands or I'll have you removed.

They watch a moment.

MR BEEM: So—I am curious to know what it is like to be famous.

SMITH: It's a drag, man. Creeps like you are always buggin' the shit out of me.

MR BEEM: Well, bear in mind, we don't mean to be pests, we're simply grasping at straws, looking for clues—and by we, of course, I mean those of us who have not yet solved our lives—and I should think it would be quite natural to expect us to look upon someone famous as someone who has a few answers, someone who is focused and on the right track, someone who is getting on with their life and not stuck way back at the basic question. That, sir, is why I am a tennis fan—because while I frankly do not believe most people who appear to have the answers I do believe in someone like—well, like Miss Bogdan. She has obviously found her niche. She plays the game as if it were a matter of life or death, as I think you noticed.

SMITH: Yeah—well—I agree with you there.

MR BEEM: As I said—tennis is my calling.

Crowd cheer.

Nice shot, Miss Bogdan! Precisely placed and smartly executed!

REFEREE'S VOICE: Will security please escort that gentleman from the stands.

MR BEEM: No no—I'll leave—I understand—I'm an annoyance, a distraction—I can't sit here quietly and confidently like the rest of you.

Farewell, sir, nice meeting you. I'm glad you agreed with me on the point I made about Miss Bogdan—it's not often people agree with me, especially someone so famous they are forced to wear sunglasses to disguise themselves from people like me—creeps was the word I believe you used—yes, creeps like me.

[*As he exits.*] All right—good luck, Miss Bogdan—I'm a big fan you know—perhaps we might talk sometime—I'm an excellent strategist—I could offer you some tips—tennis is my calling.

Radio static.

Fade to RAND.

RAND: Hi honey—Tibet didn't work out—neither did Bali—but my wanderings are over—I'm standing in one of the wildest places on earth—a region called Bird's Head—at the western tip of Irian Jaya. A lot of bugs, but really an amazing place. The only way in here was by missionary helicopter - leave it to the missionaries to find all the primo places. The people here are pretty much stone age—they live in tree houses, carry spears and wear penis sheaths.

But I wish you could just be here and breathe this air, honey. It has really transformed me—such mystery—it's an almost tangible presence—at night it gets so dark here, honey, so incredibly dark that it lets you believe in almost anything—it's so powerful—so deep dark powerful—it puts things in perspective—

Tibet was a bust, by the way—full of religious hypocrites—boy did they have me fooled—and Bali was a big orgasm—at first—I fucked everything that moved and ended up trying to bite some poor jerk's eyebrows off in a Dionysian frenzy—I thought I was having a real sexual mystical revelation but…well…guess I just hadn't had sex in a year or two.

But getting back to this place, honey—I've never felt like this—not since I was a kid waiting up to see if I could hear Santa's reindeer—I mean, there's something I wanna convey to you about…you know…me and…It's hard to put my finger on it—it's just that—well—you and me in that house together I couldn't… I could never seem to breathe—I almost feel like I can just sort of magically become… anything…like there's this whole untapped region of myself that… Shit—I'm having a hard time communicating this—I feel like you're on some other planet—

Anyhow, for all I know you don't even pay attention to all these tapes anymore and are happily married to another woman and could care less about what I'm doing but in case you're still interested I thought I'd let you know where I was and how I was doing. This will be the last tape you'll get from me. I plan to grow old and die here in this magical place. I hope you're happy for me. I promise I won't bother you any more. Good luck with your life and everything. I'll miss you. Bye.

Phone rings.

Fade to JUDD *on the phone.*
A man breathing is heard.

JUDD: HELLO? ALEX? IS THAT YOU? Listen—I'm very disturbed by all this. Can't you talk? I'd like to know where I stand. Alex? Why do you just breathe like that? Like you were lying on top of me...the way you do after making love...remember? You're not with someone...as we speak, are you? That would be cruel. It's one thing to do things behind my back but to... Oh Alex, can't you say something? You're such a strange man. I don't know what goes on inside you. I sometimes think I know you and then I'll see you eating breakfast or something—the angle of your face—the way the light hits it—and I suddenly feel you're someone completely strange to me. Do you feel that way towards me? That we exist with each other with some kind of easy familiarity but that at heart we are not in each other's confidence, that we actually have quite separate—agendas—as you would say. Honestly Alex, I don't want to feel like that towards you. I don't like to lie next to you—naked as a baby—and feel this pain—this sharp pain in my side—anxiety I guess—but...well, since I'm telling you this much—there have been times when we were making love that for a moment I had the horrible feeling you were someone else. Alex? You're not mad are you? I can never tell. Alex? Won't you say something? I can feel that you want to—I think things would be so much better—so much more comfortable—if we could confide in each other—we did at one time didn't we?—Alex? Alex! I won't be left hanging like this—I won't be—I have a right to know!

Goodness—you probably think I don't trust you. I'm sorry.

ALEX? I WISH YOU'D SAY SOMETHING—IT UNSETTLES ME SO—I JUST NEVER KNOW—I JUST NEVER KNOW...

Alex....?

Fade to CLAUDE.

CLAUDE: No place to go—no place—bang bang, clang clang—everything is...

Voices sing.

...beautiful—where is that sound—those voices—do you hear?—do you hear that my baby? So beautiful—so beautiful—from where does it come?

A light from below.

Ohhh... Yes—of course—deep—down deep—from...from where the water...goes down—sanctuary...

Fade to WOODARD, *unconscious—dressed in camouflage, black face, several cuts, burn marks on his skin and uniform.*

A tinny sounding transistor radio is suddenly heard overhead. A commercial jingle—"The Club Med Vacation—the antidote for civilization"—repeats.

WOODARD *suddenly springs up, a bloodied knife in his hand.*

The radio flips to a baseball game.

WOODARD *focuses overhead.*

WOODARD: Hey. Jesus Christ. Shhh. Come on, boy. Get—get outa here. [*Makes as if to throw his knife.*]

The radio fades away. Monkey screeches.

What is this?—fuckin' Disneyland? [*Into his walkie-talkie.*] Hello—Rat's nest—
come in—do you read me—hello—this is Night Force.

VOICE: [*Over the walkie-talkie.*] We read ya Night Force—where ya been—what's happened?—where's the chopper?

WOODARD: It's down, man—Dean, Festus, Rovey—they all bought it—I'm the only
one left—they were chasin' me all night—If Alex is still alive they still got him. Over.

VOICE: Forget about Alex—you just get yourself to the secondary pickup point and
we'll get a chopper in to…

The overhead radio: the news in Spanish.

What the hell's that? Over.

WOODARD: It's a monkey. With a radio.

VOICE: A what?

You okay, man? You been hit? Over.

WOODARD: Yeah—I'm okay—I'll meet you guys at the secondary pickup point.

WOODARD *clicks off the walkietalkie.*

Noise of the jungle grows.

WOODARD: [*Half hums, half sings*] …THE ANTIDOTE FOR CIVILIZATION. THE
CLUB MED VACATION.—

Dabs a bit of blood onto his face like warpaint.

Fade to KLARI, *exhausted.*

KLARI: Okay—good—I am ready—tomorrow—the quarter finals—one step closer—
no mistakes—sleep—sleep tonight yes sleep—no sound of tennis balls—in my
head—no girls with no faces—one step closer—one step closer—they will all see—
Klari Bogdan—I will be champion I will be champion—

Okay—good—I am ready—tomorrow—the quarter finals—ONE STEP
CLOSER—ONE STEP CLOSER—no mistakes—sleep—sleep tonight yes sleep—
no sound of tennis balls—in my head—no girls with no faces—ONE STEP
CLOSER—ONE STEP CLOSER—they will all see—Klari Bogdan—I will be
champion—I will be champion—

TOMORROW—THE QUARTER FINALS—ONE STEP CLOSER—NO
MISTAKES—SLEEP—SLEEP TONIGHT YES SLEEP—NO SOUND OF
TENNIS BALLS—IN MY HEAD—NO GIRLS WITH NO FACES—ONE
STEP CLOSER—ONE STEP CLOSER—THEY WILL ALL SEE—KLARI
BOGDAN—I WILL BE CHAMPION—I WILL BE CHAMPION—I WILL BE
CHAMPION—

Fade to JUDD *and* CLAUDE.

CLAUDE: Sanctuary, you see—I have been looking every place—to Roosevelt Island I
went—

JUDD: The newspapers seem to think my husband is dead. I find it disconcerting. Especially when he calls.

Roosevelt Island?

CLAUDE: Pigeons—a wild goose chase. But now—I find it—just by accident—walking on the street—

JUDD: It's just an infatuation, I'm sure. You don't live with a man all these years and then lose him to some harmless little fling.

What have you found?

CLAUDE: Forget about your stupid rat of a husband—let him go—

SANCTUARY—DEEP DOWN DEEP—I KNOW IT IS THERE—AND I AM GOING—

JUDD: You don't just forget someone you've been intimate with for all these years.

I can tell he wants to confess—but well—now that it's become an international incident—I'm sure he's worried about phone taps and so on—he doesn't say a word—

CLAUDE: Listen to me—right here—under the city—under our noses—sanctuary—I know—I have heard the voices—

JUDD: I WISH HE'D COME BACK THOUGH—YOU CAN'T HELP BUT WORRY—

You reach a point where…well…you get tired of waiting—where you feel you have to…do something…

CLAUDE: From out of the drains I hear it—so far away—so deep below—beautiful voices—singing—down deep—

JUDD: The sewer?

CLAUDE: Beautiful singing—below the subway—below the clang and bang—deep—very deep—there must be some hidden place—some hidden beautiful place—sanctuary—sanctuary—

JUDD: Oh stop—please—the sewer is…the sewer—you must be out of your mind—

CLAUDE: No—I am going—you could come—you could come too—

JUDD: Go. Just go. I don't know who you are anymore. You've let this whole business warp your mind. It unsettles me. Just go. Goodbye. Please—

BIG MUSIC.

Fade to SMITH *in the studio.*

SMITH: Okay, we're back.

You know, there are times, my friends out there, when I get such a rush from life—I mean it—like listening to the end of Turandot—my body shakes—I pace around and get red in the face—Turandot, the ice princess—finally conquered by love—the last lines are: I know the stranger's name! His…

Cut it, man—cut the music—

His name is…love!—and the orchestra and chorus like a huge tidal wave that's been building and building since the first act comes crunching in like a million pounds of humanity and they sing:

LOVE! O SUN! LIFE! ETERNITY!

LIGHT OF THIS WORLD AND LOVE!

WE REJOICE AND CELEBRATE WITH SONG IN THE SUNSHINE

OUR GREAT HAPPINESS

GLORY TO THEE! GLORY! GLORY!

—and by that time, man, I am a ruin, a puddle on the floor, I can't take it, I just can't take it—it sounds stupid explaining it but when you hear it full tilt it just

sweeps you away—it's so big—there's just such a relentless, unstopable faith behind it, I guess—I mean that's what gets to me, I think—that against all reason to
believe in anything there nevertheless has always been this blind urge, like sap
through the trees—people giving birth, people dying, making wars, acting cool,
building ships, raising kids, getting old, falling in love—and I hear all that, you
see—this massive, turbulent, churning, insistent crush of humanity—and it makes
me wanna just run up to people on the street and shout and scream with them like
a wild man and lift them in the air and we all just spontaneously realize our predicament, our human dilemma, our common bond, this great unstopable love of
life that holds the universe together—that makes us all allies and lovers and bells
ring, horns honk, traffic stops, and we weep, we weep like new born babies, like
we'd all just won the lottery and we sing—we sing, man, like with big giant voices—
we sing the end of Turandot—millions of us—all out in the streets of New York—
we sing—and out of our mouths come the voices of every human being that has
ever lived—yeah—like we're the cumulative voice of the human race—and it shakes
the ground—and vibrates right down into the marrow of our bones—of our
bones—and the sky cracks open and a giant face looks down at us and is amazed—
amazed at our bravado, that we persist and flourish and stubbornly go on with the
blind faith of inspired idiots. [*Cues sound engineer.*]

    End of Turandot—*loud.*

    He listens over the head phones—ecstatic.

All right. There it is. The morning rampage. We'll be back—right after this.

    Fade to KLARI *in a nightgown with a tennis racket.* BEEM *is nearby.*

KLARI: I MUST GET UP—I MUST GET READY—I MUST GET OUT ON THE
COURTS—which way to the courts?—I am ready—I am ready—tell the photographers which one is me—they forget, I think—I don't know why—how can they
not know which one is me?

MR BEEM: Ah…Miss Bogdan—excuse me—I happened to be parked outside your
lovely home here—I wanted to speak to you—you might remember me…

KLARI: My face—you must recognize my face—how can you not recognize my face—
ask those girls over there who I am…

MR BEEM: What…girls?

KLARI: OH LOOK LOOK LOOK—do you see?—that woman—look in her hand—
the steel wool—you see how she does it?—ERASES EACH FACE—CLEAN AND
SMOOTH—LEAVES NO FEATURE—LEAVES NO FACE—

MR BEEM: Miss Bogdan—if I could speak to you a moment— I'm a big fan of yours,
actually—

KLARI: LOOK HOW KLARI SERVES—LOOK HOW KLARI MOVES—LOOK
HOW KLARI WINS—Don't you see who I am?

MR BEEM: Yes—as I just told you I'm a big fan—and I've been parked outside here—
waiting to see you actually—that's a bit irregular perhaps but…

KLARI: The quarter finals. No mistakes. FOREHAND, FOREHAND—BACK-
HAND, BACKHAND—

MR BEEM: Yes well that's what I wanted to speak to you about—I am something of a strategist—I consider it my calling in life—and I think you would do well to hire me on in some capacity as an advisor—I could send hand signals to you from the stands—I know it's late but if we spent a few hours tonight going over some of my ideas it would be of great advantage to you in tomorrow's match.

KLARI: You think I am kaput, finito—I know—I READ THE PAPERS—but you will see—I WILL BE CHAMPION—I WILL BE CHAMPION—I WILL BE CHAMPION—

MR BEEM: There are certain people in this world faking it, Miss Bogdan—you are not one of them—you know what you want—you're getting on with your life—I admire that—

KLARI: I MUST GET UP—I MUST GET READY—I MUST GET OUT ON THE COURTS—which way to the courts?—I am ready—I am ready—tell the photographers which one is me—they forget, I think—I don't know why—how can they not know which one is me?

MR BEEM: Miss Bogdan, I really think you should allow me to walk you back to your house—I believe I can be of great service to you—I really do—but we have a great deal to discuss before your match tomorrow and...

KLARI: Center court! Klari Bogdan. Do you hear? They call my name—me K-Klari.
Runs off.

MR BEEM: Miss Bogdan! Wait! Please! Miss Bogdan! [*Runs after her.*]
Rat squeaks.
CLAUDE *appears with a flashlight.*

CLAUDE: Oh my god—thousands—thousands—fierce little eyes—
SANCTUARY—SANCTUARY—
Yes—I am like you—I need SANCTUARY—up there—the banging and clanging—the dirty little men hiding the poor dead pigeons—we cannot live up there—oh, my little friends, my horrible little friends—down deep—down deep below—have you not heard it?—the sweet voices?—down deep—under the garbage and subways and pounding—we must find it—yes—through the deep hidden tunnels—yes, all of us will go—up there they trap you and kick you and poison you—no—come deep with me—yes—oh yes, my horrible ones—we cannot waste a moment—not a moment—we need sanctuary—SANCTUARY—it won't be long my wretched ones—it won't be long—
Rat squeaks grow in volume.
Fade to RAND.

RAND: I am standing near the Acobamba Abyss where I am kayaking the headwaters of the Amazon flowing from the Andes. The Inca descendants who inhabit this region stand flabbergasted along the shores when I glide past in my bright red high-tech kayak. I won't bore you with why Bird's Head didn't work out or my adventures getting here to this place—I'm sure you're not interested anymore in a restless woman like me—we never should have married, of course, I suppose that's obvious—I'm a very hard person to please, I'm coming to realize—

I was in town actually, just before making this expedition—I suppose I should have called you—got tied up with other things, I guess—I wish I had though, 'cause in a way I'd like to know if we really are still married or not—I mean, I'm assuming we're not—I certainly wouldn't expect you to be waiting around for me, god forbid—but I have to admit, I think I would find it kind of comforting if we were—not that I'd want to go back to L.A. and live with you or anything—I mean, I'd explode, honey—literally—my body would just explode like some terrorist bomb—no offense—but like I was saying it would be cool if we were still married just 'cause like up here when it's freezing cold and I see the silhouette of some baffled curious Incan standing up on the cliff looking down on me all night—it MAKES ME KIND OF... I mean, it seems that I'm so UTTERLY—TOTALLY... ANYWAY—

Anyway—I'm looking forward to the lower Amazon—that great teeming rain forest—the mother of them all—home to, I think, something like half the species on earth—So long honey—oh—and the kids—Jesus—little Martha and what's-his-name—Thomas. Give them a hug and a kiss for me. I hope they remember me. Ciao.

Fade to WOODARD, *wearing foliage in his hair, looking more savage, sharpening a stick with his knife into an arrow.*

The radio is heard overhead. First Mozart, then:

SMITH'S VOICE: [*over radio*]—and the sky cracks open and a giant face looks down at us and is amazed—amazed at our bravado, that we...

Static—flips to:

VOICE: —twenty seconds and we'll give you the world.

Tennis star Klari Bogdan has died in a bizarre traffic mishap—the young star who captured the heart of America when she defected from Rumania was struck by a car near her home in Connecticut—

WOODARD: Shit.

VOICE: Police say a possible abduction was in progress which may have caused the accident—a suspect is under arrest. Today Miss Bogdan was to have played in the semi-finals at the U.S. Open against...

Radio flips to easy listening music.

WOODARD: HEY! TURN THAT BACK! Dammit. God dammit. Jesus—Klari Bogdan—that's a shame—

VOICE: [*Over walkie-talkie.*] Hello—Night Force—this is Rat's Nest—do you read? Over.

WOODARD: Yeah. What's up. Over.

VOICE: Where are ya? You gonna get outa there or not? Over.

WOODARD: Yeah—it's just that I lost my bearings a bit—jungle just seems to be gettin' deeper—and this god damn monkey with the radio...

VOICE: Listen man, you're delirious—you gotta pull your shit together and get outa there—understand?—you're losin' control—you're fadin', man—get control of yourself—are you hit?—are you losin' blood? Over.

WOODARD: I'm fine—only thing that scares me is that I'm not scared at all—[*Static over the walkie-talkie.*] Hello? Hello—you there?—hello?

> *Radio static.*
> BIG MUSIC.
> *Fade to* KLARI, *under a sheet.*
> SMITH *enters.*

VOICE: You're not allowed in here, sir.

SMITH: Wow. That's wild. Just got smacked by a car huh. Just like that.

VOICE: I said you're not allowed in here.

SMITH: No, you don't understand—I'm a fan. A big fan. Yeah—I'm a big fan of hers. I watched her play once. And I found it touching, m'am. She touched my—how shall I say—heart. No—not romantically—almost more like religiously—yeah—I was so moved by the sincerity and conviction of her performance that I pulled out some of my old opera records.

Being human—being human, you see, taking that leap of faith—like a good actor—if you'll excuse the tired metaphor—but don't get me wrong—I have nothing but contempt for her—for you—for all of it—not that I wouldn't trade places in a second—

VOICE: Please leave immediately or I'll have to call for...

SMITH: Like I was saying—I heard on the radio and I just thought I'd...

[*Pulls out a gun.*] Listen, you oughta get out here right now cause I'm gonna make kind of a mess.

> *Phone rings.*
> *A man breathing is heard.*
> *Fade to* JUDD *on the phone.*

JUDD: HELLO—ALEX—IS THAT YOU—listen to me—this has gone on long enough—you can't keep me hanging like this forever—I'm terribly upset—Alex? ALEX?—I have to know, Alex—one way or the other—I'm always in the dark—I have to know—I can't lie next to you at night—naked as a baby—I just don't know who you are anymore—it's not a comfortable feeling, Alex—I want us to be comfortable—Alex? Alex? [*Dial tone*] ALWAYS IN THE DARK—I JUST DON'T KNOW—WHO YOU ARE ANYMORE—ARE YOU THERE, ALEX—OH ALEX—ARE YOU THERE—WHY DON'T YOU SAY SOMETHING— YOU'RE SUCH A STRANGE MAN—OH ALEX—PLEASE ALEX—JUST SAY SOMETHING—CAUSE I'M TIRED—SO TIRED—FLOATING AROUND IN MID-AIR—ALWAYS IN THE DARK—ALWAYS IN THE DARK—

> *Fade to* MR BEEM.

MR BEEM: Your honor—I think I can explain this whole ridiculous situation—I am quite aware, you see, that I am something of a pest—I tend to annoy people—but that is a far cry from abducting someone—especially Miss Bogdan, whom I admire—she ran from me, yes—out into the traffic—but she was actually asleep, you see—oh!—oh, okay—fine—you're smirking—you're all smirking—you think I don't realize what I'm saying—or that I'm lying—well, I admit I am a liar—truth is not an obsession of mine—nevertheless, I am quite capable of discerning whether a woman is running from me or whether she's sleep walking and I am here to tell you that Miss Bogdan was definitely sleep walking—she had, you see, no reason to run from me—we were in fact just agreeing on my becoming her advisor—I am a tennis strategist by trade, you see—so the woman would hardly be running from me—I resent the implication, to be frank—of course, I suppose I'm an easy target—I realize I happen to look suspicious—that is, that I have a sort of offkilter feel to me—an edginess—believe me, I know—if I were a novelist writing this story I would certainly cast myself as the lonely drifting mild mannered maniac who killed the poor tennis star and than tried to worm his way out of it—but don't be misled by my inability to sit before you calmly and confidently and to speak with the authority and easy assurance that all you gentlemen seem to have mastered—I MAY BE SOMETHING OF AN UN-ANSWERED QUESTION—a loose cannon on the deck, so to speak—but I am perfectly sane—and I am certainly not a murderer…

Well I can tell by all your faces that I've perhaps said too much—my lawyer advised me not to speak but I…well I thought…but perhaps he was right—I am aware of the effect I have on people but I thought in this one instance it would be best to speak up for myself…however…I SUPPOSE I HAVE NOTHING LEFT TO SAY, YOUR HONOR, OTHER THAN THAT I AM—even though none of you apparently believe me—COMPLETELY INNOCENT!

Uh…do I get down now or is someone going to ask me questions?

Rat squeaks.

Fade to CLAUDE.

CLAUDE: IT WON'T BE LONG—MY WRETCHED ONES—IT WON'T BE LONG—

Oh kick—how she kicks—how she kicks—she wants out—you must help my horrible ones—we cannot let her be born here—we have come so far—so deep—maybe you could carry us—yes—oh please, my rodents—we are so tired—you could carry us—on your little backs—yes—to sanctuary—

Yes—come—all of you—my horrible ones—lift—yes—lift—Oh… careful—be gentle—that's it—yes—that's it—we go on—closer and closer—deeper and deeper—to SANCTUARY—

Fade to SMITH *and* KLARI *lying down, covered by sheets.*

SMITH: Hi kids—we're back—how 'bout a death update—want an update on what it's like to be dead? Well—it's…it's not all its cracked up to be. That just in from the Suicide Supercopter.

KLARI *bolts upright.*

KLARI: My match—I'm late—

SMITH: Relax—we are both, as they say, done deals.

KLARI: Who are you doing here? What is going on?

SMITH: You're dead. The game is up.

KLARI: No—I have a match—I MUST GET UP—I MUST get ready—

SMITH: Applying a purpose to life is the trick we play on ourselves to help us maintain interest—that just in from the…

KLARI: Where is my clothes! I am wasting time—I have a match—me—K-Klari—FOREHAND, FOREHAND—backhand, backhand—

SMITH: Your head's crushed, your face is an unrecognizable mess—it hurts just to look at you.

KLARI: My face?—no—she takes off the face of those other girls—not me—I am Klari Bogdan—I fight and I fight and I fight—

SMITH: I'm a big fan of yours, by the way—Marv Smith—maybe you've heard me on the radio—

KLARI: I must get up—I must get ready—

SMITH: I just stood over your body and blew my brains out in a kind of desperate perhaps misguided last ditch symbolic effort to artificially inject some final meaning into my existence.

KLARI: I am dreaming—this is a dream?

SMITH: It seemed to make sense at the time.

KLARI: I must get up—I must get ready—

SMITH: What for?

KLARI: Listen to me—Mr. whoever you are—all those girls back in Rumania—no one knows who they are—no one—they are erased—kaput, finito—they are dead—and maybe you are dead—but not me—me—I am Klari Bogdan—I have a tournament to win—

As she exits, wrapped in the sheet.

SMITH: Oh Miss Bogdan—have a good match.

Fade to WOODARD, *a complete savage, stretching a just completed bow, testing it with an arrow.*

The walkie-talkie lies on the ground. WOODARD *hums* THE CLUB MED VACATION.

VOICE: [*From the walkie-talkie*] Hello—Night Force—this is Rat's Nest—do you read me—hello—Jesus, man—come in—please—Woodard, man—come in—can you hear me—hello—where are you, man?—do you read me—hello—come in, come in—

The overhead transistor radio clicks on: Vienna Choir Boys.

JUDD *enters with a safari hat and cigarette.*

JUDD: Alex? Hello? Surprise. I'm here. Come out come out where ever you are. Alex? Are you there? Come on, buster, get your ass out here!—I haven't got all day—and I'm not a real big fan of hot sticky jungles—Alex? I'm beginning to wonder about you, Alex. Ten minutes tops and then I'm outa here and you can kiss my ass goodbye. Alex?

RAND *appears.*

RAND: Well honey, finally—this is it—

I am standing somewhere north of the Amazon River—several days ago—or weeks ago, I guess—I left my kayak behind and pushed further into the jungle on foot—I guess the only word I can use to describe it here is immense—I feel like I'm in the center of the world—it's so…so incredibly…incredibly overwhelming—I'm like some tiny albino ant crawling my way deeper and deeper into the heart of this endlessness—there is nothing like this anywhere, honey—everything is drenched— sometimes I think I'm in some enormous womb—I haven't seen the sky for weeks— or months—I wish…wish we had thought of coming here for our honeymoon—I guess I never really felt comfortable with you—or…well…with anyone…myself even, for that matter—

ANYWAY—THIS IS IT—NO FALSE ALARM THIS TIME HONEY— THIS IS IT—I better go—gotta build a home you know—GOTTA BUILD A HOME—THIS IS WHERE I BELONG—THIS IS WHERE I BELONG—

> *The jungle grows louder.*
> *Fade to* KLARI.

KLARI: Hello—ref—it's me—Klari Bogdan—what is that girl doing out there—this is my match—don't you see who I am—that is supposed to be me—

[*Watching the match.*] Oh—good shot—push—push—forehand forehand— backhand backhand—yes—beautiful - that's the way—look at them—look at them—those girls are alive—look how beautiful—look how beautiful—those girls are alive—alive—alive!

> *Rat squeaks, loud.*
> *Fade to* CLAUDE, *staggering.*

CLAUDE: Oh, my rodents—my horrible ones—don't be angry—I know—you are so hungry—so tired—so deep we are—so deep—so close—just a little more—

IT WON'T BE LONG—MY WRETCHED ONES—IT WON'T BE LONG—

Spit vomit gag! Oh—don't kick, my baby, don't kick—WE ARE GETTING CLOSE, SO CLOSE—

> *Voices singing.*

Yes—Yes!—Do you hear?—Listen, my horrible ones—listen—sanctuary— SANCTUARY—

Oh my poor rodents—Do you hear how close?—they will greet us—Yes, my hungry ones—take us in their arms—bathe and feed us—oh we will sparkle, we will shine—SANCTUARY—SANCTUARY—yes, even you my filthy ones—even you—

IT WON'T BE LONG—MY WRETCHED… You…bit…me…

My god—you are…you are just…rats… I am down in…down in the sewer with…rats… My baby—my god—my baby—I have taken my baby to be born with filth and rats—

Get away—get away!—you cannot have her—she is mine—and if she cannot be born with beauty than she will not be born at all—[*About to stab herself.*]

> *The light becomes brighter, voices sing.*
> *She is transfixed, radiant.*

Fade to MR BEEM.

MR BEEM: HELLO MR. WARDER, SIR—I WON'T TAKE A MOMENT—I simply wanted to say that—well, I understand that I'm up for parole this month but if I may I'd like to decline—if that's allowed—you may think that's a bit unusual—I know my fellow inmates do—but being allowed to work with the educational program here—I mean to say—I enjoy it here—teaching men who have never read a book in their lives some of them—IT'S BEEN THE BEST THING THAT EVER HAPPENED TO ME—I think I'm something of a born teacher, you see—and I believe I serve an important function for the men here—I seem to have a knack for reaching very tough unreachable types—for whatever reasons—I don't know—but anyway—well—YOU MAY THINK IT ODD—BUT I LIKE IT HERE—AND I'D LIKE TO STAY—IF THAT'S ALL RIGHT—

YOU MAY THINK IT ODD—BUT I LIKE IT HERE—AND I'D LIKE TO STAY—IF THAT'S ALL RIGHT [*Repeat*]

KLARI, JUDD, RAND, CLAUDE, *and* WOODARD *join* BEEM, *all repeating til a crescendo is reached.*

WOODARD: THE CLUB MED VACATION—THE ANTIDOTE FOR CIVILIZATION—

CLAUDE: SANCTUARY—SANCTUARY—

KLARI: ERASES EACH FACE—CLEAN AND SMOOTH—LEAVES NO FEATURE—LEAVES NO FACE—

JUDD: ALWAYS IN THE DARK—ALWAYS IN THE DARK—

RAND: THIS IS WHERE I BELONG—THIS IS WHERE I BELONG

SMITH *appears at the microphone. Howls.*

SMITH: Hit it!

BIG MUSIC.

He dances.

THE END

Suzan-Lori Parks

∾

*Imperceptible Mutabilities
in the Third Kingdom*

Imperceptible Mutabilities in the Third Kingdom premiered at BACA DOWNTOWN, Brooklyn, New York, on September 9, 1989, with the following cast:

> Edward Baran
> Jasper McGruder
> Madeline McCray
> Maggie Rush
> Mona Wyatt

Directed by Liz Diamond; Set Design by Alan Glovsky; Lighting Design by Pat Dignan; Costume Design by Laura Drawbaugh; Slide Design by Phil Perkis

PART 1: SNAILS	PART 2: THIRD KINGDOM	PART 3: OPEN HOUSE
The Players:	*The Players:*	*The Players:*
MOLLY/MONA	KIN-SEER	MRS. ARETHA SAXON
CHARLENE/CHONA	US-SEER	ANGLOR SAXON
VERONICA/VERONA	SHARK-SEER	BLANCA SAXON
THE NATURALIST/	SOUL-SEER	CHARLES
DR. LUTZKY	OVER-SEER	MISS FAITH
THE ROBBER		

THIRD KINGDOM (Reprise)	PART 4: GREEKS (or THE SLUGS)
The Players:	*The Players:*
KIN-SEER	MR. SERGEANT SMITH
US-SEER	MRS. SERGEANT SMITH
SHARK-SEER	BUFFY SMITH
SOUL-SEER	MUFFY SMITH
OVER-SEER	DUFFY SMITH

PART 1: SNAILS

A *Slide show: Images of* MOLLY *and* CHARLENE. MOLLY *and* CHARLENE *speak as the stage remains semi-dark and the slides continue to flash overhead.*

CHARLENE: How dja get through it?

MOLLY: Mm not through it.

CHARLENE: Yer leg. Thuh guard. Lose weight?

MOLLY: Hhh. What should I do Chona should I jump should I jump or what?

CHARLENE: You want some eggs?

MOLLY: Would I splat?

CHARLENE: Uhuhuhnnnn . . .

MOLLY: Twelve floors up. Whaduhya think?

CHARLENE: Uh-uh-uhn. Like scrambled?

MOLLY: Shit.

CHARLENE: With cheese? Say "with" cause ssgoin in.

MOLLY: I diduhnt quit that school. HHH. Thought: nope! Mm gonna go on—go on ssif nothin ssapin yuh know? "S-K" is /sk/ as in "ask." The little-lamb-follows-closely-behind-at-Marys-heels-as-Mary- boards-the-train. Shit. Failed every test he shoves in my face. He makes me recite my mind goes blank. HHH. The-little-lamb-follows-closely-behind- at-Marys-heels-as-Mary-boards-the-train. Aint never seen no woman on no train with no lamb. I tell him so. He throws me out. Stuff like this happens every day y know? This isnt uh special case mines iduhnt uh uhnnn.

CHARLENE: Salami? Yarnt veg anymore.

MOLLY: "S-K" is /sk/ as in "ask." I lie down you lie down he she it lies down. The-little-lamb-follows-closely- behind-at-Marys-heels....

CHARLENE: Were you lacto-ovo or thuh whole nine yards?

MOLLY: Whole idea uh talkin right now aint right no way. Aint natural. Just goes tuh go. HHH. Show. Just goes tuh show.

CHARLENE: Coffee right?

MOLLY: They—expelled—me.

CHARLENE: Straight up?

MOLLY: Straight up. "Talk right or youre outta here!" I couldnt. I walked. Nope. "Speak correctly or you'll be dismissed!" Yeah. Yeah. Nope. Nope. Job sends me there. Basic skills. Now Job dont want me no more. Closely-behind-at-Marys-heels. HHH. Everythin in its place.

CHARLENE: Toast?

MOLLY: Hate lookin for uh job. Feel real whory walkin thuh streets. Only thing worse n workin sslookin for work.

867

CHARLENE: I'll put it on thuh table.

MOLLY: You lie down you lie down but he and she and it and us well we lays down. Didnt quit. They booted me. He booted me. Couldnt see thuh sense uh words workin like he said couldnt see thuh sense uh workin where words workin like that was workin would drop my phone voice would let things slip they tell me get Basic Skills call me breaking protocol hhhhh! Think I'll splat?

CHARLENE: Once there was uh robber who would come over and rob us regular. He wouldnt come through thuh window he would use thuh door. I would let him in. He would walk in n walk uhround. Then he would point tuh stuff. I'd say "help yourself." We developed us uh relationship. I asked him his name. He didnt answer. I asked him where he comed from. No answer tuh that neither. He didnt have no answers cause he didnt have no speech. Verona said he had that deep jungle air uhbout im that just off thuh boat look tuh his face. Verona she named him she named him "Mokus." But Mokus whuduhnt his name.

MOLLY: Once there was uh me named Mona who wanted tuh jump ship but didnt. HHH. Chona? Ya got thuh Help Wanteds?

CHARLENE: Flies are casin yer food Mona. Come eat.

MOLLY: HELP WANTEDS. *YOU GOT EM?*

CHARLENE: Wrapped thuh coffee grinds in em.

MOLLY: Splat.

B   *Lights up onstage with canned applause. At the podium stands* THE NATURALIST.

THE NATURALIST: As I have told my students for some blubblubblub years, a most careful preparation of one's fly is the only way by in which the naturalist can insure the capturence of his subjects in a state of nature. Now for those of you who are perhaps not familiar with the more advanced techniques of nature study let me explain the principle of one of our most useful instruments: "the fly." When in Nature Studies the fly is an apparatus which by blending in with the environment under scrutiny enables the naturalist to conceal himself and observe the object of study—unobserved. In our observations of the subjects subjects which for our purposes we have named "MOLLY" and "CHARLENE" subjects we have chosen for study in order that we may monitor their natural behavior and after monitoring perhaps—modify the form of my fly was an easy choice: this cockroach modeled after the common house insect *hausus cockruckus* fashioned entirely of corrugated cardboard offers us a place in which we may put our camera and observe our subjects—unobserved—. Much like the "fly on the wall."

C   MOLLY *and* CHARLENE *onstage.*

MOLLY: Once there was uh me named Mona who wondered what she'd be like if no one was watchin. You got the Help Wanteds?

CHARLENE: Wrapped thuh coffee grinds in um.—Mona?

MOLLY: Splat. Splat. Splatsplatsplat.

CHARLENE: Mm callin thuh ssterminator for tomorrow. Leave it be for now.

MOLLY: Diduhnt even blink. I threatened it. Diduhnt even blink.

CHARLENE: Theyre gettin brave. Big too.

MOLLY: Splat!

CHARLENE: Mona! Once there was uh little lamb who followed Mary good n put uh hex on Mary. When Mary dropped dead, thuh lamb was in thuh lead. You can study at home. I'll help.

MOLLY: Uh-uhnn! I'm all decided. Aint gonna work. Cant. Aint honest. Anyone with any sense dont wanna work no how. Mm gonna be honest. Mm gonna be down n out. Make downin n outin my livelihood.

CHARLENE: He didnt have no answers cause he didnt have no speech.

MOLLY: Wonder what I'd look like if no one was lookin. I need fashions. "S-K" is /sk/ as in "ask." The-little- lamb-follows-Mary-Mary-who . . . ?

CHARLENE: Once there was uh one Verona named "Mokus." But "Mokus" whuduhnt his name. He had his picture on file at thuh police station. Ninety-nine different versions. None of um looked like he looked.

MOLLY: Splat! Splat! Diduhnt move uh muscle even. Dont even have no muscles. Only eyes. Splat! Shit. I woulda been uhcross thuh room out thuh door n on tuh thuh next life. Diduhnt twitch none. Splat! I cant even talk. I got bug bites bug bites all over! I need new styles.

CHARLENE: Once there was uh one named Lutzky. Uh exterminator professional with uh Ph.D. He wore white cause white was what thuh job required. Comes tuh take thuh roaches uhway. Knew us by names that whuduhnt ours. Could point us out from pictures that whuduhnt us. He became confused. He hosed us down. You signed thuh invoice with uh x. Exterminator professional with uh Ph.D. He can do thuh job for $99.

MOLLY: Mm gonna lay down, K?

CHARLENE: Youre lucky Mona.

MOLLY: He thuh same bug wasin thuh kitchen?

CHARLENE: Uh uhnn. We got uh infestation problem. Youre lucky.

MOLLY: He's watchin us. He followed us in here n swatchin us.

CHARLENE: I'll call Lutzky. Wipe-um-out-Lutzky with uh Ph.D. He's got uh squirt gun. He'll come right over. He's got thuh potions. All mixed up. Squirt in uh crack. Hose down uh crevice. We'll be through. Through with it. Free of um. Wipe-um-out-Lutzky with thuh Ph.D. He's got uh squirt gun. He'll come right over.

MOLLY: Uh—the-cockroach-is-watching-us,-look-Chona -look! Once there was uh me named Mona who wondered what she'd talk like if no one was listenin.

CHARLENE: Close yer eyes, Mona. Close yer eyes n think on someuhn pleasant.

D THE NATURALIST *at the podium.*

THE NATURALIST: Thus behave our subjects naturally. Thus behave our subjects when they believe we cannot see them when they believe us far far away when they believe our backs have turned. Now. An obvious question should arise in the mind of an inquisitive observer? Yes? HHH. How should we best accommodate the presence of such subjects in our modern world. That is to say: How. Should. We. Best. Accommodate. Our subjects. If they are all to live with us—all in harmony—in our modern world. Yes. Having accumulated a wealth of naturally occurring observations knowing now how our subjects occur in their own world (*mundus primtivus*), the question now arises as to how we of our world (*mundus modernus*) best accommodate them. I ask us to remember that it was almost twenty-five whole score ago that our founding father went forth tirelessly crossing a vast expanse of ocean in which there lived dangerous creatures of the most horrible sort tirelessly crossing that sea jungle to find this country and name it. The wilderness was vast and we who came to teach, enlighten, and tame were few in number. They were the vast, we were the few. And now. The great cake of society is crumbling. I ask us to realize that those who do not march with us do not march not because they will not but because they cannot.... I ask that they somehow be—taken care of for there are too many of them—and by "them" I mean of course "them roaches." They need our help. They need our help. Information for the modern cannot be gleaned from the primitive, information for the modern can only be gleaned through ex-per-i-mentation. This is the most tedious part of science yet in science there is no other way. Now. I will, if you will, journey to the jungle. *Behavioris distortionallus-via- modernus.* Watch closely:

E *During this part* THE ROBBER *enters, steals the roach and attempts an exit.*

CHONA: Verona? Hey honeyumm home?

VERONA: Chona Chona ChonaChonaChona. Mona here?

CHONA: Laying down.

VERONA: Heart broken?

CHONA: Like uh broken heart. Thuh poor thing. I'll learn her her speech. Lets take her out n buy her new styles.

VERONA: Sounds good.

CHONA: She wants fashions.—We got roaches.

VERONA: Shit! Chona. Thats uh big one. I got some motels but. I got some stickys too—them little trays with glue? Some spray but. Woo ya! Woo ya woo ya?! They gettin brave.

CHONA: Big too. Think he came through that crack in thuh bathroom.

VERONA: Wooya! Wooya! Shit. You call Lutzky? Thuh Ph.D.?

CHONA: On his way. We'll pay. Be through. He's got uh squirt gun.

VERONA: We'll all split thuh bill. He gonna do it for 99?

CHONA: Plus costs. Mona dunht know bout thuh Plus Costs part. Okay?

VERONA: —K. Maybe I can catch uh few for our Lutzky shows.

CHONA: Once there was uh woman who wanted tuh get uhway for uhwhile but didnt know which way tuh go tuh get gone. Once there was uh woman who just layed down.

VERONA: Traps. Place um. Around thuh sink corner of thuh stove move move yer feet threshole of thuh outside door. Yeauh. Mm convinced theyre comin in from uhcross thuh hall—slippin under thuh door at night but I aint no professional—see?! Lookit im go— movin slow-ly. He's thuh scout. For every one ya see there are thousands. Thousands thousands creepin in through thuh cracks. Waiting for their chance. Watchim go. Goinsslow. We gotta be vigilant: sit-with-thuh-lights-out- crouch-in-thuh-kitchen- holdin-hard-soled-shoes. GOTCHA! Monas got bug bites on her eyelids? Mmputtin some round her bed. Augment thuh traps with thuh spray.

CHONA: Once there was uh woman was careful. Once there was uh woman on thuh lookout. Still trapped.

VERONA: Vermin free by 1990! That means YOU!

CHONA: *Wild Kingdoms* on.

VERONA: YER OUTTA HERE!

CHONA: Yer shows on.

VERONA: Great. Thanks.

CHONA: Keep it low for Mona. K?

VERONA: Perkins never shoulda uhlowed them tuh scratch his show. Wildlife never goes outta style. He shoulda told em that. Fuck thuh ratings. Oh, look! On thuh trail of thuh long muzzled wildebeest: mating season. Ha! This is uh good one. They got bulls n cows muzzles matin closeups—make ya feel like yer really right there with em. Part of thuh action. Uh live birth towards thuh end....

CHONA: You want some eggs?

VERONA: They got meat?

CHONA: —Yeauh—

VERONA: I'm veg. Since today. Kinder. Cheaper too. Didja know that uh veg—

CHONA: Eat. Here. Ssgood. Ssgood tuh eat. Eat. Please eat. Once there was uh one name Verona who bit thuh hand that feeds her. Doorbell thats Lutzky. I'll get it.

VERONA: Mona! Our shinin knights here!

MONA: THE-LITTLE-LAMB-FOLLOWS-MARY-CLOSELY-AT-HER- HEELS—

VERONA: Wipe-um-out Dr. Lutzky with uh P uh H and uh D. Baby. B. Cool.

MONA: B cool.

CHONA: Right this way Dr. Lutzky. Right this way Dr. Lutzky Extraordinaire Sir.

LUTZKY: I came as quickly as I could—I have a squirt gun, you know. Gold plated gift from the firm. They're so proud. Of me. There was a woman in Queens—poor thing—so distraught—couldn't sign the invoice—couldn't say "bug"—for a moment I thought I had been the unwitting victim of a prank phone call—*prankus callus*—her little boy filled out the forms—showed me where to squirt—lucky for her the little one was there—lucky for her she had the little one. Awfully noble scene, I thought. You must be Charlene.

CHONA: Char-who? Uh uhn. Uh—It-is-I,-Dr.-Lutzky,—*Chona.*

LUTZKY: Ha! You look like a Charlene you look like a Charlene you do look like a Charlene bet no one has ever told that to you, eh? Aaaaaaah, well. I hear there is one with "bug bites all over" Are you the one?

CHONA: I-am-Chona. Mona-is-the-one. The-one-in- the-living-room. The-one-in-the-living-room-on- the-couch.

LUTZKY: What's the world coming to? "What is the world coming to?" I sometimes ask myself. And—

CHONA: Eggs, Dr. Lutzky?

LUTZKY: Oh, yes please. And—am I wrong in making a livelihood—meager as it may be—from the vermin that feed on the crumbs which fall from the table of the broken cake of civilization—oh dear—oh dear!

CHONA: Watch out for those. We do have an infestation problem. Watch out for those.

LUTZKY: Too late now—oh dear it's sticky. It's stuck—oh dear— now the other foot. They're stuck.

MONA: THE-LITTLE-LAMB—

VERONA: SShhh.

CHONA: Make yourself at home, Dr. Lutzky. I'll bring your eggs.

LUTZKY: Can't walk.

CHONA: Shuffle.

LUTZKY: Oh dear. Shuffleshuffleshuffle. Oh dear.

VERONA: Sssshhh!

LUTZKY: You watch *Wild Kingdom*. I watch *Wild Kingdom* too. This is a good one. Oh dear!

MONA: Oh dear.

CHONA: Here is the Extraordinaire, Mona. Mona, the Extraordinaire is here. Fresh juice, Dr. Lutzky Extraordinaire?

LUTZKY: Call me "Wipe-em-out."

MONA: Oh dear.

VERONA: SSSShhh.

LUTZKY: Well. Now. Let's start off with something simple. Who's got bug bites?

MONA: Once there was uh me named Mona who hated going tuh thuh doctor.— I-have-bug-bites-Dr.- Lutzky-Extra-ordinaire-Sir.

LUTZKY: This won't take long. Step lively, Molly. The line forms here.

CHONA: I'll get the juice. We have a juice machine!

LUTZKY: I have a squirt gun!

VERONA: He's got uh gun—Marlin Perkinssgot uh gun—

MONA: Oh, dear....

LUTZKY: You're the one, aren't you, Molly? Wouldn't want to squirt the wrong one. Stand up straight. The line forms here.

CHONA: I am Chona! Monas on the line!—Verona? That one is Verona.

LUTZKY: ChonaMonaVerona. Well well well. Wouldn't want to squirt the wrong one.

VERONA: He's got uh gun. Ssnot supposed tuh have uh gun—

MONA: "S-K" IS /SK/ AS IN "AXE." Oh dear. I'm Lucky, Dr. Lutzky.

LUTZKY: Call me "Wipe-em-out." Both of you. All of you.

CHONA: Wipe-em-out. Dr. Wipe-em-out.

LUTZKY: And you're "Lucky"?

VERONA: He got uh gun!

MONA: Me Mona.

LUTZKY: Mona?

MONA: Mona Mokus robbery.

CHONA: You are confusing the doctor, Mona. Mona, the doctor is confused.

VERONA: Perkins ssgot uh gun. Right there on thuh Tee v. He iduhnt spposed tuh have no gun!

MONA: Robbery Mokus Mona. Robbery Mokus Mona. Everything in its place.

CHONA: The robber comes later, Dr. Wipe-em-out Extraordinaire, Sir.

LUTZKY: There goes my squirt gun. Did you feel it?

VERONA: I seen this show before. Four times. Perkins duhnt even own no gun.

CHONA: Once there was uh doctor who became confused and then hosed us down.

LUTZKY: I must be confused. Must be the sun. Or the savages.

MONA: Savage Mokus. Robbery, Chona.

CHONA: Go on Mokus. Help yourself.

LUTZKY: I need to phone for backups. May I?

VERONA: He duhnt have no gun permit even. Wait. B. Cool. I seen this. Turns out alright. I think....

CHONA: Juice? I made it myself!

MONA: I am going to lie down. I am going to lay down. Lie down? Lay down. Lay down?

LUTZKY: Why don't you lie down.

MONA: I am going to lie down.

CHONA: She's distraught. Bug bites all over. We're infested. Help yourself.

LUTZKY: You seem infested, Miss Molly. Get in line, I'll hose you down.

MONA: MonaMokusRobbery

LUTZKY: Hello Sir. Parents of the Muslim faith? My fathers used to frequent the Panthers. For sport. That was before my time. Not too talkative are you. Come on. Give us a grunt. I'll give you a squirt.

VERONA: Ssnot no dart gun neither—. Holy. Chuh! Mmcallin thuh—That is not uh dart gun, Marlin!!!

MONA: Make your bed and lie in it. I'm going to lay down.

CHONA: Liedown.

MONA: Lay down.

CHONA: LIE, Mona.

MONA: Lie Mona lie Mona down.

CHONA: Down, Mona down.

MONA: Down, Mona, bites! Oh my eyelids! On-her-heels! Down Mona down.

VERONA: Call thuh cops.

LUTZKY: That will be about $99. Hello. This is Dr. Lutzky. Send ten over. Just like me. We've got a real one here. Won't even grunt. Huh! Hmmm. Phones not working....

VERONA: Gimmie that! Thank-you. Hello? Marlin- Perkins-has-a-gun. I-am-telling-you-Marlin- Perkins-has-a-gun! Yeah it's loaded course it's loaded! You listen tuh me! I pay yuh tuh listen tuh me! We pay our taxes, Chona?

CHONA: I am going to make a peach cobbler. My mothers ma used to make cobblers. She used to gather the peaches out of her own backyard all by herself.

LUTZKY: Hold still, Charlene. I'll hose you down.

CHONA: Go on Mokus. Help yourself.

VERONA: *HE'S SHOOTIN THUH WILD BEASTS!*

MONA: Oh dear.

VERONA: He-is-shooting-them-for-real! We diduhnt pay our taxes, Chona.

LUTZKY: Here's my invoice. Sign here.

CHONA: x, Mona. Help yourself.

MONA: Splat.

CHONA: Cobbler, Dr. Lutzky? Fresh out of the oven????!!!

MONA: Splat.

LUTZKY: Wrap it to go, Charlene.

MONA: Splat.

LUTZKY: What did you claim your name was dear?

MONA: Splat.

CHONA: I'll cut you off a big slice. Enough for your company. Youre a company man.

LUTZKY: With backups, Miss Charlene. I'm a very lucky man. Molly's lucky too.

MONA: Splat. Splat. Splatsplatsplat.

VERONA: Cops dont care. This is uh outrage.

LUTZKY: Here's my card. There's my squirt gun! Did you feel it? I need backups. May I?

VERONA: Dont touch this phone. It's bugged.

LUTZKY: Oh dear!

CHONA: Cobbler, Verona?

LUTZKY: Well, good night.

VERONA: We pay our taxes, Chona ?

LUTZKY: Well, good night!

VERONA: We pay our taxes Chona??!!!!?

MONA: Tuck me in. I need somebody tuh tuck me in.

F VERONA *speaks at the podium.*

VERONA: I saw my first pictures of Africa on TV: Mutual of Omahas *Wild Kingdom.* The thirty-minute filler between Walt Disneys wonderful world and the CBS Evening News. It was a wonderful world: Marlin Perkins and Jim and their African guides. I was a junior guide and had a lifesize poster of Dr. Perkins sitting on a white Land Rover surrounded by wild things. Had me an 8 × 10 glossy of him too, signed, on my nightstand. Got my nightstand from Sears cause I had to have Marlin by my bed at night. Together we learned to differentiate African from Indian elephants the importance of hyenas in the wild funny looking trees on the slant—how do they stand up? Black folks with no clothes. Marlin loved and respected all the wild things. His guides took his English and turned it into the local lingo so that he could converse with the natives. Marlin even petted a rhino once. He tagged the animals and put them into zoos for their own protection. He encouraged us to be kind to animals through his shining example. Once there was uh me name Verona: I got mommy n dad tuh get me uh black dog n named it I named it "Namib" after thuh African sands n swore tuh be nice tuh it only Namib refused tuh be trained n crapped in corners of our basement n got up on thuh sofa when we went out n Namib wouldnt listen tuh me like Marlins helpers listened tuh him Namib wouldnt look at me when I talked tuh him n when I said someuhn like "sit" he wouldnt n "come" made im go n when I tied him up in thuh front yard so that he could bite the postman when thuh postman came like uh good dog would he wouldnt even bark just smile n wag his tail so I would kick Namib when no one could see me cause I was sure I was very very sure that Namib told lies uhbout me behind my back and Namib chewed through his rope one day n bit me n run off. I have this job. I work at a veterinarian hospital. I'm a euthanasia specialist. Someone brought a stray dog in one day and I entered "black dog" in the black book and let her scream and whine and wag her tail and talk about me behind my back then I offered her the humane alternative. Wiped her out! I stayed late that night so that I could cut her open because I had to see I just had to see the heart of such a disagreeable domesticated thing. But no. Nothing different.Everything in its place. Do you know what that means? Everything in its place. Thats all.

    Lights out.

KIN-SEER: Kin-Seer.
US-SEER: Us-Seer
SHARK-SEER: Shark-Seer.
SOUL-SEER: Soul-Seer.
OVER-SEER: Over-Seer.
——.

——.

KIN-SEER: Kin-Seer.
US-SEER: Us-Seer.
SHARK-SEER: Shark-Seer.
SOUL-SEER: Soul-Seer.
OVER-SEER: Over-Seer.
——.

——.

——…

KIN-SEER: Last night I dreamed of where I comed from. But where I comed from
    diduhnt look like nowhere like I been.
SOUL-SEER: There were 2 cliffs?
KIN-SEER: There were.
US-SEER: Uh huhn.
SHARK-SEER: 2 cliffs?
KIN-SEER: 2 cliffs: one on each other side thuh world.
SHARK-SEER: 2 cliffs?
KIN-SEER: 2 cliffs where thuh world had cleaved intuh 2.
OVER-SEER: The 2nd part comes apart in 2 parts.
SHARK-SEER: But we are not in uh boat!
US-SEER: But we iz.
SOUL-SEER: Iz. Uh huhn. Go on—
KIN-SEER: I was standin with my toes stuckted in thuh dirt. Nothin in front of me
    but water. And I was wavin. Wavin. Wavin at my uther me who I could barely see.
    Over thuh water on thuh uther cliff I could see my uther me but my uther me could
    not see me. And I was wavin wavin wavin sayin gaw gaw gaw gaw* eeeeeee-uh.
OVER-SEER: The 2nd part comes apart in 2 parts.
SHARK-SEER: But we are not in uh boat!

---

* "Gaw" should be pronounced as a glottal stop.

US-SEER: But we iz.

SOUL-SEER: Gaw gaw gaw gaw eeeee—

KIN-SEER: Ee-uh. Gaw gaw gaw gaw eeeee—

SOUL-SEER: Ee-uh.

US-SEER: Come home come home dont stay out too late. Bleached Bones Man may get you n take you far uhcross thuh waves, then baby, what will I do for love?

OVER-SEER: The 2nd part comes apart in-to 2.

SHARK-SEER: Edible fish are followin us. Our flesh is edible tull them fish. Smile at them and they smile back. Jump overboard and they gobble you up. They smell blood. I see sharks. Sssblak! Sssblak! Gaw gaw gaw eee-uh. I wonder: Are you happy?

ALL: We are smiling!

OVER-SEER: Quiet, you, or you'll be jettisoned.

SOUL-SEER: Duhduhnt he duhduhnt he know my name? Ssblak ssblak ssblakallblak!

OVER-SEER: Thats your *self* youre looking at! Wonder # 1 of my glass-bottomed boat.

KIN-SEER: My uther me then waved back at me and then I was happy. But my uther me whuduhnt wavin at me. My uther me was wavin at my Self. My uther me was wavin at uh black black speck in thuh middle of thuh sea where years uhgoh from uh boat I had been—UUH!*

OVER-SEER: Jettisoned.

SHARK-SEER: Jettisoned?

KIN-SEER: Jettisoned.

US-SEER: Uh huhn.

SOUL-SEER: To-the-middle-of-the-bottom-of-the-big- black-sea.

KIN-SEER: And then my Self came up between us. Rose up out of thuh water and standin on them waves my Self was standin. And I was wavin wavin wavin and my Me was wavin and wavin and my Self that rose between us went back down in-to-the-sea.

US-SEER: FFFFFFFFF.

SOUL-SEER: Thup.†

SHARK-SEER: Howwe gonna find my Me?

KIN-SEER: Me wavin at Me. Me wavin at I. Me wavin at my Self.

US-SEER: FFFFFFFFF.

SOUL-SEER: Thup.

SHARK-SEER: I dream up uh fish thats swallowin me and I dream up uh me that is then becamin that fish and uh dream of that fish becamin uh shark and I dream of that shark becamin uhshore. UUH! And on thuh shore thuh shark is given shoes. And I whuduhnt me no more and I whuduhnt no fish. My new Self was uh third Self made by thuh space in between. And my new Self wonders: Am I happy? Is my new Self happy in my new-Self shoes?

---

* "Uuh" should be pronounced as an air-intake sound.

† "Thup" should be pronounced as a sucking-in sound.

KIN-SEER: MAY WAH-VIN ET MAY. MAY WAH-VIN ET EYE. MAY
WAH-VIN ET ME SOULF.

OVER-SEER: Half the world had fallen away making 2 worlds and a sea between.
Those 2 worlds inscribe the Third Kingdom.

KIN-SEER: Me hollering uhcross thuh cliffs at my Self:

US-SEER: Come home come home dont stay out too late.

SHARK-SEER: Black folks with no clothes. Then all thuh black folks clothed in smilin.
In betwen thuh folks is uh distance thats uh wet space. 2 worlds: Third Kingdom.

SOUL-SEER: Gaw gaw gaw gaw gaw gaw gaw gaw.

KIN-SEER: May wah-vin et may may wah-vin et eye may wah-vin et me sould.

SHARK-SEER: How many kin kin I hold. Whole hull full.

SOUL-SEER: Thuh hullholesfull of bleachin bones.

US-SEER: Bleached Bones Man may come and take you far uhcross thuh sea from
me.

OVER-SEER: Who're you again?

KIN-SEER: I'm. Lucky.

OVER-SEER: Who're you again?

SOUL-SEER: Duhdduhnt-he-know-my-name?

KIN-SEER: Should I jump? Shouldijumporwhut?

SHARK-SEER: But we are not in uh boat!

US-SEER: But we iz. Iz iz iz uh huhn. Iz uh huhn. Uh huhn iz.

SHARK-SEER: I wonder: Are we happy? Thuh looks we look look so .

US-SEER: They like smiles and we will like what they will like.

SOUL-SEER: UUH!

KIN-SEER: Me wavin at me me wavin at my I me wavin at my soul .

SHARK-SEER: Chomp chomp chomp chomp.

KIN-SEER: Ffffffffff—

US-SEER: Thup.

SHARK-SEER: Baby, what will I do for love?

SOUL-SEER: Wave me uh wave and I'll wave one back blow me uh kiss n I'll blow you
one back.

OVER-SEER: Quiet, you, or you'll be jettisoned!

SHARK-SEER: Chomp. Chomp. Chomp. Chomp.

KIN-SEER: Wa-vin wa-vin.

SHARK-SEER: Chomp chomp chomp chomp.

KIN-SEER: Howwe gonna find my Me?

SOUL-SEER: Rock. Thuh boat. Rock. Thuh boat. Rock. Thuh boat. Rock. Thuh boat.

US-SEER: We be walkin wiggly cause we left our bones in bed.

SOUL-SEER, US-SEER, SHARK-SEER, KIN-SEER AND OVER-SEER: Gaw gaw
gaw gaw gaw gaw gaw gaw gaw gaw gaw gaw gaw gaw gaw gaw—

OVER-SEER: I'm going to yell "Land Ho!" in a month or so and all of this will have to
stop. I'm going to yell "Land Ho!" in a month or so and that will be the end of this.
Line up!

SHARK-SEER: Where to?

OVER-SEER: Ten-Shun!

SOUL-SEER: How come?

OVER-SEER: Move on move on move—. LAND HO!

KIN-SEER: You said I could wave as long as I see um. I still see um.

OVER-SEER: Wave then.

PART 3: OPEN HOUSE

A *Dreamtime: A double-frame slide show: Slides of* ARETHA *hugging* ANGLOR *and* BLANCA. *Dialogue begins and continues with the slides progressing as follows: (1) they are expressionless; next (2) they smile; next (3) they smile more; next (4) even wider smiles. The enlargement of smiles continues. Actors speak as the stage remains semi-dark and the slides flash overhead.*

ARETHA: Smile, honey, smile.

ANGLOR: I want my doll. Where is my doll I want my doll where is it I want it. I want it now.

ARETHA: Miss Blanca? Give us uh pretty smile, darlin.

BLANCA: I want my doll too. Go fetch.

ARETHA: You got such nice white teeth, Miss Blanca. Them teeths makes uh smile tuh remember you by.

ANGLOR: She won't fetch the dolls. She won't fetch them because she hasn't fed them.

ARETHA: Show us uh smile, Mr. Anglor. Uh quick toothy show stopper.

BLANCA: She won't fetch them because she hasn't changed them. They're sitting in their own filth because they haven't been changed they haven't been fed they haven't been aired they've gone without sunshine.

ANGLOR: Today is her last day. She's gone slack.

BLANCA: Is today your last day, Aretha?

ANGLOR: Yes.

ARETHA: Smile for your daddy, honey. Mr. Charles, I cant get em tuh smile.

BLANCA: Is it? Is it your last day?!

ANGLOR: You see her belongings in the boxcar, don't you?

BLANCA: Where are you going, Aretha? You're going to get my doll!

ARETHA: Wish I had me some teeths like yours, Miss Blanca. So straight and cleaned. So pretty and white.—Yes, Mr. Charles, I'm trying. Mr. Anglor. Smile. Smile for show.

BLANCA: Youre going away, aren't you? AREN'T YOU?

ANGLOR: You have to answer her.

BLANCA: You have to answer me.

ARETHA: Yes, Missy. Mm goin. Mm goin uhway.

BLANCA: Where?

ARETHA: Uhway. Wayuhway.

ANGLOR: To do what?

ARETHA: Dunno. Goin uhway tuh—tuh swallow courses uh meals n fill up my dance card! Goin uhway tuh live, I guess.

BLANCA: Live? Get me my doll. My doll wants to wave goodbye. Who's going to sew up girl doll when she pops?!

ANGLOR: Who's going to chastise boy doll!? Boy doll has no manners.

BLANCA: Who's going to plait girl doll's hair?! Her hair should be plaited just like mine should be plaited.

ANGLOR: Who's going to clean their commodes?! Who's going to clean our commodes?! We won't visit you because we won't be changed! We'll be sitting in our own filth because we won't have been changed we won't have been fed we won't have been aired we won't have manners we won't have plaits we'll have gone without sunshine.

ARETHA: Spect your motherll have to do all that.

BLANCA AND ANGLOR: Who!??!

ARETHA: Dunno. Smile, Blanca, Anglor, huh? Lets see them pretty white teeths. *Camera clicking noises.*

B *Onstage,* MRS. ARETHA SAXON.

ARETHA: Six seven eight nine. Thupp. Ten eleven twelve thirteen fourteen fifteen sixteen. Thupp. Seventeen. Eighteen nineteen twenty twenty-one. And uh little bit. Thuuup. Thuup. Gotta know thuh size. Thup. Gotta know thuh size exact. Thup. Got people comin. Hole house full. They gonna be kin? Could be strangers. How many kin kin I hold. Whole hold full. How many strangers. Depends on thuh size. Thup. Size of thuh space. Thuup. Depends on thuh size of thuh kin. Pendin on thuh size of thuh strangers. Get more mens than womens ssgonna be one number more womens than mens ssgonna be uhnother get animals thuup get animals we kin pack em thuup. Tight. Thuuup. Thuuuup. Mmmm. Thuuup. Count back uhgain: little bit twenty-one twenty nineteen eighteen seventhuup sixteen fifteen fourteen twelve thuup eleven ten uh huh thuuup. Three two thuuup one n one. Huh. Twenty-one and one and one. And thuh little bit. Thuuup. Thup. Thirty-two and uh half.

MISS FAITH: Footnote #1: The human cargo capacity of the English slaver, the *Brookes,* was about 3,250 square feet. From James A. Rawley, *The Transatlantic Slave Trade,* G. J. McLeod Limited, 1981, page 283.

ARETHA: 32½ Thuuup! Howmy gonna greet em. Howmy gonna say hello. Thuup! Huh. Greet em with uh smile! Thupp. Still got uh grin. Uh little bit. Thup. Thuuup. Thirty-two and uh little bit. 32½. Better buzz Miss Faith. Miss Faith?

MISS FAITH: Yeahus—.

ARETHA: Thuup. Sss Mrs. Saxon. 2D.

MISS FAITH: Yes, Mrs. Saxon. Recovering? No more bleeding, I hope.

ARETHA: You wanted tuh know thuh across.

MISS FAITH: Holes healing I hope.

ARETHA: 32 and uh half.

MISS FAITH: Is that a fact?

ARETHA: Thup. Thatsuh fact. 32 feets and uh half on the a-cross! Thats uh fact!

MISS FAITH: Thank you, Maam!

ARETHA: You say I'm tuh have visitors, Miss Faith? You say me havin uh visitation is written in thuh book. I say in here we could fit—three folks.

MISS FAITH: Three. I'll note that. On with your calculations, Mrs. Saxon!

ARETHA: On with my calculations. Thuup.

MISS FAITH: Mrs. Saxon? I calculate—we'll fit six hundred people. Six hundred in a pinch. Footnote #2: 600 slaves were transported on the *Brookes,* although it only had space for 451. *Ibid.,* page 14.

ARETHA: Miss Faith, six hundred in here won't go.

MISS FAITH: You give me the facts. I draw from them, Maam. I draw from them in accordance with the book. Six hundred will fit. We will have to pack them tight.

ARETHA: Miss Faith—thuup—Miss Faith—

MISS FAITH: Mrs. Saxon, book says you are due for an extraction Mrs. Saxon an extraction are you not. Gums should be ready. Gums should be healed. You are not cheating me out of valuable square inches, Mrs. Saxon, of course you are not. You gave me the facts of course you did. We know well that "She who cheateth me out of some valuable square inches shall but cheat herself out of her assigned seat aside the most high." We are familiar with Amendment 2.1 are we not, Mrs. Saxon. Find solace in the book and—bid your teeth goodbye. Buzz me not.

ARETHA: Thup. Thup. 2:1.

MISS FAITH: Footnote #3: The average ratio of slaves per ship, male to female was 2:1.

ARETHA: "Then she looketh up at the Lord and the Lord looketh down on where she knelt. She spake thusly: 'Lord, what proof canst thou give me that my place inside your kingdom hath not been by another usurpt? For there are many, many in need who seek a home in your great house, and many are those who are deserving.'" Thuuuuup! Thuup. "And the Lord looketh upon her with" Thuuuup! "And the Lord looketh upon her with kind azure eyes and on his face there lit a toothsome— a toothsome smile and said, 'Fear not, Charles, for your place in my kingdom is secure.'" Thup. Thuuup! Charles? Miss Faith?

MISS FAITH: Buzz! BUZZZ!
        Buzzer.

    C *Dreamtime:* CHARLES *appears.* BLANCA *and* ANGLOR *hum the note of the buzz.*

ARETHA: And she looketh up at the Lord—

CHARLES: And the Lord looketh downeth oneth whereth sheth knelth—

ARETHA: What proof can yuh give me, Lord? I wants uh place.

CHARLES: A place you will receive. Have you got your papers?

ARETHA: Thuh R-S-stroke-26?*

CHARLES: Let us see. It says "Charles." "Charles Saxon."

ARETHA: Had me uh husband names Charles.

CHARLES: Funny name for you, Mrs. Saxon. "Charles"?

ARETHA: My husbands name. We's split up now.

---

* A common form from the Division of Housing and Community Renewal.

CHARLES: Divorce?

ARETHA: Divorce?

CHARLES: The breakup of those married as sanctioned by the book. Illegal, then. Non legal? I see. Were you legally wed, Charles? Wed by the book? Didn't—"jump the broom" or some such nonsense, eh? Perhaps it was an estrangement. Estrangement? Was it an estrangement? Estrangement then? You will follow him, I suppose.

ARETHA: He's—He's dead, Mister Sir.

CHARLES: I'll mark yes, then. Sign here. An "x" will do, Charles.

ARETHA: I dunno.

CHARLES: There is a line—

ARETHA: Mehbe—

CHARLES: —that has formed itself behind you—

ARETHA: Mehbe—do I gotta go—mehbe—maybe I could stay awhiles. Here.

CHARLES: The book says you expire. No option to renew.

ARETHA: And my place?

CHARLES: Has been secured.

ARETHA: Where?

CHARLES: Move on.

ARETHA: Where to?

CHARLES: Move on, move on, move on!
　　　Humming grows louder.

D　*Humming is replaced by buzzer buzz.* MISS FAITH *appears to extract* ARETHA'S *teeth with a large pair of pliers.*

ARETHA: How many—extractions this go, Sister Faith?

MISS FAITH: Open up. ALL. Dont look upon it as punishment, Mrs. Saxon, look on it as an integral part of the great shucking off. The old must willingly shuck off for the sake of the new. Much like the snakes new skin suit, Mrs. Saxon. When your new set comes in—and you will be getting a new set, that the book has promised— they will have a place. We will have made them room. Where would we go if we did not extract? There are others at this very moment engaged in extracting so that for us there may be a place. Where would we go if we did not extract? Where would they go? What would happen? Who would survive to tell? The old is yankethed out and the new riseth up in its place! Besides, if we didnt pluck them we couldnt photograph them. To be entered into the book they must be photographed. Think of it as getting yourself chronicled, Mrs. Saxon. You are becoming a full part of the great chronicle! Say that, Mrs. Saxon. You dont want to be forgotten, do you?

ARETHA: Thuup! I was gonna greet em with uh grin.

MISS FAITH: An opened jawed awe will do. Open? Yeauhs. Looks of wonder suit us best just before we're laid to rest. AAAh! Open. Hmmm. Canine next, I think. Find solace in the book. Find order in the book. Find find find the book. Where is the book. Go find it. Find it. Go on, get up.

ARETHA: Thuuuuup.

MISS FAITH: Read from it.

ARETHA: Thuuuuuup?

MISS FAITH: Now.

ARETHA: Thup. Thuuuuppp! "The woman lay on the sickness bed her gums were moist and bleeding. The Lord appeared to her, as was his custom, by dripping himself down through the cold water faucet and walking across the puddle theremade. The Lord stood over the sickness bed toweling himself off and spake thusly: 'Charles, tell me why is it that you....'" Thuuuuuup! "Charles" uhgain. Thup. Wonder why he calls her "Charles," Miss Faith? Now, I had me uh husband named Charles wonder if it says anything uhbout Retha Saxons husband Charles in thuh book. Still. Havin uh husband named Charles aint no reason for her tuh be called—

MISS FAITH: Open! She is named what her name is. She was given that name by him. The book says your Charles is dead. Sorry. Never to return. Sorry. That is a fact. A fact to accept. The power of the book lies in its contents. Its contents are facts. Through examination of the facts therein we may see what is to come. Through the examination of what comes we may turn to our book and see from whence it came. Example: The book has let us know for quite some time that you expire 19-6-65, do you not, Mrs. Saxon. You expire. (Footnote #5: "Juneteenth," June 19th in 1865, was when, a good many months after the Emancipation Proclamation, the slaves in Texas heard they were free.) You expire. Along with your lease. Expiration 19-6-65 with no option to renew.

ARETHA: Thuuup?

MISS FAITH: You expire. Yes, Maam!

ARETHA: Yahs Maam.

MISS FAITH: Yes, Maam. 19-6-65. Thats a fact. And now we know youre to have visitors. And now we know that those visitors are waiting on your doorstep.

ARETHA: Naaaa?

MISS FAITH: Now. 32.5, 19-6-65? Now. Open! Now. Close!

ARETHA: Now. Howmy gonna greet em? Was gonna greet em with uh smile.... Awe jawll do. I guess.

MISS FAITH: Youre expiring. It's only natural. Thats a fact. Amendment 1807,* Mrs. Saxon. A fact. You sit comfortably. I'll buzz them in.

    Buzzer.

E *Dreamtime:* CHARLES *appears.*

CHARLES: You know what they say about the hand that rocks the cradle, don't you, Aretha?

ARETHA: Nope.

CHARLES: Whats that?

ARETHA: No suh. No Mr. Charles suh. I dont.

CHARLES: Well well well. "No suh. I dont." Well well well well thats just as well. How about this one, eh? "Two hands in the bush is better than one hand in—"

---

* In March of 1807, England's slave trade was abolished.

ARETHA: Sssthey feedin time, Mistuh Charles.

CHARLES: —Go on. Feed them. Ooooh! These will make some lovely shots—give the children some wonderful memories. Memory is a very important thing, don't you know. It keeps us in line. It reminds us of who we are, memory. Without it we could be anybody. We would be running about here with no identities. You would not know that you're my—help, you'd just be a regular street and alley heathen. I would not remember myself to be master. There would be chaos, chaos it would be without a knowledge from whence we came. Little Anglor and little Blanca would—well, they would not even exist! And then what would Daddy do? Chaos without correct records. Chaos. Aaaah. You know what chaos is, don't you.

ARETHA: No suh. I dont.

CHARLES: He he he! Aaaaah! Ignorance is bliss! They say ignorance is bliss—only for the ignorant—for those of us who must endure them we find their ignorance anything but blissful. Isn't that right.

ARETHA: Yes suh.

CHARLES: "Yes suh. Yes suh." Heh heh heh heh. Hold them up where I can see them. Thaaaat's it. You will look back on these and know what was what. Hold em up. There. Thaaaaaat's just fine. Smile. Smile! Smile? Smiiiiiile—
> *Clicking of camera.*

F *Clicking of camera is replaced by buzzing of door.*

ANGLOR: Very nice!

BLANCA: Very nice!

MISS FAITH: As the book promised: very well lit, views of the land and of the sea, a rotating northern exposure—

ANGLOR: Very very nice!

BLANCA: Oh yes very nice ! Blanca Saxon—

ANGLOR: Anglor Saxon.

ARETHA: I'm Mrs. Saxon.

MISS FAITH: —Expires 19-6-65.

ANGLOR: Very nice.

BLANCA: We're newlyweds.

ARETHA: I'm Mrs. Saxon.

BLANCA: Newlyweds. Newly wedded. New.

ANGLOR: Very new.

MISS FAITH: Very nice.

BLANCA: Blanca and Anglor Saxon.

ARETHA: Thuup! I'm—

MISS FAITH: Very nice. 32.5, 19-6-65. By the book. As promised.

BLANCA: We read the book. The red letter edition. The red herring.* Cover to cover. We read the red book.

ANGLOR: We're well read.

---

* Red herring. In co-op apartment sales, a preliminary booklet explaining the specifics of sale.

ARETHA: You ever heard of Charles? He's in thuh book—

MISS FAITH: Five walk-in closets. Of course, theyre not in yet.

BLANCA: Does she come with the place?

MISS FAITH: She's on her way out.

BLANCA: She has no teeth.

ANGLOR: Haven't I seen her somewhere before?

BLANCA: Anglor Saxon!—He's always doing that. When we met he wondered if he hadn't seen me somewhere before. And he had! We had to make an Amendment.

MISS FAITH: The closets will go here here there and thar. We will yank her out to make room for them.

ANGLOR: Thus says the book. Amendment 2.1. Always liked that amendment. It's very open—open to interpretation.

MISS FAITH: We will put in some windows, of course.

BLANCA: Of course.

ANGLOR: Yanking out the commode?

MISS FAITH: Commodes just for show.

ARETHA: Just for show.

BLANCA: We might like to have a bathroom. We're planning to have a big family.

ARETHA: A family. Had me uh family once. They let me go.

ANGLOR: Meet our children: Anglor and Blanca. They're so nice and quiet they don't speak unless they're spoken to they don't move unless we make them.

MISS FAITH: This is where we plan the bathroom.

ANGLOR: You'll never guess where we met.

BLANCA: Love at first sight.

MISS FAITH: Plenty of room for a big family.

ANGLOR: Guess where we met!

MISS FAITH: We'll rip out this kitchen if you like leave it bare youll have more space.

ARETHA: Charles got you tuhgether.

ANGLOR: Close. I told you we know her, Blanca.

MISS FAITH: We'll put in the commode and rip it out then put it back again. If you so desire.

BLANCA: Guess!

ANGLOR: We're going to need someone to mind that commode. We're going to need help.

ARETHA: I raised uh family once. I raised uh boy. I raised uh girl. I trained em I bathed em. I bathed uh baby once. Bathed two babies.

BLANCA: We're childhood sweethearts. From childhood. We met way back. In the womb.

ANGLOR: We need help.

BLANCA: We're twins!

ARETHA: That iduhnt in thuh book.

ANGLOR: We're related. By marriage. It's all legal. By the book.

MISS FAITH: We will put the commode closer to the bath. Put the commode in the bath. Youll have more space.

ARETHA: We got different books.

ANGLOR: We have the same last name! Saxon! Blanca Saxon—

BLANCA: Anglor Saxon. Blanca and Anglor Saxon—

ARETHA: I'm Mrs. Saxon. Howdeedoo.

ANGLOR: Mrs. Saxon, we need help.

BLANCA: We're going to have children. We're going to breed. Weve bred two and we'll breed more.

MISS FAITH: Its all a part of the great shucking off—

ARETHA: You wouldnt know nothing uhbout uh Charles, wouldja? Charles was my husband. Charles Saxon?

MISS FAITH: The old must willingly shuck off to make way for the new. Much like the snakes new skin suit. The new come in and we gladly make them room. Where would they go if we did not extract?

ANGLOR: I don't suppose you've nowhere to go? We need help. You seem like a sturdy help type. I suppose you can shuffle and serve simultaneously? Wet nurse the brood weve bred? A help like you would be in accordance with the book. Make things make sense. Right along with the record. More in line with what you're used to. I would be master. Blanca: mistress. That's little master and little missy. Yes, that's it! Give us a grin!

MISS FAITH: Shes on her way out.

ANGLOR: Give us a grin!

BLANCA: Anglor, she's toothless.

ARETHA: Charles sscome back! I see im down there wavin—no—directin traffic. Left right left right left—he remembers me right right he's forgiven me right left right right he wants tuh see me.

MISS FAITH: Charles is dead.

ANGLOR: Thus says the book?

ARETHA: Make uh amendment. Charles ssdown thuh street. On thuh street down thuh street.

MISS FAITH: Not in my book.

BLANCA: We've got different books.

ARETHA: We got differin books. Make uh amendment. I'm packin my bags. I left him. Had to go. Two babies to care for.

ANGLOR: We know her from somewhere.

ARETHA: Had tuh go. He gived me his name. Make uh amendment.

BLANCA: We've got the same name.

ANGLOR: WE KNOW HER FROM SOMEWHERE! Too bad she can't grin.

ARETHA: Had to go. Have tuh go. Make thuh amendment, Sister Faith, Charles is back.

MISS FAITH: You need help. She comes with the place. She can live under the sink. Out of mind out of sight.

BLANCA: She's toothless.

ANGLOR: Not a good example for the breed. Make the amendment.

ARETHA: Miss Faith? Make uh uhmendment. Charless waitin—

MISS FAITH: Charles is dead! Never to return. Thus says the—

ARETHA: Buchenwald! Buchenwald! I—I showed em my blue eyes n they hauled me off anyway—

BLANCA: Stick to the facts, help! She's bad for the brood. Make that amendment.

MISS FAITH: An amendment.

ARETHA: Nine million just disappeared!* Thats uh fact!!

BLANCA: Six million. Six! Miss Faith? The amendment! I would like another child. I would like to get started!

ARETHA: They hauled us from thuh homeland! Stoled our clothes!

MISS FAITH: Amendment! Amendment XIII.† You have been extracted from the record, Mrs. Saxon. You are free. You are clear. You may go.

ANGLOR: Free and clear to go. Go.

MISS FAITH: Go.

BLANCA: Go.

ARETHA: Oh. How should I greet him? Should greet im with uh—

BLANCA: GIT! Wave goodbye, children ! That's it. That's it! They're so well mannered.

ANGLOR: Wife? Brood? Isn't this a lovely view? And the buzzer! It works!
    Buzzer.

G *Dreamtime:* CHARLES *appears.*

CHARLES: You let them take out the teeth you're giving up the last of the verifying evidence. All'll be obliterated. All's left will be conjecture. We won't be able to tell you apart from the others. We won't even know your name. Things will get messy. Chaos. Perverted. People will twist around the facts to suit the truth.

ARETHA: You know what they say bout thuh hand that rocks thuh cradle?

CHARLES: I didn't rock their cradles.

ARETHA: You know how thuh sayin goes?

CHARLES: "Rocks the cradle—rules the world," but I didn't rock—

ARETHA: Dont care what you say you done, Charles. We're makin us uh histironical amendment here, K? Give us uh smile. Uh big smile for thuh book.

CHARLES: Historical. An "Historical Amendment," Ma'am.

ARETHA: Smile, Charles.

CHARLES: Where are you going, Miss Aretha?

ARETHA: Mmm goin tuh take my place aside thuh most high.

CHARLES: Up north, huh?

ARETHA: Up north.

CHARLES: Sscold up there, you know.

ARETHA: Smile, Charles! Thats it!

---

* An estimated 9 million Africans were taken from Africa into slavery (Rawley, *The Transatlantic Slave Trade*).
An estimated 6 million Jewish people were killed in the concentration camps of WWII.

† Amendment XIII abolished slavery in the United States.

CHARLES: Chaos! You know what chaos is?! Things cease to adhere to—

ARETHA: SMILE. Smile, Charles, Smile! Show us them pretty teeths. Good.

CHARLES: I can't get the children to smile, Ma am.

ARETHA: You smile.

CHARLES: They're crying, Miss Aretha!

ARETHA: Smile! Smile! SMILE!! There. Thats nice.

CHARLES: They're crying.

ARETHA: Dont matter none. Dont matter none at all. You say its uh cry I say it uh smile. These photographics is for my scrapbook. Scraps uh graphy for my book. Smile or no smile mm gonna remember you. Mm gonna remember you grinnin.

Whir of camera grows louder. Lights fade to black.

THIRD KINGDOM (REPRISE)

OVER-SEER: What are you doing?

US-SEER: Throw-ing. Up.

KIN-SEER: Kin-Seer sez.

SHARK-SEER: Shark-Seer sez.

US-SEER: Us-Seer sez.

SOUL-SEER: Soul-Seer sez.

OVER-SEER: Over-Seer sez.

KIN-SEER: Sez Kin-Seer sez.

SHARK-SEER: Sezin Shark-Seer sez.

US-SEER: Sez Us-Seer sezin.

SOUL-SEER: Sezin Soul-Seer sezin sez.

OVER-SEER: Sez Over-Seer sez.

KIN-SEER: Tonight I dream of where I be-camin from. And where I be-camin from duhduhnt look like nowhere like I been.

SOUL-SEER: The tale of how we *were* when we *were*—

OVER-SEER: You woke up screaming.

SHARK-SEER: How we *will* be when we *will* be—

OVER-SEER: You woke up screaming.

US-SEER: And how we be, now that we iz.

ALL: You woke up screaming out—you woke me up.

OVER-SEER: Put on this. Around your head and over your eyes. It will help you sleep. See? Like me. Around your head and over your eyes. It will help you see.

KIN-SEER, US-SEER AND SHARK-SEER: Gaw gaw gaw gaw —eeeee-uh. Gaw gaw gaw gaw eeeeeee-uh.

SOUL-SEER: Howzit gonna fit? Howzitgonnafit me?!

US-SEER: Bleached Bones Man has comed and tooked you. You fall down in-to-the-sea.

KIN-SEER: Should I jump? Should I jump?? Should I jump shouldijumporwhut?

SHARK-SEER: I dream up uh fish thats swallowin me—

SHARK-SEER AND KIN-SEER: And I dream up uh me that is then be-camin that fish and I dream up that fish be-camin uh shark and I dream up that shark be-camin uhshore.

ALL: UUH!

SOUL-SEER: And where I be-camin from duhduhnt look like nowhere I been.

SHARK-SEER AND KIN-SEER: And I whuduhnt me no more and I whuduhnt no fish. My new Self was uh 3rd Self made by thuh space in between.

ALL: UUH!

KIN-SEER: Rose up out uh thuh water and standin on them waves my Self was standin. And my Self that rose between us went back down in-to-the-sea.

US-SEER: EEEEEEEE!

SHARK-SEER: Me wavin at me me wavin at I me wavin at my Self.

US-SEER: Bleached Bones Man has comed and tooked you. You fall down in-to-the-sea....

KIN-SEER: Baby, what will I do for love?

OVER-SEER: Around your head and over your eyes. This piece of cloth will help you see.

SHARK-SEER: BLACK FOLKS WITH NO CLOTHES....

US-SEER: This boat tooked us to-the-coast.

SOUL-SEER: THUH SKY WAS JUST AS BLUE!

KIN-SEER: Thuuuup!

SHARK-SEER: Eat eat eat please eat.

SOUL-SEER: THUH SKY WAS JUST AS BLUE!

KIN-SEER: Thuuuup!

SHARK-SEER: Eat eat eat please eat. Eat eat eat please eat.

OVER-SEER: Around your head and over your eyes.

US-SEER: This boat tooked us to-the-coast.

SOUL-SEER: But we are not in uh boat!

US-SEER: But we iz. Iz uh-huhn-uh-huhn-iz.

OVER-SEER: There are 2 cliffs. 2 cliffs where the Word has cleaved. Half the Word has fallen away making 2 Words and a space between. Those 2 Words inscribe the third Kingdom.

KIN-SEER: Should I jump shouldi jumporwhut.

US-SEER: Come home come home dont stay out too late.

KIN-SEER: Me hollerin uhcross thuh cliffs at my Self:

SOUL-SEER: Ssblak! Ssblak! Ssblakallblak!

OVER-SEER: That's your *soul* you're looking at. Wonder #9 of my glass-bottomed boat. Swallow it, you, or you'll be jettisoned.

SOUL-SEER: UUH! UUH!

KIN-SEER: This boat tooked me from-my-coast.

US-SEER: Come home come home come home come home.

SOUL-SEER: The tale of who we were when we were, who we will be when we will be and who we be now that we iz:

US-SEER: Iz-uhhuhn-uhhuhn-iz.

KIN-SEER: You said I could wave as long as I see um. I still see um.

OVER-SEER: Wave then.

OVER-SEER, KIN-SEER, SOUL-SEER, SHARK-SEER AND US-SEER: Gaw gaw gaw gaw ee-uh. Gaw gaw gaw gaw ee-uh.

SHARK-SEER: This is uh speech in uh language of codes. Secret signs and secret symbols.

KIN-SEER: Wave wave wave wave. Wave wave wave wave.

SHARK-SEER: Should I jump shouldijumporwhut? Should I jump shouldijumporwhut?

KIN-SEER:	SHARK-SEER:
Wave wave wave wave.	Should I jump shouldijumporwhut?
Wavin wavin	Should I jump should I jump
wavin wavin	shouldijumporwhut?

US-SEER: Baby, what will I do for love?
SOUL-SEER: Rock. Thuh boat. Rock. Thuh boat.

KIN-SEER:	SOUL-SEER:	SHARK-SEER:	US-SEER:
Wavin wavin	Rock.Thuh boat.	Shouldijump	Thuh sky
wavin	Rock.	shouldijump	was just
wavin	Thuh boat.	or whut?	as blue!
		THUP!	
Wavin wavin	Rock.Thuh boat.	Shouldijulllp	Thuh sky
wavin wavin	Rock.	shouldijump	was just
wavin wavin	Thuh boat.	or whut?	as blue!

OVER-SEER: HO!

KIN-SEER:	SOUL-SEER:	SHARK-SEER:	US-SEER:
Wavin wavin	Rock.Thuh boat.	Shouldijump	Thuh sky
wavin	Rock.	shouldijump	was just
wavin	Thuh boat.	or whut?	as blue!
		THUP!	
Wavin wavin	Rock.Thuh boat.	Shouldijump	Thuh sky
wavin wavin	Rock.	shouldijump	was just
wavin wavin	Thuh boat.	or whut?	as blue!

OVER-SEER: HO!

KIN-SEER, SOUL-SEER, SHARK-SEER, US-SEER AND OVER-SEER: Gaw gaw gaw gaw
gaw gaw gaw gaw.
OVER-SEER: I'm going to yell "Land Ho!" in a day or so and all of this will have to
stop. I am going to yell "Land Ho!" in a day or so and that will be the end of this.
KIN-SEER, SOUL-SEER, SHARK-SEER AND US-SEER: Gaw gaw gaw gaw-ee-uh.
Gaw gaw gaw gaw-eeeee-uh.
OVER-SEER: What are you doing? What'reya doin. What'reyadoeeeeee! WHAT ARE
YOU DO-EEE-NUH???!
KIN-SEER: —.—: Throw-ing. Kisses.

PART 4: GREEKS (OR THE SLUGS)

A

MR. SERGEANT SMITH: I'll have four. Four shots. Four at thuh desk. Go ahead—put in thuh colored film. Mmsplurgin. Splurging. Uh huh. Wants em tuh see my shoes as black. Shirt as khaki.Stripes as green. No mop n broom bucket today! I'll sit first. No. Stand. I kin feel it. In here. Mmm gettin my Distinction today. Thuh events of my destiny ssgonna fall intuh place. What events? That I dont know. But they gonna fall intuh place all right. They been all along marchin in that direction. Soon they gonna fall. Ssonly natural. Ssonly fair. They gonna fall intuh place. I kin feel it. In here. This time tomorrow mm gonna have me my Distinction. Gonna be shakin hands with thuh Commander. Gonna be salutin friendly back n forth. Gonnla be rewarded uh desk cause when uh man's distinguished he's got hisself uh desk. Standin at thuh desk. My desk. Sssgonna be mines, anyhow. Fnot this un then one just like it. Hands in pockets. No—out. Ready for work. Here is Sergeant Smith at his desk. Ready. Ready for work. Next, second shot: right hand on the desk. Like on the Bible. God and Country. Here is a man who loves his work. The name of this man is the name of Smith. You get the stripes in? They gonna be bars by evenin! Ha! Bars by evenin! Having a desk is distinguished. All of us have them. Because when there is danger from above, we stop. We look. We listen. Then we—dive underneath our desk (being careful that we do not catch our heads on the desk lip). Dive! Dive under our desks where it is safe. Like turtles. In our shells we wait for the danger to pass.—I don't wanna do uh shot uh that—don't want em tuh worry. Next, third shot: Here—oh. I will sit. Hands folded. Here I am—no. Arms folded. Next, shot number four. Ready? Hands on books and books open. A full desk and a smiling man. Sergeant Smith has got stacks of papers, but, not to worry, he is a good worker and will do well. Wait. Uh smile. Okay. Go head. Take it. Smiling at work. They like smiles.

Airplane sounds.

B MRS. SERGEANT SMITH *and* BUFFY. *A lovely home.*

BUFFY: Mommie, what should the Biloxie Twins wear today?

MRS. SMITH: Sumthin nice.

BUFFY: The green one with pink stripes orange and yellow fuzzy sweater sets. Blue coat dresses. Double breasted. Which one's nicest?

MRS. SMITH: They all perm press? Put em in permanent press. You don't want em arrivin wrinkled. I vote for them two sharp little brown n white polka-dotted numbers. Put em both in thuh brown n white dotted swisses.

893

BUFFY: There iduhn't any brown and white swiss.

MRS. SMITH: Perm press is best. Put em in thuh swiss.

BUFFY: I'll press em with my hands. My hands get as hot as uh iron sometimes, Mommie. Here they go—ssss—tuh! Hot enough! Press press press.

MRS. SMITH: Don't press on thuh desk. Gotta keep your daddy's desk nice for im. Use starch? Starch!

BUFFY: Starch—starchstarch! Ooooh—starch made uh tab come off.

MRS. SMITH: Sssokay. It'll hold with three tabs.

BUFFY: What if thuh wind blows her dress? What if three tabs won't hold? She'll be naked. Thuh wind'll steal her clothes and then she'll be naked.

MRS. SMITH: Ssit pressed? Bring it here. Lemmie feel. Good, Buffeena—

BUFFY: But what if her dress whips off? What if she is naked? Can't be outside and naked people will see her she'll be shamed—

MRS. SMITH: Good tuh be pressed. Don't like crinkles—

BUFFY: What if thuh wind pulls like this and this and then she is naked and then—

MRS. SMITH: She kin hide behind her twin. They look just alike, don't they. They look just alike then Miss-Naked-Biloxie-with-thuh-three-tabs kin hide behind Miss-Fully-Clothed-Biloxie-with-thuh-four. Nobody'll notice nothin.

BUFFY: Where the Biloxie Twins off to, Mommie?

MRS. SMITH: Off out.

BUFFY: Off out where?

MRS. SMITH: Off out to thuh outside.

BUFFY: Off outside when they go who're they gonna meet?

MRS. SMITH: Their Maker. They're gonna meet their Maker. Huh! Sssimportant. Last furlough your daddy had, I tooked you tuh see him. Remember? Two thousand, oh hundred fifty-three stops. Three days on one bus. Was uh local. Missed thuh express. Changed in Castletin. Most folks waited in thuh depot. We waited outside. In thuh snow. Wanted tuh be thuh first tuh see thuh bus round thuh bend. That bus tooked us to thuh coast. Last tuh get on. Sat in thuh—rear. More even ride in thuh rear. Tooked us to thuh coast. Saw your daddy. Remember?

BUFFY: Uh huhn. The Biloxie twins are gonna—

MRS. SMITH: Huh! Good memory you got.—That was before you was born. I tooked you to see your Maker. Put on my green n white striped for thuh busride—it got so crinkled. Had tuh change intuh my brown with thuh white dots. Changed right there on thuh bus. In thuh restroom, of course. There's some womens that'll change anywheres. With anybody. Not this one. Not this Mrs. Smith. I gotta change my dress I goes to thuh restroom no matter how long thuh line. Goin in thuh mobile restroom's uh privilege, you know. They let me privy to thuh privilege cause I wanted tuh look nice for your daddy. Wanted tuh look like I hadn't traveled uh mile or sweated uh drop.

BUFFY: Biloxie Twinsss gonna wear their brown and whites—

MRS. SMITH: Got off that bus at thuh coast. Sky was shinin. Real blue. Didn't see it. All I seen was him. Mr. Smith. Your daddy. He tooked up my whole eye. "Mrs.

Smith!" he yelled, loud enough for everyone tuh hear, "you ain't traveled a mile nor sweated a drop!"

BUFFY: You were just as proud.

MRS. SMITH: I was just as proud.

BUFFY: You were just as proud.

MRS. SMITH: I was just as proud. "Ain't traveled a mile nor sweated a drop!"

BUFFY: I'm gonna be just as proud.

MRS. SMITH: As what?

BUFFY: —As proud—.

MRS. SMITH: Uh huhnn. We're gonna have us uh big family. Your father's got uh furlough comin up. How'd you like uh—uh sister, Buffeena?

BUFFY: The Biloxie Twins don't need uh sister cause then they wouldn't be twins.

MRS. SMITH: We can put her in uh bed next tuh yours.

BUFFY: Where would the Biloxie Twins sleep?

MRS. SMITH: Men from thuh Effort come by?

BUFFY: 0-800.

MRS. SMITH: Whatja give em.

BUFFY: Thuh floor lamp.

MRS. SMITH: With thuh curlicues? Huh. Don't need it nohow. Whatcha need is uh—uhnother girl. You and her—you'll have uh—uh sister. Get your twins off thuh desk, Buffy. Gotta keep it nice for your daddy. Two girls'll make things even. And thuh next time your daddy comes home we'll all do it up in brown and white.

Airplane sounds rise up.

C

MR. SERGEANT SMITH: Here I am on a rock. As you can see, the rock is near water! We of the 20-5 3rd are closer to water than you can guess. We are in the water! But we are not on a boat! But, we are not on a submarine! We of the 20-5 3rd are on an ISLAND!! A big rock in the middle of the ocean. Next time your mother takes you to visit the ocean, Buffeena, look very far out over the water and give me a wave. I will waaaave back! You may have to put on your glasses to see me, and I expect that to you I'll look like just a little speck. But if you look very far, you'll see me and if you wave very hard, I will waaaaaave back! Next time your mother takes you to visit the ocean, Buffeena, throw me a kiss and I will throooooow one back! Now, Buffy, to reach me at the 20-53rd you are going to have to throw me a BIG kiss. Ask your Mother to help you. She will help you just as we here at the 20-53rd help each other, working together, to get the good job done. Here at the 20-53rd different men have different jobs. Some read maps. Some fly airplanes. Some watch guard over our island home. It is my job to keep watch over this rock. The rock I'm standing on right now. Our Commander, the man in charge, likes a clean rock. See my broom? See my mop? It is my job to keep this rock clean! My rock is very clean. My rock is the cleanest of all the rocks on our island home. I make the Commander very happy because I do a good job. I help him and in turn he will help me. My Commander,

when the time is right, will reward me for a good job well done. My Commander
will award me soon and put me in charge of bigger and more important—more
important aspects of our island home. And your daddy will then have his Distinction. And your daddy will then come home. He will come home with bars instead
of stripes and you and your Mommie will be just as proud! Well, it is time for work!
Your daddy loves you, Buffy, and sends a big kiss and a big smile.

  Airplane sounds rise up.

D MRS. SMITH, BUFFY, *and* MUFFY. *A lovely home.*

MUFFY: How come he didn't write tuh me?

BUFFY: Say "Why is it that," Muffy, not "how come."

MUFFY: Why is that he didn't write tuh me? He didn't include me.

MRS. SMITH: You got thuh ledger, Buffeena? "Subject": uh letter. Check thuh "non
  bill" column. "From:"? Write—

MUFFY: How come he didn't say Muffy too?

BUFFY: Get out from under the desk, Muff. Mrs. Smith, write "Sergeant Smith"?

MRS. SMITH: Right.

MUFFY: Duhdun't he know my name? I'm Muffy. Duhdun't he know my name?

BUFFY: Contents?

MUFFY: Duddun't he know me?! I'm Muffy.

MRS. SMITH: Write—uh—"general news."

BUFFY: General news.

MRS. SMITH: Slash—"report of duties."

BUFFY: Good.

MUFFY: He duhdn't like me. Sergeant Smith dudhn't like me Buffy. He only likes Mrs.
  Smith he only likes Buffy Smith he only likes his desk. He duduhn't like Muffy. I'm
  Muffy. He duduhn't like me.

BUFFY: He likes you.

MRS. SMITH: Signs of Distinction: —uh—uh—put "—." What'd we put last time?

MUFFY: He duhuhun't love me. HE DUDUHN'T LOVE HIS DESK!

BUFFY: Helovesyouheloveshisdesk.

MRS. SMITH: I hear you kickin Sergeant Smith's desk, Mufficent! I'm comin over
  there tuh feel for scuff marks and they're better not be uh one! Hhh. "Signs of
  Distinction"? What'd we put last time.

MUFFY: Why didn't he love me? If he really loved Muffy he'd say Muffy. If he really
  loved me he would I'm Muffy why dudn't—

BUFFY: Last letter's Signs of Distinction were "on the horizon."

MRS. SMITH: Before that?

BUFFY: . . . "Soon." Before that he reported his Distinction to be arriving quote any
  day now unquote.

MUFFY: Mm wearin my brown and white. You said he likes his girls in their brown
  and whites.

MRS. SMITH: On thuh horizon any day now soon. Huh. You girls know what he told
  me last furlough? Last furlough I got off that bus and thuh sky was just as blue—

wooo it was uh blue sky. I'd taken thuh bus to thuh coast. Rode in thuh front seat cause thuh ride was smoother up in thuh front. Kept my pocketbook on my lap. Was nervous. Asked thuh driver tuh name out names of towns we didn't stop at. Was uh express. Uh express bus. "Mawhaven!" That was one place—where we passed by. Not by but through. "Mawhaven!" Had me uh front seat. Got to thuh coast. Wearin my brown and white. "You ain't traveled a mile nor sweated a drop!" That's exactly how he said it too. Voice tooked up thuh whole outside couldn't hear nothin else. We got tuh talkin. He told me that over there, where he's stationed, on his island home, over there they are uh whole day ahead of us. Their time ain't our time. Thuh sun does—tricks—does tricks n puts us all off schedules. When his time's his own he tries tuh think of what time it is here. For us. And what we're doin. He's in his quarters stowin away his checkers game and it's dark but you're whinin out thuh lumps in your Cream of Wheat, Buffy and Muffy, you're tearin at your plaits and it's Tuesday mornin and it's yesterday. And thuh breakfast goes cold today. I redo Miss Muff's head and fasten it with pins but it ain't today for him. Ssstomorrow. Always tomorrow. Iduhn't that somethin?

BUFFY: I'll put "expected." Hows that.

MUFFY: I like his desk. I love his desk. I kiss it see? I hug it. Uuh! Hear me, Mommie, I'm kissing Sergeant Smith's desk. I am hugging it. Uuuhh! He likes his girls in their Swisses, right? Don't you, Sergeant Smith? I'm their Swisses! I'm their Swisses!!

MRS. SMITH: "Mention of Work": check "yes."

BUFFY: Check.

MUFFY: "Mention of Family": check NO.

MRS. SMITH: Check "yes," Buffeena.

BUFFY: Check.

MUFFY: Did not mention Muffy.

BUFFY: Censors, Muff.

MRS. SMITH: Scissors?

BUFFY: Censors. The Censors—they're uh family. Like us. They're uh family with Mr. Censor at thuh lead. Mr. Censor is a man who won't let Sergeant Smith say certain things because certain things said may put the Effort in danger. Certain things said and certain ways of saying certain things may clue-in the enemy. Certain things said may allow them to catch Sergeant Smith unawares. Sergeant Smith, Muff, deals in a language of codes—secret signs and signals. Certain ways with words that are plain to us could, for Sergeant Smith, spell the ways of betrayal, right, Mrs. Smith? Notice he only says "Commander." He isn't allowed to mention his Commander by name. We say "Muffy" every day but for Sergeant Smith saying your name would be gravely dangerous.

MUFFY: Muffy's not gravely dangerous.

MRS. SMITH: Muffy—Muffy—Muffy sounds like minefield. What's uh mine, Mufficent?

MUFFY: A mine is a thing that dismembers. Too many mines lose the war.

MRS. SMITH: Good girl.

MUFFY: Remember the Effort.

MRS. SMITH: Good girl!

BUFFY: We all gotta make sacrifices, Muffy.

MRS. SMITH: Wouldn't uh named you "Muffy," but they hadn't invented mines when you came along.

MUFFY: They named mines after me?

MRS. SMITH: Go put on your Brown n White. We're goin tuh thuh beach.

BUFFY: She's got it on, Mrs. Smith.

MUFFY: Sergeant Smith's comin?!?

MRS. SMITH: You're not wrinkled are you Mufficent? Comeer. Lemmie feel. Hmmmm. Ssall right. Wouldn't want tuh be crinkly for Sergeant Smith. Huh. I remember when he first saw you. We traveled for miles and—when we walked off that bus! Brown-and-White polka dots uh swiss! Lookin like we hadn't traveled uh mile nor sweated uh drop!

MUFFY: Was he just as proud?

BUFFY: He was.

MRS. SMITH: Your Sergeant ssgonna be furloughin soon. How'd my two girls like uh—uh brother, huh? Seems like three is what this family needs. He always wanted uh—boy. Boy. Men from thuh Effort come by already, huh?

BUFFY: 0-800.

MRS. SMITH: Whatyuh give em?

BUFFY: Floor lamp.

MRS. SMITH: Thuh one with thuh green brass base?

BUFFY: And thuh phonograph.

MRS. SMITH: Records too? HHH. Don't need em no how. What we need is uh—

BUFFY: Uh brother.

MRS. SMITH: Uh brother! Your Sergeant Smith ssgonna be furloughin soon. Whatduhyuh say, Buffy? Muffy? Buffy? Muffy?

Airplane sounds rise up.

E

MR. SERGEANT SMITH: I expect it's today for you by now. Last night it comed to me: there's four hours every day that I kin say "today" and you'll know what today I mean. We got us whatcha calls "uh overlap." We got us uh overlap of four hours. Times when my day's yours—and yours is mines. Them four hours happens real quick and they look just like thuh other twenty-odd so you gotta watch for em real close. That little bit uh knowledge comed tuh me last night. Along with—my Distinction. Mrs. Smith, your Sergeant Smiths now—distinguished. They're etchin "Sergeant Smith" on thuh medals right this very moment as I speak I expect. Sssmy desk. Sssmy desk, this. Hhh. I saved uh life, ya know. Not every man kin say that, Mrs. Smith. I know you're gonna be proud. Make no mistake. Just as proud. Just as proud as—. Not every man saves uh life!

Airplane sounds rise up.

F MRS. SMITH, BUFFY, MUFFY *and* DUFFY. *A lovely home.*

MRS. SMITH: You ironed thuh Sergeant's desk today, Buffeena?

BUFFY: Yes, Mrs. Smith.

MRS. SMITH: Don't want it wrinkled.

BUFFY: No, Mrs. Smith. We'll get him another one tomorrow, K Muff? Duff too.

MRS. SMITH: Another what?

DUFFY: Are turtles mammals, Mommie?

MRS. SMITH: Mammals? Waas uh mammal?

MUFFY: Live births. Nurse their young.

MRS. SMITH: Waas today, Buffeena?

BUFFY: No, Duffy, they're not mammals. Today's Friday, Mrs. Smith.

MUFFY: Mind if I yo-yo, Buff?

BUFFY: Be careful, K?

MRS. SMITH: Be careful of thuh desk. Sergeant Smith's comin home n all we need's for it tuh be scored with your yo-yo welts, you!

DUFFY: Sergeant Smith uh mammal?

MRS. SMITH: Waas uh mammal?

MUFFY: Live births—round the world—whooosh!

BUFFY: Yes, Duffy.

MUFFY: Nurse their young. Whoosh! Whoosh !

MRS. SMITH: Today Friday?

BUFFY: Yes, Mrs. Smith.

DUFFY: He said he was uh turtle.

MRS. SMITH: Turtle?! Today's Friday. Waas uh turtle?

MUFFY: Masquerade as fish, Mrs. Smith. Round the world! Round the world!

MRS. SMITH: They catch on my line when I cast it out. Today's Friday. Fish on Friday. We'll have fish.

BUFFY: When Sergeant Smith said he was uh turtle that was uh figure of speech, Duffy. Sergeant Smith was figuring his speech.

MRS. SMITH: We'll go out. Out. Out. Have fish. You'll wear your swiss, Duffy. Same as us.

DUFFY: How do they breathe?

MRS. SMITH: Same as us.

DUFFY: Underwater?

MRS. SMITH: Same as us. Same as us. Sergeant Smith's comin. Soon. Today. Sergeant Smith's comin soon today soon.

MUFFY: Soon today today soon on the horizon today soon on the horizon today soon round the world round the world.

DUFFY: All winter through gills?

BUFFY: In summer they suck up lots of air. They store it. In the winter they use the stored air. Like camels use water.

DUFFY: Camels breathe water? Camels have gills?

MRS. SMITH: Course they got gills. You heard of thuh overlap, aintcha? Overlap's up gap. Uh gap overlappin. Thuh missin link. Find thuh link. Put out thuh cat. Close thuh kitty cat flap mm feeling uh breeze. Seal up thuh flap mm feelin uh breeze.

BUFFY: Flap is sealed.

MRS. SMITH: Sscold. Mm feelin uh breeze. Mm feelin uh breeze.

MUFFY: She's feeling a breeze we're all gonna freeze round the world round the world.

BUFFY: Flap is sealed.

MUFFY: Round the world.

MRS. SMITH: Look for thuh overlap!

MUFFY: Round the world.

DUFFY: Overlap's uh gap!

BUFFY: Isn't!

DUFFY: Is!

MUFFY: Round the world round the world.

DUFFY: Overlap's uh gap!

BUFFY: Isn't!

DUFFY: Is!

MUFFY: Round the world round the—

MRS. SMITH: FREEZE!

MUFFY: —world.

MRS. SMITH: Sound off.

BUFFY: Buff-y!

MUFFY: Muff-y

DUFFY: Duff-y!

MRS. SMITH: Mm feelin uh breeze. Stop that yo-in, Mufficent, or you'll have thuh Sarge tuh answer to. Still. Still thuh breeze. Anyone by at 0-800? Whatja give em? Don't need it no how. What we need is uh—. There was uh light in thuh sky last night. Don't suppose no one seen it. You all'd gone out. Through thuh gap. I was waitin up. There was uh light in thuh sky. I stopped. I looked. I heard. Uh man was fallin fallin aflame. Fallin at midnight. There wasn't uh sun. He was comin from another world. I stopped. I looked. I heard but couldn't do nothin. It all happened so far away. It all happened before you was born. Go put on your Brown and White, son. The Sergeant likes his family in their Brown and Whites. Muffy. Walk thuh dog.

MUFFY: Walking the dog walking the dog.

MRS. SMITH: Thuh sergeant'll want to see things in order. Nothin more orderly than uh walked dog.

MUFFY: Walk the dog. Walk the dog. Round the world. Walk the dog.

MRS. SMITH: Stand me in my walker. Go on—my walker, Private! Sarge is comin, gotta snap to attention.

DUFFY: Turtles lay eggs in thuh sand at night. Then they go away. How do they know which ones are theirs? Which eggs? Thuh eggs hatch and thuh baby turtles go crawlin out into thuh sea. How do thuh parents know em? How do thuh parents know em, Buff?

BUFFY: I don't think they much care.

MRS. SMITH: TEN-SHUN!

MR. SERGEANT SMITH: Hello, honey. I'm home.

BUFFY: Daddy is home!

MUFFY: Daddy is home!

DUFFY: Daddy is home!

BUFFY, MUFFY AND DUFFY: Hello, Daddy!

MRS. SMITH: Hello, Mr. Smith. How was your day?

MR. SERGEANT SMITH: Just fine, Mrs. Smith. Give me uh kiss. Why, Mrs. Smith, you've lost your eyes. You've lost your eyes, Mrs. Smith. When did you lose your eyes?

BUFFY: What did you bring me, Daddy?

MRS. SMITH: For years. I had em lost for years.

MR. SERGEANT SMITH: When?

MRS. SMITH: YEARS. Years uhgo.

MUFFY: What did you bring me, Daddy?

MR. SERGEANT SMITH: Shoulda wroten.

DUFFY: What did you bring me, Daddy?

MR. SERGEANT SMITH: Shoulda called.

BUFFY: Daddy promised me uh china doll!

MR. SERGEANT SMITH: Shoulda given me some kinda notice, Mrs. Smith. Iduhn't no everyday uh wife loses her eyes. Where did you lose them and when did they go? Why haven't we ordered replacements? I woulda liked tuh hear uhbout that.

MRS. SMITH: Thought they'd come back afore you did. Shoulda informed me you was stoppin by.

MR. SERGEANT SMITH: I wrote. I called.

BUFFY: I'll get thuh ledger.

MRS. SMITH: What do you think of our brown and whites, Mr. Smith?

MR. SERGEANT SMITH: Who're you uhgain?

DUFFY: Duffy. You promised me an airplane.

MUFFY: I'm Muffy.

MRS. SMITH: You are Mr. Smith. You are our Mr. Smith? What do you think of our brown and whites, our Mr. Smith?

DUFFY: I'm your spittin image. Did you bring my airplane?

MR. SERGEANT SMITH: I was uh fine lookin man—like you—once. I got pictures. Uh whole wallet full. There. That's me.

DUFFY: Nope. That's me. We look uhlike.

BUFFY: They took thuh ledger. Thuh ledger was in thuh desk.

MRS. SMITH: Ssstoo bad. We needs documentation. Proof.

MR. SERGEANT SMITH: I wrote! I called!

MRS. SMITH: There's lots uh Smiths. Many Smiths. Smithsss common name.

DUFFY: You promised me uh air-o-plane!

MR. SERGEANT SMITH: I visited. We had us a family. That's proof.

MRS. SMITH: Lots uh visits. Lots uh families.

MR. SERGEANT SMITH: I got my Distinction. See? Here are my medals here is my name. They let me be uh Mister. Mr. Smith's got his bars!

MRS. SMITH: Distinction? Waas uh Distinction?

BUFFY: You promised me uh Chinese doll.

MR. SERGEANT SMITH: Uh Distinction's when one's set uhpart. Uh Distinction's when they give ya bars. Got my bars! See?

MRS. SMITH: Lemmie feel.

MR. SERGEANT SMITH: I saved uh life! Caught uh man as he was fallin out thuh sky!

MRS. SMITH: You catched uh man? Out thuh sky? I seen uh light last night. In thuh sky. From uhnother world. I don't suppose you catched it. Don't suppose you're our Distinctioned Mr. Smith?

MR. SERGEANT SMITH: Was standin on my rock. I stopped. I heard. I seen him fallin—

MUFFY: You stepped on a mine. I read it in the paper. A mine is a thing that remembers. Too many mines lose the war. Remember the Effort. The mine blew his legs off.

MR. SERGEANT SMITH: You one uh mines?

BUFFY: He lost his legs.

MR. SERGEANT SMITH: You one uh mines?

DUFFY: He lost thuh war.

MR. SERGEANT SMITH: You one uh mines?

MRS. SMITH: Why Mr. Smith, you've lost your legs, why, Mr. Smith, you've lost thuh war. When did you lose your legs, Mr. Smith, Mr. Smith, when did you lose thuh war? Men come by at 0-800. What do we give em? What we don't need nohow. BuffyMuffyDuffy? Your father's got hisself uh furlough comin up soon. That's just what we need. Uhnother boy. Always thought things should come in fours. Fours. Fours. All fours. I'll put it to him when he comes home. Whatduhyasay?

DUFFY: Are we turtles? Are we turtles, Mr. Smith?

BUFFY: Duffy—

MR. SERGEANT SMITH: No. No—uh—boy we iduhn't turtles. We'se slugs. We'se slugs.

    Airplane noises rise up.

G

MR. SERGEANT SMITH: Always wanted to do me somethin noble. Not somethin better than what I deserved—just somethin noble. Uh little bit uh noble somethin. Like what they did in thuh olden days. Like in thuh olden days in olden wars. Time for noble seems past. Time for somethin noble was yesterday. There usta be uh overlap of four hours. Hours in four when I'd say "today" and today it'd be. Them four hours usta happen together, now, they scatters theirselves all throughout thuh day. Usta be uh flap tuh slip through. Flaps gone shut. I saw that boy fallin out thuh sky. On fire. Thought he was uh star. Uh star that died years uhgo but was givin us light through thuh flap. Made uh wish. Opened up my arms— was wishin for my whole family. He fell on me. They say he was flying too close to thuh sun. They say I caught him but he fell. On me. They gived me uh Distinction. They set me apart. They say I caught him but he fell. He fell on me. I broked his fall. I saved his life. I ain't seen him since. No, boy—Duffy—uh—Muffy, Buffy, no, we ain't even turtles. Huh. We'se slugs. Slugs. Slugs.

    Airplane sounds rise up.

Tina Howe

☙

One Shoe Off

3724

•

One Shoe Off premiered May, 1993 at the Joseph Papp Public Theater/Anspacher Theater. It was produced by Second Stage Theatre and was directed by Carole Rothman. The cast was as follows, in order of appearance:

LEONARD	Jeffrey DeMunn
DINAH	Mary Beth Hurt
CLIO	Jennifer Tilly
TATE	Daniel Gerroll
PARKER	Brian Kerwin

PLACE
    A Greek revival farm house in upstate New York.

TIME
    Early November.

ACT I
    SCENE 1—early evening
    SCENE 2—a moment later
    SCENE 3—an hour and a half later

ACT II
    SCENE 1—an hour later
    SCENE 2—moments later

CHARACTERS
    LEONARD, Once an actor, 50s
    DINAH, His wife, a costume designer, late 40s
    TATE, An editor, 40s
    CLIO, His wife, an actress, 30s
    PARKER, A director, 50s

The ground floor of LEONARD *and* DINAH'S *Greek revival farmhouse in rural upstate New York. A slow moving disintegration is at work, things are starting to fragment and sink into the ground. Rooms are drifting into each other leaving mold-ings, door jams and window frames stranded. The staircase, uppermost walls and ceiling vanish in mid air. Grass, weeds and tangled shrubbery are encroaching in-doors. Saplings and full grown trees have taken root in the corners giving the place the look of a surreal ruin. It's early November around six in the evening.* LEONARD *and* DINAH *are in their bedroom trying to decide what to wear.* DINAH'S *in her slip and* LEONARD'S *in his underwear and a shirt. Both are barefoot. The bed and floor are littered with cast-off outfits. The wind howls outside.*

LEONARD: [*Holding up an old sports jacket.*] What do you think?

DINAH: [*Looking at herself.*] It's hopeless.

    The wind rattles the windows.

LEONARD: Fucking wind.

DINAH: …hopeless!

LEONARD: Just listen to it.

    They stand motionless, lost in their own worlds.

DINAH: *I don't know what to wear!*

LEONARD: One of these days it's going to blow the house down. That's all we need, to have the goddamned house flattened.

DINAH: Look at me!

LEONARD: You look great.

DINAH: But I'm still in my slip.

LEONARD: [*Nuzzling her.*] Mmmm, you're so warm!

DINAH: [*Resisting.*] Honey…?

LEONARD: You're like a little furnace.

DINAH: They'll be here any minute.

LEONARD: So?

DINAH: I've got to get dressed.

LEONARD: Who says?

DINAH: [*Heading into her closet.*] I hate this, I just hate it! [*She crashes around inside.*]

LEONARD: [*To himself.*] Forget it, she's out of here. [*He puts on the sports jacket.*]

DINAH: [*Emerges wearing a be-ribboned shepherdess dress.*] What do you think of this? [*She strikes shepherdess poses.*]

LEONARD: [*Engrossed in his jacket.*] I've always loved this jacket.

DINAH: [*Starts herding imaginary reindeer.*] On Dasher, on Dancer, on Cupid and Vixen…

LEONARD: [*Holding up two pairs of pants.*] Which pants do you think go better?

DINAH: On something and something and Donner and Blitzen!

LEONARD: The gray?

DINAH: Wait a minute, those are reindeer, not sheep! What's wrong with me?

LEONARD: Or the brown?

DINAH: Good old reindeer…

LEONARD: [*Switching them back and forth.*] What do you think? Helloooo? You there…

DINAH: What *is* it about reindeer?

LEONARD: Bo Peep?

DINAH: They're so…what's the word…? [*Pointing to the gray pants.*] Nice pants!

LEONARD: Yeah…?

DINAH: They look great, but then you look great in everything.

LEONARD: Hey, hey, what do you say? Forget the brown and go with the gray! [*He puts them on.*]

DINAH: Isolated, that's it.

LEONARD: *Isolated*…? What are you talking about?

DINAH: Reindeer. You never see them with other animals…[*Pause.*] *Oh honey, he's coming, he's finally coming!*

LEONARD: You're not planning to *wear* that, are you?

DINAH: After all this time.

LEONARD: [*Disappearing into his closet.*] And now for a tie…

DINAH: [*Catching a glimpse of herself in the mirror.*] God, look at me, I look like something out of the circus! [*She wriggles out of the dress.*]

LEONARD: Which do you think would go best? The maroon one you gave me for my birthday or the one with the crickets?

DINAH: You're so lucky, you always look great. It's not fair.

LEONARD: [*Emerging with several ties.*] Or how about the paisley one I spilled on?

DINAH: That's why I married you, come to think of it. You could wear a shower curtain and look good.

LEONARD: [*Holding it up.*] Then there's this striped number Po-Po gave me last Christmas.

DINAH: [*Putting her arms around him.*] Five hundred years later and you still take my breath away, it's uncanny!

LEONARD: Awww.

DINAH: [*Suddenly pulling away.*] He's going to cancel. You know Parker, he always cancels at the last minute.

LEONARD: I still don't understand why you had to invite those creeps over. Claribel and Thaddeus, or whatever their names are…

DINAH: Clio and Tate.

LEONARD: The guy's an ass hole.

DINAH: [*Heading back into her closet.*] How can you say that?

LEONARD: Easy, he's an ass hole.

DINAH: But you don't even know him.

LEONARD: So why did you invite him over?

DINAH: [*Emerges wearing a fringed cowgirl outfit.*] What do you think of this? [*She strikes cowgirl poses.*]

LEONARD: It's going to be a disaster.

DINAH: Remember how he used to pick you up and carry you around?

LEONARD: Who?

DINAH: Parker.

LEONARD: Parker...there's another one.

DINAH: I always loved that.

LEONARD: Dinah, what *is* that you're wearing?

DINAH: [*Whipping it off.*] I know, I know, don't even say it.

LEONARD: Stay in your slip!

        DINAH *screams with frustration.*

LEONARD: I mean what kind of name is that? Theo ..?

DINAH: Tate, *Tate!*

LEONARD: It's so pretentious, he sounds like an English butler. Can't you tell them not to come?

DINAH: [*Picking up a variety of cast-off outfits and holding them up to herself.*] No.

LEONARD: Why not?

DINAH: I just *can't!*

LEONARD: You know I don't like having people over.

DINAH: They're new here, they don't know a soul.

LEONARD: So?

DINAH: I'm trying to be nice.

LEONARD: What about being nice to me?

DINAH: What are you talking about? I *am* nice to you.

LEONARD: The evening's going to be a disaster.

DINAH: Don't worry, it will work out. Parker's cool, he can handle anything. He's a director.

        The wind howls again.

LEONARD: You hear that...?

DINAH: Remember "Cyrano"...?

LEONARD: Fucking wind!

DINAH: I've never seen so many crazy people on stage at the same time.

LEONARD: [*Sitting down on the bed.*] I can't take this anymore!

DINAH: What was the name of that love-sick actress who cried all the time?

LEONARD: Meg Benedict.

DINAH: *Eggs Benedict,* always in tears! Poor Parker, I've never seen anyone so besieged. Not that he seemed to mind. You know Parker and women.

LEONARD: Don't laugh, but I've always thought you had a thing for him.

DINAH: *Me?*

LEONARD: Your whole face lights up whenever you talk about him. I may be going out on a limb, but I've always suspected something once happened between you.

DINAH: Between Parker and *me?*

LEONARD: That's what I said. What is this, an echo chamber?

DINAH: Pull yourself together woman and *get dressed for God's sake!* [*She throws down the last of the cast-off outfits and heads back into her closet.*]

LEONARD: I'm right, aren't I? Something did happen between you.

DINAH: Between who?

LEONARD: Between Parker and you. Jesus...

DINAH: [*Emerging in a green cocktail dress dripping with beads and sequins.*] My lizard dress! What do you think? [*She darts her tongue in and out.*]

LEONARD: I think you need professional help.

DINAH: *I have nothing to wear!*

LEONARD: What do you mean, you have nothing to wear? Look at all this stuff.

DINAH: [*Taking the dress off.*] But it's not mine.

LEONARD: You designed it.

DINAH: For shows, not myself. I can't dress myself, I don't know who I am. It's tragic.

LEONARD: I wouldn't go that far.

DINAH: You're so lucky, you look great in everything.

LEONARD: I'm not lucky, I have shitty luck.

DINAH: You do have shitty luck.

LEONARD: The worst.

DINAH: Don't say that! It's just asking for trouble.

LEONARD: You're right, I'm sorry.

DINAH: If you go around saying you have the worst luck, you'll *get* the worst luck. I mean, think of all the terrible things that could happen. Colon cancer, Parkinson's disease...

LEONARD: I'm sorry, I'm sorry...

DINAH: A sudden stroke, cholera...

LEONARD: *Cholera...?*

DINAH: You ought to sink down to your knees and thank God for your blessings, I'm serious! [*Shutting her eyes and praying.*] Thank you, God, for giving us so much. Good health, beautiful children...

LEONARD: We only have *one* child, Po-Po. God, I wish we saw her more often. [*Wailing.*] Po-Po, Po-Po, I want Po-Po.

DINAH: Half an acre of land, exciting careers...

LEONARD: Speak for yourself, I haven't worked in eleven years.

DINAH: Food in the icebox, wonderful friends...

LEONARD: What friends? We don't have any friends.

DINAH: You're right, we *don't* have any friends, I forgot. [*Pause, she looks around the room.*] Jeez, look at the place...

LEONARD: We used to have friends. The minute the going gets tough, they're out of here. Take Parker for example, the man hasn't called in five years.

DINAH: Six.

LEONARD: You'd think we had the plague or something. Arrogant son of a bitch.

DINAH: It's a mess! [*She pulls a rake out from under the bed and starts raking drifts of fallen leaves into piles.*] Come on, give me a hand.

LEONARD: Who does he think he is, suddenly inviting himself over after six years of avoiding us? The prodigal son! [*He grabs another rake and joins her.*]

DINAH: [*Raking away.*] I can't keep up anymore.

LEONARD: It never occurs to him that *we* might have plans, that *we* have a life...

DINAH: Look at this, we're being buried alive!

LEONARD: You've been planning to invite our new neighbors over for months now, months. What are their names again?

DINAH: Clio and Tate.

LEONARD: They sound like a pair of goldfish. [*He stops raking and starts making fish faces.*]

DINAH: They *do* sound like a pair of goldfish, how funny. You're right, the evening's going to be a disaster, we don't even know these people. There's no telling how they'll get along with Parker or what kind of shape he'll be in when he gets here. *How did we get into this?* [*Pause.*] You know the trouble with us? We lack courage.

LEONARD: What are you talking about?

DINAH: Do you think we'll ever have to forage in the woods.

LEONARD: *Forage in the woods?*

DINAH: WE DON'T HAVE ANY MONEY!

LEONARD: Oh, that...

DINAH: Things are starting to get scary. [*She picks up a Chap Stick and starts reading the ingredients on the side.*] Petrolatums, Padimate, Lanolin, Isopropyl, Myristate, Cetyl Alcohol...

> *The telephone suddenly rings. Both race to get it.*

DINAH: It's probably Parker!   LEONARD: The telephone!
I'll get it, I'll get it!   I've got it, I've got it!

LEONARD: [*Gets there first and grabs the receiver.*] Hello?

DINAH: Who is it?

LEONARD: Hey, Parker, son of a bitch!

DINAH: I knew it.

LEONARD: You're still coming, aren't you?

DINAH: [*Trying to horn in.*] Hi, Parker...

LEONARD: Slow down, slow down, I can't understand a word you're saying.

DINAH: It's me, Dinah...

LEONARD: [*Struggling with DINAH.*] Easy, honey, easy! [*To PARKER.*] Where are you?...What...? I can't hear you over the sirens...

DINAH: [*Yelling into the phone.*] We can't wait to see you!

LEONARD: Dinah, please! [*Back to PARKER.*] I'm sorry, you were saying...

DINAH: Hey, I was in the middle of a...

LEONARD: [*To DINAH.*] Can't you see I'm talking?

DINAH: [*Imitating his rhythm.*] Nya, nya, nya, nya, nya nya!

LEONARD: [*To PARKER.*] Sorry, sorry, I'm back...What are all those sirens in the background?…Slow down, slow down, I can't hear you. [*Listening for a while.*] No…! Sweet Christ!

DINAH: [*Going ashen.*] What happened?

LEONARD: Oh no.

DINAH: *Is he all right?*

LEONARD: Stop, stop…

DINAH: *WHAT HAPPENED?*

LEONARD: Right, I understand…Hey, we'll do it another time…. Right, I will…You too. [LEONARD *gazes at the receiver.*]

DINAH: Is he OK?

LEONARD: [*Hanging up.*] Good-bye.

DINAH: *What happened?* [*Pause.*] Tell me! Honey please?

    LEONARD *covers his face with his hands.*

DINAH: I'm *dying!*

LEONARD: [*Recovered.*] I don't believe a word of it. Not. One. Word.

DINAH: [*Shaking him.*] A word of *what?*

LEONARD: What does he take me for? A half wit?

    DINAH *mews with frustration.*

LEONARD: The man's a congenital liar.

    DINAH's *mewing intensifies.*

LEONARD: A mobile home breaking loose from its trailer and careening all over the highway…? Three cars totalled and five people dead before it finally crashes into a truck in the opposite lane…. Get real!

DINAH: He's not coming?

LEONARD: He said it missed him by inches, *inches!*

DINAH: [*In a tiny voice.*] He's not coming?

LEONARD: Wreckage and twirled bodies everywhere….

DINAH: I knew he'd cancel, I knew it.

LEONARD: He stayed with the victims until help came, but now he's so shaken up he has to go home.

DINAH: He does it every time.

LEONARD: I've heard excuses to get out of evenings, but *this* takes the cake.

    There's a knocking at the door.

DINAH: It's Parker, he came after all!

LEONARD: [*Full of affection.*] That son of a bitch, he almost got us that time.

DINAH: [*Heads towards the door.*] I'll get it, I'll get it!

LEONARD: Coming, coming…

DINAH: [*Suddenly skids to a stop.*] Oh no, I'm still in my slip! [*She rushes back into the bedroom.*]

LEONARD: [*Skidding to a stop.*] Whoops, I don't have any shoes on! [*Calling.*] *Just a minute, just a minute!* [*He follows* DINAH *into the bedroom.*]

    The front door opens a crack, the wind howls.

CLIO: [*Offstage.*] Hello…?

TATE: [*Offstage.*] Anybody home…?

CLIO: [*Creeping into view.*] Are you there?

LEONARD: [*To* DINAH *from the bedroom.*] Flipper and Whosis!

DINAH: Oh no, I forgot all about them.

CLIO: [*Walking into the living room.*] Yoo hoo, we're here!

BLACKOUT

I.2

A split second later. CLIO *and* TATE *come creeping into the living room. She's breath-takingly beautiful, dressed in actressy clothes. He's rugged looking, wearing casual weekend gear. Because they've left the front door open, the wind howls louder than ever.* DINAH *and* LEONARD *are still in their bedroom.*

TATE: [*Calling.*] Louis…?

CLIO: [*Correcting him in a whisper.*] Lawrence.

TATE: [*Whispering back.*] Who *are* these people, anyway?

CLIO: Lawrence and Diana.

TATE: How did you get us into this?

CLIO: Or is it Dianne?

TATE: You know I don't like going out on weekends.

CLIO: [*In a sing-song.*] Hellooooo…? It's us…

TATE: [*Pulling on her arm.*] Come on, let's get out of here while we've still got a chance.

CLIO: [*Calling.*] Lawrence…? Dianne…? [*To* TATE.] No, I was right the first time, it's Diana. Or is it Delilah? Oh God…

TATE: [*Pulling harder.*] I want to go home, I don't like this.

CLIO: You don't like anything.

TATE: I don't like going out on weekends, you know that. It's my one chance to get caught up on my work.

CLIO: Work, work, work…Can't you ever take a break?

TATE: [*Turning to go.*] You can stay if you want, but I'm leaving.

CLIO: [*Taking in the room.*] Holy mackerel…

LEONARD: [*Suddenly comes rushing into the room.*] Come in, come in…

TATE: [*Skids to a stop under his breath.*] Shit!

CLIO: This is amazing!

LEONARD: We were just…

TATE: Too late!

LEONARD: [*Pumps* TATE's *hand.*] Tad!

TATE: Louis!

CLIO: [*Correcting* TATE.] Lawrence.

LEONARD: [*Correcting* CLIO.] Leonard.

CLIO: [*Correcting* LEONARD.] Tate!

LEONARD: [*Pumps* CLIO's *hand.*] Clara!

TATE: [*Correcting* LEONARD.] Clio!

LEONARD: Whoops!

TATE: [*Softly to* CLIO.] Thanks a lot, I'll remember his.

CLIO: I'm sure you will.

LEONARD: So glad you could make it. Come in, come in. Let me take your coats.
    They overwhelm him with coats, mufflers, hats and mittens.

LEONARD: [*Dropping and retrieving them.*] Whoops...sorry, I've got it, I've got
    it...Good old wintertime...nothing like it...Whoops, there we go...[*He exits trailing their outerwear after him.*]

TATE: Well, this is quite some place...

CLIO: It's wild.

TATE: Great trees.

LEONARD: Please!

CLIO: Just wild!

TATE: How do you get them to grow indoors?

LEONARD: [*Returning.*] You mean, how do you get them to stay *outdoors?!*

CLIO: It's such a great idea.
    Silence.

LEONARD: [*Rubbing his hands together.*] So...?
    The wind howls with rising fury.

TATE: Oh sorry, I'm afraid we forgot to shut the ding. [*He rushes over to it and slams it
    shut.*]

CLIO: [*Under her breath to* TATE.] The *door!*

TATE: That's what I said.

CLIO: No, you said, the ding...

TATE: The *ding?*

CLIO: Never mind. [*To* LEONARD.] What *is* it with the wind around here...?

LEONARD: Don't get me started.

CLIO: I've never heard anything like it.
    TATE *opens the door again.*

CLIO: Toto, what are you...?

TATE: [*Slams and opens it obsessively, finally slamming it for good.*] There we go, I just
    wanted to make sure it was shut tight.

CLIO: Well, we all have our little...

TATE: Why waste precious heat if you don't have to?
    Silence.
    DINAH *pokes her head in the room. She's still in her slip.*

CLIO: Dianne!

TATE: Delilah!

LEONARD: [*In a whisper.*] You're still in your slip.

CLIO: [*Whispering to* TATE.] What's her name?

TATE: [*Whispering back.*] How should I know?

LEONARD: [*Whispering to* CLIO.] Dinah.

CLIO *and* TATE: DINAH!

DINAH: [*Trying to enter the room but stay hidden at the same time.*] Don't pay any attention to me...

TATE: [*Starts singing.*] "Someone's in the kitchen with Dinah, someone's in the kitchen, I know ow ow ow...'

CLIO *and* TATE: "Someone's in the kitchen with Dinah strumming on the old banjo. They're strumming fee, fi, diddlio..."

DINAH: I just wanted to see what everyone was wearing. [*To* CLIO.] Ohh, what a great dress.

CLIO: What, this old thing?

DINAH: [*Dashing out of the room.*] I'll be right back.

CLIO: I've had it for years.

LEONARD: [*To* DINAH.] Hey, where are you going?

TATE: Stay in your slip, you look great.

LEONARD: She does look great, doesn't she? *Dinah come back!*
            Silence.

CLIO: It's so nice to finally meet you.

TATE: So...how long have you lived here?

LEONARD: [*Calling after* DINAH.] Honey...?!

CLIO: We've been waving at each other for months now.

LEONARD: Don't mind her, she has a terrible time dressing herself.

CLIO: Don't we all.

TATE: Speak for yourself.

CLIO: I just did.

TATE: Well, well, aren't we in good form this evening.
            Silence.

LEONARD: [*Calling in a strangled voice.*] Dinah, please!

DINAH: [*Enters dressed in a spectacular toga.*] You called?

LEONARD:	CLIO:	TATE:
[*Covers his eyes and moans..*]	Holy Moses!	[*Does a wolf whistle.*]

DINAH: "Julius Caesar." It's too much, isn't it?

CLIO: Look at you!

LEONARD: Honey, this is upstate New York, not the Roman senate.

CLIO: That's incredible...

DINAH: [*Turns to go.*] I *knew* it was too much.

CLIO: Incredible!

LEONARD: [*Grabbing her arm.*] Don't go!

CLIO: Look, Zoo-Zoo.

TATE: I see, I see.

CLIO: Where did you get that?

LEONARD: She made it.

DINAH: [*Trying to pull away.*] I've got to change.

LEONARD: Don't leave me again!

TATE: [*To* DINAH.] You made it?

DINAH: [*Struggling with him.*] Leonard...?

TATE: *Why?*

LEONARD: Because she's a costume designer.

CLIO: Of course! I knew your name was familiar!

TATE: Right, right.

CLIO: [*Pressing* DINAH's *hands.*] You're wonderful!

DINAH: Why, thank you.

TATE: Clio's an actress.

DINAH: No kidding.

TATE: On stage and off.

CLIO: [*To* TATE.] What's that supposed to mean?

TATE: If the shoe fits, eat it.

     A pause as everyone looks at TATE.

DINAH: Leonard's an actor too.

CLIO: No!

LEONARD: Was an actor.

DINAH: [*To* LEONARD.] Now, now...

CLIO: I didn't know that.

LEONARD: *Fucking bastards!*

CLIO: [*To* TATE.] Did you know he was an actor?

TATE: I had no idea.

LEONARD: *Sons of bitches!*

DINAH: He was the best, the best.

CLIO: Wow, what were you in?

LEONARD: You wouldn't remember it was so long ago.

DINAH: "Cyrano," "Richard the Second," "Uncle Vanya"...

LEONARD: *Stupid ass holes!*

DINAH: [*Putting her hand on his arm.*] Honey...?

LEONARD: [*Whirling away from her.*] *Don't touch me!*

     An awful silence.

DINAH: He also keeps bees.

CLIO *and* TATE: Bees...?

LEONARD: [*World weary.*] Dinah...?!

TATE: I love bees!

CLIO: I'm terrified of bees!

DINAH: Leonard's a naturalist.

LEONARD: I thought I was a fatalist.

TATE: My brother keeps bees.

DINAH: He has over five thousand.

CLIO: [*Rushing toward the door.*] I'm getting out of here!

LEONARD: They're not in the house, I keep them out back.

DINAH: We'll have to give you some of our honey, it's the best in the area. Leonard markets it all over the state.

LEONARD: Bees are highly civilized, they put us to shame.

TATE: Bees are the best.

LEONARD: They *are* the best!

DINAH: Well, they certainly keep Leonard busy.

CLIO: [*Hands over her ears.*] I don't want to hear.

LEONARD: I could watch them all day.

DINAH: And he often does.

LEONARD: Well, better bee keeping than acting, it's a lot safer.

TATE: I've never understood the impulse to perform.

DINAH: Me either.

TATE: It's always seemed slightly perverse. Oh well, one man's meat is another man's pistol.

CLIO: Poison.

TATE: That's what I said.

CLIO: No, you said "pistol."

> *The wind suddenly blows the front door open with a blast. The four freeze in terror.* CLIO *rushes to* TATE *who puts his arms around her.* DINAH *stands rooted to the spot, hand over her heart.* LEONARD *sways on his feet. Then just as suddenly the wind dies down.* CLIO *gasps,* TATE *releases a long breath.* LEONARD *and* DINAH *shudder.*

CLIO: What was that?

TATE: Wee Willie Winkie.

DINAH *and* LEONARD: Wee Willie Winkie?

LEONARD: God, there's a name I haven't heard in ages.

TATE: "Wee Willie Winkie runs through the town,
Upstairs and downstairs, in his nightgown;
Rapping at the window, crying through the lock,
'Are the children in their beds? It's almost eight o'clock.'"

> *They all look at* TATE. *An uncomfortable silence.*

DINAH: [*To* LEONARD.] So, how about shutting the door?

LEONARD: Right, right. [*He moves to the door.*]

TATE: [*Joins him.*] Here, let me give you a hand.

> *They hurl themselves against the door, slamming it shut.*

TATE: "Diddle diddle dumpling, my son John, went to bed with his trousers on…"

LEONARD: So, what would everybody like to drink? We've got beer, wine, vodka…

TATE: "One shoe off and one shoe on,
Diddle Diddle Dumpling, that's my John."

DINAH: Mineral water, ginger ale, orange juice…

TATE: Poised for the worst.

> *Silence, then to* TATE.

LEONARD: Well, what's *your* line of work?   DINAH: So, what do you do, Tate?

[*To* DINAH.] Whoops, after you...
    Pause.

LEONARD: Sorry, I was just wondering what *you*...
    Pause.

[*To* LEONARD.] Oh, sorry, sorry...

DINAH: So, tell us what you...
    Whoops...

CLIO: Tell them what you do, Dee-Dee!

TATE: Guess.

DINAH: Let's see...

LEONARD: Um.... you write nursery rhymes.

TATE: Close, close...

DINAH: You illustrate nursery rhymes.

TATE: You're getting warmer...

LEONARD: You *are* a nursery rhyme.

TATE: Bingo!

CLIO: He's an editor.

TATE: You got it! "The girl in the lane, that couldn't speak plain, cried, 'Gobble, gobble gobble'"...

LEONARD: And where do you do this editing?

CLIO: Raven Books.

LEONARD: [*Impressed.*] Raven Books? Wow, you don't mess around!

TATE: "The man on the hill that couldn't stand still,
    Went 'hobble, hobble, hobble.'"

CLIO: [*Putting on a funny voice.*] Hobble hobble, wiggle wobble!

DINAH: She sounds just like Enid Brill.

CLIO: Enid Brill?

DINAH: The woman who gallops around the countryside in her nightgown.

CLIO: *Her!*

LEONARD: [*Imitating her.*] She talks through her nose.

CLIO: We see her every morning.

LEONARD: She's certifiable.

DINAH: She's my idol.

LEONARD: Her husband's a crop duster. You'll hear him in the spring. [*He mimes a low-flying plane.*]

DINAH: They have eight children.

CLIO: She whips that horse as if her life depends on it.

DINAH: It does, she's fearless.
    LEONARD's *crop dusting intensifies.*

DINAH: Wait 'til you've lived here a few more years, you'll understand. Easy, Leonard, easy...

LEONARD: [*Recovering.*] Sorry, sorry.

DINAH: You know what she dressed up as at Halloween? You'll never guess. [*Pause.*] A sieve.

CLIO *and* TATE: A sieve?!

DINAH: She pulled the screen out of her back door, molded it over her head in a dome and stuck a broom handle between her legs. The year before she went as a rubber glove. Don't even ask.

LEONARD: Poor Enid Brill.

DINAH: There but for the grace of God go I. Well, I hope everybody likes carrots. [*She heads into the kitchen.*]

LEONARD: So, what would you like to drink? We've got beer, wine, vodka, mineral water, ginger ale, orange juice…

TATE: Clee-Clee?

CLIO: I'll have some white wine if you've got it.

LEONARD: You're on. And you, Todd?

TATE: Vodka sounds good.

CLIO: [*Correcting* LEONARD.] Tate, *Tate!*

LEONARD: [*Fixing the drinks.*] Coming right up.

DINAH: [*Enters carrying a mountain of carrots with their tops still on.*] I'm back, miss me?

CLIO: Holy Moses…

TATE: Look at all those chariots!

CLIO: Where on earth did you…?

DINAH: Help yourselves, I'm trying to get rid of them.

> CLIO *and* TATE *gingerly take one.*

DINAH: They grow all over the house. In the kitchen, the den, the upstairs bathroom…Dig in, dig in!

> CLIO *and* TATE *take a tentative bite.*

CLIO: Hey, these are delicious!

TATE: They're so sweet!

> *They crunch in tandem.*

DINAH: [*Offering the tray again.*] Take more, take more.

> *They do.*

LEONARD: You should have tasted the acorn squash from our bedroom last year…[*Passing out the drinks.*] Chloe? Ted?

CLIO: [*Still engrossed with her carrot.*] Ohhhhh…these are fabulous! [*To* LEONARD.] Oh thanks…

TATE: Mmmmmm…oooooohhhh…[*To* LEONARD.] Much obliged. [*More happy crunching.*]

DINAH: Well, I hope you're in the mood for turkey.

TATE: Where did you grow that? Down in the basement with the cranboobies? [*He emits a hoot of laughter.*]

DINAH: Whenever we have guests, I do Thanksgiving with all the trimmings. It's the only meal I'm really good at.

CLIO: [*Reaching for the platter of carrots.*] More, more…

DINAH: Fall, winter, spring, summer, out comes the Butterball and Stove Top stuffing.

CLIO: Tate does Thanksgiving at our house.

LEONARD: Butterball and Stove Top all the way! We love processed food.

CLIO: He's a great cook. We're talking corn chowder, oyster stuffing, zucchini pilaf…We can't move for weeks, weeks!

DINAH: An old friend was going to join us tonight, but he canceled at the last minute.

LEONARD: He came up with this incredible cock and bull story about a mobile home running amok on the highway…

TATE: [To CLIO.] Well, you do Christmas, fair is fair. That is, when you're home.

LEONARD: I mean, people aren't mowed down by houses.

DINAH: They're only buried by them.

CLIO: [To TATE.] I've never missed a Christmas with you, never!

LEONARD: What does he take us for, total idiots?

CLIO: [To TATE.] When have I ever missed a Christmas with you?

DINAH: You'd think we'd learn. He sets us up and lets us down…

TATE: Last year.

DINAH: Sets us up and lets us down.

CLIO: My plane was grounded, I was stuck in the airport.

DINAH: Six years and not a word.

TATE: For a week?

DINAH: The trick is not to let it get you, right?

CLIO: [To TATE.] As if you'd notice, you're so wrapped in your goddamned editing.

TATE: Now just one minute…

CLIO: Words, words, words…and they're not even your own.

TATE: Nice Click, very nice.

DINAH: Keep your hand on the tiller and your back to the wind! [She picks up a nearby bottle of Worcestershire sauce and reads the list of ingredients on the side.] "Water, vinegar, molasses, sugar, anchovies, tamarinds, hydrolyzed soy protein, onions, salt, garlic, eschalots, spices and flavorings!" [She slams the bottle back down.]

    Silence. CLIO and TATE resume munching on their carrots.

DINAH: [Gazing at CLIO.] You are so beautiful.

CLIO: Why, thank you.

DINAH: Your skin…[Reaching out to touch it.] May I?

CLIO: Be my guest.

DINAH: [Caressing her cheek.] Ohhhh…it's so soft. Feel, Leonard, feel…

    LEONARD hesitates.

CLIO: Go ahead, it's all right.

LEONARD: [Touching her cheek.] Mmmmmm…

DINAH: Isn't it soft?

LEONARD: Not as soft as yours.

CLIO and TATE: Awww…

LEONARD: I think you have the softest skin in the world.

CLIO and TATE: Awwwww….

DINAH: It's like burlap.

TATE: [Reaching to touch DINAH's face.] Burlap ..?!

DINAH: [*Whirling away from him.*] Please?!

   Silence. The phone suddenly rings, everyone jumps.

LEONARD: DINAH:

   [*Getting there first.*] I've got it, I've got it!   [*Racing to get it.*] I'll get it, I'll get it!

LEONARD: [*Picking up the receiver.*] Hello?

DINAH: [*Trying to wedge in on him.*] Who is it, who is it?

LEONARD: [*Into the phone.*] Parker!

DINAH: Parker…?!

LEONARD: Um hmmm…um hmmm…yeah…yeah…Wow, that's great! You sure you remember the way?…OK twenty minutes. See ya. Bye. [*He hangs up. To* DINAH.] He's coming.

CLIO: Who?

LEONARD *and* DINAH: Parker Bliss.

CLIO: *Parker Bliss?*

TATE: The director?

DINAH: You know him?

CLIO: [*To* LEONARD *and* DINAH.] You know Parker Bliss?

LEONARD: He's one of our oldest friends.

TATE: What was the name of that terrifying movie he just made?

DINAH: We've known him forever.

TATE: You know, the one based on the true story about the couple that murdered their children.

LEONARD, DINAH *and* CLIO: "Lullabye and Goodnight."

TATE: "Lullabye and Goodnight"!

CLIO: It was incredible!

TATE: I couldn't sleep for weeks.

DINAH: Us either.

CLIO: The performances he got out of those children. They were just toddlers.

DINAH: Parker's always been great with kids.

LEONARD: Except his own.

CLIO: That scene where their mother dressed them in party clothes before she threw them in the freezer…

TATE: [*Hands over his ears.*] Don't, don't.

CLIO: The look on that little girl's face as her mother leaned down and folded the cuffs of her tiny white socks, just so…

TATE: She knew what was going to happen.

DINAH: She knew.

ALL: She knew.

TATE: I couldn't go near our freezer for months.

LEONARD: When Parker called this morning and said he was going to be in our neck of the woods, we insisted he drop by.

DINAH: We figured you wouldn't mind if he joined us.

CLIO: *Wouldn't mind?* I've always wanted to meet him.

DINAH: But then he called right before you came, claiming a mobile home had broken loose from its trailer on his way up.

LEONARD: It totaled three cars and killed five people before it finally crashed into a truck on the opposite lane.

CLIO *and* TATE: Oh no!

DINAH: It missed him by inches.

LEONARD: Please! You can't trust a word the man says.

TATE: [*With meaning.*] "Jack and Jill went up the hill, to fetch a pail of water. Jack fell down and broke his crown, and Jill came tumbling after."

CLIO: Don't mind him, he's editing a new annotated *Mother Goose.*

TATE: [*With brio.*] "Then up Jack got and off did trot as fast as he could caper. To old Dame Dob, who patched his nob with vinegar and brown paper."

CLIO: Ahh Tate, ever the brilliant mind.

DINAH: Well, the important thing is he's coming.

CLIO: [*Leaning into* TATE.] Actually, you *do* have a brilliant mind, Tic-Tac.

TATE: [*To* CLIO.] Why thank you, Cliquot.

DINAH: He's coming, he's coming!

LEONARD: [*To* DINAH.] I'll believe it when I see it.

DINAH: [*Rises, freezing.*] God, look at me! I've got to change!

BLACKOUT

I.3

An hour and a half later, PARKER *still hasn't shown up.* DINAH's *slumped in a chair wearing an old-fashioned cotillion dress.* LEONARD's *pacing by the door. He keeps checking his watch.* CLIO *and* TATE *are asleep on the sofa, a mound of carrot tops at their feet. Several moments pass.*

LEONARD: 9:41…

DINAH: Honey, please.

LEONARD: [*Continuing to pace.*] 9:42.

DINAH: You're driving me crazy!

LEONARD: An hour and forty minutes late!

DINAH: Not so loud, you'll wake them up.

LEONARD: *Manipulative son of a bitch!*

     CLIO *groans and stirs.*

DINAH: Gently, gently…

LEONARD: [*In a strangled whisper.*] Who the hell does he think he is?

DINAH: He probably got lost.

LEONARD: Tell me another one.

DINAH: He'll show up.

LEONARD: [*Resumes pacing, looks at his watch.*] 9:43!

DINAH: [*Suddenly rises.*] *I can't take this anymore!*
> CLIO *and* TATE *stir in their sleep.*
LEONARD: [*As if seeing her for the first time.*] Honey, what *is* that you're wearing?
DINAH: Amanda Wingfield, the dinner party scene with the Gentleman Caller.
LEONARD: Let me out of here!
DINAH: [*Striking flirty poses.*] What do you think?
LEONARD: This is a mad house.
DINAH: Be honest, I can take it.
LEONARD: I want to go home.
DINAH: You *are* home. [*Dashing out the room.*] Hang on, I'll be right back.
LEONARD: Where are you going?
DINAH: To change.
LEONARD: Not again!
DINAH: I'll just be a sec.
LEONARD: This is getting perverse.
DINAH: [*From the bedroom.*] What did you say?
LEONARD: I SAID, THIS IS GETTING PERVERSE!
> TATE *and* CLIO *wake like a shot.*
TATE: Perverse? Who…? Where…?
CLIO: Did somebody say "perverse"?
LEONARD: [*Waving to them.*] Welcome back to the land of the living.
CLIO: [*Groggy.*] Ohh, where am I?
LEONARD: Still waiting for Parker.
> *There's a loud crash from the bedroom.*
CLIO: [*Jumping.*] What was that?
LEONARD: Easy, Dinah, easy…
TATE: [*Looking at his watch.*] Good God, look at the time.
> *A series of crashes from the bedroom.*
DINAH: [*From the bedroom.*] It's all right, it's all right, not to worry…
LEONARD: Poor Dinah, getting dressed always throws her into a tailspin. It's one of life's ironies—the costume designer who doesn't know what to wear.
> DINAH *enters swathed in a jingling harem outfit with pointy gold shoes.*
> LEONARD *covers his eyes and groans.*
DINAH: [*Brandishing a scarf.*] "Peer Gynt." What do you think?
CLIO: Heaven, *heaven!*
TATE: What happened to Amanda Wingfield?
CLIO: [*Grabbing the scarf.*] I want it!
TATE: I've always been a sucker for faded Southern belles.
LEONARD: [*Peeking at* DINAH *between his fingers.*] Sweetheart…?
DINAH: God, look at it in here! [*She grabs a nearby rake and starts raking the carrot tops.*]
LEONARD: We need to have a little talk.
> DINAH *keeps raking as* CLIO *launches into a sexy belly dance.*

TATE: Clee-Clee, this isn't the Casbah!

> CLIO *dances with rising abandon. Everyone watches, enthralled. Suddenly there's a loud knock on the door. They all jump.*

DINAH:	LEONARD:	CLIO:	TATE:
He's here,	*Well, what*	*It's him!*	*At last!*
he's here!	*do you know?*		

DINAH: [*Getting there first.*] I'll get it,   LEONARD: [*Two steps behind.*] I've got
I'll get it!   it, I've got it!

> PARKER *stomps in, shaking a blizzard of snow off his head and shoulders. He wears work shoes and a parka with an enormous fur-lined hood. He scoops* DINAH *up in his arms and whirls her around in circles.*

PARKER: Dinah, Dinah...

DINAH: [*Clinging to him.*] Oh Parker...

PARKER: Sorry I'm so late, I got lost.

CLIO: [*Gazing at him in raptures.*] Parker Bliss...

TATE: It's snowing?

LEONARD: HEY, PARKER...!

TATE: When did it start snowing?

CLIO: I'm going to die.

PARKER: [*Showering her face with kisses.*] Threads, Threads...!

LEONARD: [*Trying to horn in.*] YOU OLD SON OF A BITCH!

DINAH: I've missed you so!

PARKER: [*Thrusts* DINAH *out at arms' length.*] Hey, sweet thing, let me get a good look at you!

DINAH: [*Reaching for him.*] Come back, come back!

PARKER: [*Pointing at her dress.*] "Peer Gynt," the Olympic Theater!

DINAH: You got it!

LEONARD: "Anitra, oh thou true daughter of Eve, how can I refuse you? I am but a man."

PARKER: [*Bursts out laughing, scooping* DINAH *back into his arms.*] You're too much, too much!

LEONARD: [*To* CLIO.] Like I said, we've done a lot of shows together—Washington, Philadelphia, New York...

TATE: [*Goes to the door and gazes out.*] Boy, look at it come down.

CLIO: [*Shivering.*] Oooh, shut the door, Robert, that wind is wicked!

TATE: Robert? Who's Robert?

> PARKER *squeezes* DINAH *tighter and roars.*

CLIO: [*All innocence.*] Robert?

TATE: You just said, "Shut the door, Robert, that wind is wicked."

CLIO: I did?

TATE: As clear as a bell.

CLIO: You've lost your mind.

TATE: Not my mind, just my bearings. [*He plunges out the door.*]

CLIO: [*Starts to follow him.*] Toto, where are you going? It's freezing out there!

DINAH: [*To PARKER.*] Hold me, hold me.

PARKER: [*Squeezing her tight.*] It's been so long.

DINAH: [*Barely audible.*] My dearest, my darling…

CLIO: [*Re-entering the room.*] Don't mind him.

LEONARD: [*Dancing around them.*] When do I get my turn? I want my turn!

PARKER: [*Lifting DINAH off her feet.*] God, I love this woman!

LEONARD: [*Trying to pull PARKER and DINAH apart.*] No fair, no fair! What about me?

PARKER: [*Finally catches LEONARD's eye and starts laughing.*] Hey Handsome, how are the bees?

LEONARD: *Busy!*

PARKER: Come on, get over here.

> *They roar and pummel each other.*

PARKER: [*Grabs LEONARD in a bear hug and kisses him square on the lips.*] MAA! [*Holding him at arms' length, laughing.*] Look at you, you crazy son of a bitch!

LEONARD: I *am* a crazy son of a bitch, aren't I?

PARKER: [*Imitating him.*] "I *am* a crazy son of a bitch, aren't I?" Jesus Christ, you never change.

> *They start air boxing.*

DINAH: [*To CLIO.*] Men…

CLIO: Please!

DINAH: They're such little boys.

CLIO: You should see Tate when he gets together with his friend Walter. Forget it!

DINAH: Where *is* Tate, by the way?

CLIO: *Who knows!*

> There's a sudden banging on the front door. LEONARD *and* PARKER *stop air boxing.*

DINAH: Goodness, who can that be?

CLIO: Beats me.

LEONARD: [*Heading toward the door.*] Well, there's one way to find out.

DINAH: Careful now, there are all kinds of maniacs out there.

> *The knocking gets louder. No one moves.*

PARKER: I'll get it. Let me. [*He opens the door.*]

> TATE *stands shivering on the threshold, a light mantle of snow dusting his head and shoulders.*

PARKER: Yes, may I help you?

TATE: Ohhhhh, it's freezing out there!

LEONARD: Todd!

CLIO: Zum-Zum!

DINAH: Tate!

CLIO: There you are!

DINAH: Where have you been?

TATE: I just stepped out for a fresh of breath air.

LEONARD: Come in, come in.

TATE: [*Entering, stomping snow off his feet.*] Oooohhhh!

LEONARD: [*Introducing him to* PARKER.] Todd, Parker. Parker, Todd…

TATE: [*Extending his hand.*] Parker!

PARKER: [*Shaking it.*] Todd!

CLIO: [*Touching* PARKER's *arm.*] Tate!

PARKER: [*Finally seeing her.*] You!

CLIO: [*Staring back.*] Parker Bliss…

PARKER: Clio Hands…

DINAH: You know each other?

PARKER: *I don't believe it!*

CLIO: I'm speechless.

PARKER: I adore you!

      Silence as they gape at each other.

DINAH: When did you meet?

PARKER: We've never met. [*Takes her hand and kisses it.*]

DINAH: Oh.

LEONARD: [*Ushering* PARKER *into the living room.*] Well, come on in and stay awhile. Take off your parka, Parker. [*He laughs at his cleverness.*]

PARKER: [*Rooted to the spot.*] Clio Hands…

TATE: [*Strides over to her, pulling her close.*] Hi, Coco.

PARKER: I must be dreaming.

CLIO: Hi, Totes.

TATE: How're you doing?

CLIO: Fine, fine…

PARKER: [*To* LEONARD *and* DINAH.] Didn't you see "Tiger Bright"?

LEONARD *and* DINAH: "Tiger Bright"?

TATE: [*Under his breath.*] Here we go…

PARKER: The movie.

LEONARD: [*To* CLIO.] You were in "Tiger Bright"?

PARKER: She was a vision…

LEONARD: I didn't know that.

PARKER: A vision.

DINAH: Gosh.

LEONARD: So, you're a movie star?

CLIO: Hardly, it was my first film.

PARKER: That scene where you danced with the dwarf…. [*He groans.*] She smiled this smile…her lips started to tremble, or should I say melt…No one in the theater could breathe. [*Brushing her breast.*] It was as if she'd handed us her soul.

TATE: [*Quickly pulling her away from* PARKER.] That's my Clicker.

      CLIO *walks away from them both.*

DINAH: Well…

Silence.

DINAH: And how's Patsy these days?

LEONARD: Yeah, how *is* Patsy?

CLIO: Patsy?

DINAH: His wife.

CLIO: Oh.

PARKER: Fine.

DINAH: I love Patsy.

PARKER: Everyone loves Patsy.

DINAH: Well, she's a great woman.

PARKER: Tell me about it.

Silence.

LEONARD: Come on, take off your coat and stay a while.

PARKER *takes it off, revealing a large dried blood stain on his shirt. everyone screams.*

LEONARD:	DINAH:	CLIO:	TATE:
Jesus Christ!	Parker?!	Blood!	Are you all right?!

LEONARD: You were telling the truth!

DINAH: A mobile home *did* run wild!

TATE: Holy shit!

CLIO: [*Covers her eyes and sways.*] Oh God!

PARKER *collapses in a chair, burying his face in his hands.*

DINAH: [*Rushing over to him.*] Oh Parker…

LEONARD: Son of a bitch…

DINAH: Baby, baby…

CLIO: [*Sinking into the sofa.*] I'm going to faint.

LEONARD: I thought you made it up.

DINAH: [*To* PARKER.] Speak to me.

LEONARD: I'm stunned.

CLIO *faints.*

TATE: [*Rushing over to her.*] Darling…

DINAH: [*To* PARKER.] Say something!

LEONARD: He was telling the truth all along.

TATE: Can you hear me?

LEONARD: You could knock me over with a feather.

CLIO *comes to and groans.*

TATE: [*Grabbing her hands.*] My beauty, my sweet…

CLIO: Whoooooo….

TATE: What happened?

DINAH: [*Unbuttoning* PARKER's *shirt.*] Here, let's get you out of this.

DINAH *eases it off him. The blood has seeped through to his undershirt.*

DINAH:	CLIO:	LEONARD:	TATE:
Uughhh!	More blood!	Jesus Christ!	Oh no…!

CLIO *passes out again as* DINAH *helps* PARKER *off with his undershirt. Traces of blood linger on his chest. More horrified gasps.*

DINAH: Baby, baby, does it hurt?

PARKER: It's not my blood.

     DINAH *recoils from him with a groan.*

LEONARD: Whose is it?

TATE: [*To* CLIO.] Speak to me!

PARKER: It's from the ten-year-old boy who died in my arms.

LEONARD: Oh God!

CLIO: [*Coming to.*] Where am I?

TATE: [*To* CLIO.] Right here, safe and sound with me.

PARKER: His cat was sliced in half by the thing.

DINAH: Awful, awful…

PARKER: It was the strangest sight…seeing this *house* plowing down the highway.

LEONARD: He's cold, Dine, get him something to put on.

DINAH: Right, right…[*She exits.*]

PARKER: It was a split level ranch with redwood siding.

TATE: He's in shock.

PARKER: I saw a woman through the window. She was doing the dishes in the kitchen sink, washing this huge enamel pot. You know, one of those black and white speckled things you cook corn or lobsters in…She was scrubbing it with this yellow brush…I've never seen such a color. It was that neon yellow students underline textbooks with—only brighter. But how could that be? People don't live in those giant mobile homes when they're being transported, and they certainly don't do the dishes while they're moving. Yet I saw her as clear as day…There was no sign of her after the crash, though…Strange…It's a miracle more people weren't killed when you stop to think about it. A fifty-ton split level ranch ricocheting across a four lane highway…It's a wonder any of us escaped.

DINAH: [*Returning with an assortment of kingly robes and doublets.*] Here, I brought you some things from my collection.

PARKER: Eeeny, meeny, miney, moe.

LEONARD: Dinah, this isn't a play.

    Silence.

CLIO: [*To* DINAH.] Didn't you do the costumes for that wonderful "Hedda Gabler" we saw at The New York City Festival a few years ago?

TATE: I remember that, lots of starched linen and high button shoes.

DINAH: You saw it?

CLIO: We see everything at The Festival.

LEONARD: She also works at Baltimore Rep, the Boston Theatre Company, Altered Stages…

CLIO: You're a busy woman.

DINAH: A frantic woman!

PARKER: Ohhh, I'm freezing. [*Reaching for a robe.*] Let me have one of those, would you?

DINAH: [*Handing him one.*] God, what *was* that from?

CLIO: Ohh, it looks great.

PARKER: Yeah?

DINAH: "Pericles"? "Coriolanus"? [*Adjusting the shoulders.*] It fits perfectly.

CLIO: Well, the woman's a brilliant designer.

PARKER: Hear, hear.

DINAH: Uuugh!

LEONARD: "Richard the Second."

DINAH: "Richard the Second"!

CLIO: I love that play.

PARKER: It's the best, the best.

LEONARD: "For God's sake let us sit upon the ground,
And tell sad stories of the death of kings..."

DINAH: Talk about ancient history...

PARKER: Sold out every night.

LEONARD: "How some have been deposed, some slain in war,
Some haunted by the ghosts they have deposed,
Some poisoned by their wives, some sleeping killed..."

DINAH: You should have seen Leonard.

LEONARD: "All murdered..."

DINAH: He was so handsome, he looked like a god.

CLIO: He still does.

DINAH: [*To* LEONARD.] You hear that?

CLIO: You've got great bones.

PARKER: Why do you think I call you Handsome, Handsome?

DINAH: Ahhh, the lure of beauty.

TATE: The lure of beauty...

DINAH: It's a killer, a killer.

LEONARD: [*Grabbing a robe and putting it on.*]
"...for within the hollow crown,
That rounds the mortal temples of a king,
Keeps Death his court; and there the antic sits,
Scoffing his state and grinning at his pomp..."

PARKER: [*Unsheathes an imaginary sword and starts doing* Henry v.] "Once more into the breach, dear friends, once more, or close the wall with our English dead!..."

LEONARD: "Henry the Fifth!"

CLIO: Go for it!

LEONARD: [*Entering into the spirit.*] "But when the blast of war blows in our ears, then imitate the action of the tiger: Stiffen the sinews, summon up the blood...[*He pauses, unsure of the words.*]

DINAH: Disguise...

LEONARD: Disguise fair nature with hard-favored rage..."

PARKER: "Cry havoc and let loose the dogs of war!" [*He links arms with* LEONARD *and starts marching around the room with him.*] Hut, two, three, four; hut, two, three four…

DINAH: And they're off—The March of the Kings!

PARKER *and* LEONARD: Hut, two, three, four; hut, two, three four…

PARKER *toots an imaginary trumpet and* LEONARD *mimes playing a xylophone.*

DINAH: Don't mind them, this is something they do.

CLIO: Hey, wait for me! [*She dashes in front of them and mimes being a baton-twirling drum majorette.*]

> *They march around the room with rising gusto.*

PARKER: About…face!

> *The band switches direction and function.* PARKER *plays a trombone,* CLIO *bangs a drum and* LEONARD *becomes the baton twirling drum majorette.*

PARKER: Fall out! [*Catching* CLIO *in his arms.*] Well, you're quite an accomplished little musician.

> LEONARD *continues to march, tossing an imaginary baton.*

CLIO: I played trumpet in my high school band.

> *They lock gazes.*

TATE: [*Taking* CLIO'*s arm.*] Clio's a woman of many talons.

PARKER: So I see.

DINAH: [*Linking arms with* PARKER.] Still the same old Parker.

TATE: She acts, she marches, she plays musical elephants…

CLIO: Come on Toto, let up.

> DINAH *and* TATE *separate them.* LEONARD *keeps marching around the room tossing his baton.*

DINAH: Leonard…?

PARKER: Go Handsome!

DINAH: Don't encourage him.

LEONARD: Hut, two, three, four; hut, two, three, four…

PARKER: [*To* DINAH.] So, you're here year round now?

DINAH: This is it. Just me, Leonard and the bees.

PARKER: [*To* CLIO *and* TATE.] They used to have the most magnificent apartment on Central Park West.

CLIO: No kidding.

DINAH: Leonard inherited it from an aunt.

PARKER: Ceilings up to here, and forget the view.

TATE: We have a place there too.

DINAH: But then things got tough and we had to sell.

LEONARD: [*Whirling in the opposite direction.*] About face!

TATE: In the Beresford.

DINAH: I don't want to hear.

CLIO: What a coincidence!

TATE: The top two floors.

DINAH: [*Hands over her ears.*] Don't!

LEONARD: Double time! [*He marches and tosses in double time.*]

DINAH: Oh well, easy come, easy go.

CLIO: We've just bought a summer place here.

PARKER: Ahhh—

TATE: We're renovating the Van Alstyne mansion next door. Fourteen rooms and six fireplaces.

CLIO: It's a nightmare.

DINAH: Leonard, you're making me dizzy!

       LEONARD *comes to a stop.*

PARKER: Renovations always are. [*Pause.*] So, what do you do, Todd?

CLIO: [*Correcting him.*] Tate.

TATE: I'm a scream writer.

DINAH: Wait, I thought you said…

TATE: I write screams.

CLIO: Don't listen to him, he's pulling your leg.

       TATE *suddenly screams very loud. Everyone freezes.*

CLIO: He's an editor.

PARKER: Well, well…

CLIO: Editor-in-chief, as a matter of fact.

       TATE *screams again.*

CLIO: He's head of Raven Books.

PARKER: Whoa, that's one of the classiest publishing houses in the country!

TATE: So I'm told.

LEONARD: Well…[*Silence. Then to* DINAH.] Sweetheart, haven't you forgotten something?

DINAH: Who, me?

LEONARD: It starts with "D."

DINAH: Let me think. Um, *drinks, hors d'œuvres…*

LEONARD: [*In a whisper.*] Dinner.

DINAH: [*In a panicked little voice.*] Dinner?

LEONARD: It's almost eleven o'clock.

DINAH: Oh my God…

PARKER: Thanksgiving with all the trimmings?

LEONARD: Thanksgiving with all the trimmings!

DINAH: *Dinner!*

TATE: You need any help?

PARKER: [*To* CLIO *and* TATE.] It's the only meal she ever makes. Birthdays, Easter, Fourth of July, out comes The Butterball.

CLIO: Tate does Thanksgiving at our house.

DINAH: DINNER…! [*She hikes up her skirts and dashes into the kitchen. She starts hurling pots and pans every which way.*] Start the beans, fix the cranberry sauce, finish the sweet potatoes…

CLIO: He's a great cook.

PARKER: Lucky you. [*Drifting over to her again.*] And lucky Tate.

CLIO: [*Gazing into* PARKER's *eyes.*] Why, thank you.

TATE: Lucky Tate, that's me all right. Yes siree, Bob, I've got it all.
  "Old King Cole, was a merry old soul and a merry old soul was he,
  He called for his pipe and he called for his bowl, and he called for his fiddlers three…"
    There's a series of loud crashes from the kitchen.
DINAH: Whoops…easy does it, easy does it.
LEONARD: [*Yelling to* DINAH.] ARE YOU OK IN THERE?
DINAH: FINE, FINE, NOT TO WORRY…Open the cranberry juice, dump it into a
  bowl, add a little orange juice, cut up some celery…
TATE: "And every fiddler, he had a fine fiddle, *and a very fine* fiddle had he…"
CLIO: Don't mind him, it's stress.
PARKER: Ah, stress.
LEONARD: Good old stress.
CLIO: He works too hard.
    Silence.
DINAH: [*Rushing back into the room, wearing an apron.*] Talk, talk, everything's under
  control. It will just be a couple of minutes. [*She dashes back to the kitchen.*]
    Silence.
TATE: I've always liked Old King Cole, he knew how to enjoy life. He had his pipe, his
  bowl, his fiddlers three…I've often wondered if he was married. If there was an old
  Queen Cole in the picture. What do you think, Clee?
CLIO: I have no idea.
TATE: Maybe it was the *absence* of a wife that made him so merry. He didn't have to
  worry what she was up to all the time. What do you think?
CLIO: [*Getting upset.*] I said, I don't know.
TATE: I say he was a unencumbered.
CLIO: Totey, please…
    Silence.
DINAH: [*Re-enters the room.*] Talk, *talk!* [*She waits, the silence deepens.*]
LEONARD: [*To* PARKER.] So…
    DINAH *rushes back to the kitchen.*
LEONARD: [*To* PARKER.]…how come you never call?
PARKER: Never call?
LEONARD: It's been six years and not a word, a murmur, a snooze. I thought we were
  friends.
PARKER: We are friends.
DINAH: [*From the kitchen.*] OH NO, I DON'T BELIEVE IT!
LEONARD: I haven't worked since "Cyrano." It's been eleven years, *eleven years!* You're a
  big director now…movies, TV specials every other week…Why won't you hire me?
PARKER: I was almost killed a couple of hours ago.
LEONARD: I was your favorite actor!
PARKER: A 10-year-old boy died in my arms.
LEONARD: I need a job.
PARKER: You know what he kept saying?

LEONARD: This is a tough business, I'm not getting any younger.

PARKER: "I've got a stitch in my side."

LEONARD: I need all the help I can get.

PARKER: *I've got a stitch in my side!* "

LEONARD: I'm going crazy.

DINAH: [*Staggers in, carrying an enormous raw turkey.*] LOOK, I FORGOT TO TURN THE OVEN ON!

TATE: Oh no!

DINAH: Snow white and cold as ice.

LEONARD: Dinah supports us now.

PARKER: His legs were severed at the knee.

LEONARD: [*Indicating the turkey.*] There I am…

PARKER: They were lying on the hood of his car.

LEONARD: Dead meat!

PARKER: It could have been me, so kick up your heels while they're still attached.

DINAH: What am I going to do?

TATE: [*Taking the turkey from her.*] Not to worry, I'll just filet it into cutlets, dust them with a little rosemary and olive oil and stick them under the broiler. They'll be ready in no time. [*He exits to the kitchen.*]

DINAH: [*Near tears.*] I'm so ashamed.

PARKER: Drain the cup and dance the dance.

DINAH: Everything was going to be perfect.

LEONARD: So, it's dancing you want. I'm versatile, what are you looking for? A little soft shoe? [*Doing as he says.*] A little tap?

DINAH: My one fool-proof meal…

CLIO: [*Heading toward the kitchen.*] Well, I think I'll go see what Tate's up to.

LEONARD *taps in front of her, deliberately blocking her way.*

CLIO: Excuse me, I was just…[*Trying to get past him.*] Sorry, sorry…

LEONARD: I may not be as young as I once was, but I still have technique.

DINAH: This is getting scary.

CLIO *finally manages to escape.*

LEONARD: No, wait! I know, you're looking for something a little more south of the border. You're just a stone's throw away from Mexico these days. Why didn't you say something? [*He starts doing flamenco steps.*]

DINAH: Everything's out of control.

PARKER: Easy, Handsome, easy…

LEONARD: I'm sensitive, but I'm not a mind reader. [*He dances with rising gusto, adding yelps and hand clapping.*]

DINAH: Parker's homecoming, and look at us. I'm a wreck, you're dancing the flamenco, and our guests are making dinner!

AND THE CURTAIN QUICKLY FALLS

II.1

An hour later. Dinner is almost over and hilarity reigns. LEONARD, DINAH *and* PARKER *have just taught* CLIO *and* TATE *how to play the finger-snapping, hand clapping game, Concentration. Plates pushed to one side. They're about to start a new round.* LEONARD's *at the head of the table, with* TATE *on his left.* DINAH's *at the opposite end with* PARKER *on her left and* CLIO *on his left. They've changed into elegant 19th century Chekhovian costumes. The encroaching trees and shrubs are starting to close in on them.*

LEONARD: [*Establishing the rhythm.*] Are you ready…? If so…here we go…starting with…names of boats. [*Pause.*] The Titanic!

TATE: The Andrea Doria!

DINAH: Um, um…The Lusitania! [*Placing her hand on his.*] Parker…?

PARKER: The Normandy! [*He empties his wine glass and slams it down for emphasis.*]

CLIO: Kon Tiki.

LEONARD:	DINAH:	TATE:	PARKER:
Whoa!	Very good!	Nice!	[*touches her shoulder, making a hissing sound.*]

LEONARD: [*Picking up speed.*] Um…The Nina!

TATE: The Pinta!

DINAH: [*With a Spanish flourish.*] And the Santa Maria! Ole!

PARKER: The Mayflower! [*Reaches across* CLIO *and helps himself to more wine.*]

CLIO: The Arabella, John Winthrop's boat.

LEONARD:	DINAH:	TATE:	PARKER:
She's good.	My, my…	That's my girl!	[*Whistles.*]

CLIO: [*Helping herself to more stuffing.*] Mmmm, I can't stop eating this stuffing!

LEONARD: [*Picking up speed, in a French accent.*] The Ile de France!

TATE: [*Likewise.*] The De Grasse!

DINAH: Um, um…Help, I can't think!

ALL *except* DINAH: You're out, you're out.

LEONARD: Go on, Park, it's your turn.

PARKER: The Constitution. [*He drains his glass.*] Great wine!

DINAH: I've got it, I've got it, The Intrepid!

LEONARD: [*To* PARKER.] Glad you like it.

CLIO: The Mauretania! [*Helping herself to more.*] Ohhh, this stuffing!

DINAH: The Queen Mary!

LEONARD: Dinah, you're out.

DINAH: The Queen Elizabeth!

LEONARD: The Pequod!

TATE: The Pequod?

DINAH: The QEII!

LEONARD: From *Moby Dick.*

TATE: [*To* LEONARD, *breaking the rhythm.*] I *know* where The Pequod comes from, I thought we were only naming real boats.

LEONARD: [*To* TATE.] All boats, the more literary the better.

DINAH: The HMS Pinafore!

TATE: Then why didn't you say so at the outset?

LEONARD: My apologies.

TATE: It *is* helpful to know the rules, you know.

LEONARD: You're right, you're right, I wasn't thinking.

TATE: Who knows what I might have come up with, I am an editor, after all.

CLIO: [*Piling more stuffing on her plate.*] Ohhhh, what is it about this stuffing?

TATE: The Antelope from *Gulliver's Travels,* The Patna from *Lord Jim,* the Nellie from *Heart of Darkness...*

DINAH: [*Starts singing.*] "I am the monarch of the sea, the ruler of the Queen's Navee, whose praise Great Britain loudly chants.
And so do his sisters and his cousins and his aunts..."
Come on, Parker, help me.

TATE: [*To* LEONARD.] So the sky's the limit? You're including boats from films and lyrics as well?

LEONARD: Everything, the works.

CLIO: [*Joining* DINAH.] "And so do his sisters and his cousins and his aunts!
His sisters and his cousins, whom he reckons up by the dozens, and his aunts!"

PARKER: [*Applauding* CLIO.] Bravo, bravo! More wine?

CLIO: [*Starting to get tipsy.*] Let 'er rip!

PARKER: [*Filling* CLIO's *glass and then his.*] I've got to hand it to you Handsome, this is terrific wine.

CLIO: And forget the stuffing!

LEONARD: Glad you like it, glad you like it.

PARKER: I haven't had this much fun in a dog's age.

TATE: [*Handing his glass to* PARKER *to refill.*] Party, party!

CLIO: [*Running her hands down her bodice.*] And it's so great getting to wear these costumes!

PARKER: [*To* DINAH.] *God, I've missed you!*

DINAH: Oh Parker...

CLIO: I feel like we're all in "The Cherry Orchard" or something.

PARKER: Remember the old days?

CLIO: I've played Varya three times.

DINAH: We used to dress up every night.

LEONARD: It's true.

PARKER: Every night. [*Returning* TATE's *filled glass.*] Here you go.

CLIO: It's one of my favorite roles.

DINAH: Monday, Greek tragedy; Tuesday, Restoration comedy; Wednesday, Theater of the Absurd…God, what happened?

PARKER: Good question.

LEONARD: Life.

PARKER: Shit.

TATE: Same difference.

PARKER: Hear, hear.

> *Silence.*

CLIO: [*Reciting as Varya.*] "I don't think anything will come of it for us. He is very busy, he hasn't any time for me—And doesn't notice me. God knows, it's painful for you to see him—"

DINAH: [*To* PARKER.] You went into movies, Leonard went crazy and I…who knows.

PARKER: Leonard's always been crazy.

LEONARD: I *have* always been crazy. I wonder why.

PARKER: Because you're an actor.

DINAH: Because he lost touch.

PARKER: All actors are crazy.

CLIO: Thanks a lot.

DINAH: He can't cope, he lives in his own world.

TATE: "Hey, diddle, diddle! The cat and the fiddle, the cow jumped over the moon…"

LEONARD: "The little dog laughed to see such sport and the dish ran away with the spoon." [*To* TATE.] You're right, these little babies say it all.

> *Silence.*

CLIO: [*Reciting as Varya again.*] "Everybody talks about our marriage, everybody congratulates us, and the truth is, there's nothing to it—it's all like a dream— [*Pause.*] You have a brooch looks like a bee."

PARKER: [*Applauding* CLIO.] Nicely done.

TATE: "Hickety, pickety, my black hen; she lays eggs for gentlemen."

> *Silence.*

LEONARD: [*To* PARKER, *with sudden rage.*] *You abandoned me, you ingrate!*

DINAH: Leonard?

LEONARD: Once you left the theater, I never worked again.

PARKER: Hey, hey, you can't pin that on me.

LEONARD: No one wanted me. I was too old, too young, too tall, too short, too real, too…

DINAH: That's not true, you were offered all kinds of roles.

LEONARD: Yeah, lousy ones.

PARKER: Work is work.

LEONARD: Bad plays, incompetent directors…

PARKER: You do what you have to do.

LEONARD: I have standards…unlike some people I know.

DINAH: Now, now…

LEONARD: Not all of us sell out.

PARKER: Opportunities present themselves, things change.

LEONARD: I don't change.

PARKER: Everything changes.

TATE: "Little Boy Blue, come blow your horn, the sheep's in the meadow, the cow's in the…"

PARKER, LEONARD *and* DINAH: *Will you shut up!*

TATE: Sorry, sorry…

> *Silence.*

DINAH: Me, I'm designing six shows this season. It's insanity, but, hey, it puts food on the table.

TATE: And it was delicious.

DINAH: Thanks to you.

LEONARD: [*To* PARKER.] Why won't you cast me in a movie?

TATE: [*to* DINAH.] Please.

LEONARD: Huh? *Huh?!*

PARKER: It's a different medium.

LEONARD: You mean, you only cast stars.

DINAH: [*Suddenly clamps her hand down on her head.*] Ohhh, I just had the most massive déjà vu. Whoooooo…

CLIO: What causes those anyway?

DINAH: Ahhhhhhh…

TATE: They're small cerebral strokes, gentle prods to remind us that lunacy's just a heartbeat away.

LEONARD: Let's hear it for the crazy people! [*He rubs his finger up and down his lips.*]

DINAH: Easy, honey, easy.

LEONARD: [*Reaches a crescendo and stops.*] Ahhh, I needed that.

DINAH: The great thing about Leonard is he lets everything out. There's no holding back with him. Lucky dog.

LEONARD: It's one of my many gifts.

DINAH: It *is* a gift.

TATE: Indeed.

DINAH: I wish I had it.

LEONARD: [*Bowing.*] Why, thank you.

> *Silence.*

PARKER: Well, where were we?

> *Silence.*

CLIO: [*To* LEONARD.] You just said The Pequod.

LEONARD: Right, right…

TATE: [*Resumes the rhythm.*] The African Queen!

DINAH: The Love Boat!

LEONARD:	TATE:	PARKER:	CLIO:
Honey, you're out!	I thought she was out.	What's going on?	No fair, no fair.

PARKER: [*Picking up speed.*] The Caine Mutiny!

CLIO: Mutiny on The *Bounty!*

LEONARD: The Dixie Queen!

DINAH: The Good Ship Lollipop!

ALL *except* DINAH: YOU'RE OUT OF THE GAME!

DINAH: Ohhh, Noah's ark on you all!

LEONARD: Let's add marine figures of speech.

TATE: Um…[*Picking up speed.*] Ship of state!

DINAH: Ship of Fools!

PARKER: [*Eying* CLIO *meaningfully.*] Ship shape!

CLIO: [*Returning his gaze.*] Dream boat.

PARKER: [*Dropping the rhythm.*] Thar she blows!

CLIO: [With *rising ardor.*] Batten down the hatches!

TATE: [*To* CLIO.] That's not a figure of speech.

DINAH: And it's not your turn.

PARKER: [*Moving closer to her.*] Man overboard!

CLIO: SOS…SOS….

PARKER: Coming about!

DINAH: Hey, hey…

CLIO: Shiver my timbers!

TATE: What's going on?

PARKER: Yo ho ho and a bottle of rum!

CLIO: Heigh ho, heigh ho, it's off to work we go.

PARKER: I'll huff and I'll puff and I'll blow your house down!

CLIO: Not by the hair of my chinny-chin-chin!

DINAH: Guys ..?!

TATE: [*To* PARKER.] It's not your turn!

PARKER: [*To* CLIO.] Rapunzel, Rapunzel, let down your hair!

CLIO: My, what big *teeth* you have!

PARKER: [*Licking his chops.*] All the better to eat you with!

TATE *and* DINAH: STOP THE GAME, STOP THE GAME!
     Silence.

CLIO: [*Collapsing against* PARKER.] Ohhh, that was fun.

PARKER: You're really good.

CLIO: Well, you're not so bad yourself.
        DINAH *and* TATE *eye her angrily. She quickly straightens up.*

DINAH: So…anyone want seconds on anything? [*Silence. She rises and starts clearing the table.*] Then on to the salad!

TATE: There's more?

CLIO: I'm going to burst.

PARKER: What are you trying to do…?

LEONARD: Hold on to your hats, you ain't seen nothing yet!

PARKER: Kill us?

DINAH *exits to the kitchen.*

PARKER: [*To* CLIO.]
So...how often do you
come up here? Just weekends
or...oh sorry...sorry...
Silence.

CLIO: [*To* PARKER.]
I can't believe I finally met you!
[*Hand over her heart.*] Parker Bliss...!

LEONARD: [*To* TATE.]
So...how's the renovation
coming? I see you're stripping
the paint right down to the...
sorry...
Silence.

TATE: [*To* LEONARD.]
Tell me, when was this house built?
I figure it was more or less the same
time as...whoops...

PARKER: [*To* CLIO.]
I was just wondering how often
you...
Silence.

CLIO: [*To* PARKER *her hand over heart.*]
Boom boom, boom boom, boom
boom...

LEONARD: [*To* TATE.]
That's got to cost serious money.
I also notice you're repainting
all the...
Silence.

TATE: [*To* LEONARD.]
I've checked the records at the
County Clerk, but they don't have any-
thing before 1850 because of the...

PARKER: ...come here?

LEONARD: ...chimneys!

TATE: ...fire!

CLIO: [*Placing his hand over her heart.*] Feel it.

PARKER: [*Feeling it.*] Whoa!

CLIO: Boom boom, boom boom, boom boom!

     PARKER *keeps his hand on her heart as* TATE *shoots them murderous looks.*

CLIO: [*Putting her hand over his.*] Scary, huh?

DINAH: [*Staggers in carrying a gigantic vat of salad. She pauses at the sight of* PARKER *and* CLIO *so intimately involved and drops the salad in front of them with a resounding thud.*] UUUUGH!

PARKER: [*Pulling back in his chair.*] JESUS CHRIST...

CLIO: Look at the size of that bowl!

DINAH: I picked it fresh this morning.

CLIO: A person could take a bath in it.

DINAH: From inside the coat closet. It's like a greenhouse gone mad—mushrooms nesting in the mittons, avocados blooming in the galoshes, broccoli sprouting out the umbrellas...

LEONARD: She's exaggerating.

DINAH: A wave of vegetable lust is surging through the house, it keeps us awake at night. The pollinating and fertilizing, the germinating and foliating—you've never heard such a din...Green beans quickening, okra stiffening, zucchini swelling...

LEONARD: Dinah!

DINAH: Oh, the burgeoning and urgency of it all! [*Picks up a bottle of Wish Bone Italian salad dressing and reads the ingredients in a booming voice.*] "Water, soybean oil, vinegar, salt, garlic, onion, sugar, red bell peppers, lemon juice…" [*She shakes the bottle so violently everyone cowers in his seat.*]

LEONARD: Easy, easy!

DINAH: [*Still shaking the bottle.*] And then there's the roiling of the leafy things that wait! Swiss chard shuddering, spinach seething…

LEONARD: Don't mind her.

DINAH: Arugula unfurling on the stairs. Cabbage writhing, endive panting, hearts of palm ululating under the bed. [DINAH *pours the dressing over the salad, splashing everyone in the process.*]

LEONARD: CLIO: TATE: PARKER:
  Watch it!   Help!   Hey, what's…   Lookout!

DINAH: And don't forget the clamor of the ripening fruit. [*She starts tossing the salad.*] The crooning of the cauliflower, the pleading of the chili peppers…

LEONARD: Dinah, Dinah…

DINAH: [*Taking on their voices.*] "Yoo hoo, here I am, behind the curtains."—"Pssst, over here, under the sink…"

PARKER: [*Pushing away from the table.*] Hey, hey…

DINAH: The entreaties of the tomatoes, the yodeling of the yams…"Look up, I'm inside the light fixture.""Open your eyes, you fool, I'm right under your nose!" [*She starts heaving spoonfuls of salad onto* PARKER.]

LEONARD: [*Head in his hands.*] Jesus God…

DINAH: [*Burying him with rising abandon.*] The gasping and groaning, the clasping and moaning, you've never heard such carryings on. Cucumbers thrusting, carrots plunging…

PARKER: [*Trying to ward her off.*] What do you think you're doing?

DINAH: Eggplants crying out for more…

LEONARD: [*Grabbing her arms.*] Stop it, Dinah. Stop it!

DINAH: Tendrils snapping, seeds spattering, ruby red juices seeping through the floor…

LEONARD: *I'm begging you!*

PARKER: [*Rises, pushing* DINAH *to the floor.*] GET A GRIP ON YOURSELF!
         DINAH *lands with a scream. There's an awful silence as everyone stares at her.*

TATE: "Mary, Mary, quite contrary, how does your garden grow?
      With silver bells and cockle-shells and pretty maids fornicating in a row."
      Silence.

LEONARD: [*Overcome.*] God, oh God, oh God…

TATE: Well, that was quite a…
      Silence.

CLIO: [*Rising.*] Excuse me, which way to the little girl's room?

LEONARD: [*Pointing.*] Down the hall.

PARKER: [*Rises, pulling back his chair.*] Madame…

CLIO: [*to* PARKER.] Don't get up.

> DINAH *gets up with a groan as* PARKER *doffs an imaginary hat toward* CLIO.

DINAH: [*to* PARKER, *dusting herself off.*] Ever the perfect gentleman.

> CLIO *sashays down the hall. She throws* PARKER *a backwards glance and disappears.*

LEONARD: Well…

DINAH: I'm sorry, I don't know what came over me.

LEONARD: [*Softly.*] Po-Po, Po-Po, I want Po-Po!

DINAH: [*As an echo.*] Po-Po.

TATE: The stick of the blind man invents a new darkness.

PARKER: [*To* TATE.] What was that again?

TATE: The stick of the blind man invents a new darkness.

PARKER: Nice, very nice.

TATE: I read it on a placard in a bus the other day.

LEONARD: My pope, my pip, my little pup…

DINAH: My dope, my dip, my little dup.

LEONARD: My yes, my own!

DINAH: My bless, my throne!

TATE: [*Sotto voce to* PARKER.] Who's Po-Po?

PARKER: Their married daughter who lives in Tacoma. They're very close.

TATE: Ohh, I thought it was a pet.

PARKER: They like to shout out her name.

TATE: "Po-Po"?

PARKER: It's short for Phoebe.

LEONARD: [*Mournful.*] Po-Po, Po-Po, I want Po-Po!

PARKER: It's something they do. It's a way of staying in touch.

LEONARD: [*Waving to* DINAH.] Hi, Dine.

DINAH: [*Waving back weakly.*] Hi, Leonard.

LEONARD: How's it going?

DINAH: I don't like this anymore.

LEONARD: Me either.

DINAH: *No, I really don't like it!*

> *An awful silence.*

TATE: Well, this has been quite an evening.

PARKER: I'll say.

TATE: [*To* PARKER.] You narrowly escaped death, we met our new neighbors, had a few laughs, got through the blight. I mean, *night.* That's the hard part.

DINAH: Tell me about it.

PARKER: [*Raising his wine glass.*] To getting though the night.

> *He drinks.* TATE *joins him.*

DINAH: [*Starts clearing the table.*] So how about a little dessert?

PARKER: There's more?

TATE: I couldn't eat another bite.

PARKER: Me either.

LEONARD: When you come to our house for dinner, you *dine* right Dine?

 PARKER *groans at the play on words.*

DINAH: You got it! And now for dessert—the pearl in the oyster, the ruby in the crown…[*She plunges into the kitchen.*] Pumpkin pie, home grown, if you please!

PARKER: Dinah, Dinah…!   TATE: Holy shit!   LEONARD: My favorite!

DINAH: And…[*Returning, bearing them aloft.*] Honey nougat meringue, compliments of Leonard's bees.

LEONARD: Let's hear it for the bees!

TATE: When it rains, it pours!

DINAH: [*Setting them down with a thud.*] Gentlemen, go to it!

 CLIO *emerges from the bathroom and slowly makes her way back to the dining room.* PARKER *turns and sees her.*

LEONARD: [*Beaming at* DINAH.] Look at her! Have you ever seen anyone more beautiful? [*Pause.*] Well, have you?

DINAH: [*To* LEONARD, *embarrassed.*] Honey…?!

PARKER: [*Quickly turning back to look at* DINAH.] Never!

TATE: [*Reaching for the meringue.*] Well, maybe just a spoonful.

DINAH: [*Handing each one a server.*] Dig in, dig in.

PARKER: [*Rising from his seat.*] Excuse me, I'm afraid I'm going to have to use the facilities first…

 LEONARD *attacks the pumpkin pie and* TATE *samples the meringue as* CLIO *and* PARKER *collide in the darkened hallway.*

CLIO: Oh, hi.

PARKER: Hi.

CLIO: [*Brushing against him.*] Sorry, I was just…

PARKER: [*Suddenly grabs her in his arms.*] Ohhh, you wonder, you marvel, you shining girl…[*He pushes her against the wall.*] You destroy me! I can't see, I can't walk, I'm in flames. [*He starts kissing her.*]

CLIO: No, no don't, they'll see us.

PARKER: [*All over her, barely audible.*] I wanted you the moment I saw you…

CLIO: [*Starting to melt.*] Ohhhh…ohhhhhhh…

PARKER: Your face, your eyes, your skin, your voice…Sweet Christ, I've never seen anything like you…

CLIO: [*Returning his kisses.*] Ohhh…ohhhhhhh…

 Even though they can't see them, DINAH *and* TATE *hear every word and freeze in horror.*

CLIO: Parker Bliss…

PARKER: Clio Hands…

TATE: [*Rising from his seat.*] You son of a bitch…

LEONARD: [*Wolfing down more pie.*] Ohhhh, this is great pie, Dine, *great* pie!

BLACKOUT

II.2

Seconds later. CLIO *and* PARKER *enter the room shame-faced. No one moves.*

DINAH: [*to* PARKER.] How could you…?

TATE: [*On his feet.*] I'm going to kill you!

LEONARD: [*In ecstasies over the pie.*] Ohhhh, ohhhhh…

    A ghastly silence as everyone looks at LEONARD.

DINAH: [*Embarrassed.*] Leonard…?

TATE: [*To* PARKER.] That's my *wife,* you ass hole!

LEONARD: It's so *moist!* [*He groans with pleasure.*]

PARKER: [*Returning to the table.*] Well, it's getting late.

CLIO: [*Looking at her watch.*] It *is* getting late.

LEONARD: It's her specialty.

TATE: [*Advancing towards* PARKER.] Just who the hell do you think you are?

LEONARD: [*Gobbling down more.*] Her *pièce de résistance…*

PARKER: [*Backing away.*] Hey, hey…

CLIO: [*Threading her arm through* TATE's.] Come on, we've got to get up early tomorrow.

TATE: [*Shaking* CLIO *off.*] I don't like guys manhandling my knife. [*He pushes* PARKER *backwards.*]

CLIO *and* DINAH: [*Correcting him.*] Wife.

PARKER: Take it easy.

TATE: [*Pushing him harder.*] Make me!

LEONARD: Hey, what's going on?

DINAH: [*to* LEONARD.] Later, later…

PARKER: Are you threatening me?

TATE: [*Pushing him harder.*] What does it look like?

CLIO: [*Trying to pull* TATE *away.*] Toto!

TATE: [*Violently pushing* CLIO *away.*] *Get your hands off me!*

CLIO: [*Massaging her wrist.*] Ow!

LEONARD: [*Looking up from his pie.*] What happened?

PARKER: [*To* TATE.] Don't push her.

TATE: [*To* PARKER.] What did you say?

LEONARD: [*Louder, to* PARKER.] What happened?

PARKER: [*To* TATE.] I said: Don't. Push. Her.

DINAH: [*To* LEONARD.] Later, honey, later.

PARKER: [*To* TATE.] What's the matter, do you have a hearing problem?

TATE: No, I have an ass hole problem and it's you! [*He takes a swipe at* PARKER.]

CLIO: Tater, *please!*

DINAH: [*Rushing between them.*] My costumes, my costumes!

CLIO: Oh God, the costumes! Careful, careful…

    TATE *and* PARKER *quickly shed their costumes.*

LEONARD: Will someone please tell me what's going on?

DINAH: Forget it Leonard, just crawl back in your hole.

CLIO: They're so beautiful, it would be terrible if they got damaged.

DINAH: It's like living with a dead person. You've gone, checked out, flown the coop…

PARKER: [*Putting up his dukes.*] OK, come to Papa…

LEONARD: …"flown the coop…?"

TATE: [*Dancing around him.*] You low-life, you scum…

LEONARD: [*To* DINAH.] What are you talking about?

DINAH: It's every man for himself.

PARKER: [*Moving in on* TATE.] Pretentious wimp…

DINAH: [*rushing to shield* PARKER.] *Don't touch him!*

CLIO: [*Pulling at* TATE.] Stop it!

TATE: [*Pushing* CLIO.] Get away from me, bitch!

PARKER: [*To* TATE.] Come on, hit me, hit me.

CLIO: [*To* TATE.] Fuck you!

DINAH: [*To* TATE.] I'm warning you. [*She bares her teeth and snarls.*]

CLIO: [*To* TATE.] Just, *fuck you!*

DINAH: [*To* TATE.] Ass wipe!

CLIO: [*To* TATE.] Dick head!

LEONARD: [*To* TATE.] Scum bag!

TATE: [*To* LEONARD.] Just a minute here, he made a play for *my wife!*

DINAH: Butt wad!

CLIO: Shit face.

LEONARD: Jerk off!

TATE: Not that it's any great surprise, given her track record.

CLIO: What's that supposed to mean, "Given her track record"?

TATE: "Jack be nimble, Jack be quick, Jack jump over the blind man's stick." You'd better have quick reflexes, it's dark out there and very dangerous, in case you haven't noticed. There's a randomness at large, something wayward and unnatural.

LEONARD: One false move and you're done for. Kaput, fini…exit the king.

TATE: Mother Goose was no fool, she knew what was going on. Her rhymes are charms against disaster. Shout them out loud and often enough and you'll be safe. You should hear Clicks and me when the going gets rough…She's very good. She makes up her own.

    Silence.

PARKER: Well, I don't know about the rest of you, but I've got to get up early tomorrow. Patsy's got an opening at the Modern.

DINAH: Oh, don't go!

TATE: [*To* PARKER.] At the Modern?

PARKER: My wife's a sculptor.

CLIO: [*To* TATE.] Come on, Pooks, time to go.

    TATE *doesn't move.*

CLIO: *Pookie? !*

TATE: Right, right! [*To* PARKER.] You wouldn't be talking about Patsy Cincinnati, would you?

PARKER: You got it.   DINAH: That's her.   LEONARD: The one and only.

CLIO *and* TATE: [*Stopping in their tracks.*] You're married to Patsy Cincinnati?

PARKER: Whoops, I'd better put on some clothes here. [*He grabs his shirt and starts putting it on.*]

CLIO: Wow, Patsy Cincinnati!

TATE: She's major, her work's shown all over the world.

PARKER: [*Thrusts out his arms and bows, revealing the blood stain again.*] Meet Mr. Patsy Cincinnati.

> *They all scream with horror.*

DINAH: You can't wear that. Put the Chekhov shirt back on. [*She helps him into it.*]

> CLIO *and* TATE *look down at themselves and realize they're still in costume. They hastily start to change.*

CLIO: What's she like?

TATE: At the Tate, the Jeu de Paume, the Reina Sofia…

LEONARD: Tiny.

DINAH: And very feminine. You'd never know she was a sculptor to look at her.

LEONARD: You can practically pick her up with one hand.

CLIO: You're kidding!

PARKER: I wouldn't try it, though.

TATE: The Castello di Rivoli, the Hara Museum, the Moderna Museet…

PARKER: [*To* TATE.] Well, well, don't we know the art scene.

> *Silence.*

DINAH: She has wonderful hair.

PARKER: She does have wonderful hair.

DINAH: [*Indicating on herself.*] Corkscrew curls out to here.

CLIO: Patsy Cincinnati…Wow.

PARKER: I could drop off the face of the earth and she wouldn't even notice.

DINAH *and* LEONARD: *Parker*?!

PARKER: You know what she calls me these days? *Maestro!* She's forgotten my name. She leaves these messages on my answering machine—"Hi Maestro, it's me. How's Hollywood?" But hey, I can't complain, she's got a great eye. Look, she picked out this parka for me…[*Pulling it on.*] "I wanted to get you something warm," she said. "I don't want my Maestro shivering on the set." Well, you know Patsy and her circulation, the woman's got a perennial chill…[*Pause.*] Let's just hope I don't run into anymore runaway mobile homes on my way back.

DINAH: Oh, don't leave.

LEONARD: Mobile homes, sinking homes, no one's safe.

TATE: You can say that again. Well, we ought to be heading along too. [*Hands* CLIO *her coat.*] Here you go, Clee.

CLIO: [*Putting it on.*] Thanks Pooks. Luckily, we're right next door.

LEONARD: Well, you never know, crazed Enid Brill could always pop out of the bushes and mow you down.

DINAH: [*Clinging to* PARKER's *arm.*] Oh, stay a few minutes more.

TATE: Stop by the next time you pass the house, we could use a break.

CLIO: [*Hugging* DINAH.] Yes, do, I feel so drawn to you. You're so *there*.

TATE: [*Pulling* CLIO *toward the door.*] Come on, Clue…

CLIO: [*To* DINAH.] If I don't call you, you call me, OK? It can get pretty lonely around here, in case you haven't noticed. I've been abandonéd.

LEONARD: [*Impressed with her accenting.*] My, my!

CLIO: Stranded in the middle of nowhere.

TATE: [*Putting his arm around her.*] But with me.

CLIO: I'm never with you. You're either working or locked up with the painters and carpenters. When I walk in a room you don't even see me. I wave and it's like no one is there. Well, someday you'll take me in and when that happens…[*Getting weepy.*] Oh my…[*Recovering.*] Once we get the place fixed up we'll just be here weekends and during the summer, but Tate insists we live here while the work's being done. You know, *to keep an eye on things.* He's temporarily moved his office up here. I've never renovated a house before, so I'm not that much help. I look at wall paper, pick out paint and talk to the contractor— that is, when he shows up. Which is hardly ever.

TATE: [*Hands over his ears.*] Don't…

CLIO: He's impossible. He's also the fattest man I've ever seen. And the hairiest. He has a full beard and is covered with fur, thick brown fur. He looks like a wooly mammoth.

LEONARD *and* DINAH: Frank Flood.

CLIO *and* TATE: Frank Flood.

DINAH: She's right, he *does* look like a wooly mammoth!

PARKER: Wooly mammoths…I love wooly mammoths!

LEONARD: He's the best, the best.

TATE: But try getting him to make an appearance.

CLIO: I'm quite fond of him, actually. He's one of the few people I see. I have fantasies of leaping on his neck and galloping back to the dawn of time. Just him and me and the saber tooth tigers. [*Pause.*] Thank God I've got a film this spring. [CLIO *reaches into her bag, pulls out a scrap of paper and quickly scribbles down her phone number.*]

TATE: [*Shaking hands with* DINAH *and* LEONARD.] We had a great time. Good food, lively conversation…

CLIO: [*to* DINAH.] Now call me.

DINAH: I will.

CLIO: Don't forget.

DINAH: Wait a minute, let me give you some of Leonard's honey. [*She starts rummaging through a drawer.*]

PARKER: [*Shaking hands with* CLIO.] It was a pleasure.

CLIO: Likewise. [*She slips* PARKER *the piece of paper with her phone number on it.*]

DINAH: [*Handing* TATE *several jars of honey.*] Here you go.

PARKER: [*Glancing at it.*] Why, thank you.

TATE: Much obliged. [*Pulling her toward the door.*] OK, Coco, time to go home.

LEONARD: I'll get the door. [*He opens it, the wind howls louder than ever.*] Fucking wind!

TATE: Thanks again. Next time you come to our house. [*He pulls* CLIO *after him.*]

CLIO: [*Waving.*] Good night, good night…

DINAH: Quick, shut the door.

LEONARD: [*Slams the door behind them.*] Son of a bitch!

DINAH: Well, that was quite a…

   Silence.

LEONARD: [*To* PARKER.] Come on, take off your coat and stay awhile.

PARKER: [*Zipping up his parka.*] I've really got to go.

DINAH: [*Hanging on him.*] Stay, stay!

PARKER: I can't.

LEONARD: We haven't begun to catch up.

DINAH: Spend the night.

PARKER: I *can't!*

LEONARD: Please?

DINAH: Pretty please?

PARKER: [*Opening his arms to* LEONARD.] Come here, you lunatic.

   LEONARD *rushes into them.*

PARKER: [*Lifting him off the ground.*] Ughhh!

LEONARD: Come on, stay! You can sleep in Po-Po's room.

PARKER: [*Lets him go and opens his arms to* DINAH.] Hey, Threads….

DINAH: [*Rushing into them.*] Oh Parker, Parker…!

PARKER: That's my girl.

DINAH: [*Clinging to him.*] Don't go!

PARKER: [*Pulling away.*] I've got to, Patsy's waiting.

DINAH: Stay, I'm begging you!

PARKER: [*Putting an arm around each of them.*] Guys, it was great, just like the old days. I forgot how much fun you were. I don't have friends like you anymore. Funny how things change.

LEONARD: Hilarious.

PARKER: Here I am this big movie director and I don't have any real friends.

LEONARD: My heart is breaking.

PARKER: And then there's the work, which is a whole other kettle of fish. Or is it worms? It sure ain't Shakespeare. Oh well, we do our best. Right?

LEONARD: *Do* we?

PARKER: [*Heading out the door.*] OK, I've got to go.

DINAH: [*Reaching for him.*] Come back!

PARKER: I'll call you in a couple of days, I promise. [*And he's gone.*]

DINAH: [*Running out the door after him.*] Don't leave me…

LEONARD: Easy, Dine, easy…

DINAH: Don't leave me!

LEONARD: [*Pulling her back inside.*] Where are you going?

DINAH: Come back!

LEONARD: [*Slamming the door shut.*] It's cold out there.

DINAH: [*Getting weepy.*] He left, he left…

LEONARD: Well, that's Parker for you. Selfish son of a bitch.

DINAH: [*Throwing herself face down on the sofa.*] Oh, Leonard….

    Silence.

LEONARD: So, what did you think of the evening?

DINAH: It was a disaster.

LEONARD: It *was* a disaster, wasn't it?

DINAH: Total.

LEONARD: What did you think of our new neighbors?

DINAH: I couldn't stand them.

LEONARD: She was very taken with you.

DINAH: I'd say Parker was the one she was taken with.

LEONARD: [*With disgust.*] Parker!

    DINAH *sighs. Silence.*

LEONARD: You know, you looked really beautiful tonight.

DINAH: Please!

LEONARD: No, you did.

DINAH: Not next to her.

LEONARD: I'd take you over her any day, no contest.

DINAH: Well, Parker seemed to like her.

LEONARD: Parker…

    Silence.

LEONARD: Well, that was quite some performance with the salad.

DINAH: Salad…?

LEONARD: Talk about throwing yourself at someone.

DINAH: I don't know what came over me.

LEONARD: How do you think it made me feel?

DINAH: I couldn't stop myself.

LEONARD: [*Covering his ears.*] I don't want to hear.

DINAH: Once I started, I just…

LEONARD: I said, *I don't want to hear!*

DINAH: Sorry, sorry…

LEONARD: Give a guy a break.

    Silence.

DINAH: [*Rising.*] God, look at the place. It looks as if a bomb went off. [*She starts putting the costumes away.*]

LEONARD: Something did happen between you. It was during the production of "Cyrano." There was a real charge between you. Hello…? You there in the Chekhov outfit. I'm right, aren't I? You can tell me, it was almost ten years ago.

DINAH: Twelve.

LEONARD: Whatever.

DINAH: Twelve and half, to be exact.

LEONARD: Parker's a very charismatic guy, look what happened to Whoosis tonight.

DINAH: *Clio! Clio! Think Cleopatra, for Christ's sake! It's not that hard a name!*

LEONARD: You don't have to yell.

DINAH: [*She starts clearing the table.*] I mean, after awhile…

LEONARD: She succumbed while her husband was in the room, at least you were more discreet. Come on, tell me, I can take it.

DINAH: [*Sings, carrying the dishes into the kitchen.*] "Someone's in the kitchen with Dinah, someone's in the kitchen I know, ow, ow, ow…Someone's in the kitchen with Dinah, strumming on the old banjo…"

LEONARD: What happened?

DINAH: [*Returning.*] "They're strumming fee, fi, fiddlio; fee, fi fiddlio; fee, fi, fiddliooooo…strumming on the old banjo."

LEONARD: Well…?

DINAH: Give it up, Dinah, just *give it up.*

LEONARD: I'm waiting.

DINAH: OK…. We were in your dressing room going over some costume changes after the show one night. The theater was empty, it was just Parker and me in a sea of plumes and doublets, and suddenly he's all over me, his hands, his mouth, his tongue, anything that protrudes…And he's murmuring, "Ohhhh, you wonder, you marvel, you shining girl. You destroy me! I can't see, I can't walk, I'm in flames…Your face, your eyes, your skin, your voice…"

LEONARD: Why does that sound so familiar?

DINAH: Because he just said it to Clio five minutes ago. The only difference is she gave in and I didn't.

LEONARD: What did you say?

DINAH: I said, *she gave in and I didn't!* What's the matter, are you deaf now too?

LEONARD: Nothing happened?

DINAH: I guess I showed them. Oh yes, I showed them good!

LEONARD: *Nothing happened?*

DINAH: That's right, rub it in.

LEONARD: Nothing happened.

DINAH: And one more time. [*Waving her arms like a conductor, she mouths "Nothing happened."*] It's a shocker, but there you are.

LEONARD: I don't know what to say.

DINAH: The joke's on me. Everyone assumed it was a *fait accompli*, so it wouldn't have made any difference. Good old Dinah, ever the dutiful wife. [*Imitating herself.*] "It's not right, Leonard would never got over it, he's bound to find out, I know him. He'll see it in my eyes, he'll smell it in my hair, nothing gets past him when it comes to me."

LEONARD: You were faithful.

DINAH: If you can call it that. I wanted him, I just couldn't go through with it. Don't ask me why, I've been trying to figure it for the past eighty years. No, ask, ask…On second thought, you'd better not, it's too humiliating.

LEONARD: You didn't do it, you didn't do it!

DINAH: I lacked courage, I wasn't up to it. It's pathetic.

LEONARD: And all this time I thought…[*Folding her in his arms.*] Oh baby, baby…

DINAH: I wanted him.

LEONARD: You didn't do it.

DINAH: I wanted him.

LEONARD: It's all right.

DINAH: Oh Leonard…

LEONARD: Let it out…

DINAH: You're not listening to me. [*She starts to cry.*] I said, *I wanted him, I wanted him, I wanted him, I wanted him*…

LEONARD: I know, I've always known. I've just been lying low. But you…how you held your ground all these years…It takes my breath away. You don't lack courage, you can't contain it! You're like the cauliflower under our bed, fierce and tenacious…

DINAH: Oh Leonard…

    They look at each other and slowly embrace. The wind starts to howl.

LEONARD: Fucking wind!

DINAH: I can't take it anymore! [*She rushes to the front door and flings it open, facing the wind.*] HEY, YOU OUT THERE, LET UP ALREADY! SHOW A LITTLE RESPECT FOR ONCE. WE'VE GOT SOME SERIOUS CATASTROPHES ON OUR HANDS!

    The wind howls louder.

DINAH: A BREAKDOWN HERE, A LOSS OF NERVE THERE, A MAJOR IM-BALANCE IN THE ORDER OF THINGS…[*Pause.*] SAVINGS GONE…

LEONARD: [*Joining her.*] A BACKED UP SEPTIC TANK…

DINAH: TWENTY DOLLARS IN THE CHECKING ACCOUNT…

LEONARD: CORRODING WATER PIPES…

DINAH: TEN MORE YEARS ON THE MORTGAGE…

LEONARD: A LEAKING ROOF…

DINAH: WE'D APPRECIATE SOME PEACE AND QUIET, IF YOU DON'T MIND. [DINAH *retreats a few steps.*]

LEONARD: Bats in the attic…

DINAH: Mice in the basement…

LEONARD: Swallows in the kitchen…

DINAH: Eagles in the pantry…

LEONARD: [*To* DINAH.] *Eagles* in the pantry?

DINAH: [*Heading back into the wind, yelling with new fury.*] I'M NOT ASKING, I'M TELLING YOU. IT'S TIME FOR A CHANGE IN THE WEATHER!

    LEONARD *joins her, pulling her close. They hold their ground against the gale which finally starts to subside.*

AS THE CURTAIN SLOWLY STARTS TO FALL

David Greenspan

∾

Son of An Engineer

Son of an Engineer, produced by HOME for Contemporary Theatre and Art, premiered at Here Theatre in New York on January 12, 1994, with the following cast:

Chuck Coggins
Karin Levitas
Thomas Pasley
Lisa Welti

Characters:
TOM
PHOEBE
THE KILLIAN BOY
DIANE
THE KILLIAN BOY'S MOTHER

Directed by David Greenspan; Sound Design: Edward Kosla; Costume Design: Mary Meyers; Light Design: John Lewis; Set Design: Alan Glovsky; Stage Manager: James Kroll

Setting:
Act 1, Suburbia.
Act 2, Mars.

Note: This can be played by four. An actress doubles as DIANE and THE KILLIAN BOY'S MOTHER.

ACT ONE

Ding dong. Light illuminates the front door of a nice suburban home. Clean. Flagstone path leads to two flagstone steps up to the door. Through the picture window—drapes drawn—the interior of the house can be, at best, vaguely detected. When the facade travels, the inside will be revealed. Standing at the front door is THE KILLIAN BOY. *Early to mid-thirties, handsome, but not pretty, soft, but not fey. He is dressed simply—white tee shirt, pants, sturdy black shoes. He holds a windbreaker in one hand, a backpack droops from one shoulder. The front door opens—*TOM *is there.* TOM *is a large bear—like you see in the woods—ursidae carnivora. In one hand he holds his reading glasses and newspaper. Nice dad kind of head of the household pleasant.*

TOM: Yes? Can I help you?

THE KILLIAN BOY: Ummm…I don't know. Who are you?

    *From within the house, a woman's voice—*PHOEBE. *Pleasant, strained.*

PHOEBE: Who is it, Tom?

TOM: Some young man.

THE KILLIAN BOY: Is this the Killian residence?

TOM: It was.

PHOEBE: If he's selling something, just tell him to go away.

THE KILLIAN BOY: [*To* TOM.] What?

TOM: They've moved on.

THE KILLIAN BOY: I see.

    PHOEBE *appears at the door beside* TOM. *She's human, dresses attractively, and wears a pretty apron. Svelte. She holds a cooking fork and a dish towel. Busy day running errands. Been to the beauty parlor. Housewife. Pleasant.*

PHOEBE: [*To* TOM.] What's going on? [*To* THE KILLIAN BOY.] Hello.

TOM: He's looking for the Killians.

PHOEBE: [*To* TOM.] Oh. [*To* THE KILLIAN BOY.] They don't live here anymore.

TOM: Did you know them?

THE KILLIAN BOY: Yeah, I'm their son.

PHOEBE: Oh. [*To* TOM.] My goodness.

TOM: They didn't mention to you they were moving on?

THE KILLIAN BOY: No, they didn't.

TOM: When did you last speak with them?

THE KILLIAN BOY: About two weeks ago. They didn't leave a number or anything, did they?

TOM: I'm afraid not, son.

Phone rings offstage.

PHOEBE: Excuse me.

    PHOEBE *disappears into the house.*

THE KILLIAN BOY: My apartment was broken into the other day.

    Offstage, phone is picked up.

PHOEBE: Hello? Hi Jenny, how's he doing?

THE KILLIAN BOY: All my identification was stolen.

PHOEBE: Un huh.

THE KILLIAN BOY: I lost everything.

PHOEBE: Oh good, I'm glad to hear that. I'll tell Tom.

TOM: [*To* THE KILLIAN BOY.] Excuse me. [*Calling into the house.*] Is that Jenny? How's Frank?

PHOEBE: Wait, Tom.

TOM: Is that Jenny?

PHOEBE: Tom—wait!

THE KILLIAN BOY: [*To himself.*]I can't believe this. I grew up in this house. This is the house I grew up in.

TOM: A friend of ours was in surgery this afternoon. Good friend. [*Pause.*] You should have called in advance. You would have known your folks moved on.

THE KILLIAN BOY: I know.

    I guess so.

PHOEBE: Ok, I'll call you later. What time will you get home?I'll call you then. I'm so happy he's doing well. We're very relieved. We were worried.

TOM: [*To himself.*] Deep inside you. What do you see? Dark spots.

    PHOEBE *reappears.*

PHOEBE: It was Jenny.

TOM: That's what I thought.

PHOEBE: And he's fine. He's resting comfortably. Jenny's going to stay with him until nine, then she's going to go home. She's tired. I'll call her about ten.

TOM: You should have told her to stop by—we could have saved dinner for her.

PHOEBE: That's what I should have done. I'm going to call her back.

TOM: Can you reach her?

PHOEBE: I'll call the nurse's station. I can get the number.

THE KILLIAN BOY: Well, thanks for your help.

TOM: Where do you go from here?

THE KILLIAN BOY: I don't know.

TOM: Maybe you should come in the house.

    Silence. Uh oh.

THE KILLIAN BOY: There's no reason for that.

PHOEBE: I'll call the nurse's station. I can get the number.

THE KILLIAN BOY: Well, thanks for your help.

TOM: Where do you go from here?

THE KILLIAN BOY: I don't know.

TOM: Maybe you should come in the house.

    Silence. Uh oh.

THE KILLIAN BOY: I think I better be going.

TOM: You might find it interesting. See how it's changed inside.

PHOEBE: Tom, please, he's gotta find his family.

    Tom, please, he's gotta locate his family.

    Got to. Besides, Diane's not feeling well. A boy in the house. I don't know.

TOM: Diane's our daughter.

THE KILLIAN BOY: I feel so lost.

PHOEBE: Besides, Diane's not feeling well. A boy in the house. I don't know.

TOM: Diane's our daughter.

THE KILLIAN BOY: No, I'm gonna hit the road.

TOM: Diane's our daughter.

THE KILLIAN BOY: I feel so lost.

TOM: Then come on in.

THE KILLIAN BOY: I couldn't impose like this.

PHOEBE: I'm going to make my phone call. Tom, I think you're being a little…Well…

    PHOEBE *disappears into the house. Silence.* OK.

TOM: You don't have to come in. Don't feel obligated or under any pressure.

    You don't have to come in. Don't feel obligated or under any pressure. I just thought—

THE KILLIAN BOY: I better hit the road.

TOM: [*To himself.*] What then? What rest? Words without thought. When will we rest?

THE KILLIAN BOY: I better hit the road.

TOM: Well, good luck, son. I hope you find your family.

    Good luck, son. I hope you locate your family.

THE KILLIAN BOY: I hope so too.

    I do too.

    I hope so.

    I hope so too.

    THE KILLIAN BOY *hits the road.* TOM *watches him leave, then closes the door. Light changes, as the house facade travels.*

    Light illuminates the living room—the bar area. TOM *sets his newspaper down on a bar stool, switches on a small radio that rests on the bar, and mixes himself a martini. From the radio, comes a man's voice.*

VOICE FROM THE RADIO: Who is Daniel Greenburg? Where is Daniel Greenburg? Whatever happened to Daniel Greenburg? Daniel Greenburg has a lot of nerve. Daniel Greenburg's family was living in Beverly Hills, then moved into Los Angeles, west of Beverly Hills. Maybe they got a bigger house, I'm not sure. A nice house, sure about that. So then—but then Daniel Greenburg continued to go to school in Beverly Hills—even though he was no longer a resident of the city of Beverly Hills. I don't know how these people pull this off—fake an address or something. Perhaps Daniel didn't want to leave all his good friends at Horace Mann Elementary School in Beverly Hills—or perhaps Daniel didn't want to give up the superior education offered at Horace Mann Elementary School in Beverly Hills. Certain folks, now and again, find some way to get their kids into the Beverly Hills school system—even when they don't live in Beverly Hills.

Now I should note that Daniel Greenburg did not—to the best of my knowledge—attend Beverly Hills High School. He had by then terminated the charade and enrolled in either a Los Angeles City high school or some private institution. Either way—as far as I know—Daniel Greenburg did not attend Beverly Hills High School.

But whatever happened to Daniel Greenburg? I don't know how his life turned out. And what about Daniel Biscar? He was a genius. Whatever happened to Daniel Biscar? He was a student at Hillcrest Elementary School in Los Angeles, but his parents pulled him out—maybe to study in some special school for really smart children. Don't know what happened to him, how his life turned out. And what about Daniel Gunther? He went to Beverly Hills High School, I know that. How did his life turn out? And Danny Silver. Danny Silver was so funny—he was the funniest guy in school, just cracked me up. And he was always getting in trouble and sent to Mr. Hazzerott's office. What in god's name happened to him—how did his life turn out? All these people come and go from our lives and then we don't know what happened to them. And I'm sure those aren't the only Daniels. There are more! And what about the Alans and the Jans and the Michaels and the Sharons. Shit! And the Christophers—Chris—or no—Cliffs!—Cliffs! Cliff Curry. Whatever happened to Cliff Curry and Christopher Mulrooney—Alan Sperling and Alan Abshez? And the Rons! Ron Silverman, Ron what's his face. What happened to these people? What did they make of their lives? All moved on! Haven't heard from or about these people for twenty—some twenty-five years. Maybe some of them are dead.

Daniel Gunther, Jonathon Prince, Josh Goldstein. Oh, my god!

TOM *sips his martini. Light changes, as the living room travels.*

Light illuminates the kitchen. Black and white linoleum. A counter, center. Modern. One door leads to the dining room. Another door leads to the living room. PHOEBE is in the kitchen—getting plates, silverware and glassware ready to bring into the dining room. She calls to TOM.

PHOEBE: Honey, dinner's ready.

Immediately, TOM *enters.*

TOM: Did you call Jenny?

PHOEBE: You know, I didn't—I think she wants to be on her own tonight. She'll get home too late if she stops by here.

TOM: [*Sniffs.*] Smells good.

PHOEBE: Call Diane. I need some help getting dinner on the table.

TOM: I'll help you.

PHOEBE: No, you go and rest. I want Diane to help me.

TOM: I can help you.

PHOEBE: You've been working all day, darling. [*Calling.*] Diane, come down and help me set the table.

> From off left, above and behind, a girl's voice—DIANE.

DIANE: I'm doing my homework.

PHOEBE: You can do your homework after dinner, sweetheart. I need some help.

TOM: [*Munching on something.*] Come on down, cookie. Help your mother. You can do your homework after dinner.

PHOEBE: She was watching cartoons when I got home.

DIANE: I have a lot to do.

TOM: Come on down, sweetie.

PHOEBE: [*Firmly.*] Diane, get down here this minute.

TOM: Don't get your mother angry, lambchop.

PHOEBE: Diane, I'm warning you.

TOM: Come on, baby, come down and help your mother; she's been working hard all day to make us a nice dinner.

PHOEBE: I swear, Tom, I'll beat the living shit out of her if she doesn't come down and help me.

TOM: Did you hear that, honey? You better come down.

PHOEBE: Give me your strap, Tom.

TOM: I'll help you. Let me—

PHOEBE: No, Tom, she has to learn. Give me your belt.

TOM: Pussy, come down before your mother goes upstairs and beats you.

PHOEBE: Don't give her options, Tom. This is where the problem begins.

DIANE: I'll be right down.

TOM: There we go.

PHOEBE: I don't care. Give me your strap.

TOM: Oh, come on, relax, honey.

PHOEBE: I swear, Tom, you give me that belt, or I'm going up there with a spatula.

TOM: [*More the authoritarian, playfully.*] Hey, come on now.

PHOEBE: Don't come on me. I'm here all day like this. You don't know what it's like all day.

TOM: [*His teeth clench, his tone changing, begins play-boxing with PHOEBE—psychosis surfacing.*] What are you getting excited for?

PHOEBE: I don't know how much more I can take, Tom.

TOM: What are you talking about?

PHOEBE: All you do is humiliate me.

TOM: You're talking crazy.

PHOEBE: No, I'm not.

TOM: What are you getting yourself all worked up for?

PHOEBE: I can't take it anymore.

TOM: [*Taking hold of her wrist.*] Come on, baby, stop it now.

PHOEBE: Let go of me.

TOM: I want you to stop it.

PHOEBE: Don't do this to me.

TOM: You're acting like an animal.

PHOEBE: Don't call me an animal!

TOM: I'm not calling you an animal. I'm saying you're acting like one.

PHOEBE: Don't do this to me.

TOM: Keep your voice down.

PHOEBE: Don't tell me what to do.

TOM: Hey—

PHOEBE: I'm warning you.

TOM: You want the neighbors to hear this?

PHOEBE: Come on, Tom.

> *Phone rings offstage.*

TOM: See, that's probably Mrs. Benjamin, calling to complain.

PHOEBE: The woman's a Nazi.

TOM: [*Pounding his head.*] She was in a concentration camp. You want me to tell her that?

PHOEBE: Stop it, Tom.

TOM: The whole neighborhood knows you're an animal.

PHOEBE: I'm gonna kill you.

TOM: See that, like an animal. Let's call up Dick Edelman, and see what he thinks about that.

PHOEBE: Fuck Dick Edelman!

TOM: [*Shouting.*] Hey, Dick, did you hear that?

PHOEBE: Cut it out, Tom.

DIANE: Will someone answer the phone, I'm trying to do my homework.

TOM: [*Threatening, pounding his fist into his hand.*] You see that, your daughter's trying to do her homework, baby, and look how you're carrying on.

PHOEBE: Get away from me, you son of a bitch.

TOM: You gonna call me names, I'll slap you.

PHOEBE: You touch me and I'll kill you.

TOM: [*Pushing her toward the living room.*] Go answer the phone!

PHOEBE: Get away from me.

TOM: Answer the phone, for Christ sake. Get in there.

PHOEBE: Help.

TOM: You see what you're doing to me?

PHOEBE: Don't touch me, you piece of shit.

TOM: You see what you're turning me into?

PHOEBE: I don't know what you're talking about.

TOM: I'm this close to killing you.

PHOEBE: You're hurting me. Help.

> *Sound of* DIANE, *running downstairs to answer the phone.*

DIANE: [*Calling.*] I'll get it.

PHOEBE: Diane, your father's trying to hurt me. Come help me before he hurts me.
Sound of phone picked up.
DIANE: Hello?
PHOEBE: Diane, help me.
TOM: [*Pounding his fist into his hand.*] Shut up!
DIANE: [*After a pause.*] Dad, it's for you.
TOM: I'm telling you something, baby. [*Two fist pounds into his hand.*] You know?
TOM *exits to living room. Sound of* DIANE, *running upstairs, back to her room.*
PHOEBE *collapses on the kitchen floor. Light changes, the kitchen remains.*

Light illuminates a phone booth. THE KILLIAN BOY *enclosed within. He speaks on the phone.*
THE KILLIAN BOY: [*Rapidly.*] I don't know, Seymour, I feel like—I don't know, I feel like—Like—I don't know—like I can't…go on at all, you know. At all—I feel like—Like this—I don't know—I feel like—Like I can't…go on, you know. I feel—I think I feel when this—Feel this terror, terror, Seymour—this real—very—very real terror—you know, I feel like—I don't know, this—I just don't—I don't—I just don't think I—I don't know.

I just know—I know I can't go on like this. I can't—like this—go on, Seymour—not like this—that's all I know. A change? Not like this—there are no words. What? There are no words—to describe. No words. Don't have the words. I can't go on describing without words. Not without words. I can't. Can't without words. Can't without. There's this dread. What? Dread—terrible dread—morning, afternoon, evening—a dread. Terrible. Dread. Terrible. Do you know what I mean? As I speak now. Wait, Seymour, my dime runs out! As I speak. There's no number, they've scratched it away. I've no more change. What? Seymour, where do I go from here? Wait, where do I go? I'm just repeating, repeating! Where do I go? What's the secret? What? The secret, yes, to a happy life, a good life. My dime runs out! How do I get there from here? How do I get there? I see no sign! Seymour, they interrupt us. Are you with someone? Are you with someone? Are you with someone now? May I call you back? May I call you back?
Hold. He hangs up. Hold. He exits the phone booth. Sound of automobile traffic. He looks both ways. He smiles sheepishly.
Don't do that.
Hold. He re-enters the phone booth, sound of automobile traffic out. Hold. He picks up. Dials zero.
Hello, Operator? I'd like to make a collect call. It's a local number—can I do that? PHOENIX 9-6959. Um…The Killian boy. Tom. Thank you.
Through the phone, the sound of the number being dialed, phone ringing, phone picked up. From inside the phone, DIANE'S *voice.*
DIANE: Hello?
OPERATOR: Good evening, I have a collect call—
PHOEBE: Diane, help me.
OPERATOR: for Tom—

TOM: [*Sound of fist pounded into hand.*] Shut up!

OPERATOR: from the Killian boy.

DIANE: Dad, it's for you.

TOM: I'm telling you something, baby. [*Two fist pounds into the hand.*] You know?

> *Then the sound of a door opening, and someone running up a set of stairs.* TOM'S *voice.*

Hello?

> *Light changes,* PHOEBE *speaks from her position on the kitchen floor.*

PHOEBE: Hello, Jenny—it's Phoebe, how's Frank? It's Phoebe, how's Frank? Is Frank— how's Frank? How's Frank? Is Frank—how's Frank?

> *Light changes, as the kitchen and telephone booth travel.*

> *Light illuminates the dining room. A table, nicely set. Four chairs. A door, right, shut—it leads to the kitchen. A door, left, open—it leads to the hall. Seated, enjoying dinner,* TOM, PHOEBE, *and* THE KILLIAN BOY. THE KILLIAN BOY *sits with his back to the open door. A fourth place is empty—the setting untouched—* DIANE'S.

TOM: Aerospace.

THE KILLIAN BOY: Wow.

TOM: [*Chuckling.*] Missiles and bombers.

PHOEBE: [*Pleasantly.*] Who would like more asparagus?

TOM: ICBMS.

THE KILLIAN BOY: But what, specifically?

PHOEBE: [*To* THE KILLIAN BOY.] More asparagus?

THE KILLIAN BOY: Yes, thank you.

TOM: This is a delicious meal, by the way, baby.

PHOEBE: I'm glad you're enjoying it.

THE KILLIAN BOY: Really delicious. Everything.

PHOEBE: Tom? How 'bout you? More asparagus?

TOM: Uh, sure. Not too much.

PHOEBE: [*To* THE KILLIAN BOY.] Do you like asparagus? Because I just love it.

THE KILLIAN BOY: I used not to like it. Now I do.

PHOEBE: It's my favorite. And there's more of everything, don't be shy. Potatoes. Chicken. What about some more chicken for you?

THE KILLIAN BOY: I'm fine for right now.

PHOEBE: Tom? Chicken? Potatoes? You're doing all right?

TOM: I got plenty right here.

PHOEBE: And we have green salad when you're ready. I'm sorry to interrupt.

TOM: No, I was just saying—

PHOEBE: Tom's work is classified. It's difficult for him to talk about what he does.

TOM: [*A bit embarrassed.*] Hey, come on, baby, you make it sound important.

THE KILLIAN BOY: Oh, gee, I'm sorry. I didn't mean to—

TOM: It's nothing. I work in weights and measures.

THE KILLIAN BOY: Uh huh.

TOM: Nothing special.

PHOEBE: You know, I'm very glad you called us from the station. I didn't realize the bus stopped running this early. It was smart that you called.

THE KILLIAN BOY: Well, it's very nice of you to have me over.

PHOEBE: I just wish Diane would come down. She's not feeling well.

TOM: She should come down.

PHOEBE: [*To* TOM.] Oh, she and Gammara had some kind of fight, I don't know.

TOM: Again? She's too young to have a boyfriend.

PHOEBE: Well, I told you that. But you didn't want to interfere.

TOM: I didn't know how serious it was.

PHOEBE: Well, it's not that serious. It's just I think at this age they get kind of intense.
     [*To* THE KILLIAN BOY.] Gammara is from Japan. But he's had a very difficult upbringing. His parents are divorced—which I think is very sad—because he's such a sweet boy.

TOM: He a nice kid.

PHOEBE: He's a little violent, though, Tom—which scares me.
     [*To* THE KILLIAN BOY.] Anyway, his mother left Japan after the divorce— although she hardly speaks a word of English—which is odd—because the Japanese, in general, speak very good English—they learned after the War—but she has money—I don't think she works. [*To* TOM.] But Tom, you were talking about aerospace. What you do.

TOM: It's nothing.

PHOEBE: Tom works in weights and measures. At the Douglas plant.

TOM: When you design an aircraft, to insure that its design is aerodynamically sound—

PHOEBE: Boy, do I love asparagus. I could eat it all day.

TOM: [*After a brief pause.*] The weight and measure of each section of the aircraft…you have to calculate the weight and measure of each section to insure the aircraft is aerodynamically sound. This is determining…in designing…
     So for instance in a rocket—my unit will calculate how much, for instance, a fin…we work with the designers—to determine how much, for instance, a fin can weigh…or the length…the kind of metal used in construction… what kind of materials will weigh…their properties…So that in trajectory…in flight… So we determine—

PHOEBE: It's all so sad, isn't it? I mean, I know it's important. But if someone should actually press those buttons some day. Boy oh boy, what a mess! I sure wish there was peace in the world. [*To* THE KILLIAN BOY.] Don't you?

THE KILLIAN BOY: Oh, yes. I do.

PHOEBE: I pray for peace. I was just a girl during the War—a teenager. And it wasn't— of course we weren't subjected to what was going on in Europe. And all the Jews being slaughtered.
     [*Calling.*] Diane? Are you in your room? I wish you'd come down to supper. We have company tonight. [*To* THE KILLIAN BOY.] I'm so sorry.

TOM: Maybe I should go upstairs and get her.

PHOEBE: No, Tom. Leave her. I don't know what's wrong. [*To* THE KILLIAN BOY.] I'm sorry. I wish she'd come down for you. Nothing much we can do. When my father passed away I cried and cried for days. He was such a good man. But now what? What are we left with—after they're gone? Tom had a hard time as a kid too. When your folks split up. Very sad. Tom's mother was a bit unstable. When they divorced she left Tom and his younger brother, Sidney, with their father and moved back to Chicago—started living with her Aunt Rose. Spent the rest of her life in that house. Never left that house. Wouldn't even speak on the phone. Complete recluse. [*To* TOM.] You talked to her—what— once, twice between the time she left and when she died?

TOM: I talked to her—I don't know—once, maybe twice. Once when I was away at college.

PHOEBE: [*To* THE KILLIAN BOY.] Tom went to school in Iowa. I never met her. She was on medication for years. The pain inflicted on Tom. We got a call one day she had passed away. Tom talked about never having seen her since she left the family— the long years without her—how he misses her to this day—how he's still in mourning. Calls out Mommy in his sleep. Imagine her—and she wasn't an old woman either. But locked herself up in that house with her aunt. Never felt the light of day again. Until she died. And then only briefly. Into the earth. Who's ready for dessert? Or I forgot, we have salad.

>   *They all sense another presence—offstage. It is to* THE KILLIAN BOY's *back.* TOM *and* PHOEBE *see.*

TOM: Hey, angel. You came down.

PHOEBE: Come in, sweetie. We want you to meet the Killian boy. He used to live in this house.

>   *From offstage,* DIANE's *voice.*

DIANE: [*Shyly.*] I don't know.

PHOEBE: Oh, come on, sweetie, don't be shy.

TOM: Come on in, princess, there's nothing to be afraid of. Your supper's getting cold.

DIANE: I'm not hungry.

PHOEBE: [*Warmly.*] Yes you are, honey. You were nagging me all afternoon about how hungry you were.

DIANE: But then I had crackers. Now I'm not hungry anymore.

TOM: Diane, the Killian boy's going to be very disappointed if he doesn't get to see you.

THE KILLIAN BOY: [*Not turning.*] I really will.

DIANE: I'll come in later.

TOM: There's nothing to be afraid of, kitten. This young man isn't going to hurt you. Come in and introduce yourself.

PHOEBE: Tom, maybe we better leave her alone for a bit. Maybe she'll come in later.

>   TOM *and* PHOEBE *return to eating.* THE KILLIAN BOY *turns slowly to the offstage behind him. But as he does, light is extinguished.*

Light illuminates the cellar. Stairs ascend. The door at the top of the stairs is open—light floods in. A single illuminated light bulb hangs center. Two small windows, raised high on the back wall, peek out at the surface—grass and daylight visible. P H O E B E *stands near the top of the stairs—aproned. She holds a dish and a dish towel. In the cellar, a hospital bed—occupied. The bed is directed upstage, its upper half raised. Thus, only the top back of the patient's head is visible. Long white hair, strands cascading over the sides of the pillows. The patient is hooked up to an* IV *and several monitors that display the life signs. Standing beside the bed is* T H E K I L L I A N B O Y.

P H O E B E: [*To herself.*] Oh, dear. My goodness. And Tom at the office.

T H E K I L L I A N B O Y: [*To the patient.*] I don't understand. What happened to you? They told me you moved away. Where's Dad? What's going on here?

> *Phone rings offstage.*

P H O E B E: Oh, shoot!

> T H E K I L L I A N B O Y *realizes* P H O E B E *is above him. Looks up at her. To* T H E K I L L I A N B O Y.

Don't move. I'll be right back.

> P H O E B E *exits.* T H E K I L L I A N B O Y *takes hold of the patient's hand.*

T H E K I L L I A N B O Y: What's happening here?

> *Offstage, phone is picked up.*

P H O E B E: Hello? Oh, hi, Jenny. No, but can I call you back? Yea, I'm just a little…No, nothing's wrong. I'm just…OK, fine, I'll call you back. I wanna hear about Frank.

> *Phone is hung up.* P H O E B E *returns without dish or dish towel.*

I'm sorry. I should have told you sooner. We should have. Tom didn't want to upset you. We didn't—want to.

T H E K I L L I A N B O Y: What happened?

P H O E B E: I don't know.

T H E K I L L I A N B O Y: What is she doing here? Where's my father?

P H O E B E: I don't know. He's not here. I'm sure.

T H E K I L L I A N B O Y: Can she hear me? Ma? Ma?

P H O E B E: I don't think she can hear you. She can't speak. Doesn't speak. At least not…

T H E K I L L I A N B O Y: Is she dying?

P H O E B E: I don't know. Yes. It looks that way.

T H E K I L L I A N B O Y: Oh, my god! Why isn't she in the hospital?

P H O E B E: I don't know! I don't know! I don't know anything! Tom— I'm sure Tom can explain everything. When he gets home from work this evening, you'll ask him. There must be an explanation.

T H E K I L L I A N B O Y: She doesn't answer me.

P H O E B E: She's very sick. She wasn't sick when you last saw her?

T H E K I L L I A N B O Y: In perfect health. This sudden change.

P H O E B E: I know. It's so sudden.

T H E K I L L I A N B O Y: Why didn't you tell me my mother was here?

P H O E B E: Tom advised against it. I'm not sure.

Phone rings.

Oh, damn. I'll just let it ring. Why don't you come upstairs, sit in the kitchen with me while I do my ironing? I'll make you a cup of coffee.

THE KILLIAN BOY: I'm going to stay here with my mother.

PHOEBE: Oh, please. Please. Come keep me company.

Backdoor opens upstairs.

DIANE: [*Offstage.*] Hi, Mom, I'm home.

Phone stops ringing.

PHOEBE: Ok, sweetheart.

DIANE: Was that the phone?

PHOEBE: I don't know. Why don't you grab an apple from the fridge. And pour yourself a glass of milk.

DIANE: Do we have any crackers?

PHOEBE: Diane, please, don't start eating crackers. You're going to ruin your appetite.

DIANE: Mom, dinner isn't for hours.

PHOEBE: Diane—

DIANE: Besides, what's the difference if I have an apple and milk, or if I have crackers?

PHOEBE: I hope to god you realize some day, Diane, how much you upset me. I hope some day you realize.

DIANE: Fine, I'll have an apple!

PHOEBE: Eat your goddamn crackers, I don't care.

DIANE: Mom, don't—

PHOEBE: I said, eat crackers—I'm through with you.

DIANE: They're not my crackers, first of all, they're everybody's. You bought them for the house.

PHOEBE: Diane, I don't want to discuss it anymore. You should know, though, that when your father wants a cracker…and he can't find one…because you've finished the box—

DIANE: Oh, shut up! I'm not even listening to you anymore.

*Footsteps—*DIANE *is on her way up to her room.*

PHOEBE: That's right, Diane, lock yourself in your room. That's a fine way to deal with things.

Door slams.

Diane!

[*To* THE KILLIAN BOY.] Please, come upstairs, leave your mother. She's not going anywhere.

THE KILLIAN BOY: I can't leave her here. We should bring her upstairs.

PHOEBE: Let's wait for Tom. Please, I have ironing to do. Let me make you a cup of coffee. I promise you, things will straighten themselves out—just don't press it, right now. There's a logical explanation for what's going on. I know there is. Even if I can't articulate it. There has to be. Please, be patient with us.

THE KILLIAN BOY *looks up at* PHOEBE, *but continues to hold his* MOTHER'S *hand. Sound of a large dog, barking, pulling at its chain, fades up. Light is extinguished.*

Sound of a large dog, barking, pulling at its chain, continues. Light illuminates TOM *and* PHOEBE's *bedroom. Large four-poster, center. Left of bed, small table—on table, lamp, alarm clock. Bright, Sunday morning light streams in through window, right and left of bed. Breeze blows curtains into room. Gentle. Right of bed, the bathroom door—ajar. Man's robe hangs on inside of door. Sound of a lawn mower. In bed,* TOM *and* PHOEBE. TOM, *right,* PHOEBE, *left.* PHOEBE *lies flat on her back. She wears a blue lamé robe, visible where the cover ends.* TOM *is removing his underpants beneath the covers. Otherwise, bare. Drops underpants on floor beside bed—large, red-striped boxers.* TOM *moves toward* PHOEBE.

TOM: [*Manly.*] Hi.

    TOM *attempts to put his hand into* PHOEBE's *robe. She stops him.*

PHOEBE: No, Tom.

    Brushes his hand from her. Beneath the cover she pulls up her nightgown, adjusts her robe—makes available her vagina.

Here.

    She spits in her hand.

I've got baking to do today, and marketing.

    She puts her moistened hand beneath the cover—masturbates TOM. TOM *touches her breast. When she feels him erect, she pulls him on top of her.*

Come on, Tom.

    TOM *gets on top of* PHOEBE, *attempts to put himself inside her. She stops him.*

PHOEBE: Wait.

    She takes hold of his member, positions him correctly.

Go ahead.

    He moves inside. PHOEBE *embraces* TOM. TOM *fucks* PHOEBE. *Slow.*

[*After a while.*] Hurry, Tom. I need to start baking. I'm meeting Jenny at 11:00.

    TOM *raises himself on his hands—push-up style. Fucks more. Cums in* PHOEBE. *Great growls as he cums—his teeth exposed. When finished, he lies on top of* PHOEBE, *listens to the dog bark. Time passes.*

TOM: [*Peaceful.*] That damn dog.

    Time passes.

PHOEBE: [*Gently.*] I need to get going, dear.

TOM: OK, baby.

    TOM *pulls himself out and off of* PHOEBE.

[*Saluting.*] Thank you very much.

    PHOEBE *gets out of bed, pulls down her nightgown, adjusts her robe. She exits right to bathroom.*

PHOEBE: [*As she exits.*] Take a shower. I'll cook you eggs for breakfast.

    TOM *is getting out of bed. Huge bear penis—not completely flaccid yet.*

[*From offstage, chuckling.*] That dog is really something.

    TOM *looks out left window.*

TOM: Poor fella—he wants to go in. Why don't they let him in the house?

PHOEBE: [*With dark sadness.*] Take a shower, Tom.

    Sound of shower turned on.

I'm putting the water on for you. [*Containing a sob.*] Hurry down, dear. I've got marketing to do.

Sound of door closed from other side of bathroom. TOM *stays at left window, looks out. Turns, touches his penis.*

TOM: What's a matter, boy?

TOM *moves to the bed. Sits.* PHOEBE's *side. Hold. Holds his penis. Sits, holding his penis. Masturbates. Sits there and masturbates. Curtains blowing, sound of dog barking, sound of lawn mowing, sound of shower as he masturbates.*

Light illuminates the backyard. Sliding glass patio doors. A frosted bathroom window above. A fence. Standing center, a red rocket ship, aimed at the stars—its hatch open, a ladder descending to the ground. TOM's *legs stick out from underneath the rocket. He's making some last minute repairs with electrical equipment. Sparks flying.* PHOEBE, *aproned, slides open the patio doors. Detected vaguely through the frosted bathroom window above,* THE KILLIAN BOY.

PHOEBE: Tom, we don't have all day.

[*Calling offstage through the sliding door.*] Diane, didn't I ask you to get into the ship? We're going to be blasting off any minute—I don't want to have to leave you behind.

From offstage, DIANE's *voice.*

DIANE: Mother, would you please stop nagging me.

PHOEBE: I'm not nagging you.

DIANE: Yes, you are.

PHOEBE: No, I'm not. It's just—

Phone rings offstage.

Darn, I bet that's Jenny.

Kitchen timer rings offstage.

Oh, and my bird is done. Tom, have you seen The Killian boy?

TOM: [*From underneath the rocket.*] I think he's upstairs, shaving.

PHOEBE: Oh, boy, I hope we get out of here on time. They've launched their missiles. This is the end of the world.

PHOEBE *exits through the sliding door. The bathroom window flies open, revealing* THE KILLIAN BOY, *lathered, standing at the sink, shaving. Buck naked but for a wrist watch. In one hand he holds a razor. In the other hand, a phone—the base resting on the floor, the cord extending underneath the bathroom door. He speaks on the phone.*

THE KILLIAN BOY: I don't know, Seymour, should I go with them—what choice do I have, the world ends? So, really, there's no choice. Go with them. And my mother—I was planning on bringing her along—what do you think? Better if I could leave her behind. I don't think I can, Seymour, I don't think I can. I have tried. You know I've tried. She nears death.

Seymour, soon I'll leave the Earth. What if I don't see you again? Will you miss me? Will you miss me when I'm gone? You will?! I don't think I'll see you again,

Seymour, I don't think I will. I have your number, yes. So I'll go with them. Yes. Like the end of *Ulysses*. Yes, yes.

> *He hangs up, finishes shaving.*

How old am I? Thirty-six. A man. I'm no longer a boy. I look in the mirror. That's me shaving. A man, full grown. Hair on my body. Been there for years, but now I see it. If I live, I'll grow old. My body will continue to change. Hair will grey or disappear. My flesh will fade. Then I'll die. There'll be nothing. I'll be gone again.

> *Five knocks on the bathroom door.* D I A N E's *voice.*

D I A N E: It's me, hi. My mom is getting panicky. She wants to go.

T H E K I L L I A N B O Y: Ok, I'll be right out. Does you father need help with the rocket?

D I A N E: I don't know. Do you think I should bring my math book along?

T H E K I L L I A N B O Y: I guess so, sure. Why not?

D I A N E: Do you think you could help me with some of my problems?

T H E K I L L I A N B O Y: I'm not that good at math.

D I A N E: You are.

T H E K I L L I A N B O Y: Not really, Diane. You should get your father to help you. After all, he's an engineer. He excels in mathematics.

D I A N E: I don't like asking my father for help.

T H E K I L L I A N B O Y: Why not?

D I A N E: Because he doesn't help me solve the problem. He just does it for me.

> Last year I had to write a paper about Columbus and the discovery of America. Dad took one look at the paper and thought it was awful. We sat down together, for him to help me. He ended up writing the paper himself. There was hardly a word of mine in it. *The Discovery of America.* He wrote it. We got a B minus.

> *From offstage—as if downstairs,* P H O E B E's *voice.*

P H O E B E: What are you kids doing up there? The Earth is doomed. Hurry down.

T H E K I L L I A N B O Y: [*Calling to* P H O E B E.] We're coming. [*To* D I A N E.] Diane, when will you show yourself to me? I keep wandering. In all the time I've been here, I've never once seen you. Only your voice. There's always a wall between us.

D I A N E: Open the door.

T H E K I L L I A N B O Y: I can't right now. I'm undressed.

P H O E B E: [*Coming up the stairs.*] Diane.

T H E K I L L I A N B O Y: You better go downstairs. I'll be right down.

> *Sound of* D I A N E *heading downstairs.* T H E K I L L I A N B O Y *begins to dress. Three knocks on the bathroom door.* P H O E B E's *voice.*

P H O E B E: [*Softly.*] I didn't mean to call you a kid. I'm sorry.

> *The bathroom window descends as* T H E K I L L I A N B O Y *continues to dress.* T O M *gets out from underneath the rocket ship, wipes his hands with an old grease rag, talks to himself.*

T O M: Well, well, well, house guests, heh? And who might you be? Oh, no, no, now don't tell me. Let's see, you're a…you're traveling in disguise. No, that's not right— I…You're a…you're going on a visit. No, I'm wrong—that's rather a… You're a…you're running away!

PHOEBE *enters through the sliding door.*

PHOEBE: [*Catching him.*] For god's sake, Tom. Stop that!

TOM: [*Caught.*] What's a matter?

PHOEBE: What are you doing?

TOM: Nothing.

PHOEBE: Stop fooling around!

TOM: All right, come on now—you suprised me. I think we're ready.

PHOEBE: You still haven't told me where you're taking us, Tom.

TOM: [*Pointing into the sky.*] Look.

PHOEBE: [*Looking up.*] Oh, my god, the missiles.

TOM: Look at that. Beautiful, isn't it? The trajectory.

PHOEBE: [*Looking offstage through the sliding door.*] Oh, Tom, hurry, help him. He's got his mother.

    TOM *exits through the sliding door.*

    [*To herself, as she looks at the missiles.*] Oh, Jenny. [*A small gesture—as if plucking something from the air, bringing it to her heart.*] Bring it along.

    THE KILLIAN BOY *and* TOM *enter, carrying* THE KILLIAN BOY'S MOTHER *in her hospital bed. She is still hooked up to all the life support machinery.*

    Easy does it fellas. Tom, watch yourself, don't scrape the walls. Ada spent all day cleaning yesterday. She does such a nice job.

    [*To* THE KILLIAN BOY.] Your poor mother. I feel sorry for her. What could have caused this terrible illness? Are you sure you wouldn't rather leave her behind?

    THE KILLIAN BOY *does not respond.*

    I guess not.

    TOM *and* THE KILLIAN BOY *carry* THE KILLIAN BOY'S MOTHER *up the ladder and into the rocket ship.*

    [*To herself.*] If he were my son…Well, he is my son—in a way. Isn't he? Aren't you? Why am I talking to myself?

    PHOEBE *exits through the sliding door.* TOM *and* THE KILLIAN BOY *emerge from the rocket ship.*

TOM: Don't even think about it. She's locked in tight. It would take a great force to dislodge her.

THE KILLIAN BOY: Ok.

TOM: What's your mother's name, by the way?

THE KILLIAN BOY: April, I believe. She never told me. But fishing through her drawers, one day, I came on an old snap shot. A little girl—standing in a driveway—backed up against an auto—scrawny—hand on hip—pouting, clutching a broken doll—shadow of the photographer upon her. Scrawled in blue ink on the border, "April, 1936."

TOM: Could be the month.

THE KILLIAN BOY: Or her name. I'll never know.

    PHOEBE *enters with a large covered roasting pan.*

P H O E B E: Tom, have you seen Diane?

T O M: What?

P H O E B E: [*Calling offstage through the sliding door.*] Diane, please, you're driving me crazy. Get in the ship!

> *From inside the rocket ship,* D I A N E'S *voice.*

D I A N E: For god's sake, Mother, what do you want?

P H O E B E: What are you doing? Where are you?

D I A N E: I'm in the rocket already. For christ sake!

P H O E B E: I swear, Diane. [*To* T O M.] Tom, why didn't you tell me she was on board?

T O M: I didn't see her get on. What are you getting so excited for, baby?

P H O E B E: Don't start with me, Tom. I'm serious. I'll throw this chicken at you.

T O M: Hey, watch it now.

D I A N E: Will you two shut up, so we can get going.

P H O E B E: I'm really ready to drop dead, but let's just get the hell out of here. The missiles are upon us.

> P H O E B E *begins climbing the ladder. She hands the roasting pan to* TOM.

Here, Tom, put the chicken on board.

> T O M *carries the roasting pan into the rocket ship.*

[*To* T H E K I L L I A N B O Y.] Is your mother safely stowed?

THE KILLIAN BOY: Yes.

P H O E B E: [*Cautiously.*] You know I wish you were leaving her, and not bringing her.

THE KILLIAN BOY: Uh huh.

P H O E B E: [*Demurely.*] You don't mind, when I speak to people, if I refer to you as my son?

THE KILLIAN BOY: No, it's O K. But I'm not your son.

PHOEBE: I know. I'm sorry. Tom is not Diane's father. I was married once before. I left my first husband. He was very disturbed.

> T O M *pokes his head out from inside the ship.*

T O M: We better get going.

P H O E B E: Ok.

> P H O E B E *boards the rocket ship.*

T O M: [*To* T H E K I L L I A N B O Y.] Say good-bye to the world. Next stop, Mars!

> THE KILLIAN BOY *boards the rocket ship.* TOM *closes the hatch. Engines ignite. The rocket ship blasts off. The Earth is destroyed by missiles.*

ACT TWO

Ding dong. Light illuminates Mars. Barren, dusty terrain. Distant mountains. Cloudy sky. Wind blowing. Right of center, the rocket ship, fallen on its side, cracked open. Its landing legs are extended—either it crashed, and the legs proved useless, or it made a safe landing, but over time has been left to rust and junk. General refuse— solid waste littered about. A small encampment, left—a shabby tent—flaps blowing in the Martian wind. Near the tent, P H O E B E, topless, kneeling by a metal washtub, washing her breasts with a dish towel. She hasn't been to the beauty parlor in months. Wears the same apron over the same skirt. All gone ratty. Same shoes, but the heels have long since broken off.

P H O E B E: Been brought down. Clean my tits. Wash my jugs. The language you use now, Phoebe. If I'm lucky, I won't talk long. Something will happen. A change in fortune. That's it. I'll get out of here. Until then—wash yourself.

From within the tent, a phone rings. P H O E B E *lets it ring.*

See something else.

T O M *enters from behind the rocket ship, right. He is nude, his huge bear penis erect. He is followed by* T H E K I L L I A N B O Y. T H E K I L L I A N B O Y *is also nude.*

Observe this.

T O M: Come on, son.

T O M *kneels in the dust.* T H E K I L L I A N B O Y *kneels before him, prostrating himself, taking* T O M's *penis into his mouth.*

That's a boy.

T H E K I L L I A N B O Y *gives* T O M *oral sex.* T O M's *hand on the back of* T H E K I L L I A N B O Y's *head.*

T O M: [*To himself.*] This is what you were waiting for. Wasn't it? All these years. Then let them see it. I don't care.

P H O E B E: I grow accustomed to this. Indeed I do.

T O M: Hell, honey. I've grown accustomed to this. But how am I punished.

T O M *takes his hand from the back of* T H E K I L L I A N B O Y's *head. Puts both hands on his hips. Music sounds: Benedictine Nuns.*

[*Expounding, generally.*] Surround yourself with youth and you'll never grow old. Chow, chow, chow, chow, chow. There is a force. An energy. Make contact with it.

You begin with a point. This point is a contact. An opening. Allow it to enter you. It will open you.

It is a point of light. This light enters you. It is a goodness.

Open yourself to this goodness. You see, there's nothing to be afraid or ashamed of. This force will purify you.

PHOEBE: Once I was happy. I walked in the sun, felt its warmth on my head. Then disaster struck, and I wasn't prepared.

TOM: You establish a form by imposing a structure. Begin with a point. Establish that point in space, a point of light. Now throw a second point out into space, a second point of light. Connect those two points of light with a line segment. Feel the energy move between those two points of light. Chow, chow, chow, chow, chow, chow, chow.

PHOEBE: Once, long ago, I was happy. I walked in the light of day. Then darkness came, covered me.

TOM: You establish a third point. A third point of light. These points of light are knowledge. [*To* THE KILLIAN BOY.] Keep moving on me, boy.

   THE KILLIAN BOY *affirms vocally, as he continues sucking* TOM's *penis.* Where was I?

PHOEBE: Things began pleasantly enough, didn't they? Now look what you've done.

TOM: [*Remembering.*] The third point, yes. Three points of light.
   [*To* THE KILLIAN BOY.] That's good.

PHOEBE: We'd hoped to leave behind us all the suffering and sordidness on Earth. The horrible human race. But look what's happened. A nightmare.

TOM: [*Expounding.*] Three points. These three points connected divine a triangle. A trinity. Three points of light. Chow, chow, chow.

PHOEBE: I'll never forgive you, Tom—for bringing us here. What you promised me!

TOM: This trinity is illumination. Three points of knowledge. You experience it. It experiences you.

PHOEBE: [*Calling.*] Diane! Diane, where are you? Your mother's calling you. [*To herself.*] I hope she hasn't wandered into the mountains.

TOM: Now break form!

   TOM *puts his hand on the back of* THE KILLIAN BOY's *head, pushes* THE KILLIAN BOY *harder up and down on his penis.*
   [*To* THE KILLIAN BOY.] Really work it.

PHOEBE: I'm stuck in the mud.

TOM: [*Expounding.*] You envision a fourth point. Chow!

PHOEBE: Phoebe say shit.

TOM: You slit your triangle. The trinity dissolves. Four points now, unaligned in space. Chow, chow, chow, chow. But ah! You give meaning. You create a new form by imposing structure. From chaos, order. Stay with me!

   TOM *holds* THE KILLIAN BOY *by his hair, holds him down on his penis.*
   Now. You force these four points of light into a new alignment, a new structure.

PHOEBE: This is madness, isn't it?

TOM: [*Gesturing.*] You draw a line segment from point A to point B. Chow.

PHOEBE: Or maybe everybody lives this way.

TOM: [*Gesturing.*] Now quick, connect points C and D, another line segment. Chow, chow.

PHOEBE: Or is it like the Christians say, our little lives are but a reckless prelude to some divine afterbirth?

TOM *releases* THE KILLIAN BOY's *hair, gives him a crack on the back of his head.* THE KILLIAN BOY *resumes moving up and down on* TOM's *penis.*

TOM: Now, you're ready. [*Gesturing.*] Impose line segment CD upon line segment AB at one quarter distance from A on AB. Yes! That's it.

PHOEBE: A revelation, I'm sure.

TOM *orgasms into* THE KILLIAN BOY's *mouth, holds* THE KILLIAN BOY's *head on his penis as he orgasms.*

TOM: A cross! You lay down on it. "Oh, father, father…" Some shit like that.

[*To* THE KILLIAN BOY.] Just swallow it, boy.

PHOEBE: Forgive us. To put you through this. It wasn't my idea. The sweet Sabbath wine has turned to vinegar.

TOM: So much for him.

TOM *pulls his penis from* THE KILLIAN BOY's *mouth, pushes him aside.* THE KILLIAN BOY *buries his face in the dust, moaning, spitting up* TOM's *jism. The spitting up not visible to the audience.* TOM *squats. The music stops.*

Now, let's sit here in the dust and share philosophy. We are players, aren't we? Some rude mechanics.

PHOEBE: This is awful. I won't be a part of this.

[*Calling, as she puts on her brassiere.*] Diane! Diane, why aren't you listening to me? I hope you haven't wandered into the mountains.

PHOEBE *puts on her blouse. The phone stops ringing.*

The phone stops ringing. I hope it wasn't Jenny. To keep her waiting like this. Will she forgive me?

PHOEBE *exits into the tent.*

TOM: [*To* THE KILLIAN BOY.] Oh, yes, I suffer too. You're not the only one. Self-indulgent little whelp. Think how this affects me. The things I'm forced to do. Phoebe was right. Something she said. I can't remember.

PHOEBE *rolls out* THE KILLIAN BOY's *mother. As ever, in her hospital bed. She is still attached to her IV, but not the rest of the equipment.*

PHOEBE: I've done the best I could.

TOM: Thank you, dear. You have. Sit with me.

PHOEBE: I've done as directed. Let me go.

[*To* THE KILLIAN BOY.] It's your mother.

PHOEBE *exits into the tent.* THE KILLIAN BOY *rises, goes to his* MOTHER, *lays himself across her on the hospital bed, weeps.*

TOM: Go to your mother, son. While I sit in the desert and philosophize. Yes, it's growing dark. Night falls. I'll sit up all night and ruminate. The stars to contemplate.

Indeed, it has grown dark. The clouds have rolled by, and night has fallen by PHOEBE's *last exit. The Martian sky is filled with stars. The asteroid belt is visible. And Jupiter—a prominent dot. Most conspicuous are the two Martian moons, Phobos and Deimos. The wind still blows.*

I marvel at the universe. What a strange place.

And so it is. Light changes, as the set travels.

A mile or so from the encampment—another barren stretch of the planet. It is day—late afternoon. Dim sun. A wind. The two moons are visible—not far from each other in the sky. THE KILLIAN BOY *stands, up left, shovel in hand, a protuberance in the ground beside him. He has buried something.*

THE KILLIAN BOY: She's gone. How do we survive? No life. Better buried.

      DIANE *enters from down right. She is robed—like a patriarch—in soft earth colors. Radiant, she appears cleansed. She walks with a long staff. Time passes.*

DIANE: Hello.

      THE KILLIAN BOY *turns.*

It's me. I'm back.

THE KILLIAN BOY: [*Hardly believing.*] Diane. Diane?

DIANE: It's me.

THE KILLIAN BOY: You came back.

DIANE: Down from the mountain.

THE KILLIAN BOY: Yes. You were gone.

DIANE: [*Acknowledging the grave.*] Your mother.

THE KILLIAN BOY: Yes. She's dead. It took her a long time. But you've returned. Years since you went away. Where did you go?

DIANE: Up, into the mountains.

THE KILLIAN BOY: I waited for you.

DIANE: Did you?

THE KILLIAN BOY: Yes, every evening. I looked in all directions, hoping for some sign. Hoping you'd appear, reappear.

DIANE: My mother told me I'd find you here.

THE KILLIAN BOY: Yes. Did you see your father?

DIANE: Pretty feeble.

THE KILLIAN BOY: Yes, he's been that way. Sits on the ground, mumbles.

      [*Still hardly believing what he sees.*] Diane. I can't believe you've returned. I waited so long. And I'd never seen you. But your voice. Your voice I remember. Though it's changed. It's changed too.

DIANE: I'm older.

THE KILLIAN BOY: Yes. What did you do in the mountains?

DIANE: There are people there. I lived with them.

THE KILLIAN BOY: People? In the mountains?

DIANE: On the mountain, yes.

THE KILLIAN BOY: There are people. My god.

DIANE: Yes. I lived with them. Learned from them.

THE KILLIAN BOY: Did you?

DIANE: Yes.

THE KILLIAN BOY: What did they teach you?

DIANE: I'm going to repair the ship. I know how.

THE KILLIAN BOY: Repair the ship, really? Blast off from this dust heap?

DIANE: I have the knowledge.

THE KILLIAN BOY: Take us off this planet, Diane.

[*With longing.*] I never saw you before you went away. All that time. Only your voice. How it sounded to me! I could listen to you sing for hours. You sang, remember? For hours, listening to your voice. And now you stand before me. Radiant one. Diane.

My mother…I'll leave her here. When we blast off, I'll leave her here on Mars.

DIANE: That's best.

THE KILLIAN BOY: Where will you take us? The Earth has been destroyed.

DIANE: There are a million worlds. I have the knowledge.

THE KILLIAN BOY: Do you? Your father would be so proud of you. And your mother. Have you told them?

DIANE: Nothing yet. I've come to tell you first because…I intend to leave them behind.

THE KILLIAN BOY: Oh, no. You what?

DIANE: I'm going to leave them behind.

THE KILLIAN BOY: But—

DIANE: You dragged your mother along with you—how many years now? Until she's finally collapsed. I'm not making the same mistake.

THE KILLIAN BOY: But Diane, your parents are old and feeble. You saw. They couldn't care for themselves.

DIANE: [*Gently.*] Then let them die. You'll come with me. I have the knowledge, I promise you. Even Seymour advised you to leave your mother behind. I know what's right.

> THE KILLIAN BOY *turns to his* MOTHER's *grave.*

THE KILLIAN BOY: I had no marker to lay down. Just this mound of dirt.

DIANE: Better that way, isn't it? Let me go back. You musn't say a thing to my parents. I've told you. The ship will be ready soon. I'll take you away. Yes?

THE KILLIAN BOY: [*After a pause.*] All right.

DIANE: I'll see you back there. [*Fondly.*] I knew what you looked like. All those years. Even when you couldn't see me. I knew what you looked like.

> DIANE *exits. Time passes.*

THE KILLIAN BOY: Good-bye, mother.

> THE KILLIAN BOY *turns from his* MOTHER's *grave. As he does, light changes, and the set travels.*

> *The encampment. Years later. The rocket ship is gone. The place is cleaner, but the same old dust bowl. It is night. Clear sky. All the stars are out—the asteroids, and the two moons. Jupiter—a prominent dot. And Saturn, too—with its rings!* PHOEBE *sits on a rock before a fire, just left of center. A black kettle hangs over the fire.* PHOEBE *has changed. She is an old woman now—almost a crone—plump and white-haired. She wears a shawl. She is peeling a potato. Up right,* THE KILLIAN BOY *stands gazing into the heavens.*

THE KILLIAN BOY: Quite a night, old mother, isn't it?

PHOEBE: We live under the stars. On a little ball rolling through space.

THE KILLIAN BOY: Yes. All of heaven.

PHOEBE: I'm peeling a potato. For the soup!

THE KILLIAN BOY: Are you making a potato soup?

PHOEBE: Yes. To warm you. My old friend, Jenny, taught me this recipe.

THE KILLIAN BOY: Did she?

PHOEBE: I take it from her. A good potato soup.

> PHOEBE *chops the potato, puts it into the soup.*

THE KILLIAN BOY: We live under the stars. That was years ago that Diane left us.

PHOEBE: [*As she stirs the soup.*] Poor Jenny Woodman. She had a hard life. Her husband, Frank, was a sick man. He was a young man, but he had a crippling disease. It struck him early in life. In his thirties. And her son-in-law hung himself.

Soon you'll bury me beside Tom and your mother, out in the dirt field.

THE KILLIAN BOY: The whole place is a dirt field, old mother.

PHOEBE: That's true. A good potato soup.

THE KILLIAN BOY: I'll be alone then. My only comfort is that I'll follow you.

PHOEBE: You'll live a while longer.

THE KILLIAN BOY: I've lived a long time.

PHOEBE: Maybe you'll go up into the mountain. Like Diane did.

THE KILLIAN BOY: No, I'm not going to go up into the mountain. I just want to keep this place clean, a bit. The wind blows all the time. There are the stars. I watch the planets wander. Diane is out there some place. She left without us.

PHOEBE: That was such a long time ago. I've almost forgotten her.

THE KILLIAN BOY: Have you really?

PHOEBE: Soon I'll die. It will be good to lie down.

Come, the soup is ready. You'll eat.

> THE KILLIAN BOY *sits beside* PHOEBE. *She gives him a bowl of soup. They eat the soup.*

It's a little watery. I only had one potato.

> *Quietly, they continue to eat the soup. Light is extinguished.*

The final scene. The encampment. Morning. Bright light. Pale blue sky. Light wind. Time passes. From within the tent, the sound of a man waking—a healthy yawn. Some whistling—fragments of a tune. Then quiet. Then more whistling. Sound of water, splashed on the face. The man makes a sound as he splashes himself. THE KILLIAN BOY *emerges from the tent, wiping his face with a clean white towel. He is old now—white-haired. He stands a few feet from the tent, looks out in all directions, surveys the horizons. Whistles,* You've Changed. *Same tune he whistled in the tent. Time passes. Stands there and whistles. The vastness. Then light is extinguished.*

Lynne Alvarez

❧

The Reincarnation of Jaimie Brown

·

In memory of Peter Jay Sharp:
Thank you

Author's Note

The truth is, I wrote *The Reincarnation of Jaimie Brown* for the pure fun of it. I was taking a breather from an unbroken line of serious plays such as *Thin Air* and *The Absence of Miracles and the Rise of the Middle Class* and decided to try my hand at comedy. Of course I'd never written a comedy before, so you'll find that *Jaimie Brown* does deal with suicide, various kinds of sexuality, reincarnation, hair loss, and so on. But I was delighted to have a chance to be a relatively free spirit—at least on paper.

I've always been fascinated by the interplay of character and destiny, fate and free will—especially in a country which bristles at the mention of fate and views the concept of destiny as a ludicrous delusion. Yes, there is desultory agreement that one can be genetically "fated" to have brown hair, to be thin, gay, subject to heart attacks or sudden attacks of creativity. But for the most part we Americans feel that if it exists, we can tamper with it. In any event, I saw no reason to cease exploring this theme because I was writing a comedy. I could also indulge a writer's prerogative to include any damn thing he or she wants by using references to people I love, or art I admire—i.e. dragging in a poem of Richard Wilbur's, some favorite astrological arguments, references to jazz, rock n' roll, and some very early, very earnest poems of my own.

What's more, I could grind any number of axes under the guise of comedy including: intolerance, the difficulty of finding an apartment in Manhattan, money and art, personal property and taste, flowers, champagne, youth and old age.

What could be better?

The Reincarnation of Jaime Brown was first presented through the New Plays Program at American Conservatory Theater (Carey Perloff, Artistic Director), San Francisco, California. It was directed by Craig Slaight; costumes by Allie Floor; lighting by Kelly Roberson; music composed by Lois Cantor, and Richard Taybe was the assistant director. The cast was as follows:

JAIMIE BROWN	Stephanie Potts
JIMMY	Mike Merola
DAVID BALDWIN	Ryan Kennedy
SAN BOT LHU (SAMMY)	Sarah Hayon
HUDAN BOT LHU (HUGHIE)	Uri Horowitz
TINA, MARIE, JOYCE	Christianne Hauber
BORIS	Brad Clark
WILSON MEREDITH	Jack Sharrar

CAST In order of Appearance:

JAIMIE BROWN, 19. Street Poet.

JIMMY (JAMES HOBARTH III), 19. Juggler, or other street performer. (Educated at Princeton)

DAVID BALDWIN, 23. Singer, composer.

SAN BOT LHU (SAMMY). Any age, all ages, expert in reincarnation. Played by a woman, but appears as a man until the end.

HUDAN BOT LHU (HUGHIE). As above, but a man, dressed identically to Sammy. Always speaks in questions.

MARIE, 20s. Brooklyn, intermittent girlfriend of David's.

JOYCE, 20s. Wilson's onetime date.

BORIS (The Butler), 20s–30s. Strapping, handsome, blond Russian.

TINA, 40s. The Polish maid. Boris' wife.

WILSON MEREDITH, Late 60s. Tycoon, literal, but cultured.

All bits and crowd scenes should be played by cast members who are not in the immediate scene. No effort should be made to hide this fact. The same actress plays Tina, Marie and Joyce.

SET

All action takes place in the present at:
Port Authority Bus Terminal in New York City
Jaimie's Apartment
Wilson's Estate
The Beach
Kennedy Airport

ACT ONE

JAIMIE BROWN *enters in black. She carries a paper cup of coffee and wears a derby. She has obviously just awakened. Port Authority Bus Terminal takes shape around her. People wander by, pillars come down (obviously made of cardboard). They descend unevenly. One lands on a passerby who yelps and is extracted by two other people.* JAIMIE *dodges one.*

JAIME: Construction in New York's a bitch. [*She passes a donut stand, hands the vendor a sheet of paper and grabs a donut. He starts to protest.*] Don't sweat it, man—in a couple years that'll be worth a fortune. I sign all my copies. A small investment now could set you up for life, you know what I mean? [*People pass, she tries to sell them a poem.*] You want a poem, Miss...uh you there, Miss, how about a poem? Thanks a lot. And you sir...a poem, an adventure—

> *The man stops and looks her up and down lasciviously. Opens his raincoat and flashes* JAIMIE. JAIMIE *confronts him. As she walks forward, he walks back until at some point he turns and flees.*

not that kind of adventure, man, but thanks for sharing.

I bet you and I are thinking a lot of the same things right now.

I'm out here selling poetry, but you're walking around naked under that raincoat with the same question burning between your...ah...ears.

"What's happened to poetry in America?"

Am I right?

I mean when was the last time a poem rattled your bones?

Well here I am to remedy that.

Cast off, blast off

I'm the new wave poetry slave

I know what you're thinking—you have to study Elizabethan English to read poetry; you have to buy an arcane insane esoteric totally prosaic literary magazine available in only one bookstore on 47th street twice a year—am I correct?

Or you feel to hear a good poem you have to kneel at the knees of some MMP—Major Male Poet preferably facing his crotch.

Now tell me if that isn't true? Sad isn't it?

Well I say, no way

I give you your poetry straight

no rap, no rock, bee bop or hip hop

So how about five dollars, man?

You can afford it. Think of what you must save on clothes.

> *The flasher turns and runs.*

Yes, yes, yes
I'm the new wave poetry slave
the last living purist in America—
>   DAVID *walks by with an instrument case. She looks him over.*
Well maybe I'm not all that pure,
Hey you—superdude.
Yeah you. What's up? [*She follows him.*]
You want a poem? A touch of culture, a touch of class
Love'em and leave'em right?
I have something just for you…
A road poem, a heartbreak poem, lonesome sexy blues.
DAVID: Are you trying to pick my pocket?
JAIME: Dude, those jeans are so tight
no one could pick your pocket without a surgical instrument.
Looks good though. Don't get me wrong.
Now, how about a poem?
I'm in a difficult profession here.
I'm a major if undiscovered poet
reduced to selling original works of art on the street.
I have hundreds of poems ready made—for all occasions,
every mood, theory, relationship and philosophy of life.
Only two dollars. Five dollars will get you
an original, custom-composed on the spot, stirring, moving unique
work of art and for only one dollar—and this is an introductory
offer. I can write you a limerick as effective as a quick kick in the butt.
What do you say?
DAVID: Sorry, kid.
JAIME: Signed. Dated, limited copy.
Think of it as an investment.
Or if you like, you can pass it off as your own.
You take the credit, I'll take the cash.
No problem.
DAVID: You're broke. [*He hands her a dollar.*]
JAIME: Totally. But this isn't charity.
You get your limerick.
Now—who's this for? Sweetheart, mother, boss. The judge that let you off the hook,
what?
DAVID: A girlfriend.
JAIME: Figures. Her name?
DAVID: Marie.
JAIME: Catholic, round collars, flat shoes.
DAVID: Not quite.
JAIME: Okay. Forget it.

Marie…Marie…
Romantic, raucous, rancorous or vindictive?
I have a great vocabulary.
What mood do you want? I'm talking tone here.

DAVID: Romantic.

JAIME: Dirty or clean?

DAVID: Jesus.

JAIME: Okay, clean. Got it. Where's she from?

DAVID: I have to meet her bus, all right?

JAIME: If I were making a suit, I'd take your measurements correct?

DAVID: She's from Arkansas.

JAIME: Nobody's from Arkansas…
Okay, Arkansas, the dude wants a rhyme for
Arkansas…
Arkansas [*She's writing.*]
I like a challenge.
All right.

DAVID: Shoot.

JAIME: I'll read it for free, but it's 50 cents if you want a copy.

DAVID: [*Hands her two quarters.*] Go buy an airplane.
How long've you been doing this?

JAIME: Eight months. [*Reads*]
There's a sweet young thing
named Marie…

DAVID: Must be tough.

JAIME: No problem. [*Starts to read again.*]
There's a sweet young thing named Marie
Who I'm just dying to see…

DAVID: Have you ever thought of taking on a regular job?

JAIME: What are you talking about? I could get a steady job any day, but I believe you
are what you do, okay?
If I'm waitressing and waiting to be a poet—then I'm a waitress waiting to be a
poet. Simple, I cut the waiting.
Now let me read the damn thing, so I can get on with this.
There's a sweet young thing
named Marie.
Who I'm just dying to see
She's got what it takes
So I don't need no brakes
Cause Marie's just dying to "blank" me.

DAVID: Blank?

JAIME: As in fill in the blank…
I don't know you. So I couldn't tell how strong to make it…

so what do you want…hug, kiss, fuck?

Fill it in.

DAVID: You didn't use Arkansas.

JAIME: What do you want for a dollar?

Announcements of arrivals and departures.

DAVID: Here's five kid.

Keep the wolf away from the door.

JAIME: I got to give you a poem then. A real one. [*She finds one.*]

I personalize them.

What's your name?

DAVID: David.

JAIME: Hi. I'm Jaimie Brown.

DAVID: Gotta go.

JAIME: Right.

You're a musician, right?

Guitar?

DAVID: Synthesizer. [*He exits.*]

JAIME: Musicians are cool.

A mugging is going on.

There must he a better way to make a living.

JIMMY *walks by, also in black. Pale, thin. He carries a small bag.*

Stops nearby, opens his bag. Starts juggling. He puts a hat on the floor. The muggers come by. Stare and then throw him some money. The muggee comes by and takes it out angrily. SAMMY *comes in wearing a suit, tie, etc. Watches* JIMMY *and throws in a coin.* JAIMIE *starts her routine.*

JAIME: Okay, all right.

Poems for sale.

Poetry

the real thing

right from me.

Choose the topic, choose the tone

Buy a poem

that's all your own.

No rap, no haiku.

SAMMY *watches standing close, peering.*

Look buster, if you don't want a poem, move on.

Okay?

SAMMY: You have a mole on your face.

JAIME: Mole! What mole? That's a beauty mark.

Get lost.

SAMMY: Are you an orphan?

JAIME: Look I'm not a runaway. Okay? Or a crook, or a hooker.

There's no poster out on me no photo on a milk carton, got it?

SAMMY: I'd like a poem.

JAIME: Two dollars ready made and five bucks made to order.

SAMMY: What do you have already made up?

JAIME: I have hundreds of poems.

I mean I have everything—suicide to seashells.

I have lots of love poems. People usually want love poems.

Do you have any idea what you want?

SAMMY: What kind of love poems do you have?

JAIME: Let's see. Ecstatic, dramatic, trivial, passionate…

SAMMY: No other kind of love?

JAIME: Right. Weird.

I should have known. Look.

I deal with heterosexual love.

If you want me to work it around a little

I'll have to charge you.

SAMMY: I see. No love of God, love of mankind, nature, beauty, truth, a rose and so on?

JAIME: Oh.

SAMMY: Yes?

JAIME: How about me writing you one on the spot.

SAMMY: Fine.

JAIME: Five dollars though.

SAMMY Fine.

JAIME: You choose the topic, but I write what I want. And if it goes over 10 lines, there's an additional fee plus 50 cents for giving you a written copy.

SAMMY: Fine.

JAIME: So. You want one on love, right?

SAMMY: No.

JAIME: Okay. What then?

SAMMY: [*Meaningfully.*] The number one.

JAIME: The number one.

As in one, two, three, four, five…?

SAMMY: Yes.

The number one.

JIMMY *has stopped juggling and has come to watch.*

JAIME: Half up front.

Don't wander off. This'll take a minute.

SAMMY *hands her the money.* JAIME *scribbles,* JIMMY *juggles.*

JAIME: Okay. [*To* JIMMY] That beats it friend. Leave. I can't concentrate. Got it?

[JIMMY *shrugs and walks away still juggling.*] Look, I have your poem Mr…

SAMMY: San Bot Lhu.

JAIME: Yeah. I personalize my work here. I put a dedication "to" and your name.

Now San Bot what?

SAMMY: Sammy, put Sammy.

JAIME: Great. [*Writes it in.*] This is heavy. But I write what comes out, okay?
You ready?

SAMMY: [*Crosses his arms.*] Sure thing.

JAIME: [*Reads*] To Sammy
One bears witness
disguised as the enemy
among us.
The burning stake
the bloody pike is his
the mother covering her
child's eyes.
One watches and remembers
One is the tower and the well,
the woman rocking in the street,
One is the empty house, the empty pocket,
the glass about to be filled.
    A moment of silence.

SAMMY: You don't look like you'd write a poem like that.
    Takes the poem.

JIMMY: Appearances are deceiving.

JAIME: What do you know?!

JIMMY: You're not a bad poet.

SAMMY: Are you here every day?

JAIME: When the sun's out I'm in Central Park. Rain, snow, frost, hail— I'm here.

SAMMY: I see. [SAMMY *exits.*]

JIMMY: Are you all right?

JAIME: I'm fine. Why?

JIMMY: That poem was pretty depressing.

JAIME: Sue me.
I've had a lousy life.
Don't just stand there. This isn't a freak show.
You make me nervous.

JIMMY: What?

JAIME: It's a big planet. Feel free to explore it.

JIMMY: We'd do better if we stuck together.

JAIME: No way.

JIMMY: [*Juggling.*] Who'd cross the street to buy a poem?
Really.
But juggling has high visibility.
    Juggles high.
Get it?
Juggling draws a crowd.

Bingo. They see me, hear you,
their hand's already in their pocket,
voilà.
JAIME: It won't work now.
Business is lousy.
JIMMY: So we'll go somewhere else.
JAIME: This place has always been lucky for me.
Just the last couple of days have been rotten.
JIMMY: Last couple of days?
JAIME: Yeah, the pits.
JIMMY: Mercury retrograde.
JAIME: Mercury retrograde. What's that? Metal pollution?
JIMMY: My dear, my dear...
Metal pollution.
You're a poet...think of the planets—Venus, Mercury;
think Romeo and Juliet; think starcrossed;
think getting into the bathtub and the phone rings:
think sending a letter and forgetting the zip code;
think bounced checks, stalled cars, accidents, strikes
misunderstandings—that's mercury retrograde.
Mercury rules communications. When it goes retrograde—
miscommunications—thus people lose things or fight.
JAIME: Shit. That bad?
JIMMY: The only good attribute of Mercury retrograde is...
Finding lost objects and people from the past.
Mercury retrograde brings them back.
JAIME: So how long do I have to look forward to everyone fighting and striking and
whatever—
JIMMY: It goes direct in three weeks. At noon I believe.
JAIME: Three weeks. No money for three weeks?!
JIMMY: Two hats are fuller than one. James Hobarth III. Jimmy to you.
And?
JAIME: Jaimie Brown, here.
JIMMY: Jimmy and Jaimie...unfortunate.
But then, it could be quite vaudeville.
Jimmy and Jaimie.
Okay, try Jaimie and Jimmy...
          SAMMY *returns dragging* HUGHIE. *They are dressed exactly alike.*
Dear Heart, speaking of duos...
HUGHIE: This is her?
SAMMY: Ask her for a poem.
HUGHIE: Will you write me a poem? [*He holds out money.*]
Is this enough?

SAMMY: Look at the mole.

  HUGHIE *peers at* JIMMY.

JIMMY: [*Touches his face, he has a bandage on his cheek.*]
   How did you know I had a mole?
   I cut it off shaving.

SAMMY: Not him. Her mole.

      HUGHIE *peers.*

JAIME: Beauty mark, man.

HUGHIE: Are you an orphan?

JAIME: [*To* JIMMY] Can you believe this?
   [*To* HUGHIE] Look, tell me what kind of poem you want.

      SAMMY *and* HUGHIE *strike identical poses, identically dressed.*

      JAIME *looks at them.*

   No. No.
   Let me guess.
   You want a poem about the number two, right?

HUGHIE: How does she know that?

SAMMY: What did I tell you!

JAIME: Just give me a minute.

JIMMY: I can do a routine about the number two. [*He juggles two balls.*] And number
   three. [*He juggles three balls.*] Number four. [*He juggles four.*] Should I go higher?

SAMMY: Yes. Yes.

JIMMY: Watch. [*He juggles the four balls very high.*]

JAIME: All right you guys,
   you dude…

SAMMY: She wants your name.

HUGHIE: Why?

SAMMY: This is Hudan Bot Lhu.
   Call him Hughie.

JAIME: To Hughie…
   Here we go.
   Two is always hungry,
   the doublebarrelled shotgun
   propped against his chin
   the knock on the door
   the stillness of night
   Two is the black horse and rider
   the streak of horizon
   Nose to nose and belly to belly
   Two is always hungry
   and in mortal danger.

HUGHIE: [*Excitedly*] Did you hear?

SAMMY: Yes! The shotgun!

HUGHIE: How about the "knock on the door?"

SAMMY: The stillness of night!
  The suicide
  That's just how it was.
  Amazing.
HUGHIE: You wrote this?
JAIME: No I dreamed it.
  Two fifty plus twenty five cents.
SAMMY: [*Hands her the money.*] We need your birthdate.
HUGHIE: When were you born?
JAIME: Off limits. Sorry guys.
SAMMY: We are experts in reincarnation!
  We need information.
JIMMY: Reincarnation—a perfect Mercury retrograde activity. Finding lost people!
SAMMY: I assure you we are legitimate.
HUGHIE: Are there not wine connoisseurs who from the mere taste and appearance
  of a wine, can tell you the site of its vineyard and the year of its origin?
  Are there not antiquarians who by a mere glance at an object, can name the time,
  place and individual maker?
SAMMY: And we, given certain details, can tell what your last incarnation was. We
  have clients. We are searching for someone in particular now.
JIMMY: Give them your birthdate.
  What can it hurt?
JAIME: February 25, 1976…
JIMMY: I was born on February 25th!
HUGHIE: And where were you born?
JAIME: On a farm in Missouri.
JIMMY: He needs the city.
JAIME: How do you know?
JIMMY: This is very exciting.
JAIME: I was born near Jefferson City.
JIMMY: What time?
HUGHIE: What time?
JAIME: How would I know?
SAMMY: [*Whips out cellular phone.*] Call your mother and ask.
JAIME: She's dead.
SAMMY *and* HUGHIE: Ahhhhhhhhhh.
HUGHIE: Are you an orphan?
JIMMY: Go ahead. Admit it.
  I'm an orphan. No big deal.
JAIME: Okay. All right.
  I'm an orphan.
  [*To* JIMMY] What is this, a club?
  [*To* HUGHIE] So how can I tell you what time I was born?
HUGHIE: Were you born in the morning?

JAIME: How would I...

Wait—My mom always said I was born an early riser...

SAMMY *elbows* HUGHIE.

SAMMY: This has been very interesting. Thank you.

HUGHIE: What's your name?

JAIME: Jaimie.

SAMMY: Jaimie. James.

HUGHIE: You see?

JAIME: So who was I?

SAMMY: We'll be in touch.

They exit.

JAIME: You can have this place. It's too weird.

JIMMY: We've seen the hand of God.

We've just seen fate at work.

JAIME: We?

JIMMY: Now I know why we hit it off.

We're both Pisces.

Giving, sensual, sensitive.

JAIME: Are you hitting on me?

JIMMY: No. [*He turns abruptly and juggles away.*]

JAIME: Sensitive is right. [*Goes after him.*]

So what's your problem?

JIMMY: I need a place to stay.

JAIME: Hey, I only have one room, no running water.

JIMMY: No problem. It's warm out.

Point me to a park bench.

I'm cool.

JAIME: You're crazy. Where are you from?

JIMMY: Boston.

JAIME: In New York, you can't just sleep anywhere.

JIMMY: Don't worry about it. It's not your problem.

JAIME: Yeah. Sorry.

DAVID *walks by, arguing with a girl in a tight, short leather skirt, with tank top and spiked red hair. She has a heavy Brooklyn accent.*

DAVID: I'm here, aren't I.

MARIE: So what? I'm supposed to be ecstatic?

I wake up and you left a note pinned to my chest.

You call that romantic?

DAVID: I knew if I said anything, we'd argue.

MARIE: And whaddaya call this?! [*She slaps him hard and walks off.*]

JIMMY: Typical.

Mercury retrograde.

Never leave a note.

JAIME: [*To* DAVID] Class act.

    You always pick them like that?

DAVID: I like women who are hard to handle.

    If they're too easy, I get bored.

JAIME: I guess she doesn't bore you, then. She seems like a three-ring circus.

DAVID: Actually, she's pretty predictable. She'll call me tonight between six and seven.

JAIME: So that's Arkansas.

DAVID: Via Brooklyn. [*Hands her back the limerick.*]

    I didn't have a chance to give her this.

JAIME: Sorry. No refunds.

DAVID: Store credit?

JAIME: Read it to her when she calls.

DAVID: What if I'm not home?

        JAIME *shrugs.*

    What if I'm out with you, darling?

JIMMY: He's hitting on you.

JAIME: [*To* JIMMY] Mind your own business.

    [*To* DAVID] You're not going out with me.

DAVID: I like feisty women.

JAIME: You didn't ask me out.

DAVID: Will you go out with me?

JAIME: I don't know. What would we do? Hang out?

DAVID: Sure. Go to the park, drink wine, listen to music.

JAIME: Your treat?

DAVID: Why not?

JAIME: Okay.

    [*To* JIMMY] I'm going to take your advice. Why fight the stars, right? The joint's
    yours.

JIMMY: Thanks.

DAVID: Do you have everything?

JAIME: Yeah. Just a sec.

    [*Goes to* JIMMY] Look. You can't stay in my room. I need my privacy.

    But you can stay in the hall.

    The lady I take care of lives right across, but she won't mind.

    Here's the address. [*She writes it out for him.*]

    Ring the bell. I can see you from the window. Second floor, left front, there's tomato
        plants on the fire escape—and don't pick any!

    I'm pretty sure you're safe, but I sleep with a knife, got it? So, keep out of trouble.

        She exits with DAVID.

JIMMY: I knew it.

    Pisces are a soft touch.

        WILSON's *Estate. Paneled room with many windows looking out over grounds.*
        Sunlight. WILSON *is listening to Gregorian chants. His girl of the moment,* JOYCE,

in a two-piece thong bikini, with a bright luxurious scarf knotted as a skirt, jewelry. She's bored. BORIS THE BUTLER *in white slacks and pale pink polo shirt is serving drinks.* BORIS *is stoic,* JOYCE *flirts outrageously when she thinks* WILSON *isn't looking.*

WILSON: Joyce—this music is magic, it's time travel, it's immortality, don't you think?

JOYCE: Divine.

WILSON: These Gregorian chants date from the 8th century. I can smell the damp ancient stone, the incense; I can see the brown-robed tonsured monks. Primitive. Extraordinary.

The eighth century experienced now in the twentieth!

Boris, Dewars please.

> *He holds out his glass.* BORIS *rushes over and fills it.*

JOYCE: [*Stretches so* BORIS *notices.* WILSON *admires her too.*]

Mmmmmmmmmmmmmmmmmmmmmmmmmmmmmmmmmmm.

WILSON: Do you know what they call these?

JOYCE: Sure. Gregory chants just like you said.

WILSON: Antiphonal psalmody. Plain chants. So many names. It reminds me of my son. He was a monk you know. The only way I can understand his calling is to listen to this music, ascetic grave. This music has given me hope through its own immortality. It expresses the possibility that my son is also immortal. Somewhere I believe his spark of life has been transferred to a new and startling soul—

just the way a song lives on by being passed from mouth to mouth down through the ages. My son too, lives on, reincarnated—and I will find him if it's at all possible. Do you think it is, Joyce? Possible?

JOYCE: [*Runs her hands over* BORIS' *thighs.*] Anything's possible. That's my motto.

My mother said those were my father's first words when he saw me as a baby. What do you think he meant?

WILSON: Joyce dear—I'm a very rich man and I can afford to have the best—and the way I determine the best—is through a series of tests and you my dear…

JOYCE: Yes. Tell me.

WILSON: Have failed. [*He takes her glass.*]

The only reason I keep a butler who looks like a porno star is to separate the wheat from the chaff. There's a helicopter waiting for you on the lawn.

> JOYCE *gets up to leave.*

JOYCE: Wilson…

WILSON: Now. Now. Let's not spoil a perfectly superfluous weekend with attempts at insight.

A lovely weekend, Joyce.

> *He kisses her cheek. She exits. He savors his drink.*

BORIS: Sirrr…

WILSON: No need to apologize.

I'm a capitalist. I believe in competition.

You can bring in the boys now.

BORIS *exits and returns with* SAMMY *and* HUGHIE.

WILSON: [*Without turning. Facing the ocean.*] Did you know that if you stay near the ocean and in the proximity of young women, you never get old? Passion—the elixir of youth!

HUGHIE: [*Very interested.*] Really?!

SAMMY *elbows him.*

WILSON: Would you care for anything after your travels? Champagne, perhaps?

HUGHIE: [*Delightedly*]Champagne?

SAMMY *elbows him.*

Do you have something to eat?

WILSON: Of course, of course.
Bring some carrots.

SAMMY: We're starving.

WILSON: And some celery.
Would you like that with salt or plain?

HUGHIE: Salt?

SAMMY: Plain.

WILSON: And turn down the music as you leave. [*To* SAMMY *and* HUGHIE] Isn't it extraordinary?

SAMMY: Extraordinary.

WILSON: So gentlemen.
What do you have for me?

SAMMY: We have three candidates. All born within three years of your son's death. All orphans, discovered at the same latitude 40 North and longitude 73 West within a radius of 66 miles from his death.

HUGHIE: Don't you think it should be from his birth?

SAMMY: We've discussed this.

HUGHIE: Have we?

SAMMY: Yes. But we don't agree.

WILSON: I thought you were experts.

SAMMY: We always disagree over beginnings. But we never disagree at the end.

HUGHIE: Didn't we guarantee, no results, no payment?

WILSON: Yes you did. No results, no payment.

HUGHIE: And weren't our references impeccable?

WILSON: You wouldn't be here otherwise.

SAMMY: The Dalai Lama himself and the Maharajah of Jaipur.

HUGHIE: Didn't we also get a prelate from the Orthodox Church?

SAMMY: No.

HUGHIE: Prince Charles?

SAMMY: Enough.

WILSON: Enough.

HUGHIE: [*Stage whisper.*] Could I have a mint julep?

SAMMY *elbows him.*

WILSON: You two are my last hope of locating my son's reincarnation. I've already used psychics and numerologists and astrologers, white magic, black magic and psychotherapy. I've behaved like a dotty bereaved eccentric of the worst kind. Yet I know, I sense that I can find my boy. I can find him.

But if I can't, if you two who are deemed the best in your field cannot find him, I'll accept defeat as gracefully as I can. I'm prepared to will my entire estate to a series of worthy causes— although to see my life's blood in the hands of lawyers and trustees is almost more than I can bear to imagine...

HUGHIE: [*Trying to be sociable. Holding a drink, slightly tipsy.*] Really?

WILSON: Does he always ask questions?

SAMMY: That's how he talks.

He distrusts reality. [*To* HUGHIE, *cueing a set speech.*]
Hughie?

HUGHIE: Why aren't questions enough?
Why do people insist on answers if all answers
fall short of reality?
Don't people see that questions are a journey?
Why must people insist we end the quest with finality?

BORIS: Another mint julep?

HUGHIE *takes it and smiles.*

SAMMY: Our candidates, sir.

WILSON: Yes.

SAMMY: Each candidate had a quality that was extremely pertinent to your son's life and character.

HUGHIE: Aren't there three?

SAMMY: Three. Yes three. The number of full expression; Number one became a successful stockbroker at 15.

HUGHIE: Didn't your son take his vows as a novitiate at 15?

WILSON: Yes.

HUGHIE: How could an adolescent take a vow of silence?

SAMMY: Number two specializes in illumination of sacred texts in gold leaf. He also adores skeet shooting.

HUGHIE: Like your son?

WILSON: Yes.

HUGHIE: What about the girl?

WILSON: A girl?
Discount that one.

SAMMY: Unlikely perhaps, but your son did like men.

WILSON: Yes, he was a homosexual.

SAMMY: This girl likes men. She is also unusually attuned to mystical poetry.

WILSON: My son would never come back as a woman.

SAMMY: We think that this was his first incarnation as a man and therefore...

HUGHIE: We?

SAMMY: And therefore it was something of a shock to find himself a man and he left before his incarnation was completed…

HUGHIE: Wouldn't it be far more logical to conclude that his next incarnation would be as a woman and therefore he was preparing himself…?

SAMMY: In any event, finding himself in a man's body proved extremely agitating to him and before he could fully learn this life's lesson— what it is like to be a man who loves men—he…

WILSON: Propped a shotgun against his temple and pulled the trigger.

SAMMY: Yes.

HUGHIE: Perhaps we should look for someone suicidal?

> SAMMY *elbows him and* HUGHIE *doubles over.*

WILSON: Your conjectures don't interest me.

> I want results.
>
> No results, no money.
>
> We have agreed on the criteria…

SAMMY: Yes. The size of the cranium, slant of the ears, the mole, the nails with no half moons, coincidence of preferences, identification of your son's favorite ring, walking stick and mare.

HUGHIE: Mayor? Was he political?

SAMMY: [*To* HUGHIE] Mare. Mare. A horse.

> [*To Wilson*] Moreover the person must be a Pisces, the ruling sign of your son's fourth house, the house of endings…

HUGHIE: Wouldn't you think…?

> SAMMY *covers* HUGHIE's *mouth.*

WILSON: I'm very anxious to see these people.

> I'm actually nervous, can you believe it?
>
> There are many strange and wonderful things in the world and yet…
>
> How will I know—without a doubt—that this person is my son reincarnated? I can't imagine what proof could possibly convince me absolutely that I have found my son.

SAMMY: First,

> discard the idea of proof.
>
> Proof refers only to causality; results produced by an observable and logical sequence of classified and isolated phenomena.
>
> The only thing proof gives you is objective correlation; statistical proof.
>
> So discard proof.
>
> Accept—coincidence.
>
> Coincidence is more than chance.
>
> Coincidence is the interdependence of all events in a single moment in time. Synchronicity!
>
> And we, who are trained in this field, will find for you the one detail in the moment of coincidence that reveals the absolute truth.

When you find the absolute truth—there is no doubt.

I promise you. It will be a true revelation.

WILSON: Shall we toast the truth?

>   *They hold their glasses aloft.*

To revelations.

HUGHIE: Revelations?

SAMMY: Revelations.

>   *They wait.* WILSON *is lost in thought.*

WILSON: My poor son died for passion,

>   while passion gives me something to live for. [*He exits.*]

HUGHIE: [*Takes more champagne from* BORIS' *tray.*] Another toast?

SAMMY: To what?

HUGHIE: Passion? [*He toasts and drinks by himself.*]

SAMMY: You drink too much.

HUGHIE: [*Toasts by himself again.*] Isn't the body the tavern of the living spirit?

SAMMY: Temple.

The body is the temple of the living spirit.

HUGHIE: Ahhhhhhhhh.

>   *Later that evening, the street.* JAIMIE *and* DAVID *returning from the park. A couple of bums are lying around as parts of* JAIMIE's *small room are being assembled. They grumble and are pushed aside. One bum grabs a bag from the other. Bum One yells "Help". Police come. Bum Two yells "Stop, Thief" and points ahead of himself. Police run off. Bum Two saunters across stage.*

JAIME: This neighborhood is the pits.

They always ask if it's affordable. No one asks

if it's livable. [*The apartment or rather room is assembled.* JAIMIE *points to different corners.*]

No bathroom. But McDonald's is two doors down and they're open all night.

DAVID: Starving artist, eh?

JAIME: Yeah.

I find it therapeutic to refer to different corners

of the same room as the living room, dining room, kitchen…

DAVID: Bedroom.

JAIME: Yeah. It's the bedroom. So?

DAVID: Nothing. [*Pointing to a poster.*]

Who's that?

JAIME: Rimbaud. The French poet.

DAVID: Didn't Sly Stallone do him? [*Imitates Rambo with a machine gun.*]

JAIME: You're thinking of Rambo you jerk—

DAVID: I know honey. I know.

JAIME: Well I like him. He did his best work by 21, quit to run guns and leave graffiti on the pyramids.

Great poets die young you know. I'm going to die when I'm 27, maybe 28 tops.

DAVID: Really?

JAIME: And this is…

DAVID: Let me guess.

JAIME: Shut up.

DAVID: My psychic energy, my spiritual guide tell meee…Bob Dylan. Greatest rock poet ever born…

JAIME: And a great outlaw. I love outlaws.

DAVID: [*Checking out her windows.*] You must. These windows are an open invitation to any outlaw who happens by. Put some bars on the windows—eh. Then you can chose which outlaws come into this pad.

JAIME: How sweet. You want to protect me.

DAVID: Do you bring just anyone up here?

JAIME: Do you go up to just anyone's pad—dude?

DAVID: You seem pretty sure I'm not going to jump you or anything.

JAIME: You seem cool. I'm a good judge of character.

DAVID: So was Jesus and Judas nailed him.

JAIME: Right.

DAVID: That was a joke.

JAIME: I know. It was good. Smart.

DAVID: Hey. What's up?

JAIME: Nothing. I'm great.

DAVID: We were having a great time and now you're like…

JAIME: Like what?

DAVID: Down, beat. I don't know. Shall I leave?

JAIME: No.

DAVID: Fine.

> *They stand awkwardly.*

JAIME: I'm nervous.

DAVID: What's the matter?

JAIME: I like you.

DAVID: [*Moving closer*]Great!

JAIME: I mean really.

And now that I got you up here, I don't know what to do.

DAVID: What do you usually do?

JAIME: Usually? Are you nuts?

With all the disease-ridden, murderers, punks, pimps and perverts out there do you think I'd be stupid enough to bring anyone to my room? Let alone have them know where I live?

DAVID: So I'm the first?

> *He moves away from her.* JAIME *nods.*

JAIME: Don't sweat it. I've been deflowered.

Cowboys.

DAVID: Cowboys?

JAIME: [*Hooks her fingers in her jeans.*] Walllll ma'am, been real nice, but I gotta be
movin' on.

Cowboys!

How about you?

DAVID: Me?

JAIME: Are you in love now?

DAVID: Let's just say I'm a cowboy, ma'am.

Better steer clear of me.

JAIME: Really?

DAVID: The only thing I know how to do is play music.

JAIME: So play.

DAVID: Right. [*Takes out his keyboard.*] Just happen to have my little keyboard.

JAIME: What kind of stuff do you play?

DAVID: Sorta post-punk, semi-funk, hillbilly-hardcore with a bluesy edge.

JAIME: Oh.

DAVID: [*Setting up.*] I have a new song.

JAIME: Groovy.

DAVID: Groovy? What's this sixties shit?

JAIME: I'm a purist. I'm trying to preserve classic language. Play.

DAVID: It doesn't have a title yet. [*He plays.*] So…what do you think?

JAIME: I think you're the real thing.

DAVID: Thanks.

JAIME: It's in your blood, isn't it?

DAVID: Yeah I guess. My dad was a jazz drummer. You know the kind in bars, plays,
smokes pot with his friends—what people in jazz do.

Didn't really know him too well.

JAIME: My mom was into country. She was an Elvis freak. We're pretty different.

DAVID: Very. [*He goes to kiss her.*]

JAIME: Do you believe in love at first sight?

DAVID: You're going to spoil this, aren't you?

JAIME: I thought that was romantic.

DAVID: Romantic? Love?

Love's a responsibility.

Now sex—that's romantic.

JAIME: I don't just go around saying that, you know.

DAVID: Why did you just say it now?

JAIME: Cause that's what I was feeling.

Cause I thought you'd dig it.

I've never been in love before.

DAVID: And you're not afraid to tell me this?

JAIME: Well shit, yeah!

DAVID: Jaimie, you're too open. You got to protect yourself. Look, I don't have a lot of
experience with heart-on-the-sleeve kind of people. Maybe I should leave.

JAIME: Maybe you shouldn't take it so hard.
   Maybe I was just trying to nail you against the wall to see what you'd do—rip your
   skin off a little before I decide whether to put salt or ice cream on you.
   Do you want to leave?
DAVID: No.
JAIME: I could read you some of my stuff?
DAVID: No love poems.
JAIME: Right.
   This one's great.
   I based it on a man I overheard downstairs… [*Reads*]
   "I just like to see'em fall, slow
   like in the movies,
   drops of blood spread,
   sailing through the air
   as if they don't belong nowhere
   and land, spla—a—at, like rain
   on the river…"
DAVID: Uh…no. I don't think so.
JAIME: That's just how he said it.
DAVID: I believe you.
JAIME: You said no love poems.
DAVID: You need a sense of humor.
JAIME: I thought that was kind of funny. "Spla—a—a—at, like rain on a river."
DAVID: But you're talking about blood, sweetheart,
   What's this?
JAIME: Don't read it now.
DAVID: I don't like women who tell me what to do. [*He opens it and reads.*]
   "When you are old"
   When did you write this?
JAIME: In the park.
   Look…
DAVID: "When you are old
   And mysterious to me,
   a dim figure on a
   fragile horizon,
   Think back
   Across the years,
   That on one summer night
   we broke out of ugliness
   and fled
   Two conspirators
   with bottles full of
   Wine and joyous music

on the radio
and remember,
if
you
can
That it was right and
fine and sometimes
More, and we left
Pain.
That interminable fire,
only scorching
Our heels."
    Silence.
JAIME: It's not funny.
DAVID: No. [*He kisses her.*]
    They move to the bed. A pale face appears at one of the windows. It's JIMMY. *He
    taps on the window.* DAVID *and* JAIMIE *spring apart.*
JIMMY: Hey you guys. [*Taps*]
JAIME: Just tell me, [*Covers her face with her hands.*]
    Does he have a gun?
DAVID: It's the guy from the terminal…the little guy that juggles. Should I let him in?
JAIME: Oh God. Mercury retrograde.
DAVID: What?
JAIME: Bad timing.
    Crossed stars.
    Romeo and Juliet.
    Never mind.
    Let him in.
    JIMMY *comes in through the window.*
JIMMY: I guess you guys didn't hear me throwing pennies at the window.
DAVID: Guess not.
JIMMY: [*Looks at them, half undressed.*] I'm sorry.
JAIME: Yeah. [*Starts dressing.*]
    You want some wine?
JIMMY: I could use it.
JAIME: You have to drink it from the bottle…
DAVID: The bathroom's down the street.
    At McDonald's.
    Look. I better be on my way.
JIMMY: Don't leave on my account,
    I'm really sorry.
    I'm just not good on the streets.
    I was juggling along the way…

attracted quite a crowd…only I looked up and
noticed quite a few were sexual deviants and psychopaths.
Not that I'm prejudiced.
It's live and let live with me, but I don't think we
shared that philosophy so I…uh…ran.
But I'll be out of here in a moment.
Just let me catch my breath.
Oh God, I can't believe I did this.

JAIME: David?

DAVID: I have a gig at eleven anyway.
I'm a disk jockey
Strangers in the Night on Staten Island.
Power pop and yuppie rock.
Best sound goin' round
etcetera, etcetera.

JAIME: He's really an artist—he writes songs.

DAVID: [*Gives her a light kiss on the cheek.*] It was sweet.
See you around.
Ciao good buddy.

JAIME: [*Following him to the door.*] Can I see you again?
Maybe I can come down to the club.

DAVID: I don't like women who pursue me. [*He leaves.*]
Be in touch, babe.

> JAIMIE *stands at the door. Her back to* JIMMY.

JIMMY: Perfect timing. James Hobarth III does it every time.

JAIME: You probably did me a favor.
You just don't have a one night stand with someone you love.

JIMMY: Bad omen.

JAIME: What?

JIMMY: Wrong place. Wrong time.

JAIME: I thought we were just experiencing Mercury retrograde.

JIMMY: We are…it is but…
How can I have a fabulous new beginning under Mercury retrograde?
It does not bode well.
Here I was ready to strip my life to its barest essentials; to live without a past, without a dime.
Yes. I was going to be self-reliant, complete unto myself and what happens? I freak!
One look at that park—the black trees, the moonless night, the quiet pierced by occasional screams—
I couldn't hack it.

JAIME: Don't be so hard on yourself. A person doesn't sleep on a bench in a city where mugging's considered a rite of passage. You did the right thing.
Have some more wine and sit down.

JIMMY: Then I stumble over here and fuck things up.

JAIME: Just shut up and relax.

JIMMY: I'm not good on the streets. I need a home. It's okay if I sleep here?

JAIME: You're not going to rob or rape me, are you?

JIMMY: No really, I never…

JAIME: I'm joking.

Cool it.

It's fine.

I could use the company tonight.

You okay?

JIMMY: Yeah. [JAIMIE *gets into bed.*]

JAIME: [*Sighing*] I'm messed up.

Do you have an aspirin?

I have a monumental headache.

JIMMY: Cheap wine?

JAIME: Cheap date.

JIMMY: You know I bet you and I are a lot alike.

We need someone to love.

But we keep choosing crazy people, idiots, sociopaths, the lame, the maimed, the married, right?

JAIME: Right.

JIMMY: If I make one more bad choice. it's over.

I swear. Plug pulled.

Lights out.

JAIME: Things'll get better I'm sure.

JIMMY: It's not a sure thing at all.

[*Tragically*] I have Venus in Pisces.

JAIME: Oh, I see.

JIMMY: You don't.

If Venus is what you want

And Pisces is the sign of the martyr

That means I want to be a martyr. God!

Oh well, Good night.

> *Next day. Wilson's Estate. We hear the helicopter taking off.*

JAIME: So is white slavery a possibility?

Will I wake up in Saudi Arabia in a duffel hag?

JIMMY: I doubt it.

JAIME: Man. I could live like this.

A helicopter, a pool,

the ocean.

I mean there's less bugs on this lawn than there

are in my apartment.

JIMMY: I must say, being airlifted is quite an experience.

JAIME: So is being paged at Port Authority. The only other place I've had my name called in public was at the dentist.

Can you believe it?

It's enough to make you believe in reincarnation.

> BORIS *walks in with a tray of champagne.* JIMMY *gives him an appreciative look which* BORIS *returns discreetly.*

JIMMY: [*Checks his watch.*] It's ten o'clock and that's champagne.

JAIME: Shit. What a life.

BORIS: Would you care for a mimosa?

JIMMY: [*Looking at the label.*] Krug Brut '76…not bad…terrific, actually.

I'd rather not spoil it with orange juice.

BORIS: Excellent decision.

JIMMY: Thank you.

BORIS: Do you know wines?

JIMMY: A little.

BORIS: I could sneak you a little "Taitinger Blanc de Blanc."

JIMMY: Fantastic.

BORIS: I know you'd appreciate it. And you Miss?

JAIME: It's questionahle whether I should drink given the circumstances. Oh what the hell. Sure give me a glass. [BORIS *serves her and winks to* JIMMY *as he leaves.*]

JAIME: So you appreciate good wine, eh?

JIMMY: Another life, dear

A previous life.

JAIME: Yeah, a life where you're fluent in astrology and wines.

JIMMY: Princeton '96…

Educated to ponder the universe and such questions as—

If the subways in New York are air conditioned, but no one has ever felt air conditioning, is the subway really air conditioned?

But not to worry. I'm just folks.

I was summarily disinherited when I was fifteen.

My father caught me…let's say, he loathed my lifestyles.

Then he died and we were never able to patch it up properly… Oh well… [*He sips his champagne.*]

BORIS: [*Enters*] They'd like to see you now, Miss.

JAIME: If I turn out to be this man's son, all this will be mine, right?

JIMMY: Right.

JAIME: Groovy. [*She exits.*]

BORIS: We have 500 species of the rhododendron.

JIMMY: Lead the way!

BORIS: We have skeet shooting if you like.

JIMMY: [*As they leave.*] You're Scandinavian, aren't you? I'd say Danish. The Danes have eyes the color of blueherries.

> *They exit.*

A half hour later. Enter WILSON, SAMMY, HUGHIE, *and* JAIMIE, *single file.*

SAMMY: Her ears are the right size.

HUGHIE: And did you see—she was missing part of the right lobe too?

JAIME: A dog bit me. I told you.

SAMMY: And she has the mole.

JAIME: Beauty mark.

SAMMY: Nails with no moon showing; she identified the cane, the photograph of his mother and his worry beads.

> JAIMIE *wanders around the room as they talk. Flipping open books; opening boxes, etc.*

WILSON: And she's one in three chosen from the entire world's population as the probable reincarnation of my son. Hmmmmm.

SAMMY: You haven't seen the others.

HUGHIE: Do you think you should be looking through Mr. Wilson's things?

WILSON: No. No let her. I want to see what she picks out.

JAIME: Oh wow, you have Richard Wilbur. Great poet. [*She thumbs through the book.*]

WILSON: Yes. He was my son's favorite.

Do you know him?

JAIME: Oh yeah. He wrote the single greatest poem I ever read!

WILSON: My son was an avid reader.

JAIME: Oh I don't read much—it clouds your mind, but I do know Richard Wilbur.

WILSON: Is there a poem you'd like to show me?

JAIME: Are you kidding? [*She shows him.*]

WILSON: "Love Calls Us To The Things Of This World"

Oh my... [*He takes out his handkerchief.*]

HUGHIE: What is it?

SAMMY: What is it?

JAIME: What is it?

WILSON: There's something here I tell you. There's something definitely here.

HUGHIE: Yes?

SAMMY: Yes?

JAIME: Yes?

WILSON: This was my son's favorite poem. His very favorite. My God!

"Bring them down from their ruddy gallows
Let there be clean linen for the backs of thieves;
Let lovers go fresh and sweet to be undone
And the heaviest nuns walk in a pure floating
Of dark habits
keeping their difficult balance"

> *He turns away.*

Excuse me.

JAIME: Wow.

I'm sorry.

WILSON: No, no dear. You've brought my son to me. I felt him nearby today.
Gentlemen. I'm convinced she's the one.

HUGHIE: But the others?

SAMMY: I agree. You must see the others.

HUGHIE: Emotions might be clouding your judgment, don't you think?

SAMMY: I agree.
We must always offset emotional mysticism with mental balance.

WILSON: No. I tell you—intuitively, and by all the rules of your game—she is the reincarnation of my son. The percentages of correct answers are astronomical. I believe it was one hundred percent. Not one wrong guess, not one wrong move and now this...this... [*Holding up the book.*]

HUGHIE: Would you like a drink?

SAMMY: Hughie!

WILSON: You see? I have both intuitive and statistical proof, congratulations gentlemen.
I'm ecstatic.
Boris! Boris!
Of course there will be a longer period of examination, but I feel it.
I feel it just as you two said. A revelation.
Boris! Boris!

> TINA *comes out.*

TINA: [*She is Polish*] You called sir?

WILSON: Where is your husband?

TINA: I don't really know. I believe he's showing someone the grounds, sir.

WILSON: Never mind. Bring me my checkbook. It's on top of my desk.
[*To* SAMMY *and* HUGHIE] You've earned your fee.

SAMMY: No!

HUGHIE: [*To* SAMMY] Are we refusing it?

SAMMY: Yes! This is incomplete. We do not do incomplete work.

WILSON: I'll make out the check and you can do with it what you will.

SAMMY: It's not that we're so certain the girl is not your son.
We're just not sure she is.

JAIME: [*Haltingly*] I have to tell you all something...

WILSON: Yes?

HUGHIE: Yes?

SAMMY: Yes?

JAIME: I don't feel like a man. And I don't remember consciously anything about this place.

SAMMY: You wouldn't necessarily remember.
You share a soul with the old James. The soul is the unit of evolution.
The soul is old. But the personality is brand new and the personality is the unit of incarnation. So you wouldn't necessarily remember anything.

HUGHIE: Do you think that's quite true?

SAMMY: Of course that's what I think. I said it, didn't I?

HUGHIE: Not a trace of past lives? Not a preference carried over? Not a talent? Not an interest? What about the cane? The ring? The poem?

SAMMY: All right, a trace. There's a trace of previous lives.

WILSON: Why don't you wait for me in the library, gentlemen. I want some time alone with Jaimie.

SAMMY *elbows* HUGHIE. *They exit.*

[*To* JAIMIE] So, what do you make of all this, my dear?

JAIME: Mercury retrograde.

WILSON: I beg your pardon.

JAIME: This could be a terrible mistake.

WILSON: Not so terrible.

Why don't we agree to give this a little time.

JAIME: All right.

WILSON: Three weeks?

JAIME: I guess.

WILSON: Anyone I should notify? Anyone you want to call?

JAIME: There's one dude…but no. Let him stew. It'll be good for his ego.

WILSON: Fine. Tina will show you to your room.

JAIME: What do I have to do?

WILSON: Be a poet, I imagine.

JAIME: I am one.

WILSON: Yes I know. So was my son.

JAIME: This is really spooky.

WILSON: It is eerie isn't it?

JAIME: It's too much. I can't see myself living here.

WILSON: Oh I see. You have a prejudice against money.

So did my son.

He couldn't imagine himself here either.

He went into a monastery.

JAIME: I'm different. I could never be a monk…I mean a nun. Whatever. I believe in sex.

WILSON: So did my son.

He was a Franciscan—of course.

Truly mystic. A fatal paradox.

He was a passionate boy who took a vow of chastity; a sensual person who lived in poverty; a romantic who engaged in affair after affair each sadder and more desperate than the last. He always chose someone inappropriate—a drunk or a married man. He was a homosexual who never made his peace—except with a double barreled rifle at the end.

JAIME: I'm sorry.

WILSON: I loved him very, very much.

JAIME: I'm sorry.

WILSON: So—where were we?

Three weeks.

Give it a chance.

Immerse yourself.

Try an external approach to inner development.

Try the clothes, the food, the freedom, the richness, the color, sound, the perfume.

Let yourself awaken to the possibilities.

This is not preposterous.

Look at yoga—by adopting certain outer physical postures a resonant chord can be struck in the inner soul.

JAIME: I'll do it.

WILSON: Just relax, let this experience wash over you—

money isn't evil, you know.

Lord, how many times did I say this to my son.

Money is time, space, loveliness—I can take money

and create a garden full of flowers and color and streams

and moss…I can take money and have musicians play

day and night, or have composers write music,

or architects build dream houses for the poor.

I can take money and change the direction of rivers,

or cure the sick…money is godlike in the right hands

It can even help poets…

That's why this money, this wealth I've

somehow impossibly accumulated, must end up in the right

hands.

So stay. If you can't believe. Don't disbelieve.

And we'll see.

I feel this inexplicable tenderness towards you.

JAIME: Your son could've come back as a woman. Then he wouldn't be so torn up about loving men.

WILSON: You'll stay then? Wonderful. Go upstairs and see if Tina's around.

JAIME: I think your son had Venus in Pisces. [*She exits.*]

> HUGHIE *and* SAMMY *march in very determined.* TINA *follows with the checkbook.*

HUGHIE: Would you please listen to us for a moment?

SAMMY: Yes.

We want to talk to you alone.

> SAMMY *pulls* WILSON *aside.*

We feel what you're doing is wrong.

We feel quite strongly about it.

WILSON: Do you agree, Hughie?

SAMMY: We agree.

We always agree about conclusions.

We won't take the check.

HUGHIE: How could we risk our reputation?

How could we betray our gods and our talent?

How could we permit you to mistake passion for perspective?

WILSON: You needn't worry. I'm not about to hand over my fortune to a charming little street poet—no matter how charming.

If in three weeks Jaimie has doubts, and I have reservations—I'll call off the search and create a foundation.

HUGHIE: Why three weeks?

SAMMY: Three is the number of full expression;

WILSON: Because that's sufficient.

Now I must find Boris. We have some excellent recordings of the Tango, Gardel himself, 1928, Paris.

The tango of course—it's a Latin American dance in duple metre—much like the habanera. [*He exits.*]

HUGHIE: What about the other candidates?

Tina enters. BORIS *and* JIMMY *are outside.* JIMMY *is shooting at geese. We can't hear him fire.*

TINA: Oh, there's Boris.

She taps on the window and waves. BORIS *waves back. She exits.*

HUGHIE: Are you positive the girl's not the one?

SAMMY: I'm as convinced as you are.

We can't let him do this.

We must find the right person and bring him hack here.

HUGHIE: And if we can't?

SAMMY: Fate.

This person is doomed to repeat his mistakes over and over and over until he is ready to redeem the qualities that destroyed him in his previous life.

HUGHIE: Does that mean, perhaps?

SAMMY: Suicide.

HUGHIE: Ahhhhhhhhhh.

He puts his arm around SAMMY's *shoulders in comradely fashion. Behind the glass doors, in full view,* BORIS *gently takes the rifle from* JIMMY, *leans it against one of the glass doors and embraces him passionately.*

END OF ACT ONE

ACT TWO

Three weeks later. JAIMIE'S *room. Also we see part of the street outside. Inside* JIMMY *has his juggling paraphernalia around.* JIMMY *is stripped to the waist, wearing sweat pants and juggling first three and then four balls. Rock music. In the street,* DAVID *is walking. There is also another couple; the woman with a fur boa. A dummy falls at their feet. The Woman: "Quick Charles, up here. I do believe we've finally found a vacant apartment." She yanks him off stage.* DAVID *steps over the dummy. He goes to the window over the fire escape and taps loudly on it, but* JIMMY *can't hear. He taps harder and shouts.* JIMMY *is startled and makes a big show of almost dropping all the balls, but then recovers.* DAVID *indicates* JIMMY *should open the window.* JIMMY *still juggling, manages after several attempts to turn the radio down with one hand.*

JIMMY: [*Yelling*] It's open!

Just lift it. It's open.

DAVID: [*Climbs in.*] Well what do you know. Jimmy the juggler.

How's tricks?

JIMMY: Wonderful. I'm in love.

DAVID: I see. Congratulations.

JIMMY: I highly recommend it.

DAVID: Is...ah...Jaimie around?

JIMMY: Oh no, no, no, no, no.

DAVID: Don't worry, I'm here for a signature, not a seduction.

JIMMY: She's not here. She's living with a millionaire.

DAVID: Hold on. I thought you were in love?

JIMMY: Oh, you thought Jaimie and I...? No.

She's hit an incredible streak of luck.

For that matter so have I.

We have a truly karmic connection. Both Pisces.

Born on the same day.

She has a mansion. I have this apartment.

She's got Daddy Bigbucks and I—have a brand new friend.

DAVID: What's she doing with this millionaire?

JIMMY: I don't know—what time is it? Just kidding.

DAVID: Let's go find out what she's up to.

I assume you know where she is.

JIMMY: My my, aren't we headstrong.

What's the hurry?

DAVID: Here's your hat. Let's go.

JIMMY: I don't need a hat.

Actually I don't wear it any longer. It weakens my hair follicles.

Does it look like I'm losing my hair?

I'm only nineteen, but the brush looks full…

DAVID: You look great.

JIMMY: [*Puts on a shirt—rather Hawaiian.*] I'm wearing colors now.

I always wore black.

But I feel like a prism these days.

Light passes right through me…ah love…

Are you sure my hair doesn't look thinner? I can see the scalp.

DAVID: Is Jaimie in love too?

Seeing as you have such a karmic connection.

JIMMY: If I'm in love, she's in love.

DAVID: Are you ready?

JIMMY: Wait!

DAVID: Why?

JIMMY: Sorry.

DAVID: What?

JIMMY: Today's out of the question.

Momentous decisions are pending.

She can't be interrupted. No. No. Impossible.

I'll tell her you called.

DAVID: I have to see her now.

JIMMY: Now? After you waited three weeks, it has to be now, right this minute no
matter whom you inconvenience or—destroy?

DAVID: Right.

JIMMY: Well you're no Pisces!

DAVID: Not on your life.

JIMMY: Don't tell me, don't tell me. Let me guess… [*Walks around him.*]

Reddish tinge, brash, headstrong.

Headstrong. You're an Aries, right?

Aries rules the head.

You're headstrong.

Brash, romantic…

If you want fireworks, take an Aries. Romeo was probably an Aries.

DAVID: So does that get me your recommendation?

JIMMY: No. Aries are romantic—but have no follow through.

Give me a Taurus. Steady. Built.

I'm in love with a Taurus.

I have the most beautiful, sweet, exotic big blond Russian Taurus you ever laid eyes
on.

Silver white hair, blue eyes, skin like a rosebud

And best of all—silent.
One of those one word Taurus wonders like Gary Cooper—the original "Yuuup"
man.
There was a Taurus.
They're so terrific. Like stoked fire
Always burning and just stir them up a little...
But oh, I do go on...
DAVID: Where do we have to go to find this millionaire?
JIMMY: So do you love her?
DAVID: I like her.
JIMMY: "Like"... "like"...how paltry.
I don't even remember "like."
I've never been in love like this before.
It's a three ring circus with four clowns
and my head going 'round like a four ball shower. [*He does a four ball shower and tosses the balls into a canvas case.*]
DAVID: This has got nothing to do with love.
We co-wrote a song together.
A major label is making interested noises.
I want to talk to her about rights and money.
JIMMY: Not love?
DAVID: Definitely not love.
JIMMY: Look, I know you're an Aries and it's hard, but think of someone besides yourself.
DAVID: Fuck you.
JIMMY: I shouldn't complicate things for her. Certainly not for "like."
Now if you had been in love with her...
DAVID: I can say the word if that's what you want.
JIMMY: I'd do quite a lot for love.
I understand passion, but business [*He shrugs.*]
I mean this fellow is cultured, civilized, rich...
DAVID: And old. All that goes with old.
JIMMY: Seasoned. Well I won't take you. You'll queer the deal.
DAVID: I'm sure I'd have no effect on her.
She's probably deeply in love with this man.
Didn't you say you two were so cosmically attuned that if you're in love, her heart's going pitter pat as well?
JIMMY: Actually, I know for a fact she's in love.
DAVID: Good for her.
JIMMY: Well, it may not be. But she has a mentor.
Poets need mentors.
Us jugglers, on the other hand,
we're independent—there's the street, the circus, bar mitzvahs— n'est-ce pas?

But a poet?

What can a poor poet do?

You don't have a lot to offer her.

DAVID: I have a voice that can kill a cow at a hundred yards.

I have talent, management ability…

JIMMY: And money?

DAVID: I don't buy into a billboard mentality—money equals happiness—buy this, buy that, own it all and you'll turn into a cougar, jump on top of a billboard, screw the girl in the black velvet dress and ride off into the sunset. However, if this deal goes through, they may offer me quite a bit of money.

JIMMY: But it won't help you. Sorry.

DAVID: [*Pushes* JIMMY *against the sill. He drops his juggling balls.*] Looking to get your balls busted, buster?

Let's go.

JIMMY: All right. All right.

I respond to passion as well as the next man. In fact I was going there anyway.

Mercury goes direct today at noon. All this will be straightened out.

No more Mercury retrograde.

Thank God. [*He gets his things.*]

I'm waiting until five past noon myself and then,

I'll ask my Taurus to live with me.

We'll walk by the ocean, hold hands, kiss, caress, embrace…

My God,

And I thought I'd die young, poor and

alone.

There's hope I tell you.

There's always hope.

Well follow me, what can you do with an Aries?

> DAVID *exits first.*

Typical Aries—always has to lead even if he doesn't know where he's going! [*He exits.*]

> *Later that same morning.* JAIMIE's *bedroom on the second floor. A canopied bed. A desk piled with papers. A full length mirror and a large glass door opening onto a balcony. We only see sky beyond billowy curtains. Hints of luxury.* TINA *the maid enters with a stack of lingerie. She steps out onto the balcony for a moment and catches sight of someone.*

TINA: There you are you tomcat, you rooster.

I know you have a lover, you lovesick bull, you peacock,

I won't put up with this. I tell you…

JAIME: [*Enters wearing jeans, a tee shirt, a flamboyant headdress.*] What is it, Tina?

TINA: I will not put up with this! [*She puts the lingerie on the bed and preens in front of the mirror.*] I don't have to.

My father was a calvary officer in the Polish army and my uncle was a prelate in the

Catholic Church.

I didn't have to settle for a Russian serf, a vulgar bulgar, a peasant always in heat!

JAIME: A love spat, right?

TINA: A love spat! I'll kill him.

No. I'll kill her!

The laundress found a note in his pocket.

signed your "adoring, worshipful servant," imagine!

In his trousers

And after all I've done.

I left my family, my country, my training for him.

I was trained as a ladies maid. A fine ladies' maid. No one else could fold lingerie or arrange drawers the way I could.

My ladies never had a pleat out of place,

a button missing, a spot on their lace—

and although I was always slimmer, taller,

more naturally elegant—

all of my ladies went out feeling like a million bucks.

And now?

Cotton underwear for Miss Bluejeans.

What's more—

I answer doors, announce guests, set the table—all to cover for...

She shoves the note under JAIMIE'S *nose and quickly withdraws it and reads.*

You see, here's the note.

Can you believe...

"Never have I been so in love, so enthralled, so overwhelmed.

We'll meet on the beach at noon there is so much to say..."

Can you believe?

Well, she'll believe.

I'm going to confront her, this woman, this girl.

I'll tell her to her face that Boris is mine, married

in the Church in front of all the saints. I bet Boris the Bull did not tell her that!

I betcha!

She'll see. And let her "overwhelm" herself someplace else!

Your lingerie is clean. [*She stalks out.*]

> JAIMIE *is in a good mood. She sits at a table and puts her hair up. Tries it different ways. Then she puts on makeup. She is wrapped in a towel. She turns the radio up. There is a soft knock on the door. Another knock.* WILSON *lets himself in carrying a stack of books.*

WILSON: Jaimie...

JAIME: Oh Wilson, I'm not ready yet.

WILSON: I'll stay here and wait. May I?

JAIME: Sure. [*She turns the music down.*]

Hope you don't mind rock.

WILSON: No as a matter of fact I was reading about rock and roll. Did you know it's a commercial amalgam of the styles of American White country music and Black rhythm and blues?

JAIME: [*Putting on some huge sapphire earrings.*] Yeah. [*She looks at herself. Takes another sip of champagne.*] Wow! Not bad.

WILSON: Yes. And Rhythm and Blues is particularly interesting. Did you know that the 12-bar melodic and harmonic pattern and the three line stanzas are now common to much of the popular music of recent decades?

JAIME: Yeah. [*Wrapping a long piece of black silk around her until it forms a slinky dress with one strap.*] I'm almost ready Wilson.

WILSON: I think the idea about these get togethers to share interests is a splendid idea. I wish I had been able to do this with my son—originally that is.

JAIME: [*Steps out.*] Ta Da!

What do you think?

Pretty hot, right?

Watch out Vogue—here I come.

I feel like a peacock.

WILSON: You look like a bird of paradise.

JAIME: These earrings are devastating.

WILSON: They belonged to the last Raj of Sinukhan who presented them to my mother who was a very beautiful woman.

She'd be pleased to see them on you. She wanted them to go to a daughter if I had one, or to my son's wife if he married.

JAIME: Wilson. I can't keep these.

WILSON: We'll see.

JAIME: You're not treating me like a son.

WILSON: Like a daughter.

I can't ignore the fact that you've come back to me as a girl. You look absolutely beautiful.

JAIME: [*Changing the subject.*] So our topic for today is…

WILSON: Oh yes—our topic of conversation for today.

JAIME: [*Taking the books.*] Emily Dickinson, Elizabeth Bishop, Anne Sexton—Women poets.

WILSON: Like you—blessed by the Greek literary goddesses Calliope, Erato and Euterpe no doubt.

JAIME: No doubt.

WILSON: You make me want to show off.

JAIME: All women poets, eh?

WILSON: I wanted to do something of special interest to you.

JAIME: So because I'm a woman I'm interested in women poets?

WILSON: I suppose that is a bit simplistic isn't it?

Well, I'm only a businessman puttering around in the arts.

JAIME: You're very kind, Wilson.

WILSON: Kind? Kind? I meant to be exciting.

Well—in any event you really should read more. You have a fine untutored mind.

JAIME: I like being untutored.

Every time I write, I'm an explorer.

WILSON: But you need heroes.

JAIME: My friends are my heroes.

WILSON: How gallant.

JAIME: You're my friend. My gallant friend.

I'm going to miss you.

WILSON: You know, Jaimie—I was thinking.

JAIME: Yes.

WILSON: Although the three weeks are up at noon, I really think we should prolong this experiment. We both have doubts still and I see no reason why you can't stay a few more weeks. You should be here to see the ocean in the Fall—it would inspire you. It's grainy and tempestuous. I've found I can learn all the seasons through the ocean's lens. You see—it even inspires me to wax poetic—"ocean's lens"—not bad. Just think what it would do for you.

JAIME: I don't know what to say.

I love it here. This is so decadent.

I grew up in the Midwest.

I shouldn't feel this way.

WILSON: Do you really think it's harmful for an artist to have money? Do you think you'd be the first? What about Baudelaire or James Merrill or Tolstoy? Do you think Bob Dylan's starving in a garrett or Baryshnikov is without a sinecure? Please— you sound like my son.

JAIME: Wilson…

DAVID *appears on the balcony and sees the embrace. He stays hidden.* DAVID *enters.*

WILSON: [*As he exits*] Think about it. We'll discuss this at lunch. Today the three weeks are up in any event and we should discuss the future. I'll see you at noon then. Wear what you have on now.

He kisses her cheek and embraces her tightly.

There's a reason we've been brought together. Can't you feel it?

Fate is at work here, Divine Providence.

We should explore it together.

DAVID: Some outlaw.

JAIME: What?

DAVID: You look like you belong in a harem.

Have you fucked him yet?

JAIME: David? What are you doing here?

DAVID: Ditto.

JAIME: How did you find me?

DAVID: Cosmic intervention.

Stand up. Let me take a look at you. [*Whistles*]

JAIME: Get out of here.

He'll hear you.

DAVID: Have you fucked him yet?

JAIME: You're really a limited person, you know that.

DAVID: Yes. How boring. I relate to life through my cock. They all say that. [*He languishes on the bed.*] But what's a poor boy to do?

JAIME: Did anyone see you come up?

DAVID: Not to worry.

All my years of seeing married women have paid off.

JAIME: What the hell do you want now?

DAVID: Now?

You sound hurt. Did I wait too long? Of course I haunted Port Authority in my off hours.

I climbed your fire escape on several occasions.

You don't seem to have a phone or a fax—or a brain in your head. How was I to know you'd been reincarnated during the last three weeks?!

He goes to kiss her. She moves away.

Well, I just dropped in to say "Howdy, Ma'am."

JAIME: David…

DAVID: Not to worry little lady—I'm here to complete your streak of luck. I have good news. I'm frontman in a new band, Harm's Way.

JAIME: So glad you dropped by to tell me.

DAVID: And our first hit single will be none other than "Conspirators."

JAIME: Great.

DAVID: You should be happier than that. It's going to make you rich— although I see you're quite comfortable already. And here I thought you were a waif shivering in the woods.

JAIME: Hold on a minute. I don't get it.

Why should this song make me rich?

DAVID: It's our song. The song we wrote.

JAIME: What "we" is this?

DAVID: As in you and I—we.

JAIME: What are you talking about?

DAVID: I took that poem you gave me. Did a little editing. Now it's a rock song.

JAIME: Are you kidding?

DAVID: Cut a demo with some of the guys at the club; sent it to Pacific Records. They loved it. Soooo we're gettin' a contract. All you have to do is sign on the dotted line.

JAIME: I didn't say you could use it.

DAVID: You gave it to me.

JAIME: It was private. Special. I wrote that poem just for you.

DAVID: And I wrote this song just for you.

JAIME: Yeah, you and the guys had a good laugh, I bet.

DAVID: Will you at least listen to it for chrissakes?

He plays the demo tape.
We are…we are…we are
conspirators
against the past
armed with bottles full of wine
lost for time
with joyous music blast-ing
on the radio
so did you know
we are conspirators
we are, we are
conspirators
breaking out of ugliness and
fleeing
just you and me
conspirators.
We take what life deals
take back what it steals
we love and leave
pain—that interminable fire
only scorching our heels.
We are conspirators…we are…we are…
conspirators.
     Pause.

JAIME: I didn't hear from you for a long time.

DAVID: You disappeared. What was I supposed to do—consult an astrologer to find you? At least, can I have your signature?

JAIME: No.

DAVID: Why? Revenge?

JAIME: It's not revenge.

DAVID: Look. I won't fuck with your karma, if that's what you're afraid of.
I'll just copyright this song and send you some checks.
You love my ass. You won't pass this up.

JAIME: Drop dead.

DAVID: I didn't need to come here to find you. I could've cashed in all by myself.

JAIME: I would have found out and sued your ass.

DAVID: So sue me. [*He holds her.*]
Call the cops.
You're really gorgeous, you know.

JAIME: You dig sapphires and silk.

DAVID: I dig skin like silk and eyes of brilliant blue.
Jaimie—come on tour with us. We could write other songs.
I won't pressure you. If you want you can be one of the boys.

JAIME: One of the boys with extra holes, right? Don't come on to me because you want to use my lyrics.

DAVID: Fine. Forget the come-on. Sign this, you'll have real financial independence. You won't have to lay around with an old geezer and eat bonbons.

JAIME: You're so stupid.

I've been working.

DAVID: Good. Let's see what you've been up to. [*He grabs some papers off her desk. He reads.*]

"Black ivy in a wasteland of debris…"

Hmmmm not quite…

Let's see. [*He reads.*]

"Her dreams are made of plasterboard and paste."

That's hearty.

Oh, yeah, here,

How about

"The faulty skein of sky and road has strung me out from place to place"

Glad to see you're so happy here.

JAIME: I always write sad stuff.

DAVID: You write sad stuff because you're sad and have sad things to say. Not much has changed here. On paper.

JAIME: I haven't digested this experience yet.

DAVID: Right.

Besides which,

you're his son.

JAIME: Jimmy told you.

DAVID: Son.

JAIME: Yeah. But we're going to talk more about it. Today in fact.

DAVID: Well there's nothing to talk about…it's perfectly obvious you're this guy's…this guy's…I can't say it, honest-to-God—

JAIME: Son.

DAVID: Whore.

JAIME: [*Slaps him hard*] You asshole.

DAVID: I thought you were different than anyone else I'd met.

Free, open, out to conquer the world.

But I see I was wrong. You talk a good game

but all you're looking for is shelter, safety, a harbor in the storm.

That's great if you're protecting babies—but not if you want to be out there—being an artist. Sorry.

You've lost your nerve.

  TINA *knocks.*

TINA: Lunch, Miss.

DAVID: [*Falsetto. Imitating her.*] Are you coming, dear?

JAIME: [*To Tina*] I'm coming.

DAVID: I'll be at Kennedy Airport. My flight leaves at five thirty-six for L.A.

JAIME: What? You snap your fingers and I jump? No way!
>   *Grabs the paper from* DAVID. *Signs it and thrusts it into his hands.*
>   Here. Buy yourself another girlfriend!
>   And don't put my name on the song. We never met.
>   *She starts to leave.* DAVID *stops her.*

DAVID: Now we know what love at first sight means, don't we!
>   It sure ain't love at second sight!

JAIME: You shit! [*She exits.*]

DAVID: Ditto my love. Ditto.
>   *He exits from the balcony. Empty room. Curtains billow. An exaggeratedly long dining table half set. Noon.* SAMMY *and* HUGHIE *sit side by side.* BORIS *and* TINA *come in and out arranging the table setting. Everything* BORIS *puts down* TINA *rearranges.*

BORIS: Stop! Enough!
>   You think I am uncompetent.

TINA: Incompetent!

BORIS: [*Checks his watch.*] Ten before noon. I must go for a walk.

TINA: No!

BORIS: You do luncheons.

TINA: Don't go.

BORIS: I'm tired of your not founded jealousies.

TINA: Unfounded.
>   It's not unfounded!
>   I am not a fool.

BORIS: You are the only woman I ever love. I swear. I promise.
>   Boris is many things, a sportsman, a wanderer, a great lover but never a liar. You are the only woman I love. [*Checks his watch again.*] I must go.

TINA: Those are your last words?

BORIS: Yes.

TINA: Fine.
>   I will be right back. [*She flounces off.*]

BORIS: Where are you going?

TINA: Ahh, my big Russian bloodhound.
>   Don't worry so much. I only go to little ladies room.
>   *She exits.* BORIS *storms out and then returns. Throughout,* BORIS *continues setting table and waiting impatiently.*

SAMMY: I'm glad we don't fight.
>   HUGHIE *says nothing.*
>   We talk things over.
>   For instance, there is the matter of failing Mr. Meredith.

HUGHIE: Have we failed?

SAMMY: We've failed.
>   The girl is not the right person…

HUGHIE: Ahhhhhhh.

SAMMY: You're no help. We've failed. Where are your suggestions?

HUGHIE: Where are your suggestions?

SAMMY: We've found the person.

    We always find the person. But we haven't identified him!

HUGHIE: Or her?

SAMMY: We have the big picture.

    Orphans, Pisces, mid-town Manhattan, August.

    Eighth house of legacies in a water sign.

HUGHIE: Wasn't it the fifth house of hidden karma

    in a fire sign?

SAMMY: No! Well, maybe…But that's not it.

    There is something we've overlooked.

HUGHIE: Do you really think we've failed?

SAMMY: We've failed.

    It's the beginning of the end.

HUGHIE: Of what?

SAMMY: Of us, you nincompoop.

    We don't work well together, we've run out of rope, out of ideas,

    out of steam.

HUGHIE: Are you kidding me?

SAMMY: I need someone decisive, energetic,

    Someone who can come up with answers, make statements,

    take the bull by the horns.

HUGHIE: Do you mean that?

SAMMY: Tell me something!

HUGHIE: What?

SAMMY: Something. Anything.

BORIS: [*Worriedly*] Tina! Tina!

HUGHIE: What do you want from me?

SAMMY: Decisions. Action.

HUGHIE: Don't you know by now what I'm like?

    Do you know what you're asking?

SAMMY: Yes.

HUGHIE: Sure?

SAMMY: Yes.

    I'm asking for…

HUGHIE: What?

SAMMY: My needs are different.

    We're facing a crisis. I need someone who confronts reality. I need someone different.

HUGHIE: Haven't we always worked well together?

SAMMY: Until now.

HUGHIE: Why throw out a perfectly good partnership?

SAMMY: Is that all you can say?

HUGHIE: Do you want me to leave?

SAMMY: Do you want to leave?

    Answer. Yes or no. Do you want to leave?

HUGHIE: [*Crestfallen*] Why are you doing this?

    Can't you see you're making me miserable?

    Aren't you miserable too? Don't you have any feelings?

    What's wrong with you?

SAMMY: That's it?

    All right.

    I can't stand it.

    Leave. Go. Get.

HUGHIE: Do you really mean it?

SAMMY: Fight for what you want, you fool!

    Can't you say anything?

HUGHIE: [*Leaving sadly*] What's there to say?

    HUGHIE *exits.* SAMMY *slumps in his seat.* JAIMIE *enters.*

JAIME: Hi guys…guy…what's wrong?

SAMMY: Nothing.

JAIME: Okay.

    Nothing's wrong with me either. [*She sits primly.*]

BORIS: [*Enters*] Have you seen Tina?

JAIME: No.

BORIS: She went to the little girls room. But

    now she's late…

    This is special lunch for you and Mr. Meredith.

    Big decisions. Big deal. BIG deal. Believe me.

    He wants everything special. And if there's no service, Tina and I both be fired. For

        sure. NO doubt. Kaput!

JAIME: Sammy?

SAMMY: I don't know anything about this. I'm no mindreader.

JAIME: I see. Well. Don't count on Tina being on time.

        She sits. BORIS *stands.* SAMMY *sits.*

    Nice day.

BORIS: Yes.

    No.

    Miserable day.

    People suffer.

SAMMY: Yes.

    People suffer.

BORIS: Why do you say Tina is late?

JAIME: I didn't say she'd be late.

BORIS: You know something. Tell me.

    It's your friend who will suffer.

    Your friend? [*He does juggling action.*]

JAIME: Jimmy?

It's about Jimmy?

Oh no.

BORIS: Tina is a strong lady, a very strong lady. Jimmy is tender, too tender. He will be upset, destroyed.

Do you know what I mean?

JAIME: Yeah, sure I got it.

You creep.

BORIS: Is Tina on the beach?

JAIME: She found a note.

BORIS: My God.

JAIME: The laundress.

BORIS: My God.

JAIME: I take it, Jimmy doesn't know about Tina.

BORIS: My God. [*He exits.*]

JAIME: My God. [*She exits after leaving her high heels on the table.*]

     SAMMY *sits dejectedly.* WILSON *enters. Pressed starched white shirt, blue and white striped pants, blue blazer. Perfumed, pomaded. Excellent.*

WILSON: I see I'm early.

SAMMY: You might enjoy a walk along the beach.

WILSON: I'll just wait.

Thank you...Hughie?

SAMMY: Sammy.

WILSON: Would you care for a drink?

SAMMY: No. Thank you.

     They wait.

WILSON: Yes. Well.

Did you know the scale most typical of Chinese music is the pentatonic scale?

SAMMY: I see.

WILSON: You are Chinese?

SAMMY: No.

WILSON: I see.

Well, I'll tell Boris.

He'll find some books on it.

Boris?

Tina? [*He waits.*]

How strange.

SAMMY: My highly developed intuition tells me you would gain great insight into your present circumstances if you went for a walk along the beach.

WILSON: [*Picks up* JAIMIE's *high heels.*] Why? Has something happened on the beach?

SAMMY: It will.

     WILSON *exits.* SAMMY *sits.*

Along the beach. We hear water and gulls. JIMMY *is sitting on a dune, pant legs rolled up, bright sweater knotted around his shoulders. Picnic basket by his side. Peaceful. Tina awkwardly making her way carrying a rifle. Two tourists obviously from Manhattan by their dress, with some minor adjustments to the beach such as jacket slung over one arm, or carrying shoes. Perhaps they are a large woman and a small man. Woman speaks as they make their way across the stage: Woman: "You call this a beach? You call these waves? You call this is a vacation? Where have you been all your life?" Continues as they walk offstage. The Man meekly behind Woman: "You call these birds? You call this a stroll along the shore? You call this fun? You call this romance? You call this… " We hear a thud. The man returns alone. Tips his hat at* TINA, *who has now reached* JIMMY, *and exits.*

TINA: Excuse me. Do you have the time?

JIMMY: Yes. Certainly.

It's almost noon.

TINA: Good.

JIMMY: Aren't you from the house over there?

TINA: Mr. Meredith's. Yes.

I'm the maid.

JIMMY: I thought so.

TINA: You're a friend of Boris's and the young lady.

I've seen you.

JIMMY: Yes.

Hello.

TINA: Listen. I am looking for a young lady. Have you seen her?

JIMMY: No one's come by, but what's she look like? I'll keep an eye
out for her.

TINA: No, that's all right.

Can I wait with you?

JIMMY: Sure.

Want a sandwich. Chips? A coke?

TINA: No. I have lost my appetite. Believe me!

JIMMY: You're upset.

TINA: So sensitive. Such a nice young man.

Too bad about your hair.

JIMMY: My hair?

TINA: A nice young man like you. But women don't mind baldness in
a man. Mature women don't, that is.

JIMMY: Thanks. That's good to know.

TINA: But yes. I'm upset.

Love is so sad.

JIMMY: You've had a fight with your lover?

TINA: My husband.

We always fight.

I love him and he loves me. But we always fight.

He's unfaithful.

JIMMY: You know how men are.

TINA: Yes.

I would make him jealous too.

JIMMY: Why don't you?

TINA: Too tired. [*She sighs.*]

I am ruining your picnic.

JIMMY: No. I'm waiting for someone.

TINA: A lover. Lucky you.

Boris and I were lovers once. My wild Russian bear, my love.

He is a bit younger than I am, twelve years or so…

JIMMY: Boris?

TINA: Boris. Your friend. My husband. The butler over there…

I cannot stand to have him running around so…

It makes me sad, so sad.

JIMMY: Boris.

TINA: Yes.

Do you have a tissue?

JIMMY: I. No.

Boris.

TINA: You are surprised.

I know.

He does not give the appearance of being married.

JIMMY: I have a napkin.

TINA: [*She wipes her eyes and nose.*] But he loves me. In his way. He loves me so much.

He lets me know what he is doing. [*She holds out the note.*]

JIMMY *takes it and gives it back, dazed.*

JIMMY: He gave this to you?

TINA: Yes.

We share everything.

He is loyal, but not faithful.

It is my cross to bear.

JIMMY: Yes.

TINA: No. I make you sad.

I'm sorry.

This girl has stood him up!

Hah!

JIMMY: It happens.

TINA: I say, Hah! on you my Soviet stallion.

Hah!

I leave you waiting for your lover.

And I give you advice, be firm, but quick too.

You're young, but you're losing your looks.

Even men need their looks. I'm glad I have a full head of hair,
not one grey strand. I really don't look so much older than my Boris, do I?

JIMMY: No.

TINA: That comes from having a stallion for a husband.

My Russian stallion.

Well, you look like a sad boy, but I wish you luck. [*She exits.*]

JIMMY: [*picks up gun to tell her she's forgotten it, but changes his mind.*] I really must do
something about my life.

I really must

I can barely breathe, all of a sudden…

The sky, the ocean, the wind is catching my breath…

He didn't even come.

Perhaps he sent her.

Jim you idiot, you stupid idiot. Be a man. Do something.

> *He takes up the gun.*

Why don't you shoot something

Some poor dumb gull. [*He sights something and follows it.*]

Some poor dumb, dumb [*He lowers the gun, sits down, holds it between his knees. He
props the barrel against his forehead.*]

creature.

> JAIMIE *comes running up the beach.*

JAIME: Oh, Jimmy, stop!

JIMMY: Get away from me.

JAIME: Jimmy, please.

Put that gun away.

Nothing can be that bad.

JIMMY: Does the whole fucking world know?

What a laugh!

Everything I thought was beautiful and private
is a public joke.

JAIME: Hey dude, come on.

JIMMY: Dude?!

JAIME: Yeah, 70s, "dude." You're a major dude. You can work it out.

Man to man.

Talk to the guy, will you?

JIMMY: [*Gets up.*] Don't follow me.

JAIME: [*Follows him.*] This is no time to tune out. I mean you just turned a corner and
ran smack into the love of your life. Who knows what'll happen next.

JIMMY: Just say I can't stand the suspense, all right?

JAIME: This is a minute in your life. It'll pass. Let it pass.

JIMMY: It won't pass. This minute resembles too many others.

I told you I either get them sick. Maimed or married. I'm stuck.

Next time around, things'll be different.

Now turn away for Christ's sakes. [*He kneels.*]

God's in his heaven and all's right with the world. [*He points the rifle at his temple and closes his eyes.*]

> BORIS *lumbers up, quite out of breath.*

BORIS: Jim, stop.

> JIMMY *freezes but keeps the gun in place.*

JIMMY: Please.

BORIS: Tina talks with you. I know.

She exaggerates.

JIMMY: Exaggerates! How the hell do you exaggerate being married.

BORIS: Things are mixed up.

You don't understand.

We can talk.

You told me. Mercury is straight now. It's noon.

Everything be all right.

JIMMY: Mercury is what?

JAIME: Retrograde?

JIMMY: Not anymore. It's direct.

You're right. Mercury is direct.

That's why I came here.

BORIS: So now we get things straight. You know. We talk.

JIMMY: [*Opens his eyes.*] How could you give Tina my note?

BORIS: What note?

JIMMY: The note where I said I loved you.

BORIS: Ay...yayayayay

In my pocket. The laundress found it. [*He walks over and gets* JIMMY *up. Takes away the gun gently.*]

It was a mix up.

Come on. We can talk. Boris is a big man, full of feelings, but not smart.

JIMMY: I don't know, Boris.

BORIS: Boris is dumb. I love you. I love Tina and everyone is mad. How can love produce madness?

JAIME: That's the question of the century.

BORIS: [*Puts his arm around* JIMMY.] You see?

You explain it to me.

> *They walk down the beach.* HUGHIE *comes running up.*

HUGHIE: Where is everyone?

JAIME: Walking down the beach into the sunset, Hughie.

HUGHIE: And your friend...?

JAIME: Jimmy?

HUGHIE: And Jimmy...is with...?

JAIME: Boris.

HUGHIE: He's with Boris? With a man?

A man with another man?! Delightful, no?

And this, Jimmy, is short for James?

JAIME: You got it.

HUGHIE: Ahhhhhh.

Don't you think that's perfect? [*He trots after them.*]

WILSON *comes up, perfectly groomed.*

WILSON: Jaimie, Jaimie dear. Wait a moment.

I've had an epiphany.

JAIME: Wilson, I have to talk to you.

WILSON: I know dear.

Oh I'm glad.

I thought you were leaving me.

Here—sit with me.

They sit.

The waves are pounding. How perfect. [*He presses her hand to his heart.*] I must tell you, Jaimie. I've made a mistake.

JAIME: Yes, I know.

WILSON: You're not my son.

JAIME: I know.

WILSON: Strangely I feel my son is near.

I feel his passionate presence. That sensitivity. But not in you. However, all those feelings I've had for you are real. Those stirrings. That tremendous excitement and tenderness.

It all became clear when you kissed me.

I tell you. When I saw you, it was love at first sight.

JAIME: Love at first sight!

WILSON: You believe in love at first sight too?

JAIME: Yes. Yes, I do.

WILSON: I knew it!

What poet could resist it!

And this life, this opulence, this sumptuousness hasn't put you off completely, has it?

JAIME: No, but Wilson...

WILSON: There's hope...like a delicate bud...Oh forgive me—I sound like a greeting card.

JAIME: Wilson...

WILSON: And I haven't told you how magnificent you look. You can change so—wrapped in a bit of silk and those sapphires—you look so mysterious, a quiet fire...how's that? Less like a card. I think. My son would have been proud. He never knew me like this, you see.

JAIME: Wilson.

WILSON: Yes?

JAIME: This is all wrong.

WILSON: Oh I know it's doomed, but who cares. You don't have to love me. I love you enough for both of us now. I feel like a giant. I could straddle continents and oceans and lift mountain ranges and polar caps for you.

Yes. Yes and I'm so much older. I'll die soon and you'll be rich.

If I can't find my son, I want you to have the money.

JAIME: I've got to be real careful here.

I can't take what's not mine.

It would make me weak.

What would my life be if I were saved before I've ever been in danger?

WILSON: You're right. You're right. Whatever you want.

No money. No things.

I understand that too.

You see, that's part of my epiphany.

How lovely.

I understand finally. The curse of things.

All these years in love with the beauty and power of money

the supreme luxury of it all.

But now, because of you

I understand the greatest luxury may be freedom

from the clutter of possessions, their care, the fear of their loss.

I understand my son. At last.

Because of you.

He was wise, not foolish.

He wanted to be free and let his spirit soar

and now that's what I want as well.

Jaimie—you've given me a new life; nothing short of rebirth.

And you'll be my perfect companion.

JAIME: Wilson.

WILSON: I bore you. I terrify you. I disgust you.

JAIME: I love someone else.

WILSON: Oh.

JAIME: I'm sorry.

WILSON: Don't. Don't. [*He takes out a handkerchief.*]

JAIME: It was love at first sight.

         HUGHIE *comes back nearly dancing.*

HUGHIE: And Sammy?

WILSON: We're talking.

HUGHIE: Do you have a moment?

WILSON: Not now. [*He turns to* JAIME.] It is good-bye then.

JAIME: Yes.

WILSON: I see.

JAIME: I'm terribly sorry Wilson—that I wasn't your son and that I can't share your passion.

WILSON: Passion! Who wants passion!

I can see why it runs young people ragged.

JAIME: I would have missed a whole world if I hadn't met you. [*She kisses him.*]

WILSON: It's strange.

HUGHIE *and* JAIME: [*Simultaneously*] What?

WILSON: I feel closer to my son than I ever have—although the search has failed and you're leaving me.

HUGHIE: Do you have a moment?

WILSON: Not now. [*To* JAIME] How will you get home?

JAIME: Your helicopter?

WILSON: Of course.

JAIME: Groovy.

> WILSON *hugs her and then turns his back.*

Good luck Hughie. [*She exits.*]

WILSON: Stupid girl. [*He wipes his eyes.*]

Just delightful.

HUGHIE: Ahhhhhhhhh.

WILSON: What are you "ahhhhhing" about?

HUGHIE: Don't you see?

WILSON: See what?

HUGHIE: You have your wishes, don't you?

WILSON: Wishes? What are you babbling about?

The bottom has just dropped out of my world.

HUGHIE: Don't you feel young? Didn't you say young women make you feel young? Didn't you say passion makes you feel young? Didn't you want passion?

WILSON: She doesn't feel passionate about me, you fool.

She walked away, didn't she? You saw it.

Passion. How can you babble on about me getting any sort of wish about passion when I'm the one who… [*Looks at* HUGHIE.] Yes, I'm the one who feels passion. Ahhhhhh.

HUGHIE: And you wanted to find your son?

WILSON: Please.

> BORIS *and* JIMMY *approach arm and arm.*

HUGHIE: And who's that?

WILSON: Boris?

No.

That young man?

HUGHIE: Can you guess his name?

WILSON: James?

James.

Ahhhhhh.

Lights dim.

Kennedy Airport. The next day. Flights being announced. People walking to and fro. JAIMIE *looking for* DAVID. *A tour guide with some extremely foreign people huddled in a group walks by giving instructions. Tour guide: "When you get to New York, never establish eye contact with anyone. Babies are technically okay, but follow your instincts."* DAVID *walks by with* MARIE. *She is dressed for tropical weather and wears sunglasses.* JAIMIE *approaches.*

JAIME: [*She comes up behind* MARIE.] Hey you.

Beat it.

MARIE: I can't believe it.

Are you talking to me?

Hey David, get a load of this!

DAVID: Jaimie!

JAIME: Howdy, good-lookin'. Jus' thought I'd stop by and give my fondest regards.

DAVID: Jaimie.

MARIE: You know this broad?

Great.

Terrific.

JAIME: Either of you have a quarter?

MARIE: [*Digs through her purse.*] Here. Call the zoo and tell them you escaped.

JAIME: Thanks… Listen. I have the perfect limerick for you guys. Half price. A real deal.

Are you prepared?

"There was a young dude name of David

Who liked all his women stark naked."

MARIE: This is offensive.

JAIME: "Who liked all his women stark naked.

When one of them balked

He got up and walked

And lost out on the best damn thing he ever had

in his whole life."

MARIE: Look sweetie…

handle this.

I got my ticket. *People Magazine*

I'm all set.

I'll see you at the gate.

[*To* JAIMIE] You know sweet pea—

David and I have known each other for years.

We're steak and potatoes

and you're just a candy bar.

Exits.

JAIME: I like how you really step in and take over.

DAVID: I like women to fight over me.

JAIME: So?

DAVID: So what?

JAIME: So what should I do besides stand here feeling like a total idiot?

DAVID: Excuse me—but you did walk into the middle of my life unannounced and started making demands.

JAIME: Tsk, tsk, tsk. Do I believe my ears?

Are you talking double standard?

I thought that dialect was defunct.

DAVID: Marie's waiting.

JAIME: I thought you invited me?

DAVID: I thought you were otherwise engaged. If I'm not mistaken, your last words to me were—"We never met."

JAIME: Right. Well.

Great. We're even.

Nowhere together.

I thought you like women who give you a hard time.

DAVID: Sure. I like women who give you a hard time.

I couldn't love a woman like that.

JAIME: I should've seen this coming.

Lord have mercy—

You want a sweet young thing.

DAVID: Right.

JAIME: With a heart of gold.

DAVID: Helps.

JAIME: What other specifications?

DAVID: Gold…I like gold. Maybe some silver…You got fillin's ma'am?

JAIMIE *nods.*

Maybe some copper in her hair…

JAIME: Oh, I get it.

DAVID: You do?

JAIME: To find true love…

DAVID: Yes?

JAIME: You need…

DAVID: Yes?

JAIME: A metal detector.

DAVID *kisses her. People walk up including the tourist group of foreigners with their leader…all of whom are walking very carefully single file staring at their shoes. Suddenly a large cutout of a mountaintop descends. It should hit with a thud.*

SAMMY *is sitting crosslegged meditating.* HUGHIE *approaches.*

HUGHIE: So how're you doing?

SAMMY *looks up then ignores him.*

Are you deaf?

SAMMY: Only to counsel.

HUGHIE: What?

SAMMY: I thought we were through.

HUGHIE: Why?

SAMMY: After what I said.

HUGHIE: We solved the case, didn't we?

SAMMY: Yes.

HUGHIE: Aren't you glad?

SAMMY: Delighted.

HUGHIE: So?

SAMMY: We're not meant for each other.

HUGHIE: It comes to that?

SAMMY: Yes.

   We have irreconcilable differences.

HUGHIE: Sammy, would you explain what's really going on?

   Don't you know you're hurting me?

SAMMY: Not enough.

HUGHIE: What?

SAMMY: I said not enough! I'm not hurting you enough.

   Now get away. You're ruining my meditation.

HUGHIE: What do you want?

   Why can't you tell me what you want?

   Isn't it important to discuss things, openly, fully?

   Haven't we always treated each other that way?

SAMMY: If you ask one more question, I'll punch you in the face.

      Rises.

HUGHIE: [*Backsaway.*] Ahhhhh.

   So, you want me to change my whole philosophy?

SAMMY: Tell me you love me.

HUGHIE: [*Pulls out a flask.*] How about a drink?

SAMMY: Hughie!

HUGHIE: [*Drinks*] Do I insist that you alter your behavior for me?

   Change your approach, your outlook on life?

   Just for me?

   Do I?

SAMMY: Coward.

   Take a stand.

   Express a belief.

   Make a commitment.

HUGHIE: What's gotten into you?

SAMMY: I'm serious.

HUGHIE: Is it too much time in the West?

SAMMY: If you don't do it right now, this minute…

HUGHIE: [*Crosses his arms on his chest.*] Yes?

SAMMY: We're finished.

HUGHIE: Have you thought this through?

SAMMY: Life is change.

HUGHIE: But if I make a statement, don't I lose my posture as a seeker of truth, a humble observer and prober?

Don't I, with a simple statement, wed myself to a specific reality?

SAMMY: Yes. Me.

HUGHIE: Ahhhhh.

SAMMY: Life is change. [SAMMY *takes off her cap. Her hair flows to her shoulders. Her mannerisms become more womanly.*]

We're changing. [*She faces* HUGHIE, *challengingly.*] So?

HUGHIE: Yes? [*He copies her stance, but takes a quick sip from the flask.*]

SAMMY: So tell me you love me.

A long, long, very long pause.

Hughie?

HUGHIE: [*Guiltily*] What? [*He can't meet her eyes.*]

SAMMY: Never mind. [*She wipes her eyes and turns away.*]

HUGHIE: [*Taps her on the shoulder.*] I do love you, you know.

Black out. Lights up.

END OF PLAY

Murray Mednick

୶

Switchback
or
Lost Child in the Terror Zone

A Jazz Operetta

•

CHARACTERS

TONY: A young street Prince (25); dressed in white.

RITA: His mother; forties; good-looking, hip, shell-shocked.

BRENDA: Girlfriend of Tony's; (20s) beautiful, high-strung, street-wise; dressed to look like a boy.

C.C.: Street warrior; late 20s, early 30s; known as the Preacher; dressed in army fatigues.

SHEILA: Girlfriend of Tony's and C.C.'s; late 20s; sleek.

For Brian

The interior of a building partially destroyed by artillery fire; this is presently a neutral area in the Terror Zone. Maybe it was once a health club, as there is a swimming pool behind the audience. The stage rear wall has a hole in it, or a large window, revealing a switchback walkway. The switchback could be built onstage, be an image to scale, or a video-tape so as to depict c.c.'s *entrance and the finale. The baby carriage is of the old-fashioned type. The plane is to scale—a toy model guided from offstage—or video. Down right is a bench; on it, sitting quietly, all in white, is* TONY. *Gunfire.* RITA *rushes in with the baby carriage, as* BRENDA *enters from the opposite direction on a bicycle.*

BRENDA: He tried to run me over! He doesn't even know me! I am meat! I am garbage! [*Gunfire*] I am fun! Fun target! Fun! Fun to shoot! [*Gunfire. Shouts off*] You bag! You fart! You maniac! I hope you die!

RITA: Quiet!

BRENDA: I coulda been killed! Me!

RITA: Shut up, Brenda!

   Gunfire stops.

BRENDA: This was a safe neighborhood!

RITA: You look like a boy now!

BRENDA: Do I resemble Tony?

RITA: You look just like him!

BRENDA: There's water in the pool!

RITA: Oh!

BRENDA: Is this the place?

RITA: This is the place!

BRENDA: There's water in the pool!

RITA: This is it!

BRENDA: Who said?

RITA: C.C.!

BRENDA: Okay! Where is he?

RITA: He's on his way! [*Looks off*] That must be he!

BRENDA: Do I resemble Tony?

RITA: What I say? [*Looking off*] C.C.! He's coming in—here he comes!

BRENDA: Who is this guy?

RITA: You know C.C.

BRENDA: What's C.C.?

RITA: Curtis Craig, or Craig Curtis.

BRENDA: How can he?

RITA: He can cross boundaries, he.

BRENDA: Say how?

RITA: He has connections on the other side. [*A plane appears*] That be he!

BRENDA: Up there?

RITA: That far: perspective.

BRENDA: You know him?

RITA: Yeah.

BRENDA: Say when?

RITA: Before.

BRENDA: Say who?

> *The plane circles.*

RITA: I said.

BRENDA: Say what?

RITA: Tony's friend. A dearest boy. A bosom pal. A companion. You know him well. They call him Preacher.

BRENDA: A drug dealer and a pimp. Say?

RITA: I would say.

BRENDA: Okay. When do we run?

RITA: 7:30.

BRENDA: And the baby?

RITA: Baby, too.

BRENDA: Baby, too.

RITA: Act right.

BRENDA: Say where?

RITA: Right here. Try to relax. And don't start confessing.

BRENDA: "Don't start confessing!"

RITA: He's coming in! There he is!

> *An orange parachute appears in the sky. The plane makes a pass or two and flies off.*

BRENDA: Let's step on it! Squash him!

RITA: Here he comes!

BRENDA: Is that him?

RITA: What I say?

> *Enter C.C., folding an orange parachute, wearing army fatigues, a portable phone, and a .45. He throws the parachute aside.*

C.C.: Greetings on a good day!

BRENDA: Good night, Sir!

C.C.: Surprised.

BRENDA: Pleased, Sir.

RITA: Be joined. [C.C. *and* BRENDA *perform an elaborate handshake.*] Grateful. Happy.

C.C.: I bring wishes for child.

RITA: Thoughtful.

BRENDA: Poignant. And now?

C.C. *pops* BRENDA *on the nose*

C.C.: Whim. [*Broad smile*] Fantastic. [BRENDA *falls away to compose herself as* C.C. *speaks into his portable phone*] Poolside. 7:35. Smacked Brenda. Hello?

———————— *On the bench, find* BRENDA *joining* TONY

[*past*]

BRENDA: You ever use? You used, didn't ya?

TONY: What?

BRENDA: You. You used.

TONY: Yeah, I'm clean now.

BRENDA: Hey, what do I care? When?

TONY: I'm cleaned up now. I don't do nothin'.

BRENDA: When?

TONY: Before.

BRENDA: Hey, who hasn't used? Crack?

TONY: I don't do nothin' now, not me.

BRENDA: Crack?

TONY: Hey, fuck that shit. I drive a cab. I got the word. Fuck that shit.

BRENDA: In school?

TONY: Who went to school? I went to jail. I went to jail school. I got reformed.

BRENDA: The word?

TONY: I got the message. I got the news.

BRENDA: Say?

TONY: I was fourteen at the time, maybe fifteen. I told nobody.

BRENDA: Say?

TONY: Who wants to say something? Who wants to know? People talk too much.

BRENDA: You don't wanna kill nobody either.

TONY: I take precautions. I watch myself.

BRENDA: Are you sick?

TONY: I'm only twenty-four, but I feel like I'm aging. I'm not escaping like I thought I would. I drive my cab. I eat good. I watch myself. I could get on TV. Then maybe I could say something.

BRENDA: Are you sick?

TONY: I feel great. I feel fine. People in a session, in the joint, everybody is trying to look like they're listening, but all they wanna do is talk their shit, they gotta listen to their own shit...Now I go to groups, I go for counseling, it's the same, I could hear myself...

BRENDA: You wanna see me ever?

Out.

————————

C.C.: [*Into phone*] I gave you the goods. You got the goods. The count is right. No. The count is not short. The count is right. Excuse me? [*Clicks off*]

RITA: [*Big breath*] Ah. [*Rocks baby carriage*]

C.C.: [*Of* BRENDA] She can't go.

RITA: No?

C.C.: Just you.

RITA: And the baby?

C.C.: No. Kid stays, Brenda stays, you go.

RITA: Say?

C.C.: Price: Baby.

RITA: Say?

C.C. They.

RITA: Who?

C.C.: Other side.

RITA: That's not what you said.

C.C.: What I say?

RITA: Family go!

C.C.: No deal. Only you.

RITA: No!

C.C.: Tony had a lady on the other side. Sheila. You know Sheila?

RITA: I don't know no Sheila.

C.C.: She liked Tony.

RITA: So?

C.C.: She wants his child.

RITA: Why?

C.C.: Love and retribution.

RITA: Love? Retribution?

C.C.: My word is my deed.

RITA: Say?

C.C.: Exactly 8:15. Remember, 8:15. Only you. You alone. 8:15.

RITA: Alone?

BRENDA: [Crossing] Apologize!

C.C.: [Laughing] I'm sorry.

BRENDA: [As TONY, with big strut] Drop dead you cunt-suckin' fuck!

C.C.: Fine.

RITA: [Of BRENDA] That's Tony!

BRENDA: [As TONY] I hope you eat shit for the rest of your life, you punk!

C.C.: Keep talking dirt. See what good it brings you.

RITA: Shut it, Tony! Brenda!

BRENDA:[As TONY] I hope you drown!

C.C.: [To RITA] Okay, that's enough from him.

RITA: Time out, Bren'.

BRENDA:[To C.C., as TONY] Hey! How come you got walk-about money and others
    don't? Are you smarter?

C.C.: I am.

BRENDA:[As TONY, big strut] They may bleed![Of the phone] And them things is kill-
    ing machines! Am I right? They eat blood!

C.C.: They are clean machines. And they don't breed.

BRENDA: I said bleed!

C.C.: An' they don't eat.

BRENDA: [*As* TONY] Them money machines is fed on blood, Sir.

C.C.: They are electrical machines, Boy. Electro-mathematical.

BRENDA: [*As* TONY] No! Why you walk about with money while we get only chits?

RITA: Stop it, Brenda! Tony!

BRENDA: [*To* RITA] How can he?

RITA: He gets views. He gets satellite info-mation.

C.C.: One hand washes the other.

BRENDA: [*To* C.C.] Explain!

C.C.: I'm a warrior businessman, me. I'm the Captain of Swords, the Commander. One of you I'll spare and save from grief.

BRENDA: Explain!

C.C.: People need different things. One needs this, the other that. I give you something, you give something back.

BRENDA: Example!

C.C.: Some people have nothing. You're one of them.

BRENDA: I have a child! I have a baby!

C.C.: You're mental, Brenda.

BRENDA: [*As* TONY] Don't say that, you dumb fuck!

C.C.: I'll have you shot. Are you ready?

BRENDA: Shoot!

C.C.: [*Into phone*] You see the little one with the hat? Yeah, that one. [*Pause*] Shoot him.

BRENDA: Okay, I'm sorry!

C.C.: [*Into phone*] Hold your fire. But keep an eye on them. Thank you. [*Walks away, singing*]

——————— *On the bench, find* TONY *and* SHEILA

　　　　　[*past*]

SHEILA: What you got, Guy?

TONY: What you got, Girl?

SHEILA: I don't have.

TONY: I got something.

SHEILA: It's hard these days, crossing over.

TONY: I got something nice.

SHEILA: I can't cross over.

TONY: I got Colombia Red. I got buds and flowers.

SHEILA: Oh, how good!

TONY: Came through the line today!

SHEILA: Oh, how fine!

TONY: Not much, but some.

SHEILA: Wanna trick me for it?

TONY: Say?

SHEILA: Are you deaf?

TONY: I'm not deaf.

SHEILA: Wanna trick me for it?

TONY: I can't right now.

SHEILA: No? [*Laughs*]

TONY: Next time, maybe.

SHEILA: You give me the goods?

TONY: I got no problem with that.

SHEILA: Then we'll see next time. How I feel.

TONY: You like poetry?

SHEILA: You silly boy.

    Out.

C.C.: [*Beckons to* BRENDA] Come here, Girl.

BRENDA: [*Aside, to* RITA] I'll try. [*Goes to him*]

C.C.: What I do is, I take me an area and I develop a market, a demand. I set up supply and distribution. I study the laws, the procedures. The police. I guard my turf and I watch my back. It's hard work.

BRENDA: Are there bodyguards? Are there dogs?

C.C.: Yes. And I have an army, too. Me!

BRENDA: Okay, I forgive you. What's your racket?

C.C.: I have soldiers. I have a crew. I have dependents, I have clientele. I love it. I'm the Man, they come to me. Be a business, and I'm the power. Be research and development. Be psychology, be marketing.

RITA: Good mood.

C.C.: Be oratory. Be preachery.

BRENDA: You're a fucking gangstah!

C.C.: I've gone to a great deal of trouble on behalf of this lady here.

BRENDA: Why?

C.C.: Because of Tony, who was a friend of mine. Now gone.

BRENDA: Now gone!

C.C.: [*Charging her*] Blame?

BRENDA: [*Quickly*] No blame!

C.C.: Who the fuck do you think you are?

BRENDA: Do I remind you of someone?

C.C.: Yeah.

BRENDA: Who?

C.C.: Tony.

BRENDA: Ha! I am BRENDA!

C.C.: No shit. I knew you once, and you're still a head case. [*Walks away*]

BRENDA: Hey, Curtis!

C.C.: Craig.

BRENDA: Hey, Craig! [*Pointing*] You live over there now? Other side?

C.C.: Where else could I be the Man? And earn five thousand dollars a day?

BRENDA: [*To* RITA] He makes forty million dollars a year!

RITA: We get chits. Chits is all we get.

BRENDA: Chits and bullets and a fast death.

RITA: There are too many people and they must eat. An absolute horror. Are we worms? I look at virtual reality, I see worms sliding, giving expressions, thrusting their noses into the camera. Are we worms?

C.C.: Worm-like, I'd say.

BRENDA: "There are the working poor and the very poor, which is us. We are the left behind, we. Plus fire, flood, quake and riot."

C.C.: Such is nature, Girl.

BRENDA: What I say?

RITA: [*To* C.C.] Do you like parks and pools?

C.C.: What time is it?

RITA: Say?

C.C.: I like parks and pools. [*Tries to grab baby, foiled by* RITA]

BRENDA: Kidnapping? Baby stealing?

RITA: Shut up, Tony/Brenda.

BRENDA: [*To* C.C.] What's your business there, Curtis?

C.C.: There are extraterrestrial substances, be always in demand. They are: the coca, the poppy and the tobacco. The opium poppy is a funny looking blue plant from another planet. Some places here it grows like a weed. Not from Earth. Strong. Addictive. Invest. Now for earth substances. They are: alcohol, coffee, wheat, hemp, and water. Invest.

RITA: Alcohol?

C.C.: Invest.

RITA: Water?

C.C.: Invest.

RITA: Extraterrestrial?

BRENDA: Police?

C.C.: We got a system here, they don't want to talk to anyone who knows. You have to start with the leaders. We're strictly into supply and demand. It's like we got one economy on Mars and another in the neighborhood. Nobody wants to talk about real things. They'd have to see themselves in it all.

BRENDA: Police?

C.C.: The police know. But what are the police gonna do? They throw one guy away and ten more are lined up to fill the hole. They're locked into a vicious game, goin' nowhere. No winners, no losers. Police suffer.

BRENDA: Can I go to the bathroom?

C.C.: And they'd have to face my private army. And shit has to move. Police got to eat, too. [*Into phone*] Don't fire. Remember, Gentlemen, I have my army. And they are waiting. And they are watching. And they are nasty. [*Clicks off. To* BRENDA] Go take a leak.

BRENDA: Thank you. [*Leaves*]

——————— *On the bench,* BRENDA *discovers* TONY.

   [*past*]

BRENDA: Tony!

TONY: Yo!

BRENDA: What you doin' here, Boy?

TONY: I'm movin' in wit you.

BRENDA: Say?

TONY: You gonna be my girl friend. I'm tired of hanging here by myself. You're a little strange—but who am I, right? I'm off the streets, and I should have a home. Am I right?

BRENDA: Marry me?

TONY: Later we'll get married. Now we'll have an apartment. Me and you. You won't have to worry.

BRENDA: Oh!

TONY: I'll take care. You make it nice. I'll drive, I'll bring home the goods. One thing only: You gotta stay on them head pills, B.

BRENDA: I know that. Sex?

TONY: I take precautions. I watch myself.

BRENDA: Family?

TONY: Don't go so fast.

BRENDA: Will you die, Tony?

TONY: Not me.

BRENDA: Tony?

TONY: Not me.

BRENDA: Oh!

TONY: Don't worry about it, B. I'm feeling fucking great.

   Out.

——————

RITA: What was on earth before?

C.C.: I was not here before.

RITA: Where were you, C.C.?

C.C.: I was unborn.

RITA: How old are you? We were ALL unborn! There's fifty-four billion more unborn than born! Are we talking the transmigration of souls here? Where are all the fucking people coming from if they weren't here before if you're talking transmigration of souls? And if they were here before, where were they?

C.C.: So I don't know.

RITA: How did they get here?

C.C.: What time is it?

RITA: Them drugs!

C.C.: Through the sky. So. You get life and freedom. A home. Safety. They get the kid.

RITA: Not mine.

c.c.: Let go.

RITA: Oh, no.

c.c.: Do it for me, Rita.

RITA: Why? I hardly know you, you!

c.c.: I watched over your son, Tony. We did time. And he was a pal of mine.

RITA: You weren't there!

c.c.: [*Manipulative*] I'm interested in you. I care about you. I feel a deep rapport. I'd like to save you before you come to grief.

RITA: Bullshit. You flew in here to steal the child. For the other side!

c.c.: Not true, darling. [*As* TONY, *with strut*] This is the last time, Mom. I promise. I swear to God, that's it. I'm gonna clean up and go away to another country. Mom? Death goes where I go, Mom. Death is inside of me. It is dormant, it is waiting. I'm trying, Mom. I love you, Mom. I'll make friends with death.

RITA: Tony! And Brenda?

c.c.: [*As Tony*] She's trying, Mom. [*Walks away*]

———————— *On the bench, find* TONY *and* SHEILA

[*past*]

SHEILA: You crossed.

TONY: Here I am.

SHEILA: What you bring me, Boy?

TONY: I got words. [*Recites:*] "I hate and love. And if you should ask how I can do both, I couldn't say; but I feel it, and it shivers me."

SHEILA: Hate and love.

TONY: Catullus. He was a Roman.

SHEILA: Nasty boy.

TONY: He'd put his mouth on anything.

SHEILA: I'll slap you.

TONY: They killed your friend, Terry.

SHEILA: C.C.?

TONY: They caught him crossing over to your side. C.C. had to put a bullet in his head.

SHEILA: Dirty dog!

TONY: He had a good time.

SHEILA: Watch out.

TONY: He likes you.

SHEILA: C.C.

TONY: He likes you.

SHEILA: He'll never fuck me. [*She shivers*]

TONY: Are you cold?

SHEILA: No. Where I come from, it's cold. This is not cold. Where I come from, this time of year, it's cold. You wanna get inside?

TONY: Yeah.

SHEILA: Trick me?

TONY: Where?

SHEILA: Inside. Over there.

TONY: You don't owe me.

SHEILA: Life's too short, and death is sudden.

TONY: You want revenge?

SHEILA: Why? You offering?

TONY: I'm asking.

SHEILA: Not today.

        Out.

———————

C.C.: I cared about the cunning little sonofabitch.

BRENDA: [*Re-entering*] Yo, Rita!

C.C.: [*Aside to* BRENDA] I was hoping you fell in.

BRENDA: "Darling!" [*Holding out a hand*] Give us money! Shake it out! All we get here
    is chits!

RITA: And bullets.

C.C.: Money is not free.

BRENDA: How much?

C.C.: Twenty-two.

BRENDA: That's high.

RITA: That's high.

C.C.: That's tough.

RITA: Okay.

BRENDA: Have a heart, you cheap oaf.

RITA: Money for the road! Money for the journey!

C.C.: Leave the child? Leave the baby?

RITA & BRENDA: No!

C.C.: Forget about it.

BRENDA: Interest rate's too high. Twenty-two is high.

C.C.: Yes, it is.

RITA: Let's try and forget about it.

BRENDA: If the rate was frozen, I could go along with it.

C.C.: Market forces decide the rate.

RITA: Then what's to keep the Asians back?

C.C.: The army. What I say. [*Walks*]

      ——————— *On the bench,* TONY *and* SHEILA.

        [*past*]

TONY: I heard you did time.

SHEILA: C.C. told you?

TONY: Yeah. What?

SHEILA: Screaming and crying.

TONY: Trade?

SHEILA: Yeah. I saw the money and it was not real. Scared?

TONY: Not me.

SHEILA: You wanna do something?

TONY: We can do things.

SHEILA: First: You have a girl over there? Other side? Brenda?

TONY: We two have an apartment.

SHEILA: How nice for you.

TONY: I could be big. Disks and tapes. MTV.

SHEILA: Money is shit: Sigmund Freud.

TONY: Who?

SHEILA: You don't know?

TONY: I heard of him.

SHEILA: You can barely read English.

TONY: I'm a poet. Authentic.

SHEILA: Grungy old Jew.

TONY: Anti-semite?

SHEILA: You're not Jewish.

TONY: I am half-Jewish.

SHEILA: I can't read him, Freud. Like Karl Marx, I can't read him, either. [*Gunfire*] What is that fucking music?

TONY: Be machine guns. Stay right here. Don't go away. Don't move.

> *Out.*

BRENDA: Sun coming down through holes in the sky! The sun be burning down us!

RITA: Be calm, Brenda!

BRENDA: Meta-Murder! And Marxism can't save us! [*Laughs*] Religion! Perhaps Mormonism! Or: Water vapor could fill the holes. Cloud formations. Water and ice.

RITA: [*Baffled*] The oceans?

BRENDA: Make new ozone. Go to Mars, grab some ice. Manufacture ozone. Invest in water. Must find the cool, bring the cool to the hot.

> *Two gunshots, near misses.*

C.C.: [*Into phone*] Not now, gentlemen. Ha, ha. Yeah! It's the military death disco! Be shoot-to-kill-die-young-America! [*Waves*] Take a moment to enjoy yourselves! [*Clicks off*]

BRENDA: [*To* RITA] Are you burning? The skin be a soft and delicate substance. Be careful.

RITA: Am I peeling?

BRENDA: Uh, no. Question: Does the sun have a skin? Does it have a membrane, like a skin? Answer: Yes. It is the solar system. Sunspots flash and the rabbit population goes up! [*Laughs*]

C.C.: Thing about the genes. What a man wants: pump his genes.

RITA: We know all about it.

C.C.: Bodies. Look out: people staring inconsolably at bodies, at imagery.

RITA: Don't look.

C.C.: I don't do that anymore. I feel remorseful about looking. I keep my head down now. I keep my eyes straight now. [*Walks*]

——————— *On the bench, find* TONY *and* SHEILA
          [*past*]

TONY: [*Recites or sings* Catullus #32:]
   I beg of you, my sweet, my Ipsitilla,
   my darling, my sophisticated beauty,
   summon me to a midday assignation;
   and, if you're willing, do me one big favor:
   don't let another client shoot the door bolt,
   and don't decide to suddenly go cruising,
   but stay home & get yourself all ready
   for nine—yes, nine—successive copulations!
   Honestly, if you want it, give the order:
   I've eaten, and I'm sated, supinated!
   My prick is poking through my cloak & tunic.

SHEILA: Whoa! I like that one. I liked it. Ummmm. Nine times. Catullus.

TONY: Him again.

SHEILA: But that was not Lesbia. That was some filthy hooker.

TONY: The Romans, they had a lot of troubles. They didn't take care of their poor. They were afraid of their poor. Am I right?

SHEILA: You read this? You looked it up?

TONY: I learned it. I take classes.

SHEILA: So why ask me?

TONY: Because you're smart.

SHEILA: No. Because you're bragging on yourself. Next time bring your own. And bring some other shit, too.

TONY: What you got?

SHEILA: You can trick me for it. [*Laughs*] But don't tell the Preacher. What you do. Bragging on yourself.

TONY: He wouldn't hurt me. Man's a pal of mine.

SHEILA: Yeah, yeah. You should come over to my side.

TONY: No.

SHEILA: Why not?

TONY: My mother. My people.

SHEILA: Brenda. You're all gonna die over there.

TONY: We're all gonna die anyway.

SHEILA: Not me, Tony. Not so fast. Let's go. Let's go into one of these buildings.

TONY: Wait. Snipers.

          Out.

———————

RITA: Man says, "I have a feeling of hope." He may mean the opposite: "I have a dread feeling." He don't know. He say. Then he don't know and I don't know. He thinks you mean what he means. She say, "That ain't you. That your Mama talkin.'" Dreams, they act like memories. Projections, they seem virtual.

C.C. *pulls his gun.* BRENDA *ducks.*

C.C.: Tony played games with the other side. Dope games. Mind games. He liked that shit, Tony. I'll take the child.

RITA: Shoot!

C.C.: Would you like a bullet through the head?

RITA: I have seen the dirty face of death.

C.C.: I know you have.

RITA: So fuck off. [*Pause*] There is day and night and there is the sky, and that's all there is.

C.C.: And the child?

RITA: And there is a child.

C.C.: But it doesn't belong to you, Rita.

RITA: Yes, it does. A Jewish child.

C.C.: Brenda's not Jewish.

RITA: Tony's child. [*Pause*]

————— *On the bench,* BRENDA *joins* TONY.

[*past*]

BRENDA: Hey, Tony.

TONY: Yo.

BRENDA: What's the matter?

TONY: Mom be always on my bubble.

BRENDA: What for?

TONY: Viruses. Whatever.

BRENDA: You told her?

TONY: Don't I go for counseling?

BRENDA: You told her?

TONY: I could be on TV.

BRENDA: No wonder.

TONY: I could tell my story. I could sing it. [*Big strut*]

BRENDA: She knows.

TONY: I am no bullshit white boy, me.

BRENDA: Where you goin'?

TONY: Cab time.

BRENDA: You cross over, Tony?

TONY: Who?

BRENDA: You. You cross over? In your cab?

TONY: You're thinking about other people, B. You're not thinking about me.

BRENDA: You. Tony.

TONY: Not me.

BRENDA: Don't lie, Tony.

TONY: Get it out of your head, B.

BRENDA: You going cabbing, or for class?

TONY: I'm working, then I go to class.

BRENDA: You got extra money coming in.

TONY: I get tips, don't I? I rap to the fuckers. They love that shit.

    Out.

C.C.: [*Of the child, as* BRENDA *re-joins them*] Give it to me and you can go.

RITA: No! Brenda?

BRENDA: NO!

C.C.: Brenda. More wired than awake, more frenzied than alive. Unfit, wouldn't you say?

RITA: I wouldn't say.

C.C.: Give up the child. Fresh start. Good life.

RITA: And she?

C.C.: Back to the hospital. You go free. I take the child.

RITA: Be a Jewish child.

C.C.: What they want.

RITA: Half-Jewish!

C.C.: What they want.

RITA: For what?

C.C.: Raise it up. Blood offering.

RITA: Slave! Sacrifice! [*He is about to fire into* RITA's *head—when* C.C.'s *phone rings*]

C.C.: [*Into phone*] It's not time yet, people! I am the Preacher. Sheila? Don't ask me stupid questions! And don't call me—I'll call you! [*Hangs up. To* RITA] Dumb fucks. They call me the Preacher.

BRENDA: We know!

RITA: Our fathers cut into the equatorial rain forests, and the Viruses came out. [*Breaks into uncontrollable tears.* C.C. *looks on helplessly.*]

BRENDA: Tony was a poet! He loved to talk his shit! He walked his talk! [*To* C.C.:] Do you?

C.C.: I taught the sucker everything he knew. Am I right?

BRENDA: You're not Jewish!

C.C.: So what? [*Laughs*] I could be. I might be. You never know.

RITA & BRENDA: You're not Jewish. You can't be Jewish. There's nothing Jewish about you. You have not one Jewish cell in your body. If you were Jewish, you would know it and I would know it. You would be intelligent, for one thing. There would be no question. As it is, you're not, so forget about it.

C.C.: I'm restless and eager to do. I love life and God. I make a lot of money.

BRENDA: Ha! You hear that?

    Rapid gunfire, off.

C.C.: Stay right here. Don't go away. Don't move. [*Exits to pool*]

BRENDA: [*Of the shooters*] Psychopaths, like him.

RITA: They are not sane.

BRENDA: They shoot to kill. They shoot for fun.

RITA: It's true.

BRENDA: Let's run.

C.C.: [*Off*] Shut the fuck up! Cut!

> *The firing stops.*

RITA: [*Of* C.C.] A strange creature. Exotic creature, he. An odd duck.

BRENDA: Is he judging me?

RITA: Yes.

BRENDA: Do you feel he likes me?

RITA: No. I believe he thinks we have a real relationship.

BRENDA: You and me?

RITA: No. He and I. What's he doing now?

BRENDA: He's taking a dip.

RITA: Maybe he'll forget to breathe and drown himself.

BRENDA: Do we snap him?

RITA: Man's a preacher, knows stuff, feels bad.

BRENDA: Let's snap him!

RITA: He has employees. They—

BRENDA: Let's snap him, grab his phone. Where's his guards? [*Pause, sound of baby*] Hear the baby?

RITA: Sounds good. [*Rocking*] Excellent baby.

BRENDA: Wonderful baby.

RITA: They want the baby.

BRENDA: What for?

RITA: Trade. We go, baby stay.

BRENDA: Drop dead.

RITA: Wonderful baby.

BRENDA: What's he doing, sneaking nips down there?

RITA: Get your juice today? Take your pills today?

BRENDA: Yeah, yeah. I've had enough. [*As* TONY] I've had enough. Long line. Biological failures. Hoarse whining. Yellowish complexions. Childish demands. Hassling of nurses. I've had enough.

RITA: Tony!

BRENDA: [*Of* C.C.] Did he call you, "Darling"?

RITA: He wants the child. He wants the baby.

BRENDA: Let's snap the fucker.

RITA: He's kind sometimes.

BRENDA: I'm the mother.

RITA: You're not a mother.

BRENDA: So let go.

RITA: No.

BRENDA: It's mine. Uh, oh. [*Of* C.C.] He's coming back.

> *Re-enter* C.C., *wet.*

C.C.: Did you miss me?

RITA: No.

BRENDA: Sneakin' nips are ya?

C.C.: [*A bit tipsy*] Ah, refreshed. Public pools: reward. Provide amusement parks and pools, beach-front pleasure, hoops, hip-hop, chits for the indigent, and so on.

RITA: A horror. [*To* BRENDA] Watch out for the mood change.

BRENDA: [*To* C.C.] We thought you drowned. Ha, ha, ha.

C.C.: I could drop you down the sewer, Brenda. No trouble at all. Drink your fuckin' junk-juice, Brenda. Fuckin' shit was invented by Hitler. You're not clean. Go back on the rack an' climb the fuckin' walls.

RITA: There it is.

BRENDA: Be hard.

C.C.: Ha, ha, fuck you.

BRENDA: I got drunk in high school a lot.

C.C.: I'm not drunk.

BRENDA: My parents gave me tranquilizers. And then I took to crank. One thing led to another. Then I got on the program.

C.C.: Junk-juice program.

BRENDA: Where I met my Tony.

C.C.: You are not Jewish.

BRENDA: I know I'm not.

RITA: I AM. Thank God.

C.C.: Not you.

BRENDA: I'm Italian.

RITA: My husband was Italian.

C.C.: Jewish parents are not poor. Jewish parents do not give their children drugs.

RITA: Long gone.

C.C.: Were your parents your parents?

BRENDA: My parents WERE my parents.

C.C.: Not you.

RITA: My real name is Rita Burns. I got tired of being a waitress. I did know you once.

C.C.: I'll help you find a home, Rita.

RITA: We were poor, and my mother was psychotic. Unbearable stress. There used to be a vacant lot. I played on the fire escape. Strangers came. There was an Aunt who smelled like talcum powder and an Uncle who smoked. I needed help, but it came too late. I forget to breathe. I'm always holding my breath, me, waiting to get whacked. I was undernourished. Trouble to breathe. My mother, she tried to starve us. In the morning, hard bread and tea. In the afternoon, porridge. Leave me alone, she said, and hoarded dollars in socks. Psychosis lay waiting, like a virus, waiting. She was mean and cold. We are talking child murder here.

C.C.: Be handed down in the family, like with Tony. Am I right?

BRENDA: Sir, you are a bag!

C.C.: I could have you hanged on a clothesline, Brenda. Time is running out. You're a junk-juice suckin' junkie and Rita doesn't love you.

BRENDA: You don't know! But I know the truth of you! You are no hero, you! You are no savior! You are no Preacher! [*Hides under the parachute*]

C.C.: Good. Tony used to be with her. I wasn't in the picture. They set up housekeeping. Brenda, she was clean and sober in every way, and the Virus didn't matter, because Tony was A-symptomatic. And then one day Brenda stopped taking her pills. She had to be alone. Tony freaked, he OD'd on crack, he fell down gasping. Say?

RITA: I won't say.

C.C.: They found him on the floor, coughing. Pneumonia. That's it. They had to plug him into the respirator. And now?

RITA: Now he is ashes.

———— *On the bench, find* TONY *and* SHEILA

[*past*]

SHEILA: You don't see me.

TONY: I don't see you?

SHEILA: I'm the class of this city but you stay on your side with crazy Brenda.

TONY: It is not safe over here.

SHEILA: Scared?

TONY: Ain't it me who comes over?

SHEILA: Scared?

TONY: Not me!

SHEILA: Scared?

TONY: No!

SHEILA: Scared and run! You're still a baby.

TONY: I seen it all already.

SHEILA: Get over it. Enjoy. Take no prisoners. Life's too short and death is sudden.

TONY: Who was serious?

SHEILA: Go ahead and die if you want to. With her.

TONY: Not me.

SHEILA: What you want.

TONY: I'm feeling fucking great!

SHEILA: My people, you see them, it gets like ten below zero, they're freezing to death in cardboard boxes along the railroad tracks. [*Silence*] I want you to bring something over to your side for me. Some money. Some food.

TONY: For you, no problem.

SHEILA: My father kicked my mother out of the apartment. She's over there now. Your side. I could see her leaving from my window, down in the parking lot, in the brown slush, crying. She was all by herself. Just one car in the lot, holding my mother. Snipers—from both sides. Everything around grey and black and old snow—Winter, bitter, my mother down there hunched over with her face in her hands. My father came running up behind me and grabbed my hair. I could see he was terrified in his fuckin' eyes. He started to run to bring her back, but he couldn't run fast enough. [*Snaps her fingers*] I looked down onto the parking lot and she was gone— just a big dead, dirty corner lot, empty and wet. Bullets slamming into the icy slush.

TONY: I'll talk to the Preacher.

SHEILA: You can't trust C.C.! How many times!

TONY: Forget about it.

SHEILA: Check her out yourself.

TONY: Okay, I will.

SHEILA: Thank you, Darling.

TONY: Don't call me Darling.

SHEILA: I'll give you love. Not like that madwoman, Brenda.

     Out.

C.C.: Tell Brenda I can crack her: change her spine forever, me. Result: permanent backache.

RITA: Brenda!

C.C.: Alternative: burn down the neighborhood. A little kerosene and a match: out she comes. Ha, ha, ha.

     BRENDA *comes out of hiding.*

BRENDA: Okay!

C.C.: They are waiting for you, Brenda.

BRENDA: [*As* TONY] I hope they all die. I hope they are mangled. I hope they burn.

RITA: Why our child? A Jewish child? Tony's child?

C.C.: I told you. Love and retribution.

BRENDA: When a child is born, death is defeated!

RITA: Love comes streaming down then. God shows his love then!

C.C.: Over there, no more Jewish people. None left. No survivors. I'll tell you what they did, them. Say?

RITA: No.

BRENDA: Say.

C.C.: War. A round-up. Four hundred Jewish people, they ran them through the slaughterhouse. [RITA *gags and weeps*] Where I come from, nobody loved nobody.

BRENDA: It shows!

C.C.: Me and Tony, we came up together. We did time together. We ran the neighborhood, him and me. But Tony was playing with the other side. He insulted the wrong people. Now for the payment.

RITA: No!

C.C.: Is it yours?

RITA & BRENDA: Yes!

C.C.: I'll take it.

RITA & BRENDA: No!

C.C.: [*Into phone*] Time?

RITA & BRENDA: No!

C.C.: [*Into phone*] Time?

RITA & BRENDA: No!

C.C.: [*Into phone*] Time?

RITA & BRENDA: No!

C.C.: [*Into phone*] Put Sheila on. Hello? I want an extension. Are you deaf? I'm tired. What? [*Clicks off. To* RITA *and* BRENDA] Be clear to me now, clear as shadows on a bright day.

BRENDA: Oh, yeah?

C.C.: Hostile?

BRENDA: Give an example.

C.C.: Be with one, fall in love with she. Lose both. Repeat, repeat.

BRENDA: I didn't follow that.

C.C.: Emotions and desires: ephemeral. Fade. Can love endure?

BRENDA: I have the intelligence to understand that.

C.C.: Okay, listen up. There is a woman with a baby. She loves it to pieces. She's totally attached to it. She'll do anything for it. She's a slave to it and a martyr.

RITA & BRENDA: Say?

C.C.: She is jealous of the baby so she won't allow help. Though the baby is difficult and needs a lot of care, she doesn't let anyone else get too close to the baby.

RITA & BRENDA: And?

C.C.: Before the authorities, she weeps and laments. Who among us can resist a mother's martyrdom?

RITA & BRENDA: Not one of us.

C.C.: And so she continues in thrall to the baby, and the baby in bondage to she. [*Pause*] Be only one problem.

RITA & BRENDA: Say?

C.C.: It's not her baby.

RITA & BRENDA: Conclude?

C.C.: The baby must be separated from this woman and restored to her rightful blood.

RITA: A parable?

C.C.: No.

RITA: A riddle?

C.C.: Think it over. You have five minutes. [*Exits to pool*]

BRENDA: What the fuck?

RITA: That was rude!

BRENDA: Sheila? [*Of the carriage*] We have minutes, so let go.

RITA: No.

BRENDA: Are we alike at all?

RITA: You're not Jewish.

BRENDA: We have nothing in common but Tony.

RITA: We know what's what, the Jews. It's in the Bible.

BRENDA: Sheila? [*Off, splashing from the pool. Of* C.C.] I think he likes to wash himself.

RITA: He thinks he's beautiful for a worm-like creature.

BRENDA: He's a water freak. We snap him.

RITA: [*Rocking the carriage*] You can do what you want, you.

BRENDA: Let's run.

RITA: Not we.

BRENDA: Why not?

RITA: Not we.

BRENDA: You blame me?

RITA: I'm trying.

BRENDA: You blame?

RITA: No.

BRENDA: I'm trying.

RITA: I know.

BRENDA: Forgive me? [*Pause*] When I met Tony, I had tracks all over, like the pox. I was hookin' for fixes. I got on the program and took my pills. He started cracking, Tony. He knew he was going to die, he. Virus—no forgiveness. Tony. Just a boy. He cracked. I knew he knew he was going to die. He fell down. I? I was panicked. I wanted to go into hospital. I wanted to be alone, me. Nobody dying. Me alone. Tony cracked. He fell down. Me. He made friends with death, Tony. We—a good life. We—a family. We—a future. He—he made friends with death. Say?

RITA: I forgive you.

BRENDA: Say?

RITA: I forgive you.

BRENDA: Say?

RITA: I forgive you.

> *Re-enter* C.C. *all wet.*

BRENDA: Here he comes. [*To* C.C.] Who is Sheila?

C.C.: Hey! Man must live and enjoy the flaws. Pussy by the pool, and so on. But I keep my eyes down now. That is, I try.

BRENDA: Who is Sheila?

> ———————— *On the bench, find* TONY *and* SHEILA
> [*past*]

SHEILA: You don't look good.

TONY: I feel great.

SHEILA: Are you using?

TONY: Not me.

SHEILA: Okay, Tony.

TONY: You don't know what you're looking at.

SHEILA: Do you have money?

TONY: I don't have any money.

SHEILA: What do you do with it all?

TONY: I have responsibilities.

SHEILA: Are you sick?

TONY: No.

SHEILA: I don't believe you.

TONY: Shoot me.

SHEILA: Not so fast. I heard of a story. There's a swordsman, he liked to pick up girls. There's a carnival, where he goes to find one. There's a strange girl, and they see each other. She's dressed funny, you know, like revealing. She could be the love of his life, his one true love. She warns him: I might be crazy for all you know, maybe you don't want to go dancing with me. Let's go dancing, he says, and see what happens. They have a wild time—until the men from the asylum come. She fights like a tiger but they beat her down. She's killed three men, they tell him, in a breakout to go dancing. Two men she stabbed, the other she decapitated. Remind you of someone?

TONY: Brenda!

SHEILA: Is she pregnant?

TONY: Who?

SHEILA: Brenda. Is she pregnant? [*Pause*] You don't know?

TONY: Yeah.

SHEILA: Yeah, you know, or yeah she's pregnant?

TONY: Yeah she's pregnant.

SHEILA: How?

TONY: How?

SHEILA: You heard me—Yours?

TONY: Mine.

SHEILA: I don't think so. I'd like to slap you.

TONY: Go ahead.

> *She slaps him.*

SHEILA: I'll kill her. Then I'll rip the child out of her stomach.

TONY: I don't think so.

SHEILA: After you die, Tony. Once you're dead, I'll take care of it.

TONY: I won't die.

SHEILA: Revenge and retribution.

TONY: No reason, then.

SHEILA: What I say.

> *Out.*

RITA: Calm down, Brenda.

BRENDA: Fifty times a day I'm wrong! Am I imagining things? [*Sulks*]

C.C.: Decision?

RITA: Yes.

C.C.: Will you give me the child?

RITA: No.

> C.C. *takes* BRENDA *aside.*

C.C.: Fucking ants are taking over the planet. And they bite.

BRENDA: Are you nice now?

C.C.: You're cute.

BRENDA: How many of you are you?

> *Off, baby crying.*

C.C.: I'll tell you about Sheila.

BRENDA: You're not a bad guy, really. You're nice sometimes.

C.C.: Pay attention. I was dealing hemp, I was just getting started in business. I brought her a nickel bag. I didn't realize she liked me. She wore a see-through gown. She was skinny but cute. She lay down seductively, offering her body in exchange for grass. "Will you trick me for it?" said she.

BRENDA: Say?

C.C.: I said I couldn't do it at first, loyalty and so on. Shy and confused. I could taste her pussy but I was afraid of dishonor. Once we took a ride on a motor-scooter and necked on 59th street. A man shouted at us to get out of public view. Sex seemed dirty then.

BRENDA: I have problems in that area.

C.C.: Sure you do, Brenda. I let it alone and Tony grabbed it.

BRENDA: Are you mean now?

C.C.: Then a connection is made. Any good: substances exchanged. Lasts: forever. Mysterious, permanent.

BRENDA: Babies are born from it, too.

C.C.: That's right, Brenda. How?

BRENDA: I know how.

C.C.: Good for you, Brenda.

BRENDA: But not now. [C.C. *laughs*] I have a tendency to want to be alone. But I've enjoyed this part of the conversation.

C.C.: Good.

BRENDA: You can be just a regular guy, seems like.

C.C.: You want attention.

BRENDA: I suffer that. Along with the feeling of being wrong.

C.C.: Where I grew up, they strung up cats on clotheslines, and tried to fuck the younger ones in the ass. Where did you grow up?

BRENDA: Brooklyn, USA. [*To* RITA] This man's cool. Honey, this man's been baptized, or something.

RITA: Light's changing.

BRENDA: Man could be a friend of mine.

RITA: This is a special light. I love it. Brenda?

——————— *On the bench,* BRENDA *joins* TONY

[*past*]

BRENDA: What you got, Boy?

TONY: [*Sings:*]
If any pleasure can come to a man through recalling
decent behavior in his relations with others,
not breaking his word, and never, in any agreement,
deceiving men by abusing vows sworn to heaven,
then countless joys will await you in old age, Catullus,
as a reward for this unrequited passion!
For all of those things which a man could possibly
say or do have all been said & done by you already,
and none of them counted for anything...

BRENDA: What's that?

TONY: Poetry.

BRENDA: Are you sick?

TONY: How do I look to you?

BRENDA: You need to build up something that could fight it off.

TONY: What for?

BRENDA: You could fight it off.

TONY: Okay.

BRENDA: You're in very good shape.

TONY: They'll have cars that talk to you and fly. You'll have a home address, it'll be a cubicle with a bed and some shelves, there'll be a number—that's your home—be a gigantic barracks!

BRENDA: She thinks she's in charge, she thinks she can drive right over me, say? She thinks she can fox me and tell me what to do!

TONY: Who?

BRENDA: She!

TONY: Who?

BRENDA: Rita! Yeah, well I'm outa here sweetie, I'm gone baby, you no longer run my life, you bitch!

TONY: Wait! The baby!

BRENDA: Not yours!

TONY: Say?

BRENDA: Mine!

TONY: Where you goin'?

BRENDA: Virus, remember! Precaution, remember!

TONY: No! Wait, you!

      Out.

RITA: Brenda?

BRENDA: Yo, Rita! [*To* C.C.] Ha, ha—fuck you.

C.C.: Fuck you—ha, ha.

BRENDA & RITA: You don't know anything. You're a performer, you, a politician, a hipster philosopher, an artiste. The real horror—you don't know it. The real death—you don't know it. The real abuses—you only dream them, you!

C.C.: Ha, ha, fuck you.

RITA & BRENDA: We don't talk the same talk! We don't walk the same walk! We're not on the same ground! We're on different sides of the world! We're on different angles! We on a different edge! The shape is not the same shape! You are in a parallel world, you!

C.C.: Swim-time! [*Exits to pool*]

RITA: He's got us, Brenda. No ID. No money. Insecure and homeless. What he wants, he gets.

BRENDA: Can we have an exchange about this?

RITA: Speak.

BRENDA: We couldn't handle the responsibility. We can't provide stability. For example, I would have to get off the junk-juice.

RITA: Of course. You wish to stay bloated? You wish to stay medicated? You wish to segue to the junk-juice boat every single sunny day? Is that the proper atmosphere for child-rearing or parenting?

BRENDA: It's not done. It's impossible. Be in the bones.

RITA: What I say?

BRENDA: I'll try.

RITA: Okay. I'll make plans.

BRENDA: But not today.

RITA: I'm always holding my breath.

BRENDA: Say?

RITA: Remember Tony. Last gasp, and death.

BRENDA: Take care.

RITA: Say?

BRENDA: A person could string out on that.

RITA: You don't know. Blame?

BRENDA: No.

RITA: Blame?

BRENDA: No.

RITA: I was his mother.

BRENDA: No blame.

RITA: Say?

BRENDA: I forgive you. [Pause. Splashing, off. Of C.C.] Guy's got a real problem with water. Did ya notice? [As TONY] Time now to snap the fucker.

RITA: Ah. I'm breathing.

BRENDA: [As TONY] Snap his fuckin' neck, snatch his phone, flee to the Yucatan.

RITA: Sarajevo was the place to be. Twenty years from now, people will have said with pride, "I was in Sarajevo in the 90s."

BRENDA: They'd like to be sniped and starved?

RITA: They will have suffered and endured.

BRENDA: Kids, they learn fast what's what. Survive first, be nice later. Kids are sticking it to each other everywhere. Rio, Brooklyn, L.A.—What time is it?

RITA: Remember Tony. No one remembers very long, do they? Life dropped him like he was a bunch of bananas.

> Re-enter C.C., wet.

C.C.: Speaking of me again?

RITA: We don't always talk about you, C.C.

C.C.: Say?

RITA: Tony.

BRENDA: I'll tell you what happened. They lock you away and you're alone. You're alone and you got time to think and there's no action. You start to look at yourself.

Visiting day, you get to see the ruins—my Tony and me was the same. We did the same and acted the same. Only he was out and I was in, he was loose and I was tied. He got the Virus, not me. Only he it was who died the dirty death.

RITA: [*To* c.c.] She's trashing his life. [*Sigh*] That's what he's used to. Tony was a junkie. Once a junkie, always a junkie. Tony?

——————— *On the bench,* TONY—*lying down*—*responds to* RITA.

[*past*]

TONY: Mom?

RITA: Tony!

TONY: Get me out of here, Mom.

RITA: I told you a hundred times, Tony. Give it up or it will kill you—and it did.

TONY: No one knew, which spoon, which point—no one even heard of it.

RITA: You stupid kid.

TONY: I was ripping off your goods, Mom. I'm sorry.

RITA: I forgive you.

TONY: I'm sorry, Mom.

RITA: I forgive you.

TONY: Get me out of here.

RITA: I can't, Tony. Pneumonia, Tony.

TONY: Therapy. Group counselling. School and cab, Mom.

RITA: First they have to clear the pneumonia, honey, and then you can go.

TONY: You don't believe me, Mom?

RITA: I believe you.

TONY: Rita.

RITA: I believe you.

TONY: My feet are swollen.

RITA: They are swollen, Tony.

TONY: I fell down on the floor, Mom.

RITA: I know you did. [*Weeps*]

TONY: Don't worry, Rita. I have made friends with death.

RITA: [*Gagging*] Ah!

TONY: Where's Brenda?

RITA: She's in another hospital, Tony.

TONY: Is she coming?

RITA: She's coming soon.

TONY: She's a head case, B. She has demons.

RITA: She loves you. She loves you very much.

TONY: Love, Mom?

RITA: She loves you.

TONY: Time?

RITA: Not time.

TONY: Time!

RITA: Not time yet, Tony.

TONY: Time!

RITA: Say?

TONY: Time!

RITA: Not yet, Tony.

TONY: My shot! Where's my shot? It's time!

     Out.

———————

RITA: Brenda?

BRENDA: [*As* TONY, *big strut*] Shut the fuck up! I'm trying to change. I want to change. But you can't force change, you can't will change, and you can't act changed!

RITA: [*To* BRENDA] You're hysterical!

C.C.: And the child?

RITA: You want love and you can't buy it or steal it!

C.C.: "Mom be always on my bubble." [*Laughs*]

BRENDA: That's what Tony used to say!

RITA: He was a good kid!

C.C.: Five percent of the time.

RITA: He used to watch for the white-coats. He kept one eye out. Time for his shot. Time for his shot. He'd move you out of the way. Time. Time for my shot, Mom. Get out of the way. Time. Then they put him on a morphine drip. [*To* C.C.] Have you no capacity for grief?

C.C.: "I have made friends with death."

BRENDA: That's what Tony said!

RITA: Poor Tony. He could not breathe with his own lungs. The respirator breathed him. [*Weeps*]

C.C.: Tony was great. The ace of street kids. The King. I miss him. Even though he ripped me off every chance he got. Manipulative sonofabitch.

BRENDA: He always made sure the lights were out and there was food in the refrigerator. He took care. And he was a hustler. I liked that. He would take a job. He drove a taxi-cab. Something came up through my uncle, a pallbearer, whatever, he was ready. I liked that about Tony. He wasn't one of those young guys: "Excuse me, but don't bother me."

RITA: He was a good kid!

C.C.: He would try to manipulate you in any way he could.

BRENDA: We had a good time. He was sweet.

   ——————— *Find* TONY *on the bench, his face contorted.*

     [*past*]

TONY: What is that fucking music?

RITA: Respirator, Tony.

TONY: Good times.

RITA: Oh, yeah.

TONY: Good times.

RITA: Oh, yeah.

TONY: C.C.?

RITA: No, Tony.

TONY: C.C.?

RITA: No, Tony.

TONY: Action, Mom.

RITA: He is at war.

TONY: The Commander.

RITA: Quiet now, Tony.

TONY: I can't talk.

RITA: You shouldn't talk.

TONY: Get this thing out of my mouth.

RITA: They won't let me, Tony.

TONY: Please get this thing out of my mouth.

RITA: I can't, Tony.

TONY: I'll never make it out of here alive, Mom. [RITA *gags*] Mom?

RITA: Rest now.

TONY: Father?

RITA: You have no father.

TONY: Where?

RITA: Nowhere.

TONY: Prison, Rita.

RITA: I don't know.

TONY: Dad?

RITA: Not here, Tony.

TONY: I forgive you.

RITA: Say?

TONY: I forgive you.

RITA: Brenda!

BRENDA: [*Off*] Here I am. [*Out*]

RITA: We sat with him for months. Respirator music. Incessant. He vanished into it. We fought to have it removed. Then they made us ask him four times: Are you ready to be unplugged, Tony?

BRENDA: Are you ready to be unplugged, Tony?

RITA: If yes, blink with one eye, then the other. Four times.

C.C.: And did he?

RITA: I couldn't tell. But the white-coats thought he did. They removed the machine from his throat. We held him in our arms. Twenty minutes later he gasped and died. They turned him over like refuse. They asked us to leave. He was now inanimate matter. Brenda cried with me. When a child appears, he comes from heaven. Even his shit is sweet. Is that so, Preacher?

C.C.: That is so.

RITA: Then I have the following questions: What is the sacred? When does it start?

C.C.: Now we are here, we live. Before: parents.

RITA: That is an answer, but that is not what I asked. That is an an answer to a question I did not ask. Is there a sacred? When does it start? When does it end? Was Tony's death a sacred death? The white-coats said, "Ask four times. If yes, then blink an eye. Tell us if you are ready to die or not." Are you ready to die, Tony? I couldn't tell if he blinked. Four times. They unhooked the machine, finally. They turned the switch, they pulled the tube. He struggled to breathe and then he breathed his last. I wanted to sit quietly, but they rushed in and started cleaning it up. [*Pause*] What an awful disease, a dreadful disease, a disgusting disease. He was a boy of twenty-five. Who did he shoot up with in some filthy hallway? In some tenement dump? In what fucking dope-filled project?

BRENDA: What's a virus, Craig?

C.C.: A virus be a moving thing, they aim to replicate. One aim: make copies. Repeat, repeat. But must have living cells. Are parasites. Nature's way: correction. Like war and famine, like quake, riot, fire and flood.

RITA: Did he notice?

C.C.: Say?

RITA: Tony. The moment of death. Did he notice it?

C.C.: I don't know. I wasn't there. Time, please?

RITA & BRENDA: Oh! The time!

C.C.: You have missed your appointment.

RITA: Light changing.

C.C.: Pay attention. I know these people. They won't stay with this much longer. Game: blood and bodies. Exchange of living or dead. They shoot to kill.

BRENDA: The time!

RITA: Be dark again. This is what I remember.

BRENDA: Say?

RITA: The feeling at twilight.

C.C.: Who is the mother of this child?

RITA & BRENDA: I am!

C.C.: When was the kid born?

RITA & BRENDA: When Tony died!

C.C.: What did you give for him?

RITA & BRENDA: Nothing! [C.C.'s *phone rings*.]

C.C.: Hello? I told you not to call me. I know what time it is. I'm not a kidnapper. I'm not a baby-stealer. I'm trying to do the right thing. I've had a harder life than any of you. I've earned every penny, every honor. I am the Captain, I am the Commander. I am organized, and I am true. Chance has nothing to do with it. You're a bunch of drunken, homicidal maniacs who belong in mental institutions under heavy guard. [*Pause*] You heard me.

BRENDA: Uh, oh.

C.C.: [*Into phone*] You can't give people things or try to help—causes hatred and confusion. That you, Sheila? Fuck you, ha, ha. Time passes while we have this conversation. I hope you can afford it. I see—you may want to be killed anyway. No? It's thrilling to murder people? Hold your fire. [*Clicks off. To* RITA *and* BRENDA] Last chance for exchange of child. [*Silence*] Done. You're on your own.

BRENDA: Wait, Preacher.

C.C.: What is it, Brenda?

BRENDA: They built a great blaze, and they put Tony into it. There was a silent burning, save for the hissing of steam.

C.C.: Say?

BRENDA: There was a condensation in the Spirit World, a gathering of force—like clouds, like rain.

C.C.: Where?

BRENDA: In the atmosphere. Cleansing, redemption. Say?

——————— *Near the bench,* C.C. *and* TONY.

[*past*]

C.C.: Tony!

TONY: Yo, Preacher! [*Elaborate handshake*]

C.C.: How you doin', Man?

TONY: I'm feeling fucking great.

C.C.: That's Tony!

TONY: How's the Preacher Man?

C.C.: Hey, I'm goin' to war, Pal. I'm going to straighten out the issue! I will finalize it, me! Are you there?

TONY: I am with you, C.C.!

C.C.: Am I right?

TONY: Right as rain, Preacher!

C.C.: Will they make up poems about the Preacher? Will they make an epic about the Preacher Man?

TONY: I don't think so.

C.C.: I'm sad about the whole thing and I'm sorry. Forgive me?

TONY: I forgive you.

C.C.: It's the women, Tony. They're on a different path.

TONY: No blame.

C.C.: The child be on its own now.

TONY: I'm the child.

C.C.: Say?

TONY: I'm the child.

Out.

———————

C.C.: [*Into phone*] Get off the line, I'm calling my mother. Hello? Mom? Once I was a handsome young street prince, Mom, I believed in romance, or: Sex was too much for me, and close-ups confused my mind. Is everything on tape? Me, immense ego, low self-esteem. White Nigger. Commit: Spiritual Crime. Did I? I? Falling.... Close-ups. Two-shots. Result: Fear. Result: Confusion. Just listen. I'm in a hurry. No, be close-up, intimacy: self-love. Be action, fast: revenge, adventure. Heroes, beautiful dames. [As TONY] Inside: little boy, little white nigger boy, nobody loved nobody, white nigger Jew boy, slave boy, just a boy, frightened, lonely boy. [*Clicks off*] Dream on. [*Starts off*]

RITA: Wait, you!

C.C.: The core of the earth is molten rock, or liquid metal. It is hotter than the surface of the sun.

RITA: Say?

C.C.: I'll be finishing my thought, which is: the core of the earth is hot, and the crust of the earth is thin, and the sun and the moon.

RITA: Be what?

C.C.: When you look at what a man be.

BRENDA: I see what he's saying.

RITA: Say?

C.C.: Be dust. [*Pause*] It's time. This is for the record. [*Into phone*] Whoever makes it up the switchback and lives—she is the mother.

RITA: And you? Where are you going, you?

C.C.: Well, I just have a feeling of fate. I feel like there are waves, and one of them's got my name on it. [*Into phone*] Last word: Ha, ha, fuck you. What else? Nothing else. Next time I see you, come out firing. We shoot on sight. [*Goes*]

RITA: I realize there's an end to my story. There's a be-all and end-all, built in to the story. BE: the End. World collapse.

BRENDA: Say?

RITA: What if I didn't believe that? Suppose the world goes on and on? Population: no problem. Viruses: cured. Forests: re-born. America: eternal. What then?

BRENDA: The time!

RITA: We're escaping together!

BRENDA: I have hypertension. I have Angst.

RITA: What time is it?

BRENDA: I believed in C.C. for a minute because he had something to say.

RITA: Electro-mathematics, I think it was.

BRENDA: The Way of the Psychopath.

RITA: That's it. [*Gunfire*] Oh! A battle!

BRENDA: He is shooting! He is fighting!

RITA: Oh! What now!?

BRENDA: He's going into the water.

RITA: Look at him swim! [*Battle ends*]

RITA: They got him.

BRENDA: Is he flapping?

RITA: He is flapping.

BRENDA: Is he floating?

RITA: He is floating. [*Pause*] He was a good man, basically. He could see his end coming in a wave.

BRENDA: He was loyal, but he had a bad side to him.

RITA: When I die, I hope people say nice things about me.

BRENDA: He couldn't tell the difference between what he did and what he saw in his head.

RITA: I see now that I don't have my own fate. My fate is my Mom.

BRENDA: Maybe there ARE no reasons. People like to interfere with the pleasures of others, or to inflict torture upon them.

RITA: Let's go.

Pause. BRENDA *grabs the baby carriage and races up the switchback. Gunfire.* BRENDA *makes it to the top, then falls, shot. Pause.* RITA *trembles with indecision, then rushes up the switchback, retrieves the carriage and rushes away.*

Mac Wellman

The Hyacinth Macaw

The mysteries current among them, the [...], initiate them into impiety.
—HERACLITUS

Or he said:
"Passing to the point of the cone
You begin by making the replica."
—EZRA POUND,
from CANTO XXIX

.

The Hyacinth Macaw was first performed at Primary Stages Company, Inc. (Casey Childs, Artistic Director) on May 13, 1994 with the following cast:

SUSANNAH	Francie Swift
MISTER WILLIAM HARD	Yusef Bulos
DORA	Melissa Smith
RAY	Steve Mellor
MAD WU	Bob Kirsh

Directed by Marcus Stern; Scenery & Lighting by Kyle Chepulis; Costumes by Robin Orloff; Sound by John Huntington; Composer: David Van Tieghem; Production Stage Manager: Kristen Harris; Dramaturg: Marc Robinson; Associate Producer: Seth Gordon; Production Manager: Andrew Leynse; General Manager: Gina Gionfriddo; Press Representative: Tony Origlio; Public Relations Director: Anne Einhorn; Associate Artistic Director: Janet Reed

Icons for the Scenes

NOTE: The occasional appearance of an asterisk (*) in the middle of a speech indicates that the next speech begins to overlap at that point. A double asterisk indicates that a later speech (not the one immediately following) begins to overlap at that point. The overlapping speeches are all clearly marked in the text.

ACT ONE

Sunrise by the porch of an American type house. A WOMAN (DORA) *opens the door, walks out on the porch, whistling a tune. She smiles and looks about, surveying the morning with evident satisfaction, then re-enters. The* DAUGHTER (SUSANNAH) *runs down the steps of the porch to the backyard, where a clothesline is hung. She plucks the line as if it were the string of a cello, or some other musical instrument. We hear the sound of a plucked string (we do; she doesn't). A* MAN [MR WILLIAM HARD] *appears carrying a suitcase (which he does not set down until indicated). He is dressed in an ordinary business suit, but has loosened his tie, and his jacket is hung over his shoulder. He has been walking for some time. He spots the young* WOMAN (SUSANNAH) *before she realizes he's there. When she does she freezes. An uncanny pause.*

SUSANNAH: Good morning, Sir.

MR WILLIAM HARD: Orphans ought to be sent back
    where they come from. They ought
    to be beaten with sticks.

SUSANNAH: I am not an orphan,* sir.

MR WILLIAM HARD: I didn't say you were. I was
    expounding philosophy, young lady.

SUSANNAH: My parents are presently in the house,
    asleep. Except for my mom.* She's up
    and about.

MR WILLIAM HARD: My philosophy of orphans, my girl,
    orphans in whom the urge for a true
    homeland will never be assuaged.
    Pneumatically speaking…
        Pause.

SUSANNAH: But I am not* an orphan.

MR WILLIAM HARD: Indeed, the spectacle of such an
    egregious orphan like you, why
    disremembers me, of how and
    when and wherefore* I made this
    world…

SUSANNAH: Mom, there is a man here who wants
    to ask you something I don't know.
        To him.
    Are you…a writer?

MR WILLIAM HARD: No, young lady, but I am a variable
  in the mystic sirocco of our disbelief.
SUSANNAH: Mother, please come.
  Her MOTHER *appears.*
MR WILLIAM HARD: Good day to you, ma'am.
  She starts hanging laundry.
DORA: If you are who I think you are
  you can wait. Standing idle
  is all your kind can do anyhow.
  The rest of us must toil.
MR WILLIAM HARD: You don't
  know me. You never heard tell of
  anyone like me.
  What you truly know you can go ahead
  and tell, but what you don't! Hell!
  you can't even name the name of it.
  That's why the orphans in these parts
  are orphans. The name for what a
  person doesn't know is a terrible
  thing. I've come a whole helluva
  long way just to say "hello" because
  I know the full absurdity of trying
  to right a wheelbarrow while you are
  sitting in it, ass planted North.
  Land of evening. Land of the Adversary.
  Do you understand?
DORA: Not one word. In this part
  of the country it is customary
  to jawbone a little on the subject
  of the weather. Sure, jawbone
  on the weather…
  Working at the clothesline.
  That and talk of vacations, photos
  of friends and relations while
  doing the best we can to not
  bring up the subject of who
  did what. Got cancer and died
  of it, or broke back tumbling
  down the cellar stairs. We are
  polite. We are polite out of need.
  Sweet, sweet reasonableness's need
  to catch no ill crutch of roach.
SUSANNAH: Mom, he said I was an orphan. Why
  would he say a thing like that?

MR WILLIAM HARD: He would say so to mark time.

DORA: He would say so to mark time, all
because he doesn't know how to
be properly appalled.

SUSANNAH: He looks like…I don't know…
Something sheer awful.

MR WILLIAM HARD: I've had some hard times. Been had,
so to speak. Messed up with politics,
which I never had no talent for.
Simple speaking has always been my
mosthow there shitfor. Certainly.

DORA: So: are you saying you are hearing
what we are saying, or not? Which?

MR WILLIAM HARD: I am hearing what you are not saying,
which is what I came here for, and
you two, both. It figures, because
I am from far away, a place you'd
never recognize. Bug River, the sign
here says. I'd never post that. It'd
be too much an abject certainty, and
I'd be like to lay about and grow…
tantamount. Same as a big, horror bug,
all myself a whorled mystery. Cheesy.
See, where I come from's on no map.
You could call me Vincent Hat, or
Johnny Sock, but the real name, the
one I answer to unquestionably is
"Mister William Hard." That's my moniker.

SUSANNAH: Bug River has nothing to do with bugs.
We have a gym, a school, malls, all
the normal things. American-type things.
We act as if nothing strange had ever
occurred here, which it has fucking not.
I want to attend Junior College next Fall
and learn the names of things, packaging.
Packaging's got a true forward momentum.
I believe in it. That's the metaphysical
reason I don't equal an orphan. That's
my philosophy of drift. Mom's too.
Right, Mom?

DORA: Right too, Squeezre.

MR WILLIAM HARD: A kid's name.

SUSANNAH: So what. It's mine.

MR WILLIAM HARD: It's yours all right.

SUSANNAH: Yes, it is. Mine. All mine. All I got, practically.
   An awkward pause. All shift about. Another pause.
MR WILLIAM HARD: That means I was right. You
   are an orphan. A yanked up
   rootless thing. Adopted.
DORA: She's not adopted, she's adapted.
   Squeezre, go get the man a road map
   while I make him a sandwich. He
   must've mislaid his topology.
   Going to be too hot today for conversation.
   Besides, you don't know anything, and
   Mister "Johnny Sock" seems to know it all.
   Therefore you're matched for life, and
   oddly so. Therefore, too, you're safe
   with him, the way I see it,* so I'll
   just go....
SUSANNAH: Mother, you are extremely uncouth.
DORA: Squeezre, be quiet. You're rattling the bugs.
SUSANNAH: Yes, and I suppose you don't!
DORA: Behave. Show respect.
SUSANNAH: Respect is for the birds.
DORA: The man's a stranger.
SUSANNAH: Our family's more stranger.
DORA: So: behave. Be quiet.
SUSANNAH: Our strangeness must show. It's got to.
DORA: It must be hidden.
SUSANNAH: Explain what you mean.
DORA: Hidden things can be healed.
SUSANNAH: Hidden things are hurts.
DORA: Healing takes time. It's slow.
SUSANNAH: Hurts too are slow. They also grow. Slowly.
DORA: Behave. I'm your mother.
SUSANNAH: We are both human people.
DORA: Sometimes I wonder.
MR WILLIAM HARD: Maybe you are crows.
DORA: Keep your two cents out of this please.
MR WILLIAM HARD: Yes, ma'am. Sorry.
SUSANNAH: I demand to say what I will.
DORA: Demand anything.
SUSANNAH: What do you mean?
DORA: While you're here you'll behave like one of us.
SUSANNAH: So I am an orphan!
DORA: That's ridiculous!

SUSANNAH: It's true. Say so. Admit.

DORA: Why would anyone adopt a person like you?

SUSANNAH: I've had an inkling this was true.

DORA: Just because you can do basic reasoning.

SUSANNAH: I knew all along* I was different. Separate.

DORA: Now you're an embarrassment. Stop.

SUSANNAH: Separate. Apart. Out of place.

DORA: Stop.

SUSANNAH: An entrechat of enthymemes.

DORA: Stop talking strange.

SUSANNAH: You're strange. I'm normal.

DORA: You're an enigma. Behave. Quick.

SUSANNAH: Okay. Okay. Quick. It goosewillies me.

DORA: Squeezre?

SUSANNAH: Quick. Behave. Stop being a…a girl.

DORA: Behave. Stop. React.

SUSANNAH: Quick. Okay. Stop. Okay. Goosewillies . .

DORA: Are you listening to me? Squeezre?* Are you?

SUSANNAH: I am listening to a different drummer* and it…

DORA: Squeezre, for Christ's sake, be quiet.

SUSANNAH: It tells me to honor the quick and the dead.

> *She plucks the clothesline. We hear it. Pause. The music is atonal. Aleatoric. Non-Chekhovian. The* MOTHER *goes out (or, rather, in).*

MR WILLIAM HARD: Progress. Progress has come to the
land of evening.

> *He goes to put down his suitcase, but hesitates. Pause.*

Mind if I put this down, young lady?

SUSANNAH: Squeezre's the name if you don't mind.

> *Pause. He stands straight up.*

MR WILLIAM HARD: Mind if I tell you the true tale of the
Sistine Ornithologist, Squeezre?

SUSANNAH: My name's not "Squeezre." That's my nickname.
An intrafamilial verbal sight gag. Old hat.
Boring. When I was a toddler I used to squeeze
up my face and hands. Like this.

> *She demonstrates.*

Or so I was told. Hence: Squeezre. My
name is Sue. Susannah. You're a stranger,
so act normal. You are acting too strange
for a stranger. You are acting truly
strange. Like family almost. Goosewillies
me…

> *Pause. He puts down the suitcase.*

Besides, I know that story.
Besides, I've got a full
dance card.
An entrechat of enthymemes. So make it quick.
MR WILLIAM HARD: The Bird-maker flew in with the wind
one day. The same wind that bears the
mystic seeds from China. Which died
with sun-up, as it's wont to. Promised
a new dispensation to the assembled
quacks. All odd ducks, people. Tribe
of paradox. So-called humanity. They
were at sixes and sevens. Gabbled amongst
theyselves. In the gloaming, his shadow clawed across
them like a tool. A terrifying implement.
An axe to grind…
SUSANNAH: Ha. Ha.
MR WILLIAM HARD: You laugh.
SUSANNAH: La. La* la.
MR WILLIAM HARD: You laugh, and they did too. The suckers!
All they craved was the drug of authenticity.
Sad self-similarity. But he was a true
Bird-maker. Apocalyptic. Sistine. Even
a little lupine. Wolfish, that is. But
the world of gradualness is a sucker for
images. The resistless clamor of the new
world for images of itself. Its own folly.
Follow me?
SUSANNAH: Can't follow the thread of your…tale.
La. La.
MR WILLIAM HARD: Because it is a deliberate tangle. So.
True tales are tangled. Especially in the
evening. Especially in the land of evening.
Mind if I smoke?

> She rolls a cigarette. Gives it to him. Lights it for him. He smokes. Pause. Both look
> over their shoulders at the sun. Both turn back. She snaps out of it, as if out of a spell.

SUSANNAH: Now, why in hell did I do that? I don't
even know the man.* I don't know how
to roll a cigarette. I don't even smoke.

> She rolls herself a cigarette, and lights it while he continues.

MR WILLIAM HARD: So: Even came. Eventide. The Evening of
Sixty Days. He spoke in the darksome
wilderness. He convinced them their joys

were nothing but gloom inverted, sophistries,
invented geegaws, idolatries from a former
world. He said they knew not from whence
they ushered. Nor what dark wind uttered
them. Feathered them, and put them all
in cages. Up on perches, like a brace of
hyacinth macaws. Cockatoos. Cockatoos,
hornbills and toucans. Cockatoos of cockatrice.
In the old birdpark at Jurong. Forever chattering.
Chatting twaddle. Entrechats of enthymemes,
as you put it, in the language of your town.
Gradual, population 1990. Circa now.

SUSANNAH: And then?

MR WILLIAM HARD: He took up archeology and flea circuses.

SUSANNAH: No I meant the people he changed. What happened
    to them?

MR WILLIAM HARD: That remains unrecorded. An historical
    ellipsis. An error in the wilderness
    of what we suppose we're here for, but
    don't know. The outcome is lacking in
    the element of decidability I mean.

    He puts out his cigarette.

SUSANNAH: Now Mom's mad and I'm to blame.

MR WILLIAM HARD: For shame.

SUSANNAH: You're mocking me. You have no right to.

MR WILLIAM HARD: Indeed. I have no rights period.

SUSANNAH: Just what are you driving at.

MR WILLIAM HARD: What's real has no name. None.* Whatever.

SUSANNAH: What?

MR WILLIAM HARD: None. What's real, that is.

SUSANNAH: What's that supposed to mean?

MR WILLIAM HARD: You asked me. You go figure. Now you know.

SUSANNAH: I know nothing. Mom's right about that.

MR WILLIAM HARD: Neither do I.

SUSANNAH: What's your name again?

MR WILLIAM HARD: Bill. Bill Hard.

    She holds out her hand. They shake hands.

SUSANNAH: Hi, Bill, I'm Sue.

MR WILLIAM HARD: Hi, Sue, I'm delighted to meet you.

    Pause. They smile. MOM *enters. They unshake their hands.*

DORA: You still here? Thought you'd be off by now.
    Squeezre, don't you have errands to do?

SUSANNAH: Yes, ma'am. Feed the neighbor cats.

DORA: Then go do it. Sun's coming up. Now.

SUSANNAH: Yes, mother.

DORA: Right now.

SUSANNAH: Okay. I'll go. Good-bye, sir.

MR WILLIAM HARD: Good evening, young lady.

     Off she goes. Pause.

DORA: So what is it you've come for precisely?

MR WILLIAM HARD: Time to get around to it, I suppose.

DORA: I'd say so. And? So?

MR WILLIAM HARD: Appears to be a case of pneumatic
redundancy. Unnecessary replication…

     Pause.

DORA: When it becomes clear to you I'm sure
you will let us know. It would be a
shame not to. We have a right to know.
Things do happen slowly around here.
Knowledge sprouts as slowly as the mystic
seeds from China that Mad Wu talks about.
One thing about the devil, he moves fast.
Knows all that's on your mind before you
do. Take Susannah, our daughter, now.
She has signed a ninety-nine year lease
to feed the neighbor cats. I don't
know how long they'll be away. Years for
certain. Our neighbors are missionaries
in…some far place. A long-playing
record of woe, disease, drum-playing,
taboo, bamboo and vice. Maybe China.
Maybe Shenango. Years aplenty. Maybe
not a whole century, but it's the idea
of responsibility that works on you, grows
like a worm in a green apple. Susannah'll
grow up with this daily task until…
marriage, a job at the crocodilarium,
or junior college. Already I can sense
a change in her. I think I can, in only
six years. Her eyes have changed color,
from grey-green to topaz. What she says
makes more sense, and her vocabulary's
improved. She uses words like "redundant,"
"paradox" and "pathological" now. Before
she fed the neighbor cats she never would've

used a word like "pathological." Except
to spite me, or someone else. Eldridge,
or Sandoval, the man with the thing in his
backyard. The thing that goes *whump,*
whump when he winds it up. At night
when he puts on his raincoat, and
lights all those lanterns. He runs all
around his house shouting, and the big
heavy thing, it's made of iron, I suppose,
it goes *whump whump,* and then it goes
clank clank, clang. And then he sings:
"Hallelujah" and takes off his trousers,
and runs three times around the house, in
the rain, in his boxer shorts. That's
what he does. I am not sure what it all
means, only it must possess a...signification.

MR WILLIAM HARD: I'm sure it must. Sounds like a
device like the one I witnessed back in,
back in, was it Powerdive?

DORA: Oh yes. I think I remember that. Yes,
it was Powerdive. East Powerdive.
It was Mister Phelps who invented it.
He never showed it to anyone. Called
it an "Equilateral Spiritual Triangulator."

MR WILLIAM HARD: I have some papers here in my pocket...
somewhere...

    He fumbles about in his pockets.

DORA: I was madly in love with Mister Phelps,
when he was young and Harry...So
was I, young and Harry...Oh, not that,
Harry Phelps was his name. Also invented
the thing that you put in the wheelchair
between the wheelbug, and the wheelwhang.
"The whang provides the necessary whammy,"
he used to say, Harry. We would go for
long walks on the bank of Bug River, talking
about what the Adversary was up to, what
happens when the coffin is too big for the
hole; or at night in the zoo when the
big cats can't get to sleep; what life
would be like without a set of fixed
points to navigate by;

    She looks down.

...and prolonged abstinence, and how it
feeds the fires of belief. Harry talked
a lot about the value of prolonged abstinence
and the relation of this to the fear of the
world. True trepidation. Then we would
take off our clothes, wade off in the
river, and listen to the larks and jays
rattling about in the reeds and grasses.
Rattling about in the cat-tails and willow.
    Pause.
I have always thought that faith
had more to do with moments like that.
Long-playing moments like that. Long-
playing loganberry moments with nervous
fingers and no longevity. Moments of
pure revelation, regarding a birth mark,
a scar, another person's belly-button...
Never mind ministrations of the dying.
    She snaps out of it.
You don't need faith to do the dying
in a foul bed, howling. You don't need
faith to crush the neck of a woodpecker
with a broken wing the cat brought in
to the wilderness of the kitchen in a
fit of patriotic fervor. You don't need
to grasp the full profundity of god's
love to know what's got *you* in its jaw,
shaking you to death, when it does.
When it's your turn, there is no escape.
There is no escape. That knowledge
is as sexual as all the hennaed works
of wicca, where devil fucks devil and the
long greensnake yawns and whips the wind-
tasting feather of his lolling, laggard,
lazily-serene lizardtongue. You don't,
in my opinion. You don't.
    He hands her a letter. She takes it. She looks up at him. He gestures for her to
    open it. She does. It take her a long time to read the letter. He shifts from foot to foot.
    Adjusts his necktie. He looks at the sunset. Pause. He looks at his watch. Finally she
    looks up. Pause.
What does "tantamount" mean?
MR WILLIAM HARD: To amount to as much.
DORA: What does "to amount to as much" mean?

MR WILLIAM HARD: It means that the force of the malfeasance
   has the same effect as.
DORA: Oh. I see. I guess.
      She looks a little bewildered.
MR WILLIAM HARD: You have to go on a bit. It becomes clearer
   towards the end.
      Now he looks confused.
   Oh, I didn't give you the other page. Shit,
   where is it?
      Looks in the envelope.
   Not there.
      Goes through all his pockets.
   Nope. Shit.
      Looks sheepish.
DORA: What is "tantalum"?
      *He recites the following while he goes flapping and flailing through the tall weeds
      and grass near the house. She looks at him, totally mystified.*
MR WILLIAM HARD: A very hard, heavy, gray metallic element
   that is exceptionally resistant to chemical
   attack below 150 degrees centigrade.
   Specific gravity 16.6; valences 2,3,4,5.
DORA: What about six?
      He stands up, in the middle of poison ivy, in a fury.
MR WILLIAM HARD: WHAT ABOUT SIX? WHAT
      THE HELL DO YOU MEAN!?
DORA: Does Tantalum also have a valence of six?
MR WILLIAM HARD: Did I SAY it had a valence of six?
      Irritated pause.
DORA: Well, no, I thought it might, though.*
   I mean, it doesn't seem all that implausible
   to me. If 2,3,4,5, why not six? You tell
   me, I don't know. Okay. Okay. Just
   drop it. I don't care. I really don't care.
MR WILLIAM HARD: If it HAD a valence of six it would say so
   in the letter. Does it say so in the letter?
   No, therefore tantalum does not have a valence
   of six. Okay? Where did I drop that damned
   second page? Shit.
      Stands up in horror. She goes back to the letter.
   What happens if I left it back at the
   office? They'll crucify me. They'll raise
   hell, and I'll never hear the end of it.
   Shit, now my rotator cuff is acting up again.

Again, I should've had it taken care of when
I still had Elective Surgery through Blue Cross
Blue Shield. I did not believe Herb Shorter.
That'll teach me always to believe! HERB SHORTER,
I SWEAR I WILL ALWAYS BELIEVE IN WHAT YOU
    SAY, WHATEVER IT IS, NO MATTER HOW IM-
    PROBABLE IT SOUNDS,
ALWAYS LORD HEAL ME HEAL ME. HEAL ME IN MY
    UNBELIEF.
        He falls down and we see only the soles of his shoes. Pause. She still looks puzzled.
        His head pops up.
You must be thinking of plutonium. Plutonium
has a valence of 3,4,5 *and* six. When exposed to
the open air, plutonium catches fire.
        Pause. Finds the page in his hat. Jumps up, delighted.
DORA: What is a "tarboosh"?
MR WILLIAM HARD: Found it! Finally. What'd you say?
DORA: What's a "tarboosh"?
MR WILLIAM HARD: A brimless, felt cap with a silk
    tassel. Usually red. Worn by Moslem
    men, either by itself or as the basis
    of a turban. Here's the other page.
        He hands it to her, and while she reads this, he dusts himself off.
DORA: What's a "taradiddle"?* Jesus, you
    do find some *hard* words…
MR WILLIAM HARD: A "taradiddle" with one "r" is a variant
    of "tarradiddle" with two.
DORA: That doesn't clarify matters much.
MR WILLIAM HARD: A "tarradiddle" is a petty falsehood. A fib.
DORA: You are accusing my husband of perpetrating a fib?
MR WILLIAM HARD: I am not the author of this document,
    only its deliverer. Deliverer of its deliverance.
    Forgive me. I bear no responsibility for the
    contents of this message. It derives from a
    higher authority, an authority beyond rebuke.
DORA: Oh…
        Pause.
In that case, I guess I'd better call up
Ray at the office and find out
what this is all about.
        She looks at him.
I hope you don't mind if I leave you.
Would you like a cup of coffee? Or a
cheese sandwich? Looks like rain.

You might want to find shelter
under that stand of poplars. I'd
ask you in, but under the circumstances
I don't think I will.

MR WILLIAM HARD: It's all right, ma'am. I understand.

DORA: You do, sir?

MR WILLIAM HARD: Yes, I do. I think.

> *Long pause.*

DORA: Tell me, sir…

MR WILLIAM HARD: Bill Hard's the name, ma'am.

DORA: Tell me, Mister Bill Hard. Do you
think the deep woods of the human soul
are full of terrible music?

MR WILLIAM HARD: Yes, I do, ma'am.

DORA: So do I. Furthermore, I do also
believe all things have happened
before. Even the things we are not
aware of, down in China, down there.

> *She points.*

MR WILLIAM HARD: So do I, ma'am.

DORA: You do, really?

MR WILLIAM HARD: Yes, ma'am. Really.

DORA: I'll be back in an hour or two.
We've got to get to the bottom
of this, Mister Hard. Soonest mended.

MR WILLIAM HARD: Soonest mended, ma'am.

> *He tips his hat. She looks hard at him.*

DORA: Who are you? Really.

MR WILLIAM HARD: All in good time, ma'am. All in good time.

> *She turns.*

DORA: I guess. Well. Okay. See you later. Don't
go anywhere.

MR WILLIAM HARD: I'll be here, ma'am. Sunset is nice.

> *He points. Sure enough the sun's going down. A slow, picturesque black-out.*

I'll be here. In the nettles and hollyhock.
Sunset is fabulous, in the weeds and ivy.
With my heart in my throat.

DORA: See you later then.

> *Slowly she makes her way indoors. Pause.*

MR WILLIAM HARD: Good evening, ma'am.

> *We hear roars from the neighhor "cats."*

END OF SCENE

NEXT SCENE • *Scene the* ◁ *(woop)*

> *Inside the house. The* M O M *(*D O R A*) sits at kitchen table drinking coffee.* D A D *(*R A Y*)*
> *has returned home from work. He wears a normal business suit, but seems dazed.*
> *He slowly reads the letter she has shown him.*
>
> *A starry night outside. In the woods a hunger moon is rising. We can barely*
> *make out the silhouette of the* M A N *(*M R W I L L I A M H A R D*), standing motionless*
> *among the trees and bushes outside.*

R A Y: Okay. Okay. So when I was a kid
I went crazy, and they hauled me off
to a nut house.
> *Pause.*
I had written and staged a perverted
drama in boarding school. It was called
SENSITIVITY, OR THE LANGUAGE OF DREAD.
It contained many perverted passages
dwelling on the topic of lips and thighs.
And other torments and temptations.
Torments pertaining to the sex drive.
Torments which surround us. And convey
animalistic urges to us all, with
their laughing little wicked voices.
The persons of the play had foreign
names. They wore the fez, and performed
unspeakable acts. "Don't ever write
another play," the Headmaster suggested.
But I did, not heeding his warning. I
simply couldn't control my diabolical
urges. I was caned, canned, drummed
out. I was conveyed to the House of the
Mad in a conveyance, and talked to by
serious men concerning the Adversary,
and the diabolical nature of my urges.
I would talk to them about my fantasy
of performing certain unspeakable acts
while wearing a fez, or tarboosh;
> *She looks up in recognition.*
They would continue to look serious,
and recommend a long period of abstinence.
I did not know what they meant by "abstinence"
since I bore the full weight of my urge
like a gigantic boulder upon my back.

He looks down.
Then I discovered the world of higher
mathematics, and was healed. Now
I am a perfectly normal fellow. Stable.
Always, as you have no doubt perceived,
in control. My urges have largely abated.
The urges which have not abated I have
largely trained; I have tamed them with
patience, and little sweet gifts, cookies,
chocolates and the like. My urges look up
at me now, with dark, lustrous adoring eyes.
My urges nuzzle about my trouser pockets,
and rub lovingly against my pant-leg. My
urges no longer are of the School of Night.
They no longer worship the Adversary.
Through prolonged abstinence my urges
have become model citizens of my soul,
as you and I, Dora, have become model
citoyens, so to speak, of the town of Gradual.
    He looks up.
All my urges, except one. You and I
know which one, don't we, Dora?
    He whispers into her hair. She looks down.
Don't we know the fierce temptation
to enact the urge which only the
Evil One dare pronounce? Don't we,
Dora?
    She looks up.
DORA: But that has nothing to do with
    this, dear. The letter makes no
    mention of your former condition,
    your urges, nor your adolescent
    episodes of theatrical dementia.
RAY: It makes no mention of it, but the
    implication is clear enough.
DORA: You're being paranoiac, dear.
    He looks out the window and sees the MAN. *She looks out the window and sees*
    the MAN. *Pause.*
RAY: And that, I suppose, is the fellow
    who delivered the letter?
DORA: Under the circumstances I didn't think
    it was appropriate to invite him in.
RAY: He doesn't look dangerous.

DORA: He tells very interesting stories, and
   has a boyish glint in his eye. I rather
   like him. Even though he is the one
   who has delivered this letter to us.
RAY: Where is Squeezre?
DORA: She is feeding the neighbor cats.
RAY: Why does she do that?
DORA: It strengthens her mettle.
        Pause.
RAY: What is "mettle" again?
DORA: Any of a category of electropositive
   elements that are usually whitish,
   lustrous, and in the transition metals,
   typically ductile and malleable with
   high tensile strength.
        Pause. Still puzzled.
RAY: What does Squeezre need high tensile
   strength for? She's a girl.* For Pete's sake…
DORA: Don't be obtuse, Ray.
RAY: It shouldn't take her all day to feed a couple of cats.
DORA: There are more than a couple of
   them, and some are large.
   Bulky and large, one might say.
RAY: Bulky and large? Really? I wasn't
   aware of that.
DORA: She'll be back before too long, I'm sure.
        A pause of uncertainty.
   I suppose.
RAY: I don't know, Dora. It gives one cause
   to stop and think. You get a letter
   that is mostly incomprehensible, but the
   basic meaning of which seems to be—
   or boils down to—basically something
   like: "…your soul has spontaneously
   combusted, foop, just like that, and
   wiggled up the chimney in a wispy,
   dark orchid of soot, where it shall
   disperse among the lesser elements,
   in particulate form…or…gas…";
   and, well, it gives a man reason to
   stop and mull over the meaning of his
   life. It makes one feel a tad uncertain.
DORA: I'm sure it's just an unusual set

of phrases for something quite familiar.
Like death. Or taxes. Or transubstantiation.
RAY: Like death?
DORA: Like not paying a parking ticket maybe.
RAY: And what's all this stuff about
  "the presencing of beings" as opposed
  to "Being" and "whydahs" and "moonsucking
  wigglies?"
DORA: Ray, I can't tell you. I don't have
  the expertise. The man in the poison sumac out there…
      She points. The MAN *very slowly scratches his arm.*
  …he has the expertise. He knows.
      RAY *looks hard at the* MAN. *Pause.* RAY *turns back and sits down.*
  Ray?
      No reply. He just sits there.
RAY: It's *déjà vu* all over again.
      He gets up and strides out. Strides back in again.
  Interesting day at the office anyhow.
DORA: How so?
      He sits down carefully, so no reply again. Pause.
RAY: *Déjà vu* again. Wow! Oh, at the office?
DORA: You brought it up, not me.
      He looks puzzled.
RAY: Oh yeah. I know what I was thinking…
  I was somewhere else for a moment.
  Strange…
      He looks strange.
  I've become obsessed with coincidences
  lately. And today, there were no coincidences.
  So—isn't this ironic—I felt safe.
      She talks as if in a trance.
DORA: Why don't you go and ask the gentleman
  what the meaning of his message is.
RAY: Funny, the same thought just occurred
  to me. Funny how the obvious solution
  to a problem is invariably the last one
  to enter* one's mind…
      She is stern:
DORA: Do it now, Raymond.
RAY: What's his name, by the way?
DORA: Mister William Hard, Doctor of Divinity,
  Equidistance and Gradualness.
      Pause. He cheers up.

RAY: At least I'll be dealing with an educated
   person.
        She looks at him hard.
RAY: Okay, Okay.
        He goes out, slamming the screen door. She looks out the window for a long time,
        as the two MEN *talk. She turns back, in a trance.*
DORA: ...tarboosh...
        SUSANNAH *enters, wearing fez. She sings her song "Bug River":*

>   Till the Bug River bears away
>   my blues
>   I'll be there for you.
>   There in the air, with my smile
>   and miles of high hopes hooray.
>
>   Till Bug River washes away
>   my things,
>   I'll be there for you.
>   There in the air, with my wings
>   high, miles and miles above the hay hooray.
>
>   But...
>   When old Bug River fouls her nest
>   I promise
>   I won't be there for you.
>   You'll have the blues; all the rest
>   of us will fly away hooray hooray.

   SUSANNAH *sails once all around the kitchen and exits. Pause. Her* MOM *snaps*
   out of whatever state she has been in. Blackout. Sudden crash of noise, and bizarre
   sequence of lights
        All (including house) up to full, and white. Then red and violet, veering through
   the spectrum to violet and blue, then black again. Another crash (based on the
   plucked clothes-line motif of the first Scene). We see DAD (RAY) *in the door, look-*
   ing amazed. MOM *and* DAUGHTER *stand opposite, together. They regard him*
   with horror. A long pause (outside, the MAN *has vanished).*
RAY: ...he talked to me about various things...
   All in a foreign language...Mimbreland...
   the land of evening...of how the moon
   was wont to come and sit before him...on
   her footstool...like an amiable ghost...
   but now is dying...an invisible college
   of demons has instructed him...and all
   about us, crows perched on hoodoos, a

murder of crows…witnesses to what was
said…"according to necessity,"
he said, "for they pay one another recompense
and penalty for their injustices…" The
moon is very sick.
>   *Snaps out of it.*
It boils down to this, the long and short
of it, that is:
>   *Pause. He sits heavily.*
He is me. That's right. He is me.
I am him.* I'm a double. A duplicate.
An inauthentic copy. I'm supposed to
pack one light suitcase. Three pair of socks.
One hat.** Leave my credit cards behind,
because he'll need them.

DORA: Whatever did you do wrong, Raymond?

SUSANNAH: Father, how is that possible? How can
a heavenly body, a huge thing made out of
stone, get sick? I don't buy it. Nope.
Not me.

RAY: I am to pack a few things, and depart.
I am going far away. To someplace
he calls "the land of evening." It
turns out there has been an error in the
big plan. His friends are my enemies,
and vice-versa. My animalistic urges
apparently have nothing to do with
it. Even prolonged abstinence would
not have changed things. Much.

DORA: I'll go make you a sandwich.

SUSANNAH: Dad, what is "Mimbreland"?

RAY: The land of evening.

SUSANNAH: What is "the land of evening"?

RAY: Mimbreland. Don't ask me to explain.
I can't. This is really quite a shock
to my system. Sheesh.

SUSANNAH: Dad, can I have your credit cards?

RAY: No, Squeezre, sorry, but they belong to
him. He is me. I told you. I am him. A duplicate.

DORA: I called up Jack at the office.
>   *Pause.*
He said you did things. That you were
a premature-something-or-other.

RAY: Well, yes, maybe. That might be* true…

SUSANNAH: Dad, does that mean you're a fake?

RAY: I prefer the term he used. A duplicate.

SUSANNAH: Then you are a fake.* An imitation. A cheap knock-off.

RAY: Good God, Squeezre, allow me a
    shred of self-respect, won't you?* Sheesh…

SUSANNAH: Sorry, I was just trying to establish
    the facts. I have rights too you know.

DORA: Did you do the things at work, the
    things Jack said you did, did you
    Raymond? Did you?

RAY: Jack should talk. Jack is gaga.
    Today at work Jack said, "This
    is today" and I said, "What do you
    mean?" and he said "Just that:
    This is today" and I said, "Jack,
    I don't see what you're driving at,"
    and he looks me right in the eye and
    says, "I had a revelation. The Angel
    of the Lord came down out of the sky,
    during my lunch-break, on a park bench
    in Gooner Park and said: 'This is today,
    Jack, and you are so lost in your
    block-headed corporeal swinishness
    that you cannot respond with an
    open heart.' And that is what I am
    saying to you, Ray: This is today.
    This is today, Ray, and you are so
    lost in your block-headed corporeal
    swinishness that you cannot respond
    with an open heart. Respond to an
    utterance of purest, unblenched revelation.
    This is today, Ray. Think about it."
    Then he went all cross-eyed and kinda
    googly, took off his clothes, right
    down to the shoes and stockings,
    and went all around the room, singing an
    old song from yesteryear's Top 40, I
    forget, doing the Rumba.* "This is today."
    Can you believe it?

    SUSANNAH *holds up a huge* BUG *and stands motionless in a vatic pose, eyes*
        skyward.

DORA: He said you did things, that you did things
    indicating something the matter with you,

in the head. He said you always had an
excuse along the lines of this was only
coincidental and that also was only
coincidental, and that appearances deceive
and that eating red meat did not imply a
moral condition involving torpitude, animalistic
boffing* of teenage sluts and so forth, and
one's status as a premature-anti-something-
or-other; but I don't buy it. I don't buy
it at all. And neither does Squeezre; do
you, Squeezre? Do you? Pay attention, dear,
this is important...Is that some kind of
stag beetle you've got there!? Get it away
from me, you nasty child. Get it away...
SUSANNAH: Does this mean I can bring my beetle
collection downstairs? Yes? No? Maybe?
Why doesn't anybody listen to me? Isn't
anyone curious to know about my life?
Doesn't anyone care about what my day
is like, feeding those cats next door?
Those bulky, monstrous cats. With their
big, greenish, unblinking saucer eyes.
The tufts of fur on their eartips. Their
deep guttural purring, and the swishing
of their tails as they tear apart the carcasses
I fling down to them. And the huge bugs
I find in the walls, and in the wainscotting
of the neighbors' house. Big ones, like this!
Stag beetles and Rhino beetles and rare
Longhorn beetles that are not supposed to
grow in these parts. Beetles sprouted
from the mystic seeds that I found in
that shop. Seeds from China. Where Mad Wu
was born. Under a Ding-Dong tree. A
worshipper of cats and bugs and beetles.
      MOM *hisses at* RAY.
DORA: Don't you say a word against Jack. You shit.
He's a beautiful loving man with a
Christian soul, and a fine set of his
own teeth. He works hard. He dreams on
things other men merely guess at. You aren't
fit to lick the shit off his shoe.
RAY: Jack's okay.

DORA: Jack understands circumstantiality,
   and he respects me.
RAY: I did not mean to denigrate the man, Dora.
DORA: When Jack enters the room, things of
   a wispy nature gather outside, under
   the eaves and palpitate in the moon's
   spittle. And I recall my girlish circum-
   rotation. The circumflex of my innocent
   ardor...
RAY: ...
DORA: ...
RAY: You do?
         MOM *lowers her head.*
DORA: Yes, I do.
         DAD *gets up, and leaves the room. He speaks from off.*
RAY: Where's my old suitcase?
DORA: In the attic.
         We hear the attic door squeal.
SUSANNAH: Careful. I've got beetles up there. In cans
   and bottles.
DORA: Careful, Ray. She's got her beetle collection
   up there.
         A muffled yell. A muffled thump. RAY *appears with his suitcase.*
RAY: My god what EYES they have. I never knew
   insects could look at you that way.
SUSANNAH: I hope you didn't hurt any of them.
RAY: No, dear, I didn't.
DORA: So when do you go?
RAY: Tomorrow, I guess. After dinner.
DORA: Shall I get something special at the butcher?
RAY: Sure, leg of lamb maybe.
SUSANNAH: Can I go now?
RAY: Sure, go.
         Pause. He looks around, gets up and finds the letter. He sits down and reads it
         once more.
   What does "tantalum?" mean?
DORA: Damned if I know. Doesn't sound very nice.
RAY: ...sheesh...
         Slow blackout.

ACT TWO

Scene 〰〰 (gums)

The kitchen again. Again, it is evening, the next night. Tablecloth, candlelight and
a wonderful meal spread out. Sweet music from the old victrola. Toasting and mer-
riment. The MAN, RAY, DORA, *and* SUSANNAH. *It is* DAD'S *going-away-party.*
Suddenly, the MAN *becomes silent and stares at* RAY. *He* (RAY) *raps his wine-glass*
with a spoon. All become silent and look at RAY. *Pause. He realizes it is time for his*
farewell speech. He rises from the table, glass in hand.

RAY: Ladies and gentlefolk. Kind sirs and colleagues.
    Pause.
Welcome to the banquet. My farewell
solemnity, and solenoid. I propose
to salute you, wife (Dora), daughter
(Susannah), good friend from the Outer
Dark (Mister William Hard) with a sally
of good cheer, a solfatarra of deeply
felt verbal solfeggio. Tonight, my heart
is full with shreds, folded pop-ups, and
the stuff of the heart, farewell stuff,
feathers, obscure bones of small creatures,
portraits in lockets of the lesser Popes,
poop, sailboats, sentimental threnodies
from the gaslight era, odd riffs of jazz,
corny keepsakes, tufts of hair, confederate
dollars sewn into the ruffles of antique
gowns, ferrotypes of audacious perukes,
satins, lizard-skins, coral buttons, ivory
needles, silver thimbles and billets-doux
from the Pretty Times Done Did.
    Pause.
My mission has been modestly to amuse,
bemuse and defuse. I have, to the best of my
abilities, struggled to maintain a full
larder, a cheerful parlor, and a backyard

free of pests and vermin. I chose the low
way because it seemed, to me, in my dreamtime
myopia, more noble. My political thoughts
have remained primitive, but most passionately
embraced. I am a simple man beset with heartbreak. Work has been my therapy. Mathematical
unction the charm of my meat-wagon. When you
grasp the simple truth: how all things have,
well, have happened once, or more than once,
before; the fur under your collar is likely
to flatten, and not flare up, so bristly.
Such perspective ennobles the atrocious,
authenticates the truly tragic. We can
traipse into the gasworks furnace of Fate
with a gleam of what's holy in our eye, thankful.
    He looks down. He looks up.
I am...simply...aghast. For nothing ever
cries out from its true heart to me, without
my having held my hat in my hand, looking at it,
thinking it was not mine, but someone else's.
A gift, on loan. Nothing ever flies into the
plate glass of the picture window, and plops
down, thus, stunned, to the ground, without my
feeling a pang as of a pulled weed flung into
the sky, flung with great urgency, as if the
Evil One were watching from his Tower of Tantalum,
perched there on the fiery coast of Hell, his devilish
picnic laid, with cheeses, devilwine and so forth;
there, where the heart yields to weird compunction.
    Pause.
I see myself a feckless youth hardened by
prolonged abstinence and chilblains, aghast,
alone, in agony. I see myself, a young shoe-
salesman on the windy plains of West Gradual,
where the Bug River hyphenates the mighty Ohio
with its moxie doodle, a cipher, a tragic hipster,
a tramp. I encounter the notorious Mu Factor
in the sad, shanty towns of Shenango and deem
myself wise with the leer of unholy knowingness.
My cynic heart fructifies the loins of my undoing
with condoms, cigars, saltpeter, and cryptic
notes inscribed on paper towels in the cafeterias
of Junior Colleges at Shenango. I treasure the

bricabrac of the sacred Mu Factor, as I torment
the Moon with my offtune whistling.
Lira lira, lira lara, lira-lay.
> *Pause.*

> SUSANNAH *and* MR WILLIAM HARD *look at each other, then down.*

I complete my studies in Celestial Mechanics.
My dissertation on Clovis Man, and on the Creeping
Dartworm are published in the *Darkwind Almanac.*
The world west of Gradual stretches out before
me, like a rumpled bed full of golf balls. Clutching
the horrible inner truth of the Mu Factor, I am
able to grow fabulous greensward from what was
yellowish, pale, and covered with spikes and thorns.
I am able to perform certain amazing rites, rites
in the bleak char and firelight, all before the
foul nest of Promise, that lady of cheat. All my
doubts are as nothing to a nope star. I fear
no one. I thunder as I touch the earth with my pods.
> *Pause.*

Alas, the theory of the Mu Factor is refuted by
David Braithwaite, and his Meso-thermal Crabwise Digitator,
or MCD. What am I to do, a heretic with no heresy?
An inane loose screw. Useless. Arcane. Alone.
So, I look down upon my shoes, gather up what
remains of my sour circumspection, add a circumflex
to my name, learn to trot the Hilda, get up, clear out,
set off for the big cities east of here, with their
racket, wisecraft, perverted alleyways, alien custards,
bizarre hats, diddle-shoots of double-edged disregard,
and resolve to go among them, the people who dwell in
those parts, a fey joker of ill-report. A shoe-salesman
of cosmic proportion.
> *He drinks a glass of water. The others shift about in the interval. He prepares to*
> *begin once more. Rapt attention.*

From the depths of my heart I curse David
Braithwaite, and all his works. Waving my hands
to the dim roof of heaven, I will a monster
furunculosis on his abdomen, which in the
fullness of time does appear, aborting both
him and his joy. By my will, hosed down the sluice
of the Evil One's infarction.
> *Pause.*

Whether wrongly or rightly, I capsize morally.

I grow contentious, arrogant, addicted to the
kind of overdrive that afflicts those hobbled
by a tender sprain, spiritually speaking. The
ball in my pivot pops out and bounces away,
under the dining room table and hops out the
screen door. Gone. Gone forever, like all
baubles the heart grows fond upon, under
variety's banana frond. We are fools, to whom
the usages of what wiggles make wilely, with
painted stripes of Oriental wickedness. Oil
lamps, tents swooshed by the sweet simoom,
fezzes and incense, wicked ankle bracelets
of the seductress. The works of temptation.
      He gulps, looks strange.
And so, the fire of my animalistic urges
is fanned, flies up and flaps madly out the
door. In Shenango's greasy bar rooms I
enact vice. I practice my vice with surgical
precision. I practice my vice till I carry
it around with me, carry it at all times
like a hump. My depravity, my animalistic
urge to prey upon those whose goodness or
beauty or teasing, sexual tarradiddle freezes
my heart in my throat like a stovepipe hat
on the head of a nineteenth century missionary
buggering a disciple in the saturated frangipani
glade of an isle sacred to strange gods, gods
with scissors who snip the clothesline of
causal connection wherever they perceive,
in the humid air of paradisiacal archipelagoes,
a sexual suction.
      Pause.
Such are the powers of the animalistic urges
that torment me that I struggle, like Jacob,
in the grasp of the Divine Greco-Roman. Philosophy
means nothing to me, nor commerce, nor letters.
My resolve to question and to acquire, through
prolonged abstinence, the mantle of Intellectual
Hero and Demigod flattens out; and the swerve
of my second, sad undoing is accomplished.
Feverish, I jeer goodness, frankness, well-
argued narrativity. Whenever faced with truth
and sincerity, I invoke the sarcastic raspberry

of my disbelief. I do not reckon, dear friends
and family, how all things have been done before.
Done before in the precincts of a finer, better
world, with tighter tolerances, glossier paint,
and more in the way of enhanced structural impeccability.
In short, cheesiness afflicts me in all my works, and
I am dead to nuance, timeless elegance and the rigors
of three-year limited warranty. The little clock of our
father's perfect plan has, to my jaundiced eye, petered
out in the pudding. The wreck and the lure of what's
wrecked tempts me to a perception of this world as an
instance of itself only, a green bower in a green glade,
and not a paradigm, as it truly is, of the place beyond
error, where ergo equals a Coulomb Field in which every
point is so charged with forced electromagnetic energy
as to stand directly proportional to the total, combined
product of their charges, and inversely proportional to
the square of the distance between and among them. An
infinite ergo of ergots, the consciousness altering
black bread of Mimbreland…Photostated in Heaven,
by the angelic horde…So, I snivelled…
    He crouches and leers.
I snivelled, and sniggled, and sneaked away.
I smoked and niggled and slaked my lust. I
quenched the hot pods of my animalistic urges
wherever suction would permit. I perched, small,
on a remote psychic abscess of myself, ran
up and down the creaking celestial staircase,
and double-charged for half-a-plate. Nothing
foreign was not natural to me. My disciples
resembled me in their easy ways, witless saunter
and careless discharge. Cigarettes, polkas,
pinkie rings of horn and nitre, obscure deals,
black shirts and pink ties, vacations in fat lands
paid for by Bug River's most brazen delinquents,
money in stacks, bottles of acquavit, revolvers
by Smith and Wesson, lotto tickets and trick dice,
expensive shades in gold frames, stolen art works
from Eastern Europe, hen's teeth and panda's thumbs,
stuffed owls, maculate three-deckers, pneumatic
superinflatibles, bluestreak disinternments, lace,
lurchings, engineered fuddles, nude beaches, rigged
sameness, reified urchins, dead mice, scarabs, scat.

He sits down, complerely run out of steam.

MR WILLIAM HARD: The optic on all that, brothers and sisters,
  is the pornographic.

DORA: As we burn, so are we quenched.

SUSANNAH: Why, when he talks like that,
  about himself, does Dad employ such a
  fixed vocabulary?

DORA: Hush, dear, it's your father's going-away
  party, and he's had little too much to drink.

RAY: All I'm saying is I don't understand.
  I wish someone could illuminate me,
  that's all.

MR WILLIAM HARD: Raymond, there is a season for quickening
  and a season for puzzlement.

SUSANNAH: No one else's parents, my friends at
  school, talk like this.* It goosewillies me.

RAY: What are you talking about, you ninny?

MR WILLIAM HARD: We are all orphans, beneath the hieratic
  balloon of the blank. Children of nightdoingness.
  Abandoned.

  This doesn't help anyone. Pause.

SUSANNAH: Why was Dad talking about his urges like
  that? The big cats I feed next door, they
  don't whine all the time about how…well…
  animalistic they are. Those big cats just
  glow and glisten. Their deep purrs rumble
  in the twilight like a faraway lawnmower.
  I hear a powerful mower in those purrs.

DORA: He's not who he thought he was, so
  it's plain, he's just got to go, Squeezre.

RAY: [*dazed and blank*] He is me. I'm a duplicate. I am him.
  Show's over. I'm to go to some place
  called "the land of evening."* Mimbreland.
  We received notification yesterday. I am
  him, whoever that is.

SUSANNAH: But why does he have to make such a big
  deal about it? When I went to Indiana
  nobody made such a big deal about it.

DORA: That's because he's not coming back.

SUSANNAH: Why not?

  Pause.

Never?

MR WILLIAM HARD: That's right, Squeezre. A man has to take

a thing like this standing up. It's a
body blow for sure, but he's got to stand
there and take it. And not run away…

He looks at RAY *who is mouthing a wordless supplication to* DORA, *but she doesn't understand what he is trying to say. Pause.*

DORA: It's as if a very proud and important-type
American man called and asked for you.
But since you were not the person who
answered the phone, this big-type
person, someone in a position of real
responsibility; someone with values,
convictions and a complex, but highly
distinguished Curriculum Vitae, this
person got disappointed; got fed up,
and hung up. But tried again later,
only to get the same result. And kept
calling up, but since you were never
the one to answer the phone, he would
not leave the message that would save.
And because he kept calling and calling,
and leaving no message you start to get
anxious, worried and a bit perturbed.
In fact, Squeezre, you start going
through the Seven Stages of Mourning
because you start to feel like someone
you love has passed on, while you're
doing something bad in the barn, with
someone…foreign…Someone big and
stiff, with a fat lip, broken teeth,
and a really tasteless demeanor. Maybe
a fez, or tarboosh…You've never
had that feeling, have you, Squeezre?

SUSANNAH: …

She looks at RAY. *He looks back.*

RAY: …

MR WILLIAM HARD: I have a little present for Raymond,
on the occasion of his departure.

Takes out a little shiny black box. All lean over it, so we have a hard time seeing. All, except the MAN, *involuntarily fall back. It's a very bright, vermillion snake. It is very beautiful and very alive.*

Pause. All are transfixed, except SUSANNAH, *who leans forward to stroke it. She makes an odd noise of pleasure in her throat.*

SUSANNAH: Can I have one too?

MR WILLIAM HARD: This one's for your father.

> *But he's in a trance. As if, he sees the truth, in all its naked power. All eye him as*
> *he slowly stands. He stutters:*

RAY: …Shakespeare lived in this house. This
is Shakespeare's house. He wrote all his
books here. The one about geese. The
one on gardens. And the one about the
cemetery business…

> *Pause.*

…calling up and leaving no message…

> *Pause.*

He cried. She cried.

> *Pause.*

He took his trousers off.

> *Pause.*

MR WILLIAM HARD: I gave you the snake because I'm from
the Land of Evening. We worship snakes
in the Land of Evening. And that's where I'm from,
and that's where you're going.

> *He takes off his trousers. Pause. He hands the trousers to RAY. RAY looks at him,*
> *looks at the trousers, looks at his wife and daughter, looks out at us. Slowly, he takes*
> *off his trousers and hands them to the MAN. Pause.*

RAY: …and of course the one whose name
I forget. The one with that song. The
one that goes…

> *Suddenly he goes blank. Pause. He snaps out of it, puts on his new trousers (so*
> *does the MAN), adjusts his tie, puts on his jacket; and, as if unaware of the others,*
> *slips quickly and quietly out the kitchen door. At this point all freeze for a second or*
> *two. MOM produces a pitch-pipe from her pocket. Squeaks out the correct note, and*
> *all three sing, ever so softly, and with great, slow solemnity " The Battle Hymn*
> *of the Republic." Pause.*

Scene, the next: ⋂⋂ *(rabbits)*

> SUSANNAH *and* DORA *unfreeze, look about, make their way downstage and ca-*
> *sually hang out, smoking and talking. This scene, thus, amounts to an odd, little*
> *interlude. While the* WOMEN *talk the* MEN *can move around, stretch, etc, as com-*
> *fort dictates. If necessary the* WOMEN *may take their chairs downstage with them.*
> *This is a quiet, deliberate scene. Both do a lot of thinking in between their replies.*

SUSANNAH: Why did Dad have to go away?

DORA: Sometimes Susannah, you can row
out to the middle of Bug Lake.

And sometimes when the water is
very clear you can see all the
way to the bottom. And sometimes
when you look down what you see
there is a cause for…for anxiety
and fearful speculation. When
Raymond looked down to the bottom
of the lake, he saw a human face.
He recognized the face. It was his own.
SUSANNAH: I know where I am right now, but
where did Dad go? Is it far away?
DORA: The time comes when you hear the music
from another world. You know the
music is from another world because
it is so sad and strange you feel
as if you had awakened from a dream,
flung your fists out in a nightfever
and caught a living sparrow in your
hand. Only, the bird sings a piercing
wildnote threnody that drives you
unwilling straight to the center of
things. Its little heart trilling the
mysterious work of the heart. Your
father, Raymond X, Raymond X Dogsbody,*
knew this work, but could not name it.
SUSANNAH: But our family name is "Moredent."
DORA: I know, dear. I know. I was only
making an example, an example of his instance.
SUSANNAH: …oh*…
DORA: To go nameless in the heart's wonder
is to be a ghost. The ghosts all live
in a thin, hard place, hidden behind the moon.
SUSANNAH: If he doesn't like the food there, what will
he do? Are there places where he can go to
work if he misses his friends and colleagues?
Will his enemies go there too, and find him
out? Will he find another wife, and love
her, and make another child with her, holding
hands with her silently, of a summer's eve,
on the glider, on the front porch, with a
picture of the furnace of infinity emblazoned
for both of them, like a wilderness of competing
sunsets, at all the compass points? Will they

conceive and give birth to another child,
one like me? Will this one like me come
in the softness of the afternoon, and replace
me, systematically, in the hearts of those
who know me, who love me, who would kill to
protect me? Would she do all this in the name
of wormwood? In the name of what has not been
fathomed because it exceeds dimension, and
rushes off the spectral palette of all colors
we see, and hence of all things we know?

DORA: Wherever he is, he will awaken every day, and
every day he will catch the sparrow in his bare
hand, the sparrow of his own undoing.

SUSANNAH: So where do we stand, do we truly dwell
in the world we know, here in the town
of gradual, on the marshy flood plain
of Bug River? Or is it all a bad joke
perpetrated on us by blue jays, a sham, a hoax?

DORA: No, it is not what we think, at least
I don't think so. But there are many things
of which I am uncertain. This is one of them.

SUSANNAH: But then, where? I need to know?

DORA: Halfway through my life, I sat down and
cried because I knew, somehow, somehow
so obscurely that I could not fathom it,
that my life was half over. But at the
same time, I had the revelation that my
wretchedness would be compensated for.
That I should henceforth discover in
my heart the place of bounty. A place
where all the parallaxes of the parlous
are fused. The Holy Flame of victory
has welded my nameplate to this unwobbling
hub. So I am fixed here, and yea! my
tents are pitched forever by the waters
of sweet Jordan. Jordan River. Hallelujah!
In the land of evening. In the land beyond
the mathematical deconstruction of the soul.
Hallelujah!

SUSANNAH: Does this place have a name, beyond the inkling
of spiders? Or is it all like moss? Or like
fur? Or worse, is it like a coat of clothing
we can put on, and take off, at will? What
on earth did Dad mean by all that stuff?

DORA: I don't know. I don't know anything.

SUSANNAH: Sure, you do, Mom.

DORA: No, darling, I don't. To some, like me,
the human heart is as opaque as a stone.
Through a glass darkening your eye, there
is only the reflex perception of a glint.
I sometimes think of that glint as the first
morning of the world.

SUSANNAH: So, you *do* know something!

DORA: It is only a bauble thing. Like a singleton
earring from a cotillion ball of long ago. The
Pretty Times Done Did. An ivory earring of
error flung, hopeless, in a squat, stone box
of deepest jet. Useless. Classic. Mute.

SUSANNAH: Have all things truly happened before?
Even Dad's removal and departure?

DORA: Only the loving know no repetition. I think
it is a great mystery of the heart. The miracle
of loving kindness was told once, only once
and that in Olden Times and sadly no one
listened. That is why crows, of all birds,
have inherited the earth. Wastrel crows,
with hearts of pitch, given to scandal-mongering.

SUSANNAH: Does anyone love me for myself truly? Did
Dad? Do you, mother?

DORA: No, my dear, no one does. You are merely
an idol of my conceit. Your father, Raymond,
loved you for yourself only, but look where
it got him. He was a silly, old man. He was
a silly old man even when he was twenty-three
years old, wore bowties, and ventilated
straw hats.

SUSANNAH: So you don't know where we are?

DORA: I love all maps, but not for what they tell
me of the world. The world is a useless thing,
without the soul's commission. Maps tell me
the mind of humankind's a porridge of whim,
wisecracks, whimsy and flim-flam. World's
only a tinny usufruct. We die in a ditch
alone, spat upon by our social betters.

SUSANNAH: But mother, I have seen the map with the
town of Gradual written all over, and Bug
River too. A sharp, red snake of a wriggle.

DORA: The devil put it there, to delude the mapmaker.

SUSANNAH: But why?

DORA: He owed him dark blood, I suppose. The blood
   of senseless sacrifice. You think too much. You
   can't love anything, a man, a woman, a cat, a
   skink, if you think too much. Thinking poisons
   the well with choke cherries and skunk cabbage.
   In our time the presencing of beings has outmoded
   Being itself.

SUSANNAH: What kind of people are we then? Who are
   we? and why do we talk like this? Can't
   I catch the sparrow in my dream, and will
   my life turn out better than his? Why did
   he ruin his career as a shoe-salesman
   with his mad dream to climb to the stars?
   What do we know truly, if we can't even
   verify what's on the plate before us, at
   the Holy Banquet? Are we phantoms, birds
   of prey? Or are we only machines that
   rattle on all through the night because
   we can't turn ourselves off? Are we going
   to be hosed down the sluice, with David
   Braithwaite, into the devil's infarction?
   Are we animal, vegetable, mineral? Are
   we paper, scissors, or stone? Are we a key
   locked in someone else's box?

DORA: You ought to go feed the neighbor cats.
   The contract says ninety-nine years.
      Pause.
   That face at the bottom of the lake haunts
   me, that face that so resembled your
   father. Raymond had a way with practical
   jokes, when he was younger. That was a
   side of him you never saw. It's a pity
   too. He lost whatever sense of humor he
   possessed after the failure of the first
   machine he invented, the Microscopic Midas
   Tactoreceptor. Took the wind out of his
   sails, so to speak. I always suspected
   his faith was thinner than mine, and only
   a thin coverlet hiding a despair. Such
   things could not be parsed in church talk,
   and I've always felt it best with sleeping
   dogs to let be. Rabid ones you blast with
   a shotgun from a safe distance.

She laughs.

Raymond though, Raymond used to do the
most amusing things with department store
mannequins. You can't imagine! The human
body never dreamed of it, I'm sure. Once
he constructed a complete demonic diorama,
starring the Mayor, the City Council, and
ladies from the Garden Club. Our goat,
Jasper, was featured prominently also.
It did not amuse many. Or the simulated,
hacked corpses he had a way of half-hiding
in more remote regions of Gooner Park. It
was a form of humor long on dark dare, and
provocation, and short on justifying higher
purpose. That's when the "devil" talk began.

We hear a music softly.

SUSANNAH: Does any of this MEAN anything, Mom?
I mean, if all of us have an inescapable
penchant for acts that defy convention,
actions conceived in woe and bastardy,
and consummated in direct contradiction
to human nature? Aren't we standing in
a perilous relation to our own destinies
even, not to mention the high regard
of the community of Gradual, where we reside?

DORA: Don't go and get metaphysical on me, Susannah.
Keep your mind fixed on the here and now,
things like feeding the cats, and so forth.
Which reminds me, I've got to look into the
matter of Raymond's insurance, to see if it
specifically declares null and void acts of
breakthrough into insubstantiation, even if
miraculously initiated. Me oh my.

SUSANNAH: I don't understand, Mother.

DORA: Neither do I, Susannah, and that's the sad truth.

SUSANNAH: But I really want to, I really do.

DORA: Study grass. Study lace. Study the pattern
in these things. The truth is needlework. All
the rest is crotchety supposition. But the whole
world's at sixes and sevens, especially
what with this recent instance of Raymond's
translation into the fairy world of the transmundane.
Faith is garbage, hog food, slops.

She gets up suddenly, very agitated.

SUSANNAH: Mother, how can you say that?* Mother, you
   of all people?
DORA: Faith is a tale told by an idiot in a basement
   during a bargain basement tale—I mean *sale.*
SUSANNAH: Belief is supposed to make you fine-boned,
   and I'd feel anxious without any of it.
DORA: Believe me, the world goes whirling along
   quite nicely without much of it, Susannnah.
SUSANNAH: But no it doesn't, don't you see?
DORA: All I want to know is why, why things
   have got to be this way. Why I must live
   in total disharmony with nature. Why I hate
   this awful, spreading tub of dough that is
   my human flesh. Why I wish to punish my
   elders with pointless mockery, and tear
   the bread from out of their mouths. What
   I am doing on the face of this planet
   when I cannot think of a moment in my life
   that has not been shadowed by a failure
   to follow through, to answer act with
   any other strategy than timid, tactical
   inaction, by the failure to connect.
SUSANNAH: I don't know what to say, mother.
DORA: Then for the love of Christ, shut up, Susannah.*
   Just shut up.
       She sits down, terribly vexed.
SUSANNAH: I thought America was supposed to be a happy
   place. A place of bounty, and faith, and
   problem-resolution through prudent self-interest.
DORA: [*fiercely*] Cut the crap, Susannah. Don't play innocent.
   I see through your mask. Your pride and
   selfish vaunting. The devil's working his
   thick, hot, red tongue between your lips
   even as we sit here. He makes you speak
   such rot as would make me spew if I didn't
   know well enough to not listen. Behind
   those pale, thin lips. Those liquid, soft
   doe's eyes.* Those perfect pearly teeth.
SUSANNAH: I'm not what you think, Mother. I'm not
   thinking *that.* It's not true. Believe me.
DORA: Oh yes you are. I've known what you are
   since I heaved you out of my belly, bloody,
   bellowing, and full of shame.

SUSANNAH: Mother, I'm just an ordinary young
    woman. I would never think those things.
DORA: Yes, you would, you cheap slut. You
    would because you are my daughter,
    flesh of my flesh. So talk straight
    and don't fool with me. You hear, Susannah?
SUSANNAH: All right, I *do* think those things. The
    same things you think.* Only I don't say them.
DORA: The very same things I think, Susannah?
    You had better be sure they are exactly the
    same, Susannah. Because if they are not
    the very same things, then I promise you
    I shall curse heart and soul till the
    moon come down out of the sky, tear
    your heart out while you yet live, and
    you shall watch as she fry it in her skillet
    and press the fat, red flesh in her mouth.
SUSANNAH: Mother, I promise never to say them.* Again.
DORA: You promise, Susannah? Not ever?
    Are you very sure?* You must be very sure,
    Susannah?
SUSANNAH: Cross my heart. Not ever.
        Pause.
SUSANNAH: Mother?
DORA: I've answered six of seven. That's enough
    for tonight. There's work to be done. Let's go.

    They rejoin the MEN, *and the previous scene circles its square and completes itself. Pause. The* WOMEN *clear off the table while the* MAN *sits there, like an insensate thing. A boulder. Lights go down, then slowly come up on early morning of the next day. The music has of course stopped, and we hear the chirping of birds. Blackout.*

Scene the next: XX *(exxon)*

    The MAN, *seated as before, is eating his breakfast.* SUSANNAH *pours some coffee for herself and him. She has a few questions for him as well. Scene begins as he examines what's in his bowl carefully, extracts something large and dark from it with the thumb and forefinger. He rapidly conveys this to his mouth, as if he were afraid it might be alive. He tucks a napkin into his collar, and chews doggedly on this object through the rest of the scene. His face is lowered, forward and tilted down, intent upon his work; his eyes are opened wide, rolled back and staring upward.* SUSANNAH *slowly dries a dish, a saucer perhaps, with a dishtowel. Thus occupied she walks slowly, downstage, to a far corner of the kitchen; in fact, as far from him as possible, probably along the rooms's diagonal. She crooks her head over her shoulder, and in this somewhat awkward position, addresses him. Outside* DORA's *face is visible in the window.*

SUSANNAH: Do you intend to stay with us? Do you

intend to stay with us for some time?

How long?

> *Fifteen-second pause.*

MR WILLIAM HARD: Yes.

> *Five-second pause.*

SUSANNAH: Answer my question. Exactly how long?

> *Fifteen-second pause.*

MR WILLIAM HARD: For ninety-nine years.

> *He points to the suitcase.*

It says so in the contract.

> *Fifteen second pause. She points to the suitcase.*

SUSANNAH: What have you got in there?

> *He snaps his fingers. The suitcase opens. A hoard of ordinary, but very rumpled clothing falls out.* MOM *rushes in, repacks the clothes, closes the suitcase, composes herself and goes out again. Her face reappears at the window.*

SUSANNAH: What do you want from us?

> *Fifteen-second pause.*

What do you want, please tell me.

> *Fifteen-second pause. Still no reply.*

Will you sleep with my mother?

> *Her* MOM's *face disappears.*

Answer my question. Will you sleep* with her?

MR WILLIAM HARD: Yes.

> *Fifteen-second pause.*

SUSANNAH: You really intend to sleep with her?

MR WILLIAM HARD: Yes.

SUSANNAH: Will you fuck her?

> *Thirty-second pause.*

MR WILLIAM HARD: Yes.

> *Thirty-second pause .*

SUSANNAH: Will you fuck me?

> *Thirty-second pause.*

MR WILLIAM HARD: Yes, if you want me to, and I

think I can get away with it.

> *Thirty-second pause.*
> *Both look down. The room is filled with shame.*

SUSANNAH: I don't want you to.

> *Thirty-second pause.*

MR WILLIAM HARD: Then I won't.
>   *Five-second pause. Both visibly relax.*

SUSANNAH: Now that we've got that settled...
>   *They hear music outdoors. It is* MAD WU. *The* MAN *arises, takes whatever it is he's been chewing on out of his mouth, places it carefully back in the bowl, and walks to the window. He looks out, then turns to* SUSANNAH. *She joins him at the window. A fifteen second pause as both look. He puts his hand on her shoulder. They look at each other, then out the window.*

SUSANNAH: Who is that man Mom is talking to?
Why is he making such a racket?

MR WILLIAM HARD: That's Mad Wu, the Chinaman, from
the other end of the world.

SUSANNAH: Mad Wu, the Chinaman!

MR WILLIAM HARD: Don't worry. He only calls himself that.
He's a harmless vagabond. From over in Corntown.
Where they buried the angel, or was it the devil?
in the calabashes...
>   *Fifteen-second pause.*
>   *She steps away, turns back and looks hard at him.*
>   *Fifteen-second pause.*

SUSANNAH: Who are you, *really*? Tell me.
>   *Fifteen-second fade to black, as* MAD WU's *music swells.*

Scene the 𝄽𝄽𝄽 (willowy)

>   MAD WU *plays a song for* DORA *who sits on a swing nearby, obviously enjoying herself.* MAD WU *is dressed with great elegance. Evening clothes, and wireless microphone. He sings his odd song with all the assurance of a professional:*

MAD WU: When the moon comes up
Motels are full of saxophones
of bingo bingo bam bango bum bim.

When the moon comes up
I think of my darling,
Hot, in the blue light.

Out there on Bug River
Motels full of pale travelers,
Lost within sight

Of bingo bingo bam bango bum bem.
Remind me of another time
When the moon came up.

In the motel of mind
I rehearse each night a scene
Of lover's horror:

Those who betrayed us
To love another run naked
With their red tongue bright.

And I grow lonesome
Without my wicked lover's
Head upon the pillow.

I sleep in the woods
    all day, all night.
If I don't finish this song
    There is no one around
To tell me I'm wrong;
    Or, worse, that I'm right.

And the hours I lost,
Spilled like spit on the salt earth
When the good take leave

Of the Bug River dead;
When the moon comes up and mourns
For bingo bingo bam bango bem bum.

but Bug River blazes bright.
And we who taste the hour
Of bingo bingo bam bango bem bum bim.

Curse the moonlight, curse
Like devils, on the white road
Of bingo bingo bam bango bum bim.

...

But when the moon sinks
We raise high the hopeless glass
Of black wine and drink.

When the moon comes up
On our explosive heartache
Set off the bomb.

SET OFF THE BOMB.

I sleep in the woods
    all day, all night;
If I don't finish this song
    There is no one around
To tell me I'm wrong;
        or, worse, that I'm right.

As the song ends, MOM *begins her monologue.* MAD WU *continues his playing
which provides an impromptu accompaniment for her performance as well, different
as it is from his; all during this we behold a glorious sunset. While she is soliloquizinq,
the* MAN *and the* DAUGHTER *steal out the kitchen door, and into the vast, open
spaces of the unexplored back yard (this is the front yard).*

DORA: Say what you like, there is nothing like
    music to fever the soul when the chill
    of strangeness is upon it. It's like at
    the crutch factory when they installed the
    Distichous Musical Trip-hammer, or "DMT."
        Pause.
Say what you like, I should very much
like a very long vacation, a vacation
to someplace where no one has formed
the higher concept of "vacuum cleaner,"
or "dish washing" or "ironing board."
I think this place ought to be visually
hyposensitive, like certain of the cold,
dry valleys of Mars, or Antarctica, for
that matter; and be an ecological exacta
of hysteron-proteron. An edenic idyll
of hydrophane, where fruits abound, vice
is sweetly ignored, and our faithless
wonder in other people's fatuity bars
the hangman as surely as it beckons
to colorful birds like macaws and toucans,
lorries, parrots and lorikeets as they dodge
and sway, high above the vine-canopy, the
coral sea and our own wind-slathered fields
of automatic, self-harvesting wheat. I
feel a proper paradise ought to be perpetually

self-correcting, a reflexive, introspective
perpetuum mobile rather like Plato's
Republic, only with people like me,
roughly, on top. People with my tastes
roughly, on top. People with my tastes,
temper, sensitivity and degree of education.
Nothing more or less would be pleasant.
  Pause for reflexion.
As for the moon, I would have twelve
and be done with it. Each a different
size, shape, texture and color. They
would be arranged, artistically with orbits
of varying distance, ellipticality, period,
and grace. I would name them: Welk (after
Lawrence), Dorothy (after Oz), Isabella
(after the Queen of Castille), Amelia (after
the obvious), Turkey, Tonsil, Okra, Banana,
Lace, Greedy, Moth, Pretzel, Dog and Dudu.
That's two too many, but then again two
of the twelve could be double-named; or
possess a secret life while coasting around
the other end of creation.
  Pause for a bad thought.
Oh my. Identity is a hellish burden. I'm
completely fed up with the whole thing.
Parenting, wifing, the PTA, the Democratic
Party (liberalism), then the Republican
Party (conservatism), then the party of
Ross Perot (geezer politics), highways,
house paint, salad bowls, exercise machines,
aerobics, lack of exercise, the Garden Club,
license plates, television, night-vision,
VCRs, Robot cheese, coathangers, paperclips,
other people, mystery novels, romance novels,
novels period, other people, anything that
is packaged in a way safe for children,
garbage bags full of stuff, empty garbage
bags, garbage, bags, sunglasses, reading
glasses, glasses, glass, other people,
not being able to see, toothpaste, oil
for the skin, oil for salad, cooking oil,
gasoline, oil companies, hospitals, smells
that remind one of hospital smells, illness,

pain, the suffering of others, the pleasure
of others, other people. The trap of being
something definite. A woman in middle of
her life surrounded by people who feel
nothing. Who feel literally nothing! A
slight curvature of the spine. A desperation
for pocket money. A loathing for other people's
ash-trays, toenail clippings, and tendency to
burp. God contains bad stuff. One swell
foop. An embarrassment of clichés.
    She looks down at herself, and softly wails.
What bloody-minded god dreamt up
this female mishap of bad-plumbing?
Cysts, fibroids, yeast infections. Swellings
and drainings. Tumescence, cramps and
detumescences. A horror-show cycle of
fecundity, and the wobble of fertility.
The unsteadiness of having to endure
what one has not willed for oneself. Children!
Children who turn into strangers. The
once welcoming world that turns its back
once you come into your gray maturity,
once you understand your need. Baffling,
it midasizes every hope, each slender dream
into the solid elemental dross of regret.
Midas backwards transposed. So much,
everything! all that I've chosen. Even
when I chose truly, I chose wrong. The
young and female are right to put off
all choosing. Yet not to choose is
worse. Because then the choosing is done
for you, societally, institutionally,
by your family, husband, colleagues,
social betters, or those persons far
away, who design the argument of your
future needs, even before you are
aware. People far away, who never
rest, who know your heart, mind and
every little itch better than you
ever will and have the courtesy not
to tell you what they know till you've
taken the trouble to put your cash
down, plunk, on the table. True power

dropped to the subterranean layer of
taste, fashion, what clothes, what hair
color and length, this book or that
(both truly awful), this drug or that
(both with truly terrifying side-effects),
lotto number. Vibrator speed. What
docudrama or infomercial that touched
us too deeply when we were tipsy, that
plucked the fatal heartstring, once,
when your guard was down, and you went
unwary into the pandemonium of the world,
its hospitals, its supermarkets, its
country clubs. Its malls with their
vile urchins, filth and muffled din.

>   *She holds her ears. He has stopped playing and is looking at her, intently She*
>   *realizes she has been going on a little.*

DORA: This is silly. I shouldn't talk too much.

MAD WU: It sounds crazy, coming from someone like you.

DORA: I'm sorry. I should watch my behavior.

MAD WU: Your behavior can take care of itself. Leave
    it alone.

DORA: I don't have anything today for you.

MAD WU: I'm not *you*. I'm Wu. And since I come
    from China, I don't need anything. In
    China the trees grow upside-down.

DORA: Here's a dollar. Go away. You're disturbing me.

MAD WU: Look, I am a folksy and amusing antitype
    to the contemporary cliché of the homeless
    person as a pathetic, scrofulous, deranged
    drug-ravaged glossalalian *sauvage* and ultimate
    social victim. I'm invoking the previous
    cliché of the wise, mad fool, and it works.
    The poison of the latter neutralizes the poison
    of the former. My true character is conditional.

>   *He bows.*

Conditional, contingent, conventional, and
phantasmal. I am here for the purpose of
singing a song. Which I have successfully
accomplished. My mission now, that being
done, is, like yours, one of escape.

>   *He produces a map.*

I suggest we rusticate ourselves to the town
of Moon Hat, some seventeen miles down Route

6, as the crow flies, also adjacent Bug River
but further North, direction of the devil,
but closer to its source among the Ice Mountains.
I suppose you've never heard of Moon Hat.
DORA: I'll take your word for it.
MAD WU: I wouldn't if I were you. I'm a congenital liar.
DORA: If you hate America enough to make such a
   spectacle of yourself that's good enough
   for me.
MAD WU: One thing, I don't believe in flashbacks,
   freezeframes, or time-lapse cinematography.
DORA: Fine with me.
MAD WU: Everything is fine with you. How do you
   expect to get through life if you're not
   more complex? The world is complex. It
   contains things like "tantalum" and the
   large intestine; it contains things like
   the Omaha Subharmonic Lantern Wheel. Also
   known as OSL...
DORA: That's an invention of Raymond's. A dream
   of his anyway. Before he went subcritical.
   The Omaha Subharmonic Lantern* Wheel is . .
        She looks at him hard. He looks at her hard.
MAD WU: Don't get all moony on me now. I'm serious.
DORA: Wait just a minute. I want to take off my apron.
        He grabs her hand.
MAD WU: Keep it, there are dirty dishes in Moon Hat too.
DORA: I don't know if I should do this.
        He begins to play his music. She looks up at the moon.
MAD WU: The Moon Hattans are not from Manhattan.
   They are realists. They have certain down-home
   needs too.
DORA: I hunger so much for what I
   will never be able to understand.
MAD WU: Join the crowd.
DORA: What will everyone think of me
   if I just up and leave, without
   so much as a note, a hint, or
   the most perfunctory fare-thee-well?
MAD WU: They'll pack up all their belongings
   in wheelbarrows. They'll follow you.
   Escape is useless, but escape from escape
   is even worse. My, look at that moon.

DORA: So, you're teasing me?

MAD WU: Pardon me, I am from China, all
the way around the world. Your physics
means nothing to me. But I do know
I am an unnatural entity, and that
when I cease to have anything to say
the only recourse is to vacate the
premises. This distinguishes me from
all Americans. But then the theatre
of Gradual possesses other charms...
> *Pause.*

Dead dogs, for instance. Cats and rabid raccoons.
> *She throws down her apron.*

DORA: Okay, okay. I'm coming.

MAD WU: I'm going to lead you to the stars, Dora.
I'm going to take you where you've
never been, to the blackberry bog at
East Moon Hat. Where people still
wear the kilts and fezzes native to
the region, where they still employ
the Univocal Sine-Wave Perforator
to crack open hickory nuts, where folks
gather in secret to worship St Lachesis,
patron saint of legalized gambling.*
Where we shall toast to Peace, Harmony,
and Selective Immortality, at the classy
lounges and establishments of Moon Hat.
(It isn't) We shall sip silvery martinis
by an art deco mirror that reflects our
nullity and reverses our sappy question-mark
into a universal affirmation suitable for
framing, family-viewing and...so forth.

DORA: That doesn't sound like America.
> *Pause.*

I have the feeling this has all happened
before. Long ago and far away.* I'm...
so happy...

MAD WU: It most certainly did. History occurs first
as tragedy, then is repeated successively
as farce, crime, and flim-flam. Then,
when all hope is gone, as...forgetfulness.
> *It's dark now. They begin to go out.*

DORA: That's just what I mean...my word,

would you get a load of that moon? No,
I mean it's so *exhilarating** not to know…
MAD WU: You got it, baby. The well of stupidity is
bottomless. Ignorance, true ignorance
shames the infinite with its extent, its
sheer maximal scope. Embrace your
ignorance. It'll never let you* down.
DORA: Look, look at the moon!
MAD WU: Why, what for?
DORA: It looks so real it almost looks fake.
MAD WU: You can say that again.
DORA: …Looks so real it almost looks fake…
MAD WU: I've heard that before.
DORA: What's that supposed to mean?
MAD WU: …could be…
DORA: …jerk..
    Go out arm in arm.
    Blackout is complete.

Scene: /\/\/\/\\ (*tigertiger*)

    Lights up in the backyard. The man is lugging his suitcase talking all the while to
SUSANNAH *who is guiding him carefully with a flashlight.*
MR WILLIAM HARD: …and the corn of Asaph was buried
in the ditch with Japeth and Gamaliel;
and they are come into the Land of Evening
and lay down upon the ground; and Garth
and Starfish went to Zenith with Altazimuth
and begat the tribe of Starfish;
and these too are come into the
Land of Evening where they all
lay down upon the ground; and
fishhead Curry talked with Tobit
concerning the doings of Ashtaroth,
and it grew even to the Seventh
Hour of the day, then She came—
She, in her gown of nitre and wormwood—
and they were pacified; and threw
down their idols of wood and tantalum,
and drove their flocks into the Land
of Evening whereupon they all took
off their shoes, and lay down upon

the hard ground; but Moab
met with Zechariah and Nebuchadnezzar
with Shenango, and all took an oath
under the shade of Whelk and Wheelbug,
and they knew the worm from what the
worm eats, and by this knowing they
cast lots, and Ishmael spoke to
Susannah and Suwannee in pidgin of
pignuts in pigpens, of pygmies in
saris kneeling before Sasquatch in
the sassafras, and knew by Worm-Hole
the wonders of worm-fence and caused
a worm-gear to be builded upon the
sand of Isfahan and Durango; these,
too, they all dropped their tools
in the ditch and walked with slow, mystic
tread into the Land of Evening and there
they rested.

SUSANNAH: Bill? Why do you need a shovel? Are you
going to dig up something? This is where
I buried my goldfish when I was a kid.
This is where I buried the angelfish.
And this...

    Another spot.

...is where Dad buried Richard M. Nixon
when he was excommunicated by the House of
Reprehensibles, in New Pork City...
New York City, I mean. That was back
in '77. Dad didn't actually bury the
President, it was only an effigy, a
Richard M. Nixon doll. We walked around
the house: Mom, Dad, Simon, and me. In
the dark. Like now. Beating on roasting
pans and buckets with soup spoons and
rolling pins. Dad mutilated the effigy
in horrible ways while I smeared ketchup
all over it. Then by torchlight (we
had made improvised torches out of brooms,
tar and kerosene) we buried it here,
howling. We trampled on the grave with
our pants down. Dad told us not to tell
anyone at school. Especially at the
Guidance Office. So I didn't. It was

really neat. And yuky—neat and yuky—
at the same time. It goosewillied me
severely.
>   *His wild eyes are bright.*

MR WILLIAM HARD: This must be where they buried the Angel.

SUSANNAH: Angelfish. I told you.

MR WILLIAM HARD: No, no, no. It's from an old prophecy.
From the Book of Folding Chairs. The
High Molality of Sacro Lumbar. An angel
fell here, the book says: "…twenty
snake-skins from the Bug River by the
town of Whangdoodle…"—and that's
Gradual, in the parlance of the Torrid
Zealots. So it's got to be here…
but where?
>   *He looks about.*

Saint Modred the Tormentor. A very wicked
saint from Shenango who began his days in
the dry goods business, and was known in
the period before his conversion as the
inventor of the Semi-Square Nickel-Plate
May-Wine Pile-Driver, used to send telegraph
messages to those hypothetical beings we
call "the niggle-carp people," at the
center of the world. In the boiling atomic
madness of the core. Right through the
Mohorovicic Discontinuity and everything,
and that takes some technological knowhow,
I assure you. Then he went mad.* Then he…

SUSANNAH: That was no angel, that was my brother,
Simon,
>   *But he's not listening.*

MR WILLIAM HARD: He also invented the Pygmy Klein Bottle.
But Mister Klein had the better attorneys,
and patented it first.

SUSANNAH: I told you—that's where we scattered Simon's
ashes.

MR WILLIAM HARD: Your brother was Saint Modred the Tormentor?

SUSANNAH: No, he was Simon Moredent, of our family,
of the family of Moredent. He was dealing
drugs at Gradual High. He was a genius,
but his talents went to waste. He died
one night in June. His girl friend broke

off with him because he was destroying his
mind with drugs.

MR WILLIAM HARD: Drugs are a terrible thing.

SUSANNAH: He was so desperate he stole a semi from
the A&P. On top of that he took an
overdose of crack cocaine. On top of
that the truck jack-knifed up on Route
6, in the rain. On top of that he was
struck by lightning as he lay there,
dying, all broken and bloody, all zonked
out on drugs. It was terrible. He was
a genius. When he wasn't on drugs he
was the most beautiful person in the
world. He wrote a little poem for me:
"When the moon comes up
... "

     He looks very wild. He cuts her off. Pause.

MR WILLIAM HARD: What do I care about your damnable brother?

SUSANNAH: Well I did, and do.

MR WILLIAM HARD: Life goes on, Susannah. Get over it.

     She sighs.

SUSANNAH: Want to hear my theory?* I think all things...

MR WILLIAM HARD: Susannah, look at the moon and what
do you see? Look! Look hard...

SUSANNAH: I see the moon. Big deal. What's so special
about that?* Can we just move on...

MR WILLIAM HARD: No, Susannah, that is *not* what we see.
That is what we think we see, but, alas
the optic on the lunar is not a true appearance.

     Pause.

It's flim-flam.

SUSANNAH: What are you suggesting, Bill?

     Fifteen-second pause.

     Slowly, he points at the moon.

MR WILLIAM HARD: It's all a hoax.

SUSANNAH: A hoax?

MR WILLIAM HARD: A swindle, yes.

SUSANNAH: A swindle?

MR WILLIAM HARD: Yes, I would say. A deception.

     Pause. She laughs.

The optic on the lunar possesses
an aspect of moonliness, but not
its essence. It's a fake. I'll show you.

She doubles up with laughter as he scrambles up stage. By dint of much clambering he nears the moon. He taps on it with his fingernail. We hear auditory proof that BILL *is correct: this moon is a fake. She is stumped.* SUSANNAH *holds her cheeks in her hands.*

SUSANNAH: Wow.

He climbs down, straightens out his clothing, and comes downstage to her. He hands her a letter. Pause. She opens and reads it.

MR WILLIAM HARD: It's a fake. A duplicate. A mere replica.

She looks at him hard.

SUSANNAH: What happened to the moon? The real moon,
   I mean.

MR WILLIAM HARD: The real moon is dying.

Thirty-second pause.

SUSANNAH: Oh.

He leans close to her.

MR WILLIAM HARD: I've come from the Land of Evening, here,
   with the moon in my suitcase. The moon
   has nearly expired, and I am—with
   your assistance—going to bury the moon
   on the spot. According to an ancient rule…

She looks back at the letter. She reads. Pause.

SUSANNAH: What's a "tarboosh"?

*He hands her one. She takes it. He puts on his own. Pause.
She puts on hers.*

Tell me more. This is fascinating.

He begins to dig the grave. She holds the flashlight for him.

MR WILLIAM HARD: In the time of Zed and Zeph people were
   stupid and slow, but because of gradualness
   they were graceful.

SUSANNAH: Wait a minute. You opened your suitcase
   for me. Before. I saw what was inside. I'm
   not so stupid. What was inside was clothes.

MR WILLIAM HARD: False-bottom.

She looks at him hard.

SUSANNAH: Show me.

He looks down, thinking. He looks up.

MR WILLIAM HARD: When the time comes.

SUSANNAH: Show me now.

Fifteen-second pause.

MR WILLIAM HARD: All right.

He opens, very slowly, the suitcase, only a sliver. A terrible light bathes them both for thirty seconds. We hear the ancient melody of YU KO. He closes the suitcase. Both stand.

SUSANNAH: Wow.

MR WILLIAM HARD: Ultimately, Susannah, to doubt is to do
    a very bad thing with your head.

SUSANNAH: Maybe we're all duplicates.

    He takes up the shovel and starts to work.

MR WILLIAM HARD: The philosopher Plato thought so.

    He digs for some time.

SUSANNAH: My theory is that all people give off
    a glow. A strange, barely perceptible
    glow. This glow is the furnace of life.
    Over the ages the glow will slowly
    become brighter and brighter, and more
    apparent. Then one day each one of us
    will slip out of our mortal human body,
    and drop it to the ground, like an old
    sock or glove. Like a garment we no
    longer need. The world will be called
    "Ding-Dong" and people will glide high
    above the surface of the earth, like the
    angels once did, walking light on the
    spongy pathways of aire!

MR WILLIAM HARD: Hallelujah!

SUSANNAH: Like box-kites with a brain. Or like
    big, ectoplasmic bats. Fabulous bats.

    He goes back to work. Pause.

    In some people the glow is more pronounced
    than others. In some the glow is very dim.

MR WILLIAM HARD: Devil raise a hump upon this hard earth.

SUSANNAH: I can see the glow on my skin, sometimes,
    on my belly. On my cheeks and arms.

MR WILLIAM HARD: The glow is also a gradual process.

SUSANNAH: People who are dim are disgusting. They
    crouch low and huddle in the square boxes
    of their shabby lives. I think people
    who have no glow ought to be exterminated.
    Shot in the streets and be left to molder
    there, or be cast down with John Moldy,
    in his basement.

MR WILLIAM HARD: —

SUSANNAH: —

    Pause. Sky becomes bright for a moment. Then it darkens again. Pause.

    …wow…

MR WILLIAM HARD: The Great Vegetarian thought so too.

SUSANNAH: Who was the Great Vegetarian?

MR WILLIAM HARD: Adolf Hitler.

SUSANNAH: But he was a very bad man.

MR WILLIAM HARD: Yes, he was, Susannah.
  He digs very hard.

SUSANNAH: They are to be shot. Strangled. Stabbed
  with the long, silvery spindle of a dagger.
  In the heart.

MR WILLIAM HARD: Only what is slow can absorb all
  the poison we emit. Poisons of the
  head. Poisons of the heart. In a
  million years none of this will matter.

SUSANNAH: I don't care about what the world
  will be like then. Do you need some help?

MR WILLIAM HARD: I need you to hold that flashlight.

SUSANNAH: What's that thing down there?
  Pause.

SUSANNAH: Guess the moon doesn't need a coffin.
  Pause.

SUSANNAH: So...what do you think of my theory?

MR WILLIAM HARD: We are all sleepwalkers in a boiling
  furnace of flame.
  She shivers.

SUSANNAH: It's getting chilly. Will you be done soon?

MR WILLIAM HARD: Okay, we're ready. I need your help.

SUSANNAH: What do I do?
  He opens the suitcase. Light!

MR WILLIAM HARD: It's very heavy. And I've brought a towel.
  Hold it through the towel. Otherwise
  you'll burn your hands. Even in its
  current state the moon is very hot.
  She touches it gingerly.

SUSANNAH: Wow, it sure is.

MR WILLIAM HARD: Ready?

SUSANNAH: Well, okay.
  Together they lift the moon, wrapped in a bath towel. It is about the size of a
  basketball. Even wrapped the moon glows with odd intensity.
  God, it's heavy.

MR WILLIAM HARD: It is heavy. Lead, nickel and antimony mainly.
  And tantalum...
  Slowly they lower the moon into the grave. It takes some doing owing to the
  spherical shape of the moon, and the need to keep it covered.
  Easy, easy...

SUSANNAH: Have you got it?

MR WILLIAM HARD: Okay, you can let go.

SUSANNAH: …goosewillies me…

Pause. He secures the moon where he wants it to rest.

MR WILLIAM HARD: Good. We're almost done.

Both stand up and straighten out their arms and legs. They stretch.

SUSANNAH: Do you…have you ever done things like this…before?

He looks at her.

MR WILLIAM HARD: —

SUSANNAH: —

MR WILLIAM HARD: Now just a little shoveling and we'll be done.

She turns to face out, as the MAN shovels dirt in the grave. Slowly she raises her arms, and pronounces a mock benediction in a quiet voice.

SUSANNAH: Let the Parsley rejoice with Dinoflagellate;
For the dip-needle knows nothing of the Crow.
Let the Sultanate of Swish be florous with Alphabets;
For Amoebic Dysentery is awash with Amatol.
Let Comparison Shop walk with Depressor Nerve;
For Paragoge is wink and wingnut with Kemal Ataturk.
Let Borax be titanous with tidbit and tizzy;
For all the names of Shenango are gradual.
Let Forenoon worship with Calamity Jane;
For the Quizmaster quits in the name of Sheboygan.
Let Spun Glass and Sprocket speak with Leland Stanford;
For Grandma Moody officiates in panic and panfry.
Let Pangloss worship with the Erie Canal;
For Panic Button panhandles the Photogravure.

He's done now as the blackout begins. Both look down at the grave with respect. They both cross themselves. He lays the shovel on the grave. She holds her hand over her heart.

MR WILLIAM HARD: Now we all, each and every one, are orphans.

Pause.

SUSANNAH: May Misrule and Hepcat be conjugate….with…
The Hyacinth Macaw. Ipso Facto. La. La la.

Black out.

END OF PLAY

Kier Peters

The Confirmation

I felt that I had to tell the truth.
—PROFESSOR ANITA HILL

I have never, in all my life, felt such hurt,
such pain, such agony.
—HIS HONORABLE JUDGE
CLARENCE THOMAS

•

The Confirmation premiered at the Vineyard Theatre, New York City, on April 6 and 7, 1994, as part of the T.W.E.E.D. New Works Festival, with the following cast:

MOTHER	Linda Hill
GRANDMA	Nora Dunfee
SISTER	Lia Chang
CARMELITA	Cate Woodruff
BLANCHE	Kirk Jackson
HARRY	Joey L. Golden
Director	Mollie O'Mara
Lighting	Richard Schaefer
Set Design	Matt Housman
Costumes	Carol Brys
Original Music	Tom Burnett

ACT I

In the middle of a yard stands a woman with a large straw garden hat. She points at GRANDMA, *sitting on a couch.*

MOTHER: Now sit down there very nicely and be out of the way!

GRANDMA: What?

MOTHER: Sit down very nice.

GRANDMA: [*looking about*] Where is the house?

MOTHER: [*busying herself*] We will build one around you and me one day.

GRANDMA: Who?

MOTHER: The man whom I may marry then.

GRANDMA: Who?

MOTHER: You'll know him when he comes.

GRANDMA: I will?

MOTHER: And everyone will be happy in the end. [*Taking a pie out of the stove.*] As soon as it cools down I'll cut you a slice.

GRANDMA: What kind?

MOTHER: You know I've forgotten what I put in.

GRANDMA: Because I don't like cherry or apricot.

MOTHER: I don't think it's cherry and I doubt I've made apricot since it's something I've never done.

GRANDMA: And I don't like apple nor blueberry nor rhubarb mince banana raisin or chocolate.

MOTHER: Gee I don't know what to say it might be one of those it just might.

GRANDMA: Nor lemon nor lime nor peach. I completely hate peach.

MOTHER: Well Grandma what do you like?

GRANDMA: [*Screwing up her face*] I forgot.

MOTHER: [*Putting down the pie*] I'm not going to serve it then besides it wasn't really a pie. It's a cake.

GRANDMA: I like cake.

MOTHER: I guess you would with almost ninety candles to blow out.

GRANDMA: Is it my birthday?

MOTHER: You know I don't remember. When were you born?

GRANDMA: Before the War.

MOTHER: Which war?

GRANDMA: Have there been more?

MOTHER: Plenty yes. You must recall Herman your husband died in the first and his brother's son in the second one. And his son Mark died in Korea and his son Dick died in Laos.

GRANDMA: What was he doing in Laos?

MOTHER: Now that's something we never found out.

GRANDMA: Where is it?

MOTHER: One of those jungles I think.

GRANDMA: Who'd have thought.

MOTHER: Who would? I guess the military might. Their job is to think of strange places for men to die in.

GRANDMA: What was your name again?

MOTHER: Now Grandma sit down very nice.

GRANDMA: I need to stand. I need to walk about.

MOTHER: O dear that you can't.

GRANDMA: Can't what?

MOTHER: Remember you fell and broke your whole hip one night.

GRANDMA: Never did such a thing in my life.

MOTHER: Oh but you did! And the doctors said it was doubtful you would ever walk again they did.

GRANDMA: [*Attempting to rise*] Pooh on them!

MOTHER: Now Grandma what a way to talk!

GRANDMA: [*Sitting down again*] I'll talk as I walk and I'll do both just as I please thank you.

MOTHER: You've no one to thank but yourself. Marching around in the dark of night.

GRANDMA: I had to pee.

MOTHER: If this goes on I'm going to have to put a patch of tape across your mouth. Besides they found you by your own front door.

GRANDMA: I wanted to whizz.

MOTHER: [*Skeptical*] Now you're just being difficult. You've had plumbing for forty years or more.

GRANDMA: Can't get used to it.

MOTHER: Well you don't have to worry anymore at least not until I meet Mr. Right.

GRANDMA: At your age you're not going meet anyone.

MOTHER: Now Grandma that hurts where it hurts plunk through the heart. And remember you met Mr. Billingslea at 53?

GRANDMA: Who?

MOTHER: Your third husband Mr. Billingslea.

GRANDMA: He was Black.

MOTHER: [*laughing*] Now what made you think that? He was white as that lily plant with hands just as pale to match.

GRANDMA: He was a nigra.

MOTHER: Well if that was so he certainly fooled me and everyone else and you if I know you as I do who is terrified of colored men Islamic women and Indian children who talk too fast wouldn't have been marrying one of them!

GRANDMA: I'll marry anyone I like.

MOTHER: And I will too as long as he builds us a house around all the comforts we've collected for ourselves.

GRANDMA: The sun's too bright.

MOTHER: It's nearly noon Grandma love. Here take out your umbrella [*putting an umbrella into her mother's hand*].

GRANDMA: I don't remember this.

MOTHER: Well you don't remember anything anymore much it's true.

GRANDMA: I remember I don't like you.

MOTHER: You never did. Always talking Harry Harry Harry even when we were growing up never a word of praise to Mary or me or poor poor Blanche.

GRANDMA: I liked Blanche I bet I did cause I like her name still today yet.

MOTHER: Well you certainly had a funny way of showing it keeping her locked away from all the rest.

GRANDMA: Who?

MOTHER: Poor Poor Blanche.

GRANDMA: I locked her away from...you and Mary and Harry and everyone else you say I knew? I wanted her to grow up better.

MOTHER: But to teach her nothing but Norwegian really! She couldn't even communicate with us.

GRANDMA: [*smiling*] I did that?

MOTHER: Yes you certainly did you wouldn't let her communicate with anyone else.

GRANDMA: And did she learn the formal tense?

MOTHER: How would I know not knowing a single word of it. I just remember poor poor Blanche whom they took away one day when they found out what you did.

GRANDMA: Who? Who found out?

MOTHER: The authorities. The school board and the social worker and then that dreadful nurse.

GRANDMA: Pooh on the nurse!

MOTHER: Well there I agree taking away Mary who was as perfectly normal as you and me all because Blanche was treated so specially.

GRANDMA: What happened to that Mary then?

MOTHER: Now Grandma you can't pretend to have forgotten that!

GRANDMA: I remember I guess she ran away and had to get married and became a nymphomaniac.

MOTHER: What an imagination you've got!

GRANDMA: That's what I recall.

MOTHER: She was taken by a Catholic family who converted her quick.

GRANDMA: Converted her from what?

MOTHER: From Protestantism surely! At least that's what I always thought! We went to Public High.

GRANDMA: Was there a Catholic one?

MOTHER: Maybe not.

GRANDMA: So?

MOTHER: Well anyway Mary became one and then became a nun.

GRANDMA: I was a nun.

MOTHER: What?

GRANDMA: Before I got married.

MOTHER: Now Grandma you know you were not!

GRANDMA: Was so! I remember that much!

MOTHER: All right if you say so but I was brought up Protestant.

GRANDMA: By who?

MOTHER: By Daddy and you.

GRANDMA: Now I remember Harry and I think I can remember Blanche and I can even once in while imagine I had a daughter Mary but I certainly don't remember a thing about Protestantism!

MOTHER: Are you doubting my word I've had just about enough. [*Calling*] Mary come out! Come out!

> SISTER *comes out from behind tree dressed in plain simple frock.*

GRANDMA: Who are you?

SISTER: I'm Sister Bliss momma you remember me as Marie.

GRANDMA: If you've become a nun why aren't you dressed as one?

SISTER: We don't have habits anymore.

GRANDMA: Why not?

SISTER: It interferes with our calling.

GRANDMA: What is that?

SISTER: I run a clinic for wayward boys.

GRANDMA: [*Calling her over to her*] Do you know Sister Carmelita?

SISTER: [*Surprised*] Yes.

GRANDMA: [*Clapping her hands*] See Miss Smarty she was Mother Superior when I was a nun.

SISTER: O I don't think this Carmelita could have known you ever. She's fairly young.

GRANDMA: It's the outfit hides the gray hair and the varicose veins and such. A sweet face wouldn't you say?

SISTER: Well yes but....

GRANDMA: Then it's the same one! Sister Carmelita how she used to get on my case. She was the cause of my giving up.

SISTER: Isn't that strange she...this Carmelita is in part the reason why I'm leaving the order.

GRANDMA: A nasty old bitch!

MOTHER: Grandma now don't say that!

GRANDMA: Just ask Mary.

> SISTER *retreats to the swing.*

MOTHER: [*Sitting down on the couch to whisper*] Your Carmelita is not her Carmelita and your Harry is not my Harry and I'm here even if you don't think I am or ever was.

GRANDMA: [*Shouting*] What are you talking about?

MOTHER: You're going to hurt her feelings if you don't quiet yourself.

GRANDMA: Sister you come right over and shut this woman up.

> SISTER *does not respond.*

MOTHER: You're hurting her feelings and I won't let you! You just don't understand her Carmelita is not a ninety-nine year old dictator in some old convent you dreamed up she is her friend and I won't have you calling her a bitch in my house.

GRANDMA: What house?

MOTHER: [*Clapping her hands*] Come out come out!

> *Another woman,* SISTER CARMELITA, *comes out from behind a tree.* SISTER *joins her in a brief embrace.*

MOTHER: Now do you see?

GRANDMA: See what?

MOTHER: Grandma they're lovers.

GRANDMA: What's that supposed to mean?

MOTHER: [*whispering*] Lesbians.

GRANDMA: Where? [SISTER *and* CARMELITA *come forward.*]

SISTER: Here we are Mother.

GRANDMA: Who?

SISTER: Carmelita and me.

GRANDMA: [*Studying* CARMELITA *carefully*] Spittin' image!

CARMELITA: [*Smiling*] Of whom?

GRANDMA: Harry of course!

CARMELITA: [*Turning to the others*] Who's Harry?

MOTHER: Now Grandma!

SISTER: Mother!

GRANDMA: Yep. Just like him!

CARMELITA: [*Laughingly*] Who is he?

MOTHER: O nobody really at all.

SISTER: Well not exactly nobody.

MOTHER: No not nobody just somebody you don't need to worry about.

CARMELITA: But if I look like him....

GRANDMA: You sure do!

SISTER: I don't see the slightest of likenesses.

GRANDMA: You lie!

MOTHER: Grandma shush. [*Stomping her foot.*] Shame on you shush!

CARMELITA: Come on now tell me who's Harry?

GRANDMA: Harry was my....

MOTHER: [*Stomping her foot*] Grandma!

GRANDMA: Dog.

SISTER and MOTHER: [*aghast*] Dog!

CARMELITA: I look like a dog?

MOTHER: O no this was a very special dog.

CARMELITA: [*Amused but not completely*] O really?

SISTER: A Lhasa.

CARMELITA and GRANDMA: [*together*] A what?

MOTHER: Harry was a terrier.

GRANDMA: A terrier! I hate little high-strung animals of any kind whatsoever.

SISTER: Well not a terrier exactly.

GRANDMA: I pray the Lord not!

CARMELITA: [*with an uneasy laugh*] Well I don't think I look like either!

SISTER: She loved that animal so she sees certain features in almost anyone she meets.

MOTHER: In everyone she likes at least.

SISTER: Yes in everyone she likes.

GRANDMA: [*Calling to* CARMELITA] Come here dear sit by me. [*In a stage whisper*] Now tell me really truthfully did they or did they not not hire you directly off the street?

CARMELITA: [*Disconcertedly*] O no I've known Sister Bliss here—well it seems like all my life and she has often spoken of you and Betty.

GRANDMA: Betty? Who's Betty?

CARMELITA: [*Pointing at* MOTHER] She's Betty isn't she?

GRANDMA: Betty is not a name I'd give even to a pig.

CARMELITA: Well I think it's Betty. The name I mean.

GRANDMA: Couldn't be. Harriet maybe Caroline Margaret—after my mother—but Betty never Betty!

CARMELITA: [*Looking around confusedly*] Sister! [*Signaling Mary, Sister Bliss*] What's your sister's name. I've forgotten so it seems.

SISTER: Never you mind it doesn't matter really.

CARMELITA: But I thought her name was what it isn't evidently.

SISTER: To be honest I don't even recall.

CARMELITA: You don't know your own sister's name?

SISTER: Sometimes I don't even remember mine.

CARMELITA: That's different you have a different name from the one with which you were borne and bred. But Betty or whoever she is has had the same name her entire life to date. How could you forget?

SISTER: You remember Mother?

GRANDMA: I think it's Blanche she said something about Blanche.

SISTER: Blanche dear could you bring us some tea and honey cakes please?

MOTHER: Honey cakes?

SISTER: You know those little golden cakes you used to bake when you came home from school that summer.

MOTHER: [*Giving herself up to memory*] That summer! Leave you to remember it.

GRANDMA: What? What summer?

    The two sisters giggle.

CARMELITA: Well who's Betty then?

    Everyone looks completely puzzled.

CARMELITA: I must have got everything confused with something else.

MOTHER: How I remember that summer you and your John Box.

CARMELITA: [*to* SISTER] You never told me about anyone named John.

SISTER: Blanche you got it all confused you were the one engaged to John.

GRANDMA: I remember John. A tall boy with long long frozen fingers and a dick that could gag a gull.

MOTHER: Grandma!

SISTER: Mother!

CARMELITA: Really! Blanche you tell me right out were you engaged to John?

MOTHER: [*Turning to* CARMELITA] My name is not Blanche. Blanche was Sister's poor sister who had to go live in asylum.

CARMELITA: [*Pointing to* SISTER] But she called you Blanche.

MOTHER: O that's an old saw with us she always called me just anything that came into her head. But you not being family should use my Christian name instead.

CARMELITA: What is your name?

MOTHER: Well everybody knows that! I'm known round here clear through the country. Honey where have you been?

CARMELITA: I was at the convent.

MOTHER: [*Looking at* GRANDMA] Well it appears we got connections even to that—besides Sister here. Didn't they teach you anything?

CARMELITA: [*utterly confused*] They certainly taught me a lot about all sorts of things. About a life given over to Christ about the relationships between silence and sinlessness between celibacy and sainthood but I don't think they ever uttered your name. Sister Bliss used to call you Betty.

MOTHER: See what I mean? Any name that comes into her head.

CARMELITA: [*Giving up*] Do you mind if I call you...Mother?

MOTHER: Now isn't that a coincidence.

CARMELITA: Mother. I like that Mother. It sort of reminds me of what a home is supposed to be like.

SISTER: Carmelita come over here!

MOTHER: [*To* CARMELITA] Anyway it wasn't me who sat on John Box's lap.

SISTER: [*To* CARMELITA] Don't believe a thing she says!

CARMELITA: And why shouldn't I?

GRANDMA: My dear at my age you learn not to believe in anything.

CARMELITA: [*Almost in tears*] You're all daft!

SISTER: Carmelita come here!

CARMELITA: No none of you make sense. Is Harry a dog? [*No answer*] Are these your daughters? [*No answer*] Is your name Betty or Blanche? [*No answer*] [*To* SISTER] Did you have sex with John Box? [*No answer*] I want answers.

SISTER: [*Coming over to her and putting an arm about*] There aren't any answers in families don't you know that?

CARMELITA: I never had a mother or father or sister or brother.

SISTER: Well then you just gotta trust. Families don't make sense they just talk. And talk.

GRANDMA: Didn't I hear someone ask for honey cakes well where are they at?

MOTHER: I'll go bake some. I'll be back. [*She exits.*]

GRANDMA: You two really lesbians?

> *They look at her and laugh.*

BLACKOUT

ACT II

Tea has been served. And cakes. MOTHER, SISTER, *and* CARMELITA *face* GRANDMA.

MOTHER: I guess by now you've guessed my little secret Grandma?

GRANDMA: You going to leave me?

MOTHER: Now don't be silly what does it look like we're having here?

GRANDMA: Where?

MOTHER: Right here in front of you?

GRANDMA: [*Pondering it*] A conspiracy! You going to kill me?

MOTHER: O you've ruined it here we are all full of love and joy and you got nothing on your mind but suspicion and hate.

SISTER: She's just joking aren't you Mother?

MOTHER: I most certainly am not!

SISTER: I meant her! She's just trying to get a rise.

GRANDMA: Now I remember you!

SISTER: [*Surprised*] What?

GRANDMA: You're the one who always says I am saying when I'm saying anything that it is anything but what I've said. [*She tries to rise.*]

MOTHER: Now Grandma sit still and be nice!

GRANDMA: Not as long as she's here!

SISTER: [*Going over to her*] Now now mother I didn't mean anything but we're not trying to kill you surely you know we're here out of love.

GRANDMA: I like men!

SISTER: Well of course you do.

GRANDMA: [*Relaxing some*] And I don't like women kissing me or giving me a hug.

SISTER: [*Releasing her*] I won't bother you then.

MOTHER: Now Grandma behave can't you see what we're trying to do for you?

CARMELITA: She's just a bit confused.

GRANDMA: I am not! You Sister Carmelita are an evil person and I won't let you beat me with a stick.

CARMELITA: [*Extremely troubled*] O no you got everything wrong. I am not evil I'm a loving person who would never hurt you ever.

    SISTER *comes over to* CARMELITA *and puts her arms around her neck.*

MOTHER: Yes yes she gets confused.

GRANDMA: I have never been confused and I intend to stay so. You can deny everything but I know what is and what is not!

MOTHER: Now shame on you old lady you've got her in tears almost. Can't you see

1134

we're trying so hard just to please you here Sister Bliss comes clear down from the city with her dear friend and you treat her like some kind of Satan-loving scum. Either you behave yourself or I'll send you straight back to your lonely old house.

GRANDMA: Fine with me. I've had enough of this sun.

MOTHER: O no you don't we've come here to celebrate and we're going to yes.

GRANDMA: Celebrate what?

MOTHER: That's what I've been asking myself. Think think as hard as you can.

GRANDMA: That's one of the blessings of being one hundred and thirty-seven years old you no longer have to think about anything or anyone.

CARMELITA: [*Recovering and unable to control herself*] Are you that old!

GRANDMA: I am one hundred and thirty and seven yep!

CARMELITA: [*Awed*] That must be some kind of record.

MOTHER: Now you don't believe a word she says.

CARMELITA: How old are you really granny?

GRANDMA: Come here! [CARMELITA *goes over to her.*] Bend nearer dear. [CARMELITA *bends*] How do lesbians fuck?

MOTHER: Grandma!

SISTER: Mother!

CARMELITA: I don't mind really she's just curious. [*Turning back to the old woman*] We have fingers we have tools and we have tongues.

GRANDMA: Yes you're honest Harry's daughter.

CARMELITA: When did your dog die?

GRANDMA: What dog?

MOTHER: Well well I have a surprise a big surprise for all you and Grandma most! Blanche! Blanche!

     A stage type of the Yiddish-theatre, BLANCHE *comes out of the house.*

SISTER: Here comes Blanche!

CARMELITA: Who's Blanche?

BLANCHE: [*In Yiddish*] Hello hello everyone!

MOTHER: [*To* CARMELITA] She speaks Norwegian.

BLANCHE: [*In Yiddish, the only language she speaks*] I nearly fainted waiting for days and days in there for you to call me out.

SISTER: Blanche do you remember me?

BLANCHE: [*To* SISTER] You must be my mother. [*Shaking her hand*]

SISTER: [*A little confused*] Nice to see you again too.

MOTHER: [*Taking* BLANCHE *by the arm*] Here's your mother Blanche. Remember?

BLANCHE: [*Taken aback*] So you're the little mother who made me what I am!

GRANDMA: How'd you learn to speak Norwegian?

MOTHER: You taught her Grandma recollect? You said that seeing how you failed with Harry Sister and me you'd teach Blanche another tongue.

GRANDMA: [*Delighted*] I said that?

SISTER: You sure did and you wouldn't let her talk with us or anyone. Poor Blanche.

MOTHER: [*Stroking* BLANCHE'S *arm*] Poor poor Blanche.

BLANCHE: [*Bristling*] I don't like to be touched. [*She goes over to the table and sits apart.*]

CARMELITA: It doesn't sound Norwegian.

SISTER: What?

CARMELITA: It doesn't sound like it.

SISTER: Like what?

MOTHER: It's a dialect. From Bergen that's in the West.

SISTER: Mother's from Bergen.

GRANDMA: Who says?

MOTHER: Well Grandma you've always said.

GRANDMA: Pooh and poppycock.

CARMELITA: Well I had a Norwegian friend. My Norwegian was from Tønsberg and I don't know where that's at.

SISTER: In Sweden almost.

MOTHER: In Denmark nearly.

CARMELITA: O well that explains a lot.

BLANCHE: [*Rising*] Aren't you going to serve me anything?

MOTHER: See she understands Denmark. Tell us Blanche where do you live now?

BLANCHE [*Reaching for a cake*] Honey cake!

MOTHER: That means Lido Beach Long Island.

SISTER: How ever did you find her clear over there where none of us would ever go or have ever been?

MOTHER: [*Pointing at her nose*] Instinct! Hound dog instinct.

GRANDMA: And my letters.

MOTHER: [*To the others*] They're all in Norwegian but I got the postmark offen one. And here she is—voila!

BLANCHE: [*Gorging herself*] Wine?

SISTER: [*Pouring her coffee*] [*In disgust* BLANCHE *puckers her lips.*] [*To* CARMELITA] See that means coffee we all had to learn a little Norwegian to get through the years.

CARMELITA: Hvördan stor det till? [*No response*] Hvördan stor det till?

SISTER: You got something in your throat?

CARMELITA: I was speaking what my friend says when she asked how I was. [*To* BLANCHE] Is that Danish or Norwegian and did I say it right?

BLANCHE: Yes this is a good party where's the lox?

MOTHER: In Norwegian lox means salmon.

GRANDMA: I remember one time when Harry was O I'd say three four five he had hair down to his neck golden honey and as thick I used to curl it with hot bricks and spit he caught a fish.

MOTHER: Grandma everybody knows that Harry's hair was black as dark and evil as his thousands of sins.

CARMELITA: Then Harry isn't a dog?

Everyone including BLANCHE *stops.*

SISTER: No my love Harry was dog in human skin.

CARMELITA: [*Sitting down by* GRANDMA] Tell me all about him.

BLANCHE: [*Still in Yiddish*] Harry was a murderer!

GRANDMA: Harry was as sweet as sin.

MOTHER: Harry was our brother the man who everybody loved.

SISTER: Harry was a saint really.

CARMELITA: I think not everything is being said. [*Rising*] I think you are hiding a great deal from me and each other and yourselves.

GRANDMA: The spittin' image.

CARMELITA: I think none of you really have been honest with me or each other. I might very much like Harry her son I might be the spitting image really I might and I don't look like a dog or even a cat. [*To* GRANDMA] And you know as well as I do that we came together here Sister, Mother, Blanche and me to celebrate your eighty-eighth birthday or if you want your one hundred thirty and seventh one.

MOTHER: Now you stop it hear I certainly won't let anyone throw a fit.

SISTER: Carmelita shame on you shame!

CARMELITA: You're just a bunch of liars that's what you are and I'm not afraid of any of you one little bit.

GRANDMA: So that's it that's why you came and got me waiting out here in the sun. You think I'm going to celebrate I am not going to celebrate anything with anyone!

MOTHER: Now Grandma just shut up! Carmelita you come apologize to us.

CARMELITA: I will not!

SISTER: Carmelita shame!

CARMELITA: [*Turning on* SISTER] And I won't be intimidated by your likes!

SISTER: Well really!

GRANDMA: [*Screaming*] Fight fight!

MOTHER: Grandma do be quiet! [*To* CARMELITA] In a way you're right we haven't been completely honest with you. You see Harry was a sweetheart.

SISTER: Don't!

MOTHER: But we don't like to talk about him much.

CARMELITA: [*weakening*] Did he die young?

MOTHER: O very!

SISTER: O yes such a painful death.

GRANDMA: Doesn't seem so painful to me in retrospect.

MOTHER: Now Grandma sit down and be nice.

GRANDMA: Wish someone would give me a little too much gas.

SISTER: Now shut!

CARMELITA: He died of asphyxiation?

MOTHER and SISTER: [*surprised and pleased both*] Yes. Yes.

CARMELITA: O that must have been so horrible now I understand.

BLANCHE: [*Finding the tea empty*] Will you make some more tea?

GRANDMA: Understand what?

MOTHER: [*Coming over to* BLANCHE *and putting her arms about*] Yes Blanche we all loved Harry didn't we?

BLANCHE: [*Handing her the teapot*] And more cakes please!

CARMELITA: [*Going over to* SISTER *and putting her arms about*] I'm sorry I couldn't have known really could I have?

SISTER: No no you couldn't.

CARMELITA: Did he really look like me?

SISTER: [*Looking* CARMELITA *over carefully*] No not really not in the least.

FADEOUT

ACT III

When the lights come up again it is later in the afternoon and everything is golden bathed. At the center of the table a cake has been placed from which several slices have been cut.

SISTER: [*coming out of the house*] Blanche is taking a nap.

GRANDMA: Not on my bed!

SISTER: On the couch.

GRANDMA: Is she going back tonight?

MOTHER: No Grandma she's staying with me.

CARMELITA: [*Confused*] Isn't that your house?

SISTER: Well.....

MOTHER: [*For a moment nonplussed.*] No it truly isn't no. As you might have got a whiff of me and Grandma don't get on one little bit. So she lives in there [*pointing at the house*] and I here.

CARMELITA: Where?

MOTHER: Right there where you got your feet and where I stand and stood over there and over there and over there. All about.

CARMELITA: So that's why you have a couch....

MOTHER: Right in the middle of the grass! And a cupboard and a stove and a table in the yard. And some chairs. The couch pulls out at night.

CARMELITA: But doesn't it get cold?

MOTHER: I got blankets more than most and when it rains—which it hardly does ever—I cover everything with plastic and pitch a tent or go visiting on my friends.

CARMELITA: It's a little like being a homeless person isn't it?

MOTHER: But I have a house. [*Winking*] Just waiting.

GRANDMA: I'm not going to die until she dies.

MOTHER: And I won't die ever. She's tried....

SISTER: It's what keeps them both living.

MOTHER: To wear me down to wear me out. But I'm tough as leather.

CARMELITA: Couldn't you two just bury the hatchet?

SISTER: Careful Carmelita stay out!

CARMELITA: But it all seems so sad it truly does.

MOTHER: It is certainly it is.

CARMELITA: [*To* GRANDMA] Why ever do you pretend not to love your daughter who I know you really do surely since I see it in your eyes when you're just being stubborn.

GRANDMA: You read too much!

CARMELITA: That old house has so many rooms couldn't she come live in a couple?

MOTHER: O you don't comprehend! Grandma doesn't mind if I move back it's me who left and who will never sleep under the same roof with her another night.

    GRANDMA *laughs.*

CARMELITA: What on earth could have made you say that?

    Everyone momentarily grows tense.

MOTHER: I love the out-of-doors!

CARMELITA: [*Crestfallen*] O!

MOTHER: Come have another piece of cake.

SISTER: I've got some wine! [*She brings a bottle out from a nearby sack.*]

GRANDMA: Well I'd like some!

MOTHER: And I!

CARMELITA: Just a little.

BLANCHE: [*From the house, in Yiddish*] Did I hear a cork?

SISTER: A toast to mother on the eighty-eighth year of her birth. A toast to my sister who planned this surprise and a toast to my little sweet lover!

    BLANCHE *enters and observes them mid-toast.*

BLANCHE: [*Toasting*] L'Chaim!

    Everyone toasts and everyone laughs and everyone is joyful for another moment. Silence settles for an instant and crickets start and the sun dims a pale yellow.

MOTHER: Now who's going to help me with the dishes?

SISTER: I am.

CARMELITA: And I'll keep Grandma company.

    BLANCHE *pours herself another.*

GRANDMA: Come here my dear sit with me.

    CARMELITA *comes to her. In the distance the sisters giggle once again.*

GRANDMA: Now tell me truly do I look healthy?

CARMELITA: [*Looking her over quickly*] Of course you do.

GRANDMA: Come on you've got Harry's honesty.

CARMELITA: [*Looking her over completely*] Yes. Amazingly so. For a woman of one hundred thirty seven!

    They laugh together.

GRANDMA: Then why are these women hanging about?

CARMELITA: [*Thinking*] I think they thought it'd be a nice surprise. I think they love you even though they're hurt you don't show that you even know who they are or admit even a little bit that you're their mother.

GRANDMA: Who said I was?

CARMELITA: They did!

GRANDMA: Well I'm not. I'm just their aunt.

CARMELITA: [*Amazed*] Their aunt?

GRANDMA: Their mother died with the baby Blanche. I couldn't afford to keep them all so I put Blanche in Hebrew School and Mary in a Catholic one and what's her name (she changed it every month) in the Public School System where she had begun.

CARMELITA: Sister has never said anything of this.

GRANDMA: She couldn't accept her mother's death and pretends to this day yet that Emily my sister never put foot on this planet. And what's her name was furious with Emily for dying and furious with me for not.

CARMELITA: Well this is really a shock!

GRANDMA: Don't tell them I told you but it's true so I don't take at all to this malarkey.

CARMELITA: Well I have to admit even though it was forbade I brought you a little gift. [*She produces a small package.*]

GRANDMA: [*Taking it.*] You brought something for me?

CARMELITA: Nothing very much.

GRANDMA: But it's something isn't it?

CARMELITA: A little something I thought you just might like. Go ahead but don't let Sister see or she'll scold.

GRANDMA: [*Unwrapping it*] Let her! [*She pulls out a porcelain elephant.*] An elephant. A porcelain elephant. That's something I never thought I'd get. You know I'm a Democrat?

CARMELITA: O dear I didn't think of that I just liked the look of it and then I thought what a wonderful animal it is and this reminded me please excuse this of how old you are when I remembered how old elephants get. I heard of one who lived to a hundred and thirty and seven or even longer I don't recall the actual number of years before it passed.

GRANDMA: Well it's a wonderful gift even if I am a Democrat to the bone a wonderful gift. I like elephants really and have resented always the way Republicans use them. I don't like donkeys much. Do you like donkeys?

CARMELITA: No but I like cats. I like dogs. And dolphins. But I like elephants more I think than I like monkeys which are so very much like us.

GRANDMA: [*Looking around suspiciously.* BLANCHE *is blissfully involved with her bottle.*] Now I have a surprise for you.

CARMELITA: You do?

> GRANDMA *claps her hands. As she does so her head falls to her shoulders and she is as suddenly asleep.*

CARMELITA: [*Shaking her*] Grandma! [*Gently shaking the old woman*] Grandma? [CARMELITA *takes a blanket folded out of the corner of the couch and puts it around the old woman then sits for a moment alert of the crickets, the sound of which has gradually risen during the previous discussions.*]

> *From the other side of the yard* MOTHER *and* SISTER *laugh.*

> *Suddenly* CARMELITA *senses a presence near her. She looks up to discover a man standing behind the couch in close range. She starts.*

HARRY: [*Coming forward*] I didn't mean to scare you.

CARMELITA: O how dare you sneak up on a person just like that and who are you too?

HARRY: I'm Harry.

CARMELITA: [*Almost falling off the couch. She stands.*] Harry!

HARRY: [*Quickly putting his hand across her mouth.*] Shhhhhsh. Shhhhhsh. You ready? [*He removes his hand.*]

CARMELITA: Harry?

HARRY: [*Quickly puts his hand over her mouth again.* BLANCHE *lifts her head and squints her eyes at him.*] Now you have to promise me truly promise to keep still or I'll just have to go away again. Do you promise?

      CARMELITA *shakes her head.* HARRY *releases his hand.* CARMELITA *backs away for a second looking him completely down and up.*

CARMELITA: You're a very handsome man.

HARRY: [*Bowing*] And you're a good looking woman.

CARMELITA: I wouldn't mind looking like you.

HARRY: You do. [*And indeed there is a strong resemblance.*]

CARMELITA: [*Backing a bit away*] I thought you were dead.

HARRY: Well in a way I am.

CARMELITA: In what way?

HARRY: To them. At least they want it to be.

CARMELITA: My they certainly do tell a pack of lies.

HARRY: You musn't judge! Everyone tells the truth they want.

CARMELITA: I can understand them wanting your Mother alive but why would they want you to die?

HARRY: But while our Mother lives I...am a ghost to most eyes.

CARMELITA: O but I thought your Mother died with Blanche!

HARRY: Who told you that?

CARMELITA: [*Pointing at* GRANDMA] She did! She told me everything.

HARRY: Haven't you noticed she gets all mixed up?

CARMELITA: O I have noticed yes. She called you a dog.

HARRY: That was intentional.

CARMELITA: She confused me with a mean Mother Superior she met in a convent.

HARRY: She's never even been in a church! But I've.

CARMELITA: In a church?

HARRY: In a convent.

CARMELITA: [*Embarrassed*] Were you a brother?

HARRY: Nope.

CARMELITA: A priest?

HARRY: Good heavens!

CARMELITA: [*Racking her brains.*] A bishop!?

HARRY: [*Laughs*] You can't explain everything away.

CARMELITA: [*On the verge of tears*] It's been a very confusing day.

HARRY: [*Coming over to her and putting his arms upon her shoulders.*] I know it has I know I know how it has been so difficult.

      CARMELITA *breaks down in tears to* HARRY's *caresses.*

HARRY: Cry away all you like.

CARMELITA: [*Recovering*] You are nice. All day I knew you would be although they didn't want me to know not only that you were handsome and truly might have my nose and eyes but even that you were living. Everyone agreed you died.

HARRY: [*Releasing her*] I did.

CARMELITA: Did what?

HARRY: Die. [BLANCHE *who has continued to squint her eyes at the couple stands and moves over to them.*]

BLANCHE: Harry. Is that you is that you Harry?

HARRY: [*In Yiddish*] Yes Blanche. Yes Blanche.

> BLANCHE *puts her arms out to hug him.* SISTER *and* MOTHER *head to the couch to see what all the ruckus is about and* GRANDMA *awakens.* BLANCHE *is seen in a frieze embracing thin air for* HARRY *is no longer there.*

MOTHER: What on earth?

SISTER: Blanche what's the matter honey?

BLANCHE: It was Harry Harry right here he was wasn't he?

> MOTHER *and* SISTER *to* CARMELITA.

MOTHER: Carmelita what happened what is she talking about?

SISTER: She's saying Harry she's speaking his name! Grandma please translate.

GRANDMA: I don't know Norwegian!

BLANCHE: Harry he was here.

SISTER: Carmelita tell us!

CARMELITA: [*Confused, circumspect*] I don't understand anything anymore I guess.

MOTHER: Well she's certainly agitated enough! [*Putting her arm about* BLANCHE *who pulls away.*] Come here sit down sit down Blanche.

CARMELITA: I think she drank a lot.

SISTER: [*Picking up the bottle*] I should certainly say so.

MOTHER: It must have been the DT's. [*She returns* BLANCHE *to the table*] You'll be all right Blanche you'll be all right.

SISTER: Well it's time we should go.

CARMELITA: Leave o no not yet o no. I've just met everyone and I want to get to know you better Mother and you Grandma and even Blanche....

GRANDMA: [*Winking at* CARMELITA] Come sit here beside me dear.

CARMELITA: We don't have to go home yet.

GRANDMA: No you're both of you young. Stay stay all day all night!

SISTER: I really do think we should go with all the boys waiting up.

CARMELITA: O Sister Rose will certainly put William and Paul and Ricky to sleep and Michael can stay up if he likes. And Arne will stay up anyway even if we did go home to tell him to turn out the light because he never does.

MOTHER: It seems odd it really does to think you have so many sons while I who married young have none.

SISTER: You have Mother.

MOTHER: It seems strange nonetheless.

CARMELITA: [*To* MOTHER] Do you have anything else to drink?

MOTHER: Well I can make some coffee.

GRANDMA: Sister in my dining room bureau back of the platters is a bottle of Schnapps.

MOTHER: Well I never!

GRANDMA: And won't. Go get it sister get it.

       SISTER *exits.*

GRANDMA: We shall drink to the present and to the past!

CARMELITA: Yes we shall drink to that!

MOTHER: [*Going over to* BLANCHE] Yes Blanche yes everything is going to be all right.

BLACKOUT

ACT IV

Candles have been lit lamps turned on and fireflies from time to time flit.
The sisters laugh.

MOTHER: I've got one I've got one! A farmer went into the city one day and asked a man on the street You got a daughter? Yes said the man I truly do. Can I spend the night with you the farmer asked. Don't be unreasonable said the man of course you can't. So he asked another man do you have a daughter and the man said no but I have a son. Can I sleep at your house tonight asked the farmer. There's a nice hotel just down the street the second city slicker said. Then we stopped a third man and the man said quick to the farmer You got a daughter No said the farmer You got a son No said the man Come with me we'll have some fun.

They laugh.

BLANCHE: I have a joke. Jake and Becky were a loving couple but they had one flaw. On each other they liked to play jokes. One day Becky hid from Jake and Jake who thought Becky was away hid from her and they waited and they waited and they waited for each to come. And since neither of them did they each of them sweared and got angry at the other one. Becky came out from behind the bookcase and Jake came out from behind the couch and they encountered one another right there by the front door. Where have you been Becky demanded. Where have you been insisted Jake. I've been right here. I've been right here. You're lying! You lie! And so forth and so on. Of course it ended in a divorce.

All are silent having not understood one word.

Then SISTER *begins to giggle and* MOTHER *joins in and* CARMELITA *cannot help herself.* BLANCHE *beams with success and laughs heartily along with them.*

SISTER: Can you imagine us tipsy just a little and having such a good time as this.

GRANDMA: I don't understand.

MOTHER: O you just sit back and be nice. We're having fun!

GRANDMA falls asleep while the sisters each take another drink. CARMELITA *quickly looks behind her and there* HARRY *stands. She gasps.*

SISTER: What's wrong.

CARMELITA: O just a little gas.

HARRY: Don't worry they can't see me unless they want.

MOTHER: [*to* SISTER] You tell us one.

SISTER: O dear I'm not very good at stories.

HARRY: [*to* CARMELITA] You tell one.

CARMELITA: What?

1145

SISTER: Well you know I'm not.

HARRY: Tell them a story.

CARMELITA: [*Pausing to catch her breath*] I have a story.

MOTHER: O good!

SISTER: You do?

CARMELITA: If I can remember it. [*She stops.*]

MOTHER: Go ahead honey go ahead.

> As CARMELITA *opens her mouth to tell the story* HARRY *comes and stands in front of her. In* CARMELITA'S *voice he tells the tale.*

CARMELITA-HARRY: Once upon a time there was a family, a very American one typical too if anyone is typical ever. There was a mother and father and son and a daughter and then another one. Let me call the mother Mabel and the father Abel who was indeed a good provider when he did before he went to war and died there which was everywhere except the place from where he'd come. And the family was very sad and very bereft and what was left was the mother and the brother and the sisters George Sally and Sue. [*The sisters smile and settle in to hear the rest.*] The Mother was so lonely she up and married another man quick who she knew not really very well but some. And said here is my little family with whom he would have nothing to do. He didn't like George Sally or Sue even by name let alone by reputation. George was a wild one it is true. And Sally was far too correct. And Sue was sinful and saintly in the very same step. So mostly they stayed out of sight and out of the minds of their folks which quite obviously has its effects. But George was loved by everyone still and Sally by him and Sue she. Suddenly a new baby Maggie came onto the scene and out the next second as she was kept from all the rest.

> *The sisters stir uneasily.*

MOTHER: This is certainly a long story.

CARMELITA-HARRY: Yes but it has to be told before I forget. For Mabel it is evident had already begun to forget how she had borne and bred this boy these two girls and could have cared less. She grew wicked and she grew mad.

> *The sisters get antsy.*

SISTER: What are you leading to?

MOTHER: This isn't very funny.

CARMELITA-HARRY: No it's not and soon it gets uglier yet. For Mabel thought these are dragons at her breast who needed a good old-fashioned slaying by her new noble knight. He beat George. He slapped Sally. He locked Sue up. America was no longer very nice.

MOTHER: Why don't we play charades?

CARMELITA-HARRY: And then one day...

SISTER: Carmelita where did you hear this?

CARMELITA-HARRY: I guess I'm just making it up.

SISTER: Well you should stop!

MOTHER: Let's have another drink each. Blanche do you have a joke?

BLANCHE: [*Putting out her glass*] I'll have some!

CARMELITA-HARRY: And then it happened as suddenly as that!
>   *The sisters are silenced.*
CARMELITA-HARRY: On a fair July 4th with firecrackers going off in most the houses
>   of the neighborhood in full blast and parades going by with bands and legions and
>   legions of very old men who shot bullets over everyone's heads it happened that a
>   gun went off right in Sally and Sue's room.
SISTER: Stop this right now!
CARMELITA-HARRY: A gun a gun! You can hear it whizz right by as they fell to the
>   floor and hid.
MOTHER: Stop! Stop!
>   BLANCHE *stands in alarm.* GRANDMA *wakes up.* HARRY *has disappeared*
>   *again and* CARMELITA *is left on the couch in near collapse.*
CARMELITA: [*Out of breath*] Why ever did you do that?
GRANDMA: What's happening here?
SISTER: I want to know Carmelita to whom you have been talking!
CARMELITA: [*Looking intensely at* MOTHER] It was you wasn't it?
MOTHER: Me what?
CARMELITA: Who looked up from under the bed and saw who it was.
MOTHER: [*Nearly hysterical*] Were you there too?
CARMELITA: You know I could not have been.
MOTHER: I don't know anything I don't know anything!
SISTER: [*Holding onto* MOTHER] Whatever has got into you?
CARMELITA: [*Herself in tears*] I don't know but it's true isn't it true?
MOTHER: Yes I saw him. I told Sister. I told Mother.
CARMELITA: That it was Harry.
SISTER: Please leave us!
GRANDMA: Harry tried to kill everyone of us!
SISTER: [*Comforting* MOTHER] Shssssh. Shssssh.
BLANCHE: [*In tears too*] What is everyone crying about?
CARMELITA: I'm sorry I'm sorry.
SISTER: Be quiet!
>   CARMELITA *is nearly hysterical.*
GRANDMA: Killed his own father.
SISTER: [*Turning on* GRANDMA] It wasn't his father old woman. It was your sick
>   husband who did beat and hold us in complete disgust. There's something I've
>   never told you I was glad he died!
MOTHER: [*Lifting her head*] So was I.
CARMELITA: What Harry said...I mean the way I see it....
SISTER: Carmelita shut up!
MOTHER: He was so mean to us.
GRANDMA: He was a good man.
SISTER: [*Hardly believing her ears*] How you can say that? You who tortured us too?
GRANDMA: None of you ever tried to understand. He came from quality and ex-

pected more out of you than you even knew how. [*To* M O T H E R] He wanted you to play the coronet. [*To* S I S T E R] And you would make a good stew. [*To* B L A N C H E] You were his linguist. [*To* C A R M E L I T A] And you were to be an art critic!

S I S T E R : [*Nearly spitting the words out*] Carmelita isn't one of us!

G R A N D M A : And who are we?

M O T H E R : She's not your daughter old witch!

G R A N D M A : But she's Harry's.

S I S T E R : Mother you've got everything confused.

G R A N D M A : For Harry he had no hope. Harry who was blessed with enough personality to burn for eternity in Hell had no redeeming qualities whatsoever. Harry was interested in one thing only: sex.

S I S T E R : What on earth are you talking about?

G R A N D M A : Well he truly was having sex with almost everyone he met. That's why everybody loved him so women men children his own sisters too. Your father caught him in your beds.

M O T H E R : I'm tired of this conversation it's time for me to take you in.

G R A N D M A : I don't want to go yet!

M O T H E R : Well you're going!

G R A N D M A : I won't [*As* M O T H E R *pulls the wheelchair over to her she stands and walks off.*] Put that away!

M O T H E R : Grandma you know you can't walk.

G R A N D M A : [*Walking with just a little limp way from all*] That's what you've said. But it's not true. Your memory's out of whack.

S I S T E R : That's the pot calling the kettle black.

C A R M E L I T A : Listen to her please.

M O T H E R : It was you who got us into all this. One night one night I would just like a little joy a little pleasure from this family but it doesn't know what joy and pleasure is. And you a perfect stranger coming in to take everyone's ghost out of everyone's closet go away leave us be.

    H A R R Y *suddenly reappears.*

M O T H E R : Particularly you who put us through this miserable wringer of forgiveness and guilt!

C A R M E L I T A : Can you see him too?

S I S T E R : Who who Carmelita who?

M O T H E R : When I want to. [*To* S I S T E R] It's Harry honey it's Harry. He haunts this house my yard these trees. Doesn't he ever visit you?

S I S T E R : [*Embarrassedly*] Yes on occasion he does show up. I thought I was going insane.

C A R M E L I T A : [*To* S I S T E R] You've never told me of this.

S I S T E R : There's lots of things I haven't told you and lots I never will I guess. If a person doesn't have something to keep inside who's left?

C A R M E L I T A : I just always thought you were being completely honest with me.

M O T H E R : [*To* C A R M E L I T A] What is your problem girl? What is honesty what's truth? You tell me!

CARMELITA: I look like Harry for one and for two Harry didn't try to kill you.

GRANDMA: Watch it!

HARRY: Go ahead Carmelita!

CARMELITA: [*Pausing to get up the strength*] It was someone else who shot at the two of you!

MOTHER: Who?

GRANDMA: That's enough!

SISTER: How do you know anything about any of this?

MOTHER: No let her speak!

CARMELITA: I don't Harry's telling me.

SISTER: I don't see him Carmelita and I don't think you do!

MOTHER: Well he's here he most certainly is.

SISTER: You always were subject to visions! You should have become the nun!

MOTHER: What's that supposed to mean?

SISTER: Harry was tried and hung dear sister on your testimony. It was you who saw Harry with the gun. I was under the bed! Mother was nursing Blanche.

CARMELITA: That's what Harry and I are trying to say. That afternoon Blanche didn't get much to drink. Blanche do you remember?

BLANCHE: I'll have some more schnapps!

CARMELITA: I don't know what she said but I don't think it really matters. Nobody understands Norwegian! And you [*to* MOTHER] were too terrified to follow the legs you saw go by at a run.

MOTHER: [*Breaking down*] Yes I was yes.

CARMELITA: Harry please speak!

HARRY: Now that you understand I don't need to. The dead can rest. [*He disappears once more.*]

MOTHER: What's he saying Carmelita?

CARMELITA: You didn't hear? He was cryptic very oblique but I know what he meant. [GRANDMA *has gradually made her way back to the couch.* CARMELITA *turns to face her.*] It was you wasn't it?

GRANDMA: I wasn't trying to hurt my little girls I shot over their heads! It was the judge I was trying to get! The maniac. A man who believed that people should be saints! A man who believed that being alive and living life through wasn't going to last!

The sisters are stunned.

SISTER: Then Harry didn't....

GRANDMA: O yes he did I forced him to. It was either murder my husband or face the paternity suit Sister Carmelita was threatening.

MOTHER: [*Rising*] Not again I can't take any more of this! Can't you see [*taking* CARMELITA *by the chin*] Sister Camelita isn't old enough.

GRANDMA: Not her the real one! The one who was a nun!

SISTER: Mother we're nuns.

GRANDMA: Prove it!

CARMELITA: What are you saying?

GRANDMA: Somehow he got in the convent and screwed this Sister and probably all the others. Harry was always looking for places to sin. The judge caught him red-handed with you [*to* MOTHER] and beat him until you got hysterical so that he had to hit you too.

MOTHER: [*To* SISTER] This is ludicrous!

SISTER: Is there any way to stop her?

CARMELITA: Shush shush.

GRANDMA: This particular nun unlike the other ones wanted to have Harry's kid and told Harry what he'd done. So I made a deal: the child would be paid for.

SISTER: Mother we've had enough! Harry was gay you know he was. It was the boys he was always in trouble with. He was not interested even slightly in nuns!

GRANDMA: [*Sitting*] So you've said.

CARMELITA: Go on go on!

GRANDMA: And she was paid for! We got the best abortion I could afford!

CARMELITA: [*Completely crushed*] But you said I look like Harry!

GRANDMA: I see his face in every whore!

MOTHER: Carmelita she doesn't mean that!

SISTER: Honey I told you you don't look anything like he did!

CARMELITA: But I've seen him!

SISTER: Carmelita Harry's dead.

MOTHER: I was just speaking metaphorically when I said he haunted this house. We were so young when they took us to court and put us up in front of it. I don't even know what we said but Harry was taken away to stay.

SISTER: Now do you comprehend? Harry is such a source of grief and such a souce of guilt to us. But you musn't believe anything she says.

> GRANDMA *has fallen asleep.*

HARRY'S VOICE: No you musn't.

CARMELITA: Did you kill him?

HARRY: Kill who?

SISTER: Who are you talking to honey?

CARMELITA: [*Rising in anger*] Everything changes from instant to instant but I know what I saw I know what I heard I know what I said! [BLANCHE *raises her glass in a toast.*] You saw him Blanche! You saw him too!

BLANCHE: [BLANCHE *speaks slowly in English*] Good morning to you!
> *And indeed there is a slight tinge of white in the night. And birds begin to chirp.*

CARMELITA: You're not listening!

GRANDMA: [*Waking up*] Who's making all this racket?

SISTER: Carmelita let's go.

GRANDMA: Come here dear I told you if you remember I have a gift for you.

CARMELITA: [*In tears*] Yes you did say that.

GRANDMA: [*Holding out a tissue-wrapped package*] Here!

> CARMELITA, *confused, accepts and slowly clumsily even opens it. It is the porcelain elephant completely broken to bits.* CARMELITA *turns with a smile upon*

her face almost deliberately into a bend to pick up the umbrella placed earlier beside the couch and standing up very erect brings the rolled umbrella down upon the old woman's head in a crash. She repeats the action and attempts to repeat it again but is restrained by the sisters, MOTHER, SISTER, *and* BLANCHE.

BLACKOUT

Naomi Iizuka

❧

Tattoo Girl

•

Characters (in order of appearance):

PERPETUA, a trumpeteer
PERPETUA'S HUSBAND
THE BASSOON PLAYER
TATTOO GIRL
PETER, PERPETUA'S son
PERPETUA'S MOTHER
THE PORNOGRAPHER
ROBERT, a lover
DOG
EDMUND, a grower of hops
THE REVOLUTION
MARSHAL FOCH, a French hero of WWI
HENRY, a builder of cathedrals
NADIA COMANECI, an Olympic gymnast
THE DUMB FRENCH GUY

Tattoo Girl may be performed with 6 actors.

2 women
4 men

Suggested Doubling:

PERPETUA
TATTOO GIRL (also NADIA COMANECI)
HUSBAND
PETER
BASSOON PLAYER (also PORNOGRAPHER, ROBERT, EDMUND and MARSHAL FOCH)
MOTHER (also DOG, THE REVOLUTION, HENRY, and THE DUMB FRENCH GUY)

Tattoo Girl was presented by the Annex Theatre, Seattle, Washington, on October 27–November 19, 1994, with the following cast:

PERPETUA	Julia Prud'homme
PERPETUA'S HUSBAND	Paul Stettler
THE BASSOON PLAYER/	
THE REVOLUTION	Frank Martinez, Jr.
TATTOO GIRL	Sarah Gunnell
PETER	Kevin Mesher
PERPETUA'S MOTHER/	
ROBERT/DUMB FRENCH GUY	Jason Cannon
EDMUND	Burton Curtis
HENRY	Kathleen Clark
MARSHAL FOCH/	
NADIA COMANECI	Jillian Armenante
YOUNG NADIA COMANECI	Savanah Migluri

Director	Lisa Portes
Scenic Designer	Heather Lewis
Lighting Designers	Patti West & Matt Perlman
Sound Designers	Wier Harman & Tom Utterback
Costume Designer	Camille Benda

1. HAROLD *watches TV.* PERPETUA *lives alone. She oils the valves of her trumpet.*

PERPETUA: This is the story of Nadia Comaneci who cartwheeled and tumbled and flew through the air, and balanced on a little piece of wood no wider than a large man's thumb. Four foot four. Double-jointed.

She had tiny bumps for breasts and the most perfect little pigtail. She was a little girl with spring. This was 1976 and I wanted to be Nadia Comaneci more than any thing in the whole wide world. I wanted to leap and bound and balance on my pinkie from a very great height. I wanted to defy gravity in front of a panel of gloomy Eastern European judges with names like Uta who would watch me and only me, their jaws slack with awe. I wanted to be Olympic.

HUSBAND: Perpetua?

PERPETUA: What is it, huzzband, hubbee?

HUSBAND: Perpetua, why do you hate my guts so?

PERPETUA: I don't know. Because you're cruel, because you're stupid, because you're limited in application.

HUSBAND: Not cruel not really.

PERPETUA: You lock me in rooms. You go through my things. When I'm asleep, you pull out my hair. I wake up with tiny aches in my follicles. You pretend everything is the way it's supposed to be, but it's not. I see the things you do. You're a bad man, and you're tricky, very very tricky.

HUSBAND: You're exaggerating. You're insane. Jesus, Perpetua, you're a pain in the ass.

PERPETUA: I know what I know.

HUSBAND: I'm not a bad man. You know I'm not. I'm actually pretty OK in the big scheme of things.

PERPETUA: If I stay here with you, I know I will wither like a tulip in the desert.

HUSBAND: Perpetua—

PERPETUA: WHAT?

HUSBAND: Why must everything be such a big deal with you? Why do you have to be this way?

PERPETUA: I have expectations.

HUSBAND: You used to love me. A lot.

PERPETUA: A mistake. An error. Do not nettle me with details, please.

HUSBAND: I don't know. Call me a nut. I'm looking for a woman like Debra Winger. Sensible yet sexy. Spunky yet delicate.

PERPETUA: I don't know what I'm looking for. I watch men in drug stores. They linger near cold remedies and hair care products. I undress them in my head and think about the distribution of their body hair.

HUSBAND: Perpetua, what is it about me?

PERPETUA: Many little things like little tiny pieces of lint on the vast carpet of my soul.

HUSBAND: No, I mean, really.

PERPETUA: Say good-bye to me now.

HUSBAND: Tell me one good reason why.

PERPETUA: Because I'm leaving you. Because I'm sick of the way things are. Because I'm bored. Because you bore me. Because I want to meet new and dazzling people who will make my teeth shiver with electric delight. There is no mystery here.

HUSBAND: She gives me many more reasons than I really need. We divide our things. We make preparations. And then she goes away.

Loud music ensues.

2. *Loud music ends.*

"PERPETUA smiled at the new life she saw spread before her like a red velvet map."

PERPETUA: Here there are canyons and valleys and meadows and mountains and big, kidney-shaped lakes. On the shores, tourists scan the waters for huge, snake-like sea monsters—Nessies with brains the size of chick peas. There's excitement in the air. The anticipation of supernatural hoohah. The cameras are ready. The tape is rolling. There's motion in the water. Somebody sees what looks like a tail.

The Tourists Oooh and Aaah.

PERPETUA: It's the Loch Ness monster.

BASSOON PLAYER: Ridiculous.

PERPETUA: I saw a tail and what looked like a hump.

BASSOON PLAYER: You'd like to think you did.

PERPETUA: But I saw it. Just now. I saw the tail.

BASSOON PLAYER: Scientists now believe the Loch Ness monster is a very big sturgeon.

PERPETUA *plays the trumpet briefly. It sounds like the mating call of an ancient, long extinct beast.*

HUSBAND: My ex-wife was a trumpet player. A trumpeteer. No more trumpeteers for me.

HUSBAND *scans a magazine for men. He turns the page. He comes upon a photograph: the back of a naked girl. On her back: a tattoo of Marshal Foch.*

HUSBAND: This girl has a nice back. Simple yet deep. Strong yet vulnerable. It's really incredible.

TATTOO GIRL: It's only a back.

HUSBAND: A back is something.

TATTOO GIRL: It's not enough.

HUSBAND: You're bewitching me, you know that? God, you're wonderful.

TATTOO GIRL: You only know me by my back.

HUSBAND: It's captivating.

TATTOO GIRL: It's a back.

HUSBAND: I love a girl with tattoos. I have to tell you this. I can't help myself. I'm developing very strong feelings for you.

TATTOO GIRL: Don't.

HUSBAND: I think this is something serious. Let me touch.

TATTOO GIRL: Don't.

> PETER *arrives.* PETER *is a student.*

PETER: Hey, Dad.

HUSBAND: Hello, Peter.

PETER: What are you doing, Dad?

HUSBAND: Getting to know someone new. Life goes on. What do you think?

PETER: Hard to say. Isn't that Marshal Foch?

HUSBAND: Marshal who?

PETER: Some French guy we learned about at school.

HUSBAND: I don't know. I don't care. The past is dead. She's very special to me. She's just a little shy. Please don't tell your mother. How's school?

PETER: It sucks. Hey, can I touch?

TATTOO GIRL: Don't even think it.

> HUSBAND *and* PETER *watch the Suns play the Sonics in silence.* PERPETUA
> *plays a few more notes on her trumpet.*

BASSOON PLAYER: The Loch Ness monster is a very big sturgeon.

PERPETUA: You've said that already.

BASSOON PLAYER: I don't think I can stress it enough.

PERPETUA: Is this a date? Would you call this date, this thing that we're on?

BASSOON PLAYER: I'd say this is a date.

PERPETUA: I don't know very much about you.

BASSOON PLAYER: I'm a musician.

PERPETUA: That's a start.

BASSOON PLAYER: I play bassoon.

PERPETUA: I love the bassoon.

BASSOON PLAYER: I play bassoon. I have beliefs. Belief #1: face up to reality. What we do is absolutely meaningless. Nothing we do makes a difference. Let us not delude ourselves. Art serves no conceivable purpose in the culture in which we live. Zip zero. Nobody cares. Nobody listens. We are obsolete. Lost sturgeon from another place in time.

PERPETUA: I'm proud of my trumpet.

BASSOON PLAYER: Oh?

PERPETUA: I'm expressing something unique and special. With my trumpet.

BASSOON PLAYER: Yes, but what have you and your trumpet done for the world lately? That's what I'd like to know.

PERPETUA: We are trustees of Form.

BASSOON PLAYER: Oh grow up.

PERPETUA: My trumpet—

BASSOON PLAYER: Please.

PERPETUA: Art for art's sake.

BASSOON PLAYER: What an asinine thing to say. What are you? Some kind of nine-teenth century throwback?

PERPETUA: I am a custodian of culture.

BASSOON PLAYER: Good Lord, what rock have you been hiding under? Nobody thinks things like that anymore.

PERPETUA: You're a very bitter bassoonist, aren't you?

BASSOON PLAYER: It's hard to make a revolution with a bassoon. I used to believe in my bassoon. Now I have nothing.

PERPETUA: I'm tired of talking about your goddamn bassoon. Go away. I said, go away. GO AWAY GO AWAY GO AWAY.

BASSOON PLAYER: Fine.

The BASSOON PLAYER *skulks away in his black raincoat.*

PERPETUA: I say go away—and they go.

3. *Time passes. Christmas music ensues. This is Christmas. There is snow. There is Christmas goo ga. There is* PERPETUA'S MOTHER *who clutches an over large turkey, mammoth and glowing.*

PERPETUA: Home for the holidays. Merry Christmas, Peter.

PETER: Merry Christmas, mom.

PERPETUA: How's school?

PETER: It sucks. Guess what? Dad's in love.

PERPETUA: I don't want to know.

PETER: It's kind of weird.

PERPETUA: I don't want to hear about it.

PETER: She has a tattoo.

PERPETUA: I SAID, I DON'T WANT TO HEAR ABOUT IT. Let's all speak of jolly things. It's Christmas. I want to be jolly. I want to strive towards jolliness. Everybody. Family. Let's think one thing, one very special thing, we're thankful for. I'll start. I'm thankful that I am no longer married to the ridiculous creature who was my husband. I am free free free to do anything I goddamn please. All right, Peter, your turn darling.

PETER: Uh. I am thankful for the advent of snow boarding as a recognized Olympic event.

PERPETUA: Good. Good, Peter. Mother, now it's your turn. Mother?

MOTHER: Pass.

PERPETUA: No passing allowed. Mother? Mother, please.

MOTHER: I am thankful that this is my last turkey ever. After this no more. Eighty-seven turkeys I have cooked in my lifetime. Eighty-seven. It defies imagination. If only you knew how much I hate turkey. Every goddamn holiday. Goddamn the turkey. Has no one in this family heard of ham?

PERPETUA: It's Christmas, Mother. Try.

MOTHER: I'm old, Perpetua. I get to say whatever I want. Soon I will be dead.

PERPETUA: Can we not talk about death please. It's Christmas for God's sake.

MOTHER: I should have run away from home half a century ago. Eighty-seven turkeys is eighty-seven one too many.

PERPETUA: You're ruining it, mother. You're killing the festive mood.

PETER: Can I be excused?

PERPETUA: No. Nobody is excused. We are family and this is Christmas. Snow and Santa Claus and yule logs and Christmas trees and reindeer and jingle bells and little, brown chestnuts roasting on an open fire.

PETER: Don't forget turkey.

PERPETUA: And turkey.

PETER: A big steaming butterball.

PERPETUA: That's right. Absolutely. Mother?

MOTHER: I can't.

PERPETUA: Mother, what is it?

MOTHER: I can't. I can't stand it anymore.

> PERPETUA'S MOTHER *chucks the turkey, and flees into the snowy night.*

PERPETUA: Mother, wait.

> PERPETUA *follows.* PETER *is alone.*

HUSBAND: Hello?

PORNOGRAPHER: Yes?

HUSBAND: I'm trying to get the name and address of the girl, the girl with the tattoo.

PORNOGRAPHER: I'm sorry, sir, that's confidential.

HUSBAND: What do you mean?

PORNOGRAPHER: Sir, we're not at liberty to give out that kind of information. It's private.

HUSBAND: Private? What's private? You're a porno magazine for Christ's sake. You publish pictures of women with their legs spread and their tongues sticking out. Don't talk to me about privacy.

PORNOGRAPHER: We see your logic, sir, but our hands, you see, are tied.

HUSBAND: Listen to me, fellah. If you don't do this thing, I will raise a ruckus. I will clog your phone lines. I will file frivolous law suits. Eventually I will be the lunatic with the AK 47 stalking your corporate hallways. You'll hear about me on the evening news. They'll interview my neighbors and flash footage of me being led away in shackles with a jacket over my head. Make no mistake, I will hound you till the end of all time.

PORNOGRAPHER: Your threats ring hollow, sir. We've heard it all before.

HUSBAND: But I'm in love.

PORNOGRAPHER: Love is tricky.

HUSBAND: I need to find this woman. I need to tell her of my love.

PORNOGRAPHER: What if she spurns you? What if she's already seeing somebody? What if she doesn't even like guys?

HUSBAND: I don't care. All that's unimportant.

PORNOGRAPHER: Hello? Is this reasonable thinking? Are we maybe losing sight of reality here? Come on, mister. Get a grip.

HUSBAND: I love her. I'm an adult. I know what I'm doing. Does love mean nothing in this world?

PORNOGRAPHER: Love? You're in love with an airbrushed, two-dimensional thing. Between you and me, buddy, I think you need to reconsider your definition of love.

HUSBAND: Give me her phone number, please pretty please.

PORNOGRAPHER: Sorry, no can do.

HUSBAND: Ok all right, look, fellah, let me put this another way. It's Christmas goddamnit. My wife just left me, and I'm sitting here watching *It's A Wonderful Life* for the forty-fifth time and eating a can of creamed tomato soup for one. I can't help but think this is a little thing, this thing I'm asking you for.

PORNOGRAPHER: While we cannot give you her address, we do consent to giving you her grid coordinates.

HUSBAND: Bless you.

> HUSBAND *disappears into the wilderness with a compass and a map. Christmas music grinds to a halt.*

4. PERPETUA *on a balance beam with trumpet. She makes furtive moves.*

PETER: Dear Peter: Yesterday: a movie with Larry the Lawyer. Tonight: Thai food with Bart the Banker. Next week: two stepping with Enrique the Engineer. I'm meeting new people and having lots of fun. How's school? Hugs and kisses, Mom

PERPETUA: The secret of perpetual motion: just keep moving.

> *New People flood* PERPETUA's *life. The world is all of a sudden filled with big, conspicuously friendly faces. They talk too loudly and with far too much gusto. Loud music ensues. And ends.*

TATTOO GIRL: So like I remember seeing Nadia Comaneci on this TV show, and she was giving this interview from some like Best Western in Tampa, and she had on this wild green eye shadow and she was no longer this cute Romanian chicky poo. She was like a woman, and she was with this guy, this really shady dude in this burgundy jogging suit, his name was like Sergio, and he was totally suspect, and the whole thing was so like tawdry, it made me want to cry.

PERPETUA: Who are all these people? Go away. Go away go away go away.

> *The New People disperse.*

PERPETUA: Where am I? What am I doing?

TATTOO GIRL: Are you OK up there?

PERPETUA: I used to want to be Olympic.

TATTOO GIRL: That seems kind of, you know, precipitous.

PERPETUA: Now I don't know, I don't know what I want anymore. People are strange. The world is perverse. I think: What has become of my life? Where is this all going? I think: Where does all that time go?

TATTOO GIRL: Time flies. Time stands still. Time to eat. Time to sleep. Time to go. Time to stop.

PERPETUA: You're one of those clever girls, aren't you?

TATTOO GIRL: I have fun.

PERPETUA: I play trumpet.

TATTOO GIRL: Oh yeah?

PERPETUA: I've always been, you know, kind of artistic. Are you an artist?

TATTOO GIRL: I don't know. I don't think so.

PERPETUA: What do you like to do?

TATTOO GIRL: I like getting really fucked up and then doing stuff while I'm really fucked up. I like floating. I like floating in the ocean when I'm really high. It makes me feel all see-through and jelloey like some big jelly fish. I like that.

PERPETUA: Someday I would like to be a great artist.

TATTOO GIRL: Someday I would like to pierce my nipple.

PERPETUA: You seem very modern. You must be very happy.

TATTOO GIRL: I'm really not. I posed for this photo, and now I've got all these sicko losers like totally obsessed with my back. It really bites. I got to get some money together, laser off this thing. I want to blend in. I want to disappear.

PERPETUA: You know, of course, there will be scars.

TATTOO GIRL: That's OK. I rock on scars.

> TATTOO GIRL *leaves. The sound of a symphony orchestra warming up. The invisible orchestra falls silent.* PERPETUA *is alone on stage. She faces a dark, cavernous house. She doesn't know what to do. She taps the microphone. She clears her throat. The screech of feedback.*

PERPETUA: Good evening. It's a pleasure to be here. Tonight I will be playing something very special, to me. My own interpretation of the beloved American classic: Boogie Woogie Bugle Boy. As adapted for trumpet.

> PERPETUA *plays briefly. A smattering of half-hearted applause.*

PERPETUA: Thank you. Thank you very much.

> PERPETUA *goes to bed.* ROBERT *emerges from the sheets.*

ROBERT: Perpetua?

PERPETUA: Who are you?

ROBERT: I'm Robert. Your lover. Go to sleep.

PERPETUA: I'm cold. Give me more blanket. Robert?

ROBERT: Yes?

PERPETUA: Do we have a life together? Have we shared momentous memories?

ROBERT: Ssh. You're going to wake the kids.

PERPETUA: Kids? We have kids?

ROBERT: No, Perpetua. I have kids. From my first marriage. Little people who resemble my ex-wife.

PERPETUA: Do I have kids?

ROBERT: You have Peter. I guess he counts. Now go to sleep.

PERPETUA: Robert?

ROBERT: Yes, Perpetua.

PERPETUA: Do you love me?

ROBERT: We haven't used that word yet. We're holding off. We're cautious people.

PERPETUA: I feel unease. Things seem—I don't know—not right, not the way I envisioned they'd be. Robert?

ROBERT: What?

PERPETUA: Tell me something.

ROBERT: I have to get up in four hours and go to work.

PERPETUA: No, something else.

ROBERT: I hate my job. I've made a mockery of my life.

PERPETUA: No, I mean something memorable, something from when you were little, some little thing that I can picture in my head and is real.

ROBERT: Once, when I was in fourth grade, my teacher Mrs. Fitz accused me of being "pert."

PERPETUA: Pert?

ROBERT: Pert.

PERPETUA: What does that mean?

ROBERT: Perky. Peppy. Full of gusto.

PERPETUA: Yes, but what does that mean? Robert?

5

PERPETUA: Do I know you, Robert? Do I really know you? Do you matter? Are you somebody important to me? Robert?

> PERPETUA *is alone. The Tourists are infinitesimally tiny figures on a distant shore.*

PERPETUA: My life: a map. Here there is desert. And more desert. There is sand and cactus and the occasional pit viper.

> PERPETUA *sees a* DOG *in the window of a pet shop.*

PERPETUA: Hello, little dog.

DOG: Woof.

PERPETUA: You're very cute. What a cute little dog you are.

DOG: Woof.

PERPETUA: And yet I am not charmed by your cuteness.

DOG: I talk, you know.

PERPETUA: A talking dog.

DOG: I'm very special. Pet me. Go on. Pet me.

PERPETUA: The novelty of you is already wearing thin.

DOG: Oh let me out, please. I want to run in the park. I want to pee by a tree. I want to catch a frisbee in my teeth. I want to be loved.

PERPETUA: Just what I do not need.

DOG: I would love you unconditionally. I would love you forever.

PERPETUA: Stop it. You're embarrassing me.

DOG: How could you not love me?

PERPETUA: Because you drool. Because you have fleas.

DOG: Let me lick your hand. Let me lick your face.

PERPETUA: Shoo. Go away. You smell.

     PETER *arrives.* PETER *is a bigger student.*

PETER: When I was little I wanted a dog.

PERPETUA: Peter?

PETER: I craved normalcy. Mom. Dad. Dog.

PERPETUA: Is that your definition of normal?

PETER: It'll do.

PERPETUA: But we were never normal, Peter. I played trumpet. Your father wore a penis sheath and feathers in his hair.

PETER: He did not. Dad didn't do that. Dad sold insurance. Why do you always exaggerate? Why are you so weird?

PERPETUA: I remember your father going to work in the morning, adorned in beads and feathers, his face smeared with paint, little hieroglyphs painted onto his cheeks. I remember him waiting for the train with his blowpipe and his spear.

PETER: Dad was not what you think he was. You're remembering everything wrong.

PERPETUA: Did you know your father? Did you ever really know anything about him? You were just a kid, Peter. What could you have possibly known? You were playing with Lincoln Logs. You were wearing pajamas with little feet.

PETER: Dad read spy novels. Dad had pockets full of change. On Saturdays, he swept up the leaves, and put them in dark green bags. Later, he fell asleep in front of the TV with his mouth open and his shoes off. Dad was always Dad.

PERPETUA: Your father was a mystery. He was exotic and strange. He killed his nameless enemies, and brought home their heads in little plastic bags. He roasted their hearts in the oven. He said things to me. He said—

HUSBAND: I killed them in the heat of passion. I know what passion is. I am a passionate man. Nobody understands that.

PETER: Mom?

PERPETUA: He said, he was a passionate man. He said, I watch the pretty girls. I watch them go down the street, he said. He said—

HUSBAND: they break my heart. With their loveliness, they break my heart. When I looked at you, I used to see loveliness. You used to break my heart, Perpetua.

PERPETUA: There are photos of your father and me. We have round, young faces and long hair. We're wearing clothes from another decade. We're smiling and holding hands. This was when we were happy. We were happy. I keep them in a box in the garage.

PETER: Mom?

PERPETUA: Go away, Peter.

PETER: It's going to be OK, Mom.

PERPETUA: I'm not interested in your opinion, Peter, not at all. You only make things worse. Go away. I said, go away. Go away go away go away.

     PETER *goes away.* HUSBAND *is a tiny figure in the wilderness. He has a map. It is the wrong map. He also has a little, black book.*

HUSBAND: The past is dead. The future is what I make of it. Here, it says right here:

"Victory equals *Will*...Victory goes always to those who deserve it by the greater force of *will*...A battle won is a battle in which one *will* not acknowledge oneself beaten." That's from *The Principles of War* by the late Marshal Ferdinand Foch (1851–1929). I think Foch's figured something out here. I think he's stumbled across a little, spiritual pot of gold. Call it a hunch. I have a theory. I have a map. Onward and upward. Yesss.

6. PERPETUA *is scrubbing* TATTOO GIRL's *back with a typewriter eraser.*

TATTOO GIRL: FUCK! OW! OW! STOP!

PERPETUA: It's not coming off.

TATTOO GIRL: Goddamnit.

PERPETUA: I thought you said you were going to have an operation.

TATTOO GIRL: I don't have the money. I spent it on all kinds of goodies I refuse to return. I fucking hate being poor.

PERPETUA: In time, it will disappear like a pebble carried down a mountain stream.

TATTOO GIRL: I can't wait that long. I don't want to be a wrinkled hag with some dead guy's head tattooed to my back. I fucking rue the day I got this tattoo. Jeez, what was I thinking?

PERPETUA: You were thinking: I want to be a rare and special thing. I want to be unique.

TATTOO GIRL: No. I was thinking: tequila. I wasn't really thinking.

PERPETUA: I think I think too much.

TATTOO GIRL: I think I used to think too much. I think I used to be a real thinker. My parents wanted me to be a lawyer. Isn't that a hoot? They wanted me to wear a power suit and drive a luxury sedan. I can't believe this. I think I'm experiencing regret. What a drag.

PERPETUA: Don't be silly. We're having fun, aren't we? Well, aren't we?

TATTOO GIRL: I don't know. Are we?

PERPETUA: Of course we are. Are you kidding? We're having a blast. We're free. We're unattached. We're young, relatively. We have talent. We have charm. We have promise. Carpe diem. The world is our oyster. All we have to do is shuck it.

The boulevard. EDMUND *is a tourist in the big city.*

EDMUND: Ladies.

TATTOO GIRL: Do we know you?

EDMUND: We have never had the pleasure of meeting, I don't think.

TATTOO GIRL: You're not from here.

EDMUND: I'm from Oregon.

TATTOO GIRL: Oregon? What is there to do in Oregon?

EDMUND: Oh many things. I farm. I'm a farmer.

TATTOO GIRL: Uh huh. And what's your cash crop?

EDMUND: Hops.

TATTOO GIRL: Hops?

PERPETUA: Did he say hops?

EDMUND: Hops. Yes, hops. I am a grower of hops. Two hundred acres. I'm a rich man. Hops has made it so. Would you ladies care to join me for a drink?

TATTOO GIRL: Sure.

PERPETUA: I don't feel like it. He seems a bit peculiar.

TATTOO GIRL: One drink. Come on.

In the wilderness. HUSBAND *is beginning to resemble Paul Bowles. He wears sandals. His skin is red. He squints in the photograph, indifferent to the latest trends.*

HUSBAND: I grow tired. Time passes. I forget where I am going and why. I circle the world. I ride a bus across the Orient. I sample strange delicacies. I have chronic dysentery. I smoke Thai stick on the beaches of Bali with a group of robust Australians who take me in. I am no longer what I once was. I meet a middle-aged, Slavic-seeming woman who claims to be Nadia Comaneci. She wears a sarong, and drinks American scotch. She regales me with stories of Olympic glory. And then she tries to sell me a watch. A fake Rolex made in goddamn Taiwan. What does she think I am? Some kind of tourist? I'm not a tourist. I'm a pioneer for Chrissakes. I tell her to go to hell.

The bar. EDMUND, PERPETUA *and* TATTOO GIRL *sit in the darkness, drinking. There is bar music. There are sullen, lipsticked faces in the shadows.* EDMUND *is recounting the history of hops. He has been speaking a very long time.*

EDMUND: ...Hops, or humulus americanus, is an herbaceous twining perennial, cultivated throughout temperate regions in the Pacific Northwest, it can grow anywhere from 15 to 20 feet in height, customarily trained to high wire trellis systems secured by stout poles. Noted for its rough, clingy stems, the male and female flowers are quite separate and distinct plants, the female being less conspicuous in its youngish state, the strobile consisting of a number of small acute bracts with two purple, sessile ovaries at the base, each containing a single ovule which eventually becomes, in the fruit, an exalbuminous seed. The light dusty pollen is then carried by the wind from the male to the female flower. In addition to its use in the brewing and manufacture of beer, hops has lesser known medicinal qualities. The most serious threats to the hops crop include the Downey Mildew, the Hop Aphid, the Click beetle, and the Nettlehead—

TATTOO GIRL: You must like really love your job.

EDMUND: I love hops. You have to love something.

TATTOO GIRL: Hops. Wow.

PERPETUA: Ok, I think I'm leaving now.

TATTOO GIRL: Don't go.

PERPETUA: This situation depresses me. I don't want to hear about hops anymore. This isn't where I want to be.

TATTOO GIRL: I think he's kind of sweet. Hey—Edmund, right?

EDMUND: Edmund, yes.

TATTOO GIRL: Are you having fun, Edmund?

EDMUND: I'm on vacation in New York City. Everything seems a little kooky.

TATTOO GIRL: You want to see something really cool, Edmund?

EDMUND: Oh gladly.

> TATTOO GIRL *shows her tattoo.*

EDMUND: Oh my.

TATTOO GIRL: What do you think?

EDMUND: It's different. It's big. Who is it?

TATTOO GIRL: Ferdinand Foch. Marshal Ferdinand Foch. French World War I hero. Totally crushed the German land force. Perhaps the most brilliant strategist of his epoch.

EDMUND: I've never heard of him.

TATTOO GIRL: I was obsessed with him in seventh grade. It was like this defining thing for me. My first love. But now, I don't know, I guess I'm having second thoughts. I mean it's on my body, you know, for life. That's a pretty tall drink of water, if you know what I'm saying. What do you think?

EDMUND: I think it's beautiful and strange. I think you're beautiful and strange.

PERPETUA: What are you doing?

TATTOO GIRL: What?

PERPETUA: Is there something happening here?

TATTOO GIRL: What do you mean?

PERPETUA: I mean, are you falling for this weirdo?

TATTOO GIRL: I don't know. I think he's kind of cool.

PERPETUA: Are you cracked? He could be an axe murderer.

TATTOO GIRL: Edmund's not an axe murderer. He's a hops farmer. Edmund lives for hops.

EDMUND: I love hops.

PERPETUA: I can't believe this. This is insane.

> *The phone rings.*

PERPETUA: Hello?

THE REVOLUTION: Perpetua?

PERPETUA: Yes.

THE REVOLUTION: Do you still play trumpet?

PERPETUA: On occasion, yes.

THE REVOLUTION: Do you have your trumpet with you now?

PERPETUA: Not right at this moment, no. Who is this?

THE REVOLUTION: Do you still believe in art for art's sake, and other little retrogressive maxims?

PERPETUA: To be honest, I haven't given it much thought. I don't have much time to think about aesthetics these days.

THE REVOLUTION: Are you struggling to survive?

PERPETUA: You could say that.

THE REVOLUTION: Are you disgruntled and alienated from the world around you?

PERPETUA: If only you knew.

THE REVOLUTION: We're putting together a compilation CD—songs for the revolution. All proceeds will go to the revolution. It's a terrific project, and we'd like for you to contribute a song or two.

PERPETUA: Really?

THE REVOLUTION: We're thinking a march. Maybe a stirring socialist ballad.

PERPETUA: That sounds promising.

THE REVOLUTION: We're very excited. What do you say, comrade?

PERPETUA: Well, I don't know. I guess. Sure. I mean, yes. Yes. Yes.

> *A ship in the middle of the Indian Ocean.* HUSBAND *and* MARSHAL FOCH *share a cabin. The floor of the cabin is covered with miniature tanks, soldiers and weaponery.* MARSHAL FOCH *is playing war.*

MARSHAL FOCH: This is a *Sturmgeschütz* of the 1945 period. Regard the bullet nicks. Tremendous, is it not? The effect is recreated by the application of a small dab of gray paint with a burst effect, you see, of flat white. For these small holes in the armor, here and here, I pierce with a hot nail. Very authentic. Boom. Boom.

HUSBAND: I'm going home. I'm tired of traveling.

MARSHAL FOCH: Ridiculous. What kind of soldier are you?

HUSBAND: I'm not. I don't know what I am.

MARSHAL FOCH: We are all soldiers here. WoooooKPAAAH!

HUSBAND: I miss my ex-wife. I wonder if she's happy. I bet she's found deep contentment by now. I bet she's living the goddamn life of Riley. I don't know. What do you think?

MARSHAL FOCH: Women are sturdy, as a rule. EeeeeWHUUUUM!

HUSBAND: You look familiar.

MARSHAL FOCH: I was famous once. I won medals. I don't have them with me now.

HUSBAND: It's your face. I've seen your face before.

MARSHAL FOCH: Really? Perhaps you were a soldier in the war, and I was your commander. Perhaps you fought bravely on the shores of Normandy. You were wounded, say. But you lived. Your only lasting symptom: bouts of chronic forgetfulness. This could be, don't you think?

HUSBAND: I don't know. I don't know anything anymore.

MARSHAL FOCH: You've forgotten it all.

HUSBAND: I'm miserable. I'm at my wit's end. I've peeked into the abyss.

MARSHAL FOCH: Buck up.

HUSBAND: You have no idea. I've been cosmically unproductive. I've accomplished nothing.

MARSHAL FOCH: You're a little foot soldier in the army of life.

HUSBAND: Yes, yes, precisely.

MARSHAL FOCH: Well, every army needs little foot soldiers. Not everyone can be a big important general. Oh don't be so gloomy. At least you have your arms and legs. Do you want to play?

HUSBAND: Ok, yeah sure.

MARSHAL FOCH: WeeeeeeeKSHHH.

HUSBAND: YeeooooowKSHHH.

> HUSBAND *and* MARSHAL FOCH *play war on their hands and knees somewhere in the middle of the Indian Ocean.*

7. PERPETUA *plays music of the revolution on her trumpet. A little girl in a leotard dances on a beam. She dismounts with aplomb and runs off into the void.*

    PERPETUA *continues playing.* HENRY *enters.*

HENRY: Hey. HEY.

    PERPETUA *stops.*

HENRY: No more, OK? Put your trumpet away.

PERPETUA: I have a new lease on life. I'm making music for the revolution.

HENRY: Honey, the revolution came and went. Where have you been?

PERPETUA: I've been here. I don't know. What do you mean "came and went"?

HENRY: I mean: Burger Kings in Beijing. I mean: ex-KGB types taking the wife and kids to Magic Mountain. Ivan's on the Matterhorn chowing down on corn dogs. Face it: nobody cares about the Revolution. The Revolution is history.

PERPETUA: They called me. The Revolution. They wanted me to contribute a song. I was making a contribution to the cause.

HENRY: Wake up and smell the coffee, will you please.

PERPETUA: OK all right. You've made your point. I think I need to be alone for a while.

HENRY: Alone? Hey, wait. Where are you going? Don't go. I'd like to be a friend. Let's you and me be friends in Christ.

PERPETUA: Look, I'm really not interested.

HENRY: You seem lost. You seem hungry, you seem hungry for the Word.

PERPETUA: Go away.

HENRY: Maybe I can help.

PERPETUA: Don't you dare ask me about my life with Jesus. I will become very agitated if you ask me about my life with Jesus.

HENRY: So what is it you have against faith?

PERPETUA: I don't like extremists.

HENRY: Let me guess. They make you antsy. You clutch your purse. You avoid making eye contact.

PERPETUA: Something like that, yes.

HENRY: I'm not a nut.

PERPETUA: I'm sure you're not.

HENRY: At some point, and I mean this, you're going to have to find something, something bigger than your own puny, little life to believe in. You're going to have to find some kind of transcendent meaning.

PERPETUA: Please leave me alone.

HENRY: This isn't a Christian thing. I happen to be Methodist by inclination, but that's a piddly detail when you look at the big picture, which is what He does when He looks at our tiny tiny lives. What I'm talking about is a big picture kind of experience. Do you know what I do? I bet you'll never guess. Guess. Go on. Guess.

PERPETUA: I don't know.

HENRY: GUESS.

PERPETUA: Herbalist? Chiropractor? Mortician?

HENRY: I build cathedrals. I build cathedrals where there have never been cathedrals. Places like Twayne, Nebraska and Yuba City, California. Because I know, in my heart, cathedrals are the way to go. Awe and grace. Awe and grace. Cathedrals feed a nation's soul. Mine are completely authentic. They have sextons and bellringers and beadles and archbishops. They have arches and buttresses and pretty little rose windows. They have Poet's Corners where anybody who was a poet, anybody even suspected of being a poet can be entombed, just like in Westminster Abbey. I live for Dedication Days. I can't even begin to describe the feeling. Crowds of faithful. The long lines of little girls carrying bouquets of flowers, the Elks Honor Guard with their M-16s reassembled just for occasions such as these, and the band playing Albinoni "Adagio in G Minor" which must surely be the saddest piece of music ever written by mortal man, and all the while sunlight is streaming through the stained glass windows, the awe so thick you could cut it with a knife.

PERPETUA: What do you want from me?

HENRY: Faith. Maybe a small tax-deductible contribution. Nothing big.

PERPETUA: I'm sorry. I am. I'm very tired right now. I need to take some Advil and lie down. This is nothing personal. I'm all for cathedrals. Cathedrals are swell.

HENRY: You think about it. No rush. Remember: you're a wonderful person, and God loves you.

PERPETUA: Thanks.

HENRY: Remember: He walks with you in your darkest hour. Please, take a free color brochure, and as a bonus, here, a small piece of holy rock, absolutely free of charge.

PERPETUA: Thanks. Really.

> PERPETUA *walks into the void.* HENRY *scuttles into a distant cathedral. A brief ray of sunshine. A gust of holy music.*

8. PERPETUA *is in the void. The void is bigger than it seems.*

PERPETUA: This is the story of Nadia Comaneci who cartwheeled and tumbled and flew through the air, and balanced on a little piece of wood no wider than a large man's thumb. Four foot four. Double-jointed.

She had tiny bumps for breasts and the most perfect little pigtail. She was a little girl with spring.

> NADIA COMANECI *appears out of the blackness.*

NADIA COMANECI: Hell. It was hell. My joints ached. My muscles killed me. I was so nervous, I couldn't breathe.

PERPETUA: But you were Olympic.

NADIA COMANECI: Big deal.

PERPETUA: I wanted to be just like you.

NADIA COMANECI: Big mistake.

PERPETUA: I wanted to be Olympic.

NADIA COMANECI: You want to be Olympic? Get a good publicist.

PERPETUA: But this is your story.

NADIA COMANECI: No, my dear, this is your story.

PERPETUA: I don't have a story.

NADIA COMANECI: Untrue. False. You want to know the story of Perpetua? I'll tell you her story. True story. Perpetua, the real Perpetua was a martyr. She lived about a thousand years ago. The Romans wanted to feed her to the lions, except the thing is—this is the interesting thing—the lions wouldn't eat her. So, there she was, this little woman, in the middle of a pack of hungry lions, in the middle of a colliseum, in the middle of all these men in togas, and nothing happened.

PERPETUA: Nothing?

NADIA COMANECI: Nada.

PERPETUA: Is that really true?

NADIA COMANECI: My hand to God.

PERPETUA: So she lived happily ever after, and everything turned out OK.

NADIA COMANECI: I think they cut off her head. I forget how it ends.

PERPETUA: What do you think it means?

NADIA COMANECI: Who knows? What do I look like? I'm a retired gymnast for God's sake. Don't look to me for answers.

PERPETUA: It means something.

NADIA COMANECI: Everything means something. Don't think too hard about it. It'll give you a headache.

PERPETUA: I think I need to go. I need to keep moving. Which way?

NADIA COMANECI: Who knows? Pick.

PERPETUA: I don't know. That way?

NADIA COMANECI: Why not?

PERPETUA: Ok, well. Off I go then.

NADIA COMANECI: Off you go.

PERPETUA: It was nice meeting you.

NADIA COMANECI: Yeah, yeah, my pleasure. Ciao.

> PERPETUA *goes away.* NADIA COMANECI *is alone in the void. Blackness.*

> 9. PETER *tends to his pet snake.* HUSBAND *enters, laden with third world souvenirs.*

HUSBAND: Peter?

PETER: Hey, Dad. Welcome home.

HUSBAND: Here. It's a little Buddhist thingy I picked up in Macao.

PETER: Gee. Thanks.

HUSBAND: How's school?

PETER: I don't go to school anymore, Dad. I graduated. I'm a grownup now.

HUSBAND: Wow. We really need to catch up. It's been a long time. I want to know everything. Tell me about your life, Peter. Fill me in.

PETER: I don't know. I have credit cards. I have appliances.

HUSBAND: Are you seeing anybody special?

PETER: I don't want to talk about my sex life, Dad, if you don't mind.

HUSBAND: No, no, of course not. Do you see your Mom much?

PETER: Not really. She's been dating this French guy.

HUSBAND: Oh yeah?

PETER: He's remarkably dumb. I call him The Dumb French Guy. It pisses Mom off.

HUSBAND: Life goes on, I've found. It just keeps going on and on and on.

PETER: What happened to that girl?

HUSBAND: What girl?

PETER: You know. The one with the tattoo.

HUSBAND: Oh, I don't know. I don't think I ever really got to know her as a person.

PETER: She was hot.

HUSBAND: She was just a passing folly of my youth.

PETER: She had a nice back.

HUSBAND: I did not truly love her.

PETER: I thought the largeness of her tattoo, I thought that was very sexy.

HUSBAND: I try not to dwell on the past. The past is dead, finito, the end. So, uh, what is it you do these days?

PETER: I'm a neurosurgeon.

HUSBAND: Really?

PETER: Just kidding. A joke. I temp actually. I'm a temp.

HUSBAND: Uh huh. And how is that?

PETER: It sort of sucks.

HUSBAND: I don't know what to say.

PETER: It's OK. Lots of things sort of suck. It's not the end of the world.

HUSBAND: So what's the little fellah's name?

PETER: This is Curtis. He's very serene. If I feed him and keep him warm, he'll live until I'm seventy three. It's weird. I always wanted a dog, but I don't know. Snakes are cool. Snakes are zen. Did you like have adventures while you were gone?

HUSBAND: I had fun. I don't really remember much.

PETER: I like your sandals.

HUSBAND: Thanks.

PETER: So, Dad, I have a question I need to ask you.

HUSBAND: Yes, Peter, anything. Ask me anything. Whatever it is. Talk to me. That's what I'm here for.

PETER: I just, I don't know, I just wanted to know if maybe you like had any pot?

HUSBAND: You mean, on me now?

PETER: Uh huh.

HUSBAND: Well, yes. Yes, I do, as a matter of fact.

PETER: Brilliant.

> HUSBAND *and* PETER *share a joint, and watch the Hornets play the Knicks in silence.*

> *In the blinding brightness of the future.* TATTOO GIRL *has no more tattoo. She has a back like any other. She is surrounded by a brood of babies wrapped like little mummies. She waits for the flash.*

TATTOO GIRL: Dear Mom: I married a farmer named Edmund, and moved to his farm in Oregon. Edmund grows hops. Edmund loves hops. I think hops is OK. I'm living happily ever after now. That's all. Love, Moira.

> TATTOO GIRL's *babies begin to wail.*

> EDMUND's *hops farm in Oregon. As far as they eye can see: fecund fields of hops.* EDMUND, TATTOO GIRL, THE DUMB FRENCH GUY *and* PERPETUA *are drinking.*

EDMUND: Here's to happiness.

THE DUMB FRENCH GUY: To happiness.

EDMUND: Here's to hops.

THE DUMB FRENCH GUY: To hops.

EDMUND: Will you do something about the kids, please.

TATTOO GIRL: I'm trying. Ssh. Ssh. All of you, ssh.

EDMUND: Why do they cry so much?

TATTOO GIRL: They're babies, Edmund. Babies tend to do that.

EDMUND: Don't smart off at me, Moira. Do something. Feed them. Rock them. Provide them some solace goddamnit. What kind of mother are you?

TATTOO GIRL: All right OK. Rock-a-bye baby on the treetop, when the wind blows, the cradle will rock, when the bow breaks the cradle will fall, and down will come baby, cradle and all. OK all right. Hush little babies, don't you cry, momma's going to sing you lullaby, and if that mocking bird don't sing, momma's going to—fuck, what is momma going to do, wait wait—SSH. ALL OF YOU, SSH.

> *The babies fall instantly asleep. Silence. Then a hiccup.*

THE DUMB FRENCH GUY: Ah. I love the countryside. So quiet. *Salut.* I am from Lille. It is a big city. Very busy. Rushing rushing oh my.

EDMUND: More?

THE DUMB FRENCH GUY: Please.

PERPETUA: What happened? Where did it go?

TATTOO GIRL: Where did what go?

PERPETUA: You know.

TATTOO GIRL: Oh. I had it removed.

PERPETUA: But why?

TATTOO GIRL: I don't know. Because I wanted to. Look, it's not a big deal.

PERPETUA: I miss it.

TATTOO GIRL: Jeez, I don't. Really. I really don't.

PERPETUA: It was beautiful.

TATTOO GIRL: It didn't fit anymore. It didn't make sense.

EDMUND: Moira, where is the fruit and cheese plate?

TATTOO GIRL: Edmund, I'm having a conversation.

EDMUND: Oh excuse me. Please. God forbid I interrupt anything important.

TATTOO GIRL: Some days I want to drive a spike through his face.

EDMUND: When you girls find a natural pause in your very important conversation, maybe we can all get a little fruit and cheese.

THE DUMB FRENCH GUY: If this is France, Lille is here. Nobody knows Lille. Everybody say: Paris oh Paris. I think Paris stink *peeuw.*

EDMUND: More?

THE DUMB FRENCH GUY: Please.

PERPETUA: They're very cute babies.

TATTOO GIRL: They're OK.

PERPETUA: Peter used to be cute. Now he's big. He has secrets. He has a snake. I think he's closer to that snake than he ever was to me.

EDMUND: Some fruit and cheese in this decade maybe?

TATTOO GIRL: Did I ever know Peter?

PERPETUA: Nobody ever knew Peter. He was sort of on the periphery of things.

TATTOO GIRL: Baboons are supposed to be great moms. I saw a thing on the Discovery Channel. They love their young.

EDMUND: Moira.

PERPETUA: I really wanted to be friends with Peter. That was something I hoped for.

EDMUND: Moira. Earth to Moira.

PERPETUA: I wanted to recognize things in him, I wanted to have delightful phone calls, and long dinners where we laughed and drank wine, and talked about life, but that's not how it is.

TATTOO GIRL: Baboons have snouts and bright pink butts. And they really really love their young. Now, turtles, turtles are another story. Turtles dig a hole in the sand and drop their eggs. Then they go away. After that, the baby turtles are on their own. Who the hell knows where the mom got to. She's out of there. She's gone. So anyway, this is the thing I'm wondering: am I a turtle or am I a baboon? That's the breakdown, the way I see it. Turtle, baboon. Turtle, baboon.

EDMUND: MOIRA.

TATTOO GIRL: What?

EDMUND: Fruit. Cheese. Fruit *and* cheese. Figure it out, Moira.

THE DUMB FRENCH GUY: I love cheese. Camembert: the best. Gouda it's nice. Havarti: so so.

TATTOO GIRL: I hate fruit and cheese. I also hate hops. Every where I look: hops hops hops. I'm fucking sick of hops.

EDMUND: I'm sick of you.

TATTOO GIRL: I don't know why I married you. I don't know what I'm doing here.

EDMUND: You're lucky I put up with your crap.

THE DUMB FRENCH GUY: *Salut.* Good friends.

TATTOO GIRL: You're lucky I don't torch your goddman hops farm.

EDMUND: I gave you a home. I gave you a family. When I met you, you were a weirdo, Moira. You were an impoverished freak.

TATTOO GIRL: And now I live in fucking Oregon and I'm married to some fucking hops farmer from fucking Oregon—What is *that* all about?

> The babies commence crying. The cries resemble air raid sirens ringing across the land.

EDMUND: I saved you, Moira. I gave your life meaning and depth.

TATTOO GIRL: You gave me nothing but boredom and aggravation.

EDMUND: All right. That's enough. Party's over. Go home, Jacques.

TATTOO GIRL: Don't fuck with my guests, Edmund.

EDMUND: Don't use language like that around the kids.

TATTOO GIRL: FUCK FUCK SHIT PISS FUCK.

EDMUND: What's the matter with you? What the hell is the matter with you?

TATTOO GIRL: I hate you, Edmund. I hate my life.

EDMUND: What are you saying?

TATTOO GIRL: I want out, Edmund. I think this phase of my life is over.

EDMUND: People make commitments, Moira.

TATTOO GIRL: Fuck commitments.

EDMUND: You think it's that easy? You think you can just wake up one day, and say: "OK. This was fun, but now it's done. Have a nice life. See ya"? You think that's how it works?

TATTOO GIRL: Yeah, I think that's exactly how it works.

EDMUND: Well, I have news for you, Moira. Life is not that simple.

TATTOO GIRL: No, see, I disagree. I think it's very simple. I'm leaving. I'm taking the kids and I'm leaving. And if you try to stop me, I will tear off little pieces of your flesh with my teeth.

EDMUND: OK, all right, look, Moira. Deep breath. Take deep breaths. Things, things are not as bad as they seem. We can work it out. I really believe that. The two of us. We can do it. All we need to do is try. What do you say, Moira?

THE DUMB FRENCH GUY: Where is the wash closet please?

EDMUND: Moira. Honey? Sweet pea? Sugar cube?

TATTOO GIRL: Shut up. Shut up. All of you, just shut up.

A Flash. The babies' cosmic howling ceases. No human voice. A silence only astronauts know. A photograph of people PERPETUA used to know. They are tiny and alien. Darkness. PERPETUA is somewhere else faraway.

10. PETER's *place. A smoky haze.* PETER *and* HUSBAND *are watching* TV. PERPETUA *enters.*

PERPETUA: Peter?

PETER: What's up, Mom?

PERPETUA: Who is that?

HUSBAND: *Konbanwa,* Perpetua.

PERPETUA: My god, is that you? What are you doing here?

HUSBAND: I've come home, Perpetua. Here I am. Home. With my son. We've been having a real heart to heart. I love my son. I love you, son.

PERPETUA: Are you drunk? What is that smell?

PETER: You missed a great game, Mom.

PERPETUA: I was busy. I was doing other things.

PETER: Where's the Dumb French Guy?

PERPETUA: I don't want to talk about it. Where is the snake?

PETER: Curtis?

PERPETUA: Yes. Curtis.

PETER: He's around.

PERPETUA: Where "around"?

HUSBAND: Sit, Perpetua. Be comfortable. Peter, why don't you go get your mother refreshments.

PETER: I don't have any refreshments.

HUSBAND: Make something up. Go go.

PETER *goes.*

PERPETUA: What is that you're wearing exactly?

HUSBAND: This is traditional Javanese evening wear. What do you think?

PERPETUA: It's bold.

HUSBAND: You look lovely, Perpetua. Youthful, trim, untouched by the cruel years.

PERPETUA: This is not going to be a romantic scene. Don't even try.

HUSBAND: Not a problem. So, where's your trumpet?

PERPETUA: It was crushed by a bus.

HUSBAND: I'm so sorry.

PERPETUA: I lie. I mean, it's not true what I just said. It wasn't really crushed by a bus. I just don't play anymore. I gave it up. It was—I don't know. It's a long story. I wasn't very good. Somebody should have told me.

HUSBAND: I liked it when you played. It was nice.

PERPETUA: You don't have to flatter me. I can take the truth.

HUSBAND: No, I'm serious. It was nice. Wait. Here. For you.

PERPETUA: What is it?

HUSBAND: A bamboo whistle thingy from Canton. Try it.

PERPETUA *blows her whistle. She grows bold. She plays a little, atonal ditty.*

HUSBAND: Very nice.

PERPETUA: Thank you.

HUSBAND: Perpetua—

PERPETUA: Yes?

HUSBAND: Did you, would you—would you say that you had a nice life?

PERPETUA: I don't know. It was OK, I guess.

HUSBAND: Me, too.

PERPETUA: I mean, I don't know why I'm speaking in the past tense. It's not like I'm dead.

HUSBAND: No. Of course not.

PERPETUA: My life goes on. I go on. I have a body. I have a brain. I have opinions and ideas. I have life experience. I have my freedom.

HUSBAND: You have a little whistle thingy from Canton.

PERPETUA: Yes. That, too.

HUSBAND: I'm not, of course, but some days, I personally feel dead.

PERPETUA: I'm tired. I'm really tired.

HUSBAND: Some days, I feel like a thousand year old egg. I think I've sustained permanent sun damage.

PERPETUA: Everything I've ever done is stupid and beside the point.

HUSBAND: I'm losing my hair. I'm gaining weight.

PERPETUA: I've known so many silly men I can't even keep track.

HUSBAND: I've partaken of outrageous amounts of pot.

PERPETUA: I haven't been truthful. I haven't been brave.

HUSBAND: I've dithered. I've been a remarkable ditherer.

PERPETUA: I have no real female friends.

HUSBAND: I have no lover.

PERPETUA: My son baffles me.

HUSBAND: Everything seems foreign and strange.

PERPETUA: I don't believe in anything.

HUSBAND: I never did what needed to be done.

PERPETUA: I can't remember the last time I felt delight.

HUSBAND: At least I have my arms and legs.

PERPETUA: I think I'm losing my mind.

HUSBAND: My memory is shot to hell.

PERPETUA: I don't know what to do now. I've wasted so much time.

HUSBAND: What did you just say? What were we talking about?

> PETER *returns with a bag of food and drink.*

PETER: Here. Have a beer. Have some cheese-filled combos.

HUSBAND: Tasty.

PETER: Move over, Mom.

PERPETUA: Peter?

PETER: Yeah?

PERPETUA: I'm home. Your father and I. We're both home.

PETER: Uh uh.

PERPETUA: We love you.

PETER: Love you, too, Mom. Here, Dad, give me the remote.

PERPETUA: Peter?

PETER: Yeah?

PERPETUA: Is it going to be OK, do you think? Is everything going to be OK?

PETER: I don't know. Yeah. Sure. Why not? So what do you guys want to watch?

HUSBAND: I want to watch Letterman. I want to watch "Gunsmoke." I want to watch "60 Minutes." I like Ed Bradley. He inspires trust.

PETER: It's too late, Dad. That stuff's all over.

HUSBAND: "The Mary Tyler Moore Show." The old one. I like Lou. I like Lou a lot.

PETER: Cancelled, Dad. Kaput.

HUSBAND: Oh, well then. Anything, I guess.

PERPETUA: Peter?

PETER: Yeah, Mom? What is it?

PERPETUA: It's just, there are things, there are so many things, all kinds of things—I wish—I want—I hope—I don't know. Never mind.

> PETER, PERPETUA *and* HUSBAND *scan the airwaves for something to watch. It's late late into the night. Nothing is on but cheesy movies with Linda Blair.*

From the edge of a freeway on the other side of the continent, TATTOO GIRL *waits for a passing ride. She is surrounded by her brood of* TATTOO BABIES. *The Babies have turned into strange owl-eyed marsupials never before spotted in any hemisphere. They have fur. They have claws. Their eyes glow in the dark.*

TATTOO GIRL: Dear Mom: I'm on the road. I left Edmund in Hopsville. Me and the kids are hitching to Vancouver. I'm saving up for a new tattoo. I don't know what comes next. Will write when we get to Eureka. Love, Moira.

And then there is only the freeway. Loud music ensues.

THE END

Tony Kushner

∾

Reverse Transcription

Six Playwrights Bury a Seventh
A Ten Minute Play That's Nearly Twenty Minutes Long

•

CAST:

HAUFLOTE, a playwright in his late thirties. He writes beautiful plays everyone admires; he has a following and little financial success. He was Ding's best friend, the executor of his will and his wishes.

ASPERA, a playwright in her early thirties. She writes fierce splendidly intelligent challenging plays, frequently with lesbian characters, and cannot get an American theater to produce her for love or money. So she lives in London where she is acclaimed. She is cool and is beginning to sound British.

BIFF, a playwright in his late thirties. Scruffy, bisexual, one success, several subsequent failures, cannot stay away from political themes though his analysis is not rigorous. He is overdue; he should be home, writing; he should not be here.

HAPPY, a playwright in his late thirties. His early plays were widely admired, then one big success and he's become a Hollywood writer, TV mostly, rich now, a little bored, but very happy. He plans to go back to writing for the theater someday.

OTTOLINE, a playwright in her fifties. African-American, genuinely great hugely influential experimentalist whom everyone adores but who is now languishing in relative obscurity and neglect, though she continues to write prolifically. She is the best writer of the bunch and the least well remunerated. Hers is a deep bitterness; the surface is immensely gracious. She teaches playwrights and has a zoological fascination, watching them. Ding was her protégé, sort of. She is an old friend of Flatty's.

FLATTY, a playwright in his late forties. Colossally rich. An easy target for negativity of all kinds though he is in fact a good writer, hugely prolific, very hard-working and generous to his fellow 'wrights.

DING, a dead playwright wrapped in a winding sheet. A very talented writer, whom everyone admired for wildly different reasons.

The play takes place in Abel's Hill cemetery on Abel's Hill, Martha's Vineyard, in December near midnight. Abel's Hill is a real place, a spectacularly beautiful mostly 19th Century Yankee graveyard; it's way too expensive for any mortal to get a plot in it now. Lillian Hellman and Dashiell Hammett are buried there. So is John Belushi, whose tombstone kept getting stolen by fans till Dan Ackroyd put a gigantic boulder on Belushi's grave, too huge for anyone to lift. From the crest of the hill you can see the ocean.

Everyone has shovels, and several have bottles of various liquors.

The night is beautiful and very cold.

They are writers so they love words. Their speech is precise, easy, articulate; they are showing off a little. They are at that stage of drunk, right before sloppy, where you are eloquent, impressing yourself. They are making pronouncements, aware of their wit; this mustn't be pinched, crabbed, dour, effortful. They are having fun on this mad adventure; they relish its drama. Underneath is a very deep grief.
They all really loved DING.

High atop Abel's Hill, a cemetery on Martha's Vineyard. Just athwart the crest. Tombstones all around. As the voice of the playwright is heard on tape, with an accompanying obligato of a typewriter's clattering, BIFF, HAPPY, ASPERA, OTTOLINE *and* FLATTY *gather, facing downhill.* HAUTFLOTE *appears, carrying the body of* DING, *wrapped in a winding sheet.* HAUTFLOTE *places the body before them, then runs off, then returns with six shovels. The other playwrights look about uneasily, and then sit. They have come to bury him illegally. It's nearly midnight.*

THE VOICE OF THE PLAYWRIGHT: Dramatis Personae: Seven characters, all playwrights. *Biff,* scruffy, bisexual, one success, several subsequent failures, cannot stay away from political themes though his analysis is not rigorous. He is overdue; he should be home, writing; he should not be here. *Happy,* his early plays were widely admired, then one big success and he's become a Hollywood writer, TV mostly, rich now, a little bored, but very… um, well, happy. He plans to go back to writing for the theater someday. *Aspera* writes fierce splendidly intelligent challenging plays, frequently with lesbian characters, and she cannot get an American theater to produce her for love or money. So she lives in London where she is acclaimed. *Ottoline,* African-American, genuinely great hugely influential experimentalist whom everyone adores but who is now languishing in relative obscurity and neglect, the best writer of the bunch and the least well remunerated. She is an old friend of *Flatty,* colossally successful, colossally rich. An easy target for negativity of all kinds though he is in fact a good writer, hugely prolific. *Hautflote,* writes beautiful experimental plays, has a small loyal following and little financial success; the best friend and the executor of the estate of *Ding,* a dead playwright wrapped in a winding sheet, very talented, whom everyone admired for wildly different reasons. Seven characters are too many for a ten minute play. It'll be twenty minutes long! Fuck it. One of them is dead and the others can all talk fast. The play takes place in Abel's Hill cemetery, a spectacularly beautiful mostly 19th Century Yankee graveyard, way too expensive for any mortal to get a plot in it now. On Abel's Hill, Martha's Vineyard, in December near midnight.

When the voice is finished, HAUTFLOTE *goes to a nearby headstone, on the side of which is a light switch. He flicks it on; a full moon appears in the sky.*

HAUTFLOTE: Ah!

The play begins.

Here. We should start digging.

ASPERA: Athwart the crest. Facing the sea. As Ding demanded.

OTTOLINE: Isn't this massively illegal?

FLATTY: Trespass, destruction of private property, destruction of a historical land-
mark I shouldn't wonder, conveyance of tissue, i.e. poor Ding, in an advanced state
of morbidity, on public transportation…

HAUTFLOTE: He's been *preserved*. He's hazardous to no one's health.
He traveled here in a steamer trunk. The porters helped.

BIFF: [*apostrophizing*] O please come to me short sweet simple perfect idea. A seed, a
plot.

HAUTFLOTE: He's under a deadline.

BIFF: I'm doomed.

HAUTFLOTE: Now shoulder your shovels…

BIFF: There's no dignity, have you noticed? In being *this*. An American playwright.
What is that?

OTTOLINE: Well, we drink.

HAPPY: No one really drinks now. None of us, at least not publicly.

FLATTY: I can't remember something.

HAPPY: We're… [*Looking for the word*]

FLATTY: A name.

HAPPY: Healthier!

HAUTFLOTE: What name?

FLATTY: The name of the country that makes me despair.

HAPPY: But tonight we are drunk.

BIFF: In honor of Ding.

HAUTFLOTE: What letter does it begin with?

BIFF: Poor Ding.

> They all look at DING. *Little pause.*

ASPERA: "And Poor Ding Who Is dead."

> *Little pause. They all look at* DING.

FLATTY: R.

HAUTFLOTE: Rwanda.

FLATTY: *That's* it.

OTTOLINE: How could you *forget*, Flatty? Rwanda?

FLATTY: I've never had a head for names. Not in the news much anymore, Rwanda.

OTTOLINE: We are afraid to stick the shovel in.

HAUTFLOTE: Yes.

OTTOLINE: Believing it to be a desecration.

HAUTFLOTE: Of this holy earth.

OTTOLINE: Not *holy*: Pure. Authentic.

HAPPY: Yankee.

OTTOLINE: Pilgrim.

HAPPY: Puritan.

OTTOLINE: Forefatherly. Originary.

ASPERA: Oh fuck me, "originary"; John Belushi's buried here!

FLATTY: And he had enough drugs in him when he died to poison all the waters from here to Nantucket.

OTTOLINE: And the people steal his tombstone.

FLATTY: No!

OTTOLINE: Or the hill keeps swallowing it up. It doesn't rest in peace. A pretender, you see.

ASPERA: Lillian Hellman's buried here. She's a playwright.

HAUTFLOTE: Appropriate or no it's what Ding wanted.

OTTOLINE: And that's another thing. It cost two hundred thirty seven dollars and fifty cents for a round trip ticket. From New York. This is an *island*. Martha's Vineyard is an *island*! Did Ding *realize* that? One has to *ferry* across. Fucking Ding. Maybe *you all* have money. For ferry passage. I don't have money. I've got no money.

FLATTY: I told you I'd pay for you.

OTTOLINE: Well we all know *you've* got money.

BIFF: O come to me short sweet simple idea!

FLATTY: I want something magical to happen.

BIFF: A plot. The Horseleech hath two daughters. It's a start. And these daughters... Do.... What?

HAPPY: They cry!

OTTOLINE: Give, give!

BIFF: Brecht in exile circumnavigated the globe. Berlin. Skovsbostrand. Stockholm. Helsinki. Leningrad. Moscow. Vladivostock. Manila. L.A.. Quick stop in D.C. to visit the HUAC. New York. Paris. Zurich. Salzburg. Prague. Berlin. An American playwright, what is that? Never in exile, always in extremis. The list of cities: AIDS, loss, fear of infection, unsafe sex he says gazing upon the corpse of a fallen comrade, I fuck men and women. I dream my favorite actor has been shot by the police, I dream I shoot Jesse Helms in the head and it doesn't kill him...

FLATTY: Eeewww, *politics*.

BIFF: I dream we are intervening in Bosnia merely to give Germany hegemony over Eastern Europe. Why, I dream myself in my dream asking myself, do you dream that? You do not dream a play, you write a play. And this play is due, and there's [*pointing to* DING's *corpse*] the deadline. I write in my notebook that I am glad we are sending troops to former Yugoslavia but I [*he makes the "in quotes" gesture with his fingers*] "inadvertently" spell troops "T-R-O-U-P-E-S" as in troupes as in theatrical troupes, traveling players, we are sending *troupes* to former Yugoslavia.

HAUTFLOTE: I don't think we can avoid it any longer. The digging.

FLATTY: I imagine it's worth serious jail time for us all.

HAPPY: Incarcerated playwrights. Now *that* has dignity. Until it's learned what for.

BIFF: I repulse myself, I am not of this earth, if I were more serious I would be an essayist if I were more observant a novelist more articulate more intelligent a poet more... succinct more *ballsy* a screenwriter and then I could buy an apartment.

HAUTFLOTE: Fuck the public. It's all Ding asked for. He never got his own, alive.

ASPERA: Poor poor Ding.

HAUTFLOTE: He grew obsessed with this cemetery, in his final months. We visited it years ago. On a day trip, we could never afford…to *stay* here. Or anywhere. Or anything. Health insurance. "Bury me on Abel's Hill." His final words.

HAUTFLOTE: I think he thought this place would give him a retroactive pedigree.

OTTOLINE: That's it, *pedigree*, not *holiness*. Blood, genes. Of which we playwrights are envious. We're mutts. Amphibians.

ASPERA: Not of the land not of the sea. Not of the page nor of the moment.

HAPPY: Perdurable page. Fleeting moment.

FLATTY: Something magical should happen now.

HAUTFLOTE: Ding wanted to belong. Or rather, he never wanted not to. Or rather he never didn't want to, he *wanted* to not want to, but did. In his final months he grew finical.

ASPERA: When I saw him he wasn't finical, he was horrible. He looked horrible and he screamed at everyone all day and all night and there was no way he could get warm, ever. It was quite a change. I hadn't seen him in months, I was visiting from London WHERE I LIVE, *IN EXILE*, PRODUCED, APPLAUDED, *LAUDED* EVEN and NO ONE IN AMERICA WILL TOUCH MY WORK, but anyway he was somehow very very angry but not bitter. One felt envied, but not blamed. At Ding's deathbed.

HAUTFLOTE: Ding Bat. Der Dingle. Ding-An-Sich.

HAPPY: I remember being impressed when I learned that the HIV virus, which has robbed us of our Ding, reads and writes its genetic alphabets backwards, RNA transcribing DNA transcribing RNA, hence *retrovirus,* reverse transcription. I'm not gay but I am a Jew and so of course I, too, "read backwards, write backwards"; I think of Hebrew.

FLATTY: You're not gay?

HAPPY: No.

FLATTY: You're *not*?

HAPPY: No.

FLATTY: Everyone thinks you are. Everyone wants to sleep with you. Everyone. *Everyone.*

Oops. You were saying?

HAPPY: I was saying that in my grief I thought… Well here I attempt a metaphor doomed to fail… I mean here we are, playwrights in a graveyard, here to dig, right? So, digging, I think: HIV, reverse transcribing, dust to dust, writing backwards, Hebrew and the Great and Terrible magic of that backwards alphabet, which runs against the grain, counter to the current of European tradition, heritage, thought: a language of fiery, consuming revelation, of refusal, the proper way, so I was taught, to address oneself to God… [*He puts his hands on* DING's *body*] Perhaps, maybe, this backwards-writing viral nightmare is keeping some secret, subterraneanly affianced to a principle of… Reversals: good reversals and also very bad, where good meets bad, perhaps, the place of mystery where back meets forth, where our sorrow's not the point, where the forward flow of life brutally throws itself into reverse, to reveal... [*He lies alongside the body, curls up to it, head on* DING's *shoulder, listening*] What? Hebrew always looked to me like zipper teeth unzipped. What awesome thing is it we're zipping open? To what do we return when we write in reverse? What's relinquished, what's released? What does it sound like I'm doing here?

ASPERA: It sounds like you're equating Hebrew and AIDS.

HAPPY: I'm...

ASPERA: I'm not Jewish but I am a dyke and I think either way, AIDS equals Hebrew or the reverse, you're in BIG trouble. I'm going to beat you up.

HAPPY: Not *equals*, I... I'm lonely. I'm among playwrights. Back East for the first time in months. So I get to talk. And none of you listen anyway. In Culver City everyone listens, they listen listen listen. They take notes. They take you at your word. You are playwrights. So be inattentive. If you paid attention you'd be novelists.

FLATTY: Aspera has spent five years in London. She's acquired the listening disease.

OTTOLINE: Soon, unless she watches herself, she will be an American playwright no longer but British, her plays will be all nuance, inference.

FLATTY: Yes, nuance, unless she's careful, or a socialist feminist.

BIFF: Everyone hates you Flatty.

OTTOLINE: Oops.

FLATTY: [*unphased, not missing a beat*] And then there will be no nuance at all.

ASPERA: *Does* everyone hate you?

FLATTY: No, they don't.

ASPERA: I live in London now, I'm out of the loop.

FLATTY: They don't hate me, they envy me my money.

ASPERA: [*To* HAPPY] I wouldn't *really* beat you up.

FLATTY: I could buy and sell the lot of you. Even *you* Happy and *you write sitcoms*. There. I've said it. I am wealthy. My plays have made me wealthy. I am richer than essayists, novelists, at least the respectable ones, and all poets ever. Envy is rather *like* hatred but as it's more debilitating to its votaries and votaresses [because it's so inherently undignified] it's of less danger ultimately to its targets.

BIFF: I don't envy your money. I envy your reviews.

HAUTFLOTE: I think we should dig now and bury Ding. This ground is patrolled. The night doesn't last forever. Ding's waiting.

OTTOLINE: [*Softly, firmly*] Ding's dead. I love this place. It was worth two hundred and thirty seven dollars and fifty cents to get here. Yes Flatty you can pay my way. Send me a check. Biff's got a point. It's the reviews, isn't it. I've worked tirelessly for decades. Three at least. What I have done no one has ever done and no one does it nearly so well. But what I do is break the vessels because they never fit me right and I despise their elegance and I like the sound the breaking makes, it's a new music. What I do is make mess apparent or make apparent messes, I cannot tell which myself I signal disenfranchisement, dysfunction, disinheritance well I *am* a black

woman what do they expect it's hard stuff but it's life but I am *perverse* I do not
want my stories straight up the narrative the narrative the miserable fucking narrative the universe is post-Cartesian post-Einsteinian it's not at any rate what it's
post-to-be let's throw some curve balls already who cares if they never cross the
plate it's hard too hard for folks to apprehend easy so I get no big money reviews
and no box office and I'm broke, I'm fifty or sixty or maybe I've turned eighty, I
collected the box at the Cafe Cinno yes I am THAT old, and poor but no matter, I
have a great talent for poverty. Oblivion, on the other hand, scares me. Death. And
this may shock you but [*To* FLATTY.] I ENVY you... your RENOWN. [*Roaring.*]
I DON'T WANT ANOTHER OBIE! *I want a hit! I want to hit a home run!* I
WANT A MARQUEE! I'm too old to be ashamed of my hunger.

BIFF: O come to me short sweet [*He blows a raspberry*]. There's just no dignity. I am
oppressed by theater critics.

FLATTY: I gave up on dignity *years* ago. I am prolific. That's my revenge. If you want
dignity you should marry a lighting designer.

OTTOLINE: Perhaps now we have worn out our terror, or at least winded it.

HAUTFLOTE: At darkest midnight December in the bleak midwinter athwart the crest
of Abel's Hill on Martha's Vineyard six moderately inebriated playwrights stood
shovels poised to inter...

FLATTY: Illegally.

HAUTFLOTE: ...the earthly remains of a seventh.

HAPPY: Who might at least have agreed to the convenience of a cremation.

HAUTFLOTE: Being a creature of paper as well as of the fleeting moment Ding naturally had a horror of fire. *I knew him best.* For a long time now. I loved him.

OTTOLINE: We all did.

HAUTFLOTE: Yet not one of us dares break ground.

HAPPY: Wind perhaps, but never ground.

ASPERA: Wind for sure but not the Law. But is it the law or what's underground
which immobilizes us? Incarceration or an excess of freedom? Enchainment or
liberation? For who knows what dreams may come? Who knows what's underneath? Who knows if anything is, if the shovel will strike stone, or pay dirt, or
nothing whatsoever?

BIFF: It's the Nothing stopping me. I can speak only for myself.

FLATTY: Bad thing in a playwright.

BIFF: The horseleech hath two daughters. There's a play in there, somewhere, of course.
I used to say: it won't come out. Fecal or something, expulsive metaphor. I was
stuffed, full and withholding. In more generous times. Before the fear... of the Deficit,
before the Balanced Budget became the final face of the Angel of the Apocalypse.
Now instead I say: I'm not going to go there. A geographical metaphor. Why? *I'm
nearly forty* is one explanation. "*There*" meaning... That bleachy bone land. Into
that pit. That plot. To meet that deadline.

OTTOLINE: The play is due?

BIFF: Day after yesterday.

HAPPY: Rehearsals starting...?

BIFF: *Started.*

ASPERA: What, without a script?

BIFF: They're *improvising.*
> *Everyone shudders.*

FLATTY: You shouldn't be here! You should be home writing!

BIFF: Did I mention how much I hate you, Flatty.

FLATTY: Marry a lighting designer. It worked for me. Sobered me right up.

HAPPY: I never meant... This reverse transcription thing. I'll work on it.

ASPERA: You do that.

HAPPY: I never meant to equate Hebrew and... It's just the words: reverse transcription. *Thinking* about it. Something I can't help doing. Writing began with the effort to record speech. All writing is an attempt to fix intangibles—thought, speech, what the eye observes—fixed on clay tablets, in stone, on paper. Writers *capture.* We playwrights on the other hand write or rather "wright" to set these free again. Not inscribing, not *de*-scribing but... *ex*-scribing [?]... "W-R-I-G-H-T", that archaism, because it's something earlier we do, cruder, something one does with one's mitts, one's paws. To claw words up...!
> HAPPY *falls to his knees beside* DING, *and starts to dig with his hands.*

HAPPY: To startle words back into the air again, to... evanesce. It is... unwriting, to do it is to die, yes, but. A lively form of doom.

ASPERA: Ah, so now you are equating...

HAPPY: It's not about *equation.* It's about the transmutation of horror into meaning.

ASPERA: Doomed to fail.

HAPPY: Dirty work... [*He shows his hands.*]

ASPERA: A mongrel business. This Un-earthing.

HAUTFLOTE: For which we Un-earthly are singularly fit. Now or never.

BIFF: I'm nearly forty. My back hurts.

FLATTY: Whose doesn't? No dignity but in our labors.
> *They hoist their shovels.*

ASPERA: Goodnight old Ding. Rest easy baby. And flights of self-dramatizing hypochondriacal hypersensitive self-pitying paroxysmical angels saddlebag you off to sleep.

BIFF: [*apostrophizing* DING's *corpse.*] Oh Dog Weary.

HAUTFLOTE: Many of these graves are cenotaphs, you know, empty tombs, honorifics. Sailors lost on whalers, lost at sea, no body ever found, air and memory interred instead. All other headstones in the graveyard peristalithic to these few empty tombs, whose ghostly drama utterly overwhelms The Real.
> HAUTFLOTE *waves his hand in the air, a downbeat. Ella sings "When They Begin The Beguine"*

OTTOLINE: Dig. Shovel tips to earth.

They are.

OTTOLINE: The smell of earth will rise to meet us. Our nostrils fill with dark brown, roots ends, decomposing warmth and manufactory, earthworm action. The loam.

FLATTY: I don't want to go to jail. Doesn't David Mamet live around here somewhere?

OTTOLINE: Push in.

They do.

THE END

EDWARD ALBEE is one of the most distinguished of American playwrights and a multiple winner of the Pulitzer Prize. He was born in 1928 and thirty years later began to write plays. His works include *Who's Afraid of Virginia Woolf?*, *Three Tall Women*, *The Sandbox*, *The Death of Bessie Smith*, *Zoo Story*, *American Dream*, *Tiny Alice*, *A Delicate Balance*, *Everything in the Garden*, and *Seascape*.

At the age of thirty-one, LYNNE ALVAREZ visited the Puerto Rican Traveling Theatre and was inspired to write plays. Her first, *Graciela*, was performed by the Puerto Rican Traveling Theatre and another, *Guitarron*, brought her a National Endowment for the Arts fellowship. *Hidden Parts* won her the Kesselring Award and with *The Wonderful Tower of Humbert Lavoigent* she won both the Le Compte De Nouey Award and the FDG/CBS Award for Best Play. *Thin Air: Tales From a Revolution* was commissioned as a one-act play by the Actors Theatre of Louisville and her later full-length version won her a Drama League Award and a Rockefeller fellowship in 1988. *The Reincarnation of Jaimie Brown* was created for the American Conservatory Theatre and was published in *Women Playwrights: The Best Plays of 1994*. In 1994, she was also awarded a New York Foundation for the Arts grant. Alvarez has been commissioned to do translations and adaptations including *The Damsel and the Gorilla, Don Juan of Seville, The Red Madonna, Decameron,* and *Rikki Tikki Tavi*. Most recently she has written the play *The Absence of Miracles and the Rise of the Middle Class*. She has also had two books of her poetry published.

AMIRI BARAKA (LeRoi Jones) was born in New Jersey in 1934 and has written over twenty plays including *Dutchman, The Slave,* and *The Toilet*. He became a figure of the Beat movement, editing the avant-garde literary journals, *Yugen* and *Floating Bear*. In 1964, he became nationally recognized when his off-Broadway play *Dutchman* won an Obie Award. Since the death of Malcolm X in 1965, he has committed his life to Black Nationalism and the African-American community's cultural and political activities and causes. He has received grants from the Rockefeller Foundation and the National Endowment for the Arts, as well as the Langston Hughes Award from the City College of New York. He has also written three jazz operas, several non-fiction books, a novel, and many volumes of poetry. He is currently a professor of Africana Studies at SUNY-Stony Brook.

LEE BREUER is co-founder and co-artistic director of Mabou Mines. He has created twenty-five works for Mabou Mines as a writer, director, performer, and producer. He directed *Peter and Wendy* for an extended run at the New Victory Theater, winning five Obie Awards. He directed his adaptation of Samuel Beckett plays for Mabou Mines, which received three Obie Awards. The numerous plays he has written include *The Shaggy Dog Animation,* which received a 1978 Obie Award for Best Play, *Sister Suzie Cinema,* which was televised on the PBS series "Alive From Off Center," *A Prelude to a Death in Venice,* which won Obie Awards for both direction and script, *The B Beaver Animation,* and *The Red Horse Animation.* He also won four Obie Awards for his adaptation of a gender-reversed *Lear*. *Gospel at Colonus*, conceived, adapted, and directed by Breuer, premiered at the Next Wave Festival, was broadcast on PBS, won an Obie Award for Best Musical, and then opened on Broadway. Some of his numerous grants and awards have been from the National Endowment for the Arts and the Guggenheim, McKnight, Rockefeller, and MacArthur Foundations. He currently is on the faculty at Stanford University.

ED BULLINS, a Philadelphia native, is a much celebrated playwright. He was instrumental to the development of Black theater during the 1960s and 1970s. Much of his work was written for the New Lafayette Theatre, which was a prime location for the new voices of Black theater. *The Corner* was performed at the New York Shakespeare Festival and his many plays include *Goin' a Buffalo, Dialect Determinism* (or *The Rally*), *It Has No Choice, The Helper, A Minor Scene, The Theme is Blackness, The Man Who Dug Fish, Black Commercial #2, The American Flag Ritual, State Office Bldg. Curse, One-*

Minute Commercial, A Street Play, Street Sounds, A Short Play For a Small Theater, and *The Play of the Play. The Taking of Miss Janie* was awarded the New York Drama Critics Circle Award for Best American Play of 1974–75. He has received Obie Awards for *In New England Winter, The Fabulous Miss Marie,* and *The Taking of Miss Janie.* He has taught for over twenty years in the Black Studies Department at San Francisco State University and is currently Acting Director of the Northeastern University Center for the Arts in Boston. He has also written a novel, *The Reluctant Rapist,* and a collection of early fiction and prose, *The Hungered One.*

RICHARD CALIBAN is artistic director and co-founder of Cucaracha Theatre in New York as well as a director and playwright. At Cucaracha he has developed and produced over seventy-five productions and written and directed many of his plays including *Homo Sapien Shuffle, Performance Piece #27, Budd, A Vast Wreck, Famine Plays, Rodents and Radios, Oedipus in Kansas,* and *Internal Combustion.* Cucaracha received an Obie Award in 1989 under Caliban's directorship for its achievements as an emerging company. He has collaborated as director on a number of projects with Mac Wellman including the Outer Critics Circle Award and Obie Award-winning *Crowbar.* In Los Angeles, his one-act play *Gladiator* was produced at Act One. He was the recipient of a Rockefeller Foundation grant for the production of his play *Suburban Romance.* He also received a grant from Arts America to direct two plays in Hungarian for the R.S. Theatre in Budapest where he was in residence for two months. He wrote the text for a dance/theater piece with the Randy Warshaw Dance Company at the Joyce Theater that also toured Europe. He was awarded a MacDowell fellowship and is also a panel member of the New York State Council of the Arts.

CONSTANCE CONGDON is well-respected as an inventive American playwright with comic sensibilities. Her plays have been produced both in the U.S. and abroad. They include *Tales of the Lost Formicans, No Mercy* (commissioned by the Hartford Stage Company), *Casanova* and *Losing Father's Body,* which received grant awards for New American Plays from the W. Alton Jones Foundation. She has also been awarded playwriting fellowships from the National Endowment for the Arts, the Rockefeller Foundation, and the Guggenheim Foundation. She has won awards from Oppenheimer/ Newsday and the L. Arnold Weissberger Playwriting Competition. She is an alumna of New Dramatists and has taught playwriting at Amherst College.

Since the early 1960s ROSALYN DREXLER has been prolific in the visual arts, writing of drama, fiction, art and film, and teaching. In general, her work explores issues of women, sexual politics, art and society, and societal pressures to conform. Among her many plays are *Home Movies, The Line of Least Existence, Starburn, Delicate Feelings, She Who Was He, The Writer's Opera, A Matter of Life and Death, Room 17C, Occupational Hazard, El Diente Azucur (Sweet Tooth)* and *Dear.* Her numerous awards include a Pollack-Krasner Grant in Visual Arts for painting, a National Endowment for the Arts grant for playwriting, a New York State Council on the Arts Playwriting Award, and three Obie Awards (for *The Writer's Opera, Home Movies,* and *Transients Welcome*). She has also received four Rockefeller grants for playwriting, a Guggenheim fellowship, and an Emmy in writing excellence for WCBS TV's Lily Tomlin special, *Lily.*

ERIK EHN is married to scenic artist Pat Chanteloube. His plays include: *Beginner* (published by Sun & Moon Press), *Ideas of Good and Evil, Angel uh God, The Imp of Simplicity, No Time Like the Present, Tailings, Little Rootie Tootie, Moira McOc* and *The Saint Plays.* His works have been produced at The Undermain Theatre in Dallas, Sledgehammer in San Diego, The Annex Theatre and The Empty Space Theatre in Seattle, 10,000 Things in Minneapolis, BACA in Brooklyn, Intersection in San Francisco, Portland Stage Company in Maine, and Frontera in Austin. His recent play, *Erotic Curtsies,* was produced by Bottom's Dream in Los Angeles. Ehn is the recipient of the Whiting Award and a McKnight Fellowship. He is a member of New Dramatists.

RICHARD FOREMAN is an avant-garde playwright and founder of the Ontological-Hysteric Theatre, founded in 1968. He has written over forty plays since 1967 and has also directed and designed over half of them. Some of his plays are *Angelface, Total Recall (Sophia =(Wisdom): Part 2), Hotel China, Eddie Goes to Poetry City, The Mind King, Samuel's Major Problems, I've Got the Shakes, Classical Therapy* or *A Week Under the Influence, Pain(t), Rhoda in Potatoland,* and *Elephant Steps.* He also staged *The Threepenny Opera* at the Vivian Beaumont Theater of Lincoln Center and has collaborated with composers on other musical productions as well. He is a six-time Obie Award winner.

MARIA IRENE FORNES is a playwright, director, translator, and lyricist. Born in Havana in 1930, she first came to the U.S. at age fifteen and then lived in France, returning to New York at the age of thirty. One of America's foremost playwrights, her works are written in English, her second language. She has written more than twenty-five plays and musicals including *Fefu and Her Friends, Mud, Doctor Kheal, Evelyn Brown, A Vietnamese Wedding, The Danube, Sarita, The Conduct of Life, The Widow, Tango Palace, Promenade, Molly's Dream, The Successful Life of 3, Abingdon Square, And What of the Night?, The Summer in Gossensass,* and *Oscar and Bertha.* Her works were performed at the Judson Poets Theatre in the 1960s and since then have been performed nationally to critical acclaim. Fornes is the recipient of seven Obie Awards and in 1982 she received one for Sustained Achievement in the Theatre. She has also received a National Endowment for the Arts Distinguished Artists Award, Rockefeller Foundation grants, a Guggenheim grant, and a New York State Governor's Award. From 1973 to 1979, she was the managing director of the New York Theatre Strategy. She directs most of her own plays and has directed plays by Calderon, Ibsen, and Chekhov as well. She has been a TCG/PEW Artist-in-Residence at Women's Project & Productions for two years and conducts playwriting workshops across the country. She is a member of the American Academy and Institute of Arts and Letters.

DAVID GREENSPAN is a playwright, director, and actor. His plays include *Jack, Principia, The Home Show Pieces, 2 Samuel 11, Dead Mother, Dog in a Dancing School, Four Dialogues of a Monologue,* and *Son of an Engineer.* They have been performed in New York, Chicago, San Francisco, Minneapolis, London, Glasgow, and Berlin. At the Public Theater he directed his own plays and productions of Congreve's *The Way of the World* and Chikamatsu's *Gonza the Lancer.* He has received fellowships from the Rockefeller Foundation, the Jerome Foundation, the New York State Council on the Arts, and the McKnight Foundation. From 1987 to 1990 he was the playwright-in-residence at HOME for Contemporary Theatre and Art. Also, from 1990 to 1993, he was the resident director at the New York Shakespeare Festival Public Theater. His acting credits include Charles Ludlam's *The Mystery of Irma Vep* at The Cleveland Play House, Elizabeth Egloff's *Phaedra* at the Vineyard Theatre, and Hal Hartley's film *Amateur.* He recently received praise for his performance in *Boys in the Band.*

JOHN GUARE is a noted American playwright who has had numerous plays produced. They include *The House of Blue Leaves, Six Degrees of Separation, Four Baboons Adoring the Sun, Landscape of the Body, Lydie Breeze, Gardenia, Women and Water, A Day for Surprises, Muzeeka,* and *Marco Polo.* He also wrote the screenplay for Louis Malle's *Atlantic City.* Guare was elected to the American Academy of the Arts and Letters in 1989 and is a council member of the Dramatists Guild.

TINA HOWE was born in New York in 1937 and graduated from Sarah Lawrence. Her plays include *The West, Birth and After Birth, Museum, Approaching Zanzibar, The Art of Dining,* and *One Shoe Off.* She received a Tony nomination for *Coastal Disturbances* and an Outer Critics Award for *Painting Churches,* which was also televised on *American Playhouse* in 1986. She has received an Obie Award for Distinguished Playwriting, as well as a Rockefeller Foundation grant and a National Endowment for the Arts fellowship.

HOLLY HUGHES is a popular and controversial playwright and performance artist. The themes of female sexuality and lesbian desire are present in most of her works. She received her first Obie Award for her play *Dress Suits to Hire* and her second Obie Award for the solo performance piece *Clit Notes*. Her other plays include *The Well of Horniness* and *The Lady Dick*. In 1990, Hughes received national attention when she was de-funded by the National Endowment for the Arts because of her controversial work. She has received a McKnight fellowship, as well as numerous awards, commissions, and grants from the New York Shakespeare Festival, the Walker Art Center, Performance Space 122, the New York Foundation for the Arts, the Rockefeller Foundation, and the Ford Foundation. She has also been a writer-in-residence at the Intersection for the Arts in San Francisco. Her work has been performed throughout the u.s., England, and Canada and she also teaches and lectures in universities throughout the country.

NAOMI IIZUKA is a founding member of Theater E in San Diego and a playwright. Her play *Tattoo Girl* was adapted from "Perpetua" by Donald Barthelme. Her other plays have been produced in New York, San Diego, Los Angeles and elsewhere and include *Carthage, Marie Why and the China Thing, Lizzie Vinyl, And Then She Was Screaming,* and *The Battles of Coxinga*. She received her BA from Yale and her MFA from the University of California San Diego. She teaches playwriting in San Diego.

LEN JENKIN is the author of over twenty plays, including *Kitty Hawk, The Death and Life of Jesse James, Grand American Exhibition, Mission, Gogol: A Mystery Play, Kid Twist, The Five of Us, Limbo Tales, Dark Ride, My Uncle Sam, American Notes,* and *Poor Folk's Pleasure*. More recent plays include *Pilgrims of the Night* and *Careless Love*, which was presented at the SoHo Repertory Theater in 1993. His works also include several very free adaptations that stand as plays themselves: *Candide, A Soldier's Tale,* and *A Country Doctor*. He has also adapted two children's novels into the plays *Ramona Quimby* and *The Invisible Man*. He is the author of the novel *New Jerusalem*, which was published by Sun and Moon Press in 1996 to critical acclaim. He has received a Guggenheim fellowship, four National Endowment for the Arts fellowships, three Obie Awards, a Rockefeller Foundation Playwriting Fellowship, and numerous other awards. He also writes for the movies and television, for which he was nominated for an Emmy award. He has served as the American representative at the Toga International Arts Festival in Japan and was selected for an international exchange by USIA and the Russian Theater Worker's Union in Moscow. Jenkin lives in New York City, where he teaches in the Dramatic Writing Program at New York University.

JEFFREY M. JONES is a playwright whose works include the series of "Crazy Plays": *Write If You Get Work, The Endless Adventures of M.C. Kat, Crazy Plays Que Fumar, The Crazy Plays, Annunciation With Wranglers,* and *Office Work*. He has also written *Love Trouble*. His plays have been produced by Cucaracha Theatre, Manhattan Theatre Club, HOME for Contemporary Theatre and Art, New Dramatists, Creation Production Company, and the New York Theatre Workshop. He is also the author of *The Confessions of a Dopefiend, 70 Scenes of Halloween, Nightcoil,* and *The Fortress of Solitude*. Since 1985, he has directed and usually designed his New York premieres. He has received a National Endowment for the Arts Playwriting fellowship, a Bay Area Playwrights Festival grant, and a Thomas J. Watson Foundation fellowship, as well as support from ArtMatters and the Peg Santvoord Foundation. From 1980 to 1987, he was a member of New Dramatists and also attended the MacDowell Colony in 1991. He has been a site evaluator for the NEA Theater Program since 1984 and a panelist member for several arts councils, as well as a lecturer at several universities.

ADRIENNE KENNEDY began her career as a playwright in the 1960s. *Funnyhouse of a Negro* won her an Obie Award in 1964 and was broadcast on BBC and Radio Denmark, as well as translated into several languages. Her many other plays include *The Owl Answers, A Lesson in Dead Language, A Rat's Mass*, first performed in Rome, *Sun*, commissioned by the Royal Court Theatre in London, and *A*

Movie Star Has to Star in Black and White, produced by Joseph Papp in 1976. She has also written adaptations of *Electra* and *Orestes,* both commissioned and produced by the Julliard School of Music in 1980. Her works have also been commissioned by the Public Theater, Jerome Robbins, and the Mark Taper Forum. She has been a visiting lecturer at Princeton, Brown, Yale, and the University of California at Berkeley. Her autobiography *People Who Led to My Plays* was published in 1987.

TONY KUSHNER is a playwright whose truthful, serious, yet humorous dramas are known world-wide. His plays include *Reverse Transcription, A Bright Room Called Day, The Illusion* (freely adapted from Corneille), *Slavs!,* performed at the Actors Theatre of Louisville, and *Angels in America, A Gay Fantasia on National Themes, Part One: Millenium Approaches, Part Two: Perestroika.* He has also written adaptations of Brecht's *The Good Person of Setzuan,* Goethe's *Stella,* and Ansky's *The Dybbuk.* Kushner has received numerous awards for *Angels in America,* including the 1993 Pulitzer Prize for Drama, two Drama Desk Awards for Best Broadway Play, two Tonys for Best Play, two LAMBDA Literary Awards, and an Outer Critics Award for Best Broadway Play. *Angels in America* has been produced in over thirty countries. He has also been awarded a Whiting Foundation Writers Award and an Arts Award from the American Academy of Letters and Sciences. He wrote the book *Thinking About the Longstanding Problems of Virtue and Happiness: Essays, A Play, Two Poems, and a Prayer.* Recently, his play *Terminating* has been performed at the Public Theater.

CRAIG LUCAS has written numerous plays, many of which premiered at The Production Company in New York. He collaborated with Norman Rene as director on *Missing Persons, Blue Window, Prelude to a Kiss,* and *The Scare.* He has had plays commissioned from South Coast Repertory and American Playhouse. His musical play, *Three Postcards,* co-authored with Craig Carnelia, was awarded Best Musical by the Burns Mantle Theater yearbook. He has also written two opera texts, *Cousin Lillie* and *Orpheus in Love,* with the composer Gerald Busby. Lucas has been awarded the George and Elisabeth Marton Award, the L.A. Drama Critics Award, a Drama-Logue award, and Guggenheim and Rockefeller Foundation awards. He has also collaborated with Norman Rene on two films, *Lifetime Companion* and *Blue Window.* He has been a member of Circle Repertory Company.

Born in Floral Park, New York in 1943, CHARLES LUDLAM attended Hofstra University. In the 1960s, living on the Lower East Side, Ludlam encountered the plays of director John Vaccaro and playwright Ronald Tavel, who, collaborating with Andy Warhol on his films, had turned to theater, founding with Vaccaro the Play-House of the Ridiculous. Ludlam performed in their premiere production, *The Life of Lady Godiva,* and later performed in his first drag role as Nora Desmond in Tavel's *Screen Test.* Soon after Tavel and Vaccaro quarreled and parted, and Vaccaro returned to Ludlam for material. The result was Ludlam's *Big Hotel,* which was followed over the years by numerous other plays of his own Theatre of the Ridiculous, which were presented in repertory. These include *Turds in Hell, The Grand Tarot, Bluebeard, Eunuchs of the Forbidden City, Corn,* and *Camille,* which became one of the company's earliest successes. Among his other plays are *Isle of the Hermaphrodites, Der Ring Gott Farblonjet, The Ventriloquist's Wife, The Enchanted Pig, Reverse Psychology,* and *The Mystery of Irma Vep.* Ludlam died of complications from AIDS in 1987 at the age of forty-four.

Veteran playwright MURRAY MEDNICK was born in Brooklyn, New York. For many years he was playwright-in-residence at New York's Theater Genesis, which presented all of his early works including *The Hawk, The Deer Kill, The Hunter, Sand,* and *Are You Lookin'?.* He was Artistic Co-director of Theater Genesis from 1970 to 1974. His plays produced since then include *Iowa, Blessings* (for the PBS series, "Visions"), *The Coyote Cycle, Taxes, Scar, Heads, Shatter 'N Wade, Fedunn, Joe and Betty, Switchback, Skinwalkers, Baby, Jesus!, Kesler's Defiance, Sixteen Routines,* and *Freeze.* He founded the Padua Hills Playwrights' Workshop/Festival in Los Angeles in 1978 and was Artistic Director until its closure in 1995. *Dictator* won the 1997 L.A. Weekly Playwriting Award. He has been the recipient of two Rockefeller Foundation grants, a Guggenheim Fellowship, an Obie Award, and several Bay Area Critics Circle Awards. He also received a 1992 Ovation Award from the L.A. Theatre League Alliance for his outstanding contributions to Los Angeles theater. He is a member of New Dramatists.

CHARLES M. MEE, JR. is a playwright and historian and his many works include the play *The Investigation of the Murder in El Salvador* and a radical adaptation of Euripides' *Orestes*, which was workshopped at the American Repertory Theatre and premiered in a site-specific production in New York City. Some of his plays have been produced and commissioned by ISA.

RICHARD NELSON is a well-known playwright and has also been a literary manager at the Brooklyn Academy of Music, dramaturg at The Guthrie Theater, and associate director at the Goodman Theatre. Some of his plays include *An American Comedy, Some Americans Abroad, Principia Scriptoriae, Between East and West, Rip Van Winkle or The Works, The Killing of Yablinski, Bal, The Return of Pinnochio,* and *Conjuring an Event.* He has also translated and adapted numerous plays. His plays have been produced by Playwrights Horizons, The American Place Theatre, Mark Taper Forum, Arena Stage, Yale Repertory Theatre, and numerous theaters in Europe. He has been awarded a Guggenheim fellowship, a Rockefeller Playwriting grant, two National Endowment for the Arts Playwriting fellowships, and a Playwrights USA Award. He is also a two-time Obie Award winner, as well as recipient of the *Time Out* London Theatre Award and a Giles Cooper Award.

JOHN O'KEEFE is a California playwright and performer, and a founding member of one of the San Francisco Bay Area's important theater groups, the Blake Street Hawkeyes. Among his many plays are *Chamber Piece, Jimmy Beam, The Saints of Fr. Lyons, Ghosts, All Night Long, Bercilak's Dream* and *The Deatherians.*

ERIC OVERMYER has established himself as one of America's wittiest playwrights. His plays include *Dark Rapture, The Dalai Lama Goes Three for Four, Native Speech, Mi Familia Tropicana, Hawker, On the Verge, In Perpetuity,* and *Throughout the Universe.* He has also written the book and lyrics for the off-Broadway play *In a Pig's Valise,* with music by August Darnell. He has been awarded grants and fellowships by the McKnight Foundation, Le Compte De Nouey, the New York Foundation for the Arts, the National Endowment for the Arts, and the Rockefeller Foundation. He has also written for television's *St. Elsewhere, The Days and Nights of Molly Dodd,* and *The "Slap" Maxwell Story. Kafka's Radio* was written for WNYC. He has also been associate artist of Center Stage in Baltimore.

OYAMO (Charles Gordan) has written numerous plays including *The Resurrection of Lady Lester, I Am A Man,* and *Let Me Live.* His works have been performed at Yale Repertory Theatre, Goodman Theatre, Manhattan Theatre Club, Arena Stage, Public Theater, the Kennedy Center, the O'Neill Theater Center National Playwrights Conference, and at several other theaters. The Working Theatre, The Seattle Children's Theatre, and The Children's Theatre Company in Minneapolis have commissioned his works. He has also written a musical, *Famous Orpheus,* with choreography by Garth Fagan. He has been awarded a Guggenheim fellowship, a Rockefeller Foundation Playwrights-in-Residence grant, a McKnight fellowship, an Ohio Arts Council Award, a New York State Council on the Arts fellowship, a McKnight Foundation fellowship, and three National Endowment for the Arts fellowships. He received his MFA in playwriting from the Yale School of Drama and has taught at Emory University, Princeton, and at the University of Iowa Playwrights Workshop. He is currently associate professor of Theatre at the University of Michigan.

SUZAN-LORI PARKS' itinerant childhood is, she believes, why she became a writer. She has written many plays, including *Imperceptible Mutabilities in the Third Kingdom, The America Play, Venus,* an historically true tale co-commissioned by The Women's Project and Productions and Life on the Water, and several others. She has received two Obie Awards, a Whiting Foundation Award, a CalArts/

Herb Alpert Award, a grant from the Kennedy Center New American Plays Fund, and two grants from the National Endowment for the Arts. She has written radio plays as well and wrote the screenplay for the Spike Lee film, *Girl 6*. Parks studied writing with James Baldwin at Mount Holyoke College and teaches playwriting all over the country and at the Yale School of Drama. She is also a member of New Dramatists.

KIER PETERS is the author of nine plays, including *The Confirmation, Past Present Future Tense, Intentional Coincidence, A Dog Tries to Kiss the Sky, The Intruders, Family,* and the musical *Flying Down to Cairo. The Confirmation* premiered in the T.W.E.E.D Festival at New York's Vineyard Theatre. His *Past Present Future Tense* premiered at Common Cultural Practice in San Francisco in 1995 and the same play, as *Still in Love,* was performed as an opera, with music by Michael Kowalski, in New York's Roulette in 1996. Common Cultural Practice also performed his *A Dog Tries to Kiss the Sky* in 1997. He lives in Los Angeles.

PEDRO PIETRI is an accomplished playwright and poet who describes himself as a "native New Yorker, born in Ponce, Puerto Rico." He is well-known for both his plays and poetry, often read at the Nuyorican Cafe in New York. His one-act play, *The Masses are Asses,* premiered at Miriam Colon's Puerto Rican Traveling Theatre in New York. He also has written a book of poems, *Traffic Violations.* He is a member of New Dramatists.

JACK RICHARDSON is famous for two plays in the early 1960s, *Gallows Humor,* which was first performed at the Gramercy Arts Theatre in New York City in 1961, and *The Prodigal.*

Born in 1943 in Illinois, SAM SHEPARD is an award-winning American dramatist. He has written over forty plays and won ten Obie Awards. His first one-act plays were *Cowboys* and *The Rock Garden* performed at St. Mark's Church. His first full-length play, *La Turista,* was produced at The American Place Theatre and won him an Obie Award in 1967. In 1979, *Buried Child* won the Pulitzer Prize for Drama. His other plays include *Fool for Love, Red Cross, Angel City, Up to Thursday, 4-H Club, Rocking Chair, Icarus' Mother, Fourteen Hundred Thousand, Chicago, Geography of a Horse Dreamer, Action, Cowboy Mouth, Melodrama Play, Seduced,* and *Curse of the Starving Class,* which was produced at the New York Shakespeare Festival in 1978. He also wrote a rock-drama, *The Tooth of Crime,* which was written in London, during his four-year stay there. He was playwright-in-residence for many years at the Magic Theatre in San Francisco and wrote for them *Killer's Head, Inacoma, Tongues,* and *True West.* In 1984, Shepard was nominated for an Oscar for his performance as Chuck Yeager in the movie *The Right Stuff.* He acted in several other movies and won the Golden Palm Award at the Cannes Film Festival for his screenplay for the Wim Wenders' movie *Paris, Texas.*

JOHN STEPPLING has long been an important influence on theater in southern California, particularly as an original founding member of the Padua Hills Playwrights/Workshop Festival and as the founder of the Los Angeles theater company Empire Red Lip. He has written over thirty plays including *The Dream Coast, The Shaper, Standard of the Breed, Teenage Wedding, My Crummy Job, Deep Tropical Tan and Theory of Miracles,* and *Sea of Cortez.* In 1996, Sun and Moon Press published his collection, *Sea of Cortez and Other Plays.* A four-time National Endowment for the Arts grant recipient for writing and directing, Steppling has also received a Rockefeller fellowship, two *L.A. Weekly* awards for Best Play, and a Pen-West award for drama. His plays have been produced in San Francisco, New York, Louisville, and London, to international acclaim. He has also written several screenplays and has traveled extensively.

RONALD TAVEL's numerous plays include *Gorilla Queen, The Life of Juanita Castro, The Life of Lady Godiva, Kitchenette, How Jacqueline Kennedy Became the Queen of Greece, The Last Days of British Honduras, Gazelle Boy, The Ovens of Anita Orangejuice: A History of Modern Florida, Success and*

Succession, My Foetus Lived on Amboy Street, Tarzan of the Flicks, Indira Gandhi's Daring Device, Shower, Estrella Verde, Thick Dick, The Understudy, Arenas of Lutetia, and *Boy on a Straight-Back Chair.* He has also written many screenplays for Andy Warhol. He has received grants from the Creative Artists Public Service Program and the National Endowment for the Arts. He currently lives in Bangkok.

Poet, playwright and lyricist ARNOLD WEINSTEIN is the author of numerous plays and musicals. His play *Red Eye of Love,* first produced in 1961, has attained a legendary status. It was first read in 1958 at the Summer Five Spot in East Hampton, a home to jazz musicians, artists, and writers. With the help of investors and contributions from the sales of his friends' paintings, *Red Eye of Love* was produced at The Living Theatre in New York in 1961. It has since been performed at local and university theaters in the U.S., Italy, France, and Scandinavia. His plays and musicals include *Fortuna, Under Cover Lover* (written with Frank O'Hara), *Dynamite Tonight,* and *Casino Paradise.* He has written librettos for several operas, including the Chicago Lyric Opera production of *McTeague,* composed by William Bolcom and directed by Robert Altman. He also wrote *Schlemiel,* which was performed at the American Conservatory Theater and at the Lincoln Center Theater's Serious Fun Festival in 1995. He collaborated on *What Did I Do? The Authorized Autobiography of Larry Rivers.* He is a Harvard graduate as well as the recipient of a Fulbright Scholar Award.

Described by the New York Times as "a playwright intoxicated with words," MAC WELLMAN has written over thirty plays, two novels, and several collections of poetry. Among his plays are *Tallahassee, The Sandalwood Box, 7 Blowjobs, Energumen, Sincerity Forever, Three Americanisms, Crowbar, Albanian Softshoe, Cleveland, Cellophane, Whirligig,* and *Terminal Hip.* Publications of his plays include *Bad Penny, The Professional Frenchman, Dracula, Swoop, A Murder of Crows,* and *The Hyacinth Macaw* (all by Sun and Moon Press), *The Bad Infinity: Eight Plays,* and *Harm's Way.* His plays have been performed in New York, San Diego, Minneapolis, and at the Berkshire Theatre Festival. Wellman won Obie Awards for *Bad Penny, Terminal Hip, Crowbar,* and *Sincerity Forever.* In 1994, he won The America Award for *The Hyacinth Macaw.* He has also edited several collections of plays, including *Theater of Wonders* and *7 Different Plays.* Wellman has published collections of poetry as well: *In Praise of Secrecy, Satires,* and *A Shelf in Woop's Clothing.* His novels, *The Fortuneteller* and *Annie Salem* were published by Sun and Moon. He has received numerous grants, including a McKnight award, a Rockefeller Foundation award, National Endowment for the Arts fellowships, and Guggenheim Foundation fellowships. He is also a member of New Dramatists.

TENNESSEE WILLIAMS, the great American playwright, was born in 1911. He is best known for his plays *A Streetcar Named Desire, The Glass Menagerie,* and *Cat on a Hot Tin Roof.* His other plays include *Summer and Smoke, The Milk Train Doesn't Stop Here Anymore, Kingdom of Earth, Small Craft Warnings, In the Bar of a Tokyo Hotel, Sweet Bird of Youth, Period of Adjustment, The Night of the Iguana, Suddenly Last Summer, Orpheus Descending, Camino Real, The Rose Tattoo, The Eccentricities of a Nightingale, Battle of Angels,* and *The Gnadiges Fraulein.* He also wrote several books of poetry and prose. Williams died in 1983.